JEFFERSON DAVIS

JEFFERSON DAVIS

The Man and His Hour

William C. Davis

LOUISIANA STATE UNIVERSITY PRESS   *Baton Rouge*

Copyright © 1991 by William C. Davis
LSU Press edition published by arrangement with HarperCollins
 Publishers
All rights reserved
Manufactured in the United States of America
Designed by Alma Orenstein
ISBN 0-8071-2079-0 (pbk.)

Louisiana Paperback Edition, 1996
05 04 03 02 01 00   5 4 3

Library of Congress Cataloging-in-Publication Data

Davis, William C., 1946–
  Jefferson Davis: the man and his hour/William C. Davis.
    p. cm.

  1. Davis, Jefferson, 1808–1889.   2. Presidents—Confederate States
of America—Biography.   3. Statesmen—United States—Biography.   I.
Title.
E467.1.D26D32   1991
973.7'13'092—dc20   90-56352
[B]

The paper in this book meets the guidelines for permanence and durability
of the Committee on Production Guidelines for Book Longevity of the
Council on Library Resources. ∞

For M. Jefferson Davis,
who is not named for this man
but who bears some of his finest qualities,
and for Rebecca Mahala Davis,
who would have loved the man in spite of himself

Contents

PART TWO The Hour

Illustrations follow page 400.

Preface

Historians are sometimes a superstitious lot. It used to be said that no one who started to write a biography of Henry Clay would live through the task. Then there was the notion that those who delved too deeply into the Lincoln murder could expect unusual and sometimes sinister happenings in their own lives. And others have long believed that anyone writing a life of Jefferson Davis was only asking for trouble, for no biography of the man would ever be considered a good one.

Maybe the fault lies with the man. Even in his own time associates considered him cold, aloof, an "icicle," obstinate, petty, enigmatic, vindictive, and bitter—all of which he certainly was in varying measure. He was also warm, painfully sensitive to his own feelings and those of others, affectionate, witty when it suited him, very intelligent, absolutely impervious to physical fear, and loyal literally to a fault. His best side he kept hidden from all but his family and most intimate friends—a circle that unfortunately excludes twentieth-century historians—thus, for generations, our finest biographers have turned their talents to more sympathetic characters like Lincoln and Lee. The result is that the Davis we have been given in print has come chiefly from an unbroken string of second- and third-rate biographies, from the vituperativeness of E. A. Pollard's to the cloying worshipfulness of Hudson Strode's and the antiseptic brevity of Clement Eaton's.

Maybe the fault lies with the historians, who have so consistently baffled themselves by approaching Davis as if he were a molded icon who somehow, when cooled, failed to match the cast. "The Sphinx of the Confederacy," they have called him, "an enigma," "a mystery," and more. Historians have consistently failed to look on him as they would on other men. Instead they have seen only a man of great attainments, thrust into a great position, who failed to act like a great man. Frustrated by this, they have decided that he is an insoluble mystery. Yet there is nothing at all mysterious about Jefferson Davis. We have all known him in bits and pieces of ourselves and others in our lives, and it asks little more than a good grasp of human nature to come to grips with the man.

Perhaps no one is at fault. Some figures of the past—and the present—defy good biography. By their character or temperament, or the times in which they live, they leave a record that simply cannot be interpreted satisfactorily in fairness and justice to the subject and the reader. What Davis is to the biographers of today, Richard Nixon may be to those of the next century. Both were complex men whose roles in turbulent times seem to defy adequate delineation.

Whatever the cause, biographies of Jefferson Davis never seem to give universal pleasure, and undoubtedly this one will not prove an exception. Sheer volume will have something to do with that, for this is a massive book, a lot to read for most people whose only knowledge of Davis is the vague notion that they will dislike him. Those who nevertheless essay the task are entitled to a few words of explanation about some aspects of what they undertake.

Some will perceive what seems to be an imbalance of coverage. Nearly a third of the book deals with his life up to 1861; half is devoted to the next four years; then a fraction covers his remaining twenty-four years. Moreover, his childhood and early youth receive more attention than do substantial portions of his senatorial career. His Mexican War service occupied more ground than did his role in the crisis of 1860, while in the chapters on the Civil War years, his first eighteen months as president of the Confederacy get almost as much space as does the balance of his tenure. Meanwhile, his oft-vaunted service as secretary of war in 1853–57 is passed over rather speedily.

It is all a matter of perspective. The fact is that there is one reason, and only one, for writing or reading a biography of Jefferson Davis, and that is his quadrennium as leader of the Lost Cause. Without this vital element, few if any Americans would ever have heard of him, or wanted to. Who remembers any of the secretaries of war prior to World War II? How many of the hundreds of senators and congressmen who have served in the past two centuries are truly worthy of biographies? Davis created no significant legislation, and even in the march to secession he played a secondary role. His years in the war office generated nothing we remember or care about today, other than vaguely held notions that he tried a seemingly whimsical experiment with camels. As for his post-war years, once he left prison there was nothing to set his life apart from those of the hundreds of thousands of other former Confederates trying to rebuild their lives—nothing but the fact that he had been their president.

In short, nothing in this man's life would attract more attention than a thesis or dissertation had he not been chosen to take an oath in Montgomery, Alabama, in February 1861. Thus the preponderance of this biography looks at the four years that followed that oath. As for his prewar life, it is chiefly important only for what it reveals of the making of the president in 1861—how his attitudes and values developed and how his character took shape in the fashion that left such a distinctive mark on the Confederacy. It is for this reason that his early years are so important, including the West Point and Mexican War days that distinctively influenced his thinking on military matters. As for his senatorial career, much less space could actually have been devoted to it, for once his ideas and opinions took shape in the 1840s, they rarely if ever changed. Indeed, the balance of his political career in the old Union was little more than a constant repetition of those ideas. And as for the opposite end of his life, his years after 1865 have little value outside the contexts of Davis's reflections on the war and of his symbolic role as a leader of the Old South embarking into a new one. In the Civil War years themselves, meanwhile, the first eighteen months reveal the development of Davis to the highest point he achieved as a chief executive. By the end of 1862, the decisions, the strategies, the appointments, and the loyalties and antipathies by which he would conduct the balance of the conflict had been set in place.

This book is a "life," not a "life-and-times." Already substantial, it would be much more so if extensive background were interwoven on every political contest, every campaign or battle, and each of his many personal feuds. Enough has been provided to illuminate either Davis's direct participation or his influence. Similarly, his remarkable wife Varina Howell Davis does not spend much time at center stage. By any measure she was an unusual individual, very much a twentieth-century woman. But thanks to the limitations of the era in which she lived, she remains important to us today for no reason other than the fact that marriage changed her name to Davis. She exerted considerable influence on him at times, for good and ill. Moreover, as first lady of the Confederacy she shared with him as no other the burdens of his responsibility, and to the extent that she had an impact on her husband she appears here. This unusual woman deserves serious study in her own right.

A few words are in order about the sources used to write this study. Previous biographies have hardly been used at all, nor are there many references to the wide body of modern literature dealing with Davis. Excellent works have appeared in recent years by scholars like William

Cooper, Frank Vandiver, Paul Escott, Ludwell Johnson, and others. However, from the first, the intent in this book has been to work as exclusively as possible from sources contemporary to Davis. Should this portrait—which emerges directly from the man himself and those close to him, uninfluenced by the opinions and theses of other latter-day historians—in large part agree with their own conclusions, it is because we have looked at the same raw materials and drawn the same lessons. Similarly, little reliance has been placed on the later memoirs and reminiscences of Davis's associates, for most are unreliable, either tainted by extreme partisanship or expressions of extreme prejudice.

Happily, the superabundance of Davis correspondence for so much of his life means that there is little need to rely on other sources for more than corroboration and color. The editors of the Papers of Jefferson Davis project at Rice University estimate that perhaps fifty thousand such pieces of correspondence have been located, with more coming to light continually. Indeed, it is to those editors, Lynda Laswell Crist and Mary Seaton Dix, that the greatest debt of gratitude is owed, for this massive work could not have been done without them. For more than a year their hospitality and encouragement have been nothing less than exceptional. They have freely opened their staggering collection of Davis papers from all over the country almost without reservation, providing the most comfortable of working quarters—and the most delightful of companions—all while continuing their own work, which has set such a high standard for documentary editing projects. I shall miss looking for barbecue in Houston, nibbling chocolates from Neiman Marcus, and those wonderful luncheons at the Rice faculty club.

Indeed, similar debts are owed to many others. Dozens of libraries and historical societies have allowed the use of their collections. Every one is listed in the bibliography, and to recount them here would only be repetitive, besides which the gratitude thus expressed would only be inadequate to the contribution they all have made. Thanks are also due copy editor Susan H. Llewellyn, whose efforts made a marked improvement in the text. Reviewing her queries was almost fun, rather like a stimulating conversation. (It is perhaps proper to point out here, by the way, that nineteenth-century spelling, punctuation, and capitalization were most inventively idiosyncratic, even among the educated like Jefferson Davis. However, rather than clutter the text with a long procession of [sic]s after each infraction, I have preferred to let their letters and words stand as they are so long as their meaning is clear. When it is not, brackets have been used to include missing vital elements.)

Similarly, many private individuals have graciously given assistance, including Percival Beacroft of Rosemont Plantation, Ernesto Caldera of the Davis Family Association, Mrs. Wert Chapman, James O. Hall, Jefferson Hayes-Davis, Amelia Rodrigue, and Richard J. Sommers.

To have been associated with all of these people has been delightful, and for that I am almost sorry that this book is done.

But it is done, and I am thankful for that. "We were told long ago that of making books there was no end," Jefferson Davis wrote to his publisher when fairly launched on the preparation of his *Rise and Fall of the Confederate Government.* "I am making the first experiment in that manufacture and am very desirous to bring it to an end."

I know how he felt.

PART ONE

The Man

1

There My Memories Begin

Childhood is all too often the lost chapter of biography. During those precious years when mind and memory offer blank pages hungry to be filled, every thought, every experience, is imprinted without scruple over its worth. As time drives people farther from their youth, the ensuing years of maturity inevitably erode the earliest memories, making way for those that follow. Always some special recollections—often trivial and signifying nothing—stay locked in the mind well into the twilight of a life. Yet, in the last years, looking back, trying to clasp and hold the fleeting images of early days, the tired and inevitably saddened old reader can find little more on those yellowed pages than blurs, smudges, and blanks. And few as the memories of childhood may be, the actual records of youth are fewer still—little more than slender shafts of light through a forest of shadows. If Wordsworth was right, if "the child is father of the man," then few indeed are those men who truly remember, truly know, their "fathers." Growing up makes orphans of us all.

One such "orphan" was Jefferson Davis. Throughout a long life he never knew with certainty the year of his birth. The date, June 3, he knew well enough, but as for the rest he could only plead, with a faint sparkle of wit, that "I am not a competent witness in the case." In his forty-ninth—or fiftieth—year, he said, "Having once supposed the year to have been 1807, I was subsequently corrected by being informed it was 1808, and have rested upon that point because it was just as good, and no better than another."[1] His cavalier unconcern is oddly out of character for a man already famed for his punctiliousness in all matters of record. Yet Davis, whose whole public career would be spent looking backward rather than forward, showed little interest in his own origins. Personally he focused on where he was going, not where he had been.

Indeed, Davis did not even know if his paternal grandfather was a native-born American and probably erred when he declared that Evan Davis had come from Wales. Another Evan Davis, probably born about 1695 or earlier, and most likely in Wales, had come to Philadelphia in the early years of the eighteenth century. He left little behind to remember him. Most of his life he worked as a drayman hauling others' goods. Perhaps the familiarity thus gained with the needs of men of the road in early Pennsylvania led him to his later, and last, occupation, innkeeping. He neither read nor wrote more than a crude mark for his name. He married a woman named Mary and by her fathered six children, one of the youngest being his namesake Evan, born in the mid-1720s almost certainly in Philadelphia. This was the grandfather of Jefferson Davis.[2]

For all that he ever passed on to his grandson, Evan Davis might as well have been born across the ocean and never come to America. He lived only to his mid-thirties and died perhaps a full half century before his grandson's birth. When barely more than twenty-one, the young Philadelphian went to South Carolina with his brother, and there he met and married a widow named Mary Emory Williams. Then, almost immediately, he moved again, this time to Georgia, and even as they journeyed into that colony, Mary Emory Davis may already have been carrying the only son who would survive her husband. There, in an unknown spot in the Georgia wilderness, on an unknown date in a year that was probably 1756, she gave birth to Samuel Emory Davis. And that is all that Samuel's son Jefferson ever knew of his ancestry. It was as much as he cared to know.

Fortunately, Samuel Davis proved to be a considerably more visible and substantial influence on his own future son, though more than fifty years passed between their births. In later years he told his children of his experiences as a teenager during the Revolution, serving in Georgia and South Carolina before raising his own militia company and leading them, when just twenty-three, in the defense of Savannah in December 1779. When the conflict ended, Samuel Davis returned to his home to find it ruined by the war and his mother deceased. Unbeknownst to him, he was still entitled to a share in the estate of his grandfather Evan, but the chances are strong that the Davises back in Philadelphia did not even know of Samuel's existence, while he, orphaned in infancy by his father, very likely knew next to nothing of his family in Pennsylvania. Thus the inheritance went unclaimed, and Samuel Davis left his boyhood home near Augusta, Georgia, and settled on a twelve-hundred-acre land grant not far from what would become the small village of Washington.[3] There he farmed for a time. There, perhaps, he continued studies begun as a boy, which left him unusually literate for his time and place, and there, probably, too, he met brown-haired Jane Cook, four or five years his junior, and in about 1783 they married.[4]

Thanks to his education as well as his war service, Samuel Davis soon assumed a minor position of leadership in his rural community. Fellow citizens, valuing his ability to read and write with ease and skill, made him their county clerk. His horsemanship won him the respect of his neighbors, and certainly his efforts at taking a living from the ground showed him to be an industrious young man willing to sweat for his bread. Yet within no more than a decade of marrying and starting to farm, Davis gave up on Georgia. Like so many others he looked to the west, to the storied fertile wilderness of Kentucky. No more than a year or two after the "dark and bloody ground's" admission as a state in 1792, the Davises gave in to that tickling in their feet felt by so many young Americans. Only the passage of westering miles beneath their soles could calm the itch.[5]

As he moved northwestward across the Tennessee River, then over the Cumberland and into Kentucky, Samuel Davis could reflect that he had been successful at least in one endeavor. He and Jane were wonderfully fertile. Not much more than a year after their marriage, on December 10, 1784, they had produced their first son and named him Joseph Emory. A few years later came Benjamin, followed by Samuel; then a daughter, Anna Eliza; and not long before their move to Kentucky came Isaac Williams. Jane Davis bore five children in less than ten years, and moving to a new home slowed but did not stop her productivity. As the family alighted for a time in Mercer County, whose fabled bluegrass naturally attracted the horseman in her husband, Jane soon became pregnant with Lucinda Farrar, who may not have been born before Samuel took them all off again toward the country in the southwest part of the state around the Green River. There, in what would one day become Christian County and later Todd County, they settled again.[6]

Here Samuel built what was probably their best home yet, and certainly one in keeping with the frontier homes of their neighbors. Just off the crude road that ran from Elkton to Hopkinsville, he cut on his own property the timbers from which his log house emerged. Davis built a typical frontier home, two cabins about twenty feet apart, with two rooms apiece, and connected by a "dog trot" or "dog run"—nothing more than a roofed-over open space that was probably enclosed in later years to make more rooms. And while he set about raising tobacco on his six hundred acres, and breeding well-reputed horses, the four rooms of the Davis house became increasingly crowded as Jane steadily gave birth to more children. Amanda arrived sometime around 1799, and Matilda a year or so later. Mary Ellen came next. And then, sometime in the fall of 1807, Jane felt yet again what by then were the familiar old signs. Another child was on the way.[7]

For all that they loved their children, Samuel and Jane must have looked on this impending arrival with conflicting emotions. He still was not deriving as much as he had hoped from his land. Indeed, with his family growing beyond his means, he also began charging travelers on the Hopkinsville road for overnight lodging. As for Jane, anticipating her tenth childbirth in twenty-three years, and this when she was almost forty-seven, the thought must have crossed her mind that sooner or later this had to end. Thus it was with a touch of humor, leavened by wishful thinking, that the boy born to her on June 3, 1808, found himself endowed with the middle name Finis, testimony to his father's familiarity with Latin and both parents' hope that this baby would be their last. In honor of one of Samuel's revolutionary heroes who had become president of the young United States, the boy's given name would be Jefferson.[8]

A small child, he surely needed more care than Jane—with nine other children, a husband, and perhaps one or two slaves to look after—could devote to him. A neighbor woman came to the house to be his nurse and became much attached to "little Jeff," as she called him. Under the old locust and walnut trees around the house, she played with him as he grew from infant to toddler. The more attached she became, the harder it must have been for her when the boy's peripatetic father heeded the wanderlust once more and decided to move. News came to him of good land to the south in the Louisiana Territory. Thus, in 1810 or 1811, while his oldest son Joseph stayed in Hopkinsville to study law, Davis took the rest of his family on the road once more. Down along the course of the great Mississippi they trekked, and then off west of the river to the sparsely settled flatlands along Bayou Teche. Their stay was short, even for Samuel Davis. This was malaria country, the uncountable mosquitoes thriving in the heat and humidity. What could not thrive there were Davis's children, perhaps especially the youthfully susceptible Jefferson. His father looked yet again, this time for a place "higher and healthier," as his son remembered. Other Kentuckians had come back to Christian County with stories of the beautiful rolling hills and fertile soil of the Mississippi Territory, along the great river a few miles above St. Francisville, Louisiana. Samuel was in his mid-fifties. All he had to show for almost thirty years of striving was his family. It was time to find a home and stay there. Perhaps he could find it in Mississippi.[9]

Again they moved. By now "little Jeff" had become a favorite with his older sister Anna, some sixteen years his senior. When their mother was ill, Anna looked after him and rocked him to sleep in his cradle. No doubt she entertained and kept him out of mischief as the family crossed to the east bank of the Mississippi that year and traveled to the little settlement of Woodville. There, perhaps a mile east of town, Samuel and Jane Davis settled for the last time. There on several hundred acres he would grow cotton. There atop a tranquil poplar-covered rise he would build his home and call it Poplar Grove. "And there," his son Jefferson recalled three-quarters of a century later, "my memories begin."[10]

Samuel built what came to be called a Mississippi planter's cottage, a one-and-one-half-story Federal house with a wide center hall flanked on either side by two rooms on the lower floor, with two more and a sitting room beneath the sloping dormered roof of the second floor. He covered the wooden frame with cypress siding and built wide porches front and back. They appointed and furnished it simply at first, to the limits that Samuel could afford. In the fashion of the time, he and Jane probably slept in the bedroom at the rear of the first floor, perhaps behind the dining room. The daughters would have stayed in one of the large dormitory rooms upstairs, and the boys in the other. "Little Jeff," probably about four years old when his father and older brothers completed the house, surely stayed upstairs with the rest. If Samuel made the dormers an original feature of the house, then perhaps the little boy was already tall enough to stand at the windows of his room and look out on the rose gardens that his mother began to plant even before the house was finished. Mary Ellen's daughter Ellen, born sixteen years after Jefferson, would later pine that "the memory of the old home is to me 'like dew on a parched and withered garden.' "[11]

They all spoke of memories after the decades had taken their toll. With his life all but done, Jefferson Davis looked back to where his memories began and found little he could recall. He remembered, or was later told, how three of his brothers went off to serve when war with Britain broke out again. In 1814 an enemy invasion threatened New Orleans. The men of Woodville and Wilkinson County responded willingly to the call to arms. "One fact retained in my childhood's memories," Davis would write seventy-four years later, "is of [their] unparalleled devotion to their country." In fact, the county had to act to ensure that enough men remained home to protect women and children. He knew nothing of the particulars of the event or the war itself, "of which I have only the recollection of what a child would hear." What he retained of the event most of all was the knowledge that Southern men leapt to the defense of their hearths when threatened. Very possibly, too, in 1813 his father or brothers spoke at table of the summertime massacre at Fort Mims in Alabama, where some four hundred settlers fell to the clubs and axes of the Creeks because they were unprepared and betrayed. If young Davis thrilled or shuddered to stories of the tragedy, he came away from them with little prejudice toward the Indians; if they taught him a lesson in preparedness, he never afterward said.[12]

Meanwhile the happier memories of childhood grew. His next eldest sister Mary Ellen, called Polly, became his special friend. When the weather turned sour, the wide center hall of the house gave them ample space for play. But most often it was warm and sunny in southern Mississippi, and those days the children took the run of the cotton fields and poplar groves surrounding the house. Little Jefferson delighted in searching the orchard for the best and ripest fruit to give to his sister Lucinda. They climbed in a large pear tree in the garden corner, played on the wide front gallery, and, being children, they probably did not notice the ever-present fragrance of Jane Davis's rose hedges. Certainly everyone else did, enough so that Poplar Grove in time came to be called "Rosemont." So it remained.

The family must have been a warm one in the main. Certainly for the youngest child, being surrounded by all those older brothers and sisters virtually guaranteed him attention and affection. He became closest to his sisters, excepting only his eldest brother Joseph Emory, twenty-three years his senior and soon to practice law in Natchez some distance upriver. As for his parents, Jefferson Davis said very little in after years. Perhaps he merely took his model from his father, who said little of his own parents and relatives. Years later a young ward of Jefferson Davis recalled that "he had an utter contempt for what he called frippery (meaning genealogy) and never alluded to his progenitors." Davis never spoke at all of the grandfather Evan or of uncles that he knew of but never knew. To be sure, he spoke occasionally of his father Samuel, but whenever he reminisced with "deep and warm affection" he was talking about his brother Joseph.[13]

The problem, of course, to the extent that there was one with Samuel as a father, is that he was at least fifty when Jane presented him with Jefferson—more than old enough to be the boy's grandfather. Orphaned at an early age by the death of Evan Davis, he had enjoyed little or no fathering himself as a child, while the rapid growth of his own family, added to his constant moves and struggle to make a living, surely diminished the time and attention he could pay to being a father himself.

Certainly there was nothing brutish in Samuel Davis. He chose to instruct his children instead of punishing them. "His admonitions," remembered son Jefferson, "were rather suggestive than dictatorial." He taught by leading his offspring to make the right decisions—as he saw them—on their own without resort to the rod. Many decades later one of Jefferson Davis's children found the same trait in him. "My father was studiously careful to leave a power of decision with the very youngest, when it was possible," Winnie Davis recalled, "and even where that was not the case his commands were always given in the form of a suggestion that left us with the flattering sense of having freely chosen to do his will."[14]

Yet undoubtedly sometimes Samuel Davis did more than suggest. When children become parents themselves, they react in two ways to the parenting they received: Either they emulate it or they react against it by rejecting what they found mean or hurtful. For all Samuel's forbearance, some childhood behavior he did not tolerate well. One item, undoubtedly, was a little boy's reluctance to eat what was put before him while his elders ate something else. "If it is impossible for adults to deny themselves what is injurious to children when they are both at the same table," Jefferson Davis later told his own children, "it is unreasonable to expect children to suffer such a prohibition patiently." Perhaps Samuel was adamant about sending his children to their beds whether or not they were ready. With already "too much legislation in the world," his son later declared, "a healthy child's own instincts" were sufficient for him to know when to eat and sleep. Obviously, at a very early age "little Jeff" felt a well-developed spirit of independence and at least suspicion, if not resentment, of an authority that sought to curb what he conceived of as his rights.

He learned other things from his parents. He regarded lying as a crime and gluttony as a disgrace. He learned from hurts—real or imagined—suffered in his own youth, to feel empathy for what all children endure from adults. Perhaps it was being forced to run errands in the night, though afraid of the dark, that made him resolve never to compel his own children to do the same. Perhaps restriction to his room as punishment for some offense was what later made him look on the incarceration of children, for any reason, as "incomprehensible cruelty."[15] So much of those lost years of childhood consists of "perhaps."

Samuel Davis's aloof and sober manner with his children is fact. "My father was a silent, undemonstrative man," wrote Jefferson. "He was usually of a grave and stoical character, and of such sound judgment that his opinions were a law to his children." And real or assumed, there was a coldness in the man. He spoke very little with his family, and almost not at all among outsiders. Though he seemed capable of deep and affectionate feeling, Jefferson believed, "he sought to repress the expression of it whenever practicable." So seldom did Samuel openly show demonstrative love for his children that it took them by surprise when he did. In later years, when Jefferson spoke of his father, he revealed a natural desire to take pride in his parent by mentioning Samuel's reputation as a horseman and his respected place in the community. Yet it is clear from the little Jefferson Davis said, and from what he said, that he knew barely more than the shell of his father.[16]

Open love, warmth, affection—those came to him from his sisters, his brother Joseph, and from Jane Cook Davis. True to character, Jefferson said little of her either, but all of it he limned in words of tender recollection. Always he remembered her cheerfulness and kindness, her "graceful poetic mind." To the end of his life he cherished "a tender memory of the loving care of that mother, in whom there was so much for me to admire and nothing to remember save good."[17]

Samuel Davis preached to his children that "knowledge is power." He and Jane believed heartily in education, being well educated themselves for their time. Consequently there was never a question that young Jefferson would go to school. Unfortunately, in the Mississippi Territory schools were scarce and indifferent. Half a mile from Rosemont, near Woodville, stood a rude log schoolhouse, where, when he was six or seven, Jefferson went with his sister Polly. Any education there proved basic at best, and if anything he learned made an impression on the boy, he never thought it worthy of mention. Indeed, the only recollection he left behind from those school days dealt not with learning but, characteristically, with independence and bravery. Their daily path to the school took the boy and his sister through a dense wood on a dark and narrow road. As children often do, the boys and girls of Woodville settled on an odd local character as an object of mystery, rumor, and fear. A chair mender, fond of his dram, he was often seen wandering drunkenly along local roads with his day's work stacked atop his head. He was rude and difficult to the children, though never harmful, yet still they feared him.

One day as the two Davis children walked through the wood to school, carrying their lunch in a basket between them, they saw on the road ahead, dimly lit in the forested gloom, the telltale chair legs high in the air, portending the chair mender's approach. Most children would have taken to the trees. Not Jefferson Davis. "We will not run," he told his sister. Instead he took her hand and they stood still, awaiting the terror's approach. Soon fright turned to surprise as the supposed chair legs proved to be antlers on a magnificent buck who walked close to the two, looked curiously at them for a moment, then disappeared into the woods. It was not quite what his brothers had done in defending New Orleans against the British, but still "little Jeff" Davis had stood his ground. That meant a lot to him.[18]

If he approved of his son's mettle at that early age, Samuel Davis did not care for the rudimentary education available in Mississippi. Back in Kentucky there were good schools, even a university. Despite his accustomed reticence, Samuel discussed with Jane the idea of sending the boy away. Though she was adamantly opposed to having her youngest darling taken from her, in the end her opinion did not matter. Sometime in May or early June 1816, Samuel learned that Major Thomas Hinds would be taking his family to Kentucky. Without telling Jane what he was doing, and presumably without allowing her even to say farewell to her son, he sent his nine-year-old "little Jeff" away with the major and his family, off into the great wilderness along "the devil's backbone," the Natchez Trace.[19]

They made a small party, just Hinds, his wife, her sister, a niece, a maid, and a slave and young Howell Hinds, about Davis's age. The two boys rode ponies, and the whole party slept under the stars on their journey, living during the several-week trek on the supplies they had brought along. First they stopped in Natchez, just thirty-five miles north of Woodville. There they saw Joseph Davis, and perhaps he made up for his mother's inability to give Jefferson a warm and affectionate send-off. Here, too, his younger brother saw for the first time some of the increasingly grand mansions being built by the wealthy ruling elite, inaugurating a love for the high-ceilinged square rooms and wide porticos of the typical Southern planter that remained ever after his favorite architectural form.[20]

And then they were out on the Trace. It was the first great western wilderness road, built years before, out of necessity rather than convenience. Merchants and traders from Nashville and middle Tennessee found lucrative markets for their wares and produce in faraway New Orleans. They built flatboats of logs and floated themselves and their cargoes down the Cumberland and Tennessee rivers to the Ohio, then along it to the Mississippi, and down the great river. But for the return trip, they could not go upstream on their flatboats, and steam navigation would not be introduced until 1812. To get these flatboatmen back home, an inland highway was needed. Young America found it in a series of lesser paths that dated back to the time of the discoverer DeSoto and earlier. Even before the national capital moved to Washington, Congress haltingly provided legislation to improve this track, connecting Natchez with Nashville. Over it thousands moved to the growing Deep South; others returned to Tennessee, Kentucky, and the North; and at least a few took their living by preying on the travelers in either direction.[21]

When Major Hinds and his party set out from Natchez, as the Trace snaked slowly northeastward, they soon entered the so-called Choctaw Nation. Every day they met flatboatmen making the tiresome journey back to Tennessee. Indians, now peaceful for the most part, occasionally crossed their paths. The Choctaws, especially, could be considered safe since they made a boast, remembered by Davis, that they had never shed white blood.

Most nights the Hinds family simply wrapped themselves in their blankets and slept in the open. Occasionally they came to a "stand," a log inn or layover operated by frequently unscrupulous but always colorful characters. The first they encountered, just a few nights out of Natchez, belonged to one D. Folsom. Folsom's Choctaw wife quite possibly presented Davis with his first view of a racial intermarriage. A few nights later he found intermarriage again at Louis LeFleur's stand on a bluff overlooking the Pearl River, near latter-day Jackson, and yet again a few nights later in the stand at French Camp, another LeFleur cabin. When they finally left the northeast corner of Mississippi and crossed briefly into the corner of the Alabama Territory, they stopped at the stand and ferry operated by George Colbert on the Tennessee River. Colbert proved to be half Chickasaw. Perhaps Davis remembered it most because Colbert's house was so out of the ordinary for this frontier. One traveler likened it to "a country palace with its abundance of glass in doors and windows."[22]

Davis later recalled nothing more of this stretch of the Trace than that he had traveled it, and he mentioned nothing at all of the balance of the route through Tennessee to Nashville, not even of passing Grinder's Stand, where just seven years earlier the noted explorer Meriwether Lewis had died a violent and still-mysterious death. But perhaps all these memories made way as later events demanded space in Jefferson Davis's recollections, leaving room only for one transcendent experience he never forgot: Andrew Jackson.

Thomas Hinds had commanded a battalion of Mississippi horsemen under Old Hickory in the Battle of New Orleans and determined to visit his old commander at his home, the Hermitage, outside Nashville. So cordial was their host, and so pleasant the camaraderie, that an intended brief visit lasted into weeks, much to the delight of young Davis. "I had the opportunity a boy has to observe a great man," he recalled, "a stand-point of no small advantage." He found the hero "unaffected and well-bred," temperate in his language and behavior, and generous in the hospitality of his spacious log home, his grander mansion not yet built. He asked a blessing before each meal, and encouraged young Davis, Howell Hinds, and his own adopted son Andrew Jackson Donelson at all sorts of play, restraining them only from wrestling. "To allow hands to be put on one another," he told them, "might lead to a fight." Almost seventy years later those boyhood contests still stood out for Davis in "my remembrance of those early days." As for General Jackson himself, "little Jeff" always recalled that he was "very gentle and considerate." "In me he inspired reverence and affection that has remained with me through my whole life." Perhaps already the little boy sorely missed his mother, for as much as Jackson impressed him, Rachel Jackson seems to have left an even deeper, more personal imprint. "I have always remembered with warm affection the kind and tender wife who then presided over his house," Davis would write. "A child is a keen observer of the characteristics of those under whom he is placed, and I found Mrs. Jackson amiable, unselfish, and affectionate to her family and guests, and just and mild toward her servants."²³

With such associations setting his young mind swimming, Davis reluctantly resumed the journey northward into Kentucky. Finally in mid-July they reached Springfield, on the fringes of the "bluegrass" region forty miles southwest of Lexington. There on July 10, 1816, Hinds, or perhaps Charles Green of Mississippi, who acted as the boy's guardian while they were in Kentucky, deposited Jefferson Davis with the friendly dominies of St. Thomas College. With him went a payment of sixty-five dollars toward his first year's tuition.²⁴

St. Thomas was a Catholic boys' school run by Dominicans, and apparently run well. Though only about eight years old, it already held substantial property in fertile fields, livestock, a flour mill, and several slaves. Why an indifferent Baptist like Samuel Davis sent his son to a Catholic school is uncertain, but if it was for the stern discipline notorious at parochial institutions, he would be disappointed. "From whatever reason," his son recalled, "the priests were particularly kind to me." Perhaps it was because of his youth or the fact that he was the smallest boy in the school. Maybe it was because they chose to show more forbearance to one not of their faith (he was the only Protestant in the student body). Certainly the priests' treatment of him did not spring from a hope that he would convert to Catholicism. Young Davis himself first broached the subject. Thinking that he would do well to fit in better with the other boys by adopting their creed, he went to see Father Thomas Wilson. He found him just starting his simple meal and stated his intent. The kindly priest, soon to become another of the boy's idols, smiled and told him that conversion was a serious matter that could wait and handed over a biscuit and a bit of cheese, suggesting that Davis be satisfied with "some Catholic food."

One of the priests took a special liking to the little boy from Mississippi and put a small bed for Davis in his own room. Thus Father William Tuite may have felt a bit betrayed when "little Jeff" became party to a prank organized by the older boys. They persuaded Davis to blow out the light that burned in the room one evening. Then, in the darkness, they threw all manner of vegetables and biscuits, anything that came to hand, through the door and windows, bombarding poor Tuite. Of course, when the priest relit the light and looked for the culprits, all the boys appeared to be asleep—all but Jefferson Davis. "The priests interrogated me severely," he recalled, "but I declared that I did not know much and would not tell that." Even when Tuite strapped the boy to a cot used for punishing offenders, Davis remained mute, and the priest so loved the boy that he hesitated to strike him.

"If you will tell me what you know, no matter how little, I will let you off," said Tuite, thinking he had found a way out for both of them.

"Well," said Davis, seeing another way out. "I know one thing, I know who blew out the light."

Tuite seemed delighted, eagerly promising to let the boy go in return for any bit of information.

"I blew it out," said the boy. It was not what Tuite had hoped to hear, yet he could not go back on his promise to let Davis go. But before he freed him, the priest lectured him so sternly that Davis was reduced to tears and left too fearful or ashamed to be a party to any more such schemes.

By not becoming involved in pranks, the boy found more time for his studies, and there apparently he pleased everyone. His grasp of Latin and Greek astonished professors in his later schools, and he never lost his familiarity with ancient languages and literature. Certainly Samuel Davis saw sufficient progress in the boy to renew his tuition in May 1817 for another year, but as that second term closed, Jane Davis apparently became adamant. She wanted her son back, and her husband, for whatever reason, yielded.[25]

Much had happened by the summer of 1818. For one thing, Mississippi was no longer a territory but a state. More significant for the nation as a whole, the past year had seen steam navigation of the great river become safe, easy, and reliable. Thus there would be no long trek over the Natchez Trace for his return. Jefferson Davis took the steamboat *Aetna*, 360 tons and just three years old, out of New Orleans. Before leaving Louisville, the eleven-year-old showed his bold and unintimidated nature when a local thought to take advantage of the presumably ignorant boy. The man wagered nine cents that his pig could outspell Davis. The boy took the bet, went to meet the "learned pig," and discovered, as Davis later said, that "the pig spelled as well as his master could and no better." Nine cents richer, he embarked at Louisville on a "slow and uneventful" voyage down the Ohio, then south on the great Mississippi. Still it amused him to see the steamboat arouse such great curiosity that many people boarded it just to travel a few miles downstream before getting off and riding home in carriages. He watched the captain, a former seaman, and smiled at the speaking trumpet and spyglass that he still used from his oceangoing days. As for the scenery itself, Davis noted or remembered little of the river that would play a large role in the most important events of his later life. On his last day of the trip, with Natchez just eighty miles downriver, he probably did not even notice a wide westerly bend in the stream that enclosed choice wooded acreage ripe for cultivation. Years hence it would be called Davis Bend, but in 1818 it was just another loop in the river between him and Rosemont.

His brother Isaac met him at the landing, and together they walked into Woodville, where Isaac proposed a gentle sort of prank. While he remained behind, Jefferson walked on his own to Rosemont, intent on concealing his identity to see if his parents would recognize a boy who had grown considerably in two years. As he approached the house, the scent of the roses met him once more, and sitting out in the gallery was Jane Davis. Trying to maintain calm despite his throbbing heart, he said, "I asked her if there had been any stray horses round there." The only "stray" she had seen, she said, was this boy, and then with unconcealed emotion they leapt into each other's arms.

More remarkable was Samuel's reaction. Jefferson and his mother took a few minutes to regain their calm, and then the boy learned that his father was in the fields working with the slaves, as was his practice. The boy found him and took Samuel so much by surprise that the elder Davis forgot his usual grave and distant manner. "He took me in his arms with more emotion than I had ever seen him exhibit, and kissed me repeatedly." It was the only spontaneous gesture of unrestrained affection that Jefferson Davis ever recalled from his father. At the time, though, he mainly wondered "why my father should have kissed so big a boy."[26]

Of course, schooling was not over for young Davis just because St. Thomas lay behind him. His father sent him to Jefferson College in adjacent Adams County, not far from Natchez. "Little Jeff" did not stay there long, and it is just as well, for one of his few memories of the place was of an instructor whose chief method of teaching was to whip any boy who did not quickly learn his lessons. No doubt it pleased him when Woodville's citizens organized the Wilkinson County Academy and he could live at home and attend the new school. Thus, late in 1818 perhaps, he came back to his room at Rosemont and embarked on five years of daily studies.

The new academy impressed the student very favorably, chiefly because of headmaster John A. Shaw of Boston. "He was a quiet, just man," Davis remembered, "and I am sure he taught me more in the time I was with him than I ever learned from any one else." Shaw's arrival inaugurated a new class of teachers in the region, men who taught by logic and example, and not by the rod. When Davis compared him to the ignorant, teaching-by-rote men in the usual log schools of the day, Shaw shone like a star. Unlike the others, he was a university man, and under him mathematics, language, history, and perhaps the classics took on the air of something more than crude memorization of facts.

Still, the committing to memory of substantial information remained an integral part of education at the Wilkinson Academy, and on at least one occasion young Davis decided that he had been assigned more than was in his power. His teacher persisted in the assignment, however, and the next day, when Davis still had not mastered the material, there was talk of punishment. In his early teens by now, the boy gave one of the first manifestations of the willful independence that later caused him much trouble. He took his books and left the school, announcing to his father that he would not return.

Where many parents would have applied the birch themselves, Samuel Davis, in his accustomed way, told his son, "Of course, it is for you to elect whether you will work with head or hands." But, he said, "My son could not be an idler." More cotton pickers were needed in the fields, so he gave Jefferson a bag and sent him out with the slaves, where Samuel himself worked under the hot sun from dawn until dark. For two days the boy filled his bag, the conviction all the while growing stronger in his mind that this was not how he wanted to live. It was too hot, the work exhausting, and "the implied equality with the other cotton-pickers" soon convinced him that school was by far the preferable evil. He so stated to his father, who sent him back to the academy the next day with the admonition that "a man, gently bred, suffers when choosing a laborer's vocation."[27]

Education would not always be so troublesome for young Davis, and while he studied on at the academy he found other advantages that offset any discomfiture. His beloved sister Anna had married in 1816 and moved to St. Francisville, and he often rode the twenty miles to her home, Locust Grove, to visit and stay the night. Best of all, he was at home with his mother. Too old now to follow at her apron the way he had before he went to St. Thomas, still he could learn from her things that contributed to the formation of his character—her regard for truth, for justice, and for patience and generosity. Also, after his brother Joseph moved to Natchez, he had more and more opportunity to see and learn from him, to study Spanish with his neighbor and friend John Quitman, and to build a relationship that soon had Jefferson looking on his brother more as a father, perhaps more so than he looked on Samuel. "He was my beau ideal when I was a boy," the student recalled years later, "and my love for him is to me yet a sentiment than which I have none more sacred."[28]

There was also time to be just a boy in southern Mississippi—and few places better for it. He loved his dogs and horses; he could ride, and rode well; and of course Samuel Davis always had good mounts. Of fishing there was plenty, and good game for hunting, too, not all the deer looking like a drunken chair mender. He wrestled with the young slave men for fun, and he had his share of boyish confrontations with others of his age, revealing, as in the episode with the deer, that he was undeniably brave and combative and would not back down. Hunting one Saturday with his fowling piece, he ran out of shot and soon encountered a neighbor boy, Bob Irion. He, too, was hunting, but he was out of powder. Each had what the other needed, but when Davis asked for the loan or gift of some shot, the other boy refused, then became abusive, and finally threatened with his gun that, powder or no powder, he might shoot Davis anyhow. It was foolish teenage posturing, but Jefferson Davis could respond in kind. With a charge of powder already in his own weapon, he reached into his pocket, took out a small knife, dropped it down the barrel onto the powder, and leveled it at Irion. "Now, Sir, I'm ready for you," he said. "I dare you to shoot!" In the end the boys gave up the nonsense and exchanged powder and shot to their mutual satisfaction. His youthful presence of mind also revealed itself when a dog believed to be rabid bit a brother's leg, and Jefferson immediately sucked the presumed poison from the wound. How many other such episodes went unremembered no one said, but clearly Jefferson Davis's unyielding character was already well formed.[29]

The years passed quickly. At the academy Davis continued to stand out in Latin and Greek. His difficulty with memorization behind him, he mastered substantial lessons with relative ease and attracted the notice of Principal Shaw. The quicker his mind became, the more time that left for being a boy, and a friend recalled, "If there was any mischief afloat, he was always ready to take a hand." Yet he seems never to have forgotten his own sensitivities and how easily hurt he must have been when younger, for he refused to participate in pranks that might cause real pain, physical or mental. He stayed out of fistfights, mindful of Jackson's warning about laying hands on people. Instead he found himself called on frequently to arbitrate the disagreements of others. If he made enemies, he could not remember them. Though usually put in classes with older boys, still he was liked and accepted. That was important to him and always would be.[30]

By the spring of 1823 he was sixteen, still growing in mind and body, and outgrowing the Wilkinson Academy. That summer his father—apparently learning at last of his distant Pennsylvania relations —went east to Philadelphia in the hope of getting something out of the inheritance due his own father Evan Davis, though the matter was then more than sixty years old. Before leaving, however, Samuel arranged for his son to return to Kentucky, this time to Lexington, to continue his studies at Transylvania University, perhaps the most distinguished school west of the Alleghenies. Young Jefferson wanted to follow his brother Joseph into the law, and Transylvania was the perfect place to start.

As it happened, Samuel started his journey before his son did. About May 1, 1823, he and his servant James Pemberton said their farewells and prepared for the seven-week-long ride to Philadelphia. Though the elder Davis was then sixty-seven, he mounted his tall, restless horse by simply vaulting straight into the saddle. Then he was off. Jefferson Davis could not know then just how many farewells he was saying. He was never to see his father again, and when he left for Transylvania he would never again return to Rosemont as his home. Though only sixteen, he was bidding his boyhood good-bye.[31]

Boys, Put Away That Grog

Lexington, Kentucky, was a charmed place. Surrounded by lush meadows of bluegrass, it boasted the very cream of Western society. Here lived the Breckinridges and the Todds, the Morgans, the Hewetts, and a host of other local and national luminaries, not least of whom was the "great pacificator," "Harry of the West," Henry Clay. Its broad streets displayed scores of splendid mansions and town houses, while the farms and tobacco and horse plantations nearby offered homes that rivaled many of those Davis had seen in Natchez. The city was a center of trade, politics, and, most important, learning. Often called the Athens of the West, it boasted a university when most of the rest of the South was still unorganized territory and when Kentucky was still a part of Virginia.

The Virginia Assembly chartered the Transylvania Seminary in 1783, and the school itself opened six years later. The new Transylvania University finally opened its doors on its own land, right in the center of Lexington, in 1799, but endured years of financial and management difficulties until the selection of Dr. Horace Holley as its president proved to be its salvation. A brilliant administrator and educator, Holley soon attracted outstanding faculty and students, expanded the curriculum to the point at which it competed with some of the best Eastern colleges, and put the school on its way to financial stability. All this he accomplished in just the six years prior to the May or June 1823 arrival of one of his newest students, Jefferson F. Davis.[1]

The boys attending Transylvania did not board at the school but instead rented rooms in the homes of townsfolk. Young Davis hired lodging on the corner of High and Limestone streets in the home of

Joseph Ficklin, an old friend of Samuel's, just commencing his second year as Lexington's postmaster. In the cosy, two-story brick residence, Davis found a warm home. Mrs. Ficklin took a special liking to him and fed him well, ever regarding him as a "dear boy." Still, both Ficklins noted that, though only sixteen, he seemed dignified and formal beyond his years, more like a man of thirty. That was his father in him.[2]

That assumed air of dignity may also have been the result of nearly finding himself classed with boys younger than he, whereas he was accustomed to being the youngest in his class. Thus his mortification at discovering upon arrival at Transylvania that his mathematics were so deficient that the school wanted to admit him as a freshman. "I felt my pride offended at being put with smaller boys," he confessed. The only remedy was for Davis not to enter the school immediately but to take private lessons in math, improve his grasp, and then pass an examination in the fall that could put him where he belonged, with the entering juniors. Davis set himself a tough program but—helped by a kindly professor who gave him a lot of special time and pushed by his own determination to keep studying even when the professor fell ill and then went away during the summer recess—he persevered. Consequently, in the fall of 1823 he passed his examination and proudly entered the junior class.[3]

Lectures at Transylvania took place in the school building on Gratz Park, where four hundred students of all levels gathered each day to open their minds. More than half of those boys came from Kentucky, and of the balance all but forty came from slave states. A few of them also lived with Davis at the Ficklins', including James Monroe of Frankfort; Charles Morehead and Euclid Covington of Bowling Green, Kentucky; and a fellow Mississippian, Francis Richardson of Wilkinson County. Perhaps they all got along, but for his special friendships young Davis looked to others. He formed lifelong attachments with David Rice Atchison of Missouri and George W. Jones of Indiana, both several years his senior. Another student who greeted Davis was his playmate of several years before when he had visited the Hermitage, Andrew Jackson Donelson. Certainly he did not want for companionship.[4]

But of course he was there to learn, and when he actually began studies as a junior that fall, he faced a daunting curriculum. A junior's school week included classes in Latin, Juvenal, Livy, Latin verse, Greek, surveying, ancient and modern history, natural philosophy and astronomy, chemistry, writing, and speaking. That was a heavy load for a teenager from the Wilkinson County Academy. Fortunately, Davis's early grounding in Latin and Greek put him well ahead in the classics courses, and he found that he much enjoyed listening to Professor John Roche, who had studied at Trinity College in Dublin and whose pronunciation of the ancient languages the Mississippian found to be "the purest and best of our time."

Davis also did well in his history studies, being naturally inclined toward the subject and further inspired by Professor Robert H. Bishop's depth of knowledge and the keen insight he showed into human characteristics. Since Bishop taught biblical history as well, his fundamentalist concept of religion naturally manifested itself in his assertion that the Scriptures were to be taken literally in all things. Some of the boys disagreed, and when one giggled or mumbled during his religious lectures, Bishop gravely announced that "sobriety becometh the house of God." If a boy went too far, Bishop grasped a large ruler, laid the offender—despite his size—over his knee, and paddled him. To protests that university rules forbade the whipping of collegiates, Bishop declared that "every rule has its exceptions." Though Davis was never the boy being paddled, his own rules for conduct were still in embryo, hence these episodes made an impression on him.[5]

Every week the juniors made oral presentations, or "declamations." Ten were selected, so Davis must have been called on about ten times during the course of his junior year. Very probably it was his first experience at formal public speaking, aside from the recitations required at the Wilkinson Academy, and they were not speeches at all. No one recalled how well he did at Transylvania, though in later years he rarely showed either hesitation or shyness about addressing multitudes at length. In this respect, as in several others, Transylvania trained men for public life, and it is no wonder that future governors, senators, vice presidents, and presidents issued forth from Gratz Park.[6]

As a student Davis impressed his friends and fellow scholars by his studious application to his lessons. His friend Jones remembered him as "the most active, intelligent and splendid-looking young man in the College." Jones first met Davis in October 1823 and years later said that "at that time young Davis was considered by the faculty and by his fellow-students as the first scholar." Theodore Lewis, another classmate, also recalled the Mississippian as a "devoted" learner. "He was a good student," said Belvard Peters, "always prepared with his lessons, very respectful and polite to the President and professors." No one remembered that Davis was reprimanded for misbehaving or being unprepared, and even if their glowing recollections should be somewhat discounted for the passage of time and the reverence these men felt for Davis in their old age, it is clear nonetheless that in some degree he impressed his faculty and fellow students.[7]

Yet there were differences in how they saw him otherwise. Peters recalled that, though amiable, "he was rather taciturn in disposition" and rarely took part in sports and games. "Perhaps he did not choose to lose his time from his studies," Peters suggested. Or perhaps, like his father, young Davis found difficulty in being open and relaxed with others. To his innermost circle of close friends—and at Transylvania that meant Jones, Atchison, and Waller Bullock—he showed another personality. Only Jones left any account, but he declared that "at college, Mr. Davis was much the same as he was in after-life, always gay and buoyant of spirits." Already, though not yet seventeen, young Davis left people with very differing views of his nature. But there is little mystery as to which was the real Jefferson Davis, taciturn or gay. He was both—the one to informal acquaintances, and the other to his few intimates.[8]

Certainly he behaved at times like any teenager. While friends later claimed that he refrained from all manner of vice—drinking, smoking, gambling and the like—it is altogether likely that they sanitized their recollections and that Davis enjoyed at least some of the racier frolic most boys indulged in away from home, especially considering his behavior a few years after leaving Transylvania. The boy undoubtedly liked a good prank now and then, especially if it discomfited someone who assumed an air of importance or superiority. One such person, though not a student at the school, boarded for a time at the Ficklins'. He seemed to Davis to be "penetrated by esteem and respect" for himself, which naturally aroused his indignation.

One day an advertisement came to the *Lexington Reporter*, signed anonymously by "Many Voters" and appealing that the Ficklins' self-important lodger run for county sheriff in appreciation of his many gifts and attainments. Households everywhere in Lexington, including Joseph Ficklin's, buzzed with the question of who "Many Voters" was (or were). Meanwhile, at table, the object of all this controversy puffed himself up even more and commented haughtily that he had known that in time people would naturally think of him for an important office. At that remark, Ficklin happened to look at Davis. He saw the boy's red face and twitching jaw muscles as he suppressed a laugh and immediately guessed the authorship of the advertisement. When he called Jefferson out of the room, the boy confirmed his suspicions. It was the kind of prank or humor that Davis seemed to like, knowing something himself and watching others try to figure it out, just as he had tried to fool his mother on his homecoming from St. Thomas.[9]

As they will when men are young, the months passed speedily at Transylvania, and in later years Davis remembered far more of his friends than of his days of study, recitation, and examination. He learned as much as the faculty expected of him, however, for when the time came for the oral examinations each boy had to pass for admission to the next class, Davis presented himself well prepared. The examinations lasted for well over seven hours, with only a break for lunch. Even the townspeople turned out, making it a public event and adding an unfortunate extra measure of pressure on the boys, who had to "perform" in front of an audience as well as before their professors and fellow students. On June 4, 1824, when the examinations took place, Davis found himself a candidate for honors in at least one of his subjects. Attaining it, he was so proud that in later years it was one of the few achievements of which he modestly boasted. A reward for that honor was an invitation to deliver a speech at Transylvania's June 18 Exhibition, when the school annually displayed its faculty and outstanding students to the public. After preliminaries, eleven essays, critical dialogues and orations would be delivered. Davis was slated as the third speaker on the program, right behind a boy talking on the Love of Glory. For his own text, the Mississippian chose—or was assigned—an address on Friendship, a subject of which he had learned much at Transylvania. Nothing of his speech survives, but four days later the *Lexington Monitor* reported that "Davis on Friendship made friends of the hearers."[10]

Davis himself needed his friends just then. Only a few weeks earlier he received news from Mississippi that his beloved sister Mary Ellen, the "Polly" of his childhood, had died of unspecified causes on March 2. The first death in his immediate family, it was an especially hard one to bear as it always is for those too young even to imagine the grave. Yet how much more difficult the news must have been when followed at the end of July by a letter from his sister-in-law Susannah, Isaac Davis's wife. Much had happened back in Mississippi while he was away. Indeed, some of it had taken place while he was still at the Wilkinson Academy, though the taciturn Samuel Davis may not have shared much with his children.

Desperate financial difficulty faced Samuel Davis in 1822, thanks to his having agreed to act as security for a debt owed by his son-in-law Robert Davis. As a result he stood more than five thousand dollars in debt, and the only remedy he saw was to sell Rosemont and his few slaves to his prosperous lawyer son Joseph. Samuel still owed two thousand dollars from his own purchase of the plantation, and that plus the debt he had to pay because of his son-in-law's default was almost enough to ruin him. But then Joseph seems never to have paid out more than about five hundred dollars to his father for the property, and nothing for the slaves at all, leaving Samuel in even worse condition. It was in the vain attempt to improve his fortunes by tracking down that old inheritance from Evan Davis that Samuel left Rosemont and went to Philadelphia in the summer of 1823. The trip netted him nothing. "If I had applied some thirty year ago," Samuel wrote to his son at Transylvania that summer, "I might now have been immensely rich but I fear all is lost here by the lapse of time." If only he had known more, he lamented, explaining his admonishment to Jefferson to "use every possible means to acquire usefull knowledge as knowledge is power the want of which has brought mischiefs and misery on your father in old age."

His spirit broken by his misfortunes, Samuel Davis, now sixty-eight, worked in the spring of 1824 to put in another crop on the 256-acre plantation that now belonged to his eldest son. Joseph already owned another, larger plantation of several thousand acres in the great sweeping curve of the Mississippi his brother Jefferson had steamed past a few years before. Now people called it Davis Bend. When Samuel Davis fell out with his other son Samuel, the only boy remaining at home to work the cotton, he decided to take his field hands and go to Joseph's plantation. They reached the new city of Vicksburg, probably traveling overland, and were descending the Mississippi the few miles to Davis Bend when Samuel became very ill. Six days later, as Susannah Davis's letter now informed Jefferson, his father died.[11]

The news came as a blow that few seventeen-year-olds, even in those rough times, had to endure. Now Jefferson Davis remembered that the last time he had seen his father, Samuel had told him that they might not meet again. And in the sad, disturbing letter he sent his son from Philadelphia, he also mentioned the possibility that he might "never return or See you any more." Then on July 4, 1824, he had died. Perhaps the last words Jefferson Davis ever received from his father were the closing thoughts of that letter, a letter that, even twenty-three years later, he could not read without being so moved as to leave the room if anyone was present. "That you may be happy & shine in society when your father is beyond the reach of harm," wrote Samuel, "is the most ardent desire of his heart." When he signed it "Adieu my Son Jefferson," he clearly felt it might be his last farewell.[12]

Adolescence is often a time of melancholy for even the gayest of youngsters, but news like that borne by Susannah's letter sinks an especially heavy blow to the spirit. Jefferson Davis's reaction was anything but predictable. When he wrote to his sister-in-law to thank her for telling him, he devoted not more than four brief sentences to his father, and even those in such formal terms as, "In my Father I lost a parent ever dear to me," and, "I cannot describe the shock my feelings sustained, at that sad intelligence." Indeed, he did not try to describe his feelings. In those moments he was Samuel Davis's son, unable or unwilling to express his feelings, adopting the formal, taciturn manner his father invariably used at emotional moments. But then the facade broke down for a minute. As he confessed how hard it was to get this news so soon after the loss of Polly, he declared that "if all the dear friends of my childhood are to be torn from earth, I care not how soon I may follow." There, at least, his heart spoke.[13]

The hurt and confusion brought by the death of Samuel Davis only compounded what had already been an unsettling summer, unfortunate after the high spirits in which Jefferson's junior year closed. Barely two weeks after delivering his honors address on friendship, young Davis received an envelope from the national capital in Washington City that called for a decision. For unknown reasons, even before Jefferson went to Transylvania, his brother Joseph had for some time wanted him to attend the United States Military Academy at West Point, New York. Seeing the reverses suffered by their father, Joseph must not have wanted the uncertain life of a planter for his brother, though he went into planting himself. Tiring of the law, perhaps he did not want his favorite brother to follow him in that direction, either. The military was well on its way to becoming an acceptable and socially distinguished career for a Southern gentleman, and maybe Joseph sought that avenue of advancement for the boy. And it may simply have been that Jefferson's parents could not afford to keep him at Transylvania, while at West Point the government bore the expense of a student's education. Efforts to secure an appointment began in January 1823.

The student in Lexington wanted to finish his senior year there with his friends, and then perhaps move on to the University of Virginia to study law. But Joseph persuaded him sometime that spring that if an appointment could be secured, then young Jefferson should give the academy a try for one year. "It was no desire of mine to go," he said, but when Joseph urged, "I was not disposed to object." If he did not like it, then he could go on to Charlottesville. That was enough for his energetic older brother. Not without influence in Mississippi, thanks in part to his role in drafting its constitution, Joseph secured the appointment, and on March 11, 1824, Secretary of War John C. Calhoun issued Jefferson Davis a commission as a cadet. Because it was sent to Natchez first, it only found its way to Lexington in the first week of July, but Davis promptly made his final decision and wrote back to Calhoun accepting. Only in later years could Davis reflect that this simple note to the secretary of war marked the beginning of a singular relationship with Calhoun that shaped his destiny.[14]

He did not leave Lexington right away but remained until the latter part of August, hoping, no doubt, to enjoy a few last weeks with his friends. News of his father's death marred that, of course, and also Davis worried about his status as an incoming cadet. Here at Transylvania he would have been commencing his senior year. By going to the academy he would be reverting to the status of a freshman. It was certainly not the last time that he fretted over his position versus others.

Whatever the reasons he delayed leaving for West Point, he almost waited too long. Most cadets entered in June, and staff expected all to be present by September 1, when they assigned classes. Davis arrived sometime after that date, to find that all the candidates had been admitted before him and were already at their studies. He faced an inflexible rule that barred any late admissions. Only the fortuitous intercession of Captain Ethan Allan Hitchcock, who met Joseph Davis during a tour of duty at Natchez, remedied the impasse. Because another former cadet who had been in France for a year was being given a special examination for reentry, Hitchcock persuaded the superintendent to allow Davis to be examined at the same time. Passing the examination would get him admitted despite the rules.

Hitchcock took some special pains instructing Davis what to expect. Mathematics, particularly, concerned him, and he gave the boy a book, probably the Frenchmen Lacroix and Bezout's *Treatise on Plane and Spherical Trigonometry*, then in use at the academy for first-year cadets. But Davis barely started to look through the book when the order summoning him before the examining board arrived. To his immense relief, the "examination" proved to be almost rudimentary. The professors asked a few questions about algebra and geometry that he answered easily. He demonstrated a fair command of French, more than they expected. And when he showed his fluency in Greek, the professor forgot that he was supposed to be testing the lad and launched into a discussion with him about the construction of the language. Superintendent Sylvanus Thayer had to interrupt it, and that ended the session. Stunned at how little knowledge he felt he had displayed, Davis thereafter "never believed that an examination formed a very conclusive rule of decision upon the qualification of a person subjected to its test." Perhaps so, but conclusive or not, that "test" made Jefferson Davis a cadet.[15]

The military academy had endured a troubled career since its founding in 1802. Perched high above the Hudson River at a spot once used as a military installation by Washington during the Revolution, it almost succumbed to petty squabbles among army officers and the parsimony of a Congress and people who always distrusted a professional military and objected to giving free education to boys who got their appointments by political preferment. The performance of the first graduates in the second war with Britain helped to change that attitude, and the arrival of Thayer as superintendent turned the school around even more. He found and recruited generally outstanding professors, modeled the curriculum on the most current European, and especially French, patterns, and dramatically improved the discipline of the corps of cadets. By 1824 the academy had become an institution in which Thayer and the Congress took pride, and it was attracting the sons of the finest families in the nation.

There were 259 cadets including Davis when he began his studies at West Point. They lived three and four to a room in one of the barracks, issued little more than their uniforms and a paltry sixteen dollars per month in pay with which they had to buy everything else—furniture, personal items, buckets, brooms, and mops. They also received an additional twelve dollars per month for "rations," though regulations severely limited what they might bring into their rooms. Indeed, regulations governed their every moment. They were told when they could rise, when they must put out their lights and go to bed, where their brooms had to be kept, how to clean their floors, how to clean and keep their bedding, how to wear their hair, and even what they were allowed to read. Any failure to meet these regulations, at any time, constituted an "offense" that went on the cadet's record. In his very first month at West Point, September 1824, Davis appeared on a list with eighty-three other cadets who were "distinguished for Correct Conduct" with no offenses. Of course, for him it was a short month, and he rarely afterward saw a month with no demerits.[16]

In that first year at West Point, Davis and the other incoming cadets studied mathematics and French exclusively in their nonmilitary curriculum. Six hours every day they had to devote to algebra, calculus, geometry, trigonometry, and analytic geometry. In French they spent three hours a day, studying grammar and vocabulary and then reading Voltaire's history of Charles XII. In addition they translated much of their French reading into English, largely, no doubt, to enable them later to read and master the French military manuals that most nations then regarded as preeminent. Only aside from those nine hours in the classroom did Davis have time for the drill and details that formed the military part of a first-year cadet's day. It was a grueling pace, and intentionally so, designed to weed out the weak or uncertain and to instill an instinctive obedience and unquestioning acceptance of commands.[17]

Jefferson Davis gave ample proof that the spirit of independence in these boys died hard. On October 17, in his first full month at the academy, he disobeyed an order and was cited for an offense, while twice missing a guard mounting. In November he disobeyed another order, and two times an officer caught him in another cadet's room during study hours, when regulations required that he remain in his own quarters. In December and January 1825 he may have gotten by with no offenses at all, but a year passed before he again attained a spotless record. The kinds of offenses he committed are ample testimony to a spirited, willful, and somewhat careless young man. He was often absent from his quarters or caught in the rooms of other cadets. He arrived late at parade drill or else missed it altogether. He did not keep his quarters in order, misplaced his fireplace fender, failed to close his door, and forgot to put up his cot in the morning after reveille. Even though regulations allowed a cadet a considerable amount of freedom in choosing how to wear his hair, still on April 24, 1825, he earned a demerit for having it too long, most likely because he could not afford to have someone cut it.[18]

In fact, like most of the cadets, Davis found that he could not live on the pay and allowance he received. Eventually many of the young men went into debt to the tailors who made their clothing and the local merchants from whom they bought food and other items. In part their pay was insufficient; also, being young, they squandered much of it. By January 1825, even though regulations forbade receiving any outside funds, Davis was financially embarrassed and wrote to his brother Joseph requesting some cash. Just why Jefferson needed the money he did not say, but he may have given a hint when he said to Joseph that he hoped generally that his monthly pay would meet his needs, "which however depends entirely upon the company I keep." He did not say just who he kept company with, though he made it clear with whom he did not associate. "The Yankee part of the corps find their pay entirely sufficient," he wrote, "but these are not such as I formed an acquaintance with on my arrival . . . nor are they such associates as I would at present select." It was his earliest statement of any perceived differences between the men of North and South, and he did not see the Northerners flatteringly. "You cannot know how pittiful [sic] they generally are," he said in an expression that betrays more of immature overstatement than deep-rooted prejudice.[19]

If Jefferson Davis did not associate in that first year with young men from the North, however, he could only have taken as his friends cadets from the South. Implicit in his statement to Joseph is the hint that these boys lived a looser, freer, more expensive kind of life at West Point, as indeed many of them did. Davis's own roommate was Walter B. Guion of Mississippi, who would be dismissed three years after he and Davis began their studies, and who at one point apparently attempted to shoot Captain Hitchcock. Another roommate was A. G. W. Davis of Kentucky. Three of his close friends would later be dismissed for drinking, while fellow classman R. C. Tilghman of Maryland, and a friend in the next class, Thomas Drayton of South Carolina, were also frequently in trouble for insobriety. Fortunately, Davis formed some close and lasting friendships with upperclassmen who provided better models of conduct. Albert Sidney Johnston of Kentucky, five years Davis's senior, had left Transylvania University just a year before the Mississippian arrived there. Somehow the two discovered at West Point that they had that school in common, and this was sufficient introduction to begin a friendship destined to grow through the years. Johnston, in turn, introduced Davis to his close friend Cadet Sergeant Major Leonidas Polk of North Carolina. Proudly Davis later recalled that "we belonged to the same 'set,' a name well understood by those who have been ground in the

Academy mill." That even in his last years Davis spoke of Johnston's early friendship with pride betrays the reverential admiration and love he felt then for the older cadet who befriended him, and for Polk as well. These were not merely friends a youth skylarked with; they were idols to whom the Mississippian looked up, proud and flattered to be allowed into their "set."[20]

Davis should have spent more time admiring Johnston and Polk and less under the influence of his younger and less-disciplined companions. Among the offenses that steadily mounted on his record appeared other, more serious, infractions than a misplaced fender. Teasingly, perhaps, he wrote to Joseph in the fall of 1824 that he might find himself in trouble if his offenses continued, and his brother re-:ponded with a warning, perhaps just as good-natured, about staying out of the guardhouse. Even while breaking regulations by asking Joseph to send him money, Jefferson promised that "I trust ever to have enough prudence to keep from being confined." It was a misplaced trust.[21]

By the spring of 1825 officers cited Davis for being absent from his quarters for long periods of time—up to four hours. He missed parades and drills. In April, starting from a perfect record the previous September, he found his name on a list with fifteen others as having the greatest number of offenses in the corps. Just where Davis went on those absences no one said, just as the cause of his running short of money remains a mystery, but chances are that both had something to do with Benny Havens.[22]

In West Point's early years, arriving cadets stayed at Gridley's Hotel before moving into their barracks, but frequently when on leave they returned to Gridley's for good meals and drink. The food at the academy, after all, had little to recommend it. One of Davis's friends, Cadet Ormsby M. Mitchel, wrote that their soup was bad, they were given molasses that was "filthy," and for dessert were presented "some black looking stuff contained in a tin pan which was honored with the name of pudding." No wonder the young men sought something better off the post, but then the government bought Gridley's to make it into a hospital, and the boys were left with an entertainment vacuum. Not for long. Benny Havens kept a small house down on the bank of the Hudson. His business had not included much from the academy until the closing of Gridley's. "From this time," Cadet Albert Church remembered, "he became *an institution*." At once the cadets rushed to Benny Havens's establishment, and for years he held a virtual monopoly of their off-post food-and-drink custom. The only problem was that off post was also off limits.[23]

Davis knew better. On May 21, 1825, six cadets turned up missing. Captain Hitchcock found them at Benny Havens's and arrested them.

Brought before a court-martial, all were dismissed, though by order of the president they were all allowed to remain with a reprimand. Leaving the post violated the 1415th paragraph of the General Army Regulations, and the 1408th paragraph forbade bringing alcohol onto the post or going into any public house off the post without the superintendent's permission. The regulation clearly defined what was prohibited as "wine, porter, or any other spiritous or intoxicating liquor," and it specified dismissal for any infraction.[24]

On July 31, 1825, with classes over and the corps in its summer field encampment, a heavy rain drenched the ground and flooded Davis's tent as well as those of others. When the bugle sounded for the young men to disperse due to the rain, the Mississippian encountered four other cadets "who like myself," he said, "were at a loss to know what to do." Thus, he continued, "urged by circumstances," they "wandered too far." They "wandered" two miles to Benny Havens's tavern. There at least most of them spent a jolly time drinking wine, porter, and cider, missing their evening parade, and at least a couple showed visible intoxication when Captain Hitchcock suddenly walked into the taproom and confronted them. Each reacted in his own way, but Davis immediately exhibited "extreme embarrassment bordering upon weakness." While Hitchcock saw the other cadets with drinks before them, he did not certainly see Davis with a glass, but the captain inferred from the cadet's behavior, not to mention his associates and surroundings, that he, too, had been drinking. At once he arrested them and put them where Jefferson Davis had thought himself too prudent to be—the guardhouse.

The next day, the infraction having taken place on a Sunday, the post adjutant formally arrested the five offenders, and on August 2 their court-martial began, presided over by Captain William J. Worth. Davis first appeared in the role of a witness for the defense of one of the other cadets, and in cross-examination declined to say more than that he had been with that cadet on that day. "I cannot answer further without criminating [sic] myself," said Davis. Then he went on to testify that he had never seen Cadet Theophilus Mead take a drink during the past year. When the trial continued the next day, Davis elaborated by saying that he believed Mead did drink wine, cider, and porter, "which, of course I did not understand to be spiritous liquors." It was like the prank of the vegetable bombardment at St. Thomas years before when "little Jeff" blew out the light. He split hairs, just as he had in his "confession" to the priest, only this time he adhered to a strict definition of "spiritous" to mean distilled spirits. A few minutes later, when it came time for his own case, he went even farther in trying to pettifog over tiny points. Charged under regulations just a few weeks old, he maintained he had not seen them. These were the regulations that specified "wine, porter, or any other spiritous or intoxicating liquor" as being forbidden. He

believed that he should be tried under the 1823 regulations that prohibited "wine or spiritous liquors" and visiting establishments that sold
them. The distinction, if any, was a fine one, and in any case the court
decided that the new regulations should apply.

Faced with the charges against him, Davis pleaded guilty to going
beyond the limits of the post without permission and to visiting Benny
Havens's. However, he pleaded not guilty to drinking "spiritous and
intoxicating liquor." As was the custom, Davis conducted his own defense, extracting from Hitchcock an admission that he had not *seen* Davis
with a drink, only that he *appeared* to have been drinking. At the same
time Hitchcock also testified that the accused's behavior previously had
been good and gentlemanly. There matters remained until the next
morning, August 4, when Davis delivered his defense.

He complained that he spoke "with feelings of the greatest embarrassment," not because of his infractions but because he was being tried
ex post facto by regulations he had been unaware of at the time of his
visit to Benny Havens's. In short, he argued that ignorance of the law
was an excuse. He then maintained that the rain that Sunday in some
measure justified him in leaving the post and suggested that their arrival
at the tavern was more by accident than design. As for his embarrassment and visible distress when Hitchcock entered Havens's, "the fact of
being caught was certainly enough to have confused any Cadet," and this
argument was well made. Unfortunately, by his use of the word "caught,"
Davis clearly revealed a sense of having committed some kind of offense,
which rendered almost ludicrous his next argument, namely that Benny
Havens's was not strictly a "public house."

It would not be difficult to imagine his judges smiling behind their
scowls as the defendant admitted that liquor was sold at Havens's, but
that he thought that "a matter of the smallest importance." Declining to
apply a "strict construction" to regulations, as some Southern statesmen
were already arguing should be done with the Constitution, he opted for
an implied construction that the wording of the regulation prohibiting
cadets from visiting public houses was really meant to apply only to those
who "visited such a place and *bought* spiritous liquors." There was a hair
thinly sliced to be sure, and the court did not buy it, even after his
concluding appeal that they remember the maxim, "Better a hundred
guilty should escape than one righteous person be condemned." The
court quickly found him guilty on all charges and ordered him dismissed.[25]

It convicted all the others as well, though it recommended pardon
for Davis and one other, and Secretary Calhoun approved. Despite
spending all of August under arrest, even then Davis managed to garner
one offense. The evening of his last day before the court-martial, having
heard himself pronounced guilty and sentenced to dismissal, Davis must

have been confused or resentful. At evening parade he got into the wrong rank in the formation and was caught. It was a rather discouraging time for a cadet who had only recently learned that back at Transylvania that spring, during a holiday celebration, his old friend Waller Bullock had proposed a toast "to the health and prosperity of Jefferson Davis, late a Student of Transylvania University, now a Cadet at West Point—May he become the pride of our country, the idol of our army." Just then, the pride of that idol felt pretty wounded.[26]

At least there had been a few more cheerful events in the past year. For one, there had been the September 1824 visit of the Marquis de Lafayette, one of the greatest living revolutionary heroes. His reception was the first real military pageant Davis would have witnessed. The marquis reviewed the entire corps of cadets, and with him came leading army officers, a number of militia officers, and other venerable veteran officers of the War of Independence. General Jackson, too, soon to be president, inspected the corps. Just a few weeks before Davis's debacle at Benny Havens's was the annual July 4 dinner given by the cadets, to which they invited their officers and professors. Authorities lifted the ban against alcohol for such an occasion, leaving many a boy the worse for the evening, and giving some of them a taste for Havens's wares. The date also marked the first anniversary of Davis's father's death, and he needed a diversion.[27]

Certainly the Mississippian found no cause for melancholy in his academic performance. He never led his class in anything, but he gave an acceptable account of himself in mathematics at the end of his first semester, ranking fifty-fourth out of ninety-one in his class, and earned a nearly outstanding nineteenth place in French. By the end of his first year, twenty members of his class had dropped out or been dismissed, and he stood forty-third in math and eighteenth in French. By the weighting system then employed at the academy, Davis finished his year with an overall standing of thirty-second, just into the top half of his class. It was not easy to get there. The examinations given the young men could be daunting. The questions they faced included being asked to "determine the figure of the voussoir of an annulo-radient grain," or to "analyze a curve from its most general equation, find the points of rebroussement, of inflection, and where the tangents are parallel or perpendicular to the axis of Abscipa." They also had to demonstrate similar practical knowledge of the application of math in such things as determining the working of canal locks.[28]

It was a lot for young men their age to master, but Davis did it well enough to pass from the fourth class up to the third on July 1, 1825. Two weeks later a real treat came to him when he obtained a six-day leave. The past January his brother Joseph had written that he would be coming to West Point to visit in July, and an anxious Jefferson Davis, his leave in his pocket, eagerly awaited his arrival. Watching for the boat that brought his brother up the Hudson, young Jefferson ran down to the landing and literally caught Joseph in his arms. Then, recovering his composure, and perhaps remembering how his father would have behaved, the cadet simply slipped his arm inside Joseph's and sat down next to him, with no further signs of feeling or affection thereafter except an occasional silent squeeze of his arm. Joseph and his friends, Mr. and Mrs. William Howell of Mississippi, saw in the lad a boy "very stout" (by which they surely meant "tall" or "strong") and "florid," with blue eyes and a strong figure. Margaret Howell was struck by his "open bright expression," while her husband remarked that he seemed a "promising youth." The visit, all too brief, was surely the highlight of Cadet Jefferson Davis's summer.[29]

He was nearly fully grown by now. Though almost no contemporary description of him survives, he probably fulfilled the recollection, years later, of one of his classmates, who remembered that "his figure was very soldier-like and rather robust; his step springy, resembling the tread of an Indian 'brave' on the war-path." Though he may have had a bit of growing still ahead of him, he must already have been what most observers called "tall," somewhere approaching six feet. One thing that certainly the academy impressed upon him was erect carriage. For the rest of his life, even into old age, acquaintances remarked on his ramrod-straight posture.[30]

Perhaps his experience with Benny Havens taught the young man a lesson for a time, for his conduct during his year as a third classman was, if not exemplary, somewhat better. Most of his demerits came from missing drills, keeping his quarters messy, skipping chapel, and putting his belongings in improper places. His youthful spirits got the best of him at least once; on May 2, 1826, he injudiciously fired his musket out his barracks window, probably into the air, and quite likely on a dare. Still, in January 1826 he managed an entire month without an infraction—or without being caught—and did so again in February. His classwork also showed improvement, as drawing had been added to the French and mathematics of the previous year. Midway through the term he stood thirty-fourth in math, sixteenth in French, and twenty-third in drawing, out of a class of fifty-three. At year's end, in June 1826, he moved up two places in math and one in drawing, placing himself twenty-ninth overall in a class that now numbered forty-nine. French remained his best field of performance, and he never lost his French, though it was a reading command only. He always pronounced it as if it were English. His standing in math, plus the shrinking size of the class, combined to put him a little over the line into the bottom half, but still he did well enough to receive an appointment as fourth sergeant of his company for the summer encampment.[31]

He made more friends. Sidney Johnston graduated in 1826 and left for active service. Polk still had another year at the Academy. Meanwhile Davis formed a close attachment with Alexander D. Bache, a great-grandson of Benjamin Franklin, and found that this natural-born educator had "a power of demonstration beyond that of any man I ever heard." Davis believed that Bache shared the genius of his distinguished ancestor. Another close friend, Cadet William H. C. Bartlett of Missouri, denied any genius at all, though he led his class. Davis should have profited by the example of these more serious students, for his third, or second-class, year almost proved to be his undoing and even his death.[32]

He began it with a prank when he and twenty-one other cadets were detailed for a week's duty at the laboratory presided over by Lieutenant Zebina Kinsley. For whatever reason, Davis believed that Kinsley had previously taken a dislike to him on sight, the sort of instinctive prejudice that a boy often imagines in a strict or too-exacting professor. Davis even believed that the lieutenant intentionally attempted to catch him in errors of recitation. Since Kinsley enjoyed considerable popularity with the other cadets, the most logical explanation would be that any animosity, if it truly existed, came from something in Davis's behavior and not from a prejudice. Certainly, if the Mississippian tried any of the haughty hair-splitting that he used with his court-martial, the professor could well have decided to deflate this sometimes priggish young cadet if given the chance. One day he did certainly make a pointed reference to the subject of presence of mind, and seemed by word and gesture to indicate that he doubted that Jefferson Davis possessed much.

Then came their week at laboratory. Kinsley instructed the class on the making of incendiary fireballs. Accidentally one of them took fire when Kinsley was not looking, and Davis himself pointed to the flame and asked, "What shall I do, sir?" Kinsley's only response, apparently, was, "Run for your lives," after which he ran for his. Davis, meanwhile, showed a fair amount of presence of mind and simply threw the fireball out a window before it posed a danger of igniting all the other explosives in the laboratory. The act won him the admiration of many, including his friend Thomas Drayton, who believed that "Jeff, by his presence of mind, saved many lives and also the building from being demolished." These were the kind of stories that schoolboys reveled in remembering and expanding on in later years, and there was still some schoolboy in Davis and his classmates.[33]

Perhaps too much. His brush with Kinsley in the laboratory occurred in July 1826. Not more than a month later he gave in to the lure of Benny Havens's again. This time he went with his friend Cadet Emile La Sere. They had in mind "a little frolic" and naturally did not have leave to indulge in one. How much "frolic" they enjoyed is not known, but when a report that a professor was approaching the tavern reached their ears, the two of them ran from Havens's at full speed. Not wanting to risk the main lane, since the professor would likely approach that way, they took a shortcut up a steep bank. Perhaps Davis had enjoyed a bit too much of what he defined as nonspiritous liquor—cider, wine, or porter—or maybe he simply lost his footing. Either way, he plummeted sixty feet down the bank, only breaking his fall by grasping a tree as he flew past. It tore his hands severely, while the fall itself probably left him at least with a concussion and probably some internal injuries as well. La Sere yelled down, "Jeff, are you dead?" Davis felt an initial desire to laugh at the ridiculous question but suffered so much pain that he could do nothing more than signify, by raising one of his bleeding hands, that he was still among the living.

Just how Davis explained his serious injuries, without "criminating" himself for another visit to Benny Havens's, he never said. Certainly he did find himself confined to the post hospital for most of the next four months, where for a time he believed "I was about to die." So serious did the doctors find his condition that they severely limited even visits from his friends, until in November he showed signs of recovery. At least the hospital stay kept him out of mischief, and from August through October he enjoyed a spotless record for behavior.[34]

Apparently only hospitalization or death could have kept him out of trouble that year. Christmas, and tradition, almost finished him at the academy. For years cadets had been in the habit of giving parties on Christmas morning, before reveille. Superintendent Thayer tried to suppress the practice but with only indifferent results. As 1826 drew to a close, the frolic started on Christmas Eve, when Davis and several other cadets were not in their rooms after church, as regulations required. Several days earlier some of the cadets had laid plans for their party and appointed Davis and Tilghman to "procure such articles as were necessary for a drinking party," which they would hold in Robert Sevier's room. That is probably where Davis was on Christmas Eve, down at Havens's buying the whiskey and eggs and such for the traditional eggnog. Somehow that night they brought the ingredients back into their barracks, and very early the next morning, perhaps as early as 1 A.M., the mixing and drinking began. Certainly it was still dark when Davis offered Sevier his first cup. Though no one later testified to seeing Davis himself drinking, it is certain that he did. After dawn, between 6:00 and 6:30 A.M., Cadet Edgar Lacey heard considerable noise coming from the room next to his—Davis's. "From the language he used I supposed him to be intoxicated," said Lacey, and almost surely he was—perhaps very intoxicated, and that drunkenness may just have saved him.

Around 4 A.M., with the party in full swing, the ever-vigilant Captain Hitchcock heard a lot of walking in the halls of the barracks and decided to investigate. In time the noise led him to Room Number 5 on the second floor of the North Barrack. Stepping inside, he found some thirteen cadets, including Sevier and Davis's roommate Walter B. Guion. Hitchcock ordered all the cadets who did not belong there to return to their rooms, and some of them may have left. Then he looked around the room and asked that some trunks be opened, no doubt expecting to find the liquor there. Just as he was doing so, Jefferson Davis came running into the room and did not see the captain, who stood at the back of the crowd. Davis ran up to the fireplace and anxiously announced, "Boys, put away that grog. Capt[ain] Hitchcock is coming." Only then did he discover that Captain Hitchcock was already there. The officer walked up to Davis and ordered him to return to his room immediately, under arrest. Meekly the young man did as he was ordered and was soon asleep, except for a few minutes later in the morning when Lacey heard him talking, or perhaps being ill, in his quarters in Room Number 19 in the South Barracks. Meanwhile the other cadets had not gone back to their rooms. Instead a virtual riot broke out in which they used clubs and other weapons to drive the officers out of the barracks or into their own quarters. As Davis slept, his roommate Guion came to their quarters and took a pistol, apparently intending even worse mayhem.

Only after considerable difficulty, and a lot of damage to the barracks, did officials quell the "egg-nog riot." They arrested twenty-three cadets and placed them in confinement. The subsequent court of inquiry took a great deal of testimony, including Davis's, which contributed little to the case other than the fact that Guion had taken out a pistol. Late in January a general court-martial sat in judgment on nineteen of the boys implicated in the riot. Davis narrowly averted inclusion thanks to ample testimony, including Hitchcock's, that he had gone to his room before the riot broke out and did not participate. All nineteen were dismissed. Clearly the entire episode was a great embarrassment to Davis for years afterward. He spoke of it at all only to most intimate associates, and even then he gave an account highly flattering to himself, maintaining that he got in trouble for refusing to name Guion and therefore "was implicated unjustly." In fact, he pointed the finger at Guion twice when questioned, an act that the code of honor he lived by in later years would have damned as reprehensible. Rather than admit that he had, after all, only told the truth under oath, he chose instead either to invent a fiction or else to put the truth out of his memory.[35]

Certainly Davis remembered at the time how close he had come to being among those dismissed. All he got for his part in the affair was six weeks' arrest, and for a time the experience scared him thoroughly. From January through March 1827 he received but a single demerit. At his examinations in January he finished twenty-ninth of forty-three classmates in natural philosophy, twenty-third in chemistry, and thirty-ninth in drawing, clearly in the bottom half everywhere. By the end of the year

his standing had changed very little, and he finished twenty-ninth overall, in a class now down to thirty-seven. All in all it had been a terrible
year.[36]

Thankfully, in his last year he stayed out of serious trouble, though
there was a rumor that he got into a fistfight with second classman Cadet
Joseph E. Johnston of Virginia, over Benny Havens's daughter.
"Johnston, being heavier but not so tall," said the rumor, "gave Davis the
worst of the fight." Perhaps—but if so, it is the only instance of Davis
breaking Jackson's advice about avoiding fights. Otherwise he kept
mostly to his studies, which now included tactics, fencing, and more
"Pyrotechny" with Professor Kinsley. Still, he could not stay entirely out
of trouble, and on June 5, 1828, with the year and his West Point attendance virtually completed, he absented himself from his quarters after
the evening taps. No doubt by this time in their West Point careers, a lot
of fellow first classmen felt like celebrating the end of their years as
cadets. The watchful officers like Captain Hitchcock managed to catch a
few, and among them Cadet Davis, who did not return to his room until
midnight. The next day the post adjutant ordered him placed under
arrest and confined to his quarters. It was not exactly a distinguished
end to his academy days, but then his had not been a very distinguished
career there: repeated infractions, several arrests, one court-martial conviction and very nearly a second, a mediocre academic record, and the
near loss of his life when breaking the rules. To be sure, there was
nothing unique in his performance. Almost every cadet transgressed at
least occasionally. The grimy interior of Benny Havens's probably saw a
majority of the young men at some time or other in their academy
career. For most, as for Davis, these were their first years away from
home, and even if military discipline could be much more severe than
parental controls, they all felt the natural urge to exert some independence. Good, bad, and indifferent, they were all boys becoming men.

Probably it occasionally troubled Davis that he did not finish with
an exemplary record like that of his friend Sidney Johnston, who graduated 8th in his class, or that in every respect he finished way below the
two Virginians in the class behind him, Joseph E. Johnston and Robert
E. Lee. The Mississippian's final standing for his four years was 23rd in
a class that had dwindled down to thirty-three. That put him in the
bottom third. Worse was his standing for conduct in the corps as a
whole, 163rd out of 208, well into the bottom fourth. But he was done.[37]

Before he got there, Jefferson Davis never desired to attend the
military academy. When he did go, it was chiefly to please his brother
Joseph, and then only for a year's trial. He amply demonstrated in his
record of offenses that he resented substantial authority and could not
yet control his own spirit of independence. When caught and questioned
on his conduct, he never admitted actual wrongdoing but rather ratio-

nalized his behavior and resorted to fine points or technicalities to exonerate himself. If haughty and prone to be priggish, he also loved fun, made close and lasting friendships, and was one of those looked to for active participation whenever his friends concocted some new scheme for mischief. While he came close to excelling in French, he never conquered mathematics and gave equivocal performances in engineering and other sciences. But that did not matter greatly. West Point was a test of, and training ground for, character. It changed men or helped them to find themselves. It changed Davis. "The four years I remained at [W]est Point made me a different creature from that which nature had designed me to be," he told a sister less than a year after graduating. Just what he felt nature had intended him to be, he could not say yet, but for better or worse, now he was convinced that West Point had made him into a soldier.[38]

3

Something of a Martinet

He would be an infantryman. Men who finished in the lower ranks of their classes at the academy always were. His actual promotion came on July 1, 1828, a brevet second lieutenant of infantry. Brevets were an odd sort of rank. In the tiny United States Army of that time, with only a few regiments, Congress strictly limited the number of officers. Thus newly commissioned West Point graduates waited until a vacancy opened in their branch of service before receiving their regular army commission. While waiting, they held brevet rank only. Sometimes the wait could be a long one. For Davis it lasted nearly three years.

To give the young officers a much-needed rest after their four years of discipline, as well as allowing the army time to decide what to do with them, a lengthy furlough after graduation became traditional. Late in June the academy sent Davis off on a sixty-day leave, and soon thereafter the War Department in Washington extended the furlough through October 30. Instead of going home right away, however, Lieutenant Davis went to Lexington, Kentucky, and remained at least through most of September. After so many years away from Woodville and Rosemont, it seems odd that he would not return immediately. No one knows where he went on his way to Lexington. Perhaps he saw a little of New York City. Maybe he stopped in Philadelphia to see where his grandfather was born, and where his father Samuel met heartbreaking disappointment over his inheritance. He may have visited with the families of fellow cadets along the way, enjoying the northern summer. As for going to Lexington, all of his Transylvania friends graduated a year or so before at least, so most likely he went to see the Ficklins. By

39

late August he still had not left for Mississippi, and now the advent of the annual fever season made traveling farther south dangerous. As a result, he requested from Major General Winfield Scott an extension of his furlough until the end of December. Early in September the order granting the extension came to him, issued by Scott's aide, Samuel Cooper.[1]

Just when Davis reached Woodville, and how long he stayed, is unknown. He found much changed there since he left in 1823. Only his mother and his sister Lucinda Stamps and her family still remained at Rosemont. Jane Cook Davis was sixty-eight by now and ever more dear to her youngest son. Certainly the young man visited with his brother Joseph on his growing plantation at Davis Bend, but the sweet days of a Southern fall could not linger indefinitely. Probably just after Christmas, the prodigal son left once more to start his life as a soldier.

Orders took him to Jefferson Barracks, a two-year-old encampment just below St. Louis, Missouri. All fresh academy graduates destined for the infantry went there first, to the "Infantry School of Practice." There they learned the practical applications of much of their West Point instruction. Davis's arrival on or around January 1, 1829, reunited him with many old friends, among them Thomas Drayton from his own class, and Sidney Johnston. One other friend he brought with him—Samuel Davis's former slave James Pemberton. The army allowed an officer to keep a servant with him and even provided pay and ration allowances. Pemberton remained with his young master for years.[2]

But Jefferson Barracks afforded only a brief stopover. Even while he took part in infantry practice, he received notice that his first assignment would be to the First Infantry, stationed at Fort Crawford, way up the Mississippi beyond Illinois, in the Michigan Territory. Davis finished his training in Missouri and by late March arrived at his first frontier post. This was an important occasion for a young brevet lieutenant. About to meet his first commanding officer at his first posting, Davis had little use even at this early age for sycophancy, or at least for practicing it himself. "Though it may be beneficial," he said, it "is not necessary to success." Still, he wanted to make a good impression. Thus, when he came ashore at the landing, he donned his best full uniform, admitting himself to be "something of a martinet." Bravely he marched to regimental headquarters, only to discover that, both being absent, he could not present himself to his commanding colonel or to the lieutenant colonel. He could only find Major Bennet Riley, whom he encountered at the commissary's office, sitting alone at a table, playing solitaire. The lieutenant gave his best West Point salute. The major nodded and told him to sit down while he continued his game.

"Young man, do you play solitaire?" Riley finally spoke after a few minutes. "Finest game in the world! You may cheat as much as you please and have nobody to detect it." It was Davis's only welcome to active service.[3]

Another speedy introduction to army life came when his commander ordered him to go up the Wisconsin River to Fort Winnebago, a post only six months old, built where a portage connected the Wisconsin with the Fox River. White miners, seeking the lead in the Wisconsin hills, were causing increasing confrontations with the Sauk and Fox Indians in the region, and the army felt it wise to establish a line of posts starting at Fort Howard at Green Bay and then extending to Fort Winnebago, halfway between Green Bay and Fort Crawford on the Mississippi. Davis probably reached his new posting early in May, only to discover no immediate assignment for him to undertake. In a few days the post's commander, Major David E. Twiggs, detailed him as assistant commissary of subsistence, and throughout May and June his first services to his country were the purchase of army beef at $5.75 a pound.[4]

No wonder that when his birthday came in June, the now twenty-two-year-old junior officer felt something less than euphoria over his prospects in his chosen profession. He liked the beautiful countryside, but that was about all. His fellow officers struck him as uninspired men "of light habits both of thinking and acting." They had "little to care about and less to anticipate," he found, and the almost hopeless expectation of promotion robbed them of ambition. A new lieutenant might wait eight years to make first lieutenant, and another ten for captain. Ten more, on average, could see him a major, and yet ten again to become a lieutenant colonel. All told, the average expectations of reaching colonel and commanding a regiment were fifty-eight years, which for Davis would have meant 1886. For Davis and his comrades of the First Infantry at Fort Winnebago, that was hardly an attractive prospect. No wonder he found little enthusiasm there or within himself. "Promotion does not depend on merit at all," he wrote on his birthday, "and the duties being plain there is but small inducement to study." At least he found his companions men of good character, without the dissipation, especially alcoholism, so prevalent in frontier commands.

With less than a year's service behind him, Lieutenant Davis confessed, "I cannot say that I like the army but I know of nothing else that I could do which I would like better." Indeed, he had serious second thoughts about his decision to stay at West Point after that first year. In retrospect his original intention to go to the University of Virginia and study law looked better and better. "I might have made a tolerably respectable citizen," he said, "but now I do not believe I could get along well with citizens." Deciding to make the best of his situation, he ordered some books from New York to be sent to him, including a few elementary law texts, and looked forward to his next posting, hoping that it would put him closer to a library or school where he could study in earnest.

"I think I would prefer the practice of law to any other profession," he declared to his sister Lucinda, and it is evident that the arrival of his birthday left him unsettled about where his life was headed. In his boyhood daydreams he had seen himself by then wealthy and powerful. Yet now "I am 22 and the same obscure poor being that I was at fifteen." He had little hope of a career in the military, though he comforted himself that it was an honorable profession. At least, he said, it was better than being a politician, "whose struggles begun in folly are closed in disgrace."[5]

He did not have to wait long for something more interesting to do than buy beef. With Fort Winnebago still unfinished, Twiggs ordered Davis to take a work party out to cut timber on the upper Wisconsin, then float the logs down to the portage and bring them overland to the fort at the headwaters of the Fox. Late that summer, taking with him two-man whipsaws for cutting the trees, Davis set out. When the time came to bring the logs back down the Wisconsin, however, he found that summer rains had so swollen the stream that it was in flood and its waters actually surged into the Fox as well. Thus he saved himself and his men a lot of work when he tied the logs into rafts and floated them across the portage to the fort on the flood waters. The expedition offered Davis his first experience with Indians in the wild, for he believed that he and his men, with their saws, presented quite a curiosity.

Indeed, the Indians may have been more than curious, if the stories Davis told later of his adventures are to be believed. On one occasion a considerable number of canoes approached while the men were cutting and, taking their occupants for hostiles, Davis and his men hid in the woods. Davis himself lay concealed within a few feet of the river bank, right where one canoe came ashore briefly, but he was not seen. During this same expedition, another party of apparently friendly Indians hailed Davis and signed that they wanted to trade for tobacco. Only the warning of Davis's guides saved the party from a surprise attack when he and his men rowed ashore to make the trade. Quickly the soldiers moved back into the stream—the braves in hot pursuit and gaining on them until Davis rigged a makeshift sail on their rowboat to add the wind to his oars. "The Indians seemed to me to be legion," he recalled later.[6]

On his return from the timber-cutting expedition, Davis enjoyed a brief taste of power when he assumed temporary command of Company B of the First Infantry from September through October. At the same time he took on recruiting assignments, though the fund of available men in and around Fort Winnebago was slim indeed, and he only signed on a single recruit. But then he received another assignment to independent command, a modest expedition to look for deserters. His route took him and his men eastward, toward Fort Dearborn on Lake Michigan and the fledgling village of Chicago. Somehow he got lost and ran out of rations. Years later he claimed to have gone ten days without food and three without water until he killed a pheasant and its brood. When he came to the side of the river opposite the fort, Davis stopped and saw a white man paddling out onto the river in a small wooden canoe. It proved to be Lieutenant David Hunter. Curious at seeing another white across the river from the fort, Hunter felt compelled to investigate. For both of them the chance encounter presented such a novelty in the dull life of the frontier army that Hunter had Davis lie down in the bottom of the boat while he paddled the two of them back to Fort Dearborn. There the Mississippian ate heartily and remained as Hunter's guest for several hours until "refreshed," when they paddled back again and Davis rejoined his small command and returned to Fort Winnebago. For more than thirty years Davis retained a fondness for Hunter.[7]

It had been nearly a year now since Davis reported to Jefferson Barracks. Entitled to a leave, he obtained thirty days' furlough on December 22 and soon left the post. There was hardly time to return to Mississippi without having to turn right around again, so instead Davis mounted his horse and rode off toward Sinsinawa Mound, some fifty miles distant. Somehow Davis had learned that his close friend from Transylvania days, George W. Jones, lived there in a log house and engaged in lead mining. It was well after dark when the young officer finally rode up to his old friend's door. Calling inside he asked if this was where Mr. Jones resided. When Jones answered, Davis once more showed that peculiar amusement he found in knowing something that others did not. Instead of identifying himself right away, he asked if he could stay the night. Jones offered the meager hospitality of his corral for Davis's horse and a bunk in his cabin for the officer himself. Only then did the lieutenant start to give hints. He asked if Jones had ever attended Transylvania. When Jones said he had, the voice in the dark spoke again.

"Do you remember a college boy named Jeff Davis?"

"Of course I do," said Jones.

"I am Jeff."

Overjoyed, Jones leapt out of his house and dragged Davis off his mount, bringing him inside where they lay awake nearly through the night talking and laughing over their old college times. Davis remained with Jones for several days, "and after the unconstrained manner of early frontier life," Jones recalled, "we had a delightful time."[8]

Indeed, the isolation of frontier life quickly taught young Davis the importance of friendships. In the next year, when the opportunity afforded, he visited Jones frequently, while back at Fort Winnebago he formed other close attachments. Captain William S. Harney of Company K especially befriended Davis. They raced their high-spirited horses together, fought their dogs against wolves, went spear fishing and boating on the Fox, and kept each other company as Harney worked devotedly in his company garden. Yet Davis also showed a temper that could supersede the bonds of friendship, as when he nearly came to a duel with Harney over a dogfight, perhaps the earliest manifestation of an inability to control his ire once aroused.

Social activities on a remote post could be very few, but still a few settlers in the region occasionally held parties called "gumbo balls." Accompanied by a hearty stew and quantities of fresh bread, the respectable young women of the neighborhood danced with the officers to the tune of a fiddle. No doubt, on such occasions, as he had for a few balls during his brief stay at Jefferson Barracks, Lieutenant Davis wore on his blouse a diamond pin given him by Lucinda. It always attracted no little attention, leading him to wonder if the girls did not see in it evidence of his being a wealthy cotton planter. Speculating on how disappointed they would be to find that he owned nothing, he playfully wrote to his sister, "I did not of course put myself to the trouble of telling them this."[9]

The arrival of any new officers and families was always a cause for some celebration. When the new Indian agent, John Kinzie, and his wife, Juliette, arrived, Major Twiggs gave a party in their honor and soon thereafter showed them to their quarters in one of the new buildings whose construction Davis had supervised. Apparently the officers built most of the furniture as well. In the bedroom, Mrs. Kinzie found "a huge, unwieldy bedstead, of proportions amply sufficient to have accommodated Og, the King of Bashan, with Mrs. Og and the children in the bargain." Even as they laughed out loud at the bizarre piece, they soon stared in wonder at another monstrosity Davis himself had specifically supervised. Neglecting to build closets into the quarters, Davis and his carpenters made mammoth three-sectioned armoires, with separate compartments for clothes press, storage, and china closet. For this last, Davis thoughtfully provided an abundance of shelves, but located them so close together that nothing taller than a plate would fit. "We christened the whole affair," said Juliette Kinzie, "in honor of its projector, a 'Davis.'"[10]

When frolics were too few at the fort, Davis and the other officers sometimes rode to Dodgeville, forty miles away, for a social gathering. Traveling such long distances for a little diversion was more than worth the effort of breaking the tedium of regular post duty. In April 1830 Davis became acting quartermaster, adding this to his other duties involved in the construction of the stone-and-wooden barracks at Fort

Winnebago. The latter he handled very well, but as a quartermaster he nearly got himself into trouble with Captain Joshua B. Brant at the quartermaster's office in St. Louis. Apparently Davis failed to follow the proper procedure in issuing a draft for payment of government funds to a local merchant or failed to clear it with Brant in St. Louis. When he presented news of this to Brant, the indignant quartermaster honored the payment but informed the lieutenant that "no draft of yours will hereafter be paid by me at this Office" unless handled properly beforehand. Any such statement as that was guaranteed to affront the dignity of someone like Lieutenant Davis, who had revealed his thin skin when criticized in his West Point days. Receiving Brant's letter, he promptly returned it to him, "not wishing to retain your letter in my Office." It was an act intended to end any further communication between people, an option this lieutenant did not have with a superior officer. Haughtily, Davis went further by assuring Brant, "I Shall avoid making any call on you, which it may be optionary with you to grant or refuse." An affronted Brant promptly sent the whole correspondence to Washington as evidence of Davis's "insubordinate and highly disrespectful" behavior, and the quartermaster general turned it over to the commanding general of the army, Alexander Macomb. "The conduct of Lieut. Davis is so repugnant to every sound principle of service," wrote Thomas Jesup, "that I hope it will not be allowed to pass without the animadversion it deserves."[11]

Apparently it did pass. Macomb knew the frontier service, how boredom and isolation and stagnant careers made otherwise sensible men turn petty matters into controversies and even feuds. He took no action against Davis, perhaps because the lieutenant's work on building at Fort Winnebago was well done. Nor did Jesup apparently say anything to Davis, though the two corresponded regularly in relation to the building. Some things were best left alone.

The work of building Fort Winnebago's permanent barracks, magazine, stables, and other structures occupied a good deal of Davis's time, especially since some of the materials needed, like horse hair for the plaster, he could not readily procure. Well into 1831 the work continued as weather allowed, along with his duties as acting quartermaster. His combative nature resurfaced in the rough frontier atmosphere when he confronted a massive carpenter who towered over him by several inches. Though the big man could box, he proved clumsy, and Davis jabbed and feinted, then delivered a heavy blow that failed even to stun the man. He grabbed and squeezed Davis nearly to fainting. The lieutenant flipped himself over the carpenter's back, landed prone on the ground, then kicked the man in the stomach when he approached. At this point Twiggs separated them, but Davis was not to be calmed, and Twiggs put him in arrest for the night. Only Harney's intercession prevented Davis from renewing the fight the next day. Years later Davis would look back and admit that "in my youth I was overwilling to fight."

The only bright spot in the tedium was the receipt late in March or early April of his commission as second lieutenant, signed by President Andrew Jackson. At the end of April he also received his permanent posting to Company B of the First Infantry, but still he had to act as quartermaster, and also as commissary of subsistence, making him responsible for procuring rations as well as material supplies.[12]

A brief taste of excitement came in the late spring when war threatened to break out with Indians led by the Sauk chieftain Black Hawk. Much of the First Infantry went to Rock Island on the Mississippi to be ready for fighting, but another treaty averted bloodshed just in time. Yet if he did not see adventure this time, there were other opportunities. Probably sometime prior to the move to Rock Island, his colonel ordered Davis and seven others, accompanied by an Indian guide, to trek north through the territory toward Lake Superior to find a detachment of the regiment. Unfortunately the guide proved to be ignorant and soon left them lost in the prairies of grass. The soldiers wandered for days. The provisions they took with them had anticipated only a two-day journey, and when this gave out they went on hungry and thirsty. Three days' exposure to the scorching summer sun took their toll. One by one Davis's men either fell by the wayside or else deserted, thinking they could do better on their own. In the end just Davis and one other soldier came to a muddy pond. After resting for some hours, Davis decided to press on, but the soldier refused and would not move until the lieutenant threatened him with a pistol. Happily, they reached Lake Superior a few hours later and found food and care at a friendly Indian village. Though ill for some weeks thereafter due to exposure, Davis had demonstrated a determination and presence of mind that would have made Professor Kinsley proud of him.[13]

Certainly he was well recovered by late July when orders came directing him to superintend a sawmill on the Yellow River, west of Fort Crawford and across the Mississippi. Soldiers under his direction turned logs into planking for the building of a new Fort Crawford. Lumbering was not exactly what the lieutenant had bargained for, but at least it meant the end of his commissary and quartermaster days, and it got him out into the country. It also nearly killed him. For the first time in his professional career, Davis evidenced a tendency to overwork. Perhaps it was because this mill had been entrusted to him for a specific task, and he wanted no backbiters like Brant questioning his actions or results. Perhaps it was because the enlisted men under him knew little of what they were doing, or were reluctant to work. Indeed, Davis repeatedly felt that he had to prove himself to his men. When one soldier, just discharged, announced that he intended to thrash the first officer he met, meaning Davis, the young officer jumped atop a log and knocked the man senseless without warning. The bully left without further trouble. For whatever cause, he worked himself near to exhaustion. That and ever-present dampness brought on a severe illness, probably pneumonia. For weeks he lay ill, lost weight, dehydrated, and all the while tried to continue directing from his cot the work at the mill. Pemberton looked after him constantly, even carrying the emaciated lieutenant to a window to see progress at the mill. If what Davis later claimed was true, the local Indians formed an admiration for him, no doubt moved by his determination when so ill, and perhaps because he learned their language, customs, and traditions. Never a hearty or robust young man, he lost so much weight that the Indians called him Little Chief. Until this episode Davis apparently enjoyed excellent health all his life, other than the normal childhood diseases he would have contracted at school. Yet this pneumonia savaged his constitution, perhaps permanently. Certainly from this time on the Yellow River onward, he battled sicknesses and discomforts for the rest of his life.[14]

By early September Davis returned to Fort Crawford but remained little more than a month before the regimental adjutant ordered him to relieve an officer stationed at Dubuques Mines in the Iowa territory. By treaty, white men were to stay out of that region, leaving it to the Sauk and Fox Indians. Lead mines there provided a considerable temptation to would-be miners, however, and increasing clashes between them and the Indians could, it was feared, lead to another outbreak of hostilities. Davis went immediately, and soon saw enough to convince him that the Indian lands were being regularly visited by miners. To further confirm his findings, Davis made repeated personal reconnaissances out into the prairies looking for evidence of intrusions. The report that he filed with his commanding officer, combined with his other services to date, made a sufficient impression that, in forwarding Davis's report to Jefferson Barracks, he added that the Mississippian was "a young Officer in whom I have much confidence." It was his first official compliment.

That confidence also got Davis a five-month assignment keeping the peace at Dubuques Mines and apprehending trespassers. Once he followed a trail in the snow for twenty miles, tracking offenders, and another time he camped beside an Indian lodge, creeping inside to sleep, only to discover in the morning that he had spent the night with a dead Indian. The miners could be difficult to handle. Assuming that treaties with savages counted for little, like most whites of the time, they could not understand why their government would try to keep them from the riches of a territory there for the taking. Thus Davis tried to deal carefully with them, not unmindful that most were armed. The first time he confronted a number of them, it became plain that their minds were set on staying and they resented, even to violence, his orders to move them out. Some actually plotted to waylay and murder him. He went one by one to their homes to attempt to reason with each, promising that in time they would get their access to the lead in the ground, but if only they remained patient, all might be accomplished without violence. He even resorted to buying rounds of drinks to win their regard. In the end, by cajoling and threats intermixed, Davis persuaded almost all to leave and await the settlement of a new treaty with the Indians before returning to their mining claims.[15]

While Davis confronted the miners, the government gave him a furlough in January, to take effect when he left Dubuques Mines on March 26, 1832. He requested it, he said, because of "private matters" in Mississippi. Those "matters," besides a desire to see his family again, consisted in the main of an attempt to find a position that would enable him to leave the army. Somehow out on the plains and prairies of the northwest word came to him of a new railroad being chartered, probably the West Feliciana Railroad Company. It sought to run a standard-gauge line from St. Francisville to Woodville, not a long distance, but one that would connect Mississippi cotton planters more directly with steamboat traffic to New Orleans and beyond. Despite his uninspired performance in mathematics and engineering studies at the academy, Davis felt he might have a chance at obtaining a position as engineer with the new line, no doubt to oversee its construction. Perhaps his work in running the Yellow River sawmill and overseeing the building of much of Fort Winnebago convinced him that he could manage the task.

Davis surely looked into the post shortly after his April arrival at Woodville. When nothing became immediately apparent as to his chances, he took advantage of his option to apply for a four-month extension of his leave late in May. The time in the warm Mississippi spring with his mother and Lucinda's family must have seemed a blessing, especially after the rigors of his last year. As for the railroad position, inevitably he turned to Joseph for help, freely admitting, as he later put it, that his older brother "occupied to me much the relation of a parent." More than just his advice, however, Joseph could offer his influence, as he had become increasingly prominent as a planter at Davis Bend on the plantation he called Hurricane.

Indeed, as with going to West Point, young Jefferson almost let his decision of what to do rest with his brother, a responsibility Joseph declined to take. It was a "Matter that deeply concer[n]s your future life," he wrote his young brother. "No One can judge for an other." The youthful lieutenant was considering a move that would affect the rest of his life, yet Joseph feared that he sought only an immediate solution to his boredom with the army, rather than what would benefit him most over the long term. As for the proposed West Feliciana line, he repeated what he had told Jefferson some time before, that he did not think it would be successful. In this last he proved prescient. If Davis was determined to leave the military to become an engineer, Joseph preferred that he do so for the government, and even considered a trip to Washington for either or both of them, presumably to contact friends with influence about procuring a position. In the end, rather in the manner of their father Samuel, Joseph simply reiterated his conviction that Jefferson must find and stay with a good profession, and that "I wish you to decide for yourself." It was good advice.[16]

Jefferson read the hint in Joseph's skepticism about the proposed railroad. He did nothing further in the matter, and the railroad never came to be. Suddenly other things claimed his attention. His furlough did not expire until September 26, but well before then came exciting news. Black Hawk and many of his Sauk had crossed the Mississippi into traditional tribal lands again in April, only to be turned back by the army in a bloodless show of force. But then local volunteers, beyond control of the army, caught several of Black Hawk's braves in May and killed them, only to lose twelve of their own number to the Sauk braves. Thus commenced, such as it was, the Black Hawk War. Through June and July the army tried to bring the chieftain to bay without success. Just how much news reached Woodville, and how quickly, is uncertain, but undoubtedly Lieutenant Davis knew of the campaign under way by June at the latest, though at first he took no action to rejoin his command. Of course, he was still considering leaving the army for the railroad enterprise. How long he waited to make up his mind after Joseph discouraged him in early July is uncertain, but by the middle of the month, though no order had come recalling him from his furlough, he decided on his own to return to his command. Having determined to stay in the army, he could not miss this opportunity for active field service.

In fact, he missed it almost entirely. Davis did not actually rejoin his regiment until August 18, after the so-called war ended. Though that is when he physically reported at Fort Crawford, very probably he had actually gone straight to his company or to other regular or volunteer forces already in the field some time earlier. Since he was still officially on furlough, he had no reason to report at headquarters first, and so it was as a "vacationing" soldier that he witnessed the last days of the conflict. Just when he met with the forces in the field is uncertain. He could not have reached them by July 21 for the Battle of Wisconsin Heights, though years later he reminisced about witnessing a very similar engagement. Confusion and failing memory probably helped him mistake it with the Battle of Bad Axe, just north of Fort Crawford. There on August 2 came the last engagement of the brief war. Black Hawk and a few others escaped, while most of his followers died in the battle or drowned trying to reach the far side of the Mississippi. Davis may have been there to witness this dying gasp of the proud Sauks, but it is most improbable that he took an active part in the battle.[17]

Davis's disappointment at missing the war probably did not last long. No great reputations were made in brief and wholly one-sided contests like that. Indeed, Davis himself, like many officers, believed the whole episode unfair to the Indians and unnecessary, the fault of undisciplined territorial volunteers, many of them the miners he had previously persuaded to leave Dubuques Mines. It is ironic, then, that having missed any chance at glory from the active campaigning, Davis still emerged from it all as one of the very few officers to have performed services of note. He became Black Hawk's jailer.

Escaping the debacle at Bad Axe, Black Hawk and a few remaining followers took refuge on an island in the Mississippi. Within only a few days a report of the Sauks' whereabouts filtered back to Fort Crawford, where the new commander of the First Infantry, Lieutenant Colonel Zachary Taylor, immediately determined to apprehend them. He ordered Davis and a small party to go on a scout and, if possible, bring back the fugitives. On reaching the island, Davis saw abundant signs of habitation, though the Indians themselves were nowhere to be seen. Just then Black Hawk and his people appeared on the east bank of the river, having gone ashore for food. Seeing his only refuge occupied by his foes, the old chieftain quickly raised a white flag and surrendered.

Black Hawk asked to be taken to Joseph Street, the Indian agent at Fort Crawford, but Davis took him to Taylor instead, and the sad chieftain was immediately put under lock and guard. Taylor decided to send Black Hawk to Rock Island. Since Davis had captured him, he should act as guard and escort. On or around September 3 Davis and a good friend, Lieutenant Robert Anderson of Kentucky, took receipt of sufficient stores for the journey, including a ball and chain, handcuffs, and a leg shackle in case the chief proved unruly. It is even possible that Black Hawk had been shackled while in the fort's guardhouse, but if so, Davis removed his chains when he took him aboard the steamboat for the trip downriver.

General Winfield Scott had come to Fort Armstrong at Rock Island when the war broke out, and here he expected to receive the prisoners. However, an epidemic of cholera met Anderson and Davis when their boat arrived on September 5, and Scott decided that the prisoners' safety required that they be taken farther south to Jefferson Barracks. Aboard the *Winnebago*, they made the slow but calm passage down the Mississippi. The trip may have taken a week altogether, and it gave Davis and Black Hawk time to become acquainted. Davis's direct personal encounters with Indians had been limited to those who lived at or near his frontier posts, and certainly none bore the legendary reputations of this old Sauk. He found him fascinating, just as he found interesting the clash of cultures that made certain forms of discussion unwise. "Never joke with a child or a savage," he would say in after years: "They will not understand, and you will only destroy their confidence in you." Surely he did not gain this knowledge at Black Hawk's expense, for by the end of their journey the Sauk looked on the "young war chief," as he called Davis, as "a good and brave young chief, with whose conduct I was much pleased." Especially pleasing was Davis's consideration of the Indians' feelings when the boat landed briefly at Galena. Scores of citizens flocked to the wharf, wanting to gawk at the captives. "Knowing from what his own feelings would have been if he had been placed in a similar situation, that we did not wish to have a gaping crowd around us," said Black Hawk, Davis kept the curious away. It was an empathy well placed; thirty-two years later, Davis would know that feeling all too well himself.[18]

He returned to Fort Crawford by mid-September and very shortly left again to complete his furlough, spending at least some of his time in Memphis and not returning until January 1833. With the Sauks pacified, the life of the army returned much to normal. "The summer season on the upper Mississippi is in all respects pleasant," he would say in later years. "The green prairies, open woods and cloudless skies remain to me an enchanting memory."[19]

For a young man like Davis, with little else to occupy his days and nights, diversion and romance came easily to mind. Forty years later highly colored stories appeared of his attending dances and wedding frolics, "his tall form . . . conspicuous among the dancers," stepping first in the French fashion, then imitating the Indians, then swirling into a Kentucky hoedown. There were even stories of him becoming fascinated with a young Indian woman, of drinking too much and making to her "a dishonorable proposition." Only the intercession of other officers prevented her outraged brother, knife in hand, from battling with the pistol-brandishing young lieutenant. There were also later stories of his drinking and gambling, even of cheating at draw poker and declining to defend himself when caught and slapped, but, like the tale of his impropriety at the dance, these are almost surely fable. One of the local people of Prairie du Chien, near Fort Crawford, B. W. Brisbow, later denied the stories, in which he was supposedly involved himself. He recalled that when he knew Davis "he was a perfect gentleman" about whom no such stories ever circulated in the 1830s. Yet if the stories were false, being told a half century after that winter at Fort Crawford, there may still be at least a germ of truth in their portrayal of a gay young lieutenant who had not left his West Point ways entirely behind him.[20]

*   *   *

Then he met "Knoxie." When Zachary Taylor came to take command of the First Infantry, he brought his family with him to Fort Crawford. Among them were three daughters and a son, Richard Taylor. The middle daughter, Sarah Knox, immediately shared one thing in common with Jefferson Davis. There was an uncertainty about her year of birth, whether 1814 or 1815. Diminutive, perhaps pretty though hardly beautiful, Knoxie Taylor came quickly to Lieutenant Davis's attention. Quarters at Fort Crawford were cramped, some officers living in tents, and Lieutenant Samuel McRee and his wife turned theirs into a local social rendezvous. Inevitably Davis had already become fleetingly acquainted with Colonel Taylor during and after the Black Hawk capture, but quickly his interest turned far more to Taylor's daughter. The two frequently met at the McRees' tent, and thrown together as they were by circumstances, friendship quickly grew into love. By the coming of spring in 1833, Davis was ready to ask her father if the two could wed.

Few things in Jefferson Davis's life became more clouded by myth and misconception than this courtship. The bare facts are that Taylor did not object to Davis as a man, being quoted as saying that "he had nothing but the kindest feeling and warmest admiration" for him. The only trouble was Davis's uniform. Taylor knew from his own experience, and the pleas of his wife, how hard marriage to an officer could be, and he determined that he did not want any of his daughters to marry military men. In the end, naturally, they all did, but for the moment Taylor's answer to Davis was a firm but friendly no.

Not long afterward, Taylor, Davis, and Captain Thomas F. Smith received orders to sit on a court-martial. For some unknown reason, Taylor and Smith disliked each other. When it came time for the court to convene, another officer, recently arrived from Jefferson Barracks had left his full-dress uniform behind. Regulations required that officers sitting on courts-martial appear in full dress. In the circumstances he naturally asked the court to relax the rules a bit and allow him to continue in his regular uniform. Taylor, who was known for his informality about uniform dress, voted against the exception to the rules. Smith, perhaps just to goad Taylor, voted in favor. And Davis sided with the unfortunate young lieutenant.

If anything came of it at the moment, no one said, but soon thereafter "a mean fellow," as Davis described him, went to Taylor and apparently suggested that Davis's vote was intended as an insult to the colonel. Taylor believed him and upbraided Davis severely, accusing him of ungentlemanly motives. Of course, that was all it took to arouse Davis, who was always testy when called on his behavior. Years later, with what was for him an infrequent personal insight, Davis recalled that "I became wrong as angry men are apt to be." Undoubtedly he bristled at

Taylor's insinuations, made some insulting remarks himself, and stormed out of his commander's quarters with his ears echoing Taylor's declaration that he should not only not marry Knoxie, but that henceforth he was forbidden from visiting her at home. His always-tender pride stung, and his heart frustrated at the situation that now seemed to bar forever his hopes of marriage, Davis stormed to McRee's tent and asked him to act as second if he challenged Taylor to a duel. McRee calmed him, pointing out how unwise it was to attempt to kill a man Davis hoped would be his father-in-law—and his commander at that. Davis curbed his anger, though never his conviction of having been wronged. "I was right as to the principle from which it arose," he maintained more than thirty years later, "but impolitic in the manner of asserting it." Indeed he had been impolitic. Already he revealed a pattern of behavior that traced back at least to that boyhood episode when he was ready to shoot his knife at another. Challenged, he would not back down; assailed verbally, he could not control an instinct to respond in the same coin, and in a tone that escalated the confrontation, even with a superior officer. After the fact, though he might confess yielding to the heat of the moment, something in his character stopped him short of admitting error. "I was right," he said, and would say again and again.[21]

Right or wrong, Davis almost abandoned his hopes for Sarah in the wake of his falling out with Taylor. In a small frontier post, strained relations between officers quickly become common knowledge, and the confines of the grounds seem to become smaller and smaller. Thus, though saddened to leave Knoxie behind, Davis must have felt at least a little relief when otherwise exciting news arrived sometime late in March or early April. Congress had just authorized the raising of a new regiment of dragoons, and the secretary of war on March 4 commissioned Davis a second lieutenant in the unit. While his actual commission did not catch up with him for some time, an announcement of his appointment reached him in general orders, and by the end of April he was off for Lexington, Kentucky, where it would be his task to recruit for his new company. Certainly the leave-taking from Sarah came hard; leaving her father behind was another matter. At least the lovers could write, and possibly Taylor gave his daughter one ray of hope: If she and Davis felt the same way in two years, he would not oppose them.[22]

Just how this new appointment came to Davis is unknown. He may have applied for it, though most likely the War Department simply parceled out the commissions to junior officers in each of the serving infantry regiments. Certainly the return to Lexington must have been a happy one. Arriving in May, he stayed through late June or early July, and a cholera epidemic that fortunately left him unharmed. Yet caring for his recruits at this rendezvous, keeping them fit and fed, and most of all keeping them from fleeing the disease-ridden city, was no mean task. More than five hundred people died in Lexington that summer. Perhaps by devoting himself tirelessly to his work, though he risked exhausting himself, Davis could at least remove his heartache from his mind occasionally. His family back in Mississippi surely knew of his disappointment over Knoxie Taylor, for even a young niece at Hurricane wrote to him in June that he should "cherish ambition, cherish pride, and run from excitement to excitement, [as] it will prevent that ever preying *viper* melancholy, it will blunt your sensibilities, and cause you to be unmoved amidst all afflictions." He still had reason to "look for happiness," she wrote, "and that you may gather its sweet blossoms to your bosom at last, I do fondly pray." Wise words from a fifteen-year-old girl, and perhaps Lieutenant Davis heeded them.[23]

His task done and the company recruited, Davis took his men to Jefferson Barracks by early July. His company was soon followed by others. For the next four months the dragoons' officers trained the men and organized the unit. Their colonel was Henry Dodge. Some of the captains included Nathan Boone, son of Daniel Boone, Stephen Watts Kearny, Edwin V. Sumner, and Davis's friend from Fort Dearborn, David Hunter. His fellow lieutenants were old friends like Lucius B. Northrop and Theophilus H. Holmes, and on the whole the days at Jefferson Barracks were pleasant ones. Davis immediately liked the mounted service, his taste for horses and riding showing him always to be Samuel Davis's boy. Often he was seen around the parade ground on his dark brown horse, named Red Bird after an Indian warrior up in the Michigan Territory. He wore white drill pants, wide at the thigh and tapering closely to the boot in the most fashionable military style, with his undress coat buttoned smartly to the chin. "As you rode through the Parade ground," one of his men recalled, no one "would have made a more gallant and dashing Dragoon" than Jefferson Davis.[23]

But Davis was not entirely content, and this time it had nothing to do with Sarah Taylor. When his commission as second lieutenant in the new regiment finally caught up to him, he was distressed to see that three academy cadets who had been barely senior to him at West Point were now first lieutenants in the dragoon regiment, while two of them had actually been junior to him as second lieutenants. Ever watchful for a technicality or to jump on an action that denied him his due, Davis brought the case to the attention of the secretary of war. At least he was diplomatic enough to assert that, regardless, "I am as an Officer ever ready to render my best services wherever the Government may require them, not doubting but that I shall receive all to which I am entitled." When Colonel Dodge made Davis his regimental adjutant on August 29, he soon thereafter took up the lieutenant's case as well, perhaps urged by Davis himself. Major Richard B. Mason also endorsed the request for promotion, as Davis was "every way worthy of it." The War Department promised to consider their request.[24]

Other devils drove Davis this season. To date he seems to have lived in a political vacuum, leaving behind no expressions of sentiment on the issues of his day and quite possibly having few well-developed thoughts or opinions. Certainly he did not think highly of politicians, as he told his sister in 1829. And he did not hold a high esteem for "Yankees" at West Point, though that prejudice apparently grew out of distaste for their behavior rather than a dislike for their region. Squabbles between North and South in the political arena had existed, of course, almost since the formation of the Republic, most recently boiling over in the controversy on the admission of Missouri as a state. Only the Missouri Compromise of 1820, by which a line drawn across the Louisiana Territory decreed where slavery should and should not exist, settled the ferment for the moment. It did not, however, address permanently the deeper issues that underlay the acrimonious debate.

It all arose again in different guise in 1828 with the so-called Tariff of Abominations, a protective measure that hit hard at the cotton-growing South in particular. John C. Calhoun, now Jackson's vice president, advocated that Southern states resist the tariff by exercising their sovereign right to "nullify" the law. Thus he introduced his notion of the "concurrent majority," and with it the doctrine that a state, being part of the Union by its own consent, reserved the right to declare null any of that nation's acts within its borders. The controversy stopped short of a confrontation, and by 1832 a new tariff softened the impact of its predecessor, but not enough for Calhoun. Early that year, at Calhoun's instigation, South Carolina declared both tariffs nullified and further asserted that should President Jackson attempt to force compliance, then the union between that state and the United States would be dissolved. Jackson fought back with the Force Bill of March 2, 1833, empowering him to use the military to enforce the laws of the United States.

Naturally, through the long months of 1832 and the early weeks of 1833, men in the army watched anxiously as events over which they had no control played out in Washington and South Carolina. With so many officers hailing from the South, the possibility of being ordered to use force in South Carolina made them look within themselves to see where their loyalties lay. That choice faced Davis. Though he left behind no record of it at the time, years later he remembered his feelings as he "looked forward to the probability of being ordered to Charleston in the event of actual collision." Fifty years later, when memory conveniently glossed over his ambivalence and discontent with the army, he recalled that "by preference I was a soldier," and just thirteen years later he said much the same, arguing, "I desired to remain in the army," when the fact is that at the time of the controversy he was already thinking of leaving it for railroading or some other pursuit. Jefferson Davis had cast his very first vote for Jackson in 1828 and probably did so again in 1832, but he could not countenance the Force Bill. Thus, as that bill approached passage, Davis faced a choice.

How he made it at the time is uncertain, but by 1850, in the midst of an even greater sectional crisis in which he was an active participant, he declared unequivocally that "much as I valued my commission, . . . that commission would have been torn to tatters before it would have been used in civil war with the State of South Carolina." Despite his lack of candor—or poor memory—over his attachment to his commission when he looked back on the events of 1833, there seems little reason to doubt his sincerity about resigning rather than take arms against fellow Southerners. Happily, the new Tariff of 1833 compromised the issue sufficiently to negate the need for force, and the tempest subsided once more, though it was destined to reemerge again and again.[25]

To men on the frontier, whose concerns were more immediate, politics back in Washington otherwise seemed like stories from another land. With the regiment of dragoons still in embryo, Colonel Dodge arrived to take command on October 2 and immediately chose Davis to act as his staff officer, not just for the dragoons but for the entire post, of which he was senior officer. The assignment lasted only three weeks, but still Dodge and Davis became well acquainted and perhaps found that they did not particularly like each other, as later events would demonstrate. That dislike probably resulted from Dodge's ill-advised decision late in November to take his regiment out of Jefferson Barracks and march it more than three hundred miles southwest, across Missouri and Arkansas to Fort Gibson in the unorganized territory that would later become Oklahoma. Only the first five companies of dragoons were organized, and two of them did not yet have their horses. Arms and uniforms had not arrived as promised, though the men had discarded much of their civilian clothing in anticipation. With winter approaching, it was altogether an unwise decision.[26]

Dodge and his command left on November 20. Three days out a heavy snowstorm hit them, and the journey worsened after that. Apparently the estimate of rations needed for the trek proved faulty, and in the last days of the three-and-one-half-week march they had almost nothing to eat. Reduced to cornbread, Davis never forgot one of his men, Littlebury Hawkins, who hated the stuff yet became so hungry that he would not trade one chunk of cornbread, exclusively his own at one meal, "for a barrel of white flour." By the time they all staggered into Fort Gibson on December 14, "weariness and extreme fatigue were depicted upon every countenance," wrote one dragoon. During the last two days of the march, their provisions gave out entirely.[27]

Perhaps as a result of the exertions of that march, Davis almost immediately came down with what the regimental surgeon diagnosed as a chronic "affection of the lungs." Almost certainly it was pneumonia again, and it broke the lieutenant's health for some time. Indeed, he could not even keep up his correspondence with his family in Mississippi. His mother threatened to come to the territory to see him if he did not write, and Joseph's second wife, Eliza, complained that Jefferson gave more attention to his dog Basto than he did to his family. The lieutenant did not particularly approve of Eliza, who was twenty-seven years Joseph's junior and had been just sixteen when she married him in 1829. With the self-importance of young men his age, Jefferson had called her "silly" and ignored her letters. She craved the friendship and approval of the brother who stood like a son to Joseph, however, and she kept writing to him anyhow. "I have Sometimes felt unpleasantly that I shared so little of your affection, as to make it a matter of indifference to you Wether or not you heard from me," she wrote to him during his illness. Perhaps because he looked on Joseph as a parent, the lieutenant resented or even felt jealous that his brother had married so young a woman. At least her letters brought him news of home, of his horses cavorting in the fields, and of his mother. It was the only comfort to be found out on the frigid prairies in that winter of sickness.[28]

As spring approached, Davis improved, though his weakness surely helped persuade him to resign his appointment as Dodge's adjutant— sickness and a disgust with the foolish journey that had made him ill. That left him without an assignment, since he officially belonged to the still-unformed Company F. During March and April, as he was able to do duty, he was attached temporarily to Companies A and E.[29]

Shortly after reaching Fort Gibson, Dodge's command moved to a spot nearby and began laying out Camp Jackson, and Davis was there when good news finally caught up with him. On May 10, 1834, President Jackson had signed his commission as first lieutenant. He had beaten the averages, at least a little. Instead of taking eight years to make this promotion, Davis achieved it in slightly less than six. Perhaps the boost given by his newfound status helped put renewed vigor into him after his recovery, for at Camp Jackson he soon impressed his friend Northrop as "strictly and rigidly military." Indeed, "too rigid in the minutiae of the service." Davis rarely left camp at all, even though other officers often went out hunting or into Fort Gibson for recreation. He protested that he thought it "wrong for officers to be frequently away from the command to which they were attached and being out of the way of any duty that might arise." His major, Richard Mason, also commented upon Davis's "soldierly feeling in relation to the welfare of the Regiment of Dragoons."

But if Davis was trying to be a model officer, he came up a bit short, for Mason also complained later that the Mississippian occasionally had to be reminded of his duties. Perhaps so, but Mason, though still on very friendly terms with Davis, began exhibiting signs of the martinet and of an unruly temper as well. On one occasion, during mounted training, he thought Davis directed a critical remark at him and immediately called his subordinate to account, until he learned that Davis had been speaking of another officer. The frustrations of this remote service made even mild-tempered men irritable and short.[30]

Fortunately, there were diversions. Wolf fights became popular, pitting the officers' dogs against wild wolves in a savage, if exciting, contest to the death, and Davis attended at least two. Then there was the novelty of seeing Jackson's old friend Sam Houston, until recently governor of Tennessee, and now living with an Indian woman at Fort Gibson and telling stories in return for drinks. Davis found him to be "a worthless man with some good points," an "enigma." As the weather got better and his stamina returned, he surely raced his horses with others on the post and spent the quieter hours reading what few books were available. But then came orders for their first real service as dragoons. The government wanted the military to contact the remote Indians of the south-central plains, the Kiowa, Pawnee, and Wichita. It was time for a peace meeting between them and the whites, and it was also hoped that two white captives could be recovered. Though not intended as a hostile campaign, the journey of several hundred miles would nonetheless be hazardous.[31]

The column left Camp Jackson on June 15, though the command hardly stood ready. All along the way on the first days' march, the surgeon sent men back to their base for being unfit. One of the new companies had only reached Camp Jackson two days before they left and was still exhausted from the arduous journey from Jefferson Barracks. Their uniforms, received at last, were too heavy for the hot weather on the plains. As usual, estimates of rations proved faulty and food ran low.

Still, for the officers at least, it went well. When they met passing herds of bison, some men went on the hunt, chasing the beasts on horseback, though Davis, like his friend Northrop careful of his horses' condition, probably did not join the hunts. A number of Indian guides and interpreters accompanied the five-hundred-man expedition, along with a German botanist, a herd of cattle, and the artist George Catlin. He described how the mile-long column, seen from a distance, took on "the appearance of a huge black snake, gracefully gliding over a rich carpet of green." They moved first to Camp Rendezvous at the mouth of the Washita River. By July 7 they had covered nearly two hundred miles, but at a terrible cost. The expedition commander, General Henry Leavenworth, injured himself in a fall while chasing a bison, and his health quickly declined. He turned command over to Dodge. Worse, nearly 150 fell by the wayside sick, and another 109 had to be left on the Washita to build and man a new post. Thus only six reduced companies continued the march, and now Dodge assigned Davis to Company E. With ten days' rations, they set out on July 9 for the worst part of the journey, another two hundred miles ahead of them.

Now the worst of the summer heat hit them. Their beef gave out, and the command had to rely on bison meat for weeks at a time. To Davis, the flesh of the great shaggy beast of the plains became "the most distasteful of all food." He tried to make soup with the dried meat, but there was no flour to thicken the broth. His slave James Pemberton tried, to no avail. "No one can make soup without flour," Davis decided; "it is simply water." As for the assistance of the bison meat to the dish, "it was only tea, no matter how much buffalo meat was put in." Water also became a prime concern, and sometimes Davis was ordered away from the column to find a stream or spring to bring water back to the command. Once both the rations of water and whiskey disappeared before they found a stream, and his men wanted to turn back to the regiment. As he had done on his trek to Lake Superior when serving at Fort Winnebago, however, Davis insisted they had to press on, giving the men his own whiskey to help their parched throats, and perhaps as a bit of a bribe.

In time Dodge's command reached the Toyash villages nearly on the border with the future Republic of Texas, though it took two weeks of hard marching. The Indians gave up one of their white captives and agreed to send some representatives back with the soldiers to talk peace at Fort Gibson. While Dodge parleyed with the Indians, he sent Davis off on a reconnaissance to the northeast, toward the southern reaches of the Rocky Mountains. There, looking for stragglers from the column, he saw a large bear rush from a gully to run away. Davis spurred his horse after the animal, only to have it turn on him, frightening his mount into a mesquite bush. Undaunted, Davis recovered, went after the bear, and killed it.

This expedition to the Indians took a terrible toll on the men. Leavenworth died from typhus or dysentery, and another 150 of his command did the same before the haggard and exhausted column once again reached Fort Gibson in August. The illness bypassed Davis, happily, though he never forgot the rigors of the campaign. On his return to the fort he met with another hardship, a letter from Mississippi informing him that his sister Matilda had died on June 18. This young man, just twenty-seven, was seeing altogether too much death and woe. He dealt with it as he felt a soldier should, stoically, in silence, inside himself—the way Samuel would have.[32]

No sooner did Davis return to the fort than Dodge sent Mason and three companies off to build a new post twenty miles north of Fort

Gibson, near the Creek Indian lands along the Arkansas River. The men needed a healthier climate, and in this new position, in the log cabins they were to build, with good stables for their horses, Mason hoped to see them improve. The companies composing Mason's "squadron" were E, F, and K, and thus Davis set off with the rest on September 2 for what they would call Camp Jones. Solicitous of his men as always, Davis found one of his troopers, John Doran, in the Fort Gibson hospital, pronounced by the surgeon too ill to leave. Fearing what would happen if Doran remained, Davis personally interceded and insisted that he be brought with them. The soldier lived for decades to express his gratitude.[33]

Happily, the move improved the health of Mason's ragged soldiers, and the months spent constructing Camp Jones proved to be restful ones on the whole. But beneath the surface a growing discontent churned among his officers, including the lieutenant from Mississippi. By year's end it would erupt at the worst possible time for Jefferson Davis, a time when he should have been transported with joy. He was going to marry Sarah Taylor at last. But he would have to be court-martialed first.

Dreams Are
Our Weakest Thoughts

Colonel Henry Dodge may have set the tone for the trouble with his officers by the ill-advised winter march to Fort Gibson. It shook the faith of many, and some openly showed their disillusion. In April he complained to Davis's friend George W. Jones that "I find More treachery and deception practised in the Army than I ever expected to find with a Body of Men who Call themselves Gentlemen." He accused Davis of being among the first to attack him, declaring that "Major Mason and Davis are Now two of My Most inveterate enemies." He did not say if harsh words passed between them, but added that "they dont want to fight," making it clear that the kind of fight he had in mind happened on a duelling field.[1]

While Mason and Davis appeared to ally against Dodge and got along very well before the Leavenworth expedition, the spirit of dissension spawned by this acrimony soon found other targets. Mason, in other respects a fine officer, increasingly demonstrated an exactitude in orders and a demanding attitude toward his subordinates that Davis approved in himself but resented from others. As they built the barracks and stables of Camp Jones, Mason required that officers attend the construction site all day, as well as the grooming of the horses and the cleaning of the stables, though Lieutenant James Izard declared that "they were of no possible use" there. Later that fall when Northrop fell ill and on his own went to Auguste Chouteau's trading post forty miles distant to recuperate, Mason ordered Davis to take two armed dragoons to arrest him. When Davis asked if there was really a need for arms, Mason insisted. The coming of the cold weather seemed to make Mason even more difficult. On December 7, when two enlisted men inadvertently lost control of a horse, Mason ordered Davis to punish them with a ride on the "wooden horse," a painful and humiliating treatment out of proportion to their offense. Davis suggested the excessiveness of the punishment, and Mason ordered Northrop, now out of arrest, to do it instead.[2]

By December 20 relations deteriorated rapidly. Davis and Northrop received orders to supervise men working on new barracks at Fort Gibson, the squadron having returned there in November. Off duty men started a horse race not far away, and though the two officers could have watched it from a distance where they were, Northrop suggested that they go to the track for a close look at the entrants to see who could pick the faster horse. When Mason found them absent from their work parties, he sent his adjutant to arrest them, but Davis showed that he had left a subordinate officer in charge of his work party, so only Northrop was confined to quarters. When Northrop left rebelliously to go to dinner that evening, Mason decided to press charges.[3]

As for Lieutenant Davis, Mason found him missing roll calls, presumably neglecting his stable duties, and giving "repeated instances" of inattention to duty, even while Davis loudly condemned such dereliction in others. Thus the major felt in no amenable mood when Davis asked for leave to go to a warmer climate for fear the cold and damp winter would bring on a recurrence of his apparently chronic lung ailments. Mason's response persuaded Davis to "say nothing more about it." Then Mason ordered Davis to take the men of his company and commence laying the floors of their company barracks. During the next several days the major visited the work site. Afterward he said that he repeatedly found the laborers idle, the work progressing slowly, and Davis himself absent. Only by ordering that a company officer be present at all times, he felt, could he keep Davis on the job.[4]

If Davis was concerned about his growing problem with Mason, he showed no awareness to his fellow officers. He rode his horses, played with Basto, and most of all daydreamed of Sarah. Even in his sleep he dreamed of her, confessing when awake that "by *dreams* have I been lately almost crazed." "Dreams," he wrote to her, "are our weakest thoughts," and Sarah was his weakness. It did not help that another officer at Fort Gibson repeated a rumor heard in St. Louis that Colonel Taylor was forcing her to marry some doctor. But then, on the night of December 15, he had a different dream. He saw her standing in the Kentucky home of Taylor's brother, her uncle. He saw her walking toward him on the arm of their friend Captain McRee, and then McRee turned her over to him and she whispered in Davis's ear that her father had withdrawn his objection to their marriage.

The very next day brought a letter from Sarah, and to the lieutenant's amazement, she told him in her own hand what she had said to him the night before in his dream. Nearly two years had passed, she had told Colonel Taylor, and in that time he had found nothing to question in the honor or character of her beloved. Just as strong-willed as her father, she announced that she would marry Davis with or without consent. Perhaps in her letter Sarah named the time and certainly the place. It would be Kentucky, at the home of her aunt Elizabeth Taylor near Louisville, and not at Fort Crawford where her parents were.

The news left Davis ecstatic. "Kind, dear letter," he wrote that night, "I have kissed it often and it has driven many mad notions from my brain." "Whatever I may be hereafter," he declared, "I will ascribe to you." Still he sorrowed for the breach opened between her and her father, and that she felt forced to be wed far from her parents for fear of making the gulf even wider. He hastened, too, to erase from her mind a little twinkle of jealousy over a gift he had supposedly received from another woman when he was recruiting in Kentucky, assuring her that all the woman gave him was a warm tribute to Sarah's charms. He wrote a lover's letter, from start to close, like many he had sent her during the past two years. But this one closed with hope turned to certainty, and his heart was beyond restraint. "My dear Sarah My betrothed," he exulted, "no formality is proper between us." For such a letter, only the language of love seemed apt for closing. "*Adieu Ma chere tres chere amie adieu.*" ("Farewell my dear, very dear friend, farewell.")[5]

Probably Davis had already announced his hope for an engagement to his family in Mississippi, for a letter received from a niece not long before Sarah's arrived chided him that her "advice was to be asked before you entered into *engagements* of any kind." Indeed, writing in anticipation that Mason would give him a winter's leave, he had suggested that he would be home for Christmas and mentioned a hope that Sarah might be there with him. Joseph's wife Eliza, still trying pitifully to please him and win his affection, boasted that she had herself cleaned Jefferson's room, put a "scrap" of new carpet on the floor, and hung doors in the doorways, wishing that "when they are opened it would be for yourself—& one equally as dear to you."

But there would be no trip to Mississippi this December, no opening of doors, no visit by Sarah. They would have to wait. Maybe Davis even hinted to Sarah about the difficulties before him at Fort Gibson when he spoke of "how I long to lay my head upon that breast which beats in unison with my own, to turn from the sickening sights of worldly duplicity." Certain it is that when Christmas came that year, Jefferson Davis was under arrest.[6]

Christmas Eve dawned cold and rainy, the ground saturated with water. It was the sort of weather that the post surgeon told Davis might be bad for his lungs. When the time came for morning reveille, Davis remained in his dry tent. He well knew that regulations required all officers and men to assemble outside for the morning roll call, but he also remembered a stipulation that "in bad weather, permission may be given to the chiefs of squads, to make the call in tents or quarters." Mason had to give that permission, but Davis just assumed that staying in his tent would be allowable without actually asking the major. His recent experience with Mason encouraged him not to bother, while his pride recoiled at inviting another refusal.

When everyone else appeared in the rain for the roll, Mason sent an orderly to fetch the missing lieutenant, and when Davis arrived his commander asked why he had been absent. Wary of Mason, Davis immediately adopted what he called "a guarded manner."

"Because I was not out of my tent," answered the lieutenant, "and the Regulations require when it rains that the roll shall be call'd in quarters by Chiefs of squads."

Though he never admitted it, Davis was goading Mason intentionally. His pride wounded at being summoned in such a manner before the major, he immediately assumed an attitude that, by his own admission, he knew was best calculated to infuriate his superior. "A calm, collected bearing before him is likely to irritate him," Davis said to Captain David Perkins a few weeks later, and that is the bearing Davis took on the morning of December 24. Making things worse, his answer to being asked why he was not on parade—"because I was not out of my tent"—was flippant at best, if not insolent. And last, as he had several times before and would all his life, Davis relied on a strict construction of the law, in this case, regulations. There he felt impregnable. However, his command of the rules was not as infallible as he thought. Whereas he smugly stated that the regulations "required" roll call in quarters when weather was bad, in fact they specifically said that "permission may be given." It was an option only, and one that lay with Mason in this instance.

Mason bristled almost at once. "You know it is my order that all officers of this command attend the Reveille roll call of their respective companies," he said.

Davis said nothing in response but turned on his heel and walked away. At some point before, during, or immediately after that about-face, he muttered in a stage whisper, "Hum!" in a manner that Mason found "highly disrespectful, insubordinate, and contemptuous."

Immediately Mason called him back and upbraided him for acting in such a fashion when being spoken to on a point of duty. He ordered Davis to go to his quarters under arrest. The lieutenant stared him straight in the face and said nothing. Mason repeated his order again, and now Davis's own company, finished with their roll call, marched past, well within earshot. Being upbraided by a commander in front of his own men added humiliation and indignation to Davis's already wounded pride. Still he stared at Mason.

"Now are you done with me?" Davis asked in what Mason characterized as "a disrespectful and Contemptuous manner." Yet again Mason repeated his order that he go to quarters under arrest, and this time the lieutenant obeyed.[7]

On the way back to his tent, his now-soggy uniform an added reminder of his encounter with Mason, Davis ran into Northrop, and the two went into his quarters. Northrop, who fancied that "I can infallibly detect any irritation in any man of Lieut. Davis's character," believed that his friend was perfectly calm. Even smiling, Davis described his brief contretemps with the major as nothing more than a passing irritation on Mason's part and expected that nothing more would come of it than his brief arrest. If Davis really believed the affair would pass that easily, he misjudged the major even more than he misinterpreted the regulations. No more than three days later Mason wrote and delivered to Brigadier General Matthew Arbuckle charges and specifications against Davis.[8]

And so for Jefferson Davis there would be yet another court-martial. Most immediately he chafed at being confined to his quarters. Perhaps to test Mason's seriousness, he asked his major to relax the restriction, but Mason refused. All Davis could do then was appeal to Arbuckle, who asked Mason to allow Davis the freedom of the post, saying that the lieutenant's offense really did not warrant such close confinement. Indeed, there were those who believed that the whole episode warranted neither arrest nor court-martial. When Arbuckle notified the adjutant general in Memphis, the response advised that "a difference of the nature which this appears to be" had no business going to a court and should be arranged between the warring parties by the post commander. Arbuckle's superior, General Edmund P. Gaines at Jefferson Barracks, agreed, and personally asked Arbuckle to mediate. He spoke to Mason, who had long since calmed sufficiently to say that he had no real desire to prosecute and would drop his charges if Davis apologized. It was a reasonable request. But when Arbuckle visited the lieutenant in arrest, Davis declined. "I then felt that an examination into the charges should wipe away the discredit which belonged to my arrest," the Mississippian said, protesting that "the humble and narrow reputation which a subaltern can acquire by years of the most rigid performance of his duty, is little worth in the wide world of Fame, but yet is something to himself." To save his reputation, which really meant his pride, Davis would go to trial.[9]

On January 15, 1835, an order from Memphis named a court though, ironically, a trial of Davis had not yet been decided, and this court was to try Northrop, with Davis as a member of the panel. Shortly the Mississippian's name went on the docket, however, and at 11 A.M. on February 12 the trial of Davis commenced. The charge against him read "conduct subversive of good order and Military discipline," followed by the specification. In the latter appeared a brief account of the encounter with Mason. Davis, who by custom conducted his own defense, challenged whether the charge and specification really constituted any criminal offense, but the court decided that it had been a military offense, and that was sufficient grounds for trial. That done, Davis entered pleas of not guilty on both.[10]

For the next eight days, with a two-day adjournment in the middle, Davis tried to confute Mason point by point. On the smaller issues he did a capable job throughout. From Mason himself he extracted an admission that no standing order requiring officers to turn out regardless of the weather had been promulgated; Mason simply believed his attitude was common knowledge, but other witnesses supported Davis that it was not. From several fellow officers Davis got testimony that Mason was known to be sometimes "harsh and disregardful of the feelings of those under him" and himself characterized the major's demeanor at times as one "which would prevent any man of pride" from enduring it. He even got from Mason an admission that on the whole Davis had been a good officer and generally attentive to his duties, though the major pointed out several occasions on which he had had to call Davis to his responsibilities. Even then he protested that if only Davis had been civil and subordinate that morning, matters would not have come to a head. Just then a rather perceptive member of the court asked a question: "Might not the usual manner of the accused be considered disrespectful or even contemptuous by one not well acquainted with him?" It was a question that would be asked about Jefferson Davis for most of the rest of his life.

Davis managed pretty ably to do away with most of Mason's charges, though after his initial pleading he never directly addressed the issue that began the whole sorry mess—his failure to appear at roll call that Christmas Eve morning. When he interviewed another officer, Lieutenant James Izard, who had also failed to report at roll call, Izard initially seemed to support Davis's contention that sick officers were commonly allowed by Mason to remain in their quarters in poor weather. But a question by Lieutenant Dixon S. Miles, special judge advocate on the court, revealed that Izard himself believed that such an "indulgence" from Mason was specific and not general. Mason had granted it to him, but not to Davis, thus weakening the defendant's case.[11]

Finally, on February 17, all the testimony came to an end. Davis asked, and received, a day's delay to prepare his final defense, and at 10 A.M. on February 19, he arose to address "Mr. President and Gentlemen of the Court." Aside from his lecture on friendship at Transylvania, this defense was probably the longest speech yet made by young Davis, and is certainly the earliest of which a substantial record survives. It reveals much of the formation of the character and perceptions of the twenty-seven-year-old officer. If it contains little of the eloquence that he sometimes achieved in later years, certainly it shows a number of other traits, good and ill, that characterized him for the rest of his life.

Davis revealed a ready grasp of facts and events, each link in the chain of accusations against him recited in order, and each one broken, so he thought, by the evidence he produced. It was the same style of oratory that he would practice for the next thirty years, restating an opponent's position or arguments and then demolishing them point by point. The methodical, almost scholarly approach appealed to him and, as he saw it, offered the most convincing way of demonstrating the correctness of his own view and the error of others'. Yet at the same time Davis revealed a tendency to misstate his opponent's case in a form more easily countered by his own arguments, and in making his own case he either glossed over or ignored what contradicted him, sometimes introducing irrelevancies in order to add seeming weight to his presentation.

The first substantive statement in his defense was Davis's demonstration, by means of a witness, that when Mason's summons to the roll call arrived, the lieutenant had not been asleep but was awake and out of bed, a point that had never been argued and that was no part of Mason's accusation. That done, Davis pointed out that he had ably shown that his health was precarious, that the weather on the morning in question looked threatening, and that Mason himself knew of Davis's previous illness. But then the lieutenant presented his own assumption as if it were fact. "Therefore," he said, he "had a right to expect from my commander, a care similar to that by which he attempted to account for not noticing the absence of Lt. Izard from the Reveille roll call of the same morning." Davis completely ignored Izard's own testimony that Mason knew he had been on sick report for several days—which Davis had not—and that he had reported to Mason first before being specifically told that he could stay in his tent at reveille. Davis never made any such request of his commander, and now in his summation again took refuge in his mistaken understanding of regulations. If he knew of his mistake, he glossed over it.

But then Davis steered back onto the path of accuracy and demonstrated with some effect what appeared to be a case of Mason singling out him alone for the required attendance at reveille, and making some capital out of Mason's inability to recall the specific dates of the numerous occasions on which he charged Davis with missing roll call. Unfortunately, having gotten into an area with firmer ground under him, Davis abruptly leaped off into the absurd, devoting the greatest portion of his defense to the issue of the word "hum!"

After accusing Mason of seizing on "an isolated meagre interjection" and magnifying it "into an importance worthy the most significant word in the English language," Davis proceeded to do exactly the same thing, devoting more time to it than to any other point in his defense. He argued about tone and manner and how they signify the meaning of words such as *hum*. He tried to profit from Mason's uncertainty as to precisely at what point in the affair Davis had uttered the offending syllable. Davis even implied that he ought to be commended for his forbearance in meeting Mason's ire with only a *hum* and silence, despite his own earlier testimony that he believed such a bearing was the best way to provoke the major. As for staring Mason in the eye when the major became aroused, then turning on his heel abruptly, Davis did not deny it, but he denied that it was censurable. "Is it part of the character of a soldier to humble him self beneath the haughty tone, or quail before the angry eye of any man?" he asked. Of course, it was just that tone and that eye that Davis had turned on his superior.

Finally Davis attacked the accusation that Mason had to order him three times to go to his tent under arrest, and here he returned again to sounder logic on a worthwhile point. And with restraint, he refrained from imputing to Mason any ungentlemanly motives in bringing charges against him. Mason's ire, rather, grew out of his being "a man biased by strong feelings." "His irritation committed him to the course he has taken against me," said Davis. "Had my self respect allowed me to make to him those explanations which through witnesses I have made to the court," said the defendant, he believed that Mason's course would have been a different one.

Even here, as he concluded by denying that Mason had malign intentions, Davis revealed something about himself. He could have averted all this, he said, if he had made "explanations" to Mason. "Self respect" would not allow him to do so. Indeed it would not, though what Davis saw in himself as self-respect looked more like pride—an excessive pride that would not admit error, that would not explain when questioned, and that did not apologize. Davis preferred to go through eight days of court-martial, weeks of arrest beforehand, a tense examination and cross-examination, and a statement of facts and opinions almost certain to poison any future relations with his commander rather than explain his behavior on the spot at the time of the incident. And through the whole court-martial, Davis never once even hinted at apology for his actions; not once did he admit any poor judgment or wrongdoing on that ill-starred Christmas Eve.

Already the mold of the man was set. While he did not seek confrontation, he would not step aside to avoid it, regarding personal self-respect—pride—as paramount to whatever problems that confrontation might yield, and no point was too small or insignificant if Davis felt that it touched on his honor or conduct, even the meaning of the word "hum." In almost every other context, friends and family found him a warm, witty, even charming companion during his army days. But when a word or an action appeared to reflect criticism of any kind on him, his mind took on a single purpose, to prove himself right—completely right—even if in his conviction of righteousness he overlooked, discounted, or misstated to his purpose views and evidence to the contrary. It was not dishonesty so much as it was a blindness to his own fallibility. Davis often argued in future years that he was the first to admit error, yet such admissions would be few, and he made none now. Unshakably convinced of the correctness of his conduct, his mind simply could not countenance the possibility that other points of view on an issue might be valid.

The court-martial proved to be not quite as charitable to Davis as he was to himself. The courtroom was cleared while Miles read to the members all of the past days' proceedings. There followed a "mature deliberation" over the case. Finally they called Davis and Mason back before them, and General Arbuckle, president of the court, read the verdict. In reviewing the specification of the charge against him, that he had acted as Mason charged on December 24, 1834, the court removed the words "highly disrespectful, insubordinate and contemptuous conduct" where they appeared, and found him guilty of all the actions that Mason charged. However, they attached no criminality to those actions, as indeed there was none in a military sense, and therefore found him not guilty of the actual charge of conduct subversive of good order and military discipline. The court therefore acquitted him.[12]

Though he never commented upon it, Davis cannot have been entirely pleased with the verdict, for it was equivocal at best. His acquittal on the greater charge removed any stigma of criminality, yet the verdict on the specification made it very clear that the members of the court did not agree with Lieutenant Davis that his conduct on Christmas Eve had been beyond reproach. Surely that stung his tender pride as it never had been hurt before. Indeed, it may have stung so much that it prompted the sort of response that only hurt pride can elicit: Eleven days after the verdict he wrote his resignation and gave it to General Arbuckle.[13]

Davis may have been considering resigning anyhow as his marriage to Sarah Taylor approached. It cannot have matured into a fixed idea by this time, though, or Zachary Taylor would not have continued to object to the wedding, his sole objection having been that he did not want his daughter marrying into the army. Had Davis announced an intention to resign, then all grounds for Taylor's refusal to endorse the marriage should have disappeared. Certainly the lieutenant's resignation did come within a few months of his wedding vows, yet nothing, in either his surviving correspondence with family in Mississippi or his heartfelt December letter to Sarah a few days before his arrest, even hinted at an intent to leave the army at this time, nor did he have an immediate occupation to replace the military. In later years Davis apparently told family members that he resigned to get married, but the plea does not ring true. Though he rarely did anything hotheaded or impetuous, Jefferson Davis did so now. Rather than stay in a regiment and at a post where he could not face those who had heard him criticized by the court—and perhaps fearing that his career would be stunted despite his acquittal—he chose to abandon the only profession he knew. Just how much the guilty verdict on the specification hurt may never be known. Fifty-five years later, after his death, a memoir by his most intimate life's confidante did not hesitate to recount some of his escapades at West Point and even told—though flatteringly—of his court-martial at the academy. Of the court that tried him at Fort Gibson, however, that memoir is absolutely silent, as if it had never happened or Jefferson Davis had never revealed it.[14]

Even in his hurt pride, Davis postponed an irrevocable choice. In fact, once or twice in the past he had shown a tendency toward indecision. It was Joseph's will, not Jefferson's, that had sent him to West Point. Less than a year after graduation, Davis was already thinking and talking of leaving the service, though he did nothing about it. Then came his flirtation with railroading, again apparently influenced in the negative by Joseph. Now, though he wrote his resignation on March 2, Davis gave it to Arbuckle undated and asked him to hold it and not date and forward it to headquarters for six weeks. The day before, Davis had applied to Mason for a leave of absence, "that I may give that attention, to individual interests, which my future welfare requires, and which family transactions imperiously demand of me to render." Since the only "family transaction" he then contemplated was his fall nuptials with Sarah, and his leave extended only from March 10 to April 20, clearly Davis was really asking for time to think over his future. If he did not return by April 20, he told Arbuckle, then the resignation should be dated and sent through army channels.[15]

Before he left, Davis gave a champagne party for Northrop and other chums, and in less than two weeks he had reached Mississippi. Word of his coming preceded him and caused quite a stir at his brother's Hurricane plantation. According to tradition among the Davis slaves, Joseph went to work prettying the house and grounds while the young ladies, especially his wife Eliza, toyed with the idea of filling the house with attractive belles to welcome the soldier home. If so, Eliza soon thought better of it. "I know your aversion to good company," she had written to her brother-in-law four months before, and besides, they all knew about Sarah by now. Thus, when the steamboat put in at Davis Bend and the lieutenant walked ashore, there was only his family to greet him, and Joseph's hand was the first that he took. His servant Pemberton got off with him, along with a favorite black horse named Oliver, and astride his steed Davis rode with his family up from the landing to Hurricane. As he approached, several of the little slave children ran to the gate to see the Davis they had heard of but never met. To the first one at the gate, little Florida Ringgold, Davis gave a bright silver dime. He was home.[16]

Indeed, Joseph Davis now intended that Davis Bend should be his brother's home, even while the lieutenant himself grappled in the coming weeks with whether or not to return to Fort Gibson at the end of his leave. If the recollections of little Florida may be believed, Joseph had discussed with his family his intention to make a planter of Jefferson even before the soldier reached Hurricane, despite the disinclination Jefferson had shown for field work when his father Samuel made him work with the slaves some years before. Now that the brothers were together, they rode out in the early mornings over the fields of Hurricane, Joseph pointing out what he had done already and what he intended for the future. Certainly during their rides he showed his brother a parcel of 800 acres that he owned, densely covered with cane and briers. Joseph suggested that he could give this land to his brother "in consideration of his leaving the army," as he later said. There he could make a new profession, plant cotton, and prosper. And if Jefferson Davis did not care a lot about becoming a wealthy man, still there were other advantages to planting. Joseph may not have said exactly what Florida Ringgold later recalled him saying, but surely it occurred to his brother anyhow that a planter was "absolutely independent, without a superior officer on earth to give orders." There would be no Major Masons to deal with at Davis Bend.[17]

While he settled his mind on his future, Davis probably learned of the March 15 ruling by General Gaines that approved the findings of his court-martial, both the good and the bad. Perhaps that finally decided him on resignation. He made no communication with General Arbuckle of any kind and simply stayed on in Mississippi well past the April 20 expiration of his leave. By May 12 Arbuckle had no choice but to conclude that Davis was not returning, and consequently he dated the signed resignation April 20 and sent it on to higher authority. He did so with regret. "Lieut. Davis is a young officer of much intelligence and great promise," he lamented. Only recently Twiggs, now a colonel at New Orleans, had suggested that Davis be sent to him to build a new barracks, thinking him "well, *if not better* qualified for that duty, than any officer of my acquaintance." Important men of substantial rank felt kindly toward the lieutenant, and even now Arbuckle hoped that Gaines might have heard something that would induce him not to accept the resignation.

No such word came forth, and at the War Department in faraway Washington City, the resignation of Lieutenant Jefferson Davis took effect as of June 30, 1835.[18]

By that time he was a married man. In late May or early June a steamboat brought Sarah Taylor to St. Louis. She left with her parents' consent, despite later stories of an elopement, but when she spoke with her father one last time aboard the vessel before its departure in an attempt to reconcile him to her marriage, he remained unswerving in his opinion. Thus she left under a cloud, but it soon lifted when she changed boats at St. Louis and found herself disembarking at Louisville, where her aunt Elizabeth Taylor met and took her home to Beechland.

Just when Davis arrived is unknown, though he came alone, and probably visited with old friends in Lexington on the way. Now the young couple advanced the date for their wedding to June 17. On the morning of the appointed day they were both busy. Davis, oddly enough, allowed his mind to turn to the army. Though he had left it, so he thought, for good and was about to be married, still here in Kentucky, on his wedding day, he thought to write to the treasurer's office in Washington inquiring about the status of the final reconciliation of his accounts with that department when he had been acting assistant quartermaster the year before. It was a peculiarly routine thing to do on such a special day, revealing a quirk in Davis's nature that impelled him to take care of business even at times of high emotion. As for Sarah, she wrote to her mother that morning. Davis had persuaded her that they need not wait until the fall as earlier planned. Davis Bend was "quite healthy" at this time of year, he told her. Regretting that her parents could not see her married, she thanked her father for the money he had sent her, which would no doubt get the couple off to a start on their life together.

That early afternoon Sarah wore her best bonnet and traveling dress. Jefferson and her uncle Hancock Taylor that same day obtained the marriage license. Now, in a parlor of Beechland, they exchanged their vows in a civil ceremony, surrounded by Sarah's aunts and uncle, and others of her more distant kin. Then at 4 P.M. they left immediately for Mississippi, having already decided that Davis Bend was where they would make their home.[19]

The people at Hurricane anxiously awaited the arrival of the newlyweds, and much was made of the new Mrs. Davis when her in-laws met her. "She was a little slim woman," remembered Florida Ringgold, and for some reason the slaves, and perhaps their masters, came to call her Miss Orry. Hurricane was hardly the sumptuous plantation mansion of legend, but still it offered comforts unheard of at the frontier posts where Sarah had lived with her father. Joseph Davis and his family found his new sister-in-law to be refined and intelligent, of an open and engaging character, even-tempered and sincere. Quickly they all took to her, and she to them.[20]

Apparently the new Davis family stayed at Warrenton, a few miles upriver from Davis Bend, off and on during the summer, but certainly most of their time was spent at Hurricane. Now that he was a married man, it was imperative that Jefferson Davis start to make a living. If Joseph had not completely persuaded him to take up planting at Davis Bend before the marriage, certainly he did so now or else his brother quickly made up his own mind. Joseph still owned five thousand of the eleven thousand acres he originally purchased at Davis Bend in 1818. The eight-hundred-acre piece that was to be Jefferson's, immediately downriver from Hurricane, was "an old burn," as he described it, "with stumps of trees, some cane & many briers." Joseph wanted Jefferson to clear the land and make it into a plantation of his own. Joseph would keep the actual title to the property, but in all other ways it was to be his brother's, Jefferson's share of their father's estate. Perhaps uncertainty over his brother's commitment to farming, or a concern that the land might be lost should Jefferson not prove to be an able planter, prompted Joseph to retain legal title to the property. Certainly Joseph had seen his brother's occasional indecision and recalled his tendency to live beyond his means when at West Point. Once again, as so often before, Joseph Davis acted the part of a father, making opportunity for his brother but also maintaining a measure of control over him.[21]

Jefferson Davis seemed delighted with the arrangement, though it would cause him grief in future years. Perhaps it was the dense briers that covered so much of the land—and the additional one thousand acres that would come his way in time—that made him decide to call his plantation Brierfield. There he would clear the land, build a house, plant cotton, and create for himself and his new bride a little piece of the South all their own.

First he needed labor. All he had in that line was James Pemberton, his old servant. Once more Joseph stepped in, giving his brother a loan and taking him to a slave market in Natchez, where together they bought ten blacks and took them aboard the steamer *Magnolia* back to Hurricane. There, with the summer's cotton crop coming into bloom, they helped Joseph's other slaves in harvesting while Jefferson laid out his planned house, slave cabins, and outbuildings and began the work of clearing his land. Apparently Joseph had built a small cabin on the Brierfield property back around 1832, so his brother at least had a place for himself and Pemberton to stay.[22]

Just how much actual work the young would-be planter finished that summer is uncertain. The thick cane and briers proved too dense to cut or uproot, so they burned them instead. By all accounts Davis went at the work with a will, perhaps helping his slaves with digging the shallow holes in the earth into which they placed the cotton seed for the next year's crop. There were trees to fell, and perhaps he even commenced work on a new and larger log house to be home for him and Sarah until future crops enabled him to build a grander mansion house.[23]

As for Sarah, she settled effortlessly into Mississippi life and the Davis family. In mid-August, almost two months after her marriage, she gloried in a beautiful colt given her by her husband. She played the piano at Hurricane, sometimes providing music for the slave girls to dance a jig, and in idle hours wrote to her mother at Fort Crawford, evidencing an understandable bit of homesickness for the sights of her girlhood, watching Margaret Taylor feeding the chickens or skimming the cream from the cows' milk. Sarah Davis was happy. If the summer's heat and the bite of the mosquitoes that swarmed about the plantation bothered her, she did not complain. "Do not make yourself uneasy about me," she wrote her mother on August 11. "The country is quite healthy."[24]

Five weeks later she was dead. The country was not at all healthy at that time of the year. Those teeming millions of mosquitoes carried parasites that produced both malaria and the deadly yellow fever. While symptoms favor the former, it could have been either of the two diseases that some hungry insects brought to Sarah and her husband. Most likely they were bitten in late August or early September, along with hundreds of other people in the Mississippi Valley who regularly died every year of the brutal fevers. They may still have been at Hurricane, though it is just as probable that they had already gone farther south to West Feliciana Parish in Louisiana, near St. Francisville, to visit with Jefferson's sister Anna Davis Smith at her home, Locust Grove.

Davis later recalled that he became ill first and Sarah the day after, quite likely meaning that a single mosquito became their agent of pain and suffering by biting them as they slept together. A tradition among the Hurricane slaves said that Sarah immediately became the more ill and had to be carried on a litter to the boat landing for the trip to Locust Grove, her husband, himself pale with the disease, walking alongside to shade her with a parasol. Once under Anna Smith's care in Louisiana, however, Davis himself appeared to be the more endangered. To ensure that they got as much undisturbed rest as possible, Jefferson and Sarah lay in different rooms, lapsing into delirium. Mercifully, neither knew the perilous condition of the other. But then Sarah declined rapidly. On September 15, during a brief spell of consciousness, Jefferson Davis heard his wife's voice coming from her room, singing a song they both loved, "Fairy Bells." Painfully he struggled from his bed and staggered toward her voice, only to hear it stilled as the fever took her life.[25]

That very afternoon, or the next day at the latest, poor Sarah Davis was buried in the small family plot at Locust Grove. Though one tradition claims that her husband insisted her funeral service be held in his own sickroom, it is probable that he was himself too ill to accompany her body to its resting place. Jefferson's older brother Benjamin already lay in that plot, along with Anna's husband, Luther Smith. Her grave was covered with brick, and sometime later a simple marble slab was erected, atop columns, with the inscription "Sarah Knox Davis, Wife of Jefferson Davis, Died Sept. 15, 1835, age 21." Nothing more could be done for her.[26]

The greater concern now was the widower. With heartbreaking grief added to his own very serious case of malaria, he wavered between life and death for a few days afterward, and for fully a month after Sarah's death Anna and the rest of the family alternately felt hope and despair for his recovery. But slowly he improved. Never a fleshy man, he now looked cadaverously emaciated. Spasms of coughing frequently racked his body. Yet by mid-October his strength revived sufficiently for his family and physician to send him home to Hurricane. Pemberton carried his master to the boat landing in his arms.

The slow passage upriver preceded more than a month of further convalescence. By the middle of November, Davis could at least attend to a few simple matters like correspondence, and focused sufficient attention to settle one or two remaining matters from his military service. Writing may not have come easily to him now, for he began to notice an intermittent problem with his left eye, probably not serious or even very alarming considering what he had been through in the past months. He put it down to a side effect of the malaria, though it is quite possible that he may have had problems with it even before 1835. Later developments revealed it to be something quite different—and more serious.[27]

Even though he seemed to improve, still the family worried about his continuing weakness. Though Mississippi is hardly a cold climate, Joseph Davis nevertheless recommended—or decided—that his brother spend the winter somewhere warm and dry. Seeing the dejection that plagued Jefferson even while the ravages of the malaria slowly abated, Joseph no doubt believed that a major change of scene would take the patient's mind away from his terrible personal tragedy. They decided to send him to Cuba. The warmth of the Caribbean, its deep blue waters, and the lazy pace of life on the tropical island all should calm and soothe him in mind and body.

Some time prior to Christmas young Davis left Hurricane, steamed downriver to New Orleans, and, accompanied by Pemberton, boarded a sailing ship bound for Havana. The voyage probably took no more than a week, yet Davis felt himself improving almost from the first. Daily he bathed on deck as Pemberton doused him with cool seawater from a bucket, and the sight of the simple pink-and-white stuccoed buildings of Havana as he entered the harbor gave at least some promise of new experiences. By his manner and probably his expression, he made it clear that he did not want to mix with local society. He needed time to himself, and as he regained more and more strength he used it in solitary walks about the city. Its ancient fortifications especially interested him, awakening his recollections of recent years in the army and of his studies of military history at the academy. He found solace in walking around the old stone walls or sitting on the hills with sketchbook and crayon making drawings of the forts and watching the local troops march on parade. Though young, Davis had not yet uttered any serious political thoughts or given evidence of paying much attention to public affairs. Still—as a Southerner—it is unlikely that he was ignorant of the tension already filling the air between the United States and Cuba's Spanish masters. Certain increasingly vocal liberation advocates wanted to free themselves of their European rulers and align the island with the Union, while a few men in Washington, chiefly from the South, saw in Cuba a position of strategic importance in the defense of the Gulf coastline, as well as a suitable candidate for another slave state. Seeing Cuba for himself, Davis agreed.

Thus it should not have surprised him that Spanish officers, seeing an Anglo sketching their fortifications, became suspicious. Though dressed as a civilian, he obviously walked with an erect military bearing and gait. One day as he observed the troops drilling, an official approached him and politely but firmly warned that if he was seen again watching them or sketching the fortifications, he would be arrested and imprisoned. Davis's protestations availed him nothing, and though he no doubt fumed at being treated in a highhanded and authoritarian manner, still he prudently ceased his innocent pastime. Unfortunately, this left nothing to do that appealed to him, and soon thereafter he left Cuba out of boredom. He returned to Hurricane.[28]

Jefferson Davis could not know what lay ahead of him as 1836 dawned. He knew that he grieved more sorely than he could have imagined. His broken health was nothing compared to his broken heart. All his prospects seemed dim. He had left the only true profession that he knew. Cruel fate took his beloved from him after just three months of their life together. Even his "plantation" taunted him. Still mostly briers and canebreaks and barely improved, the land itself was not even his own, but on loan from Joseph. Yet right now the land was all he had, all he could grasp and put himself into. Perhaps he might bury his sorrows in the earth of Brierfield. At the same time, having chosen a new life outside the military, this young man who not long before confessed that he felt himself unfit for civilized society realized that just as he reshaped his Mississippi bottom land, he would have to reshape himself for his new life. At least once before, overseeing the training of his company of dragoons, Jefferson Davis exhibited deep reserves of discipline, a capacity for intense application of all his faculties toward a goal.

Now in his despair he summoned those reserves for an even greater purpose. He mustered them to conquer his grief, to turn Brierfield from a wilderness into a plantation, and to make Jefferson Davis into a gentleman.

Toughing It Out

For the next two years he rarely if ever left Davis Bend. He lived in the
big house at Hurricane with his brother Joseph, and now more than ever
looked upon the elder Davis as his mentor. Truly a remarkable man for
his time and place, Joseph Davis read widely in literature and the law as
well as in history and government. He brought to his plantation management ideas that could only be considered very liberal and advanced
for the 1830s. They grew in part from reading, but also out of the
influence of a chance stagecoach encounter with the British industrialist
and utopian Robert Owen in 1825. Among Joseph's other seemingly
innovative ideas was the notion that men responded to their treatment
and surroundings, that humanity and generosity bred character and
loyalty. Owen, of course, applied his theories to the lower-class industrial
workers of England. Joseph Davis saw in those same ideas a way to
manage slaves on his plantation, making both a better life for them, and
a more profitable and happy living for himself.

The slaves at Hurricane lived in comfortable two-room cabins with
large fireplaces and comfortable porches front and back. Rather than
ration the blacks, Joseph allowed them to take as much from the plantation stocks of grain and meat as they wished to eat, and gave them
chickens to keep and feed for themselves. Almost nothing in the plantation larders was off limits. Moreover, he clothed them better than most
slaves elsewhere in the South, and in his treatment of them personally he
was distinctly out of the ordinary. Running entirely contrary to the prevailing notion that order and discipline with slaves could only be maintained by keeping them meek and subjugated, he gave them almost

unheard-of freedoms. The whip and lash caught dust on their shelf from lack of use, if indeed Davis even had instruments of punishment on the premises. Instead he left it to the slaves themselves to judge and punish transgressions by their fellow blacks. Every Sunday, in a building the slaves came to call the Hall of Justice, the slave court met to deal with offenders, much as a regular civil court. Davis acted as judge, and when he interfered at all in the decisions of the juries it was to lessen sentences.

Moreover, Davis encouraged his slaves to challenge and expand themselves by studying special skills and crafts. Slaves could work extra hours and make money by selling their wares to other planters. Others earned bonuses for surpassing cotton-picking quotas, and all the plantation blacks profited collectively by selling their chickens and eggs. He brought in his own doctor to treat their ailments and sent them to specialists in New Orleans when a malady became too serious. When there was a slave wedding, Joseph gave the bride a dress, and birthdays and holidays or other special occasions seldom passed without a party.

In every respect save one, Hurricane became a utopian community, and that exception, of course, was that its citizens were property. Davis did not at all regard the Negroes as equals. His was an entirely paternalistic little society geared to his belief that "the less people are governed, the more submissive they will be to control." Still, some slaves received considerable freedom and responsibility from Davis, and none more so than a teenage boy he bought in Natchez the same year that brother Jefferson returned from Cuba and started to work on Brierfield in earnest. Benjamin Montgomery ran away at first, but Joseph got him back. Where other planters would have whipped or branded him, Davis asked the boy why he ran and talked almost father-to-son with him. Recognizing the youth's quick mind, Davis opened his considerable library to him at a time when planters elsewhere in the South were already enacting laws to prevent literacy in slaves. In time Ben Montgomery would become virtual business manager of Hurricane and an entrepreneur in his own right, all with his master's enthusiastic blessing.

Joseph Davis also had the vision not to be a one-crop planter. Cotton brought the big money, and his was generally conceded to be of the best quality, but he also grew several varieties of corn and other vegetables, planted fruit trees, and devoted many of his acres to livestock to make the plantation self-supporting, as well as to give the land a rest from the exhausting effects of cotton cultivation. Rather than going for the greatest profits in the shortest time, Joseph Davis took the long view, nurturing and building, and still profiting handsomely. He was not greedy, but his methods allowed him and his slaves to have a better standard of living than did any of his neighbors. As his brother's father-in-law Zachary Taylor declared, Joseph Davis "made himself a little paradis[e]."[1]

Without Joseph Davis, there never would have been a Jefferson Davis. Just as the older brother guided the younger in his youth and education, so now he became the model for the young planter-to-be. Through much of the day Jefferson rode with Joseph over the fields of Hurricane, watching, learning, and applying what he had seen to his own slowly clearing fields at Brierfield. More to the point, Jefferson readily adopted his brother's ideas in the treatment of his slaves. He began with an attitude already sympathetic in the main. From youth, Davis had shown a tenderness of feeling for others. However imperious or cold he could become when challenged, still he evidenced great reluctance to give pain or offense to anyone, especially those who could not fight back. Years later a daughter would recall that her father would "almost invariably side with a child or slave against what he called 'irresponsible authority,' " an attitude entirely in keeping with Joseph's. Rather, he shared his brother's faith in the power of persuasion and common sense. Unfortunately, though he rarely if ever directed it at his slaves, he also shared Joseph's inability to understand how someone could differ with him after he had explained an opinion and the reasons behind it, as evidenced in his court-martial. The slaves, of course, were probably wise enough simply not to disagree.[2]

Pemberton, however, may have enjoyed that privilege, as he quickly became to Jefferson Davis what Montgomery was to become to Joseph. A deep and warm bond existed already between the two men. Pemberton had been with Davis since his youth, had nursed him through a terrible sickness in the northwest, and attended him again with his malaria. Very quickly the black man took charge of the rest of the slaves on Brierfield, acting virtually as overseer in carrying out Davis's wishes. Pemberton spoke very little, and that quite respectfully, while his master invariably addressed him simply as James. "It is disrespect to give a nickname," Jefferson Davis explained, and invariably he showed that respect to his servant. "They were devoted friends, and always observed the utmost ceremony and politeness in their intercourse," wrote one who intimately observed them both. Whenever Davis left the plantation, he gave Pemberton a cigar. They sat at the same table occasionally, and though Pemberton never presumed to sit uninvited in his master's presence, Davis always asked him to and sometimes himself brought forth a chair.[3]

Moreover, Davis showed the same consideration to the rest of his slaves, and this must have come as much from his own nature as from his brother's example. Rather than nicknaming them, he allowed his blacks to choose the names that they preferred themselves. As at Hurricane, there was to be no corporal punishment at Brierfield, and when one of his own slave juries found a defendant guilty and sentenced the culprit to the whip or lash, Jefferson Davis generally commuted the pronouncement to extra labor or even just a probationary warning. And whenever one of his slaves was accused, regardless of the source, white or black, he refused to take immediate action. "I will ask him to give me his account of it," Davis invariably said, and allowed the black to defend himself. "How can I know whether he was misunderstood, or meant well and awkwardly expressed himself." At times Davis seemed so solicitous of the goodwill of his slaves that he actively tried to placate them when he thought they were annoyed with him. And his corn crib and fruit trees, like Joseph's, were to be open to the slaves. He also learned that they could be relied on to fight if given proper—white—leadership, after he led a group of them against some lawless neighborhood whites.[4]

Certainly he was patient with their inefficiencies. Perhaps as a result of years of army fare, or because his illness had robbed him of appetite and Sarah's death robbed him of interest, Davis began to show an almost complete indifference to food and drink. Years later he would claim that it was "unworthy of a man to care much what he ate, except so far as his choice should be dictated by his digestion." As a result he consumed whatever was put before him, with barely a complaint over quantity or quality. Bringing a new mulatto woman to cook for him, he quickly found her considerably lacking. She forgot to make his breakfast, so he satisfied himself with drinking milk. When time for the evening meal came around and she had prepared nothing, he merely said, "Do not trouble yourself; just give over trying to-night and catch up for breakfast." In the end his only requirements were that he have corn pone or hoecake with a meal. Whatever taste he had enjoyed for strong liquor as a cadet or out on the frontier seems now to have left him. Perhaps his invalid's stomach could not tolerate it; perhaps with Sarah gone, it was just one more thing in which he found no pleasure.[5]

As Jefferson Davis surveyed his spreading fields in those two years and looked with fond pride on the happy and thriving little community of blacks, the changes in Brierfield mirrored the changes in its master. The year of Sarah's death became more and more obviously a watershed in his life. The youth who once loved to roam over the gentle Mississippi hills hunting small game with his rifle now enforced a prohibition against all shooting on his plantation. Birds and beasts alike were to be protected as he came to feel an abhorrence that "any innocuous creature should be killed without some useful end, or on account of a misplaced trust in man." Perhaps death of any kind was too disturbing in the aftermath of what death had taken away from him.[6]

A greater change still came in the way he spent his time away from the fields. By all accounts he buried himself in Hurricane's library. He read voraciously and on almost every subject. For several hours a day he studied whatever was available. He read widely in the works ancient and modern, especially of the eighteenth century and the first third of the nineteenth. He loved Virgil, but Milton bored him. The poetry of Byron and Burns and the novels and poems of Walter Scott he so mastered that years afterward he could recite from them by memory. In the tragic heroes of Scott, particularly, he seemed to see something of himself in his current bereavement. He read Cervantes but could not see in Don Quixote anything ridiculous but, rather, "a noble mind distraught." He also savored James Fenimore Cooper's writings, perhaps for their Indian characters. Much as he remained distraught himself, he could only use novels to drive more serious matters from his mind. He read the Bible, though he, like Joseph—and many Jeffersonians—maintained a discrete distance from organized religion. Far more meaningful to him were the works of Shakespeare, whom he revered above all others. After digesting over and over again the plays and the sonnets, he concluded that in them "one might find a symposium of all human wisdom if one only knew the exact places to look for it." He felt the same for the Song of Solomon and looked on portions of the Book of Job as the finest poetry in any language.

Davis's reading explored beyond literature into history and government and political economy. On Joseph's shelves he found the *Federalist Papers*, works on the Constitution, reports of congressional debates, and the several works written on the controversial Virginia and Kentucky Resolutions of 1798 and 1799, in which Jefferson first proposed the notion that a state might set aside laws of the federal government that it found objectionable. And when he had finished his readings, he could sit up for hours talking with Joseph, discussing and debating his readings, throwing out his impressions and conclusions, and hearing the rebounding views from his brother's remarkably fertile and open mind. Mild, good-humored, often prone to color his arguments with a keen, if satirical, wit, Joseph Davis was the perfect sort of intellect to guide the formation of another's views while still allowing them to take shape for themselves.[7]

Certainly Jefferson Davis found plenty of time to talk and read, for he did not sleep, or at least not a planter's sleep of early to bed and early to rise. Later he teasingly complained that he had been "obliged to get up to reveille for so many years that he had never been able to make up for his lost morning naps." As a result he could not rise early in the morning. The real reason, of course, was insomnia. He could not get to sleep at night, often until after midnight. Thus he read and talked to fill the lonely hours of darkness. There is no mystery over what kept him awake: It had to be ·Sarah. Yet beneath the tragedy of her loss ran deeper currents, past shadows darker even than he himself may have realized and flowing in directions that profoundly changed Jefferson Davis for the rest of his life. For in those sleepless midnight hours he met other foes than heartbreak and loss. Arrayed against him on that battlefield he found the more formidable, and more sinister, armies of guilt.

Sarah Taylor had revealed many things in the letter she wrote her mother on the morning of her wedding day. "You will be much surprised, no doubt my dear Mother," she wrote on June 17, 1835, "to hear of my being married so soon." Obviously when she left Fort Crawford in May she did not expect a June wedding. And in a previous letter that Sarah referred to on June 17, she still had not anticipated either being married or moving to Mississippi for some time. "I had no idea of leaving here before fall," she said, "but hearing the part of the Country to which I am going is quite healthy I have concluded to go down this summer." Beyond question, from her own words it is clear that she originally intended to stay in Kentucky through September or October in order to avoid the fever season on the lower Mississippi. Clearly, before June, she had heard and believed that it would be dangerous to go south in the summer, and just as clearly—"hearing the part of the Country to which I am going is quite healthy"—someone persuaded her in June that it would be safe. Who was there in Louisville that June familiar enough with Mississippi to offer convincing arguments as to its safety? Who was there who could want to persuade her not to wait until fall to wed and go to Davis Bend? Only Jefferson Davis. And the agonizing knowledge that had to claw at him now in his midnight anguish at Hurricane was that he had known all along from his own experience and observation that Mississippi in the summer months was not safe at all.[8]

All through his childhood in Mississippi, young Davis had seen and heard of the deaths of hundreds every summer from malaria and yellow fever, especially in the months of July and August. There had been summertime deaths in his own immediate family, very probably from the fevers, and certainly he knew others at Woodville and later near Vicksburg and Davis Bend who succumbed. By the 1830s his brother Joseph may already have commenced his practice of taking his family to the North every summer to escape the danger, and in August 1828 Lieutenant Jefferson Davis himself, just after graduating from West Point, asked for an extension of a furlough from October 30 until December 31 in order to visit his family. "It would be unsafe for me to visit Missi.," he said, prior to October. Concerned as he was for his own health in 1828, seven years later he would persuade Sarah to go to Mississippi in June, knowing full well that the fevers started to appear in July and got steadily worse in August and September before disappearing by the end of October.[9]

Why would Davis have convinced Sarah to move up their wedding date and move to Davis Bend more than three months before they originally planned? The answer is simple enough to anyone who has been young and in love. Already he had waited nearly two years for her, most of that time on lonely frontier outposts with nothing but her letters to keep him warm. His own plantation at Brierfield awaited him, and October could be too late to start clearing land for a first crop. He was tired of waiting. Looking ahead to a new life, with the anxiety and impetuosity of youth, he wanted Sarah for his wife now, his wife in his bed, and his bed at Brierfield.

Thus he took a risk. His eagerness getting the better of his judgment, no doubt he rationalized that the risk was not so great. Yes, hundreds died every summer—but thousands lived. And Davis Bend was isolated. They would encounter few people, and thus—not knowing that the lowly mosquito was the messenger of death—he could conclude that they would be unlikely to contract a fever from others. In short, he allowed his passion to overcome his prudence. He convinced himself of things he knew to be untrue, and then he convinced Sarah, and it cost her life.

Even in the unlikely event that someone else gave Sarah to believe she ran no risk, Davis obviously did nothing to persuade her otherwise. Marriage is not a unilateral relationship, and since it was his home they went to, there is no question that he could have taken decisive action to stop her from coming had he wished. In the aftermath of September 15, Jefferson Davis had to believe that Sarah's death rested heavily in his hands and on his conscience.

People cope with such burdens in ways that reflect their characters. For some, the realization of a mistake so momentous is simply crushing, and they never recover. For Davis it would be quite different. Long before Sarah's death he had given ample evidence that his was a nature that only rarely admitted error and that he could stretch logic to some lengths to avoid doing so. Now faced with the most terrible kind of mistake imaginable, one that had cost the life of his beloved, he must have fought terrible battles in his mind and heart. Many others have engaged similar foes, and very often they emerge just as he did. The only way to live with the results of their actions is to convince themselves somehow that they are faultless after all. The telltale sign is rationalization on even the most minor issues, for to confess fallibility in small matters automatically opens the door—one they want closed forever—to self-doubt about the greater issue. Not a single word or thought survives from Davis's hand that he felt or accepted any responsibility for Sarah's death. To keep that door closed, he adopted a posture that cost him dearly in years to come. From this time to the day of his death, Jefferson Davis would never say openly, categorically, without qualification, "I was wrong."

These long days and longer nights at Hurricane brought other profound changes in the man. Years later he wrote that "few things were in my younger days more sad to me than the mirth of a professed clown." He did not see how someone could hide unhappiness behind a smile or a laugh, and he could not do so himself. Yet overcome by grief as he was, still Davis was too proud to wear his heart on his sleeve and let his anguish show. He cloaked it beneath a stoical application of will and self-control. It came naturally to him. After all, his father Samuel lived behind much the same facade for most of his life, only occasionally allowing deeper feelings to escape, as when he hugged Jefferson on his return from St. Thomas College. Now the son did the same, cultivating an attitude of dignified reserve to hide the turmoil beneath. Many who knew him both before and after 1835 commented on the change. The exuberant, unruly, mischievous, gay young man of West Point and Fort Winnebago all but disappeared, or at least to those outside his immediately family and very close friends. Of course he could still be witty, would love again in time, and even occasionally engaged in a small frolic, but the walls he erected to contain his grief in the first months and years after Sarah's death soon imprisoned other emotions as well. Though not yet thirty, from this time forward he impressed new acquaintances as being older than his years. Only after these reclusive days at Hurricane would the adjective *cold* begin to occur to those who met Jefferson Davis.[10]

Now, too, his views of the outer world began to change. Unable or unwilling to accept imperfections in himself, he developed a preoccupation with what he perceived as imperfections elsewhere, whether in people or things. He may not yet have commenced his later practice of lecturing people at length on their conduct and deportment, but certainly he already showed signs of an inclination to ruminate at length on failings that perturbed him. He much admired art, having demonstrated no mean skill in drawing at West Point, yet now when he saw in a book an engraving that he liked, still he could not help but look for and find some deficiency that in his eyes marred the artist's work. "Any fault of this kind in an object he approved seemed to worry him strangely," wrote one who observed Davis in later life, "and he would often mention it in conversation long after we supposed he had forgotten the existence of the thing to which he referred."[11] It was but one aspect of a budding preoccupation with a rigid sense of right and wrong, truth and error.

Thus for two years after Sarah's death Davis faced the demons within him by night, while he worked in his fields with Pemberton by day. Gradually both body and mind improved. By the spring of 1836 he was ready to think of traveling to Woodville to see his mother if she could not accept his invitation to come see Brierfield. That summer he again turned his attention to his still-outstanding accounts with the army, and during the winter most probably heard from his friend Northrop the satisfying news that his old nemesis Major Mason was himself going through a court-martial on charges brought by Northrop and based, among other things, on Mason's treatment of the two of them. While his correspondence with his family farther south was sporadic, still he enjoyed visits from some of them, even undertaking to counsel his sister Lucinda Stamps's sickly son Hugh. It was all part of forcing himself to get over his woe, to conquer adversity by perseverance—a process he called "toughing it out."[12]

One thing in Davis's makeup did not change during this period of intense remolding: his streak of restlessness and indecision. In 1835 he had decided—at Joseph's urging—to leave the army behind him and become a planter. After Sarah's death and his own slow recovery, he renewed his commitment to his plantation. Yet by the fall of 1837, after less than two years on the land, he found himself bored with growing cotton or else needful of a change of scenery. Word came to him, no doubt from old friends still in uniform, that one or more new infantry regiments might be created by Congress. Davis remembered the good fortune that came his way when the creation of the dragoon regiment resulted in an accelerated promotion. Now he determined to attempt to return to the army by applying for a commission in one of the new units. Perhaps he could even reenter the service with another promotion, a captaincy or better. With the movement of American settlers into the Oregon Territory heating boundary disputes with Great Britain, with others putting pressure on relations with the Mexican owners of California and the Southwest, and with white-Indian confrontations continuing on the central and northern plains, there could be plenty of opportunities for a young officer to see action and excitement and to get ahead. Certainly it would be more exciting than farming. Just what Joseph thought of this is a mystery. It is likely that he did not approve. If he did, it could only have been for the therapeutic effects a major change might have on Jefferson.[13]

He left sometime that fall, going first to New York, where he visited with Joseph's brother-in-law Watson Van Benthuysen, before continuing on to Philadelphia. Already the journey overtaxed him, and between Philadelphia and Baltimore he began to feel unwell. He recuperated a day or two in the Maryland city, venturing out into the countryside to look at some newly imported cattle that he found very interesting, then proceeded on his way to Washington on Christmas. After he reached the capital the next day, fevers, chills, and coughs kept him bedridden for almost a week. Only on New Year's Day did he venture out of his room, and then he went down to Pennsylvania Avenue to an open house at the Executive Mansion. President Martin Van Buren literally opened the house to any and all comers. As a result Davis found it so crowded, and felt so weak, that he could not make himself enter the bustle to circulate, see the house, and shake the president's hand. "I hung like a poor boy at a frolick about the empty corners for a short time," he wrote, "and left the House without being presented." He felt more welcome when he went to Dowson's boarding house on Capitol Hill. There his old friend George W. Jones, now a congressman from the Iowa Territory, shared rooms with Thomas Hart Benton and other representatives from the western states and quickly persuaded Davis to board with him during his visit. The familiar old company was delightful, of course, and Jones and the others as well might prove helpful in his petition to obtain a commission in one of the new regiments. He also called on the two Mississippi congressmen to solicit their influence early in January, and then resigned himself to the old Washington game of waiting for news.

Meanwhile, as his health allowed, Davis actually tried to enjoy himself with Jones and other friends, one of whom was Franklin Pierce of New Hampshire. Running with Jones, however, could be a hair-raising experience, and in February—when he acted as a second for Representative Jonathan Cilley of Maine in a duel with William Graves of Kentucky—Jones brought Davis to watch the meeting, and they both saw Cilley killed. Then, later that same month, or in March, fate very nearly touched Davis yet again.

One evening Jones, Davis, and two others from Dowson's went to a reception given by Secretary of War Joel R. Poinsett. Around midnight, when Jones and one of the others went home, the insomniac Davis remained for a late supper and champagne with John J. Crittenden of Kentucky and others. Crittenden promised to bring the Mississippian back by carriage. Sometime later Jones heard voices and footsteps outside his bedroom, and then saw Senator William Allen of Ohio help a blood-soaked Jefferson Davis into the room. There was a deep cut in his head, and mud and water dripped from his face and clothing.

They had decided to walk back from Poinsett's after all, and since Davis was still new to the town, Allen led the way. Unfortunately, a heavy infusion of champagne led Allen that night. Missing his way in the dark, he accidentally walked off a bridge over the Tiber Creek and fell in, without harm. Davis followed right behind him. His friend Jones, as friends do, claimed that the Mississippian was quite sober, and perhaps he was, though certainly Jones saw him drinking some champagne that night. As he later described the incident, Davis felt himself lose his footing and tried to recover by diving headfirst into the Tiber. Unfortunately, it was so shallow that he struck his head against a rock and nearly killed himself. Allen fished him out of the stream and dragged him back to Dowson's, meanwhile drunkenly reciting over and over again a campaign speech.

His friends cleaned and dressed Davis's wound, then put him to bed, not realizing that he had probably suffered a concussion. The next morning Jones found him unconscious, and only after several hours of attention could they revive him. One doctor present suspected that if Jones had not discovered his condition that morning, Davis would have died. Perhaps so, but in the days that followed his recovery seemed quick, and before long Davis was able to continue the rounds of meeting important people. Pierce even got him an audience with President Van Buren, and together they shared breakfast one morning. Certainly they spoke of the army, and no doubt Davis pressed his case for an appointment. They spoke as well of politics and other subjects, but as time went on Van Buren's eyes kept wandering to Davis's New Orleans shoes. Finally he asked where Davis had had them made. Meeting the president was an impressive and memorable experience, and Davis remembered Van Buren and admired him politically for several years thereafter, even if the New Yorker seemed more interested in his feet than in his ambitions for a command.[14]

By early April there was no definitive word on his application, or else Davis may already have received inklings from his congressional friends that only one new regiment would be created and that new officers would not be needed. At the same time his health returned to normal, and there seemed no point in tarrying longer. Soon it would be time to start planting again. Davis left on April 5 for Philadelphia and then went to Pittsburgh to catch a steamboat for the long trip back to Davis Bend. All he had acquired on his trip was a pair of pistols from Baltimore. Yet certainly the trip had done him good, accident and all, for he renewed old friendships of youth that, at an age like his, could be very powerful restoratives. And he formed new acquaintances with men who would figure in his future, and for the first time felt the thrill of standing face to face with the great men of the day. It was a feeling he surely liked.[15]

So he was to remain a planter. Davis and James Pemberton moved into the old cabin on the Brierfield property and continued the work of cultivation and harvest, the endless cycle of the farmer. "I hope My Dear Uncle," his niece Florida McCaleb wrote that summer of 1838, "that you have not found the time hang heavily on your hands." Perhaps it did not. There was much work, there was Joseph's library to occupy his long evenings, and more and more he found himself willing to leave Davis Bend to visit family and friends and work himself back into the normal routine of life. He talked of visits to Louisville and to Hot Springs, Arkansas, that summer. He oversaw both Brierfield and Hurricane when Joseph's family went north for the fever months, though when Jefferson decided to remain in Mississippi for the season, Joseph cautioned him against something he had seen in his brother: "an attempt at *too much*."

As officers observed at Fort Gibson, when Jefferson Davis decided to put himself into something, he did it sometimes to extremes, pushing himself to (or beyond) his limits.

That winter he agreed again to leave Davis Bend, to take his niece Ellen Davis to the Nazareth Academy near Bardstown, Kentucky. He did not make the trip after all, but as 1839 dawned he already contemplated other journeys. That coming summer he planned to return to the scenes of his early army days and visit Jones at his home at Sinsinawa Mound in Wisconsin. He also looked back to other long-neglected old friendships, no doubt finding in their renewal a renewal in himself. Seeking out a schoolmate from his days in Kentucky, Davis found him in Natchez late in 1839 anxious "to talk about those *gone by days—when our spirits were high* with *future hopes*, days: before care, *or the* mishaps, or *misfortunes, or perplexities* of life, had eaten Canker like upon our fortunes." Davis knew all too well the bite of that "Canker."[16]

By the summer of 1840 Davis could write to William Allen, whom he loved despite having nearly been killed by him, that "I am living as retired as a man on the great thoroughfare of the Mississippi can be." Indeed, now he had time to divert his thoughts by worrying about his brother Joseph for a change. As early as the fall of the previous year friends had commented to him on their concern for the "depression & melancholy" they all saw in the elder Davis. The exact cause is uncertain, but beyond question at least part of it was marital. Eliza Davis, highly strung and continually lacking self-confidence, seemed at the point of nervous exhaustion. She and Joseph traveled north again in the summer of 1840, but things only got worse, and by July her husband was sending her to New York to her relatives, while he remained in Kentucky. In anguish she wrote to Jefferson of her fears for her sanity "if Mr Davis leaves me." There must have been much cause for discontent between a fifty-five-year-old husband and a twenty-nine-year-old wife, yet if Jefferson recognized the problems that such a difference in age might cause, still he drew no conclusions. As for Joseph and Eliza, whatever their differences, they passed through them, with many long years of marriage ahead.[17]

Gradually Brierfield grew, and with it Davis learned the vicissitudes of a planter's life. By the summer of 1840 his initial dozen slaves had multiplied to forty, twenty-nine of them devoted to working his soil. In another five years he would have seventy-four. Meanwhile he managed a small herd of twenty cattle, and his improved acreage produced good cotton crops. Indeed, he produced too much, so that in 1840, like most other planters, he saw the bumper crop result in falling prices. He clearly saw that prices would only rise by limiting production, "an event which the embarrassed condition of cotton planters in this section will not allow them to consider." Very quickly he learned to look anxiously at published price indexes like the *Liverpool Circular* to see what he could expect the European buyers of his cotton to pay. Happily, later in 1840 the price went up again, and the planters of Mississippi breathed easier.[18]

But something new claimed more and more of Jefferson Davis's attention after his return from Washington. Perhaps brushing sleeves with those politicians, hearing the debates in Congress, and seeing where issues that affected the entire Union were argued and decided awakened in him something of which he had previously been unaware. He became increasingly interested in politics. No doubt his long discussions with a very politically sensitive brother had laid a foundation, but it is only after his Washington visit that talk of politics first enters his correspondence— not that he entertained any very high opinion of its practitioners. Less than a year after his visit to Washington he looked on the capital as "that hot bed of heartlessness and home of the world's worldly." Nor did he pretend any very sophisticated grasp of public affairs. "When I write of politics," he told Jones, "I am out of my element and naturally slip back to seeding and ploughing."[19]

Davis balanced his interests between national and local affairs and probably derived his opinions largely from Joseph. Ardent Jeffersonianism guided both brothers, putting them in the mainstream of the Democratic party. Andrew Jackson, recently retired from the presidency, remained an idol to them, even though he was an ardent nationalist. His successor Van Buren, a craftier but less gifted executive, commanded their respect, and Davis felt at least some fondness as a result of Van Buren's hospitality at the White House. Their rising hero, however, would be John C. Calhoun of South Carolina, himself formerly a leading nationalist who, by the 1840s, had progressed far down the road to become a champion of localism.

Interestingly enough in the light of his own history of indecision, Jefferson Davis chiefly expressed unhappiness with Van Buren for the same fault. "As the head of the democratic party I wish him success," Davis wrote to Jones, "but he has sowed indecision." Van Buren tried too hard to accommodate too many factions in order to retain popularity, he believed, and that would cripple a leader. What Van Buren seemed to lack, as Davis viewed it, was that sense of ironbound certainty of rightness that he and Joseph shared. That summer of 1840 every steamboat, stagecoach, rail car, and barroom echoed to electioneering voices as men spoke of nothing but "Hard Cider Log Cabin," as Joseph put it, referring to the campaign slogans and totems of the William H. Harrison camp. Harrison, the hero of Tippecanoe, led the Whig assault on Van Buren's reelection attempt, and his victory in the fall brought to an end a twelve-year Democratic hold on the White House.

To the South especially this represented a blow, for Van Buren had run on a conservative constitutional platform that implicitly favored the protection of localism and noninterference by the national government in state matters. Already, though not a major issue in the 1840 campaign, states' rights had come to be a euphemism for slavery. Joseph Davis, spending the summer in Kentucky, actually saw some of the major campaigning in person, since the grand old Whig Henry Clay lived in Lexington. And he heard another Clay, Cassius Marcellus, one of the early and ardent Southern opponents of slavery. Kentucky put a law on its books that prohibited bringing new slaves into the commonwealth for sale. This Clay supported the law and contended that it was not an abolitionist measure. But Joseph wrote to Jefferson that "any interference with the unqualified property of the Own[er] in a Slave was an abolition principle." There is no reason to doubt that his brother felt exactly the same by this time. Moreover, Cassius Clay advocated keeping a distance between the people of Kentucky and the cotton and sugar planters of the lower South, because the latter were so wholeheartedly intertwined with slavery, an institution "that the whol[e] Civilized world was opposed to."

Joseph Davis found that shocking, and his opinion carried much force with his brother. "You may readily Suppose the feeling of any Southern man on hearing Such principles in Such a place," he wrote from Lexington. He intended to respond himself, declaring it a "duty to. apprise the South of the opinions entertained and advocated by the *whigs* in a State where they expected funds, and when the necessity occurs they may be prepared to act as men." Joseph Davis was no more explicit than that, but in his words there lay the germ of a belief that if the Democrats' political opponents on the topic of slavery put that opposition above their common Southern heritage, as Cassius Clay suggested, then trouble could follow, and true Southerners might have to "be prepared to act as men."

If Joseph Davis ever actually discussed the subject of resistance to federal authority or secession with his brother prior to this time, neither recalled it, but almost certainly the topic occupied some of their conversation during those evenings at Hurricane. After all, the memory of the South Carolina nullification crisis still remained strong. Davis had been resolved then to resign his commission rather than take arms against fellow Southerners. Joseph, though far out of the mainstream in the management of his slaves, still shared the overwhelming majority opinion of other Southerners as to slavery itself and their constitutional rights to that kind of property. As a good Democrat, Jefferson Davis wholeheartedly admired President Jackson for standing up to the nullifiers. "Resistance to the laws it was his duty to suppress by all the means at his command," he would say of Old Hickory in a few years, "and when loud and deep were heard threats of disunion, . . . he resolved, cost what it might, to save it." But as a good Southern rights man, Davis also honored Calhoun for the stand that resulted in that crisis. Such even-handed empathy with men on both sides of a sectional issue was rare in 1840; in a few more years it would be rare in Jefferson Davis.[20]

The art of public oratory also gained more and more of the young planter's attention. Though he probably never practiced it himself other than in school—and in defending himself in courts-martial—still, by the summer of 1840 he avidly read the published speeches of leading public men and analyzed their strengths and weaknesses, finding his friend Allen a model orator, and the much admired Calhoun at times too "sententious." Even family members took notice of his increasing interest in public affairs and public men. In Kentucky that summer, Joseph Davis and one of his daughters talked about the presidency, and the fact that to date Mississippi had not sent a native son to the White House. Davis confessed perhaps the state never would, but his daughter Caroline blurted out that "Uncle Jeff would be President after [a]while."[21]

The next two years, though peaceful ones for the master of Brierfield, saw his attention turn increasingly away from planting and toward matters beyond Davis Bend. By the end of 1842 Jefferson Davis was thirty-five, a settled and secure farmer whose tragedy now lay seven years behind. Though he and others later claimed that he spent almost a decade in perfect seclusion, rarely leaving Brierfield, seeing almost no one, the facts are otherwise. He made at least one trip to the East, possibly a second; planned several other visits to friends and family from Wisconsin to Arkansas, which he may have made; certainly traveled to New Orleans more than once either with his cotton crops or at least to buy his shoes; and carried on a widespread correspondence that paid increasing attention to national affairs. Far from turning inward, Davis, after two and one-half years of isolation, had started looking outward. While nothing survives to testify to his social intercourse in and around Warren County, Mississippi, it is clear that by December 1842 his friends and neighbors, and especially fellow Democrats, knew him sufficiently, and thought well enough of his judgment, that they selected him to go with his brother Joseph and others as a delegate from Warren to the Democratic State Convention to be held in Jackson on February 22, 1843.

He may have done nothing more than observe at that three-day convention. Joseph, much better known to Mississippi Democrats, sat on a central committee. But even if Jefferson only became known as Joseph's brother, it would have earned him some respect. In his own right, however, the young planter's erect and dignified military bearing, added to the reserved demeanor he developed during his bereavement, must have impressed some of the delegates. Jefferson Davis walked and acted like a man confident that he was born to command. As evidenced by his involvement in the formation of the Vicksburg Jockey Club a week later, he was also willing now to be an active participant in public affairs. Such men could do well in politics.[22]

The Democrats of Warren County found themselves in turmoil in the summer and fall of 1843. The cause was a complex and controversial economic issue—the repudiation of state debts. To ease financial strains in the late 1830s, Mississippi authorized the incorporation of the Union Bank and the issuing of bonds at interest to raise capital. But the bank nearly failed, leaving bondholders without either their investments or their interest. In the crisis the legislature, by a partisan vote—the Whigs being opposed and the majority Democrats in favor—repudiated those bonds. A public outcry followed immediately, for the incorporating legislation and subsequent enactments clearly made the state liable for both principal and interest in the event of a failure. The Democrats won wide support in the 1841 election on the basis of repudiation, since the majority of taxpayers had little interest in seeing their revenues reimburse relatively few investors, but in the ensuing two years the issue would not die and became increasingly divisive, as Whigs pointed out quite rightly that repudiation amounted to bad faith at best and theft at worst.[23]

With the fall election of legislators approaching in 1843, the Whigs put up two candidates in Warren County against the Democrat John B. Williamson, himself a repudiator. But then he became involved in an embarrassing public quarrel with a newspaper editor that seriously compromised his credibility and lost him the support of many in his own party. On October 30, with the election only a few days away, he withdrew his nomination, leaving the Democrats without a candidate.

Someone, perhaps Williamson himself, approached Jefferson Davis. "I have informed Maj. Davis, if he would become a candidate I would support him and urge his election," Williamson wrote in an open letter to the press on November 1. In the process, with a typical Southern informality where titles were concerned (perhaps hoping it would win a few extra votes), he "promoted" the onetime lieutenant two grades. However Davis learned of the plan to make him Williamson's replacement, he accepted the offer, and in a hasty convention at Vicksburg that same day the Warren County Democrats gave him the nomination.

Davis never said why he took the nomination, for it was a forlorn hope, as any could see. Whigs outnumbered Democrats in the county, and they must have been so certain of their majority that they allowed two of their candidates to run and still expected that one or the other would beat the Democratic repudiator Williamson. Perhaps this explains why the underdogs turned to Davis, for, though a Democrat, he opposed repudiation, his position not materially differing from the Whigs'. That might make him acceptable enough to the opposition to attract some voters away from their party candidates, and certainly this threat was not lost on the Whigs. Immediately after Davis's nomination, one of their candidates withdrew. They would not risk splitting their votes. The withdrawal of the second Whig candidate made Davis's defeat certain, "at least so I regarded it." Nevertheless, the Whigs obviously felt that they needed added security for their majority. They called on one of Vicksburg's most noted citizens, and one of the state's acknowledged master orators, Seargent S. Prentiss, a former congressman, prominent attorney, and a friend of Davis's through their mutual involvement with the Jockey Club. While he was not a candidate, he would debate with Davis in two meetings at Vicksburg, the only opportunities the Democrat would have to speak publicly before the election.[24]

Seldom does a political candidate find himself in a battle more uphill than the one that faced Jefferson Davis. It is unknown how long before November 1 he had an inkling that he would be a candidate, but it cannot have been more than a few days, and not more than two weeks before the November 11 election. Certainly he had some knowledge and opinions on most of the issues of the contest, especially repudiation, but that is far different from being prepared to debate them, especially with an experienced orator like Prentiss. Davis had never made a political speech in his life. "The friends of Prentiss anticipated for him an easy victory," recalled another Mississippian, Reuben Davis. But one of Jefferson Davis's nobler traits was that he never quailed at accepting a daunting challenge or championing a forlorn hope. Whether it be winning Zachary Taylor's consent to marry his daughter or competing for this seat in the state legislature, he went into the contest to do his best.[25]

The meetings with Prentiss would be perhaps his only chance to place his real views before the people, for the two Vicksburg newspapers, one aligned with the Whigs, failed to publish any formal statement of his position on repudiation until after the election. Knowing Prentiss and being on good terms with him, Davis met with his opponent shortly before their first debate on November 4 to set some rules. In the interest of time, they agreed not to bring up points on which they did not differ. One of those was repudiation. If Prentiss is the one who suggested that they leave it out, then it worked to his advantage, for by this agreement, the planter's position on that critical issue would be absent from the rostrum as well as the press.[26]

They met first in the barroom of one of Vicksburg's hotels. Prentiss, an old hand at stump speaking, went on for three hours. The subject of repudiation did come up, but only peripheral issues and technicalities that did not affect his basic position. When it came time for Davis to speak, he occupied a mere thirty minutes, and refrained from the flights of oratorical grandeur that Prentiss indulged. "Mr. Davis is a more classical and chaste speaker than S. S. Prentiss," reported the Democratic *Daily Sentinel*. Standoffish because Davis had broken with the party on the repudiation issue, still the paper asserted that "it is not presumption in Mr. Davis' friends to anticipate for him a proud and honorable career, should a sphere for the display of his talents once be presented." Two days later, when Davis and Prentiss met a second time, they improvised a stand on the steps of the Warren County courthouse and went at it again. It became evident to Reuben Davis that in the very brief time since his nomination, the Democratic nominee "had made himself as familiar with the subject in hand as it was possible for a man to be." "Less brilliant in oratory than Prentiss, he was always fascinating and charming, and had much more strength as a debater."

Later reports found Prentiss at his best, referring to him as "the gigantic Goliath" with whom Davis, "our little David," contended. Yet one journal claimed that Davis emerged from that struggle "untouched and unscathed." Moreover, it concluded that "Major Davis is no *ordinary man*." As for Davis himself, he marvelled at Prentiss during these, his first political speeches. Prentiss "impressed me deeply with his capacity for Analysis and logical induction," he said, more "than by any other effort I knew him to make." Finding merit in one's opponent was not always a feature of politics in those times, nor would it always in the future characterize Jefferson Davis.[27]

The election returns a few days later brought no surprise. Of the five voting precincts in the county, Davis carried only one, the little community of Milldale. His opponent Jefferson Nailer took the rest, though he won the largest precinct, Vicksburg, by a margin of only 11 votes. Countywide, Davis captured 512 out of 1,197 votes cast, a very respectable 43 percent. More to the point where his future was concerned, he impressed the local party leaders by his last-minute effort on their behalf—an accomplishment they would not forget.[28]

It had been a big year. The convention in February drew him away from Brierfield for his first organized political involvement. The county election put him before the people for the first time and revealed that he could toe the line on the stump and win votes. Both proved to be turning points for a man clearly ready to end conclusively his so-called retirement after Sarah's death, what some would call the "lost period" of his life. Yet 1843 had one more turning point in store for him before it gave way to the new year. On December 19 Joseph gave his brother a message and asked him to deliver it to Diamond Place, the plantation of his daughter Florida McCaleb. It was an invitation to pay a visit to Hurricane, and Jefferson was to give it to a visitor there. The stop was not out of his way, as Davis had already embarked on yet another political mission, this one a caucus in Vicksburg to select delegates to the forthcoming Democratic State Convention on January 8.

Davis rode up to Diamond Place on horseback, and there, for the first time, he met Varina Howell.[29]

How Little Do We Know
That Which We Are

Though the two had never met before, each at least knew of the other's existence. Varina's father, William B. Howell, owned a handsome house, the "Briers," high on the bluff at Natchez, and he had met Jefferson Davis. He and Joseph shared an old friendship and rode together on that stage when Davis met Robert Owen. William and Margaret Howell accompanied Joseph Davis when he visited West Point to see his brother, and both Howells left behind favorable recollections of the young cadet. They made that visit in the summer of 1825. On May 7, 1826, Margaret Howell gave birth to their daughter Varina. Thus the young woman Jefferson Davis met at Diamond Place was halfway through her eighteenth year, making him, at thirty-six, just over twice her age.

They talked for awhile before he remounted his horse and left for Vicksburg. It is probable that Joseph Davis sent Varina an invitation to come to Hurricane, and sent it by Jefferson, with the explicit intention that the two should meet. He had managed so much else in his brother's life that he would hardly hesitate to do a little matchmaking. By his other activities in the past year, Jefferson had clearly showed that he was ready and even anxious to return fully to the bustle of the world, and at his age and with a growing plantation to manage, it was time he found a wife and helpmate. Despite his own difficulties with a spouse many years his junior, Joseph apparently saw no serious drawbacks in such diverse ages in a union. His brother, as usual, found unobjectionable whatever Joseph found unobjectionable.

If any such thoughts were on the younger Davis's mind when he delivered his message, the face-to-face encounter with Varina herself

96

almost immediately usurped his thoughts. Neither plain nor beautiful, she had a strong face, a sultry complexion, and a handsome figure and carriage. She showed everyone a strong will and an independent nature—reminders of Sarah, perhaps—and brought an alert and cultivated intellect to her conversation. She could be haughty and imperious one moment and contrite and submissive the next, and she was an altogether challenging and complex young woman, the more so to a man nineteen years older.

Davis left no recollection of their first meeting, but Varina Howell did. That same day she wrote a letter to her mother that revealed just how perceptive she was. She found Davis's voice "peculiarly sweet" and his manners winning and agreeable. She did not know his exact age and could not quite guess. "I do not know whether this Mr. Jefferson Davis is young or old," she wrote. "He looks both at times; but I believe he is old." Though she found him "a remarkable kind of man," still she detected in him an "uncertain temper" and did not at all like his way of "taking for granted that everybody agrees with him when he expresses an opinion, which offends me." "The fact is," she said, "he is the kind of person I should expect to rescue one from a mad dog at any risk, but to insist upon a stoical indifference to the fright afterward." This remarkable teenage girl, in a single afternoon's conversation, read Davis's character to the letter and saw in him both the strengths and weaknesses that would elevate and bedevil him for the rest of his life. Davis always fancied himself an excellent judge of character, though the years revealed few examples of any such insight; certainly he never read anyone himself so quickly and accurately as Varina Howell, that December day, read him.[1]

"I do not think I shall ever like him as I do his brother Joe," the girl told her mother. Jefferson Davis felt no such doubts. It may not have been love at first encounter, but undoubtedly he rode off to Vicksburg with his thoughts full of her, and he hurried back to Hurricane after his political meeting caucus concluded, knowing that Varina had left for Davis Bend the day after their meeting. She stayed for several weeks, probably well into February 1844, and much enjoyed her visit. She listened to Joseph and Jefferson in the evenings when they sat in the office and talked of the law, planting, and politics "and made and perfected theories about everything in heaven and on earth." Jefferson Davis read aloud to Joseph from copies of congressional debates and sometimes asked Varina to share the reading with him. No doubt the two walked together in the rose garden behind the house or strolled through the fruit orchard nearby. Certainly they rode, and Varina immediately noted how both Davis brothers fawned over and spoiled their horses "and talked of them in the most affectionate tones."

For Jefferson Davis, Varina's stay raced past all too quickly. He had to feel a boiling turmoil inside as long-dormant emotions reawakened. If he had paid any attention to other women during the years since Sarah's death, he never spoke of it. Quite possibly he had avoided all such social contacts, and Varina may have been the first eligible young woman he met. He saw in her some traits that reminded him of Sarah, to be sure, but there was much that was different, as Davis himself was different now. He acted with an impetuosity suggesting either a heart carried away by uncontrollable passion or else a man bent on taking the first opportunity of finding a wife that presented itself. The subsequent courtship revealed elements of both.[2]

He courted her almost from the outset. By the time Varina returned home in February 1844, Davis had either proposed already or at least discussed with her the possibility of marriage. Surprisingly, considering her earlier reservations about his age and his "uncertain temper," Varina met his suit with encouragement. She claimed later that they were actually engaged when she left Hurricane, though certainly much remained unsettled between them as he saw her off from the steamboat landing. Once again, as years before, there were fears of a problem—this time, with parents who might not approve because of the age difference. Varina herself hesitated. When Davis asked her to write to him, she frankly said she might not. It was all happening very quickly for a girl not yet eighteen, and Davis doubtless pushed his case almost to the point of overwhelming her. She, too, must have worried about the difference in their ages. Perhaps she even wondered at the nature of Jefferson's sudden love, for in much of his discourse he spoke to her often more as a father to a daughter—instructing, reproving, judging—just as Joseph Davis dealt with his younger wife Eliza. When she stood on the bottom deck of the steamboat waving farewell to Davis and others, she could not have been entirely certain in her heart of the man who looked so forlorn at her leaving. She did know that she felt somehow desolate at parting. For himself, Jefferson Davis stood there wishing that by some word or gesture she would beckon him to join her on the boat.

But she did not, and Davis returned to a Hurricane that he found dull without her. Every time he entered a room in which they had been together, she entered his mind, and he even imagined that others in the house thought of her whenever they saw him. Varina obsessed his thoughts, leaving him melancholy and diffident. He told her before she left that he intended to come to the Briers himself before long to propose formally to her there after honorably securing her parents' permission. Yet as the days passed and he did not hear from her, his confidence eroded. Thus early in March when a letter from Varina finally arrived, he exulted that "it came to dispell my gloomy apprehensions." After a battle of her own, Varina had concluded that she loved him, too, though she implored him not to come to Natchez just yet.

There must have been some reluctance from William and Margaret Howell, and she needed time to work on them. Frustrated but still overjoyed, Davis agreed that "I am willing in this matter to be guided by you."

Interestingly enough, Varina had been amused or troubled enough by one little incident in Natchez to tell Davis of it in her letter. One day, addressing her father, she called him "Jefferson." Was it because her suitor was constantly on her mind, or did it have something to do with the paternal manner he sometimes assumed with her? Davis himself, answering her letter with an outpouring of almost lawyerlike address interspersed with expressions of love, closed with fatherly admonitions not to keep a candle burning in her room all night or to stay up too late or read after dark. One reason she did stay awake, as she told him, was out of a fear that he would censure her.[3]

Thus the courtship progressed. He treasured her letters. When she posted them she pressed between their pages flowers she had worn or a lock of her hair, and Davis kept them all in a concealed place at Hurricane away from prying eyes. By the middle of March, Varina herself had definitely consented to his wishes and had persuaded her mother to withdraw any objections to the marriage, thus leaving her suitor free to come to Natchez. Later that month he made the trip, spoke with the Howells, and secured their permission and Varina's formal assent. Their engagement was announced. Once again for Davis it would be a long one, though not so frustrating as his long-distance engagement to Sarah Taylor. They set the time a year off, in the spring of 1845. The reason, no doubt, was that for much of the rest of 1844, Jefferson Davis would be in the grip of politics.[4]

At that meeting of Warren County Democrats back in December, Davis and a number of others received appointments as delegates to the state convention. On January 8, 1844, Davis walked into the representatives' hall of the statehouse and took his seat. This was a national election year. Mississippians had to choose their delegates to the Democratic convention in Baltimore and instruct those delegates which presidential and vice presidential candidates they were to back. They also had to outline the stand Mississippi Democrats wished to take on platform issues. Interestingly enough, when a committee including Davis met to discuss all the platform issues—a litany of anti-Whig positions opposing internal improvements, a national bank, and federal assumption of state debts and an ardent statement that the national government had no power to interfere with domestic institutions of the states, meaning slavery—Davis and the others deliberated and then returned that afternoon to recommend that all platform matters be tabled and only the matter of the party nominees be dealt with.

Davis could not have been entirely happy with his committee's decision, if not for ignoring platform matters, then for the candidates that it recommended to the convention as a whole. As Warren County's chosen representative on that committee, he had been instructed by fellow delegates from his home county to cast his vote in favor of Martin Van Buren, and indeed the committee had recommended instructing delegates to the Baltimore convention to vote for Van Buren for president and James K. Polk of Tennessee for vice president. But during the committee meeting Davis ignored his instructions and proposed Calhoun instead of Van Buren, and now in the debate that followed the committee's report he made a lengthy speech advocating Calhoun.

He took nothing away from Van Buren, said Davis. He simply thought Calhoun's position on certain important issues better founded, and now for the first time in public Davis revealed the extent to which his years of reading, his talks with Joseph, and his own natural inclinations as a Southerner formed his attitudes. He believed that the executive branch in Washington had become overblown and cumbersome and that Calhoun would cut it back and streamline its operations. As a cotton planter, he favored free trade and opposed restrictive tariffs, as did Calhoun. Davis hoped for the speedy annexation of the Republic of Texas, which had won its independence from Mexico a few years before, as a state. Calhoun, like most Southerners, agreed, for as a result of the Missouri Compromise, Texas would come into the Union as a slave state. Calhoun favored building more navy yards on the Southern coastline, and Davis agreed.

Most of all, intertwined with almost all of these and other positions, Davis stood with Calhoun on the growing controversy over the rights of individual states, the threat of minority status in Congress for Southern states, the growing sentiment for abolition in the North, and other issues that all had at their root slavery. "Daily we are becoming relatively weaker," he declared, "and with equal step is the advance of that fanatical spirit which has for years been battering . . . the defenses with which the federal constitution surrounds our institutions." He said no more now, but two things he made abundantly clear in his address. One was that, like Calhoun, he stood in the ranks of those "strict constructionists" who rigidly opposed any federal interference in state matters not specifically granted under the Constitution. The other was a short memory, or an imperfect reading of history, for Calhoun, now the champion of states' rights, had been an ardent nationalist thirty years before when the South held comfortable control in Washington. More recently Calhoun ardently supported the internal improvements program of the 1820s and 1830s, from which the South had much to gain, even though it violated a host of states' rights. Calhoun's values shifted as the South went from majority to minority status, showing at best a fickle belief in democracy and the will of the majority.

Davis shifted right along with him, yet his activity here at the convention did reveal one trait not generally found among other strict constructionists. They as a rule regarded elected or appointed representatives as essentially bound to represent the will of the electorate. Yet in championing Calhoun in the committee deliberation and again on the floor of the convention, Davis not once but twice went directly against the instructions of the majority of the Warren County delegates. Faced with a conflict between his own judgment and the will of those who chose him their representative, he would follow his own counsel. As so often before, he had thought the subject through, decided the correct course for himself, and if the will of the majority said otherwise, then the majority was wrong. Even with his speech done, and when the convention had chosen Van Buren and Polk as their favorites, Davis rose to offer a resolution endorsing Calhoun should Baltimore fail to nominate Van Buren. This, at least, the Jackson delegates approved, and they went on to appoint Davis, William Gwin, Jacob Thompson, Henry S. Foote, Robert J. Walker, and others to go to Baltimore in May. Further, the convention also appointed Davis and five others to be its candidates for electors in the fall.[5]

Davis catapulted himself deeper into politics almost at once. Just the day after the Jackson meeting, he and Foote and John A. Quitman, his onetime Spanish teacher and a neighbor on Davis Bend, made public addresses advocating the annexation of Texas. Shortly thereafter he began acquiring copies of prominent speeches and annual reports of executive departments in Washington. "I have mingled but little in politics," he explained to William Allen, "and . . . have an arsenal poorly supplied for a campaign." It would not be that way for long, and as always he devoured and digested everything in detail. "Labor is expected of me and I am willing to render it."[6]

Render it he did. Davis took it upon himself to write directly to Van Buren and query him on questions he felt sure to come up during the campaign in Mississippi: where Van Buren stood on the Texas question, his view of Congress's power to legislate over slavery in the District of Columbia, and his true position on the hated Tariff of 1828 that had led to the nullification crisis. After his March visit to the Briers to ask for Varina's hand, Davis set off on horseback for a grueling season of stump speaking at political rallies covering much of the state. Indeed, as the campaign escalated with the coming of summer, he nearly exhausted himself, and more than once the rigors of riding long days in the hot sun brought about brief recurrences of his malaria.

And even in the midst of this hectic activity, Davis still found time to visit Natchez occasionally, as well as to involve himself in some nonpolitical public affairs like the organization in May of the Mississippi Antidueling Society. In response to two duels in as many days in Vicks-

burg, he and other citizens met in protest. Most favored adopting resolutions that condemned the carrying of concealed weapons and the
issuing or accepting of challenges: some proposed the arrest of participants and even legislative action. Davis and his brother Joseph declined
to go quite that far. He offered counterresolutions that still condemned
concealed weapons and public brawls but then went on to suggest that
they should only seek "to prevent, *unnecessarily*, a resort to deadly weapons, and to regulate such a resort, when it cannot be prevented." In
short, not all dueling was bad. It was an odd position for Davis, of all
men, to take. Present when George Jones acted as a second in the Cilley
affair, he knew the cost to Jones's political career after a public outcry.
For Davis, now embarking wholeheartedly into politics, if he had any
expectation of seeking and holding elective office himself, he should
have profited by Jones's example.[7]

The next five months were a whirlwind: at least two stump meetings in June, sixteen in July, eleven in August, and three in September,
with more speeches right up to the eve of the November election. Conveniently, one of his first meetings was in Natchez; then came one in
Vicksburg. After this, however, Davis departed on tours that kept him
away from home for weeks. On July 1 he started at Port Gibson, just a
few miles south of Davis Bend, then commenced a two-week-long canvass that took him straight north, county by county, from one seat to the
next, speaking every day but two, until he reached Davis Mills, fully two
hundred miles from where he started, and just below the Tennessee
border. Then, with only a week off, he started again on August 5 at
Columbus, in Lowndes County on the border with central Alabama,
then zigzagged across the center, southern, and southeastern counties
until September 2. All told Davis addressed crowds in more than twenty
counties, from border to border, and even made one speech in northern
Louisiana. On horses, stages, carriages, and steamboats, he traveled
more than five hundred miles. He rendered good service indeed. He
also made his name a familiar one to Democrats in every corner of
Mississippi.[8]

These political meetings were almost all of a type—the rowdy, exciting, thoroughly democratic stump speech venue—the political barbecue. The dates were well publicized in advance, so that a wide local
populace could attend the event, a favorite rural entertainment. "For
weeks before the appointed time," Reuben Davis recalled, "the notable
housekeepers of the land were busy in preparing food for the multitude." Tables swayed beneath the weight of the roasts and chops, the
mounds of vegetables, pies, and cakes. In nearby pits, pigs and beefs had
been cooking slowly over coals since the evening before. Everyone
turned out on the appointed day, regardless of any interest in politics.
This was American democracy, Jacksonian democracy, at its best, the

people seeing and hearing their candidates and advocates face to face
and having a great time in the bargain.[9]
Generally the speaking came first, sometimes a debate between
candidates and at others just a platform of speakers supporting the same
men or issues. In the early days of this canvass Davis traveled and spoke
with Foote, though to gain maximum coverage of the state—and because
of some personal dispute—they split from time to time before rejoining
for the larger barbecues. The men spoke as long as their texts, or their
stamina, lasted, sometimes exceeding four hours of largely extemporaneous fulminations from a single speaker. Davis, fortunately, proved far
more temperate in his use of time, in part because he was still a neophyte
at this business but also because the rigid and orderly way in which he
tried to organize his thoughts into speech encouraged economy.

From all indications Davis probably wrote his speeches, or more
likely a single basic speech that he repeated with variations at each stop.
Before long he found this ill-suited to a stump forum. The audience
wanted the orator talking to them, not reading from sheets of paper.
There were also problems with the way he couched his thoughts. Davis's
readings and brief experience, as well as his inclinations, made his style
too classical for these rough-and-tumble forums. His quotations from
poetry and fiction were largely lost on his uneducated audiences. Having
committed to memory so much literature, he tried to demonstrate his
prowess by recalling a lot of it. Quickly he learned to reshape his arguments in a plainer and more assertively forceful cast, though he would
never be able to speak down to the masses sufficiently to be regarded as
one of them.

On the stump Davis also had the good sense to look his auditors in
the eyes. "While speaking," Varina recalled, "he took in the individuality
of the crowd, and seeing doubt or a lack of confidence with him in their
faces, he answered the mental dissonance with arguments addressed to
the case in their minds." Varina was not an impartial witness, of course,
but others agreed. When Reuben Davis heard Jefferson Davis on the
stump for the first time at Holly Springs on July 24, he was not impressed when the speaker took the stand. "I remember thinking as he
made his salutation," said Davis, "that there was nothing particularly
imposing in his appearance or manner." Yet as the speaker went on, that
opinion changed. Reuben Davis found Davis's voice soft and mellow, his
arguments lucid, and even liked the poetic flourishes that Jefferson
Davis had not yet given up at that stage of the campaign. "Dignified and
commanding, soft and persuasive, his speech was from beginning to end
a finished piece of logic and oratory." The next day at Davis Mills, the
speaker from Warren County again seemingly left "every man present
entranced by his words."[10]

As he gained more and more confidence during this canvass, Davis relied less and less on his written address. At the same time, as thoughts or recollections sprang into his mind while he declaimed on a point, he developed a tendency toward parenthetical speaking that was entirely absent from his written discourses. On the stump it proved to be no handicap. However, one other trait probably did cost him at least a few of his hearers, just as it bothered Varina. "He talked 'on the stand,' " she said, "as he did at home." Indeed, Varina had spotted and objected to it the first time she met him. "He sincerely thought all he said," she wrote, "and, moreover, could not understand any other man coming to a different conclusion after his premises were stated." That trait, already pronounced in 1844, would only become more so in the years to come. Varina believed that this "sincerity of opinion" accounted for his opponents thinking him to be domineering and closed-minded. For the most part those opponents would be right, yet Davis never understood why. He was surprised and sometimes even hurt when others did not see—as he so clearly did—that, having thought through a matter, it naturally followed that his conclusion was the correct one.[11]

Davis could also hold the stand for awhile, sometimes up to two hours or more, though, as he liked to say, he "gave close attention to the necessity of stopping when he was done," unlike Prentiss and many another garrulous orator. Though commentators noted a certain coldness or aloofness in his addresses, they liked his mild manner, finding him chaste, intellectual, and Socratically logical. "Could he only animate the perfect, but somewhat inanimate statue of his eloquence with some of the strong outlines of passion," lamented one sympathetic editor, "could he, after he had convinced the judgment by his inimitable style of passionless argument, rouse the will and the passions, enlist the feelings and captivate the imagination, he would rank among the foremost of our Mississippi orators." He hoped that Davis would lose his coldness during the frequent exposures to the public offered by the canvass. A Whig editor agreed on Davis's pleasing manner and his "musical and well modulated voice." But that was all. "These, and these alone, in our opinion, comprise all his 'oratorical' abilities, for his speech resembled, in every other respect, a school boy declamation." Allowing for partisan bias, still evidently everyone picked up that detached, unimpassioned, cool attitude in Davis's address. It reflected much of the man he had become, outwardly, and he would never lose it. His words could always touch intellect but rarely passion.[12]

Certainly his audiences believed in Davis's sincerity. "It is truly impossible," wrote a member of the crowd at the Holly Springs meeting, "to hear him without being convinced that the principles he advocates, are sincerely believed by him necessary for the welfare of our country." And in time, as he gained experience on the stump, he appears to have become looser, more confident, and occasionally at least a little impassioned. By mid-July another listener lamented that he did not have "more animation and warmth of action while speaking," and at Davis Mills he was still using "clas[s]ical beauty point and finish," yet still he was winning some voters. "He is the greatest man for soft words and hard arguments ever listened to," one Democrat declared, and by the beginning of his August tour audiences actually called for him though he was not scheduled to speak. By September Davis himself realized that his approach to the stump was changing. "As public speaking was a new thing to me," he told Varina, "change was to be expected and in more particulars than one has no doubt occurred." "How little do we know that which we are," he told her with a rare personal insight. As for public speaking, "It is as far from being agreeable or desirable to me as ever." No doubt this disinclination also contributed to the impression of coolness as he spoke.

Yet Davis showed that he had learned—or would allow to work in his favor—a few of the tricks of the stump orator. If a man could win the personal regard of the audience, usually by showing that somehow he was one of them, then he had gone a fair distance in winning them to his position as well. Davis would never be one of the common folk, but early in the campaign he let it be known that he was devoted to Mississippi as "the land of his birth." Of course it was not true. If he did not make the claim himself, neither did he issue a correction by announcing his Kentucky nativity. Though he refused to engage in any of the inflammatory verbiage then popular on the stump, still by August he resorted increasingly to sarcasm in his attacks on Whig positions, and the electorate liked it. In his last speech at Vicksburg, just two days before the voting began, he even came close to name-calling when he exclaimed that "the Whig party claim to be the decency party, raise their coons and roll their balls, but they remind me of a certain *insect* which rolls its ball backwards and down hill." In the last presidential campaign the Whigs had originated the phrase "get the ball rolling," which quickly became a part of the language. But Davis, in using their slogan, referred sarcastically to the first usage of the term back in 1837, when a critic compared Thomas Hart Benton to a dung beetle that rolls its ball of dung backward and uphill. Calling his opponents dung beetles was a far cry from the chasteness for which Davis had been complimented early in the campaign. "His taste has become corrupted by bad association," a Whig editor concluded.[13]

On November 4–5 the voters spoke. How much of an impact Jefferson Davis had on the outcome could not be measured empirically, but the general sense was that it had been considerable. Of the more than twenty counties where he spoke for Polk and George M. Dallas, the final nominees of the Democratic party, the Democrats carried all but five. All but one of those lost went by narrow margins, Claiborne County by as few as five votes. Statewide the Whigs took a beating, carrying only fifteen of fifty-nine counties. Thus Mississippi's electoral votes, of which Jefferson Davis would cast one, were to go to the Democratic nominees. Polk and Dallas won the national election as well.[14]

Just what Davis thought of the nominees during his canvass, he did not clearly say. Indeed, in the end he did not actually make the trip to the Baltimore convention that May, though the Jackson convention in January certainly nominated him as a delegate. On May 27, the day the convention began, Davis was in Vicksburg meeting with the Antidueling Society. None of the newspaper accounts published after his speeches during the ensuing campaign have Davis even mentioning Polk's name. Was Davis piqued because neither of his first two choices, Calhoun or Van Buren, got the nomination? Perhaps a bit, but there is no argument that he ardently supported the platform on which Polk ran—annexation of Texas and Oregon, opposition to a national bank, and reform of the tariff laws. These topics, especially Texas and the tariff, dominated Davis's stump speeches all through the summer. Thus, like most other Democrats, while Davis knew little at all of the true "dark horse" candidate, Polk, he did know that he agreed with him on the great issues of 1844. The Davis who attended a celebratory Democratic ball at Vicksburg's Prentiss House hotel on December 5 must have been a happy man—happy with his candidate, happy with the vote he cast as an elector the day before that made Mississippi's stand in the Polk camp official, and happy that the campaign was over. Now he could get married.[15]

The campaign had made visits with Varina all too few and too brief, perhaps as few as three or four over the course of many months. "Whilst attending to the public," he wrote to her in June, "my private affairs had got much out of joint." She, of course, stood uppermost in those affairs, and she frankly complained to him of his distraction with politics. Still their courtship continued, and by November they had agreed on a date, probably early in 1845. Some matters of discord did arise during those months. One was where they should go after their marriage. Apparently Varina did not want to live at Hurricane, or perhaps even on Davis Bend at all, as Brierfield's house was not what she had been used to in Natchez. They discussed the subject more than once, Davis protesting that they had no choice but to reside at Brierfield. "We are contro[l]led by a master not likely to regard either your wishes or mine," he told her in late November, without saying who that master might be. Perhaps he meant fate, for he had no economic prospects other than planting, and thus no choice but to stay at Brierfield, or perhaps he meant Joseph. There was doubt whether Joseph would attend their wedding, which at least hints at the possibility that some difficulty had erupted between him and the Howells. Certainly Varina's opinion of Joseph changed rapidly, accounting not only for her disinclination to live at the spartan Brierfield but also at the more sumptuous Hurricane. In later years Joseph would have little good to say about many of her kin, and Varina would find him "bitter at times against all his family, except his wife, and at times engaged in controversies of very irritating character."[16]

Anything more is speculation, yet when Jefferson wrote to her on December 11, barely three weeks later, a sudden coolness appeared. He addressed her simply as "Dear Varina," rather than his customary "Dearest." He closed with a hasty "I am as ever your," and not his usual "Farewell my own sweet Wife." What this or the businesslike tone of his letter suggests is unclear, though it may be significant that he wrote it on a steamboat during a trip from Davis Bend to New Orleans that took him right past Natchez without stopping for a visit. However, Varina was ill and had been for some time. Perhaps he refrained from visiting in order not to tax her health, and for no deeper motive.[17]

Whatever their differences, within a few weeks all discord, if any, submerged, and early in February Davis boarded a steamboat. This time he got off in Natchez, but not before another old wound healed. Quite by chance he met on that boat, for the first time in more than a decade, Zachary Taylor. In what might otherwise have been a difficult and embarrassing encounter, Taylor cordially approached Davis, extended his hand, and at once erased all ill feeling between them. Taylor had already visited Sarah's grave some time before, and now journeyed to the Texas border where troubles with their Mexican neighbors threatened. The reconciliation truly delighted Davis, who went ashore at Natchez with no idea of how soon they would meet again.

Unfortunately he found Varina still very ill and so went back home, waited three weeks, and then came again. This time he did not leave a bachelor. The day before their wedding he sent her an emerald ring along with a teasing admonition to "be calm and meet the contingency of this important change as becomes you." He signed his note "Uncle Jeff." On February 26, 1845, at ten in the morning, Davis and Varina stood before her family at the Briers. Varina wore her new engagement ring and a set of inexpensive but prized jewels inherited from a grandmother. David Page of Trinity Episcopal Church performed the ceremony, and, that done, the whole assemblage sat down to a breakfast.[18]

Their honeymoon proved unusual for several reasons. Leaving after the breakfast, they boarded a steamer for Locust Grove, where undoubtedly Davis, at least, stood at the grave of his first wife no more than a day after marrying his second. If Varina minded or thought it inappropriate, she did not complain. Then they went to Woodville and Rosemont, where Davis's aging mother, now into her eighties, lived out her last few months. "His dutiful attentions to her," Varina wrote of Jefferson and his mother, "impressed me greatly." Just two years before

Jane Cook Davis had been confirmed in the Episcopal church by none other than Davis's old West Point friend Leonidas Polk, now bishop of Louisiana.[19]

Leaving Woodville, the newlyweds went on to New Orleans, and all told spent nearly six weeks before they went upriver to Brierfield to begin their settled lives as a planter and his wife. There the modest house that Davis and Pemberton built some years before became their first home. Its design had been an experiment by Davis to test his thoughts on architecture and efficient design for the climate. Built in a style similar to that of the old Spanish colonial houses, the house stood in the middle of a grove of large oaks. In later years Davis maintained that "in his ideal dwelling the internal plan should be declared by the position of the outer walls." Perhaps such notions governed the floor plan of the Brierfield house, though his chief innovative feature was outer doorways six feet wide. They were his special pride, designed to admit as much cool breeze as possible, only Varina found that when they were opened "the [whole] side of the house seemed to be taken down." Indeed, there were a few such "Davises," as they had been known at Fort Winnebago: He miscalculated on his windows, with the result that the sills were at chest height, and the fireplaces looked almost Elizabethan in size, big enough "to roast a sheep whole." Still, it was a cool and comfortable house, with large rooms, and the Davises would be happy there for nearly five years. "We are living so humbly," Davis wrote to Margaret Howell soon after their arrival, "that we may well expect happiness."[20]

Yet if Jefferson Davis expected to retire to life as a farmer, he would be disappointed, and it seems likely that, given his history of tentative commitment to any occupation, he probably welcomed the Mississippi Democrats' refusal to let him leave the public arena. In June, on the announcement of the death of Andrew Jackson, Vicksburg citizens called on Davis to deliver a formal eulogy, even though he had already spoken on Jackson briefly a few days earlier. Then, one day later, the Warren County Democratic Convention met in Vicksburg to appoint delegates to the July 7 state convention in Jackson. Predictably Jefferson and Joseph both were chosen as delegates, and the former acted on the committee that drafted resolutions condemning the tariff, opposing state reimbursement to bank stockholders of insolvent banks, and other matters. But then, perhaps unexpectedly to the others present, but undoubtedly with the foreknowledge and assent of the master of Brierfield, Dr. George McElrath arose and proposed that the delegates to Jackson be instructed to propose Jefferson Davis as a candidate for Congress in the fall election. The motion passed unanimously.[21]

If Davis did not actively seek that candidacy, certainly others had suggested it prior to the convention. And he appeared to be prepared for it, for within days he took assertive action aimed at securing the

nomination. On June 30 the *Daily Sentinel* published an anonymous letter that asked Davis, yet again, for his views on repudiation, and specifically on a piece of legislation called the Briscoe Bill. Essentially the issue
was whether the state should take measures to prevent fraudulent bank-
ruptcy in order for banks to escape debt or else require that a bank's
borrowers be held legally liable for the bank's debts, thus guaranteeing
its creditors at least some protection and allowing bondholders to escape
an absolute loss of their investment in the event of a bank failure. By
1845 Mississippi Democrats supported the former, consistent in their
repudiation stance that the state should not act on the behalf of investors. Of course, Davis, who opposed his party on the issue of repudiation, was being forced by this letter—just as he sought the party's
nomination—to publicize yet again his difference.

To his credit, Davis replied on July 5 with a bold restatement of the
fundamental reasons why he differed with the majority of Democrats.
Likely he never gave it a second thought or even considered temporiz-
ing. It was yet another case of having thought a matter through and
come to the inevitably correct decision. If his party did not like it or it
damaged his chances for Congress, so be it. "As I have no opinions
which I wish to conceal," he responded, he gave a full account of the
issue and his stance, which had not changed. Yet he was not entirely
frank about his reason for responding. Complaining of "an unwillingness to appear before the public," he begged that his published response
"shall not be construed into an admission of my being a candidate for
any office." It was the old political device of pretending to be dragged
into the public arena by popular demand rather than personal ambition
or desire. If Davis did not want to be a candidate, all he had to do was
refuse when it was proposed several days earlier. He did not.[22]

Davis's reply would not appear in the Vicksburg press until July 8,
the day after the state convention was to meet in Jackson. This troubled
him, for he feared that it might appear that he had withheld expressing
his attitude toward the Briscoe Bill until after the nomination for the
congressional seat. As a result, he approached the editor of the Vicksburg *Daily Sentinel* to ask if his letter could be typeset, and copies run off,
for distribution in Jackson in advance of its appearance in the newspaper. Unfortunately, the *Sentinel's* staff was too occupied with its regular
work of getting out the next issue. Only after Davis stayed up much of
the night of July 5–6—writing out his text and handing it directly to the
typesetters—could the copies of his letter be printed as small pamphlets
for him to take to Jackson. The *Sentinel's* editor, John Jenkins, who had
been lukewarm toward the planter in 1844, could not help but compliment him for his determination that "no charge should ever apply to
him that he had kept back his opinions through policy," though Davis
confessed to him his belief that so doing "he thought would cause his

defeat." By that last confession, Davis also made it quite clear, protestations to the contrary, that he wanted the nomination.[23]

He need not have worried. When the convention met on the morning of July 7, Davis had probably already distributed copies of his Briscoe letter to the other delegates. Nothing was done about the congressional nomination that day, but in the evening the delegates unanimously nominated Jacob Thompson for reelection to the United States Senate. After that day's adjournment, Davis, Quitman, and others made speeches to the delegates and citizens of Jackson, in approval of the recent ratification by the Republic of Texas of an annexation treaty with the United States. Whether planned in advance or spontaneous, such a speech (on a topic universally popular among Democrats) certainly did not hurt a man who might be nominated for an office the next day.

On the morning of July 8 the delegates convened again and first nominated candidates for congressional seats from Mississippi's north- and southeastern regions. Then came the southwestern region, and Brigadier General W. C. Hale rose to nominate Jefferson Davis. Four other names, including William Gwin's, went into nomination, though one candidate promptly withdrew. Thus it became a four-man race. Balloting commenced immediately, and at the end Davis held a plurality, with forty-two of ninety-three votes, but no majority. Gwin stood just behind him with thirty-three. H. T. Ellett then withdrew, freeing his fifteen votes for the next ballot, and nine of them went to Davis, only one to Gwin, and for some reason seven other delegates in the hall did not vote at all. Nevertheless, with fifty-one out of eighty-six votes cast, Davis became the nominee. It had been a tense nomination, one delegate regarding it as the "most exciting" part of the convention. The business of the nominee's break with the party on Briscoe surely contributed to the high feeling in the hall. Gwin accused Warren County of sending an outsize delegation in order to lobby for Davis, and a Gwin supporter accused the next day that Davis threatened to break up the convention should Gwin be nominated, "& resisted his nomination in the most violent manner." That sounds out of character for Davis, as does the same supporter's claim that the rancorous and irascible Gwin "acquiesced with cheerfulness" when Davis won.[24]

And so there would be another summer's campaign, more long rides, more daylong barbecues, and more even longer-winded orations. Just how Varina felt about this is not hard to guess. Barely nineteen, a bride for just five months, she was about to give up her husband to weeks, even months, on the hustings. "Then I began to know the bitterness of being a politician's wife," she later recalled, "and that it meant long absences, pecuniary depletion from ruinous absenteeism, illness from exposure, misconceptions, defamation of character; everything which darkens the sunlight and contracts the happy sphere of home."

Having been courted so ardently, she may well have wondered how Jefferson could now divert that ardor into another direction. Perhaps she did not yet fully grasp the force of the phenomenon when Jefferson Davis committed himself to something or someone.[25]

For a man who pretended to dislike electioneering, the nominee set himself a grueling pace. He began on August 4 in Amite County, at the very bottom of the state, and thereafter spent much of August and virtually all of September working his way county by county all the way to Holly Springs and Davis Mills again, at the top of the state. In October he also canvassed briefly in some of the eastern counties. Mississippi did not as yet have mandated congressional districts. All representatives were elected from the state "at large," meaning that all the candidates had to curry votes throughout the entire state. Eight candidates, four Whig and four Democratic, received nominations, though one of the Whigs quickly pulled out of the race before it really began.

In his own campaign, Davis appeared before at least twenty-one political meetings and barbecues in at least eighteen of Mississippi's fifty-nine counties. He ignored substantial portions of the state, especially the whole southeast corner bordering the Gulf of Mexico and all the river counties north of Warren to Tennessee. Many of these had overwhelming Democratic majorities in their voting population and were being covered by other fellow Democratic candidates. Others were Whig bastions, but with too few votes overall to be worth attacking. Besides, there was plenty to do in the rest of the state.

With only five exceptions, Davis made his appearances in counties where substantial numbers of Whig voters either posed a real challenge or actually enjoyed a good majority, though Whigs in the state as a whole were heavily outnumbered. Trying to continue the pose of being rather dragged into running, he played on the suspicion that many of the time felt of a man who actively sought public office. "He wished it to be understood," he told people in Amite in his first campaign speech, "that it was not soliciting votes" that brought him there; "he merely wished to become acquainted with the people and know their wants." Davis tried to support his claim to disinterest by pointing out that he was the candidate for southwestern Mississippi, when of course, in fact, he was a candidate from the state as a whole. In this Whig bastion where he commenced his campaign, he wisely avoided the divisive issues of repudiation and the Briscoe Bill. Once in safer territory such as Port Gibson, where the parties split voters' allegiance almost evenly, he discussed both, chiefly to erase misrepresentations of his attitude. He opposed all special legislation in favor of banks, arguing that they should stand or fall on the laws in existence at the time of their charter. In Vicksburg he made it even clearer that he only disagreed with Briscoe on a point of law, that legislation should not in principle be used to aid banks to evade their responsibility. Otherwise he and Briscoe, who was believed to have supported Davis's nomination at Jackson, stood in perfect accord as Democrats.[26]

He raised the subject himself because, for the first time, Davis found himself misrepresented in the press, and attacked by anonymous letters. It was all part of political life, then and later, but he did not stand it well. "Base insinuations," as he called them, even implied that he was in one of the banks' pocket. One by one, at length, Davis replied to the published letters against him, as he always replied to critics. In future years, as now, he would not always be able to dismiss such attacks as just a part of politics. To him they would be personal, and as such they could occupy enormous amounts of his time as he attempted to destroy them with unassailable logic.[27]

In late August he spent a few days at Brierfield to rest and recover from an attack, perhaps of malaria. When he returned to the canvass on September 1, Varina saw that "he looks very badly," a double meaning she did not intend. He did not appear well, to be sure, but he also did not see well. His eyes appeared inflamed, and the left one showed itself entirely red when he left. These attacks in his left eye were becoming progressively more pronounced, and more painful, as they continued to be in future years. Davis and his doctors blamed them on his malaria, and perhaps the lung afflictions he suffered in the army. Latter-day diagnosis suggests, however, that his real eye problem was due to herpes simplex, the same virus that caused so-called "fever blisters" on the mouths of its victims. Whether Davis also suffered from such blisters is not known, but his eye complaints consistent with herpes simplex went back as far as his frontier service. How he contracted the virus is anyone's guess, though it is easily transmitted to the eyes by the fingers and can be passed to a baby during birth should the mother have it. But judging from the absence of any mention of eye problems early in his life, it is more likely that Davis contracted it quite innocently as a young man. Unfortunately, the best ways to invite attacks were lung infections, fevers, stress, tension, and long exposure to the sun, all continual companions of Jefferson Davis, especially when campaigning. Like all varieties of herpes, it was incurable and would not go away, and of all places where the infection could produce damage, the eyes were the most vulnerable.[28]

As in his canvass the year before, Davis found himself misrepresented in another fashion when he returned to the road in September, though this sort of error he took no pains to correct. Southerners enjoyed a positive penchant for military titles, even if they represented nothing more than some honorary local militia position. It gave an added sense of cachet to a man, which earned favor in the voters' eyes. Now and in the days ahead Davis once more found himself referred to as

"Captain Davis," "Major Davis," and even "Colonel Davis," substantial exaggerations of his onetime status as a lowly first lieutenant. One newspaper even called him Judge. Regardless of his title, Davis revealed development as a backwoods stump speaker. While listeners faulted him repeatedly the year before for his unimpassioned manner, only rarely in this canvass did any commentator remark on his "argumentative, dignified statesmanlike manner." Yet neither did he become a haranguing, fire-eyed orator. That was not in Jefferson Davis. He stated his views, answered his opponents, and relied as always on what he viewed as his fair examination of the issues and his presumably unassailable logic. Before these voters in this election, at least, the electorate seemed persuaded.[29]

Repeatedly he outlined the vital issues of the day as he saw them. The tariff, the national bank, and an independent treasury system in its place that would get federal deposits out of private and state banks where they were endangered by defaults. He opposed the 1841 distribution bill that took funds from the sale of government lands and scattered them to the states. Expansion, especially that of Texas and Oregon, of course, earned his ardent support. Texas he regarded as effectively a member of the Union already, and as for Oregon, "the whole . . . country he considered ours," reported one journal. He opposed allowing England to have any foothold either in Oregon or anywhere else on the continent. As an expansionist, he also hoped that the people of California would rise up against their Mexican rulers so that "she too, should be received in the sisterhood of States." Indeed, his ideas on expansion, he said, were to "extend the 'area of freedom,' until we had reached that point where man is incapable of self-government, and destitute of those principles which elevate him above the brute creation."

He was willing to see the army used to aid and enforce expansion, if necessary. While on military matters, he also advocated a national policy of establishing a number of local military academies at the federal forts scattered around the country, there to train citizens for the militia. "Thus we would always have men among us qualified for an effective discharge of the duties of a soldier," he said in Ripley on September 22, "yet with the feelings and pursuing the occupations of the m[a]n of peace." As border tensions mounted, the notion of a future conflict with either Great Britain or Mexico cannot have been far from his mind.[30]

He argued these and other, lesser issues in meeting after meeting, returning most often to the tariff and his belief in using it only to raise revenue and not to protect one industry or another. Audiences found him persuasive. In Tippah County, where Democrats already enjoyed a heavy majority, he rose to speak just after most of the crowd had disappeared during his Whig predecessor's harangue. "As soon as his voice was heard," however, "the people flocked in again to hearken to his words." A friendly reporter in Lafayette County said that "he left behind him fame as an orator and statesman," predicting for him a place as "another star to the galaxy of Southern talent in the councils of the nation." Often editors referred to Davis's favorite weapons: "incontrovertible facts and arguments." There was more applause, more spontaneous indication of the audience being with him, than the year before, and clearly he was more effective this time around. He even took his first stab at pork-barrel politics by opposing the new navy yard about to be constructed at Memphis, arguing that the federal government ought instead to locate it on the Gulf Coast, the ideal location naturally being somewhere on Mississippi's scant forty miles of shoreline.[31]

It proved to be a tough campaign, not for the closeness of the contest but for its physical toll on Jefferson Davis. Yet he received much for what he paid. Two days before the voting, in his last campaign speech, he turned loose once more "his trumpet tones, his eagle look, and bold, free 'form and gesture.' " Editor Jenkins declared him then to be "the impersonation of the true spirit of the South." By that, of course, Jenkins meant that Davis personified Southern values. In future years some would indeed accuse Jefferson Davis of trying to assume to himself the single voice of—to impersonate—the South. For now, Jenkins suggested another more tangible and immediate impersonation. "We predict that he becomes the Calhoun of Mississippi."[32]

The voters decided that on November 4–5. Given the Democratic majority in the state as a whole, few doubted the outcome. Not a single Whig won a seat. More interesting than the Democrats' sweep of the four positions available was the individual vote. Jacob Thompson, best known of all the candidates, received the largest number of ballots. Of the other three new congressmen-elect, two had been judges, and one of them speaker of the state house as well. Yet Jefferson Davis outpolled both of them, standing just three hundred votes behind Thompson. In five of the counties where he campaigned, Davis gained more votes even than Thompson, and in fifteen of those counties he bested both of the other two Democrats. Clearly something in this thirty-eight-year-old "reluctant" politician spoke to the voters of Mississippi in a voice or a manner that they liked. Little could they know that in sending Jefferson Davis to Congress in this election, they were beginning to bind their fortunes to his own for the next two decades.[33]

I Make No Terms,
I Accept No Compromise

There is a delicious irony in the fact that, following his election, the very first public act of this new "Calhoun of Mississippi" was the delivery of the major reception address in Vicksburg two weeks later when the real John C. Calhoun visited the state. Calhoun was en route from New Orleans to Memphis for a commercial convention and expected to stop in Vicksburg on November 10. Despite Varina's later claims that he and Davis had been acquainted "with some degree of intimacy" since 1836, most probably they never met at all prior to 1845, unless Jones introduced his friend to Calhoun during that visit to Washington in 1838. Certainly Davis wanted to meet Calhoun now, even postponing his own departure to take his seat in Congress. Moreover, Davis carefully planned his address, limiting it to half an hour and dictating it to Varina. In the presence of such a noted old orator as the South Carolinian, Davis clearly wanted to make a good impression, especially now that he was himself embarked on a career in that same Capitol wherein Calhoun had created such legends. He returned to all the old poetry and high-flown rhetoric that he wisely left out of his stump speeches. "The speech," said Varina, "had an amount of pretty imagery and lofty rhetoric in it, that, to my girlish taste, was as wonderful as it was charming."[1]

Alas, on the appointed day there was no Calhoun. A problem with his steamboat resulted in his visit being postponed for a full eight days. Just how important it was to Davis to see Calhoun, be seen by him, and be seen with him is evident from the fact that he again delayed his departure for Washington, even though this gave him only until November 30 before the House of Representatives convened the following

115

day. But Davis was a man who honored commitments regardless of the personal cost. During the past campaign, news that his mother had died on October 3 reached him a few days later. Immediately he cancelled a speech to rush to Woodville, where he was "much overcome" by her death. After the funeral he rode some forty miles to Natchez, where Varina visited with her family. He spent but an hour with her, then left again, rushing back to the hustings. Perhaps this, too, was some of his father in him. He felt hurts and losses deeply, but he would not allow them to deter him from other responsibilities.[2]

Davis could not have made a better decision than to honor his commitment to welcome Calhoun, even if it did make him late in Washington. When Calhoun arrived, welcomers took him to the Prentiss House, and finally Davis delivered his laboriously prepared address. Varina sat in the audience, hearing him speak publicly for the first time, and she could see that he was nervous. For his part, Jefferson asked her not to look at him during his talk, no doubt for fear it might distract him or make him self-conscious. Varina's brother Joseph Howell and Davis's niece Mary Bradford were also in the crowd, adding to his ill ease. When he started to speak, his words came slowly and even hesitatingly, despite the excitement others had seen in him all day. Doggedly he tried to remember the words he had committed to memory after Varina wrote them down, and that is part of what threw him off his normal timing and manner on the stump. Before long he abandoned his memorized speech almost entirely, and then his tempo and address improved markedly. He went to familiar old ground, the tariff, expansion, strict construction of the Constitution, and the nature of the Union. Joseph Howell found it a "beautiful and appropriate address," as did Varina, though she was chagrined that almost nothing of what she had laboriously written at his bidding was actually used.

Calhoun appreciated it too, though he sidestepped Davis's oratorical efforts to stimulate him into replying at length on those issues. Instead he made only a few general remarks of thanks and then stepped out into the crowd to be presented and shake hands. Dancing followed, but observers noted that Varina and Jefferson did not dance, because Calhoun was obviously smitten by her and never left her side for the balance of his afternoon's visit. "The old man indeed seemed quite struck with her," Joseph Howell wrote three days later. "He walked with no one else, talked with no one else, and seemed to have no use for his eyes except to look at her and Mr. Davis." As for Mr. Davis, who behind his smile was deciding that—after his near embarrassment that day—he would never again attempt to bind himself by writing out a speech in full, he beamed at Calhoun's attentions. The elderly statesman told Howell that his brother-in-law "was a man whose talents were of the highest order," and the fact that Calhoun paid so much attention to Davis certainly appeared to confer on the new congressman his hearty approval and endorsement. Of course, Calhoun could have known little more of Jefferson Davis than that he was a recently elected Democratic candidate for the House. On that basis alone it behooved him, as a grand old man of the party, to show him public favor and approval. Yet the degree of attention Davis received, besides owing much to Calhoun's infatuation with Varina, probably revealed also a more personal and less political bonding. Though they never had an opportunity to become personal intimates—Calhoun carried on a long correspondence with Varina but not with her husband—still the two men began that day a relationship that, in the public mind at least, constituted mentor and student. Certain it is that with Jackson dead and Van Buren fallen from grace, Davis admired Calhoun more than any other public man of the era, and the men he admired—as with brother Joseph—he emulated. Without the John C. Calhoun of the 1840s, the Jefferson Davis of the 1850s would not have existed.[3]

Once Calhoun departed, the Davises had no time to waste. Joined by Varina and Congressman-elect Robert W. Roberts, Jefferson boarded a steamboat bound upriver to the Ohio, and thence to Wheeling, Virginia. But the passage up the Mississippi proved torturously slow, with fogs impeding progress. It took five days to reach Cairo, Illinois, at the mouth of the Ohio, and by then Davis despaired of making it to Washington in time. He became even more pessimistic when he saw the low water in the river and the huge chunks of ice floating downstream, endangering the boat. Still they tried to go upstream, only to be frozen in by the ice. With nowhere to go, they stayed aboard for a week hoping for a thaw, and when that did not come, they transferred to a smaller boat that might make it through the ice, but after steaming all night it only reached the opposite side of the river.

Undeterred, Davis and his party put their trunks aboard a wooden sled, sat on their bags, and bumped over rough roads as horses pulled them to Wheeling, once tipping over a bank and sending passengers and baggage careening down a hillside. Varina took some bad bumps, and Roberts broke a rib. In time they reached Wheeling, a little the worse for the journey, and then had to take a stage overland to Brownsville, and thence by river once more to Pittsburgh. Often on the journey Davis jumped out of the coach to help push or lever the stage out of ruts and snowdrifts, not at all what a new congressman from the temperate climes of Mississippi expected when he sought public office.

Yet Davis showed considerable good cheer throughout the arduous journey. "We'll tough it out till morning," he said time and again. As the travelers' own store of victuals gave out, they faced meal after meal of the ubiquitous rural sausage, brightened by nothing more than maple syrup. When he could, Davis left the party briefly to visit some roadside inn to buy candy or fresh milk. He even jested when they had to eat hard-boiled eggs without salt. His endurance and patience all who knew him would have expected. His good humor and occasional flashes of wit, however, would have seemed out of the ordinary to those who remembered only the sad master of Brierfield from years past. Davis was excited at going to Washington.[4]

The whole trip took perhaps three weeks. Upon arrival he learned what surely he already knew, that he and Roberts had missed the opening of the session. Quickly the Davises took temporary lodging at the National Hotel, and on December 8 he walked into the hall of the House of Representatives, swore an oath to support the Constitution, and took his seat.

Being a freshman congressman, Davis, along with Roberts, found himself in the very back row of desks, far to the right of the Speaker's stand. Roberts sat to Davis's left, while in front of Davis sat Armistead L. Burt of Abbeville, South Carolina. There were few who remarked the new representative's arrival, for he came with no reputation outside Mississippi, yet one man at least, Henry Hilliard, remembered Davis on his first day. "His appearance was prepossessing," Hilliard recalled. "Tall, slender, with a soldierly bearing, a fine head, an intellectual face; there was a look of culture and refinement about him that made a favorable impression from the first."[5]

Within less than a week of his arrival, Davis moved himself and Varina to Mrs. Potter's rooming house on the south side of Pennsylvania Avenue between Second and Third streets. Half of Washington, it seemed, engaged in lodging all the politicians who came to Congress, for the city teemed with establishments like Mrs. Potter's, most of them charging the same rates. Davis found an interesting and convivial group at Mrs. Potter's. Their "mess," as they borrowed the military term, included fellow Mississippians Jacob Thompson and Stephen Adams and, briefly, George Jones. Another acquaintance of Davis's was Augustus C. Dodge, son of his old commander Henry Dodge and now a representative from Iowa. Davis probably did not previously know Democrat Henry D. Foster of Pennsylvania or Senator Ambrose Sevier of Arkansas. Undoubtedly he had never heard of first-term Senator Simon Cameron of Pennsylvania. Nevertheless, they all formed a convivial group, and many of them paid the same board of $1.50 per day or $10 a week that Davis paid for meals at nearby Gadsby's.[6]

Immediately Davis threw himself into the routine of being a representative, and for the first time in his life he dealt with a volume of paperwork, much of it of minor importance. Indeed, he appears to have buried himself in his official correspondence, going out very little, often reading or writing until two or even three in the morning despite the fact that colds and fevers troubled him from the day of his arrival in

Washington. Earaches at times almost incapacitated him, and Varina could see again that his eyes looked "so red and painful." Yet he kept himself at his work and kept her at it as well, as he dictated to her his replies to the requests, protests, and every other manner of communication sent him by constituents. Within only a few weeks, by the end of January 1846, Varina already feared for him. She had dreaded his going into public life before his election but now confessed that those fears "were nothing like the reality." Certainly her husband was with her, and that meant much, "but he is not so happy as he used to be." "His mind wants rest," she went on, but he refused to take time away to go to the museums and other places of amusement where he might get some relaxation.

Instead he buried himself in the minutiae of his job, making little or no distinction between matters great or small as they claimed his time. In short, he exhibited all the signs of an insecure administrator who, fearing that some detail or other may get the better of him, chooses instead to immerse himself in that detail and thus enslaves himself. For the rest of his life Jefferson Davis's experience in public office would not change from what Varina saw within the first month in Washington—a race between the expiration of his term and the exhaustion of his stamina. Only to her mother did Varina confide the depth of her fears as she saw him exhausting himself. "I feel so fearful—so uneasy," she wrote. Davis, of course, said nothing. "You know how patiently Jeffy always bears suffering."[7]

Constituents wanted his help in getting military pensions. Others asked his aid in securing land grants or appointments to the military and naval academies for their sons. Almost everyone called on him for what most Americans then felt was their right to receive complimentary copies of a host of government documents and printed congressional debates. He also experienced that sudden reacquaintance with old friends not recently heard from that almost every congressman encountered. In January came a letter from Albert Sidney Johnston, asking Davis to use his influence in securing a regimental command, and a month later Stephen W. Kearny, who once tried to intercede on Davis's behalf with Zachary Taylor, sought his aid in gaining promotions for officers of his old First Dragoons. Inventors asked his help with patents or with getting the War Department to adopt their designs for new engines of war. They were all the routine business that any congressman tried to cope with—and cope with successfully if he looked forward to reelection. Yet it swallowed his time ravenously and left him ill-inclined to waste time on social or frivolous invitations. Willing to concentrate far too much on inconsequential correspondence, he would spare no time at all for inconsequential dealings face to face. When the somewhat imperious but much-liked Senator Jesse Speight summoned Davis to his presence once with the terse message "Come over," signed "Speight," the representative responded in kind. "Can't," he wrote. "Davis." Later they often laughed together, but when Davis wrote that response, it was not good-humored.[8]

Almost the only social engagements that Davis allowed himself were those of political importance. When President Polk invited him and Varina to the White House for an evening, of course they went. They made their first appearance at the Executive Mansion on January 13, along with thirty or forty other congressmen and their wives. Varina did not care for the president. "Polk is an insignificant looking little man," she wrote two weeks later. "I don't like his manners or anything else." Davis left no impressions of the man, but most probably he agreed with Varina, finding the simple Polks rather too overwhelmed by their importance and inclined to be ostentatious.[9]

Far less exalted than presidents, few representatives made much of an impression in their first terms. Jefferson Davis proved to be an exception, in part because of who he was and also as a result of the times. He delivered his maiden speech on the floor of the House just ten days after taking his seat, and that in itself was out of the ordinary. As a rule, freshmen congressmen were to be seen and not heard, listening and learning before venturing into the debates. But they lacked what Davis always possessed in abundance, a rock-hard assurance of the certainty of their position. Thus, when resolutions arose that touched on the naturalization of immigrants, Davis knew exactly where he stood without study.

The resolutions owed their introduction to the rising Native American Party in the North, a xenophobic coalition of anti-Catholics and others who feared competition at the ballot box from the hundreds of thousands of recent European immigrants. The resolutions sought to extend the wait for naturalized citizenship from five years to twenty-one and provided that only native-born Americans could hold public office. The debate on them began on December 15, and three days later Davis rose to request the floor. At once he denounced the Native American Party "for its sordid character and its arrogant assumption," proclaiming that articles such as these "deserved at the hands of this House no reference anywhere." So far as he was concerned, the naturalization laws should be modified, but only "that they might be simplified, and that the process of naturalization might be more easily accomplished." Make it easy or withhold it altogether, he declared. "If we admitted foreigners, and yet denied them the enjoyment of all political rights among us," he said, "we did but create enemies to our Government, and fill our country with discontented men." It was an enlightened opinion and a bold stand at a time when a wave of nativism was about to sweep across the nation, a wave that cost the Democrats dearly in future elections. No wonder that one Washington newspaper correspondent wrote of this address that "Jefferson Davis earned a wreath of fame." It was an excellent start for a career in national politics.[10]

From the favorable reaction to his first address on the floor, Davis went on to yet another small triumph. Varina herself complained in late January that "I hear nothing but Oregon—notice—notice—war." While she went to the House often, especially if "Jeffy" was to speak, she lamented that most of the time she heard nothing but "empty vapouring about our abilities, or power to whip England." As far back as 1818 the United States and Great Britain agreed to a joint occupancy of Oregon, and it worked well for a time, but by the 1840s American immigration to the region placed increasing pressure on Washington to evict Britain and annex Oregon. For the Democrats, Davis among them, this position became a foundation of their creed when Polk ran in 1844 and, more than just demanding that the British leave the portion of the territory then occupied by the United States, they wanted all of the country up to and beyond the fifty-fourth parallel. The first step in any such program would be to terminate the congressionally mandated joint occupation, and in January the debate began.[11]

Davis addressed his colleagues on the subject on February 6. All his oft-repeated feelings on expansionism were heard, as was his acceptance of the notion that the United States had a "manifest destiny" to occupy the continent from sea to sea. He went considerably beyond the difficulty with the British, however, to survey all his aspirations, including California and the Southwest, and at first devoted much of his speech to the current difficulties with Mexico, referring not only to that country's "amicable relations" with its northern neighbor but also to "the most delicate and difficult of questions" remaining between them, their boundary. Showing considerable restraint for an ardent expansionist, Davis counseled caution in dealing with Britain, not out of fear of war but because, seeing the possibility of conflict between the two English-speaking nations, Mexico might be heartened to take a more belligerent attitude itself. Indeed, he mildly rebuked the war hawks in his own party who took the most extreme stand on both Mexico and England and advocated war, if necessary, to gain the disputed territories. "It is true that republics have often been cradled in war," he said, "but more often they have met with a grave than a cradle." "An appeal to arms should be the last resort, and only by national rights or national honor can it be justified."

But having said that, he added another objection for attempting to nullify the joint occupation treaty—the Union did not stand ready to back its decision with force. "That nation negotiates to most advantage which is best prepared for war," he declared, and America was not ready for war with England, especially with its navy. Instead he suggested that Oregon should be settled more aggressively, that military roads be built to connect the territory with western forts, and that the local Indians be cultivated to win their friendship. Then, and only then, he said, would the United States be ready to fight the British in the Northwest. "The party must succeed which has bread within the country," he concluded. It was the old quartermaster and dragoon combined in him that spoke, perhaps with the memory of the starving Dodge expedition.

He also disagreed with many in his party who asserted a claim to the line of 54°40′, pointing out that any such extreme demand guaranteed war. Regarding the United States' claim to Oregon as not entirely ironclad anyhow, he suggested that the best true claim lay only up to the forty-ninth parallel, for there had been no American settlement beyond that line. And in one of the best examples of dispassionate, even-handed treatment of an issue that he would ever display, Davis asked Congress to look at the matter from the British side. "We cannot expect, we should not require, our adversary to submit to more than we would bear," he said. Would they allow Britain to occupy all of Oregon without a fight? Of course not. Why, then, should not the reverse be true? Given the option of part of Oregon with peace, or all of it—maybe—after an armed conflict on their northern borders while Mexico postured to the south, he knew his preference.

This said, he turned to the inevitable question of sectionalism. Why was it that those who now clamored for war with England to gain all of Oregon—all of it above the Missouri Compromise line that barred slavery—also opposed the peaceful annexation of Texas, whose location obviously destined it to be a slave state? He felt the answer was obvious enough, and yet he could not agree with the "malign predictions" of Joshua Giddings of Ohio, who earlier had declared that this constant agitation over expansion would one day lead to disunion as the sections fought over new territories. Such an outcome was unthinkable, especially since the streams and rivers that grew out in the new western lands—the Missouri, the Arkansas, and more—eventually flowed into the Mississippi. Their waters inevitably would bring their produce to the rest of the nation by Southern cities and ports on that mighty watercourse, and thus any attempt to somehow separate the South from the new West must be futile.[12]

It had been an excellent address, and when Davis sat down to considerable applause, he did not yet appreciate the impact of his words and what lay behind them. In an era when Southern statesmen made increasingly strident and categorical statements, becoming more and more extreme and uncompromising in their stance, Davis revealed a dispassionate and conciliatory pose toward all sides of the Oregon question that was uncharacteristic, even of himself. He never concealed his still-considerable interest in military matters. While he did not say so, it is still quite probable that if somehow a high commission in the army were to have been offered him early in 1846, he would have left his House seat and returned to uniform. The prospect of war should have made his military ardor rise even more, especially since he might hope to win glory in real campaigning. Certainly his commitment to being a representative was not so great that it would stop him. Yet he did not join all those other fellow Southerners clamoring for a hard stance toward Britain. He counseled against war, against extreme territorial demands, and for empathy for the English position. Jefferson Davis characteristically told himself that he examined all sides of a matter before deciding what was right. In discussing Oregon he genuinely did so, and for that he won richly deserved plaudits from all sides.

The response from fellow congressmen was immediate. Men clustered around his desk and grasped his hand, without distinction of party. Certainly the ardent advocates of expansion at any cost may not have been pleased, but those who agreed with Davis in what Varina called his "contempt for illiterate clamor and demagogical attempts to influence legislation" hailed him for his moderation and statesmanship. There is no question that Davis found such attention flattering and gratifying. "He liked to receive the applause" of his fellow members, an intimate acquaintance recalled.

Even more gratifying to Davis was the reaction of one special representative, a Whig from Massachusetts. After yielding the presidency to Jackson, John Quincy Adams had gone on to a distinguished career in the House. With only two years of life left to him, he reigned as its grand Old Man Eloquent, and as such he took it on himself carefully to weigh and judge new members, particularly since he might have to debate them one day. When Davis began to speak, Adams drew his chair closer, fixing his gaze on him. As the speech progressed, Adams moved yet closer. "It was difficult to say which interested the old members most," wrote an observer. "The conduct of Mr. Adams or the eloquence of the orator." When Davis finished, Adams stepped up to him with extended hand and offered fulsome compliments. To others, this aged veteran gave predictions that "we shall hear more of this young man" and that "that . . . gentlemen, is no ordinary man. "He will make his mark yet, mind me." As for Davis, he never forgot Adams's words and kindness and for the rest of his life treasured a friendship for the old man. In years to come, he often told friends of "the pleasure he had received from the compliments of John Quincy Adams, who called him an orator."[13]

Davis and Adams already knew each other slightly thanks to some of the less inflammatory business of the House. On December 19, Representative Robert Dale Owen, son of the utopian whom Joseph Davis met on the stage years before, presented a bill to take the $508,000 bequest of Scotsman James Smithson to the United States and use it to establish a "Smithsonian Institution," for "the increase & diffusion of knowledge among men." The funds had sat around for years before Owen's bill finally forced serious consideration of the establishment of such an institution, and now the Speaker appointed a select committee of seven to consider the bill. He named, among others, Adams, Davis, Owen, and David Wilmot, and in the course of their deliberations Davis would form an enduring regard for Adams, despite their political differences.

It helped that the two found themselves so thoroughly in agreement on the benefits that would accrue from the Smithsonian. While Davis denied that the federal government had the right to take charge of education, lauding the normal-school system in the states and praising the "uniformity in our language" stemming from the widespread use of Noah Webster's "spelling-book," he also denied that the Smithsonian would in any way constitute government control of education. "Knowledge was the common cement that was to unite all the heterogeneous materials of this Union into one mass," he said. Smithson's bequest would help to collect and diffuse that knowledge. A surprising amount of debate took place on the bill finally presented by the select committee, mostly having to do with funding. Davis himself offered an amendment that failed to settle the issue, and when Adams presented a whole new bill, Davis offered yet another amendment to help that one along. In the end neither bill passed, but another, offered at the end of April, did get through the House and the Senate and was signed into law by Polk in August, though this would not close Jefferson Davis's association with the Smithsonian.[14]

Thereafter, when Davis spoke, men of consequence listened as they might not otherwise have done with a freshman representative. Yet he did not rise often. As his old friend from Transylvania, David Rice Atchison, now a senator from Missouri, observed, "Davis differed from all the others . . . You never heard anything foolish from his lips." Davis rose at his seat only when he had something of substance to say and avoided the casual and often time-consuming petty debate that many members indulged in. Only two subsequent issues prompted him to take the floor for an extended period of time, both dealing with national defense, and one touching very directly on Mississippi.[15]

Davis showed a keen interest in rivers and harbors, their commerce and defense, almost from the first—naturally so as a representative of a state tied to the rest of the world by the Mississippi River and with a little piece of the Gulf Coast thrown in. He presented a petition to clear a sandbar that impeded coastal traffic through the Mississippi's waters between New Orleans and Mobile and later offered a resolution inquiring of the secretary of the navy the suitability of Ship Island, off the Mississippi coast, for a navy yard and of the fortifications needed for its defense. Then on February 24 came a bill for the improvement of rivers and harbors.[16]

Democrats had split over the issue of internal improvements. Those from west of the great river, representing vastly underdeveloped waterways, favored such bills, while Deep South men like Davis opposed them as violations of the Constitution. Significantly, here Davis broke with Calhoun, a proponent of the rivers and harbors bill, who maintained that the Mississippi was so vast that it should come under federal jurisdiction just like all the other major coastal harbors at Boston, Charleston, and elsewhere. On March 16, just four months after his fulsome welcome to Calhoun at Vicksburg, Davis rose to side against him on this issue. He argued from the outset the "question of strict or latitudinous construction" of the national compact and then attacked one by one each of the arguments in favor of the bill. At times it became almost a normal-school lecture, as when the bill's defenders cited the federal government's powers "to regulate commerce" as entitling them to regulate the waters plied by commerce. Davis reminded the House that the Latin root of the word was *regula*, meaning "rule." Ruling commerce was fine, but trying to "create" it by using federal funds to make waterways navigable was not. If the government could "create" commerce by making new harbors, why then could it not create commerce by building its own merchant ships and other enterprises that would even put it in competition with private business? As for another member, who suggested that the bill should be approved out of faith in the federal government, Davis sarcastically responded that "faith, sir, is the belief in things not understood."

He could not stay away from states' rights. The government had no natural authority. "It is the creature of the States," he said. "As such it could have no inherent power, all it possesses was delegated by the States." The Constitution consisted not of limitations on the government's power but of grants of power to that government. Using the inevitable "ship of state" metaphor that most new politicians resorted to, he declared that he preferred to "see our vessel stranded there, with the flag of strict construction flying over it, . . . rather than have a peaceful voyage, by hauling down the ancient motto of our faith." That "faith," of course, was the states' rights creed of strict construction. Did he not recall that only a few minutes earlier he himself had declared faith to be "the belief in things not understood"?

The bulk of Davis's speech got down to matters of more local concern to a Southerner and a member from Mississippi. The bill called for a disproportionate share of the appropriation going to Eastern and

Northern states. He pointed out the lack of attention given to the defense of the Gulf Coast. He suggested again how ideal—from his viewpoint—Ship Island would be for military and naval defense and maintained that his advocacy came out of "the distinction between great national and little local objects." He condemned the improvement of a harbor on Lake Erie, more work on the one at Chicago, the landing at St. Louis, and other proposed projects. "Can any other argument be found for this expenditure than the advantage it will bring to the trade of the locality?" he asked. However, spending federal money on Ship Island—in his state—would be to the benefit of the nation.

This was but the fulfillment of the promise he made when campaigning to advocate having the proposed navy yard at Memphis moved to the Mississippi coast instead, along with the fortifications needed to protect it. Beyond doubt Davis believed what he said. To his opposition, it sounded like the usual pork barrel. And when one member asked him if he would vote for Great Lakes appropriations if his own request for federal spending on the Mississippi coast should be approved, he almost indignantly exclaimed, "Sir, I make no terms, I accept no compromises." If Davis presented an appropriation and the purpose were shown to be "proper and the expenditure constitutional," then, he said, "I defy the gentleman, for his conscience' sake, to vote against it." There it was again—the Mississippian's iron certainty that if he concluded that he was right, no one could in good "conscience" disagree.[17]

Though it was not a speech up to the standard of his Oregon address, Varina liked it well enough. She stayed away from the House on the days that he made such talks, however. "I always keep away when I know he is to speak," she explained, "for it is so trying to the feelings to hear remarks which persons around make to each [o]ther." Thus she did not hear firsthand his other remarks of substance on a bill to raise regiments of riflemen. It might have seemed odd that a man who had been so diffident and often dissatisfied while in uniform could later assume such a proprietary attitude toward the army and military affairs, yet the fact is that Davis never emotionally committed himself to being a soldier until after he left the service. Now in Congress he became a champion of its cause. Back in December he had introduced his pet project of turning forts into military schools, another of his campaign promises, and the House Military Affairs Committee did consider the proposal, though it progressed no farther. In February his acquaintance Kearny had lobbied him for positions in a proposed new regiment, and Davis had already shown his attentiveness to the requests of old friends.[18]

Thus, when debate on a House bill to raise those two regiments commenced on March 23, 1846, Davis was ready to speak the very next day with a question in the debate and then took the floor to meet the objections of many to the bill. Reducing—in his mind—the matter to two issues, he dealt with each. Asking if there was a real necessity for two more regiments, he pointed out that both England and France already had riflemen in service, whereas American soldiers still used the less-effective and inaccurate smoothbore firearms that were largely unchanged from the days of the War of 1812. They "who were literally the rifle people of the world, who were emphatically skilled in the use of the rifle, were now falling behind." For that reason, if for no other, he argued that they needed a rifle regiment. As to how the increase in the army should be made, he favored the suggestions of others that men of the western states and territories should be enlisted because of the "qualifications of western men for this particular kind of service." In the end Davis and the rest of Congress accepted and passed a revision that allowed the president to raise the size limitations of companies in existing regiments, accomplishing much the same goal.

But almost immediately a bill from the Senate came to the House, this one proposing a regiment of mounted riflemen, the unit Kearny had heard of. This, too, met stiff opposition, and Davis immediately leapt to its defense. Eventually the bill passed and became law on May 19, 1846. When Polk signed it that day, the atmosphere in Washington and in Congress had changed dramatically where military bills were concerned. The nation was at war with Mexico.[19]

On April 25 Mexican troops crossed the Rio Grande into Texas. Still not acknowledging the legality of either Texan independence or its annexation by the Union, the Mexicans postured constantly along the border for months prior to actual hostilities, and Polk happily postured back, sending General Zachary Taylor to protect the Rio Grande. As it happened, the Mexicans struck Davis's old dragoon regiment, commanded now by his friend Colonel David E. Twiggs. Almost two whole companies of the regiment were killed or captured by the attackers. "Hostilities may now be considered as commenced," Taylor reported to Polk, who got the news on May 9. The next day the president announced to Congress that the United States was at war.

Davis supported Polk wholeheartedly. The day after the declaration, when an amendment to a bill authorizing Polk to accept volunteers for the war came up, Davis proposed changing a clause that authorized Polk "to resist" foreign aggression, to a much more assertive statement "for the vigorous prosecution of hostilities." Davis had not been anxious for war, but now that it had come, he would hold back nothing. On June 4 he received a personal letter from Twiggs, declaring that "we have war in earnest on the Rio Grande," and deploring the lack of "officers of rank in the field." By the time Twiggs's letter arrived, Jefferson Davis was already well on the way to becoming one of them.[20]

That old itch, the restlessness or indecision or lack of commitment—call it what one would—acted on Davis the congressman as it had on Davis the soldier and planter. As far back as January 20, after only a few weeks in Washington, Davis wrote a note to Robert J. Walker that might indicate his being interested in the appointment to the unexpired Senate term that Walker left when he became Polk's secretary of the treasury. If Walker took the hint—if a hint was intended—nothing came of it. But the growing tension with Mexico, and the increasing likelihood of an armed conflict, certainly left Davis with no doubt that, when war came, there would be an instant need for volunteer regiments from the several states to meet the emergency. There was an opportunity he could not resist. Even before Polk declared war, and perhaps even before word of hostilities actually reached Washington, Davis confided to a friend that "in the event of war I should like to command a Warren regiment."

Now, May 12, the day after the discussion on the volunteer bill, Davis wrote an open letter to the *Vicksburg Sentinel and Expositor*. "Let the treaty of peace be made at the city of Mexico," he declared, "and by an Ambassador who cannot be refused a hearing—but who will speak with that which levels walls and opens gates—American cannon." His education and prior military service fitted him to lead Mississippians in the field, he suggested. Though he realized that his fellow citizens' trust had sent him to Congress to represent them, still "I look to the movements of our forces on our Mexican border with a strong desire to be a part of them." The *Sentinel* enthusiastically endorsed him. "Major Davis," the editor said, giving his subject the usual promotion, "is the man!" In bold letters he appealed to those who would volunteer to elect "the native, gallant, glorious son of our soil—to lead you to your country's service."[21]

The War Is Probably Over

The next month was not a happy one for Varina Davis. For most of those weeks, as she told her mother on June 6, "it has been some time a struggle between Jeff, and I, which should overcome the other in the matter of his volunteering, and though it was carried on in love between us, it is not the less bitter." Worried for his erratic health when he was at home or even in Washington, she could imagine what the rigors of the field and campaigning might do to him—and that did not even contemplate the dangers of battle. Sometime before the outbreak of hostilities she extracted from him a promise that he would not volunteer, but he broke that promise with his letter to the *Sentinel*. Not only would he volunteer but actively seek high command. "He could not help it I suppose," she lamented. All she could do was hope that Polk would not accept any volunteer regiment raised in Mississippi.[1]

Actually many felt some concern about what regiments the president would accept. Almost immediately Polk called for twenty thousand volunteers from the Deep South and the states along the Mississippi and another thirty thousand from the North. This affronted some Mississippians like Quitman, first because they regarded the war as their own. "We were foremost in the cause of annexation," they said. "We look upon this as our own quarrel. . . . We want no aid from the abolitionists." Worse, by May 22 Louisiana had already called out five thousand volunteer militia, and though they were unlawfully raised, still Quitman feared that there would not be room enough left in the army for Mississippians—and that, incidentally, meant there might not be an opportunity for him to obtain a high commission. Within a few days, in

129

fact, Davis and others in Washington would send Polk a petition requesting that the president make Quitman a brigadier general of volunteers.[2]

Quitman got his brigadiership, and Mississippi got the chance to contribute one regiment of volunteers. In late May the volunteers began to enlist and make their way to their rendezvous at Vicksburg. As for Davis's hopes of a colonelcy, they must have seemed considerably dimmed by the fact that there would be only the one unit raised from his state, and Mississippi teemed with ambitious men craving a command, many with military experience much more substantial than his, and better political connections as well. All he could do was wait and attend to his House duties, which now became almost entirely consumed with military matters.

Suddenly finding itself needing an army once again, Congress largely reversed its usual parsimonious and suspicious stance toward the military and especially toward West Point. On May 28 Davis spoke in support of a recently introduced bill offering the thanks of Congress to Taylor and his army for their two recent victories at Resaca de la Palma and Palo Alto, and awarding to officers and men an extra month's pay in reward. He also responded to William Sawyer's attack on the military academy and its graduates, asserting that arms, like every occupation, required study, and where better than at a school like West Point? Pointing to Taylor's little victories, Davis asked if "a blacksmith or a tailor could have secured the same results."

It was a reasonable statement, but perhaps Davis should have made certain that there were no blacksmiths or tailors in the House that day, for such words, innocent though they were, coming from a planter, could well offend a tradesman or a mechanic. They did. Sawyer was a blacksmith in his youth, and must immediately have assumed that Davis intended his remark as a sarcastic insult. Sitting elsewhere in the House was Andrew Johnson of Tennessee, a tailor, and he, too, bristled at Davis's remark. For the balance of May 28 and much of the next day, Davis found himself on the defensive against the indignant attacks of both. His frustration at their refusal to see his point that *any* profession had to be learned, and that being a blacksmith was no better training for soldiering than being a general necessarily fitted a man to make a nail, clearly showed. It also revealed Davis's fundamental inability to see why his own words, innocent to his ears, could offend others. Not understanding the sensibilities of men at the lower end of the social or economic ladder, it baffled him that they would take offense at what was, after all, only his irrefutable logic.

Johnson, especially, bristled, responding that the "illegitimate, swaggering, bastard, scrub aristocracy" that looked down on laborers and mechanics possessed neither "talents, information, nor a foundation on which you can rear a superstructure that would be useful." Even the next day Johnson refused to let go of the subject. Davis issued as much of an apology as he ever would when he confessed that "if he knew himself, he was incapable of wantonly wounding the feelings, or of making invidious reflections upon the origin or occupation of any man." Yet Johnson persisted in complaining that Davis had singled out those two trades, when he might simply have said that no men of any calling except trained soldiers should command armies.

It was a pettifogging point not worth making, but all his life Johnson would be ultrasensitive about his humble origins and resentful of the planter aristocrats of his section who looked down on him. He and Davis went on for some time, their passions rising in the debate, which one reporter called "the richest scene of the session." Indeed, no record of all their remarks survived, because local reporters, at the request of friends of both Davis and Johnson, suggested that publication would bring distinction to neither. All they would say was that there had been a "colloquy of a personal and somewhat angry kind," while the official organ of Congress, the *Globe*, referred only to "the debate in all its stages not being of an entirely pleasant nature." Davis could not know that twenty years later the repercussions of this debate, and the enemy he unwittingly made in Andrew Johnson, would have a profound impact upon his life.[3]

Such undignified, aggravating, and, to Davis, illogical behavior must have made him all the more anxious to get out of Washington and back into uniform. If he did, it would come at a price, for the possibility of his going to war, and his obvious desire to do so despite her wishes, made relations with Varina increasingly strained. By the first week of June she turned to her mother, protesting that "I am so miserable I feel as if I could lay down my life to be near to you and Father." Seeing his determination, she admitted defeat to herself, "but god only knows how bitter it is to me." Until June 5, she still believed that Davis had not committed himself, but then that evening she learned by accident that his decision was made. What she learned is unknown, since no actual offer of a command had yet been made. Perhaps it was simply a decision to go to the war in any capacity, and not just as leader of a regiment. After all, captains and majors made reputations, too. "I have cried until I am stupid," Varina complained the next day. She confided her anguish to Walker's wife, and that estimable lady promptly gave Davis an upbraiding for his conduct. As for Davis himself, he preferred to believe that his wife was ill or that she suffered from some other cause, rather than admit that his own behavior had caused her distress. In fact, her health did trouble her considerably, no doubt exacerbated by the discord with her husband, and a few days later she left for New Hampshire to recuperate with friends. Perhaps she also left to be away from Jefferson, away from the strife that already separated them. "He is such a dear good fellow, I might quarrel a month and he would not get mad," she said. Still, a gulf had opened, their first major marital disagreement. Though Davis stayed in Washington to attend to House business, he remained solicitous of her, promising that "if my presence is necessary to you all other things must yield." He even tried to cajole her with little familiarities that would mean nothing to anyone but her, signing himself "your 'Hubbin.' "[4] That his own emotions were on edge is equally evident from the fact that somehow someone sent him, or else he stumbled across, an old letter from his father. As a curiosity, he started to read it aloud to Varina before she left, "but handed it over unread and left the room unable to speak." For all the coolness on the surface, there were hidden fires within the man, burning to vent themselves through his reserve.[5]

Little of moment remained for Davis that summer. He sat on a committee that exonerated the venerated Daniel Webster of financial misdeeds, winning plaudits for himself by refusing to use the opportunity to damage a Whig opponent. "No one could deprecate his policy more than I do," Davis told a Democrat of his feelings toward Webster. Nevertheless, "I would not make a false and partizan report or parley with my sense of justice and honor." He also spoke in favor of Congress presenting a gold medal to Taylor for his victories, and prepared himself for what he expected to be another battle and an important vote on a tariff bill. But then, on June 29 or 30, James Roach, an old friend and banker from Vicksburg, found Davis at his seat on the floor of the House and presented to him a message from home. Quite probably it came addressed to "Col. Davis, 1st Mississippi Volunteers."[6]

Men had gathered rapidly at Vicksburg, camping in a grove called Camp Independence a mile south of the center of town. By June 18 ten companies had formed, 913 men in all, and it was time to follow the time-honored custom among volunteers of electing their own officers. They started with the office of colonel, and five men's names were entered. All of them except Davis at one time or another held the rank of colonel or brigadier in the state militia, and such titles could be persuasive to a young volunteer trying to pick an experienced man. Yet of them all, only Davis had the benefit from West Point training and active Army experience. When the ballot box closed, no one emerged with a majority. General A. B. Bradford of Holly Springs showed a plurality with 350 votes, and Davis was just behind him with 300, while the others trailed considerably. But Bradford immediately declined, relinquishing his election, and pleading that the volunteers owed it to themselves to select only a man who could command a clear majority. Thus the volunteers voted a second time. Despite charges that some of Davis's friends used undue influence to prevent Bradford getting a majority, the next ballot showed a change in allegiance by some companies. Of the votes cast, Davis emerged with a majority of 147, or about 604 votes. Though Bradford's friends were disappointed, no great outburst of dismay followed. Instead, the local press predicted that "a good feeling will prevail in this Regiment and particularly among the officers—for brave men always respect each other." It was a good, if naive, sentiment.[7]

Davis wrote at once to accept the appointment, lamenting that Mississippi would not be allowed to send as many soldiers to the war as other states but hoping nevertheless that "an opportunity will be afforded to the 1st Regiment of Volunteers . . . to give renewed assurance of that which may be expected of Mississippians." Perhaps his next act was a visit to President Polk to notify him of his election. Davis intended to leave Washington as soon as he could secure weapons and equipment for his regiment, but Polk persuaded him to remain long enough to vote on the tariff bill by promising in return that he would expedite Davis's requests with the secretary of war.

The Whitney Arms Company of New Haven, Connecticut, in 1841 brought out a new model rifle much more accurate and effective than the old flintlock smoothbores then in use in the army. It used percussion caps instead of unreliable flint and powder, making it safer and faster to load and fire, and its thirty-three-inch barrel held internal rifling that could send its .54 caliber conical bullet hurtling through space for distances up to one thousand yards, and with excellent accuracy at lesser ranges. Though not yet adopted by the U.S. Army, this Whitney rifle was the latest in technology, and Davis wanted it for his Mississippians. He requisitioned one thousand of them, and Polk backed his request, even when General Winfield Scott suggested that at least six of his ten companies should carry muskets. Accustomed to the execrable marksmanship of the average United States regular, Scott reckoned without the skill with rifled hunting weapons frequently exhibited by private citizens turned volunteers. "I knew the confidence the Men I was expected to lead had in rifles," Davis recalled, "and their distrust of the musket then in use." Certainly there was no controversy between Scott and Davis in the matter, and it is unlikely that either retained any ill feeling from this, their first substantive meeting since a passing acquaintance at the end of the Black Hawk War.[8]

Davis waited in Washington until July 3, when twin events enabled him to leave for Mississippi. An order from the War Department positively ordered him to take his regiment immediately to Mexico to report to Taylor. Meanwhile, that same day the War Department directed that the regiment be mustered into service without waiting for Davis and go to Mexico under the command of its lieutenant colonel, Alexander K. McClung. Davis could join the regiment en route or in Mexico. That same day, in the House, Davis cast his vote on the tariff bill, thus relieving himself of his agreement with Polk. He left for Mississippi the next day, July 4, the seventieth anniversary of the great national holiday.[9]

He traveled as quickly as possible, first to Pittsburgh, then down the Ohio. Varina, though still far from well, went with him, planning to stay with her parents in Natchez. She and Joseph's wife Eliza could not get along, it seemed, and Davis put this down to Varina's "weaknesses which spring from a sensitive and generous temper." He did not have to say that relations between himself and Varina still were not right. His frustration showed in an increasing resort to profanity, which she protested. For most of the journey he kept his face buried in a small book on military tactics rather than pay attention to his young wife, still ill, from whom he had been parted for nearly a month and from whom he would soon be separated for much longer—perhaps forever. When Varina complained of his ignoring her, he began to talk to her, but only on the subject of "enfilading, breaking column, hollow squares, and what not." Jefferson Davis had focused his mind once again, and there was no room in his new view for anything other than the sight of Mexico.[10]

The Davises reached Vicksburg on July 13 and immediately left for Brierfield. Davis had to decide what to do about the plantation. Pemberton had managed it for him during his absence in Washington, and now the two old friends, master and slave, discussed whether or not James should accompany Davis to Mexico. Pemberton himself decided the matter by pointing out that Varina would need him there, and the place might suffer in the hands of a new overseer. Consequently, Davis borrowed another slave, Jim Green, from his brother Joseph, and left Pemberton in charge of Brierfield.[11]

There was little time. The regiment had already left for New Orleans before Davis reached home, and he did not want them to go to Mexico without him. He spent only one night at Davis Bend putting things in order—everything, that is, except Varina. On July 14 when he mounted a favorite horse, Tartar, and set out for Vicksburg again for the trip downriver, she could not conceal "what the parting cost us, and how sad it was."[12]

Davis and Jim Green stepped off the steamer *Paul Jones* on the New Orleans waterfront on July 17 and went immediately to the Mississippians' campground. Even before joining them, Davis was beginning to promulgate the usual fiction of office seekers that his election had been unsought on his part. He also gave Joseph a letter resigning his seat in Congress, but asked that his brother not send it to the governor until Jefferson had a chance to get to Mexico and see for himself the look of the war. A long conflict would require him to yield his seat, but there was no sense in giving it up too soon in case the contest proved to be brief. "This movement was unexpected," he wrote somewhat disingenuously on July 8, neatly omitting any reference to his open letter in May announcing his willingness to accept the colonelcy. While most of the rank and file in the new regiment greeted him with enthusiasm, there were those adherents of Bradford and the other aspirants who would not forget that Davis's friends may have pulled some strings to get him the commission on that second ballot.[13]

But most of the men welcomed Davis. Some were family, like Varina's brother Joseph, a six-foot-seven-inch giant she feared would make too good a target. Davis's own nephew Robert also served as a private, and of course many of the men raised in Vicksburg and Warren County, as well as a company from around Woodville, were on first-name terms with their new colonel. As for his officers, Davis knew almost all of them and had met some on the stump.[14]

Next in command was McClung, a thirty-five-year-old former lawyer and newspaperman, intensely ambitious and equally contentious. Bradford, having lost the colonelcy, won a majority in the vote for major instead. An old soldier, seventeen years Davis's senior, he was a Whig who occasionally spoke opposite Davis during the 1844 canvass, though the two were on cordial terms. A number of other men known or soon to be known to Davis filled lesser positions, including Humphrey Marshall; Carnot Posey, a lieutenant in Company B; and Douglas H. Cooper, captain of the same company. For some reason, Cooper and Davis definitely were not friends.[15]

Even before Davis joined the regiment, the men were forming their opinions of him. Word of his concern for their welfare, by struggling for the best weapons and equipment, made a favorable impression on them. A correspondent to the Holly Springs paper asserted that "Jefferson Davis, our Colonel, is no doubt a gallant officer and accomplished gentleman," though since Holly Springs was Bradford country, he went on to say that "I think the precedent bad" (that a congressman left Washington to take the field) and that "he should have been left in his position in Congress." Rumblings of the presumed unfairness of the election died hard. Davis would have been unwise and naive indeed if he expected himself to be universally liked by a small host of men who, like himself, were ambitious, sought glory, and feared only a limited time and stage on which to win it. That could make them all jealous and suspicious of each other.[16]

By all accounts Davis leapt into the work of training his new command with all the energy and singleminded application that he devoted to any endeavor that captured his attention. There was little time for formal exercises, however, for orders commanded that the Mississippians join Taylor as quickly as possible. The day after he arrived in New Orleans, Davis wrote to Varina though he had time for only two sentences, signed "Your Hubbie." Four days later three of his companies left under McClung for Brazos Island off the mouth of the Rio Grande, and another four left the next day. Davis and the last three companies did not depart New Orleans until July 26. Probably he delayed his own departure in the hope that his Whitney rifles might still arrive, but through misadventure they were shipped incorrectly, and only the influence of his friend Secretary of the Treasury Walker eventually got the guns to him in Mexico, delivered by Treasury Department revenue cutters. Perhaps in return Davis sent Walker intelligence of the state of political affairs in New Orleans, pointed out an enemy or two, and sought a little influence in favor of a friend. He had learned much of the way of things political in his short stay in Washington, and the transition from one occupation to another still found him at times with a foot in both camps.[17]

His own voyage to Brazos Island proved uneventful. The men about him on the steamer laughed and joked and whistled and kept a very careful eye on everything their colonel did, trying to take his measure. Thus Davis refrained from kissing the pages of a brief letter to Varina, though he could not keep himself from lecturing her a bit on how she should spend her time while he was away. Especially he recommended cultivating the shrubs around the Briers and suggested that "the season of our absence may be a season of reflection bearing fruits of soberness, and utility, and certainty of thought and of action." Obviously, in his assumed role as her mentor, he advised that she think over her behavior toward him in recent months.[18]

By August 3 Davis had the entire regiment together once more and encamped on the mainland near the mouth of the Rio Grande. Here they remained for nearly three weeks, and now their real training began. Some recalled it as "the most trying time that the men were called upon to endure." The incessantly hot sun burned into and reflected from the white sandy beach, scorching the Mississippians head and foot. Many men sickened, and the first exposures to camp disease began to claim lives. The change in water and diet weakened others, though Davis's own health, surprisingly, seemed excellent. To whatever degree any of his ailments were psychosomatic, as some may have been, the excitement preempted them from his mind. His challenge came from his men, for many, dispirited and resentful, murmured in their tents against him. "Colonel Davis did not have the entire love and confidence of his command," said an officer in Company E. They objected to what they felt was excessive drill, rifle practice, guard posting, camp policing, and more. Every morning and every evening Davis paraded the men at company and regimental drills "on the hot sands of this cheerless encampment."[19]

Certainly that drill was necessary. Like most West Pointers, Davis entertained an inherent distrust of the reliability of volunteers, however much he acknowledged their courage. Even now, though he confided it to few or none, he felt implicit confidence in the bravery of his Mississippians. What troubled him was how well they might remember their training in the confusion of battle. Success there relied more on coolness than courage. The only security he could have would be the knowledge that he had trained them as best he could, drumming the drills and commands into them by rote. He had to try to instill in them an instinct to follow orders, immediately and unquestioningly, to ensure their effectiveness and safety in a fight. Thus to some he would seem to be a martinet, though what dissatisfaction the officers and lower ranks expressed sometimes seemed to come as much from old political alignments as anything else.

Another reason for Davis's harsh regimen may have been an inkling that his regiment would see action before long. No sooner had Davis come ashore from Brazos Island than he received a letter from General Taylor at Matamoros, only a few miles away on the Mexican side of the river. He was moving the growing army of volunteers to Camargo, a hundred miles up the river, and very much wanted Davis with him. Indeed, he would issue orders that gave the Mississippians some preference in coming to Camargo, not making them wait to leave their encampment in the order of their arrival, as with other regiments. "I can assure you I am more than anxious to take you by the hand, & to have you & your command with or near me," the general wrote. Obviously, all tension or resentment between the two men was dead and buried with Sarah.[20]

From Taylor's letter it was not hard to conclude that the First Mississippi might soon be in the campaign. By August 16 Davis daily expected the boats that would take his command upriver. To Varina he confided that he was "much chafed by delay," and especially because most of his Whitney rifles had not yet arrived. Two of his companies already had rifles, but the rest had nothing but the promise of some old muskets in need of repair. On August 18, learning that more ships had arrived at Brazos Island from New Orleans, Davis sent his assistant quartermaster Captain Franklin Smith on the hot and miserable ten-mile trip back to the island to get the rifles if they chanced to be on one of the ships. Happily Smith found a partial shipment and returned with them to camp, but he was less than delighted when Davis sent him back again two days later to inquire after the remainder. "The Col's heart being altogether set on military glory," Smith complained to his diary, he made a wasted and uncomfortable trip. Still, the arms did arrive that day, though Davis now found himself without the percussion caps needed to fire them. Earnestly he pleaded with the ordnance officer at nearby Fort Polk to send him the caps. "If it shall not greatly promote the public service," he pleaded, "it will at least greatly oblige me, and inspir[e] some additional confidence in the men."

Only on August 22 did Davis finally have all his weapons and the ammunition they required. "We have met delay and detention at every turn," he complained in a last letter to Walker two days later before he left for Camargo. He suspected either incompetence or malice on the part of the quartermasters in New Orleans, and further laid at their feet responsibility for the fact that 178 of his men were either discharged already or on the sick roll. Had they not been delayed at this unhealthy encampment, they would have been leaving with him. More significantly, he hinted at poor morale in the outfit. A few days earlier he had already noted that percussion caps would give "additional confidence" to his men, since weapons that could not shoot otherwise were not worth much. Now, thanking Walker for his assistance in getting the Whitneys to him, Davis suggested that the Mississippians were not as "full of zeal, and vigor" as they could have been.[21]

Nevertheless, though reduced in numbers and spirits, the Mississippians began the trip to Camargo on August 24, after only three weeks of training. Davis left that day himself, the balance of the regiment following two days later, and on August 31 he stepped off the steamer *Virginia* to join Taylor's somewhat ambiguously named Army of Occupation or Invasion. When Davis reported to the general's headquarters at last, their greeting was warm and friendly. Taylor saw before him, as did others then in Mexico, a man "erect and probably six feet in height," slender yet well formed, with hollow, clean-shaven cheeks, high cheekbones, and gray eyes, one of them looking somewhat clouded while the other cast a penetrating gaze. He was not a handsome man in the conventional romantic sense, but rather in an aristocratic, high-toned, almost distant and unapproachable way. In a time when men liked to admire and comment on each other, Jefferson Davis invariably attracted attention.[22]

Very probably Taylor confided to Davis at their first meeting his anger and frustration over the way the war was being run. Indeed, perhaps no other conflict in American history would see its military operations so influenced and even dictated by political affairs in Washington. Taylor had won two small and militarily insignificant victories immediately after the outbreak of hostilities, but at once Palo Alto and Resaca de la Palma made him a national hero. That posed a problem for the Democrats, for the apolitical Taylor was thought to be a Whig, and since Polk had no intention of running for reelection in 1848, the Democrats feared losing the White House should the opposition nominate Taylor. They needed a hero of their own. General Winfield Scott was no comfort to them, for he, too, had Whig leanings and, even more than Taylor, he felt presidential ambitions. The best the Democrats could do was to try to keep either general from winning too much glory or too many headlines, while they hoped that a champion of their own would emerge.

Thus both generals would have an enemy in their rear, and now Scott, as general-in-chief, also tried to undercut Taylor by stripping from his command most of his trained regular regiments, hoarding them for his own contemplated movement against Mexico City. No one doubted that the Mexicans could be defeated; everyone worried over seeing them beaten too gloriously and by the wrong general. As a result, by now Taylor already loathed Scott, and despite being on the opposite side of the political fence, Davis easily absorbed Taylor's prejudices, as he did with those of any man he admired. His own brush with Scott over the rifles helped, and the way Taylor's army was treated by the general-in-chief only added to the impression of Scott as an imperious manipulator.

Taylor organized the troops left to him into three divisions. The first two, commanded by Major General William Worth and Davis's old friend Brigadier General David Twiggs, actually left Camargo on August 19, while the third organization, the Field Division of Volunteers, was still forming. Davis's friend Quitman, now a brigadier, commanded its Second Brigade, to be composed of the First Tennessee and the First Mississippi. This boded well, for Quitman, both a friend and a neighbor on Davis Bend, could be counted upon to give Davis any opportunity that offered itself to see action and win plaudits. After all, he owed his general's star in part to Davis's assistance in Congress and with Polk. On September 7, just three days after the Mississippi regiment was consolidated once again, Quitman's brigade marched out of Camargo. Six days of marching due west took them fifty miles to Cerralvo, and there they joined the First Brigade of volunteers, made up of a Kentucky and an Ohio regiment. The whole comprised the division commanded by Major General William O. Butler. They rested at Cerralvo for two days before marching another twenty-five miles west to Marin. There at last Taylor's entire army joined together, when on September 18 J. Pinckney Henderson's division of Texas volunteers arrived.[23]

Taylor's plan of campaign was a simple one. His role in this war was to protect the United States from invasion, while to Scott fell the task of actually conquering Mexico. Thus Taylor needed to hold a line across northern Mexico, its left anchored at Fort Polk on the Rio Grande and its right extended as far west as necessary. His first goal would be the fortified town of Monterrey, two hundred miles west of Brazos Island. Advancing up the Rio Grande to Camargo, though an indirect approach, spared his men almost half the distance to the objective, which they would otherwise have had to make by punishing march. As it was, the heat of the journey from Camargo to Marin exhausted them, but it also left them poised just twenty miles from their goal. Incredibly, with only three weeks of real training, and just two months after leaving New Orleans, Davis and the First Mississippi stood on the verge of the first real battle any of them had ever experienced.[24]

Davis moved out again on the morning of September 19, camping that night in a wood near San Domingo. The next day the operations against Monterrey commenced in earnest. Taylor sent Worth's division on a march off to the west to take possession of the road to Saltillo, cutting off the Mexicans from either retreat or reinforcement. The next morning, September 21, he marched the balance of his army directly toward the northern approaches of the city. His strategy was simple enough. Monterrey lay with its back in a crook of the Santa Catarina River. The only major access into or out of the city was the road to Saltillo, while the city itself was now trapped between Taylor's army and the river. A line of impromptu forts protected Monterrey, from La Tenería, a major fortification with two hundred men and four cannon, on the east by the river, to another called the Citadel or Black Fort above the center of town. Orchards and fields of cane and corn gave some impediment to any approach on this line, and should the Americans get past the forts, another called El Rincón del Diablo lay farther inside the city behind La Tenería. If Taylor took the forts and Worth held the road to Saltillo, the Mexicans would almost certainly have to surrender.[25]

September 21 dawned warm and bright. The volunteers arose before dawn. Soon they heard the firing far to the west, around Monterrey, as Worth commenced his attack on the forts guarding the Saltillo road. Almost immediately Taylor sent his other two divisions to a depression a mile north of the city, where an American battery already lobbed shells at the Citadel and La Tenería. Then, while the volunteer division waited in reserve, Taylor sent Twiggs's division in to attack.

Davis cut an interesting figure that morning. Unlike most of the other ranking officers of regiments and brigades, he was on foot. Tartar remained with Jim Green back at their last camp. More unusual, he wore civilian dress, probably because he never found time to have a uniform made in the rush to get to the regiment and get it to Mexico. Now he simply stood coolly in line with his men, listening to the fighting ahead of them, and perhaps occasionally seeing the flash of Mexican cannon in the distance. Like his brigade commander, Quitman, he became restless at the waiting.[26]

Quitman put Davis at the extreme left of his line, in a position that was somewhat exposed. Hearing the firing in his front grow in intensity, Davis himself went forward a little distance to reconnoiter the ground before him and to the left. Here he got his first look at La Tenería and at the fire its defenders were pouring into Twiggs's men. Before long Davis saw the volunteer regiments to his right, the First Tennessee and the First Ohio, start moving out by the left flank, passing across the front of his own regiment and heading obliquely forward. No orders had reached him, but he logically assumed that an order to advance had been given, as indeed it had. Seeing the beating Twiggs was taking, Taylor decided to commit Butler's division to the attack.[27]

Davis ordered his Mississippians up and into the line and quickly marched them to the left as well, inserting them between the Tennessee and Ohio volunteers as they moved. Before long the Ohio regiment peeled off to the front, leaving Quitman's brigade on its own. Now the volunteers came under fire for the first time. Though some distance from the works around Monterrey, still they were within range of the cannon on the Citadel and La Tenería and actually suffered a crossfire. Still they marched on at the double-quick until they found themselves facing the extreme right of the Mexican line, La Tenería itself. Quitman, already nursing a painful shell wound in his thigh, halted the regiments when they were within a few hundred yards of the fort. Davis noted that enemy musketry, though wildly inaccurate, could still reach his men and that random shots struck a man here and there while they were still too distant for his men to take advantage of the superior accuracy of their own rifles. The Tennessee regiment now stood due north of the fort's northern wall, while the Mississippians, to their right, were before the northwest face of La Tenería, almost within sight of an open rear embrasure, or sally port. When he saw a portion of the Fourth U.S. Infantry in his front, and a gap on his left between his own and the Tennessee regiments, Davis moved his command left slightly to fill out the line. There is no record that he met a lieutenant from Ohio in the Fourth U.S. Infantry, Ulysses S. Grant.[28]

Now events took over almost for themselves. Quitman intended the Mississippians to soften the defenders' resistance with volleys from their rifles and then the Tennesseans to charge the fort. Only he put off giving any orders. During the waiting back at the ravine, McClung had seen Davis pacing back and forth complaining loudly and vehemently that he had no orders. Now that the regiment was under fire, waiting could be deadly. Finally Quitman apparently did give Davis the order for his regiment to form in line and slowly advance toward the fort while firing their rifles, or else he told him to do so when he approved the filling of the gap with the Tennesseans. In either case the Mississippians went forward, McClung commanding the four companies on the left and Davis managing the four on the right, two others having been left behind on the march as a garrison.[30]

Davis ordered his men to select their targets carefully and not to fire unless they had them in their sights. "Their fine rifles told upon the enemy," he reported, and about ten minutes after the slow advance began the return fire from the fort slackened noticeably. With his regiment not more than 150 yards from the enemy works, a great opportunity seemed at hand. Having no other instructions, and later claiming that he did not know the Tennesseans were actually supposed to assault the fort, Davis ordered a charge. Ironically, over on the left Lieutenant Colonel McClung did exactly the same thing and at the same time, having concluded that Davis must have been hit or else he would have issued such an order himself.[31]

Now everything seemed to happen at once. No one seemed to know that the Tennesseans were charging at the same time. Davis himself went forward, witnesses reported, "as coolly in battle at the head of his men as if on parade." One of his privates thought him "the bravest, coolest, grandest man that I ever saw." Yelling at his men that twenty of them could take that fort with nothing more than butcher knives, he hurled them at its walls. Just then Davis saw McClung again for the first time in several minutes, now yelling wildly at his companies to follow him as he waved his sword over his head. Everyone ran at full speed toward La Tenería, "so rapidly," said Davis, "that who should reach it first was a question." In only seconds they struck the sandbagged walls of the fort, and the next sight in Davis's eyes was McClung, the first man atop the parapet, standing exultant and waving his sword in triumph.[32]

Davis's own route took him farther to the right, into the open embrasure on the northwestern flank. A lieutenant ran through before him and shot down a defender, and then Davis himself entered the fort. He saw nothing but the Mexican dead and the arms and other equipment left behind as the living defenders rushed out of the sally port at the rear. The fort was theirs. In the excitement and confusion Davis did not see or notice that Tennesseans were also streaming in over the northern parapet. No one could ever tell just which regiment actually scaled the walls and entered the fort first—not that it really mattered militarily. The fact is, the Mexicans were already abandoning their works before any Americans hit the walls. It was the sight of the Tennesseans' bayonets and the Mississippians' rifle fire coming toward them in the charge that defeated the Mexicans. The only defenders still in the fort when the Americans poured in were those too slow to get out.

Those retreating foes now claimed Davis's complete attention. He saw some of them run to a stone building that had been a tannery or distillery less than one hundred yards in the rear of La Tenería, while others ran past it across a little stream and down to the El Diablo fort. Almost without stopping, Davis gathered a few men and rushed after the Mexicans. Twiggs and his men had finally made some headway over to the right of La Tenería, and now as Davis pursued the fleeing enemy, he saw and heard Twiggs yelling after him to follow the foe closely, as if that were not what Davis was doing already. Running around the front of the building to the side door entered by the Mexicans, Davis was so hard on their heels that as the last enemy soldier went in and shut the door, Davis crashed into it with all his weight before it could be barricaded.

Inside he saw perhaps twenty Mexicans, thoroughly beaten, holding their hands in the air, while one of their officers called out that they surrendered. Seeing no other American soldiers in the building, Davis accepted the enemy officer's sword, then went outside again and closed the door, hoping to prevent any other soldiers from firing on the Mexican prisoners. He put the nearest officer, a lieutenant of Company K, in charge of disarming the prisoners, and then took twenty or thirty other Mississippians and headed after the rest of the fleeing enemy. He could not know that once again McClung had acted in unison, had entered the stone building from another side, and in the confusion of his appearance had been shot and wounded seriously by a frightened soldier.[33]

Now it was Davis's turn to brandish a sword above his head. Captured by the exhilaration of the moment, he raced on foot after the Mexicans, splashing through the shallow creek ahead of his men. Exhorting them to take cover and open fire on El Diablo, he posted himself in the open on a street from which he could shout back to the rest of his regiment to come forward. Just then a message came from Quitman ordering him to retire. When Davis seemed reluctant to obey quickly, Quitman himself rode to the stream and called to him to withdraw. Davis could not conceal his chagrin. Later, rumors in the army claimed that he wept openly at the recall order. Asked about it in a few weeks, Davis would laugh and say that, as he recalled, he had not shed tears, "but was excessively mortified." He stood before Quitman convinced that given another few minutes he could have taken El Diablo as well. "Yes sir that is true," he told Quartermaster Smith on October 22. "I feel confidant that we would have done it."[34]

Perhaps he would have, but now Quitman needed to regroup his scattered and overexcited volunteers—and their officers. Davis recrossed the stream and looked for the balance of his regiment. He found a few men but could not put together more than thirty, and with them he moved off west along one of the city streets until he and others encountered one hundred or so of the enemy in a position covered by a nearby earthwork. Davis and fellow officers were planning their attack on this new position when another order to retire ended his fighting for the day except for a rear-guard volley to keep Mexican lancers from striking his exhausted men. Before nightfall the Mississippians had returned to their encampment of that morning.[35]

It took some time before Davis could tell just how much his regiment had suffered. It finally appeared that he had lost seven killed and forty-seven wounded, three of them mortally, as well as the loss of Mc-Clung and two other officers with lesser wounds. The next day Quitman ordered both of his regiments back into La Tenería as a garrison, posting the Mississippians at the stone house. There they passed an uncomfortable day and night, without rations or heavy blankets or overcoats to protect them from a chilling north wind that blew through the night. In the darkness all they could see were the enemy's signal flares on the city, and now and then they heard the clatter of Mexican cavalry in the cobbled streets. Few slept that night. They believed themselves heavily outnumbered, knew the foe was regrouping for more fighting, and stayed almost constantly on the alert.

But dawn presented a different picture. Peering out from the roof of the tannery, Davis saw the Mexicans withdrawing from the works at El Diablo. When he told Quitman what he had seen, the general sent him out with four companies to reconnoiter, and they found the fort unoccupied and took possession. Then Davis moved out again, commencing a full seven hours of almost constant house-to-house, street-to-street fighting and sniping.[36]

From rooftop to rooftop, he posted his men as they slowly made their way along the streets toward the center of town. Davis himself often took the lead. "We have been at the heels of Davis since the fight opened," one of his lieutenants wrote two days later. "Davis is a gallant fellow." Much of the day General Henderson of the Texas division stayed with him, and he, too, later remarked on the colonel's "gallant conduct." Still another Mississippian who saw Davis in the fight declared that "it is to me a wonder that he was not killed, as he was at all times in the hottest of the fight." Even one of the enemy generals later remarked upon the "deadly execution" of Davis's riflemen.[37]

Passing as they did from one house to another, the Mississippians inevitably encountered a host of scenes both comic and pitiful. Before one barricaded hacienda Davis ordered a private to "burst open that door." The soldier beat at the door with a large rock, then lunged against it. The door flew open, and he tumbled inside. Davis and Quitman started to enter next when the private ran back out, bumping both officers.

"What!" Davis exclaimed. "Retreating, Smith!—are you wounded?"

"Yes, I am," said the hapless private. "There is a battery in here I can't attack—at least without reinforcements."

When Davis and Quitman entered they discovered that the house was one of ill repute, and each promptly exited again with a Mexican girl "vexing his ear" alternately screaming in fury and pleading for mercy. Then, at another house, he met a woman so convinced that the Americans would kill her that she tried to give him her baby. "Do not kill it but take it for your own," she pleaded.[38]

By the late afternoon Davis had advanced close to the cathedral, barely more than a block from the central plaza of Monterrey. Once again orders came to him to withdraw, and reluctantly he obeyed. Davis could not know of the turn of events elsewhere, but Worth had been successful in taking the forts on the Saltillo road and now intended to shell the city into submission. All the volunteers had to be withdrawn or else they would come under the same fire. "They were having their own fun," one regular officer said of Davis and the rest, and it was only with difficulty that they were all pulled out.[39]

That night the Mexican commander, General Pedro de Ampudia, decided that he had no alternative but to capitulate. The next morning he asked Taylor for terms, and Old Rough and Ready appointed a commission composed of Worth, Henderson, and Davis to negotiate the surrender. How the Mississippian found himself on that commission is somewhat difficult to explain. Either Taylor chose him because of his good performance in the battle—though other colonels also performed well—or else because he hoped to advance Davis by having him associated with an important event. Davis rode to see Ampudia, accompanied by his old friend Sidney Johnston, serving with Henderson's volunteers. They spent all day at negotiations, left late, and then attempted to return in the morning. Suddenly they found themselves confronted by armed Mexicans. Davis sent word to Ampudia but received no reply. Johnston quickly grabbed Ampudia's adjutant as a hostage and forced him to conduct them to the general. Davis never lost his admiration for that quick thinking. "The decisiveness of his actions," said his admiring friend, got them out of what Davis believed was "one of the most perilous situations" of his life. Whatever Taylor's motivation, Davis and the rest produced a controversial document that obtained possession of the city and all its munitions. However, they allowed the Mexican army itself to leave, along with one six-gun field battery, each officer and man taking his personal arms with him. The agreement further required Ampudia to withdraw at least fifty miles to the south or west and enjoined Taylor from following beyond that line for a full eight weeks.[40]

It was an odd agreement, but there was good sense behind it, and Taylor had the unanimous support of his commissioners on his terms. The Mexicans still outnumbered him; they still held the one major fort, the Citadel; he had no siege guns or battering apparatus to take the fort. Without the Citadel, Taylor could not hold the town. His supplies and ammunition were low. Everything suggested that Taylor himself might have to pull out. Thus, the agreement, though very conditional, still gained the Citadel; the town; all of its much-needed powder, shot, and provisions; and the withdrawal of Ampudia a sufficient distance away that Taylor could rest and refit his army. From the viewpoint of the men on the ground that day, it seemed the best they could do. "We may congratulate ourselves upon the part we have taken," Davis declared after the convention was signed that afternoon. Unfortunately Taylor would later be roundly condemned by his political enemies in Washington for these terms, though no opprobrium attached itself to Davis.[41]

An exultant Jefferson Davis wrote home immediately after the capitulation, though he wrote first to Joseph. Speaking of the terms granted, he claimed "they were whipped, and we could afford to be generous." Having heard a rumor that peace commissioners were on their way to Mexico City, Davis concluded with the overconfident prediction that "the war is probably over." Quite to the contrary, the conflict would go on for more than a year, though now the war within Taylor's army for the glory of Monterrey commenced. More sinned against than sinner, Colonel Davis nonetheless joined in the battle for laurels.[42]

Much of the fight would be in his own regiment. Joseph Howell saw only a rosy picture in the First Mississippi, but as the colonel's brother-in-law, chances are that is all he was allowed to see. "There is not a man in his regiment who would not sacrifice his life to obey him," wrote Howell two weeks after Monterrey. " 'Colonel Jeff,' as they call him, 'knows best, so hurrah, boys.' " But there were other, less admiring voices. Within days of Monterrey, new complaints about Davis's leadership emerged, accusing him of being overbearing, no doubt his old habit of seeing things only his way. Worse, as soon as he wrote his report of the recent battle, his officers immediately split into two camps, pro-Davis and pro-McClung, with splinter factions loyal to neither. Even before the contents of Davis's report were known, some of his officers spread rumors of its contents, and at least one, Captain William Rogers of Company K, believed it would be "both partial and false." "If he has done me injustice," Rogers declared before seeing it, "he must give me satisfaction."[43]

In fact, there was nothing in the report to object to, but as Rogers admitted to his diary, in the scramble for glory from what many feared would be their only battle, "there [was] much villainy." "Knowing that men are tricky it is well enough to watch them," he wrote after filing his own report. McClung, though wounded, was already making trouble, and was "as corrupt I think as frail human nature can become." As for Davis, he "made great professions of kindness" to Rogers, but still the captain did not trust him either.[43]

The problems with McClung, especially, would become both very public and very embarrassing. In his report Davis stated that he had ordered the charge on La Tenería and that he was the first inside the stone tannery, receiving its surrender. McClung claimed exactly the same things for himself. In their assertions, neither officer acted in bad faith, for each surely believed the sequence of events in the battle was as he had seen it. Unfortunately, since they rarely saw each other, neither knew what the other had been doing, and neither could know that their actions had been virtually identical and simultaneous. On reading Davis's report, McClung immediately commenced collecting statements from his friends and supporters bolstering his claim, and before the end of the year much of what they had to say started to appear in the Vicksburg press. Forced to respond, Davis collected statements of his own, never actually denying McClung's claims but stating only that he supposed they had done much the same thing at the same time. McClung never accepted that. His serious wound put him out of the war for good, so the lieutenant colonel clung tenaciously to the only opportunity for military glory he would ever have—one he could not bear to share with Davis. "He is a dangerous and wily politician," McClung wrote of his commander, "loaded down with vanity and self conceit, wishing only for his own aggrandizement." Never settled, the controversy between them raged on in the press for months and even after the war occasionally. By February 1847 McClung was telling friends that he wanted to have a duel with Davis "because I think the United States will be better off without him." A few years later the embittered man took his own life instead.[44]

The controversy did credit to neither, though throughout Davis remained quite restrained, as usual showing more in the way of surprise and hurt than anger that someone should disagree with him. Even more public, unfortunately, would be the external debate between Davis and the colonel of the First Tennessee. It seems that William Campbell believed *his* regiment had been the first into La Tenería. Finding Davis's report "most presumptuous," Campbell set out to "expose his false statements." Calling portions of the Mississippian's report "ridiculous and untrue," he went on to reveal that this controversy, too, was one of misapprehension. The Tennesseans had struck a different face of the fort, largely unseen by the Mississippians, at almost exactly the same time. In the excitement, the haze from the heat, and the smoke of their guns, neither regiment retained any organization, and neither seemed to have noticed the other. Once again, confusion led each to believe itself the first and rightful captor of the fort. "The universal sentiment of the army is against the presumptuous claim of Col. Davis," Campbell wrote a few weeks after the battle. That Davis and his regiment even got into the battle he suspected was due to favoritism from General Taylor.[45]

Thus the controversies raged, and Davis entered into the one with Campbell with vigor. "As a duty to my Regiment," he said, "I will follow this question, raised by others, until a mass of concurrent testimony from a variety of witnesses shall [have] incontestably established our claim to whatever credit attaches to the storming party on that occasion." Once again it was Davis gathering evidence to overwhelm an opponent with the weight of the truth as he saw it. Unfortunately, this time none of the witnesses wanted to play the game. Only General Twiggs gave him a fully supportive affidavit, while others evaded or, like Quitman, refused to get involved. In the end the controversy fizzled out, though Davis never put it entirely out of his mind, and the two colonels never reconciled.[46]

Just why Davis allowed himself to be drawn into these public arguments depended on the viewpoints of his critics and admirers. Some said that he merely defended the truth, and certainly that is how he saw it. Yet others could not forget that just ten weeks before Monterrey he had been a politician sitting in Congress. All these higher-ranking volunteer officers were politicians themselves. The Whig McClung would run unsuccessfully for the House in 1847. Campbell, another Whig, had already been in Congress and in 1851 would use his Monterrey battle cry, "Boys, follow me!" to win the Tennessee governorship. As for Davis himself, so far as he knew in October 1846, the war was over. Having no word as yet of his resignation from the House being accepted, he regarded himself as still being a member of Congress. Now he determined to return to the United States and if possible reclaim his seat, with the laurels of victory on his brow.[47]

9

Boys, Fire, and at Them with Your Knives!

Other considerations besides political ambition ran through Davis's mind when he left the army for a sixty-day furlough on October 19. Mixed news came from home. Varina was unwell, apparently mostly from anxiety for his safety. Her letters, addressed "Dear Banny," expressed fears mingled with expressions of love. "May God bring you [to] these arms once more," she pleaded in a letter he received about the time of the battle, "and then at least for the time I clasp you I shall be happy." Letters from Joseph told of affairs at Brierfield, with reports from James Pemberton that this season's crop was almost as good as Hurricane's. Joseph still held his brother's letter of resignation, awaiting Jefferson's authorization to send it to the governor. As always, Jefferson's decisions were conditional. He withheld his resignation from the army in 1835 pending new developments, and obviously in 1846 he did not intend to give up his House seat if the war proved short enough for him to get back to Washington for the fall session. Jefferson Davis never acted hastily.[1]

Taylor happily granted the furlough application. Davis rode Tartar to Camargo and there boarded the *Hatchee Eagle* for the trip to Brazos Island. Leaving his volunteers he declared how pleased he felt. "I always believed them brave, but did not expect them to be cool," he said. "I now know them to be both brave and cool." The prejudice of the regular officer toward volunteers had dissipated markedly. After all, they helped him win glory.[2]

By November 1 Davis stepped ashore in New Orleans once more, stopping just long enough to demand that a local editor correct a recent article crediting the Tennessee regiment with taking La Tenería. Agreeing with Sergeant Prentiss that Davis "only wished to make a little Locofoco capital at home for Miss. consumption" in the press, the editor ignored the request of the "locofoco," referring to a recent derogatory nickname for Democrats. A few days later, almost immediately after reaching Davis Bend, the colonel made a little more political capital by addressing a large assembly of citizens at Vicksburg. Offering mostly a recounting of the campaign of the First Mississippi, Davis brimmed with the self-assurance, and assurance in his regiment, that so many found overbearing. Relating an event when his regiment took the lead in the march from another unit, and that unit protested, Davis said he had told the other commander—"irritatingly, but yet truthfully—'*Their merit places the Mississippi Regiment in front.*' " It did nothing of the sort, of course. Taylor placed them there because they had rifles and because Davis came with special orders from the War Department to report directly to him and not delay. In other words, Davis's political influence with Polk "put them there." He was right, however, when he described himself as speaking "irritatingly." Yet he showed generosity toward McClung, stating that both had ordered the charge at the same time.

Less than two weeks after returning to Brierfield, Davis continued the controversy with Campbell by writing a long letter to the Vicksburg *Weekly Sentinel,* going over all the old familiar ground, and this just two days after he sanctimoniously told another editor of his reluctance to bring "this question before the public." The fact is, once Davis had the bit of controversy or contention firmly between his teeth, he could not let go.[3]

The visit was brief, for Davis returned to New Orleans again by November 20. One of the first things he learned at Davis Bend was that Joseph, not having heard from him to the contrary, had sent his resignation to the governor on October 17. The local press already carried columns devoted to a special election to fill his House seat when Davis got home. With that avenue closed, and no word that speedy peace with Mexico was coming, Davis decided quickly to return to the army. Trouble with Varina probably impelled him even more. Before leaving Mexico, he knew that she and Joseph irritated each other. The two shared much, too much to be good friends. Each jealously acted as Jefferson's protector, and that naturally put them in conflict. Further, she resented a will that her husband had drafted either before he went to Mexico the first time or now on his brief visit. It divided his estate three ways, Varina receiving only one-third, and this probably at Joseph's urging. The elder Davis had taken a dislike to the Howells despite an earlier friendship, and since the Brierfield property was still legally his, he did not want an acre of it going to a Howell other than Varina. On top of all this, Varina apparently decided that she would design and appoint the new house at

Brierfield that they had discussed for some time. (Of course, Joseph would have to pay for it.)

Finding himself in the midst of all this contention, Colonel Davis must have felt relieved to mount another bay horse, this one named Richard, to leave for a more comfortable war in which he risked nothing more dangerous than bullets. As usual he wrote to Varina on the way, his letter clearly revealing the strain between them. Nonetheless, he could not resist lecturing her to "rise superior to petty annoyances." "To be able to look over the conventionalisms of society yet to have the good sense which skillfully avoids a collision with [them] is the power and the practice I desire in my wife"—a power and a practice that often evaded Jefferson Davis, by the way, as his own recent controversies attested. Faced with an apparent sudden assertion of independence from Varina, perhaps growing out of resentment at the way he so often took Joseph's part rather than hers, Davis gave way to resignation for the moment. "You have taken upon yourself in many respects the decision of your own course." As if talking to a child, he reminded her that responsibility "is not the happy state which those who think they have been governed too much sometimes suppose it." He might have said the same thing to a slave wanting freedom. As for the house, he gave way completely. "Have such a house built as . . . you desire, & endeavor to make your home happy to yourself and those who share it with [you]."

Oddly enough for a man already not in his wife's best graces just at the moment, Davis included in his letter an account of two days spent in New Orleans with the wife of his old army friend McRee. "One of these days God willing I will give you the history of several of my female acquaintance, of whom I lost trace when I left the army and refound in New Orleans," he wrote. "When in a speculative mood they will furnish food for contemplation." That a man who had spent barely two weeks with his wife would write of the fine time he had for ten days in New Orleans with other women stretched credulity. Either his customary infatuation with cold facts got the better of his good sense, or else, just perhaps, Davis felt hurt by Varina's recent behavior in questioning his judgment. Maybe he wanted to make her a little jealous.[4]

The return trip to Taylor's army proved slow and frustrating. It took him two full weeks to get back to Camargo and another ten days or more to find Taylor, then camped near Montemorelos, as far south as his convention with Ampudia allowed. When Davis rejoined him on Christmas Day 1846, the eight-week time limit had expired, of course, but lack of supply and political interference kept the army stationary. As fall moved toward winter, Taylor decided that Washington intended to relegate him to a minor role in the war while Scott took most of the troops and saw most of the action. As a result, without exactly disobeying orders, he would stretch their latitude, pleading poor communications, to conduct a campaign on his own. After much planning, he intended by the end of the year to march against Victoria, one hundred miles south of Monterrey. He had already taken Saltillo, fifty miles west of Monterrey, and left Worth there with a mere twelve hundred men, while he took six thousand on the road to Victoria. He hoped to take that capital city of the province of Tamaulipas and thus place himself deep in the Mexican heartland from which he could strike out against the main enemy army under General Santa Anna.[5]

Taylor took Victoria without resistance, and there, on January 4, Davis finally rejoined the First Mississippi, which had come from Monterrey. And then after only ten days Taylor turned his army around and marched back to Monterrey. Word came from Scott, peremptory word, ordering Taylor to send him nine thousand troops from his area of command, most of them his regulars. As a result, by early February his army numbered barely more than 4,750. Only 750 or so, among them the Mississippians, had any experience of battle. When he returned to Monterrey, Taylor took with him only Davis's regiment, two batteries of light artillery, and a squadron of dragoons. Then he went to Saltillo, where he learned that Scott had requisitioned his best engineer as well, Captain Robert E. Lee of Virginia. Possibly Lee and Davis met here for the first time since their days at West Point.[6]

Taylor's was not the only army moving north. General Santa Anna, with some twenty thousand soldiers at his back, received excellent intelligence of the depleted state of Taylor's command and decided that here would be an easy and yet morally important victory. Defeating and destroying Taylor could clear northern Mexico of organized Americans, and then he might turn his attention to Scott's anticipated thrust toward Veracruz and Mexico City to the south. Late in January the grand Mexican army set out for Saltillo. By February 20 it stood poised at La Encarnación, just thirty-five miles south of Taylor. The next morning they marched to attack.[7]

After arriving at Saltillo, Taylor consolidated what few regiments remained to him and moved south a few miles to Agua Nueva, a spot he deemed critical since it had the only fresh water for miles around. But then came word of Santa Anna's march toward him with more than three times his strength. Having had no time to fortify Agua Nueva, and believing it to be an untenable position against such great odds, Taylor evacuated early on February 21 only hours before the Mexicans arrived to attack. He moved his army some fifteen miles to the north to the Buena Vista hacienda, left most of his tiny army there under command of General John E. Wool, and took Davis and his regiment to Saltillo that night to work on its defenses.

Up to this time Colonel Davis felt less than optimistic about seeing any more action. His regard for Taylor growing steadily, he told Joseph late in January that "I expect any honorable service which he can give us." Unfortunately, the combinations against Taylor between Polk and the War Department and Scott seemed to preclude any further fighting in the north. Scott and his Veracruz expedition held all the prospect of further action and glory. Still, Davis would stay where he was. "The desire to be in every battle fought during my term of service is strong," he confessed, "but I could not in the present condition of Genl. Taylor ask to leave him." His resentment of Winfield Scott and of politicians interfering with the operations of the army grew in proportion equal to his loyalty to his former father-in-law. Even on February 8, at Agua Nueva, he wrote briefly to Varina that "we came expecting a host and battle, have found solitude and externally peace." Two weeks later he marched to the sound of the guns, to become a national hero.[8]

Taylor selected a good spot at Buena Vista, for the hilly country-side insured that Santa Anna must approach by the San Luis Potosí–Saltillo road. At a narrow place called La Angostura, any movement by the Mexicans would be particularly restricted, their advantage of numbers reduced. Taylor or Wool placed an infantry regiment and a battery there, while the rest of the army took position in the hills to the south, east of the road. Thus they hoped to strike Santa Anna in the flank as he marched or else stand on high ground themselves if the Mexicans attacked.

The morning of February 22, a date whose significance was not lost on the men in their positions below Buena Vista, Santa Anna marched north not expecting to find resistance. When he encountered American outposts, he sent a demand for surrender. It had been a tense morning for Taylor and for Davis. They arose early and set out almost immediately from Saltillo, though not before Davis had to deal with another of his contentious subordinates. Captain William P. Rogers, already suspicious of his colonel, now refused an order when Davis told him to stay with his own and another company at Saltillo to guard their camps. Probably resentful of the acclaim Davis had won at Monterrey, Rogers fumed that his own contributions and bravery seemed to be forgotten. Now he believed that his colonel deliberately sought to keep him out of the battle to deny him any further chance at distinction. Relations between the two clearly were not good, and yet Davis relented and left another company behind in Rogers's stead. At a critical moment, he showed considerable forbearance.[9]

As it happened, even though they reached the battlefield before noon, neither Davis nor his Mississippians participated in the limited action that day, being relegated to spectators of some skirmishing that took place three hundred yards or so distant. They spent the whole day in reserve behind La Angostura, and that night Taylor sent them back beyond Buena Vista itself. He had dismissed the surrender demand and watched a day of desultory skirmishing that produced no conclusion and left him thinking that there might be no attack on the morrow. Taking Davis with him, he spent the night at Saltillo feverishly looking over its defenses, expecting the main battle to be fought here. Nevertheless, he determined to resist Santa Anna's advance every step of the way and set out before dawn on February 23 to return to Buena Vista.[10]

Ordered to leave two companies behind to guard their rear at the encampment, since Mexican cavalry had been seen in the vicinity, Davis went once more to Captain Rogers. Calmly he explained that he was the only company commander who had not previously been on detached service, thus now it was his turn. In ordering Rogers to stay behind, Davis showed unusual restraint and even empathy for a fellow officer who itched to see action. The colonel frankly said that he realized Rogers had "no kind feeling" for him but asked that in the interests of the moment Rogers lay aside his animosity and comply with the order. Playing a bit on the captain's ego, Davis also hinted that being rear guard was a post of honor and indicated that being left with what amounted to an independent command might just lead to greater glory than if Rogers served with the balance of the regiment in the main fight. Significantly, Davis could not inspire Rogers to obey by an exertion of superior force or by an appeal to logic. He could only do so by appealing to traits he knew very well in the character of upper-class Southern males— ambition, vanity, and pride.[11]

With Rogers protecting their rear, Davis's Mississippians moved out at the double-quick, just behind Taylor himself. They covered the six miles in less than two hours but before arriving heard the report of cannon that showed the fighting had already commenced. After a brief halt for water, Davis pushed the men onward, soon encountering disoriented cavalrymen and others wandering from the field. In a few minutes Davis turned off to the left, into a ravine that led to the left flank of the American army. As he approached, the first thing he saw was the Second Indiana Volunteers breaking ranks and fleeing to the rear, thanks to a confusion of orders. So far as Davis could tell, the regiment simply became demoralized, and immediately he feared that the sight would dispirit his own men. He need not have worried.[12]

While Davis directed his regiment to advance toward the position just vacated by the Second Indiana, he rode forward on Richard, through the fleeing Hoosiers, appealing to them to hold their ground. "Stay and re-form behind that wall," he said, pointing back to his regiment. Twenty or thirty, perhaps more, of the Indianians did stop their retreat, reformed under an officer, and moved into the rear of Davis's advancing column, to spend the rest of the day fighting with the Mississippians. Meanwhile Davis continued forward, oblivious of the bullets that whistled ever more frequently across the field. He found General Wool alone and trying to rally men and suggested that he would attack the advancing Mexicans if Wool sent him another regiment. Obviously the battle, still just a couple of hours old, was entering a critical moment. Taylor's left flank was giving way. If he forced it back much more, Santa Anna would have a clear approach to the Saltillo road and Taylor's base, not to mention that he would also have Taylor trapped on that road with nowhere to go. Wool agreed and went off to find support.[13]

"The moment seemed to me critical," Davis said later, "and the occasion to require whatever sacrifice it might cost to check the enemy." Ahead of him he saw a plateau between two ravines, and the Mexicans heading toward it. At once he rode back to the First Mississippi, quickly formed them into battle order, then double-quicked them forward until the enemy came within range of their Whitneys. "Fire advancing," he ordered. The Mississippians let go their first volley. Onward they moved at the quick pace, loading and firing and steadily gaining ground. Davis continued at their front, when suddenly he felt an enemy bullet strike his right foot. The lead ball drove bits of his brass spur, boot, and stocking deep into his instep, shattering bones in its path toward the heelbone. He may not have felt the pain at first, only numbness, but he calmly took a handkerchief from a pocket, bound it around the injured foot to staunch the bleeding, and remained in the saddle.[14]

Their volleys stopped the enemy advance on the plateau, and then pushed the Mexicans back. The Mississippians advanced perhaps seven hundred yards before Davis found himself too far forward and dangerously exposed. He saw enemy cavalry in the distance trying to ride around his right to his rear, and decided it was time to withdraw. The left flank of Taylor's army, though still threatened, was stabilized for the moment. As his regiment retired, Davis again rode ahead to a point overlooking a ravine the Mexican cavalry were crossing. He called to him the men within sound of his voice and at once started firing into that ravine at the struggling Mexican horsemen, putting them to flight. Then Davis continued the withdrawal, only to encounter Major Bradford glumly walking beside his own horse and exclaiming, "Shoot me! Shoot me!" When asked the problem, he cried that with the Mississippi regiment running from the foe, "I don't want to live another minute!" Davis soon relieved him of his misapprehension that they were running and shortly re-formed the regiment not far from the original position vacated by the Second Indiana.[15]

With their ammunition almost exhausted, Davis ordered a fresh issue of cartridges—conical bullets with a powder charge at the base in a paper tube. Unfortunately the men discovered that a mixup in the ordnance supply had furnished these new cartridges in a caliber slightly larger than their rifles' bores. They could not be loaded. Still mounted, the blood slowly dripping from his foot, he told the men to spread their cartridges on the ground, take rocks in their hands, and hammer the bullets to reduce their diameter. Of course, while doing so also ruined any accuracy they might otherwise have had from a close fit in the barrels' rifling, at least they could be rammed down those barrels. The Whitneys were little better than muskets now.[16]

Reinforcements finally arrived—a regiment of Indiana infantry and a field piece. Thus bolstered, the Americans fired a volley and saw the Mexican cavalry start to withdraw. Then Davis gave the order "Forward! Guide center! March!" Steadily they advanced, pushing the enemy back and clearing the plateau of lancers. Here Davis held his ground, even when a Mexican battery in the distance began to put shells into the Indiana line and forced that unit to take cover in a ravine to the left. Davis took advantage of the brief lull in close fighting to comb the field for his own wounded from the morning, for it was now past noon. This done, he moved the regiment to the ravine on his left and withdrew several hundred yards closer to the Saltillo road to guard Taylor's flank. The Indiana regiment moved along with him, down a ravine on the right side of the plateau, covered from enemy artillery.[17]

Davis never said how far he intended to withdraw if the movement came on his own initiative. So far this day he acted independently, but at some point Taylor joined him to see the situation at firsthand. Indeed, Davis worried that the general needlessly exposed himself, and tried to get Taylor off his conspicuous Old Whitey and onto the more anonymous Richard instead. Taylor would have none of it. Quite probably he gave Davis some directions about where to hold the line, a caution to watch for enemy cavalry getting around his flank, and then rode away to other parts of the field. With the Mississippians almost his only veteran soldiers, he needed to keep watch on the rest of his line.[18]

Before long, as he moved along the plateau, Davis saw perhaps two thousand Mexican cavalry come up out of the ravine in front of the position he had recently left, not more than a mile and a half distant. Forming line, they advanced rapidly toward his command. Davis thought quickly. Though outnumbered, he believed retreating to be pointless, for the enemy horsemen could run him down, and then the army would be in peril once again. The accepted formation for infantry to meet a cavalry attack was a hollow square, the mass of men at the point forcing the cavalry to break and run a gauntlet of fire from the riflemen positioned on either side as they passed around. But he did not have enough men, and most likely no one had foreseen the need to teach these volunteers such formations in any case. His own regiment, the Third Indiana, and those of the Second Indiana who had rallied probably did not number more than one thousand after the day's casualties. Thinking quickly, perhaps acting on instinct drawn from long lectures at West Point, Davis thought of one thing only—converging fire. If he could get bullets striking the advancing cavalry from two directions simultaneously, it might disorganize and repulse the foe. He rode in front of the First Mississippi. It was their most desperate moment together. Behind him the Mexicans loomed into view, handsomely equipped lancers, moving "rapidly and in beautiful order—the files and ranks so closed, as to look like a solid mass of men and horses."

He ordered the First Mississippi, not more than four hundred strong, to form a line across the plain. The men obeyed at once. They knew their colonel well; he had led them to glory at Monterrey. All day here at Buena Vista they had seen him in their front, risking the enemy fire every bit as much as they did. They saw him ignore his own wound to stay with them in the fight, and they knew a leader. "He could infuse courage into the bosom of a coward, and self-respect and pride into the breast of the most abandoned," one witness wrote two months later. Another claimed that "he could lead them into h——l." Though, as with Captain Rogers that morning, Jefferson Davis might never inspire men with words, when occasion demanded inspiration by personal example and bravery, he was magnificent. He and his Mississippians would always remember these next moments as the most glorious of their lives. In ways he could not then imagine, Jefferson Davis never got over them.[19]

Quietly the Mississippians went into their line. At the same time Davis ordered the Third Indiana to join its left to their right and, using the joint as a hinge, swing its own right forward more than one hundred yards. It nearly formed a right angle, what a nearby captain called a V. Still on Richard, Davis rode calmly along the line. "Hold your fire, men, until they get close," he said, "and then give it to them!" They obeyed, standing as still as rocks, he thought, "silent as death, and eager as a greyhound."[20]

Davis took his place near the center of the angle, while the lines waited with rifles at the "shoulder arms," ready to aim and fire at the command. The Mexican cavalry gradually slowed their pace as they approached and unaccountably came to a near halt barely one hundred yards from the Americans. The Mississippians saw one whole company of lancers mounted on beautiful white horses. Red plumes fluttered atop the Mexicans' gleaming brass helmets.[21]

As the enemy prepared to charge, a few men in Davis's line fired their rifles without orders. Some later recalled Davis yelling, *"Boys, fire, and at them with your knives!"* Over in the Indiana regiment, others thought they heard their colonel, Joseph Lane, shout, *"Now give it to them!"* Some in the Mississippi line merely remembered the word "Fire!" Davis himself said only that a simultaneous volley roared out of their lines. Captain Thomas W. Sherman had just brought up a field piece, and he added its fire to the storm descending on the lancers. They never even tried to mount a charge. Hit from two sides by fire, the horsemen almost immediately turned and fled in confusion, leaving their dead and wounded behind them. Sherman sent shells into the fleeing column, but Davis did not pursue, though later stories would be told of the Mississippians dragging fleeing lancers from their saddles to meet death at their knife blades.[22]

When more reinforcements arrived, Davis joined with them in pushing forward on the plateau once more, but then he heard an aide shouting from across the ravine on his right that Taylor wanted the Mississippians to come quickly to the right flank of the army, where the last real Mexican offensive advanced. Because of the hilly ground, Davis could not see ahead of him as he marched the regiment to Taylor, but he heard the firing well enough. After scrambling about fifteen hundred yards, he came upon three field pieces ably dealing mayhem to the enemy under the steady command of Captain Braxton Bragg. Just as a line of Mexican infantry approached Bragg, Davis brought his Mississippians up out of a ravine on the enemy flank and delivered a crushing volley. In seconds the enemy soldiers turned and retreated in confusion.[23]

It was the end of the fight for Davis, and very nearly the end of the battle itself. It had been a near-fought affair all day long, but Taylor held his ground, though losing almost 750 in casualties. Tactically it was a draw, and as the general visited his lines that evening and counted his wounded and killed, he expected the fighting to continue the next morning. One of his visits was to a hospital tent to see Jefferson Davis. By the end of the day, the pain, loss of blood, and heated excitement left the Mississippi colonel delirious and swooning in his saddle. Either on his own or with the assistance of his men, he came into the hands of the surgeons, who cleaned his wound as best they could and put him on the ground not far from the body of the colonel of the First Illinois. When Taylor arrived, he spoke with Davis, then spoke with a wounded tentmate, Captain Samuel G. French. Taylor seemed uncertain of victory on the morrow. Wool also came by and talked with Davis about the battle over on the right, admitting privately that he had almost mistakenly ordered a charge that would have been disastrous. Davis kept the secret and later advised another officer who learned of it "as to the impolicy of truth-telling always."[24]

That evening Taylor ordered the Mississippi regiment back to its morning encampment, and Davis and French and others were put in a wagon for the trip to Saltillo. Expecting the fight to be renewed in the morning, he sent the hapless Rogers and the two rearguard companies forward to the battlefield to be ready. After a very uncomfortable night, Davis himself awoke early, determined not to miss the battle. Unable to walk, he ordered himself placed in a wagon and with it stayed at the head of his regiment the next morning until they, like Taylor, discovered that Santa Anna had withdrawn from the battlefield. The victory was theirs.[25]

Davis felt elated. "The Mississippians did well," he wrote Varina the next day, though he said little else. Instead he sent a longer account written by his close friend Thomas L. Crittenden, though, significantly, Davis had him address his letter not to Varina but to Joseph. "The regiment commanded by your brother won the admiration of all," wrote Crittenden, adding that "I have been with your brother almost daily for several months, and have formed for him a great personal attachment."[26]

Initially, some rumors—which Taylor may have heard himself during the battle—said that Davis had been killed or mortally wounded. Still, when he visited Davis in the hospital tent on the night of February 23, and found one of the Mississippi captains pouring a constant stream of cold water over the colonel's battered foot, Taylor told Davis, "My poor boy, I wish you had been shot in the body, you would have a better chance of recovering soon. I do not like wounds in the hands or feet," he went on in the same merry vein. "They cripple a soldier awfully." At least Taylor was more cheering in his battle report, praising Davis and his regiment for their "highly conspicuous" bravery and steadfastness. Davis's "coolness and gallantry, and the heavy loss of his regiment on this day, entitle[d] him to the particular notice of the Government." Wool proved equally glowing in his commendation. Even one of the enemy generals paid tribute a few months later to "the flashing sword of Davis at Buena Vista." And when the noted writer Richard Henry Dana, Jr., dined with Taylor's chief of staff, William W. Bliss, two weeks after the battle, Bliss declared Davis to be "the best volunteer officer in the army." Speaking in the most laudatory terms of the First Mississippi, Bliss praised their "perfect discipline, for volunteers," and pronounced Davis's battlefield conduct "unsurpassable."[27]

Their glory came at a price. Thirty-nine died in the battle, and another fifty-six took wounds. Estimates of their actual strength going into the action range from 280 up to 360, but clearly with verified losses of 95 men, Davis suffered casualties of one-third or more, the highest of any unit in Taylor's army. Once again the inevitable jealousies arose, this time from the Indiana troops—or rather, from their officers. First, the Second Indiana hotly protested reports by Davis and others that they were running in rout when the Mississippians first came on the field, and later men of the Third Indiana protested that when the Mexican lancers approached the V, the Hoosiers repulsed the horsemen by a volley of their own before the Mississippians even opened fire. Much of this carping came from the natural desire to excuse poor behavior or to claim the limelight. But some of it also stemmed from the clear favoritism that

Taylor showed for Davis and his regiment throughout their Mexican campaigning together. That Davis returned the feeling is evident from the fact that less than a month after the battle he took Wool to task for being critical of Taylor's conduct of the battle. Persuading Wool with a threat of his "intention to make such publication as would set the matter in its true light," Davis elicited from him a disclaimer of any aspersions on Old Rough and Ready. Davis had learned from the Monterrey controversies. Henceforward he would not shrink from using the press to expose those who challenged his version of the truth or assaulted his idols.[28]

Recovery came slowly. Unable to get about without crutches, Davis recuperated at Monterrey from late March through mid-April. Unable as well to ride, he contented himself with gathering reports of the battle from his subordinates, making recommendations of some of his officers for commissions in the regular army, and attending to the other daily needs of the regiment. The twelve-month term of enlistment of the Mississippians would be expiring in June, and there were many details to attend to before he led the regiment back to the coast for the trip home to muster out.

There was also the question in his mind of what was next for Jefferson Davis. He could not have been unaware that his performance at Buena Vista, added to the reports of Monterrey, had made his name known in almost every newspaper in every state of the Union. Indeed, with the natural fulsomeness of the press, his exploits had been, and were being, exaggerated considerably, and he stood along with Bragg and Taylor as the most hailed heroes of the war to date. The V became famous in its own right, and the Whitney firm of New Haven lost forever its rightful association with its fine weapon, which would be forever known after Buena Vista as the Mississippi Rifle.

Inevitably politics came back to his mind. His injury put further service out of the question, even though rumors spoke of the raising of a Second Mississippi Volunteers, whose colonelcy he could have. Even if he sincerely did not want to return to public life, Davis was not so foolish as to think he would not be approached. His war record and his national acclaim made him electable for almost any office in Mississippi's gift. In April, Joseph wrote to advise him that another state convention would assemble in June. "If you have any view to public life it migh[t] be well to say to your friends or some of them if you desire a nomination." In fact, earlier that year the Mississippi press suggested Davis for various state offices, including the governorship. It appears that just after Buena Vista, Davis actually wrote to the editor of a Jackson newspaper and categorically declined to be a candidate while in command of his regiment. Of course, since the Mississippians were to muster out in another three months anyhow, within a couple of weeks after the state convention, his reason for declining lost most of its logic and was probably just the usual pretense at reluctance to seek office. But Davis certainly made it clear that he really did not want to be nominated for the governorship.[29]

Then events took a hand. On May 1 Senator Jesse Speight died in office. Less than two weeks later Joseph visited Vicksburg and heard several of his brother's friends talking of a desire to nominate Davis for something in spite of his professed refusal. Some wanted to see him in the House once more, others continued to speak of the governorship, and yet more thought to see him appointed to fill out the balance of Speight's term. Joseph told them emphatically that, at Jefferson's instructions, the governorship was out of the question. By excluding that office alone, however, it was implicit that the colonel would accept some other. Less than a week later a messenger from Governor Albert G. Brown arrived at Hurricane with a sealed envelope for Joseph's brother. Though it turned out to be only routine documents relating to his regiment, at first he was certain it was the senatorial appointment. Still, Joseph's anticipation, as well as the repeated conversations of men of affairs in Mississippi generally, make it certain that Davis knew he could have an office, or at least a nomination, if he wanted one.[30]

Other matters claimed his consideration at the same time. Cotton had soared in price, but inflation eroded most if not all of the increase, and the crops themselves were running behind previous years. The expense of the war, he feared, would resuscitate the protective tariff and lead to a greater issue of paper currency—feeding inflation. Along with such things, he told friends, would come "every other political quackery." Brierfield needed his attention, though Pemberton did a good job of running it for him. Varina needed him. She had spent some of the time at Hurricane despite her difficulties with Joseph and Eliza, and her health improved. Apparently so did the rift between her and her husband, though not entirely. Even the Brierfield slaves were anxious to see their master once more. And, though he would be on crutches for fully two years, still his foot seemed to be healing fast. "It is with regret that I look forward to leaving this country before the war is concluded," he wrote to Joseph on April 30, and two months later he confided to Robert Walker that "if the War continues I hope to [be] again in the field and to see the end of it." With an army under Scott even then marching from Veracruz toward Mexico City, the war certainly was not over just yet. As so many times before, Jefferson Davis was not at all certain what he would, or should, do.[31]

By the time he wrote to Walker, he was back at home again. On or about May 17 he and his men began leaving Monterrey, and ten days later they all reached the coast. Boarding sailboats at Brazos Island on

May 30, they reached New Orleans on June 6. There, besides an enthusiastic welcome, Davis found waiting for him a letter from President Polk, written two weeks before. Praising "your distinguished gallantry and military skill, while leading the noble Regiment under your command and especially in the battles of *Monterey* and *Buena Vista*," the president conferred on him a commission as brigadier general of volunteers. He would have a brigade of new volunteer regiments. Here was yet another choice thrown into the mix. Even if it was only a volunteer commission, still, being a general—of any kind—had to be a dream of any man who had entertained thoughts of a military career. Furthermore, as evidenced by what Davis had seen in his congressional race, the title of general could carry with it powerful connotations for a man seeking political office. "General Davis" must have had a pleasant sound to it as he pondered Polk's letter.[32]

Yet there was a problem—two problems, really. First, Davis did not recognize that the president had the power to appoint generals over volunteer troops. Volunteers were militia, with "a constitutional right to be under the immediate command of officers appointed by State authority." He believed this right was somehow violated by any formation in which they lost their distinctive character as state troops after they came under federal authority. There was a delicious inconsistency in his argument, of course, because at some point, volunteers *had* to come under federal authority. Obviously he believed that volunteer regiments should choose their own colonels—he had been one. Judging from his reaction to Polk's appointment, he also thought that volunteer regiments brigaded together should only be led by volunteer officers appointed by state governors, but which governor should appoint them? He had been in a brigade of one Mississippi and one Tennessee regiment. Which state would have had the right to appoint that brigade's general? Or should it have been left to the officers or the men in the ranks to make the decision? Obviously, stalemate would have been the most likely result. Or did he feel that brigades should only be composed of regiments from single states? That was fine if a state contributed more than one unit, but Mississippi sent just one in 1846, and one regiment cannot be a brigade. Even if states did appoint their own brigadiers, brigades were formed into divisions. Could the president commission a major general to lead a division, or did the states have to do that too? Like many strict constructionists, Davis would with increasing frequency find himself backed into logical absurdities by the rigidity of his views. It was the old story. Having studied an issue and made up his mind on it, he could not and would not bend—perhaps, in part, because it took him so long to make a decision. This one cost him dearly, as even he acknowledged. "My principles would not allow me to receive the commission tendered," he in-

formed Robert Walker. "Instead of seeing the end of the war, as I
desired, I am again a 'clod hopper.' "

Davis kept Polk's letter of appointment for ten days or more before
he replied. The decision cannot have been an easy one, and factors other
than his constitutional rigidity influenced his decision. He may have
known that he was not Polk's first choice for the generalcy. The president had another man in mind, but Davis's popularity was so great after
Buena Vista, especially in Mississippi, that Polk feared a political backlash if he did not give the commission to Davis. The 1848 election loomed
a year away. Davis was a Democrat, of course, and Polk feared for
Mississippi in 1848. If he did not recognize the colonel with such an
offer, the president feared that Taylor's popularity, added to the ambi-
guity of his Whig adherence, might win the state for Old Rough and
Ready should he be nominated. Giving Davis the appointment would
help keep Mississippi safely Democratic. Taylor himself, however, suspected something else behind Polk's action. In the general's view, knowing of Speight's death, Polk dangled the brigadier's commission as a way
of keeping Davis from accepting an appointment to the Senate. Davis
was too closely connected with Taylor, both personally and in the public
mind, it seemed. Perhaps he could not be trusted to stand by his party in
1848 if Taylor ran as a Whig.[32]

If Taylor communicated his suspicions to Davis, or if similar apprehensions played any part in his decision, the colonel never said. Whatever his motivations, he wrote a grateful and diplomatic letter to Polk
turning down the commission. Even before he wrote to Polk, on June 20
he addressed a crowd in Vicksburg, telling them of the appointment and
his decision not to take it. Indeed, since his arrival at New Orleans,
speaking to crowds is mostly what he did. On June 10 the people there
put on a grand parade to honor the First Mississippi and its colonel.
Hobbled as he was by his wound, he propped his leg on a chair and
thanked them for their demonstration, though he spoke more in praise
of Taylor than on any other subject. Four days later at Natchez, where
Varina met him, he spoke in the same vein, specifically denouncing the
government for its treatment of Taylor. Obviously Polk had good cause
to wonder about Davis in the Senate. Climbing into a flower-filled
barouche, he and Varina drove to the landing and were soon on the
steamboat for Davis Bend.[33]

Back at home, Davis received a long and affectionate letter from
Taylor, responding to one of his own sent back in June. Davis had asked
for advice on the brigadier's appointment—at least Taylor felt that he
"appears undetermined what course to pursue," though he thought
Davis might accept if the war should continue. Indeed, Taylor even
addressed him as "My Dear General," assuming that Davis would take

the commission. "I would consult my own feelings & interest in regard to it," Taylor advised, offering a suspicion that there be little fighting left in Mexico anyhow, and thus little reputation to win. As for the Senate vacancy, which Davis also asked about, Taylor told him to take it if offered. "It is one of the highest most dignified & conspicuous positions in the Country."[34]

Taylor's letter, written July 27, probably did not arrive at Brierfield until early September, and by that time Davis had already come to a decision. The generalship he rejected, of course, but when a letter from Governor Brown in mid-August tendered him the Senate appointment, he accepted. Actually it came as something of a surprise, for Davis believed that Brown had little kindly feeling for him. It is possible that Davis was even then still considering the colonelcy of the new Second Mississippi, made to him in July, though he may not have received news of the offer until August 18, the day after he wrote to Brown accepting the Senate seat. In any case, he would have had to decline. His foot healed slowly. He still used crutches, and any accidental jarring or bumping of the foot caused excruciating pain. Besides, it looked as if the war was all but over. Scott had reached the outskirts of Mexico City, battered its outlying defenses, and the foe had agreed to an armistice pending negotiations. Davis could not use crutches on a battlefield, but he could use them to stand and fight battles of another kind on the Senate floor. He would go back to Washington.[35]

Davis had actually found himself immersed in national politics from the very moment he returned to Brierfield, for the simple reason that he enjoyed so close a relationship with Taylor. Everyone in the Union wanted to know where the general stood politically. Was he a Whig or a Democrat? How was he on slavery? Did he want the presidency in 1848? With Taylor in faraway Mexico, from where it could take months to get a reply to a letter, many turned to Davis instead and pumped him for Taylor's views. He responded at first based on his own impressions. "I would say he is no party man," Davis told Walker in late June, "would not consent to be the candidate of a party, and probably would disagree with the ultra men of both parties." However, realizing that his own suppositions would not be enough, and urged by his onetime House messmate Simon Cameron of Pennsylvania, Davis wrote to Taylor late in July and at least hinted that he ought to express himself in order to quell rumor and misrepresentation. Davis did not believe that the Whigs would nominate Taylor and believed that Democrats would vote for him with or without a nomination. With undisguised dismay, Davis told Cameron that he believed Taylor would be supported by the South regardless of party. He did not object to Taylor, of course. What bothered him was that "we have drawn near to that which has been for many years my dread, a division marked not by opinions, but by geographical lines." He earnestly hoped that patriotism would "save the Republic from the evil consequences so likely to follow from a geographical issue."[36] When Taylor replied to his letter, the new senator could see just how difficult the coming election would be. Taylor complained bitterly of Scott's perfidy. Davis had heard plenty of this already, for the general had commonly discussed Scott with him and others at his headquarters. "I do not believe he would hesitate a moment to sacrifice me or anyone else who stood in his way," the old general declared in one letter, and Davis agreed with him wholeheartedly. As for the rest of national politics, Taylor expressed the equivocal views of a man bitten by the presidential bug but wholly unfamiliar with public affairs. He had never voted in his life and simply stated opinions without regard to party. He opposed reviving a national bank. He thought that if all of Mexico were annexed, as some Southern extremists desired, it would avail slave interests nothing, for slavery had been abolished in Mexico years before and the inhabitants would be unlikely to stand for its reintroduction. Internal improvements were inevitable as the United States sought to grow and expand its commerce and communications. As for slavery, he was a Southern man and he would stand by his rights as a slaveholder under the Constitution, "& when arguments will no longer suffice, we will appeal to the sword if necessary to do so." He made the usual denial of any desire for the presidency, followed by the inevitable caveat that if the people demanded that he serve, then of course he would.[37]

In fact, Taylor wrote to Davis repeatedly, expressing largely the same views, though occasionally referring to himself as a Whig in broad principles. That he wrote so voluminously shows not only his real desire for the White House, but also his trust in Davis as a friend and confidant. Thus the planter should not have pretended to be surprised when he learned in September that his own opinions were being misunderstood and misrepresented. How could he be, as one put it, "a Calhoun democrat, and a very strong Taylor man"? Others accused him of hostility to Polk, and many suspected his party loyalty, given his ties to Old Rough and Ready. Davis soon found it necessary to write an open letter for publication in which he made clear where he stood. He expected all along to stay with his party and support its nominees in 1848, he said. Yet he did fear that agitation over slavery might force Southern men to unite for their section, regardless of party.

His old friend David Wilmot had only recently galvanized much feeling in the nation by proposing in Congress that any territory acquired from Mexico by the war be accepted only with the proviso that slavery be excluded. Northern antislave men rallied around the proposal, while Southern proslave men, regardless of party, condemned it. Taylor regarded the Wilmot Proviso as a trifle, all fuss and no substance, because the Mexicans would not stand for the reintroduction of slavery into their territory even if the United States took it. Davis felt somewhat the same, at least privately, but now before the public he declared himself unutterably opposed to the measure, which eventually failed to pass anyhow.

He was more worried about the splitting of Democrats along sectional lines. Many Northern men were leaving the party over the issue of slavery and Southern rights, yet he hoped that when it came to the election in 1848 they would "show themselves worthy of their ancient appellation, the natural allies of the South." Indeed, if this were not enough to show that he regarded the Democratic Party as primarily the ideological property of the South, he made it even more clear. When they all met in convention in 1848, before nominating candidates the delegates from the North should formally repudiate the Wilmot Proviso; where slavery was concerned, accept the extension of the Missouri Compromise line to cover all future territory annexed to the Union; and stand up for the rights of the South. If Northern Democrats did this, all would be well and the convention would represent "every section of the Union." If they declined, then Southern delegates should withdraw from the convention, take no part in its nominations, and "under the necessity for self-preservation," he said, "party divisions should be buried in union for defense." In closing he said that, "though the signs of the times are portentous of evil, and the cloud which now hangs over our northern horizon threatens a storm," still he hoped it would blow over. If not, then "enough for the day will be the evil thereof, and enough for the evil, will be the union and energy and power of the south."[38]

It was the most extreme position Jefferson Davis had ever taken on public affairs, carrying him far beyond the immediate need to assure Mississippi Democrats that he would stand with the party in 1848. Unfortunately, as always happened when the slave issue arose, passions exaggerated men's fears and animosities. The Wilmot Proviso never stood a real chance of passage, as Davis himself admitted. Northern Democrats may in large part have opposed slavery, yet all but a few stayed loyal to the party and supported a conservative construction of the Constitution. This was not enough, it seemed. With a neat hypocrisy that he surely did not realize, Davis argued that the Democrats were and should be a party "representing every section of the Union," which he further defined as meaning that all Democrats should be "the natural allies of the South." Even while deploring what he feared would be the rise of parties based on section rather than principles, he maintained at the same time that the principles of his party should be exclusively those of his section. Whereas in late July he had privately lamented to Cameron the possibility that the old parties might be broken apart by sectionalism, now just two months later he publicly avowed the breakup of his own party if its Northern wing did not fall in line behind the slave states.

It was the war with Mexico that had done it all. Never did so minor a military affair exert such a terrible impact. The prospect of vast areas of new territory, most of it south of the Missouri Compromise line, inflamed Southern ambitions for the extension of slave states, and thereby the expansion of Southern power in Congress to counter the spread of antislave sentiment in new territories north of the line. It all came down to a balance of power. Maintain the balance, and the South maintained slavery, an enormous capital investment in slaves, a way of life, and a social order unthreatened by millions of free blacks elsewhere. Lose the balance, and regardless of all Northern promises not to interfere with slavery where it already existed, Southerners were convinced that the growing abolition movement would take hold and the laws of the Union, and even the Constitution itself, would be changed, not so much to destroy slavery as to subjugate the South politically. However irrational the fear, it was very real to the men of the South who felt it, honorable men like Jefferson Davis—perhaps especially to a man like Jefferson Davis, who with his usual certitude had long pondered the subject of slavery and Southern rights and knew that his position was right. Convinced of that, as always, he could not yield or compromise.

Now, as 1847 waned, Davis faced a phenomenon that men all across the South beheld with increasing terror. Calhoun symbolized all of them as they trembled before an ideal they once embraced—democracy. In those bygone days when Southern congressmen and Southern presidents commanded a majority in Washington, Calhoun had been an ardent nationalist and Southerners applauded democracy. But now, with the possibility of a shift—probably permanent—in the balance of power, the "will of the majority" no longer had much appeal to Calhoun or the rest. He was aging now. He had not long left to live. As the threats to Southern rights grew ever greater, the South needed a new Calhoun.

10

The Days of the Confederation Are Numbered

Once again Jefferson Davis felt relieved to be leaving Brierfield. Not that he was a happy man, for surely he was not. In September the malaria returned and put him down for two weeks or more. With it came another inflammation of his eyes that made reading or writing or even exposure to bright light painful. His health forced him to cancel appointments and turn down invitations from well-wishers wanting to see him off to Washington. His foot continued to trouble him, as much from lack of easy mobility as for the pain caused by the bone splinters that now started to work their way out through his flesh, causing frequent infections.[1]

The real cause of his unhappiness was Varina. When he first returned from Mexico that summer, their difficulties seemed on the surface to be healed. As late as the end of September, when she visited her family in Natchez, he wrote to her in warm, open, loving terms. If wounds remained between them, the excitement of his safe return from the war preempted them for a time. Then, late in the summer, Varina's own health declined enough that concern for her probably outweighed any ill will or resentment felt by Davis.

But during his last six weeks at Davis Bend before departing on November 11, it all reemerged, more strident and bitter than ever before. Anything might have been the catalyst—Varina's growing breach with Joseph, the building of their new house at Brierfield, now started or about to begin, or her husband's new will. Any or all of these could have been pretexts for a much deeper resentment on the part of a strong-willed young woman still only twenty-one, who in two years of matri-

168

mony had seen her husband repeatedly absent for extended periods. In fact, of the twenty-seven months since their marriage, he had spent fourteen away either campaigning or fighting. She was missing her youth, her husband, children, and the life she had been reared to expect as a planter's wife. No wonder she manifested increasingly frequent periods of irritability, nervousness, and bad temper. In her era these were often a woman's only acceptable weapons, and even these seemed pitiful to one of Varina's strong and independent temperament. She would never entirely accept being her husband's subordinate by social custom as well as his own decree, and that fall of 1847 she broke out in open rebellion.

Certainly Joseph irritated her, in part because of his tight clench on his brother as well as for his growingly vocal disdain for her family, particularly her spendthrift father and irresponsible brothers. The new Brierfield house also caused problems. Jefferson insisted on designing it to accomodate his widowed sister Amanda Davis Bradford and her children, whereas Varina did not care to share her house, and perhaps did not like Amanda in any case. And, according to Davis's new will, made out in 1847 by his brother Joseph, Jefferson Davis would leave his estate equally divided between Varina, Amanda, and his other widowed sister, Anna Smith.[2]

The will finally set her off. To his face Varina confronted him. She accused him of ignoring her welfare, of denying her the comfort of a home exclusively theirs, and of giving away her "*rights as a woman and a wife.*" He thought her "querulous," but she meant what she said. In an age when a woman could expect or demand few rights, she at least expected to be the sole beneficiary of his estate. Varina fully suspected Joseph of using his usual influence on his brother to make her only a party to the will rather than its exclusive recipient, and she would never forgive him. Nor did she find it in her power then to forgive her husband for so consistently heeding Joseph before her. She fought in those weeks of October and November with the only weapons she could use— reproach, coldness, and probably absence from his bed.

It was more than Davis could bear. Quite aside from the fact that his wife did not pay him the respect he thought due him as her husband, he must also have felt resentment that marital vows forced him, a man of forty, to deal with such insolent behavior from someone who was otherwise barely more than a child, and a woman as well. More to the point, as he told her often, "I cannot bear to be suspected or complained of, or misconstrued after explanation." The old trait that Varina noticed at their first meeting—the assumption that he was invariably right and that everyone must agree with him—was becoming more pronounced as he grew older, fueled no doubt by habits of command with his volunteers in Mexico. He accused her of "constant harassment, occasional reproach, and subsequent misrepresentation." With his health already bad, he could not deal with the abuse he felt she heaped upon him "at a time when a wife's kindness was most needed." On top of this, "the dread of constant strife" was so great in his mind that he feared they would not be able to conceal it in Washington society. Consequently, "with body crippled, nerves shattered, and mind depressed," he told her, he decided that she would not accompany him when he left to take his Senate seat. Their marriage was breaking down. Admitting no fault on his part, he said that if her conduct and attitude did not change, it "would render it impossible for us ever to live together." There was, he said, "a necessity for separation." "The wounds your suspicion has so often inflicted" would need a long time to heal, if heal they could.[3]

He took the usual river route via Louisville, Cincinnati, and Pittsburgh. The trip passed quickly this time, though surely the glum and depressed new senator found no pleasure in the journey, his mind filled by the battlefield he left behind on Davis Bend. The trip was made no more pleasant by his traveling companion, Henry S. Foote, Mississippi's other senator. Though they stumped together briefly in 1844, the two were never friendly. Foote defended in a trial the man accused of murdering Amanda Bradford's husband in May 1844, and though he and Davis campaigned on the same platforms for the first several weeks of the canvass that year, in mid-August they began speaking separately. Temperaments naturally put the two at odds. If they fraternized at all on their journey, it was a distant and formal association. Probably not even a chance meeting with former president John Tyler in Cincinnati put any zest in the trip for Davis. He would have felt even more depressed if he had known that in leaving one war behind him on this journey, he but rushed toward a host of battles when he reached Washington.[4]

Almost his first concern as he settled into his room at Gadsby's Hotel on Pennsylvania Avenue was mending relations with Polk, if they needed mending. The day after arriving, Davis visited the White House, no doubt to assure the president that as senator he would support the party and its candidates in the coming election, and he found Polk in good spirits and cordial toward him. At the same time Davis dealt with a potential political difficulty back in Mississippi. Speight's unexpired term ran out in only a few weeks. Since Senate seats then were filled by ballots in the state houses, not by direct vote of the people, his acceptance of the post carried with it an implicit assumption that he would be a candidate for reelection when the state legislature met in January 1848. Already his onetime friend and associate Jacob Thompson had broken with him when Thompson attacked Taylor in the press. Viewing Davis as a rival, he tried to link the colonel too closely with Taylor. Now one of the first things Davis learned in Washington, from Foote, was that

Thompson was inciting Mississippi Democrats against his reelection. Davis wanted that reelection, "a subject upon which I now feel greater interest than I should have done had I remained at home." Worse, even his Democratic friends muddied the waters at home by claiming that Davis did not want any Whigs to vote for him. "Col. Davis wishes to be elected by his *own party*," one paper said presumptuously in speaking for him. As a result, on Christmas Day a Whig congressman from Mississippi asked Davis if he would reject reelection if he got it because Whigs in the legislature joined with Democrats to give him a majority.[5]

Though he replied with his usual calm, Davis must have been incensed at what "unscrupulous and designing men" said behind his back in Mississippi. Of course he would welcome Whig votes as he welcomed any votes on his behalf, and for anyone to suggest otherwise was ridiculous. Having spent much of the last few months trying to convince Democrats that he was not too cozy with the Whigs, now he had to convince the Whigs that he did not disdain their support. Frustrated as he always would be by the closed-door machinations of men who schemed, and still irritable because of his problems with Varina, Davis spent that Christmas on a short fuse.[6]

Not long after responding to the Whig Congressman, he exploded. Already on stiff terms with Foote, Davis encountered him in one of the public rooms at Gadsby's, perhaps over a holiday drink. Several others were present, and to one, at least, it became apparent that Foote and Davis already felt cool toward one another. Then the discussion turned to so-called "squatter sovereignty," though the term was not yet in use. Just the day before, Lewis Cass, destined to be the Democratic presidential nominee in 1848, enunciated to an influential Washingtonian his belief that in any new territories acquired from Mexico or otherwise, the people inhabiting it should have the right to decide for themselves if the territory be slave or free. Some saw it as a way of setting aside the slavery controversy permanently, though others, like Davis, saw in it the possibility that regions south of the Missouri Compromise line, where most land taken from Mexico lay, could actually produce free states. He favored an extension of the Missouri Compromise line all the way to the Pacific and no alteration of the prescription for slavery below that line.

Apparently the discussion became heated. Davis, as was his wont, sounded smug and superior as he declared what was, of course, the only true position. To Foote it sounded like "presumptuous arrogance," and combative and intemperate as he always was, he responded in what Davis called "offensive language" that must also have contained a personal element. Davis snapped. Ignoring his foot, he walked—or hobbled—across the room and started pummeling Foote with repeated blows until others pulled him off. He later remembered that Foote started to leave the room and then turned at the door and declared that he had gotten in the first blow himself. Should a duel ensue, that would mean that Foote would have the choice of weapons.

But Davis did not want to wait for a duel. Shouting "liar," Davis broke free from those restraining him and shook his fist in Foote's face, promising to beat him to death if he repeated the lie. When Foote said nothing, Davis turned to walk away, and then the other senator struck him. In an instant they were both on the floor, Davis on top and beating away with his fists until pulled off yet again. In his passion he suggested to Foote that they go to his room and lock themselves inside to settle the matter, and Foote flippantly asked if he had "coffee and pistols for two." Davis said he had pistols sure enough, but then Foote declared that it would be unfair, probably fearing that, having been in the military, Davis might have an advantage as a marksman. At the suggestion of unfairness Davis started to jump on him yet again. Finally the rest of the patrons at Gadsby's persuaded them both that "the matter should be dropped as a Christmas frolic." Davis may have challenged Foote to a duel at the same time, but in the end nothing came of it.[7]

Never in his life had he been moved to such blind fury, and his assault on Foote well reveals the turmoil seething inside this terribly contained man. Unable to release emotions in a healthy way, he kept them within until they erupted beyond his control. In striking out at Foote, he struck as well at McClung and Campbell and Thompson and all the others who had sniped at him all year long, and probably most of all he struck at Varina.

Davis and Foote remained bitter enemies for the rest of their lives, as a result of which their mutual friends must have been happy indeed that the two sat so far apart on the Senate floor. Davis took his oath and his seat on December 6, 1847, and walked to the fourth and last row back from the seat of Vice President (and president pro tem of the Senate) George M. Dallas. There he turned to his right and walked, on his crutches or with a cane, to the last desk in the row. If he noticed Foote, seated at the end of the second row on the center aisle, he probably did not look at him. Better yet, as Davis sat down, he found that his old friend William Allen—who had almost killed him on his first visit to Washington—sat right next to him as a senator from Ohio. There was a happy reunion indeed. In the row in front of Davis sat R. M. T. Hunter of Virginia, with whom he would become well acquainted, and next to him Jesse D. Bright of Indiana, all good Democrats by Davis's definition.[8]

No doubt all eyes turned to Davis when he entered for the first time and took his seat. Here was a genuine national hero, really the first one created by the Mexican War, and certainly the first to owe his seat to his military feats. "He was erect and probably six feet in height," remembered one who saw him this December, "pale, thin, and wiry in appearance, weighing, perhaps, 130 pounds." Another in the hall that day noted "a piercing but kindly eye, and a gamy, chivalric bearing," while yet another remembered him as "prim and smooth-looking, with a precise manner, a stiff, soldierly carriage, and an austerity at first forbidding." No doubt he dressed, as he always dressed now, with scrupulous neatness. Though he avoided ostentatious finery, still he preferred carefully tailored black broadcloth suits and sparkling clean white shirts. Neither plain nor foppish, his attire only enhanced the air of severe dignity about his tall, lean frame. Certainly he looked like a man of note, a man unquestionably sure of himself. He looked like a senator.[9]

Little happened in his first month in the Senate, and indeed he would not be especially active for some time in its debates, for his health robbed him of the necessary stamina. Quite logically he was given appointments to the Military Affairs and Pension committees, as well as the committee on the Library of Congress. Just before the end of the year he also received an appointment to the Board of Regents of the Smithsonian that certainly met his approval, for his interest in that budding institution had not diminished since his service with Adams back in the House.[10]

Not until January 3, 1848, did Davis actually rise to speak in substance, and then on a subject they would expect him to speak on—the war. Following the end of the brief armistice the previous summer, Scott renewed his attacks, and the enemy abandoned Mexico City. Military activity of consequence had all but ceased, and attempts at peace negotiations commenced again. The conflict seemed stalemated, and a bill to raise ten new regiments lay before the Senate. The Military Affairs Committee, chaired by Cass, reported the bill, and Davis arose in its support. While some argued that the war was over and no more regular regiments were needed, he pointed out the fact that Santa Anna was hardly beaten, that American armies had been too small all along, and that these regulars would be cheaper than the volunteers that Senator John J. Crittenden, father of his friends Thomas and George, wanted to raise instead. Further, these regulars would not be for fighting battles, he said, but for preventing them. Mexico thought itself the greatest military power on the continent until Buena Vista showed otherwise, he declared pridefully. Only with a substantial standing army could the United States ensure that any new government in Mexico after peace came about would not become aggressive again. In a tie, Davis voted for the bill, and it only passed when Vice President Dallas added a deciding affirmative.[11]

This would be his only speech during his brief appointive tenure, aside from occasional remarks during the addresses of others. On January 11, 1848, the legislature back in Jackson quite predictably elected him to a full Senate term in his own right, though only by a nine-vote majority. Without some of those Whig votes, he might not have won. On February 15 he took the oath of office to begin his six-year term. He might have wondered why he bothered, for it seemed to him that the Senate bogged down "talking about minute points of history," and that the current course of Congress as a whole was focused more on the coming presidential election than on the business of government. For himself, he did not yet have close ties to any factions trying to make this man or that a candidate, though as late as April he continued hoping that Taylor might somehow emerge as the Democratic nominee.[12]

Only as spring approached did Davis take a more active role in the debates. Others in the Senate now found him "clear, forcible and argumentative: his voice clear and firm" when he spoke. "He was," said another, "occasionally vehement in manner, but always courteous." As he felt better, he threw himself into all the tedious paperwork and other duties of a senator. Every morning after breakfast he filled the time until the Senate convened by visiting the several executive departments, taking with him the petitions for appointments, pensions, land grants, and other favors sent by his constituents. It did not take long to discover that the entreaties a senator received considerably outnumbered those sent to a member of the House. So he spent his evenings as well, eschewing the dinner parties and public houses frequented by most of the others in Congress. Without Varina he took little pleasure in society, and even with her he would rarely have allowed himself relaxation when there was paperwork to handle. Tiring of Gadsby's, and probably eager as well to escape the odious Foote, Davis moved early in 1848 to a boardinghouse on Capitol Hill, and there he lived a lonely existence. Now and then letters from Varina arrived, but they did not cheer him. Her attitude seemed unchanged, and even into April her remonstrances were such as he felt could drive a man to drink or "vicious associations"—and clearly he believed undeserved. When she spoke of their "weary past and blighted future," he chastised her for not adopting a line of "conduct suited to the character of your husband, and demanded by your duties as a wife." In other words, she must learn to be subservient, not to question him or his actions and motives, and to be what a wife was supposed to be: "kind and peaceful." On those terms he would be happy to be near her.[13]

While his domestic drama dragged on, Davis truly began to assert himself. Elected now in his own right, feeling better, and with his foot hardly troubling him, he rose to the challenges of issues and debate, and he showed himself overawed by no man, not even the magisterial Calhoun. Indeed, he repeatedly though respectfully differed with Calhoun in debate, though not on the great issues of the session. When Calhoun objected to the bill raising ten more regular regiments as "mere braggadocio," Davis countered persuasively that the war was not yet won and that even after its conclusion, a larger army was needed to keep the peace. And when Daniel Webster that same day called the war odious, Davis replied with vigor. "Odious for what?" he cried. "On account of the skill and gallantry with which it has been conducted?" Citing the humanity, magnanimity, and morality with which Americans had waged the contest, he looked in vain to find odium. Men watching Davis in the debate saw him warm to the topic. "His first sentence was the signal for profound silence and attention," wrote one. "His keen eyes literally blazed as he poured forth a torrent of withering sarcasm and crushing invective." Even the press back in Mississippi praised him for his "lofty independence" from Senate giants like Webster and Calhoun.[14]

Davis's independence appeared especially on the two big topics of the year, the war in Mexico and Zachary Taylor. Unlike the other debaters in the Capitol, Davis had served in Mexico, fought with distinction, and left his blood on its soil. Buena Vista had been the greatest achievement of his life to date and his only truly independent one, not in some way due to Joseph or others. Thus he had more of a personal stake in the war than most, bristled at the suggestion that the conflict in which he won glory was odious, and recoiled when men suggested that the territory conquered from Mexico should be given back. "I hold that in a just war we conquered a larger portion of Mexico, and that to it we have a title which has been regarded as valid ever since man existed in a social condition," he told Webster. As for Taylor, Davis would not brook criticism of the general, even from fellow Democrats, and did not care if it hurt him. When he finally concluded that Taylor would not be nominated by his own party, he freely confessed, "I have been disappointed in the course of events, and look despondent upon a progress which I have no power to control or conform to."[15]

As the spring ground onward, things continued to look better for Davis. Letters from Varina showed a gradual change, an acceptance of what he saw as her role in their marriage, or more likely simply an acquiescence. Davis acquired more confidence on the Senate floor, speaking forcefully against internal improvements and repeatedly on his general view of expansionism and American destiny. A bill introduced in May would have authorized Polk to send armed forces into the Yucatán Peninsula, where a race war between whites and Indians had come to the point that the whites offered sovereignty to any nation that would intervene to put down the rebellion. Davis wholeheartedly approved the bill and went even farther to declare his belief that the United States had claim to the entire Gulf of Mexico. Citing Yucatán and Cuba as bastions controlling the gulf, "which I hold to be a basin of water belonging to the United States," Davis declared that before he saw any other power establish itself there, "I am ready, for one, to declare that my step will be forward, and that the cape of Yucatan and the island of Cuba must be ours." When threats arose of a black insurrection in Cuba and that Britain might intervene to quell the outbreak, Davis proclaimed that he would hesitate "not a moment" to go to war with England to keep them out of the gulf.

Davis felt an acute interest in Cuba. A few weeks later he took three Cubans to the White House to meet with Polk and offer their testimony that a revolution on the island seemed certain and that native Cubans desired annexation to the Union. Polk himself admitted that his reply was evasive (he was not interested in Cuba just then). America was at peace again, for the moment, after both countries' May 30 ratifications of the Treaty of Guadalupe-Hidalgo finally ended the Mexican War. Before the Senate voted on that treaty back in March, Davis tried to pass an amendment adding to the land taken from Mexico almost all the provinces that bordered on Texas and the New Mexico territory. He failed, but he left no doubt that he now stood closer than before to the front rank of the expansionists.[15]

Behind much of the expansionist urge, of course, lay slavery, and—when debate turned to the subject of potential servile insurrection—Davis found an opportunity in the midst of all this to declare on the Senate floor his feelings on the institution. "I have no fear of insurrection," he said on April 20, "no more dread of our slaves than I have of our cattle. . . . Our slaves are happy and contented." Thanks to the paternal institution in which they were kept, they actually bore a happier relation of labor to capital than did wage earners. The only source of misery the slaves of the South had was "the unwarrantable interference of those who know nothing about that with which they meddle." Further, he urged that Congress intervene to prevent abolitionists from inciting slaves to revolt, to run away. Warming to the topic, he showed that vehemence that observers remarked. "We who represent the southern States are not here to be insulted on account of institutions which we inherit," he declared. "And if civil discord is to be thrown from this Chamber upon the land—if the fire is to be kindled here with which to burn the temple of our Union—if this is to be made the centre from which civil war is to radiate, here let the conflict begin."[16]

Several months later, discussing a petition for an appropriation for colonizing free blacks back to Africa, he said even more. How regrettable it was that day after day the senators should "find themselves beleaguered by irritating questions forced upon them by individuals whose piety is so great that they must always be appropriating to themselves other men's sins." He called upon abolitionists to "cease this perfidious interference with the rights of other men." Chastising those who seemed comfortable only in "affection for the negro race," he denounced all the controversy of recent years over human rights as being in fact something that "begins, and ends, and has its middle with the negro race." He called the men of the North who raised the stir hypocrites. "You were the men who imported these negroes into this country," he charged. "You enjoyed the benefits resulting from their carriage and sale; and you," he concluded, "reaped the largest profit accruing from the introduction of the slaves."

Of course Davis erred grossly on his last point, and he knew it. How could a slave trader who bore the expense of importation and sold a black for one thousand dollars or so reap more profit than a buyer who then had the work of that man's body—and of his issue—for the rest of his life? While no one challenged his misrepresentation, he moved quickly on to the usual litany of benefits that slavery brought to the slave. "Has it made any man a slave any more than he was a slave without this institution?" he asked. Had it reduced any man from liberty to slavery? Of course it had, but Davis answered, "It has not. It benefits them, in removing them from the bigotry and the heathen darkness which hangs like a cloud over the country in the interior of Africa to the enjoyment of all the blessings of civilization and Christianity." In a beautiful bit of sophistry, he reasoned that slavery created commerce, commerce brought civilization, and civilization brought international relations and exchange "and all those mighty blessings that now bind the people of the most remote quarters of the globe together." In short, slavery in the South was the cornerstone of the modern world.

Yet if Davis's reasoning to justify slavery was as fallacious as any position he ever held, his vision of the outcome of agitation over the institution showed itself frighteningly keen. "This, sir, is the question which is to destroy our republican institutions, if indeed they are to fall." He called on men who loved the Union "better than they love the negro race" to stand up against interference with slavery where it existed, "or the disunion of this glorious Confederacy will follow."[17] Too much was happening at the same time—the war with Mexico, the acquisition of all that new land, the impending breakup of the old national Whig party along sectional lines, and the coming presidential election in which slavery was becoming the chief issue, and in which a new Free-Soil party was making its debut. There were too many influences irritating the old festering wound of slavery and Southern defensiveness over it. Even Jefferson Davis, whose previous utterances had displayed a commendably even-tempered and moderate attitude, felt propelled into an ever-more-strident and combative posture. It had not made him an extremist, but it put one of his feet in the extremist camp—probably the wounded one that bled for Mexican land and Southern rights.

The pressure showed as Davis engaged in another public argument with Henry Foote, this time on the floor of the Senate in a brief interchange over a seemingly insignificant issue—the presentation of a flag flown over the captured citadel of Mexico City. Davis seemingly accused

Foote of trying to make "political capital" out of an argument over the achievements of Quitman versus Twiggs in the war. Foote resented the implication, Davis replied with increasing heat, and reporters noted that the subsequent debate between them became "warm, and then personal in its character." In the halls of the Capitol whispered rumors of a duel soon followed, though if either Davis or Foote actually issued a challenge, cooler-headed friends soon put it to rest.[18]

Only one issue remained to be settled before the late-summer recess allowed Davis to go home to see what remained of his marriage. Perhaps he saw at Brierfield a metaphor for what he feared was happening to the Union—two partners, once loving and respectful, who found it increasingly intolerable to live together. Perhaps if he could summon what was needed to win his point on this last matter, then he could win over Varina as well.

The issue, of course, was Oregon. The subject of one of his earliest public speeches in the House two years before, it remained unresolved. Settlers had not yet formed a territorial government, and now with the new lands of California and New Mexico taken from Mexico, Congress faced the issue of three territories seeking organization. If they all formed themselves without slavery, the South saw itself in deep trouble. The Missouri Compromise line did not then extend to cover New Mexico, guaranteeing slavery there, but earlier legislation on the old Northwest Ordinance seemed to argue that Oregon would have to be a free territory. The balance of power was threatened more than ever, and then on June 23 Senator John Hale of New Hampshire introduced an amendment to the Oregon bill that would effectively preclude the possibility of Oregon organizing itself with slavery. That same day Davis responded with an amendment of his own, prohibiting the prohibition of slavery by Congress.[19]

The debate went on for days, and it became clear to Davis that this would be the overriding issue of the session. It called for herculean efforts to stop a seeming tide against the South and its institutions. If slavery were prohibited in Oregon, then Southern men—men whose toil and effort had helped win that territory—would not be able to settle in the new land and take their "property" with them. In essence, by excluding slaves, a free territory excluded slave owners, meaning that such new territories would be settled almost exclusively by Northern and antislavery men. That, in turn, meant that when the territory became a state, its constitution would certainly prohibit slavery, and thus its representatives in Congress would naturally be antislavery in their outlook. Inevitably, that would lead to a majority in Congress against the South and Southern rights. In Davis's mind, as in the minds of most slave holders, it was only a short reach to the conclusion that such a majority would then attack slavery where it legally existed. That constituted nothing less than the virtual destruction of Southern economy, culture, life-style, and social structure—the destruction of the South.

He prepared as he had never prepared before, and when he arose on July 12 to defend his amendment, he made the greatest address of his life thus far. In his clear and sparkling voice, he held the floor for nearly two hours in exactly the sort of closely argued, unimpassioned, logical, and high-toned address for which he was already widely admired. From the outset, he made it clear that to his mind, agitation over slavery had but one real goal, "which is to totally destroy political equality." His amendment, conversely, sought only to preserve Constitutional rights. He did not mean for it to force slavery into Oregon—only to prevent slavery from being forced out. For "such obligations as belong to other species of property, we claim as due to our property in slaves." As usual Davis laid an extensive groundwork for his arguments by tracing the history of the recognition of slaves as property, first in the colonies, by Great Britain, and in the new United States Constitution. It was a common debating style in the Senate, and the men in those seats listened to orators going over the same historical ground so often that their eyes glazed over in stupefaction.

So it must have been with his obligatory reiteration of the nature of the states to the Union, which powers were whose, and so forth. They had heard it all time after time, and with it all the arguments on the limitations of congressional ability to legislate over the local institutions of new territories that might seek statehood. He attacked, as well, the doctrine of "squatter sovereignty." Only a sovereign power could exclude property from a territory. If the settlers of Oregon had such sovereignty, then that was tantamount to acknowledging them to be an independent state, and thus not a territory or possession of the United States. But if it was a territory, then Congress could not turn over the decision of its institutions to its inhabitants, for a territory was the property of all Americans. It was a Jefferson Davis style of argument through and through, step by logical step, establishing a seemingly impenetrable barrier of reason. How could anybody disagree with him?

He further presented the South as a habitual underdog in the affairs of the nation. The Missouri Compromise, seen by Northerners as a great concession to slave interests, he saw as a great concession by the South, for it gave up its perfectly legitimate claim to extend slavery throughout the Louisiana Purchase territory. Even if the Missouri line were extended to the Pacific to govern all future territories, still slavery would be prohibited in three-fourths of the new ground to be organized. Were these not generous concessions? How much did the North expect the South to yield? No one interrupted to point out the frequent oratorical tricks he used, like misstating an opposing opinion in order to set it up for demolition or asserting as unquestioned fact some questionable assumptions in order to use them as the foundation of arguments. Though he could not see it in himself, he played the same game that most politicians played in their congressional seats or on their stumps and speakers' stands, and he played it well.

His most unusual argument—like the most unusual arguments of most men defending the "peculiar institution"—came when he addressed the subject of slavery. By a bizarre perversion of logic, he actually argued that if the proponents of emancipation really had the best welfare of the Negro at heart, they should favor rather than oppose the spread of slavery to new lands. Confining slavery to where it already existed meant that, as slave numbers increased, the same number of masters had more slaves, naturally became more distant from them individually, and were forced to resort more to overseers. This was when cruelty and mistreatment took place. But disperse the blacks throughout the territories, and there would be fewer slaves per master, and kinder treatment must ensue. "To confine slavery to a small district would go further than any other means to strip it of its paternal character," he said in all seriousness. "When the master would no longer know his slave, when the overseer would have the proprietor's power, then would disappear many of the features which commend it to those who have been reared amidst it; then would cease the moral and intellectual progress of the slave; then would steadily diminish the feelings promotive of emancipation, and the power to effect it."

The implication of his argument was incredible: The best way to promote eventual freedom for the slave was to promote the spread of slavery now. It was the most convoluted exercise in logic heard on the Senate floor in this session, yet quite probably Davis genuinely believed what he was saying. Like Joseph, he knew all of his slaves well. He treated them with a good measure of respect, honoring the names they chose for themselves, giving them responsibility and some independence. He regarded James Pemberton as almost akin to a brother, entrusting the management of Brierfield to him rather than to Varina. He gave his slaves education, and he and Joseph ensured that they received religious instruction. Almost certainly the slaves on Davis Bend enjoyed a quality of life exceeding that to be found on the overwhelming majority of plantations in the South. Perhaps Davis believed that Davis Bend was the norm, however.

The fact is that by 1848, this rising spokesman for Southern interests had traveled far more extensively in the North than in the slave states. He had seen only a little of Louisiana and nothing at all of Alabama, Georgia, Florida, the Carolinas, or Virginia. He had seen with his own eyes very little of slavery other than on the banks of the Mississippi from Vicksburg to New Orleans. Did he perhaps take it on faith that most other slaveholders manifested the same enlightened attitude as he and his brother? Only out of such a belief could he assert that "it has been from the association with a more elevated race that the African has advanced; it has been from their mutually kind offices that the master has in many instances liberated his slave as a mark of affection." But such good feelings could only exist where the concentration of slaves was not too dense.

Then he raised an underlying issue that grounded more of the Southern position on slavery than most would admit, and one that frightened free-state men as well. "Upon a large territory, a few blacks might be turned loose without injury to the progress of society," he said, "but on a small territory, a large number of blacks could only be released by surrendering the country to them." There he raised the specter of social disintegration: blacks competing with whites for jobs, masses of unemployed Negroes reverting to thievery or the public dole to survive, and worst of all, racial amalgamation. These, at least, were fears on which North and South united.

Instead, he argued, look at the condition of the slaves in the South today when compared to recently imported blacks to be seen in the West Indies. Compare their slaves even with free blacks in the North, he said. "You find the one contented, well provided for in all their physical wants, and steadily improving in their moral condition; the other miserable, impoverished, loathsome from the deformity and disease which follows after penury and vice." In painting a rosy portrait of slave life that never really existed much outside Davis Bend or his own mind, Davis chose not to address the reasons why slaves ran away at the rate of one thousand or more a year, though if he had he would have said, as he did on other occasions, that they did so because they were agitated and misled by abolition demagogues. It could not have been because they did not want to be slaves.

Liberty, he said, "would be their greatest curse." "Does it warrant the desire on the part of any friend of that dependent race to hasten upon them responsibilities for which they have shown themselves so unequal?" In the end it came not to the issue of slavery but of race. Blacks had to be elevated and instructed before they could be free, and then they had to be "separated from the white man, be relieved from the condition of degradation which will always attach to them whilst in contact with a superior race." In short, emancipation solved only half the black man's problem and the political conflict that tormented the country. Once free, the Negro had to be removed entirely from white society. The two races could not coexist on an equal footing because of their inherent inequality. He did not say that slavery was perpetual, inevitable. A time might well come when the competition between free and slave labor might make the latter so economically unprofitable that slaveholders would voluntarily give up their property. He even asserted that "it is quite within the range of possibility that the masters may desire it when their slaves will object."

As for slavery itself, "Its origin was Divine decree," he said. God gave man the right to enslave the heathen, and any man reared in the South amid the benevolent institution of slavery could attest that the happiness and usefulness of the slaves proved "their present condition to be the accomplishment of an all-wise decree." "It may," he said, "have for its end the preparation of that race for civil liberty and social enjoyment." Certain he was that no question of morality entered the debate over slavery, however much the abolitionists tried to introduce one. "I think there is no foundation for the presumption of moral change," he declared. The Northern states that had abolished slavery did so because slavery had become unprofitable and because their slave populations were so small that they ran little risk of masses of freed blacks disrupting society. On the contrary, the moral position was the continuation of slavery for the good of the blacks.

Finally, after denying the sincerity of the opposition's concern for black welfare or moral outrage over slavery, Davis concluded with an argument just as perceptive as his earlier ones were contrived. "The mask is off," he said. "The question is before us; it is a struggle for political power." The South had compromised enough. It was being taken for granted, its constitutional rights ignored or abused, its pride and dignity affronted. If a "self-sustaining majority" opposed to the South and its institutions continued in its course, "the days of the Confederation are numbered." And then Davis finished with what had become a pattern in his speeches and his correspondence—the threat of disunion. "We should part peaceably, and avoid staining the battle-fields of the Revolution with the blood of civil war," he said, rather than continue indefinitely this political strife. Compromise and stick with that compromise, he said. Otherwise part, like the patriarchs of old, and leave each other in peace. "Let no wounds be inflicted which time may not heal," and simply fold the Stars and Stripes and keep it in a safe place until North and South were ready to join together again.

Arguing in conclusion that if his amendment to the Oregon bill did not pass he would view it as "ominous of the future," Senator Davis sat down.[20] In the end his amendment did not pass. Instead a series of back-and-forth compromises between House and Senate finally led to the passage of an Oregon bill on the terms of the old Northwest Ordinance, though Davis opposed it to the end.

His had been a remarkable address, both for what he said and the way he said it. Never before had he spoken at such length on these subjects, nor so fully revealed either his position or its increasing militance. Never before had he so clearly demonstrated those thought processes by which he arrived at his own unshakable conclusions or the strained and sometimes fallacious logic necessary to support some of them. Never before had he shown the degree of political paranoia, the sense of being an underdog on the defensive, that he proclaimed this July day. It was only two years since he had stood in the chamber on the opposite side of this Capitol addressing the House on an earlier version of an Oregon bill, and then he himself proposed an amendment organizing it on the basis of the Northwest Ordinance and never even mentioned slavery. But that was before the war brought new lands and new battles for political power. Never before did he speak of disunion, not in advocacy but in fear, and perhaps as a threat.[21]

It is fortunate that Congress recessed when it did on August 14. They all needed time to escape the heat of Washington, both in climate and politics. Davis attended to the remainder of his more routine duties, as always, devoting considerable attention to helping his old army friends, trying to push an appointment for Kearny, reinstatement to active duty for a now-disabled Northrop, and voting for the appointment to major general of a Tennessee Democratic political hack, Gideon J. Pillow, probably for no reason other than Pillow's much-publicized feud with Winfield Scott. A recurrence of illness made it impossible for him to leave immediately after the end of the session, however, and it may have been early September before he departed for Mississippi.[22]

What he met upon his return to Davis Bend later that month can only be surmised from the fact that no more vituperative letters seem to have passed between him and Varina. As she was showing progress in conforming her behavior to his wishes in April, it may be assumed that she had progressed even more by the time he reached home. Forever afterward, both remained silent about their separation, and it would not be known at all but for their mutual habit of saving all correspondence.

As is often the case with troubled marriages, a new excitement took their minds from their domestic troubles as both directed energy and attention toward a shared enthusiasm. There was to be a new house at Brierfield. Though it had been discussed for at least two years, its planning often providing a source of discord, the Brierfield house finally started to go up while Davis was away in Washington. The design finally agreed on was a simple one, perhaps reflecting Davis's notion of the interior layout conforming to the exterior shape. They settled upon a one-story home 132 feet wide. Its central portion would have two large rooms on each side of a wide center hall, the front rooms a parlor and library, the rear ones bedrooms. Wings extended from those back bedrooms some 40 feet on either side, each wing containing another bedroom, and one ending in a study and the other in a dining room. A huge back porch ran the entire length of the rear of the house, with kitchen and other outbuildings behind it, while large front porches stood before the main house and the two wings. Fields and woods in front of the house led down a gentle slope to the levee and the river. It was not to be a grand house in the manner of the wealthy planters of Natchez or the mansions lower on the Mississippi in Louisiana. But it would be large and comfortable, and as always with Davis's ideas of a good home, breezy and well ventilated.

It would also be costly, and as usual, Joseph Davis was paying for it. He sent the same contractors who had remodeled Hurricane to do the work for his brother, and of course such an arrangement only created yet another source of irritation between himself and Varina. It may have been patterned somewhat after Diamond Place, the nearby home of Jefferson's niece, which Varina admired, and she certainly showed that she had a taste for fine things. Marble mantels were to come from Italy, and later furnishings would include a grand piano and the custom-made New Orleans and European furniture so popular among the Mississippi planter gentry. Joseph Davis quite frankly thought the house, as planned, extravagant, and estimates of its cost ran from about six thousand dollars to Varina's own statement of ten thousand dollars. When Jefferson Davis returned from Washington, he probably saw not much more than the frame of the new Brierfield, made for the most part from timbers cut on his own property. Meanwhile, he and Varina lived in the older house nearby, amid all the clutter of the furniture for the new house that was stored in it. Even though the new house was being built with room for his sister Amanda and her children, Davis probably did not know that Varina fully intended that the Bradfords should never live there. In the end she would have her way, though by Amanda's decision, not Jefferson Davis's.[23]

It was to be a brief stay in Mississippi, no more than two months, and he spent most of it at Brierfield despite the fact that there was a presidential campaign going on. As many had suspected, and as Davis dreaded, the Whigs nominated Taylor back in June. This left him in a terrible position, as he had feared. To campaign for Cass would be disloyal to his friend and hero; to campaign for Taylor would be treason to his party. The only course he could follow was to plead "considerations of a private character" and take little or no part at all in the canvass. Thus he made but five public speeches while in Mississippi, never far from home, and tried to confine himself to current public issues. He spoke of the presidential contest only with what one reporter thought was "evident reluctance" and then refused to say anything critical of Taylor. Indeed, when he spoke of Taylor, he did so with such glowing expressions of esteem that in a speech at Raymond he almost excited Democrats in the crowd to swarm the stand before he assured them that Cass would have his vote. Yet when he spoke of Cass, it was only with one shallow and backhanded compliment after another, and before another crowd he dodged the whole issue entirely by saying that he viewed it as unseemly for a senator to mingle or interfere in presidential politics. When he turned to the Oregon bill, however, and to the congressional debate over slavery, he warmed quickly to his work, and declared over and over again his apprehension that the North would exclude slavery from the territories time after time until those territories, becoming states, would swell the number of free states to the three-fourths majority necessary to amend the Constitution and abolish slavery where it already existed. He called on men of the South to band together, not because of party or ideology but because they were Southern. Having only recently deplored division of sentiment in the Union "along geographical lines," he now appealed for it. Only by so doing, he argued, could Southern institutions be maintained.[24]

Taylor won in November, to the surprise of few, and Davis must have felt mixed emotions. But there was little time to ponder, for he had to return to Washington for the opening of the second session of the Thirtieth Congress on December 4. How things were going with Varina still seemed uncertain, for in October he had declined an engagement due to "domestic affliction," and now, once more, he left her behind when he departed. Within two weeks he was back in the capital and took up new lodgings at Mrs. Duvall's boardinghouse on Missouri Avenue. His associates and "mess" there were almost exclusively Southern men from Louisiana and Alabama, and quite probably now he intentionally sought more and more the association of men of his section and way of thinking.

Mercifully it was to be a short session, with little legislation of importance coming before the Senate. They needed the rest from the controversies of the previous months. Davis took a new seat and found himself now in more exalted company. Behind him sat the dynamic senator from Missouri, Thomas Hart Benton, whom Davis once admired but now regarded with suspicion. Before him sat John Niles of Connecticut. And to his right sat the giant himself, Calhoun. Already so much a spiritual mentor to the Mississippian, the white-maned senator from South Carolina would henceforth be at his very hand, a constant model and source for inspiration. It could hardly be argued that in future, when Jefferson Davis arose to defend the South and Southern institutions, he did so unconscious of the man sitting attentively beside him. As with other men before Calhoun—Joseph, Taylor—Jefferson Davis very much wanted and needed his approval.[25]

Reappointed to his old committees, Davis got on with the day-to-day paperwork of being a senator. Military matters occupied much of his time. Still looking out for old friends, he recommended the promotion of David Hunter; opposed a brevet for U. S. Grant, whom he did not know; and tried to intercede to prevent the cashiering of his friend

Thomas Crittenden's brother George. When he rose on the floor, he was as likely as not to be speaking on matters of no public controversy. In January 1849 he stood in favor of additional appropriations to allow the Navy to make astronomical observations. He retained his interest in the affairs of the Smithsonian, then constructing its buildings. Even when speaking in opposition to Congress buying the collection of Indian paintings by George Catlin, still he paid tribute to the painter's art. He recalled Catlin well from their 1834 expedition together, and he admired his work. "He has painted the Indian as he lives, unfettered by art, untamed and degraded by the contact of the white man," said Davis. The paintings were "the extraordinary labors of a great American artist," and he opposed their purchase only because he felt the government had no business becoming a "patron of art."[26]

Southern matters occupied him more, however. Only days after Congress convened, he joined thirteen other Southern senators to discuss a united address opposing the application of the Wilmot Proviso to any territory below the Missouri Compromise line as far west as California. A few days later he joined with Calhoun and forty-three Southern congressmen in an appeal for Southern unity. Having dispensed with Oregon, not to his liking, they would soon have to deal with California, and Davis found himself appointed to a special committee to look into the admission of that West Coast empire.[27]

But most of his public attention went to the coming inauguration of Zachary Taylor. Appointed to a select committee to go through the formality of examining the electoral ballots, he was later made the official Senate teller to count those votes, and also chosen one of the managers for the inaugural ball, all no doubt because of his close relationship with the president-elect. On February 26 he and a joint committee from Congress formally called on Taylor to inform him of his election. That done, Davis then took Taylor to the White House to meet with Polk. By now his opinion of Polk had plummeted, and he regarded him as weak and hesitating. He placed more reliance in Taylor and gave his old friend and commander such advice as he could, believing that Taylor "knows very little of our public men." However little Taylor knew, he would have to make do. He counted on Davis to assist him as far as the Democrat's party allegiance allowed. On inauguration day, Jefferson Davis escorted both Taylor and Polk to the ceremonies.[28]

Two days before, with Congress hurriedly rushing through legislation in order to adjourn, the Finance Committee reported a bill to establish a new cabinet branch, the Department of the Interior. While several opposed the measure, Davis spoke ardently in its favor, not least because it was the creation of his friend Secretary of the Treasury Robert J. Walker. As the nation grew, so its officialdom needed to grow in kind. This was not an enhancement of federal power as some argued, else he would join them in opposition. Rather, the new department would relieve other departments like War and Treasury of some of their burdens, as with transferring the Bureau of Indian Affairs from the War Department. Davis did not necessarily oppose big government—just government with big powers—and expanding a bureaucracy would rarely trouble this man who, himself, had so many of the instincts of the bureaucrat.[29]

But for the calling of a special session of the Senate that lasted until March 23, he could have gone home immediately after the inauguration. But then he was off for Brierfield, and he must have looked forward to returning. Not only had this been a short, pacific session, but he had every reason to believe that Varina had become completely as he wished her to be. When she wrote to him partway through the session in January, her letter almost dripped subordination, acquiescence, and humility. "Much as I have loved and valued you," she wrote, "it seems to me I never knew the vastness of my treasure until now." Calling herself his "thoughtless, dependent wife," she flattered him with praise that sounded almost fawning and implored him to be careful of himself, not to be out late at night, nor to drink wine, or eat fruit. "Jeff, my sweetest," she called him, "my better life, my nobler self." Just what could have made this strong-willed and independent nature change so dramatically is hard to say. Perhaps it was love, or maturity. And perhaps she had not changed at all but merely decided to tell her husband what he wanted to hear, in the interests of domestic harmony.[30]

Whatever sea change came over Varina, Jefferson Davis approved heartily. Though he could not know it as he surveyed the tranquil waters of the Mississippi taking him home, he would need peace in his own house more than ever, for the next time he set foot in Washington it would be on the eve of that climactic year 1850, when the house of his fathers launched itself with a violent start into a decade of turmoil.

The Assurance That
I Am Right

It was a tranquil though busy seven months that Davis spent in Mississippi. He and Varina read books together in the evening hours, she managing to insert an occasional modern novel among the histories. There was a bit of Tennyson, too, but Davis preferred songs, whether read or sung.

The new house at Brierfield took shape as the plaster went up on the walls. Builders finished the kitchen and servants' quarters, and very probably before he left in November to go back to Washington, he and Varina moved into their new home. This alone must have gone a long way in easing their minds toward each other, though the cost of the house seems to have left some difficult feelings between Jefferson and Joseph. That, of course, would go away, for the two brothers could never be angry with each other for long.[1]

Davis also had some time to devote to his plantation and to his slave "property." His cotton crop would bring him $3,500 for the 36,389 pounds from this harvest. More than half of his eight hundred acres were under cultivation, adjudged to be worth over $25,000, and that did not count the seventy-two slaves that he owned, their numbers steadily increasing. Despite the acrimonious debate in Washington over slavery, Davis never wavered from his kindly, paternalistic treatment of the blacks at Brierfield. Whether on the streets of the capital or on his own plantation, he showed unfailing civility. "I cannot allow any negro to outdo me in courtesy," he would explain, even returning their bows when they bowed to him. In later years the young woman Florida recalled that "we had good grub and good clothes and nobody worked

hard. "Dem Davis's never would let nobody touch one of their niggers."
As a result, when Davis walked through the slave quarters, the children
gathered around him, shaking his hands and clustering around his long
legs. When he returned from Washington, he often brought gifts for the
little ones. If word went out among the slaves that Davis was coming, all
work ceased, and sometimes they rushed into the house to find him and
embrace him around the knees. With no show of irritation, he quietly
pried them off and started to ask after their families and answer their
own questions. The picture that Davis painted of the tranquil and happy
plantation life of white and black together really existed on Davis Bend,
however much it may have been a dream world elsewhere. The trouble
in Washington was that he could not make Yankees believe that it did
exist, and they could not convince him that aside from Brierfield it did
not.[2]

He spent much of the spring, summer, and fall speaking at public
meetings on the issues confronting them, his arguments the same as
before, his stridency gradually growing. Always disunion came into his
arguments. Still he did not advocate it; rather, he raised it as perhaps the
only alternative that would be left to them. He urged against hasty
action, of course, but he did tell Mississippians that Southerners were
going to have to decide soon on a stand from which they would not
retreat. "When all other things failed," he said ominously, "then was left
the stern appeal—*to arms*." The Yankees felt no solicitude for the black.
They used slavery only as a means to "political dominion." To settle all
this agitation peacefully, the South would have to take a united stand
that would awaken the people of the North to the danger their leaders
courted. He said as much when he addressed the Democratic State Convention in Jackson on June 18. Having lost the White House, Democrats
had a majority only in the Senate. In the House the Whigs outnumbered
them by five. It was imperative that the party make gains in the fall, since
they could no longer count on a presidential veto to stop odious legislation. He appealed for unity as their last hope short of dissolution.[3]

Davis's major focus as a public man was his bid for reelection. His
appointive position to the Senate, ratified by the vote of the legislature in
January 1848, expired on March 3, 1851, and the legislature would vote
to choose the next holder of that office in the coming February. While he
would not make as strenuous a canvass as in previous campaigns, still he
expected it to be difficult enough. "There are many screws which will be
tightened on me," he told a friend as the canvass commenced. He expected both Foote and Quitman to throw their support to some other
candidate, either Roger Barton or Jacob Thompson, and Davis made it
clear that he would "incomparably prefer" Barton to "Jake," should he
be defeated himself. The sectional issue would be thrown at him. His
friendship for Taylor, of course, would become an issue, but he could

live with that and do his best on the stump. Candidates for the Senate did not actually campaign for themselves so much as they spoke on behalf of the party candidates seeking election to the House of Representatives, and he was going to go out and do his best. Privately to a friend, however, he confessed that he thought politics "the meanest and most demoralizing pursuit which is followed."[4]

Nevertheless Jefferson Davis continued in that pursuit. He spoke at least nine times during September and October, his text varying in little other than nuance and illustration from his milestone July 12 speech on the Oregon bill. Indeed, that address would be the foundation of practically all his public talks for the next year and throughout the subsequent controversy over the territories. When he finished his tour at the end of October, he returned to Brierfield, there to spend a quiet three weeks before leaving to resume his seat in the Senate. It was a different leave-taking this time. Varina went with him.

When they reached the capital around December 1, they first took a room at Gadsby's before moving to the west end of the city to a Mrs. Wise's boardinghouse at Third and Pennsylvania Avenue. Varina did not care for Wise's at all. "There was a mess of clerks, and that sort of people there, and wretched living," she complained to her mother. "I really did feel lonely and dull." Because of this, perhaps, she did not stay in Washington more than a few weeks before returning to Natchez in mid-January to escape the winter or else to oversee more of the finishing work on the buildings at Brierfield. Certainly when she left there was no reappearance of the causes that had separated her from Jefferson before. Thanks mostly to Varina's willingness to subordinate herself, the marriage was growing stronger. She would be back in the spring.[5]

It is good that Varina left him alone, for he was embarking on the greatest senatorial battles of his young career. He would need the time to prepare for the fight, though he might have benefited from her soothing hand to keep him calm. Slavery became an issue immediately. He rose to oppose allowing an antislave minister a privileged seat to observe the debates in December, and then in January 1850 rose in debate with Hale of New Hampshire over slavery resolutions introduced by a Vermont senator. Almost from the first, Davis took a sarcastic tone toward Hale, and a pessimistic position on the future of the Union. "I came to this session of Congress with melancholy forebodings," he said, "with apprehension that it might be the last of our Government." Seeing the session barely commenced before antislave men began to harrass him and others with their resolutions, that foreboding was hardly allayed.[6]

When Varina saw his published remarks, she chided him. "It was a little too violent," she said. "More so than I would have liked to hear you be." Yet it could hardly have surprised her that her husband's ire was raised. He took for granted now that the hated Wilmot Proviso, or some variant of it, would actually pass. Just three weeks into the session he confessed to a friend that "my observations here have destroyed my hopes in Congress." He could only count on the president to veto any legislation inimical to Southern rights.[7]

Then the bomb went off. On January 29 the venerable Henry Clay of Kentucky, for whom Davis rarely had a good word to say, introduced into the Senate a number of proposals that he and Senator Stephen A. Douglas of Illinois had originated, aimed at putting an end to the sectional wrangling over the territories and slavery. Eventually called the Omnibus Bill because it comprehensively attempted to address every issue of contention, it set the Senate and the nation aflame.

Clay proposed eight resolutions in all. One would abolish the slave trade in the District of Columbia. Another settled a boundary question between Texas and the New Mexico territory. Yet another would admit California to the Union as a free state, while still another suggested organizing New Mexico and Utah as territories but leaving the slavery question unsettled. Finally, in response to the outcry of Southerners that escaped blacks were harbored in the North and that runaways were encouraged, a fugitive slave law would recognize the property rights of slaveholders and help to enforce recapture. For Clay, the "Great Pacificator," these were to be the last efforts of a career devoted to postponing sectional controversy, a well-intentioned attempt to settle the issues that divided North and South on the cursed subject of slavery.

Several senators reacted at once. The very day that Clay introduced his resolutions, Davis rose along with others to challenge them. Customarily, after brief debate such resolutions would be referred to a committee whose task it was to study the proposals and report an actual bill to the Senate. But the issues involved here were so great, the nerves they touched so raw, that debate broke out spontaneously.

Davis must have had some prior knowledge or expectation of what Clay would say, for his response revealed a preparedness beyond even Davis's accustomed command of a subject. When a previous speaker alluded to a resolution twelve years before on the subject of abolition in the District, Davis was armed with the exact text of that now-forgotten proposal. Revealing his usual professorial delight in making a correction, Davis immediately launched into an extemporaneous assault on Clay. A man looked to for compromise was instead, he asserted, inflaming the sectional controversy, and one by one the Mississippian attacked Clay's resolutions. The proposition to eliminate the slave trade in the District, he declared, ran counter to that previous resolution of Clay's twelve years before, when the Senate agreed that any act "designed to abolish slavery" in the capital would be hostile to Southern interests. Of course, Clay's new resolution said nothing at all about abolition in the

District, proposing only to end the buying and selling of slaves there. Masters from elsewhere would still be entirely free to come and go with their "property" as they pleased, and to live there indefinitely with their slaves. Davis viewed the closing of the slave trade, however, as but an opening of the door to complete abolition.

As for the rest of the new propositions, Davis found in them little of merit, and Clay himself he charged with assuming "as facts things which are mere matters of opinion," an interesting observation in light of the repeated testimony even of his friends and wife that Davis himself did exactly the same thing. He opposed on principle any interference with the boundary of Texas, especially if it should finish by placing a square inch of slave territory from Texas into the New Mexico Territory, which might very possibly end up being a free state. He also challenged Clay's assertion that California should be admitted as a free state because slavery would never take hold there anyhow. Working the new gold mines to which thousands flocked even as they spoke would be labor very conducive to slaves, and better handled by them than by Europeans who could not stand "the burning heat and sudden changes of the climate." Obviously, not only had Davis never been to the gold regions, but he had not troubled himself to learn anything of the northern California climate either.

His response to the introduction of the resolutions was hasty, and Davis made it clear that he spoke chiefly from a desire that the first newspaper accounts that took word of Clay's proposals should be accompanied by his immediate stand in opposition. So far as slavery in the territories was concerned, furthermore, he established his own last line of defense: "I here assert that never will I take less than the Missouri compromise line extended to the Pacific ocean," he said, "with the specific recognition of the right to hold slaves in the territory below that line." Prior to the formation of territories into states, masters must be free to take their slaves into such lands at will.

Clay felt startled at the degree of debate his resolutions stimulated, regarding Davis's remarks especially as premature and unnecessary. He suggested that whenever Davis would be prepared to debate him "at a proper time," he would be ready for him.

"Now is the time," Davis interrupted. "Now, to-day, the present time."

Clay was not prepared at that very moment, though Davis remained briefly insistent, seemingly anxious for the debate, and continued his own remarks at some length, arguing that extension of the Missouri Compromise line already represented giving away too much by the South. Clay proposed that each new territory, regardless of its location, decide the slavery issue for itself. There the matter rested for the time being, as the Senate named February 5 as the date for formal debate on the resolutions to commence.[8]

Already something very significant was manifesting itself, both for the nation and for Davis. The senators aligned themselves not so much by party as by section; moreover, they fragmented into at least four distinct groups. Northern Whigs, with two exceptions, wanted slavery prohibited in all new western territory. Most Southern Democrats, including Davis, demanded that slavery be allowed at least below the 36° 30′ line. Northern Democrats and a few of their Southern brethren advocated Clay's compromise and a "popular sovereignty" decision on slavery, and Southern Whigs leaned toward "popular sovereignty" as well. All the old lines of allegiance that bound Northern and Southern men together were breaking down, reemphasizing Davis's old fear of a geographical orientation in politics.[9]

As for Davis himself, it is significant that it was he who spoke out representing the Southern Democratic position. Calhoun stayed silent. Calhoun was dying. Though he might be counted on to make some effort in the debate to come, the frail old warrior for Southern rights had only months to live. Never by specific act or design did he seem to confer his mantle of leadership on another. Rather, Davis seems to have assumed it, probably unconsciously. As one of the most consistent and outspoken followers of Calhoun's position, Davis very likely seemed a natural successor, especially since his manner of address was much more dignified than that of many other equally outspoken Southern senators. He might seem to cloak his arguments in the same majesty that Calhoun had given them. Thus, those accustomed to look to Calhoun to provide leadership in fighting the battles for Southern rights could still look in the same direction, just one seat farther to the right.

The ensuing weeks were among the busiest, and certainly the most strained, that Davis ever experienced as a senator. Even while he gathered the documents he needed to prepare his own formal debate on Clay's resolutions, Davis could not stay out of the debates on a host of the side issues connected with the burning matter at hand. North Carolina presented a petition protesting Northern fanaticism. In response, the next day Delaware offered a petition calling for the peaceful dissolution of the Union. Overwhelmingly, the Senate declined to receive the petition, and Davis stood to argue against it—partly because of what it advocated, and also because he did not recognize that Congress had a right to dissolve the Union—only the individual states could do that. This same day, February 8, he also responded to Sam Houston, now senator from Texas, but still remembered by Davis as a drunken "enigma" at Fort Gibson. Houston averred that Mississippi had acted to initiate a proposed convention of Southern men at Nashville to take a regional stand. In fact, in the fall of 1849 Mississippians of all parties did gather in Jackson, adopting eleven resolutions that stated much the same position on slavery and the Union as did Davis and Calhoun and calling on other states to join in a convention the following summer. But other than a brief organizational function, Davis took little part in the Jackson meeting. Seeing in Houston's remarks an implication that he somehow masterminded the affair, he felt compelled to explain himself. The episode was of no consequence in itself, but Davis's response revealed an increasing sense of being personally on the defensive, a growing paranoia regarding both himself and his section. Coming events only aggravated it, even to the point that Davis attempted to lecture the vice president when he felt Senate rules were not being applied fairly to himself.[10]

Davis made his formal reply to Clay's resolutions over two days, February 13–14, 1850, in some of the longest orations of his career. Noteworthy for the sheer stamina required for delivery, if for little else, Davis's address opened no new ground, nor did it in substance say anything that he had not said previously as far back as his first speech on the Oregon bill two years before. He accused Clay of yielding everything for the South, of helping the abolition horde more than any Northern man could have done. The abolitionists he accused of nothing less than an intent to take dominion over the whole nation. "I see nothing short of conquest on the one side, or submission on the other," he declared, and Clay seemed clearly to side with those who would conquer. Yielding California as a free state, abolishing the slave trade in the District of Columbia, leaving territories below the Missouri Compromise line free to choose for themselves on slavery, all involved only concessions from the South, he argued. Even a new Fugitive Slave Law was little more than talk, since no one expected Northerners actually to obey such legislation.

From the outset the great issue was slavery in the territories. Arguing that slaveholders must be allowed to take their property into lands that belonged to all the people, he proceeded to state an opinion as if it were a fact, just as he castigated Clay for doing a few days earlier. "Every one must understand that, whatever be the evil of slavery, it is not increased by its diffusion," he said. Everyone most certainly did not perceive the problem that way, but as usual Davis did not admit of disagreement. He attacked the notion that slavery could not be introduced into California and New Mexico because their previous owner, Mexico, had abolished slavery there. He asserted that Congress had no power to abolish the slave trade in the District because it was the property of all the people, its buildings erected out of the common treasury. He brought out his old arguments that the slave trade itself had been a blessing for the African, bringing him out of ignorance and degredation to a land of Christian enlightenment where the slave "entered the temple of civilization." It was all by divine ordination that the black man had been made "a servant of servants."

At times, for a man so proud of his logic, Davis could be almost sophomoric. Now that the African slave trade itself was a thing of the past, he agreed that this was good, largely because "it is a thing which was never introduced or engaged in by the South, and one for which southern men never were and their descendants are not responsible. . . . It is odious among us now, as it was with our ancestors." Of course he would say so, since, like most Southerners, he believed in—and promoted—the myth that the slave trade had been exclusively a Northern enterprise. But when he asserted that Southerners bore no responsibility for the slave trade even if they did not engage in it he purposely ignored one vital element without which there would have been no slave trade: demand. Northerners forced slavery on the South by importing slaves, his statements implied, ignoring conveniently one of the immutable facts of free enterprise, namely that without demand there would have been no supply. Slavery itself Davis would not attempt to defend. "It is enough for me," he said, "that it was established by decree of Almighty God, that it is sanctioned in the Bible, in both Testaments, from Genesis to Revelations." Considering the indifference Davis had shown to religion all his life up to 1850, his seeking justification in Scripture—however commonplace among Southerners—is still striking.

As usual at that time, Davis raised the specter of disunion and war. If no acceptable compromise could be found—and it was up to the Northern majority to suggest such a compromise, he said—and if no constitutional guarantees of the preservation of Southern rights were established, then there would be little honorable choice left to men of the South except secession. He was willing to accept any solution that permanently settled these plaguing questions, though he warned that if secession came, the North would suffer more than the South. In his first public avowal of the power of "King Cotton," he asserted that an independent South would flourish as the world beat on its doors for "the great staple," while the industrial North, like Venice, Carthage, and Tyre in earlier times, would perish as all commercial states had perished. "Grass will grow on the pavements now worn by the constant tread of the human throng which waits upon commerce," he warned. It was a theme he had expressed before, and one that he liked. Little more than a decade later he would risk a great deal on its being right.[11]

The reaction to Davis's speeches those two days was predictable. "He ranked as one of the ablest in debate," his friend Atchison would say, and the friendly press back in Mississippi praised his defense of Southern rights. Even though they were political opponents, President Taylor looked with favor on Davis's stand. Indeed, the Mississippian was an almost-weekly visitor at the White House, and the president looked to him to counter Clay, for whom he felt no admiration. "Mr. Clay can't rule, in Congress, the Nation, as he used to do," said Taylor to a friend. *"Now there is Mr. Davis of Mississippi."*[12]

There was little time for Davis to bask in the glow of approval, however, for one week after he concluded his address he very nearly found himself on the dueling field. Congressman William Bissell of Illinois, frustrated at what he thought to be repeated Southern exaggeration of both the region's abilities and woes, rose in the House on February 21 and offered, as an example, the fact that at Buena Vista, when the Second Indiana gave way early in the day, the Second Kentucky and the Second Illinois saved the day, and that despite its grandiose claims, the Mississippi regiment was still a mile and a half away and had not yet fired a gun.

Naturally Davis heard of Bissell's comments. The next day he wrote and asked if Bissell had been reported correctly, since he had not actually seen a printed report of the congressman's remarks. Bissell responded immediately in the affirmative, and that elicited from Davis on February 23 a stiffer request for further explanation. Bissell replied curtly the same day, and in a manner that Davis found "unsatisfactory." Having sent his previous letters by his friend Congressman Samuel Inge of Alabama, Davis now had him return to Bissell with an "invitation" to meet him somewhere outside the District to settle the dispute. It was a challenge, of course, and Bissell accepted through his intermediary General James Shields, asking only two days to finish work on a speech first. On February 27 Bissell named his second, Major Osborne Cross, and that same evening Cross, Shields, and Inge met to make arrangements. By this time rumors of the impending duel swarmed around Washington and the nation. Davis believed that warrants had been issued for himself and Bissell, dueling being illegal, and he may have tried to elude arrest. Other politicians came uninvited to the February 27 meeting hoping to put a stop to any further foolishness. According to rumor, President Taylor even posted guards at the antagonists' homes to keep them from leaving to fight.

In the end Shields and the others achieved an amicable settlement, whereby Davis and Bissell withdrew their correspondence after February 22, and Bissell changed his response to acknowledge the gallant services of Mississippians at Buena Vista. To alert everyone that the crisis was over, Shields published their "approved" correspondence in the Washington press along with a notice that the difficulty had been settled, and a day or two later Davis made a point of entering the House chamber to sit beside Bissell, "indulging in a friendly chat with him." Somewhat waggishly, a correspondent of the *New York Herald* commented that "one compromise, at least, has succeeded."[13]

Meanwhile, the debate on Clay's resolutions raged on, and a host of events crowded in on Davis. On February 12 the Mississippi legislature formally reelected him for another full six-year Senate term. He took comfort in that, at least. This same month two mysterious men appeared one evening at the Davis boardinghouse and held a hushed conversation with the senator. They were Cubans, and one of them, General Narciso Lopez, remembered what he had seen and heard of Davis during the Mexican War. He had sought for years to launch a successful invasion of Cuba to free it from its Spanish masters, and now he offered Davis, for considerable money, the command of a liberation expedition. However much he wanted to see Cuba out of Spanish hands, Davis also preferred that it become a part of the United States. Such an invasion might have been a first step, but Davis did not approve of foreign adventuring by filibusters. Besides, he had important battles to fight right there in Washington. "I deem it inconsistent with my duty," he told Lopez, and suggested that instead he should approach Major Robert E. Lee. Lee also declined.[14]

But these were only diversions from the overriding issue of the day. "We are here in the midst of excitement," Davis wrote to a friend on February 25, while waiting for Bissell, "and the wisest cannot foretell what a day may bring forth." He saw the old solid Southern wall in the Senate falling apart. "Clay, and Benton have deserted us," he lamented, and even Calhoun was so old and feeble that he had "no influence beyond the circle of those who need no prompting." This realization of Calhoun's powerlessness may have helped him decide to assert himself to leadership, the more so since as he looked around the rest of the Senate, he saw that "of the men who have national reputation, and sufficient ability, all are out of position, or so embarassed as to be unable to lead." Ironically, the only man from whom he hoped much was the venerable Northern Whig Daniel Webster. A few days later, in fact, Webster did make his famous March 7 speech in which he cried out for the Union and extended the suggestion of substantial concessions to the South.[15]

But Davis believed that it was up to him to lead the continuing fight. Never did he feel a personal antipathy for Clay. They had been acquainted when Davis attended Transylvania. The elder statesman's son Henry Clay, Jr., had been the Mississippian's friend and fell in battle at Buena Vista not far from Davis. The very afternoon of Webster's moving speech, Clay and Davis met on the Capitol grounds, where Davis confessed that he liked Webster's proposal to make four slave states in the west below the Missouri line and pass a more effective fugitive slave law. Clay appealed to him to "join the Compromise men," adding that if they could agree, it might buy thirty years of peace. Davis, never willing to run away from a battle, preferred that they settle things now.[16]

In the ensuing weeks he became increasingly strident. A Swedish visitor, Frederika Bremer, came to Washington that season and found him to be "a young man of handsome person and inflammable temperament who talks violently for 'Southern Rights.' " Several noticed that he spoke on the floor of the Senate with an advancing sense of the correctness of his position. Indeed, during debate on March 6, Senator Isaac P. Walker of Wisconsin actually interrupted to observe that "the Senator from Mississippi always speaks so very positively."

"Because I am very certain," replied Davis.

Walker went on to say that Davis spoke "with an air—I say it with no disrespect—which seems to say, 'Nothing more can be said'—'I know it all'—'it must be as I think.' "[17]

Davis went on to show that Walker was right, and furthermore, observers now saw something in his address that critics complained was lacking a few years before. "There was passion in the speech," a correspondent wrote of Davis's March 8 comments on slavery in the territories. "It was concentrated into a *white heat*, that threw out no sparks, no fitful flashes, glowing with an intense, but not an angry glare." Indeed, carried away at times by his intensity of feeling, Davis argued against points not made, as when he went after Walker's comments on one of his speeches, even after the senator from Wisconsin repeatedly interrupted to tell Davis that he had discussed a different address from the one Davis was defending. He raised anew the issue of a Constitutional amendment to guarantee to the South protection of its interests in light of its minority position, and when Cass of Michigan asserted that in the end the question of the rights of slaveholders in the territories could be decided by the Supreme Court, Davis interrupted almost plaintively from his seat to say "but we cannot get there." He would have welcomed handing the whole matter over to the court, presided over as it was by the conservative Roger B. Taney of Maryland.[18]

Perhaps Davis felt himself impelled the more by the death of Calhoun. Too ill to appear for the debates, still Calhoun had read for him on March 4 his stirring appeal for equal rights and, failing that, a constitutional guarantee of Southern rights. The following day he actually struggled into the Senate chamber to defend his position. Alerted in advance, Varina was there, and as Calhoun passed he grasped her hand feebly, whispering, "My child, I am too weak to stop." Sitting next to Davis, Calhoun pitifully tried to contend with his foes, while Davis and others tried to spare him the effort, yet the great South Carolinian would not be deterred until friends actually carried him out. He returned to hear Webster's great address and then failed again and left the chamber for the last time. Confined to his bed thereafter, he died on March 31. Fittingly, Davis served on the Senate committee that arranged for Calhoun's funeral, joined the guard of honor that saw the remains back home to South Carolina, and in the Senate delivered a formal eulogy.

Moved to tears, he spoke with quavering voice of his departed friend and the South's champion. Now it was up to him.[19]

Probably just as Davis was leaving for Charleston with Calhoun's body, a Senate committee of thirteen was established on April 19 to take Clay's resolutions and, in light of all the debate, craft them into a single bill. By May 8, when the Omnibus Bill came out of committee, Davis was back and ready to renew the battle. It was obvious to him that the measures would probably pass, so now he lent his strength to amendment instead. On May 15, to debate on the provision to admit New Mexico to territorial status, Davis proposed that wording be inserted that would prohibit the territorial legislature from enacting any laws interfering with the rights of a slaveholder to take his property into the territory and enjoy the benefits of that property. Here again was a stroke at "squatter sovereignty." Davis did not argue the right of a territory to decide for itself the question of slavery at the time it became a state. His concern was excluding slavery prior to that time, which would ensure that there would be few if any proslave men living there when the time came to vote on the issue of statehood. A few days later Davis modified his amendment, then accepted a substitute proposed by another senator, but in the end they were voted down in June. With equal futility he opposed on June 8 the portion of the Omnibus Bill that would settle a boundary dispute between Texas and New Mexico by taking a strip of land from the former and appending it to the latter. Texas was already a state, Davis argued, and the federal government possessed no power to take its land away or to purchase it and bestow that land elsewhere. The territory in dispute was large, composing half of what would later be New Mexico and portions of the future Oklahoma, Kansas, and Colorado. Davis frankly asserted that the motive was to take slave state land and make it subject to organization into new free states. Had boundaries been well defined when Texas applied for admission, the subsequent controversy could not have taken place.[20]

The debate continued at a hectic pace. On June 12 Davis arose again in discussion of the proposed Fugitive Slave Law and responded to an accusation that runaway slaves were jailed and sold. Davis argued that this was done out of "humanity," for selling a runaway put him in the keeping of someone who would care for him, rather than the state incarcerating him for the rest of his life as a lawbreaker. That same month, seeing the threat to the South in larger terms than just the Omnibus Bill, Davis joined sixty-three other Southern men in Washington in a call for the establishment of a pro-Southern newspaper in the capital to help present their side of the pressing issues of the time. His interest in the Nashville convention held that month revealed the same concern. "It is necessary to begin an organization of the South the want of which has left us a divided people," he had said back in April. Mississippi's legislature adopted resolutions that he introduced to the Senate in May, calling among other things for, in the last extremity, the joining of Southern states into "a compact and a union that will afford protection to their liberties and rights." That meant a Southern nation, and while Davis did not elaborate on the notion, it is clear that he agreed to its efficacy as a final option. Davis even found himself differing from Robert J. Walker, who supported the Omnibus Bill, opening a breach that widened in time and cost him a friend.[21]

When the convention of delegates met in Nashville, they did little more controversial than endorse the extension of the Missouri Compromise line and adopt a wait-and-see attitude toward the Omnibus Bill. Certainly they did nothing to promote the idea of disunion or a separate Southern nation, and this, at least, helped to remove some of the stigma that others attached to Davis for favoring the convention. Still, he reacted with increasing sensitivity to the attacks on him in the public press, complaining of the calumny he suffered from "every petty newspaper or degraded letter-writer." He claimed publicly to ignore all this. "Proud in the consciousness of my own rectitude," he said to the Senate late in June, "I have looked upon it with the indifference which belongs to the assurance that I am right." There was that ever-present conviction of infallibility again, but he was less than honest with the Senate, if not with himself, for indifference was the last thing he felt when meeting criticism. As the summer wore on, the newspaper assaults became ever more sarcastic about his protestations of a "superstitious," reverential devotion to the Union. "What kind of 'reverence for the Union' a 'superstitious' reverence is, we cannot well imagine," commented one editor. "Judging from the development of Col. Davis' course, it cannot be of a very *practical* character."[22]

In the midst of all this, another personal loss only added to Davis's frayed nerves during that cursed session. Word came from the White House on July 5 that President Taylor had fallen ill. His condition rapidly declined, and Davis went often to his bedside. Varina went with him. She had left Washington for the home of a niece in Pennsylvania late in May but all the while pined to return to her husband. The debates kept Davis in the capital so incessantly that he could not get away to fetch her, but late in June she returned. He had been terribly lonely without her. Standing beleaguered in the Senate and so seemingly alone, he needed her comfort and, to be sure, he needed her acquiescence that in all things he was right. Now, with Taylor dying, he needed her all the more.[23]

At 3 P.M. on July 9 a messenger called on the Davises at the White House. The senator told him that Taylor seemed better, but his stomach was "irritable" and his pulse raced. Varina and her husband sat at the bedside, along with Taylor's family, throughout the day. Shortly after ten that night, the president spoke to Davis in his delirium. "Apply the Constitution to the measure Sir regardless of consequences." They were to be Taylor's last intelligible words. Four days later he lay in his casket in the East Room, with his onetime son-in-law, faithful subordinate, and ever-loyal friend Jefferson Davis seated beside the bier.[24]

At times it seemed that this cursed year only grew worse. Just days after Taylor's death, Davis and Varina enjoyed an all-too-infrequent quiet interlude together, playing and teasing and she scolding him for always looking at the mail before showing it to her. With a smile he handed her two or three unopened letters just received and then watched, helpless, as her laughter turned to tears when the first one she opened announced the death of her little brother George Howell. For the next several days he stayed with Varina every minute possible when he could escape the debates in the Senate.[25]

But escape was never more than temporary. Even other duties of his office could not take his mind entirely from the daily confrontations in the Capitol. Davis became chairman of the Military Affairs Commit-tee, much to the pleasure of many observers who felt that "probably no man in the country and certainly no man in Congress understands better the uses and the abuses of that branch." From that vantage point, he introduced legislation to increase the numbers of the rank and file of the army, and even during the worst of the June debates he managed to introduce resolutions to protect the seniority of West Point graduates as they received their regular army commissions. Retaining his position as a regent of the Smithsonian, he served on its building committee and urged that it collect designs and models of ancient and modern archi-tecture, continuing evidence of his interest in building.[26]

The building that most haunted his thoughts, however, was the Capitol. Day after day he returned, and then suddenly a tide seemed to shift. During the final week of July opponents of the Omnibus Bill began to dissect it piece by piece. The troublesome portion covering New Mex-ico was eliminated by a substantial majority. A few days later a one-vote margin took out everything relating to Texas. Sensing a gathering mo-mentum, Atchison backed a proposal that took California statehood out of the bill. Clay himself walked out of the Senate in disgust, not being there to see the bill's lone survivor, the Utah Territory, receive approval. By July 31, 1850, the Omnibus Bill was dead. It had simply asked too much at one time, and a majority of the senators could not make them-selves adopt and swallow such a controversial chunk of legislation whole.[27]

Davis, of course, was delighted. The defeat of the bill, however, did not mean that its component parts could not still come before the Sen-ate, and debate on California resumed on August 1. Hoping to capitalize on their seeming advantage, Davis, Atchison, and several other Southern men met to discuss their next step. Davis favored a filibuster or other means of delay to keep the California bill from coming to a vote, and a few days later David Yulee of Florida attempted unsuccessfully to do so. Then Davis himself stood to oppose a proposal that the Senate extend its hours beyond normal adjournment in order to prolong the filibuster. He and the other Southern men committed themselves in writing to "any and every means" to prevent California's admission unless its southern boundary should rest on the Missouri line.[28]

What Davis feared, of course, is precisely what happened. Losing on the Omnibus Bill as a whole, Douglas took over managing its provisions through as separate bills. Utah had already been passed, Davis voting in favor, as a matter of fact, since that territory rested entirely above 36° 30′ latitude. Next the Texas–New Mexico boundary matter came up, and on August 9 it, too, passed, despite Davis's opposition. Senators began to wonder if Taylor's death had come at an inopportune time, for men he was thought to control in the Southern Whig ranks now defected to vote with Clay and Douglas. California came next. Preceded by heavy debate, much of it from Davis, the issue went to a vote on August 13. That day Davis and nine others, including Atchison and Yulee, signed and presented a protest against the California bill. By this time they knew they were beaten and simply wanted their position on the record one more time. They objected to California going immediately to statehood, bypassing the territorial stage in which inhabitants might decide for themselves the question of slavery. They closed with the ever-present threat of disunion. Against the outcry in the Senate to presentation of the protest, Davis defended himself from charges that he sought or advocated the breakup of the states. More and more often now he felt called on to deny that he advocated disunion, though almost his every major public address closed with the dire prediction. It was very easy, in the face of this repetition, for his listeners to wonder if he was warning of an existing threat or making one, though Davis himself could never be made to see their confusion.[28]

Despite his vote against it, California statehood passed that day. Davis knew he was beaten and admitted it. "It is not, therefore, for want of will, but for the want of power," he said, "that I have not offered further opposition than I have." Two days later he was still arguing his case, however, very nearly getting into a serious argument with Solomon Downs of Louisiana, and this on top of repeated exchanges throughout the session with Foote and even Houston. In the argument with Downs, the president pro tem of the Senate had to scold Davis for using unacceptable language, and Davis immediately backed away from the confrontation. There is no denying, however, that his patience and nerves were exhausted by the past six months of controversy.

When the bill establishing the New Mexico Territory came before the Senate the same day as his exchange with Downs, Davis did not vote at all. It passed overwhelmingly, though nearly a third of the senators abstained. Quite probably, knowing himself beaten, Davis did not object to the old custom of "pairing off" with an opposition member who, for some reason, could not attend and asked the Mississippian if he would withdraw. Thus each canceled the other's vote, leaving the relative standing of the balloting unchanged. But a week later, when the Fugitive Slave Bill came to a vote, Davis made sure to be there. Indeed, he participated in the debate leading up to the vote and on August 19, and again three days later, rose to defend the Southern position. He argued that slave-catchers going into the North and kidnapping free blacks to bring them back to servitude could not happen, because the sense of honor of Southern people would not stand for it. The kidnapping, he said, was done by Yankees who stole lawful slaves from their masters. Having lived his whole life on the frontier or in Mississippi, he really had little idea whereof he spoke, but even if Davis knew firsthand what happened along the Ohio River border states, it is unlikely that he would have argued any differently. He saw only what he chose to see, and what he did not see he did not admit to exist. "I feel no great interest in this law," he lamented, "because I have no hope that it will ever be executed to any beneficial extent." Nevertheless he voted with the majority that passed the law, and even added a few minor amendments that constituted his only lasting contribution to the so-called Compromise of 1850.[29]

By September 15, with the adjournment of Congress only two weeks distant, Davis privately complained to Varina's mother that "I am weary and more than ever before disgusted with political life." Often he told Varina that he would be happy to get back to Mississippi "just as soon as Congress d——n pleases." There was one more important vote to come, however, and Davis cast his the next day on the bill to abolish the slave trade in the District of Columbia. All but six Southerners, Davis among them, voted against the measure, but it passed overwhelmingly just the same.

Davis looked back on all that had passed in this tumultuous session with unrestrained chagrin. "For the first time we are about permanently to destroy the balance of power between the sections," he complained, leading them to "the point at which aggression will assume such a form as will require the minority to decide whether they will sink below the conditions to which they were born, or maintain it by forcible resistance." There was that reference to disunion again, and this time accompanied by a hint of violence. The credit for the final, individual passage of all the old Omnibus measures Davis correctly laid at Stephen A. Douglas's desk, while he took only hollow comfort from the fact that he had helped defeat the original Omnibus Bill, a meaningless conquest in light of subsequent events, but still he was proud that he had stood his ground and fought the fight despite the odds.[30]

Indeed he did fight. On eight major days of compromise debate, Davis rose and took the floor some fifty-four times, more than any other senator. Moreover, setting aside the substance of what he said, his words carried an impact for the way he said them. Senate reporters found his speech so dictinctly enunciated that there was no difficulty in transferring his remarks to paper. "The reporters liked to hear him," one recalled, "because his matter was always good and 'meaty,' his manner pleasing and his utterances deliberate and distinct." All commented upon his "clear, sonorous voice and a flowing style." They probably also enjoyed his frequent flashes of temper. Even on the last day of debate on the slave trade in the District, Davis got into it briefly with Foote again, this time with Foote getting the last word and even a laugh from the other senators when he referred to Davis's "excitable" nature.[31]

Despite his volcanic frustrations within, Davis kept his calm outside the Senate chamber. To almost all he presented a "genial, courteous and considerate" manner. Oliver Dyer, a reporter for Washington's *National Intelligencer*, observed how "it seemed to give him keen pleasure to do an act of kindness for any one," often taking some pains to get Dyer reports and other documents. "Such acts he did with a magnetic courtesy that went straight to my heart." Years later one of Davis's children, too, would comment on this trait in him. "He never conferred a favor as though it cost him anything."[32]

What it cost him to keep that calm, to hold his boiling passion and anger within, none could say. Truly Davis did love and revere the Union in the way that many Southern men loved it, as something to which they had attached themselves freely and conditionally, yielding a few rights in return for benefits and protection of their remaining prerogatives. But the sectional controversy of the past decades, and especially that summer of 1850, challenged his idea of democracy. Like Calhoun before him, Davis believed in the will of the majority so long as he approved of that will. He did not believe that the minority was obligated to acquiesce in it, but rather that the role of the general government was to protect the rights of the minority. In a representative democracy, of course, that could not happen unless the Constitution put specific limitations on the powers of the majority. Calhoun had argued for this, and now Davis started to do the same, but in 1850 the damage was already done. He could not, or would not, see slavery and Northern opposition to it as a moral issue. It was not such in his own mind, and therefore could not legitimately be so in the minds of others. The outcry against slavery that produced all this discord, and now this so-called compromise, stemmed so far as he was concerned from nothing more than the grasping for political power and hegemony by the rising abolitionist party of the

North, who cared nothing for the true welfare of the Negro and used him solely as a vehicle to power.

In fact, Davis was just as out of touch with the sentiments of Northerners as he was unfamiliar with the true nature of slavery outside Davis Bend. Abolitionist politicians certainly did use slavery as an issue to attain power and could be callous in manipulating it to their ambitious ends. But the people who elected more and more of them to office in successive elections sought no such power nor could they gain or use it for themselves. Their votes were the incontestable voice of a growing revulsion for the abetting of slavery by living in a nation where it existed. Davis neither saw this nor would he have understood it if he had. It was foreign to him because in his mind, and in the world he saw, the true morality lay in keeping blacks in slavery. Unable to countenance assaults on the institution as anything other than attacks on the South, his mind could conceive the compromise measures only as attempts to continue the political containment and subjugation of the South begun in 1820 by the Missouri Compromise. The fact that the bulk of the civilized world felt the same distaste for slavery as did the North did not signify with him. Like the Yankees, he would say, Europeans did not understand slavery in the South and therefore should mind their own business.

It all contributed to the sense of being besieged on all sides that Davis first seriously revealed after the Mexican War. By the end of the debates in 1850, he had passed through all the stages from surprise to hurt to anger to determination. Now and in the future when others accused him of being a disunionist, he saw not that the charge stemmed naturally from his own repeated references to secession as a last resort, but only that once more he was being attacked and his motives misrepresented. Now that he began to talk of the possibility of forcible resistance, he opened himself to even more criticism, but he would never understand why. He *had* to raise the specter of resistance to make the North aware of how serious its assaults on the South's rights were. He was not saying, "We *will* do this," but rather, "Push us too far, and we may *have* to do this." He saw the difference, and could not understand why others did not, just as he never recognized that men who opposed the spread of slavery into new territories did not necessarily want to attack it where it already existed. In an era of exaggerated fears, misunderstood motives, and resorts to illogical conclusions on all sides, Jefferson Davis was right in the mainstream.

In the South, however, he stood at the forefront. Where two years before his Mexican service had made him a national military hero, now his self-assumed leadership of the anticompromise forces made him a sectional political hero. His debates in the Senate, reprinted throughout the Southern press, made him easily the best-known states' rights advocate since Calhoun, and Calhoun's timely death left him the unchallenged senatorial spokesman for the South as a whole. It is significant that he attained that position not as an actor on the public stage but as a reactor. He introduced no new legislation, championed no new movements. This was not part of his makeup and never would be. He rose only to respond to the acts of others. It was a defensive posture, one symbolic of the South itself. It gave Davis added stature among those in his part of the nation and subtly reinforced in his mind and theirs that they truly were under attack, that the North was waging a kind of war against them.

When Jefferson Davis left Washington early in October after the adjournment of the session, these thoughts must have spun around like a carousel in his mind. Disgusted with politics he definitely was, though chiefly because he found himself on the losing side, and Davis did not like to lose. He left more angered by public events than ever before in his life, and in a way more frightened, too. Certainly in his own thinking 1850 was a watershed. Previously, the South, though its rights were imperiled, still had an expectation of extending its institutions and thereby the balance of power. Now all that was changed. California tipped the scale in favor of the free states, and the application of the "squatter" or "popular sovereignty" principle to the Utah and New Mexico territories bade fair to see slavery excluded there, too. If so, the slave states would be hemmed in geographically and doomed to an ever-diminishing minority status. In the outlook from such a position, Davis could see nothing but gloom. As he boarded the steamboat *Fanny Smith* on the Ohio for the final leg of the journey to Brierfield, he already knew that his labors had just begun. Having lost in Washington, Southerners must now resist by the constitutional right they enjoyed as sovereign states, perhaps even to the point of secession. He would not quail from that eventuality, though he did not welcome it either, for it would bring in train a host of dangers. In the end that would not matter. As always, Davis knew but one way to deal with a problem, and that was to face it squarely and manfully, with an unshakable conviction that he acted for the right.

These and other thoughts and plans for the coming months were probably still on his mind when he steamed down the Yazoo River toward Vicksburg on October 19. Along the way he passed the spot where, five days earlier, a steamboat had sunk near Satartia. Her owners had called her the *Jeff Davis*. With the lazy waves of the Yazoo rolling over his namesake as he passed the wreck, Jefferson Davis may well have wondered if in the days ahead a similar fate awaited him.[33]

12

I Will Meet Force with Force

Even before leaving Washington, Davis decided that his brief two-month hiatus during the adjournment would not be a restful one. Instead, he would use that time to speak to the people of Mississippi, to arouse them to the dangers they faced, and urge them to organize both among themselves and with other Southern states for the defense of their rights. While on his way to Davis Bend, he stopped to make a speech in Lexington, Mississippi, and just three days after returning to Brierfield he addressed a crowd in Vicksburg. Thereafter he spoke several times throughout central Mississippi, and almost everywhere from the same text. He was not a disunionist, no matter what others said. But that did not mean that he would not resist the recent enactments of Congress. Governor Quitman had called for a special session of the legislature to discuss the recent events in Washington, and Davis heartily endorsed that call. Moreover, he pledged that he would abide by the dictates of that session, whatever they might be, even should they require him to leave his seat in the Senate "to take his place on a new field of duty in Mississippi." He did not say what he thought that "field" might be, but he emphatically proclaimed himself in favor of "resistance." There were many ways to resist, of course—meetings and protests, nonintercourse with the North, and more. He withheld saying that he advocated "the resistance of FORCE," but left the decision on how to take a stand to the people through their legislature. Declaring his utter disgust with every one of the bills recently passed, he asserted that "the South would be infinitely benefitted by a dissolution of the Union." Still, he was not a disunionist and hoped that Southern rights might be preserved within the United States. The South should demand guarantees of its future security and protect those rights "in the Union if she can and out of it if she must."

Addressing the crowds, he asked again and again, "What are we to do?" "That's it, that's the question," his listeners responded. Of course, Davis had an answer for them. Every Southern state should follow Mississippi's lead, call a convention, and send delegates to a general Southern convention. Then that body could proclaim the guarantees that Southerners demanded to protect their rights. "A body thus chosen would carry with it a moral force," he said, "which the fierce abolitionists dare not oppose." If Northerners ignored that convention's mandates, then the South would have to leave the Union.[1]

Attendance was spotty at his appearances. At Raymond on October 25 only four of the scheduled six speakers showed, and almost no audience. The debate was postponed to the following day, and then sixty or seventy citizens appeared. Elsewhere reporters noted that "but few were in attendance, and but little interest manifested to hear the speakers." Partly out of frustration at the apparent lack of interest, and also because of the heat he felt over the subject, Davis occasionally became aroused, and when angered he tended to make more strident statements, as at Raymond when one listener thought he "shadowed forth views of a disunion character." Appearing along with him were speakers supporting the recent compromise measures, and occasionally one or another of them seemed to calm him.[2]

Davis's program was for him, or for any Southern politician, a far-seeing one. He urged Southerners to determine to make themselves independent of the North. They should build railroads to stimulate the growth and transport of their agricultural products. They should encourage immigration from the North and from abroad to increase their population and wealth. They should commence expanding Southern manufacturing capabilities in order to make their own consumer goods from the cotton they grew, as well as to make their own shoes, hats, blankets, and every other purchasable article in order to keep Southern money at home. They should commence a system of liberal, state-supported higher education to keep students in the South "and preserve them from the contaminations growing out of an education acquired in the free States." On top of all this, he urged that the South build a stockpile of arms and munitions and establish the manufacturing capability to make them.

In short, Jefferson Davis suggested nothing less than the virtual remaking of the South—and, except for the one issue of slavery, largely in the image of the hated North. He proposed taking a rural, pastoral, semiliterate region and transforming it into a modern, industrial, self-sufficient "nation." Achieving this, he said, then the South "may apply the last remedy—the final alternative of separation, without bloodshed or severe shock." There lay the essence of his plan. He would make the South like the North not for its intrinsic betterment, but so that it could beat the North. If the South met its antagonist from a position of military, industrial, economic, and agricultural strength, then the abolitionists could be bluffed into guaranteeing Southern rights and secession need not occur. Ironically, in conceiving what would have been a brilliant future for his beloved region, he did so solely as a means of preserving an institution of the past.[3]

Davis was speaking right up to the day before he left to return to Washington on November 22. He complained that the abolition majority had reduced the South to a "permanent minority" in Congress and in the Electoral College, implying, without saying so, that somehow he felt the Union had an obligation not to allow any special interest group to achieve a majority. Perhaps he felt that states should only be admitted in twos, one slave and one free, in order to keep a parity in the Senate at least. If so, it was a naive expectation and an impractical one at that. But he took it seriously. As he boarded the *General Scott* for the return journey to Washington, he declared that "the time has arrived when all who love the Union or the Constitution should unite to throw an adequate shield over the minority; before it is driven to seek in arms that protection."[4]

A sectionwide convocation never came to pass. With an alacrity that distressed Davis, Southerners quickly acquiesced in the compromise measures, and in the end only Mississippi, Georgia, and South Carolina actually held state conventions, producing fulminations, resolutions, and nothing more. By that time he was back in the capital, without Varina this time, since the session would be a short one. He took a room at Mrs. Henry Hill's house, resumed his seat on December 5, and confided to friends the hope that the Senate would "work more and talk less in this session than last."[5]

Mercifully the session passed quickly, barely more than three months, and everyone seemed to take a breath after the tension of the previous sitting. Davis spent as much time on Smithsonian matters as he did in debate, and on the floor of the Senate he was as likely to speak for inventors' rights on patents or a defense of the coastal survey as on any of the more heated issues in the country. Twice he did rise to talk about the Fugitive Slave Law, and he also opposed a measure to keep American seamen from indulging in the slave trade in other countries. But more often than not he stayed in his seat. He, too, was tired, and sick and tired of the attacks on him whenever he spoke. "It is not my good fortune ever to find my opinions quoted on account of their value," he complained, "but only by some one who intends to show what is required by consistency, or fix me to some particular issue." He was tired of being quoted and misquoted and clearly evidenced a mounting suspicion of the press that afflicts many public men.[6]

Yet there were a few flashes of raised feeling, especially when a resolution was introduced in February to confer on Winfield Scott the honorary title of lieutenant general. Davis bristled, arguing that this would raise Scott above even the rank held by Washington, but his real opposition stemmed from his enduring loyalty to Taylor. If such honors were to be conferred on "individuals to gratify their just pride," then he argued that "he who beat the regular armies of Mexico, and disorganized her military power"—meaning Taylor—had a better claim to such an honor than "he who met the fragment of a beaten army"—meaning Scott. He paid a backhanded compliment to Scott, having had "some cause to remember him kindly," but had to add that "I might have some objection to particular acts of his." Nevertheless, he opposed the promotion on grounds of military principle and not because of personalities. Indeed, he always acted on principle, Davis declared, declining to engage "in any personal controversy as to [the] merits of individuals." Of course, he said that only a few minutes after he introduced the invidious comparison between Taylor's Mexican War achievements and Scott's. As usual, Davis never saw in himself what he condemned in others.[7]

Others were not so patient, and a few weeks later Henry Clay took Davis to task for lecturing the Senate during a discussion on a rivers and harbors bill. In fact, Davis first accused Clay of lecturing, but then Clay responded by asking "who most often endeavors to fill the lecturer's chair, that Senator or myself?" Davis denied that he ever did more than exercise his right as a Senator. His temper immediately flared, and it was Foote, of all people, who appealed for calm. 'We are getting on extremely well and very calmly," he said. "Nothing should excite us now." Of course, any such words from his enemy Foote were bound only to antagonize Davis, just as years before he had used calmness himself to antagonize Major Mason. Caught up in his outburst, Davis soon had to be reproved by the chair for referring to Clay's supporters as a "trained band." It was in the final hours of the session; important appropriations bills and a report from Davis's own Military Affairs Committee languished unattended, and his frustration got the better of him. Indeed, as he feared, a weeklong special session had to be called on March 4 to attend to unfinished business.[8]

No wonder he took comfort in his military and Smithsonian duties. There he was comfortable, unchallenged, and could feel not entirely powerless. He discussed with the other regents a plan to improve the Mall extending from the Capitol toward the Potomac, hoping to see it become "an extended landscape garden" with graveled walks and carriage drives. As for military matters, he was interested in the possibility that the camel, until then an object of curiosity exhibited in New York and elsewhere, might have a practical use in the desert areas of the Southwest. On January 21 he introduced a resolution that his committee be instructed to look into the propriety of using them for army transportation. By the end of the session, that resolution had become an amendment to the military appropriations bill, seeking $30,000 to buy fifty camels and their equipment and to employ ten Arab handlers for a year. The Senate rejected his amendment with some laughter, and resultant indignation on Davis's part, but he did not give up the idea. He rarely gave up.[9]

Davis had one last reason to rise in debate in the Senate on March 11, when he protested a bill appropriating $37,800 for sending 750 blacks captured from a slaver to the colony in Liberia. Years before, the American Colonization Society, an early emancipationist group, obtained a substantial territory on the west coast of Africa. There, in 1822, they created the Liberia colony, its capital at Monrovia named for then President James Monroe. Their plan was for voluntarily manumitted slaves, and those purchased for emancipation by philanthropists, to be repatriated to their ancestral continent, to what would eventually become their own country. Liberia did indeed become independent in 1846. However, its dual intent of being a means to end slavery *and* to remove free blacks from the United States to avoid racial tension and intermixture was never practical. Most slave-state leaders opposed the spending of any federal money on the experiment, and thus Davis now joined with Hunter of Virginia. They had nearly killed the appropriations bill a few days earlier, and now he tried to show that freed blacks sent back to Africa were being indentured by their so-called benefactors of the American Colonization Society. His objections were of little consequence in the end, and as he sat down he could hardly have expected that his voice would not be heard again in the Senate for another six years.[10]

By the end of March, Davis was back at home in Mississippi, thoroughly pleased to be out of Washington for several months, though he was hardly out of the maelstrom of politics. Already distressed by other states' failures to follow Mississippi, Georgia, and South Carolina by calling conventions, he saw Georgia retreating and believed that Mississippi would probably follow suit. More galling still, his archrival Foote had not been content with ardently supporting the 1850 Compromise measures. After being censured by the Mississippi legislature for his actions, Foote returned home and organized a new Union Democratic party, consisting of Union Democrats and old Whigs, which was determined to make a run for the governorship that fall. However much Davis deprecated Foote's policy, he could not underestimate the wily politician's abilities. Only South Carolina seemed to be standing true for Southern rights. Given this state of affairs, Davis considered his hopes of an assertive and powerfully united South to be moot. ("We are the defeated party," a friend lamented in April, "and, therefore, in no condition to make demands.") He decided that "we must wait, keeping our souls in patience." The agitation over slavery had only just begun, he believed. In time the oppression would become so great that the Southern people would reawaken to the danger; only then they would not seek remedies in the Constitution, and by then it would be too late.

Quitman was to run for the governorship again that fall and was already making suggestions that Mississippi should secede now. Davis asked friends what his course should be, and the wiser counseled caution, that he not identify himself with Quitman's premature notions. Secession might come, but the time was not now. When the Southern temper was right to act, the South would do so decisively and would not forget Davis. Indeed, one associate that year predicted to Jefferson Davis that ten years hence, in 1861, he would be hailed as the "President of a Southern Republic."[11]

Still, Davis felt that he needed to speak to the people of Mississippi to explain his actions as their senator. As usual, he scheduled an exhausting series of twenty-four public addresses from early May to mid-June, often speaking with Democratic candidates for office or other prominent Southern rights men. So hectic was the schedule that he often had to write to Varina from the speakers' stand itself.[12]

If Davis's public declarations that spring and summer may be believed, he had sickened of politics and expected to do no more than serve out his Senate term before returning to private life. Until then he would speak as loudly as his breath allowed for what he believed to be the rights of the South. To do so he started on a new course not previously seen in his speeches, and illustrating just how desperate he found the situation. He appealed to the poor whites of Mississippi, asserting that they must stand and be counted lest abolition elevate the Negro and thus place him on a level of equality. A white might now be poor, but he was still better than a black. Wealth did not distinguish between men in the South, he said, only color. "There is no such thing," he said, "as a distinction of property." Preservation of slavery was necessary for the preservation of "the *equality* of the *white race*." It was the closest thing to a demagogic appeal that Davis ever made, exactly the kind of rhetoric that he repeatedly condemned earlier. He had never mingled with, or spoken to the level of, the poor whites before; he had hardly needed them, for the political decisions in Mississippi in those days rested chiefly with the educated and the more affluent. But he needed the poor now, and he appealed to them on a level certain to claim their attention.

He continued to argue for his scheme of Southern growth and improvement to stand against the North, and he also still urged seeking to stay within the Union. But secession was a remedy available to them, and when asked if Mississippi should go to South Carolina's aid if it seceded and Washington attempted to use force to keep her in the Union, Davis did not equivocate. "I answer yes!" he said. *"I will meet force with force."* Meanwhile, there was a state convention coming in June, and wherever he spoke he urged the voters to send to that convention men determined to resist federal usurpation, men determined to oppose Foote and the so-called "submissionists."[13]

Davis, too, went to the convention in Jackson on June 16 and 17, and at once he found himself in an internal controversy. Quitman spoke too loud and too soon for secession, and that made him unpalatable to a fair segment of the party that wanted now more than ever to quell accusations of disunion sentiment, which would dilute the strength of their arguments against federal power. The nominating committee approached Davis to ask if he would take the nomination if Quitman withdrew. Then, as a sop, Quitman would be appointed to Davis's vacated Senate seat, for to run for governor Davis would have to resign. He agreed, leaving the question to Quitman, but the old general, whether out of ambition or the continuation of early strained feelings toward Davis, declined. Meanwhile, rumors of the proposed deal leaked out of the convention, and observers regarded with wonder that Davis might even consider such an "act of self-martyrdom" as accepting the nomination. The sentiment against a strident stand and for Foote's moderate position ran so high that many despaired of any Democrat winning the governor's mansion that year, even Davis. Almost certainly he felt the same.[14]

Nevertheless, though suffering from a relapse of his old fevers, Davis embarked yet again on the canvass for Quitman, scheduling fifteen meetings in the month after the convention adjourned. Already the summer sun and exhaustion worked on his eyes and his illness, but he pressed on. To his distress he found that many of the voters seemed not to grasp what he thought was the true intent of the compromisers in 1850. The rising swell of Unionism in Mississippi distressed him. "Foote is as industrious as a bee," he lamented, and that only contributed to the disinclination to take a strong states' rights stand. He believed only a few weeks into the canvass that Quitman could not be elected, or at least not by Democratic votes alone. For himself, he still hoped that a new state convention in the fall would repudiate the compromise.[15]

At least Davis took personal comfort from the manifestations of esteem that he saw everywhere. He spoke from stands with banners proclaiming THE HERO OF BUENA VISTA, TRUE TO THE SOUTH in bold letters. People suggested to him that in the next presidential election they would like to see him on the ticket as vice president, while yet others continued to proclaim that they felt Davis should be president of "a Southern Confederacy." Meanwhile, to those trying to fathom the man personally, he remained as elusive as ever. "This man Davis is a riddle to me," wrote one reporter that June. Seldom smiling, he could still get laughter or tears from an audience. "No perceptible emotion is ever seen to thrill his frame," and though "apparently stiff, starchy and affected, he is yet beloved." Joining the chorus of others who puzzled at Davis's aloof and unimpassioned manner, he concluded that "you mistake him for an icicle."[16]

Certainly Davis stayed cooler on the stump than he had in the Senate, repeating constantly his objections to the compromise measures, his disavowal of being a disunionist, his avowal of the right of secession if necessary, and the need for Southern states to band together in mutual support. But if Davis remained subdued, it was largely because of his increasingly frail health. Late in July he had to leave the canvass for several days, and then again in mid-August the fevers struck him so severely that he withdrew for over a month. His eyes, especially the left one, became dreadfully inflamed, and for some time he remained at the home of a friend, living in darkness. When finally he returned to Brierfield, Varina found him to be "a shadow of his former self." Light caused terrible pain to either eye, and for weeks he slept during the day, then paced the floors of Brierfield at night. In light so dim she could barely make out the furniture in the room, Varina sat up with him as he dictated to her his correspondence.[17]

Much happened while Davis recuperated. Foote gave Quitman a beating on the stump over the disunion issue, and the two literally came to blows in front of an audience in August. Worse, Unionists soundly defeated the states' rights candidates for the state convention by an overall majority of 7,500 early in September, making it obvious even to Quitman that he stood no chance at all of being elected in November. As a result, he resigned his candidacy on September 6. Two months before an election, the Democrats had no candidate.[18]

Immediately discussions began among the party managers. Several candidates were considered, but by mid-September a nominating committee in Jackson settled on Davis. By this time old Quitman had already called on the convalescent at Brierfield. Telling him that "I carry my State rights views to the citadel; you stop at the outworks," Quitman urged Davis to accept a nomination should it be proferred. By September 16 the party did offer him the position, and now Davis faced a personal dilemma. He had declined to consider the governorship in June and again in 1848, when an appointment had been offered. Clearly he was not intensely interested in the job. The overwhelming majority by which candidates sympathetic to him had been defeated in the September balloting obviously suggested that Foote would win no matter who opposed him. Worse, to run for this office, Davis would feel compelled to follow the convention of resigning his Senate seat, even though Foote had not resigned his. There seemed to be nothing at all to gain. But his party needed him. Someone had to stand before the voters to represent the views he felt so strongly. Someone had to uphold the principles that he knew in his heart to be right.

Thus he decided to accept. It may not have been so much of a sacrifice after all, for back in July he confided to Yulee that if the state convention to be elected in September endorsed the 1850 Compromise, he would be happy to "seek that post of honor which is found in a private station." Unwilling to represent the expressed procompromise sentiments of his state in the Senate, he may have been glad of this opportunity honorably to escape that duty by seeking an office he could not win. Thus he would be out of the dirty business of politics entirely without compromising his conscience and honor, and without abandoning the trust placed in him by Mississippians.[19]

Davis accepted the nomination on September 17 and six days later resigned his Senate seat. His friends received the news with undisguised joy and even began to predict victory. Many Democrats boycotted the polls in September, and the compromisers won with substantially less than a majority of the total number of eligible voters in the state. A popular man like Davis could bring the disaffected and discouraged back to the polls in November, and that 7,500 majority against the states' rights position might be turned around. Knowing him to be ill, party managers took it on themselves to draft an address for him, but when Varina read it to him in the dark he became frustrated at its turgid language and finally threw it out and dictated a paper of his own.[20]

The nominating committee promised Davis that they sought only the use of his name, and that they did not expect him to leave his sickbed to take the stump. Indeed, when they saw him they could hardly have expected him to leave home. Emaciated, apparently exhausted, he was all but blind in his left eye and so sensitive to light that he could not emerge outdoors without that eye being patched and bandaged and without wearing thick, green glass goggles to protect both eyes from sunlight. By late September he was still unable to leave home for a trip to a specialist in New Orleans. Through rest and darkness, the sight of his left eye slowly returned, though not fully. He washed it daily and took quinine and happily noted that a cloud once spread over the cornea had receded. Still, he was hardly in a condition to stand outdoors on a speaker's platform or a courthouse portico in the sunlight for hours, addressing a crowd and looking them eye-to-eye as was his wont. Yet he could not restrain himself. The competitive urge so much a part of his nature, added to growing feelings that the election might just be winnable after all, inevitably lured him out of his darkened room into the sunlight. By mid-October, with only three weeks of the canvass remaining, and with rumors actually circulating that he was dead, Jefferson

Davis took the stump to show Mississippi that he and the principles he stood for still lived.[21]

Davis left home for Jackson on or before October 20, and thereafter spoke in Columbis, Athens, Aberdeen, and Holly Springs, most of his speeches being in those eastern counties where voters had been told he was dead. He said the same things he had been saying for months, adding that he was not dead and "did not intend to die (politically) before the November election." As for Foote, he refrained from making substantial attacks on his opponent personally, though one potentially embarrassing issue arose late in the day. The Senate authorized its members to claim reimbursement for what it termed "constructive mileage," that is, payment for travel not made to and from home for special sessions when the senator was already in Washington. Davis and others opposed this in principle, but nevertheless it was allowed, and Davis himself, therefore, claimed the usual eight dollars for every twenty miles supposedly traveled. Here arose the issue, because Foote lived only forty miles from Davis, which would have entitled him to an extra sixteen dollars, yet he put in a claim for an additional five hundred dollars. The issue appeared too late to make much difference, and Davis and Foote argued it for years to come as a part of their perpetual personal feud.[22]

From elsewhere in the nation came support for Davis's uphill battle, especially from South Carolina, which now stood alone in its avowedly anticompromise and prosecession posture. Senator Robert Barnwell wrote to encourage Davis "in behalf of all true lovers of Southern rights" for keeping alive the flame in Mississippi. "You are still my file leader," he said, just as in the Senate. "I look to your prudence & courage to mark out the course of our struggle." As election day approached, many others watched as well, for despite all his denials, Davis was a leader now in the spiritual movement toward secession. He did not yet advocate its actual practice, but for more than a year now he had raised it as the only alternative should the majority in Congress not offer protection to Southern rights. By his repeated private declarations that such guarantees would never be forthcoming, his policy was a de facto advocacy of disunion. Without his admitting it—perhaps without his even realizing it in his own heart—Jefferson Davis by 1851 had become the premier champion of secession in his section. Others spoke much more stridently in their own states, as with Quitman and Barnwell, but only Davis now spoke for the South.[23]

Perhaps this helped to defeat him on November 4, but he lost by only a slender margin. Early returns showed Davis with a surprising majority in some counties, making it obvious that a number of Union Democrats were voting for him. The count proceeded slowly, and by November 6 it appeared possible that he might win. Even as late as November 12, with several counties still to tally, Foote held only a 1,000-

vote lead. Nevertheless, when the final totals appeared, Davis lost by the tiniest of margins: 999 out of 57,717 votes cast.[24] Considering that he had only three weeks to campaign, his friends felt assured that he would have won if nominated back in June. Even though they lost the governorship, Democrats took heart. Davis had reduced that 7,500 majority against them in September to almost nothing, and turned out thousands of previously apathetic voters at the same time. "His name was a magic sound in the ears of all ranks," Reuben Davis believed. "He was stronger in the State of Mississippi, not only than any man, but than any principle." Heartened, his friends expressed anxiety to "fight, under your standard, another political battle," said Reuben Davis. The defeat was a moral victory for the candidate, and made him "the head and front of the Democracy in this State and the whole South." Inevitably, he said, Jefferson Davis would one day be a president.[25]

Davis may have thought he would get a rest now. Only a week after the definitive tally came out, he told a fellow planter that "separated from the exciting strife of politicians we may the more profitably look on the whirl of their bubbles, and perhaps better than they see when and why their bubbles will burst." But if Davis thought he was out of that whirl, then his own bubble burst very quickly. The Democratic State Convention would meet in Jackson on January 8, 1852, to select its delegates to the national nominating convention in June. Naturally Davis attended as a delegate from Warren County, and it is no surprise that convention managers called on him to make the keynote address. Having turned down an offer of reappointment to his vacant Senate seat from outgoing Governor James Whitfield, Davis was still a private citizen, but easily the most influential in the state. Thus his appeal to all Democrats to come home to their party and the states' rights principles that had been its foundation attracted wide approval. They had to unite with all Democrats in the nation to "wrest the administration from the imbecile hands into which it had fallen," meaning Taylor's Whig successor, Millard Fillmore. Another imbecile, whom Davis termed a "mere demagogue," was Foote, elected to the governorship in a campaign he characterized as "Fraud and Falsehood and Free-Soil and Foote and Fillmore." To erase the stain of Foote on Mississippi, Democrats had to reassert states' rights in their choice of national candidates.[26]

Without realizing it, Davis thus commenced with Foote what became known as the "newspaper war." Foote responded in his inaugural two days later, causing Davis to charge in January that he had resigned his Senate seat when Foote had not, and that Foote had used that seat to attack Davis for being a disunionist. Foote responded in the press with a veiled impugning of Davis's vaunted military career and a return to the disunion charges. Davis in turn called Foote a slanderer and liar, and Foote then accused Davis of getting only a rump nomination for governor from a little group of "secessionists." Davis called the attacks "one of the coarsest and most scurrilous productions which has ever disgraced the newspaper press of the South." Of course, Davis could not let Foote's slanders stand, coming as they did from "an habitual defamer." He wrote and published a massive rejoinder in mid-February, concluding that he was heartily weary of the whole controversy, which, of course, he had started in his keynote address. Foote ended the rather embarrassing exchange by refusing to continue the newspaper salvos, and the Democratic press of the state was heartily glad that he did. "Unless you cease your bickering," one editor said in print to both men, "we will select others under whose guidance we can secure more harmony and good feeling."[27]

When the furor abated, Davis actually enjoyed a period of retirement to private life. Only from afar did he watch national public events. Friends kept him apprised of sentiment toward potential nominees that summer, Douglas and Cass both being mentioned, along with James Buchanan of Pennsylvania. Now and again a suggestion of Davis for the vice presidency emerged, though he probably did not entertain the idea seriously. Besides, as Varina said, they needed to "put our home in order." The new house at Brierfield was finally completed, but through their continual absence much had suffered. "What isn't broke is crack," said a servant, "and what isn't crack is broke." Davis, always fond of trees and shrubs, ordered apple, plum, pear, and peach saplings to plant in his orchard. He and Varina worked together happily in the garden for much of the day, Davis especially finding joy in the roses that no doubt reminded him of his mother and Rosemont in his youth. Almost every day they rode when possible, entertained visiting neighbors, or retired to read quietly on the veranda, where the air was "redolent of the perfume of the moss, flowers, wild crab-apple and plum blossoms."[28]

Varina could see her husband letting down, relaxing as the tensions of tumultuous years slowly drained away. All was well between them now, and that surely helped. "Winnie," as he called her, read such books as *The Guide to Social Happiness* and other works designed to show women their proper role, telling her husband that "it will help 'Winnie' to be 'Wife.' " Davis himself confessed that caring for his slaves, building the plantation, and raising his small herd of cattle all made the time pass with unaccustomed pleasantness. "Do come and see Jeff for the first time with no political troubles," Varina wrote her mother in March, "and see how agreeable he is."[29]

Even while his plantation and his contentment grew, something else was growing as well. Jefferson and Varina had conceived a child early the previous November, indeed, within days of the election, and as the spring of 1852 progressed they watched her pregnancy advance. By early July, Varina's time was near, and they ordered a special low bed and material for diapers from New Orleans. Later in the month many of Varina's family came to be with her, while other affairs took Davis away from Brierfield, and she chided him that "your wife's courage is giving out about your staying away at such a time." But he came home in time to be there on July 30 when his first child was born. They named him Samuel Emory Davis after the grandfather the baby never saw and the father Jefferson Davis barely knew.

It was a touching scene that day. Every slave on the plantation came to the house with little gifts for the baby boy. They offered eggs and baby chicks from their private flocks and yams from their little plots. Each of the slave women kissed the little one, hailing him as their "little massa" and declaring that he would never have to work.

Sadly for his father, the baby did not receive good wishes from one very special slave. James Pemberton died that summer, and in him Davis lost a friend whom he never replaced. Henceforth Ben Montgomery from Hurricane would attend to Brierfield at times, and Davis himself would go through a seemingly endless string of white overseers, finding fault with each, usually over their treatment of his slaves. He would not allow his blacks to be whipped and insisted that their health be of paramount importance to his crops. Consequently, his income from Brierfield, especially when he was absent, sometimes dwindled alarmingly. Yet it was characteristic of him to champion the defenseless, even at his own cost. Varina, as so often, put her finger on the essential truth of him. "The truly generous temper of my husband was best exhibited toward his inferiors," she said. Slaves, children, women—all responded warmly to Jefferson Davis, and he to them. What they all had in common was that in their place and time, they were subordinate to a white male. On that basis of inferiority, Davis could deal with them openly and generously, because in the end they always had to be deferential, and something in his makeup needed deference. When Varina did not adopt that attitude some years before, he left her and became miserable. It also explains his increasingly frequent confrontations in public life. Other white males stood every bit his equal. They paid no deference to anyone if they did not so choose. Davis's pride and his rigid belief in the superiority of his positions and conclusions left him ill equipped to accept with equanimity the dissent of others. In short, he could not handle strong-willed men like himself; he could not deal with equals.[30]

The interlude Davis enjoyed away from the arena of those confrontations proved, as usual, to be all too brief. Indeed politics took him away from Brierfield during the last month of Varina's pregnancy. Early in June the Democrats met in national convention to choose their nominees. The balloting for president ran long and inconclusively until, on the forty-ninth vote, a complete dark horse captured the nomination, Franklin Pierce of New Hampshire. In the subsequent vote for vice president, William R. King gained the nomination, though not before New York and Illinois had cast their ballots for Davis. The news delighted the Mississippian. For fifteen years he and Pierce had been close, since their meeting during Davis's first trip to Washington. He regarded the nominee as a true friend of the South and of Southern rights, a man sound on every issue. Indeed, Davis may already have commenced with Pierce the same mental sanctification he conceived for Taylor and Calhoun. Certain it is that this was a candidate Jefferson Davis wanted to see in the White House.

As soon as word of Pierce's nomination reached him, he left for Jackson to address a large meeting of state Democrats. Hardly able to contain his elation at the nominees, and at the apparently confused state of the Whig opposition, he called for a united effort to regain the presidency. A month later he commenced a series of speeches in support of the national ticket, even going out of the state to Memphis, and returning home only for Samuel's birth. Through much of August and more of October, he stayed on the stump. When Winfield Scott became the Whig nominee, Davis finally abandoned his previous restraint when discussing the general and gave vent to the frustration he still felt from the days of the war. He spoke for Taylor now, as well as for Pierce, when he called Scott's actions in 1847 "peevish" and Scott himself "proud, petulant, vain and presumptuous."

Davis tried to withdraw somewhat from his outspoken position on secession and a Southern confederation, now that Pierce's candidacy seemed to lessen the threat to slavery. When asked if twenty years hence there would be "a Southern Republic," he replied that he believed not, nor did he want to see it. In the dark depths of the summer of 1851, he might have felt that might be the only course left for Southerners, but now he saw hope in Pierce.[31]

His eyes kept Davis off the road in September. The disease appeared in May and got steadily worse, aggravated considerably by problems at Davis Bend that even the appearance of his son could not erase. For the first time in their lives, Jefferson and Joseph had a serious falling out over an issue that Varina thought to be of "a very irritating character." Even before Samuel's birth, Davis spoke of moving away from Brierfield and buying a home elsewhere. Then, when his brother made a new will after the baby arrived, Joseph became excited, especially when he heard a rumor that Jefferson intended to sell the plantation—which, of course, was not his to sell. Seriously upset, perhaps resentful of his continuing reliance on Joseph, and frustrated by his eye problems, Davis seems to have let all these influences combine to run down his system. Even his Mexican War wound caused him trouble, and one friend reported seeing him on crutches about this time. Varina complained that he ate barely enough to sustain a child. His eye problem lasted well into the fall, and his ire with Joseph perhaps considerably longer, for in January 1853 he bought from Varina's parents a place near New Orleans. It seemed inconceivable that he should think of leaving Mississippi, but believing himself possibly out of elective office for good, he could continue the fight for Southern rights in any venue, even Louisiana.[32]

But Davis never moved to the new property. As always, relations with Joseph calmed as the bond between them refused to be broken. Undoubtedly the excitement of politics grasped him again as it always did, especially with the potential for a friendly man in the Executive Mansion. Davis even believed that the state legislature might likely elect him to the Senate post Foote had vacated for the new term commencing in March 1853. A trip to New Orleans to see an eye specialist and to look at the property he would buy probably kept him away from home on election day. If not, he certainly voted for Franklin Pierce. To his delight, for once he stood with the majority, albeit a slim one. Pierce outpolled Scott handsomely, though four other candidates took more than 170,000 votes from both, leaving Pierce with a margin of just 50,000 of the total votes cast. But he carried every state but four, and his victory in the Electoral College was crushing.[33]

Quite likely Davis wrote to his friend congratulating him on his victory. However, he may not have expected the letter he received from Pierce in mid-December, even as he sought to recover from another bout of the fevers and eye inflammation. Referring with warmth to their close friendship, the president-elect said that "I much desire to see you." He wanted Davis's advice on a number of issues, not least being selections for his cabinet. Then he offered a very circumspect hint. "I am not permitted to know, that you would accept a place in it if desired," he said, but the mere fact of his raising the question was no doubt intended to prompt Davis to indicate whether or not he would be amenable. Seemingly obsessed with secrecy, he even suggested to Davis a simple code by which he could telegraph his willingness to come to Washington. He asked that any mail be addressed to a third party.[34]

Varina begged Davis not to accept. They had a new baby, a new home they had hardly inhabited, his health was frail, and she wearied of sharing her husband with Washington. She did not need to plead too hard, for Davis himself felt tired of public life. Many men thrived on it, and intellectually so did he, but the way he threw himself into it—as into anything—took a terrible toll on him physically and emotionally. The decision, then, may have come easily, and on December 27 he wrote cordially to Pierce and asked that he not be considered for a cabinet post. He would certainly come to Washington in March for the inauguration, but after that he would return to Mississippi.[35]

When Pierce received Davis's letter, he accepted almost apologetically the latter's reasons for declining. He also gave evidence that his efforts at secrecy were well founded, for he wrote on January 12, 1853, that "politicians seem to have troubled themselves very much on account of the friendly relations supposed to exist between us." Indeed they did. Days before, on January 1, Albert Brown wrote to Davis from Washington that men generally believed that Pierce had offered the Mississippian a cabinet portfolio. More than that, most suspected that Davis would be secretary of war, and men who met with the president-elect came away with the feeling that his mind lay fixed in the matter. A number of Davis's friends in Washington, without his knowledge, actually pushed an appointment on Pierce. R. M. T. Hunter of Virginia even went to New Hampshire to press the case, partly out of friendship for Davis and also from a conviction that Southern rights men should be represented in the cabinet. Where Davis was concerned, of course, Pierce needed no persuading. As for Brown and the others, "It will satisfy me fully," he said, "if he so far respects the wishes & feelings of the State Rights men of Mississippi as to appoint their recognized leader to a cabinet office."[36]

Undoubtedly more communication took place between Pierce and Davis, and the door to a cabinet post, closed in December, reopened. Too many men spoke of it, too many in the South wanted it, and Davis himself may have begun to feel a growing compulsion both from a sense of duty to the South as well as a meaner motive. Mississippi was entitled to a place in the cabinet. Davis was first choice, obviously, but if he declined, then probably any appointment would go to Brown. The two were uneasy friends at best and would hate each other before the year was out. Davis may very well have reconsidered his position in order to keep Brown from getting the appointment. In either case, Davis's mind cannot have been entirely fixed in the matter when he left Brierfield on or around February 22. Indeed, communicating through Pierce's intermediary, Davis at least discussed being in Washington three weeks before the inauguration, with no discernable purpose other than to confer with the president-elect. Events prevented him from doing so, however, and in fact he reached the capital on March 5, the day after the inauguration. He went to the White House to greet and congratulate its new occupant, and Pierce devoted much of the day to convincing Davis to accept the war portfolio. In the end, the president had his way, and on March 7 the Senate confirmed the appointment and Davis took his oath of office.[37] Little could he or the nation know that in taking charge of an executive department for the next four years, he would, thought many, be taking charge of a weak and ineffectual executive as well.

13

I Am Paying Dearly Indeed

The day after taking his oath, Davis met formally with the leading officers of the army, including such men as Generals Twiggs and Persifor Smith, John E. Wool, and of course Winfield Scott. The Scott meeting must have been a bit stiff after Davis's remarks about him during the past campaign, but any real strain between them did not surface publicly. As usual in Washington, everyone was still too excited over the change in government. There were balls almost every night, a White House dinner for departing President Fillmore, and a host of scurrying office and patronage seekers. Pierce held his first formal cabinet meeting on March 9, and then Davis met the rest of the men with whom he would share the president's time and trust for the next four years.

Most of them he already knew. William L. Marcy of New York held what was usually considered the premier position as secretary of state. He and Davis were destined by nature not to get along well, for they shared some common traits. "He was not a genial man," Varina said of him, "and too much in earnest to spare time for social intercourse." James Guthrie of Kentucky held the Treasury post, and Davis knew and liked him from the days of his youth at St. Thomas Academy. Massachusetts Brahmin Caleb Cushing would be attorney general, and he and Davis formed an instant alliance of like minds, for Cushing—like Pierce—stood with the Southern rights men on the Constitution. Postmaster General James Campbell came from Philadelphia, but he and Davis became cordial friends who, between them, could never remember more than one disagreement. Pierce owed much of his nomination to James C. Dobbin of North Carolina, and accordingly gave him a post as secretary of the navy. He, too, would enjoy excellent relations with the secretary of war. The Department of the Interior went to Robert Mc-Clelland, a Michigander with whom Davis had only a passing acquaintance.[1]

The salient feature of this cabinet was the preeminent standing of Marcy and Davis. The aging Guthrie was never a forceful man in public life. Dobbin was already frail and of nervous disposition and would barely live past his term of office. Campbell, like most postmasters general, was a cipher on the national scene, and McClelland, having been governor of Michigan, seemed to have little ambition left in him. Only Cushing enjoyed a rising national reputation, and it did not at all measure up to Davis's. From first to last, these three men—Davis, Marcy, and Cushing, in that order—would be the prime influences acting on the president.

Even while getting to know his fellow cabinet secretaries, Davis had to reacquaint himself with the War Department. As often as he had dealt with it as an officer, and later on the Military Affairs Committee, now he saw it from the inside. Standing second only to State in seniority, the War Department consisted of a number of general staff departments or bureaus, each administering separate functions of the army. Most had self-explanatory titles and incumbent chiefs who had been in place seemingly forever. The adjutant general handled correspondence and record keeping, recruiting when necessary, the assignment of officers, and the formal promulgation of War Department orders. Colonel Samuel Cooper had held the post just a few months when Davis arrived. Davis first met Cooper on his 1837 trip to Washington, and the high recommendation given then and later by Franklin Pierce was enough to win Cooper's esteem. Now they forged an even closer union as the adjutant impressed the secretary with his fairness and lack of prejudice. They would be friends for life. The inspector general managed every variety of inspection on order, and Sylvester Churchill had been doing it for more than eleven years. Judge Advocate General John Lee took office in 1849 and administered the legal affairs of the military. Henry Craig headed the Ordnance Department that obtained and managed weaponry, and, as commissary general, George Gibson oversaw Subsistence, where for thirty-six years he had fed and clothed the army. Thomas Jesup ran the quartermaster general's office. Surgeon General Thomas Lawson was in his sixteenth year of directing the Medical Department, while Paymaster General Nathan Towson did just what his title implied. The Corps of Engineers answered to Joseph G. Totten and had done so for fifteen years, just as long as John J. Abert directed the Corps of Topographical Engineers, which made maps and studied positions likely for military defense of the coastline.[2]

Many of these men Davis knew at least by passing acquaintance from his own army days, especially Cooper, who had served on Scott's staff in the 1830s. A few were superannuated officers far too long in place, though the army had no set retirement policy and, in the absence of one, Davis would not attempt to force them out of office immediately. He would work with what he had, and most of them, being deskbound by career, proved to be the pliable sort who deferred to the new secretary's wishes.

The army itself had changed little from his own days in uniform. Authorized to number 13,821 men and officers, it really mustered little more than 10,000 at any time, most of them scattered across thousands of miles of frontier and coastal fortifications. With America's traditional suspicion of a large standing army in peacetime, the old regular service was constantly kept bouncing between the needs of an expanding territory and the parsimony of a Congress that rarely saw the need to spend money on the military when the country did not face the threat of war.[3]

Managing such a charge could be a thankless task, made easier only by the fact that most cabinet secretaries of the era attracted little notice from the people and entered and left their posts as almost forgotten men, at least so far as their cabinet service was concerned. Indeed, many worried that by taking the war post, Davis would be eclipsed just at the time when his star on the national scene shone the brightest. "Worse than a crime," a New Orleans editor responded to the early rumors of Davis's acceptance, "it would be a mistake." When rumors said that Free-Soiler John Dix might have a seat in Pierce's cabinet, the Southern press howled. Davis should not sit at the same table with such a man, they cried. "Just think of Jeff Davis and John A. Dix sitting at the same council board discussing a question growing out of, or connected with slavery!" Even once the cabinet appointments were definitely fixed, many expected Davis to clash with Marcy, who had himself been secretary of war in a prior administration.[4]

In large measure they all underestimated Davis. Despite his strong and often strident beliefs, he rarely made them a personal matter and enjoyed cordial relations with a number of his most outspoken political opponents. Yet he did face a host of foes in the years ahead, most of them within his department and a few within himself. Most immediately he confronted an administrative challenge that would have overwhelmed many others with his limited executive background. He had been a quartermaster occasionally, a staff officer, and managed a plantation intermittently, but none of this constituted real preparation for the War Department. Besides himself and General-in-Chief Scott, his offices in a red-brick building just northwest of the White House contained ninety-two clerks, ten messengers, and even five watchmen, not to mention a ten-thousand-volume library. With this staff he had to manage all the affairs, paperwork, and maintenance of the army in the field.[5]

In his very first days in his office, Davis discovered one of the facts of life in a cabinet post—patronage. With a new administration in town, a host of Democrats expected a piece of the "spoils"—a term coined some years before by Marcy, as it happened. A crowd of office seekers descended in the second week of March, forcing Davis to make probably his first substantive policy decision. There would be no spoils. Good clerks already in place would keep their jobs, despite their politics, so long as they performed satisfactorily. He told the crowd that when incompetent clerks were removed, he would then consider new applicants not for their politics but on their "merits." Early in April another band of some forty office seekers called on him with a testimonial and a petition some three feet long, demanding their rewards as Democrats. Demands were the last way to approach Jefferson Davis. He listened quietly, coldly, and then told them that only death, resignation, or incompetence would put any of his clerks out of a job. They all left disappointed, but the word soon spread around Washington not to expect this secretary to play by the usual rules.[6]

Indeed, Davis very quickly revealed an instinctive reaction to attempts to pressure him, no matter what the source, and the attempts were many. When a number of Southern congressmen sent him a petition suggesting Captain Randolph B. Marcy for command of a survey of a proposed railroad from the Mississippi to the west coast, Davis bristled at "the attempt to influence, by political considerations, my selection of officers." It may not have helped that the captain was a relation to William Marcy. In June members of the new California legislature made an effort to have Colonel Ethan A. Hitchcock, the same man who had arrested Davis a couple of times at West Point, removed from his command of military forces in the Pacific Division. Again Davis bristled. "You need have no apprehension that in my administration of the War Department, officers of the Army will be viewed through a political medium," Davis assured Hitchcock. At the same time, however, Davis stood for equal opportunities for Democrats. When he learned that some Whig officers refused to employ civilian laborers on the basis of their politics, Davis directed that the practice be stopped immediately. He would not give a job to a man because of his political affiliation, and neither would he allow that cause to prevent a man's employment.[7]

Greater concerns confronted him in the organization of his own department. He had not finished his first three months in office before clashes with some department heads tainted relations. Since officers obtained those positions by seniority, they became essentially permanent incumbents. They left only when they died or chose to retire, regardless of age or competence, and they devoted a considerable effort to perpetuating themselves. He saw how the service suffered under this rigid application of seniority, and tried unsuccessfully to correct the problem, hoping to implement a rotation system between staff and line officers, allowing him to appoint men to head his departments for limited tours of duty. The reaction was predictable. Congress declined to authorize his efforts, and the senior men in the army became incensed. Foes attacked his "specious arguments and dogmatic assertion," accusing him of trying to gratify "personal aims, prejudices, or a spirit of nepotism." Indeed, if he had succeeded in his plan, quite probably old friends like Northrop and Johnston would have found themselves with staff assignments, but even if this would have gratified a temporary desire on Davis's part, the permanent abolition of these virtual appointments for life would still have done lasting good for the service.[8]

These clashes, at least, remained relatively behind the closed doors of Congress and the department. Unfortunately, Davis's encounters with others, including some of his leading officers, became much more public, sometimes embarrassingly so. In 1854 he feuded with Commissioner of Indian Affairs George Manypenny over the blame for a small massacre by the Sioux near Fort Laramie, and eventually the feud found its way into the press, with rumors flying that Davis threatened to resign if Manypenny were not dismissed.[9] More serious was the battle Davis carried on with General John E. Wool. The two knew each other from their days in Mexico, and though seventy years old in 1854, Wool remained an active and energetic officer. Their relations were good up to the time that Davis took office, and in 1853 he appointed the general to command of the Department of the Pacific. Then things began to go bad. At San Francisco in February 1854, Wool reportedly made remarks critical of the Pierce administration that got into the press. Immediately the secretary's correspondence assumed a cool and formal tone, the more so when Wool took it upon himself to arrest locally organized filibusterers intent on seizing more of Mexico. When the 1850 Compromise seemingly put an end to hopes of new slave states from the existing territories, the acquisition of Cuba and more of Mexico—by conquest if necessary—became for Davis an acceptable alternative, though obviously the government could never do so. Some even speculated that he took his cabinet post partially in the hope of being able to aid in the annexation of Cuba. While he would do nothing overt to aid in such adventuring, Davis did not work actively to hinder it either.[10]

Throughout 1854 Wool repeatedly attempted to restrain filibusters, sending Davis a series of pleas for more men and equipment for the purpose. By August Davis called Wool to account for his attitude of complaint and reproach, reminding him that while he held a high commission, "you assume an obligation to render due respect." A month later Davis told Marcy that if he could make use of Wool in some diplomatic employment, "I could bear to be deprived of him." By October the San Francisco papers carried reports that he was persecuting Wool, and soon thereafter Davis wrote him lengthy lectures that must have taken hours to compose, each one reciting the history of their relations, with dates and times, rules and regulations, and all the other hallmarks of a Davis case in presentation. Their correspondence became increasingly vituperative, and in the end, the controversy sank to petty levels. In 1854 Congress authorized the presentation to Wool of a magnificent gold-and-silver mounted sword for his career services. At the time, Davis endorsed the idea and told Wool to expect it in due time. By the fall of 1855 the sword sat in the hands of the War Department, and Davis promised that it would be sent soon. But the sword never left his office. For more than a year Davis kept Wool's saber, and in the end the general did not receive it until 1857, after Davis left office.[11]

But of all Davis's feuds in his military family, surely the most publicly damaging, and personally unflattering, would be his enduring battle with Winfield Scott. In 1853, when Davis took office, relations between them were already formal at best. Davis's well-known association with Scott's bitter enemy Taylor, and his uncomplimentary comments about the general during the 1852 presidential canvass, certainly combined to leave Scott with little good will toward the man now placed over him. Scott's own vanity, hauteur, and resentment of any authority other than the president himself did the rest. As for Davis, in private he probably had detested Scott since 1846 solely from his affection for Taylor. The general's standing in opposition to Pierce, another of his heroes, did not help. As a result, now that he was in a position of some authority over the general, Davis would not go out of his way to be obliging. Probably even in his most introspective moments, Davis never admitted that he might also be exacting a bit of revenge.

They clashed quickly. In May, Davis disallowed Scott's application for reimbursement of travel expenses, and on this issue alone the two argued for the next two years. Later Davis took Scott to task for more than $20,000 still unaccounted for that he had disbursed during the war with Mexico. A year later Davis challenged Scott's claim to additional pay because of his brevet rank as lieutenant general. By this time, Scott had already taken his headquarters and, in a fit of petulance, removed it to New York, just as he had done when Taylor was president.[12]

The open warfare broke out in July 1855 when Davis learned that Scott had given Hitchcock a four-month leave of absence without, he thought, sufficient grounds. Davis asked for an explanation. Scott replied in a childishly petulant tone, called Davis's letter "dogmatic," and implied that Scott was really only subject to the president. Of course this was exactly the tone best calculated to arouse Davis. He soon responded, escalating the pettiness, calling Scott "peevish" and giving him a lecture on the proper relation of the general-in-chief to the secretary of war. Davis's response had been three times the length of Scott's offending letter, and Scott quintupled that in his sarcastic reply. He accused Davis of aggrandizing his own authority by trying to usurp duties and responsibilities that regulations reserved for the commanding general. "Your object," he accused, "is evidently to crush me into a servile obedience to your self-will." "I know your obstinacy," said Scott. Davis responded a few days later in a letter, written privately and not in his official capacity, which, sent to a younger man, might have provoked a challenge. Calling Scott's assertions "malevolent, and . . . utterly false," he said little else. Scott, however, was not to be ignored. He came back with a threat to make their letters public as an "example to be shunned by your successors," protesting that he was an innocent party and that their controversy was entirely of Davis's making.

This only provoked Davis more. With all that he had to do in his office, he spent much of the next month composing what Scott contemptuously called "the book," a letter that filled twenty-seven foolscap pages with glistening venom. He called Scott "a vain controversialist, defeated, and a false accuser exposed." There followed the lecture of all lectures. As was his custom, Davis restated Scott's arguments in his own words, thereby often altering their intent, that he might better attack and demolish them.

Scott responded with a "book" of his own, point by point. He called Davis's reasoning "criminal," a manifestation of "tyrannical will," filled with "stabbing innuendos and other outrages, without regard to truth, honor, or law." Davis referred the correspondence to date to Pierce, suggesting that things would run much more smoothly if army headquarters were moved from New York back to Washington. Scott's "persistent disobedience" could be overcome if henceforward all orders relating to the army should come exclusively from the War Department. In effect, Davis would treat Winfield Scott as if he did not exist, and the fact is that during his entire tenure in the War Department, Davis never saw his general-in-chief in person more than once or twice.

Meanwhile the secretary of war continued the scramble for the last word, blissfully unmindful that he and Scott were both behaving like children. Now he sneered at Scott's 1810 court-martial, then called him a thief in everything but name for keeping money taken from Mexico at the end of the late war. In January 1856 Scott responded, accusing Davis of a recklessness that stemmed "from one whose low ambition is flattered with the title of *The Favourite*." The shameful affair did not end until the spring of 1856, after the exchange of several more increasingly infantile letters. Indeed, Scott accused Davis of trying to taunt him into a duel, and Davis responded by referring to the general's unwillingness in an affair years earlier "to act upon the sentiment which makes a gentleman responsible to any one whom he assails." In short, Davis implied that Scott was a coward. "Your petulance, characteristic egoism and recklessness of accusation have imposed upon me the task of unveiling some of your deformities," said Davis, "marked by querulousness, insubordination, greed of lucre and want of truth." Scott replied in kind, even hinting at the ridiculousness of their exchange by calling a letter from Davis "more last words," and closing his own with the almost teasing sentiment, "what next?" Poor Hitchcock became a casualty of the feud, resigning his commission late in 1855, sick of the controversy and sick of Jefferson Davis.

By May 1856 the antagonists had done everything but stick out their tongues at each other. Longer intervals separated their letters as each, no doubt, tired of the fun. Scott's final blast came on May 21. "Compassion is always due to an enraged imbecile," he said. No one could get the last word on Davis, of course. In a single paragraph he closed their correspondence, gratified to be "relieved from the necessity of further exposing your malignity and depravity."[13]

Of course it all got into the newspapers, even while the letters were being written, and the press had a delicious time with it. Which of the two of them provided it to editors is uncertain, though since each threatened to make it public, probably both made good the threats. In time, though, the press tired of it, and even became itself embarrassed by the almost infantile nature of the exchange. "It is deeply to be regretted," *Harper's Weekly* said in an otherwise complimentary profile of Davis not long afterward, "that his disagreements with the Commander-in-chief . . . were ever suffered to see the light." An editor back in his own Mississippi minced no words at all. "We regard the correspondence as disgraceful to both parties concerned," as indeed it was. Few who knew him would have disputed any of the flaws in Scott's character; the correspondence with Davis only confirmed them.

But for Davis it revealed aspects of his character only hinted at in his previous dealings, and to depths that few previously would have suspected. Worse, it revealed them to the public. From the whole sorry business, nothing good can be said for the secretary of war. Vanity, obstinacy, imperiousness, pettiness, petulance, and more all revealed their substantial presence in his makeup. All that kept them in check was that same veneer of dignity that kept all his other passions and emotions under control, and it took nothing more than the challenge of a strong-willed man for them to burst their bonds. It should have been a severe embarrassment for Davis in 1857 when the Senate, having seen portions of the correspondence in the nation's press, asked for copies of the entire exchange and then published it. It should have been an embarrassment but, convinced of his blamelessness, Davis quite probably felt no dismay at all, thinking that it made only Scott look like a fool.[14]

Even if Winfield Scott is set aside as an extreme and special case, still Davis was not popular with a number of the officers in the Army, and more than a few regarded him as high-handed and even imperial. Part of the problem came from the fact that he was the most active, energetic, and involved secretary of war in decades. Davis went about this post exactly the way he approached everything else he undertook, thoroughly, methodically, and perhaps a bit to excess. Previous war ministers were most often career politicians with no experience of the military and no interest in it. Davis marked a radical change, which meant that an entrenched military system accustomed to having its own way with little or no interference from a cabinet member was bound to react unfavorably. Scott and Wool were only the most visible examples.

From the outset, Davis looked at the officer corps itself. He might not be able to achieve his goals with the staff department commanders, but he could make his influence felt lower down the line, out in the field. He involved himself directly in appointments, promotions, and retirements, and almost every other species of task. Working out of his small office behind the stairway, midway along the south side of the building, he calmly chipped away at the problems of the Army as he saw them, and with his characteristic indifference to—or inability to see—the sensibilities that his acts might offend. He was only doing what was right and logical, therefore no one had any legitimate reason for complaint. Yet very soon rumors went through the army that only his favorites got the promotions and choice appointments. "Jeff Davis and his crowd conferred all such favors on a coterie called the 'Coburg families,'" complained Godfrey Weitzel, an 1855 Academy graduate.

It was more rumor than truth. Certainly Davis looked out for Johnston, his old friend and hero. When he succeeded in getting Congress to approve two new mounted regiments, Davis took a large hand in choosing their officers, and he gave Sidney Johnston the colonelcy of the 2d Cavalry. Indeed, critics would later charge that Davis filled the ranks of the regiment's field officers with old friends and fellow Southerners. The accusation carried a germ of truth, perhaps, greatly exaggerated. Johnston's next in command was the Virginian Robert E. Lee. Majors were Virginian George H. Thomas and Georgian William J. Hardee. Captains included Earl Van Dorn and Edmund Kirby Smith, and in the ranks of the lieutenants were such younger men as John B. Hood. Yet there were nearly as many Yankees represented in the commissions granted, and of all of the officers, only Johnston could certainly be regarded as a favorite of Davis's. He got the appointment even though other senior officers were available, just as Davis's old dragoon associate Edwin Sumner got the colonelcy of the First Cavalry. Davis would argue that he chose men on the basis of their ability and not their seniority.[15]

The balance was the same in the First Cavalry, and in the two new infantry regiments also created in 1855. What caused more of an outcry was the number of men given direct commissions from civil life, almost all of them politically motivated, and probably the cost Davis and Pierce had to bear for winning congressional approval. Almost half of the officers in the four new regiments, mostly lieutenants, would be such appointees, and they aroused bitter hostility in the regular ranks and among West Pointers. Even these "creatures" of Davis's, as they were called, came from all across the nation, revealing little or no sectional bias.[16]

Davis went after reform everywhere. He tried unsuccessfully to circumvent the seniority system and introduce promotions on the basis of merit alone. He tried, again without success, to correct the confused system of awarding brevet, or honorary, rank to officers when no real vacancies existed at higher levels. It led to unending confusion and problems of proper pay and allowances. For the enlisted men, Davis succeeded in getting a four-dollar-per-month increase in pay, with bonuses to encourage reenlistments.[17]

In overseeing the War Department, Jefferson Davis managed a total annual expenditure of nearly twenty million dollars, all of it with little complaint and hardly a penny unaccounted for. It amounted to almost a third of the entire appropriation for the running of the whole government. The soldiers that he kept in the field were scattered throughout six major departments west of the Mississippi, and the massive Department of the East on the other side of the river. During his four years in office, he oversaw the increase of the effective strength of the army from 10,417, with 8,378 in the frontier service, to a total of 15,562. Besides looking out for their welfare while in uniform, Davis steadily pressed for a system of pensions for the widows and orphans of those who died while in the service. He also implemented new designs in uniforms and equipment, one of which, the "Jeff Davis" hat, would carry his name throughout its years of service. Understandably, considering his own experience with the Whitney rifle in Mexico, he took a keen interest in the newest technological developments in arms. In the rifled shoulder weapon he saw an end to the need for light-caliber field cannon, for rifles would now be more useful against personnel. He supervised experiments on a host of things, from wrought-iron carriages instead of wooden ones for cannon to the metal used in the cannon themselves. For the foot soldiers, he introduced a standard rifled weapon that used the hollow-based conical minié bullet and a special priming system for speedy and effective fire, and ordered all the older flintlock muskets converted to this same or a percussion-cap system and rifled as well. "The propriety and necessity of using only the best and most effective arms is obvious," he told Pierce in 1856. He also took an interest in even-faster-firing breech-loading rifles, but none were available for practical tests before he left office.

Moreover, Davis began the construction of new arsenals and armories, enhanced the nation's coastal fortifications, stretched military road construction on the frontier, and also oversaw the explorations by parties looking for the most practical route for a railroad to the Pacific. He issued training manuals to the several state militias, continuing his old preoccupation with making more effective the local defense forces of the country, especially since he believed that in case of insurrection, the army and navy should not be used except as a last resort.[18]

Davis oversaw a surprising amount of all this himself. He visited the testing grounds to observe experiments, inspected many of the arsenals in the East, and maintained a regular correspondence with almost all the leading officers in the field. In order to keep abreast of the latest developments in warfare, he took a special interest in the events in the Crimea. When war broke out there in March 1854, he placed a map of the region on the wall of his office and thereafter followed its course in the press and diplomatic dispatches with a keen eye. He traced in red on the map all the movements of the several armies, especially the siege of Sevastopol, and delighted in lecturing visitors on the varying ways of making war practiced by the English, French, and Russians. To obtain better information, and in order to study the newest developments in tactics, he sent three leading officers, including the promising young George B. McClellan, to the Crimea on an official mission to observe everything from supply and transportation to weapons and fortifications. They left in April 1855 and did not return for fully a year, and on their arrival in Washington, Davis immediately sat with them for an extended report. Their later published reports provided a small library on the latest state of the military sciences.[19]

One of the things Davis charged them with was observing the use of camels by the military. He never gave up on an idea once convinced of its usefulness. Even though some in the Senate had laughed in 1851 when he introduced his resolution to experiment with the "ship of the desert" in the American Southwest, he remained undeterred, and his position as secretary of war allowed him to put his idea to the test. In the fall of 1855 he sent a ship to Egypt, then to Turkey, charged with bringing back the odd beasts. Ten dromedaries came from the former and another forty-four from the latter. They all arrived in the spring of 1856, and Davis meanwhile devoted many of his evening hours to translating a French book on camels for the instruction of the animals' American handlers, who would be assisted by several Arabs hired to train them. Many still ridiculed his experiment, but early in his time in office one editor magnanimously concluded that "as we cannot discover that these camels and dromedaries have anything to do with the great national issues between the Cabinet and country, let them be brought in." In the end the experiment withered and died from apathy after Davis left office. Soldiers disliked the ill-tempered beasts, preferring their horses and mules, and later the coming of the railroad preempted the need for them. Nevertheless the camels proved their effectiveness and adaptability; the timing of their introduction was simply unfortunate. Ironically, this one comparatively insignificant experiment, of much lesser importance than any of his efforts at modernizing weapons and instruction, would become the second-most-remembered episode in the life of Jefferson Davis.[20]

This same western expanse that the secretary thought would accept the camel occupied most of his strategic planning during these years. It was an enormous territory, largely unmapped and even unknown. Davis sent parties of exploration through much of it, especially the departments of California, New Mexico, Utah, and Oregon. For defense as well as to initiate settlement, he worked to establish a network of frontier forts that eventually numbered more than sixty by the time he left office, from Fort Yuma in the Southwest, to Camp San Juan Island above Washington's Puget Sound, to old Fort Ripley in Minnesota, to Fort Brown at the southernmost tip of Texas. Two major east-west trails were established to connect the Pacific Coast with Fort Leavenworth, in latter-day Kansas; and Fort Smith, Arkansas, and a host of lesser routes interconnected the major pathways with the other outposts. To meet the needs of this expanded frontier defense network, Davis struggled with Congress to get his four new regiments. Having fought so many political battles over all this territory, he acted with his remarkable sense of duty paramount to personal preference to see that the region would be safe for settlement, even though the people who would populate it might in all probability make free states out of every acre.

An equal or greater challenge, especially with the expectation of settlement, lay in the indigenous population. Frontier clashes with the Plains Indians had been relatively infrequent prior to the Mexican War. But now, faced by an expanding white civilization, the Indians of the new territories began fighting for their homeland. The 1854 massacre of a party in the Nebraska Territory near Fort Laramie inaugurated the first really serious hostilities with the Sioux. Davis sent an expedition under Colonel William S. Harney the following year to subdue the hostiles, and after a battle at Blue Water, negotiations for a peace treaty commenced. Even earlier, just after Davis took office, Shasta Indians began depredations on working parties along Oregon's Rogue River. The Treaty of Table Rock speedily ended that uprising, but only temporarily, and in 1855 another, more serious war broke out with Yakima, Walla Walla, Rogue, and others.[21]

These and other hostilities confronted Davis with a problem never faced by a previous war secretary. He had to oversee a limited, highly mobile form of guerrilla warfare across a truly continental stage, against foes that, combined, outnumbered his own forces alarmingly.

Devoting considerable thought to the problem, Davis proposed to Pierce a revision of military policy. He suggested that "instead of dispersing the troops to form small garrisons at numerous posts," the regulars should be concentrated in larger numbers at a few major installations connected by rail or steamboat with the East. This would make supply quicker and cheaper. Then, every spring, large columns should be sent out from these posts "to hunt up and chastise" any recent offenders. Moreover, such columns would be moving over the major trails at the same time as the spring and summer immigrant trains, affording them protection.[22]

It was a well-conceived scheme, not entirely original to Davis. He soon discovered for himself the political impracticability of concentrating large numbers of soldiers, however, when he tried to do so in 1854 and heard protests from the settlers in areas that would have been left unprotected. In the end, no change in policy came about, but Davis had taken a strong role in stimulating a strategic debate and at the same time learned a far-reaching lesson that in a defensive conflict, whether for better or worse, civilians and their leaders expected every inch of ground to be fought for and protected. He would remember that.[23]

Indeed, Davis generated a lot of debate. No one argued that he did not attend to his duties. Barely a month after taking office, he told Varina that "I am paying dearly indeed for public honors, worn out by incessant boring." In fact, he hardly found time to write to Varina that first spring of 1853. He snatched moments at his desk, but rarely wrote for long without an interruption. Even when he announced that he would see no more visitors and tried to have a few quiet moments, one of his department heads would appear with official business that he could not turn away. Sometimes Davis wrote to his wife while others stood in the room reading papers. When there were no visitors, and when he did not have to pore over endless drafts of legislation for the department or waste hours writing to Scott and his other foes, Davis kept a ruthlessly vigilant eye on his staff. After less than two years on the job, he was actually counting the lines of copying done by his clerks in a morning's work and threatening the slow ones with discharge. Though apparently not a harsh superior, he still expected every man to give the government its money's worth.[24]

Many came to feel that Davis allowed his authority and power to get the better of him, aided by the widely held perception that he could do no wrong in Pierce's eyes. Certainly Scott believed this, but after 1853 so did an increasing number of other less partial observers. Albert Brown would exclaim before the end of Davis's incumbency that it was "hardly possible for Davis and myself to be friends." He condemned the secretary's imperious manner, declaring that Davis tried to "play the 'big man me and little man you' all the time." Such complaints came louder and louder and from more quarters than ever before, and not surprisingly. Davis held a position from which he could exercise an influence on the professional lives of thousands. When he saw something that he believed needed doing, he went about doing it, not disregarding the feelings of others involved but wholly oblivious of why they should object if he did it his way, that way being the best.[25]

Thus came the accusations that he usurped power and appropriations even from outside his department when he took over the management of civil works in the capital itself. The Capitol building could not contain its occupants any longer. House and Senate, their committee rooms, offices, and support staff needs, almost literally overflowed the building. A major expansion of the structure was necessary. At the same time, Congress, in the wake of a disastrous fire in 1851 that ravaged the Library of Congress, mandated the creation of a water system in the city, its source to be the Potomac and the water to be brought in by a massive aqueduct. All this officially fell under the responsibility of the Interior Department, but not for long. That department itself was new, with no building of its own and its branches parceled out elsewhere. Further, with Secretary of the Interior McClelland charged with the construction of those new quarters, Davis saw little progress and expected less. McClelland he found to be "a man of fair ability, conservative democracy, and rigid integrity," though he later maintained that the Michigander was true only to the first and last. He also thought him slow, apparently, for Davis despaired of the new Interior Department offices ever being completed.[26]

How much of this influenced Pierce is unknown. On March 19, 1853, only two weeks after the new administration took over, McClelland asked Davis to detail to him an engineer to supervise the Capitol and Patent Office construction, and perhaps other public works as required. Almost certainly Davis objected to having one of his officers removed from his authority or in any way made subject to someone else. He may have taken the matter to Pierce, or perhaps not. They did meet in a cabinet session on March 23, and that same day Pierce issued an order directing that henceforth all such construction work would be handled by the War Department. In future, appropriations for the work naturally went to War as well.[27]

High-handed or not in acquiring the responsibility, Davis threw himself into it with the same energy and fascination that characterized all his architectural efforts. He appointed Captain Montgomery C. Meigs of the Corps of Engineers to oversee the work, and in April added the proposed new aqueduct to his schedule. Meigs reported directly to Davis himself. "Mr. Davis was a most courteous and amiable man," said Meigs. "He was a man, too, of marked ability, and I quite looked up to him and regarded him as one of the great men of the time." The secretary of war involved himself at every stage, from selection of design to inspecting samples of floor tile, marble, and even the interior decoration. Davis himself turned a spadeful of earth at the November groundbreaking for the aqueduct and made his first actual speech, albeit brief, in Washington since leaving the Senate. Though the project would not be completed until 1864, it accomplished all that was hoped.[28]

As for the work on the Capitol, its massive scale guaranteed that it would not be completed during Davis's tenure. The plans included whole new Senate and House wings extending from their smaller existing chambers, a massive new dome to replace the little one then in place, and a marble-columned portico. Furthermore, a host of internal details had to be settled, and Davis looked into all of them, even inviting studies on the acoustics in such structures to make certain that speakers would be heard clearly. He considered ventilation and heating systems, windows, even the color and pattern of carpeting.

When designs for a statue to crown the dome came in, Davis involved himself. The initial design showed Liberty as a goddess with the Phrygian cap on her head. Davis objected, pointing out that the liberty cap, among the Romans from whose architecture the Capitol derived, symbolized "freedom obtained by manumission—that is, of *freed slaves.*" Americans were not freed slaves and never had been. Without saying so, he probably also disliked the general suggestion of manumission. Another design came in, this with a laurel wreath. Again Davis objected, for that symbolized peace, and liberty could not always be maintained without war. Finally Davis himself proposed that the goddess's headgear be composed of eagle feathers shaped like a helmet "without being a helmet (for that symbolizes war) and to serve as a *cap* without being a cap (for that belongs to manumitted slaves)." This design was adopted and eventually crowned the Capitol years after Davis left office.

Nothing could symbolize Davis himself better—a design derived from pettifogging steeped in classical imagery and amended to remove any suggestion of freedom for slaves. As for the building itself, it would not be entirely completed until the mid-1860s, and remained for some time controversial. The House moved into its new chamber late in 1857, and the Senate in January 1859. Reactions were mixed, some praising the building's beauty and others complaining about the poor ventilation, for the windows did not open. Years later a senator would still be haranguing Davis bitterly "for cooping up the Senate in this iron box covered with glass." As for the ornamentation, beauty lay in the eye of the beholder, though at least one complained that the decor satisfied no one but the secretary of war. So far as some were concerned, he had only succeeded in creating another "Davis."[29]

Measured in their entirety, the Mississippian's four years as secretary of war stood unparalleled for the vastness of the shadow he cast, for the scope of the responsibilities he assumed, and for the influence he exerted. None of his predecessors approached either his achievements or the intent and breadth of thought and imagination he displayed. Some of this, certainly, Davis owed to the times. A whole new military technology was exploding in the 1850s, just as he took office. At the same time came the challenges of a vast new frontier, supporting his arguments for a larger and more modern military, and giving him the stage on which to put his ideas into practice. But the fertile mind, the sense of innovation, the willingness to experiment, the fascination with the new and progressive—all these belonged to Davis. The United States Army was still a tiny cadre of professionals when he left office, but half again as large as it had been when he started, and better trained, better equipped, better supplied, and better organized as well.

What Davis revealed of himself during those years is even more significant. There are many kinds of administrators, but chiefly there are those who delegate and those who do not. Davis was not a delegator. He assumed the attitude that the secretary of war was literally responsible for everything that took place in his department, and no one ever took any responsibility more seriously. Combined with his temperament and his obsession with being right, this attitude compelled him to decide everything himself. Leaving lesser decisions to others opened the door for them to make mistakes for which he, as secretary, would ultimately be responsible, and that he could not have. While he advanced a few favorites like Johnston and used his position to badger old foes like Scott, he maintained to the world—and persuaded himself—that in all cases he acted solely for the good of the department, and in the main this was true. Certainly he saw his duty clearly, and carried it out regardless of his personal political feelings in most instances, rejecting the spoils system and, despite later accusations, showing little sectional favoritism in granting appointments and promotions.

Another thing he showed, if anyone had been close and visionary enough to see it, is that he was not a progressive executive. He did too much himself. He let his passions and weaknesses control him in situations, like those with Scott and Wool, in which his duty would have been served better by self-control. His coolness to many prevented him from leading by inspiration, and instead he had to use raw authority enough that many accused him of being imperious. He succeeded in getting much of what he wanted from Congress, though not without clashes, and largely because he had Pierce's implicit backing.

None of this meant, however, that he was not an outstanding secretary of war. Great as they were, the demands of the office in his time could still be met by a man of Davis's temperament. Indeed, up to his time, many who exhibited similar characters held higher office, including the presidency, successfully. Even while Davis toiled late into the night in his tiny office behind the stairway, voices across the nation began for the first time seriously to call his name for such a higher station. How clearly he heard them is arguable, for during his four years in the War Department events in his old detested realm of politics inflamed the country as never before. Millions of voices echoed from ocean to ocean, punctuated by the sound of guns, and all the old arguments and divisions were only amplified. The nation was on the road to a crisis, and any man who would be president in the days ahead would have to be able to master more than rules and regulations. He might have to be superhuman.

14

Hasten Slowly, and Be Temperate in All Things

Throughout his years as secretary of war, Davis endured an unsettled and at times frustrating life, touched with tragedy. It began with leaving Varina back in Mississippi with little Sam. Davis took lodgings in the famed Willard's Hotel on Pennsylvania Avenue when he first arrived in the capital, but soon thereafter moved and by summer Varina and the baby joined him. Still they kept looking for somewhere better to reside, and by October, after considering more than half a dozen places, Davis confessed that "I have been so annoyed about a house that I cannot sit down in quiet."[1]

Perhaps because Varina was only with him occasionally, leaving to visit friends and family from time to time, he did not push the issue of a house as much as she wished. Besides, he made a number of entertaining trips of his own, often in the company of Pierce. In July 1853 he joined the president, Cushing, and Guthrie on a trip to New York to open the new Crystal Palace, and on the way Pierce repeatedly urged Davis to accompany him to New England. They passed through Baltimore, and in Philadelphia Davis addressed a crowd at Independence Hall. He gave them the inevitable reminder that he came from the strict-construction school where the Constitution was concerned but touched on sectional politics no more than that, instead turning his theme to an appeal for support of the proposed Pacific railroad. Davis's remarks won considerable applause, and even praise, in the hated Northern press. When he returned to Washington, Varina found him refreshed in mind by his journey, though so stiff from rheumatism that he could barely move one shoulder.[2]

As always, the secretary's health caused more-or-less-constant trouble. Just two months after assuming office he suffered a bout with neuralgia, at the time a loosely used term that could have covered a variety of muscular ailments, but which in Davis seems to have related to severe pain on the left side of his face. A host of causes might have stimulated its recurrence, but quite likely it was symptomatically tied to the frequent infections of his left eye and the occasional ulceration of the cornea. The late hours he worked did not help, and his New Orleans eye specialist had even warned that this might happen if Davis stayed in public life. He had noted that Davis's "very peculiar constitution—is not nervous . . . but is controlled by his will." That will kept him at his work, and yet, after this episode, Davis enjoyed a long period of relatively good health, even escaping his usual attacks of malaria. People meeting him were not, as often before, struck by his sickly or emaciated appearance. To be sure, he still stood ramrod straight, "a tall, thin, nervous-looking man," thought one, with "the tread of an Indian brave." Most now commented on his "light though manly form," and many, like Virginia Clay of Alabama, wife of Senator Clement Clay, found him distinguished in bearing. By 1855 and afterward, though, many noticed that a thin, cloudy film seemed to cover his left eye, the advance of the affliction that would all but blind him on that side.[3]

Tragically, before long Davis had other cares than his own health to burden him. The house hunting continued through the fall until late in 1853, when they settled on a house on Fourteenth Street, within easy walking distance of the War Department. Here Davis gloried in having little Sam near him. When he had to leave on a trip, he resisted the compulsion to keep running back to "kiss the dear boy." While away from him, he thought constantly of "Le man," as he called him. "There is little which does not associate itself in my mind with him." Varina herself noted warmly that "he was Mr. Davis's first thought when the door opened, and the little fellow would wait as patiently as possible, sometimes a quarter of an hour, at the door to kiss his father first." Jefferson Davis never denied his son the demonstrative love that an earlier Samuel had denied to him.[4]

All of which made the tragedy of June 1854 the harder to bear. Late in May, little Samuel sickened, perhaps with measles, and lay ill for weeks. Doctors seemed able to do nothing. They watched as the little boy, just short of two, slowly declined. On June 13 he died. Two days later they held a funeral in their home. President Pierce attended, no doubt moved by the recollection that hardly more than a year before he had seen his own son killed in a terrible train accident. They buried "Le man" in nearby Georgetown and then faced their grief. If any bond were needed to bring Davis and Pierce closer, surely this tragedy did so. Pierce's wife, still distraught from the loss of her son, had almost adopted little Samuel in his stead. Though she and the president could not have felt more empathy for the bereaved parents, their sadness was as nothing compared to Jefferson Davis's. He had looked forward to growing old with his eyes full of Samuel, dreaming of "the strong young man on whose arm, had God so willed it, I might have leaned and gone down to my grave." But the prophecy of the old slave woman at Samuel's birth had been cruelly fulfilled. This little boy would never grow up to labor, or to lend an arm to his father. For months after his son's death, Davis fought to contain his grief as he always reined in his emotions. Yet the sudden cry of a child in a street could instantly melt all his defenses. Catching him unawares, the sound "well-nigh drove him mad," said Varina. All he had during the day to take his mind from his loss was his work, in which he buried himself with renewed frenzy. At home on Fourteenth Street, denied the escape of his desk and papers, he walked the empty rooms halfway through the night.[5]

Within a year they moved from that house, perhaps unable to bear its memories, and took lodging with several congressmen on G Street near Eighteenth, and soon thereafter finally settled in the former home of the noted orator Edward Everett, farther down G between Thirteenth and Fourteenth streets. Here they remained, and here, too, a measure of happiness returned. Indeed, when young Sam died, Varina may already have noticed the signs of pregnancy, and in February 1855 a new child came, called Margaret Howell. Meanwhile, the Davises traveled, especially enjoying the White Mountains of New Hampshire, where they vacationed with their old friend Bache. Probably their first outing after Samuel's death was a trip to Old Point Comfort on the Chesapeake. Time healed their wounds, and even a sense of humor returned after awhile. In May 1855 Davis made a trip back to Mississippi to address a state convention and took the occasion to travel for the first time by rail through the South. During the ride between Branchville and Atlanta, Georgia, Davis sat in what he thought was an unoccupied compartment. When he woke a little girl sleeping on the bench in front of his, he apologized for disturbing her, then spoke to her pleasantly for several minutes. He did not know that beneath a trunk beside her sat a carpetbag holding $2,500 or more. Getting off the train the next morning at Augusta, he was startled to find himself approached and arrested by a law officer. The carpetbag had been found missing, and the conductor, not knowing Davis by sight, remembered seeing him in the car the night before. Ever dignified, Davis quietly protested his innocence, explaining that "I am Jefferson Davis, Secretary of War." Only by producing official papers and being identified by the city's mayor did Davis convince them of his identity. It seems that the conductor who identified Davis was himself the thief. Despite what could have been an embarrassing predicament, Davis "laughed as heartily as the rest at what liked to have proven an awkward blunder," noted a reporter.[6]

Davis could accept such an incident with good humor, most probably because he was away from Washington, where by this time the political atmosphere was charged with a painful tension. Unwittingly, he found himself becoming a political issue in the city, as more and more observers commented on the extraordinary closeness between him and the president. Most perceived Pierce as a weak man, easily swayed by states' rights arguments toward which he naturally leaned in any case, and this perception convinced many that Davis himself led his friend. "Being a man of strong will and limited information," one unfriendly editor said of Davis, "he is not often troubled with doubts, and walks straight ahead." Others accused Davis of surrounding himself with "a host of admirers," basking in the power he radiated. He was "the autocrat of the Cabinet," said the *New York Times* when the Scott correspondence leaked to the press in 1855. Convinced that in any event Pierce would ultimately be influenced by Davis, the newspaper again called him "the ruling member of the Cabinet." Just how true this was depended on the observer's bias, but in a few very crucial moments the influence of Davis on Pierce would be undeniable, as would the way the president acted when his secretary of war was not available for counsel.[7]

Davis should have known that being shelved in a cabinet post would not keep him out of the heat of controversy in Washington, and that he would not be able to keep himself out of the political broiler. Only months after taking office, he learned that his acquaintance—they were never close friends—Robert Toombs of Georgia had denounced Pierce for giving cabinet appointments to men who opposed the Compromise of 1850, and more particularly that Toombs had publicly accused Davis of being "a disunionist sitting in the councils of the nation." Davis replied publicly, saying, "It is false," and calling Toombs "radically false and corrupt." Typically, Davis overreacted, unable to control his compulsion to lash back quickly and fiercely. As it happened, Toombs's comments had been misreported and he said so, but he could not contain his own temper at Davis's insults, and compared his behavior to that of "swaggering braggarts and cunning poltroons." Toombs was still in Georgia, due to arrive in the capital in January 1854, and soon the Southern press buzzed with rumors of a duel.

It never came to pass, but Davis and Toombs remained hostile to each other for more than three years to come before mutual friends patched their differences with a pledge that "all past controversy shall be no more regarded by either of you—that when you meet, you shall receive, speak to, and treat each other as is common among gentlemen." It was almost such a pact as parents enforced on misbehaving children, and observers definitely began to think that Davis did at times behave childishly. The affair with Toombs constituted at least his fourth near approach to a duel in the past six years. Even the most reasonable men occasionally lost their tempers or said injudicious things. In the session of Congress just about to commence, John C. Breckinridge of Kentucky, a moderate man in all things, and one with whom Davis would in time form a close professional relationship, became so caught up in the heat of a debate with a New York congressman that the two nearly finished on the dueling green. It was the only time for Breckinridge, and most other public men, even the most high spirited, rarely got themselves into such a mess more than once or twice. Davis did it too frequently, and the fact that none of his threatened duels ever came to pass does not mitigate the seriousness of his loss of self-control. Barring settlement beforehand, he would have appeared on the field and exchanged fire with Foote, Bissell, Toombs, or anyone else who angered him.[8]

Part of Davis's sensitivity—beyond that normal to his temperament —probably came from finding himself in the awkward position of being very prominent in public affairs, yet having no forum in which to defend himself or speak his mind. A cabinet secretary, for all his importance, could not debate in Congress, and the demands of his duties would not allow him to go out on the stump. Accustomed as he was to being heard, Davis must have found the war portfolio personally stifling. Almost from the first, he made it clear that he would be willing to resign the post if another presented itself.

Just about a month after he took office, Davis heard from friends in Mississippi that he was being spoken of as a candidate for the next available senatorial term, and he lost little time in letting them know that his name "is, as it has been at their service." At the same time he warned Varina that "events in Missi." might change their plans for finding a house, and through the summer there came more and more expressions of hope from Democrats at home that Davis might be elected in the coming winter. At the same time, however, other friends warned him not to be too hasty in becoming a candidate. Foote, his ubiquitous foe, was believed to intend a candidacy, and should Davis suffer another defeat at his hands it would be a blow to the whole Southern rights movement. Yet, by late summer, even the state press assumed that Davis would try for his party's nomination, which would probably be contested by Albert Brown, his friend-turning-foe.

Davis did little more to encourage his selection than allow friends to fight for him in the January 1854 state caucus of Democratic legislators. They thought his election a certainty, but then confusion, and perhaps trickery, set in. The word that he would be willing to resign if elected had not reached everyone, or not all were convinced. As a result, they voted for Brown. Worse, actively campaigning for the post, Brown characterized Davis as sitting back in Washington in an easy chair lazily awaiting his election while Brown was out in the ninety-degree heat campaigning. If rumor may be believed, Brown even won some votes by promising that he would support Davis for the next Senate seat available two years hence (which he did not do). For some or all of these reasons, Davis lost the nomination by two votes. Foote crowed in the press that Davis was "a beaten man," though Reuben Davis wrote to the secretary from Jackson that "those who voted against you did it almost in tears."[9]

No sooner had the question of a Senate seat diminished than opponents began to speculate that the real motive behind Davis's creation of the four new regiments lay in an appended provision for an additional brigadier general in the service. By March 1855 the New York papers speculated that Davis had done so in order to maneuver the general's star for himself, using it as a base from which to launch a grab for Scott's position as general-in-chief. Davis repeatedly denied any such intent; he had another candidate in mind for the post all along, William S. Harney. Not content with this, the rumor mill went to work again that summer, when Davis made his trip through Georgia to the Mississippi Democratic State Convention. Now, tongues wagged, he came as a candidate for the governorship again, though there seems to be no reason to think that was his intent.[10]

By late 1855, with a national election due the following year, more and more people began to suggest his name as a candidate for one of the highest offices in the land, usually the vice presidency. Speculators paired him with George M. Dallas, James Buchanan, Augustus Dodge, and others. The vice presidential suggestions flattered but did not interest him. It was an office "I would not have," he told his friends, "an office which, however dignified, affords no sphere for the display of administrative talent or powers in debate." Obviously Davis believed that he possessed both, and just as clearly, he never wished again to be in a position that did not employ at least one of them, preferably the latter. As for the few mentions of his name in connection with the presidency itself, he dismissed the idea as "not to be thought of, and a man's friends should not make him look ridiculous." "I prefer the office of senator to any other," he said. As early as October 1855, Mississippi editors began proposing him for the next Senate seat, to commence on March 4, 1857, coincidental with the day Davis's cabinet position expired. This time he made it completely clear to his friends at home that he wanted the post, and they had no trouble nominating him on January 14, 1856, with fifty votes to Jacob Thompson's thirty-five. Two days later, from a field of nine candidates, the legislature elected Davis by a virtual landslide. Finally he looked forward to a time when once more he could speak out.[11]

But if Davis felt himself gagged by his cabinet post, still he exerted no small influence in public affairs. Indeed, for all the outstanding work he did in his official capacity as secretary of war—and it is difficult to estimate too highly the worth of his contributions—the fact is that his behind-the-scenes efforts as an adviser to Pierce proved to be of transcendent importance and lasting impact. He may not have been the "power behind the throne" that the opposition press alleged—indeed, with Pierce's spine not in high repute generally, several men, including Breckinridge, were thought to be dominating him—but on a few crucial issues, Davis made a difference.

The besetting nightmare of the Pierce administration, as of most of the decade, would be the organization of the new territories, especially Nebraska. It was an old issue for Senator Douglas, who repeatedly in past Congresses sought to see the vast tract of land organized and opened for settlement. He foresaw lucrative land speculation and the possibility of a transcontinental railroad passing through that section. All the prior efforts came to nought, in part because of the opposition of slave-state senators who feared that any states to come from the territory would prohibit slavery, thus further tipping the balance of power against them in Washington. Indeed, the Missouri Compromise expressly prohibited slavery in any of Nebraska, and this was the stumbling block. From a variety of motives, some personal, some political, Douglas thought he had in Nebraska an issue that, if successful, would reunite the Democratic Party, end the sectional controversy over slavery in the territories, and quite possibly make him president. His notion was hardly original, but he made it literally his own—popular sovereignty. If the decision of slavery could be left to the inhabitants of a territory at the time it was organized as a territory, then Congress would be out of the equation and vox populi would settle the issue. Southerners could not complain that their rights were being trampled by an abolitionist majority in Washington, and free-state men could not complain that Congress was looking out for the slave interests. It would all be up to the people.

The problem was the Missouri Compromise. When Douglas introduced his newest Nebraska bill on January 4, 1854, he tried to get around it, suggesting that the issue of slavery should be settled there when Nebraskans formed their constitution and prior to any application for admission to statehood. He suggested that the Compromise of 1850 had made the Missouri line inapplicable anyhow and then questioned its constitutionality as well. Several days later he added an even more explicit section to his bill, specifying that Nebraska should settle the slavery matter entirely on its own, with Congress having no part in the decision. Until such a time, of course, the Missouri Compromise would be in effect, preventing slaveholders from taking their property into the territory, but any subsequent action by Nebraska would take precedence. In effect, Douglas treated the 1820 Compromise almost as if it did not exist.[12]

Southerners immediately saw the problem with Douglas's bill. With the Missouri restriction still in place prior to a vote by the inhabitants of the territory, no proslave men would settle there, and thus their voice would not be heard in any such ballot. That amounted to a de facto exclusion of slavery from the outset. Douglas thought that a repeal of the Missouri Compromise was implicit in his bill, he said, and passage of his measure would solve the problem. Breckinridge disagreed, as did Atchison and a number of others in both houses. Instantly the Southerners saw an opportunity to win back what they had lost not only in 1850 but in 1820 as well. They would put an explicit repeal of the Missouri Compromise into the Nebraska bill. If it could be passed, it would open not just all of the remainder of the old Louisiana Territory to the formation of slave states, but set a precedent whereby the rest of the western lands covered in the 1850 measures might be fairly contested as well. Three decades of seeming Southern defeat could be redeemed in a single legislative act.

Douglas required some persuasion, but the Southerners urged that a repeal would "put a stop to agitation and preserve peace and harmony to the country." Finally Douglas gave in, if reluctantly. Pierce, meanwhile, favored the bill and thought the Missouri line unconstitutional, but he remained standoffish when Northern Democrats raised a cry. Caught in the middle, the president seemed unsure which way to turn. Quite possibly he discussed his dilemma with Davis, though to no conclusion. This was the first session of Congress during his administration, and the Nebraska bill the first major legislation. If he opposed the repeal to keep harmony with Northerners, he would forfeit the support of much of his Democratic majority and might doom any cooperation from them for the next three years. Yet to side with the repealers would open him to a torrent of abuse. Pierce tried to get out of the fix by drafting himself a revised version of the bill that left the Missouri Compromise decision to the Supreme Court, but the leading Southern senators rejected it out of hand. They wanted explicit repeal by Congress. Thus it stood on the evening of Saturday, January 21, 1854.[12]

The Senate had scheduled consideration of the bill for the following Monday. Douglas needed to have it in a final form. Postponement might mean that it could not be passed in this session. Without a repeal the bill would not pass, and Pierce seemed to oppose the bill with an explicit repeal. Breckinridge decided that the only way out of the problem was to get Pierce to endorse the bill with a repeal. Unfortunately, Pierce was well known for his reluctance to transact any business on the sabbath.

Sunday morning, even before the church bells of Washington began to chime, a small group of men appeared at the door of Davis's house on Fourteenth Street. When they were shown into the parlor,

Davis saw a number of senators and congressmen, with Douglas and Breckinridge their respective spokesmen. They explained to him the dilemma, of which he was well aware, and showed him the final draft of the bill that they wanted to introduce in both houses simultaneously the next day. Davis read it and saw that it contained an explicit repeal. Manifestly he approved. Asking their purpose in bringing it to him, he heard tacitly from their own lips what so many in Washington and the nation believed. No one stood closer to the president than he. They needed to see Pierce that day and asked Davis to presume on his relationship with the chief executive to get them an audience.

Apparently without hesitation, Davis agreed. He joined Douglas and Atchison in a carriage and drove to the White House, while the others walked the few blocks. Davis left them all in an audience chamber while he went to speak with Pierce in private and apprised him of their mission. Pierce did not like having his own version of handling the Missouri line issue rejected by them and tried at first to stand on his well-known rule about business on Sunday, declining to grant them an interview. When Davis brought that word back to the repealers, they responded through Atchison that in that case they would assume that Pierce supported the repeal and introduce it the next day as an administration measure. When Davis took that message back, Pierce found himself boxed in, for once they introduced the bill it would be embarrassing for him to try to back away from it. He told Davis to allow them to join him in the library. Coldly formal, Pierce talked with them for two hours or more, and in the end they persuaded him to draft in his own hand the repeal amendment declaring that the Compromise of 1850 effectively superceded the Missouri Compromise, making it "inoperative and void." Inhabitants would henceforth decide the slavery issue for themselves in their territorial legislatures and in their constitutional conventions, before statehood. Any questions would be settled not by Congress but by the Supreme Court.[13]

Thus did Douglas present his bill the next day, though now it proposed splitting the territory in two, Nebraska and Kansas. Of course Davis did not frame the bill or even the repeal. He had spoken in favor of a repeal in a cabinet meeting prior to that Sunday at the White House, but apparently that is all he did. And even that Sunday, he acted largely as a go-between. Yet if he had not backed the plan, if he had not enjoyed a relationship with Pierce that allowed him to call on him that day, and if he had not argued the repealers' case with Pierce in their behalf, the Kansas-Nebraska bill might never have become an administration measure, with what consequences no one can know.

The fact that Pierce endorsed it did not guarantee a smooth road ahead for the legislation. Congress debated it well through March in the House, and into May in the Senate, before Pierce signed the final law on

May 30. Through that period, Davis worked frequently behind the scenes with Douglas and Breckinridge, especially in wooing wavering votes in the House. The issue there was close, coming down in the end to a matter of seven crucial votes. Forty-four of the eighty-six Northern Democrats voted for the bill, and several of them might not have done so but for the removal of an amendment that prevented foreign immigrants from voting in territorial elections, its backers fearing that such people would be antislave. Davis sensed that the amendment was dangerous and distasteful to Northern Democrats and consulted with several who assured him they would vote for the Kansas-Nebraska bill if that offending amendment could be removed. This Davis communicated to Breckinridge, and the bill's managers in the House managed to have it removed. It is just possible that Davis's good offices secured enough of those Northern Democrats to make that slim seven-vote majority.[14]

Certainly rumors of Davis's activities circulated in the nation's press and in the drawing rooms of Washington, especially after his combined efforts with his old Transylvania friend. Instead of ending turmoil over slavery in the territories, Douglas's Kansas-Nebraska legislation only aggravated the controversy, especially in Kansas as free-soil and proslave settlers flocked to the prairies to claim the new territory for their own. Hoping to show his even-handed attitude, Pierce appointed a Northerner, Andrew H. Reeder of Easton, Pennsylvania, to be territorial governor of Kansas, but almost immediately the faults in his choice manifested themselves. Reeder was no statesman and, despite his Yankee birth, shared Pierce's wholeheartedly Southern viewpoint. Worse, he saw in his appointment an opportunity for personal gain through land speculation. Once he arrived in Kansas, he devoted more attention to his private fortunes than to organizing the territory in a way to suit Atchison, Davis, and others of like mind.

As a result, by the spring of 1855, the vexing question of Kansas had become worse than ever. Atchison demanded Reeder's replacement by someone who would be more than just sympathetic, and there was no question that Davis sided with him. The press speculated that any decision by Pierce would ultimately be influenced by the Mississippian, and the *New York Times* declared that Davis and Atchison "will settle Kansas matters pretty much in their own way without hindrance of the President." When Davis spoke publicly on the question, he made it clear that he felt Reeder should never have been appointed in the first place, as close as he ever came to criticizing his friend Pierce. The president never revealed how much influence, if any, his secretary of war exerted on his decision, but by the summer of 1855 he had had enough and dismissed Reeder.[15]

No sooner did one problem recede than another erupted in its place. By the fall of 1855, Pierce had to decide what to do about the coming year and another nomination. He kept his intentions mostly to himself, though observers noted that he spent long hours in frequent conferences with Davis. A host of issues complicated the next election. The Kansas-Nebraska legislation had galvanized antislave factions—old Whigs, Free-Soilers, and others—into forming a new Republican party that immediately became a well-organized, potent threat to the Democrats in 1856. Worse, in a pivotal state, New York, the free-soil wing of the party that had bolted in 1848 still had not come back. Men like Marcy favored compromising with them and came to be known as "soft-shells" or "softs," while those opposed to taking the antislave Democrats back into the fold were called "hards," with Davis among them. It could mean the difference between winning or losing New York in the next election, and with all its electoral votes, that could mean the election itself. As usual, Davis preferred principle over expedience, and he and Marcy finally fell out publicly on the issue. The two argued it in cabinet meetings, and after one particularly long and late session, Marcy came out declaring that the administration was "bound to go to the devil" if Davis prevailed. Pierce needed unanimity in his cabinet if he hoped to win another presidential nomination, and quickly he extinguished the fire between his two secretaries, though the two never enjoyed warm relations thereafter. With the help of his cabinet, he drafted a platform for the coming year. He saw two real issues. One was British adventuring in Central America, which had led to a lot of posturing on both sides, with Davis himself thinking that war with England might ensue. The other was the ever-present bugbear of sectionalism and disunion over slavery in the territories. Here his position matched that of Davis. The Missouri Compromise had been a bankrupt enactment once Northerners refused to extend its line to the Pacific. The Kansas-Nebraska legislation provided for territorial sovereignty over matters such as slavery, and would work smoothly if only abolition fanatics let it. The new Republican party represented the gravest danger to constitutional freedoms and protection yet seen. On such a foundation he hoped to hold onto the White House for another quadrennium.[16]

Perhaps not much to Pierce's liking, a few of his cabinet ministers were themselves being touted in the press as possible candidates for the 1856 nomination, Davis among them. Of the bunch, only Marcy and the Mississippian would have made serious contenders, and one rumor in the capital claimed that when all the cabinet members vowed late in 1855 to withdraw their own candidacies to support Pierce, only Davis refused. It is too out of character to be credited, though it reveals both the sense of unrest both inside and outside the Pierce administration, and also the perception that Davis was the administration's most willful member.[17]

Pierce lost the nomination. Kansas almost killed it for him single-handed. Open warfare broke out on the prairies between free and pro-slave factions, with Lawrence being sacked in May 1856, just before the Democratic convention. In the end the party chose James Buchanan of Pennsylvania, with Breckinridge of Kentucky as his running mate. Davis played no role at all in selecting the nominees, other than expressing to friends and associates his preference for Pierce. He did, however, declare that if Pierce could not get the nomination, then he hoped that a Northerner of like mind would. The slavery question had to be settled "at the North," he said, and that could best be accomplished by a Yankee. When men suggested his name for the nomination, Davis opposed talk not only of himself personally but of any Southern man. In short, he still thought there was a basis for compromise and harmony between the sections.[18]

Yet, as always, as the decade raced toward 1860, everything seemed only to aggravate sectional feelings over the slavery issue. At times Davis seemed willing to use his position to enhance prospects for Southern expansion of institutions and influence. There were widespread rumors that Davis persuaded Pierce to select James Gadsden as his envoy to Mexico to negotiate the purchase of a strip of land along the border of the New Mexico Territory. Some claimed that Davis actually instructed Gadsden to go far beyond his mandate by negotiating for the acquisition of most of northern Mexico—the provinces of Tamaulipas, Nuevo León, Coahuila, Chihuahua, Sonora, and all of Baja California. The obvious implication was that several new slave states would naturally be formed. No such dreams were realized in the final purchase, and Davis probably never made such a suggestion to Gadsden, but certainly Gadsden did feel that he owed his appointment mainly to Davis's influence, and during his years in Mexico he kept the Mississippian constantly apprised of his activities.[19]

At the same time Gadsden also kept a close eye on another, much more volatile area and frequently sent his thoughts to an equally interested Davis. Cuba remained a tantalizing Caribbean dream to Southerners. Certainly Davis coveted the island. "The acquisition of Cuba is essential to our prosperity and security," he argued to a friend in Mississippi. Indeed, he regretted that in joining the Union, the Southern states had forfeited the right to make treaties and acquisitions on their own, or Cuba would already be another slave state. Every time discussion of acquisition arose in Congress, Northern antislave forces prevented its going anywhere.

Other Southern men, frustrated by this, launched one expedition of conquest after another. Even Davis's old neighbor and sometime friend Quitman sought to gain the island by force. Yet Davis "officially" opposed such filibustering expeditions and exerted substantial influence on Pierce to condemn them as well. Davis's attitude may have come in part from his current antipathy for Quitman, yet his position towards filibusterers in general seems to have been consistent. Should some adventurer succeed in taking control of a American country, he would deal with him as de facto ruler (as he would suggest doing with William Walker a few years hence when that "gray eyed man of destiny" briefly held Nicaragua). But he would not officially or personally countenance such expeditions beforehand, however much he wanted new Caribbean territory. In any case, he preferred negotiation and purchase and scarcely concealed his disappointment in 1854 when talks for acquisition came to nothing. He never lost the Cuban dream and as late as 1859 said it would be indispensable should the Union fall apart. A new "separate confederacy" would need that island to protect its back door on the gulf.[20]

Kansas remained the most constant aggravation. Davis's friend Atchison organized a group he called the Border Ruffians and used them to support proslavery settlement of the territory, at the same time exhorting Southerners to emigrate to Kansas, bringing their shotguns with them. Events quickly got out of hand as free-state men brought their weapons as well. Soon the whole nation spoke of Bleeding Kansas, especially after the destruction of Lawrence by men of Atchison's stripe and the massacre a few days later of proslave men by the abolitionist John Brown at Pottawatomie. As the summer of 1856 wore on, slave men prevented free-staters from voting in a territorial election for a legislature, thus guaranteeing a slavery majority. Free-state men held their own election and created their own rival government, only exacerbating the open warfare on the border. Davis saw his duty clearly, despite his sympathy with Atchison, and ordered the army in the territory to enforce the law without respect to the combatants' position on slavery. He even asked Illinois and Kentucky for two regiments each of volunteers to aid in putting down the insurrectionaries on both sides.[21]

That Davis's own passions rose with the events surrounding him is evident in his endorsement of the cowardly action of Congressman Preston Brooks on May 22, 1856, when the South Carolinian strode into the Senate and attacked Senator Charles Sumner of Massachusetts with a cane, beating him unconscious until the cane itself shattered on the defenseless man's head. A retaliation for Sumner's recent attack on South Carolina's role in the Kansas controversy, Brooks's action attracted widespread outrage, but Davis looked on such criticism as "vilification, misrepresentation, and persecution," because Brooks had resented a "libellous assault upon the reputation" of his state. In less troubled times Davis might have thought better of endorsing such an attack, but then (considering several of his own fights in the army), it is apparent that he never hesitated to attack—sometimes without warning—when he felt threatened or insulted. In such circumstances he obviously found nothing dishonorable in striking first or against a disadvantaged opponent. Aroused passion outweighed the ordinary forms of violent exchanges between men.[22]

Indeed, Davis's ire rose frequently during these years and, as so often, he could turn it on friend and foe alike. Only as he left office in March 1857 did friends finally smooth over temporarily the breach between him and Toombs, and then it took the intervention of several who rightly believed that with Davis reentering the Senate immediately, the South could not afford disharmony within its congressional ranks. Meanwhile Davis had even feuded with his brother Joseph for many months during 1855. Hot letters passed between the brothers, with Jefferson accusing Joseph of making "reckless denunciations & accusations" of the sort that, from any other man, would lead him to demand "information," a euphemism for the preliminaries to a duel. Even when Joseph seemed conciliatory, still his brother—compelled always to have the last word—could not restrain himself from writing at the bottom of Joseph's letter, "Bah," and expressing his own anger with the polite expletive "Fudge."[23]

He wearied of being so much out of the real scene of action, the Senate. By his own statement, he never once set foot in that chamber during his tenure as secretary of war, until the final day of his office as he prepared to resume his seat. He chafed at being trapped in his dreary office at the War Department, badgered endlessly by office seekers and importuners of all sorts. He longed at times to see people who wanted nothing from him. During the summer of 1855, outside the White House, he chanced on Daniel Ammon of the Navy, an old acquaintance. "How is it you never come to see me now?" asked Davis. Ammon protested that he did not want to add to the burden of all those callers who constantly badgered Davis for patronage. "That is just the trouble," the secretary told his friend. "It is truly a great relief to see anyone who has nothing to ask in the way of favors."[24]

Adding to his frustrations were veiled hints and accusations, occasionally appearing in the press, that he had used his position at the War Department to divert weapons to Southern arsenals and otherwise weaken the ability of the army to put down a rebellion should secession come. Late in 1856 one editor charged that Davis was sending troops away from Virginia in order to lay it open to insurrection, expecting that this would somehow threaten the North into voting for Buchanan instead of his Republican opponent John C. Frémont. It was nonsense, of course. In fact, when Governor Henry Wise of Virginia decided to prepare his state for resistance should Frémont win, Davis refused his request to exchange old militia weapons for newer rifles from the U.S. arsenals. Not that Davis wanted to discourage Southern states from being ready to defend themselves if necessary; in October 1856 he advised one Georgian that "we should make all the preparation proper for sovereign States—should hasten slowly, and be temperate in all things." How they should "hasten slowly" he did not say, but it was evident that he believed that Frémont's election would "embolden the North," making the likelihood of "a resort to force" all the greater.

That same season Davis received a visit from one George G. Henry, who frankly confessed that if Frémont won, he wanted to form a new Southern government and make Davis the president. In the secretary's own office at the War Department, Henry advocated treason, advising Davis to concentrate arms, men, and munitions in the South just in case. "Take care of the jewels, eh!" said Davis, not taking Henry at all seriously. Yet the talk of arming for resistance was now all too widespread, and though Davis might joke about it to Henry and decline to use his office unlawfully for its promotion, still he applauded Wise's attempt to give his militia the "greatest possible efficiency." Davis was not over the edge on secession yet, nor was he close to it after Buchanan won the presidency in November 1856. But he had advanced close enough to the precipice to see it by now. Like so many unknowns, once seen, that edge became familiar and gradually held less and less terror. For more and more of his fellow Southerners as Davis left the War Department, it did more than lose its fearfulness—it became inviting.[25]

15

A Pretty Good Secessionist

When Jefferson Davis left the War Department for the last time on March 4, 1857, he had many reasons to be thankful. A position he had loved occasionally, yet one that had stifled his voice at a time when he felt the South needed to hear him, was now a memory. He had done much good. Indeed, on his last full day in office he used his remaining powers to act on behalf of a few deserving officers and friends, recommending brevet promotions for Harney and several others, almost all of them from his beloved old mounted service. Better yet, as he did so, he knew that when he returned home he would find Varina well. On January 16 she had given birth to a new son, Jefferson Davis, Jr., only to come close to death from complications. She spent weeks convalescing, attended tenderly by her husband and visited often by Pierce, while others like William Seward of New York showed them both special considerations. Much improved, on March 2 she hosted her last reception as a cabinet wife. Two days later, at nine in the morning, Davis met with Pierce to tender his resignation.

It was a touching scene. Already Davis had expressed to his old friend the wish, "May your days be many, your happiness great, and your fame be in the minds of posterity as elevated and pure as the motives which have prompted your official action." Davis even kept copies of his correspondence with Pierce to pass on to Jefferson, Jr., "in remembrance of your much valued confidence and friendship for his Father." Now came Pierce's turn for sentiment. As he accepted Davis's resignation, he grasped the hand that offered it, saying, "I can scarcely bear the parting from you, who have been strength and solace to me for

255

four anxious years and never failed me." At noon that same day, Davis once more took his oath and seat as a United States senator.

Davis found little to do in the next few weeks. A special session of the Senate met until March 14, its chief act of interest to him being his immediate reappointment to the chairmanship of the Military Affairs Committee, a well-deserved recognition of his military services both in and out of uniform. With no business before the Senate, Davis did not speak other than to cast a few votes on international treaties. No doubt to his dismay, he discovered that the deluge of office seekers he had hoped to escape in leaving the War Department followed him to the Senate. He was now too prominent a public man ever to avoid them. The rush to his door, he said on April 9, "exceeds any thing which has been previously seen here." Meanwhile he helped oversee the inaugural celebrations and then set about closing down the large house on the corner of Eighteenth and G Streets. Since henceforward he would only be in Washington when the Senate was in session, he had no need of a permanent residence. He and Varina auctioned almost everything in the house from carriage and horses to curtains, carpets, china, and "an excellent assortment of Kitchen requisites." But as soon as they moved out of the house, Davis and his son both took ill, as did little Margaret. As a result, they could not leave Washington until April 24 to return to Brierfield for the first time in years.[2]

The trip proved to be a troubled one. Both children showed unmistakable signs of chicken pox before they boarded an Ohio River packet at Wheeling, and even then, peacefully steaming downriver toward home, the impending crisis to the nation could not be escaped. "The fate of the Union" would be decided in the next four years, Davis had told his friend Edwin DeLeon two weeks earlier. Now he found almost all conversation among travelers riveted on the subject. It was either on this trip or on another packet boat that season that Davis dined with Joseph B. Lyman, a Yale graduate who found the Mississippian "most fascinating." "His manner has a tinge of military exactness and formal courtesy," said Lyman, "but once engaged in conversation no public man could be more lavish of his mental stores or more agreeable in his mode of displaying them." What struck Lyman the most, as he remembered their talk six years later, was what Davis said even more than his way of saying it. Davis outlined to him his hope for "the splendid future of an Independent South." "Stimulate domestic manufacturing & local commerce," said Davis. Thus Charleston and New Orleans would vie with Boston and New York as commercial centers. Though Davis was only reiterating his oft-expressed wish for economic and cultural independence from the North, Lyman became convinced that Davis spoke of hopes for an independent Southern nation. "There are no traces in his language of thorough literary culture," Lyman recalled with a bit of Yale condescension, "nor is he a deep and original thinker on the great problems of state-craft."[3]

Certainly the people of Vicksburg disagreed, for when the Davises arrived on May 5 the city gave them a grand welcome, going even further two weeks later in a special barbecue held in Davis's honor. Invitations to speak came from several quarters, as Mississippians wanted to hear again from Davis after his long silence. At the barbecue he obliged them, and again in Jackson on May 29. He looked back on the administration just ended, praised its accomplishments, and lamented its few failures, such as the aborted attempt to acquire Cuba. He hoped William Walker would succeed in Nicaragua, where the reintroduction of slavery promised to spread Southern institutions to Central America. He lauded Pierce's action in repealing the Missouri Compromise and offered thanks that the Republicans—a "faction, grown up to the colossal proportions of a sectional party"—had been defeated in the presidential contest. Buchanan would stand by constitutional principles, he told them. But, as he had said to De Leon, the emergency was not past. "In 1860 the monster crisis was to be met," he told his audience. He hoped for the best, but warned them to prepare for the worst. They must press the work of building a railroad from Jackson to Memphis, thus linking Mississippi with Charleston and the Atlantic seaboard. Mississippi must build factories, he said, "*public* factories for arms and ammunition." He spoke not for rebellion, he declared, but for defense, and when danger came, he would share it with Mississippi. Its peril was his own. He would help his state in overcoming it, "or with her he would perish."[4]

A month later Davis spoke at the Democratic State Convention in Jackson, and here his break with his onetime friend Robert J. Walker came out in the open. Buchanan had appointed Walker territorial governor of Kansas, and almost at once the Yankee-turned-Mississippian appeared to lean too much in favor of the free-state men. Davis sided with those who passed a resolution censuring Walker and later told Pierce that he had felt that the convention was "entirely on my side."[5]

As usual, Davis felt it his duty to take the stump to support the gubernatorial nominee, in this case William McWillie, and to enter the fight for the congressional seat in his own home district. He announced an ambitious seventeen-day schedule through mid-September and early October, with speeches slated for all but five days and a few scattered appearances before the main tour began. The canvass started well enough, with Davis even retaining a good measure of humor at a little boy who chided him for speaking ill of his old enemy Foote. And when two boys at a coach stop, one Whig and the other Democrat, got into a fight over issues they no doubt understood little or nothing about, the senator broke them apart and calmed them with his gentle manner. It was not yet time for blows. Yet, on only his second appearance, at Holly

Springs on September 12, Davis's health collapsed. He had suffered chills the day before, appeared "quite feeble" to his listeners, and immediately had to leave for Memphis to return home.[6]

Of course this did not deter him for long. By October 2 he was back on the stump, speaking at Mississippi City and going on from there to Pass Christian and then to Jackson for a final address on November 4. His text remained much the same as earlier in the summer, only longer and more fulsome. Kansas claimed most of his attention, always Kansas, and on it, as on all issues of the day, he proclaimed his position fixed. Indeed, he declared that, being the result of "deliberate conviction," his opinions "he had no power to change, unless the course of events had shown him that he was in error." It was as neat an admission of his oft-criticized inflexibility as he ever made.

Of Kansas he warned them to be ready for more. That summer free-state men boycotted a territorial election for delegates to the constitutional convention then meeting in Lecompton. Thus it was expected that a proslave constitution would be forthcoming. If such were the case, it could only become law when Congress recognized it and admitted Kansas as a state. But if a Northern majority in Congress should reject the constitution because it countenanced slavery, then the South would have to resist. Yet he chastised "the brainless intemperance" of those who clamored for disunion. They must strive to preserve that Union, he said, so long as in honor and dignity they could remain a part of it. Beyond that, he said, "Give me liberty, or give me death." As part of that liberty, he urged again his notion of a Southern "system," internal improvements, building factories, even reforming education to eliminate all textbooks that contained opinions at odds with his notion of the blessings of slavery. He wanted children learning from proper books that "would indoctrinate their minds with sound impressions and views," rather than allowing them to see opposing viewpoints that might corrupt their minds. Schoolteachers must be trained in the South, which for too long had relied on itinerant Yankee educators who brought concealed antislavery convictions with them. There must be more military schools, armories, and an expansion of the militia. He "gloried" in asserting the abstract right of secession, however much he pleaded for remaining in the Union, he said. But as a loyal son of Mississippi, his course would be guided by its.[7]

It is no wonder that by now the *New York Herald*, which never liked Davis, called him "the Mephistophiles of the South." He could not speak of the Union without dropping some hint of secession in his next breath. He used the two like the carrot and the stick, to persuade and to threaten both his listeners in Mississippi and those in the North whom he knew would read reports of his remarks. And when he appended his protestations of love for the country and detestation of disunionists to discourses on how the South should arm itself for resistance, his words not surprisingly had only a hollow sincerity. Ever the hairsplitter, Davis saw in his positions a difference that the rest of the South, and the rest of the nation, did not necessarily recognize. He decried "disunionists" as men who openly worked to tear the sections apart. He applauded "secessionists" as men who recognized the constitutional right to withdraw from the Union what they had given on admission to statehood. In his mind they were two very different things, though to most ears they sounded remarkably the same. Back in August he told his friend Lewis Cass that he felt himself "a pretty good secessionist." To an increasing number of Americans, that sounded as if he was a disunionist as well. Still, as one Washington editor commented, "Col. Davis is not the South." Indeed he was not—not yet.[8]

Late in November the Davises returned to Washington again, taking rooms in a house on G Street, and on December 7, when the Senate reconvened, he took his seat. Kansas waited but one day to rear its head. On December 8 Buchanan sent a message to Congress that clearly implied his support of the Lecompton constitution. Almost at once Douglas rose to oppose the Lecompton document, saying that it did not represent the true will of the settlers of Kansas on all issues, thus starting a firestorm all over again. While Davis attended a number of Democratic caucuses, no doubt making Kansas the chief topic of discussion, he spoke little on the subject on the floor other than to try to postpone debate, likely hoping that time would calm passions or at least calm Douglas so that the Lecompton constitution could be accepted. With the party appearing to fragment over the issue, it was vital to husband every vote. Unfortunately, many in the Buchanan administration looked to Toombs to lead the fight against Douglas and for Lecompton, but the Georgian hesitated out of old friendship for the Little Giant. Some speculated that Davis would have to step in for him, yet Davis was already working on a pet bill of his own to increase the army yet again by adding companies to existing regiments.[9]

But of course Davis could not stay out of the Kansas fight for long. On February 8 he rose to declare his support for Buchanan and Lecompton. He decried the antagonism he saw in the chamber, declaring that a stranger entering it might think he had stumbled into a collection of men preparing for war rather than meeting to settle the issues of the nation. He expressed his section's viewpoint when he listed the litany of wrongs inflicted upon the South, attack after attack, threat after threat, and then asked in all innocence what the South had done to deserve this. He could not understand that in the constant resort to threats of secession by himself and others, Northerners—Democrats and Republicans alike—saw hints of a design to split the Union. Neither could they understand that in their efforts to contain slavery and keep it out of the new territories, Davis and his friends saw hints of a design to weaken and strangle the South. Both sides saw what they imagined, not what was. None of this, as Davis said himself, was "the means by which fraternity is to be preserved, or this Union rendered perpetual."[10]

When Davis rose to speak again in the Senate, many more now looked to take the measure of a man widely conceded to be a leading spokesman for the South, if not in fact its preeminent advocate. They saw in him "a tall, thin, nervous-looking man, with sharp features and a keen, restless eye." Everyone commented on his slimness, and some saw in him a "stooping and not personally prepossessing" stature. Yet when he spoke, all observers confessed that everyone listened. They noted his pointed comments, his ready command of his material, and "that precision of enunciation which marks a scholar." A Boston woman admitted that he "has a strange fascination in his tone," and that she found his voice "mild, firm, gently modulated," with "nothing in his mien of namby-pamby or affected." "They say he is a fire eater," she wrote. "If so, I know he eats it *a la mode*, with a fork and napkin."[11]

Others noted how he worked the floor of the Senate when he was not debating, talking earnestly in quiet tones with this man and that, moving from seat to seat to test sentiment and support. On January 30, when Senator Hale of New Hampshire delivered an address that was characteristically antislavery in its tone, most of his opposition simply did not stay to listen. But Davis was there, along with Toombs and Hunter, and now the latter two came to the Mississippian's seat, signifying to at least one witness that they acknowledged him their leader. Davis listened attentively to each with an "easy but authoritative bearing," at the same time hearing what Hale was saying. On other occasions, annoyed observers saw Davis among the least attentive as he shuffled papers, wrote notes, sealed envelopes, and attended to all the other distracting little chores that senators indulged when they did not care to listen. Not unmindful of his lack of attention at times, Davis once jocularly announced before he spoke that he would not be offended if others left the chamber. Those who stayed remarked, as usual, on his didactic pronouncements. "He seems more addicted to the enunciation of the results of his investigation and researches, than to ratiocination," one reporter wrote. "He gives the ultimate inference, but suppresses the mental process by which he discovered it." Whether arguing for his bill to increase the army or his hopes that the transcontinental railroad would run from Texas to California, he began and ended his debates in the unshakable certitude that he and he alone was right.[12]

Davis spoke only briefly on Kansas on February 8, in part because he was not yet ready to tell the Senate what was right. More to the point, however, he did not feel like speaking. Already he felt the onset of what proved to be a major collapse in his health. Around February 12 he came down with a cold and then laryngitis, which quickly brought on an attack in his left eye once more. Rapidly his condition worsened, to the point at which doctors and friends worried seriously whether he would recover. For seven weeks he stayed in his bed in a darkened room, often unable or unwilling to speak. To Varina he communicated his thoughts and wishes by scrawling messages in chalk on a slate at his bedside. Daily his eye swelled ever larger until she believed it "was in imminent danger of bursting." So great was the pain that when Varina urged him to eat something, he emitted a muffled scream and cried, "I am in anguish, I cannot." In time the swelling began to subside, though the primitive treatments administered by his doctors did little to aid him. Leeches certainly did nothing, and the atropine doses he took may even have worsened his condition in the long run, contributing to a possible secondary glaucoma in addition to the herpes that already ravaged the eye.

Visitors constantly offered their good wishes, and they came from all across the political spectrum, demonstrating that Davis enjoyed the personal goodwill even of many of his public foes. Seward called almost daily, sometimes more than once a day, telling Davis all the news of the Senate and delighting in repeating the speeches from both sides of the aisle. Colonel Sumner called repeatedly, talking of old days in the army on the frontier to take the sufferer's mind from his ordeal. William J. Hardee, commandant of cadets at the Military Academy, paid his respects, as did foreign diplomats and dignitaries. Davis's new friend Clement Clay of Alabama sometimes sat up with him all night, giving Varina time to rest while he ministered to the invalid. All were deeply affected by Davis's suffering. Seward sometimes left the sick chamber with tears in his eyes.

Not until March did some little bit of strength return to him, though his left eye remained all but blind. When he could move—though against Varina's and the doctors' wishes—he struggled to the room above his where his young brother-in-law and namesake Jefferson Davis Howell lay ill with scarlet fever. There Varina found him, with the boy's head cradled in his arms, softly whispering "bear stories" to the child.[13]

Reports of Davis's condition went out in the press to the nation at large, only enhancing the sympathy felt for him. Most affecting of all, however, must have been the manifestations of friendship that transcended party bounds. Late in March the bill admitting Kansas as a state under the Lecompton constitution faced a challenge when Crittenden proposed a substitute bill that would resubmit the constitution to the settlers of Kansas in a supervised election free from frauds or boycotts. Naturally Davis opposed any such resubmission, and even though his health was still precarious, he announced his intention to be in the Senate on March 23 when Crittenden's substitute came to a vote. Varina and his doctors pleaded with him, but his resolve remained fixed. Only one thing could keep him out of the Senate, and that would be for some Republican senator to observe the oft-honored courtesy of "pairing" with him. Davis let it be known that he would stay home and not risk his life if an opponent would pair with him. One Republican stepped forward, his old friend from Pennsylvania, Simon Cameron. Perhaps it helped that the defeat of Crittenden's substitute was a foregone conclusion, but still Cameron took considerable criticism for his act.[14]

Davis could only look on from his darkened sickroom as the Kansas battle continued into April without him. Seeking some sort of compromise, the Senate and House created a conference committee that on April 23 reported a possible solution. Leaving the matter of slavery untouched, the committee proposed that the proposed land grant for the new state be severely reduced, and that on this basis Kansas should go to the polls. If they accepted the shrunken state boundaries, statehood would be granted under the Lecompton constitution, slavery and all. If they rejected the measure, statehood would be postponed pending more population.

The English Bill—named for its framer, Indiana Congressman William English—outraged many Republicans and Democrats alike, but it put them in a serious dilemma. The bill clearly provided an opportunity for all Kansans to accept or reject slavery, but only indirectly, as a by-product of the land-grant issue. Still, in the eyes of Davis and many Southerners, it gave Kansans a chance to decide their domestic institutions for themselves at the time of statehood, which he argued was the only point at which slavery could be decided upon in a territory. Thus, even though most assumed that such an election in Kansas would result in the defeat of the English compromise, and thus delay statehood, the men of the South by and large supported it.

The vote on the English Bill came on April 29, and fearing that it would be close, Davis determined to be present at any cost. On the appointed day he had himself carried to the Senate chamber, where he took his seat and listened to some of the debate before finding that the vote would not come until the next day. On April 30 he returned. This time he walked in, Varina supporting him on one side and his doctor on the other. All eyes turned to watch him as with faltering tread he made his way down the aisle. One observer found him "a pale, ghastly-looking person, his eye bandaged with strips of white linen, his whole aspect denoting feebleness." He had taken a small hand in this bill, having consulted with Alexander H. Stephens of Georgia, who exerted much influence in the conference committee, and he was not about to let it go down to defeat without voting in its favor. When the tally was final, the English Bill passed by nine votes and did the same in the House. Davis was elated, calling it a "triumph of all for which we contended." Several months later Kansans voted down the land-grant reduction, effectively killing the Lecompton constitution, slavery, and statehood for the time, but still Davis felt that a principle had been vindicated, and if Kansas was not a slave state, at least it was not a free state either.[15]

By early May, the spectral form of the senator from Mississippi began to assume more and more of its old stature and animation. Though still effectively blind in his left eye, he felt well enough to start attending sessions regularly by the tenth, and a day later he stood up once more to enter the debate, though with Kansas out of the way there was little to occupy his voice other than bills on fishing boundaries and legislative appropriations.

Yet almost as soon as he took his seat, Davis revealed a side of himself that few admired, and one no doubt severely aggravated by his recent terrible illness. Rarely patient with opposition or disagreement, he became increasingly belligerent and even offensive. It helped that almost everyone was losing his temper by that summer. Senator Gwin of California and Senator Henry Wilson of Massachusetts got into a shameful verbal brawl on June 10, and a challenge was issued. Only the personal intervention of Davis and Seward averted bloodshed. A few weeks later Davis's brother-in-law Joseph Howell fought a duel in New Orleans with a Nicaraguan filibusterer and got carried away, ignoring rules and decorum and firing until he hit his antagonist twice. And by this time Davis himself had almost become involved in at least two "affairs of honor."[16]

Of course Davis was instinctively combative when challenged or offended and, as he occasionally admitted, he provoked confrontations by the jugular instinct that seized him when he got into a heated argument. His reputation in some quarters, as 1858 began, was for being "quarrelsome, petulant, hot-headed, turbulent." Back in February he had gotten into a verbal exchange with William Pitt Fessenden of Maine that attracted notice for its hostility. Then, on June 3, having returned to the Senate from his sickroom, he became even more confrontational with Zachariah Chandler of Michigan. When Chandler asked a perfectly reasonable question, Davis replied contemptuously that it was "impertinent and silly." Chandler countered that "your answer is impertinent," and then, a few minutes later, when he complained of it again, Davis responded, "You know your redress."

Seward intervened to keep the argument from going to a challenge, but already observers complained about the breakdown in decorum in Washington. "I do not know that I can conscientiously assert that Congressional manners are deteriorating," wrote a correspondent for the *New York Times*, "but certainly they are not improving." An acquaintance of Davis believed that, in his case at least, recent illness probably explained "his frequent outbursts of temper and spleen," while other friends felt at a loss to explain or excuse his behavior. They were really left wondering after yet another exchange on June 8, in discussing the adoption of breech-loading arms by the military, a subject on which Davis felt himself preeminently competent and therefore least likely to brook opposition. The dissent came from his friend Senator Judah P. Benjamin of Louisiana, and it was civil enough. But Davis immediately overreacted and then sneered condescendingly, leaving Benjamin to reply that Davis's "manner is not agreeable at all."

"If the Senator happens to find it disagreeable," said Davis, "I hope he will keep it to himself." Even more hostile words, not reported or later expunged from the Senate journals, passed between them, and that evening Benjamin apparently sent Davis a challenge. Again Seward intervened, aided by John Slidell of Louisiana and Clay of Alabama, and even Davis apparently realized how far he had overstepped proper bounds. He tore up the challenge and issued an apology the next day.[17]

For a man of such storied self-control, Davis showed in his life an alarming penchant for leaping to violence, even with friends. Though he never went to the dueling ground, still in the past twenty-five years he had come close to it with his friend Harney, with Foote twice, with Bissell, with Toombs, and now with Chandler and Benjamin, not to mention close calls with Fessenden and Scott. For all his praise for being a moderate, and for all his own claims of being a temperate man above petty matters of personality, the fact is that he had probably been involved in as many—if not more—near duels than any other man in the Senate. Varina could see it. "If anyone differs with Mr. Davis he resents it," she wrote, "and ascribes the difference to the perversity of his opponent." To her husband himself she would say that "you have not been a conciliatory man in your manners always," and Davis himself had to admit his fault after the Benjamin fiasco. "I have an infirmity of which I am ashamed," he said. "When I am aroused in a matter, I lose control of my feeling and become personal." Obviously, there were moments when Jefferson Davis could be penetratingly objective about himself, but those moments were few, and despite admitting his "infirmity," he could never entirely control himself. The bitter confrontation with Benjamin would not be his last, only the one that most glaringly revealed the thoughtless passion that seethed within him, always ready to erupt at a pinprick.[18]

When Congress adjourned on June 16, Davis must have realized that he was not as much recovered as he thought. Troubled in mind as well as weak in body, he needed to get away, just as his physicians had been advising him for some time. The summer in Washington could be almost as hot as in Mississippi. Rather than return to Brierfield, where he would only further exhaust himself trying to mend his faltering plantation, he would go north to New England, to the cooler climes and the welcoming hand of his old friend A. D. Bache. When he left the capital with Varina on July 2 or 3, he would not return for nearly four months—months that remained in his memory for the rest of his life as among his most tranquil and soothing.

They boarded the steamer *Joseph Whitney* in Baltimore on July 3 and were at sea the next day when Captain S. Howes suggested that they celebrate the Fourth with a speech from the ship's most distinguished passenger. Davis obliged in fine style, looking back on the early glorious history of the country that the day commemorated. Going further, he condemned recent British adventuring on the seas, continuing a long-held Anglophobia, and then proclaimed Americans an undivided people. "Trifling politicians in the South, or in the North, or in the West, may continue to talk otherwise," he said, but they could only annoy the Union, not destroy it.[19]

It was a noble sentiment, at odds with much of what he had said in recent years, yet he repeated substantially the same sentiments elsewhere during his vacation. Arriving in Boston, he received a cordial public welcome and then went on to Portland, Maine, where an even warmer reception awaited him. Here the senator and his family remained for most of his time away from Washington, traveling, exploring, resting his body and mind. In September he went to stay with Bache at a Coastal Survey camp, where they all lived in tents outdoors. There were picnics and clambakes, and Varina could see that "happy in the society of intelligent men of bright minds and cordial manners, Mr. Davis hourly improved, and found here entire rest and recreation." On the plateau atop Mount Humpback, they joined Bache with a cook, fresh local vegetables, tenderloin steaks brought in from Bangor, books aplenty, and a new music box that played several songs from the most recent Verdi operas. Nothing relieved Davis so much as being so far away from the noise and bustle of Washington that at night he could hear the leaves falling. Even a measure of sight returned to his eye, while the strength came back to his limbs.

Everywhere, sometimes to his astonishment, Davis met with friendship and smiles. This was not the North of men like Chandler and Wilson and Fessenden. Indeed, shortly after his arrival at Portland, Maine, Bowdoin College even bestowed an honorary LL.D. degree on him. Davis made more speeches, repeated his sentiments about "trifling politicians" and the stability of the Union, and even came to believe that the people of Maine were not like other Yankees. Given their preference, he concluded, they would like to secede and attach themselves to the more congenial Canadians to their north and west.[20]

In the latter part of August he learned that not even in Maine could he escape politics, and that his public comments excited much discussion elsewhere. His old foe the *New York Herald* applauded his sentiments, saying it was agreeably disappointed that this ultra-fire-eater expressed such pacific sentiments. "It is free from all sectional and party bias," the *Herald* said of one of his speeches, "free from ultraisms of every kind, and is thoroughly marked with good sense and patriotic feeling." Davis might come to outshine all other Southerners and loom even higher on the political horizon if he continued on such a course. Farther to the south the *Richmond Enquirer* echoed those sentiments. Complaining that Northerners had until then called Davis a "nullifier, disunionist and fire-eater, . . . and the most terrible and dangerous man in the Senate," the editors proudly printed his speeches that everyone might see the true "benevolent and enlarged spirit of nationality" of the man. And far away in New Orleans, the friendly press applauded him for seeing through the "disunion-at-any-cost gentry" and their doctrine, though admitting that his speeches must surely leave them "distressed at the gallant gentleman's defection."[21]

Distressed, indeed. The *New Orleans Delta*, always fickle toward Davis, sneered at his patriotic sentiments. Elsewhere among ardent Southern-rights editors he met with even harsher criticism, but nowhere so severe as in Charleston. "Of all the signal examples of startling Southern defection that the venality of the times has afforded," said the *Mercury*, "there is none that can at all compare with this." The *Mercury* never cared for Davis and never would. He was too moderate for its tastes. "The Jefferson Davis that we loved is no more!" it said. "What a pitiable spectacle of human weakness and political tergiversation!" That he would denounce disunionists, who had all along supported him as a champion of the South, was the worst sort of treachery. Disgusted, the editor of the *Mercury* concluded that Davis should "not only go to Boston but stay there." Obviously, just as Davis's repeated enunciation of the abstract right of secession branded him a disunionist in the eyes of his Northern foes, any expression of fondness for the old Union made him equally despised by the ultra-fire-eaters of the South. Neither side fully understood the man, or else both heard only what they wanted to. As for Davis himself, he stood far closer to the *Mercury* than he or its editor realized.[22]

The Davises did stop in Boston on their way back from Maine and there encountered another outpouring of welcome and sympathy when their son Jeff Jr. fell ill. Davis visited the home of the late Daniel Webster and toured the harbor and its fortifications. On October 11 he accepted an invitation to address a Democratic meeting at Faneuil Hall and showed how recovered he felt by speaking for well over an hour. A week later he addressed another party crowd in New York. On both occasions he showed none of the ardent states rights' spirit that characterized his debates in the Senate or on the hustings in Mississippi. Clearly Davis tailored his remarks for the crowd, no doubt adding to the suspicion in some quarters that he was really touring New England not for his health but to test support for an 1860 presidential bid. This Davis emphatically denied, lamenting that already "the land swarms with Presidential candidates." But neither would he respond to the surprisingly warm feeling shown him in the North by haranguing his hosts. In his mind, he was seeing the true people of the North. The problem in national affairs was that they were not accurately represented by their men in Washington; he would save his venom for them.[23]

By late October, Davis was back in Washington, but only for a week before leaving for Mississippi. The fever season had passed, his own health was much restored, and he needed to look to Brierfield before he returned for the winter session. During the past several years overseers had managed the plantation for him, and none met his standards of conduct or management. The overseers let the house run down, mistreated the slaves, and did not keep up the crops—which would have been poor in any case. The river ran high repeatedly, and as recently as the past June much of Davis's plantation sat under water. Though he was home for barely three weeks in November, still he had much to do if his livelihood as a planter was to continue.[24]

Meanwhile, he had to take measures to repair his relations with his Mississippi constituents, as well as others in the South at large, who felt disturbed by his speeches in New England. On November 11 he spoke to a massive assemblage in Jackson, and though he showed his age—now fifty-one—and the ravages of his recent illness and recuperation, still his baritone voice range out as strong as ever. It was the Davis of old who spoke to them. After defending his decision to go north for his health rather than return to Mississippi for the summer recess, he explained his remarks there as kindness for kindness. Then he proceeded to outline once more his ardent states' rights beliefs, his denunciation of the so-called Black Republicans, and of Douglas and other Northern Democrats who did not stand by the South in asserting its rights. He warned that after the next elections, the antislavery people would control a majority in the House of Representatives, and that Southerners should expect legislation injurious to their interests. And, should a Republican win the White House in 1860, it would not be an election but "a species of revolution by which the purposes of the Government would be destroyed and the observance of its mere forms entitled to no respect." In that event, he recommended, Mississippi should leave the Union and be ready to defend itself. Though disruption of the Union would be a great calamity, he confessed, it would not be the greatest. It would be far worse to live in a nation ruled by one sectional party bent on using the powers of government to infringe on the rights of another. Again, he said, Build your armories, make your weapons, expand your railroads so that in time of peril the forces of the Southern states can be combined to meet an enemy.

Even the *Charleston Mercury* should have taken some satisfaction. Back on his home soil, Davis showed what lay within him. He did not call for secession now as an end in itself, as did the fire-eaters of South Carolina. But, predicating the action on a specific event, he called for it in two years and moreover stated that he expected disunion to meet with resistance, and that the South should be ready to meet that resistance with force. Jefferson Davis may have thought of himself as a moderate, even conciliatory, man, but almost everywhere else in the Union except South Carolina his sentiments put him near the forefront of the secession movement. For every word he said for the Union, he uttered ten for the impending necessity of secession and self-defense.

Were there to be any doubt of the direction in which his views inevitably led it was erased in a farewell speech he made in Vicksburg late in November before his return to Washington. "Col. Davis does not yet despair of the Union," a listener reported. For yet another uncountable time he went over his West Point education, his service on the frontier, his fighting for the flag in Mexico, and all the other items in the litany of associations that, he said, bound him to the Union. And then, as always, he continued with a "but." He advised the people of Vicksburg not to feel a false security and to make "immediate preparations for our defence." If an "Abolition President" should win the White House in 1860, he said, Southerners should make certain that the man "should never be permitted to take his seat in the Presidential Chair." The Union would be dissolved by such an election, he said, and he "would be in favor of holding the city of Washington, the public archives, and the glorious star spangled banner, declaring the Government at an end, and maintaining our rights and honor, even though blood should flow in torrents throughout the land." To live under Republican rule would be a disgrace. "As for himself," said Davis, he "would rather appeal to the God of Battles at once than to attempt to live longer in such a Union."[25]

Of course, Davis may have been incorrectly reported in the local press, though as a rule he showed a penchant for accuracy and often demanded corrections when misreported. He issued no such correction after this speech appeared in print. Within himself, for the moment at least, he had crossed a moral divide. In the debates on Lecompton, he made it clear that an election was an election, regardless of how the losing side felt. But that was because he favored the result of that election. Now, in anticipating an unfavorable result in 1860, he advocated insurrection to prevent the winner of such a contest from taking office, even to occupying forcibly the national capital, though he always argued that it was the property of all the people and therefore its occupation by Southern-rights soldiers would constitute an act of piracy. Davis backed

away from this extreme pronouncement before long, but for an afternoon in Vicksburg in November 1858, he actually stood abreast with or
ahead of the *Charleston Mercury*, advocating not just defense but aggression.

If Davis wavered across the disunion line that fall and winter, it
may have been because he was not as indifferent toward his own presidential possibilities as he pretended. Having seen the office firsthand
during his intimate years with Pierce, he always maintained that it was a
position that he would not want under any circumstances. It was a killing, thankless job, made especially so by the lack of harmony in the
nation. Yet Davis certainly appeared to be speaking to the sentiments of
both sides of the political battlefield that season, though the two were so
obviously incompatible—ardent pro-Union words in Boston and Maine,
radical secessionist sentiments in Mississippi. Furthermore, in December, when he returned to Washington, one of his first acts—after the
usual protest that "public duty required a course different from that
which personal preference would indicate"—was to authorize the collection of a number of his speeches into a pamphlet to appear that spring.
Significantly, it included his arguments against the Compromise of 1850,
his Union speeches in New England, and his semi-fire-eating address in
Jackson the past November. Thus he spoke to all the political factions.
Motivation can be found in part in the fact that his enemy Brown now
worked at getting the presidential nomination himself—or his friends
did so on his behalf, and they claimed that Brown's "big trump" was his
opposition to Douglas. Davis stood considerably ahead of Brown in that
department, and his pamphlet would show it. Perhaps Davis was sincere
in denying he had presidential aspirations, though, of course, he habitually denied seeking any office. The office always "sought" him. Perhaps, having seen the feeling in New England that he could excite, a
natural ambition arose within him, along with a sincere hope that he
might be the man who could reunite the two quarreling sections. Most
likely of all, as so often before in his life, Jefferson Davis simply was not
certain at all of what he truly wanted.[26]

Mercifully it was a short session of Congress, lasting only until
March 3, with a week-long special session of the Senate to follow. Most
of his participation in the debates related to the pending Pacific railroad
bill, for which he always felt ardent support. Some in the Senate politely
accused him of showing an unwarranted bias in favor of a Southern
route—citing his efforts to explore and open the southwest during his
days as Secretary of War—but this Davis denied. A northern route could
be just as feasible, he argued, though it would be "vastly expensive." "I
believe a road is necessary," he said. "I ardently desire to see a road built
somewhere." Davis even protested that if the government finally chose a
southern route, it would not result in benefit to the South, for "it would

bring those hordes of 'carpet-bag men,' who are always dangerous to the slave population of the country with which they are mingled." No one across the aisle accepted his protest of unbias. "I know of no man in the Senate or the country," said Wilson of Massachusetts, "who is more biased by sectional feeling." Putting his finger deftly on the point Davis could not see, Wilson went on to suggest that "he is, I doubt not, unconscious of it."[27]

Davis spoke for several days in succession for the railroad, even though at times he stood almost alone, as most of his Southern compatriots opposed it as unconstitutional for the government to build anything on state property. Toombs of Georgia did say he would favor the road if it ran through the southern part of the country, for then after secession, it would be the South's railroad, but Davis did not take up that line of argument, neither endorsing nor condemning it. Even the subject of the presidency came into play, when Andrew Johnson of Tennessee and others lamented that any man speaking in favor of measures that expanded the Union—like the railroad to California—was accused of politicking for a nomination. Certainly a few suspected Davis of such motives in pushing the bill, especially when he did so almost alone and unsupported by his Southern colleagues. Yet there was nothing at all inconsistent in Davis's stance with the attitude he had taken for years, long before anyone spoke seriously of him for the White House.[28]

No wonder that, in the midst of the railroad debate, Davis confided to Pierce that "we are dragging on here in a manner significant of no good to the country." "Each day renders me more hopeless of effecting any thing for the present or prospective benefit of the country by legislation of Congress." More than ever men spoke extreme opinions. If there was hope now, he said, it lay with the public. His New England trip had opened his eyes. "The field of useful labor is now among the people. . . . Temperate, true men could effect much by giving to the opposite section the views held by the other," he said. "The difference is less than I had supposed." There was the statesmanlike wisdom and temperance that Davis frequently showed yet so often could not sustain.[29]

As always, and especially when he evidenced flashes of rising above his sectional compulsions, Davis attracted the admiration of most who heard him. "He must have had great depth of character," a Senate page recalled. "He seemed always to be absorbed in things above the common level." Another declared that "cool criticism will place Mr. Davis nearer to Mr. Clay than any speaker in the Senate." By the "splendor of his talents," she wrote in 1859, Davis had "raised himself to an eminence of consideration, not only in the public position he fills, but throughout the entire country." True enough, Davis could still appear uncommonly severe, and "often unintentionally offends," said one observer, yet most agreed with the Senate reporter who found Davis "a favorite with the majority."[30]

To his credit, Davis enjoyed excellent social relations with men of all political hues during his years in the Senate. His closeness to Seward and to Cameron and even a passing acquaintance with Sumner showed that he could leave the heat of the debates in the Senate chamber. Indeed, at times during the years in Washington, when health allowed, Davis could be what Varina thought "the life of the party," singing Indian songs learned on the prairies, giving dinners for old army officers, and even mingling socially with Southerners like Toombs, whom he did not particularly like. When Varina felt well enough, they gave parties matching the best the capital social scene offered. This puzzled some of those who knew him, wondering as they did how a man so pleasant and warm one moment could be so cold, unyielding, even hostile the next. Davis's social cordiality, like his support of the Pacific railroad, had little or nothing to do with his presidential ambitions, though many others in Washington that year strove to bind old wounds. It was a side of his nature to be open, courteous, and inviting, just as the other side produced obstinacy and venom.[31]

Nothing brought out the latter as did Kansas. Like the disease in his eye that never healed, it subsided for a time, then returned painfully once more. On February 22, 1859, the Senate discussed it yet again, as men sought a way to bring the territory into the Union even before it achieved the constitutionally mandated population required to justify a congressional delegate. Douglas took the floor, protesting the South's incessant insistence on "pretty controversies in relation to African labor" and declaring that the Democratic party was being split fatally. Davis leapt on him, denying that Kansans had any right to act against slavery, even when word reached the chamber during his speech that the territorial legislature had done just that. "Never will I consent to abandon a constitutional right at the mere bidding of popular prejudice," said Davis. Not stopping there, he accused Douglas of abandoning true popular sovereignty principles in order to curry favor for the Democratic nomination in 1860's convention in Charleston. Douglas "is now as full of heresy as he once was of adherence to the doctrine of popular sovereignty," said the Mississippian. Fortunately the debate ended before his expressions could become more heated, for Douglas—though a Democrat—was one of those Northerners with whom Davis did not, and would not, get along.[32]

Davis left Washington less than a week after the end of the special session, with nothing settled on the railroad or Kansas, and returned to Brierfield. Varina was pregnant again, and on April 18 she gave birth to another son. Because her time was so near, she had remained in Washington, and her husband received word of the new baby several days later, his joy tempered by anxiety, since her pregnancies always seemed to leave her health precarious. Yet she came through the ordeal better than before, though to her mother she confessed that she wept for five days because her husband wanted to name the boy after his uncle Joseph Davis. She had to admit that the infant favored her brother-in-law, though "I pray he may grow out of the resemblance." Obviously that wound had not yet healed, but Jefferson had his way, and the baby would be named Joseph Evan Davis.[33]

Much of Varina's anxiety was for her husband, too, for the reports from Brierfield were anything but good. The water rose dangerously high again in late March, with the levees not expected to hold, while heavy rains threatened to ruin the cotton crop. On April 9 the levee gave way not far from Brierfield, and all the livestock from both Davis plantations had to be evacuated by boat. Some later called the river an "inland sea" that season, and Jefferson Davis found that he could step from the porch of Brierfield directly into a boat and row all the way to Hurricane through what used to be Eliza Davis's garden. "I have never known Jeff so distressed and broken down," Varina lamented. When his letters arrived describing the devastation of much of their plantation, she thought she saw evidence that tears had fallen on the pages as he wrote. "I have been necessarily much exposed," Davis said of himself, "and can but feel the depressing circumstances by which we are surrounded."[34]

In the midst of this woe, a telegram reached him reporting that Varina was ill. Immediately Davis returned to Washington, having done what little he could for Brierfield, and by May 1 he was at her side once more, finding her not so bad off as he had believed, or at least not physically. Varina at times affected a kind of hypochondria, exaggerating her illnesses perhaps as a way of competing for attention with her husband, about whose bouts of ill health no doubt existed. But this time her misery was mental. She could not accept the name of the new boy, and almost certainly there were serious and strained discussions when Davis reached her. She wanted the child named for her father, though she did not question her husband's "perfect right" to choose the boy's name. With resignation, she acquiesced. "I could never participate in paying, in my opinion, the highest compliment in a woman's power to a man whose very name was only suggestive to me of injustice and unkindness from my youth up to middle age," Varina told her mother. "I come so near hating him." But Joseph Evan the boy remained just the same.[35]

The Davises stayed in Washington until early June, when the senator finally to surgery for his left eye—quite likely an incision into the cornea to relieve a buildup of fluid that caused him pain. For several days he recuperated and then took the whole family to Oakland, Maryland, for a vacation. Here Varina rested while a nurse took care of the children. Davis himself did not remain long, leaving before the end of the month to return to Mississippi. There was much to prepare for, with a convention due in Jackson on July 6. Even as Varina chided him to remember that while he was only part of a powerful party, "you are all to your wife and babes," he hurried to prepare a major address for the convention.[36]

After detailing the usual history of progress under safe Democratic leadership, the customary justifications of slavery on legal, moral, and racial grounds, he went on the offensive against the Republicans for their "sectional, fanatical hostility," their attempt to take control of the government for the ends of abolition or emancipation. Blacks were born to be slaves, he said—they could be little else. The experiment in Liberia with freed Negroes had failed miserably. They were a "subservient race" and always would be. They could not found civil governments, and would not seperate themselves from their white masters. He pointed to the fact that freedmen in the North had not moved into the new western territories to start their own towns and states. Slaves could never survive if freed, and therefore Southerners needed to have guarantees from the federal government that their rights in all forms of "property" would be recognized and protected.

He returned to the perennial subject of Cuba and how much it needed to be a part of the Union. He would not seize it—he favored negotiations and purchase from Spain, but he warned that if ever it fell into hostile hands (and he thought at the moment of Great Britain) then it should be taken by force at once. Obviously it would become a slave state. At the same time, he admitted that if an attempt were made to acquire portions of Canada, certainly destined to be free states, for the Union, he would not assist in their acquisition and therefore declared that they should not ask for or expect Northern help with Cuba. Davis could be a hypocrite on many issues, but this was not one of them. "We should not expect or claim more than, under like circumstances, we would grant," he said.

In the end he reached the inevitable conclusion to all his speeches. The Northern mind had been "perverted" and alienated from the fraternity "due to the South." Every day in Congress he heard the epithets hurled at Southerners and their institutions. "Can pigmies look down upon your colossal sons?" he asked Mississippians. "Your sons have set at the table builded by their fathers; and if it shall ever be possessed by an unclean presence, from which they cannot expurgate it, then it will devolve upon them to construct another." Two choices lay before them and their fellow Southerners, subjugation or freedom. If the Republicans won in 1860, then the Union must be dissolved. "I love and venerate the union of these States," he said, "but I love liberty and Mississippi more." Their only hope for 1860 was reconciliation by the election of a good Northern Democrat of conservative principles. The alternative was probably war.[37]

While the weight of his words settled into the minds of his hearers, Davis returned to Brierfield to continue the seemingly hopeless task of repairing the recent damage. Late in July he went to Washington, falling ill once more on the way, and only rejoined his family in Maryland around mid-August. There he remained, resting, playing with his children, and enjoying such as he could the respite from national troubles. Varina remained unwell, and Davis himself feared a relapse in his own health. Still he watched and felt the national pulse and advised Pierce that, properly managed, he believed the ex-president might just secure the nomination in Charleston, now less than a year away. Certainly Davis hoped for it, for he saw in Pierce exactly the man he told the Jackson convention could keep the Union together. At the same time, seeing Douglas's and Seward's obvious politicking for nominations by their parties, he felt only disgust. As always adhering to the increasingly antique notion that a man should never actively seek office, he condemned the "low chicanery" they practiced. The presidency could never be filled "by one who has sought it in the mode and by the means known as electioneering."[38]

All the standards by which Davis had lived were breaking down before his eyes. As he had feared, the old Union, composed as it had been of two largely national parties, lay split along geographical lines by a sectional issue. A new party flourished, born in that issue and nurtured exclusively in one section that felt hostility toward a cherished right of the other. Now, sensing power, statesmen were abandoning the time-honored tradition of being called to office in favor of gracelessly seeking it. And all because of slavery, a benevolent institution that raised blacks morally and intellectually beyond anything they could ever be on their own. It preyed on Davis's mind even as he vacationed, as he returned to Washington for a few days, and as he left for Mississippi again on October 14. There was more work to do, more speeches to make, more bolstering needed of Mississippi's resolve in the coming crisis.

Yet even with the breakdown of the old order that he saw, still Davis was not prepared for the telegraphic news that flashed across the country two days after he left the capital. It probably reached him as his steamboat made a stop on the Ohio. In the culmination of several years of bloody bushwhacking against slaveholders out in "Bleeding Kansas," abolitionist fanatics led by old John Brown had come east and on October 16 attacked the United States arsenal at Harpers Ferry, Virginia, attempting to incite an uprising, arm the slaves, and create a general black revolt in Virginia and eventually the South. The arrival of marines led by Colonel Robert E. Lee quickly put down the insurrection and killed or captured Brown and his followers. The slaves themselves never responded as hoped, and the whole episode in the end appeared almost comically inept if not for its tragic impact. Shots had been fired, blood spilled. Could there be any stopping the march of disunion now? And could disunion be stopped short of open war?

We Have Piped But They Would Not Dance

Twenty years later Jefferson Davis looked back on the Harpers Ferry raid and decided that it had been "insignificant in itself and in its immediate results." However, "It afforded a startling revelation of the extent to which sectional hatred and political fanaticism had blinded the conscience of a class of persons in certain states of the Union." Davis and others easily believed the rumors that Brown had received substantial financial assistance from prominent New Englanders. A few ardent abolitionists did, in fact, furnish arms and money to Brown, but their number was a mere handful. Slaveholders, their paranoia running at a fever pitch, saw in the raid confirmation that masses of Northerners were willing to countenance, even actively encourage, unconstitutional and violent means in order to attack Southern institutions.[1]

Davis did not go to the same lengths as many in the excited crowd. He saw Brown's raid largely for what it was, an ill-advised and ineptly conducted isolated act by a fanatic, backed by other fanatics who did not represent the majority of true Northern feeling. Following his speeches in Mississippi in November, in which he said little that was new other than a promise to "hug her to his heart" should Mississippi decide to secede alone in the event of a Republican victory in 1860, he returned to Washington and almost immediately spoke out. On December 6, as the Senate reconvened, it appointed a select committee of five men, including Davis, to investigate Brown's actions and see who had been behind them. Almost immediately senators from the Northern states rose to disavow any participation in or approval of Brown's act. This pleased Davis, but he saw in the words of some of those men a desire to cripple the investigation, and that made him suspicious. "I believe a conspiracy has been formed," he said, extending even to antislavery interests in England, who contributed money and military expertise to both the troubles in Kansas, and the Harpers Ferry raid. He asserted that there was a financial motivation behind some Northerners' support of the raid. With the disruption of the slave labor force in the South, the cotton crop would be injured, reducing supply and driving up the price of bales already owned by Northern merchants. Of course, no such conspiracy existed, as Davis himself would realize after investigation, but like many he was ready to believe almost the worst.[2]

The committee would investigate Harpers Ferry for fully six months before its final report appeared on June 15, 1860. At least one prominent Bostonian, Amos Lawrence, contacted Davis to protest that while he may have given money to Brown, he never knew the fanatic's intent. He appealed to Davis for help in not being called to Washington to testify, and since he never was, perhaps Davis gave him some aid. If so, he showed a restraint practiced by few Southern leaders in the fevered days after the raid. More than thirty others did have to testify, while considerable evidence was gathered on the money Brown received and from whom. Davis attended the interrogation of most or all of the witnesses, examined the evidence personally, and took a special interest in an elusive Englishman named Hugh Forbes, whom he believed to be the military expert sent to train Brown. In fact, the Forbes trail led nowhere, and by the end of six months of study, Davis and the others concluded that "it was simply the act of lawless ruffians, under the sanction of no public or political authority."

It is a credit to Davis that he set aside his aroused passions to see clearly through the maze of testimony. Many others refused to abandon their wild speculations, so useful in inciting passions and congenial to their preconceived notions of Northern perfidy. Davis, ever the lawyer at heart, would not let his own prejudices color the facts before him, just as years before he refused to allow his political opposition to Daniel Webster to seduce him into condemning falsely his financial dealings. As for conclusions and lessons to be drawn from the inquiry, Davis and the rest suggested that in future the states must guard against any more such outrages. "The Committee can find no guarantee elsewhere for the security of peace between the States of the Union."[3]

Davis and the committee met at least thirty times in that six months, and the Harpers Ferry investigation occupied more of his time than any other legislative item of the session. There was other business, of course. As always, Davis spoke for the army on its appropriations bills, and for West Point as well. He continued his campaign to allow U.S. arsenals to sell weapons to volunteer companies in the states, and certainly in this his foes saw a design—real or imagined—to arm the states for secession and resistance. He continued his career-long campaign for economy, protesting the abuses of public officials. As with the old constructive mileage issue—on which congressmen could claim reimbursement for travel expenses they had never incurred—now he attacked the abuse of the franking privilege, by which some senators like Douglas sent—at no cost to themselves—literally hundreds of thousands of pamphlets and copies of their speeches to constituents, obviously to bolster their grasp on their seats.[4]

Yet his chief legislative concern in this session was his answer to the impending crisis, aggravated by the Brown raid. On February 2, 1860, he introduced a series of resolutions designed to define the relations of the states within the Union and under the Constitution. There was nothing original in his resolves, which were more a statement of opinion, a staking out of ground on a line of no retreat, than an actual suggestion for legislative action. They could have come from Calhoun or any of a number of his other states' rights forebears, but in this Congress and at this critical juncture, Jefferson Davis was the man the South expected to present its case. Furthermore, the message Davis hoped to get across may well have been aimed more at any nominee from the forthcoming Democratic convention than at the Senate, though most of the leading contenders—Douglas, Vice President Breckinridge, Davis himself—sat in that body. In effect, Davis attempted to set a basis for the convention platform, an ultimatum that this was the least the South would accept, and that any nominee must live by these resolutions or lose the slave-state vote, the election, and probably the Union.

In six resolutions, Davis declared that in accepting statehood, the several states did not abandon their sovereignty over their internal domestic institutions. Any meddling by citizens or combinations of other states in the affairs of another, whether on political, moral, or religious grounds, violated the Constitution and weakened the Union. Furthermore, as to slavery in particular, the Constitution recognized it, and the states themselves approved it, long before the Union was formed. Any change of heart or opinion on the part of one combination of states afterwards did not offer just grounds to interfere with it where it persisted or to attempt its overthrow by political or other means. The Senate itself bore a special responsibility to ensure that states did not interfere with or discriminate against each other and their property. No power, he said, held the right to legislate for or against slavery in the territories, and it was the duty of the government to guarantee the free exercise of the rights of slaveholders in those territories. Only when the population of those territories legally formed a constitution for admission to statehood could they themselves decide the slavery issue. And finally, the several fugitive slave laws, dating back to 1793, were the law of the land.

The individuals and state legislatures in hostile states had no right to subvert those laws but, rather, an obligation to obey them.[5]

Davis hoped to see his resolutions voted on individually in order to get a detailed expression of the opinion of the Senate, but also, no doubt, to force Douglas—whom he now detested—out into the open on each issue. Actual debate on the resolutions did not come for a month, but in the meantime the Democrats in the chamber met repeatedly to work on changes in the resolutions that would allow as many as possible to unite behind them. After the first caucus, a committee went to work on substitute resolves, just in case, while Davis himself called on President Buchanan to seek support. As the caucuses continued throughout February, it became increasingly apparent that those in control of the resolutions were out to stop Douglas at the convention. In the end, very few changes were made, merely splitting one resolution in two and removing Davis's usual threat of secession from the fugitive slave resolution.[6]

He made his first set speech on behalf of the resolutions on May 8, holding forth on all the well-trodden ground that supported his ideas. That done, he went after what he saw as a growing "trade" in antislavery activities in the North. Men actually profited by the agitation, while others set aside portions of their income to support it and to send "vagrant lecturers" out to promote agitation and mischief. As always on a subject on which he had decided for himself what was right, he would not admit an honest difference of opinion or moral feeling on the part of his opponents. The writings of prominent men like Ralph Waldo Emerson, Elijah Lovejoy, Hinton Helper, and others of the abolitionist faith he did not countenance as sincere moral outrage and scarcely gave notice of having read them, if read them he had. Men who opposed slavery were greedy, wanted power, wanted to crush the South, and cared not a farthing for the African. As always, he offered the threat of secession and civil war if Southern rights were not recognized. The North had already declared war on the South, or at least the Republicans had done so, he felt. Should Southerners wait passively while the foe gathered strength before they themselves prepared to resist? "The power of resistance consists, in no small degree," he said, "in meeting the evil at the outer gate." As always, after thus rattling his saber, he protested that the opposition would twist his words, maintaining that in merely expressing a determination to maintain his rights, he was making threats. "It is not a threat," he said, "but a warning." Take heed, he said. "This temple is tottering on its pillars." If they did not all rush to hold it up in this perilous time, they might all be crushed when it fell.

Debate continued on several later occasions, and finally on May 24 and 25 the resolutions came to a vote. Acted on individually, as Davis had wished, each passed, Democrats voting almost unanimously in approval and Republicans against. Significantly, Douglas absented himself from the chamber those days and did not vote. By that time, however, it was too late for him to avoid losing the Southern support he hoped for. The Democrats had already met in convention in Charleston and left in disaster.[7]

There was never any question that the coming presidential campaign would be the focus of the year and, as Davis had predicted for some years, the watershed of the sectional controversy. His own interest in the nomination was consistently negligible, despite what appeared to be some water testing in New England two years before. He knew that many in the South, and even the North, looked with favor on his candidacy, and there would be some logic to his nomination. He had been so close to Pierce, and had run a cabinet department that accounted for fully one-third of the government's administrative duties and budget so well, that few questioned his capacity for the presidency. He knew much of foreign affairs and possessed an intimate grasp of domestic matters, especially relating to the preeminent matter of expansion in the West. Even his opponents granted his stature as a public man. He would bring dignity to the office, and he had shown flashes of remarkably nonpartisan sentiment on some issues. He may have been a states' rights ideologue, but he was capable of standing on principle above party from time to time. Most of all, of course, he would keep the South in the Union. He might not be entirely acceptable to the ultras in South Carolina, like Robert B. Rhett, owner and editor of the *Charleston Mercury*, but in all the other slave states his election would have been hailed as the coming of a savior.

Tangible evidences of the possibility of a nomination had surfaced nearly two years before. In January 1859, during a discussion on a steamboat on the Mississippi, one man expressed the opinion that Davis was "the first statesman in the country." At the end of that year, delegates to a Democratic convention at Jackson voted overwhelmingly to endorse Davis as their preferred candidate at the coming Charleston convention. Yet to every such manifestation, however much appreciated, Davis offered the same reply. "My opinions," he wrote in January 1860, "would be sufficient to defeat any efforts of my friends to nominate me at Charleston." He knew himself to be too "radical" an advocate of Southern rights to get the Northern votes necessary for victory in the general election. As always, he favored Pierce or, as second choices, men like Hunter of Virginia, Guthrie of Kentucky, or even former Vice President Dallas of Pennsylvania. Unfortunately, they were all weak men for whom few felt enthusiasm, and therein lay the crippling weakness of his party. At its most critical moment, its strongest spokesmen—Douglas, Davis, perhaps Toombs—were all sectional in identification and therefore almost completely unelectable.[8]

As the April 23 convention approached, Davis finally decided to send to the Mississippi delegation an explicit request that they not place him in nomination. To discourage further any use of his name, Davis himself decided not to attend the meeting and attempted to exert little other influence there beyond the possibility that he urged Mississippi to withdraw from the convention in case Douglas actually got the nomination.[9]

No one got the nomination. Douglas sent a large group of well-organized supporters, while backers of the current administration, led by Slidell of Louisiana, immediately set out to block Douglas. Many favored Breckinridge, but he declined to be considered so long as fellow Kentuckian Guthrie was before the delegates. Other names echoed in the hotel rooms and parlors of Charleston, but none of them would leave with a majority of the delegates behind them. Douglas's people had enough votes at the outset to get control of the platform and rules committees, and then they adopted a platform that ignored the Davis resolutions and instead offered the South only the sop that questions of slavery in the territories would be decided by the Supreme Court. The South wanted federal guarantees of protection of property, and in response to the Douglas platform, six of the slave-state delegations walked out of the convention to form a meeting of their own. As a result, when it came to balloting, no candidate could get the required two-thirds of the original convention membership. Douglas led for thirty-five ballots, but not by enough. Despite their wishes, Davis's, Breckinridge's, and several others' names were placed in nomination, and Davis consistently received the votes of old friends like Cushing and Benjamin F. Butler of Massachusetts.

The departure of the Mississippi delegation from the convention upset Davis. He had hoped they would not do so, believing that the best hope of defeating Douglas lay in keeping the party together in spite of the platform. But he could not control them. When the main convention adjourned to meet in Baltimore in June to try again, the "bolters," as they were called, voted to hold their own convention in Richmond on June 11.[10]

It took no great wisdom to see what would happen. Splitting itself in two, the party almost guaranteed its defeat in November. Immediately Davis tried to persuade the bolters to go to Baltimore and meet with the whole party. He admitted that the bolters were "compelled to withdraw" and expressed admiration for their "lofty manifestation of adherence to principle, rising superior to all considerations of expediency, to all trammels of party, and looking with a single eye to the defence of the constitutional rights of the States." Of course he had to say that, even if in private he disapproved of what they had done. To criticize their actions would prejudice his attempt to persuade them, as he did now in an open letter on May 7, that the rest of the convention delegates would be willing to back away from the Douglas platform and accept an amendment recognizing principles allowing a harmonious reunion in Baltimore. They had a duty, he said, to return to the rest of the party. Should Baltimore not produce a platform and a nominee satisfactory to the bolters, then they could still withdraw. Postpone the Richmond meeting, he urged. Davis and eighteen other Southern congressmen signed the address, though just who wrote it is unclear. Certainly it agreed with Davis's known views. No one listened.[11]

Some of the bolting delegations did attempt to go to Baltimore, but the Douglas men were so firmly in control there that they denied Alabama and Louisiana admission. That led to another walkout by Virginia, Arkansas, Texas, and Mississippi, along with California and Oregon and parts of the delegations from Massachusetts and Kentucky. More than a third of the delegates left, and Douglas was quickly nominated in their absence. The bolters decided not to wait for another date but immediately convened in another hall in Baltimore and proceeded to their own platform and nomination. They adopted Davis's resolutions almost verbatim and then went on to nominate Davis, Breckinridge, Joseph Lane of Oregon, and Daniel Dickinson of New York. Only Breckinridge and Dickinson received votes on the first ballot, and soon thereafter the Kentuckian became the unanimous choice, and soon accepted by those original Charleston bolters who later met in Richmond. Now the once-mighty Democratic party stood shattered, with two nominees, and not a chance of victory.

But Davis did not abandon hope. Indeed, in one of the most statesmanlike efforts of his career, he tried to avert calamity by taking the same sort of managerial hand in affairs that he exercised in the Missouri Compromise repeal. Two days after the Baltimore nominations, Davis invited Breckinridge and Cushing to his home for dinner. That same day he had spoken at a ratification meeting endorsing Breckinridge and his platform, and condemning Douglas, whom he privately called now a "grog drinking, electioneering Demagogue." Already he had congratulated his old friend Cushing on his honorable part in the Charleston and Baltimore conventions, but now over dinner he spoke earnestly to his guests of the future. Breckinridge needed no convincing and neither did Cushing. The Republicans had nominated Abraham Lincoln of Illinois in May, and he was assured of victory in November if the Democrats presented two tickets. Worse, a coalition of old Whigs and other disaffected Democrats calling themselves the Constitutional Union party had nominated yet another candidate, old John Bell of Tennessee. Essentially they stood for nothing more than an appeal to the Union and wishful thinking, but they would siphon more votes away from anyone who might have a real chance of defeating Lincoln.

Breckinridge had not wanted his nomination, and as late as the day before the dinner with Davis and Cushing he announced to his closest friend that he would not accept it. But now, perhaps at Davis's urging, Breckinridge agreed to take the nomination after all. Toombs may have been at the dinner as well, or else joined them all later in the evening, and he, too, attempted to persuade Breckinridge not to decline. The reason was not in the hope of electing the Vice President. Quite to the contrary, Davis's plan called for an attempt to get all of the nominees— Breckinridge, Bell, and Douglas—to agree to withdraw in favor of a compromise candidate on whom Democrats could unite to defeat Lincoln. But first Breckinridge had to accept. Later that same night, they all went over to the Kentuckian's unfinished home on I Street. A brass band soon appeared to serenade the candidate, and he spoke in acceptance of his nomination. Davis and Toombs spoke as well, the whole business having the appearance of a genuine send-off for a campaign. Yet it was all a sham. Breckinridge had never spent so much as a single night in his new house. The house next door was finished, however, and its owner was probably there—Stephen A. Douglas. The whole demonstration was staged to impress on Douglas the division in his party and the fact that he would lose the South to Breckinridge and the Democrats thus would lose to Lincoln.[12]

Now they had to go to work securing the withdrawals. Breckinridge, of course, accepted only in order to withdraw. Toombs went to work on Douglas's running mate, Benjamin Fitzpatrick, and by a mixture of bullying and falsehood, persuaded him to withdraw. Meanwhile Davis approached Bell, and he readily agreed to withdraw as well. Thus the field was reduced to Douglas, who now had no running mate. Davis went to Douglas himself. However much the two differed and disliked each other's politics, still they were civil, and Davis believed that the Little Giant would not receive his suggestion in anything other than a friendly spirit. Certainly Douglas listened, and certainly Davis offered every persuasion he could conceive to show the Illinoisian what must inevitably follow if the party remained divided. Douglas, alas, had been trying for years to get a presidential nomination. Now he had one, such as it was, and he would not relinquish it. All of his supporters would go to Lincoln if he withdrew, he argued. It was a delusion, and a fatal one, for in fact, as subsequent elections showed for several years, Northern Democrats felt a much greater devotion to defeating Republicans than they did to electing Douglas.[13]

Nevertheless, with Douglas's refusal, Davis could do nothing more. He had hoped to see some compromise man like Hunter or Guthrie, or Horatio Seymour of New York, make a bid. Now it was all pointless. Davis probably got Douglas's refusal within a few days after the dinner with Breckinridge and Cushing, for on June 30 the Kentuckian lamented, "I fear there is nothing left but a square fight." To Varina Davis, Breckinridge spoke both for himself and her husband when he confided, "I trust I have the courage to lead a forlorn hope."[14]

For a few weeks everyone paused to catch their breath. In mid-July Davis went to West Point and remained there for almost two months, chairing meetings of the U.S. Military Academy Commission. Major Hardee, his old friend, had often invited Davis and Varina to come to the academy, and now the Senator went, probably delighted to leave the perfidy and entanglements of Washington for the settled and familiar nostalgia of his old school. There he and others of his committee on the academy looked into the course of instruction, but just as often the cadets saw him out on the parade ground in his blue flannel suit, walking erect, shoulders squared, talking with professors who had been his fellow students in the 1820s. One young second classman always remembered Davis's "spare, resolute, and rather pleading face." Often he stood in the shade of a grove of elms talking with Hardee and one or another of the instructors, perhaps forgetting in the seductive otherworldliness of a military post the turmoil engulfing the nation.[15]

Davis took little part in the campaigning itself, having little heart for it. A major address delivered in the Senate on May 17 in response to Douglas became an influential campaign document for the Breckinridge party, rehearsing as it did all of the fundamentals of the states' rights creed on the territories, constitutional guarantees of property, and Davis's resolutions. Other than writing letters, he said little more than that until late September when he returned to Mississippi. He spoke first at Corinth on September 21 and made at least a dozen other appearances in the final weeks of the campaign. There must have been a feeling of futility about it, but duty left him no other choice than to represent his views and stand for the right, even if it were a "forlorn hope." There was much misrepresentation from the podium and the press. Indeed, it had become so great as to force Breckinridge to break with tradition and make a few self-explanatory campaign speeches, while Douglas campaigned vigorously in his own behalf. Davis deplored it in both, though far the more so in Douglas.

When he spoke in Corinth, Davis found himself confronted with a set of interrogatories called the "Norfolk Questions," put to Douglas in that city the month before, and now they were being asked of all the candidates. Did Lincoln's election justify the South in seceding? If the states seceded before any outright act of aggression was committed, should their citizens resist secession? If a state seceded without Lincoln having violated the Constitution, would it be treasonable for "loyal" citizens of that state to help federal authorities in enforcing the law?

Davis dodged the first question, which is odd considering how many times previously he had said that a Republican victory should be the catalyst for secession. Of course, the past January he had retreated from that position slightly when pressed on the same subject in the Senate, saying that the South would or should first seek remedies if a Republican violated the Constitution. Now he retreated to a resolution the Mississippi Democrats adopted the previous year, saying that a Black Republican victory ought to be regarded as a "declaration of hostility," and that the state should be "in readiness to co-operate" with other Southern states in "whatever measures" they chose to adopt.

Davis evaded the second question as well. Ignoring the explicit qualifier of secession prior to an overt act of agression, he simply asserted that he would never consent to the coercion of a state, wholly missing or ignoring the import of a question that sought to determine the justification for secession. Davis's response seemed to assert that a state could secede at any time, with or without justification or provocation. And in the same way he sidestepped the last question. A citizen of a state owed his allegiance to that state first and above all, he said. To aid in putting down secession or imposing Federal law would be treason. Again he utterly ignored the very important qualifier of secession without "adjudged violation of the Constitution."[16]

Davis made his last speech at Vicksburg on November 3. Already early elections in some of the Northern states showed the trend toward the Republicans, and three days later the dreaded result of the general voting started to come in. In the end Lincoln took barely 40 percent of the popular vote, with Douglas half a million votes behind, and Breckinridge and Bell some distance farther off. Yet Breckinridge carried all the Southern states except Virginia, North Carolina, and Tennessee. That made him second to Lincoln in the electoral count, but a distant second, which killed the last remaining hope of Southerners that Lincoln might not get a majority of the overall electoral vote, thus throwing the election into the House of Representatives or the Senate, where either Breckinridge or Lane would be the likely choice, and the crisis might still be averted.

The Deep South was inflamed by the news, and in South Carolina the "ultra" men immediately made moves toward secession. Despite all protestations to the contrary, Lincoln's election was seen as the prelude to a direct attack on slavery and Southern rights. Politicians ranted, editors verbalized, ministers pontificated, and the ground swell of paranoia after this single event achieved what decades of Southern extremists had failed to accomplish. Secession, at least in the lower South, was inevitable.

The news reached Davis at Brierfield, and even as the reports came in via Vicksburg, he received a letter from Rhett and a committee advocating resistance. However much the South Carolinian mistrusted Davis's solidity as a secessionist, he sought his views on what should be done. Davis's answer probably disappointed him. He believed that if Governor John Pettus called a convention in Mississippi at that moment, a secession proposition would probably fail. Further, if Pettus asked the legislature to call such a convention, he doubted that it would send delegates to any general convention of the Southern states. Should South Carolina secede first, he expected that Mississippi would still not act unless most of the other slave states followed suit. As for what South Carolina should do, he hesitated to advise. He did observe that he thought Georgia shaky on secession at the moment. Without that state, South Carolina would be cut off from Alabama, Mississippi, and other Deep Southern states. If delay would give Georgia time to come around, then South Carolina should wait. However, if Rhett's state seceded and the federal authorities attempted to coerce it back into the Union, then Davis felt that the South would rise up united in its defense. "The planting states have a common interest of such magnitude," he wrote, "that their union, sooner or later, for the protection of that interest is certain." "Interest controls the policy of states," he went on. Eventually all the planting states must come to the same conclusion. While some still wavered, he advised restraint and caution "before asking for a popular decision upon a new policy and relation to the nations of the earth." On the other hand, if South Carolina stood resolved on secession no matter what, then he saw no reason to wait until Lincoln took office.[17]

Clearly Davis continued stepping backward from his earlier positions. The repeated utterances advocating secession in the event of a Republican victory disappeared now in face of the actual fact of that election. Yet there was nothing inconsistent with this in light of the senator's overall policy. Time and again he had also spoken of the South being ready to stand united and independent. Virginia, North Carolina, Tennessee, and perhaps even Georgia and Mississippi were not yet ready to take the leap. Thus in counseling calm and moderation, he did so only for the moment in order to be in the best position to achieve his greater goal, a unanimous stand by all of the planting states that might accomplish a peaceful and permanent withdrawal. Certainly Davis's response did not please the fire-eating Rhett, but it was the wisest counsel for the moment.

A few days later Governor Pettus called together in Jackson the state's senators and congressmen to discuss Mississippi's course in the days ahead. For two days they talked. On the immediate question of secession, Davis, Brown, and Lucius Quintus Cassuis Lamar all argued against doing anything until other states had jumped first. Davis especially warned that secession probably could not be accomplished peacefully, and especially if the state acted alone. Unprepared for war, the South would be crushed. "Miss. had better move slowly," he said. Only once eight or ten states were ready to act together should they all call state conventions and vote ordinances of secession. Davis advised Pettus against convening a special session of the legislature to call a secession convention at that time. When Pettus nevertheless asked Davis to act as his spokesman in asking for immediate secession, Davis declined. Finally, when they discussed South Carolina, Davis again advised that Pettus counsel caution and await the rest of the states or at least wait until March 4, 1861, when Lincoln took office.

If Davis needed anything to show him how fast men and events were moving, it came here in this caucus at the governor's mansion. For the first time ever, he found himself consistently in the minority and consistently outvoted. He, Lamar, and Brown stood firm for caution. Pettus, Reuben Davis, and two other congressmen present voted for more immediate and strident action. Reluctantly Davis and the others agreed to go along with the majority to give the public the appearance of unanimity. "I was slower and more reluctant than others," Davis said in later years, even admitting that "I was behind the general opinion of the people of the State as to the propriety of prompt secession." Indeed, after he left the meeting, Pettus and the others in the majority expressed open dissatisfaction with Davis's conduct. No doubt remembering his 1858 New England speeches, some said they feared that the senator actually opposed secession and sought delay in order to prevent withdrawal. They misjudged their man, but certainly Davis was right that, for once, he did not stand in the forefront of Mississippians on this issue. Another Davis, Reuben, stood there in this caucus, and he concluded that their decision to call the legislature and push for an immediate secession "was practically a declaration of war."[18]

Pettus did call the legislature, and it issued a call for a special convention to meet on January 7 to consider secession. By then, however, Davis was already back in Washington. During the caucus with Pettus and the others, a telegram arrived from two members of the cabinet asking him to return to the capital at once. He already had some idea of the temper of affairs there from a letter just received from Varina. "There is a settled gloom hanging over everyone here," she wrote. "*Everybody is scared*, especially Mr. Buchanan." Senators talked of resigning at once or in the future, others equivocated, and few were bold enough to speak out for secession without qualification. It all confirmed Davis's belief that the time was coming for action, but that it had not yet arrived.[19]

The reason for his sudden call to Washington was a hope on the part of his friends that he might exert some influence over the weak and vacillating Buchanan, then preparing his annual message to Congress. Davis immediately called on the president, and the Pennsylvanian asked for his comments on a rough draft already prepared. Davis made a few suggestions that Buchanan readily adopted and then changed the address again afterward, probably in response to someone else's advice. Thus the senator's sudden recall had been pointless, though Congress would reconvene on December 3 in any case. At once Davis felt the tension in the chamber. When Buchanan delivered his message, blaming the crisis on the Republicans yet denying the right of secession, it pleased no one. Tempers flared quickly, and accusations flew as the Senate debated the simple questions of printing the message and in how large an edition. At once Davis abandoned the conciliatory or, more correctly, cautious role he had been playing for the past few months and stepped forward at least into the second rank of the fire-eaters. He stood there as a United States senator and expected to be treated with due respect, he said. "Before a declaration of war is made against the State of which I am a citizen, I expect to be out of the Chamber," he continued. "When that declaration of war is made, the State of which I am a citizen will be found ready and quite willing to meet it." Now again he spoke of war, and not "if" but "when."[20]

Perhaps this renewed conviction of the inevitability of conflict impelled Davis now to look again to Mississippi's armament. As far back as December 1859, Pettus asked Davis for his help in arming the state with new and modern weapons. Throughout the year the governor continued to seek his help in getting rifles and powder. On November 30, shortly after arriving in Washington, Davis contacted manufacturer Eli Whitney personally, having recommended his firm to Pettus. Whitney was not producing guns as he had contracted to do, and Davis politely and firmly demanded an explanation. Pettus himself wrote to Davis four weeks later to tell him that the outstanding invoices that had held up Whitney's work would be paid, adding the ominous observation that with volunteer companies already forming for state defense in advance of action on secession, "You will be called to command the men who will use the arms." This, quite possibly, is the first intimation Davis heard from anyone else that in the coming storm—should it come—Southerners or at least Mississippians might expect the hero of Buena Vista to lead them again in the field.[21]

As for the impending storm, Davis became increasingly and rapidly less optimistic. "It is honorable to die for ones country when the sacrifice may be useful," he told a friend on December 12. Yet everything then was "haste and confusion," and Davis himself showed some vacillation. After Buchanan's message reached Congress, both chambers voted to create select committees to look into the current crisis and report resolutions for remedies. In the Senate especially the debate turned bitter and acrimonious. On December 10 they debated resolutions introduced by Lazarus Powell of Kentucky for the formation of the committee. Some proposed giving the government more power to put down any rebellion. Others counseled doing nothing. When Davis rose, he offered them all something almost approaching apology, at least for him. There had been too much discord in that chamber over the years, he said, "in which I have taken a part perhaps more zealous than useful." He pleaded instead for a return to harmony on the part of the North. Turning to the Republican side of the room, he asked that they seek "to live up to the obligations of good neighbors, and friendly States united for the common welfare." If the great and good-hearted general population of the North could offer a declaration that they would abide by the Constitution and respect Southern institutions and property, then there was still hope of a remedy. Yet even as he appealed for that harmony, Davis and others got into heated words over present and past utterances and events, and as he closed he had to lament that, after all, they had come back inevitably to "crimination and recrimination." "There is no use in it," he lamented. They must deal with events as they presented themselves. "Angry discussion here, and the arraignment of men for the evil they have done, will serve but little good."[22]

A few days later, when debate finally settled down and a Committee of Thirteen was appointed to consider the crisis, Davis politely asked to be excused from serving. His pessimism quickly evolved into despair, aggravated by the return of his almost crippling facial pain or neuralgia. Days before, on December 10, when he learned that Reuben Davis had agreed to serve on the House committee, Davis went to ask him if it were true. Davis could not accept hypocrisy, or what appeared to him to be hypocrisy. Reuben Davis had taken a lead in the caucus to propel Mississippi toward secession. How could he now agree to sit on a committee that hoped to report compromise measures? When the congressman said he intended to do so nevertheless, out of a sense of duty, Jefferson Davis only looked at him. "Then it is useless to say anything to you," he uttered, and returned to the Senate. This was the same day Davis spoke against Powell's resolution giving more power to the federal government. Obviously the senator still wavered between hope and despair, but in the next few days he finally gave up on compromise for good, or so he thought. On December 13, Reuben Davis recoiled when his committee adopted a misleading resolution stating that it was doing well and would certainly find a measure to satisfy the South. Davis knew otherwise from his participation, and that night he called together a number of Southern men in Washington. Jefferson Davis may not have been present, but the next day he freely added his name to the declaration authored that evening by Louis T. Wigfall of Texas and James Pugh of Alabama. "The argument is exhausted," it said. "All hope of relief in the Union" had vanished. "The honor, safety, and independence of the Southern people require the organization of a Southern confederacy," it concluded, and "the primary object of each slaveholding State ought to be its speedy and absolute separation from a Union with hostile States." Barely over two weeks before, Jefferson Davis counseled caution and waiting. Now, in signing this public statement, he had gone over to the Reuben Davises and the Pettuses.[23]

Because of this personal watershed, Davis did not want to serve on the Committee of Thirteen when he was appointed on December 20. Another reason for his declining, and for his despair, was the news that same day that a convention in Charleston was enacting an ordinance of secession. In fact, word of its adoption reached Washington that afternoon or evening. It was impossible for him to serve on the committee "with any prospect of advantage." It was already a busy day for him otherwise. He opposed a resolution inspired by the opposition to inquire of Buchanan the size of the garrisons at the forts in and near Charleston Harbor, a measure obviously intended to see if resistance to secession could be made by forces on hand at the scene. Why further excite the people by such provocative and threatening discussions? he asked. Yet again Davis vacillated. Indeed, three days earlier he had written to his brother Joseph and at least mentioned the possibility of "reconstruction" of the Union. Perhaps his wavering was, after all, only a part of the indecision that had frequently plagued him when it came to determining his course in life. Now Joseph no longer tried to show him his course. He was on his own. As if reflecting the two directions in which his tormented mind was tugged, that very day, December 20, 1860, with the Union starting to dissolve, he went to the Library of Congress and took out two books: One was a history of South Carolina; the other was a history of Old Glory, the Stars and Stripes.[23]

Maybe something in that book about the flag brought deep feelings to the fore yet again, for the next day Davis changed his mind and agreed to serve on the committee, averring that he would make any and every effort to forestall calamity. Unfortunately, there was little that any of the thirteen could do. Divided into three factions, Southern Democrats, Northern Democrats, and Republicans, only by coalition could they agree on anything. Davis himself moved that nothing be adopted by the committee without receiving a majority among both Republicans and Democrats, realizing that otherwise, if the committee's Democratic majority simply overrode the opposition, Republicans at large would condemn their proposals. It was a well-intentioned move, though it crippled the committee at the same time.[24]

In several days of discussions, Davis took an active part in seeking remedies. He proposed amending the Constitution—a step he had always condemned in the opposition, saying that he preferred the document as it was while they only liked it as amended. He suggested that slaves be specifically recognized as a form of property like all others, and hence free from interference by the federal or any territorial governments. He advocated Crittenden's compromise measures to prohibit

Congress from abolishing slavery anywhere it existed, to allow the unrestricted transportation of slaves into the territories, that owners be compensated for the loss of runaway slaves when other authorities refused to cooperate in their return, and a host of other measures consistent with the positions he had taken for years. When Seward proposed a measure to prohibit Congress from abolishing or interfering with slavery, Davis heartily supported his old friend and enemy. Repeatedly, however, he opposed a measure by Crittenden to restore the Missouri Compromise line. For ten days, intermittently, the committee met and argued, achieving nothing. Finally Davis joined with others in supporting Toombs's resolution to adjourn, and on December 31 the committee reported back to the Senate that it had failed. Years later Davis would recall that "with the failure of the Senate Committee of Thirteen to come to any agreement, the last reasonable hope of a pacific settlement of difficulties within the Union was extinguished in the minds of those most reluctant to abandon the effort." When the New Year dawned a few hours after the Committee of Thirteen reported its failure, a general belief finally obtained among the representatives of most of the Southern states that all that was left to them was secession.[25]

Certainly Davis himself now sat committed, his indecision and wavering done. On January 4, 1861, he advised Pettus what would be forthcoming in the Senate. A force bill to enable the government to put down secession would be introduced, probably along with a loan bill to pay for a buildup of the army. He no longer counseled a delay on secession, only that any such ordinance should provide for the continuation of federal services and officials in Mississippi to keep essential services like the post office running while Pettus made the state independent and while the several Southern states met to form their new government. Three days later the Mississippi secession convention met, and two days later, by a vote of 84 to 15, the delegates chose to leave the Union. Pettus immediately telegraphed the news to the state's representatives in Washington, and Davis replied: "Judge what Mississippi requires of me and place me accordingly."

By that time Davis had already met in a caucus on January 5, with the senators from Georgia, Florida, Alabama, Louisiana, Texas, Arkansas, and Mississippi. They adopted resolutions expressing their opinion that their states should secede immediately and that a convention should meet in Montgomery, Alabama, on or before February 15 for the purpose of forming a new government. Montgomery was chosen in part for its position near the geographical center of the seceding states, but also because South Carolina—the seemingly more logical point—was still regarded as too extreme by some. Meeting there might put off more hesitant states like Virginia and Tennessee. At the same time, they asked their governors for instructions as to their future course while they remained in Washington. Should they maintain their seats in order to obstruct hostile legislation or should they leave? In fact, Mississippi, Florida, and Alabama withdrew even before the resolutions could be communicated to them, and senators and congressmen began leaving the capital almost at once. Davis himself declared that he wished to remain in the Senate not a moment longer after his state seceded. He did address the Senate regarding affairs in South Carolina on January 9, probably before learning of Mississippi's action. The next day he spoke again at length in regard to events in South Carolina, though by this time word of Pettus's convention result had reached him. "Events, with a current hurrying on as it progresses, have borne me past the point where it would be useful for me to argue," he told them. They must deal with facts. If the weakling Buchanan had withdrawn the federal garrison from Charleston's Fort Moultrie only a few weeks earlier, the increasing rumblings of armed conflict could have been averted. But the president did not act, and the garrison had abandoned Moultrie to take refuge in the unfinished but still formidable Fort Sumter out in the harbor. Now the presence of that garrison became an affront to South Carolina's sovereignty. At any moment the situation could explode. Indeed, just the day before, a federal supply vessel attempting to take men and matériel to Sumter had been fired upon and driven away by South Carolina batteries. It did not make the situation any the happier for Davis to know that the commander of the garrison in that fort was his old friend from Black Hawk days, Major Robert Anderson.[26]

Protesting that Congress should act to take away from the president the power to make war on a sovereign state, Davis argued that the supply attempt constituted an act of aggression. It was a feeble argument at best, but then in his mind no alternative conclusion could be reached. There can be little doubt that the tension of these days acted mightily on Davis's nervous system. Three days after this speech he fell ill with a renewed and terrible attack of facial pain that almost incapacitated him and kept him confined to his room for several days, while other senators were leaving to return home to their seceded states. Nevertheless, with much to be done before he left, he continued to correspond from his sickroom. He tried to no avail to get the arms from Whitney for Mississippi and kept on advising his friends as to their course now that "we are advancing rapidly to the end of the Union."[27]

Criticism of his January 10 speech—which matched the prejudices of its authors—reached Davis in his darkened room. While his old foe the *New York Herald* accused him of treason, the *Richmond Enquirer* said that many on both sides regarded his speech as "the ablest effort of his life." Even Douglas and other Yankees had complimented him on its tone, if not its substance. "Our soul thrilled," said a reporter for the *Richmond Examiner*, "at the subdued, yet gifted manner, by which his feelings of past devotion to the Union, under all its blessings, were attested." When Davis told the Senate that "we are on the verge of civil war," everyone listened. He denied that the South had any intention of invading or making war on the North, yet he did not hesitate to predict that great destruction in blood and property could be inflicted by armed Southerners if the North did not let them go in peace.[28]

Privately, to close friends, Davis showed how truly the crisis upset him. (Varina saw his depression after visiting Southern hotspurs left his sickchamber, his only cheer being the hope that the antislavery men would not act too soon.) He asserted that the election was not itself the cause of the calamity, but rather "the last feather which you know breaks the Camel's back." "We waited, wishfully, rather than hopefully for a reaction in public opinion which would restore the fraternity essential to the existence of our Union," but it did not come. "What then remains for us to do? but at once to proceed to put ourselves in a Condition to secure our safety." To his increasingly close friend Clay of Alabama, Davis was even more direct. "We have piped but they would not dance," he wrote on January 19, "and now the Devil may care."[29]

The day after Davis's January 10 speech, the Senate voted to take up discussion of the resolutions discussed by the Committee of Thirteen. Now called the Crittenden Compromise, they were defeated overwhelmingly, making immaterial Davis's absence due to his illness. Effectively, he was out of the Senate anyhow. He had drawn his last salary check of $940 a few days before, and thereafter he was working for Mississippi and the South. He would call secession "the separation of the sheep from the goats," and having sided with the sheep he now entered the fold fully.[30]

Davis commenced a correspondence with Governor Francis Pickens of South Carolina on January 9, when the governor wrote to tell him of the firing on the supply ship. Interestingly, as soon as that hostile act took place, Pickens thought to turn to Davis for military advice, asking him to come to Charleston for "military consultation." Other South Carolinians urged at the same time that Davis come quickly to Charleston, revealing a generally preconceived notion that Davis would be influential in any new Southern nation, and probably especially in its military planning. Davis had to beg off the trip because of his illness. Moreover, Pettus kept him in Washington as a possible commissioner to Virginia, and also pending a call to Jackson to organize the state militia. Though he could not go to Charleston, Davis offered such advice as he could. Frequently in the next several days he counseled caution. Trying to starve out the garrison might create a backlash of sympathy in the North that would not help their cause. Instead, he suggested that Pickens allow Anderson and his men to have ready access to all the fresh food and other nonmilitary supplies they needed. Indeed, Davis believed that many in Anderson's garrison were more loyal to the South than the North. Anderson himself was a slaveholder from Kentucky. Davis advised against making any formal demand or ultimatum for surrender of the fort. "The little garrison in its present position presses on nothing but a point of pride," he told Pickens. "Stand still." Meanwhile, the South could be preparing itself. "I hope we shall soon have a Southern Confederacy, that shall be ready to do all which interest or even pride demands." He expressed no illusions. "We are probably soon to be involved in that fiercest of human strife, a civil war." They must not precipitate conflict until they were ready. Pickens listened and heeded.[31]

Indeed, many looked to Davis in the days leading up to his departure from Washington, all expecting that he would be an important figure—perhaps even the most important—in any new "Southern Confederacy." As far back as December 15 a West Point cadet offered his services as Davis's aide when the senator took over as commanding general of the new nation. More requests for appointment as his aide arrived that month, and in January requests for recommendations came from young men like J. E. B. Stuart, Robert Ransom, Jr., and P. M. B. Young, all of whom would become generals in the years ahead. The speculation on his coming influence in the new nation reached the press, and by mid-January newspapers already predicted that Davis would be made "commander in chief of the army of defense." Governor Pickens confided privately to Davis and publicly to others that he hoped to see the Mississippian in that position as soon as the new government was formed. Interestingly, Pickens averred that the matter of who should be president of the new confederation "is not of so much consequence at present."[32]

By January 15 Davis was still confined to his room. Despite his facial pain, he contacted one of South Carolina's envoys to Washington, rumored to have been sent to demand the surrender of Fort Sumter, and urged on him the same caution that he asked of Pickens. Over and over Davis said to all who would listen that they should wait until their government was formed and as many states as possible had seceded. He asked for "calm and deliberate counsel with those states which are equally involved with South Carolina" without unnecessarily precipitating hostilities. The envoy agreed, advising Pickens that Davis "has much to say and I am sure would do great service to the common cause." Perhaps Davis instinctively knew what Pickens would later tell him—that in fact South Carolina was not yet ready to take Fort Sumter by force. Much work remained to make preparations should a bombardment become necessary. He would wait. As for Davis, sitting there in his darkened room, in physical pain and mental anguish, he thought incessantly in his quiet hours of Charleston. And now, perhaps for the first time, he also thought of old friends from his army days who could be useful in the coming crisis. On January 20 he recommended to Pickens Lucius B. Northrop, "an old and esteemed comrade of mine" and a man of "a high degree of professional attainment." Northrop had in fact been on permanent sick leave from the army for more than twenty years. He had been troublesome and quarrelsome, and not infrequently enjoyed Davis's intercession on his behalf during the Pierce administration. Apparently, as witnessed by his first recommendation for an appointment, Davis remembered old friends. If he was to have influence in the new order, he would use it to assist those who had always been loyal to him.[33]

Quickly enough it was time for Davis, too, to leave Washington. He got the news of Mississippi's secession on January 9 or 10. On the latter day he wired to Jackson to ask if he should resign and leave at once or wait for the official ordinance of secession. A week later, still ill, he did not yet have a copy of the ordinance and was anxious to leave, since the rest of the Mississippians had already gone. Unsure whether to go to Virginia or Charleston or directly to Jackson, Davis got his instructions from Pettus only on January 19: He must return home immediately.[34]

There were things to do, and quickly. As ever, Davis thought first of old friends. The next day he wrote to two of his closest, from whom he was now forced by politics to part—George Jones and Franklin Pierce. "I am on the eve of taking my final leave from the general government," he told Jones. The separation of the states would likely not come peacefully, he lamented, "but if the arbitrament must be referred to the sword we have resolved to meet it." Parting could not make them enemies, he said. To Pierce, all Davis could do was grieve over "the probable collision at Charleston." He was in the hands of his state. "Civil war has only horror for me," but he would do his duty and prayed that Pierce would "not be ashamed of our former connection or cease to be my friend." Also, if a friend and later Confederate may be believed, Davis also leaked to authorities word of an elaborate plot by Southern hotbloods to kidnap Lincoln before he could take office. He would not countenance outlawry. That done, he and Varina packed as hurriedly as they could and bought their train tickets to leave on January 22.[35]

One final duty remained. On January 21 Jefferson Davis arose from his sickbed, nursing an aching head, and walked into the Senate chamber for the last time. The gallery was packed with spectators, for several Southerners would be saying farewell that day: Yulee of Florida, Mallory of Florida, Clay and Benjamin Fitzpatrick of Alabama, and Davis of Mississippi. Davis spoke last, as the audience of senators and onlookers already sat moved by the high tragedy of the occasion. When he rose, they all saw him gaunt from his illness, his features held tight as he fought to hold his emotions. His doctor had advised him not to come to the Capitol that day, but Davis would not be dissuaded.

"I rise, Mister President," he began, "for the purpose of announcing to the Senate that . . . my functions are terminated here." He looked over the chamber from face to face as he spoke, remembering old friends and antagonists and a host of bonds that tied them all together. His voice faltered from weakness and emotion at first, but soon his clear baritone emerged. He spoke of Calhoun, his spiritual father, of Mississippi and its rights, but this time not stridently or with a threat. He spoke in its defense, and he spoke in warm recollection of their years together there in that building. "I am sure I feel no hostility to you Senators from the North." Whatever may have passed between them in the heat of debate, he told them now, "in the presence of my God, I wish you well." Certainly they had collided. "Whatever of offense there has been to me, I leave here." As for offenses he might have given, "I have, Senators, in this hour of our parting, to offer you my apology." That done, he said, "it only remains for me to bid you a final adieu." He sat down to thundering applause from all sides, applause that shook the tears from the faces of friends and foes alike. Varina saw him "inexpressibly sad" when he walked out of the chamber. That night, on the eve of their departure for Mississippi, she heard him praying aloud, "May God have us in His holy keeping, and grant that before it is too late peaceful councils may prevail." A few weeks later, recalling the "unutterable grief" of the occasion, Davis declared that his words had been "not my utterances but rather leaves torn from the book of fate."[36]

It only remained to board the train the next morning and leave. They moved southwest through Virginia toward Knoxville, where Davis made an impromptu speech from the train's rear car platform. Passengers on the train found him genial and seemingly in good spirits, though the conversation in the car always turned to the crisis at Charleston. At Chattanooga, Davis went to the Crutchfield House on the evening of January 22 for dinner, but as soon as word of his being there got around, a crowd quickly gathered and they called for him to make a speech. Davis could not refuse and stood on a chair placed in the center of the dining room. He said what he had said before, most of it tailored to urge Tennessee to make common cause with the rest of the South, not a popular idea in much of the pro-Union state. Indeed, during his speech the hotelkeeper's brother William Crutchfield heard him, and as soon as Davis finished, Crutchfield mounted a counter and delivered a scathing reply, denouncing Davis as "a renegade and a traitor." "We are not to be hood winked, bamboozled and dragged into your Southern, codfish, aristocratic, tory blooded, South Carolina mobocracy." Davis listened to him in silence, and when he finished denied Crutchfield's charges that the South was trying to seduce Tennessee. To his dismay, he found the crowd solidly behind his antagonist and quickly left the room and went upstairs. A tense scene, with many in the crowd armed, perhaps it gave Davis a foretaste of the problems that the new Southern nation would have with the widespread Union sentiment in its back-country and mountain regions.[37]

They finally reached Jackson on January 28, with Davis stepping from the train wearing a simple suit of homespun, "looking the embodiment of plainness and firmness." He arrived to find that he had been chosen major general of the Army of Mississippi, along with several brigadiers including Earl Van Dorn. Having no choice, despite his weariness, Davis stayed at a boardinghouse in the capital for a few days, starting the business of organizing the state's militia into a small model of the old army. Arms presented a special problem, for there simply were not enough. "We shall need all and many more than we can get, I fear," Davis told Pettus, who seemed incredulous and repeatedly told Davis, "General, you overrate the risk." Approached on all sides for his help and advice, Davis could only repeat what he had been saying for years: Prepare, prepare, prepare. "God help us," he said after visitors left his temporary office. "War is a dreadful calamity even when it is made against aliens and strangers. . . . They know not what they do."[38]

Not soon enough, the Davises finally reached Brierfield. He seemed broken down by care, unable to sleep, unable to stop talking about the catastrophe ahead, and hoping that it might be solved short of war: "A guarantee of our equal rights would bring the whole country back tomorrow," Varina remembered him saying, though he supposedly admitted that all property in slaves might eventually be lost in any case. Through the first several days of February he tried to rest, yet requests and importunities came from all quarters. Especially vexing were the repeated questions about him serving as president of the new Confederacy. With the seceded states meeting at Montgomery on February 4, speculation filled every mind. Some suggested him for secretary of war, others for general-in-chief. Most believed that Davis would be president. Perhaps he remembered now that prediction back in 1851 by Robert Ward, who said that ten years hence Davis would be the leader of a Southern republic. Varina certainly hoped not. "He did not know the arts of the politician," she said, "and would not practise them if understood." She hoped that he would get the commanding generalcy. "As a party manager," she said with keen insight, "he would not succeed."[39]

While at Jackson, on January 30 Davis succinctly expressed his view of the role he wanted in the coming government. "The post of Presdt. of the provisional government is one of great responsibility and difficulty," he wrote; "I have no confidence in my capacity to meet its requirements." If the chief executive thought him capable, "I think I could perform the functions of genl." But frankly, he said, "I would prefer not to have either place." He was writing to a delegate about to attend the Montgomery convention, and probably hoped quite sincerely that his wishes would be circulated and honored. He was fifty-three, sick of politics, and perhaps too old and infirm for war. In his heart, like the South, he wanted to be left alone.[40]

This said, he tried to rest his fevered mind and body in the shambles of Brierfield. "I found much to be done," he wrote a week after arrival, "and have entered upon me the most agreeable of all labors planting shrubs and trees and directing the operations of my field." He talked with his slaves about their future welfare in his absence, and gave the two oldest new rocking chairs to comfort their declining years. As usual, he seemed more concerned for Varina's garden than the fields that had to produce his livelihood. Its ruin in the 1850s flooding had hurt him terribly, and now husband and wife spent quiet and inexpressibly welcome hours tending to the flowers and vegetable plants. Davis himself was taking rose cuttings in the garden on February 10, 1861, when he saw a messenger approach.[41]

PART TWO

The Hour

17

I Saw Troubles and Thorns Innumerable

It came as no surprise to Davis to see someone approach him that day with an envelope. He knew that his sojourn at Brierfield would be brief. Indeed, three days earlier he had told a friend that he was "daily expecting a summons to renew my service to the public though in a different sphere." That expectation did not extend just to being major general of Mississippi volunteers. Despite his desire not to take any prominent position in the new nation, he certainly believed that he would be tendered a post as its general-in-chief. Yet no news came to him of the deliberations of the convention then under way at Montgomery, though a summons did arrive that same day from Pettus asking Davis to come to Jackson right away, prepared to go on to Montgomery. It would not be hard to speculate that the governor wanted to have Davis on the scene to press for his appointment to command the armies of the South.[1]

But other things had been happening in Montgomery, and as usual and according to his creed, Jefferson Davis did nothing to influence those events. As always, out of his notion of duty, he left his fate in the hands of others; and they proved to have ideas different from his own. Convening on February 4, the delegates from the six seceded states—South Carolina, Mississippi, Florida, Georgia, Louisiana, and Alabama—made Howell Cobb president of the convention and immediately went to work on a "provisional" constitution modeled on that of the old Union. Four days later they completed and adopted the document, which differed from its forebear only in that property in slaves was specifically recognized, the sovereign independence of the states was emphatically stated, internal improvements and funding for private industry were prohibited, and the slave trade was abolished. The constitution gave the president an item veto on bills and appropriations, and for the chief executive and the vice president it specified single six-year terms.

Meanwhile the delegates already feverishly discussed who those highest civil officials should be. Many names were whispered and shouted in the hallways of the Exchange Hotel, where most of the delegates took rooms. Many expected that Georgia, with its powerful trio of Cobb, Toombs, and Alexander Stephens, all of them present, might furnish the new president. Others spoke of Rhett or Robert Barnwell of South Carolina. Yet from the first at least a plurality of the thirty-seven delegates seemed to favor Davis. By its rules, however, the convention would give to each state one vote so that all states would be equal, and that meant a winning candidate had to carry at least four of the six.[2]

Undoubtedly maneuvering took place before the state delegations went into their final caucuses on the evening of February 8, after adopting the constitution, and men changed positions from day to day. When Howell Cobb's brother Thomas reached Montgomery five days earlier as a delegate, he found that "the strongest current is for Jefferson Davis." Others thought Toombs ran in front, and Stephens believed that his fellow Georgian was "by far the best fitted for that position." Yet Toombs suffered from an embarrassing streak of intemperance, and on several successive nights got drunk over dinner at the Exchange. Indeed, on February 6, with men already looking ahead to the voting for President, Toombs became "*tighter* than I ever saw him," Stephens wrote, "too tight for his character and reputation by far." Looking back on it two weeks later, Stephens believed that that night's performance took Toombs out of the running.[3]

Yet the Georgia delegation still stood behind Toombs when they met to decide their vote early on February 9. Thomas Cobb, however, told them that he had heard that Alabama, Mississippi, and Florida favored Davis and, carrying a slightly different story, Francis Bartow reported that Florida, South Carolina, and Louisiana supported Davis. Thus conflicting reports told the Georgians that all the other states had decided, or might decide, for the Mississippian. Other rumors had this state and that leaning toward Howell Cobb. While Cobb at once asked to be withdrawn in favor of Davis and unanimity, Toombs staggered from incredulous surprise. He would not believe that at least three and possibly four states favored Davis and wanted someone to find out with certainty. They sent a delegate to canvass the other states. Mississippi was behind Davis, of course, even though Alexander Clayton had in his hand Davis's January 30 letter disclaiming a desire for any office, keeping it to himself unless specifically asked for Davis's feelings about the presidency. The nose-counting delegate also found that Louisiana stood for Davis. While some of the South Carolinians preferred Stephens, a majority seemed to favor Davis, and the story was the same with Florida and Alabama by the morning of February 9. There had been a considerable movement for Stephens in several of the delegations, but he probably ruined himself when he said that he would be unwilling to strike the first blow if it came to war. Besides, he did not really want the position, and worse, he had been too reluctant to embrace secession. Others in his own delegation, like Thomas Cobb, loathed him for his presumed Unionism.[4]

When the news came back to Georgia of the feeling elsewhere, it left Toombs mortified but helpless. Meanwhile, anticipating that the rumors would be confirmed, Georgia had quickly acted to stand unanimously behind Stephens for the vice presidency, and the other states would readily concede it as the state's due. Indeed, the agreement on Davis and Stephens reflected the general trend of the convention, which was to step back from the most strident positions taken in favor of a more conservative stance, in hopes of wooing the large body of Unionists and fence sitters in the seceded states. Even the South Carolinians themselves seemed to realize that they were too ultra to be leaders in the new nation. Thus, ironically, a movement conceived in extremism gave birth to itself by compromise.

That morning, February 9, the states voted, and there was much excitement as a large crowd observed the historic event. It was unanimous, as all agreed the election must be. Jefferson Davis was to be president of the Confederate States of America. While most cheered, some few considered their own private misgivings. Thomas Cobb heard many discuss the troubling rumors that Davis favored reconstruction of the old Union through some form of compromise. "Many are regretting already his election," Cobb wrote on February 15. "If he does not come out boldly in his inaugural against this suicidal policy we shall have an explosion here."[5]

While the convention went on about its business that day, word of the election sped through the wires to Mississippi, to Vicksburg, whence the messenger set forth for Brierfield. When he dismounted and was greeted by Davis, he handed over the telegram, no doubt expecting to see elation at its reading. Varina saw something else. Her husband read it silently, then a look of anguish passed over his face that at first made her fear someone in their family had suffered a calamity. He said nothing for a few moments, and then, "as a man might speak of a sentence of death," he told her. Davis may be believed when he said that it truly took him by surprise. He had written his letter to Clayton expecting that its contents would become generally known, and this he had considered "adequate precautions" against being chosen. Worse, if he had to serve in any capacity, he preferred a field command—which he already had in Mississippi—though he would not have minded a commission to lead all the Southern states' forces. But it was too late for any of that now. His rigid concept of a public man's duty to respond to any call of the people left him no choice but to accept this burden, however much others might think it an honor. To himself he hoped that at least his incumbency might be temporary, and that once the government was properly organized and safely functioning, he might resign and resume command of the Mississippi militia.[6]

There was little time for preparation. Packing a few things, he said farewell to Varina the next day, then made a little speech to the Brierfield slaves, showing them only the affection he felt for them and keeping his sense of depression carefully concealed. His sad parting made him late in leaving, and Ben Montgomery and the other blacks who rowed him the three miles downriver from the Brierfield landing to where the packet boats could land soon heard the expected boat blowing her whistle. She was at the landing already and would depart before they could reach it. The only thing to do was to wait in the stream for the vessel to come up to them. While they sat at their oars, Davis talked quietly with the slaves, lamenting their lateness and complimenting the men on their hearty rowing nevertheless. "Jeff Davis was a man you couldn't tell what was in his mind," said Montgomery. "He chatted with us just the same as usual," despite the momentous journey he was undertaking. Soon the *Natchez* steamed into sight, and Davis hailed her and went aboard. Montgomery and most of the others would never see him again.[7]

He reached Vicksburg that afternoon, to be met by marching bands and military companies on parade, the tattered flag of his old Mexican War regiment at their head, and there he made his first speech as president-elect. He spoke soberly, with evident sadness, remembered the old Union and the causes that impelled them all to leave it, and expressed his fervent hope that this new nation might not have to be born in bloodshed. If it did, however, then he would stand with them "by shedding every drop of my blood in your cause." Soon thereafter he boarded a special train for Jackson. During a delay waiting for the cars, he sat in the depot talking with the state chief justice, William Sharkey. Asked if there would be a war, Davis told him frankly that "there would be war, long and bloody."[8]

Before he reached Jackson that evening, Davis saw a military company march out of town to receive him, all of them boys. To himself he wished that Varina and his children could be with him then, that in later years they might remember these moving and historic demonstrations. One of his first acts on arriving was to resign his commission, and then came a round of visits with friends and dignitaries, surrounded always by crowds. Inevitably he had to address the people of the city, speaking on February 12 to an audience that included his brother Joseph. A reporter watched the elder Davis as his brother spoke, and remarked on the "pride, hope and pleasure" that passed over his face. He heard his brother express his feelings of inadequacy to the task ahead of him, his concern over the effects of the war probably to come, and his vow that if war came, he would take it to the North. "There will be no war in our territory," he said. "It will be carried into the enemy's territory." For one so recently conciliatory, and elected on the basis of his conservatism, Davis started out with a very aggressive posture indeed.[9]

Accompanied by some of the old First Mississippi and their sacred banner, he left on February 14 when a telegram arrived summoning him to Montgomery. Along the way there would be repeated stops as each junction and rail town wanted to see the new president. All told, he made perhaps twenty-five speeches in two days, saying much the same thing wherever he stopped. He expected that England and France would grant them diplomatic recognition due to their dependence on Southern cotton, charged the North with "a hell born fanaticism," and promised that "we have separated from them, and separated *forever*." Everywhere he went he met with enthusiastic receptions, bonfires, and the firing of cannon, except when his train passed through Tennessee, where Union sympathizers gave him much the same welcome that he had received at the Crutchfield House the month before. From Chattanooga he turned southward toward Atlanta, probably realizing along the way the deplorable state of the rail system in the South that forced him to travel nearly seven hundred miles—north, then east, then south—to reach Montgomery, when that city only lay some two hundred miles due east of Jackson. That did not bode well for the rapid movement of men and supplies if war should come as he expected.[10]

Davis spoke so often that he simply slept in his homespun suit, yet he always seemed "fresh and eloquent" when he stepped off his car before the crowds. Before dawn on February 16 he reached Atlanta and delivered a half hour address there later that morning, repeating the themes familiar from his earlier speeches. Peace or war, he said, he was ready for the North, but the South's policy should be peace and "free trade," even suggesting that if the Union tried to coerce the South, then he would grant letters of marque to privateers. Given the mercenary character of Northern seamen, he suggested, he could "buy the last enterprising Yankee out of Boston!" Davis may have said something else, too. Four years later a man in Atlanta would claim that the president-elect promised to lead his armies into Washington itself to "assassinate the whole Vandal Congress," and would burn Philadelphia and New York as well if he must. The account was exaggerated or false, yet Davis had rattled his saber already on this trip and may have done so again in even harsher terms.[11]

A reception committee escorted Davis aboard his train for the next leg through Georgia, and after several stops and speeches, they turned him over to another from Montgomery for the final leg of the journey. Again his train left amid the thunder of artillery and a sea of handkerchiefs waved by the smiling women on the platform. Davis was close to exhaustion by now, but the continual manifestations of good feeling and confidence buoyed his spirits to see him through the remainder of the ordeal. He seemed to become especially animated when he spoke of the possibility of war and their power to defend themselves. In his elegant private car Davis freely entered into genial conversation with any of the host of people aboard his special train, showing an unaccustomed openness and warmth to strangers. Thomas Watts, a member of the Alabama delegation to Montgomery, rode with him as one of the reception committee, and he spoke at length with the president-elect. Like everyone else, Watts wanted to know if Davis thought there would be war. Yes he did, said the president, but he would bend every effort to avoid it. Given their mutual certainty that they must fight, Watts asked who Davis thought should be their "chief commander" in the field. "There is one man above all others—he is now in California—I have written to him—I believe he is with us," said Davis. "Albert Sidney Johnston."[12]

Finally, at 10 p.m. on February 16, Davis reached Montgomery. The delegates from the several states already being there to make a constitution, they followed the precedent of Philadelphia in 1787 by declaring the city the capital of the new Confederacy. To the booming of cannon and the shouts of a crowd at the depot, he alighted from his train, made a brief address, and then went to another reception at the Exchange Hotel, where he would stay. Here William L. Yancey met him, and here he had to make yet another speech from its balcony. Despite his exhaustion, he still found the stamina to be defiant. If the Yankees tried to coerce them, he said, they would smell Southern powder and feel Southern steel. Southerners asked nothing and wanted nothing from the Union. "It may be that our career shall be ushered in amidst storm and trouble," he said. "It may be that, as this morning opened with clouds, mist, and rain, we shall have to encounter inconveniences at the beginning; but, as the sun afterward arose, lifted the mist, dispersed the clouds, and left us the pure sunlight of heaven, so will the progress of the Southern Confederacy carry us safely over the sea of troubles."

Pleading his fatigue and hoarse voice, Davis said little more than to express his diffidence and doubt as he assumed his new office, and to hope that if events required him to leave that office to "again enter into the ranks of the soldiery," they would welcome him there too. It was his first public intimation that he might not serve out his full term but choose to resign to enter the army, or perhaps exercise his function as commander in chief by taking the field while president. This said, Davis went inside while Yancey addressed the crowd briefly. Praising the "statesman, the soldier and the patriot" who had come to lead them in this critical time, he assured them that they had the leader they needed. "The man and the hour have met," he declared "Prosperity, honor and victory await his administration."[13]

The next day being Sunday, Davis rested between the incessant visits of well-wishers and dignitaries, many of them old friends. Then on Monday, February 18, came the formal inaugural ceremonies. They commenced at noon with a procession leaving the Exchange Hotel to escort Davis to the Alabama State House, which now served as Capitol of the Confederacy as well. Davis and Stephens rode in an open carriage, with bands and mounted soldiers before them. Behind them marched a host of dignitaries, including the governors of the seceded states. Cannon fired throughout the city, and thousands lined Commerce Street bestowing smiles and throwing flowers as Davis passed in his open barouche behind six white horses. Porches, windows, even rooftops teemed with cheering spectators. When finally the head of the procession reached the State House, Davis saw perhaps five thousand gathered in the Capitol square. The barouche took him straight to the building's open porch. In the absence of a national anthem, a band played the "Marseillaise." Cheer followed cheer as he strode up the steps, and then one giant shout arose from the multitude when he reached the top step and stood in full view before them all.

Beneath a bright sun, Davis and Stephens sat down next to Howell Cobb. After a prayer Cobb announced Davis, who stood before the crowd to deliver his inaugural address. He looked out upon a sea of people with their smiling faces and their bouquets, but felt that beyond them "I saw troubles and thorns innumerable." Nevertheless, in a clear voice that carried almost to the outer reaches of the crowd, he addressed them as friends and fellow Confederates.[14]

He spoke of his humility at this great undertaking, despite his distrust of his abilities, and his confidence that he would have the wisdom of the people of the South to guide him. Referring to the fact that this was a provisional government, he offered his hope for the speedy establishment of a permanent government, with a permanent constitution and both houses of the legislature properly elected. This would give them the "moral and physical power" to meet the challenges to their nationhood.

Though the speech was brief by Davis's standards, still he was speaking to the world now, as well he knew, and thus he felt obliged to offer at least some small justification for their being there at that juncture in history. There had been no wrong on their part, he said. The "wanton aggression" of others forced them to this pass. They would be a people that wanted peace and harmony with all the nations of the world, including the North. In an obvious appeal to ears in Europe, particularly England and France, he reminded the crowd that the South was an agricultural nation whose cotton was "required" in all the manufacturing countries, and that he desired nothing less than free trade. Should an "exterior force," meaning the Union, try to interrupt the flow of cotton to foreign markets, it could only be detrimental "to manufacturing and commercial interests abroad." In short, Davis attempted to remind European nations of their dependence—so he thought—on the South's produce, his purpose twofold: an encouragement of diplomatic recognition based on the obvious economic self-interest of those manufacturing nations, and an appeal to those nations for assistance or resistance should Lincoln attempt to blockade Southern ports and interdict commerce bringing in the revenue needed for defense.

Davis even exaggerated the status of this new Confederacy for their benefit, asserting that it was born of "a peaceful appeal to the ballot box." In fact, not one of the states there represented had decided on secession by a popular referendum. Rather, their withdrawal from the Union and their presence in Montgomery now had been decided by just 854 men in the several state secession conventions—157 of whom had voted against secession—and all of them had been selected by their legislatures. Without the ballot box ever being used by the population at large, the destiny of 9 million had been decided by 697. However much Davis might hope to make it look like a popular movement, the fact is that this political revolution, like the one in 1776 which he looked on as a model, was a revolution by a middle- and upper-class minority over issues of property that only mattered to the privileged. Indeed, one of the tasks ahead to which Davis did not refer in his inaugural was that of making the people as a whole feel that this was *their* cause, and that it was not what they inevitably called it, "a rich man's war and a poor man's fight."

At the same time, Davis had to speak to the ardent secessionists in the new nation, those whose rumors of his favoring reunification had so concerned Thomas Cobb. "We have entered upon the career of independence," he said, "and it must be inflexibly pursued." Going farther that he might not be mistaken, he asserted that "a reunion with the states from which we have separated is neither practical nor desirable." Instead they must build this new nation. They had a provisional constitution and soon there would be a permanent one founded on the sacred Constitution of their forefathers. "We have a light which reveals its true meaning," he declared, and that light would prevent them from wandering as their former Northern brothers had strayed. Indeed, he suggested, blessed by this new constitution, before long others of the old United States would wish to join with them. He thought, of course, of Virginia, North Carolina, Tennessee, Texas, Arkansas, and perhaps the border states of Maryland, Kentucky, and Missouri. But he also hoped that some of the other states bordering the Ohio, like Indiana, might also choose to live under the "true" constitution. If so, he would welcome them.

But the new nation had to be ready for this growth. In addition to electing a regular congress, they must also speedily create the executive or cabinet departments to deal with diplomacy, finance, military matters, and the postal service. They must prepare especially for defense. Ordinarily they might look to their existing state militias. "In the present condition of affairs," however, they needed an army and a navy.

In fact, though he devoted fewer words to the reason for their need than to other matters, still Davis returned time and time again to the possibility of their need. Five separate times he spoke of the potential of war with the North. "If we may not hope to avoid war, we may at least expect that posterity will acquit us of having needlessly engaged in it," he said. "If, however, passion or lust of dominion should cloud the judgment or inflame the ambition of those States, we must prepare to meet the emergency and maintain, by the final arbitrament of the sword, the position which we have assumed among the nations of the earth." If denied their rights and the integrity of their territory, then "it will but remain for us with firm resolve to appeal to arms. . . . Should we be involved in war," he warned, "the suffering of millions will bear testimony to the folly and wickedness of our aggressors." Not unmindful of what he and others saw as the economically motivated Yankee mind, he threatened that he would unleash on the high seas a horde of privateers "for retaliation upon the commerce of an enemy." The way to a Yankee's good sense was through his pocketbook.

For a few moments Davis spoke of himself. Experience had taught him that ahead lay "toil and care and disappointment." They were "the price of official elevation." He would make many mistakes, and they must be prepared to forgive and tolerate his deficiencies. One thing they should not find cause to fault would be his zeal and fidelity to their common cause. He could not help but remind them, as he did with every office he ever held, that he had not wanted this post and did not seek it. Yet now he had it, and he only hoped that the confidence they felt then would still be there when he retired from office, which Davis later claimed was a reference to his hope to leave the presidency as soon as the Confederacy was on its feet and functioning, perhaps at the time of the general election of a permanent congress and executive one year hence.

"It is joyous in the midst of perilous times to look around upon a people united in heart, where one purpose of high resolve animates and actuates the whole," he said. "Obstacles may retard, but they cannot long prevent, the progress of a movement sanctified by its justice and sustained by a virtuous people." Secure in the knowledge and the blessing of the Almighty, "we may hopefully look forward to success, to peace, and to prosperity."[15]

In many ways, under less-than-favorable circumstances, it was one of the finest addresses of his life, brief, to the point, tastefully eloquent without his frequent overblown rhetoric, uncluttered with literary and other allusions, and well formed to address three audiences simultaneously—the Confederacy, the Union, and the world. It fitted the occasion perfectly in tone and content. When the applause subsided, Cobb administered the oath of office. As he concluded, Davis looked heavenward when he uttered the words, "So help me God." In his mind he already saw the myriad dangers and challenges ahead. Perhaps he recalled almost fifteen years before, when—in one of his very first speeches in the House of Representatives in 1846—he spoke of "republics cradled in war." Was that to be the fate of this new republic? "We are without machinery without means and threatened by powerful opposition," he told Varina two days later, "but I do not despond and will not shrink from the task imposed upon me." Yet the enormity of that task so filled him that during the speech itself it overcame him. Absentmindedly, still looking upward, he repeated again the words, "So help me God." Then he bent down and kissed the Bible upon which he had taken his oath. Very probably it was the same Bible with which Howell Cobb swore in the members of the convention. He resolved to keep it himself as a souvenir.[16]

Responses to the inaugural proved to be almost universally positive. Even Thomas Cobb, never disposed to like Davis, found that it removed many of his doubts. "The inaugural pleased everybody," he wrote that night, "and the manner in which President Davis took the oath was most impressive." A woman in the crowd agreed. "I think I never saw any scene so solemn and impressive," she said two days later. The next evening Davis held his first levee or reception at Montgomery's Estelle Hall, and the well-wishers came forward then in their thousands. "Everybody and his wife were there," said Thomas Cobb. All evening long people kept coming in as others left. Though the crowd became packed and the heat in the hall rose oppressively, still Davis stayed at his post, shaking hands by the thousands and accepting gracefully the kisses of the ladies. Later they all went to a nearby concert hall, where music and dancing continued well after midnight.[17]

Almost at once Davis got off to a good start with most of the ruling men in Montgomery. Every day he dined at the Exchange Hotel with the Cobbs and the rest, and he exerted effort he had rarely made before to engage in small talk, to practice some of the arts of the politician, however foreign they might be to his nature. "He is chatty and tries to be agreeable," Thomas Cobb wrote to his wife. Yet the Georgian quickly concluded that "he is not great in any sense of the term." Perceptively, Cobb saw that "the power of will he has, made him all he is." Others found him "companionable," with a disposition "that endears him to all by whom he may be surrounded." As for the broader Confederacy, the general reception to the new President was one of welcome and confidence. "No man, unless Calhoun or Quitman were living, could well dispute with him the highest place in Southern confidence," wrote a New Orleans editor. "We have yet to hear of a single discordant sentiment in our whole community in regard to the wisdom of this choice."[18]

Yet some demurred. "Neither in character nor in politics, has he any hold upon the confidence of the people," asserted a hostile Natchez paper. Charging that the new government and its president represented nothing but an oligarchy that changed everything without "the consent of the governed," it accused Davis of having schemed himself into his position. Untrue as this was, still there were those who did not let the euphoria and good feeling of the moment make them forget old traits and weaknesses rumored widely enough to give pause. Even in Montgomery some speculated on the problems they might have with the new president, including what some perceived as his egotism, especially his well-known penchant for assuming that he knew better than others on just about every issue. When guessing games began to fill the hallway at the Exchange over Davis's forthcoming cabinet appointments, suggesting this man or that, one wag corrected them. "You are all wrong," he said, citing his own personal acquaintance with the president. "I know exactly." Asked to share his insight, he happily obliged by predicting every anticipated appointment: "For Secretary of State, Hon. Jeff. Davis of Miss.; War and Navy, Jeff. Davis of Miss.; Interior, ex-Senator Davis, of Miss.; Treasury, Col. Davis, of Miss.; Attorney General, Mr. Davis, of Miss."[19]

In fact, the speculation about his cabinet appointments covered just about everyone in Montgomery *except* Davis. Thomas Cobb found the question of "who will constitute the cabinet" to be the most exciting one in town on February 20. In four general statutes adopted the next day, the Confederate Congress created departments of state, treasury, war, navy, post office, and justice, and even as the members voted, suppositions flourished. Some thought Captain Braxton Bragg, Davis's old friend from Mexico, would be secretary of war, Yancey attorney general, with Toombs and Barnwell for treasury and state. Others thought Thomas Cobb might be attorney general.[20]

If he chose to, Davis might have found it convenient that the number of cabinet departments matched the current number of Confederate states; he could apportion one portfolio to each state. Indeed, he had no choice, for every state had to be given its share of the leadership in this new government. The best he could hope to do would be to find men of ability to match this political reality, and here he was himself hampered by the fact that the only public men of the South he knew well were those he had served with in the Senate, and he had never observed any of them in an administrative capacity. In fact, he had never even met some of the men he now had to approach.

State, in the old Union (as in our day), held preeminence in esteem among the executive branches, and so treating it for the moment, Davis thought at first to give it to a South Carolinian to recognize its leadership in the movement for a new nation. Davis wanted to offer the portfolio to Robert Barnwell, an old Senate associate. Unfortunately, before he could make the offer, the South Carolina delegation called on him and made a strong appeal for the appointment of Christopher G. Memminger as secretary of the treasury. Unable (wisely) to refuse such a united appeal, Davis had to give up on the other South Carolinian. Following the perceived order of stature of the states in the secession movement, then, he looked to Georgia, and where better than to the leading disappointed aspirant for his own position, Toombs? Having thought of Toombs for Treasury, now he offered him State. Toombs balked at first. "I cannot," he responded, and even when Davis repeated his offer, the Georgian responded, "My opinion is unchanged." Still smarting from his loss of the presidency, and probably from a residual dislike of Davis from their earlier difficulty in the Senate, the Georgian wanted to distance himself. Nevertheless Davis persisted, and finally Toombs agreed to accept temporarily.

Of the most important posts, that left War to fill. Davis wanted his friend from Alabama, Clement Clay, but Clay's poor health forced him to decline. Still needing an Alabamian, Davis turned next to a man he may never have met, Leroy P. Walker, and did so exclusively on the recommendations of others whom he trusted. On February 21 he nominated these three for confirmation in their appointments. Four days later he filled the other three positions. He gave Navy to Stephen Mallory, who had chaired the Senate Naval Affairs Committee. Knowing Benjamin of Louisiana to be an able lawyer, and having some regard for his intellect, Davis made him attorney general. This left only postmaster general. Perhaps Davis intentionally saved this least significant position for last, and for Mississippi—fitting since another Mississippian now held the highest office of all. He recommended Henry S. Ellett, but then Ellett declined, and so Davis approached his old friend Wirt Adams, who also refused. Not until March 6, when John H. Reagan arrived in Montgomery along with other delegates from the newly seceded state of Texas, did he find a postmaster. Now that Mississippi could be forgotten in the cabinet, Davis settled on Reagan, a former congressman with whom he had some acquaintance. Reagan took more persuading than any of the others, but finally he, too, accepted.[21]

Thus the cabinet stood complete and represented the first instance of the kind of settlements and compromises Davis would have to accept in order to keep the Confederate States—more a coalition than a nation as yet—placated. Two were men he knew; two he had never met; two he might have killed on the dueling field; and two, at least, repeatedly declined their offices. None save Mallory offered prior experience to suggest any hope of success.

As his responsibilities consumed him day after day, Davis must have felt great relief when Varina arrived at the end of the month. He had hoped to have time to start looking for a house for them after his inauguration, but was still living at the Exchange when she came. There he took his meals, entering the long dining room quietly, sometimes sitting at the "ladies table," then frequently losing himself in discussion with one of his new generals and forgetting to eat his dinner. By this time, however, the congress had taken the matter off his hands by passing a measure to lease a house to serve as Executive Mansion, though not without the disapproval of at least one South Carolinian who thought the act a trampling of the new constitution. They settled upon the Colonel Edmund S. Harrison home, a two-story frame Federal-style house just a block away from the building that was to serve as the executive and cabinet offices. It was a comfortable place, well suited for entertaining, with a wide entrance hall, a large double parlor, a spacious dining room, a rear hall reception area, two bedrooms, and a large room that Davis would use as a study. Four bedrooms and a nursery on the second floor would accommodate the children and guests. Varina liked it immediately, even though members of Congress complained that it cost them five thousand dollars a year for the lease. In fact, as soon as the Davises took possession, there were other signs of lavishness that some found objectionable, including the thirteen-hundred-dollar carriage that he ordered from Newark, New Jersey. Yet when Varina held her levees, there were none to criticize the host and hostess for their hospitality. They entertained often, and to any who complained that this house was too costly for the public purse, Varina reportedly quipped that before long she expected to be holding forth in another Executive Mansion, in Washington.[22]

The day of Varina's arrival, Confederates first raised their new flag. Davis had opposed giving up the Stars and Stripes, partly because their own forebears had helped make it glorious, and perhaps because he still hoped the Union might give them guarantees that would allow them to return to the fold. But for now that new banner fluttered before him every morning, when, before 9 A.M., he walked down to the corner of Commerce and Market streets, where the government had taken over the second floor of a building for its executive offices. Around three sides of an open court the small offices stood arrayed, including all the departments except the post office. Davis himself occupied an inside room above Market, with Toombs on one side, and his private secretary Alexander Clitherall on the other, soon to be replaced by the "jovial, ruddy-visaged" Robert Josselyn, a Massachusetts native-turned-Mississippian. Simple hand-lettered cardboard signs were pinned to the doors to identify the several departments.[23]

Davis quickly adopted a routine for his working days, just as he had when secretary of war. While still living at the Exchange Hotel, he went downstairs at the sound of a gong for breakfast with the other occupants, coming in time to sit a little apart from the others, perhaps to transact business over his morning meal. En route to his office in the executive building, he invariably walked the short distance, occasionally receiving the cheers of a passing militia company. Otherwise he remained in the Exchange, spending the day in an impromptu reception room in one of the second-floor apartments. There he sat at a desk against one wall to write his correspondence, often rummaging in the jumble of books, maps, and papers and samples of uniform fabric, hats, feathers, epaulettes, and more on the oil-cloth-covered center table. But most often in these early weeks, he sat on the sofa, "rising up with the stately grace that never deserted him" to greet the ceaseless procession of visitors, applicants, and office seekers who faced him from the nearby lounge or side chairs. There, beneath the gaze of portraits of Clay, Calhoun, and—interestingly enough—Webster, along with an oddly out-of-place Napoleon, he labored at the worst part of being a man of high station—handling people.[24]

In his correspondence he had to deal with a flood of congratulatory letters, most of them also asking for some favor or appointment. Officers from the old U. S. Army, like P. G. T. Beauregard of Louisiana, wrote to offer their services. Friends like E. Kirby Smith, reminding Davis that "to you I owe my advancement in the present service," expected him to advance them in the Confederate service as well. Men wrote applying for consulships, and a seeming legion offered to raise companies of volunteers, even before his inauguration and before Congress had authorized him to receive volunteers. At the same time, barely were some men in the military before applications came begging to have them relieved. Less than a month after taking office, Davis was already recommending discharges for sixteen-year-old boys who had enlisted without their parents' consent. When governors and prominent citizens boasted that they were sending to him "our best young men," Davis lamented to himself and others that "society cannot support the loss of such men."[25]

Some applications went beyond the usual expectations of a chief executive, and a few approached the absurd. Everyone, even women, wanted a part in the war they expected to come. The ladies of one female school offered themselves as a company of volunteers if not enough men should join the service, while others demanded a clarification on the wartime role of the "hooped skirts." A host of military plans came in, some merely impractical, many positively foolish. To take Fort Pickens outside Pensacola, Florida, one enterprising fellow suggested disguising Confederates as U. S. troops, putting them aboard the recently captured *Star of the West*, and having them approach the fort in the guise of reinforcements. An enterprising poltroon named George Bickley maintained that he could command thirty thousand men from his Knights of the Golden Circle, all of them living in the North but sympathetic to the South. Men offered new products, some useful ones like a new invention for breech-loading cannon, while others badgered Davis to adopt the use of "McDougall's Disinfecting Powder" in army camps and hospitals. Many plans came to him for capturing Washington, one promising that it could be done in twenty days, taking Lincoln and Scott in the bargain, while another would require a mysterious "new sort of arms as yet unknown," for all the good that would do. One inventor offered a means with which to destroy ships and forts from nearly a mile's distance, "provided that you do not consider any means unfare in ware." Another even promised to build an airship that would travel at one hundred miles an hour. Almost all of them, of course, wanted the government to provide money for their ideas. Perhaps the only suggestion that didn't reflect the self-interest of the applicant was one in the local press proposing that the capital of the Confederacy follow the lead of Washington by renaming itself the "District of Davis."[26]

Meanwhile, Davis found much to do just with what he conceived within his own mind. Among his first concerns was the appointment of general officers to command the new armies of the Confederacy. By act of Congress on February 26, the several staff departments of the army were created, and on March 6 Congress authorized Davis to appoint generals to command the brigades and divisions he was allowed to create. At once a flood of applications for generalships came to him, or else influential politicians lobbied for appointments for their friends. The problem for Davis was that there was no test of who would make a good leader. Just four generals existed in the U. S. Army at that time, and of them only his old friend seventy-one-year-old David E. Twiggs, clearly too old for active service, offered his services to the Confederacy. Davis would have to look to men who were barely more than captains and majors to find his generals, and he had to keep an eye on patronage, making certain to give each state its fair share of promotions, a system not destined for the greatest good or efficiency. A year later he would admit that he made many mistakes in these early days.[27]

He did not require the recommendations of others to believe that he needed to get as many West Point graduates as possible. If most of them did not have battle experience or practical knowledge of what it was like to lead more than a company of men, at least they had a head start over volunteer officers, thanks to their education. On March 1 he sent a nomination for Pierre G. T. Beauregard to Congress, making him a brigadier general in the Provisional Army of the Confederate States. As with Congress and even the presidency, the volunteer provisional service was expected to be replaced at a later date by a regular army. A few days later Davis nominated former Lieutenant Colonel Braxton Bragg for a brigadiership. With little to go on but instincts and what he already knew of certain men, Davis continued to seek out old friends. He made his associate from War Department days, Samuel Cooper, a brigadier and on March 16 gave him the same job he had had in the United States service, adjutant and inspector general. At the same time, he sought out Northrop and offered him a post in the newly established commissary department. When others he had known approached him, he acted on what he knew of their qualities. Henry Heth resigned his Union captaincy and came to Davis, who endorsed him to Cooper as "a first rate soldier and of the caste of men most needed." To be sure, in these very early days when war was hardly a certainty, Davis looked to West Pointers and to men he knew and trusted, his friends. Though some might fault him, the fact is there was nowhere else to look.[28]

Very quickly the volume of all this business, with only one secretary to assist him, literally consumed Davis. As he had at the War Department in Washington, he felt obligated to attend to most matters personally, and soon he began apologizing to old friends that he had "no time for friendly correspondence." He did, however, manage to devote a little extra personal attention to requests from friends and old Mexican War comrades and made the time to add special endorsements to their letters noting his friendship for them and commending them to the attention of the appropriate cabinet secretary. Quickly Davis learned that he could not please everyone. For almost every appointment or commission granted, there came a whining complaint that the rank assigned was too low. Before his first month in office was done, he must have daydreamed of how much more congenial it would have been to be in the field commanding an army than here in Montgomery, commanding everything. "I hope you will not have occasion to take the field," Yulee of Florida wrote to him on March 1, "but if there is a war, . . . you have the example of Napoleon before you." Did Napoleon, he wondered, have to endure all this paperwork and endless fretting by ambitious men?[29]

Davis soon developed an informal system for dealing with the mountain of applications for military and diplomatic positions—and he needed to, for the February volume doubled in the mails of March. By

April the number rose to well over three hundred, and to each he had to devote at least enough attention to decide where to refer the applicant, while to many he responded personally. "I can give you no assurance of an appointment," he wrote time and again, "as the number of applicants from the Confederate States is already very large." More of the letters he turned over to Josselyn to answer, simply noting "ack in friendly terms" as a guideline. As for those applications referred to cabinet members for appropriate action, he soon adopted three levels of docketed comment: "referred" meant just what it said; "special" or "special attention" went on those that Davis favored; and where he felt very strongly, he wrote an endorsement himself. When a real dignitary asked for something like a commission as a brigadier, he often consulted Cooper, asking "What do you know . . . what think?" or "What can be done?" Davis was not so unattuned to the needs of mollifying factions that he would not grant an appointment for purely political reasons, as when he gave a position to the son of former President John Tyler, or even more so when he made the son of his old enemy Foote an officer, perhaps in the hope of keeping Foote himself from raising discord. Indeed, old Foote wrote to Davis repeatedly that winter saying that he wished to forget past differences and support the administration, but Davis could go only so far. Foote's son was fine, but as for the father Davis could not change his conviction that he "is perfectly destitute of any sense of truth." Perhaps unwisely, Davis refused to see him. Not for several months would Davis finally order the secretary of war to begin preparing abstracts of some of the more voluminous files for him to save time.[30]

With all this correspondence to contend with, Davis still had to find time to ponder much greater questions. On a single day, March 16, he sat down and considered such things as how to care for prisoners of war, regulations to support cotton growers, free navigation of the Mississippi, a sequestration act, the possibility of indictments against himself and others in the United States, forbidding the importation of slaves, oaths from those who supported the South, and the regulation of imports. Revealing how distracted he was by all the strains and claims on his attention, he actually put the Union indictments on his list three separate times, being either very absentminded or else very concerned about the treason charges against Southern leaders. No one could question that with all this on his plate, he was earning his presidential salary of $25,000 a year.[31]

Then there was the interminable line of visitors, whether at his reception room at the Exchange, his study in the Executive Mansion, or most often at his office in the brick State and Treasury building. With no sentries posted, anyone could enter, and indeed, the street door stood open at almost all times. Visitors who walked down the long whitewashed hall and straight upstairs to the second floor would note how little bustle there seemed to be. Then they simply walked up to the door with "The President" written on a sheet of paper affixed to it, and entered the office.

Like as not, Davis would already be in conversation with someone when the next visitor entered. He sat on the sofa or in a chair at the center table, inviting his visitors to sit as well. They invariably saw him wearing a light gray summer suit on warm days, made perhaps of homespun, or else a black broadcloth, with a black silk cravat or handkerchief around his neck. Some rumored that the adoption of gray for the Confederacy's official uniforms stemmed from Davis's personal preference for the color. When William H. Russell of the London *Times* visited with him in May, he saw in the president a man with a face that was "thin and marked on cheek and brow with many wrinkles," looking careworn and somewhat haggard. The left eye appeared to be entirely blind, but "the other is dark, piercing, and intelligent." Davis always kept his hair and beard neatly trimmed, his boots blacked and polished, and even sitting at his table presented the erect and soldierly bearing that had characterized him from youth. Still, at least to the condescending Russell, "he did not impress me as favorably as I had expected," though the Englishman felt greatly relieved to see that at least the president did not chew tobacco.

Other visitors, depending on their errands and their own deportment, found in Davis little or none of the official stiffness or reserve many expected, no affectation of "presidential" manners, but only a simple, frank, and cordial attentiveness. If the visitor had just arrived from the North, Davis showed a special curiosity to learn the latest tenor of feeling in the old Union. He was also likely to pontificate a bit, restating his own and the South's positions, even to those who already knew them. "Our people are a gallant, impetuous and determined people," he told a visitor to the Exchange in March. "What they resolve to do, that, they, most assuredly, mean to persevere in doing." The North could not bully them, and if pressed, the South would demonstrate that its warlike talk was no mere boast. "To me, personally, all violence is abhorrent," he said, but he would fight, if fight he must, to defend the sacred principle of the rights of the sovereign states. He spoke almost proudly of the fact that "as President of the Confederate States, my authority is, in many respects, more circumscribed than would be my authority as Governor of Mississippi." His national government was the servant of the states, and not the reverse. For this reason, and their common institutions, he believed that the border states like Virginia, Kentucky, and others must inevitably gravitate toward the new confederation.

He denied the charge that slavery lay at the root of this separation and the new nation. It was but one of many issues, but not, as he called it, the "all-in-all" of secession. "My own convictions, as to negro slavery, are strong," he told his visitor. "It has its evils and abuses." Nevertheless, "we recognize the negro as God and God's Book and God's Laws, in nature, tell us to recognize him—our inferior, fitted expressly for servitude." Indeed, freedom would only injure the black, for "the innate stamp of inferiority is beyond the reach of change. . . . You cannot transform the negro into anything one-tenth as useful or as good as what slavery enables him to be." He admitted that in time the black might be transformed into a "peasant," with sufficient freedom enough "not to injure the race in its usefulness," but he did not favor such a notion.

Setting aside slavery, Davis admitted that there was a possibility that Lincoln might impose a blockade on Southern ports, but if that happened it would only hasten what he felt to be the inevitable recognition of the Confederacy by the great European powers. Should they prove hesitant, then he could use cotton as a weapon by denying it to their mills, and that would raise enough outcry, especially in Britain, to impel them to side with the South and break the blockade. Yet Davis confessed uncertainty about just what Lincoln planned to do, confused by the alternating belligerent talk and seeming willingness to negotiate over Fort Sumter. When talk turned to Sumter, Davis was likely to ring a table bell near at hand to summon Secretary of War Walker to join the discussion, but those present soon saw that the Alabamian contributed little to the matter, "exhibiting a docility that did not dare say 'nay' to any statement made by his Chief," and leaving the clear impression that Davis selected him largely for this very reason.

Davis listened, often with his eyes half closed, occasionally shooting the burning glare of his one good eye at the visitor when an important point stirred him. If the conversation turned to weighty or troubling matters, Davis might knit his brows slightly, but that was all. All, that is, unless the visitor overstayed his welcome or bored the president by wasting his time on trivial matters. Then the president became quickly distracted, distant, and quite obviously uninterested. Unwilling to be overtly rude by asking the visitor to leave, Davis did not realize that his manner in such cases offended far more than would a simple announcement that the interview was concluded. These were still the early days of his administration, of course, but they set the mold for much of the rest of his tenure.[32]

Rarely did he get home before 6 P.M., when Varina found him exhausted and silent, too tired to eat and too keyed up to sleep. Still he seemed remarkably serene, believing the whole Congress and people to be behind him. A houseguest at the time, Pierce Butler, asked Varina if her husband was always such "a combination of angel and seer." But soon those close to Davis saw the first weeks take their toll. By early April one observer believed that the president was "wearing himself almost sick by harrassing public duties," though his energy seemed unaffected. After a visit to Davis's office, another in the capital believed that "care and work seem to have agreed with him." Certainly the expressions of confidence everywhere he looked helped to sustain him. The troops in and around Montgomery cheered him often, and he heard from the rest of the Confederacy that its growing forces looked upon "his mind as a council and his arm as a host." Occasionally Davis found relief from his office by leaving Montgomery briefly, as in March when he traveled up the West Point Railroad to talk with its manager. A rail clerk mistook him for a farmer, spied his watch, and yanked it from his pocket with the remark, "Fine watch—how'll you trade?" When the road manager entered and addressed the visitor as "President Davis," the poor clerk dropped the watch in Davis's lap, assumed a stupefied look, and fell backward over his desk and buried his face immediately in his ledgers.[33]

Any little break, any bit of comic relief, came doubly blessed for Davis if it could take his mind away for even a few moments from its overriding burden, one that made even the swarm of office seekers and the flood of mail pale to insignificance. Over everything else loomed one subject: Fort Sumter. From the time that Anderson occupied it, the pile of brick and mortar in Charleston Harbor had been the match waiting to ignite civil war. Even before he took his oath of office, Davis received a steady stream of intelligence—some accurate, some highly imaginative—from his new friend Wigfall of Texas, who kept his seat in Congress until his state seceded, and acted chiefly as a conduit of information between Washington and Montgomery. As early as February 15 he advised Davis that Sumter and Fort Pickens must both be seized and even counseled that Davis himself should go to Charleston. In fact, a rumor traveled widely around both South and North that Davis did visit his old friend Anderson in the fort.[34]

No one could say exactly which was the best course to follow. Davis saw two. One was to negotiate with Washington for the peaceful turnover of the fort and other federal property in the seceded states, perhaps on the basis of a purchase. The second, of course, was to continue building the earthworks and batteries around Charleston until all hope of negotiation had vanished and then to take the fort by bombardment. Just five days after taking office, Davis sent an officer to Charleston to inspect all of its fortifications. Indeed, it is somewhat remarkable that nothing erupted in Charleston even before Davis took office, for from the first the commissioners that Pickens sent to Washington to negotiate reported nothing gained. Two delegations came away empty-handed, and as Davis assumed his duties friends advised him to expect nothing from Lincoln and "make up your account *for war.*" "The independence of the new confederation will not be recognized," James Mason wrote him, "until the strength & resources of this govt. have been tested in a struggle to subdue it." One of the unsuccessful South Carolina commissioners to Washington advised Davis on the very day of his inaugural that "if the attack on Sumter is delayed a week, our harbor may be in the possession of a fleet."[35]

Unfortunately, Pickens confided to Davis two days later that "we are poorly prepared for war." This may have helped persuade the Congress, in secret session, to resolve to pursue diplomatic and military solutions simultaneously. Davis wanted to get every military means available to Pickens quickly, but what the governor said of South Carolina was true of the South generally. Davis could not find any reliable information on supplies, weapons, powder and shot, and much else that he needed to know of the available material resources in the seceded states: "Not the least of my embarrassments," he confessed to Pickens. Until he gained a better grasp on affairs, he implored Pickens to preserve peace and not risk a premature attack on Sumter, reminding him that since they were a nation, the decision to open fire did not lie with Charleston but with Montgomery. In order to extend the reach of his authority to Charleston as quickly as possible, Davis assigned Beauregard to take command on the same day that he made him a general, commending him to Pickens for his "zeal and gallantry." Should negotiations fail, he wanted to ensure the reduction of the fort "speedily and at least cost of the blood of our patriotic sons." Meanwhile, Beauregard would be charged to prevent any Federal reinforcements from reaching Major Anderson.[36]

As soon as Davis assumed direction of the Sumter matter, he decided on yet another commission to Washington, this one from the new Confederate States. He selected three men on February 25, and within two days they departed for Washington. They arrived to find the new Lincoln government suffering from divided councils. Lincoln would not receive them and had little or no intention of negotiating for Sumter. Seward, on the other hand, Lincoln's new secretary of state, believed that he might be able to influence the president and himself favored evacuation of the garrison. Though Davis felt pessimistic about the possibilities of an evacuation, Seward assumed to himself more than he should have and indirectly communicated to the commissioners the sentiment that Lincoln would soon order Anderson to leave. Wigfall seemingly confirmed this when he reported rumors to the same effect among Republicans. Yet when nothing happened for several days, the commissioners approached Seward again, receiving more assurances, along with apologies for the delay. And so Davis and Charleston waited through the end of March, with still no action. Finally they contacted Seward again, and now everything changed. Discovering that he could not move Lincoln, Seward said nothing of evacuation but instead promised that the Union would not attempt to resupply Sumter without notifying Pickens in advance.[37]

Obviously now there was no intention of abandoning Sumter and, equally obvious to Davis at least, there never had been such an intention. Unaware that Seward did not speak for Lincoln, Davis and others assumed that Seward had simply lied to buy time, a suspicion confirmed when a report came from Washington on April 3 that Yankee officers spoke openly of reinforcing Sumter and that Charleston would be "reduced to ashes." Still, as late as April 6, Davis had not entirely abandoned hope. "We have waited hopefully," he wrote. But when he learned of troops being withdrawn from the frontier to reinforce Union-held forts off the Florida coast, and when that same day he heard another rumor that a Federal fleet was going to take supplies to Sumter, his mood turned increasingly pessimistic. "This is not the course of good will," he wrote to an intermediary in Washington, "and does not tend to preserve the peace." Taking Confederate victory and independence as inevitable, he prayed that the Yankees would have the wisdom to see that they could save millions of dollars and thousands of lives by negotiating. It would be "a triumph of reason over vanity," since the result, by peaceful means or violent, must be the same.[38]

Two days later he, too, abandoned hope, however. Pickens received a message from Washington that Lincoln would attempt to resupply Sumter with provisions only. No men or arms would be introduced unless the fort was attacked. Clearly the Confederates had been misled and duped, and Lincoln intended to stay in Fort Sumter as long as possible, all the while reinforcing the other forts he still held in the Confederate States. "Negotiation was now at an end," Davis would say in later years. During the past few days many had looked to see how Davis would act in the crisis. People in Montgomery saw in him a calm and grave serenity but no panic. Rather, they noted "a presence of mind, a chastened energy." He knew now what had to be done. The Confederates had tried to deal honorably to settle the matter of the Federal forts. They asked to negotiate, even to discuss payment. Davis could not see, of course, Lincoln's point of view, nor could he see that he himself, in Lincoln's place, would never have agreed to negotiate in the face of ultimatums and naked threats of violence. In matters on which he felt that ironbound certainty of right, the Confederate president did not recognize the issue of point of view. Furthermore, in the last weeks of March and the first of April, the pressure on him to take decisive action mounted. His own honor and that of his new Confederacy demanded action—he could not lose more time trying to outwait Lincoln, especially if he hoped for recognition of Southern independence from abroad and if he wanted to secure the support of the still-unseceded border states. For Davis and his nation at this critical moment, inaction amounted to defeat.[39]

On April 8 the president and cabinet met in a session that lasted two hours or more. It was rumored that Davis urged an aggressive policy toward the Union, proposing that their commissioners in Washington be instructed to issue an ultimatum to Lincoln—surrender Sumter or see it bombarded. Others in Montgomery noted an unusual level of activity at the War Department, with constant comings and goings and the telegraph wires buzzing with telegrams in and out. The next day the cabinet met again. They knew of the plan to supply Sumter, and now they also had captured reports from the fort that indicated preparations were under way to resist a bombardment, along with a letter of Anderson's expressing his lack of enthusiasm for the position he occupied. The time to strike was now, before Anderson's defenses were stronger and while his resolve was weak.[40]

The cabinet discussion that day ran long and heated. Davis favored proceeding with the bombardment. Charleston's batteries were ready, and the South Carolinians themselves were more than anxious. Though they might be firing the first shots themselves, certainly the Federals had been guilty of aggression for months. Walker and probably the others supported the president. Only Toombs seems to have dissented, fearing the civil war that must inevitably follow. According to a friend, at one point Toombs paced back and forth in the room, then turned on Davis to declare that opening fire would be "suicide." "It is unnecessary," he said, "it puts us in the wrong, it is fatal."[41]

Davis and the majority were not to be moved. The next day, undoubtedly at Davis's order, Secretary of War Walker sent Beauregard a telegram directing him to demand the immediate evacuation of Fort Sumter or else to proceed "to reduce it." As if to reinforce the decision, Davis received a note from Wigfall the same day asserting that "Lincoln intends war." "Let us take Fort Sumter," he said.[42]

For reasons of his own, Beauregard delayed sending the ultimatum to Anderson until April 11. Anderson replied that his duty would not allow him to surrender his position. But then a tantalizing final ray of hope appeared unexpectedly. The Yankee major stated in his reply that "I will await the first shot, and if you do not batter us to pieces we will be starved out in a few days." So the Federals really were desperately low on supplies. When Walker showed Beauregard's telegram to Davis, the president saw that here might be a way out short of war. If Anderson would just state the time at which he would have to evacuate anyhow, they could hold their fire and the fort would be theirs without a shot. It was a perfect solution. The honor of South Carolina and the Confederacy would be upheld, border states and Europe would see that Davis had challenged Lincoln successfully yet showed restraint, and the Yankees would be gone with no war—at least with no first shot fired by the "Rebels."

Beauregard sent his aides, led by James Chesnut of South Carolina, out to Sumter in the early predawn hours of April 12 with the reply. Unfortunately, Anderson said he would not have to evacuate until April 15 and, worse, he added the qualifier, "should I not receive prior to that time controlling instructions from my Government or additional supplies." The relief expedition was known to be on the way. Indeed, it would arrive off the harbor mouth in only a few hours. If Sumter were resupplied, Anderson could hold out indefinitely. Wiring Walker and Davis that Anderson "would not consent," Beauregard opened fire at 4:30 A.M. that morning.

Throughout the day he sent brief telegraphic reports of events to Montgomery—of the heavy shelling, of his belief that his shots were taking effect in the fort, dismounting its guns. Every message generated renewed excitement in the capital, and rumors soon flew through Montgomery's streets that Sumter had fallen, that Fort Pickens had given up as well, and that the border states were arming to join with the Confederacy. They were nothing but rumors, of course, and Davis himself wisely discounted them all that evening by refusing to accept congratulations for a victory that he knew had not yet been won. Bands paraded in the streets and crowds repeatedly shouted huzzahs as the local militia, the Montgomery Blues, marched in formation through the town. Not far from the Exchange impromptu speakers held forth on the bright future, but the president himself refused to be drawn into making an address. While Secretary of War Walker addressed the crowd, intemperately predicting that their banners might soon wave over Washington itself, Davis lay on a sofa in his office, smoking a cigar. The few visitors besides his cabinet secretaries who were admitted found him obviously fatigued, and to one official he seemed "for the first time since his elevation to the Chieftain's chair, to be weighed down by the formidable responsibilities of the office."

Walker and Toombs had just left him to go to the celebration, and the president had summoned the whole cabinet for a meeting in an hour. Now he rested. "He felt the crisis in all its fulness," remembered one visitor. He complained that the Lincoln government had dealt with them treacherously. "They have been trimming and blindfolding in Washington," he said. "We have been patient and forbearing here." "Nothing was left for us but to forestall their schemings by a bold act." He regretted that it had come to blows. "I knew its consequences," he said with determination, "but we are ready and resolved, as a people, to abide the issue." Telegrams had come in from Virginia, North Carolina, Tennessee, Kentucky, Missouri, and even Maryland, cheering the news and wishing the Confederacy success. This could only presage more tangible support from those border states in the future. That Beauregard would take the fort he had no doubt, and Davis had already instructed him to be lenient with the men and officers in Sumter once they yielded. Indeed, on the day that a war had begun, he still could not forget his old friend who was now the target of Southern cannon. "I honor the officer in command for resisting," he said. "We are disposed to be magnanimous," he continued, pointing out his hope that in magnanimity they would leave Lincoln a "loophole" for moderation in response and a more honest negotiation. Those first guns that day would show the Yankees that the Confederates were in earnest. Davis intended to handle the inevitable victory in a way that would show "how willing we, also, are that the beginning should be the end."[43]

When the cabinet met again, there was no further news, and the townspeople of Montgomery retired to their beds too excited to sleep. The next day, the bombardment having continued unabated, Beauregard telegraphed that Sumter's return fire had slackened and that its wooden barracks were blazing. Then at 2 P.M. Davis received the telegram he waited for. "White flag up," it said. "Have sent a boat to receive surrender." They had a victory. Davis wired Pickens, "All honor to the gallant Sons of Carolina and thanks to God for their preservation." He also sent word to another old friend. "If occasion offers," he told Beauregard, "tender my friendly remembrance to Major Anderson."[44]

"There has been no blood spilled more precious than that of a mule," Davis declared when he first got the news, and that was a relief. Again there were celebrations in the streets, but again Davis did not participate. Conscious of the magnitude of what had happened, his own wavering certainty over the future took over, and he confessed to intimates that he feared the North might not take this idly. Sumter's fall, he told them, was "either the beginning of a fearful war, or the end of a political contest." That said, he simply retired to his room in the Exchange, looking, thought one observer, neither "elated or depressed." Outside, the cheering never stopped. When Wigfall arrived from Charleston a few days later, the people cheered him and the president. They cheered as each new militia unit came into the city, and they cheered the hero of the day when Beauregard himself arrived. The euphoria did not even ebb when Lincoln issued a call for 75,000 volunteers to "put down the rebellion," dashing Davis's hopes of a peaceful resolution. On April 17 Davis responded with a call for 32,000 volunteers. Amid the general satisfaction only the coolest heads began to fathom what was about to unfold. The night of Sumter's surrender, Davis hopefully said to Varina that some way might still be found for reunification with guarantees of Southern rights. "Separation is not yet of necessity final," he said. Most would have agreed with Howell Cobb, however, when he told the president, "It would seem we are to have a general war."[45]

18

We Will Make a History for Ourselves

Years later Davis would claim that "the forbearance of the Confederate Government, under the circumstances, is perhaps unexampled in history," and from his point of view that was certainly the case. He could never see the garrison in Fort Sumter as anything other than a coercive threat and Lincoln's resolution not to surrender the fort as an act of aggression. But of course, as throughout his life on any question of moment, Jefferson Davis countenanced no view other than his own. Consequently, to his mind, Lincoln's calling of 75,000 volunteers was unwarranted and unjustified, a violation of his constitutional powers. In fact, Lincoln, in opinions expressed even before he took office, had issued what Davis called "virtually a declaration of war," and his response to the bloodless taking of Fort Sumter was simply another act of wanton aggression.[1]

However viewed, that act of Lincoln's certainly worked to the benefit of Davis's new country in one regard. It put the wavering border states over the edge. On the very day that he took office himself, Davis had begun to consider what would be necessary to bring North Carolina, Virginia, Tennessee, Kentucky, Arkansas, and Missouri into the Confederacy. The first four were especially vital. Added to the already seceded states, they would give the new nation an almost unbroken water border with the North, starting with the Potomac River and the Chesapeake, then jumping a scant seventy miles from the headwaters of the Potomac to the upper Ohio, thence along that river to the Mississippi. Thus the core of the Old South would be virtually an island, with only Texas, Arkansas, western Louisiana, and Missouri beyond the water, but

326

themselves protected in some measure by the wild frontier country around them. Virginia and Kentucky were the keys, of course, though all the border states felt themselves tugged and pulled. "The true men in the border states wish the issue to be, 'which confederation will you join—the Northern or Southern,'" Wigfall told Davis on February 18.[2]

Supporters in those states went to work at once to bring them into line. Henry Wise, the erratic and irascible former governor of Virginia, promised Davis a few days later that he would "stampede the flower of the State to the South." Davis himself had spoken to the border men in his speeches on his way to the inauguration, telling them, "We will be your only friends," and saying that they would be received into the Confederacy "gladly" within sixty days. His prediction proved to be quite accurate. Sixty-two days after his speech on February 14, a state convention in Richmond passed an ordinance of secession, chiefly in response to Lincoln's call for volunteers. Wavering until then, the Old Dominion would not countenance the use of force to hold the Union together. Davis's friend James M. Mason wrote from Richmond to assure him that Virginia "is as far out of the Union" as Mississippi. "The cannon of Fort Sumter sundered the Union for Virginia." At the same time he conveyed to Davis the rumor that on April 20 Colonel Robert E. Lee had resigned his commission in the old army and was on his way to Richmond. To Governor John Letcher, Davis wrote the day after Virginia's secession, "You shall have whatever aid we can give, on the shortest notice." The next day he appointed Vice President Stephens a special commissioner to Virginia to "unite and bind together our respective countries," meaning, of course, that state's admission to the Confederacy. Within days Virginians seized state arsenals and naval facilities and themselves began to prepare for war.[3]

Attention immediately turned to the other border states. Virginians especially hoped for secession in neighboring Maryland, where Southern sympathizers certainly seemed numerous. Mason told the president, "I know a lamp will be kept burning, which when the time comes, will spread its flame through the entire state." If they could not secure its secession, at least large numbers of irregulars could be counted on to keep Maryland in a turmoil while it remained in the Union, at the same time posing a constant threat to a surrounded Washington. A virtual riot on April 19 when Federal troops tried to march through Baltimore only encouraged secession hopes, and Davis held a cabinet meeting to discuss it the next day, feeling elated that Maryland's evident sympathies might bring the state into the Confederacy. Also on April 21 Davis learned from Tennessee's Governor Isham Harris that he saw secession sentiment growing in the Volunteer State, and hoped soon to lead it into the Confederacy. Soon thereafter came a letter from North Carolina's Governor John Ellis. Tarheels had seized several Federal installations and awaited only a convening of their legislature to enact secession. "The people of my State are now thoroughly united and will adopt the speediest method of union with the Confederate States," he promised. Meanwhile he invited Davis to open recruiting stations in the state. Clearly North Carolina was with them.[4]

Davis had to adopt a policy on the border states quickly. On April 22, after the whirlwind of the past week, he met with the cabinet for four hours, and they decided that their course should be to offer all aid possible to Virginia and the others, even before they joined the Confederacy. Consequently, he would issue another levy for twelve thousand more volunteers. Meanwhile, with Virginia about to come into the fold, he favored accepting the offer of volunteer companies from some of the state's northern counties, "a good point from which to pour men on Baltimore and D.C.," as he said. Beyond this, they had to consider again the matter of admitting other states, free ones. Given the groundswell of border states moving their way, many were convinced that Indiana, perhaps Ohio, and others might choose to exchange the old Union for the new one. Toombs, Benjamin, Mallory, and Memminger opposed the notion. Walker, Stephens, and the new Postmaster General, John Reagan, favored the idea. Davis found himself undecided, though one of his close advisers, John A. Campbell, who still held his U.S. Supreme Court seat, hinted that there was at least a possibility that the entire Union might in time be reconstructed, but on the basis of the Montgomery constitution.[5]

But there was a problem. For all the support that Davis believed existed in the North, and even though the border states appeared to be coming around, still Confederate success and enthusiasm could be working against their own interests. In the flush of euphoria after Fort Sumter, the press and stump echoed with the wildest, most belligerent prophecies. Davis himself indulged in this a few times, as when he predicted the destruction Northern cities and even Washington might feel in any war to come. Now from Richmond, New Orleans, Vicksburg, Raleigh—virtually every corner of the South—came declarations that Confederate armies would soon be on Northern soil. Walker himself suggested as much in his speech in Montgomery after Beauregard opened fire on Sumter. "President Davis will soon march an army *through North Carolina and Virginia to Washington*," said a Richmond paper. Another in New Orleans threatened to drive Lincoln and his cabinet out of Washington, as far as Buffalo or Cleveland. *"There is one wild shout of fierce resolve to capture Washington,"* cried the Richmond *Examiner*. Some editors even cited Walker's speech as the inspiration for their own bellicosity.[6]

Such posturing did them only harm, however. Campbell, advising Davis from Washington, asserted that the breakup of the Union might be permanent, but still "difficulty & embarrassment" lay ahead for them, and "those embarrassments will be aggravated every moment, by the indulgence of hostilities or by acts promoting hostile feelings." They must see the issue from the Yankee point of view, weigh every public statement by its effect on the North. "I read with dismay the loose vaunts in the papers & from public men of what conquests are to be made at their expense & what suffering is to be brought upon them." Confederates must not arouse Yankee pride or make them feel despised, for if the true strength of the North were ever mobilized and arrayed against them, the South would be doomed. There might not be many in the North who would fight *for* the Confederacy, but many were undisposed to fight *against* it unless provoked.[7]

Davis perhaps felt sensitive to this even without being told by Campbell. Beyond question, it was imperative that he take some official position on the subject in order to preempt in the Northern mind the impression being left by the radical speculations, to which even he had added a share. The perfect opportunity came on April 29. The Provisional Congress had adjourned its first session in March, but Davis called them back to a second session at the end of April for a variety of business. The permanent constitution had been framed on March 11, and now all the seceded states had ratified the document. They must hold regular elections to fill all the apportioned House and Senate seats, as well as perform other business necessary to the continuing organization of the government. However, he principally called them back to deal with "the declaration of war made against this Confederacy by Abraham Lincoln" in his call for volunteers. Because of the extraordinary occasion, he said, "it justifies me in a brief review" of events leading up to the present. It was the sort of announcement that must have made hearts sink in the old U. S. Senate, when Davis rehearsed the whole history of the country time after time, as he did now.

Nonetheless, the real meat of the address came at its conclusion. "We feel that our cause is just and holy," he said. "We protest solemnly in the face of mankind that we desire peace at any sacrifice save that of honor and independence; we seek no conquest, no aggrandizement, no concession of any kind from the States with which we were lately confederated." As if this were not clear enough, he said emphatically, "all we ask is to be let alone." The moment that Lincoln ceased trying to keep them in the Union, "The sword will drop from our grasp."[8]

It was an appeal designed for Northern consumption, yet one that put Davis in a tenuous position in his own country. Even when he spoke to the delegates, a small and as-yet-unorganized minority of voices rose against him and his administration. Many outcries came from men simply disposed to dislike Davis even before his election. Few of the South Carolinians ever really cared for him. Whatever his public utterances, Toombs never liked the Mississippian, and other Georgians, especially

Thomas Cobb, felt lukewarm at best. The Charleston *Mercury* vacillated between praise and condemnation, leading Wigfall to quip that "South Carolina apparently was going to secede from the new Confederacy." A Texan in Montgomery accused Davis of "getting up a very pretty little comedy" in his handling of the early days of his administration, and James Chesnut's wife lamented privately that "men are willing to risk an injury to our cause if they may in so doing hurt Jeff Davis."

A case in point was Tom Cobb, who added to his suspicion of Davis when he saw that the president seemed to listen carefully to the counsel of the despised Stephens. "Mr. Davis acts for himself and receives no advice," he complained, "except from those who press their advice unasked." When Davis twice asked Cobb to go to Arkansas as an emissary, he refused, no doubt in part because Davis's first veto of a congressional bill came on February 28 over legislation of Cobb's devising. "I shall strive hard to pass it over his head," a resentful Cobb wrote that night. "It will do my soul good to *rebuke* him at the outset of his vetoing." When he spoke out against the veto in Congress a few days later, Cobb took a perverse delight. "I was *hot* in my heart," he said. "I think I convinced the Presdt's friends that I did not look to that quarter for office or favor."[9]

This determination in the minds of some not to be overawed by Davis, combined with the war fever fed by the Sumter success and Virginia's secession, moved many to look on his conciliatory words in the message to Congress with some suspicion. Just where did Davis stand? Unionist then secessionist, reconstructionist then Confederate nationalist—all the old uncertainties about his true position stayed alive, to be nurtured by the small but slowly growing number of men who, from whatever motives, relished a chance to "hurt Jeff Davis."

The president may not yet have been aware of any incipient opposition, or if he was he certainly ascribed it to the usual jealousy and pigheadedness of men who did not agree with him. And certainly he could not be accused of peacemongering. That sword was not yet dropped from his hand. The work of mobilizing military forces proceeded more rapidly than the nation was prepared to handle. Congress authorized Davis to raise up to 100,000 on March 6, and quickly the several states sent forth their regiments. Though Davis foresaw that any war might be a long one, Congress would only allow him to receive such units for twelve months' service, though it did empower him to appoint and assign the generals to command them. At the time of his April 29 speech, at least 36,000 Confederates stood under arms, with more coming in weekly. He favored enlisting the full 100,000 authorized. Already he had 16,000 men on their way to Virginia to join the state forces already assembling there. And though Sumter was now theirs, another trouble spot loomed—one to which he would give his personal attention.[10]

Fort Pickens, commanding the approaches to Pensacola in Florida, was almost as great a sticking point in the Confederate craw as Fort Sumter. Perhaps the chief reason that the latter provided the catalyst for sending the country to war was simply the fact that it was in South Carolina. Floridians, every bit as committed to the cause as their neighbors up the Atlantic coast, still did not feel quite their degree of heat. Further, Pensacola was not the commercial port Charleston was, though militarily it may have been more important, thanks to the large navy yard seized from the Federals. Throughout January state militia and volunteers from Mississippi and Louisiana made their way to the Gulf Coast, and early in March, Davis had made Bragg a brigadier general and sent him there to take command.

Bragg seems to have been surprised by his commission. Indeed, despite their cordial relations in Mexico, he appears to have thought Davis did not like him, though on what basis it is difficult to tell, unless it was a disagreement over the need for horse artillery back when Bragg was a captain and Davis secretary of war. Yet his suspicion was unfounded, for Davis placed him on the same footing as Beauregard and gave him a command of equal importance. Indeed, it appears that Davis was even willing that the war, if there were to be one, might begin in Pensacola and that Bragg could fire the first shot. On April 3 he wrote to the general confirming recent reports that Lincoln would attempt to resupply and perhaps reinforce Fort Pickens. The Federals would avoid firing a first shot, the president thought, so as not to outrage the border states. "There would be to us an advantage in so placing them that an attack by them would be a necessity," said Davis. "But when we are ready to relieve our territory and jurisdiction of the presence of a foreign garrison that advantage is overbalanced by other considerations." In short, Davis hoped to do at Pensacola what Lincoln had done to him at Charleston—maneuver the onus of firing first onto the foe. But when Davis went on to advise Bragg that "Your measures may without disturbing views be directed to the capture of Fort Pickens and the defence of the harbor," he appeared to be giving him the option of opening fire. Having said this, the president even went on for the first time to give extensive advice to a general on how to conduct his operations, emphasizing that "there was no purpose to dictate," and that these were merely suggestions "of your old comrade in arms."[11]

Of course, no first shot came at Pickens (and practically no shots at all) as the Yankees occupied the fort for the rest of the war. Bragg simply did not have the men or matériel to accomplish the fort's capture, and then the eruption at Charleston briefly diverted attention from Pensacola. But once the Fort Sumter issue was settled, Davis again turned his thoughts to Fort Pickens and early in May decided to make a personal visit to inspect the batteries ringing the harbor and to confer with Bragg. Mallory would go with him, both as a Floridian and as the man charged with operation of the navy yard. Varina would come as well, and so would Davis's seemingly ardent new friend Wigfall. They left on the afternoon of May 14 and arrived very late that night. The next day he went to Bragg's headquarters. Observers described the president as plainly dressed, "well and vigorous, but looks somewhat jaded and careworn." Though Davis traveled without fanfare, Pensacola became very enthusiastic when his presence was known, and soon cannon salutes boomed from the batteries along the Gulf. Most believed that he was there to conclude with Bragg a plan for capturing Fort Pickens, but if so, no plan came forth. Bragg interpreted the result of their discussions to be a lessening rather than a strengthening of resolve to take the fort. The situation had changed dramatically after the fall of Sumter. Now the Confederacy needed to concentrate troops in Virginia as quickly as possible, and few could be spared for backwaters like Pensacola. Davis commended to Bragg "patience equal to your energy and vigilance," advising him to be prepared to take the fort at any time he could do so at a small sacrifice of men and means. Other than some additional cannon to assist in a siege, should one ever come, Davis could send Bragg little else.[12]

Returned from his first trip to a "war zone," Davis felt such increased confidence in Wigfall that he asked him to serve on his personal staff as an aide, which Wigfall gladly accepted, though he preferred a military appointment. The president needed an aide to help him with the burden of the increasing responsibility of office, and Wigfall had the added advantage of having been a leading fire-eater, considerably popular with just some of those elements in Congress who were beginning to grumble.

The trip to Pensacola may have been as much a brief getaway as business, for as the appointment of Wigfall reveals, Davis was once more wearing himself down with work. The cabinet met incessantly at his request, the sessions often lasting until 2 A.M. and later. A few days before the Florida trip, an insider in Montgomery noted that Davis could not see all that he had accomplished already, but only how much remained to be done. "Consequently, his time seems all taken up with the Cabinet, planning (I presume) future operations." It became common for his cabinet members to work through the day, then return to their offices again at ten o'clock and remain until well after midnight. By May 20 one reporter in the capital could see that "the President and members of the cabinet are much fagged by their heavy duties," and another noted that Davis himself appeared "somewhat faded" by his labor. Yet he often outlasted his cabinet secretaries, and as the meetings grew later and later, they left silently, one by one, until sometimes Davis discovered that his discussants were reduced to "one weak, weary man, who has no vim to contend." Davis "overworks himself and all the rest of mankind."[13]

There was much to overwork him. The euphoria of the first victory quickly waned as problems appeared on every front and in every quarter. For the first time he was involved in a minor controversy with one of his governors, Thomas O. Moore of Louisiana, giving perhaps a hint of the ways in which the states' rights philosophy he had espoused so long as a representative of a single state could come back to haunt him as the leader of a confederation. The War Department wanted the arms in the Baton Rouge arsenal in order to equip the new recruits flocking to the banner. Moore had to remind Davis that, although Louisiana had turned over the arsenal to the Confederate States after it was taken from the Federals, the contents—the rifles—had been retained for Louisiana. Nevertheless, Moore later transferred some munitions and arms as well, "as I thought proper," but he had to remind the government that he did so at his own discretion. Moore, in fact, would be one of the most cooperative and effective of the Confederate governors, yet even he would stand on his prerogatives as the leader of a "sovereign" state.[14]

More problems came with some of the units already equipped. Barely hours after Davis left Pensacola, Bragg complained in a letter that he believed the War Department was going to take from him a battalion of zouaves—specially trained and uniformed soldiers patterned after the French Algerian military—and make them into Confederate regulars. Protesting that their officers were barely competent and the men themselves "the mere sweepings of the streets in New Orleans," Bragg urged that they remain volunteers. When Davis approved another recruitment bill on May 8 that authorized up to four hundred thousand volunteers, this time for three years or the duration of the war, more protests came to him, including one from the former leader of the Alabama secession convention, William Brooks. The first to enlist had been the most ardent, and mostly slaveholders, he argued. By the provisions of the first bill to raise one hundred thousand, those men could leave the service after a year. But this new bill requiring three years or more would affect primarily nonslaveholders, the laboring classes, who were just starting to enlist. Already prone to see a rigid division in their society, many such men proclaimed that they would "*fight for no rich man's slaves*" and would not enlist at all.[15]

Even more vexing were personality problems. Again and again Davis had to intervene in controversies between some dignitary and

Secretary Walker, who seemed to lack all tact and diplomacy. He summoned one man from Georgia and kept him waiting in his office while he saw one person after another "and left me to kick my heels in his Office while he occupied himself with other individuals coming in successively." Twice the man offered to leave and come back, and twice Walker put him off; then he finally and abruptly said he wanted him for a position in the quartermaster's department, which he promptly declined and left in a huff, to complain to Davis.[16]

Most important of all at the moment was the growing army. Davis could not appoint their regimental officers—that was done by the governors or else in elections by the soldiers themselves—but he did have to create generals to lead them. The problem facing him had not improved any since he first commissioned Beauregard and Bragg. He still had to rely on men with West Point training and old army experience as his safest appointments, and on his personal knowledge of them from his own army days both in uniform and as secretary of war. The secession of Virginia, and then the secession at last of Tennessee and Arkansas on May 6, led to the resignations of many more current officers who now took sides with the Confederacy, and the last state to secede, North Carolina on May 20, enlarged the pool of potential generals.

In some cases Davis did not wait to be asked. Just five days after Virginia's action to leave the Union, the president inquired as to the whereabouts of Joseph E. Johnston and Robert E. Lee. Johnston especially interested Davis. If they did in fact have a scuffle during their days at West Point, it was long forgotten. Johnston had as much if not more combat experience in Indian wars and in Mexico than anyone else. Holding staff rank as a brigadier in his capacity as quartermaster general in the United States Army when he resigned on April 22, Johnston stood presumably higher in rank and seniority than any other officer joining the cause except for old Twiggs. Commissioning the Virginian a brigadier, Davis immediately looked to him for information on the troops and conditions in the Old Dominion, relying upon him to confer with Lee, who by now commanded the Virginia state forces. Many shared Davis's apparent confidence in Johnston, and another man who enjoyed a great measure of the president's regard, Leonidas Polk, suggested that Johnston be made general-in-chief, a position not yet authorized by Congress.[17]

At the same time, Polk also offered his own services, the first of Davis's old set at West Point to apply for a commission, and Davis asked that he come to see him. But most of all, Davis still craved to have Sidney Johnston at his side. About the end of April he received a letter from Johnston's son William Preston, informing him that the elder Johnston had resigned some weeks before and was returning from California. Though he did not say specifically that Johnston intended to join the

Southern cause, still Davis could infer that he would, and the news lightened his heart during those laborious days in Montgomery. Davis had wanted to make Johnston secretary of war, perhaps even before he considered Clay or Walker. Feeling that he was too far away to reach in time, Davis had offered it to them instead, but now he wanted Johnston in the field leading an army. Anxiously he awaited his old friend's familiar step and hearty hand.[18]

Thus his labors continued unabated. Often when Varina held levees, Davis himself could not attend or did so only briefly. By the end of May he still worked the entire day either at his office or at home, where callers were surprised to find no guards. With no air of formality at all, a servant simply met callers at the door and showed them to the president. Frequently, when he could get away, Davis walked about the city or rode one of his horses. Not infrequently he walked along the riverbank, where he heard the steamers' calliopes playing "Dixie" and other martial airs. Northrop walked with him often, their talk ranging from science to theology, and they might pass Benjamin talking with ladies or Reagan whittling a stick. Whether men met him at home or in his office, he was prone to hold a sheaf of papers in his left hand while he spoke, and even read other documents, often nodding silently over important points.[19]

In Montgomery and elsewhere there was much nodding and discussion over a very weighty matter probably also on Davis's mind just then. Would he exercise his responsibility and prerogatives to the fullest constitutional limits by taking command of the growing armies himself? No American president had done so before, but then none with military experience had been in office during time of war. Besides, Davis was the South's greatest living military hero. Varina spoke openly of how being "general of all the armies would have suited his temperament better," and Davis himself never kept his preference a secret. With the new nation growing, and with its borders stretching across half a continent, it would call for the ablest of leaders to direct the armies of defense—or offense. In Virginia some maintained that "Mr. Davis has no intention of joining the army," but they were a minority. In Montgomery itself, most seemed to want and expect Davis to do so. "I hope it may be done," wrote a friend of Clay's early in May, "for to him military command is a perfect system of hygiene." In New Orleans it was rumored that Davis was actually selecting for himself some of the best from the incoming volunteers to form his personal guard when he took command of the armies, and in Charleston many believed erroneously that Congress had asked him to go to Virginia to take command in the field. "He will be worth 50,000 men to our cause," proclaimed one editor, and another asserted, "His presence would inspire the most unbounded confidence and enthusiasm." Noting also Davis's widely known preference for the military, the editor added that "the change of life would probably be favorable to the preservation of his health."[20]

Undoubtedly Davis felt frequently the temptation to become a soldier again, or at least he daydreamed of it to relieve the relentless pressure of trying to build a government. But nothing suggests that during his months in Montgomery he seriously considered going to lead the army. Yet he was going to Virginia. With the permanent constitution completed and adopted on March 11, and with elections set for the regular Congress the coming fall (and a regular presidential election at the same time), most of the business of the provisional congress in Montgomery was concluded. They had formally recognized the existence of a state of war. Following Davis's lead, and the threat he had made in repeated speeches before hostilities, they approved his proclamation calling for the issuance of letters of marque to would-be privateers for attacking and seizing Yankee shipping. They had authorized all the executive departments necessary for organizing the government. Moreover, the geographical situation had changed. In February, Montgomery had been almost perfectly at the territorial center of the Confederacy. Events following Fort Sumter shifted that center, especially the secession of Virginia. For many reasons, Virginia's action was a turning point. However vital all the Confederate states might be, the Old Dominion seemed always to stand in front of the rest in Confederate perceptions. The home of Washington, Jefferson, and Madison, the portal through which the Old South was originally settled, it assumed itself to be first among Southerners in a highly class-conscious "classless" society. Furthermore, it stood across the Potomac from Washington. Richmond was one of the South's few major manufacturing and transportation centers. Unquestionably, in the conflict to come—if it came—the Yankees would make Virginia one of their chief targets of invasion. Thus when the Virginia secession convention issued an invitation for the Confederate capital to remove to Richmond, the proposition met with almost instant approval. "The President favors it decidedly," Thomas Cobb told his wife, and most in Congress followed suit. The logic of having the seat of government placed close to the scene of action, where it could act and react quickly, seemed clearly to outweigh any danger of its being too close to the enemy. Besides, many still believed that there would be no war, that the chastised Yankees would never have the courage or the unity to mount an offensive.[21]

Congress debated the subject frequently until May 20, when a vote decided the matter. The next day Congress adjourned, to reconvene for a third session in Richmond on July 20. The decision having been made, anxiety set in at once to have Davis in his new capital as quickly as possible. Virginians wrote to him of the universal desire to see him there, and some hinted that he was needed more than he realized. One acquaintance told him that matters in the state were not being handled well and that "*your presence is needed here.*" Another close friend from West Point days, the bombastic Kentuckian Albert T. Bledsoe, offered even franker views. He lamented that there was no one in control of the state. Lee, commanding its militia, was a good man but appeared despondent, spoke too freely of the overwhelming might of the North, and seemed too uncertain of Southern ability to resist. "Noble and glorious as he is," said Bledsoe, "I fear he does not know how good and how righteous our cause is, and consequently lacks one quality which the times demand." That quality, of course, was resolution, and in a few weeks Davis heard similar sentiments from others. Pickens complained that "Lee is not with us at heart, or he is a common man, with good looks, and too cautious for practical Revolution." And as if this were not bad enough, Bledsoe also complained that if Lee had been inclined to act, Governor John Letcher stood in his way, and worse, Letcher was a "notorious drunkard." Lee should "usurp authority," he said, but of course would not. "We do not want two heads, but *one* great man to rule over us, in this great crisis, and, as I know, you are the man to whom all hearts turn."[22]

The press in Richmond joined the chorus clamoring for his early arrival, weeks before Congress formally changed capitals. Davis did not ignore their appeals. He had already moved decisively to defend the Old Dominion, assigning Joseph E. Johnston to take command in the Shenandoah Valley on May 15 and start raising an army. "Our enemies are active for our injury," he said, "but a brave and united people like ours, cannot be conquered." But he was above all a man of laws, and until May 20, his place was in Montgomery. Even after the Congressional vote, he still refused to leave for Virginia until his cabinet and their staffs were ready for the transition, which took another week and by which time his own safety seemed to require his departure. There were threats of assassination in his mail. A few nights earlier he had seen and chased away an armed man staring in through the windows of his house.[23]

Finally on May 26 Davis was ready. Leaving behind instructions for their furniture to be sold at auction, and leaving Varina to oversee the packing of their personal articles, Davis boarded an evening train with Toombs, the Wigfalls, Northrop, and his nephew Joseph R. Davis. The trip had something of the appearance of a royal procession, as at every town they stopped crowds gathered to cheer the president and beg for speeches. His ceaseless driving of himself had almost prostrated him, and he spent much of the journey in bed, trying to avoid as much public clamor as possible, but inevitably he could not. In Atlanta and Augusta, Georgia, he had to speak, and then again as they passed through Wilmington and Goldsborough, North Carolina. Davis left the train to take a meal in the latter city, only to find himself surrounded at his table by beautiful young women who covered him with garlands and fanned him as he ate. Soon reports went out on the wires ahead of his train that "the President is in feeble health," yet occasionally he managed to get to a telegraph office or else have Wigfall send a wire for him. Just two days before he left Montgomery, word came that Federal troops had crossed the Potomac from Washington and occupied Alexandria without resistance. Anxious over just how far the Yankees meant to go, or if they were simply establishing defenses for their capital, Davis wired to Lee frequently, asking "What news today?" On May 28, as the train paused in the Carolinas, Davis sent Beauregard a wire ordering him to come to Virginia immediately. The president might be coming to Richmond just in time.[24]

After a trip described as "one continuous ovation," Davis finally reached Richmond shortly after dawn on May 29. Guns fired in salute as his train pulled in to the Richmond & Petersburg station, and then a prolonged cheer met him as he alighted from his car. Letcher, Mayor John Mayo, and a host of other local dignitaries escorted him to an open carriage, and then they drove through street after street of cheering crowds to the Spotswood Hotel where apartments awaited him. Up Seventh Street to Main, and then down that street to the hotel, Davis had to dodge bouquets thrown into the carriage, clasp hands thrust in his face, and smile and wave in spite of his weariness and ill health. Indeed, the manifestations of enthusiasm probably cheered him measurably, and when finally he reached the Spotswood and the crowd called for a speech, he walked over to a window and gave them a few words. Then, following breakfast, he went to room number eighty-three, which the proprietor had decorated specially to serve as his parlor. There, beneath a Confederate flag and a coat of arms, he sat until five-thirty that afternoon receiving visitors and going through the obligatory social motions of statecraft that he so often protested he disliked. It may have been a relief, despite his weariness, when that evening he mounted a horse and rode with some others to the fairgrounds to review troops. Again the crowds, this time both soldiers and civilians, thronged around him. Giving in to their demands for a speech, he told them very briefly what they wanted to hear. They were "the last best hope of liberty," he said to the volunteers. They might be untrained, they might be outnumbered, but they were Southerners, and in their hands "the Southern banner [would] float in triumph everywhere."[25]

Davis probably knew better than to expect the round of official formalities to end there. Though several observers noted that he did not look well, he went on with the handshaking and the hugging. The next day after his arrival he held a levee at the governor's mansion, and those present saw in him an affable and unostentatious manner. On June 1, when Varina arrived in company with Cooper and others, Davis had to endure another procession in open carriages and more bouquet throwing. When his wife's train pulled in, someone noted that in an adjoining boxcar Varina had brought Davis's gray horse and his military saddle with a compass set into the pommel. That started anew the rumors that "there can no longer be any doubt that the President will lead the army." It all must have reminded Davis of his return from Mexico, when Vicksburg filled his carriage with flowers. When one little girl missed with her throw, the president stopped the carriage and had her flowers picked up and handed to Varina.[26]

That night another crowd gathered outside the Spotswood and serenaded the Davises, then called for an appearance. Condemning the tyranny of Lincoln, he told these Virginians that their state had the honor to become a great armed camp "from which will pour forth thousands of brave hearts to roll back the tide of this despotism." "We must at first move cautiously," he warned them. There might be many sacrifices to make, yet he promised that in the end "success shall perch on our banners." In a personal reference, he even said that they would make "the battlefields of Virginia another Buena Vista, and drench them with blood more precious than that shed there." In short, he said, "We will make a history for ourselves."[27]

Not surprisingly, among Davis's first concerns were those men whose blood he so melodramatically promised to spill in their sacred cause. Day after day he rode to the camps of the different volunteer regiments there gathered. He inspected some Tennessee troops, probably the Second Regiment, and promised them arms in response to their protest of having none. At another training camp he found the men so overjoyed to see him that one boy rushed forward, threw his arms around the president, and "kissed him with affectionate earnestness." He inspected earthworks being constructed for the city's defense, and everywhere the soldiers saw him, they waved their hats and cheered. Even those who had never seen him before recognized him, for by now his likeness had been reproduced by the thousands on everything from prints and illustrated newspapers to little paper medallions affixed to consumer goods in the stores.[28]

Recovering somewhat from his ill health, Davis impressed almost everyone in Richmond with his manner and bearing. He appeared extremely gallant and courteous to the ladies, "but stern to the sterner sex," thought one. When he welcomed a delegation from the Virginia secession convention to his apartments at the Spotswood, all seemed charmed by him. He spoke to each visitor in personal terms, remembering a previous meeting, sharing a reminiscence, offering a little flattery, or commenting on the day's news. "Making himself eminently agreeable to all," he appeared at his very best, one visitor even confessing that the president magnetized him "by one of the most irresistible smiles in the world." Perhaps it helped Davis that Varina and the children were with him again, for all evening Maggie and little Jeff flitted through the crowd, often turning up at their father's side for hugs and smiles of unmistakable devotion.

Perhaps Davis felt pleased, too, knowing that he would not be dwelling indefinitely in a hotel. Just hours after his arrival in Richmond, a local citizen named Lewis Crenshaw offered the government for Davis's use a house he owned on the southeast corner of Twelfth and Clay Streets. Locally called the Brockenbrough House after a previous owner, it offered a good view of the James River and much of the city and stood just a short walk from the Virginia State House, which would now be the Confederate Capitol. Quickly the Richmond city council entered into negotiations to purchase the mansion. Within a short time the purchase was concluded, and workmen went in to the house to repair and modify it for the Davises. Davis objected to the city bearing the $35,000 cost of the house, not to mention an additional $7,800 spent on its furnishings, and directed Memminger to lease the house from the city. Though the repairs and remodeling would last into July, still Davis looked forward to living a more settled private life before long.[29]

He needed it. The business of being president caught up with him all too quickly. Offices for the executive, along with State and Treasury, occupied the old U.S. Customs House on Main Street, between Tenth and Eleventh streets, just a short walk from the new Executive Mansion. Davis shared the second floor with the State Department, his own office being on the east side overlooking Eleventh Street and flanked by the cabinet room on one side and a room for Robert Josselyn on the other. His aides occupied a large room across the central hall, though just as often he transacted business in his parlor at the Spotswood.[30]

Davis might have hoped that the train speeding away from Montgomery would leave some of his problems behind, but it could not. Scarcely had he reached Virginia before he found those initial clashes with some of his governors recurring, and with more vigor. Well before leaving Alabama, he confided to some that he did not at all like Governor Joseph Brown of Georgia, the only man in the Confederate States whom he found persistently trying to thwart him in his endeavors. Howell Cobb saw it happening, commenting, "There is a fair prospect of a quarrel between President Davis and our *worthy* Joe Brown" over the matter of control of Georgia state troops and weapons. The sticking point seemed to be arms at first, for some Georgia rifles loaned to the general government were being sent to Virginia. Worse, volunteer regiments raised in Georgia and armed with state weapons were being accepted directly into the Confederate service, taking their weapons with them out of the state. Brown appealed to Davis to have such regiments return their guns to Georgia so that he could fully arm those regiments that he was raising. "I am doing all I can," he protested to Davis on June

7. "I deprecate any thing like conflict between State & Confederate authority." Davis sympathized with Brown, or pretended to, on the matter of the arms, but when the governor started demanding the right to offer troops on conditions, that was another matter.[31]

Early in July, Brown, who was authorized only to raise regiments, suggested that Georgia could contribute a new brigade, providing that a certain officer should command it. Davis responded, politely but firmly refusing the brigade but asking for two regiments instead. This seeming incongruity aggravated Brown, since the number of volunteers might be the same whether by regiments or brigaded together. The point, of course, was that Davis was empowered by Congress only to accept regiments. Brigading them was the War Department's function, and only Davis held the authority to appoint generals. Showing commendable patience, Davis explained all this and implored Brown to recognize that he could not really have meant to arrogate for himself one of the president's constitutional functions. On an earlier occasion Brown had dangled the offer of three regiments if Davis would make one of his friends a brigadier. Apparently it worked that time, but it would not on this occasion, and the standoff continued into August before Brown finally backed down.[32]

Even while diplomatically handling the prickly Brown, Davis began to have trouble with Letcher, a far-more-amiable cast of man. He objected to Davis's appointing the field officers and staffs of regiments raised in Virginia and descended into hairsplitting over the nature of the troops: If militia, then he had the right to appoint their leaders; if not militia, then maybe Davis could choose their officers, but under what authority did he try to raise anything other than militia in a state? Letcher also withheld from the Confederate government the rifle-making machinery taken at the capture of the Harpers Ferry Armory when Virginia troops occupied it in April. The agreement between the state and the Confederacy called for the turning over of all such machinery. Letcher cooperated in the end, but not without cajoling from Davis.[33]

The problem of making generals would not go away either. Every governor expected that his state would have its full share of generals, objecting especially to men from other states commanding its troops. Most, like Brown, had old friends to whom they owed favors, and regardless of any lack of military qualifications, they expected them to get commissions. To his credit, Davis resolutely resisted their pressure, though it cost him early. He disappointed Yancey of Alabama at the outset, and then disappointed Brown, as he later said, declining to appoint generals "on the recommendation of friends & politicians." Rather, he stood in full agreement with Beauregard, whom he had called to northern Virginia to take command of the volunteer army being organized. When Beauregard asked for more generals to be appointed for his growing organization, he specified that he wanted men "of military education & experience." That meant West Pointers for the most part, and it was a wise—though not infallible—policy to give such men preference. But the governors, some of whom had opposed the U.S. Military Academy as prewar politicians, saw in this only an example of Davis's showing favoritism and looking out for his old army friends. Incredibly, they could not understand that it took more than dash and bravery to lead men to victory.[34]

Even on the rare early occasions when Davis appointed a nonprofessional, he found himself criticized. In apportioning his commissions, the first three he gave Tennessee went to Gideon Pillow, Samuel R. Anderson, and Daniel S. Donelson. Donelson was a West Point graduate, Anderson had seen active service in Mexico, and both were generals in the state militia. If they never amounted to anything as Confederate generals, still there was a logic in their appointment. Logical, too, though only politically, was Pillow's elevation. A boastful semicompetent, Pillow schemed better in the back rooms than he led in the field, and despite having been a political general in Mexico, he would before long show a recurring streak of cowardice. Politically he was too powerful to ignore. Yet these appointments were not enough for Tennessee Governor Isham Harris. He protested that all three men were Democrats and secessionists. In a state of divided loyalties, like Tennessee, diplomacy demanded, "It is a matter of positive political necessity" that appointments go to the opposition as well. Further, Harris told the president, "you must be particular to recognize the three grand divisions *East, West* and *Middle* Tennessee," whereas the three new generals all hailed from the last.

Although Davis regarded Harris's protest as a "total misapprehension," its import was not lost on him. Indeed, considering how the president had characteristically resisted attempts to influence or persuade him in the past, especially with such implied criticism of his actions, he seemed remarkably open-minded these days. Brown took the wrong approach and did not get satisfaction; Harris protested, though reasonably, and Davis soon thereafter gave commissions to two of the opposition men he had suggested. Davis could be obstinate, but he was not unreasonable when approached properly. The political realities of a South heavily divided state from state, and even within states, also forced him to retreat somewhat from his own rigid notions for the greater good. He was compromising; he was holding his temper with men he would not otherwise have suffered gladly; he was acting more like a true statesman than ever before in his life. In short, he was, in fact, showing the makings of a president.[34]

Which made it all the more frustrating when everyone seemed to complain. No sooner did he appoint Pillow than protests of the man's incompetence came to him from Memphis, the beginnings of a questioning of Davis's judgment in his appointments of men with military experience. Worse, another of his political generals, Henry Wise, now complained that he could not stand being forced to serve under yet another politician turned soldier, former secretary of war John B. Floyd, Davis's successor in the old War Department, whom Davis made a brigadier on May 23. Both Virginians lacked any military experience and proved to be utter incompetents, yet at the same time both were a steady thorn in his heel. As the days moved on in this conflict, Davis might have formed in his mind an axiom that the less able a political general was, the more likely he was to complain.[35]

All of which made him only the more reliant on the professionals. When Beauregard arrived on May 30, Davis—acting through Lee—assigned him to command of the army rapidly growing just south of the Potomac. He pined for some word from Sidney Johnston. A few days after arriving in Richmond, Davis received a visit from another old friend, Polk. The two dined with the cabinet and sat together for at least two long private interviews. "We want & he wants Genl A. S. Johnston badly," Polk told his wife after one meeting. Both had confidence in Lee, yet each believed Johnston to be his superior. As for Polk, Davis would say, "I had a high opinion of his endowments and acquirements as a soldier," and a week later offered him a brigadier's commission, though he had been in the ministry almost since the day he graduated from West Point. At least he had the training, if not the practical experience. He was also an old and close friend, and though Davis protested time and time again that such things did not influence his appointments, he frequently showed favoritism based not on experience or performance, but upon friendship and loyalty.[36]

As June moved on into the heat of summer, the threat of the growing Yankee army in and around Washington led to increasing concern about the status of Beauregard's command now posted in northern Virginia, and of the several brigades raised and serving in the Shenandoah Valley under Joseph E. Johnston. Any Federal advance into the state would come by one of those two avenues, yet there were complaints that the soldiers were ill equipped, poorly or inadequately officered, and that there seemed to be no generally known plan of action for defending the state. Indeed, as each week went by with little or no apparent activity, the euphoria of Fort Sumter steadily waned. Confederates wanted more victories and a speedy end to what seemed so far to be an illusory war. Critics complained in the press, and defenders appeared just as readily. "So far, no mistake has been made," proclaimed the Richmond *Enquirer*, "but it is impossible for the public to know, at this time, either all that has been accomplished, or what is in contemplation." Indeed it was impossible, but that did not keep them from carping. Hoping to preempt some of the bad press, Mason suggested to Davis that the government be very careful in placing the advertisements that it constantly ran, announcing orders and vacancies. Good politics, again, suggested that such space be purchased equally from the two major journals in the capital, the *Enquirer* and the *Examiner*. Almost daily, it seemed, the tightrope that Davis must walk to keep everyone happy and behind him grew thinner and thinner.[37]

He also became aware of the possible danger of his position. Even while still in Montgomery, he heard the first of a series of rumors that some Northerners, with or without Lincoln's sanction, plotted to capture him and Stephens by some kind of treachery. He had not been in Richmond more than a few days when word of another plot, this one to stab him there in his own capital, came to his ears, and a few weeks later a friend warned him that "the Black Republican crew" were hiring an assassin to send to Richmond. Perhaps he never learned of yet another scheme proposed to Lincoln's secretary of war, his old friend Simon Cameron, for a raid to capture Davis and his cabinet. Surely the stories were all unfounded rumors, but Davis probably believed them, conditioned as he was to accept the worst about his opponents at any time. Warfare, it seemed, was degenerating rapidly into something it had not been when he was at West Point or in Mexico. He could see that in his own mail, with ridiculous yet bloodthirsty proposals coming to him almost daily for new and dreadful weapons of war, like a bulletproof locomotive sprouting revolving knives like mower blades for "killing a great number" of the enemy.[38]

Late into the evening every night Davis worked, trying to force protests and criticism, recalcitrant governors and petulant political officers out of his mind while he concentrated on the most pressing task before him. "The war draws nearer to us and daily increases in its proportions," he wrote to Joseph in mid-June. He may never have realized what a divided state Virginia was until he came to Richmond, but he saw it now. Almost the entire state west of the Alleghenies was pro-Union, and some of the northern counties bordering the Potomac seemed doubtful in their loyalty to his government. He lamented the absence of good preparation for war that he found on arriving, and of which others had warned him. In fact little had been done, even after he started sending regiments and arms from Montgomery. Otherwise, he confided, "we might now have been contending for the bank of the Susquehanna instead of retiring from the Potomac." Obviously, Davis did not view this strictly as a defensive war for the Confederacy, else there would have been no thought of pushing his army through Maryland and into Pennsylvania to the Susquehanna.[39]

But now he dealt with what he found. Confessing that Virginia's border was "long and indefensible," he still began to exhaust himself in providing for it as best he could, in the hope that before long he would be "able to change from the defensive to an offensive attitude." Beauregard's army was placed to protect Virginia's railroads, especially the vital junction at Manassas that provided a rail link with Johnston in the Shenandoah. Lee, now advising Davis in Richmond, believed that any Yankee movement into the state would head for Manassas first, and this they discussed with Beauregard on the day he reached Richmond on May 31. Even while the army steadily grew, Beauregard began building defenses along Bull Run, above the junction, to prevent any enemy attempt to cross. By mid-June his command numbered fifteen thousand or more, and he applied to Davis for permission to organize the regiments into brigades and create more brigadiers. A month later his forces swelled to eighteen thousand, and he actually thought himself ready for offensive action.[40]

Strategy for defending northern Virginia evolved gradually out of repeated meetings between Davis, Lee, and to a lesser extent Cooper, with Beauregard occasionally attending. Basically it lay upon holding the Manassas Gap Railroad that connected Manassas with the Shenandoah, and using it to shuttle troops from one side of the Blue Ridge to the other in order to combine against and defeat an invader. As early as June 12 the egotistical and sometimes bombastic Beauregard suggested that it was Johnston who should cross the mountains to join him, and then together they would advance to retake Alexandria and the southern bank of the Potomac. Whatever was done, Beauregard implored for "a concerted plan of operations." Davis wisely rejected the impractical plan, but Beauregard did not take it well. Though he kept his feelings from Davis, in the general's headquarters some of his staff officers nonetheless began referring to the president as a "stupid fool." Just as unfortunate, Davis felt displeasure with his general's haughty attitude and made fun of his self-important staff. "Whoever is too fine," he said in June, "that is, so fine that we do not know what to do with him—we send him to Beauregard's staff." Davis's friend James Chesnut heard the remark, and being as well a member of Beauregard's staff, he quickly passed it along to his commander. Nothing more than idle dinner conversation at the Spotswood, Davis's comment was unwise just the same, especially had he known Beauregard's touchy temperament better. Some speculated that the president felt jealous of the general since Sumter had made him the South's premier military hero, eclipsing a position held by Davis himself for years. They may have been right.[41]

Beyond question Davis chafed at being in an office in Richmond when there were regiments out in the field, yet he did excellent service in that office, encouraging and cajoling the governors to send more regiments, exhausting every means possible to find weapons and ammunition, and worst of all dealing with the lack of adequate provisions, which many already blamed on the inefficiency of Commissary General Northrop. Whatever might become of the army Beauregard organized out on the Manassas line, it was Davis, more than any other, who built that army and a fair share of the five brigades under Johnston in the Shenandoah as well. When time allowed, Davis visited the camps of the recruits in and around the city, often riding a fine "charger" sent to him by friends. Even those who did not like him could not help confessing that, mounted on his splendid gray, he was "a consummate rider, graceful and easy in the saddle." His plain dress and military bearing impressed the soldiers. On several occasions he took part in the ceremonial handing over of battle flags to new regiments, always leaving them with words invoking the Almighty and enjoining them not to stain the banner. There were "hardships to endure," "privations to bear," and "great deeds to do" beneath those fluttering folds of cloth, he told them. More than that, he promised to be with them if he could on the day of battle.[42]

Indeed, as the first two weeks of July brought increasing signs that a clash would take place in northern Virginia before long, the speculation renewed that Davis might take command himself, and this time he contributed materially to the rumors. As far back as mid-June, he had told brother Joseph, "When it is possible to leave here I wish to be on the lines." Indeed, he wanted Joseph to come to Richmond to take care of his family while he was with the army, and when he added that "God knows what the tide of war may bear me," he made it evident that he expected to be at risk. A month later, in presenting a battle flag to the Hampton Legion, newly arrived from South Carolina, Davis promised them that he had not come to the office he occupied for its honor, "but to share its perils"; and "when Carolina levels her bayonets for the last charge," he hoped to be with them. He intended to be "where men bleed and die."

A War Department official well acquainted with him declared six years later that "the fact is, Mr. Davis intended to take the field himself with the 'Grand Army.'" Most convincing of all, however, is the discussion Davis had with his old and intimate friend Leonidas Polk in the second week of June. Polk confidently told his wife afterward that "Davis will take the field in person when the movement is to be made." It is hardly likely that Polk would have mistaken his president's intentions after their discussions. Theirs was the kind of intimate and open friendship, going back more than thirty-five years, that encouraged the frankest of expression. While Polk did not claim that Davis actually said he would go to the army, still Polk's clear impression from their talks was that this was Davis's intention. Unsaid and uncertain, however, is what the Mississippian planned to do on the battlefield. Would he actually take command, assist and advise, or simply observe? Given the frequent and open communication between Davis and Beauregard, it seems hardly likely that the president would plan to assume actual command without stating that intention to his generals well in advance of a clash. None of his correspondence contains such notification. On the other hand, Davis was too distinguished, not just as commander in chief but also as a great Southern military hero, to act as a mere observer. Consequently it seems most probable that he hoped to be on the scene as an adviser, especially since he and Beauregard differed somewhat on strategic matters. And his expectation of being at risk meant that he would be under fire and probably in a position to assume command of at least portions of the army should the necessity arise.[43]

Beauregard reported that the foe numbered thirty thousand, with large reserves, commanded by General Irvin McDowell. Initially he expected the Yankees to advance on Manassas on July 12 or 13. Being heavily outnumbered, he concentrated his eighteen thousand at the crossings of Bull Run, affording him excellent defensive cover. He would offer battle no matter the odds, said the general, striving to the last to protect his rail link with Johnston in the valley. As for the troops in the Shenandoah, they, too, faced an advance by a Federal army of greater numbers, though it was led by the superannuated General Robert Patterson, whose timidity outweighed his numerical advantage. Johnston, too, wrote with confidence, even indulging in a bit of flattery when he said that "we require now, I think, but one thing to make speedy success certain—That you should appear in the position Genl. Washington occupied during the revolution," adding, "Civil affairs can be postponed."[44]

As anticipation mounted, so did Davis's anxiety. He sent reinforcements as fast as the rail lines could handle them, and "at a rate that makes me heart sick." "Every body disappoints me in their answer to my requisitions," he lamented to Johnston. He wanted desperately to get away to the Shenandoah to visit with this general, too, but could not escape labors on his behalf in Richmond. He gave even less attention to the pitifully small army assembling out in western Virginia, beyond the Alleghenies, where Brigadier General Robert S. Garnett tried vainly to resist the advance of Yankees from Ohio led by George B. McClellan, one of the officers Davis had sent to the Crimea years before. Indeed, on July 13 Garnett fell during what was little more than a skirmish—the first general to die—thus putting more pressure on Johnston and Beauregard to protect the balance of the Old Dominion.

This only added to Davis's frustration over lack of equipment. He could get twenty thousand men from Mississippi in a moment, he protested, and thousands more from the irritable Brown in Georgia. "To these and other offers I am still constrained to answer, I have not arms to supply you." Viewing Johnston's position with "deepest solicitude," Davis could only assure the general that he was doing all that was humanly possible, which was indeed the case.[45]

On the afternoon of July 14, Chesnut visited Davis with the latest news from Beauregard and another proposed plan of action. He found Davis ill and confined to his bed, yet the president saw him and soon asked Cooper and Lee to join them for an evening conference. To the assembled men, Chesnut outlined his general's proposal that they bring Johnston from the valley to combine with him, making an army more than thirty thousand strong, and then advance against the Yankees in their front. Defeating them, Johnston could then return to the Shenandoah and attack the hesitant Federals facing him, thereafter sending men to reinforce Garnett, of whose death they had not yet heard. Then all three generals would cross the Potomac with their separate armies and attack Washington from several sides at once.

Davis and Lee both objected to the plan as too ambitious and founded on misconceptions, chiefly a gross overstatement of Johnston's strength. Furthermore, Davis already knew that Garnett was even then in retreat and in no condition to assume an offensive. A few hours later he learned of the general's death. An offensive was out of the question. Their troops were green, still barely trained. In his highest ranks, the brigade commanders, Beauregard had men who had never led anything more than a company in action before. They were all untried volunteers. In a defensive position like the banks and fords of Bull Run, they might counter the enemy's superior numbers. But on the offensive, attacking a superior foe in his own defenses, they risked disaster, and uppermost in Davis's mind was the aching fact that he could not suffer a defeat here and now. It could lose them Richmond, and Virginia, and the entire Confederacy.[46]

Certainly Beauregard was not pleased when Chesnut reported the results of the conference with the president. Yet there was little time for any of them to lament, for on July 17 Beauregard's spies got through to him the message they had all been waiting for. That same day he wired to Davis the terse yet pregnant intelligence, "Enemy is advancing." At last the battle was coming.[47]

19

We Have Taught Them
a Lesson

Almost frantically, despite his illness, Davis redoubled attempts to support his generals after he received Beauregard's telegram. "Am making all efforts to reinforce you," he assured the general. At the same time he wired to Johnston that Beauregard was about to be attacked and issued the contemplated order that Johnston move all of his force possible on the Manassas Gap Railroad to join forces "if practicable." Johnston found it practicable and commenced the next day. Meanwhile, on July 18, the advance guard of McDowell's army made an ill-conceived approach to Blackburn's Ford on Bull Run that resulted in a sharp repulse. When Beauregard reported what had happened, Davis answered "God be praised for your successful beginning."[1]

A "beginning" is what it was, and Davis seemed to realize that. The Confederates had not defeated the enemy at Bull Run; they only turned back a halfhearted probe, and though the Yankees were content not to move again for two whole days afterward, still Davis expected that Blackburn's Ford was only a prelude. Still he saw in the small victory at hand a possibility. Should McDowell be decisively defeated, foreign powers might be convinced of the Confederacy's ability to achieve and maintain its independence. Recognition could follow swiftly. He ordered an impromptu envoy to be ready at a moment's notice to cross the Atlantic. Now he determined more than ever to get to the scene of action, hoping at least to be a participant, yet everything seemed to stand in his way. Still more regiments were arriving that he had to forward to the front. Worse, with Congress convening for its next session on July 20, he had to deliver a "state of the Confederacy" message as required by statute. "I have tried to join you," he wrote Beauregard in frustration, "but remain to serve you here as most useful for the time." As soon as he got the message out of the way, he would leave for the army.[2]

It was one of his briefest addresses to Congress during his tenure, showing clearly his anxiety to have it done and get away. He devoted almost the entire address to condemning Lincoln and his policy of coercion and conquest, and when he had finished that afternoon he hoped at last to leave Richmond. Alas, yet further vital business kept him in the capital. Even at the eleventh hour before his departure he still visited the volunteers' camps in town, drawing their cheers until, as one described it, "the whole earth seemed to tremble at the sound." And there were nagging official matters to settle as well. In the midst of this crisis, a telegram came from Johnston who, like many an old soldier, felt a more-than-ordinary concern for matters of rank. Once he joined forces with Beauregard, he asked, who should command? Both were brigadiers. However, Johnston's commission was in the Confederate regular army, whereas Beauregard's was in the provisional service. Furthermore, Congress had approved the rank of full general for Johnston, therefore, his took precedence. Quickly the president wired Johnston what he felt that general ought to know already, yet behind his confident words Davis felt a sudden apprehension that jealousy or confusion about some such matter as rank might interfere with the great work before them. Even as he told Johnston that "the zeal of both assures me of harmonious action," he hastened his own efforts to get to the battlefield.[3]

On the morning of July 21, a Sunday, Davis left his office in the charge of one of his new aides, Lee's son George Washington Custis. It was a frustrating morning, his departure delayed by an Arkansas congressman to whom he intimated unspecifically that "important events" were transpiring elsewhere. Congressman A. H. Garland could sense the president's anxiety. Finally he left with another new aide, his nephew Joseph. Given the poor condition of the track and the limited engines and cars available, it took them most of the day to reach the vicinity of Manassas Junction, less than one hundred miles north of Richmond. Looking out of his car into the distance, Davis saw first large clouds of dust and then began to hear the distant boom of cannon. When he reached the junction and left the train, the artillery was a virtual thunder. A battle had been raging since shortly after dawn barely three miles north of the junction. McDowell had succeeded in crossing Bull Run and moving against the Confederates' weak left flank. Heroic efforts by officers and men stemmed his advance, and then the generals began strengthening their line with reinforcements, Johnston doing the vital work behind the lines while Beauregard inspired the men in the front ranks. A combination of Johnston's sending reinforcements to the right points at the right time, the exhaustion of the Federals, and simple good fortune turned the battle in the Confederates' favor at around 4 P.M. or soon thereafter.[4]

Davis did not know this when he got off the train at the junction. All he saw were stragglers who had broken ranks long before, when they realized the battle was going against them. Urgently Davis implored the engineer to take the train closer to Bull Run so that he could get a horse at Johnston's headquarters and ride onto the field to help stem what he feared might be a rout. Colonel Thomas Jordan of Beauregard's staff met them, and though he offered mounts, he urged Davis not to risk himself on the battlefield. Undeterred, the president and his aide rode toward the firing some three miles to the northwest. Everwhere he saw more stragglers and chastised them that "battles are not won where men leave their ranks in such numbers as this." Davis's appearance seemed to infuse new vigor into many of the faltering soldiers. As they recognized the figure on horseback, wearing only a black suit, they raised their caps and cheered. Before long the president found Johnston on the lawn of a house he had made his headquarters. Shaking his hand, Davis asked, "How has the battle gone?" and now for the first time he realized that they had the foe on the run. Anxious to see the pursuit, Davis rode westward toward the fords fought over by the armies and to the hill where the battle was decided by resolute men including Thomas J. Jackson, soon to be known as Stonewall. Several of Beauregard's staff now joined him, along with a company of cavalry, and before long they reached the far left of the Confederate line. It was growing late, and some of the regiments were starting to stack their arms when they saw him coming. A cry of "The President!" ran along the lines, and the men sprang to attention once more. Here and there he made little speeches to the men, as when he addressed the remnant of the First Louisiana Battalion, which had done more than most to halt the Yankee advance that morning, buying time with their lives. "Brave Louisianians," he said, "I thank you from the inmost recesses of my heart."[5]

Apparently Davis even crossed Bull Run and rode some distance in the direction of the panicked Federal flight, taking some troops that he found with him. Seeing the opportunity for a crushing pursuit, he was disappointed to find that the men best placed to move were pitifully ill equipped and had not eaten that day. They were too weary and hungry to go further, a condition prevailing throughout the army. Promising them rations as soon as possible, Davis turned his horse reluctantly to the rear, recrossed the stream, and rode in the moonlight back to Johnston's headquarters after a brief stop to visit some of the wounded.[6]

Well after nightfall the president and the general sat at a table inside the house, and Johnston described what he could of the day's events. Soon Jordan joined them with a report that the Yankees were in full flight to Washington. At that, Davis began writing a dispatch to

Cooper. "Night has closed upon a hard fought field," he wrote. "Our forces have won a glorious victory." Then he turned to Jordan and suggested that it was not too late for a pursuit that might crush the routed enemy and perhaps even retake the Potomac heights overlooking Washington. For some reason Johnston did not participate in the conversation, and Jordan asked Davis to issue the necessary order. Johnston may have felt that, by his presence, Davis commanded now. Davis dictated the order, but Johnston suggested the delay of pursuit until the following morning, and Davis acquiesced. Then he concluded his telegram to Cooper, and instead of asking one of the generals to sign it, he signed it himself. There was no reason that he should not, yet Beauregard later recalled feeling that the president might be trying to assume to himself thereby some of the credit for winning the battle. "My conclusion was," he recalled, "that we had to deal with an ambitious man."[7]

Davis remained on the field the next day, viewing the scenes of battle and the awful price in blood and misery paid for the victory. He felt a personal measure of that cost when he went looking for his wounded nephew Edward Anderson. Davis found his corpse in a hospital only hours after the seventeen-year-old expired, and never spoke of the moment without a trembling voice and tears. That same day, in recognition of his achievements, Davis informed Beauregard that he, too, would be made a full general in the regular army. After conferring again with Johnston and Beauregard that night, they concluded that a serious pursuit was not possible. Washington was too well defended, and the heights of Arlington and Alexandria were probably well fortified. Their green army had already achieved far more than they might have expected and was almost as disorganized and damaged as the enemy. As a result Davis concluded that there was no further need for him here in the field and that he should return at once to Richmond to continue the work of reinforcing, feeding, and supplying his generals that they might consolidate their position and be ready either to meet another advance, or make one of their own.[8]

Crowds thronged about Davis when he returned to the capital on July 23. Inevitably he had to make speeches, and when he did so he paid high tribute to the heroism and sacrifice of the Confederate soldiers and the leadership of their generals. "We have taught them a lesson in their invasion of the sacred soil of Virginia," he proclaimed, "and a yet bloodier and far more fatal lesson awaits them unless they speedily acknowledge that freedom to which you were born." After speaking at the train station, he spoke again at the Spotswood. Now, as in his speeches after the Mexican War, he outlined the battle for the crowd. Privately he admitted that, though beaten, the North could easily replace men and matériel and might march again. Still, he thought that Manassas might be the beginning of the end of the war.

According to one reporter, "the President, in a delicate manner, alluded to his own appearance upon the field." Davis spoke only of the wounded cheering him and of the stragglers who returned to the ranks at his urging. Within only a few days, however, exaggerated reports began to appear in the press. A week after the battle one story claimed that Davis assumed command of the army on his arrival and turned the battle into a victory. Such unsubstantiated reports found an expectant audience, since many had assumed that he would do so. Indeed, John B. Jones, a chatty clerk in the War Department, believed that it was with this in mind that Davis had been made president. "Our noble warrior President," Davis was called in some of the journals, and it was not until the end of the month that the newspapers began to sort out what Davis had done from what he had not. A week later Davis himself approved a resolution from Congress honoring Beauregard and Johnston for their victory.[9]

However much the elation of the victory and being on the battlefield may have buoyed the president, his health remained a problem, and hardly had he returned to Richmond before he took a turn for the worse. "I never saw a person so sadly changed," Joseph's wife Eliza wrote during a visit early in August. "He rarely smiles, and has not spoken to me except at table to hand something, although I sit next to him." Worse, so many people called at his apartments at all hours that he rarely enjoyed a meal uninterrupted. As the month wore on, he did not improve, leading to rumors that his illness was terminal. Despite a brief apparent recovery late in the month, by September he was bedridden again, and Varina had to screen callers to allow only those on the most vital business to see him. Once in August and again early in October he left the capital to go to a farm in the country, hoping to find solace and remedy in escape from Richmond and its woes.[10]

As usually happened, Davis's temperament underwent a change during his illness, becoming short, impatient, even confrontational, just as his old colleagues in the Senate had noted how much more combative he became when feeling unwell. In the aftermath of the great victory, everything seemed to go wrong. Though he cancelled a pursuit of the Yankees to commence the day after the battle, he had announced on his return to Richmond that Confederate forces were probably well on the way to recovering northern Virginia, only to learn later that Beauregard and Johnston did not follow at all. Worse, subsequent intelligence began to reveal that a concerted pursuit might well have achieved much, for the enemy was more disheartened and disorganized than they had realized.[11]

Equally troubling was the condition of the army around Manassas. Johnston had very little cavalry and needed it desperately. His artillery wanted better organization, and in Beauregard's command there was a need for yet more generals. No one seemed to care for the officer he had appointed to replace the slain Garnett. Johnston reported that the victory "disorganized our volunteers as utterly as a defeat would do in an army of regulars" and that it took him weeks to reassemble all the men and impose discipline. At the same time Johnston worried about affairs back in the Shenandoah and repeatedly sent Davis reports to which he expected, but did not receive, answers and instructions. In his camps the sick lists were growing for lack of good water, and furthermore Johnston now added his voice to Beauregard's in the complaint of inadequate rations, suggesting incompetence in Northrop's office. By the end of August the two generals had 45,000 men, almost a fourth of them sick, with facilities in camp for making only enough bread for 5,000, and not enough of either meat or flour coming from Richmond.[12]

Then there were the problems in his cabinet. Davis had known from the first that Toombs chafed in the State Department and, worse than that, the Georgian became increasingly critical of the president. "Davis works slowly, too slowly for the crisis," he told Stephens a month before the Battle of Manassas. A few weeks later he complained to Governor Brown that cabinet members other than Walker had almost nothing to do but look on idly while Davis and a few generals ran the war. By July 24 he had had enough and resigned. In accepting his resignation, Davis acceded to Toombs's desire to enter the military by making him a brigadier, and then he probably felt immediately sorry when the new general started sending him ill-advised plans for grand campaigns to capture Washington and complaining that he would rather report to Beauregard than to Johnston. Hunter of Virginia took over the State portfolio, but within only a few weeks Walker began to grow restive in the War Department.

His problems may have stemmed in part from Davis's appointment of his old friend Bledsoe to be head of the War Office, one of Walker's bureaus, without consultation with the secretary himself. In August, when Walker returned from a trip to find what Bledsoe had done in his absence, he simply shut himself up and would speak to no one. When the clerk Jones entered his office, he saw on the table an envelope addressed to Davis in Walker's hand. It sat there day after day, though Jones at least became convinced that Walker intended to leave. By September 10 the envelope finally went to Davis, and it proved to be a resignation, effective a few days later. Walker and Davis had not been a particularly good team, the former resenting the occasional interference of the latter and feeling more than a little sensitive to the criticism heaped on him for the problems in the army. Thus neither grieved at the parting. Davis made Walker, too, a brigadier, and promptly moved his increasingly close confidant Benjamin over from his post as attorney general to assume temporary management of the War Department, a post Benjamin may have been maneuvering to get for some time.[13]

Such frustrations did nothing to ease Davis's discomfort in his illness or to improve his mood. His family gave him almost his only solace. "If he has any weakness," said one of his friends at this time, "it is an excess of fondness for his wife and children." His occasional visits on his better days to see the soldiers also cheered him greatly. When they saw the ramrod-straight figure in his plain gray suit, mounted on his iron gray mare, they invariably cheered. In response he asked after their wants and promised to do his best for them. "There is nothing too trivial for his attention," wrote one, "and nothing escapes his notice that can promote another's comfort." When word reached one camp that he was coming, a regimental band struck up the popular tune, "Ever of thee I fondly am dreaming."[14]

It helped, too, in the first days of August, that the family finally moved into the refurbished Executive Mansion, soon to be called the White House. Though society at the Spotswood had its glittering moments, the Davises could hardly help but notice a certain condescension toward them—directed especially at Varina—by the members of the old "first families." For them she was too plump, too dark, and too impressed with her exalted position, and a few found both her and her husband "anything but well bred." One matron compared Varina to a refined mulatto cook, "a fine, portly, graceful woman, with darkish visage, thickish lips, bright eyes, and a most intelligent, if not a pleasing cast of countenance." "She has a somewhat masculine grasp of thought," said an old friend of the president's. "She frequently says strong things in strong words; but, then, she has a strong mind." Many saw her independent nature, her impulsiveness. "With a lofty if not a hasty temper, she does not hesitate to do or say what it suggests, when it suggests it, and regardless of consequences." Behind her back some called Varina "the empress," while others close to the executive office declared that she was in effect "the power behind the throne." When generals' wives fell out with her, the president seemed to fall out with their husbands. Her favorites seemed to become his. Certainly some of this was true. Just as certainly, more of it was perception rather than substance..But that she was his special helpmate, as she had been throughout most of his career, no one doubted. She had his ear as no other, and that alone gave her an influence that commanders and cabinet ministers envied. More than one, Benjamin especially, took pains to cultivate her goodwill. And when Davis became uncommunicative due to pique or illness, as he did late in July before moving to the new house, Varina was his only spokesperson. Certainly his condition could go up and down with alarming frequency.

One morning James Chesnut's wife, Mary, felt pleasantly surprised to meet Davis in the Spotswood's hallway and find him very cordial. "Things must be on a pleasanter footing all over the world," she concluded. "When he jokes it is a good sign." Four weeks later, in August, visitors to the Executive Mansion saw a president so weak that "mere conversation flushed his face and raised his fever."[15]

Beauregard and Johnston could not have picked a more inopportune time to challenge their commander in chief. The Virginian began the fray on July 24, just a day after Davis left the army at Manassas, and over an issue for which Davis, in earlier years, would have shown much the same attitude as Johnston—rank. On May 16 the Montgomery Congress had authorized a new rank, which the growth of the army seemed to require. In the old U.S. regular service there had been but two grades of general, brigadier and major (with Scott holding a brevet, or honorary, lieutenant generalcy). Having first created regular brigadiers back in March, Congress in May provided for a so-called rank of full general, bypassing major and lieutenant grades presumably out of a desire not to imitate the enemy. Exercising his presidential prerogatives, Davis nominated to the Congress for confirmation five officers for the new grade, and for purposes of seniority he himself selected their effective dates of commission.

He made Cooper the ranking general of all, his commission to date from May 16, the date of the authorizing legislation. Next, revealing his enduring hope to see Sidney Johnston wearing Confederate gray, though no one knew for sure where he was at that time or his actual intentions, Davis nominated his old friend, effective May 30. Following Johnston came Lee, to date from June 14, and then Joseph E. Johnston, his appointment effective July 4. Beauregard he appointed later, on the day of the Manassas victory. Unfortunately, by the terms of the law, Davis should have made all appointments effective on the same date, a requirement that he sidestepped, and for good reason. Fully expecting the possibility that more than one army might combine against a foe, he could not have a quarrel over who was to assume supreme command. Congress foresaw this problem, too, and in its legislation provided that such officers would determine their relative rank by reference to their former commissions in the United States Army.[16]

Neither Davis nor the War Department seems to have published these promotions or otherwise made them known to the army at large, and thus Johnston naturally assumed that he was, in fact, the ranking officer in the entire Confederate service. Naturally, that is, because of all of them he had held the highest rank in the old army. Sidney Johnston had been a colonel with a brevet brigadier's star. Lee and Cooper had been full colonels. Beauregard, of course, had been a mere major. But

Joseph E. Johnston had been elevated to quartermaster general of the army in 1860, with the staff rank of brigadier. Therefore, by the terms of the new law, Johnston should have held precedence over the other three, yet Davis had made him fourth in seniority, subordinate to the others except for Beauregard.

Johnston first got a hint of the problem on July 24, when an officer arrived at his headquarters with an appointment to act as his adjutant, by Lee's direction. Johnston bristled. Since he ranked Lee and everyone else, no one could choose his staff officers but himself. He wrote an indignant letter to Cooper refusing to accept the officer and asserting that he was "myself the ranking General of the Confederate Army." Cooper passed it along to Davis, who read it and then wrote at the bottom the simple endorsement, "Insubordinate." Five days later, after more orders had come to him from Lee—his friend, by the way— Johnston complained again. "Such orders I cannot regard, because they are illegal," he asserted, and again Davis penned on the message, "Insubordinate."[17]

The situation grew worse. Johnston did not learn that he was outranked by the other three until the second week of September, and when he heard of it, he did what no one should do to Jefferson Davis—he wrote a long, lecturing letter. Mortified and offended, he recited all the justifications for his having outranked the others in the old army, and therefore his claim to be the premier general under the laws of Congress in the new one. He accused Davis of "trampling" on his own and Congress's action. Under the March legislation authorizing five brigadiers in the regular army, only he, Cooper, and Lee had been appointed and confirmed. (An ailing Twiggs was offered the first appointment but declined.) The May 16 act specifically made all the brigadiers appointed under the March act full generals and at least implied that their commissions should be effective immediately. Thus Johnston, Cooper, and Lee were all generals as of May 16, but Johnston still ranked the other two thanks to having outranked them in the Federal service. According to the letter of the law, his arguments—however intemperately stated— were perfectly logical.[18]

When Davis received Johnston's letter, it outraged him and he responded angrily. "Its language is, as you say, unusual," he wrote, "its arguments and statements utterly one-sided; and its insinuations as unfounded as they are unbecoming." The correspondence ended there, and though Davis never gave Johnston an explanation of his position, he attempted years later to justify his ranking of the generals in a decidedly rationalizing and unconvincing manner. It turned, he said, on the difference between staff and line commissions. Johnston was a brigadier as quartermaster general, but it was a staff position in Washington, and by law staff officers were prohibited from exercising that rank over troops in the field. Thus Johnston would have reverted to his line rank of lieutenant colonel if for some reason he had been forced to leave Washington and go on active service. As such, Cooper, Lee, and A. S. Johnston would have outranked him. Furthermore, Davis declared, Johnston did not go directly from the United States to the Confederate States Army but after resigning first took a position in the Virginia state forces, transferring into the Confederate service when Virginia entered the new nation. In the Virginia army Lee had ranked Johnston, just as he had at every point in their prior careers. Thus, Davis concluded, there was every reason for Johnston to rank fourth behind the others in his new commission.[20]

Not since the fumbling of his understanding of regulations during his court-martial back in 1835 had Davis—usually the master of rules and laws—so misconstrued and misinterpreted statutes that were, in fact, quite explicit. The congressional act of March said nothing at all about differences between staff and line rank in the old service. It said only that "in cases of all officers who have resigned . . . from the Army of the United States, . . . the commissions issued shall bear one and the same date, so that the relative rank of officers of each grade shall be determined by their former commissions in the U.S. Army." Nor did any later legislation creating the rank of full general speak of such distinctions. Davis himself created the difference. Neither did any of the laws say that intermediate service in a state army in any way negated the preservation of seniority from the Federal service. This distinction, too, Davis invented, and if he had not, Sidney Johnston, who was made a full general directly from the old service, should have ranked all of them including Cooper. Indeed, since Cooper's colonel's rank in the Union might have been argued to be a staff position as adjutant general, while his line rank was captain, all of them should have ranked him, even Beauregard. Though the subject did not come up at the time, even more inconsistencies in Davis's policy appeared in the case of old Twiggs. A full line brigadier general, with a major general's brevet, in the old army, he was the highest-ranking United States officer to join the Confederacy by any measure. Though Davis had offered him a regular brigadiership back in March, later he did not give him an appointment in the regular army at all, making him a major general in the provisional, or volunteer, army, and thereby subordinate to all these men who had been his juniors.

Davis's actions were hardly capricious, however, Behind them lay an easily discerned intent. There were already stories at the time, going back for some years, suggesting a long history of cool feelings between him and Joseph E. Johnston. Many, like the rumored fight between them in their West Point days, were probably either fabrications or exaggerations that emerged after their current imbroglio. Still, there is enough genuine evidence to suggest at least an ambiguous relationship, if not actual animosity between them. For one thing, they were too much alike—proud, obstinate, and pettifogging. In February 1854 they had a brief exchange of letters when Davis was secretary of war, in which Davis did not altogether approve of Johnson's handling of funds for snag boats on the Arkansas River. Nevertheless the exchange ended amicably, and Davis defended Johnston later that year against an accusation of carelessness in the loss of government animals. In May 1855, when Davis issued a social invitation to Johnston, the officer accepted it "with great pleasure."

But then a few months later arose a harbinger of the specter that would poison their future relations: rank. In July 1855 Johnston raised the issue of a brevet, or honorary, promotion to colonel he had received during the Mexican War. Davis's predecessor in the War Department had declined to recognize it, and now Davis did the same. That was a great blow to a man like Johnston, but surely Davis softened it when he gave the Virginian a lieutenant colonelcy in one of his new regiments, the First Cavalry. Unfortunately, Johnston had been a lientenant colonel back in 1847–48, commanding a small special company. When it was mustered out at the end of the war, his rank reverted to captain. Now, even though he was given that rank yet again, he protested over seniority. The new colonel of the First Cavalry, Edwin V. Sumner, had not been made a lieutenant colonel until 1848, after Johnston was first raised to that rank. Arguing that his own commission should rightfully date from 1847 would make Johnston, technically, Sumner's senior in grade, and therefore first in line for the colonelcy and the command of the regiment. Davis ruled against him, as had his predecessor. Four years later, however, Johnston was still pursuing his claim, convinced that it was valid, and upsetting other senior colonels in the process.

Yet if these encounters seriously strained relations, there was no sign of it in June 1860 when Quatermaster General Thomas Jessup died and General Scott suggested four officers as possible successors: Albert Sidney Johnston, Joseph E. Johnston, Robert E. Lee, and Charles F. Smith. The Senate Military Affairs Committee, which Davis chaired, was to make a choice and recommend it to the whole Senate for confirmation. Davis might have been expected to support his idol Sidney Johnston, but he did not, most likely because saw it as a dead-end post and preferred to stay in a field command. Davis supported the other Johnston instead. Eighteen years later he even claimed that Johnston's nomination "met serious opposition, and that all my power and influence were required to prevent its rejection." The fact that the nomination was approved by the Senate on June 28 by a margin of 31 to 3 argues otherwise, but certainly Davis did cast his own vote for Johnston, and thus the contentious officer became a brigadier general with staff rank. Certainly that should have left him with nothing but kindly feelings toward Davis, while the senator's support of him rather than Lee or

Smith suggests at least any past disagreements with Johnston had not left deep marks. Nevertheless, there were other rumors even at this time claiming that Mrs. Johnston believed that Davis actually hated her husband, yet their wives were close friends now, and if Davis did feel cool toward Johnston, Varina's influence could be considerable with him in turning his favor toward those she liked.

One motive, and one motive only, adequately explains the rationalizations to which Davis resorted in order to create a framework of justification for his actions—friendship. When Davis was secretary of war, old Cooper had never disappointed him, and between them grew a sincere and deep regard that extended to their families. He trusted Cooper, and Cooper rarely if ever challenged him, an important attribute in retaining Davis's goodwill. He could count on his friend to do his bidding as adjutant general almost without question. There was no need for an adjutant and inspector general to hold high rank. He did not in the old Union army, but then there had been a general-in-chief who acted largely through the adjutant. With Cooper as senior general of the entire military establishment, Davis eliminated potential problems, such as the ones he had experienced with Winfield Scott, with imperious generals-in-chief. Cooper's otherwise inexplicable and legally unjustifiable elevation can only be rationalized as an attempt to solidify Jefferson Davis's control over his armies. Davis could act through Cooper, and the rank insulated Cooper from question. As such, it was not necessarily a bad move, just one that flaunted the law.

And friendship—friendship approaching idolatry—explains the other anomaly. At the time that he appointed the first brigadiers in the regular army, Davis did not even know where Sidney Johnston was, and did not know with certainty that his old friend would join the Confederacy until late in August, when telegrams probably arrived from Texas informing him that Johnston was there and on his way to Richmond. Significantly, Davis did not submit his rankings of the five full generals until August 31, by which time he knew that Johnston was coming and that he would take arms for the South. Indeed, it must have been the need to have such certain information that induced him to delay the nominations, which should have been sent in immediately after the May 16 legislation or else as a first order of business when Congress reconvened on July 20. The inescapable conclusion is that Davis delayed to be certain that his friend would be with him in the cause, and to ensure that this Johnston would be the highest-ranking general in the field. He knew and trusted Lee and probably thought well of Joseph Johnston professionally at least. But he worshipped Sidney Johnston as he did no other man in his life. He was, said Davis, "the only man he felt able to lean upon with entire confidence," believing that his "consistency of action and conduct and his equanimity were different from any other man he ever saw." Johnston must be his premier general. As for the other Johnston, Davis's placing him behind three others in his August 31 nomination may just have been a bit of punishment for the general's haughty attitude in his "insubordinate" letters in July and his carping about Davis's friend Northrop thereafter.[21]

Though relations between the president and Joseph Johnston were never to be wholly open and cordial after this, the general concealed his feelings rather well and, as later actions and expressions demonstrated, Davis may have forgotten the episode almost entirely. Or perhaps the Johnston mess was pushed out of his mind by an even more aggravating controversy with Beauregard that arose even before the Johnston affair fizzled in mid-September. Prior to Manassas the Creole and the president had showed signs of cool feelings for each other. But then after Manassas the general renewed his complaints about Northrop, and intemperately took his carping outside military channels to congressmen. But for Northrop, he said, he would have been in a condition to advance and take Washington right after the battle. Instantly the growing number of Davis's opponents in the legislature used the letter to create a minor cause célèbre to embarrass the president. How could this have happened? they demanded.

While trying to satisfy Congress with assurances that Northrop knew his job and that Beauregard was the author of much of his own trouble, Davis tried to appease the general with a remarkably affable and conciliatory chiding for what was, in fact, a serious breach of military etiquette. "Some excitement has been created by your letter," he said. He reminded Beauregard of the condition of his army on the evening of July 21 and that he had then agreed that their best information suggested that the enemy would be heavily defended around Washington. "Enough was done for glory," the president cajoled, "and the measure of duty was full."[22]

Beauregard hardly showed contrition over his behavior. "I accuse no one," he said. "I state facts." Though he backpedaled on his earlier assertion that he could have taken Washington if properly supplied, still he seemed defiant. He continued writing to prominent civilians, complaining to Chesnut that his army was starving, and the press stood solidly behind him (as it did everyone in the army that gave them a victory). Indeed, by that fall many spoke openly of Beauregard and not Davis for the presidential election on November 5. Considering his oft-expressed desire to leave office as soon as reasonably possible, Davis may not have held this against the general as some believed. Quite probably he would have been happy to trade places with him.[23]

The carping about Northrop continued, the commissary general becoming a focal point for those who opposed Davis. "The most cussed and vilified man in the Confederacy," Mary Chesnut called him. "Of

[Northrop's] many crimes," she said facetiously, the chief and most often stated was "his having been a classmate and crony of Jeff Davis at West Point." Beauregard himself declared that it would be a "national good" if Northrop could be sent away as an ambassador to China or Japan. But now the general made trouble for himself in another quarter, with the attorney-general-turned secretary of war.[24]

Judah P. Benjamin, affable, unctious, sycophantic, and supremely pragmatic, was the ideal cabinet minister for this president. Whatever happened, he would get along with Davis. Early in August, with Walker still in the War Department, one of his subordinates saw this in the smiling Louisianian. "Mr. Benjamin, unquestionably, will have great influence with the President, for he has studied his character most carefully," the clerk noted on August 10. "He will be familiar not only with his 'likes,' but especially with his 'dislikes.' " Indeed, just a week after Davis sent his conciliatory letter to Beauregard, rumors went through the War Department of a breach between president and general, and Benjamin at once let it be known that he, too, was "inimical to Gen. B." Once Benjamin took over the War Department, he showed an apparent delight in thwarting Beauregard's suggestions and treating his correspondence in an officious and offhanded manner, further infuriating the general. By the latter part of October, their quarrel was well out in the open, and some suspected that Benjamin's ire grew out of the talk of Beauregard as a rival of the president for the coming election. Thus, said an observer, the Louisianian "commends himself to the President." For all his many strengths, Davis was never better than an erratic judge of character in his friends. Unable to see the sycophancy in some of those who agreed with him and always deferred to his judgment, he made himself prey to the influences of men like Benjamin. Davis could see through a gross flatterer—though not always—but men of Benjamin's subtlety and chameleon character could insinuate their way into the president's confidence and thereby acquire a power and influence with him that he sometimes denied to better men. In Benjamin's case it seems it was enough that he made Davis's friends his friends and Davis's enemies his enemies.[25]

Benjamin was not the only member of the cabinet tiring of Beauregard's behavior. Mallory complained of having "our fate in the hands of such self-sufficient, vain, army idiots," and perhaps his influence added to Benjamin's. Still, Davis showed uncharacteristic patience with the general, just as he had with Johnston, even when Beauregard went over Benjamin's head and communicated directly with the president. "My dear sir," Davis implored, "let me entreat you to dismiss this small matter from your mind." Sending expressions of undimmed confidence, Davis received in response only more complaints. The situation worsened on October 1, when Davis went to confer with the two difficult generals at Centreville, not far from Manassas. The army had finally advanced slowly toward the Potomac, and Beauregard, as usual, had a plan for a major offensive.[26]

When the president reached the army, he made a few speeches, telling the men that he had "come to bear with them his part" in any coming campaign, and apparently indicating that he would personally lead them "to glorious victory or a patriotic soldier's grave." Certainly both generals had repeatedly expressed their desire that he come to take charge personally. "Leave for two months the drudgery of your civil duties," Johnston had urged. "Command the army." Beauregard said much the same, though just how sincere either of them was can only be surmised. Fed up with their complaints and pettifogging, Davis may well have intended to assume the command whether they liked it or not.[27]

But he did not. "The condition of things here is not as good as I had expected," he wrote to Varina from Centreville. It looked no better after that evening's council of war with Beauregard, Johnston, and Major General Gustavus W. Smith. They met at Beauregard's headquarters, where Davis lodged, and after some general conversation, Smith asked bluntly if they could not get the army in condition for an offensive. They all agreed that army strength was as great as it was ever likely to be for the foreseeable future, that the men felt ready to fight, and that they must do so before winter came on or else wait until spring. Smith appeared to be acting as Beauregard's mouthpiece, for the plan then suggested certainly bore nothing of Johnston in it and much of the Creole. Already in some disfavor with the president, Beauregard quite probably felt that his ideas would stand a better chance of an impartial hearing if they came from the lips of another. Unfortunately, he did not know that Davis and Smith had had a small collision a few years before, leaving Smith under the distinct impression that Davis opposed him in the old army.

Smith suggested a massive concentration of all available Confederate manpower, even at the risk of inviting defeat elsewhere, in order to build the army in northern Virginia to sufficient strength to advance. "Success here at this time saves everything," he argued. "Defeat here loses all." They could lose a part of Tennessee without disaster to the cause, but the loss of the country north of Richmond, he argued, would cost them the war. It was the first substantial assertion of a "Virginia first" strategic approach that many then and later believed dominated Confederate thinking for the rest of the conflict.

Smith said they needed fifty thousand men in their army to make an offensive across the Potomac to defeat the Yankees. Beauregard and Johnston said they thought it should be more like sixty thousand, and they would need a great deal of additional supply and transport to enable them to move at that strength. Davis agreed with them all that simply sitting along the Centreville line and waiting for the winter would be a bad policy. They still had some advantage from their victory at Manassas, if nothing more than an emotional and psychological upper hand, now supported by recent battlefield successes in Missouri. This was the time to strike before the foe consolidated his shattered army and augmented it from the inexhaustible resources of the North. Time was lives.

Davis himself had no fixed idea of the strength necessary to enable this army to take the offensive. However, he professed surprise when he learned that the effective number present for duty was under forty thousand. He had been forwarding new regiments as they arrived in Richmond ever since the battle, but sickness and other causes unfortunately depleted all the units out on the line. Just as bad, the number of arms available in the army was clearly inadequate, and of this Davis complained bitterly. If he succeeded in finding more volunteers for Johnston and Beauregard, they would not have sufficient rifles to arm them.

Seeing this, Davis felt ill disposed to consider seriously Beauregard's proposal for an offensive into Maryland to threaten Washington and force the Yankees to make a fight to protect their capital. With neither enough men nor arms to give it a fair prospect of success, the plan must meet failure. The president reminded the generals that he had to think of the defense of the entire Confederacy. Being military men, they did not have to see beyond the enemy in their front. Davis had to consider an enemy on every front, as well as the repercussions within the country should he strip one part of it to aid another. Beauregard could speak casually of the insignificance of losing a part of Tennessee; Davis could not—and for a host of political and military considerations that Beauregard had the luxury of ignoring.

No, they could not go with the Creole's plan. But grasping readily enough the benefit of some successful offensive movement, Davis suggested that good morale effect might be had by making raids on a couple of exposed Yankee brigades posted in isolated positions on the other bank of the Potomac, and perhaps by striking and damaging the Chesapeake and Ohio canal "and making other rapid movements wherever opportunity presents, to beat detachments or to destroy lines of communications." Years later Beauregard and Johnston—who agreed on next to nothing in those years—would speak as one that they could not believe that Davis, presumably a military mastermind and their commander in chief, would propose for the occupation of their army an operation so insignificant as mere raiding. Beauregard or Smith argued the impracticability of Davis's plan by observing that the enemy's ships controlled the Potomac and that any raiding parties would be in danger of having their route of withdrawal cut off by enemy gunboats. Beauregard did not seem to recognize that precisely the same eventuality applied to his more grandiose scheme, and if it had gone through, his plan might have cost the Confederacy its largest army, whereas Davis's proposal risked only portions of that army.

Faced with the united opposition of the generals to his suggestion, Davis yielded the point, though he would propose it once or twice again later that month, leaving the matter entirely to the generals. The conference, though only two hours long, must have shaken his confidence in their judgment in at least one regard. Two of his four highest-ranking field commanders—Cooper being deskbound in Richmond—men to whom he looked to lead his armies, had shown themselves politically and militarily naive, or at best myopic. They could not see beyond themselves and their own army. What would happen should Congress mandate a general-in-chief to coordinate all Confederate strategy, and someone like Johnston or Beauregard fill the position? Davis probably left Centreville with a rising determination to retain as much control over grand strategy as possible.

He may also have faced squarely for the first time a difficult fact of life. For all of the best and most logical reasons, he and Congress had given high command to the men—Cooper excepted—who by any measurement should be most expected to bring to it skill and judgment. The two Johnstons and Lee were the most eminent career officers in the nation prior to 1861, excluding superannuated old generals like Scott, Wool, and Twiggs. Regardless of who became president of the Confederacy, these were the men who would have been given the highest positions, and Beauregard, by his success at Fort Sumter and Manassas, unquestionably earned a place with the others. Yet two of his top four men in the field had shown themselves by October 1861 to be flawed. Contentious, vain, and prideful, hesitating in Johnston's case and impractically grandiose in Beauregard's, they shared many of the same character traits that others found in Jefferson Davis. Men of such character, rather like the positive ends of two magnets, could never in the long run do other than repel each other.[28]

And that is what they proceeded to do. Incredibly, affairs worsened in the following weeks. At the Centreville meeting Davis suggested a reorganization of the Army of the Potomac, as they styled Johnston's command. Thanks to the intermittent way in which regiments had reached it prior to Manassas, troops from several states found themselves brigaded together. Davis wanted to see the regiments from each state kept in separate state brigades, if possible to be commanded by brigadiers from that same state. It touched on a point of local pride, to which he always felt sensitive, and also promised to improve morale. In fact, he proposed the idea even before October 1, and simply reiterated it at the council and asked if anything had been done. Congress made state organization a law, whenever practical, and the widespread complaints of the volunteers to being commanded by men from other states made it a matter of import. Beauregard had done some work in this direction, but for the most part organization remained as it had been that summer. Davis continued attempts to persuade the generals to comply even after his return to Richmond, and for some months thereafter. As late as May 1862, Johnston still resisted the order or else simply would not get around to obeying.[29]

At least Davis received the usual manifestations of the confidence and goodwill of the soldiers during his visit to the army, and this always cheered him. Indeed, he rarely felt better than when with the soldiers, and as always he spoke to them, concealing his doubts and frustrations and praising Johnston and Beauregard. The men responded, some saying that Davis's being with them was "a guarantee that the hour is close at hand when they will be permitted to strike a blow." Unfortunately, Davis did not stay with them long. On October 3 news reached him that Varina and Mrs. Joseph E. Johnston had suffered a dangerous carriage accident, and immediately he returned to the capital. The latter suffered a fractured arm, while the president's wife escaped with only a minor cut and a contusion on her right shoulder. The chief concern for Varina lay in her being several months' pregnant, but a doctor's examination suggested that the unborn infant suffered no injury.[30]

It was a poor time for the murmurs of criticism of Davis to increase in volume. "He was abnormally sensitive to disapprobation," Varina would say. "Even a child's disapproval discomposed him." Moreover, given his conviction of rightness in all matters, he always felt himself unfairly accused in any criticism, "and the sense of mortification and injustice gave him a repellant manner." The complaints of Johnston and Beauregard, echoed by hundreds of soldiers, about scarce food and supplies reached the press and circulated throughout the Confederacy just as Davis went into his period of illness in September and his frustrations with the generals. Davis's own defense of Northrop began to appear as well, with the lines clearly drawn and the commissary general the issue of contention. "The President does not countenance any insinuations of his incapacity," said a Charleston journal, and when Northrop did manage to send quantities of foodstuffs to the forces in the field, the press was notified, probably at the behest of the administration. Indeed, Davis was already trying to counter the evil influences of a growing hostile press, particularly in Charleston but also in Richmond, by having the War Office clerk John B. Jones author articles favorable to the government, articles that Davis himself sometimes read and edited before submission.[31]

The criticism soon became more personal. As the public and the press grew impatient over the passage of months after the Manassas victory, with no activity by the Army of the Potomac, the frustration found expression in attacks on Davis, as if he were responsible. "We should have gone to Washington," proclaimed the Charleston *Daily Courier*. That they had not was due to "the miserable political jugglery of President Davis." The *Mercury*, always an implacable foe, went farther. Just the day before Davis arrived at Centreville to meet with Johnston and Beauregard, it accused him of holding back the generals, of never consulting with them in a council of war. Moreover, it maintained that the generals opposed their policy of inactivity and claimed that "we have information" that "within a few days" Beauregard had proposed an offensive to Davis, and the president had refused. Given his connections in Charleston and his demonstrated affinity for taking his private complaints to public forums, it is not hard to see Beauregard's hand in the "information" furnished to the *Mercury*. If so, that made all the worse the paper's further assertions that Davis had ordered the pursuit after the Manassas rout stopped, and that only he had prevented a march on Washington. Reports even circulated that Davis opposed any invasion of Maryland's soil.

In fact, Davis felt ambivalent about invasion. As evidenced by his proposal for raids across the Potomac, and several earlier speeches about taking the war to the North, he seems to have felt no problem justifying an invasion. Yet in his inaugural he had spoken of only wanting to be left alone and of having no designs on the rest of the old Union. In that case, how could he justify invading "foreign" soil? Vice President Stephens appears to have opposed invasion while most of the cabinet favored the idea, but the decision rested with Davis, and despite the soundness of his reasons for not going ahead with any of Beauregard's plans, still the president found himself charged with sloth and indecision.[32]

Then, just three weeks after the Centreville conference, Beauregard escalated the controversy. Frustrated at inaction, and realizing that nothing would happen in Virginia before winter, he asked for transfer to New Orleans. Davis politely refused. Still addressing him as "My Dear General," a form he had also used with Johnston, the president asserted that he could not spare the general from a post that he knew so intimately. Continuing to show an uncharacteristic patience with someone as contentious as Beauregard, Davis even closed with a bit of flattery about "my appreciation of you as a soldier and my regard for you as a man." Then Davis disappointed the Creole again when he declined to endorse Beauregard's suggestion for a revised command structure in the army. The Creole's vanity chafed at being second in command to Johnston, though the two got on well enough. He had commanded an army of his own before Manassas. He proposed now that the single army be divided into two corps, with himself commanding one of them. Benjamin refused, in an irritating manner, and Davis sustained the secretary of war, in a conciliatory one. Unfortunately, Beauregard did not know when to let a matter drop. He kept pressing, his tone and choice of words becoming increasingly confrontational. Late in the month, Davis still addressed "My Dear General" with calming words and a mild suggestion that the Yankees made a better enemy for him to fight than Benjamin.[33]

Then Beauregard overstepped the bounds of Davis's unaccustomed patience. Acquiescing in Benjamin's role, he expressed the hope that the secretary of war would not tie the hands of the army with his legalisms. When Davis responded on November 10, "My Dear General" was gone from his salutation. The president had taken enough. "Sir," he began. "You surely did not mean to inform me that your army and yourself are outside of the limits of the law. . . . I cannot recognize the pretension of anyone that their restraint is too narrow for him." It was a stern rebuke, and one with added incentive, thanks to another revelation of the previous few days.[34]

Davis and the War Department had waited some time to receive Beauregard's report of the battle at Manassas. The public almost clamored for it, yet he took some months to gather all the necessary reports from his subordinates before he composed his own. Finally on October 14 he sent it to Richmond, where the War Department received it the next day. Unaccountably, Benjamin and Cooper did not tell Davis of its arrival, and the president only learned of the report when a synopsis appeared in the Richmond press on October 29. It outraged him. The synopsis claimed that Davis had overruled the general in a plan for a battle south of the Potomac and prevented him from attacking Washington and Baltimore and from conducting a campaign to "liberate" Maryland.

At once Davis asked Benjamin for the actual report, and there he saw what, to his eyes, confirmed the insinuations of the synopsis. Beauregard did state that on July 13 he sent Davis a plan for a campaign to take Washington and free Maryland. What he read sent Davis into a fury, and immediately he wrote to the general demanding an explanation of what he viewed as "an attempt to exalt yourself at my expense." He had seen no such plan as that outlined in Beauregard's report. Worse, the clear impression left by the report and the synopsis was that, had Beauregard's supposed plan been adopted, the victory at Manassas would have suggested that the Confederates could have accomplished the much more complex and speculative maneuvers in the plan and now have Washington and Maryland for their own. In an instant, Davis reverted fourteen years to the days after Monterrey, when there was another scramble over credit for a victory. The same day he wrote to Beauregard, the president devoted himself to gathering evidence from

Chesnut, and in the following days he wrote to Cooper and Lee as well.[35]

Ordinarily Davis might not have reacted so strongly to the report. But hearing himself criticised for weeks for supposedly keeping the army inactive and for not ordering an invasion of Maryland, it was simply too much now to be charged with actually preventing an invasion. Beauregard's report tended to confirm the wrongful accusations. Just as the Louisiana general brought out the best in Davis—months of patient and conciliatory stroking of Beauregard's ego—so now did the Creole bring out the worst in the president. In a contest for the last word, Davis would never accept defeat, and thus commenced a controversy that only ended decades later with both men's deaths.

Beauregard retreated instantly, not from what appeared in his report but from any intention to injure the president, whom he now proceeded to flatter almost obsequiously. But Davis would not be mollified. He overreacted to the report, to be sure, his chief argument being that Chesnut had given him only a verbal report of what Beauregard suggested, not a written "plan" of campaign. Even if such a plan had been submitted, however, he would have rejected it for its impracticability, and there Davis stood on firm ground. For the rest, his objections mostly amounted to minor pettifogging over definitions of words. It is clear that in the sudden explosion of ire, Davis was doing more than reacting to Beauregard's report. He was releasing the months of pent-up frustration with this troublesome general and his all-too-vocal supporters in Congress and the press, and with his own critics. Chesnut seemed to realize this, for even as he gave Davis his recollections of the July 14 conference at which he outlined Beauregard's proposal, he added a prayer that they all avoid controversy and heed neither the "unwise babbling of some, nor the deliberate malice of many." Davis and his generals must be above all that, he said. It was good counsel, but wasted on the president and all too many of his commanders.[36]

The failure to see the report in full in the press only fanned the rumors of a confrontation. The *Mercury* stirred the pot by speculating on why the full report was being kept confidential. "What does this report contain so terrible that the people are not permitted to know it?" asked the paper. It assumed that the report must be "prejudicial to Mr. Davis." In the War Department itself, Benjamin frankly admitted that he had decided to withhold the report from publication because Davis objected to the inclusion of any mention of the abandoned plan of campaign as inappropriate. Indeed it was inappropriate, and Beauregard suspected that someone in that department—likely Benjamin himself—had been responsible for writing and issuing the synopsis to the press, for he ever afterward denied doing it himself. For Benjamin, it was all a part of his own war with the general to show him, as the secretary put it, "who was *strongest* with the President."[37]

It had been a terrible autumn for Davis. Circumstances largely beyond anyone's control cost them the opportunity to follow up on the great success at Manassas. Relations with one of his leading generals and an immensely popular Southern hero broke down almost completely, and his rapport with Johnston stood impaired. Walker and Toombs had resigned, Varina was hurt, and all of it was made the worse by his poor health. In those early days of September especially, it took all his strength simply to write a letter. So little came to encourage him that when Sidney Johnston's son William Preston Johnston arrived on August 20, Davis kept him all day, cheered by the news that young Johnston expected his father to arrive in Richmond at last around September 10. With Davis even then losing confidence in his generals in northern Virginia, he needed his old friend beside him more than ever.[38]

That first week of September saw the president's health so debilitated that on many days he was confined to his second-floor bedchamber at the Executive Mansion, the blinds drawn to keep out the light, his wife and aides keeping all but the most important visitors away as the invalid tried to rest. As usual, he could not sleep, his mind alive with the great matters that pressed on him incessantly. While so much of the attention of North and South had been focused on Virginia, events were starting in motion to make the Mississippi Valley the next scene of activity and peril, and out there the Confederacy was more vulnerable than anywhere else. With all this keeping his nerves and perceptions on edge, he heard every sound in the house. One afternoon there came a ring of the front door bell. Perhaps he heard muffled voices as Varina or the doorman spoke with the caller.

But most of all he heard the distinctive tread of a man's boots on the entrance foyer floor, and recognized them at once.

"That is Sidney Johnston's step," he called out. "Bring him up."[39]

20

Sidney Johnston's Step

Remembering his old maxim that the internal design of a structure ought to be dictated by its outer walls, Davis applied the same theory to the military organization of the Confederacy. The "outer walls" of his new nation posed for him an enormous problem by the time Tennessee, the last of the states to do so, seceded. For a start, some 3,500 miles of the South's border were Atlantic and Gulf coastline, from Virginia's eastern shore to Brownsville at the southernmost tip of Texas. It was an enormous expanse to defend with almost no navy, though at least the Confederates did control the former United States fortifications that protected the principal harbors. Nevertheless, there were so many harbors, and a far greater number of acceptable places for amphibious landings, that the coastline almost everywhere was susceptible to invasion.

Virginia, fortunately, gave the Confederacy a northern water border with Maryland, along the Potomac, and from Wheeling down the Ohio to the Kentucky line. Then came the first big problem. Kentucky did not secede. Bitterly divided, the state tried to adopt a Swiss policy of neutrality, which it maintained well into the late summer of 1861. Since Governor Beriah Magoffin allowed armed forces from neither side to enter the commonwealth, its neutrality at least worked as a de facto defense of Davis's central-northern line from West Virginia to the Mississippi. Unfortunately, should neutrality end or Kentucky actually secede, there would be a mad scramble of regiments from both sides to take control. Davis would much have preferred to have Kentucky's people and produce and livestock, and most of all its Ohio shoreline, on his side from the first. Then he would have had an almost unbroken Confederate water border from Brownsville all the way around the South, counterclockwise, to Columbus, on the Mississippi. Though he believed that rivers made poor boundaries, still any invasion across water, whether ocean or river, would be difficult and more dangerous and offered manifest potential for cutting an enemy off from his communications and lines of supply and retreat.

But from this point onward it got messy. Missouri, across the river from Kentucky, stood terribly divided in sentiment as well, but its more settled eastern reaches, centered on Saint Louis, remained firmly in Union hands, with no policy of neutrality to prevent the Federals from consolidating their grip. Thus the border of genuine Confederate territory rested on Arkansas, an indefensible straight line almost 300 miles long that, worse yet, ended abruptly at the edge of unorganized Indian territory, and then turned ninety degrees south another 200 miles to Texas. Then there was the Lone Star State itself, with almost 1,200 miles of border, three-fourths of it unprotected by any sort of water or other barrier. Almost anywhere from El Paso on the Mexican border to the northeastern corner of Arkansas on the Mississippi, the Federals could invade the Confederacy simply by walking across the line.

When President Jefferson Davis and Secretary of War Leroy Walker looked at a map of the Confederacy, first in Montgomery, then later in Richmond as more states joined, they saw some immediate problems. The new nation was too long, about 1,700 miles from Norfolk, Virginia, to El Paso, and too thin, nowhere more than 450 miles deep, excluding the Florida peninsula. Anything too long and too thin stands in danger of being broken into pieces, the more so when there is already a crack. And the Confederacy was cut virtually in half by a major fissure—the Mississippi. It very neatly sliced Texas, Arkansas, and all but a small part of Louisiana away from the rest of the nation. Though he never said so, Davis might well have thought how much better it would have been for the balance of the Confederacy if those states had *not* seceded. Then the Mississippi would not be a crack in his defenses but perhaps his most formidable barrier.

He had to deal with the reality of the geographical puzzle before him. What sort of defensive strategy should he adopt, and how should he implement that decision? One thing was certain at the outset. Davis interpreted his "protect and defend" oath just as literally as did Lincoln, to mean that he must hold every inch of Confederate soil. There could be no abandonment of one portion of the nation in order to strengthen another, even though in later years a dispassionate observer might have noticed that the territory west of the Mississippi acted as a drain on resources that could otherwise have strengthened the Confederate heartland east of the river. Davis had to hold it all.

Having settled that matter—though for political and other reasons it can hardly have been a difficult decision to reach—Davis had to determine *how* to hold everything. In the spring and summer of 1861, leading up to the fight at Manassas, any sort of offensive was impossible. He was still building his army a regiment at a time, struggling to feed and equip the men. Moreover, uncertainty over Federal intentions made a settled strategy impossible for Davis. For Sumter's fall did not necessarily mean that the Yankees would invade or even fight. Many in the South, like Davis's friend Armistead L. Burt of South Carolina, believed that there would be no war, and Burt waggishly volunteered personally to drink all the blood shed as a result of Sumter's fall.

For all these reasons, Davis found no alternative but to react rather than act, conforming his military movements to what he saw the enemy doing. It was the only policy available to him when he took office in February, and would remain such until victories in the field gave him other options. Indeed, Davis's initial grand strategy was quite probably fixed in his mind even before he took office. Having feared and at times predicted a conflict like this for years, it would have been strange indeed if a military-minded man such as he had not often daydreamed about what would have to be done when threats of war became fact.

It is arguable how much of his overall strategy he brought with him to Montgomery and how much evolved in the ensuing months. Never did he consider abandoning a part of the Confederacy, as he made clear to Beauregard and Johnston in rejecting the plan offered in October. Nor was he willing to consider any risk-all offensive into the enemy's country, such as Beauregard's sweeping Napoleonic proposal of July 14. Yet Davis did speak frequently of taking the offensive, and in his expressed hopes for a resolute pursuit of the Yankees after Manassas he revealed his instinct to take advantage of the opportunity presented. Indeed, opportunity soon manifested itself as the salient feature in his concept of what the Confederate military could achieve given its limitations and the enemy's resources. When Davis proposed raids across the Potomac in the October 1 council of war with his generals at Centreville, he made this clear. They could not mount and sustain a massive offensive into the foe's territory: They did not have the resources and could not afford the risks. Yet neither must they remain in a strictly defensive posture. Instead they must hold all the ground possible and keep themselves primarily in a position to meet and counter the thrusts of their more numerous and better-supplied foe. However, when an opportunity for a stroke or counterstroke appeared, they should prosecute that opportunity vigorously though prudently. Davis called it an "offensive defensive," and in 1861 it was the wisest course available to him, offering the hope of the greatest gain with the least risk. It also dovetailed handsomely with diplomatic efforts to enlist European aid. To win formal recognition, it was far more important to maintain the integrity of Confederate soil than it was to win battles on Yankee ground. Furthermore, a posture taken to protect Confederate territory coincided far more legitimately with Davis's announced desire to be left alone than did large-scale invasions bent on capturing and holding cities and states outside the Confederacy. It was important that in world opinion Lincoln, not Davis, appear as the aggressor.

Having settled on his policy and determined the overarching principle of his strategy, Davis looked again at the map in the spring of 1861 to decide how to organize and disperse his resources. Familiar as he had been as secretary of war and later as chairman of the Military Affairs Committee in the Senate with the strength and distribution of the regular army, Davis could confidently expect that he would face little in the way of serious threats from the frontier borders of Texas and Arkansas. Confederate volunteers in those states would be more than sufficient to protect themselves for some time. Nor did Missouri pose much of a threat, for though the state was more or less in Yankee hands, so much turmoil still prevailed that an invasion from that quarter seemed unlikely. Meanwhile, the ocean borders could be expected to be secure for quite some time. The major ports all stood under the guns of powerful forts at Wilmington, Savannah, Charleston, Pensacola, and elsewhere, and even though Lincoln had declared a blockade of the entire Confederate coastline, it was well known to Davis and Mallory that the Union Navy was yet too small to mount a serious assault.

A careful and logical scrutiny of the whole geographical situation sifted the points of concern down to three. The line of the Potomac above Virginia obviously offered one. Its proximity to both capitals guaranteed that the Yankees would have to contest this ground, and soon. Davis did not formally organize it as a territorial command until after Manassas, when he designated it the Department of Northern Virginia on October 22. Recognizing the special nature of the ground, Davis divided the department into three subdistricts, one covering the Shenandoah, another the bulk of the territory between Richmond and the Potomac, and a small third district on Acquia Creek covering the lower Potomac. Johnston commanded the entire department.

The second sector for concern was the mouth of the Mississippi, the important port of New Orleans, and the Gulf Coastline of Louisiana, Mississippi, and Alabama. Davis had control the lower river, especially at Baton Rouge and New Orleans. Indeed, one of the first departmental commands he created—and one of only two generated from the Montgomery capital—embraced this area. Designating it Department No. 1, he included all of Louisiana and the southern portions of Mississippi and Alabama up to the Florida border. To command it he selected David Twiggs, whose health recovered sufficiently to allow him to accept a major generalcy in the provisional forces. Davis enjoined him to take special care for the so-called Mississippi Sound, connecting New Orleans with Mobile. Realizing at last his oft-stated concern for Ship Island, Davis ordered it occupied as a part of the defensive barrier.[1]

The third and most vital region that demanded immediate attention was the rest of the Mississippi, from the Mississippi state line near Wood-ville north to the Kentucky and Missouri borders. This would be the life-line by which men and matériel from the interior of the Confederacy would be moved to New Orleans or equally critical imports sent upriver to railheads for dispersal. At the same time the river had to be held to keep open communications between the Confederacy east of the stream and to the west. Loss of the river would cut the South in two. Consequently, Davis made this area the scene of Department No. 2, which he created on July 4 and assigned to his old friend Major General Leonidas Polk. It included all the river counties in Mississippi, Louisiana, and Arkansas, along with several hundred square miles of western Tennessee between the great river and the Tennessee River, which flows northward through the state to empty into the Ohio near Paducah, Kentucky.

The Tennessee, and to a lesser extent the nearby Cumberland River, offered a natural pathway of waterborne invasion from the Ohio deep into the heart of the Confederacy, slicing clear across Tennessee, then turning east near Pittsburg Landing to course across northern Alabama, cutting the northwest corner of Georgia, and then flowing up into Tennessee again to Chattanooga. The Cumberland, which cut across only a portion of north-central Tennessee past Nashville, seemed less vital for defense for the moment. Recognizing the indispensability of holding the Tennessee, Davis included a slender finger of territory covering its path across northern Alabama. Polk took command, with head-quarters at Memphis, on July 13.[2]

The only other department created in these early months of the war was the Department of Texas, on April 21, assigned to Davis's old friend from Mississippi, Earl Van Dorn. The balance of the Confed-eracy—there being no immediate threat and he having few enough regiments to send to danger spots like Virginia—the president left un-departmentalized for the time. There were some puzzling aspects to his appointments for the department commands, however. The seventy-one-year-old Twiggs had been a distinguished soldier in the Mexican War, but now his health nearly incapacitated him. Indeed, it had earlier prevented him from taking Davis's offer of a brigadier's star in the regular service, which would have made him the ranking general in the entire army when the full generalships were passed out. The defense of New Orleans was vital to holding the Mississippi, yet Davis entrusted it to a man clearly lacking the vigor and stamina for active command. Relying largely on two massive masonry forts on either side of the river below the city, the president perhaps felt that they would do the work of protecting New Orleans, and Twiggs would not be required to perform any rigorous service. Van Dorn also was a curious selection for department command. He graduated almost last in his West Point class, and though he fought well in Mexico, he did not rise above lieutenant until 1855, when Davis made him captain of a company in the new Second Cavalry, Sidney Johnston's regiment. He was familiar with the frontier, but the responsibility of commanding a department was a far cry from commanding a company. Davis liked the foppish, high-living Van Dorn. A fellow Mississippian, he had been on Davis's staff briefly when he commanded the state militia before becoming president. In this personal association probably lay the root of Van Dorn's appointment.

There can be no question of anything other than friendship to account for Davis's appointment of Polk to Department No. 2. Leonidas Polk had never served a single day as an officer in his life. He graduated at West Point in July 1827, went on furlough, and resigned his commission in October before his leave expired. He spent the ensuing thirty-four years in the ministry, yet when he offered his services to the Confederacy, Davis tendered him a brigadiership, then a few weeks later made him a major general in the provisional army in June 1861. Indeed, Davis sought him out, and now—to a totally inexperienced man who had never even held a permanent commission as second lieutenant—he entrusted the defense of the vital Mississippi. With scores of officers of higher rank and years of service available to him, the president gave the department to a favorite schoolmate.

It was easily Davis's worst and least explicable command decision of the year—unless, that is, Davis had deeper motives. For one thing, he quite rightly believed that the Mississippi would be safe from invasion at least until the end of the heat and fever season. "I think it is in no present danger," Davis told Polk in May, and events proved him correct. Thus he could gamble on Polk for a time, and time may have been what Davis was buying, putting one trusted friend in charge while waiting for another—Johnston—to arrive. But still it was a foolish choice, for if Lincoln had somehow mounted an offensive to take the river, the Confederacy's hopes would have rested on a man little better than an amateur.[3]

Nevertheless, Davis would have good cause to regret giving Polk so much responsibility. During the three months that Polk held command, more happened than they expected. He made the politician-general Gideon Pillow his second in command and almost immediately alienated him. Then came indications of a faster Federal buildup in southern Illinois and Missouri than they anticipated. In a puzzling response, Davis proceeded to expand Polk's command, giving him all of Arkansas and Missouri as well, with the small armies led by Generals Sterling Price, Ben McCulloch, and William Hardee, all of them experienced and battle-seasoned veterans who must now report to an amateur. Worst of all, however, Polk became convinced that the Federals intended to violate Kentucky's neutrality by moving troops from Cairo, Illinois, across the Ohio to Paducah and down the Mississippi to occupy Columbus. With the latter as a base, they could launch land or river expeditions south into Tennessee. Deciding to beat them to it, Polk sent Pillow into Kentucky on September 3 to occupy Columbus.[4]

It was a stupid move. Kentucky's neutrality was not destined to last indefinitely, and the Yankees spoke seriously of violating it themselves. But as long as it lasted it worked to the advantage of the Confederacy. Polk's action ended neutrality abruptly, and Davis was not pleased. Through the secretary of war, he ordered Pillow to withdraw at once, while informing others that the general had acted entirely without authorization. Davis seems not to have responded directly to Polk's move, other than to admonish him that "the necessity must justify the action," though Polk chose to regard this as "the necessity justifies the action," implying approval. In fact, whatever the president's initial chagrin may have been, he quickly came around. Three days after the occupation of Columbus he was already defending his friend against critics who voiced what he called "stupid censure of General Polk for marching into Ky."[5]

Enter Sidney Johnston, and the timing could not have been better. Not more than a week after Polk ended Kentucky's neutrality, Davis heard those footsteps that he knew so well and saw again the handsome face of the friend he almost worshipped. "I knew Sidney Johnston, I believe, better than I know any other man," said Davis a year later. "He came and by his accession I felt strengthened and reassured." They must have talked long and intimately, as much as Davis's illness at the time allowed, and certainly they discussed Johnston's role in the days ahead. He did not know until Davis told him that now he held a full general's rank, second only to Cooper. Yet at the moment Davis had a noncombatant's role in mind for him. Leroy Walker was ill and had not pleased Davis as secretary of war. Criticism in Congress of the management of the War Department and interference in its workings by the president persuaded Walker to resign, and though he did not do so until September 10, Davis knew for at least several days beforehand that it would happen. The cabinet seemed to favor Gustavus Smith, or perhaps John C. Breckinridge, just now fleeing Federal authorities in Kentucky and on his way to Richmond. But Davis saw in Johnston the perfect replacement. Vigorous and healthy, he not only had more high-command field experience than any other officer, but also had served as secretary of war of the Republic of Texas prior to statehood. He would be perfect for the job. Even better, it would keep him in Richmond close to Davis, and yet with his general's rank, he could also take the field should he choose, just as Davis might still exert active command. The president probably saw the pair of them as warrior-statesmen.

Unfortunately, the press of affairs demanded otherwise. As recent events had shown, he needed someone very capable in Department No. 2. Now that Polk's ill-advised action brought neutrality to an end, Kentucky was fair game for whoever could take it. Johnston was himself a Kentuckian, and that would help in winning support and recruits in the Bluegrass. With the enemy certain to contest the state and try to move south for Tennessee and the Mississippi, Davis could no longer trust the defense of all that vital territory to a neophyte like Polk. The department was so far away and so important that Davis had to have in command there someone whom he trusted completely. Johnston was the ideal man. "It was not without a severe struggle," said the president, that he ordered his friend away from him to the West.[6]

Actually, a small clamor for Johnston's assignment to the region preceded his arrival in Richmond. A number of prominent citizens at Polk's headquarters in Memphis wrote to Davis asking for Johnston, and Polk himself, perhaps recognizing his own limitations, advised the president back in August that their old schoolmate was the only man who could handle this vast and crucial post. It was good that Johnston came when he did, for now Davis could relieve his mind of worries over Department No. 2 and turn his attention to a host of other pressing problems and challenges.[7]

Department No. 1 offered an immediate concern. Governor Thomas Moore, always one of the most cooperative and supportive of the governors, warned Davis early in September of a rumored enemy advance on New Orleans. Twiggs agreed, and so did George Hollins, commanding the small Confederate naval squadron on the lower Mississippi. Worse, Louisiana had sent so many regiments off to the war zone in Virginia and elsewhere that insufficient forces remained to guard the state, and there were no arms for equipping any more. "We are inadequately prepared for an invasion here," Moore warned, and in a prophetic observation on September 7 he told Davis, "I wish I may be mistaken, but I do think too little apprehension is felt for the safety of *this* place." Privately, he also confided that they needed a younger and more energetic commander than Twiggs. "Send an active commander here," he implored.[8]

Davis may already have had this in mind, and perhaps even decided on the "active commander." Gustavus Smith, after leaving the North to join the Confederacy, advised Davis in that hectic first week of September that his friend and associate Mansfield Lovell, son of a one-time surgeon general of the army, intended to "go South." "He has been like a caged lion," Smith said of the Mexican War hero. Lovell might be the solution to the problem, since Davis had received enough complaints of Twiggs's incapacity to convince him that he was "unequal to his command." Interestingly enough, however, Davis did not admit to himself or anyone else that he had erred in appointing Twiggs. He did so, he told Moore, because he "yielded much to the solicitation of the people of New Orleans," and now he shifted to them the responsibility for "the mistake they had made." Though customarily Davis protested that he made his military appointments on the basis of merit alone, and with a deaf ear to popular clamor, he was only too happy to blame others when a man like Twiggs proved a failure. The president did not, could not, make a mistake.[9]

Davis also protested the criticism that he ignored New Orleans. He made Lovell a major general on October 7 and immediately assigned him to replace Twiggs. Lovell's first report on inspecting his new command was anything but favorable. The city's defenses depended primarily on large-bore cannon in the forts and batteries guarding the approaches on the Mississippi, yet Lovell had barely more than three tons of powder when he arrived, and half of that he gave to Hollins for use in a very successful attack on the enemy blockading fleet at Head of Passes on October 12. It broke the blockade, but only briefly, and left Lovell with hardly enough powder for his forts to fire more than a few rounds if a Yankee fleet tried to come upriver. He had no trained and properly equipped troops and had to depend on local militia armed with their own shotguns and squirrel rifles. Everything of military utility had been stripped from the city. "It will be a mountain of labor to put things in shape," he told Davis, though he believed that he could hold the city "notwithstanding our deficiencies." Davis soon had good reports of Lovell's energy and enterprise, and unfortunately these only contributed to his belief that fears for New Orleans were exaggerated. Chiding Moore for being an alarmist, the president trusted that "a discriminating public will acquit this Government of having neglected the defenses of your coast, and the approaches to New Orleans." Serenely confident in Forts Jackson and St. Philip downriver, and apparently even more so in Hollins's ability to keep enemy vessels at bay after his little victory, Davis could not believe that New Orleans faced any real threat. If danger did come, it would probably come from upriver, and there he had Johnston to protect him. Thus Davis continued to send new regiments elsewhere and trusted New Orleans to defend itself.[10]

But if Davis seemed unconcerned for the Crescent City, it did not mean that his thoughts did not constantly turn to the region that men then referred to as the West. The border states particularly attracted his concern, especially with the end of Kentucky neutrality. Now that the state was fair game, he must have it. Back in June, Davis complained that "the condition of Kentucky is embarrassing enough." Should the state join the Confederacy, then "our power to repel invasion and *to maintain a long war* would be greatly increased." As a further expression of his confidence in Sidney Johnston, on the day Davis assigned him to command Department

No. 2, he also expanded again its territorial limits to include as much of Kentucky as he could take, along with even the Kansas and Indian Territories. The active courtship of other prominent Kentuckians commenced with vigor. Simon Buckner, formerly commander of the Kentucky State Guard, immediately found himself commissioned a brigadier, and in October, when Breckinridge arrived in Richmond, Davis made him, too, a brigadier, after briefly considering appointing him to the War Department to replace Benjamin, whose posting there was always intended to be temporary. He, like Buckner, and several other fellow Kentuckians, would be most valuable with Johnston.

Indeed, the move to take Kentucky was well under way. A week after his assignment, Johnston advanced into the state to Bowling Green, where he established a major camp for recruiting and training. Buckner, Breckinridge, and others would be powerful persuaders in bringing the state's young men into the army. Meanwhile, Davis undertook to order a subordinate military movement of his own, one that actually encroached on the command of his friend Johnston. The president wanted to send a column from Tennessee into southeastern Kentucky through the Cumberland Gap, and late in October he offered its command to George B. Crittenden, the brother of his old Mexican War friend. A man with an excellent army record, Crittenden resigned as a lieutenant colonel, the same rank held by Lee in the old army, yet the best Davis did for him in the Confederate service was a brigadiership in the provisional forces. Now he wanted him to drive toward the center of Kentucky. Thereafter Crittenden reported to Johnston, but it was Davis who selected the officer and put his mission before him. Perhaps he discussed it with Johnston beforehand; if not, it was a serious breach of the integrity of Johnston's command.[11]

While Kentucky looked uncertain for the Confederacy that fall, Missouri looked far better, and Davis felt real hopes of taking and holding it for the Confederacy. The past May he met with Lieutenant Governor Thomas C. Reynolds to discuss the situation. Even before then Davis had sent a few cannon to Governor Claiborne Jackson to aid in taking the Saint Louis arsenal. A state convention in March declined to pass a secession ordinance, but Jackson, Reynolds, and other sympathizers still hoped to bring the state into the Confederacy, by force if necessary. Rioting in Saint Louis in early May seemed a good start, and Reynolds privately told Davis that "our leading Southern men resolved on immediately throwing the State into a general revolution and trusting to *guerilla* war until you could send us aid." They even hoped that their actions might help propel Kentucky into the Confederacy as well. While Jackson seemed to waver, Reynolds kept alive hope that he could call another convention in the summer, where he felt confident of secession's passage.

Unfortunately, Reynolds and others misread the Missourians. A new convention did meet late in July, and though Southern supporters fought hard in the debate, they saw their inevitable loss before them. The convention deposed Jackson, Reynolds, and the whole legislature, calling for new elections in November. This virtually made exiles of Jackson and others. He and Davis's old friend Atchison were in Richmond visiting the president when the convention acted, and on his return to Missouri on August 5, Jackson issued a rump declaration of independence. Two weeks later the Congress in Richmond went through the sham of admitting Missouri to the new nation, and on December 10 they would do the same for Kentucky, acts that clearly bore no legitimacy since both secessions came without either popular referenda or properly empowered state conventions. It is ironic that Davis, usually so punctilious about the sovereign exercise of the rights of a state, would countenance such irregular actions. But they served his purpose, agreed with his overriding sentiment to have these states with him, and he could rationalize that their extraordinary manner of admission was due to the coercive presence of enemy forces within the states' borders. In short, in special cases he could justify bending his rules.[12]

It looked as if events would justify those acts in Missouri, for quickly the Federals all but abandoned the interior of the state below the Missouri River. Just five days after Jackson's declaration, a small army of Missourians led by Sterling Price and Ben McCulloch met and defeated Federals along Wilson's Creek, near Springfield. Then in September another army of Missourians laid siege to and captured a Federal garrison at Lexington, on the Missouri River. It looked as if the whole state might belong to the new nation before year's end. Confederate sympathizers even managed to gather a group of former legislators into a convention to pass a genuine secession ordinance in October, with another formal admission into the Confederacy the following month.

Then arose the problems and carping that dogged every success of 1861. Complaints came to the president that McCulloch became careless after his victory, and that he resented and interfered with Price's command. Before the end of the year Davis found the command argument right in his lap as Missourians squabbled over who should hold high rank. Reynolds wanted it for himself, while Price and McCulloch detested each other. Price, with the senior commission, won out, but then in October a Yankee advance forced him to abandon Lexington and, soon thereafter, much of the interior of the state as well. At once there came complaints that the government in Richmond was not paying enough attention. Davis protested that he held Missouri as dear as any other star in the Confederate flag. Seeing the discord in Missouri ranks by the hostility between Price and McCulloch, Davis decided to turn once more to a West Point–trained officer, Colonel Henry Heth, now commanding a regiment in western Virginia. He called him to Richmond and asked him, "Young man, how much rank can you stand?" When Heth replied that only the president should judge of that, Davis replied that "I will make you a Major-General and send you to the Trans-Mississippi; Price and McCulloch are fighting each other over there harder than they are fighting the enemy." It was not an unwise move, militarily, for sending a total outsider to command both of the quarreling generals would at least not smack of factionalism. But the new Missouri congressmen in Richmond exploded in protest, and though Davis would have been quite willing to press on in the face of complaint, Heth quickly decided not to take the post. "I have, long since, learned to bear hasty censure in the hope that justice if tardy is sure," Davis asserted in the midst of the uproar, "and in any event find consolation in the assurance that all my ends have been my country's." Nevertheless, though he had not backed down, Davis was thwarted temporarily. Still committed to the idea that only an outside third party could make Price and McCulloch work in harmony, the president sent Van Dorn to command them in January.[13]

Amid these challenges on the northern border of the Confederacy, Davis had also to deal with threats and annoyances in the Deep South. Late that fall he sent Lee to South Carolina to take charge of constructing and strengthening its defenses, and despite an initial prejudice against the Virginian, Governor Pickens seemed to be pleased, complaining now only of what he took to be Lee's "over caution." In late November the Union Navy occupied Port Royal Sound, capturing Forts Walker and Beauregard and promising in time to offer the threat of a land invasion into the South Carolina interior. The governor announced a shortage of everything and dissatisfaction with almost all the other generals assigned to the state and raised anew the widespread lament of inaction on the Potomac line, which freed the enemy to invade South Carolina. Now that the Yankees had a foothold on the Southern coastline, neighboring Georgia chimed in. Georgia had sent away too many regiments and too many arms to be able to defend itself and begged for the return of the ten regiments it had given, especially since Brown and others questioned the constitutionality of the May 11 law that allowed Davis to accept units directly without their having to be raised officially by state authority. When enough independent private companies presented themselves, Davis had simply accepted them, combined them into regiments, and put them into service, along with appointing their officers. To all this, Brown objected. To his objections, Davis gave not an inch.[14]

Amid the aggravation, Davis had to perform a constitutional duty on November 18, when Congress reconvened. He presented a message full of more hope than might reasonably have been expected. In every clash of arms thus far the Confederates had emerged at least the victors, and at worst with no significant loss of territory. Only the falling back from Lexington posed a serious ceding of ground. Seven months into the war, they had new states; manufacturing was growing, turning out munitions of war; the army stood well organized and growing; and the navy, though small and ill-equipped, had enjoyed some limited success. "If we husband our means and make a judicious use of our resources," he advised, "it would be difficult to fix a limit to the period during which we could conduct a war against the adversary whom we now encounter."[15]

Davis now had to turn his attention to matters other than the military conduct of the conflict—matters that faced him all along and to deal with which he had to struggle to rob time from his armies and generals. Somehow the Confederates had to finance their new nation, and the theme for their first efforts was put in place even before the Montgomery delegates elected Davis president. The Alabama legislature made a $500,000 loan to the Confederate Congress on February 8, 1861. Three weeks later, on February 28, Congress authorized another loan of up to $15 million, with the first issue of certificates for one-third of that amount becoming available to private citizens on April 17. How much influence Davis exerted over fund-raising policy is arguable. Direct taxation would have been the preferred method of filling the Tresury, but there was no apparatus in place for assessing or enforcing taxes. Loans offered the only immediate source of hard currency, and Davis seems to have followed Memminger's lead in inaugurating the policy.

It worked well at first. The first day of the offering, an agent reported an enthusiastic response from the people. "With plenty of money, we shall have no difficulty under your good management in whipping the Yankees," he assured. Just three days after the certificates went on sale, Memminger told the president that the $5 million was already oversubscribed, and he got Davis's approval to extend it to $8 million. Interest due to noteholders would be paid from an export duty on cotton. In the wake of the mobilization that followed Fort Sumter, Davis authorized extending the subscription for the balance of the full $15 million, and by October 15 every certificate had been sold. A wonderful response to the government's call for funds, it heartened Davis greatly.[16]

Even before this loan was realized, Congress authorized yet another, a so-called "produce loan," to be subscribed up to $50 million. Some believed that Davis originated the idea, though he gave Congress the credit. Knowing that planters would not have cash in large amounts until after the summer cotton crop came in, this loan provided that they could subscribe a portion of their crops in lieu of cash. When the crop came in, the planter sold that portion pledged to the government, and in return for the proceeds was given twenty-year bonds at 8 percent interest. Response to this loan, too, so encouraged Davis that he believed the summer crop of cotton alone would fulfill the entire $50 million. As a result, in August, Congress authorized yet a third loan, this one for $100 million, accepting produce, hard currency, foreign bills of exchange, and even Confederate Treasury notes. At the same time as the first three loans were mandated, Memminger had secured authorization for the issuance of Confederate paper money, both to raise additional funds and to attempt to establish a uniform currency throughout the Confederate States. By November 1861 more than $17 million had been approved and put in circulation—in effect, promissory notes. The purchaser bought them for hard coin, and the government promised to redeem them after the end of the war. Moreover, the government itself used them as legal tender in payment for the services and supplies it needed, in some cases promising to pay interest at the time of redemption. Important as the original loans were, Treasury notes quickly came to be the predominant means of paying the mounting debts of war.[17]

Not a little of the money went overseas to pay for necessary military supplies not manufactured in the Confederacy. Davis established purchasing agents in several Caribbean ports to which cotton and tobacco could be shipped through the blockade, and selected a commercial house in Liverpool, England, to manage Confederate finances abroad. Much of the specie originally subscribed to the first loans was sent to Europe to buy munitions and arms and to outfit and equip commerce raiders to torment Yankee shipping. As specie became more and more scarce in the late fall of 1861, Davis began to think of negotiating foreign loans, using cotton as security for the credit. Inevitably it had to come to that. "Cotton is our big gun," a friend told Davis that summer, and indeed many regarded it as such, and not just for raising funds, either.[18]

Regardless of having a secretary of state to oversee such matters, Jefferson Davis from the first took a leading hand in the foreign relations of the Confederacy, with but two goals in mind: recognition of the independence of the Confederacy by the major European powers, especially England and France; and financial, material, military, and naval assistance from those powers. Unfortunately, he faced a problem symbolized by Robert Toombs's uneasy wearing of the State mantle. The South had never been a particularly fertile source of good diplomats. When he made his first appointments, Davis showed his own uncertain grasp of what constituted effective diplomacy—not surprising given his own oft-demonstrated lack of diplomatic finesse. On March 16, 1861, though Toombs made the actual appointments, Davis was certainly behind the selection of the awkward triumvirate delegated to the courts of England, France, Spain, Belgium, and Russia.

Granted the dearth of real diplomatic talent in the Confederacy, they were still a poor choice. De facto head of the mission was Yancey, a powerful orator and a distinguished man, who yet bore the stigma of being one of the loudest proponents of slavery, an institution increasingly distasteful to England and France. Accompanying him would be Pierre Rost of Louisiana, whose only qualification seems to have been a good command of French. Only the third member, Ambrose Dudley Mann, had any diplomatic experience, and that was of the minor sort. Yet he displayed an incredible naïveté and an utter inability to judge men and events. Somehow he had become a good friend of Davis, who seemed to repose much confidence in him.[19]

Assigned to approach England first, then France and the other powers, the commissioners took with them what amounted to an article of faith. Since the Industrial Revolution the factories of England and France had become dependent on American cotton to keep their world-encompassing textile industry running and tens of thousands of their citizens employed. A disruption of the millions of bales provided by Southern planters each year would cause economic and social chaos. So important was Confederate cotton to those powers that they would have to recognize the new nation as a matter of self-interest, and should Lincoln's blockade interfere with their needs, then they would inevitably use their powerful navies to break that blockade and bring guns and supplies in exchange for cotton. There was much logic in the argument, but unfortunately it ignored a few vital problems. Recent bumper crops had left something of a surplus of raw cotton in British warehouses, and the development of new sources in Egypt and elsewhere reduced the dependence on the South. Furthermore, English and French opposition to slavery ran deep, deeper than Confederates wanted to countenance. Most of all, France was already militarily overextended by recent military adventuring in Mexico, while England was enjoying an era of unexampled peace and prosperity. War with a powerful United States posed a greater threat than the loss of Southern cotton.

As a result, Yancey, Rost, and Mann had more working against them when they arrived across the Atlantic than they ever realized, before or after. Worse, they divided their efforts. Rost stayed almost exclusively in Paris. Mann took residence in London, and Yancey bounced back and forth between the two capitals. Barely had they arrived before the theatrical Mann lamented that he was alone in London. Immediately the problems that would plague Confederate diplomatic efforts thereafter became evident. Learning that Southern states like Mississippi had repudiated their foreign debts for the duration of the war, some prominent Englishmen opposed granting formal recognition. Then there was slavery. Mann found the British public more strongly opposed to siding with slaveholders than he had expected. Indeed, Englishmen wrote directly to Davis proposing that the Confederacy give up slavery if it wanted British recognition. Davis, of course, rejected the notion out of hand.[20]

But his diplomats did confirm the conviction that cotton offered a key to opening Europe to recognition. From Paris Rost told him that the Europeans' only concerns were getting their hands on cotton and paying for it. He told Frenchmen that there would be millions of bales in Southern ports that fall—all they had to do was come get it, blockade or no blockade. Mann seconded this conviction from London. Davis's old friend Edwin DeLeon, then living in London, believed that the two great nations would not act independently but only together, and that the weaker France looked to Whitheall for leadership. "The pressure on the Cotton Men is great and increasing," he told Davis. "In England they are quaking with terror."[21]

Toombs's resignation boded well for the State Department, though his successor Hunter showed only a little more enthusiasm for the post. Yet by late September, Davis and Hunter both realized that their early hopes for speedy recognition by the great powers would not be realized. Davis may not have questioned or changed his original convictions of the reasons why he expected recognition. Probably he blamed the failure on a combination of Federal diplomatic chicanery and the ineffectuality of the Yancey-Rost-Mann mission. Recognition would require more effort and on a more structured basis. As a result, he decided to send Mann on to Brussels and Rost to Spain. Yancey wanted to resign. In their place he appointed James Mason of Virginia minister to England, and John Slidell of Louisiana to France, as permanent envoys.

Once again Davis showed his own diplomatic naïveté. Removing and replacing his envoys just six months after sending them implied to Europeans a lack of confidence in them—probably quite correct—and suggested something less than harmony in Richmond. It also cost him whatever of experience had been built by sending Mann and Rost to other postings, rather than keeping them in place to work with Mason and Slidell. Then there was the matter of the two new diplomats. Mason was the least diplomatic of men, as Davis should have remembered from seeing him in the old Senate. Domineering and crude in mannerisms, he was another leading proslavery advocate and actually the author of the Fugitive Slave Law of 1850. Slidell, meanwhile, possessed far more polish and finesse and had been an unsuccessful envoy to Mexico for Polk years before. Between the two of them, their appointment said little for their diplomatic skills; it spoke volumes for the want of able potential ambassadors in the Confederacy.[22]

Their appointment also offended Yancey, not so much for his being replaced—since he had resigned anyhow—but for the apparent lack of confidence in his efforts that their coming implied. But then all smaller considerations such as this found themselves overshadowed on November 8, ten days before Davis's message to Congress, when a Yankee warship stopped the British mail steamer *Trent* and seized the two envoys as they traveled to Europe. The resulting diplomatic furor promised at first to work decidedly to Davis's advantage, and he and Confederate publicists played it for all it was worth. Immediate protests reached Washington from London, accompanied by stiff demands for the release of the commissioners. To take them from the deck of a British ship was tantamount to kidnapping them on the streets of London, said Davis.

Unfortunately, Washington wanted war with London no more than the English wanted a conflict with the Union. Within a matter of a few weeks, a face-saving arrangement was worked out whereby Lincoln could return Mason and Slidell to the British without publicly admitting error in their initial seizure. In January 1862 they completed their trip to England to assume their duties, and though publicly jubilant that Lincoln had backed down, privately many Confederate observers lamented the peaceful resolution of the crisis. The furor had brought Britain far closer to making common cause with the Confederacy than any diplomatic efforts ever had, or would, and several saw the end of the so-called "*Trent* affair" with sinking feelings. "Now we must depend upon our own strong arms and stout hearts for defense," wrote John Jones.[23]

The release lay in the future as Davis addressed Congress on November 18, but already the president looked to another diplomatic pretext to win European recognition. "Blockades to be binding must be effectual," an international declaration made at Paris had affirmed some years before. Proclaiming the "utter inefficiency of the proclaimed blockade of our coast," Davis began gathering evidence to show to England and France the number of ships that penetrated Lincoln's slender cordon of blockaders, hoping that this might convince them that the blockade was illegal, and therefore challenge them to declare it void. Another diplomatic crisis might ensue, or at least a concerted attempt by those powers to pass through the blockade with their own vessels to get to the cotton they so badly needed. Unfortunately, not until years after the war would Davis finally realize that with a two-year supply of the staple in their warehouses, England and France did not have to risk the blockaders. With that realization far off, the president could do little but continue in the effort to lure someone, anyone, into granting recognition to the Confederacy.

Even as he gave his message to Congress, Davis found himself the object of increasing attacks on his policies, his decisions, and even his day-to-day work habits. In just the matter of raising volunteers, he could please no one, it seemed. Everyone wanted him to accept units for short terms of service, a year or less. The trouble was, by the time a unit was trained and equipped, much of its year could be gone, and at Manassas, on the eve of battle, the Confederates had come up against the potentially crippling eventuality of units whose time had expired going home just before a battle. Moreover, with arms in perpetually short supply, Davis quite rightly believed that they should be put first in the hands of men who would stay with the armies for three years or the duration of the war. "The enrollment for short terms has great disadvantages which passing events have made manifest," he protested in September. Yet at the same time, Davis also preferred not to accept any volunteers under the age of eighteen, and this, too, caused him to be criticized. "In making soldiers of them," he argued, "we are grinding the seed corn." They would need those young men to be the postwar generation to plant and build.[24]

Always his appointments bought him critics. By January 1862 some complained that he had appointed drunkards and cowards. Reports came to him of Crittenden's intemperance and that of generals in his command. Other officers raised an uproar when not given the promotions they felt they deserved. W. H. T. Walker of Georgia started a bitter controversy that he took to the newspapers when he resigned his brigadiership in pique that others his junior had been elevated to major general. It did not matter to him that Davis was under no mandate to preserve seniority among officers appointed in the Confederate service, only the old Union service. And when Davis transferred Walker from a brigade of Louisianians to a brigade of his own fellow Georgians, Walker saw not a logical move designed to improve the efficiency and elan of the service but only a case of favoritism and nepotism, for in his place Davis assigned his former brother-in-law Richard Taylor. The Charleston *Mercury*, always delighted to fan the fire under the president, complained that "President Davis is the victim of petty jealousies and prejudices of which the South could never have entertained a suspicion." Charging him with "narrow-minded favoritism," the *Mercury* did its best to encourage the slowly rising opposition to Davis in Congress.[25]

Unfortunately Davis did intermittently practice favoritism, though he could never see it. His elevation of Cooper and his convoluted reasoning to keep Sidney Johnston ahead of Lee and the others in seniority attest to this. He always denied being influenced by friendships and former relationships, though usually when dealing with men he did not particularly care for in the first place. To one annoying commission seeker who called upon former favors rendered, Davis replied coldly that he recognized "no 'political relationship' such as before stated." Nevertheless, when Northrop asked for the president's help in finding his nephew a commission on active duty, Davis complied. When a relative of Governor John Ellis of North Carolina asked for a commission, through Mrs. Ellis, Davis recommended him to the secretary of war.

Richard Taylor, with no military training or experience at all, he made a colonel, then a brigadier. And almost every surviving company officer from the First Mississippi Rifles achieved a colonelcy in a Mississippi regiment. He often noted that an applicant was "a personal friend" and as such was "entitled to special consideration." Looking at Taylor, the president's denial of favoritism wears thin, and looking at the relatives of old friends—at Polk and others—his argument that he appointed men well known to him solely because of their military talents and experience dissolves.

Critics also pounced quickly on Davis's immersion in the minutiae of his executive departments, especially the War Office. He passed his good right eye over seemingly every document—passes and transfers, promotions and assignments, complaints of every description, and even minor civil matters. Much he referred to Benjamin, but almost always with a request for inquiry or report, which meant that it all wound up back on his own desk eventually.[26] "Affairs of this sort engrossed his time, his thoughts, and left little for matters that legitimately belonged to his high functions," charged Thomas Jordan. Even allowing for Jordan's prejudice as a member of Beauregard's intimate circle, still the accusation was all too true. Much was directed to the president by mistake, and much more was sent to him by Judah Benjamin, who refused to handle it or feared to. But the greater fault was Davis's, for instead of reforming the inefficiency, he encouraged it. Indeed, despite his protestations of the burden of this work, Davis, ever the bureaucrat, clearly enjoyed it. When his health was good, Varina could hear him when he worked in his second-floor office at home, actually singing while attending to his papers.[27]

Thus, wearing himself out tracking down missing rail cars, lecturing those who questioned him, and gathering material for the campaign against Beauregard, the president fell ill again in September.[28] Yet he still kept his long office hours and could not find repose at home when applicants came to call at any hour from 8 A.M. to 10 P.M., often without notice. Soon a servant insulated Davis by telling unscheduled callers that he was out even when he was not. If met with insistence, the black lost his temper and declared, "I tell you, sir, Marse Jeff 'clines to see you."[29] The birth of another son, William Howell, on December 16, plus the usual concern for Varina's condition, added to his own ill health and exhaustion, made him short tempered and confused. He absentmindedly forgot things said to him repeatedly. He referred two separate propositions for submarines to the War Department instead of the navy. By January 1862 he intemperately complained to Benjamin of the "stupid vaporing" of his generals, and at a New Year's reception, though he looked well and tried to act friendly, some visitors found him distracted and insincere, one calling his forced cordiality "a lie."[30]

The president's immersion in details disturbed his closest advisers. "The amount of attention which he habitually bestowed upon details which are usually devolved upon subordinates" disturbed Mallory especially. Davis "encumbered his table & occupied his time" with "a vast amount of such business," most of which could and should have been left to his bureau chiefs. But such matters, "however minute, rarely failed to command his patient industry."[31]

Davis's office in the Treasury building was small, barely eighteen by twenty-four feet. Visitors allowed in when he rang a bell to summon Josselyn found him working at one of his two tables, his hands full of papers, and probably looking up at the military maps covering the walls. Though his aides used a neighboring room, one or two were usually to be found in his office, especially his close friend and most trusted aide at the moment, Colonel William N. Browne, probably the greatest intellect near the president, despite his ridiculously bulky figure in full colonel's uniform. Davis devoted one hour each morning to receiving visitors, and to those who came to discuss public business he appeared attentive and interested. But the majority of his callers sought some personal favor and, increasingly, Davis could not conceal his impatience from these people. Postmaster General Reagan observed that the president expected visitors to be direct and come straight to the point "and was not at all times patient with such persons as sought to occupy his time in general conversation." Mallory said it even better: "No man could be more chillingly, freezingly cold." When men came without appointments or took his time on personal matters, Davis sometimes kept his eyes on the mountain of papers on the table before him. He said few words, none of them encouraging cordiality, and made such callers feel distinctly uncomfortable and anxious to leave. The only time in such interviews when Mallory saw the president approach a smile was when he saw his visitors leave. And there were those out of favor whom he would not see. One day Josselyn sent in calling cards from Floyd, then Wise, then Milledge L. Bonham. Davis pleaded being too busy to see any of them, then lost his temper. "You know the sort of people that I want to see," said Davis. "All right, sir," replied Josselyn. "Then see that it is all right, and do not bother me any more." The old tendency to profanity reemerged. Josselyn found refuge from such tempers in a not-infrequent glass.[32]

Then there were the frequent interruptions by his cabinet members, most of whom called on him at least once a day. Two or three times a week he gathered them all for a formal meeting that might last up to five hours or more, "far longer than was required," thought Mallory. The problem was that Davis would digress. Time after time he wandered from the subject at hand to what Mallory called "episodical questions." A favorite topic was the Mexican War, about which Davis never tired of reminiscing. It did not help that Davis seemed habitually unpunctual, not only wasting his ministers' time while in cabinet session but also keeping them waiting for meetings to start. Yet they liked the president. "He had two characters," said Reagan, who found him "all gentleness and kindness." Mallory thought Davis "naturally genial & social," despite the more commonly held impression of a cold, aloof man. When with his secretaries, he would light a cigar and sit back to talk of anything that came to mind, relieving frustrations, sharing enthusiasms, simply relaxing in the company of men whom—for the most part—he trusted. At these times the others found him especially engaging, as his conversation revealed the depth of his reading and his wide experience. No topic came to hand but Davis could draw some anecdote from his past or a quotation from literature to punctuate a point. When feeling especially open and free, he revealed a ready sense of humor and sometimes even indulged his old frontier delight in mimicry and imitation.[33]

But it all cost valuable time. Even when he got down to a meaty subject, Davis still frustrated the others by his lawyerlike penchant for dissecting the matter to infinity, just as he had buried himself in details in his senatorial speeches. Here he felt comfortable, deriving a sense of security from taking a subject apart. "His disposition to analyze & exhaust, not only the probable, but the possible arguments of questions under consideration," said Mallory, ran counter to "the just value & economy of time." Yet this trait seemed to work against him when it came time to make a decision. Having studied so many sides of a question, and given his inbred compulsion always to be right, Davis proved slow to reach conclusions. "By all who have ever been associated with him in public affairs," said Mallory, "he is probably known to be singularly cautious, if not dilatory in these respects." Of course, from Davis's point of view, hastiness or rash action did not just risk making a mistake—it courted disaster for the Confederacy.[34]

Yet even Mallory could not fault the care that he saw Davis devote to the preparation of his important state papers and messages to Congress. He made them "singularly pure in style & language," methodical, neither too long nor too brief, and correct and concise in all their parts. Davis began working on such a document a month beforehand, when he brought the cabinet together and spent several hours discussing with them the topics he should cover. This done, the president might devote the next week to drafting the message. Davis found it—or made it—a tortuous process, for in his compulsion for the ultimate in precision, he repeatedly struck out words and rewrote almost every line at least once. Then he gave it to the cabinet again, and they discussed its merits, suggested additions, and even offered criticisms. Then Davis made those revisions he felt necessary, sent the paper to be carefully inscribed by a secretary, and reread it a last time before yet another meeting. Even then more changes might be made, as every word seemed to come under scrutiny, and when one cabinet member or another presented a good case for deleting a line or a paragraph, Davis showed considerable open-mindedness, reverting to yet another reminiscence of his days in Pierce's cabinet. "I agree with Mr. Marcy," he said, "who, in Mr. Pierce's Cabinet was always ready to strike out, because, as he said, you could never be held accountable for what you did not put in."[35]

Yet the ministers had to show some care in how they criticized Davis and what he did. Fortunately, with them at least, the president showed considerable self-control. Whether listening to the announcement of a military loss, or to a disappointing dispatch from his ministers abroad, or even to the increasingly hurtful news that old friends were joining his opposition, he met the news with seemingly perfect calm, only the flush of his face giving away his inner feelings. He kept his voice calm, only sitting a little more erect in his chair, and often simply pressed his lips together as he fought and won the battle with his own temper. Unfortunately, later reflection often persuaded him to action, but never precipitately. The imbroglios with Joseph Johnston and Beauregard presented ample evidence of that. The feuds surprised many in the cabinet, and Mallory personally tried to heal the breach with Johnston, though never with complete success. It did not help that one member of the cabinet, Benjamin, made it his business to feed Davis's resentments. "He never lost an occasion or an opportunity to express his want of confidence in their skill," said Mallory, "& Benjamin's favorite theme was their want of capacity." Though the president did not ordinarily allow the opinions of others to sway his feelings toward men, especially old friends like Polk and Northrop, still by the end of the first year of the Confederacy, Mallory believed that Benjamin had acquired sufficient influence with him that Davis never had an opportunity to judge many men impartially. "Mr. Benjamin's influence, constantly exerted, kept his feelings against them constantly refreshed."[36]

And, of course, having made up his mind about a man or an issue, Davis could not change it, a trait he had recognized in himself. Thomas Watts had seen this at the outset, calling Davis "a man of strong convictions, clear judgment, and deliberate in the formation of his conclusions, and when formed, rarely changed." Reagan saw this, though he chose not to regard it as obstinacy. Davis considered everything, he said. "After doing this and reaching his conclusion the matter was settled with him," said Reagan. "He had not time to reconsider questions upon the same facts." Indeed, Mallory lamented that if Davis "indulged an erroneous estimate it generally continued to govern his actions. . . . It was ever difficult for him to change an opinion."[37]

Nor could he change an old habit, born of instinct and nurtured in public life. As Varina so freely admitted, and as he did himself sometimes, Davis did not possess the arts of the politician. "While he was ever frank & cordial to his friends & those whose conduct he approved," wrote the secretary of the navy, "he would not, &, I think, could not, sacrifice a smile, an inflexion of the voice, or a demonstration of attention to flatter the self love of any who did not stand well in his esteem." He refused to practice the little courtesies and even shams that a great man must use in order to cultivate from others the skills that he needs to use. Barely one hundred miles north in Washington, Abraham Lincoln was revealing himself to be a master of making use of men he did not necessarily like, by subordinating his own feelings to the greater need. In Richmond, another president could not.[38]

Carrying the burden of the war, and often making that weight the heavier by his own habits and temperament, Davis had to seek some escape from his cares. Often he simply walked about the streets of Richmond, some thought "as unconcernedly as if he was on his own plantation," though they could not see what lay within. In a beaver hat and his habitual black or gray suit, he became a familiar sight, especially mounted on his gray mare. In these early days of the war Davis dined around four in the afternoon, riding afterward, and he liked to have a companion. Most often he invited Clement Clay to join him, sometimes quipping that "I think you would be benefitted by a shaking to day." Occasionally his son Jefferson, Jr., came instead, mounted on his own little pony. Stepping out of the Executive Mansion, Davis mounted his mare while a crowd of respectful citizens gathered to watch, lit a cigar, lifted his hat to the onlookers, and trotted off. Often he rode long into the evening out on the country roads surrounding Richmond, and when he returned there might be a late meal and then time alone with Varina and the children. It was not a lot by way of relaxation, considering the pressures on him, but it was all that Davis could take or would allow.[39]

Nor would this burden be lifted from him as he had hoped when he first assumed it at Montgomery. The speedy foreign recognition and Northern acquiescence in secession that he expected to secure the Confederacy a safe place among nations did not come about. The crisis continued. However much he might have hoped to leave office when the permanent government was elected in November 1861 and installed in February 1862, those hopes were to be dashed. Certainly opposition to his administration grew steadily, especially in the doldrums after Manassas. Yet that opposition remained unorganized, and the Confederacy remained essentially a democracy with only one party. Hunter was talked about as a possible successor, and Beauregard had to discourage those seeking to advance his name, but no challenge of any kind ever really emerged, and when the citizens voted for their presidential electors that November, there was never any doubt that they were electing Jefferson

Davis to the six-year term. Indeed, some observers commented on how little notice the whole affair attracted, calling the "public indifference" a manifestation of "the public unanimity."[40]

Three months later a joint committee of Congress officially notified Davis of his election. The ceremony itself came on February 22, Washington's birthday. Davis went to his office early that morning, then returned in a heavy rain to his house to prepare for the inauguration. Varina found him on his knees praying before they went the short distance to the Capitol. Everyone gathered at first in the hall of the House; then the procession moved slowly to the great equestrian statue of Washington on the public square. There, beneath an awning, Davis delivered his address and took his oath of office. He looked pale and emaciated, his face hurt him, and in heart and mind he felt a sense of depression. He might well have agreed with Varina at that moment, when she likened his taking the oath to a "martyrdom." Indeed, as he took the oath his wife found herself consumed by the image of a victim on a funeral pyre, and she quickly got into her carriage and left the ceremonies.[41]

As Davis arose to speak, he looked out not on thousands of faces uplifted to hear his words but at a seeming sea of black umbrellas raised against the rain, hardly a good omen. Through the drizzle and the pattering of the drops on the umbrellas, he made himself heard, weak though he felt. He gave the usual recitation of the wrongs suffered by the South, of their hopes for peace dashed by a vindictive Lincoln, and of their remarkable progress thus far. Yes, they had had to sacrifice much, and more would be demanded of them in the days ahead. Yes, mistakes had been made and surely more would be forthcoming, yet they were holding out, winning victories. Inevitably Europe must come to their aid, he said. Maryland must soon join with them. With confidence, with patriotism, they must inevitably prevail.[42]

Many approved of the address, though it was repetitive, apologetic, and not one of Davis's better efforts. Yet hearers admired his poise and candor. "I like these candid confessions," clerk Jones wrote that day. "They augur a different policy hereafter, and we may hope for better results in the future."[43]

That hope lasted only a few hours before the telegraph wires to Richmond sang with news from the West, and in a cruel irony, a broadside printed with Davis's inaugural address had just enough empty space left at the bottom to carry the latest news. Sidney Johnston's "step" was being heard again. Only this time it was the sound of his army evacuating most of Tennessee, abandoning it to the enemy. Clearly those dark days of sacrifice and testing the president warned of in his address were upon them in earnest.

21

The Drooping Cause
of Our Country

Matters seemed to go wrong with Department No. 2 almost from the first. Johnston arrived to find his resources far less than he expected or needed. Once he took Bowling Green, he told Davis that his force needed to be at least doubled if he was to have a chance of holding his position in Kentucky. In short, he overextended himself, taking a gamble that he could raise enough recruits and receive enough reinforcements to keep his ground before the enemy mounted an offensive against him. It was a very great risk indeed, for Bowling Green represented the center of Johnston's whole defensive line established to protect Tennessee and the Mississippi. He anchored that line on his far right at the Cumberland Gap, with a small army led by Felix Zollicoffer, to which Davis soon sent Crittenden to take overall command. On the far left, Johnston's line rested on the Mississippi at Columbus, where Polk commanded and to which, in January, Davis happily sent the troublesome Beauregard, who begged for reassignment away from the inactivity in northern Virginia. Perhaps Davis felt that placing the Creole under the majestic Johnston would give him an example to emulate and at the same time relieve the president of his carping and of the widespread advocacy he enjoyed in the Eastern press.[1]

Essential to Johnston's line was the protection of the Tennessee River and, now that he was advanced into Kentucky, the Cumberland as well. If the Yankees got possession of them, their gunboats could steam upriver in his rear and cut him off in Kentucky via the Cumberland and in Tennessee via its namesake stream. To stop a Yankee advance, powerful earthworks had been commenced the previous summer at the

395

point where each river crossed from Kentucky into Tennessee. Fort Henry on the Tennessee was not advantageously situated and did not progress well, remaining unfinished as the winter wore on. Fort Donelson on the Cumberland enjoyed far better placement. If enough time allowed for them to be completed and armed, Johnston might hope to stop the enemy, but he realized that the forts were not in the best positions and were vulnerable both to land and naval attack.

Davis offered what aid he could send from Richmond, though it was not enough. To Johnston's repeated entreaties for more men, Davis could spare only a few. When the general said he needed thirty thousand arms, the president could send only one thousand. When Johnston tried to raise troops himself from Tennessee, Mississippi, and Arkansas, Benjamin told him to stop because it violated regulations. Worst of all, Kentuckians did not flock to the banners. No more than a few regiments were formed at Bowling Green.

Frustrated with Benjamin and uncertain that his friend Davis truly appreciated the magnitude of the problems faced in this department, Johnston sent an aide to see the president. Colonel St. John R. Liddell found Davis at home on January 14 while snow blanketed Richmond. He handed him a letter from Johnston and then watched as the president read his friend's plea for troops to be stripped from other unthreatened areas—even from Virginia, Charleston, and Pensacola, not to mention New Orleans. To Davis it sounded not unlike the same impractical plea for concentration that he had rejected at Centreville the prior October. His chagrin showed on his face. Liddell, who already thought Davis careworn and troubled, looked across the table and in the light from a lamp suspended above saw the president's features contract "as if from pain or, perhaps, anger."

"*My God!*" Davis erupted. "Why did General Johnston send you to me for arms and reinforcements, when he must know that I have neither?" Surely there were men enough in Tennessee, even if armed only with shotguns or even pikes, he argued. Liddell tried to calm him and defend Johnston, but Davis asked, "Where am I to get arms and men?" When Liddell suggested that the army at Manassas was not occupied, Davis flared up again, reminded that Virginians already criticized him sharply for sending Floyd and his brigade to Johnston. When Liddell suggested Charleston and Pensacola, the president "petulantly" interrupted him. Over and over again, Davis exclaimed "My God!" and "Why repeat?" protesting that he had heard similar suggestions from others. He could not satisfy them and he could not now satisfy Johnston, though certainly his outbursts revealed frustration that to Johnston, of all generals, he had to say nay.

Forcefully Liddell argued Johnston's desire for concentration of all available forces in Kentucky and Virginia, the two danger zones, in order that they might attack rather than try to hold inferior forces all along the northern border waiting for the enemy to choose the place and time of attack. Davis did not argue the wisdom of the course and even hinted that he already entertained ideas of mounting offensives but that the time was not yet right. Liddell formed the distinct impression that Davis was not entirely comfortable with his own views and even less inclined to accept those of others, another sign of the indecision that Mallory so lamented. When Davis invited Liddell to come for dinner, the colonel accepted, and late that evening he was surprised to find a completely different man as his host. Cordial, genial, Davis spoke long and warmly of earlier days, of friends they had in common, of West Point and the frontier. As was his wont, he would not discuss business over dinner, turning aside the conversation whenever Liddell tried to return to Johnston. Only at the end of the evening, as he helped Liddell with his overcoat and took him to the door, did Davis say to him, "Tell my friend, General Johnston, that I can do nothing for him; that he must rely upon his own resources." "May God bless you," said the president, as he saw Liddell back out into the cold.[2]

Before long the enemy began to move against Johnston's overextended line. A minor battle at Belmont, Missouri, opposite Columbus the previous November had changed nothing. But then on January 18, 1862, the forces of Crittenden and Zollicoffer met a defeat near Mill Springs, Kentucky, and were driven back to the Cumberland Gap, itself now threatened by the Yankees. The right anchor of Johnston's line was bent and perhaps about to break. Frantically he asked Richmond again for reinforcements. All Davis could send were two brigades from Virginia, and Beauregard, along with some suggestions for subdistrict organization within the department—the last thing Johnston needed just then.[3]

It only got worse. In February, Brigadier General U. S. Grant, commanding Union forces in and around Paducah, began a combined army-navy move up the Tennessee toward Fort Henry. Ill-prepared and undermanned, Fort Henry fell to him easily on February 7, before his land forces even got into the fight. Immediately he put them on the move for Fort Donelson, just ten miles away. Perhaps Davis now had cause—if he were willing to reflect on it—to regret making Polk a major general and persuading him not to resign the same day that Fort Henry fell. The previous summer the construction of those forts had been his responsibility, and though neither Johnston nor Davis would criticize an old friend, still Johnston at least was not pleased with the progress on the forts when he took command. The fall of Fort Henry cannot be blamed entirely on Polk, but he was certainly a contributor.[4]

During the week after the bad news reached Richmond, tension in the Executive Mansion mounted over the fate of Fort Donelson. Still, when Davis learned that Johnston's son William Preston was then in the city, sick, he called on him and showed him special attentions. For his part, the younger Johnston felt awe in the presence of his father's old friend. "He is a very great man," the invalid told his wife. "The labor he performs is incredible." "No scheme is too broad, no detail too minute for his ready apprehension." It was the beginning of a very close association that would last for the rest of the war, made even more intimate by events unforeseen but all too soon to come.[5]

Another blow fell on February 16 when Fort Donelson surrendered. Johnston had been able to do nothing to stop Grant. Worse, the ranking commanders in the fort, Floyd and Pillow, showed themselves cowards and abandoned their men, leaving Buckner in command to go through the humiliating ceremonies. For Johnston it spelled disaster. After talking with Beauregard, he concluded that his whole advance line in Kentucky would have to be abandoned, including Columbus and Bowling Green. Otherwise he risked being flanked via the Cumberland Gap and having his rear threatened by Grant's gunboats on the two rivers. He would pull out of Kentucky and all the way out of western Tennessee and into northern Alabama and Mississippi, abandoning one state and most of another. Worse, he lost a fourth of his army with the surrender of Fort Donelson.

The news hit Davis like an earthquake. "Inform me of your condition & plans," the president frantically wired to Johnston, and the general almost immediately sent an officer to Richmond with a confidential dispatch. Before the messenger could arrive, however, Davis got the news late on February 22 that Nashville was being abandoned, probably his first hint of the extent of Johnston's withdrawal. Incredibly, he remained calm, giving no sign at his inaugural levee that evening of what he felt.[6] But the storm broke on him almost immediately afterward. From every quarter in Tennessee came protests that the people had lost confidence in Johnston and Polk, soon followed by similar clamor from Mississippi and Louisiana. They wanted even Johnston's subordinate Hardee replaced, and the population generally seemed to demand a clean sweep of all the commanders in the department except Beauregard. But as one man, all the protesters urged Davis himself to come and assume supreme command.[7]

In fact, as soon as he heard of the loss of Fort Donelson, Davis's first instinct was to go immediately, not to take command but to work to reassure the people of the West. He did not believe that "I could materially aid the able commanders in Tenn.," he protested, and when the Tennessee congressional delegation in Richmond called on him on March 8 to remove Johnston, saying he was "no general," the president responded that if Johnston was not a general, "we had better give up the war, for we have no general." He still wanted to go to the army to do what he could, but he reassured them that "much has been done and is doing to repel the enemy."[8]

Part of the reason Davis could not leave immediately was the same that had kept him from reaching Manassas in time for the battle. On February 25 he had to deliver a message to the newly convened first session of the First Confederate Congress. While he may have begun work on it a month earlier, the events of the previous two weeks forced him to revise his first draft radically. There was no way to gloss over the disaster in the West. Thus he opened with an uncharacteristic admission of error: "Events have demonstrated that the Government had attempted more than it had power successfully to achieve," he declared. By trying to protect every inch of Confederate soil, they spread themselves too thin, allowing the enemy to penetrate their borders in Tennessee and on the Atlantic coast. Having said that, he passed quickly to his pet grievance of the moment, short-term enlistments, even suggesting that that policy bore much of the blame for their recent reverses. He had warned of this, he said, but to no avail. Fortunately, almost all the new regiments now coming into service were committed to longer periods. Fortunately, too, efforts at building a navy were on the way to yielding some success. Yet throughout the brief address—one of his shortest—that refrain of defiant optimism he had sounded so often before was not to be heard. Davis was shaken.[9]

Soon an aide from Johnston brought more details on the loss of the forts, and on the behavior of Floyd and Pillow, and later each of the two cowardly generals would visit Davis to plead his case and blame everything on the other. The president found both men unsatisfactory. In fact, Davis summarily removed Floyd, whom he had never liked, the senior commander, on March 11, and the Virginian never held command again. Though he did not trust Pillow, still Davis seemed willing to forgive. Perhaps his influence in Tennessee, a state already furious with Davis, was too great to flaunt. The president removed him from command for six months, but the old politico would reemerge later in the war to show his white feather again. Seeing Davis's discomfiture over these men who let him down, William Preston Johnston observed that "the President must submit like other men to the touchstone of greatness—*success*."[10]

Others having failed him so badly, Davis needed success now from Johnston more than ever. In his first experience at coping with a major defeat, Davis showed his patience and self-command. He did not despond. He told Johnston of the criticism against him and told how his old friend "made for you such defense as friendship prompted, and many years of acquaintance justified." There was exaggeration everywhere—in the press, in the public mind, and especially on the part of friends of Floyd and Pillow. All the outcry had "undermined public confidence and damaged our cause," said the president. He begged Johnston to send him full information so that he could mount an effective defense before the people. At the same time, he planned to come to the department himself as soon as possible, not to take command, but to work to arouse the populace and enlist men to their banners. Meanwhile, now that it was too late, Davis did what Johnston had asked in January—he sent him Bragg and reinforcements from Pensacola and ordered newly commissioned Major General Edmund Kirby Smith and the small command he raised in eastern Tennessee to cooperate with Johnston. Furthermore, he hoped soon to have a small "fleet" of converted commercial steamboats ready to assist in protecting the rivers. He even suggested that Johnston might consider using the fleet to strike up the Mississippi to Cairo if the Yankees moved too far away from their base there, but Davis would not interfere more than that in the strategic planning of his commander on the scene.[11]

Other repercussions closer to Richmond manifested themselves while Johnston frantically tried to regain his footing. For one thing, on March 14 Davis vetoed a congressional act to create the position of commanding general of the Army. Cooper, of course, was senior officer, but he played no role in field planning and operations. The position mandated by Congress provided that Davis should appoint the officer in question and that this commanding general should customarily function in Richmond to control all military operations, even taking the field himself when he saw fit. In vetoing the act, Davis professed agreement with the idea of having a single military head at Richmond to direct all these affairs, but then he leaped ahead to wholly unwarrantable conclusions as to that general's taking the field, asserting that such an officer could take the field and take command of any army or armies he chose, with or without Davis's consent. The result, he said, would be to negate the president's constitutional power as commander in chief to assign army commanders himself. The argument was painfully thin, for the act specifically said that all the commanding general's acts should be "under the direction of the President." Nothing in the bill gave the commander any unilateral powers to act against the chief executive's wishes. The unspoken reason for Davis's veto lay elsewhere, partly in his conviction that his own military judgment surpassed that of most others and perhaps more so in the matter of whom he could appoint if he approved the post. Sidney Johnston, of course, would be his first choice, but at that moment this general was one of the least popular men in the Confederacy. That left the untried Lee next in line, and should Davis pass him over, he would have to select Johnston or Beauregard, hardly attractive alternatives. The only way to avoid the problem was to veto the act, perhaps waiting until later, when his old friend out west had vindicated himself in battle and his appointment would not start an uproar.[12]

Probably the earliest likeness of Jefferson Davis, taken from a portrait made in 1839 or 1840, when he was still a reclusive planter at Brierfield. (Southern Historical Collection, University of North Carolina, Chapel Hill)

Perhaps the greatest influence on Davis's life was his brother, Joseph E. Davis, a remarkable man in his own right. (Museum of the Confederacy, Richmond, Virginia)

An early portrait of Jefferson and Varina Howell Davis, from a daguerreotype made about 1849. Varina's subdued expression is belied by the independent spirit that drove Davis to leave her at least once. (Library of Congress, Washington, D.C.)

Jefferson Davis knew this view well, looking toward the garden cottage at Hurricane, the ground he daily rode with his brother during his years of solitude. (Mississippi Department of Archives & History, Jackson)

DAVIS BEND

Some of the Davis slaves, Joseph's and Jefferson's, stand beside the garden cottage at Hurricane for a photographer in 1865. Though now free, some would remain on the plantation for years, eventually owning much of it. (Mississippi Department of Archives & History, Jackson)

Secretary of War Jefferson Davis posed during his tenure for one of his favorites, Montgomery C. Meigs, builder of much of the extension of the Capitol, and amateur photographer. (Library of Congress, Washington, D.C.)

Varina Howell Davis, photographed around 1860. Her plumpness and dark features led many of Richmond's society dames to ridicule her, but she was perhaps the most remarkable of them all. (Museum of the Confederacy, Richmond, Virginia)

THE MAN AND THE HOUR MEET

At one o'clock on the afternoon of February 18, 1861, Montgomery, Alabama, photographer A. C. McIntyre focused his camera on the front portico of the Alabama State House to capture the inauguration of Jefferson Davis as president of the Confederate States of America. (National Archives, Washington, D.C.)

President Davis, probably about 1862, his features already showing the strain of his abominable health, his sleeplessness, and the weight of his office. But there is still a fire in his good right eye. (National Archives, Washington, D.C.)

William Browne, whose wit and Irish brogue amused Varina. (Library of Congress, Washington, D.C.)

G. W. C. Lee was courtly enough but showed no interest in Margaret Howell, and he opened Varina's mail. (Museum of the Confederacy, Richmond, Virginia)

DAVIS'S OFFICIAL FAMILY

Joseph Ives was too much a dandy for some, too snoopy for Varina, and too dissipated for presidential decorum. He was also a New Yorker. (T. C. DeLeon, Belles, Beaux, and Brains of the Confederacy)

The president's nephew Joseph R. Davis was a good aide but a liability when Davis made him a general and was accused of nepotism. (Museum of the Confederacy, Richmond, Virginia)

James Chesnut of South Carolina is best known for being married to the South's greatest diarist. His connections with Beauregard kept Davis from entrusting too much to him. (Museum of the Confederacy, Richmond, Virginia)

Francis Lubbock of Texas was the last aide appointed, used mostly to monitor affairs west of the Mississippi. (Museum of the Confederacy, Richmond, Virginia)

Davis's nephew by marriage, John Taylor Wood, brought a piratical dash to the Executive Mansion and the president a loyal friend during the last dark days of the Confederacy. (Chicago Historical Society)

Davis's clear favorite was Colonel William Preston Johnston, son of his beloved friend and a constant companion on his daily rides. (Museum of the Confederacy, Richmond, Virginia)

POWERFUL ENEMIES

Joseph E. Brown symbolized the problems that Davis was to have with many of his governors, only Brown made matters worse. A born controversialist, he relished argument for its own sake. (Library of Congress, Washington, D.C.)

Louis T. Wigfall, onetime friend, a man who instinctively lashed out at any who opposed him, became a bitter foe. (Texas State Archives, Austin)

P. G. T. Beauregard, the earliest of Davis's military enemies in his own camp, was in a passive way the most damaging. Davis's aversion to Beauregard dominated much of his command thinking for the war. (Library of Congress, Washington, D.C.)

Davis's hatred of Beauregard forced him to turn again and again to his other worst enemy in the high command, Joseph E. Johnston, a man constitutionally unsuited for high responsibility and a controversialist in his own right. (William A. Turner Collection)

POWERFUL FRIENDS

Braxton Bragg, loyal to Davis to the end, received nothing but loyalty in return, thereby tying Davis's fortunes and those of the South to this ill-starred commander. (U.S. Army Military History Institute, Carlisle, Pennsylvania)

Judah P. Benjamin, controversial from the first, became Davis's most trusted confidant in his cabinet. Nothing could shake the president's confidence in this born diplomat. (Museum of the Confederacy, Richmond, Virginia)

The most dependable friend of all, General Robert E. Lee. Rarely did such an excellent political-military team emerge in any conflict, in any era. (University of Texas, Austin)

Secretary of War John C. Breckinridge, first a general, became Davis's chief confidant in the last months of the war. He effectively took over management of the escape from Richmond and the government itself, gently maneuvering Davis toward surrender. (U.S. Army Military History Institute, Carlisle, Pennsylvania)

Capitol Square in Richmond in 1865. Davis's daily walks to his office often took him past the statue of Washington, whom he tried so hard to emulate. (William A. Turner Collection)

The old Brockenbrough house on East Clay Street became the Executive Mansion of the new Confederacy. It was the scene of gaiety, comradeship, and tragedy, and would ever after be linked with Jefferson Davis. (William A. Turner Collection)

The British artist Frank
Vizetelly accompanied Davis
and the fleeing government
after the fall of Richmond
and caught the proud, up-
right bearing of the president,
mounted second from left,
and his cabinet. (Civil War
Times Illustrated Collection,
Harrisburg, Pennsylvania)

The president's own cos-
tume during the flight of
the government later be-
came a topic of considerable
speculation. He posed in it
afterward, his usual suit of
Confederate gray. He was
still ever the erect cavalryman. (T. C. DeLeon, *Belles,
Beaux, and Brains of the
Confederacy*)

Davis's attempt to elude his pursuers and reach the Trans-Mississippi came to an end near Irwinville, Georgia, on May 10, 1865. Beside this thicket the Federals surrounded and captured him. (Louisiana Historical Association Collection, Tulane University, New Orleans)

Days after his capture, Davis and Varina were brought into Macon, Georgia, in this ambulance, surrounded by an often rude and hostile escort. (Library of Congress, Washington, D.C.)

THE LATER YEARS

After his release from prison in 1867, Davis went to Montreal. He still stood ramrod straight despite the hardships of the past seven years. (Museum of the Confederacy, Richmond, Virginia)

Reunited with Varina, he would spend more than twenty years trying to rebuild his fortunes and his reputation. (Museum of the Confederacy, Richmond, Virginia)

Even in old age, he remained a fiery combatant, unyielding and uncompromising to the end. (South Carolina Confederate Relic Room and Museum, Columbia)

Finally he put his own story on the record with his books, written largely in this study at Beauvoir. Much of Confederate history—and myth—was created here. (Library of Congress, Washington, D.C.)

In his last years, Davis stands on the tranquil steps of Beauvoir, the one home where he finally found a measure of peace and stability after a life of changes, challenges, and tragedies. (Louisiana Historical Association Collection, Tulane University, New Orleans)

PEACE AT LAST

In Confederate gray to the end, Jefferson Davis achieved after his death a measure of beloved admiration that he seldom knew when alive. (South Carolina Relic Room and Museum, Columbia)

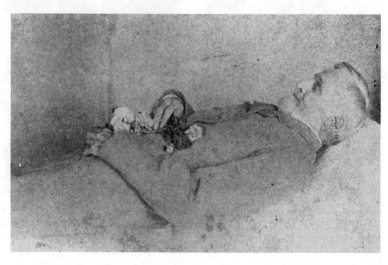

While waiting to see what Johnston would do, Davis confronted other challenges and showed a gradual hardening of his attitude toward the necessities of war. Faced with the infestation of the mountains of western Virginia by Yankees, he pronounced "worthy of attention" a scheme to inaugurate guerrilla bands to hunt down and kill the foe. Moreover, in response to the fear of civil unrest and the outspoken Unionism in some quarters, and the imminent threat of enemy attacks in others, he began to impose martial law on a spot-by-spot basis and frequently at the request of local Confederate authorities. At Fredericksburg, Virginia, on the Rappahannock, as Federals threatened northern Virginia; in southwestern Virginia, where toryism ran rampant; at Mobile, Alabama; in the lower river parishes around New Orleans; in parts of North Carolina; and even in Richmond, he put the military in charge of maintaining order. Yet Davis did not show himself to be overzealous in the application of martial law, sometimes declining requests for its imposition when he did not see sufficient justification. Nevertheless, accusations of usurpation and tyranny were not long in coming from pulpit, platform, and press.[13]

Indeed, the press itself was increasingly on Davis's mind, in direct proportion to the growing intensity of attacks on himself and his administration. Of course, he could always count on sheets like the *Mercury* and some of the old Vicksburg papers that had always opposed him to be critical. But the long idleness after Manassas, followed by the reverses in the West, gave rise to a whole new generation of hostile editors. Davis never devoted any energy to cultivating a friendly press—an action foreign to his nature. In the very early days of the conflict rumors circulated that he enjoyed some special relationship with the Richmond *Enquirer*, even to the point of personally writing some of its editorials, which of course was nonsense. Though the president did at least edit some of Jones's articles for the papers, beyond that he did little if anything, and appears never to have allowed himself to be cultivated by any of the Richmond correspondents sent to the capital by dozens of newspapers throughout the country.

Worse, Davis should have at least been at pains to enjoy good relations with the major Richmond dailies, for their stories were broadcast throughout the whole Confederacy. But though the *Enquirer* stood by him, the rival *Examiner*, under the editorship of John M. Daniel, gradually became one of his most outspoken opponents. It termed his inaugural so insignificant that the day's ceremonies would have been better off without the speech. It called his cabinet secretaries "mere clerks" and charged Davis himself with responsibility for much of their predicament in the spring of 1862. When nothing happened in Virginia after the Manassas victory, Daniel proclaimed that "the Confederacy has had everything that was required for success but one, . . . namely, *talent*."

Davis showed "puerile partiality" in his appointments. "We must get more talent in that Confederate Government or be ruined." Commenting on the proposal for a commanding general, Daniel said frankly that what they needed was not "more officers, but more brains." When Davis reorganized his cabinet late in March, largely in response to popular clamor against Benjamin and as a result of Hunter's resignation, Daniel condemned the changes as a sham. With one exception, all the players were the same, though he conceded that now the administration had a chance of making a name for itself, since any little success in a government from which the people expected nothing "will be a clear gain."[14]

In response to attacks like the one in the *Examiner*, one ardent Confederate urged that Davis suppress the paper for treason. In fact, the several executive departments were very sparing with what they released to the press, but Davis never seems to have considered imposing anything more than censorship of military information, allowing the editors to rant as they pleased. Perhaps he understood the uproar that would inevitably follow any attempt to stifle criticism, yet he left a potent enemy in his rear, one that gained strength as the war progressed.[15]

Indeed, the outcry against Benjamin as a result of the Beauregard inbroglio and especially the loss of Roanoke Island, North Carolina, and Forts Henry and Donelson, all in February, impelled Davis to yield to popular pressure, which he rarely did either before or after. Yet he showed his independence by not removing Benjamin from the cabinet entirely. Hunter's resignation to take a seat in the Senate conveniently left State vacant, and late in March Davis gave his friend and confidant that portfolio. To assume the War Department, he summoned Brigadier General George W. Randolph, a Virginian—which the cabinet needed— and a military figure of small but favorable local reputation. There were rumblings in the War Department that Benjamin lay behind Randolph's selection, hoping that, though out of office, he could influence and manipulate the new secretary. If such were his hopes, he was destined to be disappointed.[16] No secretary of war came into office at a more critical time.

Late in February and through March, Johnston consolidated what troops were available to him in and around Corinth, Mississippi, with Davis's approval. Indeed, late in March the president reassured his general, "My confidence in you has never wavered." Moreover, Davis said he breathed easier now that Johnston had concentrated all his strength, along with the reinforcements that Richmond ordered to him. Johnston advised him that two columns of Yankees, one under Grant, and the other led by Don C. Buell, were advancing toward him. Grant was moving down the Tennessee toward Pittsburg Landing, almost at the Mississippi border, while Buell was some distance away at Nashville, intending to join Grant. Johnston apprised Davis of the opportunity thus presented to attack Grant before Buell reached him and then turn to meet and defeat the Nashville column. Davis told his old friend confidently that if this plan worked, "The future will be brighter." If Johnston failed, then they could only hope for a mass civilian uprising to aid them in repelling the combined enemy forces in their advance on Corinth.[17]

Davis still hoped to be with Johnston for the coming battle. As late as March 26 he wrote to the general promising to come if he could. A few days later the president received from Van Dorn an urging that he should "be with us in the Great Battle of Corinth," though, ironically, Van Dorn himself would not be there. Even though Johnston was his superior and Van Dorn's command in Arkansas clearly fell under Johnston's jurisdiction, the Mississippian refused to heed an order to bring his forces across the river to Corinth for the concentration. Instead he launched his own campaign, designed to clear the enemy out of Arkansas and then march on for Saint Louis and the recovery of Missouri. Whether Johnston approved the plan is uncertain, but Van Dorn met with a sharp defeat at Pea Ridge on March 6–8—a repulse that would keep the Confederates out of Missouri for more than two years and seriously threaten Johnston's far left flank beyond the Mississippi. Worse, when Johnston ordered Van Dorn to him after the defeat as part of the concentration at Corinth, again the irresponsible general failed to comply.

Finally Johnston set his plan in motion. Beauregard would be his second in command, as he had been to another Johnston at Manassas. He divided his army into four corps, commanded by Polk, Bragg, Hardee, and Breckinridge, and on April 2 ordered them to advance. He intended to make a surprise attack on Grant at Pittsburg Landing, on the ground that surrounded Shiloh Church. If he struck quickly enough, he could bag Grant before Buell arrived and then crush the latter as well.[18]

Davis entirely supported Johnston's offensive strategy. It was one of those cases in his "offensive-defensive" concept of what was achievable for the Confederacy when an opportunity presented itself. Having approved the general's plans, and once advised that the campaign was under way, Davis could do little more. Johnston send him word when he could. On April 5 the president read a telegram announcing that the army, forty thousand strong, pressed forward. Buell was known to be nearing Pittsburg Landing, but "hope engagement before Buell can form junction." Davis responded immediately that he hoped the battle could be fought and won before the enemy columns united, adding, "I anticipate victory." That evening, a Saturday, the president and his family entertained at dinner a distinguished visitor, Camille Armand Jules Marie, prince de Polignac, a French nobleman now serving as a lieutenant colonel in the Confederate forces. He would be leaving in five days to take his place on Beauregard's staff, and undoubtedly Davis and the prince discussed the situation then unfolding in Johnston's department, the imminent battle, and the future defense of the Mississippi.[19]

Perhaps on Sunday some fleeting word came to Richmond that a battle was being fought out in the West. Varina could see that her husband felt keenly anxious for news, and as the day wore on he became more and more concerned, even depressed. "I know Johnston," he supposedly told her, "and if he is alive either good or bad news would have been communicated at once." Perhaps the president overlooked the fact that Johnston was on the move and might not be near enough to a telegraph line to send word of events. But the next morning came a telegram from Colonel William Preston, Johnston's brother-in-law. The general was dead.[20]

All through that day Davis tried not to credit the first report. "Victory however great cannot cheer me in the face of such a loss, and God grant that it may not be true and that he yet lives." All that sustained Davis during the anxious hours of waiting were the initial reports that Grant had been driven back. But then came definitive word, not from Johnston, but from Beauregard as second in command, and that confirmed it. Johnston bled to death the day before from a minor wound. When he got the news, Jefferson Davis broke down and wept.[21]

He had lost his best friend, he told those around him. "The cause could have spared a whole State better than that great soldier," he cried. The blow was made the worse by subsequent word that it was not a victory after all. On the first day's fighting, despite Johnston's death, the Confederates had pushed Grant back to the Tennessee. But that evening Buell arrived, and when Beauregard, now commanding, tried to renew the offensive the next morning, he met stiff resistance and decided to withdraw, leaving the surprised and battered Yankees in uncontested possession of the field. By nightfall of April 7 the Confederate army was in retreat back to Corinth.[22]

Once again the criticism poured forth, the old complaints against Johnston renewed. Now Davis did not just have to explain away another defeat, he also had to defend the memory of the friend he loved more than any other. It did not help that Johnston had not fought a good battle or that his conduct of the concentration and the resulting campaign had been loose and at times almost cavalier. Indeed, he probably died only because he unwisely ignored his wound and let his lifeblood flow into his boot and out on the ground. Latter-day "sofa generals" began asking if there had ever been any real justification for all the confidence placed in Johnston in the first place, and though everyone in the Confederacy had clamored for him a year before, now most critics seemed only to remember that he had been Davis's special friend and that it was the president who had appointed him.

Davis had to put the best face on the situation. Striving for heroes, he gave a round of promotions, making Breckinridge a major general and appointing Bragg to the rank of full general in the regular army, filling the gap created by Johnston's death, though Bragg would be junior in seniority to Beauregard. A few weeks later, as a bitter reminder of his loss, Davis received a lock of Johnston's hair, and then early in May he offered Johnston's son William a position as one of his aides. He already had three by then—Joseph Davis, young Lee, and Colonel William Browne. But young Johnston brought something special to Davis's official family—the last remaining tangible presence of his dead father. It was obvious to young Johnston, a month after Shiloh, just how great a toll the general's death had taken. "I felt an emotion stranger when I saw him," Johnston said of his meeting with Davis, "than I have felt since Shiloh, after the first shock." Others also saw the "thin and haggard" look of the president in those days.[23]

Before long, that look became one of grim determination. Still stinging from the controversy over his Manassas report and its long delay, Beauregard, as senior general, filed a report on the Shiloh campaign on April 11, just four days after the close of the fighting. In the entire document Beauregard mentioned Johnston a scant four times, making it sound as if he had been entirely peripheral to the campaign and battle. Worse, a strong argument began to emerge that Beauregard had lost his nerve. The night before the opening of the fight he wanted to cancel the advance, but Johnston refused. After Johnston fell, when the Creole assumed command, he called off the advance, even though at that point the Confederates had Grant pinned against the banks of the Tennessee River and by a desperate effort might have inflicted a disaster on the foe before Buell arrived later that evening.[24]

If any patience for or confidence in Beauregard still remained in Davis, this eradicated it forever. Defeat was bad enough, but to deny his friend's preeminent part in the battle that cost his life was unforgivable. Young Johnston's presence added to the president's hostility, for the son resented the slight to his father every bit as much as Davis did, and he fed Davis's prejudice. "That Newspaper Idol," Johnston called the hero of Manassas. "Beauregard is a vain creature and a little Frenchman," he went on. "He is moreover a newspaper hero and a humbug." The final insult came when rumors filtered back to Richmond that Beauregard was actually speaking critically of Johnston and averring that he himself had planned the whole campaign—as indeed he had exerted much influence in its conception.[25]

Davis was livid. He denied any scenario that did not have Johnston, as he said, "fighting the battle as he intended." When Preston sent William Preston Johnston a letter on the campaign, the aide read it aloud to the president to pass on its criticism of Beauregard and its vindication of General Johnston. Davis at once involved himself in yet another controversy over credit by requesting that Preston write directly to him and send along a copy of his own report on the campaign and battle. Publication of the report should settle Beauregard and do it in his own favorite medium, the press. Meanwhile Davis ordered Preston Johnston to go to Corinth on a tour of inspection of the Western army and to report its condition directly to him. It was, of course, a perfect invitation for a biased and critical evaluation, but for Davis the matter of Beauregard had passed beyond prejudice. On that man his mind was made up and would not—could not—change.[26]

The word from young Johnston, naturally, proved to be gloomy. "I fear Beauregard has thrown away the campaign in the West," he told his wife, and his report to Davis proved much the same, though more temperately stated. Indeed, the instructions given Johnston by the president almost begged for a critical report. He sent a set of specific questions that he wanted answered by the general. Late in May, Beauregard decided to evacuate Corinth, Mississippi, in the face of a powerful but sluggish Federal army that showed little inclination to attack. He pulled fifty miles south to Tupelo, in the process abandoning the Confederacy's rail link to Memphis, and thereby Memphis itself, along with forts on the Tennessee side of the Mississippi. Now the president demanded to know why, and why he had not built defenses around Corinth instead. Why had there been no offensive against the Federals' extended line of communications, and why, when Confederate gunboats were available, had Yankee vessels been allowed to steam south to take the city? In addition to this information from Beauregard, Davis instructed Johnston to inspect the care, condition, organization, and administration of the Army of the Mississippi, as Johnston's father had designated it.[27]

Davis's own conclusions on Beauregard were already formed before he sent his inspector. He was looking for confirmation, not information. On June 3 he had snidely referred to troops "lying in camp when not retreating under Beauregard." "It is hard to see incompetence losing opportunity and wasting hard gotten means," he said, "but harder still to bear is the knowledge that there is no available remedy." The day before he sent Johnston to the West, the president told Varina in speaking of the general that "there are those who can only walk a log when it is near to the ground, and I fear he has been placed too high for his mental strength, as he does not exhibit the ability manifested on smaller fields." Plaintively he lamented, "We must make a desperate effort to regain what Beauregard has abandoned in the West."[28]

If Davis had not already reached a preconceived conclusion,

Johnston fed his leanings admirably. Indeed, the aide took the measure of his commander in chief rather quickly. Though adoring and respectful—attitudes learned from his father and nurtured by Davis's kindness and generosity to him—Johnston also recognized Davis's occasional obstinacy, and most of all his prejudices. Since disgust with Beauregard was a shared bias, he had no trouble in matching his views to the president's, and Johnston's opinion, in turn, was highly influenced by that of his uncle William Preston, who had been with his father when he died. Now at Tupelo, he found Beauregard keeping himself "secluded and inaccessible," leaving it to Bragg, who was "endeavoring by excessive severity to establish discipline." Then Beauregard, who had been complaining of ill health for several months, simply left the army to go on sick leave. On June 14 he departed without either asking permission or even notifying the president. In Davis's mind it was little less than desertion.[29]

The president may already have entertained hopes of removing the general from command. Just the day before he told Varina of his belief that Beauregard had been given responsibility beyond his capacity, he suggested to Pickens that he might like to have the Creole back commanding in South Carolina. Beauregard had performed well there before, and the threats to be faced were few and far less consequential than in the West. Interestingly, though only Davis could make such assignments, Davis suggested that Pickens contact the general directly and offer him the post. Obviously the president had already determined to remove Beauregard from the Army of the Mississippi, but, not forgetting the general's powerful connections in the press, he hoped to avoid the furor a removal would cause by maneuvering him into requesting transfer on his own. It did not work. Beauregard declined Pickens's invitation.[30]

The whole command situation in the Mississippi Valley was an absolute mess, and now Davis tried personally to reform it. Shiloh was not the only disaster that April. Despite manful efforts by Lovell in New Orleans, Davis had turned a largely deaf ear to his entreaties for more men and guns to defend against the powerful Yankee fleet gathering off the mouth of the Mississippi. Placing inordinate trust in Forts Jackson and St. Philip, Davis also refused to believe that the Yankees would even make an attempt in that direction. He convinced himself that Union strategy was to move down the Mississippi several hundred miles to attack the city, rather than to steam upriver a mere ninety miles. Thus he gave everything he could to Johnston in the days before April, assuring poor Lovell that "New Orleans will be defended from above." Worse, when Lovell had an as-yet-unfinished powerful ironclad gunboat nearly ready to help battle the enemy fleet, Richmond ordered it away upriver, reiterating that the forts would be sufficient, even though by this time the successful passage by Union gunboats of strong forts on the upper Mississippi had recently given evidence that stationary works would not be very effective against swiftly moving armored vessels. Worst of all, as the crisis approached for New Orleans, Richmond ordered Hollins, its only successful naval commander on the river, to leave his fleet and come to the capital to give examinations to naval cadets! Admittedly stretched beyond his means on all fronts, still Davis and his war and navy secretaries—where they exerted any influence—bungled the defense of New Orleans from beginning to end. For the president it was another case of having made up his mind that events would transpire in one way and one way only and thereafter dismissing any other alternative. But David Farragut's fleet did not agree, and on April 25–26, they steamed past the forts and, with the loss of only one ship, took New Orleans. Unwilling to fight a battle that his small force could not win and that would only result in damage to the city and injury to civilians, Lovell evacuated.

Davis, of course, could not countenance his government's culpability for the loss of its largest port and with it the lower Mississippi. Years later he implied that Lovell bore most of the blame, in part for not making his defenses better and also for sending troops away from the city to join Johnston and Beauregard. He even implied that it was Lovell who misapprehended the direction from which a threat would come. In fact, Lovell warned everyone repeatedly of signs that Farragut would attack him. And it was Davis through the War Department who ordered those troops away from New Orleans. When Lovell later went before a court of inquiry convened to investigate the loss of the city, he emerged completely exonerated. Exoneration from Davis, however, would not be forthcoming. On June 14, before learning that Beauregard was absenting himself from his own command, Davis wrote directly to Bragg ordering him to leave at once to relieve Lovell of authority over Department No. 1. Lovell would never hold an independent command again.[31]

But Bragg could not go, of course. Beauregard, hiding any miffed feelings he may have had at one of his subordinates being ordered away without his being consulted, only now informed Richmond that he was leaving for four months and that Bragg must command in his stead. Davis would do better than that. He sent Bragg an immediate order to take command from Beauregard, and not just temporarily. Furthermore, Bragg was not to allow Beauregard to interfere or to reassume command without an explicit order from Richmond. Davis discussed this decision with his cabinet, but his mind was surely set before he consulted with them, for he presented the case in such a fashion that it appeared to all that the general left his post at a critical time without either leave or giving notice. Mallory even came away with the impression that Beauregard had lost control of himself, no doubt a picture easily derived from a president who now bordered on losing his own self-control where that general was concerned. If Beauregard bore the burden of the blame, Davis was nevertheless in no frame of mind after Shiloh, Johnston's death, and the abandonment of Corinth to be generous, understanding, or even patient with this nettlesome egotist.[32]

Still, this all left the Western army itself in a turmoil, with its third commander in ten weeks. Colonel William Preston lamented, "I wish to God the President was here." Even though away recovering his health, Beauregard hardly acted like an invalid. His distaste for Davis now turned into outright contempt, and at once he commenced a letter-writing campaign to recover his command. Calling Davis "either demented or a traitor to his high trust," the general went on to characterize him as "that living specimen of gall & hatred." Beauregard may not have been a very potent field commander, but as an enemy in the rear, Davis would find him far bolder than he had been at the head of his army.[33]

William Preston Johnston finished his inspection at Tupelo early in July and went to work on his report. Before doing so, however, he had a personal interview with Beauregard to put to him the specific questions asked by Davis. Bristling at first, the general finally answered, and despite his prejudice Johnston was forced to see some just cause in the general's actions. Yet he forbore from praising Beauregard, and in speaking of the recently improved condition and training of the army, he implicitly awarded the credit to Bragg.[34]

By the time Johnston returned to Richmond and handed over his report, Jefferson Davis was a man approaching physical and mental exhaustion. The unremitting story of disaster in the West had turned the spring of 1862 into a nightmare: Forts Henry and Donelson, Shiloh, the fall of New Orleans and Memphis, the loss of Corinth, the defeat at Pea Ridge. Not a single victory brightened the tale of disaster. Almost as bad, in the newly created Trans-Mississippi Department, containing all territory west of the Mississippi, his generals were fighting each other more than they battled the enemy. Van Dorn had disappointed him repeatedly, both by failing to support Johnston when ordered as well as by losing much of Arkansas at Pea Ridge. He tried a new commander, Major General Thomas C. Hindman of Arkansas, who promptly alienated much of the population by declaring martial law, impelling one of his own subordinates to publish a circular denouncing the order. Davis had to scold the offender personally. Meanwhile, disturbing personal news arrived from Brierfield, where in May some of his slaves robbed the house and ran away and the overseer could do nothing about it. With Federal gunboats threatening to come upriver to Vicksburg, the local Confederate commander ordered all cotton burned rather than see it confiscated by the Yankees. That included cotton at Davis Bend, and brother Joseph implored the president to except their crops from the order, but he refused. Then came reports that the Federals had actually reached Davis Bend in late June and were burning houses and outbuildings.[35]

Though the report of Brierfield being burned proved false, it hardly lightened the president's burden. Before his own eyes he seemed to be seeing his new nation falling under the invader's heel, while at the same time the quiet plantation to which he dreamed of retiring was perhaps being pillaged by that same rapacious foe. Back in February he had predicted to Joseph that "I am the object of such special malignity" that Davis Bend would suffer "because of my residence there," and so it did. Trusted old friends were letting him down—though never Sidney Johnston, of course. Polk had not done well, Van Dorn was proving a disappointment, and in May even his old Army friend Theophilus H. Holmes, a West Point schoolmate, complained that he felt himself totally incapable of exercising his command at Goldsboro, North Carolina. "This field is entirely too comprehensive for my capacity," he said with a personal insight rare in Davis's experience with his generals. He begged to be relieved. The president reacted in a manner characteristic of his dealings with old friends who did not quarrel or complain. Major General Holmes asked to be relieved of command of a small department that he could not handle; Davis promoted him to lieutenant general and assigned him to the mammoth Trans-Mississippi. It would be the most completely incomprehensible assignment he made as president, explicable only as an example of Davis's frequent poor judgment of men, his reliance on even inexperienced or demonstrably weak West Point graduates, his unswerving loyalty to friends from his own army days, and most of all to the confusion and desperation of this terrible spring. For disaster did not limit itself to the West. By the time he assigned Holmes to a department he could not handle, the Confederacy had come perilously close to losing Richmond, and perhaps the whole game.[36]

Back in mid-February Joseph Johnston had complained to Davis that he found his army at Centreville weaker than at any time since Manassas. Many of his generals, including Beauregard and Van Dorn, had been assigned elsewhere, and many of his short-term regiments had mustered out of service. He relied heavily on his next senior officer, Major General Gustavus Smith, but Johnston doubted that even with his assistance his advance line north of Bull Run was tenable. Davis called him to Richmond for a meeting two days before his inauguration, and there the two discussed the options available. McClellan was building a massive Yankee army with which to invade Virginia. Johnston expressed a certainty that he would be too weak to oppose him, and certainly at so advanced a position as the Centreville line.

Yet he could not fall back just then without severe loss of army equipment due to the cold weather and bad condition of the roads. Davis may have asked him where he would choose to set up a new line of defense, and if Benjamin can be believed, Johnston surprised everyone present by pleading that he knew too little of the countryside between Richmond and Centreville to take the responsibility for making such a decision. According to Benjamin, Davis expressed considerable chagrin. The discussion lasted from morning until late that night, and though no definitive plan emerged—showing that Davis was not the only one who suffered from indecision at times—the general claimed that he left in the clear belief that he was to fall back as soon as possible. Davis, however, had quite a different understanding. Still suffering from "a great shock to my confidence in him" because of Johnston's admission of failure to learn the nature of the ground to his rear, the president believed they had concluded only to get all the baggage, heavy guns, and other impedimenta to the rear as soon as the roads allowed, leaving the army itself in place "to advance or retreat as occasion might require." As they later looked back on the conference, the two principals agreed only on the decision respecting the baggage and guns. Each had obviously failed to communicate clearly to the other his intent.[37]

A few weeks later, on March 10, Speaker of the House Thomas Bocock called at Davis's office to find him in a cabinet session. Bocock sent in word of a rumor that Johnston and his army were falling back from Centreville. The news stunned Davis. Since the February 20 conference, he and Johnston had corresponded several times, Johnston frequently referring to "your plans" and "your instructions" without specifically saying what those were. Obviously Davis believed that Johnston referred to the removal of the wagons and heavy guns, for when he responded he gave no indication of any confusion and yet said nothing of any withdrawal. Indeed, he spoke of concentration of forces and stopping an enemy advance, even adding that "the military paradox, that impossibilities must be rendered possible, had never better occasion for its application." Thus his surprise at Bocock's news. Immediately Davis told Benjamin, still interim secretary of war, to look into it, and again, later that day—showing an impatience he almost never directed at this cabinet member—he repeated, petulantly, "Have you *not yet* sent an officer to *learn* the *facts* and *reasons?*"[38]

It was a classic case of missed signals. Indeed, the same day the president sent Johnston word that reinforcements were on the way to help him hold his position and "resume first policy" when weather improved, obviously referring to some discussion of an offensive. Now, when the general reported his withdrawal, Davis confessed being "at a loss to believe it," the more so since "I was as much in the dark as to your purposes, condition, and necessities as at the time of our conversation."

Certainly it had been Johnston's duty to keep Davis fully informed of his plans in advance. It is equally certain that a president had a duty to take steps to inform himself if subordinates did not keep him so informed, rather than complain afterward of ignorance. Both men failed, though neither would admit it. (Years later, Davis relented enough to admit that he could understand how Johnston might "very naturally mistake" pressure to get off guns and mobilize the army as advocating retreat.) Davis at least learned something from it all, however, as evidenced by his later dispatching of young Johnston to Tupelo to gather first-hand knowledge of the condition of an army and its commanders' plans. Hereafter the president would frequently employ his private aides on missions to find out for himself exactly the kind of information Johnston failed to give him now.[39]

That was only the beginning. While Johnston set up a new line near Fredericksburg along the Rappahannock River, fifty miles north of Richmond, McClellan failed to follow, but instead boarded his army on transports, steamed down the Potomac to the Chesapeake, and on to Fort Monroe at the tip of the Virginia Peninsula. Landing them there, under the protective guns of a fort still in Yankee hands, he had to move but 110 miles up the Peninsula, past Yorktown and Williamsburg, to reach the environs of Richmond. More than six months before, a friend had proposed to Davis that the Union's best route of attack on the Confederate capital would be to seize Norfolk and move up the Peninsula, and obviously now the enemy intended just that. Davis had hoped that one of Mallory's innovations, the ironclad warship CSS *Virginia*, would be able to impede or even turn back Yankee gunboats and troop transports. On March 8 she destroyed two enemy warships and panicked others in Hampton Roads. However, her March 9 meeting with the Federal ironclad USS *Monitor* in the same waters, between Norfolk and Fort Monroe, resulted in her being unable thenceforward to do anything other than protect Norfolk, and that tenuously. Thus McClellan faced little opposition in gaining a foothold on the Peninsula.[40]

Worse, to Davis it appeared that he would meet little opposition from Johnston either. On March 22 the president and General Lee, now back from Charleston and acting as an advisor to Davis, went to Johnston's army on the Rappahannock to talk with the commander. Together they reconnoitered the river's south side and concluded, as Davis put it, "to use a slang phrase, your town of Fredericksburg is right in the wrong place." The city could not be defended, they said—an interesting finding for Lee to concur in, considering events on this ground nine months later. Nothing conclusive came out of the discussion, and they agreed to leave the army where it was. Happily, they also decided not to recall the small command under General Thomas J. Jackson then out in the Shenandoah, where he guarded the vital left flank of Johnston's army, and of Richmond itself. In the ensuing weeks he would win a string of victories that electrified the continent, and give much needed relief to Davis.[41]

Any such good news was easily overshadowed by the first reports of McClellan landing on the Peninsula. Two days after the conference with Johnston, Davis received the first intelligence of the enemy landings. Instantly he saw the danger. Confederate defenses on the Peninsula were pitifully weak, just twelve thousand at Yorktown commanded by General John B. Magruder, and thirteen thousand at Norfolk under General Benjamin Huger. Initial reports said that McClellan had at least 35,000 men, and every subsequent word magnified his numbers. Within a few weeks, in fact, McClellan would have more than 100,000 with him.

On March 25 Davis asked Lee to determine how many men from the Rapidan line could be brought immediately to the Peninsula, though he preempted a low estimate by declaring that at least 20,000 to 30,000 would be needed. Furthermore, Davis advised Johnston—through Lee—that he should be ready to move all but a rear guard, and that at any time an order directing him to "Move at once" might be forthcoming. Johnston responded forcefully and positively by suggesting that all of his forces be moved at once, excepting only a thin line to shield his movement from the enemy in northern Virginia. Davis continued to show commendable restraint in dealing with Johnston, restraining himself from giving absolute orders and leaving it to Johnston to use his own judgment, and repeatedly asking for the general's views. It helped, perhaps, that Davis had Lee with him now, and his confidence in this Virginian steadily grew. Another reason that the president withheld taking decisive action in moving Johnston's army was that no one could yet tell McClellan's objective. Still marshalling his army around Fort Monroe and Old Point Comfort, he could move either up the peninsula toward Richmond, or else across Hampton Roads against Norfolk. Until he knew more, Davis feared acting hastily, for if he pulled Johnston entirely out of northern Virginia, it would endanger the rail link with the Shenandoah and Jackson.[42]

Thus far, while waiting for the threat to develop, Davis acted with judgment and restraint. Instinct might have led him to give direct orders to Johnston, and his critics would have expected it from him. Yet he did everything in daily consultation with Lee and frequent personal or telegraphic discussion with Johnston. However, Davis seems to have bypassed Secretary of War Randolph in all the important communications. Indeed, only a few days after the news of McClellan's landing, the ever-unstable Henry Wise declared that "there is no Secretary of War." Randolph, he said, "is merely a *clerk*, an underling, and cannot hold up his head in his humiliating position." This was not so, but certainly Davis left only the matters of lesser import for Randolph to handle—such things as removal of baggage and supplies. At the same time, the president also frequently took naval matters out of Mallory's hands. When he saw a threat to the Confederate navy yard at Gosport, near Norfolk, he issued orders directly to the naval commander in the vicinity for erecting defenses, not bothering to go through Mallory. It was all less a conscious policy than a spontaneous hour-to-hour coping with the developing emergency. At least Davis seems to have kept his cabinet ministers informed of what he was doing, no doubt in the almost daily meetings that now occupied themselves exclusively with the growing emergency.[43]

Finally on April 4 McClellan moved, and Davis at last knew that Richmond was his goal. Orders immediately called Johnston to the capital and most of his army to the Peninsula. In return Johnston asked Davis to direct Magruder and Huger to place themselves between McClellan and Richmond around Yorktown. Johnston himself reached Davis almost at the same time as the crushing news of the loss at Shiloh and the death of Sidney Johnston. Straining every ounce of his will to maintain himself in the face of the news, Davis must have felt an inner bitterness at the contrast between the Johnston lost and the one before him. Yet he displayed only confidence and affection, concealing his doubts and his anguish. Lee met with them and held Johnston's hand a long time in sending him off to the Peninsula. Joseph Johnston had a history of being wounded that went back almost thirty years. Indeed, during the Mexican War, Lee had teased that a little lead did fellows like Johnston good. But now, after the tragic loss of Sidney Johnston, Lee and Davis admonished this general to take care of himself.[44]

The news did not get better. Even while clinging to the desperate hope that Sidney Johnston might still live, Davis feverishly culled Virginia for more reinforcements for the Peninsula. "We are in expectation of a great battle at Yorktown," he told Van Dorn on April 7. He desperately needed a little time. "If we have a few days then success is probable." Then on April 12 came news that Fort Pulaski, protecting Savannah, Georgia, had fallen to the enemy, and that the city itself, a major blockade-running port, was endangered. Two days later Johnston returned from his first inspection of the Peninsula defenses, and brought with him a gloomy tale. The Peninsula could not be defended, he said. He should pull his army back to Richmond itself, concentrate there all of the forces from Virginia, South Carolina, and Georgia, and prepare an offensive to drive McClellan into the Chesapeake once he had advanced and extended his lines of supply and communication. Davis listened, apparently in silence, then withheld judgment until another meeting that afternoon, this time with Randolph, Lee, Smith, and others. Increasingly Davis kept Smith, Johnston's second in command, involved in discussions, perhaps fearing a repetition of what happened when Beauregard took over from Sidney Johnston and did not follow through on his commander's plans.

In a lengthy discussion, Johnston again outlined his proposal, but almost all present voiced serious objections. Abandoning the Peninsula meant abandoning Norfolk, their best shipyard. Lee argued that the Peninsula offered good opportunities for defense. In the end Davis made the decision. He turned down Johnston's plan and also refused to go ahead with another one submitted by Smith, a wholly impractical suggestion to barricade and defend Richmond with as few troops as possible while the bulk of the army invaded the North. In this, one of the most important strategy conferences yet held by Davis, he listened fully to the views of all present and then made up his own mind and stood with Lee and Randolph.

It is hardly likely that he did not lean this way even before the meeting commenced. How could he risk exposing Richmond to capture? He had been refusing repeated proposals for massive concentrations in the past, including from Johnston and Smith. With his major army in the West under Beauregard now in retreat, he was hardly in a position to sustain an invasion of the North in the East, and besides, he had heard repeated grandiose proposals for such movements from Beauregard and Smith. Their fatal flaw was that they ignored every ramification of concentration and invasion not directly involving the army itself. What of the areas thus left exposed? The fall of Fort Pulaski showed that the Federals were vigilant to find weak spots on the South's coastline. Politically, the withdrawal of substantial troops from less-threatened areas would be suicidal, costing confidence in the government, which could translate into reduced enlistments and withheld crops and money. These generals saw only what generals were likely to see. In casting a wider gaze, Davis acted presidential and entirely consistent with his military policy to date. They would fight for the Peninsula.[45]

Johnston protested the decision but acquiesced, partially because he expected that McClellan would soon outflank him and compel Richmond to see things his way anyhow. But the Federal general soon showed what he was made of and how little there was of it. Outnumbering Johnston by at least two to one, McClellan never attacked. Fooled by Confederate bluff, he contented himself with a month-long siege with only occasional assaults on the well-prepared Confederate defenses. Indeed, until late in April, when signs indicated that McClellan was about to overcome his own caution. Davis had begun to hope that he could hold the lower Peninsula indefinitely. On April 27 Johnston sent word that Yorktown might have to be abandoned at any time. At once the president ordered preparations at Norfolk to get the ships and shipbuilding machinery safely brought away. Yet there were severe limitations to what could be done, and when another message from Johnston arrived on May 1 that he would have to retire that night, Davis expressed surprise and begged Johnston to hold out longer. At the same time, fearing a threat to the small force on the northern Virginia line, he directed that Johnston send either Smith or Major General James Longstreet to take command there, at the same time rejecting yet another plan from Johnston for a concentration and invasion. Agreeing that an offensive could produce much good for the cause just then, he had to confess that in their current beleaguered condition, it was clearly impractical.[46]

In the face of the Federals' movements, Johnston held out only two more days, evacuating late on May 3 and moving back to Williamsburg. There, two days later, McClellan made a poorly planned attack resulting in a battle that neither side really won, yet it halted the Federals' progress and gave Johnston time to continue his withdrawal toward Richmond. The question in the mind of Davis, as in the minds of all Richmonders and Confederates, was where Johnston would stop, and when. The abandonment of Yorktown made imperative the evacuation of Norfolk as well. Davis sent Randolph and Mallory to help oversee the removal of supplies and machinery, but only a peremptory countermanding of an order of Johnston's by the secretary of war brought enough time to get guns and other matériel away before the city surrendered on May 10.[47]

Disaster surrounded Jefferson Davis. In the span of barely more than a month he lost Sidney Johnston and Shiloh, saw Beauregard in retreat, suffered reverses at Island No. 10 and Plum Point Bend on the upper Mississippi that led to the fall of Memphis, felt a Yankee spear in his Atlantic coastline at Fort Pulaski that helped tighten the blockade, suffered the momentous loss of New Orleans, and now came the abandonment of the lower Peninsula and the Yankee capture of Norfolk. The only bright spot in the panorama of gloom was a minor victory in the Shenandoah by Jackson, yet any long-range benefits from that remained as yet unclear.

It is no wonder that Davis became increasingly morose and depressed in April and early May. He sought refuge in the company of young William Preston Johnston, whose presence at dinner he now requested almost every day. With him there, Davis could somehow lighten his burden and even for a few minutes leave his growing fears and doubts behind. Johnston wrote on May 8 that he found the president's "manners are so gentle and dignified and his conversation so instructive & agreeable." Moreover, Davis sought another solace now. Never especially religious, he had attended Episcopal services to please Varina since their marriage. He did not even know with any certainty if he had ever been baptized.[48]

Now Varina wanted to see him confirmed in her church. It must have helped convince her when Davis came home at 7 P.M. from his office during the efforts to evacuate Norfolk. He seemed to stagger up the curving stairway from the entrance foyer to the second floor; then he walked with heavy tread to his private office and collapsed onto a sofa. He would take no dinner. Varina knelt at his side, begging to know what bore him down so, and for almost two hours he poured out to her his burden. In desperation he declared that he would give his arms and legs to have "someone with whom he could share it." All that night she read to him to take his mind from his responsibilities, but she talked to him, too, persuading him that there was another with whom he could share his heavy load.

For some time they had attended St. Paul's Episcopal Church in Richmond. At Varina's urging, Davis agreed to be baptized and confirmed. The Rev. Charles Minnegerode came to the Executive Mansion at 9:30 in the morning on May 6 and there baptized him "hypothetically," uncertain if there had been a previous baptism. At noon that same day Davis and Varina went to St. Paul's, and there Minnegerode's bishop called several candidates to the chancel. Davis rose first and strode to the ceremony. Already in his public documents and speeches, Davis had taken to using increasing references to divine purposes and aid. Now, as in all matters to which he committed himself, the president undertook to demonstrate in his own faith that he and his cause deserved the kindly eye of the Almighty.[49]

He performed one last act to ease his mind. He sent his family away from Richmond. Nothing better reveals his fear growing to a conviction, that Richmond would soon come under fire than the activities at the Executive Mansion during the first week of May. Baptism and confirmation interrupted a steady routine of packing books, pictures, clothing, and other personal articles. Their black coachman, William Jackson, believed that he saw in the president more than the usual querulousness, a downhearted spirit, and an inclination to complain of lack of support in this hour of trial. Varina, said Jackson, actually remarked to her friends that she thought "the Confederacy was about played out," and Davis himself expressed fears that if the Federals advanced from northern Virginia they might trap Richmond between themselves and McClellan moving up the Peninsula. This was why Davis had thought it so imperative to have Smith or Longstreet to command on the Fredericksburg line.[50]

With this unhappy eventuality haunting his mind, Davis sent Colonel Browne of his staff to Raleigh, North Carolina, on May 8 to look into the organization and arming of state troops, but also to find a place for Varina and the children to escape the danger of Richmond. That same day the Davises held a reception at their Clay Street home. In the middle of the evening a courier brought Davis word that Yankee gunboats were ascending the James River, getting around Johnston's flank and approaching the river defenses at Drewry's Bluff. If they got past those batteries, nothing lay between them and Richmond. When Davis returned to the drawing room, Varina saw the look in his eye, and he whispered the news to her. Later, after the guests departed, he told her she must leave the next morning. It was a melancholy parting, made no less somber by the growing signs of panic among Richmonders. Varina would not be the only refugee fleeing the capital. The Confederacy, it seemed to many, truly was about "played out."

But there would be no fleeing for Jefferson Davis. He had never run from a battle in his life, and now, at the most critical moment in his young nation's existence, he knew where he belonged. Indeed, many, including Varina, began to believe yet again that he would take command in the field himself. That remained to be seen, but his preoccupation with army affairs, which had already absorbed all of his time this spring, now redoubled. No situation would ever be so desperate that the president would abandon hope. The day after saying farewell to Varina and the children, he was consulting once more with Johnston, looking for ways to reverse what he forthrightly called "the drooping cause of our country."[51]

22

We Could End the War

Jefferson Davis did not send all of his "family" to Raleigh. The same day that Varina left, the president invited young Preston Johnston to move into the Executive Mansion with him. "I have a fine room in the third story, with a fine view," the aide wrote the next day. Obviously flattered at the special attention he received from Davis, Johnston almost fawned on his every word. Yet before long the aide discovered that he himself enjoyed a considerable measure of influence with his father's old friend. " 'Dobbin' always was sterling," Davis would say of him, using the young man's family nickname. Observers in the War Department saw that Johnston was "beyond all question . . . the most popular and useful of the lot," despite his reputation for being clumsy on his feet. Davis seemed to trust and confide in him more than any of the rest of his official family, placing Johnston in an excellent position to further goals of his own—and he had goals, to be sure. Like almost all Kentuckians in the Confederate service, he longed to see the commonwealth wrested away from the Union. Johnston's desk henceforward became almost a clearinghouse for correspondence from and plans by Kentuckians seeking to influence the president and Congress. As for his other goal, Johnston cherished his father's memory, and as the controversy with Beauregard heated in the late spring, he would be ever ready to condemn the Creole to the president. On this point, of course, Jefferson Davis needed no prompting.[1]

In a few days the president's staff received a final addition when Joseph C. Ives of New York joined him. Under an act of April 2, Davis was allowed to commission all his aides colonels. Johnston found them a genial lot. Ives had a "pleasant, friendly address." The 240-pound Browne, an Irishman, was "a jovial good fellow." The president's nephew Joseph Davis was "a splendid fellow." Johnston did not comment on G. W. C. Lee, yet they all seem to have gotten along well, and their circle became complete when young Burton Harrison accepted an appointment as Davis's permanent private secretary, after Josselyn's drinking reportedly led to his reassignment. "Dapper, sparky" young Harrison was better adapted to handle Davis's moods and tempers and soon became so welcome at the Executive Mansion that Varina was rumored to have made him a "domestic do-all." One thing they all shared was a profound respect for the president, whom they soon began referring to among themselves as "the Chief."[2]

Johnston did not at first believe that Davis or his staff would remain in Richmond for long with McClellan approaching, yet as the May days rolled onward their office routine of 10 A.M. to 5 P.M. or later continued without interruption. Indeed, so did the president's interest in all things military, even those not directly affecting the situation on the Peninsula. He revived yet again the subject of reorganization within the army, staying with it—and staying patient—even when Johnston continued to ignore his orders or responded in a petulant and haughty tone. "I have been much harassed and the public interest has certainly suffered by the delay," Davis chided the general on May 11. "Some have expressed surprise at my patience when orders to you were not observed," he went on, and he showed a bit of despondence when he implied that Johnston had not appreciated his efforts to sustain him. The general showed his own frayed nerves when he responded saying that reorganization would have to wait and revealing pique that his repeated assertions of more important matters claiming his attention apparently had not gotten through to the president. Nevertheless, though strained by the intense pressure of their predicament, both men strove to maintain cordial relations during the crisis.[3]

Davis himself rode to Johnston's headquarters on May 12 to see the situation. The general had pulled back to the line of the Chickahominy River on the south, and extending through New Kent Court House on the north, to the York River. That put Johnston only thirty miles from Richmond. There Davis spent the night, and though happy to see the soldiers' good spirits, still he felt dismay at seeing how much of their artillery and ammunition they had abandoned at Yorktown. Privately he blamed Johnston for not being better prepared for the evacuation, and it weakened his confidence in a successful defense of Richmond. "I know not what to expect when so many failures are to be remembered," he wrote Varina on returning to the capital, "yet will try to make a successful resistance."[4]

Almost daily now he rode to inspect troops or look over the defenses along the James. Happily, on May 15 Drewry's Bluff turned back a gunboat attack, thus heartening Davis and the city. The president, reaching the bluff and its fortifications shortly after the firing ceased, found the troops elated. As for Richmond itself, the little victory ended for a time the panic, and he heard people begin to speak of seeing the city destroyed rather than give it up. To such talk Davis replied that he would try to beat McClellan on the Peninsula, but he would never allow Johnston's army to be "penned up" in the city. Having stopped the Yankee gunboats, he hoped to be able to move against the enemy's infantry, defeat it, and pursue it back into the water.[5]

Yet, as the days moved on, Davis could not tell when Johnston would meet the enemy. "We are uncertain of every thing except that a battle must be near at hand," he wrote Varina on May 19. Anxiously he waited for Johnston to communicate his plans. During discussions with that general, as well as with Lee, Davis could form no clear idea of what Johnston intended to do other than stand his ground on the Chickahominy and await McClellan's attack. Johnston intentionally did not tell the president more. "I could not consult him without adopting the course he might advise," the general said eighteen months later, no doubt remembering the times that he had proposed concentrations and invasions only to have Davis turn them down. Better to propose nothing, he reasoned, though by so doing he kept his commander in chief in the dark and hindered Davis's ability to sustain him in the field.[6]

When Johnston fell back yet again, abandoning the Chickahominy and bringing his army into the actual suburbs of Richmond itself, Davis held his calm, though a certain fatalistic tone crept into his letters to Varina as he prayed that their children should "love one another." Many of his words seem written with a consciousness that any one might be his last.

In fact, Davis at first expected that in crossing the Chickahominy, Johnston would take a position on its near bank and defend against McClellan there. He sent young Colonel Lee to him with instructions to deliver a letter Davis wrote on May 17. In it he expressed the necessity of defending Richmond "outside of the city," though stating as well the obvious questions of "where and how?" The president proposed a couple of alternatives, all contingent on the enemy's movements, yet emphasized that, "as on all former occasions, my design is to suggest, not to direct." He expected that Colonel Lee would be used to communicate Johnston's immediate intentions to him.[7]

Probably the next day, as he left his office, Davis saw Postmaster General Reagan passing and asked that he join him later on for a trip to the Chickahominy to see Johnston. Cryptically Reagan replied that he "would not have to go to the Chickahominy to see the General." Either Davis did not hear or else did not take the meaning of Reagan's remark.

But when the two rode out after dinner that evening, the president saw soon enough. No sooner did they reach a hill in Rocketts, one of Richmond's suburbs, than Davis saw tents stretching out half a mile in front of them. Even when Reagan, who had visited those soldiers the night before, told him that these were portions of Johnston's army, Davis remained incredulous. "No!" he exclaimed. "General Johnston is down on the Chickahominy." It took some persuading before Reagan made him realize that Johnston had pulled back from the river almost into the city limits of Richmond. "The look of surprise which swept over his face showed a trace of pain," Reagan recalled.[8]

Accompanied by Ives, Davis rode immediately to the brick house that now served as Johnston's headquarters. Their meeting was a tense one as the president demanded to know the reason for this withdrawal. Johnston pleaded that the water was better here, his army needed provisions, and that he could defend the city more ably from this position. Davis may have asked if Johnston was willing to give up the capital without a fight, and Ives later told Reagan that the general equivocated. At this, said Ives, Davis threatened to replace Johnston with someone who would fight. Perhaps so, but Johnston must immediately have stiffened his resolve, for nothing further was said of relieving him.[9]

Instead Davis returned to Richmond and called a cabinet meeting, with General Lee present. Anxiously he asked Lee for advice on the best course to pursue if Richmond were to be abandoned. Lee replied with some warmth that Richmond should not, could not, be sacrificed. Either at this or a subsequent meeting, Lee asked Davis what he thought they should do. The president favored an offensive, attacking McClellan before his army crossed the Chickahominy, and Lee concurred. Finally they agreed that, Johnston being reluctant to communicate freely with Davis, Lee should ask the general for his plans.

More than once during the next few days, Lee asked Johnston to present his intentions and also to come in person to confer with them. He got silence in return, and by May 22 Davis still did not know anything. That day he rode out with young Johnston to Drewry's Bluff and then to Mechanicsville on the Chickahominy, just five miles north of Richmond. Even though firing took place, none of the field commanders in the vicinity knew what they were supposed to be doing. Under considerable danger himself from the firing of enemy artillery, Davis finally agreed to move his small party out of range, but his real concern was a fear that a concerted Yankee attack here would puncture Johnston's line and leave an open road to Richmond. Testily he brought this to Johnston's attention.[10]

By now Davis approached the point of showing too much patience. Johnston persistently kept him in the dark, even defying his and Lee's instructions to provide information regularly. Distant, occasionally surly, he clearly regarded Davis as his enemy as well as McClellan. Despite the president's order to defend the Peninsula, Johnston repeatedly kept quiet until he could plead that circumstances forced him to withdraw, thus tacitly achieving his own original design of abandoning the line south of Richmond. He bordered on the insubordinate. The disagreement with Davis the year before over rank still distressed him, perhaps, but this behavior on the Peninsula was altogether a different matter. This was not revenge or game playing—this was Johnston's nature. Whatever responsibility Davis bore for their initial poor relations the previous summer, this went beyond personalities. Johnston was endangering the capital and the cause itself, and Davis had been patient too long. Now he found himself trapped, stuck with a general whose views clashed with his own and who would not act as a willing subordinate. Yet to relieve Johnston at this critical hour would mean even greater danger, for not another general within reach had actually commanded an army in battle on this scale. Now he could only hope that Johnston would indeed stand his ground before Richmond, but the situation made him more than ever uneasy for the immediate future.

Not surprisingly, Davis began to make almost daily inspection visits to the army: If Johnston would not tell him the state of affairs, he would see for himself. And in the back of his mind there surely lurked the possibility that he would have to take command himself should Johnston prove unequal to the moment. Varina somehow divined the possibility from his letters, for she wrote pleading, "Don't expose yourself." "I tremble for you in a battle," she cried. "Pray don't try such a thing."[11]

By May 29 the skirmishing grew more frequent as McClellan approached Johnston's line near the village of Fair Oaks, also known as Seven Pines. Davis rode out that day, expecting the big battle, as Johnston had finally told him that he intended to attack this day. Yet nothing happened, and some portions of the army did not even seem to know that an offensive had been planned. Meanwhile, the Yankees began to cross the Chickahominy, and McClellan sent a portion of his army against Johnston's position at Fair Oaks. Early on the afternoon of May 31 Davis heard firing and kept an ear tuned to it throughout the afternoon as he stayed at his work in the capital. By 4 P.M. he could wait no longer. Asking Johnston and Ives to join him, he mounted and rode four or five miles from town, passing large numbers of soldiers hurrying to the front. By 5 P.M. they saw Generals Johnston and Lee, and the president approached the latter to ask what was happening. Neither Davis nor Lee knew of any intention by Johnston to attack, but the army commander had seen and seized a sudden opportunity to strike two isolated Yankee corps. Unfortunately he did so in poorly timed and executed assaults that lost much of their force. Worse, Smith and Magruder did not perform well, and the former exhibited a possibly psychosomatic illness that developed whenever pressure or great responsibility was thrust on him. William Preston Johnston suspected that it might be simple moral cowardice.

Davis saw with alarm that his generals knew little of the enemy's positions, showing poor reconnaissance by Johnston. Still, the Confederates fought well and drove the foe before them, capturing encampments and batteries, under the heaviest fire the president ever witnessed. Davis and his associates kept up with the advancing Confederates, riding into an abandoned enemy camp to find it being plundered by blacks and camp followers. Then the president saw the foe drawn up at the edge of an open field and watched as an ill-advised assault charged across the plain into a wall of fire. Davis sent several appeals to Magruder to send a brigade to reinforce the attack on the left, where his own reconnaissance revealed an opportunity to take the enemy in flank. Finally Davis left to find Magruder and also to escape the heavy artillery fire falling around him and his staff. Lee was still with him, and now Postmaster General Reagan rode up and scolded the president for exposing himself so recklessly. He had just left Johnston, who was himself under a heavy fire.

Davis never found Magruder but, informed that a brigade was on the way, he returned to the field after about twenty minutes of fighting to find that the Confederates had been repulsed with heavy losses. Now he and Preston Johnston went to work with a will to rally the survivors. Both of them calmly exhorted the men to stand and re-form. While they did so, Davis saw something that made his heart sink. Stretcher-bearers carried a wounded officer to the rear. Davis saw that it was General Johnston. A bullet had struck him in the right shoulder, and then a shell fragment hit him in the chest. Davis rode over to him as the general's bearers were about to load him into an ambulance. Animosities and frustrations were quickly forgotten, for Davis could not help but honor any brave man who suffered. When the president spoke, the general opened his eyes and extended his hand. He did not know how badly hurt he was, though at the moment he feared his spine might be injured. At once Davis offered to have him taken to the Executive Mansion, but Johnston's staff preferred other accommodations.

Much still remained to do. Johnston's wounding made Smith the next in line of command. Lee gave him some instructions and then joined Davis in helping to stabilize the line as night fell. Having gotten separated from Preston Johnston and Ives, Davis rode back to Richmond with Lee, arriving around 9:30 and passing his aides in the darkness without recognizing them. When they came in a couple of hours later, they all sat up until 2 A.M. talking and eating a late supper. Among the topics discussed was General Smith, in whom no one seemed now to feel much confidence. His illness or mental anxiety was apparently well known. Worse, Davis now believed that it was advice from Smith that had prevented an attack on May 29, when advantages of surprise and position would have favored the Confederates. Smith had stopped it all by declaring—on the basis of faulty reconnaissance—the enemy position near Mechanicsville impregnable. The performances of others undoubtedly came under discussion as well. Preston Johnston thought Magruder "a maniac" and repeated rumors that Toombs, now a brigade commander, ran away under fire and was about to face a duel with General D. H. Hill, who called him a coward. Most of all, though, Davis must have been unable to sleep for the reawakening of feelings long forgotten—the exhilaration of battle. President or not, he was still a warrior at heart.[12]

The battle resumed the next morning, and Davis and Colonel Johnston rode back to the field. The president had already decided that he would not leave Smith in command of the army. It may have been suspicion of the man's nerve, or it may have been his association with Beauregard and Johnston, but more likely Davis's decision rested on Lee's superior rank. It required a full general to command one of the two major armies of the Confederacy, and clearly Davis did not have sufficient confidence in Smith to elevate him to that rank. Lee already held it, and after talking with an ailing Smith at his headquarters, Davis informed Lee of his new assignment. It would be the best decision of his presidency.

Soon thereafter they left Smith and rode together to join Longstreet, then engaged in desultory fighting on the Williamsburg road. Quite a gathering of notables accumulated there, as military and civilian officials alike came to see the fighting. Besides the president and Lee, there were Longstreet, J. E. B. Stuart, Holmes, Howell Cobb, Secretary of War Randolph, Mallory, and even Reagan, who picked up a dropped rifle and fired a round at the enemy. "No important result was gained" from the day's fight, Davis wrote to Varina the next day. Mostly, even as the Yankee artillery fire fell around him, he thought that it was a Sunday, and while he was braving the danger of enemy fire, Varina would be at church praying for him and sharing the communion. He missed her more than he could say.[13]

What were they to do now? The day after putting Lee in command, Davis rode again to the front, where he joined a council of war that left him feeling little but gloom. The generals seemed despondent, feeling that McClellan would inevitably use engineering and spreading entrenchments to gradually push them back. Davis could not help saying how disappointed he was to hear such defeatist views, and Lee agreed with him. A disheartened president left the meeting to ride to the front, where Lee shortly joined him, asking what he thought it best to do. It was an act more symbolic than either ever realized.[14]

*   *   *

Prior to those first days of June 1862, Lee and Davis had had little more than a formal, though cordial, acquaintance. They knew each other at West Point, where the very proper Lee refused to take part in the egg-nog partying, and when Davis was too full of admiration for Sidney Johnston to countenance any other. Very possibly, the proud and inse-cure Mississippian might even have resented somewhat the aristocratic Virginian. Moreover, Lee's being one of Scott's favorites during the Mexican War would not have enhanced him in Davis's eyes. During his tenure as secretary of war for Pierce, Davis knew Lee chiefly as super-intendent of the U.S. Military Academy. During this last period the two became better acquainted. Davis made Lee a lieutenant colonel in one of his new cavalry regiments and then immediately inquired as to his where-abouts when Virginia seceded.

Davis did not love Lee as he did Sidney Johnston, but he respected his ability, and after working closely with him during the first weeks in Richmond in 1861, he believed that he could rely on him. Lee served him well during the days preceding and following Manassas. Even though Lee's first active command in western Virginia failed that fall, still Davis stood by him, sending him to South Carolina to see to its defenses and then calling him back to Richmond in March 1862. Indeed, before Davis vetoed the bill establishing a commanding general of the Army, many expected that he would appoint Lee to the post. Of course, Davis would have appointed Johnston had he been able, but—seeking to achieve the benefits of having a commanding general without the sur-render of executive prerogatives that Davis saw in Congress's bill—he went ahead and appointed Lee on March 13 to act as de facto command-ing general, "under the direction of the President" and "charged with the conduct of military operations in the armies of the Confederacy."[15]

Robert E. Lee proved to be a far-more-astute judge of character than most of the South's leading generals, and better than Davis. He had seen the published correspondence during the Scott feud. He knew of the feuds with Wool and other officers before the war. He observed firsthand the breakdown in relations between the president and Joseph Johnston and Beauregard and Walker's frustration at the War Office. In none of these disagreements did Davis hold exclusive title to blame, but he owned a good share in all of them, and for a man of Lee's keen insight into character, a lesson could be drawn. A man could get along with Jefferson Davis if he observed a few simple rules: Do not question him unless he invited criticism. Do not challenge him. Keep him fully informed at all times. Do not assail his friends or cronies. Have nothing to do with the press, and eschew public controversy. Avoid politicians, especially those in the growing anti-Davis camp. Most of all, remain loyal. This is what Davis required of anyone if they were to get along, and especially in a subordinate. Happily, in almost every respect these requirements accorded with Lee's notions of the proper deportment of a general to his commander in chief.

As a result, Robert E. Lee was ideally suited to be Davis's commanding general, even though the position consisted largely of title. From March until June 1, Lee found little more to deal with than paperwork and details. Davis made all the big decisions and handled all the dealings with the major armies himself. Lee advised long and often, but Davis, and only Davis, decided. Lee bore the frustration and did not complain publicly, and all the while he came more and more to see into the man he worked for. Thus, when Davis released him from his chains and gave him the army on the Peninsula, Lee was better equipped than any other man in the Confederacy to manage both that army and that president. In short, though he might not have realized it, Lee was a better politician and statesman than Davis. He knew how to subordinate his own pride to the greater goal of getting what he needed from men, whether his subordinates or his superiors. He even knew how to be a sycophant at times, giving Davis more flattery than any did other general of the war—and on Davis's most prideful topic, his military prowess.

Lee started off in exactly the right way that June 2, when Davis left the generals' meeting and Lee followed him. Beauregard would have told the president in the boldest terms what he would do next. Joseph E. Johnston would have told him nothing at all. Gustavus Smith would have proposed some great, impractical maneuver. Robert E. Lee asked the president what *he* would do. That made all the difference, and William Preston Johnston almost immediately felt some glimmer of hope. "The trouble is we have no *Generals*," he complained to his wife that same day, but now he hoped for much from Lee. "I believe he has more capacity," the colonel wrote. In answering Lee's question, Davis showed that he felt much the same. He agreed with a plan proposed by Lee earlier, that Jackson should be brought back from the valley to strike McClellan's right flank, while Lee prepared such defenses in front of Richmond as would allow them to be held by a skeleton force, freeing the bulk of the army for an offensive to move in concert with Jackson. To achieve this, Lee needed time to entrench and to allow Jackson to meet the threats still before him in the Shenandoah. Would McClellan give them that time?[16]

"General Lee rises with the occasion," Davis wrote to Varina with hope, "and seems to be equal to its conception." Joyfully, the president also saw Jackson more than rise to the occasion in the Shenandoah, as with his small army he battled and defeated three Yankee hosts and cleared the valley by mid-June. Meanwhile, by deft feints, Lee managed to keep the timid McClellan so fearful of overwhelming Confederate numbers that he did not press his advantage on the Peninsula. Frantically the Rebels dug their defensive earthworks, and just as feverishly Davis worked himself toward exhaustion trying to cajole more reinforcements, more weapons, and more supplies out of the rest of the Atlantic states.[17]

As the weeks of June wore agonizingly onward, Davis struggled with his own loneliness and sense of isolation. Young Johnston stayed constantly at his side, still marveling at the president's "generous and noble nature." Not infrequently an ill or wounded friend was taken into the Executive Mansion to recuperate, as much for the company as out of charity. Dinner guests came doubly welcome, though Mr. Eggling, who managed the house for the Davises, might have protested at the strain on the already lean larder. It saddened Davis to see Rose Greenhow—a friend and erstwhile spy for the Confederates in Washington during the days before Manassas—when she arrived after captivity in the North. Davis rather preferred that his visitors not come to talk about the war. Over wine and juleps, he spoke instead of his old days on the frontier, of planting cotton, of everything he did when younger and free from all this care. At dinner one evening with William C. Rives of Virginia and young Colonel Johnston, the president turned his mind to animals, and "talked and talked about the instincts of cows, and calves, and horses and dogs and sheep and pigs." He stayed on the theme until after 10 P.M., when Johnston gave up and went to bed, expecting that the conversation would reach cats by midnight.[18]

Yet inevitably every night came the lonely hours when everyone was in bed, the guests were gone, and there was only the president. Unable to sleep, as always, he roamed the big, empty house. "I am quite desolate," he wrote to Varina, "and at every look meet something of yours & of the children to remind me that I am alone." He found the house painfully dreary. Just as in the daytime a chance encounter with a child on the street made him think of his own little ones, now as he wandered into the large nursery on the second floor next to his office, with the midnight bells of the nearby churches in his ears, he could not repress his sadness. "I go into the nursery as a bird may go [to] the robbed nest," he lamented, "but man's tenacious memory preserves the pain." Varina shared his anguish from afar. "The vision of your beloved form wandering in our nursery among the empty beds is too much for me," she wrote him early in June. Indeed, the two must have come close to sharing the same thoughts simultaneously, for she comforted him on his loneliness in the nursery on the very same day that he wrote to tell her of it. Truly, in the years since their near estrangement, they had grown incredibly close, thinking almost as one.[19]

However much his spirits declined in the dark hours, Davis remained alert, attentive, and perpetually active during the day. "I think the President must have been a very combative man in his earlier days,"

Preston Johnston observed that June. "If he cannot successfully conduct this Revolution, then no man can and we are a failure." Once again reports circulated that Davis would take the field. Those closest to him could not form a definite opinion. In May it appeared that he would not, and young Johnston actively opposed it for fear that, should a defeat be suffered, it would be disastrous to the nation's confidence in the president. By the end of that month, however, Johnston believed that Davis would take the active command, "though he has never said so." But after Lee took over the matter seems to have been settled. A week later Johnston told his wife, "You need have no fears that the President will take the field in person." "He has perfect confidence in Genl. Lee and sees no good that could arise from his assuming the nominal command, especially as Genl Lee acts in accord with him."[20]

Yet, if he decided not to take command, still Davis spent almost as much time with Lee and the newly designated Army of Northern Virginia as he did at his office in Richmond. "At the sound of guns," Burton Harrison noted, "Mr. Davis was in the saddle and off, in a moment." He rode a favorite horse, Kentucky, perhaps symbolic of a dream that always lay in the back of his mind, and Harrison noted that Davis wore out his staff day after day as they tried to keep up with him, while the president himself never seemed to tire on his long rides. He pocketed his own pass to get through the guards on Richmond's roads, carrying the simple advice that "the bearer is President Davis."[21]

Every morning he called Johnston or Ives or one of the others, and off they went for up to four hours or more in the saddle. It was not unusual for him to cover thirty miles, and all along the way he regaled his aides with stories of his old days in the army. He showed an obvious pride in his horsemanship, and the Samuel Davis in him often revealed itself as he talked knowledgably and at length about the fine points of horses and dogs, of racing and dog fights. Frequently he rode out again in the evening to inspect the progress of the fortifications. Occasionally he might ask Johnston or Browne if they were tired, but neither had the heart to say they were, which guaranteed that Davis might lead them on for another ten or twelve miles before returning. Inclement weather seemed not to bother him in the least. Even when he and Johnston saw a heavy rain approaching, Davis determined to ignore it and press on, and when the sheets of water began to fall, he did not hesitate to plunge Kentucky into a swollen stream and took it for granted that Johnston would be right behind him. In fact, the colonel thought that "the Prest seemed to enjoy it and the wetter he became the higher his spirits rose."

Indeed, on these daily rides Davis opened up to his young friends, Johnston finding him "more talkative and communicative than usual." Most often he spoke of horses, "a theme of which the President never tires, and he really has great knowledge." Yet on a few occasions he turned more contemplative. "It is strange," he told Johnston during their ride on June 8, "that a man should be so much in public affairs, who is as averse to them as I am." He never wanted to be in public life, he confessed, "and I have acquired no taste for it since." Johnston may have sensed that this was the politician in Davis, denying his ambition, and he suggested that once Davis was out of office he might find that he missed it. The Chief disagreed, remembering his brief interlude of private life before Pierce made him secretary of war and how he "dreaded the idea of going into office again." Only "circumstances & a sense of duty" impelled him to return to Washington in 1853. Now he feared that, with Brierfield endangered by the Yankees, he might be so impoverished by the war that he would have to serve his full term in the presidency. Otherwise, once peace came, he thought he might resign. He wanted to be with his family, on his plantation, and away from the public cares and turmoil that had claimed half his adult life.[22]

Until that peace came—however it arrived—he must drive himself unrelentingly. Many evenings he stayed out on the lines late into the night, conferring with Lee and inspecting the works. The muddy roads, which impeded transportation of supplies and men from point to point, concerned him. Warily he looked across the lines to see the earthworks being thrown up by McClellan, suspecting that the enemy planned a slow approach to Richmond, protected at every step by successive lines of entrenchments. With a bit of grim humor directed at those who criticized him for his reliance on U.S. Military Academy graduates, he noted that the Federals employed that same "reviled policy of West Pointism" by using professional engineering instead of the blood of their men to achieve ground. "We must find if possible the means to get at him without putting the breasts of our men in antagonism to his heaps of earth," he told Varina. "I will endeavor by movements which are not without great hazard to countervail the enemy's policy." Davis anticipated forcing McClellan to meet him in the open field, out of his protective works. "I have much confidence in our ability to give him a complete defeat," he said on June 11, even expressing the hope that before long the North would feel what it was like to be invaded. "The issues of campaigns can never be safely foretold," he confessed. "It is for us to do all which can be done and trustingly to leave our fate to Him who rules the universe."[23]

As the month wore on and Lee's preparations advanced, the president felt that the time grew short before an explosion of arms. At the same time, his own spirits and confidence increased. A few weeks before he had confided to his inner circle that he felt himself "struggling against almost certain defeat," as his secretary Harrison recalled. By the third week of June, however, he began to feel hope. "We are preparing and taking position for the struggle which must be near at hand," he wrote to Varina on June 21. "I am hopeful of success," he said, though he confessed that "the stake is too high to permit the pulse to keep its even beat." A few days later he tried to reassure her that "we are better prepared now than we were on the first of the month and with God's blessing will beat the enemy as soon as we can get at him." Indeed, he already turned his thoughts out to the West, to where Beauregard had abandoned so much. A victory against McClellan would allow him to shift his resources to try to regain what had been lost in Tennessee, and he thought of sending Joseph E. Johnston there to command. "I wish he was able to take the field," Davis confessed, and with considerable charity went on to say, "He is a good soldier, knows the troops, never brags even of what he did do and could at this time render valuable service."[24]

The storm hit two days later. Lee started planning an offensive almost from the day he took command, keeping Davis fully informed at every step. Quickly Davis approved his plans and left pertinent decisions almost entirely to the general. On June 25, with the commencement of what came to be called the Seven Days' Battles, Lee attacked McClellan day after day until July 1 in a series of bloody encounters that in large measure followed the original plan proposed by Johnston back in May, and refined by Lee and Davis. After four days, the Confederates got around the Yankees' right flank and rear, and McClellan began to retreat from the Chickahominy. Lee pursued. There would be no repetition of the failure to follow up on the Manassas victory, yet McClellan protected himself well as he retreated down the Peninsula, and faulty staff work, lack of good maps, and the usual confusion of battle combined to hamper Lee's effort to cripple his foe.

Davis, of course, could not stay off the battlefield. On the first day of fighting, near Oak Grove, the Chief appeared near the battle line and did not leave until Lee himself asked him to leave the field. Three days later, as McClellan began to withdraw down the Peninsula, Davis visited the bivouacs along the Chickahominy and urged the troops to be vigilant of an opportunity to pursue. The next day, after the armies clashed at Savage's Station, Davis learned that an old friend, Brigadier General Richard Griffith, lay badly wounded. He sought him out and leaned over him as he was carried away, saying, "My dear boy, I hope you are not seriously hurt." Davis had repeatedly wanted to give Griffith some promising position in the War Department, but now he could only watch as yet another dear friend was carried away to die.

On several of these battle nights, Davis slept in the field with the army, and on June 30 at Frayser's Farm, he once more came personally under fire. Only moments after he heeded Lee's urging to leave a house in the line of artillery fire, shells riddled the dwelling. Later that day, after the main battle was done, Davis reformed some disorganized stragglers just as an enemy shell exploded in a tree overhead, showering him with branches and iron fragments. Soon thereafter the president, in turn, had to remonstrate with Lee for exposing himself unnecessarily to Yankee fire. Too many generals had been lost already; this one he could not spare.[25]

Finally came the Battle of Malvern Hill on July 1, and the end of the week of fighting. On the morning after the sanguinary battle, Davis tried to buy whiskey from neighboring farmers to give his soldiers a stimulant, but none could be found. Almost not to be found was McClellan, who had pulled back in the night. Davis immediately asked his generals if they could pursue, yet all but Jackson regarded it as impossible. Their army was almost as battered as McClellan's. The following day Lee did pursue, but weather, lack of supply, and the exhaustion of his army all persuaded him that further attacks would be unwise.

Still, in a week of gallant exertion, the Confederates had lifted the threatened siege of Richmond, removed the danger to the capital, and sent McClellan scurrying back down the Peninsula to Harrison's Landing, whence he would never advance again. Six weeks later he would evacuate.[26]

Best of all, after a season of brutally unrelenting disasters, the Confederacy had a victory once more. It did not matter that the battles were near-fought affairs or that missed opportunities abounded. Lee was a hero, and even Davis could bask in some of his reflected glory. The president's earlier doubts now cleared. Lee's successes convinced him, as Burton Harrison recalled, "against his own judgment, that the South could conquer an independence." Indeed, now the Chief could even indulge a little humor, and a few days after Malvern Hill, when Lee came to meet with the cabinet, Davis recalled the general ordering him away from the battleline and joked that he had thought that *he* was commander in chief. To Varina, Davis confided his disappointment that they had not destroyed McClellan utterly, but he assigned little or no blame. "Our success has been so remarkable that we should be grateful and believe that even our disappointments were ordered for our gain." Indeed, he felt bold enough to assert that "if our ranks were full we could end the war in a few weeks," boasting that there were "some things they have not dreamed which we may do." The victory raised anew his hopes of recognition from England and France, and though on balance he admitted that "our troubles you perceive have not ended," still "our chances have improved."[27]

It had been an incredibly tense time for Davis as well as for his family. From her position hundreds of miles away in Raleigh, Varina could only cling to his letters and to the occasional notes that Colonel Johnston sent her. Indeed, she relied on the young man for information she knew her husband would not give her. Between them they agreed that if the Chief should become ill, Johnston would telegraph her without his knowledge and she would come to Richmond right away, even if she had to brave Davis's displeasure. Joseph Davis joined with Johnston in watching over her "precious Banny," probably a "lover's talk" shortening of *husband*. Yet she could not hide her anxiety. "When I contemplate you in your beleaguered city surrounded by difficulty worn out by responsibilities, and tossed by doubt," she wrote him early in June, she thought he was "the noblest object I ever contemplated." When she knew that fighting was going on at Fair Oaks, she dreamed at night that she and Jefferson stood before a large crowd saying farewell to each other, but that he could not leave her, and kept running back to kiss her again and again, even though the onlookers laughed. When he did send her news, it made her heart stand still to think of the issues at stake in the fight for Richmond. "What if you should fail?" she asked. Learning of Johnston's wounding and Griffith's death—and remembering Sidney Johnston—she moaned, "Why are our best friends killed?" It only impelled her the more to implore him to "dismount your officers, or keep them out of the thickest of the fight." As for himself, he must not expose himself. "The President is much to me, but the love of my youth still more."[28]

It did not help that Varina's news was just as unsettling to her husband as his was to her. Little William remained very ill through most of the late spring and early summer, and every letter from Varina brought more news of his suffering from boils and perhaps even cholera. He reacted badly to a vaccination, and the administration of opiates and calomel hardly did him any good. Only by late June did he start to recover, yet even then the boils plagued him. Still Varina could finally advise her husband to "be easy about us." And when the news came of the repulse and withdrawal of the Federals, she exulted, not without a little dig at Lee's recuperating predecessor. "McClellan is like Gen Johnston," she teased, "great in retreat."[29]

The relief of July 1862 came sorely needed to Davis. The Shenandoah was safe, McClellan still stood on the lower Peninsula but obviously was going nowhere, and only the formation of a new Federal army around Washington, to be led by General John Pope, posed a serious future threat to northern Virginia. Out on the Mississippi, Farragut's fleet did safely steam upriver and pass the growing mass of batteries at Vicksburg, but the city remained secure. Bragg seemed to have the Army of Mississippi well in hand, and was already starting to talk about an offensive to regain some of Tennessee. Threats still loomed everywhere, but the aspect of absolute gloom of a few weeks before had shifted in the glow of Lee's victory. A cavalry raid led by John Hunt Morgan was even coursing through Kentucky doing mayhem to the Federals and helping keep alive Confederate hopes for the Bluegrass.

It all gave Jefferson Davis a little precious time to breathe easy, if not to relax. The pressure and tension of the past few months put enormous strains upon his concentration and his constitution. Inevitably his health suffered, and the daily rides, the exposure to sun and heat and rain, did not help. Yet as he often did, Davis seemed able to will himself to stay at his work, face his office table for many hours a day, and then ride to the front. Indeed, the nervous excitement of the field and the battlefield may have exercised a therapeutic effect on at least that part of his ill health caused by nerves. On his horse and in the presence of an army, Davis relaxed. As the Seven Days' Battles began to rage, he even told Varina that he felt "almost well again."[30]

23

The Vicious and the Selfish

It is good that he did, for the respite was brief. Indeed, there was no rest at all, for one war that Davis had to fight was almost constant now—its weapons words, its battlefields the newspapers, and governors' mansions, and halls of Congress.

In founding the Confederacy no one ever suspected that implanted within it were the seeds of bitter internal discord, seeds actually carried within the minds and hearts of the men who led the secession movement and championed it in legislatures and at the head of regiments, brigades, divisions, and armies. Southerners, by their very nature as men representative of their section and time, were doomed to try to tear down what they had themselves built.

Jefferson Davis himself illustrated some of the mores and impulses that now worked against him in the breasts of others—intense pride, punctilious insistence on personal rights, ambition for military glory, a disposition to be intensely critical of opposition, and the tendency to react rather than act. All these and more elements not present in Davis— boastfulness, petty greed for power, spite, and even malice—fermented in the brains and hearts of thousands.

Unfortunately, in forming the new Confederacy, its founding fathers could not leave behind their careers as mid-nineteenth-century Southerners. Ambition, boastfulness, even arrogance, were traits often admired and even cultivated by men of the time, and well illustrated by someone like the bombastic Beauregard. No greater opportunity for the boastful could ever have been imagined than the war growing out of secession. Almost every man of any prominence—regardless of his experience—felt impelled to become a great leader. How else could he display his presumed brilliance? Yet there were too few positions and opportunities, and the president gave most of those to West Point men. Thus an ambitious host of would-be Bayards saw their hopes thwarted by Davis's presumably narrow policy of giving commands to professional soldiers. They could not see that putting trained men in command was the only sound policy; they saw only favoritism and cronyism as the president looked after his own kind.

The reverses of early 1862 gave such critics a mountain of ammunition. What had the professionals achieved? Shiloh, New Orleans, Forts Henry and Donelson, the failure to follow up on Manassas, Johnston's retreat before McClellan, Van Dorn's failure in Arkansas. The disappointed would-be generals regarded this as proof enough of the foolhardiness of Davis's policy.

Then there were the politicians. For more than a generation, Southern politicians had grown up in the mold, not of policy makers, but of policy critics. Like Davis in the Senate, they proposed little significant legislation themselves. Rather, they followed a course of condemning the congressional acts of others, becoming in many instances little more than reactionary gainsayers. After so many years of feeling on the defensive in Washington, their constant instinct was to assail those in authority, to attack and tear down, and all too often without concern for the ultimate effects of their actions. Southern politicians, in effect, had evolved into professional adversaries, fractious, factious, and disregardful of consequences.

Then there were the men who came to some power in the new Confederacy who brought with them old animosities, men like Henry S. Foote, whose prewar hatred of Davis became part of his new religion as a Confederate. Not far away stood some of the original fire-eating secessionists, chiefly men of the South Carolina stamp like Rhett of the *Mercury*, men who objected to one so lukewarm on secession now being entrusted with leadership of the great cause. Governors chafed at being sent orders from Richmond, when they thought that the cause they were fighting for stood grounded on the supremacy of the states, not the national government. Most numerous of all were the people themselves, people who saw nothing but victories in 1861 and could not understand why the war had lasted long enough for the disasters of 1862. It seems not to have occurred to them that Lincoln and the Union had anything to do with prolonging the war. With Confederate armies ascendant everywhere in 1861, it must have been Confederate leadership that prevented a victorious end to the war.

All these and yet more factions festered in the struggling young nation, and even as the victories on the Peninsula should have given cheer to all, these elements saw the Confederacy's cup—like its commissary—not half full, but half empty. The harping over Davis's military appointments echoed incessantly. With Johnston wounded and out of the way, and Lee eminently successful, it focused chiefly on Polk and Van Dorn. Even the president's brother Joseph joined the chorus against the latter, declaring that "when Van Dorn was made a General it spoiled a good captain." Worse, Van Dorn represented a policy that outraged many state leaders, especially Louisiana Governor Thomas Moore. In creating the military departments over which his generals exercised authority, Davis did not make them in any way subordinate to the civil authorities of those states. In many cases, his commanders showed due tact and consideration, but a few did not. When Van Dorn took command at Vicksburg that summer, Mississippians began to complain of the "tyranny of little viceroys of Departments, who assume powers the President does not claim."[1]

Indeed, Van Dorn almost led to a breach between Davis and Moore, one of his most steadfast supporters among the often troublesome cadre of Confederate governors. Davis could count on trouble from Joseph Brown, and even from Pickens in South Carolina, especially on the always-tender subject of the use of state arms and the raising of volunteer regiments. But with Moore it was—or should have been—another matter. Van Dorn and other officers under his command virtually seized state arms without permission, and the general then published a proclamation amounting to martial law in Mississippi and eastern Louisiana. Moore protested in heated words this "illegal exercise of authority" and even promised that he would resist anyone's right, Federal or Confederate alike, to confiscate state property. Moore's protest stung Davis, already smarting from his problems with the other governors, and must have brought home to him how serious his problems with gubernatorial relations could become when one of his staunchest supporters like Moore became so outraged. Moore later withdrew his protest and apologized, and Davis, for his part, ordered Van Dorn to return the weapons. Meanwhile, when Van Dorn was ordered east of the Mississippi to reinforce Bragg and to take command at Vicksburg, Governor Henry Rector of Arkansas issued a proclamation denouncing Richmond for abandoning the states west of the river. Thus it seemed that those who lost Van Dorn wanted him, and those who had him would prefer to lose him.[2]

The rise of criticism and unrest heard in the state houses of the Confederacy found even more expression in their presses. Here, again, old prewar animosities and suspicions played their part. Certainly Charleston and the *Mercury* had never been overfond of Jefferson Davis, becoming probably his first and most vocal critic in the days after the formation of the Montgomery government. The failure to pursue the Federals into Washington after the victory at Manassas gave Rhett even more fuel for his distrust of the Mississippian, and thereafter his pages rarely lost an opportunity to strike a blow, often descending to insult. "Jeff Davis now treats all men as if they were idiot insects," it asserted during the dark days of May. James Chesnut's wife thought she saw a measure of thwarted ambition in this. If Rhett had been made president instead of Davis, or if Davis had made him secretary of state, "We might have escaped one small war, at least—the war the *Mercury* was now waging with the administration."[3]

Elsewhere other editors took up the same cudgel, their attacks based on the same complaints—usurpation of authority, cronyism, the failure to press a vigorous pursuit after Manassas, and Davis's presumed hauteur. Even in the capital, Davis was not safe from it, as John Daniel's *Examiner* quickly assumed the form of an antiadministration sheet. As early as August 1861 people noted that Daniel seemed to attack Davis in his pages almost every day. By September he asserted that any of a number of men would have made better presidents than Davis—even Toombs, Cobb, and Slidell—and the following winter claimed that if the Yankees were getting the best of the conflict after the fall of Fort Donelson, it was because they "have outwitted us." "Us," of course, meant President Davis. And then, as if to show that no matter what Davis did he could not win everyone's approval, the *Examiner* declared that he should act almost as a dictator. While the governors clamored for their rights, while civil authorities protested the imposition of martial law where it existed, Daniel said "to the dogs with Constitutional questions and moderation." After Hunter's departure from the cabinet and the shifting of the increasingly unpopular Benjamin to State, Daniel went so far as to assert that Davis held on to lesser men as his ministers because he was "jealous of intellect." Daniel even ridiculed Davis's confirmation in the Episcopal church. He had proclaimed several days of fasting and prayer for divine assistance, and Daniel saw little good to be accomplished. "These devotional proclamations of Mr. Davis have lost all good effect from their repetition," he wrote, and "are regarded by the people as either cant or evidences of mental weakness."[4]

The press clamored for action and even for retaliation. Late in July, Pope declared that male Virginians within his lines who refused to take an oath of allegiance to the Union would be expelled from his command, and if they returned they would be shot as spies. Davis countered at the end of the month with an order that any of Pope's officers captured should be treated not as honorable prisoners of war, but as felons. This was not enough for many editors, who criticized Davis for not declaring a policy of no quarter instead.[5]

More than any other single subject, the press attacked the administration—meaning Davis—for the inaction after Manassas that so many believed cost them an early victory in the war. And when that policy of staying on the defensive persisted into 1862, and seemingly left them vulnerable to the losses of the past spring, the attacks became even more bitter. Ridiculing Davis's recent confirmation, Daniel declared that "when we find the President standing in a corner telling his beads, and relying on a miracle to save the country, instead of mounting his horse and putting forth every power of the Government to defeat the enemy, the effect is depressing in the extreme." The *Mercury* went just as far in lamenting the aftermath of Manassas, saying it hoped "when another battle was won, we would not have to wait half a year for wagons or for Jeff Davis to recover his health."[6]

Davis had his defenders on this score, and most perceptive observers realized that it was easy for the ignorant or ill informed to say what should be done or what they would do, when they bore no responsibility and did not know all of the facts. Mary Chesnut saw in the attacks of the *Mercury* the making of "something of a party" against Davis, based on this one issue. "They, far removed from the seat of war and ignorant of what reasons prevent a forward movement, deem themselves far more competent to judge of what is proper to be done than those who, bearing the brunt and seeing everything, are." The fact is, his defensive posture frustrated the president almost continually. It ran counter to his basic nature as well as to his ideas of how to win a victory. Preston Johnston complained of the actions of men like Beauregard and Joseph E. Johnston, protesting that if allowed, "We would not stop retreating short of the gulf of Mexico." Davis himself called it a "crawfish policy," and though he argued strongly against it with his generals, still he found himself blamed for it. "It cannot be helped," young Johnston confided to his wife in private. "He cannot proclaim that he and his Generals are at variance," and indeed Davis could not. His policy, wisely conceived and showing considerable restraint, was to let the commander on the scene— the man most familiar with the ground, the troops, and the situation— make the final decision to attack or retreat.[7]

Only occasionally did Davis speak out to defend his strategic actions, and even then he did so without calling attention to the differences of opinion between himself and his generals. For almost a year after Manassas he listened to the criticism of what happened—or did not happen—in its aftermath. The entire South, it seemed, wanted to see Confederate soldiers invading Union territory, destroying their crops and barns, taking the hard hand of war to their farms and cities. They protested what one colorful Confederate called "the dunghill policy of fighting at every State's threshold."[8]

Davis protested it, too. "There could be no difference of opinion as to the advantage of invading over being invaded," he told a friend just two weeks after McClellan's retreat. From the outset he had hoped to "feed upon the enemy and teach them the blessings of peace by making them feel in its most tangible form the evils of war," and he joined with those in the Confederacy who advised a meek policy in hopes of not exciting the hatred of the Yankees. Yet an offensive required more than will. It needed means and power. By July 1862 the president conceded that there might have been occasions when an invasion could have been undertaken or when attacks could have been launched against isolated Yankee commands. His generals thought otherwise. "I have thought it proper to defer much to the opinions of commanders in the field, and have felt the hazard of requiring a General to execute what he did not favorably entertain." Davis had fought vigorously the false reports that he prevented Johnston and Beauregard from pursuing after Manassas, though a year later critics still charged him with responsibility for what his own generals told him their army could not do. "I have borne unjust criticism in silence and allowed vain men to shift the responsibilities of their grievous failures upon me," he said, no doubt referring chiefly to Beauregard. He did not do so, as critics charged, because he was deaf to public opinion, but to prevent open quarreling with his commanders, and his "true friends" understood that, or he felt they did. Those who did not so understand his stance he characterized as men who "make issues for selfish ends and talk for popular effect."

In fact, Davis was in a difficult position. The people at large, understanding little of military affairs, could hardly see beyond the fact that they had large armies in the field. They did not see the problems of food and transportation, supply and logistics. "The people have generally no measure of military operations," he declared. But if he publicly explained what restrained his generals—their relative weaknesses compared to the enemy—that information would invite the foe to take advantage. To preserve vital security, therefore, Davis had to keep from the public his reasons for staying on the defensive, even though doing so brought a heap of unjust censure on him. He never "preferred defensive to offensive war," he declared, "and if I could to-night issue orders to an army adequate to the work of invasion," he would do so.

"I love approbation," Davis confessed, "and will toil on though it be through evil report, to deserve, with the hope that I may gain it." Unfortunately, he made no effort to cultivate the press but instead retreated from the fourth estate out of suspicion and resentment. Being told nothing of the president's plans, the press in time assumed that he had none and itself adopted a hostile attitude.[9]

Disappointed place seekers added to the chorus. By the spring of 1862 Davis almost ceased making generals of amateurs. The pressures to keep governors and congressmen happy still influenced some appointments, but a year of war had identified enough capable colonels to give him a pool of deserving candidates. He could do little with some already commissioned, but he cashiered Floyd and tried to put Pillow where he could do no harm.[10] But other generals remained to cause problems, many of them joining his opposition. Milledge Bonham from South Carolina fell out with him over seniority and instead went to Congress to make himself troublesome. General W. H. T. Walker feuded with him when he saw old army juniors promoted over him and his own brigade reassigned to Richard Taylor. In an embarrassingly public controversy, backed by the Georgia delegation, Walker eventually resigned. Probably as a result of the imbroglio with Johnston, Davis ignored his own rules on seniority and his own improving opportunities to promote for merit instead.[11]

Yet even these considerations cannot explain the advancement of Lovell and Gustavus Smith. Neither rose above captain in the old army, and both left it in 1854. Smith believed that then Secretary of War Davis begrudged him his resignation, but others near Davis claimed that in 1861 he was anxious to have Smith join the cause and expressed a warm friendship for him. Certainly when they came South, he made both major generals, well over Walker and others much their senior, and put Smith in line to command Johnston's army after the latter's Seven Pines wound. Others may have influenced Davis, for Beauregard early lauded Smith, and Smith in turn sang Lovell's praises. But by mid-1862 Davis was disappointed with both of them, and then Smith launched a feud of his own when, with ironic justice, Davis made others, who had once been his juniors, lieutenant generals over him. Jackson, Kirby Smith, Hardee, and Longstreet earned their laurels, but Holmes, John C. Pemberton, and Polk owed theirs to nothing more than Davis's friendship. The situation led Smith to resign. Certainly he had not merited promotion; neither had Holmes and Polk, but the clear vision with which the president viewed his foes turned suddenly myopic when cast on his friends.[12]

It all played into his critics' hands. Toombs damned him regularly now, and young Johnston probably echoed the Chief when he branded the Georgian "a seditious, turbulent, able, shrewd, drunken, pestilential demagogue." Worse, such men sought to "wound the President through his friend[s]," said Johnston. Foote criticized Sidney Johnston over Shiloh, and others attacked Bragg. Davis begged Bragg to ignore "the vicious and the selfish. . . . You have the misfortune of being regarded as my personal friend, and are pursued therefore with malignant censure by men regardless of truth."[13]

Davis felt particularly grieved in the next few months as more attacks came from men who had been friends. During his July visit to Mississippi, "Dobbin" Johnston was shocked by the degree of criticism he heard in the South. Worse, Yancey was "insidiously attacking [Davis] in the newspapers." Indeed, another friend advised the president that Yancey had authored the attacks on Bragg. How had the man who declared that the "man and the hour" had met become an enemy?[14]

Yancey would have been alone among the fire-eaters if he had not felt uneasy with the moderate Davis from the beginning. He turned down a cabinet post and only accepted the diplomatic assignment under pressure. Bored abroad, he still resented being replaced, thinking it implied censure. Back in Richmond in April 1862, he confessed "hopeless despair" over Davis's foreign policy. Politely he complained to the president about Hunter's handling of foreign purchasing and Memminger's parsimony. To his credit, Davis replied in cordial terms, but when Yancey responded he did so stiffly, implying that Davis was out of touch with his cabinet.[15]

Again Davis maturely ignored the challenge. But on April 21 Yancey joined Clay in a month-old complaint that the latter's cousin had been denied his proper rank in the army. Davis's prior assurances that the kinsman retained the same relative rank to others that he had in the old army had not satisfied Clay. Now Yancey and Clay together sent a letter protesting that Davis had not appointed enough Alabamians to command the state's troops and pointed out that in spite of the president's announced policy of appointing only men who had "won their spurs," as he liked to say, he had made two inexperienced men from other states generals and put them in charge of Alabama brigades. Rubbing his nose in his violation of his own policy, they charged that newspaperman Roger Pryor of Virginia had now been commissioned a brigadier and given Alabama troops.[16]

There was no greater sin than catching Davis in an inconsistency. He responded immediately. He would receive suggestions from anyone, but he and only he had the power to nominate officers, and he would not debate the propriety of his decisions. When Yancey received the reply, written angrily on the back of their letter and returned to Clay, he wrote to the president in a conciliatory tone, complimenting the recent appointment of Alabamian Nathan Bedford Forrest and assuring that any suggestions from him came in his capacity as a citizen of his state and not as a Confederate senator. He had no ill will toward the president, he promised.[17]

Thereafter Yancey, though careful not to attack Davis personally, increasingly opposed the administration, and pressed constantly for apportioning generals among the states. Then came his attacks on Bragg for putting regiments from one state under generals from another. He moved in the Senate to limit Davis's nominating power and even opposed Davis's appointment of Alabamian John A. Campbell as assistant secretary of war when Campbell appeared hostile to many leading Alabama candidates for promotion. This and more soon convinced the president that Yancey's stance was not "of that measured kind that results from occasional difference of opinion." Yancey was his enemy.[18]

After a year of skirmishing, the battle joined in earnest over, of all things, a postmaster. Davis dispensed such local patronage, and customarily he allowed senators to choose the postmasters in their home towns. But when Yancey nominated a man named Glackmayer for Montgomery in April 1863, Davis sent a different name to the Senate for confirmation. When Clay twice called on the president and implored him to make this one small concession for Yancey, he erred in adding that he would not himself vote for Davis's choice, nor would the rest of the Senate. Davis exploded. These men would not "dragoon him into nominating their choice," he fumed. Clay went away hurt and baffled. "He is a strange compound which I cannot analyze," he told Yancey. "He will not ask or receive counsel, and, indeed, seems predisposed to go exactly the way his friends advise him not to go." "If he survives this war and does not alter his course," said the wounded friend, "he will find himself in a small minority party."[19]

Yancey immediately severed all relations with the president, even demanding the withdrawal of a request for his son's commission, charging that Davis's appointments were "conferred as rewards to friends and refused as punishment inflicted upon enemies." When Yancey accused him of "personal enmity," Davis denied it but immediately began accumulating evidence for a protracted written lecture that he soon sent Yancey. The exchange of letters continued until July 1863, despite Clay's efforts to mediate, which only left him the more puzzled. In one breath Davis spoke of Yancey "with offensive and opprobious epithets and innuendoes" and then with the next denied any hostility toward him—a claim that Clay asserted no one who had heard Davis during the past year would believe. Davis showed all the correspondence to Clay at one point, but to the Alabamian it was apparent that he did so hoping "that I would say something to justify him to himself."

Davis could not admit even to himself that now he disliked Yancey, just as he always disliked strong-willed men who challenged him and would not submit. Confessing hostility would allow reasons other than duty and the public good to explain his actions, and that he could not countenance. Clay, who remained a friend by staying submissive, lamented to Yancey in June that the president's "official course grows daily more inscrutable, and the more I see of him the less I understand him." As late as July 25 Davis still professed friendship for Yancey. "I think he begins to find himself in want of *friends* or *adherents*," said Clay, and with crystalline perception added, "I do not know, really, which he wishes." Davis himself never knew, and he never fully grasped the difference between the two.[20]

Personalities, pride, priggishness, and the strains of the war conspired to make enemies of friends. Davis had needed Yancey's support, but he could not bend or compromise even a little to keep it. Henry Clay's declaration that he "would rather be right than be President" may have been apocryphal, but the sentiment described Jefferson Davis perfectly. Certainly Yancey did say that "the man and the hour have met" in February 1861. When his death on July 27, 1863, ended the feud, he went to his grave convinced now that the man and the hour had missed.

Even as he protested his innocence in the Yancey affair, Davis almost ranted that he was "misunderstood and maltreated" and that Congress, especially the Senate, opposed him at every step. In fact, he had lost the goodwill of many in the Capitol, but not entirely by his own doing.[21] Davis had been farseeing before the war when he decried the emergence of geographical parties, but he did not count on their crippling a president of the new nation. Only one thing united Confederates—their regional hostility to the old Union. Once they were out of the old compact and the enemy—politically at least—lay beyond their borders, their commonality as Southerners was not enough to bind them. There were no platforms, no agendas, no party loyalties to hold them in line and build stability through practice and tradition. Instead, centrifugal forces sent them flying apart. The group became almost nothing, the individual everything. "*Big-man-me-ism* reigns supreme," said James Hammond of South Carolina, "& every one thinks every other a jealous fool or an aspiring knave."[22]

No real organized parties emerged. Instead, like the universe after the "big bang," the explosion of secession ended the old political order by ending the issues that had bound it, creating in its stead a host of competing stars, each seeing the new universe only from its own vantage. Statesmen, generals, border-state men, and office seekers all saw the Confederacy as a means to *their* ends, and those ends as legitimate goals for the Confederacy. They could never agree, not even to disagree. They formed no parties, only factions. The irony is that Jefferson Davis, the prewar spokesman for localism, emerged from this chaotic soup as the leading champion of nationalism. For all his flaws, only he seemed to see the universe as a whole. For the rest, the absence of parties spared them the inconvenience of establishing platforms and setting agendas. Instead they risked and proposed little or nothing, blaming all ills on Davis without submitting alternatives to the ballot box. Worse, without the restraints of party, the demagogic were left to press personal feuds unchecked.

The opponents emerged soon and venomously. Thomas Cobb had started back in February 1861 and now called Davis "an obstinate stupid fool." "He is obstinate as a mule," said Cobb, asserting that by January 1862 Davis had lost Congress and took pride in being a leader of the opposition. Thwarted ambition chiefly motivated Cobb, an amateur who aspired to high military command. He accused Davis of being a "monomaniac" in his preference for West Point men, and called then Secretary of War Benjamin a "Jew dog" for not giving him a command. Howell

Cobb and Toombs felt much the same; all sought high commissions, none were professionals.[23]

Yet these three could not conform their ambitions with those of another powerful Georgian who became a leading critic. Alexander Stephens, too, decried the "West Pointism" in the army, agreeing with Hammond that "West Point is death to us & sick Presidents & Generals are equally fatal." But Stephens stopped short of Hammond's call for impeachment and making Toombs, or even the coward Floyd, dictator.[24] Nevertheless, he distanced himself from Davis, refusing to speak at the inauguration, visiting the Capital only occasionally, and chiefly writing letters and speeches critical of the administration. Instead of binding him to the Cobbs and Toombses, however, Stephens's actions only won him accusations of being a "selfish demagogue," Thomas Cobb asserting that Congress would depose Davis but for the fact that Stephens would be the successor.[25]

Along with Governor Brown, these men arrayed most of Georgia's influence against Davis. Hammond, Rhett, and sometimes Pickens did the same for South Carolina, and to varying degrees the factions from other states joined the outcry, much of it over personal and local, not national, issues. Thus Davis learned how quickly friends could become enemies. In the early days, no one had seemed closer than Wigfall, the trusted aide who even shared Davis's carriage in the triumphal arrival parade in Richmond. But then their wives fell out, as happened with several generals' wives. In time, Charlotte Wigfall, a South Carolinian, complained of Varina's "objectionable" habits and in August 1861 called her a "coarse western woman," comments that got back to the Davises.[26] Meanwhile, Wigfall wanted to be a brigadier, but Davis made him a lieutenant colonel. Then Davis failed to take him on the trip to Manassas on July 21. In the controversy over the failure to pursue McDowell's defeated army and the squabble over Johnston's seniority, Wigfall sided against the president, at least in Richmond's drawing rooms. When Davis heard of it, he cooled toward his aide, but a reconciliation soon followed, and with it Wigfall's brigadiership—evidence of Davis's goodwill, for the Texan earned it no other way.

But Wigfall resigned in February 1862 and took a seat in the Senate, where he immediately and publicly charged Davis for the disasters in Tennessee, continued to champion Joseph E. Johnston, and tried to push the government into launching an offensive. He even urged Johnston to disobey Davis and take the offensive on his own, saying it was fruitless to urge "such a dish of skimmed milk to an honorable action."[27]

The breach widened rapidly as the intemperate Wigfall often launched into drunken speeches at local hotel bars, always attacking

Davis's military policy. Then in October Davis vetoed a Wigfall bill that would have taken away the president's prerogative of appointing staff officers. At a social gathering soon afterward, Wigfall's daughters pointedly snubbed Davis when he approached them and everyone noticed. From such small rills, said the hostess, Mary Chesnut, "flowed the mighty stream which has made, *at last*, Louis Wigfall the worst enemy the president has in the Congress."[28]

If friends like Wigfall and Yancey could become Davis's enemies, how much easier was it for men unlike Clay, men who never got the chance to know and like him in better times? As early as the summer of 1861, influential South Carolinians abandoned him. Lawrence Keitt called him a failure, and William Trescott claimed that "disintegration has already begun." Mrs. Wigfall asserted that by August of that year the anti-Davis coalition was forming and that Clay was his only friend in Congress.[29]

In fact, Davis did have good friends in Congress, men like Clay and Benjamin Hill of Georgia, but his supporters were just as unorganized as his opposition, and he made no effort to bind them to his policies. Worse, he could not spare a few kind words to make or keep a friend when these men came to call. His meetings with a congressman or a delegation could be forbidding. Even "Dobbin" Johnston admitted by the summer of 1862 that "the President, like other mortals, was somewhat irascible." "Though generally calm externally," said a War Office man, "he was peevish; worse than that, he was afflicted with strong and bitter prejudices." Burton Harrison, equally loyal, said, "A stranger, judging from appearance only, would have thought him cold and austere." Postmaster General Reagan explained that Davis "had two characters, or rather two methods of thought and action"—kind and gentle in private while "in the discharge of his public duties he seemed to be guided almost wholly by a sense of duty."[30]

Unfortunately, that air of performing an impersonal public act in meeting with members of Congress appeared to them to be nothing more than hauteur and intentional offense. It did not help that Davis developed an early distrust of Congress, not unlike many another American president before and since. He got on wonderfully with the original provisional group, composed of the best statesmen the South had to offer. But not all of them won seats in the regularly elected first Congress that met in Richmond in 1862. Some did not seek office, others failed to win it, and more were in the field as officers by then. As a result Davis faced a group of men inferior to those who strove so hard to subordinate themselves for a show of unanimity in Montgomery. Davis did not suffer lesser men any better than he handled criticism, and when these congressmen showed an early inclination to attack his administration after the disasters of February–April, he promptly adopted a policy of telling them no more than he had to. Given his lack of diplomatic skills, Davis could not see that such a course guaranteed only increasing criticism.

When he met them in person, his manner only made matters worse. To supporters like Hill or Burgess Gaither of North Carolina the president showed courtesy and even occasional affability. But more often his habitual demeanor in any such meeting was diffidence. Even getting an audience with the president became difficult. A clerk in the War Department noted that whereas the year before, Davis had been accessible to all, now he had a host of aides screening visitors first and allowing only certain ones to see him. "This looks like the beginning of an imperial court," he complained. "What a change in the Executive Department!" More than once he had to explain his inability to meet with the honorable members. Considering more than one hundred Congressmen, added to the generals and messengers, his cabinet, and other government officials, all vying for his time, he protested that "the entire official day is inadequate to their reception." "It thus happens often that gentlemen of the two Houses find me pre-engaged." Worse, when they did get in to see him, they found him preoccupied and distant. Mallory saw it repeatedly, as congressmen walked out of the president's office complaining bitterly of his being ungracious and irritable. When they called to suggest some man for promotion, or some policy for aiding the war effort, Davis listened quietly, then stated in the most economical words possible just why he could not agree with them. "In his manner & language," said Mallory, "there was just an indescribable something which offended their self esteem & left their judgments room to find fault with him." Even close friends sometimes left shaking their heads or fists, red with anger and determined never to call on him again. To Mallory it seemed a terrible loss. Friends tried to persuade Davis to use a little gentleness, to be more conciliatory and friendly toward such visitors. "It was of no use," lamented the navy secretary. "He could not do this, it was not in his nature." Davis recoiled at anything that smacked of seeking popularity, and "scorned to believe it necessary to coax men to do their duty." He could not see, as Mallory did, that "a wound to their self esteem affected their action in public affairs, & Mr. Davis' sins in this respect towards them, real or imaginary, were seen in their votes & speeches."[31]

Young Johnston saw it at even closer hand and more repeatedly. He saw Davis's habitual reserve, his unwillingness to sit still when bored or importuned by a congressman. The president so clearly knew his own mind in all matters, felt such contempt for politicking, dodges, and subterfuges, that Johnston easily saw that "this is not a man or a character to be popular with the common run of politicians." As a result, he said, [Davis] "I fear is a little too impatient of opposition—a quality that makes opposition." "I fear he does not concede or conciliate enough this powerful class of society," Johnston wrote in May 1862, "for though contemptible as individual men, they are powerful in numbers and in holding the key of the popular mind." The Richmond editor Edward A. Pollard put it even more succinctly when he lamented in 1865 that "no man could receive a delegation of Congressmen, or any company of persons who had advice to give, or suggestions to make, with such a well-bred grace, with a politeness so studied as to be almost sarcastic, with a manner that so plainly gave the idea that his company talked to a post."[32]

The result was predictable to almost everyone but Davis. Boyce came away believing him a stuffed shirt. Toombs believed the president too impressed with his own importance. A Tennessee delegation once stormed out of the president's office in a huff, and in 1863 a fight nearly broke out when a North Carolina contingent of congressmen visited and Senator Edwin Reade called Davis dictatorial. Cooler heads calmed the antagonists, and at the end of the interview Davis shook hands with all of them, even Reade. In a rare moment of self-insight the president had told Varina the year before that "I wish I could learn just to let people alone who snap at me; in forbearance and charity to turn away as well from the cats as the snakes." But of course he could not.

Even Varina saw how desperately in need of reaching out to these men Davis was, yet she could not make him do it. They entertained only infrequently at the Executive Mansion, and then usually at breakfast with close friends like Clay. Early in the war they tried to have some evening entertainments, but too often messengers arrived with news of some disaster to Confederate arms or the death of a relative of a guest. It all upset Davis too much. Varina described him as a "nervous dyspeptic by habit," and if he ate while upset or excited, he remained ill for days. Thus he stopped having officials to his home for dinner. He could either "give entertainments or administer the Government," he told his wife. He could not do both.[33]

Varina could see that he should be cultivating these men, but it was not in him. "He was abnormally sensitive to disapprobation," she would recall; "even a child's disapproval discomposed him." Unwilling to explain himself to Congress, and unwilling to communicate with them or open up to them, he felt their resultant criticism unjust, "and the sense of mortification and injustice gave him a repellent manner." Thus in his own temperament and his own insecurities, Davis gave birth to, and then nurtured, exactly the atmosphere best calculated to escalate the outcries against him, and his own increasingly obdurate response. It was precisely because of his "super-sensitive temperament," as Varina called it, that she felt so downhearted at his being called to the Presidency.[34]

Occasionally Davis made little attempts to reach out, but he would not have seen them thus, and they came more by accident than design. He passed brief idle conversation with a congressman if they met by chance on the street, though it was so infrequent as to attract comment from witnesses. He always answered their written communications in unfailingly polite terms, and when he and Varina did hold a reception, congressmen were included. Yet these were minor by their nature and availed him nothing. "So little by little the Congress became alienated," Varina would recall, without attempting to excuse her husband from responsibility. As the gap between Executive and Congress widened in 1862 and beyond, Varina could see it "gnaw at his vitals." With his usual resignation to the folly and weakness in others, Davis told her that "if we succeed we shall hear nothing of these malcontents; if we do not, then I shall be held accountable by the majority of friends as well as foes." With the faint touch of self-assumed martyrdom that occasionally emerged in his melancholy periods, he concluded that "I will do my best, and God will give me strength to bear whatever comes to me."[35]

But he did not bear it in silence. By the summer of that year he complained to his friend General Kirby Smith, with obvious disingenuousness, that "a long experience has somewhat blunted my sensibility to undeserved censure." Yet to his brother Joseph he complained in June of being drowned in a "sea of troubles," and apparently laid the blame to men in Congress who had been disappointed in their applications for special favors from him and others in the executive branch. "I hope my dear brother you may surmount them all," Joseph encouraged him, and after the successes at Vicksburg and in Virginia that summer, Joseph even advised his brother that in the West the feeling of disaffection seemed less evident and "the opposition seem more moderate." Bravely Jefferson told Joseph that he was "not annoyed by their unprin[ci]pled clamor," but of course that was not true.[36]

The president's attitude spread to his aides and official family as well. Preston Johnston complained in August of Davis having had five "stupid senators to dinner" one evening, and would go on a few days later to generalize that "this Congress is a weak body." Clearly adopting the president's attitudes, Johnston particularly noted old Foote, "a nuisance and an obstruction to public business." Decrying the dissatisfaction with the administration felt by the politicians, Johnston went on to speculate—as did Davis—that much of its basis lay with malcontents from Missouri, Tennessee, and Kentucky. Representatives from those border states, the first and last not even seceded, had no constituents to hold them responsible and hammered at Davis repeatedly that his first priority must be retaking their homes from the enemy. That same summer Johnston even thought he saw a concerted plot among these men, along with disappointed office seekers, "violent revolutionary extremists of the South Carolina school," reactionary politicians, and a knot of "factionists" led by Foote, to overthrow the government. Verily he believed they would not stop at assassination, and lamented that "the President is one of those men, whose personal gallantry and disregard of self, prevent him taking the proper precautions against such a nest of vipers."[37]

Friends tried to do what they could to aid the beleaguered president. Defenders wrote to him to decry his critics' "dunghill policy of fighting at every State's threshold," as urged by "shallow politicians too weak to see beyond the door, and too cramped in patriotism to go beyond it." Those closer to him even tried to do what Davis would not do for himself. Young Johnston contacted newspaperman W. N. Haldeman, an expatriate Kentuckian, hoping to persuade him to come to Richmond and publish a pro-administration sheet. Almost certainly Davis neither knew of nor approved the scheme, which never came to fruition. And for all of the president's good supporters elsewhere in the press and in Congress, his foes always seemed to speak louder, and more often, as their numbers continued to grow. Back in November 1861, when the anti-Davis factions were first beginning to feel their might, some of their press complained that their problem would be in getting their point of view across to the people, especially when the time came for elections. Hoping that he might be defeated for election to a full six-year term, the *Mercury* had complained that "there is no particular person upon whom the popular thought may converge and concentrate. . . . The people know not where to look for a suitable man." Were the choice up to Congress at that time, "Mr. Davis would be flung high as a kite."[38]

But another Charleston editor, that of the *Daily Courier*, took a more objective view of the situation, and one that obtained throughout the rest of the war just as well as it fit the situation that November. Characterizing the opposition as being composed of two classes, petty politicians disappointed in seeking higher office, and prominent men who found Davis's ear deaf to their grand schemes, the *Courier's* Richmond correspondent confirmed that "the anti-Davis men rally under no acknowledged leader." Indeed, "there is no leader that one could name that the other would be satisfied with." "They possess no statesman in their ranks who could command a tithe of the affection and confidence that the people have in Jefferson Davis." Instead, the little men in their plotting factions stood on street corners and in hotel lobbies and on the floor of Congress, and sought only to tear down without offering to build some better alternative. They "strive to destroy," to "spread the distrust." "The present opposition is generally formed as all oppositions to existing Administrations," said the correspondent, and he could not have been more correct.[39]

However much Jefferson Davis contributed to their animosity, theirs was the greater shame. To be sure, in his unwillingness to bend and accommodate, in his refusal to communicate with them and take them into his confidence, and in his prideful and even smug attitude and refusal to do a little harmless cajoling, the president demonstrated just how temperamentally unsuitable he was to be a chief executive. In a position, especially in time of crisis, that required great human skills, he possessed pitifully few when it came to governing and inspiring men. What he could do with a regiment on the battlefield, he could not do with a legislature in the Capitol. Worse, when proud, ambitious, and often petty men—men much like himself in ways—recoiled at his treatment and demeanor, he showed his tragically inadequate grasp of human nature when he naively complained of his hurt and shock at their behavior. It was also a bit hypocritical, since Davis himself often behaved just as they did under similar provocation.

But the actions of his opponents in all their factions was measurably the worse. Even Davis's bitterest foes did not deny that he worked hard for the Confederacy and that he dedicated himself to the cause, even as they accused him of glorying in power and thirsting for more. Their transcendent sin is that the destruction of Davis became their cause. In attacking him and his measures, they came to do so almost solely for the sake of the attack, and without a consistent program or alternative to propose of their own. Worse, they could not see that in targeting their president, they weakened his effectiveness, and thereby weakened the one and only authority vested with the responsibility to unify and coordinate the paramount attempts to defend and maintain Confederate independence. Like crazed cannibals, they could not see that in their frenzy of blood thirst they were consuming themselves along with Jefferson Davis.

Ironically, the issues over which they attacked him mattered much less to the Confederacy than did the fact of their assaults. One of their first sallies had been the bill to create a commanding general, its authors hoping thereby to divide the president's powers, leaving him with civil control but placing the military primacy with Lee. Davis, of course, vetoed the measure. Later his archrival Foote moved a vote of no confidence in Benjamin and Mallory as war and navy secretaries, chiefly as a way of striking at their chief. Though it failed, the motion served as a rallying point for the growing opposition, and the hostile press soon took up the cry against Davis's subordinates, both of whom would remain centers of controversy for the balance of the war, with even Preston Johnston agreeing so far as Mallory was concerned, calling their navy an "expensive and useless luxury."[40]

Though the first session of the first Congress met for only two months between February and April 1862, still it found a number of other issues about which to differ with him. The declaration of martial law in troubled or endangered areas became a great concern during the crisis that spring and early summer, and Davis found himself importuned by many to exercise military authority almost indiscriminately. Resisting this, he tried to be judicious in its application, repeatedly protesting that "the order I want is the order of liberty & law," not military order. Yet when he did impose martial law, often as not he found himself damned as a tyrant. Between March and May he issued such declarations for Norfolk and Portsmouth, Richmond, Petersburg, and twenty Virginia counties, all of eastern Tennessee, and a substantial portion of South Carolina. The outcry from local representatives was predictable. When the newly baptized and confirmed president also began to issue frequent proclamations of days of fasting and prayer, they were at first solemnly observed, but when he overdid the practice critics sneered that he spent too much time on his knees praying, and not enough fighting. Even cabinet ministers joked about it, but Davis took it earnestly, and when Hunter and Benjamin once teased that some time had passed since a fast day, the president missed the twinkle in their eyes and actually issued another decree.[41]

During that summer, when the Yankees threatened central Mississippi, friends advised Davis to save his cotton crop and send away his slaves and livestock. Joseph Davis did remove some of their mutual property from Davis Bend, but rumors soon spread that the president was using his influence to save his own property specifically to the exclusion of that of his neighbors, a false calumny Davis had repeatedly to deny. "The President of the Confederacy," he said, "could not send men to take care of his private property." Though always scrupulous not to abuse his high position for his personal benefit, and though the war would cost him far more in property than it did most Southerners, still his detractors did not scruple at misrepresenting him to the people.

They did the same on an admittedly more sound footing when it came to the charges of favoritism, and Davis unwisely fueled them on October 8, 1862, when he appointed his aide and nephew Joseph R. Davis a brigadier general. The younger Davis had not a whit of military experience other than a few months as colonel of the Tenth Mississippi, with no active service. As a result, when the president's nomination reached the Senate, a howl of outcry over nepotism erupted from members of the opposition. At first the Senate rejected the nomination and only reversed itself after two days of debate, during which Davis's trusted friend William Browne asserted that Davis had to promise a postmastership in Georgia in return for votes for confirmation. The uproar so upset Joseph Davis that he seriously considered not accepting the commission.[42]

Of all the legislation proposed by Davis during the first session of that Congress, only the Conscription Act aroused a real national uproar;

yet here, ironically, some of his most consistent congressional opponents like Yancey and Wigfall stood with him. The act grew out of the disasters of February–April. There were not enough volunteers to replace both the men lost in those military reverses and the twelve-months' regiments first enlisted in early 1861 and now ready to muster out. Though he probably discussed the proposal with some congressional leaders before-hand—or should have—he first publicly proposed it on March 28 in a message to Congress, asking that all able-bodied white males between eighteen and thirty-five be subject to a draft. Moreover, it made all of the men currently in the old twelve-months' regiments—more than 140 of them—liable for conscription as well, offering them furloughs and financial bounties if they would reenlist instead.[43]

An outraged Thomas Cobb decried the proposed bill as a necessity "caused by the imbecility of the government," accusing "Davis and his toadies" of ignoring him when he warned earlier that something had to be done to lure those 1861 volunteers into staying in the service. Compelling them in this fashion was not the way. Yancey agreed but saw no choice, as the South must have men for its armies. As for Wigfall, he actually introduced the first bill based on Davis's recommendation, though he did so out of no love for Davis. Committed to the military and preoccupied with pushing the war vigorously, he saw a draft as the only means to his own ends. Though his ardent states' rights friends broke with him for the most part, still two-thirds of the Congress voted with him, and on April 16 the act became law. That done, the controversy and acrimony would continue for years over the classes of men who were to be exempted from conscription, and over Davis's power to decide on those exemptions. Wisely, the president quickly directed that staff in his executive departments should come from men too young or too old for the draft. As for the exempted classes, they were to include national and state officials—hence the president's decree, in order to avoid charges that he kept eligible men from the army—those engaged in transportation and communications, ministers, miners, printers, educators, doctors and nurses, druggists, and manufacturers at the government's discretion. The exemptions made excellent sense, for they allowed the necessary infrastructure of the civil Confederacy to continue, but the categories would soon see much abuse by those seeking to stay out of uniform. The exemption statutes would be changed and amended several times in subsequent years, but always the abuses remained and, as always, the complaints were directed at Davis.[44]

Jefferson Davis must have felt considerable relief when that first session adjourned soon after passing the conscription act. It would not reconvene for its next session until August 18—just as well considering the danger in Richmond that spring and summer—and Davis did not fail to note that while he stayed in the capitol and faced the enemy, most of his detractors scurried to the safety of their home states. The past year had been a terrible one, commencing with the inability to follow up Manassas, the falling out with Johnston and then Beauregard, the losses at Forts Henry and Donelson, Shiloh, and New Orleans, the failure of diplomatic efforts to achieve speedy European recognition, the exhaustion of the Confederacy's initial financial base, and worst of all the near loss of Richmond and the death of Sidney Johnston. The growth of a vicious internal opposition and the seeming treason of some who had been friends only worsened his cares. "Mr. Davis is peculiar, and painfully sensitive about his friends fealty," Varina told Preston Johnston that August, and she was right. So unquestioningly faithful to friends himself, he could not understand or accept seeming acts of betrayal from those who, once in agreement, changed their views and opposed him. He never changed his own mind, being the slave of his consistency, and when a friend altered attitudes in one instance, Davis was likely to assume the man false in all things. "All men are not built like martyrs," he would say, thus unconsciously implying that Jefferson Davis was.[45]

Yet somehow he came through the incredible ordeal. Predictably the anxiety took a toll on his health, with all of his old ailments recurring intermittently, yet this awful time actually saw him incapacitated far less than was usual. As when he was in the field in Mexico, Davis and his constitution both rose to meet adversity, and his iron will seemingly did not admit of infirmity. During the darkest hours of May in Richmond, he actually seemed buoyant as he rode daily to face the grim prospect of McClellan's army. When the situation demanded courage and determination, he was at his best. "He bears the marks of greatness about him beyond all persons I have ever seen," a lieutenant wrote after seeing the president in church in August. "A perfect head, a deep set eagle eye, an aquiline nose, and mouth and jaw sawed in *steel*." The ever-admiring Preston Johnston, from a closer and more intimate vantage, felt much the same after witnessing Davis during his trials. "The President is fit to be the leader of our people and the exponent of our cause," he wrote in August. "He is one of the few men who seems better the closer he is viewed." Johnston found the Chief to be "just and yet merciful & long suffering." "He is sagacious wise & prudent and yet pure and honest." Johnston had no problem in proclaiming him "a grand man." Moreover, the aide marveled at his president's unwillingness to be a dictator, even when some of his friends in Congress urged that measures be passed vesting him with supreme civil and military power. Davis argued that a president should have only moral force, telling Johnston that if he assumed absolute power, "then the principle for which we contend is a failure."[46]

Even without dictatorial power, Davis had accomplished much. Despite his growing opposition in Congress, most of his administration measures passed, and none of his vetoes was overridden. Especially with the conscription act did he strike a major blow for continuing the war. For all his unwise appointments, he stood by Joseph E. Johnston despite their falling out, and then supported Lee even though his record to date in the war had been lackluster. Indeed, his forbearance with the crusty Johnston continued to be uncharacteristic, and creditable, just as his patience with Yancey and even Beauregard until Shiloh did not sound like the man who had so readily feuded with Winfield Scott a few years before. If he failed to pay sufficient attention to New Orleans, certainly he recognized the equal significance of Vicksburg and redoubled efforts to make it impregnable. He supported his infant navy in spite of criticism and was rewarded with limited success in protecting some of his vital harbors. And most of all, he kept alive in the face of a long season of gloom the Confederate determination for independence. If many of the vocal leaders of the young nation chose to attack him, by and large the common people who followed their plows and shouldered their rifles still believed in him.

Jefferson Davis never possessed the temperamental, managerial, or interpersonal skills necessary to be a great chief executive. In time of peace, running an existing nation not faced with crisis, he would have been about as effective as his friend and model Pierce. But in a situation such as the one in which he found himself after 1861, nature left him ill equipped for the task. No one saw this better than his most intimate observer, Varina, and Davis himself instinctively understood his inadequacy. Yet time after time during this last terrible year, he rose above himself—above his health, above his wounded pride and fragile ego, even at times above his woeful inability to manage men. In spite of the odds against him, in the face of the constant attacks from within and without, still on occasion he showed flashes of what he might have achieved had he been better suited to his position. Though the cumulative effects of this year would show in the months ahead, and as he began to retreat from himself once more and relapse into his weaknesses, there were nevertheless moments during these months that he never again equaled—moments when Jefferson Davis was truly presidential.

There could be no better proof of what the man was made of, and of what he could muster, than the fact that in that August, after a season of near misses and defeats, he was ready to attack in the boldest concerted Confederate effort of the war.

24

To Strike Another Blow

Through the hottest months of the summer, Varina and the children remained in Raleigh. Though she longed to come back to him, the president feared for her health during that season. "So like a dutiful wife," she told young Johnston, "I shall stay here in contentment." At least they were all well now. Billy's boils had gone, and little Jeff and Margaret, whom her father called Polly, flourished. But Varina was troubled. Colonel Ives had been sent to look after them all, and she did not like him. Worse, as August passed on, she dreamed of her husband. She saw him leading an army in battle, and no doubt awoke in a fright when she saw an enemy take him prisoner after lopping off his hand with a sword.[1]

By the middle of the month she could stand no more and prevailed on Davis to let her come to Richmond. The children remained in Raleigh, kept company by Polly's kitten Stonewall and Jeff's little black terrier Nicky. The youngster also had two small goats, one black and the other spotted, that pulled him about in a little cart, so the children would be well occupied. Their mother rejuvenated the life in the Executive Mansion upon her return. She found better food for them all, including peaches and pears; began to hold social breakfasts once more, starting with the Reverend Minnegerode and other divines; and considerably lightened the atmosphere in a house that had known only tense, exhausted men for several months. Even young Johnston, for all his admiration of the Chief, admitted privately that "I feel much easier with her than with the President."[2]

The life in Davis's small personal circle continued much as before.

He continued to ride every day, most often in the evenings now, and almost always asked Johnston to go with him as he cantered along the towpath beside the James River. As much as possible, Davis kept Johnston with him. When he needed a report on the condition of the small army in western Virginia, he sent Colonel Davis. Ives remained in Raleigh for a time, and Browne occasionally performed investigating errands as well. Frequently this left just the president and Johnston "to entertain the bores who come in every evening." The young aide watched his Chief and admiringly commented that "he earns his living." "What a relief to retire from stupid people and see nobody!" Johnston told his wife when he wrote to her in the late hours after a full day of the "bores."[3]

Occasionally local brass bands gave the president a serenade in the evening, and that helped to lighten the daily grind of routine, for Davis kept his aides busy wherever they were. To Johnston he assigned the task of preparing synopses of battle reports from his generals, perhaps to reduce his own load of official reading. When houseguests came, usually members of Varina's family, Johnston had to bunk in a room with Colonel Davis, and all the aides usually dined together. Browne lived nearby with his wife and sometimes entertained Johnston and others at his home. Then, in October, Joseph Davis got his promotion to brigadier and command of a Mississippi brigade with Lee, and Chesnut of South Carolina accepted a position on Davis's staff in his place. But Chesnut took his own apartments nearby, leaving William Preston Johnston the one permanent fixture on Davis's formal staff, along with his secretary Harrison. It was a mixed blessing. "I have here all the considerations & inconveniences the President's friendship bestows," Johnston wrote to his wife. Often, especially when active military operations were under way, he stayed up writing letters and reports until midnight and later, then rushed to write to his Rose. "You do not wonder I turn to this sheet for relief," he wrote her. Yet for all of those inconveniences, Johnston felt an unyielding loyalty, to the point that he would not ask for leave to go see his wife for fear "the Prest. should consider himself half served."[4]

Of course, as busy as Davis kept his aides, he worked himself even harder. Serious matters vied for his official notice. Everything from feuds between his generals to local affairs in Richmond, including problems with liquor, begged his attention.[5] Six months after passage of the first conscription act, the abuses and expansion of the exemption system became more and more of a headache, and a host of applications for exemption came to his desk, from blacksmiths, druggists, and even bucket makers who regarded their civilian pursuits to be vital to the war effort. A natural concomitant to the draft and the waning of the initial enthusiasm that produced the first volunteers was an upsurge in the desertion rate. Those caught and returned for military justice often found themselves condemned to death. In many if not all cases, applications for clemency came to the president, and he referred almost every one to Randolph for an immediate inquiry. When Davis could find any reason, however slight, to intervene in a deserter's or a coward's case, he used his authority as executive to set aside the sentence. He had been a soldier. He knew the pressures and temptations a soldier faced, and he knew that men could be afraid, though he never felt that fear himself. In days ahead his foes would even attack him for his unwillingness to condemn offenders to death, yet like that other president across the Potomac, Davis possessed an ennobling understanding that not all men could be supermen in a crisis.[6]

He was also capable of using his power now and then for nothing more than acts of gracious sentiment. That summer a South Carolina girl, with more heart than grammar, wrote to ask him to let her betrothed "Jeems" of the Fifth South Carolina come home from the army to marry her. "Jeems is willin', I is willin', his mammy says she is willin', but Jeems's capt'in, he ain't willin'," she complained. "Now when we are all willin' 'ceptin' Jeems' captain, I think you might let up and let Jeems come." She promised to make her beloved return to the army as soon as they exchanged their vows. Before he forwarded the letter to the secretary of war, Davis wrote on the back of it, "Let Jeems go." There was a gentle, sentimental side to the president that all too few of his people ever got to see and that he was too proud to show in an era when men were not expected to be so sensitive. Six months after Sidney Johnston's death, Davis still strove to do something for his friend's widow, even seeking to provide a home for her if possible. But then, as with young Jeems's wife-to-be, Davis could always be kind to women.[7]

At times he had to be careful with his own wife, however, for Varina was subject to prejudices and little personal feuds of her own. Sometimes they exerted a considerable influence on Davis, as perhaps with the wives of Wigfall and Johnston, but at other times he resisted her. Colonel Joseph Ives presented a case in point. Varina did not care for all of her husband's aides, and Ives and young G. W. C. Lee never met her approval. There were rumors that she had favored the handsome young Lee for her sister Margaret Howell, but Lee failed to develop any interest in that direction, thus losing Varina's goodwill. She thought Lee careless and absentminded and felt outraged when he opened private letters addressed to her by the president. At first she charged this to nothing more than inadvertent oversight. But when Ives opened some of Davis's letters to her that summer, she accused him of "gross carelessness." Ives did not just open her mail, she said, but he read it even when he could tell it was of a private character. Unfortunately, one of

Varina's good friends was the wife of Colonel Jeremy F. Gilmer, then chief of the War Department's engineer bureau, and Mrs. Gilmer felt a violent loathing for Ives. She remembered that the native New Yorker actually took an oath of allegiance to the United States in the summer of 1861, before he subsequently resigned his commission and joined the Confederacy. This, plus his Yankee nativity, convinced her that Ives was a spy, and his occasionally publicized problems with drinking and womanizing did not help. All of this Mrs. Gilmer forcefully impressed on Varina, and she in turn tried to persuade Davis that Ives was dangerous. He refused to listen and rebuked Mrs. Gilmer when she also tried to turn him in his opinion.[8]

Ives was profligate, nicknamed "Miss Nancy" by the others for his addiction to show, liquor, and high life. Yet he was a good engineer, and, with his charming wife, Cora, useful for entertaining visiting foreign dignitaries. Still, Davis eventually dismissed him. Certainly Ives was not a spy, however intemperate and indiscreet he may have been, but Davis should have been more concerned about security than he was. As far back as February, Joseph E. Johnston began to withhold information from Richmond in part because he heard supposedly confidential intelligence bandied about freely in railroad cars and hotel lobbies. Johnston blamed this on the "indiscretion of the members of the cabinet," no doubt especially Benjamin, yet they were all indiscreet, even the president. Though back in March he had sent Sidney Johnston a special dictionary, of which he kept a duplicate, along with instructions for a crude cipher based on page, column, and word numbers in the book, Davis all too frequently discussed important military matters in letters entrusted to the mails or to couriers subject to capture. Later in the war more and more of his confidential correspondence with his generals would be in increasingly sophisticated codes, but for now he was overtrusting of Postmaster General Reagan's mails. Worse, he gave at least hints—and sometimes more—of important affairs in his personal correspondence to Varina and his brother Joseph, including in July the news that Captain Raphael Semmes, formerly commander of their very successful commerce raider CSS *Sumter*, would soon take command of a newer and more powerful ship being built in England, destined to be the *Alabama*.[9]

Davis had need of security, for as the pressure on Richmond waned after the Seven Days' Battles and the withdrawal of McClellan, he turned his thoughts to what his critics had been demanding for fully a year—an offensive. The organization of the Confederacy's military departments and commands now looked considerably different, reflecting the realities of the past year and Davis's expectations for the future. Now all of the country west of the Mississippi had been consolidated into the massive Trans-Mississippi Department. Sidney Johnston's old Department

No. 2 now comprised eastern Louisiana and all of Mississippi and Alabama and the western two-thirds of Tennessee. South Carolina, Georgia, and Florida made up another department. Most of North Carolina stood by itself, while its western counties merged with the rest of Tennessee to form the Department of East Tennessee. The southeastern counties of Virginia would be merged with North Carolina, while the southwestern counties formed their own department, along with whatever could be held of western Virginia. Lee's Army and Department of Northern Virginia were responsible for the rest of the state as far as the Potomac, if they could hold it.[10]

There was much that was obvious and sound in the way Davis segmented his domain. Lee's position in Virginia was natural, considering the constant threat to Richmond and the proximity of Washington. His command needed to be no larger than it was, especially since he also controlled the subdistrict of the Shenandoah and could expect Davis to coordinate for him, or subordinate to him, the forces on his far westward flank beyond the Alleghenies. The Department of East Tennessee also addressed a reality, namely that the geographical importance of the Cumberland Gap and the vital East-West link of the railroad between Chattanooga and Lynchburg, Virginia, were far more important than the territorial boundaries of Tennessee or North Carolina, from which he carved the department. Moreover, this same region provided a hotbed of disloyal Unionists, or "tories," who posed a constant threat of sabotage and unrest. This was a department designed solely for defense, yet well poised for assistance to its neighbors on either side should Davis so direct.

With little as yet occurring in the Atlantic seaboard states, Davis's division represented administrative convenience more than it did a conscious policy for defense. But as for the rest, the Trans-Mississippi and Department No. 2, the president continued even in the face of awful past experience to cripple organizationally the one region of the Confederacy that he knew best. If the loss of the forts in Tennessee and the disaster at Shiloh had anything to teach Davis, it was the necessity for unified command in that vast expanse. Repeatedly the plans of Johnston and then Beauregard and Bragg had been hampered by their inability to order at will forces from one side of the great river to the other. Johnston, at least, had exerted authority over Arkansas, but his subordinate there, Van Dorn, proved resistant to cooperation, and inept on the battlefield at Pea Ridge. Apparently the president believed, not illogically, that combining Department No. 2 with the Trans-Mississippi would simply make too great an area for any one man to command. The trouble was that no one could securely control one bank of the river without controlling the other. At the same time, with troops spread too thin everywhere, successful defensive or offensive operations along that line must inevitably require the shifting of units back and forth across the river. By making the Mississippi a boundary between departments, Davis ensured that such cooperation could only be imposed by himself, and then from such a great distance in Richmond that he could hardly enforce his orders.

Worse yet, Davis regarded the Trans-Mississippi as something of a dumping ground, and in the summer of 1862 he began a war-long policy of sending discredited or incompetent generals there to command or using it to shelve personal favorites who had become too controversial to keep in the East. In June 1862 he had a perfectly good man there, Thomas C. Hindman, but the Arkansan was not West Point–trained and was not well liked for his high-handed methods. Worse, he was a political man who owed his commission to the need to appease his state's influential leaders. Davis felt he had to place someone better trained and more experienced in such an important command.

Apparently his first choice was Magruder, who fell into considerable disfavor both with Johnston and Davis after the Seven Days. Just a month older than the president, Magruder had known him at West Point, thought not intimately. Despite any unhappiness with this flamboyant general, Davis still could not overlook his professional training, his long service in the old army, and his excellent record in the earlier stages of the Peninsula Campaign. But then a problem arose. The same month Richmond saw the return of the vain and pompous old Sterling Price of Missouri, and he came to lobby for the command for himself. Davis met with him on June 16 and listened in silence as Price made his case. The president told him to submit his views in writing for further consideration. A week later they met again, and this time it was evident that Davis had merely been putting the Missourian off. He told him that he had already decided to assign the department to Magruder.

"Well, Mr. President," the general exploded, red-faced. "Well, Mr. President, if you will not let me serve *you*, I will nevertheless serve my *country*." He promised to resign his Confederate commission, return to Missouri, raise another small army among his many friends in that state, "and win new victories for the South in spite of the Government."

Davis became an icicle. "Your resignation will be promptly accepted, General; and if you do go back to Missouri and raise another army, and win victories for the South, or do it any service at all, no one will be more pleased than myself, or—more surprised." Price slammed his fist on the table in the center of Davis's office so hard that he made the inkwells on it bounce into the air, shouted "Then I will surprise you, sir!" and stormed out. Price did resign, but Davis soon cooled enough to see the political wisdom of keeping him in the service. He returned his resignation and promised to make him second in command in the Trans-Mississippi. It placated the old Missourian a little more to receive Magruder's promise that the retaking of Missouri would be a first priority.[11]

But then Davis changed his mind about Magruder. In July, even while the general was on his way to his new command, Davis called him back. Charges of misconduct during the Seven Days had come to light, and until they were resolved Magruder could command nothing. Moreover—and this may have been the president's controlling motive—he had someone else for the position now. His old friend of thirty years, Theophilus Holmes, needed a place. He did nothing at Manassas, then commanded for a time in North Carolina, and came back to do almost nothing during the Peninsula fighting. His men called him "Granny," some thought him feebleminded, and he admitted himself that he was so deaf he could barely hear gunfire. At least one doctor thought he suffered from "softening of the brain." But he was Davis's friend. Lee did not want him, yet he was a major general exactly equal in seniority to Magruder. The Trans-Mississippi seemed to be the perfect place.

The only trouble was, Holmes did not want it. Well aware of his own manifest infirmities and incapacity, he tried to turn down the command. Unfortunately, he was also so weak willed that he could not decline firmly, and only a little pressure from Davis changed his mind. Magruder naturally protested, even pointing to Holmes's well-known reluctance, but the president responded only with the fatuous remark that "diffidence at large undertakings" did not mean that men did not want them. When Magruder protested that even Missouri's congressmen wanted him to have the command, Davis agreed but assured him that it was only because Magruder had promised not to interfere with Price. "They care nothing for you, General," he said. "It is Price they wish for." When Holmes assumed his command in August, his attitude should hardly have encouraged Davis to believe his maxim correct. "I accepted this command with very great diffidence," the general wrote from Little Rock, "and you will do me the justice to believe that it arose from a sincere distrust of my strength." In a long, whining, pessimistic report, he pleaded to have Johnston, Beauregard, or Gustavus Smith assigned in his place and begged Davis not to "permit any feeling of personal consideration to prevent you from sending one of them to command me."

What Holmes did not know, of course, is that this was precisely the approach best calculated to achieve exactly the opposite. Sick to death of ambitious, bragging, demanding officers like Price, Davis seemed invariably to place confidence in men like Holmes, Bragg, and Kirby Smith—men who never complained, never made demands, and always assumed a self-effacing manner with him. Holmes would stay. Moreover, in October Davis made him a lieutenant general. Holmes, of course, promptly declined the promotion but left it to Davis to decide. Davis persisted.

Holmes backed down, and the Trans-Mississippi was left in the hands of a man who wanted neither his rank nor his command.[12]

Almost as bad, Holmes's subordinates were inadequate. He had only two brigadiers of consequence and trusted neither. One of his subordinates, Davis's old companion from the First Mississippi, Douglas Cooper, was charged with "habitual intoxication." Albert Pike, in charge of relations with the Indians, had made a mess of his affairs and was reputed to be either a traitor or insane. Another troublesome Missourian, the colorful partisan M. Jefferson Thompson, continually lobbied to be made a brigadier. While Davis never put the Trans-Mississippi out of his mind—as he might have wished—it obviously received only his secondary attention and the secondary and even tertiary military talents available to him. He might have done well to pay more serious heed to the proposition of the French consul in Richmond that Texas, at least, be given a separate nationality. Would that he could have done it with the whole Trans-Mississippi.[13]

In those uncountable hours when Jefferson Davis sat in his office and stared at the maps on his walls, however much his good eye may have paused on the land west of the great river, inevitably it was drawn back again and again to Virginia, Vicksburg, and Bragg's army. All summer long fears for Vicksburg mounted. His brother Joseph echoed the "alarm & agitation" felt over the feared abandonment of Mississippi. Van Dorn and Lovell had done much to strengthen Vicksburg, but they built little confidence among the people. Lovell was still discredited after the loss of New Orleans, and Van Dorn alienated most with whom he came in contact by his foppish airs and open intemperance. Joseph Davis found him slow and uncomprehending, telling his brother that "he may be a good fighter but—"[14]

When Davis readjusted his departments out west, Mississippi, Vicksburg, and Van Dorn all became a part of Bragg's overall command. Yet no sooner did Bragg assume this additional responsibility than he quickly preoccupied himself with affairs in his own immediate front. As a result, he happily left the defense of Vicksburg and the lower Mississippi to Van Dorn, aided by an interested President Davis, who carried on a more frequent correspondence with Van Dorn than with any other subordinate commander. It helped that he was constantly importuned by Governors Moore of Louisiana and Pettus of Mississippi to take steps to drive the Yankees from their territory. As a result Davis endorsed Van Dorn's plan early in August to send Breckinridge and his tiny division south to attack the Federals at Baton Rouge. If successful there, and aided by the powerful ironclad Arkansas on the Mississippi, the Confederates might drive even farther downriver to challenge the enemy for New Orleans. Davis tried to find Van Dorn some supports from

Lee's army, as well as from Holmes and others, promising that "the importance of the object at which you aim cannot be overestimated." Of course, Bragg should have been doing this, but he had his own matters to handle. Better yet, an overall commander east and west of the Mississippi could have coordinated everyone. In the absence of such a person, Davis orchestrated it from Richmond. As it happened, Breckinridge achieved only limited success, thanks to the malfunction and subsequent loss of the *Arkansas*, which much dismayed Davis. Still, Breckinridge moved a few miles north of Baton Rouge and started the fortification of high bluffs on the river at Port Hudson, commencing the establishment of a southern bastion on the Mississippi that would rival Vicksburg and keep a vital hundred-mile stretch of the river inviolate for the Confederacy.[15]

Meanwhile, Bragg departed northern Mississippi on a campaign of his own, leaving a subordinate in command—Sterling Price. The turbulent Missourian had not yet returned to the Trans-Mississippi; and his command now formed, along with Van Dorn's separate force at Vicksburg, the major Confederate presence in the state. With no one on hand to coordinate their actions, the two acted as almost independent entities. Van Dorn, the senior, wanted Price to join him in an attack on the twenty thousand Federals at Corinth. Price had other ideas, and meanwhile Breckinridge chafed down at Port Hudson, anxious to get out from under the odious Van Dorn and rejoin Bragg's army on its new campaign. Tragically, Bragg, to whom all three ultimately reported, left Mississippi without giving Van Dorn any clear instructions and without making his wishes—if he had any—evident to them all. Breckinridge, at least, acted as a proper subordinate, but Price virtually refused to do as Van Dorn wished.

It was command chaos, and once more Davis felt that he had to step in. "A want of co-intelligence and co-operation among the generals of the several columns," he said, threatened disaster. "I am at a loss to know how to remedy evils without damaging your plans," he wired to Bragg, making it clear that his general had failed to inform either him or his subordinates of what should be done. Hastily Bragg advised that he wanted Breckinridge to join his movement, while Price should join with Van Dorn and threaten northern Mississippi, and Davis himself issued orders, through Randolph, for Van Dorn to assume command immediately of everyone in Mississippi, concentrate them, and prepare to advance northward into Tennessee. By this time, alas, it was too late.[16]

The biggest offensive in the West to date was under way. Davis and his generals never lost the dream of regaining all of Tennessee, and even more, by taking Kentucky as well, of claiming the Ohio as their border. There were very sound strategic reasons for wanting it to be so. Moreover, a conviction remained in Richmond that the Bluegrass State in particular fretted under the Yankee yoke and only awaited the coming of a liberating Rebel army to flock to the colors. Preston Johnston spoke often of the loyal men of Kentucky who refused to yield to "the Beelzebub—the Devil of flies—the God of filth—the Government of the besotted bastard and blackguard Lincoln." It helped that a powerful and extremely vocal Kentucky lobby resided in Richmond, led by its congressmen and aided continually by having a highly placed partisan—William Preston Johnston—literally a door away from the president. Many spoke of the aide as Davis's "confidential friend," and Johnston himself did not scruple at using his access and relationship with the Chief toward his ends. Through much of 1862 he pushed to have his ambitious uncle William Preston made a brigadier, hoping to arrange for a Kentucky delegation to visit Richmond and demand it of Davis. Johnston's efforts to have Haldeman start a paper in the capital also had as their goal a press campaign to push for an invasion to liberate Kentucky. He often received visiting Kentucky generals like Buckner and Lloyd Tilghman, to help them plead their case with the president. And, on his own, Johnston started as far back as July, and perhaps even in June, to influence the administration to send Kentuckian Breckinridge and his division—including two largely Kentucky brigades—to Chattanooga. He could make it a base for a campaign into their homeland. Johnston won Samuel Cooper's support, but the Chief proved tougher to handle. "The Prest is too wary a soldier to interfere with his generals in the field," Johnston wrote that July, "by ordering so important a change without the approbation of Bragg." The aide had to be cautious in attempting to influence the president, confessing that "I have meddled more than usual."[17]

In fact Davis opposed neither the movement to Chattanooga nor an attempt to retake Kentucky. He wanted an offensive, and politically he needed an offensive. The trouble was, Bragg had only commanded the army a few weeks. Bragg, too, wanted to move, but logistical problems mired him through June and July, and Yankee strength in northern Mississippi was such that he could not confidently advance in that direction. Indeed, it was this stymie that first made Bragg consider a change of base to Chattanooga, by which he would sidestep the Yankees in his front and perhaps be able to march into Kentucky, leaving Van Dorn and Price to defend against the Federals at Corinth. He proposed this on July 12, though the idea appears to have been yet immature in his mind, but it reached Richmond at the same time that Preston Johnston was lobbying Davis for essentially the same movement, and the Kentucky host clamored for something to be done for their state. Within a week the idea gained shape, helped by news that a Yankee army commanded by General Don C. Buell was making a leisurely advance on Chattanooga itself. On July 21, just the day after Preston Johnston lamented that he could not press the president more for an active campaign, Bragg put his army on the move.[18]

However much Davis favored the offensive, he unwittingly hampered it from the start by his adherence to his old friends. Just three weeks before taking command, Bragg notified Richmond that of all his major generals commanding corps, only Hardee of the III Corps "can now be regarded as a suitable commander." He asked for changes, for some of the other high-ranking generals were "incumbrances and would be better out of the way." He did not offer names, but the obvious inference was Leonidas Polk and Samuel Jones, commanding respectively the I and II Corps. Davis had already shown his ill-placed favoritism and confidence in Polk, and though he seems not to have been close to Jones, still he would sustain this lackluster officer in one command after another throughout the war. Davis asked Bragg for specifics of the "incumbrances," but Bragg wisely backed down without making an issue of it. That was good for Bragg but terrible for his army.[19]

By mid-August Bragg had his army in Chattanooga well ahead of Buell, who now turned away. Everything looked wonderful for an advance into Kentucky, and the initiative clearly lay with the Confederates, but then it bogged down again thanks to another command confusion, this one the fault of Davis's policy of the rigid independence of his departments. Bragg had expected that the troops from East Tennessee would join with him in his campaign, but he did not know that Davis had made it a separate department commanded by Kirby Smith. The region deserved to be a department, demanding the full-time attention of a resourceful commander. But when a major army on an offensive through neighboring territory needed all the assistance it could get, Bragg should have been able to exercise superceding authority. As it was, the president had to notify Kirby Smith of the proposed movement, though Smith had independently suggested the same thing to Bragg on July 24, just three days after Bragg started to move toward Chattanooga. Better yet, Smith freely offered to place himself under Bragg's command, apparently forestalling what could have been a difficult situation. Davis encouraged his friend Smith, assuring him a few days later that "the junction with Genl. Bragg if effected in time will I trust enable the two armies to crush Buells column and advance to the recovery of Tennessee and the occupation of Kentucky."[20]

In fact, Davis believed the junction so important, and the possibilities of this campaign so great, that he wanted to come to Chattanooga himself but could not leave Richmond. Since Bragg was as yet untried as an army commander in battle, he may also have wanted to reassure himself that he had placed the army under the right man and perhaps see for himself more of the matter of those "incumbrances." Happily, Smith and Bragg met in person on July 31 and agreed to cooperate on a plan whereby Smith would take the Cumberland Gap from a small group of Yankees while Bragg consolidated his army. Then Smith would rejoin Bragg, and under his command their combined forces would advance on Buell. Unfortunately, no sooner did Smith return to his command than he had second thoughts and alternating visions of glory and self-doubt. One moment he asked Davis to replace him, and the next he devised a plan for his own independent campaign to take Kentucky while leaving Bragg to deal with the powerful Buell on his own. Had Davis been willing, he might have regarded it as another Van Dorn–Price impasse, with two independent commanders, each pursuing his own ends and dependent for cooperation wholly on willingness or else peremptory instructions from the president. He gave no such instructions, and it would be a long time before Bragg and Smith met again. Meanwhile, reports came to Richmond that Bragg was not moving even though he had his army in hand. "Why does not Bragg attack?" Preston Johnston puzzled on August 15. "Will he never attack?"[21]

Much of the reason that Davis did not intervene lay in what Johnston had observed earlier—an unwillingness to interfere with his generals in the field. Ignorance due to poor communications helped, and Smith's disingenuous implication that Bragg approved his idea for an independent move into Kentucky made it worse. Even more compelling was another matter. All the while that he tried to arrange for command in the Trans-Mississippi and faced command confusion and crisis in Mississippi and Tennessee, the president stared full in the face yet another threat to Virginia and Richmond.

As McClellan sat meekly at Harrison's Landing through the summer, another Yankee army commanded by John Pope grew rapidly in and around Washington. Designed initially to protect the Federal capital, this Army of Virginia soon took on offensive ambitions as Pope promised to meet and whip Lee, and on July 14 he advanced southward into Virginia. With lightning swiftness, Lee decided what to do, and Davis supported him. "We hope soon to strike another blow here," Davis wrote Kirby Smith on July 28, "so as to hold one army in check whilst we strike the other." Faced with a timid McClellan in his front on the Peninsula, Lee decided to ignore him and take the bulk of his army to meet and repulse Pope. Otherwise he risked being pinched between the two Federal forces. Lee conducted a brilliant campaign, aided greatly by Stonewall Jackson. Jackson himself moved like the wind, met and defeated portions of Pope's army at Cedar Mountain on August 9, and then moved to join with Lee himself in smashing the Army of the Potomac. Having learned that McClellan was finally evacuating his army from the Peninsula, Lee knew that he must beat Pope before McClellan could join him. On August 28–30, he did just that on the old Manassas battleground and sent Pope and his army scurrying back once more to Washington.

Throughout that remarkable six weeks, Davis was more an observer than a participant, showing both his distraction with Congress and events west of the Appalachians and also his confidence in Lee. When Lee asked for troops, Davis sent them, even when doing so left Richmond unprotected. "Confidence in you overcomes the view which would otherwise be taken of the exposed condition of Richmond," the president assured his general, and Lee rewarded his trust.[22]

It had all gone so smoothly, so successfully, that Davis could now indulge a dream. Kentucky was not the only siren beckoning to Confederates. Maryland, too, teemed with Southern sympathizers, had organized regiments in the Rebel service, and promised fat cattle and bulging granaries. Davis hoped that Marylanders might still seize control of their state and join with the South if a conquering army were there to give them spirit and support. On a more immediate and practical level, Lee's quick campaign against Pope left him in an advanced position, without adequate supply, in a region of Virginia exhausted by constant occupation. He could not stay where he was, his army needed fresh supplies, he had the enemy off guard and fearful for the safety of Washington. Necessity and advantage combined to make an invasion of Maryland appear to be his best option. Moreover, as Lee tactfully suggested to the president, with an invading army in Yankee territory, Davis might have a good platform from which to offer Lincoln a chance to make peace terms recognizing Confederate independence. To his credit, Davis did not bristle at receiving from a general a suggestion that touched on his civil authority. From *this* general, Davis would accept much because this general gave him much. It was a sign of how well Davis could work with a man on the rare occasion when he found one who suited him.[23]

Three days after putting Pope to rout, Lee proposed his invasion to Davis. Significantly, Davis seems not even to have replied or communicated with Lee for at least four days. Lee was well on his way, and already across the Potomac and in Frederick, Maryland, when Davis's first letter reached him, and it contained only a proclamation to the people of Maryland stating the Confederates' aims in invading. Nothing could better signify the fact that the president was leaving this campaign entirely in the hands of the general who gave him victories. And when Davis told Lee that he wanted to come to the Potomac to meet with him, he uncomplainingly accepted the general's polite but firm advice that it would be too dangerous. Sensitive to the president's anxiety for news, Lee sent almost daily reports of his movements as the invasion progressed, and they presented encouraging stories of the people of the state offering kindness and succor. Unable to stay quietly in Richmond with such a promising campaign under way, and denied the opportunity to go to Tennessee to be with Bragg, Davis left Richmond on or around September 11 to go to Leesburg in hopes of seeing Lee. Perhaps he even believed that he would join the army in Maryland. After all, he tried to be with his men at First Manassas, and he was on the firing line at Seven Pines and with Lee during the Seven Days. Probably only Davis's frail health at the moment, and Lee's rapid movement, prevented them from meeting. Disappointed, Davis returned to Richmond to await news from his general.[24]

He awaited news now from all his generals. All across the Confederacy's northern line, from the Potomac to the Mississippi, Southern arms advanced against the enemy. For all their ragtag appearance, haphazard arms, and uncertain supply and equipage, the armies of Van Dorn, Price, Bragg, Kirby Smith, and Lee afforded a magnificent effort. More than one hundred thousand men in butternut and gray surged northward across a front six hundred miles long, the most ambitious military operation yet seen in the hemisphere, and none of it would have happened without Jefferson Davis. To be sure, he had not planned such a sweeping coordinated offensive. Lee's invasion was almost a spontaneous reaction to unexpected opportunity and necessity. Van Dorn and Price's movements were byproducts of Bragg's campaign, as was Kirby Smith's now-independent drive into the Bluegrass. Only Bragg's move to Chattanooga and subsequent advance into Kentucky represented a planned effort, probably stimulated from the Executive Mansion and the powerful lobby in Richmond. Yet Davis sustained Lee when he proposed his Maryland campaign. Davis tardily but eventually imposed some degree of coordination on Van Dorn and Price when Bragg did not, and Davis put Kirby Smith into the Kentucky campaign.

Moreover, for good and ill, the president put bits of himself into all those offensives. He showed outstanding flexibility and a willingness to make speedy and decisive conclusions in approving Lee's proposal, the same kind of decisive thinking he had shown on the battlefields at Monterrey and Buena Vista. He recognized the vital necessity of making maximum effort with his limited resources by putting almost all of his available forces between the Appalachians and the Mississippi into the Western offensives. A year before he resisted risking too much in the grandiose proposals of Beauregard and Smith for concentrations. Those plans had been impractical and Davis knew so, but the opportunity presented by the isolation of Buell's small army offered a different case, and Davis in the meantime had grown in his willingness to accept a great risk with some prospect of success. If any of his detractors still thought him too timid now, they should have looked again. Using two small armies in Mississippi to hold in check one larger Yankee force at Corinth, he was sending Bragg and Lee against the enemy's remaining two armies, against greater odds, in a bid to beat them on their own ground and wrest from Lincoln not only all that had been lost in the spring, but also to amputate two whole states from the Union, and by doing so he would naturally reacquire most of western Virginia as well.

If these armies also marched without the fullest and best measure of coordination, that, too, could be laid at Davis's feet. There was no problem for Lee in this regard, but clearly Bragg could not control Kirby Smith, and no one seemed able to control Van Dorn and Price, for all the orders that came out of Richmond. Davis's department system worked against him. So did his favoritism for Kirby Smith, Van Dorn, and Polk. If they all succeeded, charges of cronyism would be lost in the euphoria of success. If they failed, the Chief could expect to hear the jackals barking at his door.

It all turned to dross, and with a simultaneity that robbed the South of its breath. After a letter of September 13, Davis apparently heard nothing more from Lee, who became too engaged with the enemy to write. On September 14–15 he lost small scrapes at Crampton's Gap and South Mountain but captured Harpers Ferry. An anxious Davis sent his aide Colonel Lee off to join his father and report, but even before he could reach him, garbled reports filtered back to Richmond on September 21 of a major battle near Sharpsburg, Maryland, along Antietam Creek. At first there were only statements of losses, but then a Philadelphia newspaper brought the word that Lee had been repulsed. McClellan managed to catch him with his back to the Potomac and his army split in half. On September 17 the Federals attacked and in a badly managed battle hammered him in what proved to be the bloodiest day of the war. Only McClellan's ineptitude and timidity, the desperate fighting of Lee's men, and the last-minute reuniting of Lee's forces saved the Confederates from destruction. A few days later Colonel Lee met the army as it retreated into the Shenandoah. The roads choked with stragglers, and junior officers spoke of the men having been worn out by their hard marching and too "shaky" to fight when they met McClellan. "They got the worst of it," young Lee reported. His invasion a failure, General Lee began the task of reforming and refitting his army in the Shenandoah. Davis evidenced no great dismay at the result—indeed little reaction at all. Probably he chose to look on the invasion as a success for having taken the war to the enemy on his own ground. They never intended to remain north of the Potomac indefinitely; Antietam simply propelled Lee back sooner rather than later. Several days after the fight he complimented Lee and his army "for the deeds which have covered our flag with imperishable fame."[25]

Price and Van Dorn fared no better. Still refusing to cooperate with his superior, Price was supposed to be helping hold U.S. Grant's forces at Corinth in Mississippi, preventing them from reinforcing Buell, who would be facing Bragg. But Grant moved on Price instead, and at Iuka, two days after Antietam, he bested him in a day-long fight. Stung by this, Price at last conceded that he would join Van Dorn for a concentrated movement against Corinth, and on October 3 they attacked. At first they enjoyed some success, but the next day their assaults weakened, and in the end they could not drive the Yankees from their position. They pulled back, their campaign, too, a failure in its mission to drive Grant out of northern Mississippi and western Tennessee. They did, at least, keep Grant from reinforcing Buell, but Davis soon received a flood of protests, especially about Van Dorn and his intemperance. Predicting disaster if this continued, influential Mississippians demanded a change in commanders.[26]

For whatever good Van Dorn and Price did for Bragg, he did very little for himself. The Kentucky campaign started auspiciously, with reports reaching Richmond in late August that Bragg was handling himself and his army ably. His subordinate Hardee complimented him highly, and even the president's usually pessimistic brother in Mississippi expressed "high hopes of brilliant events." Better news came on August 30, with word that Kirby Smith had won a small fight at Richmond, Kentucky, and was driving for Lexington in the very heart of the Bluegrass. Buell had no choice but to pull back to meet him, uncovering much of southern and central Kentucky for Bragg's advance. Two weeks later, even while Lee courted disaster at Antietam, Bragg's subordinate Buckner forced the surrender of a four-thousand-man garrison at Munfordville.[27]

But then the disquieting rumors began filtering into the capital. The ever-ambitious politician William Preston complained that Bragg was not properly coordinating the troops available to him, and in an obvious grasping maneuver asserted that he should himself have the command of all troops raised during the invasion. Moreover, he claimed that if Davis did not intercede personally in managing the campaign, all would be lost. Indeed, Bragg's advance slowed down, and he actually allowed Buell—on whom he had the jump at the start—to beat him to Louisville and the Ohio River. Still, on October 4 Bragg briefly took the state capital at Frankfort and installed the Confederate "governor" Richard Hawes. Almost at once Bragg began retreating as Buell advanced, and four days later, near Perryville, elements of their armies met in a small and tactically indecisive battle. Nevertheless, Bragg decided to withdraw toward the Cumberland Gap and eastern Tennessee. Like all the other offensives that fall, the Kentucky campaign had failed.[28]

"We have had a bad day," Preston Johnston wrote to his wife when he heard the news of Perryville. "Our affairs are everywhere critical," he said; "our people seem asleep to the crisis." In the War Department, the clerk Jones spoke of a "day of gloom." There had been confusing early reports that Van Dorn was successful at Corinth, but they were soon dispelled, and then came the same conflicting accounts of Bragg's movements. Not until October 21 did the War Department have definitive news that Kentucky was lost. Even then, Davis sought to encourage and sustain Bragg, just as he did Lee after Antietam. "The brilliant achievements of your army claim the thanks of the country," the president wrote on October 17, perhaps not yet knowing that the campaign was all lost. He continued to express the hope that the presence of influential Kentuckians like Buckner would encourage large enlistments in their native state. In fact, thanks to command confusions and Van Dorn's foot dragging, some prominent Kentuckians, including Breckinridge, the most prominent of all, never got to join Bragg, and barely a small-size brigade of men from the Bluegrass actually enlisted—hardly the tens of thousands expected.[29]

Then came the hard truth. "The results in Ky. have been to me a bitter disappointment," the president confessed at the end of October. Immediately the public outcry against Bragg commenced. Worse, complaints from his subordinates started to reach Davis, probably the first coming from Kirby Smith, who asked to be allowed to come to Richmond for a personal interview and begged that he never have to serve under Bragg again. Predictably the Kentucky lobby raised the loudest outcry. "All in Kentucky was loose, incoherent and pointless," charged Preston. He begged to come to Richmond to tell Davis his side of the campaign. George B. Hodge, a Kentucky congressman whom Davis tried repeatedly to get confirmed as a brigadier, represented Kentuckians as outraged by Bragg's conduct. Even Preston Johnston quickly turned against the Chief's general. "I think Bragg in Ky a signal failure," he wrote.[30]

At first, when friends with the army notified Davis of the retreat on October 20, they urged the president himself to come to Knoxville to save the situation. Davis could hardly do so. He was already thinking of visiting Lee at Winchester but could not get away for that, either. Instead, he ordered Bragg to come to Richmond right away, and when the general arrived they immediately went into a six-hour conference on October 27, following breakfast. Davis greeted him warmly, and during all of their subsequent interviews he continually sustained Bragg. Indeed, Davis may already have been disposed to defend Bragg even before he learned from him any of the details of the campaign. The uproar in the press, and from the politicians and armchair generals, came from the lips of Davis's own opposition of the past year. Able to dismiss their carping about himself as meaningless, the president easily dismissed their complaints about his high-level appointees, too, especially when he became convinced that the jackals attacked his friends as a means of getting at him. Loyalty from and to those he trusted meant a great deal to Davis, and he was determined now to remain loyal to Bragg, especially when the general evidenced "the most self denying temper in relation to his future position." It was Theophilus Holmes all over again. Davis felt an instinctive affinity for a man who, like himself, denied ambition, did not seek high place, and expressed doubts about his capacity.[31]

Still, even though he sent Bragg on his way with expressions of unbounded confidence, Davis wanted to know more. There were too many unsettling stories leaking from inside the general's army. He tried first to quell Kirby Smith's discontent by relating to him the encomiums Bragg had bestowed on him—largely undeserved, given Smith's unco-operative behavior, and almost certainly embellished by Davis in the retelling. Then he asked Smith, Polk, and Hardee all to come to Rich-mond for personal interviews to give their views of the campaign. Smith jumped at the chance, arriving November 2 or 3. Polk came a few days later. Both had the temperament, and plenty of personal interest, for political intrigue in army affairs, and each candidly told Davis that Bragg had botched the conduct of the campaign and that the rank and file of the army felt no confidence in him. Hardee, a better man and a better general than all of them, had no stomach for such backbiting, and de-clined to come. He did admit that in the main his views coincided with Polk's, saying that "the President has no doubt learned from others all that I could tell him." But then he saw through the accusations and the ambitions to the central question facing Davis. "Bragg has proved a failure, it is true, but he has learned wisdom from experience," said Hardee, "and have we any body who will do better?"[32]

Davis's sentiments echoed Hardee's. "I could make good use of him *here* in Richmond," Davis told Polk when they spoke of Bragg, perhaps thinking of him as a possible chief of staff or even general-in-chief. And he confessed that in Bragg's army "another Genl. might excite more enthusiasm, but as all have their defects I have not seen how to make a change with advantage." Of the other men of suitable full general's rank, Cooper was out of the question, Lee was needed in Virginia, Johnston was still recuperating from his wound, and Beauregard "was tried as commander of the Army of the West and left it without leave when the troops were demoralized and the country he was sent to protect was threatened with conquest." Davis hastened to point out, while on the subject of Beauregard, that Bragg's retreat from Kentucky was "not so bad" as that other general's abandonment of Corinth. He begged Polk and Smith to be forbearing and give Bragg their support. He also made each of them a lieutenant general, perhaps to recognize their services—which had not been exemplary—and perhaps to buy their cooperation. Indeed, so solicitous was Davis of Smith's goodwill that he actually re-linquished some of his jealously guarded executive power to him. On

November 19 Kirby Smith presumptuously notified Davis that, on his own authority, he had made Colonel Abram Buford a brigadier general and wanted the president to confirm it by the constitutional process of appointing Buford and submitting the appointment to the Senate for confirmation. For more than a year Davis had jealously, and at times imperiously, notified all parties, even his secretaries of war, that he and he alone could decide who should be so nominated, and that no one but he had the power to appoint generals pending nomination and confirmation. Yet now he accepted Smith's impertinence without a whimper and made the nomination ten days later.[33]

Davis had greater matters on his mind. Everywhere west of the Appalachians the uproar for changes in command continued, along with demands to know what the government intended to do to retrieve the situation. Militarily, even with the failures in Mississippi and Kentucky, Confederate arms in November stood about where they had in August, but status quo was death for an underdog. In Mississippi they begged to have Joseph E. Johnston sent to replace Van Dorn, an accused "seducer, drunkard, and libertine." Believing that the troublesome general would have to be superseded, Davis never even considered turning to the odious Price. Johnston was yet too unwell for an active command, Beauregard was out of the question and safely buried in South Carolina, and Davis wisely decided to send someone from outside the region to command, someone free of its politics and any stigma of prior failures. Unwisely, however, he turned—as he did frequently—to an unexplainable choice. John C. Pemberton was a native of Pennsylvania who went with the South and an obscure major general who had preceded Beauregard in the South Carolina command. In his favor—to Davis's eye— were his West Point training and a distinguished record for bravery in the war with Mexico. In the same days that he created a host of other lieutenant generals for Lee and Bragg, Davis made Pemberton one as well and assigned him to take control of old Department No. 2, now dubbed the Department of Mississippi and Eastern Louisiana. Davis trusted that Pemberton would be able to prevent any further Yankee advance southward "and in due time take the offensive." He even hoped that Pemberton and Holmes might cooperate for a joint drive on both banks of the Mississippi, driving Grant out of Tennessee and reopening the way for the taking of Kentucky and Missouri.[34]

As for affairs in central and eastern Tennessee, Davis had already made his decision, though prominent Kentuckians continued to protest to Preston Johnston that "General Bragg is either stark mad or utterly incompetent." Worse, Hardee was seen as weak spined, and Polk as a blowhard who would best be stationed on a "chronic Court of Enquiry." From all quarters came pleas for Davis himself to take charge. "Unless that great and good man, Mr. Davis, speedily gives his attention to affairs in this Dep't.," wrote one Kentuckian, "disaster & ruin will overwhelm us."[35]

People in Richmond persisted in expecting that the president himself would take the field to remedy the situation, yet following the dramatic days on the Peninsula the previous spring, Davis seems never again to have seriously considered doing so—and he may never have contemplated it at all. He did counsel with Bragg on a strategy for retrieving the situation, and they agreed that the Confederates should move into middle Tennessee "to resume the offensive," as Davis informed Kirby Smith. Though this was bold talk for a man who had just sustained defeat all along his active front, it was also sound thinking. Two more months of acceptable campaigning weather remained before winter would close out all movement until spring. Lee faced terrible odds in the remnants of Pope's and McClellan's armies, now united under the latter once more, and there was always the danger of Yankees from Buell's army coming to reinforce McClellan for an overwhelming numerical superiority even that weak-willed general could use to advantage on an offensive. Then, too, Buell had shown himself to be a general easily outdistanced by Bragg, and when Lincoln replaced him with a new man, William S. Rosecrans, in November, Davis had no reason to expect any change in Yankee sloth. The president did not discuss details of the plan to move into middle Tennessee when he and Bragg spoke in late October. Rather, having outlined the goal, he left it to the general to determine how it should be achieved. That was good executive behavior. Unfortunately, it required a good general in turn.[36]

Davis may nonetheless have had some lingering questions. Certainly he knew that Bragg felt doubts, both about himself and his difficult subordinates. Bragg even claimed that during his interviews with the president, he suggested appointing Johnston to a "super command" of all the forces between Chattanooga and the Mississippi, making him Bragg's immediate superior. He did so in order to avoid command confusions such as occurred with Kirby Smith. Davis politely refused, probably offering no reason other than Johnston's health. But when Polk came to see Davis in early November, he brought with him Bragg's renewed plea, and then, coincidentally, on November 13 Johnston arrived in Richmond and presented himself to Randolph at the War Department, ready for duty. Davis had made up his mind. Though he did not tell Johnston directly, he told Randolph to notify Johnston that he was being assigned to command the newly designated "Department of the West," to comprise the departments of East Tennessee, Pemberton's command, and Bragg's Department No. 2.[37]

The move showed that Davis had been thinking seriously and soundly about much of what hampered the fall campaigns out there.

"The arrangement," he said a few months later, "was intended to secure the fullest co-operation of the troops in those departments, and at the same time to avoid delay by putting the commander of each department in direct correspondence with the War office." Unfortunately, in his second clause Davis showed the weakness in his concept, for to avoid delay the department commanders should have been communicating directly with Johnston and not bypassing him in favor of Richmond. Thus, in taking a step toward the laudable goal of unified command, Davis took a step backward by making its procedures cumbersome. There could be many reasons. One, naturally, was his unwillingness to be out of direct touch with his department commanders. Another was a desire to prevent Bragg from being "overslaughed" by Johnston. Another could easily have been a lingering distrust of Johnston's fighting spirit after the spring. And surely one more would be the troubling lack of unanimity on strategic thinking between Johnston and Secretary of War Randolph. [38]

However well their relationship had commenced when Randolph took office back in March, he and Davis had come increasingly into conflict as the months passed. There were many petty annoyances. Benjamin's meddling in War Department affairs and the favoritism shown in appointments—even to recommending candidates for generalship because Varina knew them—aggravated the Virginian. Some of Davis's friends, especially Kirby Smith, became imperious with the secretary. While generals like Magruder could not appoint their own staff officers, Davis allowed Polk to do so and even indulged Kirby Smith when he actually appointed generals, merely passing the appointments on to Randolph without consultation. Preston Johnston exerted more influence on appointments than did Randolph, counseling promotion seekers to get recommendations from Joseph Davis as the surest course.[39] The arbitrariness of this gnawed at Randolph, especially when he tried to move on his own in small matters, only to be rebuked by the president for "acting without consultation & without authority." Soon Davis complained to young Johnston of the ills done "through the negligence of the Secty of War and without the knowledge of the President."[40]

Davis's obsession with pointless paperwork drove Randolph almost to distraction. Late in October one minor document went from Davis to Randolph, back to Davis, then to a clerk who referred it back to Randolph, who sent it to Davis once more, who then directed it to Cooper, having determined from all this that the item deserved to be filed. The president "lacks system," lamented the secretary, "is very slow, does not discriminate between important and unimportant matters, has no practical knowledge of the working of our military system in the field, and frequently mars it by theories which he had no opportunity to correct by personal observation, and in which he will not permit amendment from the experience of others." A man in Northrop's office was more pointed when he said he "used to think Jefferson Davis a *mule*, but a *good mule*," but had now "come to think him a jackass."[41]

Davis was no happier with Randolph. He was too independent, too prone to make quick decisions, joining with Mallory in silent rebellion at the interminable cabinet meetings where nothing was settled. Though always cordial, Randolph avoided the president to escape the endless discussion that Davis required to make up his mind. He also sinned by bringing Northrop's deficiencies to Davis, referring his own controversies with the commissary to Davis, and probably taking perverse delight in turning the tables by wasting the president's time settling petty issues like the price of salt.[42]

Sick of it all, Randolph decided to resign in September, but critical operations in Maryland and Kentucky forced him to postpone action. But in late October, after Davis spoke theoretically of the need for cooperation with Pemberton, Randolph sent Holmes authority to leave his department and cross the Mississippi if necessary. Davis rebuked the secretary, then lectured him in writing about taking action on his own. When Davis responded icily to another issue over Northrop, the secretary endorsed it, "He has forgot a conference on this subject at which Gen Lee was present." He filed the document, knowing that Davis might well come across an endorsement that would infuriate him by pointing out his own error, but Randolph did not care.[43] On November 15 he resigned—"in a huff" thought Preston Johnston—and Davis happily accepted. Some believed that Randolph manufactured the Holmes imbroglio to give himself an excuse to resign. Alfred T. Bledsoe, who had left the War Department some time before, told Davis a few days later that Randolph's departure did not surprise him, "though if I should assign the reasons which influenced him, it is probable they would be different from any mentioned by himself."[44]

Randolph had been a good adviser, certainly the best war secretary Davis had had to date and one especially keen to the needs of the Western theater, a helpful commodity when pressing events right before Richmond could preoccupy the president. Davis misused him, as he almost always misused administrative subordinates; Davis felt challenged and in some wise intimidated by him, as he always felt when up against men with wills as strong as his own. He felt compelled to dominate him with lectures and reprimands, to show Randolph—as he had shown Winfield Scott and all the others—that Davis was unassailable in his rectitude and that his constitutional oath required him to husband all power to himself.

That was all very well and good. But in the middle of November of 1862, Davis suddenly found himself in yet another command crisis, even as he had tried to prevent them. In Tennessee Bragg faced another impending campaign. In northern Virginia the tardy McClellan had been replaced by a new general with orders to move against Lee. Joseph E. Johnston had been given a new command, yet with no instructions, and now the Confederacy was without a secretary of war who, clerk or not, was necessary to do at least that part of running the War Department that Jefferson Davis did not do for himself. It had been a year of crisis—winter, spring, summer, and fall—and now with the winter of 1862–63 approaching, it looked as if the cycle was about to repeat yet again.

25

I Mourn over
Opportunities Lost

Once more Davis found himself attacked from several sides, though as the clerk Jones in the War Department noted, "the people and the press seem inclined to denounce the President, for they know not what." Randolph had been no more popular during his tenure than his predecessor, at least outside the military. The generals seemed to think more highly of him, especially Johnston, but to the people at large and to Davis's ever-ready critics, he was nothing more than yet another clerk.[1]

Despite his growing dissatisfaction with Randolph, Davis was obviously not prepared for a resignation or a dismissal, for he had no one ready to take Randolph's place. Indeed, the resignation took the president so much by surprise that he did something otherwise inexplicable. He gave the post to General Gustavus Smith, with whom he was already feuding. "Well, the President is a bold man!" exclaimed clerk Jones. Davis never meant the appointment to be anything more than temporary, of course, but he had to have someone there quickly, for a new enemy offensive against Lee seemed imminent, and Smith at least had the advantages of being available and familiar with Lee's army. He appears, in fact, to have done little more than shift a large pile of papers from his office to Cooper's before his permanent successor arrived on November 22, and it is just as well, for his onetime friendship with the president was irrevocably destroyed.[2]

The question of whom to entrust with the secretaryship did not occupy Davis for more than two days, evidence that he could make decisions quickly at times. Though nothing suggests that the outcome would have been any different had the president taken more time, he made an unfortunate choice. Several names were suggested to him, Bledsoe even making the ridiculous assertion that Leonidas Polk should be considered. "His talent is executive," said Davis's friend, "and he would be a great worker." He would have been a disaster, and Davis wisely ignored the advice. But he also ignored Bledsoe's counsel against another candidate. James A. Seddon was a Virginian, which would preserve the geographical and patronage balance in the cabinet. A congressman before the war and a member of Virginia's secession convention, he was also chronically ill, and frail health had kept him entirely out of public affairs throughout the 1850s. Though only forty-seven, he looked older, almost cadaverous. Bledsoe predicted that "Seddon would be a failure." His feeble health would kill him and, worse, "he is, neither by nature nor habit, a worker."[3]

But Davis was attracted to Seddon. They had formed an acquaintance during the previous year, founded perhaps on Seddon's subservient demeanor and his support of Davis in the Confederate Congress. Moreover, Seddon had been a moderate on secession, rather more so than Davis, and as the war progressed the president drifted farther and farther away from the troublesome fire-eaters. And Davis seems to have had an undeniable affinity for men who, like himself, suffered more-or-less-constant poor health. As the close of 1862 approached, many of the president's most trusted friends had constitutions as frail as his own. Bragg, Holmes, Northrop—all complained of chronic ailments. Even Lee suffered the onset of heart disease, and both Walker and Randolph were in poor health. Many of the experienced men needed for high civil and military posts were well along in their careers, into their forties and fifties, ages at which the incidence of infirmity, and sometimes the effects of rigorous service in earlier days, would start to manifest themselves. But Davis did not consider that ill health disqualified men from responsible positions. It is no surprise. After all, he needed to look no farther than himself to see that a determined and patriotic man could perform herculean labors in spite of sometimes crippling physical maladies. Half blind, unable to eat or sleep, his face sometimes contorted with pain, or his body racked with fever, still he managed to run the country. Surely men with lesser ills could handle lesser tasks. Besides, there may have been a slightly sinister side to the matter. Sick men could be dominated. Even Randolph never really challenged Davis's prerogatives until close to the end. These men did not complain or criticize. They did as they were told, and as Davis now commenced his retreat from the executive strengths he had shown in 1862, he would become more and more appreciative of—and susceptible to—sycophancy.

He offered Seddon the post on November 17, and the Virginian promptly accepted, though not without expressing reservations that his health would allow him to perform well. If Davis did not heed the warning, those in the War Department quickly saw its worth. Noting Seddon's frailty, Jones believed that he would not last long if he tried to perform all the duties of the position. Just three weeks later, Kean in the Bureau of War observed that Seddon "stagger[ed] under his load," appeared weak, and despite his obvious intelligence was so unaccustomed to rigorous work that he moved slowly and did little.[4]

Certainly that boded ill, for a new brace of campaigns approached that would require vigor and energy, elements entirely missing from the new secretary's makeup. Certainly their coming did not surprise President Davis. Late in October he commented that "an idle winter is not anticipated for the army of N. Va!" The buildup of the combined armies of McClellan and Pope, and the assignment of Ambrose Burnside to command the reorganized Army of the Potomac, suggested that another campaign would move toward Richmond before winter halted operations. Burnside's initial movements seemed to confirm such fears, and on the very day that Seddon took office, Lee advised Davis that he believed the enemy intended to advance against Fredericksburg. He moved quickly to the Rappahannock River himself to block the move, immediately fortifying the heights above the city on the south bank of the river. Lee did something else that he had done during the Antietam campaign. He wrote to the president almost daily at times, keeping him completely informed even when there was little to tell. Lee knew how to keep his commander in chief content. Davis craved information and rightfully expected it, thus his chagrin at Johnston's secretiveness back in the spring. Lee's openness proved a double blessing now. It relieved much of Davis's natural anxiety, and it also gave him enhanced confidence in his general, which meant that the president interfered with him not once during the imminent fighting. Indeed, so completely did Davis trust Lee's judgment, and his plans as outlined in detail in Lee's correspondence, that during the ensuing campaign, leading up to the largest land battle ever fought on the American continent in terms of numbers engaged, the president only wrote to his general twice, to offer assistance with men and guns.[5]

Davis hoped as usual to leave Richmond and go to the army early in December, to be with Lee when the battle came. But unfortunately, in another theater of the war, the ideal relationship between a president, his general, and an army did not work so perfectly. All across the region now under the ill-defined command of Joseph E. Johnston, the men in the ranks and the civilian population felt deep doubts and dissatisfaction with Bragg, Pemberton, and their prospects. Davis received frequent entreaties asking him to come to the West in person to inspire confidence, the most recent on December 1 from Pettus of Mississippi.

Though he had hoped that Johnston's appointment would quell disharmony and encourage cooperation between his armies in the region, Davis now concluded that he would have to go himself, even if his health was not equal to the journey. He told Pettus that he would leave immediately, but business delayed him for several days. He studied the organization of Bragg's army, noting some changes of assignment he intended to make. He decided to take his nephew General Joseph Davis and Colonel Lee along with him, much to the dismay of Johnston, whom the president told he urgently needed in Richmond to act as his communication link with Lee. Finally, on December 10, expecting to return by the new year, Davis boarded a train and left for Chattanooga.[6]

The trip passed pleasantly and uneventfully, and along the way Davis gave most of his thought to his hope that he might inspire men to join the armies "and to arouse all classes to united and desperate resistance." When he arrived in Chattanooga late on December 11, Davis immediately impressed those who saw him with his unassuming simplicity. He traveled with a single leather valise, the initials "J. D." printed on its side, and only Joseph Davis, Lee, and a servant for company. Those who met him at the depot remarked on his figure and stature, his "features decidedly handsome for a middle-aged gentleman," his good humor and graceful manners. They saw the gray that liberally sprinkled his hair and chin whiskers, for after a lifetime of being clean shaven, Davis had in the past year adopted a modest beard that yet left his cheeks bare.

The next morning the small party boarded a special private train for the balance of the journey to see Bragg, Davis all along the route taking in the wild and grand scenery along the Tennessee River. Even a minor accident that delayed him briefly did not spoil the journey, which proved to be almost relaxing, especially since the crowds at the stations along the way gave him warm welcomes. At Bridgeport, Alabama, his car had to be detached from the train, loaded on a barge, and floated across the Tennessee, where it joined another locomotive that took it on to Murfreesboro that evening. As Davis approached the town in the darkness, he saw the thousands of twinkling campfires that spoke of the massing of Bragg's forces barely thirty miles southeast of Rosecrans's army in Nashville.[7]

The president spent December 13 with the army, consulting with Bragg and making several appointments and promotions. Apparently Davis was becoming a little weary of the demanding Kentucky lobby back in Richmond. When he left he had intended to give the insistent Preston command of a Kentucky brigade that had only a colonel at its head. Now, however, he reviewed that brigade, declared himself much pleased with its proficiency, and instead left the colonel in command and gave him an immediate promotion to brigadier. Other promotions ensued as the president inspected the entire army, led by that First Kentucky Brigade. Bragg, Polk, Hardee, Breckinridge, and all the other generals were present. With obvious pleasure, Davis rode along the length of each division standing at attention, the division commander riding on his right, and both at full gallop. Flags waved in the breeze, bands played, and the bright sun took the chill from the brisk air. It was the sort of day a soldier like Davis daydreamed about. Having finished his inspection, Davis took a position at the edge of the parade ground, surrounded by the generals, and the army passed in review. "I fancied his eye to kindle and his features to lighten up with the natural enthusiasm of a soldier when he looks upon such a scene," noted a correspondent. Before him, Davis saw division after division of men, well armed and equipped, though their uniforms betrayed their states' haphazard efforts to clothe them and Richmond's inability to do so uniformly. He wrote happily of their "fine spirits" and took reassurance from his talks with Bragg. That evening Davis joined Bragg and his corps and division commanders for dinner and what General Joseph Wheeler regarded as an "uninterrupted flow of wit and repartee."

Indeed, he took too much assurance. Fearing a Federal buildup facing Pemberton, Davis had already informed Johnston that he wanted part of Bragg's army sent to Mississippi. Johnston resisted, noting that Bragg's 47,000 faced more then 60,000 Yankees at Nashville. Johnston told Davis that what remained of Tennessee in Confederate hands might be forfeit if Rosecrans advanced against a weakened Bragg, and Bragg argued that Pemberton was strong enough to defend himself. The president listened in silence, and then proceeded to issue the orders he had undoubtedly decided upon well before reaching Murfreesboro. Johnston was to take nine thousand men and leave immediately to join Pemberton. Should Rosecrans advance against Bragg, "fight if you can," said the president, "and fall back beyond the Tennessee."[8]

Davis interfered far more than normal and, worse, compromised the very position he created for Johnston, who left for Mississippi thoroughly frustrated and confused. He was supposed to bring about unity of command and exercise overall authority, yet Davis preempted his powers within a week of Johnston's arrival. The general himself wanted to have Holmes move to support Pemberton, strategically a sounder approach, and considering Holmes's proximity, more easily and quickly achievable. And Holmes faced no serious Yankee threat of invasion in his department, whereas Bragg's scouts daily saw the enemy army menacing his grasp on central Tennessee. But Davis had resisted this plan for at least a month, as far back as his scolding of Randolph for ordering exactly the same thing. Pique at Randolph may account for part of Davis's lapse of good strategic judgment. Surely the clamor coming from

Mississippi influenced him even more, along with inner doubts about Holmes's fortitude for rigorous campaigning. And Bragg and the others may have done themselves a disservice when they told the president that they entertained "much confidence" that they could repel a Yankee advance from Nashville if it came. Most of all, however, Davis clearly decided that his initial war stragety of holding every inch of ground was impractical. He had neither the men nor the resources. The losses earlier that year due to his unwillingness to weaken one spot in order to concentrate on another had taught him a dear lesson. His appointment of Johnston and the ill-defined mandate to press for cooperation and concentration showed Davis's evolution in thinking. Now he went farther, coldly assigning priorities, and deciding that Vicksburg and a hold on that stretch of the Mississippi were more important than middle Tennessee. When he told Bragg to fight if possible or to fall back to the Tennessee around Chattanooga, Davis authorized the abandonment of hundreds of square miles of the Volunteer State at a time when he needed its volunteers. Maintaining communications with the Trans-Mississippi took precedence. Furthermore, Davis believed from Bragg's reports that Rosecrans did not intend to advance that winter, and that impending cavalry raids would so disrupt supply and communications lines for Rosecrans in Tennessee and Grant in Mississippi that all offensive movements might be halted.[9]

Something else distracted him as well—Lee at Fredericksburg. When Davis left Murfreesboro early on December 14 to return to Chattanooga, he knew nothing of affairs in Virginia. But that night upon his arrival he found a telegram from Seddon informing him that Burnside had attacked on December 13. Immediately the president wired to Richmond for more information but none came. "You can imagine my anxiety," he wrote Varina the next day. He considered cancelling the remainder of his trip and returning to the capital, though he felt it extremely important that he visit Pemberton as well. Next day came the relieving news that Lee had repulsed all of Burnside's attacks and that Fredericksburg was safe and the Yankees severely beaten. Once again Lee had rewarded his confidence.[10]

Buoyed by news of the victory, Davis continued his journey as planned, his health and spirits actually improved from what they had been a few days before in Richmond. He left for Mississippi on December 15 and within a few days reached Vicksburg, in time to learn the great news that a raid by his old friend Van Dorn had destroyed Grant's supply base at Holly Springs and virtually brought to a halt the Federals' advance south into Mississippi. So uplifting was the news that Davis even took a brief respite from his official duties to buy 1,500 acres and some hogs not too far from Brierfield. Then he visited with Pemberton and set about inspecting the troops in their positions in advance of Vicksburg, along the Yazoo River. He created something of a sensation that some soldiers thought encouraged the troops, who otherwise felt themselves forgotten by Richmond. His conversations with Pemberton and inspection of the river batteries convinced him that more heavy cannon were needed, which he telegraphed Seddon to expedite as quickly as possible, and at the same time he somewhat reversed his own position of just a week before by writing to Holmes and asking him to cooperate with forces on this side of the Mississippi. He did not make Holmes subordinate to Johnston, but he did ask him to send reinforcements for the defense of Vicksburg and the Mississippi, terming the city's possible loss to be a much greater calamity than would be the loss of Richmond, which aside from its factories possessed mainly symbolic importance, he said. "We can not hope at all points to meet the enemy with a force equal to his own," Davis told Holmes, "and must find our security in the concentration and rapid movement of troops."[11]

Davis clearly showed himself to be wavering, the indecision that many complained about. A week earlier he had rejected Johnston's proposal for cooperation between Pemberton and Holmes and gave direct orders to Bragg to send a full division of his army to Mississippi. He also rejected, at least in part, Bragg's contention that cavalry raids could slow or stop Grant on their own. Now, however, he largely went over to Bragg and Johnston. Van Dorn's raid had stopped Grant, at least for the moment. Holmes did not face any major threat in his department that would prevent him from cooperating with Johnston and Pemberton, and so now Davis directed that the Trans-Mississippi commander do something in that direction. However, where Davis gave Bragg explicit and direct orders, he gave Holmes nothing more than suggestions, leaving precise actions up to the general's judgment. To some extent he adapted his policy to what he saw, and for the first time the president saw with his own eyes the actual condition of affairs in Mississippi. Perhaps this, more than anything else, impressed him with a sense of urgency not felt before. Yet he would not violate his department organization. He could order Bragg to reinforce Pemberton even though each commanded a separate department, because they had been loosely combined in Johnston's Department of the West. But Holmes was not a part of that division, and even though Davis still could have issued specific orders, he chose to suggest rather than demand cooperation.

It was also politic to try to get Trans-Mississippi troops to help. To quell the uproar of the past year, Davis had to convince Mississippi that he felt a commitment to defend the river. After spending Christmas in Jackson, he addressed the legislature the next day in his first clearly political speech to the public since taking office. The intent to defend his administration while he was at it became immediately apparent, showing just how much Davis's self-imposed policy of silence to most of his critics really disturbed him. He might claim to Kirby Smith and others that he turned a deaf ear to those who attacked his administration; his speech to the legislature made it clear that the president heard every word they said and did not forget.

Davis reminded the legislature that, given his own way, he would rather have been leading Mississippi troops in the field than be president. He reminded them, too, that he had predicted that war would result from secession, though admitting at the same time that even he had not foreseen the proportions that conflict would assume. He castigated the North as no better than a "den of thieves," saying rather disingenuously that he had with his own eyes seen the horrors inflicted by the Yankees, the insulting of women, the destruction of property, and the carrying off of the elderly for imprisonment. Yankees and Southerners could never again live in any kind of harmony, for the foe had revealed himself as the homeless, traditionless offspring of Cromwell and his Roundheads, bred in the bogs and fens of Ireland and northern England. Confederates, descendants of the bold and chivalrous cavaliers of old, were a different sort altogether. It was a blatant myth, of course, and one that Davis had never before indicated that he believed. He may not have believed it now, though finding it useful to stir passions and prejudice to arouse the citizenry.

That said, Davis declared that from the beginning his policy had been for the Confederacy to fight its battles on the enemy's soil, yet another assertion that he wanted to make offensive, not defensive, war. The power of the foe prevented that, of course, and Davis declared that in the face of the overwhelming odds and resources against them, "The wonder is not that we have done little, but that we have done so much." Yet more remained to be done, and having defended his primarily defensive policy, Davis went on to defend the more controversial aspects of his administration. He spoke of conscription—the need to get "sluggards in the cause" into uniform—and complained of the harsh criticism it had received. He spoke especially of the subsequent acts that established categories of exemption from the draft and tried to show the unfairness of the resultant outcry. The recent "twenty Negro" act, by which those owning twenty or more slaves were to be exempted, particularly outraged many. Some charged that this favored the wealthy, another example of the conflict being a rich man's war and a poor man's fight. "The poor do, indeed, fight the battles of the country," said Davis. "It is the poor who save nations and make revolutions." But he said that the rich were fighting too, and tried to show that the only reason for this controversial exemption was to have experienced men behind the lines on the home front in case of an insurrection, "to keep our negroes in control."

Conscription he could defend as was his wont, logically and factually. But when he tried to put the best face on Confederate experience in campaign and battle, the president indulged in "big lie" rhetoric. "In spite of disparity of numbers," he declared, "we have always whipped them." He did not mention Forts Henry and Donelson, Shiloh, New Orleans, Pea Ridge, Corinth, Iuka, Perryville, and more. In fact, he even claimed that Antietam had been a Confederate victory. Yet they could not expect always to overcome heavy odds, said Davis, returning to reality, and he urged all Southerners to frown on those who came with tales of defeat and called on the women to use their influence to sustain their men's patriotism. To all Mississippians he issued a call for renewed volunteering to fill the widening gaps in the ranks of their state's regiments.

Naturally his audience felt particular concern about Vicksburg and Port Hudson and the river itself, and Davis did not delude them. He believed these to be the primary objects of Yankee operations in the West and begged them all to fly to the defense of the two bastions "and thus conduce more than in any other way to the perpetuation of the Confederacy and the success of the cause." With less than commendable adherence to accuracy, he asserted that Memphis and New Orleans had been "admirably defended" and their loss came as a surprise to him. Be that as it might, he would not make at Vicksburg the mistakes he made before, advocating even a "scorched earth" policy if necessary.

The issue before them was a simple one. "Will you be slaves or will you be independent?" he asked. "The question is only one of time," he assured them. The end might not come soon, though he believed that in a contest so immense, "the contestants must be soon exhausted." Yet it was impossible that Confederates would be the first to cry "hold, enough." There was still much in their favor, but they must be realistic. "Put not your trust in Princes," he said. Foreign intervention had not happened, despite all his efforts, and he confessed that he could not understand why England and France withheld their friendship. Of course, Davis's distrust of Great Britain dated back publicly nearly two decades and probably went farther, to stories his brothers told him in childhood of the War of 1812 and the Battle of New Orleans. France seemed more amicably disposed, however, and he promised that any hand extended in friendship would not be turned away. However, being realistic, Confederates should not fool themselves. "This war is ours," he told the legislature. "We must fight it out ourselves."

Convinced of this, Davis tried to persuade his listeners—and the thousands throughout the Confederacy whom he knew would read his speech in the press—that "in all respects, moral as well as physical, we are better prepared than we were a year ago." Their troops were experienced, battle had distinguished the good leaders from the bad, and he expected that they would and could meet the enemy expecting success despite the odds.

Repeatedly Davis came back to the threats to Vicksburg and Port Hudson, imploring everyone in the state to lend aid. He tried to reassure them that he and Johnston felt as one in their determination upon a successful defense, and spoke of the resolution that he had seen among the soldiers when he inspected them in their camps. Beyond that, he still held out the hope of reclaiming Missouri and Kentucky, and closed by yet again asserting that the new nation stood in better condition, with fairer prospects of eventual success, than the previous December. Everyone was showing resourcefulness in making do in the face of shortages. He thought the women actually improved in looks when wearing homespun, and the men looked more manly. Moreover, piousness and morality permeated his people, undoubtedly winning the approval of the Almighty. "On their valor and the assistance of God I confidently rely."

Only once, and briefly, did Davis allude to the storm of protest and criticism that had arisen in the last year. "When misrepresentations of the Government have been circulated," he said, "when accusations have been brought against it of weakness and inefficiency, often have I felt in my heart the struggle between the desire for justice and the duty not to give information to the enemy—because at such time the correction of error would have been injurious to the safety of the cause." It was the same argument that he always used, and now punctuated with the example of his beloved Sidney Johnston, who never responded to criticism.[12]

It was a remarkable speech, not so much for what Davis said as for the fact that he said it at all. Gone was the high-flown rhetoric, with barely more than a slim handful of literary or classical allusions or quotes. Though the speech was delivered to legislators, the president clearly aimed it at the people and the soldiery. Davis never had the gift of inspiring men with words, yet here he tried. Almost always faithful to accuracy, even when it hurt, here in Jackson he strained every bit of ingenuity to make the case that the South really was better off than a year earlier and that they really were beating the enemy. Though he still did not offer excuses and reasons for the Confederacy's failures, at least here for the first time he publicly gave his reason for not revealing those excuses. In every way the address to the legislature was something Davis had never done before—a yielding response to popular clamor and a clear attempt to use the public press to improve both his own image as president and confidence in the cause.

No more than a day or two later Davis left Mississippi for his return trip, stopping in Mobile, Alabama, on December 30. He actually reached

Richmond again on January 4, 1863, and the next morning his Jackson speech appeared in the capital press. Readers found it "patriotic and cheering," and, anxious to capitalize upon and enhance the good feeling in the public engendered by his printed address, he made another one from the steps of the Executive Mansion that evening. Captain J. B. Smith's "Silver Band" came to celebrate his return with a serenade, starting with "Listen to the Mockingbird" and playing several more songs until a crowd had gathered to hear the president's expected response.

When he spoke, Davis attempted to continue the patriotic and encouraging theme he had taken up the week before in Jackson. The Yankees were "the offscourings of the earth." He repeated his charges of the outrages committed by the foe, devoting nearly a fourth of his extemporaneous address to Federal atrocities, much exaggerated. But then he turned to recent glorious news, some of it still coming to him. Lee had already beaten Burnside at Fredericksburg. In a rare attempt at public humor, Davis commented that a few Yankees who had cried "on to Richmond" actually got there—as prisoners. But even as he reached the capital, Davis had received the good news that on December 29 an enemy force attacked Chickasaw Bayou north of Vicksburg, and Pemberton repulsed them handsomely. Then on December 31, Bragg had attacked Rosecrans, and the latest telegrams from that army indicated a glorious victory.

"In every combat there they have been beaten," the president proclaimed, "and I trust they will be beaten in future." Preston Johnston sat inside the house at a window where he could see Davis and listen. "Every aspect of his voice fell with peculiar and startling sweetness," he wrote, becoming even more enrapt as the president clearly gloried in being able to announce good news. Johnston found his voice "flute-like" and declared that "fate-compelling language flows from him." Now Davis did, indeed, speak of the fate made on those recent battlefields. The triple defeats would increase disaffection in Indiana, Illinois, and Ohio, he promised. Soon much of the old Northwest would break away from the rest of the Union, leaving each section too weak to prosecute a war with the South. "Then for us," Davis predicted, "future peace and prosperity."

As if to show just how conscious he had become of the need to reach out, if only a little, Davis went on to apologize for being for the most part a stranger to the people of Richmond. By way of explanation, he pleaded "constant labor in the duties of office, borne down by care, and with an anxiety which has left me scarcely a moment for repose." He prayed for a time when the fighting would be done, peace secured, and he could come to know them all better and share with them "the social enjoyments that pertain to a time of peace."

Regarding the war itself, while he decried it as "an evil in every form," still he asserted that the Confederacy had to be "tried in the severe crucible in which we are being tested, in order to cement us together." Once peace came, that cement would hold, and the mutual assistance of the war years would become a permanent bond "to develop the great political ideas upon which our Government is based." Davis may even have seen in the repulse of the enemy all along the line in December a hint that the conflict would end soon. "If the war continues," he said as if there were some doubt, "we shall only grow stronger and stronger." They were already more united and powerful than a year ago. In the wake of recent victories, "an unconquerable spirit nerves every arm," sustained by the noble women at home. Davis could only conclude that "we are invincible."[13]

He spoke too soon. In an agonizing repeat of the disaster of the previous October, Bragg's hopeful news of victory turned out to be a fiction. Despite initial reports, Rosecrans, not Bragg, was the aggressor in the campaign as the Yankees advanced to Murfreesboro. Each planned to attack on December 31, and the Confederates only beat Rosecrans by minutes in opening the fight. Nevertheless, that first day Bragg appeared to gain a clear advantage, and when darkness fell he sent a telegram to Richmond announcing that he was driving the enemy before him. But the next day the two armies did little more than stare at each other. Bragg did not know what to do, and when the fight commenced again on January 2, he launched Breckinridge on a suicidal attack that Rosecrans repulsed bloodily. Late that night Polk advised Bragg that they should retreat, for the army was too exhausted to fight again. Speaking with Hardee several hours later, Bragg learned that he, too, advised withdrawal. The retreat did not stop until the army stood along the Duck River more than thirty miles from Murfreesboro.

When word of the retreat reached Davis, barely hours after his confident and congratulatory speech, the president could do little more than put the best light possible on the disaster. It did not work. Though in private Davis "seem[ed] contented" with Bragg, thought Preston Johnston, the public outcry against the general was immediate. Johnston himself confided to his wife a belief that Bragg possessed "the instincts of a drill-sergeant, but not the genius of a General." From the army itself came complaints of Boomerang Bragg, as Preston called him. Showing his astuteness as a "tooth and nail" politician, Preston also hinted that Bragg had recently said unkind things about Sidney Johnston, perhaps hoping that the story would get back to Davis, with the same result that attended Beauregard's criticism of the president's hero. Polk wrote directly to Davis to explain his criticism of his commander, as well as to defend his own conduct against a campaign that Bragg soon launched to shift blame for the loss. Rumors spread that Bragg would try to make

Hardee a hero, and Polk and Breckinridge scapegoats for the failure, and in fact before long open warfare broke out between Bragg and his generals, with Breckinridge requesting—and not getting—a court of inquiry. General Roger Hanson, killed in the battle, had spoken of simply shooting Bragg before the charge in which he was mortally wounded, and Breckinridge was now being urged by some to challenge his commander to a duel.[14]

Davis immediately faced a dilemma. During his visit to the army at Murfreesboro, he saw little or no evidence of disaffection from Bragg even after the Kentucky failure. But now it came oozing out of every division and corps. He needed to know more, and from an independent source outside the Army of Tennessee. After ordering Bragg to select a strong position to defend should Rosecrans advance, the president directed Joseph E. Johnston to go to Bragg at once to survey the situation. Inexplicably, Bragg had actually asked his top commanders for reports on the state of feeling in their commands. "Why General Bragg should have selected that tribunal, and invited its judgment upon him, is to me unexplained," said Davis, but it made obvious the need for Johnston's presence. In fact, Bragg lost his nerve in the battle, and now was losing his grip on himself. "My confidence in General Bragg is unshaken," Davis told Johnston, but if he had lost the support of his subordinates and the men in the ranks, he might have to be relieved.[15]

Unfortunately, in sending Johnston to look into one troubled command situation, Davis learned of yet another. Apparently during the confusion after Randolph's sudden departure from the War Department, and with Davis himself ill at home, the president and Johnston did not have an opportunity to discuss fully and freely just what Johnston was expected to do. Perhaps even as Davis ordered him to go to the Duck River line, Johnston wrote to ask Davis for clarification. Pemberton and Bragg were so far apart, he protested, that he could not exercise any general control. He could only take command in person of one or the other, yet he believed that Davis did not intend him to do so and felt himself that it would be disruptive. He asked for reassignment to some other position.

But then came Davis's order to go to Bragg. Meanwhile, Pemberton complained of confusion and asked for a clarification of Johnston's authority, especially when Davis authorized the latter to order troops away from Vicksburg to support Bragg. It was all becoming too complicated, and when Johnston sent his first tentative report from Bragg's headquarters at Tullahoma, matters did not improve. He portrayed most of the subordinate generals as dissatisfied, but he wanted to await inspection of the troops. For himself, Johnston expressed continued confidence in Bragg but asked that if Davis did have to remove the general, then he should not replace him with a man already in that army "or engaged in this investigation." Obviously, Johnston referred to Polk, Hardee, and himself.[16]

Quite possibly at Davis's urging, Seddon tried to clarify for Johnston his mission, asserting positively that he was expected to assume command of one or the other of the armies when occasion demanded. Moreover, Seddon, at least, seemed to feel that Johnston should always place himself in direct command when battle threatened, expressing dismay that Johnston did not command at Chickasaw Bayou and Murfreesboro. Yet Johnston still did not seem to comprehend the president's intentions on February 12, when he sent a full report. He reported the confirmation of the ill feeling among the generals but sustained Bragg all the same and even complimented his handling of the recent campaign. Yet again Johnston urged that Bragg be retained in command, and that if he was superseded, he himself should not be the replacement. At the same time Johnston complained that Pemberton was not communicating with him, apparently ignorant that he had the authority to compel Pemberton to keep him informed.[17]

Davis almost lost his patience and almost certainly lost some of his remaining store of confidence in Johnston. It did not help that just a few weeks before, writing from Richmond to her husband in Tennessee, Varina told him that every day in drawing rooms she heard of Johnston's "disaffection to you" and his backbiting. "Take care of him," she warned, "and see that he does not do what he pleases out there." Unfortunately, Davis could not get the general to do anything "out there." When he got the general's report, he replied rather testily that he was embarrassed at having Johnston attempt to preclude himself from succeeding Bragg should Davis decide to remove the latter. As far back as January, Davis had told him in his instructions that when Johnston reached Tullahoma, he automatically assumed command by right of his senior commission and as overall theater commander. Moreover, if Johnston would not agree to supersede Bragg, said Davis, "you will perceive how small is the field of selection if a new man is to be sought whose rank is superior to that of the lieutenant-generals now in Tennessee." Cooper could not take the field. Lee could not logically leave his army in Virginia. If Bragg had to be replaced and Joseph Johnston ruled himself out, that reduced the "field" to only one man—Beauregard. Therein lay the real reason that the president thought Johnston's position "embarrassing to me." He would have preferred any alternative to giving an important field command to that man again, especially the army that he had "deserted." The only other solution would be to make one of his existing lieutenant generals a full general, but that would have meant robbing Lee of Longstreet or Jackson, the only likely men outside the Army of Tennessee who had sufficient experience and demonstrated skills to risk in army command.[18]

As a result Davis found himself boxed into a no-win situation. Though he did not question Bragg's skill, he feared that without the confidence of the troops, the general would be powerless. He could keep Bragg in spite of the public outcry against him, in spite of the disaffection within his own army, in spite of the war Bragg waged with his own generals, and in spite of Davis's own growing doubts. Or he could replace Bragg by robbing Lee of one of his chief lieutenants and thereby possibly cripple his only successful army commander. Or he could make what would amount to a public confession of error by reinstating Beauregard, rewarding a man who had left his post and, worse, tried to stain the memory of Sidney Johnston and steal his laurels. There was nothing to do but keep Bragg and hope for the best.

It was a flawed decision, but perhaps the best Davis could make. Beauregard had courage, but his reputation outstripped his merits. A child could have taken Fort Sumter. Johnston was the real hero of First Manassas, and Lee and others had actually planned the strategy of concentration before Beauregard set foot in Virginia. Once in command at Shiloh, Beauregard lost his nerve and quite possibly walked away from a crushing victory on the evening of April 6, while his record thereafter had been one of retreat, first from Corinth and then from his own army. Even allowing for Davis's well-developed prejudice against him, there was sound logic for not returning Beauregard to command of this army. Leaving Jackson and Longstreet with Lee was eminently sound, and none of the other lieutenant generals—Holmes, Smith, Pemberton— had ever commanded more than a small division in battle. Moreover, Joseph Johnston himself expressed unshaken confidence in Bragg, and Davis agreed. His confidence was misplaced, but his decision at this time and in the face of the alternatives available was the right one.

That still left the problem of Johnston's seeming unwillingness to understand what Davis expected of his command in the West. As late as March, the general finally began to suggest that he may not have understood the president's intentions—and this after repeated letters from Davis explicitly stating that Johnston was expected to assume command of Pemberton's or Bragg's army when present, or at critical times. Even if Davis's original instructions had been unclear the prior November, there was no excuse for the general's pretending to be confused four months later, and after the two had been together at Jackson in December, when Johnston could have aired his confusion. Davis should have wondered by now, if not before, about the resolution of the man. Mary Chestnut's uncle Hamilton Boykin knew Johnston well from youth, and remembered that "never in his life could he make up his mind that everything was so exactly right, that the time to act had come." Though reputed to be a crack shot with a rifle, when Johnston went hunting he always complained that the bird flew too high or the dogs were too near—always some excuse for not committing himself. "He was too fussy, too hard to please, too cautious, too much afraid to miss and risk his fine reputation for a crack shot." While everyone else banged away, missing often and occasionally bagging a bird, Johnston kept on with his excuses—he never did "miss," but only because he never shot. He had been much the same late in 1861 and on the Peninsula, and indeed his most bellicose posturing during the months after Manassas stopped when Beauregard was transferred, suggesting that there was far more Beauregard than Johnston in their grand proposals for offensives.[19]

However much he may have wondered about the fiber of this general, Davis sustained him. Again, the only alternative would have been Beauregard. Thus, ironically, the one man the president wanted to keep out of influence in the West entirely actually played a dominant—if passive—role in the arrangement of the region's high command. The president's support of Johnston, in spite of increasingly disturbing signs of indecision and a want of inner conviction, could be interpreted as patience, and indeed he had been uncharacteristically patient in the past. From now on, however, the specter of Beauregard would be ever before Davis in his decisions on Johnston. As for Bragg's retention, while the Creole played the same passive role there, still Davis was happy to keep his friend in command. "The Prest is always loth to yield a General to the popular clamor or sacrifice one for failure," Preston Johnston noted even while Davis was studying the situation in the West. "He always hopes for better luck next time." "But," the aide confided to his wife, "Bragg is incompetent."[20]

Little wonder, then, that after a season of failure, brightened only by Fredericksburg and Holly Springs, Jefferson Davis's health relapsed while the Bragg controversy raged. About February 5 he went down again with "neuralgia in the head," and then an abscessed tooth or gum inflicted terrible pain on him for several days more. For the rest of February, except for a few days when he felt well enough for an afternoon ride, Davis confined himself to his house and often to his bedroom. During this time, his aides had to carry much of the burden of paperwork that the president often handled. James Chesnut joined the staff officially in January, and later that month Davis appointed his onetime nephew by marriage, John Taylor Wood, to replace another nephew, Joseph R. Davis, who left to take command of a brigade. Preston Johnston handled most of the ceaseless applications for interviews, keeping all but the most essential from disturbing the president's convalescence.[21]

Political affairs, of course, always intruded. Part of the reason for

Davis's hurry to return to Richmond in January had been the need to prepare an address before the opening of the next session of Congress on January 12. Young Johnston actually believed now that he was "managing Members of Congress" in a way to win support for the president. "I feel sure if we can take care of his interests, he can take care of the country." Davis himself put the best face possible on the current situation, saying much of Lee in Virginia and little of Bragg and Tennessee. He devoted more than half of his address to foreign affairs—or more accurately to the Confederacy's lack of foreign affairs. In a clear appeal to convince Britain and France logically that their neutral position should be abandoned, Davis went on at length about the illegality of the Yankee blockade, underlining the vital common interests Europe shared with the South. Yet there was little hope of foreign recognition in his words, but rather a resort to his old habit of stating what was "right" and hoping that others would have the good sense to recognize it. As he had said in Jackson, this fight was to be fought by the Confederacy, and they should not count on outside help.

Beyond this he turned his attention to the by-now-common recitation of enemy atrocities, though there was a new one to draw his special notice. Lincoln had issued his Emancipation Proclamation, declaring free all slaves in areas then in rebellion. In it Davis saw confirmation of the belief he and others had long held: that the ulterior purpose of the Republican party from its foundation had been forced abolition. Davis could not, and would never, believe that secession and war had anything to do with it. Rather he saw the war as confirmation of the lengths to which those people would go to free the slaves. Consequently, he said, "an inferior race, peaceful and contented laborers in their sphere, are doomed to extermination." He intended to ask that all Union army officers captured in the South be turned over to state civil authorities to be charged and tried according to the applicable laws covering incitement to servile insurrection. Enlisted men he would treat as simple prisoners of war, since they only followed orders. Happily nothing came of his recommendation, or the retaliation and counterretaliation might speedily have escalated to alarming and bloody proportions.

The president spoke but little of finance, following his oft-uttered policy of leaving that to Memminger and Senate Finance Chairman R. M. T. Hunter. More loans and more taxes were needed, and that was enough said. Of the War and Navy departments he spoke highly but briefly, again defending conscription yet showing some sensitivity to popular outcry when he asked for reform in the exemption system. In the end he pleaded for relief for those civilians who had lost their homes due to enemy depredations, complimented the sacrifice and resourcefulness that had sustained them thus far, and called for even more to bring the war to a close and win their independence.[22]

Happily, whether through the efforts of young Johnston or other-wise, the Congress gave Davis a brief reprieve during much of this session. It helped, perhaps, that Vice President Stephens decided to stay at home in Georgia through the winter. His increasing disaffection from the administration would have worked up considerable controversy in Richmond—not that he did not manage to do so from his home.[23] Davis could not escape controversy, of course. He had to put reins on Bragg after the general seized a state railroad in Georgia and brought down the wrath of Joseph Brown. He got into the middle of a battle over payment for the printing of Treasury notes and later found himself having to codify rules for the appointment of military courts-martial. The load of trivial tasks that he undertook, on top of his recurrent illness, left him at times confused and perhaps disoriented. The case of Colonel John Dunovant of South Carolina, cashiered for drunkenness, led Davis to generate scores of documents and to an attitude that wavered from declarations that the case was out of his hands to assertions that Duno-vant should be reinstated. When a Mississippian suggested on February 20 that Davis declare a day of fasting and prayer, Davis referred it to Seddon for consideration, yet he referred an identical suggestion re-ceived the next day to Memminger. By early March Davis had trouble remembering just who he had promoted to general during his visit to Mississippi.[24]

It was inevitable that irritability took over at times. He scolded Seddon for tardiness and shoddy preparation of civilian applications in February and apparently made a final break with Pillow the same month, after Tennessee and Alabama congressmen asked for his promotion to major general for "gallantry" at Murfreesboro, when the fact was that Pillow turned coward and hid behind a tree until Breckinridge ordered him to join his men in the fight. Only by the first week of April did the president seem once more to be recovering. He began riding regularly again, asked Clay to breakfast with him, and tried haltingly to renew his social associations with both Clays as well as others. And he never forgot those beyond his reach. Through all his ills, he continued to look out for Sidney Johnston's widow, undertaking to act as trustee for money do-nated by concerned citizens. Jefferson Davis, who felt such a peculiar sensitivity to loyalty from his friends, was himself perhaps the most loyal friend any man could have.[25]

The hard circumstances of many more than Mrs. Johnston came dramatically to the president's attention just as he emerged from his winter and early spring illness. During the past year inflation had turned consumer goods into luxuries and made Confederate currency increas-ingly worthless. Scarcity of almost everything thanks to the armies' pri-ority demands only added to the problem. The cost of feeding a family had increased tenfold since 1860, and while the War Department was a major purchaser of agricultural produce and livestock, it paid only about half of the current market value. Discontent rose proportionately, and when Davis declared March 27 to be a national day of fasting and prayer, one clerk in Richmond declared in disbelief, "Fasting in the midst of famine!" That same day Richmonders read accounts of a recent riot in Salisbury, North Carolina, where soldiers' wives demanded—and got— store goods at the same low prices paid by the government.

Richmond women also felt those pressures and frustrations and probably got their cue from their sisters in Salisbury. After an organizational meeting on April 1, they set out early the next morning, Easter Thursday, heading for the markets to "find something to eat." It started peacefully enough, but some women came armed with knives, and the leader declared that she would have "bread or blood." Throughout the morning their numbers grew steadily as first they went to the governor's mansion. Getting no satisfaction, they went on to the grocery stores on Cary Street. There, finally, their discipline broke down and they commenced breaking into stores with hatchets and axes and looting them. Governor John Letcher tried to control them, with only limited success. As the mob meandered on through the city, Major Joseph Mayo arrived, and in the vicinity of the public square he confronted them with several armed police. He gave them five minutes to disperse before his men opened fire.[26]

The president might well have heard the shouts of the crowd only a few blocks from his home. If not, surely someone came from the War Department to tell him what was happening. He was already in a sad mood, for during the night a thief had gotten into his stables and stolen one of his favorite horses. Now the women of the capital—those same women to whose patriotism and self-sacrifice he had appealed in his speech in January—were rioting in the streets. Davis immediately saw beyond the crisis before him to the greater danger. This had happened in North Carolina; now it was happening in Virginia. If the fever spread, the whole Confederate home front could explode spontaneously, and with the spring and summer campaigns only weeks or days away. Shortly after 11 A.M. he left the Executive Mansion himself to find the mob.

Davis found them while Mayo still counted off his five minutes. Climbing atop a nearby wagon and shouting for the crowd's attention, he got a quick response. Sensing the tension, Davis showed that same personal calm and self-command he had displayed in Mexico. Quietly he chided them for crying that they were after bread, when he saw in their hands jewelry and fabrics. However just their cause, they would disgrace it and their city by becoming mere plunderers. He promised that food would be given them if only they would disperse, adding that if farmers heard what was happening in the city, they would not send their produce into Richmond, making the shortages even worse. Varina Davis later claimed that Davis emptied his pockets and threw what money he had to the crowd. Perhaps so, but when he had finished speaking he also took out his watch and repeated Mayo's threat to have the armed guards open fire if they did not disperse in five minutes. "We do not desire to injure anyone," he said, "but this lawlessness must stop." Behind him the captain of the guard commanded his men to load their rifles, and in the face of Davis's determination, his promise of relief, and those loaded guns, the women finally dispersed and went home.[27]

For the next few days small groups of women continued to gather at street corners, but no more disturbances took place and rice and other foodstuffs were distributed to the most needy. Davis himself "seemed deeply moved," thought one onlooker. Always better able to relate sympathetically to women than to men, the sight of those hungry, angry wives and sisters whose men were in his armies distressed him considerably. Equally disheartening was his fear that news of the bread riot might stimulate similar outbreaks elsewhere. He had Seddon require that no telegraphic news of the event get out of the city, while also asking the local press not to mention it, "for obvious reasons," thought War Department clerk Jones. Davis should have known better. The *Examiner*, always his foe, published full accounts of the event and the later trials of the leaders.[28]

Happily, the perverse pendulum of war fortunes swung in a good direction for Davis almost immediately. On April 5 reports of an enemy gunboat fleet massing for an attack on Charleston started coming into the War Department. Then on April 8 Seddon sent the president compliments on his improving health and as a "tonic" enclosed news that Beauregard's batteries had decisively repulsed the fleet, disabling more than half of the ironclads. In the War Department, some believed that the victory would make Beauregard the most popular man in the South, except for Lee. Davis, always wondering about Beauregard, immediately sent his aide Colonel Lee to Charleston, to be of what use he could to the general as well as report fully on affairs to the president. In fact, Davis kept his aides busy that spring inspecting his armies all across the Confederacy. Late in March he sent Preston Johnston to Tullahoma and Ives to Pemberton at Vicksburg, then on to Port Hudson. Johnston found Bragg away with his ill wife, and Joseph E. Johnston actually and finally in direct command of the Army of Tennessee. The army appeared in the best condition yet seen, well armed and equipped, and suffering only from want of subsistence, "living from hand to mouth."

More ominous, however, was what the colonel found at headquarters. Neither Bragg nor Johnston expressed any plans for a forthcoming campaign and revealed only a vague notion that if Rosecrans did not advance upon their front, then they would have to do something, possibly another march into Kentucky. Just as bad, General Johnston complained repeatedly of Pemberton, of his being uncommunicative and uncooperative, and even insubordinate. And again Johnston asserted that because of the size of his overall command, his two armies in Tennessee and Mississippi "could not co-operate." As for Ives, what he said of his visit to Mississippi is lost, but for all his reluctance to communicate with Johnston, Pemberton corresponded constantly with Davis, and thus the president heard directly. Pemberton needed more cavalry and heavy guns, and Grant was advancing against him both overland and on the river, yet by mid-April he could report that "I see nothing unfavorable in present aspect of affairs."[29]

Others felt less sanguine. After his visit to Tullahoma, Preston Johnston returned ill at ease with what he had seen in Joseph Johnston and Bragg. "There is nobody competent to the command of the Western Army," he told his uncle. Their only hope would be for Davis himself to take the field, and the colonel had not stopped urging him to do so. "I feel satisfied that if he would, in sixty days we would be on the Ohio River." Yet there is no evidence that the president any longer entertained even fleeting thoughts of taking command in person, if he ever did. Instead, his health continued to bounce up and down as the spring wore on. In mid-April illness again confined him to his house and prevented personal interviews. Even the sight in his remaining good eye started to fail, and for ten straight days he did not go to his office at all. Then his throat swelled until at times he was speechless. Again there were fears for his life, and war clerk Jones believed that some took secret joy in his sufferings. "I have seen some officers of rank today," he wrote, "who sincerely hope the President will not recover." It was not until early May that he reemerged, still pale and feeble. Even then, however, he continued his vast correspondence from his sickbed.[30]

By now the inevitable spring and summer campaigns became imminent, and all across the Confederacy, as Davis returned to his office and stared at the maps on his wall, he could see the impending danger. The least-threatened area appeared to be the Trans-Mississippi. After visiting Vicksburg and Port Hudson, Ives had gone on to Louisiana and Texas, and brought back reports that, if not glowing, at least showed that commanders out there were cooperating. Magruder sent nearly a third of his command in Texas to reinforce Port Hudson, and his only real complaints were want of heavy ordnance. He faced few threats. In the overall department west of the great river, however, command continued to be a problem. Davis had approved a suspension of habeas corpus at Holmes's request back in January, and it proved to be very unpopular. Hindman continued to be effective, though even more unpopular, as commander of the subdistrict of Arkansas, and only Magruder seemed to enjoy the confidence and good opinion of the people. Before Gustavus Smith resigned his commission, Davis thought of sending him out to command the department, or a portion of it, but then he himself put an end to Smith's further service by sharing the general's haughty correspondence with Western political leaders like Thomas Reynolds, prejudicing them against the troublesome officer. Price, "a puffy, conceited old humbug," as Preston Johnston called him, was out of the question for higher command. Finally an appeal from the Arkansas congressional delegation begged that Kirby Smith be sent to supersede Holmes, helping Davis to settle matters. With Holmes himself continuing to complain, with the press and people against him, he begged to be relieved. On February 9 Davis gave in, assigning Kirby Smith to command of the Trans-Mississippi. Holmes reacted by telling the president that he was "greatly obliged" to be replaced. Smith immediately took a firm hand, set about making the department self-sufficient, and reported himself in improving condition, even while promising to send portions of his forces to aid in the defense of Port Hudson and Vicksburg. The Trans-Mississippi was in good hands at last.[30]

Of course, the president never felt any question about the opposite flank of his line being in good hands. By early April, Lee reported that the Army of the Potomac, now commanded by General Joseph Hooker, appeared about to cross the Rappahannock on another drive into Virginia's heartland. Davis, though ill, did what he could to reinforce Lee, sending him more cavalry and trying to improve his dwindling supplies. But otherwise the president remained almost entirely a passive observer of the campaign that then unfolded. As always Lee kept him almost daily informed of events in his front, of Hooker's final crossing of the Rappahannock on April 29, and of Lee's determination to fight him despite almost two-to-one odds. On May 3 Lee sped Davis's recovery with news that he was beating Hooker decisively, thanking "Almighty God for a great victory." Having commenced his campaign ably by confusing Lee as to his intentions, Hooker forfeited his advantage by losing his nerve and going on the defensive once the fighting began. Sensing this, Lee proved his daring by dividing his army and sending Stonewall Jackson on a flank march that surprised and routed much of Hooker's army on May 2. Though the battle still continued when Lee wired Davis, the victorious outcome was assured. The next day, even as he emerged from his sickroom for the first time in days, Davis sent to Lee his hearty thanks "for this addition to the unprecedented series of great victories which your army has achieved." He took a carriage ride and displayed "the finest spirits." Once again Lee had saved Virginia, reaffirming Davis's conviction that here he had at least one great general. But Lee's telegram also brought disturbing news: Jackson had been seriously wounded; in the following days his condition deteriorated. Deeply concerned, Davis kept a servant at the telegraph office constantly to bring him the latest reports on the general, even sending servants to meet incoming trains should they have news. By May 9 the outlook was grim, and Davis sat silent at home until midnight or later, unable to take his thoughts from Jackson. When he died the next day, the body was wrapped in a flag sent by Davis and brought to Richmond for the funeral. Davis rode in a carriage just behind Jackson's hearse, still looking "thin and frail in health." When the body lay in state at the governor's mansion, the Davises stood beside the casket, and Varina saw a tear escape her husband's eye and fall to Jackson's face. "You must excuse me," Davis said later after silently ignoring a fellow mourner's conversation. "I am still staggering from a dreadful blow. I cannot think."[31]

If only Davis had had such great generals in the West. Pemberton took some time to realize that the Federals moving toward him meant real business. Soon after assuring Davis that his situation was good, he reported that he thought Grant was actually withdrawing, then at the end of April reported the startling intelligence that Grant had not withdrawn but in fact had crossed the Mississippi above Vicksburg, traveled down the Louisiana side, and then recrossed the great river below Vicksburg. Even then the Yankees were marching through the interior of Mississippi heading for Pemberton's rear, trying to trap him with his back to the river. On May 1 Davis confessed that he felt "intense anxiety" over Pemberton's situation.[32]

It only got worse. The complaints about Van Dorn continued unabated, even after Pemberton assumed command, and finally the general's own indiscretions solved the problem. In the habit of visiting a doctor's wife when her husband was away, Van Dorn did so openly and with disregard for the consequences. On the morning of May 7 the doctor walked into Van Dorn's headquarters, found him sitting with his back to the door, and shot him in the head. "The General had great weaknesses in such matters," a friend told Davis in reporting the murder. Hard on the heels of the death of his old friend, Davis learned that Grant was steadily pushing Pemberton back toward the defenses of Vicksburg. Worse, Johnston was being almost no help at all. Davis insisted, and wisely, that both Vicksburg and Port Hudson must be held, while Johnston favored concentrating the defenders of both places against Grant. That was fine, but another Yankee army also threatened Port Hudson from the south, and if it fell while Pemberton tried to meet Grant, then Vicksburg was as good as gone as well, for the Confederates would then be caught between two Federal armies. Furthermore, given the goal—the seeming necessity—of keeping communications open with the Trans-Mississippi via the ninety-mile stretch of the Mississippi that still belonged to the Confederates, it was essential to hold both points. The loss of either made the loss of the other only a matter of time and would have effectively reduced Davis's zone of control of the river to nothing. Johnston, perpetually preoccupied with the doctrine of concentration, could not—or would not—see this, taking it for granted that if Pemberton concentrated his forces against Grant but then lost Port Hudson in the process, "Success will win back what was abandoned to win it." The trouble was, Johnston did not take into account what would happen if Pemberton could not beat Grant.[33]

Through much of this, Davis seemed strangely uninvolved. He should have known from experience going back more than eighteen months that he and Johnston did not communicate well with each other. Time after time, either the president did not clearly state his goals and instructions, or else Johnston inadvertently or intentionally did not take his meaning. The general still resisted assuming the responsibility Davis had given him, preferring to sit idly at Tullahoma with no foe in his vicinity, while Grant and Nathaniel Banks advanced steadily toward Vicksburg and Port Hudson throughout the spring. Johnston could and should have left Hardee in command of the Army of Tennessee until Bragg returned, and gone to Mississippi himself in April or even earlier instead of carping to Preston Johnston and Davis of how Pemberton was not telling him anything and would not obey instructions. Once again Johnston showed himself unwilling to risk firing his gun and missing. Unfortunately, the president let him get away with it until May 9, when he finally ordered him to go to Vicksburg and take personal command. Worse, he told him to take a mere three thousand men with him, a paltry reinforcement, and coming from an army doing nothing and facing no threat from the enemy.[33]

They all waited too long, and then Johnston compounded the problem by moving slowly and hesitantly. Finally on May 19 Pemberton was pushed back too far. After trying to advance farther than he thought advisable, to form a junction with Johnston who had reached Jackson, Pemberton met with a defeat at Champion's Hill on May 16 and another at Big Black River the next day. Opposed to Johnston's order for a junction, he had dragged his feet, and Johnston did not rush to help him. But the situation was almost entirely out of their hands now, for neither was a general to match Grant and his subordinate William T. Sherman. If Johnston had left for Mississippi two weeks earlier, he could have effected a junction with Pemberton. If, on his own authority as commander of the Western division, he had taken a division or more with him, instead of a mere brigade, Johnston might have been able to cut his way through to his subordinate even as late as he did move. As events unfolded, after the repulse on the Big Black, Pemberton withdrew to his defenses around Vicksburg and Grant quickly closed in for a siege. Conceiving it to be "the most important point in the Confederacy," Pemberton begged for assistance. Two days later, a friend wrote to Davis that he could hear the sound of cannon, and warned that "if stormed Vicksburg will fall." Again the protest against Pemberton erupted. "The loss of confidence is universal," wrote one Mississippian.

Davis, too, must have felt his confidence ebbing, though more toward Johnston than Pemberton. "No effort was spared by me to prevent an invasion such as has occurred," he wrote to Joseph even while Grant's batteries ringed Vicksburg. He lamented the failure of his generals to unite for an attack on Grant, for "thus alone was a complete victory expected." In fact, of course, Davis had spared some efforts. He did not have to leave Pemberton in command after Johnston's repeated complaints of lack of proper subordination and obedience. But then Davis had formed an attachment for Pemberton, and that meant that attacks on this general were attacks on the president and not to be heeded. Seeing that Johnston showed his usual indisposition to move or act decisively, Davis could have given a direct order to go take command in Mississippi much earlier, not waiting until Grant was already across the river and deep in Pemberton's vulnerable rear. But Davis, wisely in the abstract but unwisely in this instance, resisted interfering with a commanding general's management of affairs in his own department.

The overriding problem was that Johnston refused to manage those affairs either, leading to the other "effort" the president could have made—removal of Johnston. Entirely setting aside their personality differences, Davis had seen more than enough evidence of the general's incapacity for high-level command: his pride and vanity, his unwillingness to accept responsibility, the ease with which others like Beauregard could dominate him, his uncommunicativeness, his blatant backbiting of the president and willingness to be used as a tool by Davis's enemies like Wigfall, his obtusity over his orders, his sloth, and his apparent inability to compel obedience from subordinates like Pemberton. To his great credit, Davis had shown more patience with Johnston than with any other similar character in his life. By May 1863 he had been patient too long, but by then, too, there was more to it than patience. The fact still remained that the only alternative to Johnston was Beauregard. Riding high again after his repulse of the fleet at Charleston, the Creole would have been a likely and popular replacement, either for Pemberton in a subordinate capacity or for Johnston as overall commander. Cursed with a full share of flaws of his own, Beauregard would still have performed better than the former, and could hardly have done worse than the latter. But, as always, Beauregard could not be considered for any important command, and thus passively, negatively, Davis's animosity toward this one general continued to influence, perhaps even direct, the course of the war in the West. Davis's unhappy and largely unwilling adherence to Joseph E. Johnston would be his greatest mistake of 1863, and one of his greatest of the war.[34]

Throughout May the president watched the gradually tightening siege at Vicksburg progress, and Johnston's largely futile efforts to build another army in Mississippi to help break the siege, even tardily drawing more brigades to him from Tullahoma now that it was too late. Still Pemberton held out, and by the end of the month Governor Pettus told Davis that the enemy's dead blanketed the earth in front of Vicksburg's earthworks. He even predicted that Pemberton would be able to hold out. Yet in his office in Richmond, Davis did not feel sanguine. Writing to his brother Joseph, he lamented, "I would that my arm were with you to strike though it were it's last blow." But, of course, he would not go to take command himself. Yet he lamented his situation, and no doubt had Johnston, Beauregard, and perhaps even Bragg and Pemberton in mind when he almost plaintively told Joseph, "A *General* in the full acceptation of the word is a rare product, scarcely more than one can be expected in a generation, but in this mighty war in which we are engaged there is need for half a dozen."[35]

At the moment he had only one, Robert E. Lee. Davis well recognized the fickle nature of the public and even the soldiery, whom he believed regarded a Confederate general as either a genius or an incompetent. Much the same could be said of his cabinet officers, especially his secretaries of war, and now Seddon was finally starting to feel the barbs of public criticism as his predecessors had before him. Of course, the current situation in Mississippi would help account for that. Yet because he did have that one great general, Lee, the president could hope to retrieve fortunes on a variety of fronts. He needed to follow up the victory at Chancellorsville before the enemy could mount another campaign against Richmond. He needed to relieve the pressure on Vicksburg, perhaps buying Pemberton time by forcing Grant to lighten his grip to reinforce other theaters. He needed to demonstrate to Europe that the Confederacy was a mighty power in its own right, able to defend itself, and worthy of recognition. Moreover, well aware of mounting war weariness and dissent in the North, he could hope to feed the fire in Lincoln's rear if he could achieve another victory, especially one on Yankee soil. Still remembering his impression of Maine from his prewar visit, Davis even believed that its people, "a hardy, thrifty, seafaring population," might even secede to join Canada, thus further weakening the Union. All this might be achieved if the South could strike and strike decisively.[36]

Of course Lee was the one to do it. Even before Chancellorsville, Lee envisioned another invasion of Maryland and even Pennsylvania, but Hooker's advance precluded further action. Two weeks after his victory, however, Lee and Davis sat in several discussions at the president's office, and what emerged was a plan for such an invasion. Then came word that Pemberton was bottled up in Vicksburg, and that generated another meeting on May 26, in which Davis invited Lee to meet with the entire cabinet. Davis felt some hesitation now about launching an invasion, preferring to send men from Lee directly to Mississippi to help face Grant, but an overwhelming majority of those present sided with Lee and Davis willingly yielded. Yet for some reason confusion remained, as often seemed to happen with his generals' understanding of what Davis intended, for a few days later each discovered that the other had a different idea of what they had concluded to do. Happily they soon cleared up the misunderstanding, and then the president, as before, left virtually all the planning for the campaign to Lee himself.

As before, Davis devoted himself to doing what he could in Richmond to bolster and sustain his general. He called on the governors yet again for more volunteers, fifteen thousand from Georgia and North Carolina alone, to be ready by August 1. They would replace the regiments withdrawn to reinforce Lee, and the general constantly now asked for more men, even as he advanced through the Shenandoah toward the Potomac. In fact, Lee and Davis occasionally became a little stiff with each other as the tension of the great endeavor was felt by all involved, but they never lost their abiding faith in one another. Lee wrote to the president almost daily, and if Davis remained nervous and apprehensive, it was only because so much rode on those banners of the Army of Northern Virginia. On June 19 Lee started crossing the river. Within days his advance elements marched into Pennsylvania, the only truly unsettling element of the campaign so far being Lee's suggestion that a new army be formed in central Virginia, made up of all remaining available brigades from Virginia and North Carolina. Such an army would protect both states from invasion while he was in the North. The idea may have been impractical, and in any case Lee doomed it from the start when he suggested to Davis that it should be commanded by Beauregard.[37]

Once again, Davis had to be a spectator from afar. He could not go to Lee in Pennsylvania, and he could not even think of going to Mississippi. This last made all the more agonizing the word that filtered back to him of Yankee depredations on his own property and that of his brother and friends. "We have to deal with savages possessing the power of civilized people," he lamented when he learned in late June that Federals had taken several white civilians prisoner and allowed their slaves to run free. Then came word that Joseph had nearly seen his house burned by Yankee raiders and, though the house escaped, so did 137 of his blacks, with that many more drifting off in the next few days. Still Joseph Davis refused to flee to his other land in Arkansas, intent on waiting to see the outcome at Vicksburg. By this time, only six black adults and a few slave children remained at Brierfield. Most of Davis's books and personal papers, along with some furniture, was removed to be hidden at the home of a friend, but with the Yankees roving all over the country, Davis could not be at all certain of their safety.[38]

As the end of June approached, the president chafed at sitting in his office, no closer to the scene of action than looking at the pins in his maps. Everyone wanted reinforcements, and he had few or none to give. He mourned especially that he could do no more "to give aid to the defenders of my home." "But that is not my only duty," he consoled himself and others. Meanwhile, he looked backward and forward. "I mourn over opportunities lost," he said on June 24, "and as I may will endeavor to repair the injury."[39]

Soon enough there was even more to mourn and more than even he could repair. That same day Joseph Davis wrote to plead, "is it possible to reinforce Johnston or must Vicksburg fall?" The next day he still declared that "it is not too late," yet several days before Johnston himself telegraphed to Seddon that the situation at Vicksburg was "hopeless." Then it all hit at once. Davis had recovered his health during much of the month, even resuming his afternoon rides and looking "vastly improved" to Colonel Johnston, while others who saw him on horseback declared that he sat "as straight as an English King." But by July 2 Davis was ill again, too much so to go to work. The cause was unknown, but two days later, July 4, the president's physician expressed serious concern, and rumors in the War Department soon countenanced even the possibility of his death. And even though on July 6 Davis arose from his bed once more, still one observer believed, "His health is apparently gone, and it may be doubtful whether he will ever be quite well again."[40]

Much of the cause may have been anxiety, but if not, then news from the fronts placed an oppressive burden on him when it arrived. July 5 brought word that Lee had fought a great battle at Gettysburg, but in following days no dispatches arrived from Lee to tell with certainty of the outcome. Only vague reports from Northern newspapers offered any news, all of it inconclusive and most interpreted to indicate a crushing Rebel victory. But then, while awaiting definitive word from Pennsylvania, Davis received a note from Seddon on July 7 enclosing a report from Vicksburg. "With the deepest regret at being compelled to inflict the pain of such disastrous intelligence," the secretary of war gave the president the incontrovertible news that Pemberton and Vicksburg had fallen. After forty-seven days of siege, he was starved out, even as Johnston was finally marching to try to break through to him.

Poor Seddon, clutching at any chance to pass on good news, the next day gave Davis a report indicating that Lee was pushing the Yankees before him and even then marching on Baltimore. He prayed that the president "may share the hopes inspired by such good news, worthy I trust of acceptation, though not fully authentic." Davis would have been delighted to share that hope, for acute anxiety wracked him constantly now. In the face of the disaster in Mississippi and the apparent success in Pennsylvania, he was ready to give up on Johnston. "If I could take one wing and Lee the other," he told Varina, "I think we could between us wrest a victory from those people." But then came July 9, and a message penned by Lee five days earlier finally arrived. After three bloody days at Gettysburg, he had been forced to retire. A second invasion of the North thus ended in failure.[41]

Two consecutive disasters in as many days: Gettysburg on July 3 and Vicksburg on July 4. Would these dreadful misfortunes never cease?

The Clouds Are Truly Dark over Us

As the hot July days followed one another, the dimensions and repercussions of the losses became apparent. Lee, as usual, recovered quickly.
Soon he was back in northern Virginia, ready to rebuild his army, which
had lost almost a third of its numbers in killed, wounded, and missing.
Gettysburg had been his worst battle, largely out of his control and not
well fought by him, especially on the third day. Lee felt this without
having to hear any of the murmurs of criticism, and on August 8 he
asked to be allowed to resign. Davis felt touched when he read his general's letter. Instantly he thought of Sidney Johnston, and of how he
always said that "success is the test of merit," and how he bore in silence
the "senseless clamor" of uncomprehending critics. Now he saw it happening to Lee. "My dear friend," Davis responded. "There is nothing
which I have found to require a greater effort of patience than to bear
the criticisms of the ignorant." From his greater experience at being the
object of calumny, he advised Lee to ignore it. As for resignation and
replacement, Lee had no equal, much less a superior. "To ask me to
substitute you by someone in my judgment more fit to command," said
Davis, "is to demand an impossibility." Lee must remain.[1]

But in the West more attention must be paid if anything was to
retrieve the situation. Pemberton surrendered his entire garrison of
twenty-nine thousand. Wisely, Grant did not send them north as prisoners but paroled them instead. That left them in Confederate service,
though unable to participate in active operations on pain of death if
captured until formally exchanged for Yankee prisoners. In effect, having taken them out of the war, Grant now left them as an additional

unproductive burden on the South, expecting that most would simply desert and go home. Pemberton feared exactly this and asked for immediate furlough for his army, expecting that otherwise they would simply disappear and never reassemble again. Worse, almost ten thousand of them were sick, and having surrendered all weapons to Grant, he had no arms to compel the men to remain. Davis sent Colonel Lee to inspect the situation personally, and he reported the men all in pitiable condition. Capping the misfortune, and as expected once Vicksburg fell, Port Hudson's days were numbered. On July 8 its seven thousand defenders also surrendered, adding more parolees to the burden, and giving Lincoln undisputed control of the whole Mississippi.[2]

A storm of indignation swept across the Confederacy. Already unpopular before the surrender because of his Northern birth, Pemberton found himself pilloried afterward. Letters of protest flowed into Davis's office from all quarters, but especially from Mississippi, where nominally, at least, Pemberton still commanded. But as soon as Pemberton himself was released from parole, Davis sent him to the rear to prepare his report and assigned Hardee to his place. Pemberton hoped for a court of inquiry to look into all the circumstances of the loss of Vicksburg, meaning mainly Johnston's conduct.[3]

In fact, the president himself wanted to look into some things— Port Hudson, Vicksburg, the loss of Jackson, the causes of these failures, and the failure to make corrections. Pemberton he saw as largely an innocent victim. Publicly he supported him, asserting that Vicksburg fell not from want of provisions but from the exhaustion of the men. The president sent repeated assurances of the high regard in which he held Pemberton. "My own judgment places him among the ablest of our Generals," Davis told Bragg, and to Pemberton himself Davis said, "You did right to risk an army for the purpose of keeping command of even a section of the Mississippi." Moreover, knowing the temper of the armchair generals, Davis went on to say, "Had you succeeded none would have blamed, had you not made the attempt few if any would have defended your course."[4]

But Davis knew in his heart the real reason for the loss of the Mississippi. Chief of Ordnance Josiah Gorgas commented to the president that Vicksburg fell from want of food. "Yes," said Jefferson Davis, "from want of provisions inside, and a general outside who wouldn't fight." Many around him saw Davis's visible bitterness toward Johnston, and several shared it. Just a week after news of the surrender reached Richmond, Preston Johnston urged the president to replace Joseph Johnston with Hardee. Davis hardly needed much persuading. Incredibly, on July 5, with Vicksburg surrendered, Johnston was still debating by telegraph with Davis over the nature of his command and responsibilities. Because Davis had been forced to order Johnston to Mississippi to get him to be an active participant, Johnston chose to assume that this meant he no longer had any authority over Bragg, a misapprehension confirmed when Richmond directly ordered reinforcements from Tennessee to Mississippi. Johnston interpreted this as meaning that he did not himself have the power to do so, whereas Davis more likely did it from conviction that Johnston did not have the will to do so. And as always, Johnston complained that "an officer having a task like mine, far above his ability, cannot in addition command other remote departments." "No general can command separate armies." If he was right, it was only in that strained modesty about it being "above his ability."

Then came Johnston's dispatch of July 5, repeating all the old business yet again. Davis received this one the same day as the news of Vicksburg's fall, and it sent him into a rage. He fired back a stiff telegram promising to "notice" Johnston's mistakes in a letter to follow, but then complained that "I have remained without information from you as to any plans proposed or attempted to raise the siege." It was the same with any scheme to save Port Hudson. "I have to request such information in relation thereto as the Government has a right to expect from one of its commanding generals in the field." Disingenuously, Johnston replied that "I have never meant to fail" in keeping Richmond informed, though in fact it had been his own stated policy for more than eighteen months to tell the War Department as little as possible for fear of spies.[5]

The receipt of that July 5 telegram, on top of the losses at Vicksburg and Gettysburg, was too much for Davis. He had to fight and win at least one battle, and now he turned to a field on which he felt he always emerged victorious. He wrote to Johnston a fifteen-page letter reminiscent of the correspondence years before with Winfield Scott. He combed all their prior correspondence for his evidence, then stated his case, and in terms far more measured and judicious than had been his custom in past controversies. He quoted order after order, dispatch after dispatch, all showing that Johnston was vested with full control of all forces in his command, subject only—as all commanders were—to superseding instructions from Davis as commander in chief. Incredibly, Johnston had not been able or willing to see the simple facts of such statements from Davis as "you, as commandant of the department, have power so to order." Yet where Davis said nothing at all, as with his direction to go to Mississippi, Johnston then delved for hidden or implied meaning, such as that going to help Pemberton meant that he no longer commanded Bragg as well. And throughout his review of their months of correspondence over the matter, it was apparent to Davis that Johnston would not yield a desire to have Davis reduce his command to either Tennessee or Mississippi, but not both.

There probably lay the real reason for the general's apparent obtuseness. Joseph E. Johnston was not a stupid man. He had to understand what Davis intended. The trouble was, he did not like it nor did he like Davis, or at least he was surrounded by those who did not—his wife, his staff, his close friend Wigfall. So the general decided to resist the president's wishes for this supercommand by finding flaws, dragging his feet, and refusing to comprehend, in effect using stalling and deliberate confusion to demonstrate the basic impracticality of it all. Later in the war others would show just how practical it could be, and on an even grander scale. It was impractical only for a man of Johnston's insecurity.[6]

Naturally Johnston replied, and in the main he refused to understand Davis's letter just as he had declined to understand his previous instructions. Repeatedly, in the face of explicit statements, Johnston spoke only of "the inference" or "the impression" he had drawn from Davis's communications, and those inferences were consistently erroneous. At the same time, Johnston repeatedly ducked the matter of his responsibility and authority to weaken Bragg to support Pemberton by shifting it back to Richmond. "It is for the Government to decide," he said again and again, refusing to accept the responsibility Davis kept telling him he had. Even though Davis, as usual, sent a reply to Johnston's reply, the two avoided a protracted letter war and, officially at least, their relations continued to be polite. Johnston even protested that he could not understand why the president felt aggrieved toward him, though Davis was less discrete and openly discussed his disappointment with friends and in the hearing of others who passed rumors around the capital. Davis did relieve Johnston of responsibility for half of his command when, on July 25, he created the new Department of Tennessee and gave it to Bragg. Thus, in the end, Johnston had his way.[7]

But matters did not end there. At the close of July someone on Johnston's staff published a very critical account of the campaign, laying blame fully at Pemberton's feet. At once Davis brought it to Johnston's attention and asked that he investigate the matter, especially since the letter lauded Johnston to such an extent that not even Davis could believe the general himself had anything to do with it, as indeed he did not. Davis also warned Pemberton that he must be wary, and even gave him some advice on points that should be countered in his report of Vicksburg operations. For Davis, Pemberton had now become another Bragg, another Holmes, another Sidney Johnston, even, in light of recent events, another Lee. To some good men, said the president, "it is decreed that their success shall be denied or treated as a necessary result; and their failures imputed to incapacity or crime." Then there were men like Joseph Johnston, for whom "it is given to be commended for what they are expected to do, and to be sheltered when they fail by a transfer of the blame which may attach." Davis assured Pemberton that "Genl.

Lee and yourself" were of the former, better sort. "I am no stranger to the misrepresentation of which malignity is capable," said Davis sadly, "nor to the generation of such feeling by the conscientious discharge of duty." He could only assure the sad general that his own confidence in him was undimmed.[8]

Soon there were rumors that Johnston's own brother had authored the offending letter, probably an honest confusion since it had been addressed to a John M. Johnson. Certainly such confusions did nothing for relations between the president and his third-ranking general in the service. A few men attempted to patch things up between them, but for Davis it had already gone too far, and probably for Johnston as well. His wife spat venom in her letters, calling Davis and Varina the "Royal Family." Wigfall suggested to several that Davis was losing his mind, for "no sane man would act as he is doing." Johnston himself simply said that he was above Davis's accusations. He served his people, not Jefferson Davis. As for the president, he could not but see in the Johnston imbroglio a consistent design on the general's part. That he was mistaken did not matter, nor is it likely that anyone could have convinced him that Johnston was not involved in a deliberate campaign to discredit Pemberton. In time the general would actively seek to build a case against his former subordinate, but for now, like many another man whose reputation outstripped his merits, he chiefly sought to avoid blame for himself. This was lost on Davis. He had seen the same pattern too often before. He knew that men attacked him by attacking his friends. He knew that his best friends were quiet, uncomplaining officers who eschewed using the press for their own benefit. Johnston and Pemberton each fitted perfectly the two distinct molds in Davis's mind by which he now measured men, molds that were firmly set and immutable, formed by Sidney Johnston and Polk and Holmes and Bragg on one side, and by Beauregard, Gustavus Smith, and Joseph E. Johnston on the other. When men seemed to fit those molds, Davis felt that he knew as much of them as he needed to and closed his mind to anything that countered the cast. As always, in his mind he was right, his judgment of men's characters beyond question.[9]

As the burden of his cares wore him down again that July, Davis suffered another, more personal blow to make him resent Johnston's performance in Mississippi even more. Joseph Davis had moved into the interior of the state the previous summer and bought properties both for himself and his brother. Johnston's announcement of the loss of Vicksburg made even these small plantations vulnerable to the enemy, and so Joseph moved again, into Alabama. There had not been time to repack all the president's library, personal papers, furniture, and the rest. As much as could be concealed they put in the attic of a friend's house, and left it in the care of another trusted friend. When Pemberton passed through on his way late in July, he wrote to the president that his private papers were safe, but he related only what Joseph was able to tell him, and neither knew of the visit of Yankees to the property near Fleetwood on July 11. Questioned about reports of Davis's personal property being in the Dr. Owen Cox house, the hapless man in charge knew nothing. But then a slave appeared, the same one who had informed the Federals of Davis's books and letters. At once he commenced pointing out places in the attic and elsewhere that "Old Jeff's books," as the Yankees called them, could be found. At the first discovery, news spread rapidly, and soon perhaps hundreds of soldiers appeared. They carried boxes out into the yard, broke them open, and scattered their contents to the wind. Finding his carpets from Brierfield, they cut them to pieces as souvenirs and saddle blankets and took his draperies for their tents. They drank his wine, took special delight in capturing his walking sticks, and continued their plundering until two days later when an officer finally appropriated all that remained of any military usefulness. All they left were some dining room chairs, a battered writing case, two vandalized sofas, and a broken card table. The man left to guard it all boxed what he could retrieve from the fields and woods and wrote to Davis giving him the sad news. He could not help but add that a particular object of interest was a small portrait of Davis, which the Yankees stabbed again and again with their knives until it disintegrated.

The news must have devastated the president. His entire past had been in those books and papers. Now his early letters to and from the departed Sarah were objects of curiosity in some Yankee's saddlebag. His correspondence with Varina during their courtship had suffered the same fate, along with his early speeches, much of his Mexican War military papers, and the precious correspondence containing what little he knew of his father. It was a hard blow, softened only by the knowledge that Varina was safe. She had been visiting in Mississippi and had herself assured Pemberton and others that her husband's papers would never be found. He could reflect now that it had done him little good to buy those fifteen hundred acres the previous December. Ironically, while the enemy left Brierfield standing, they burned and plundered everything on his newer property, freeing his slaves in the bargain. And now, in the months ahead, he must suffer seeing his personal letters published as curiosities in Yankee newspapers and hearing of them being read publicly for the entertainment of the enemy. Somehow this, too, he could almost lay at Johnston's door, though from several sources he knew that the real culprit was a faithless slave whom everyone had mistakenly trusted. It only confirmed his belief in the untrustworthiness and perfidy of blacks removed from the oversight of their masters.[10]

Quite coincidentally, the subject of blacks was appearing on Davis's desk almost daily just as enemy soldiers in Mississippi still gleefully exhibited the mementos taken from that attic. The only bright word in the misfortunes of July had come, of all sources, from Beauregard. Commencing an eight-week siege to take Battery Wagner on Morris Island, protecting Charleston, the Federals launched a major assault on July 18. Though it failed, still it attracted national attention because the regiment leading the charge, the Fifty-fourth Massachusetts, was the first all-black unit to see major action for the Union. At first, people looked to Davis to settle the question of how captured blacks in uniform ought to be treated, though he had already tried to deal with that a year before by declaring that former slaves in uniform should be returned to slavery, that free blacks under arms should be put at hard labor, and that white officers leading them would be tried and probably executed for inciting insurrection. But in April 1863 Lincoln announced that his government would retaliate in kind for mistreatment to any Union soldier, white or black, and thus the Confederacy's attempt to discourage blacks from fighting against it was stymied.[11]

Immediately in the wake of the able performance of the Fifty-fourth Massachusetts, and with the memory of disastrous losses at Vicksburg and Gettysburg and Port Hudson before them, many in the South revived a different policy toward blacks that some had proposed back in February 1861. Almost at once a small flood of propositions came to Davis suggesting that blacks, free and slave, should be used in the Confederacy's own military. Some saw it as a last resort, but others pointed to the current "alarming" state of affairs and counseled not to wait. "Gloom overspreads" the country, said one proponent. "Cannot we who have been raised with our Negroes and know how to command them, make them more efficient than the Yankees can?" He proposed drafting blacks into regiments a thousand strong, giving them white officers, and arming them with tools for fortification building or else pikes for military service. Indeed, most favored using blacks to perform more menial tasks, freeing white men for actual combat. "Negroes are easily influenced by those around them," wrote another petitioner, "and when placed in our army would make it a matter of pride to remain loyal." Pressed by circumstances, Davis yielded to the extent that he was willing to receive slaves donated by their masters, to be turned over to the army quartermasters to act as teamsters, ostlers, and company and hospital cooks and orderlies. But arming them was still too radical a step, though he did refer such propositions—even one that suggested integrating blacks into each white company of soldiers—to Seddon.[12]

The reverses of the summer made it evident that many things once thought impossible or impractical must now be attempted if the Confederacy were to retrieve the situation. "The clouds are truly dark over us," Davis wrote Holmes on July 15. Just six days before Davis had taken a dramatic step in escalating the horrors of the war. Back in May he sent

Brigadier General Gabriel J. Rains to Johnston. Rains had recently invented a system for building land and underwater mines, called "torpedoes," detonated by a variety of means, and promising great destruction for both shipping and unwary foot soldiers. After learning of the loss of Vicksburg, Davis told Johnston at Jackson that "General Rains should now fully apply his invention," even though many in the army found it offensive and unchivalrous. Even more out of the ordinary was Davis's countenancing—though he denied it—of a plan by former Baltimore police chief George P. Kane. A habitual schemer, Kane suggested back in March that he lead an expedition from Canada against Union posts on the Great Lakes, including Chicago, Milwaukee, and Detroit. Capturing them would assist the large peace movement in those states, and he could capture steamers to prey on enemy lake shipping. He also conceived a plan for releasing Confederate prisoners held at Johnson's Island off Sandusky, Ohio, but the whole plan came to nothing when betrayed by a Canadian. Kane even hoped to burn Buffalo, New York, though Davis may not have approved of this. The president still drew a line at some things not proper in "civilized" warfare, though his correspondence and utterances for a year past made it clear that he believed the enemy had abandoned all pretense of observing the ordinary usages of war. He would not countenance arson and wanton destruction of civilian property. Nor would he respond to any of the proposals that came to him that summer suggesting plans for capturing or assassinating Lincoln and his cabinet. He referred them without comment to Seddon.[13]

Knowing full well that the victories they won in July would probably not encourage the Yankees to let the rest of the summer pass without action, Davis could not long divert his attention to his feud with Johnston or the impractical schemes of dreamers. As always, he counted on Lee to look after Virginia, and happily here the foe did nothing more than posture for nearly four months after Gettysburg. But in the West, the Yankees would not wait that long. Within days after confirmation of the loss of Vicksburg, Port Hudson, and Jackson, Davis began rearranging his command system to meet the realities of the situation. The loss of Pemberton and his army already made moot the matter of the Department of the West created for Johnston. As a result Davis followed a suggestion by General Buckner to organize the Department of Tennessee under Bragg. Perhaps influenced by Bragg's earlier declaration in favor of unity of command, and obviously by the failure of such unity under Johnston, the president unfortunately did not heed Buckner's pleas not to include his own Department of East Tennessee in Bragg's new domain. Bragg suggested that East Tennessee could be a useful base for operations and, along with others, proposed that Johnston's small army—now under Hardee—his own, and Buckner's small command, should unite to drive the Federals out of middle Tennessee. Davis looked favorably on this for a time, but then the threat to Charleston caused him to consider sending Johnston's men there instead, since Grant was now leaving Vicksburg for parts unknown. Johnston himself was no help, and then, with the arrival of August, it became more evident that even if all the forces combined, they would still total little more than half of Rosecrans's reputed numbers.[14]

At the end of the third week of August, Rosecrans finally moved, his goal probably Chattanooga. At the same time a smaller Yankee army advanced toward Buckner's headquarters at Knoxville. Caught without an offensive plan of their own, the Confederates now had to react to the movements of the foe. Buckner had no choice but to abandon Knoxville, and eventually he joined Bragg. Davis, meanwhile, pursued a puzzlingly dilatory course for sending Bragg more reinforcements. Bragg appealed to Johnston, who naturally asked Richmond for instructions, and Davis did not even reply, at least not personally, leaving it to Cooper to tell Johnston to help "as far as you are able." Surely Davis should have known by now that a general who would not heed explicit instructions could not be counted on to do much with a qualified order like this. Worse, when he did telegraph Johnston, Davis only asked if he could send help, rather than ordering him to do so. The result was that Johnston kept half his small army sitting idly in Mississippi, while slowly sending the other half to Bragg. Davis also sent Colonel Chesnut to see the governors of Georgia and Alabama to urge them to send local militia to Bragg's aid, and he wrote directly to Vice President Stephens to ask him to use his influence in Georgia to secure help. And finally, against Lee's wishes, Davis authorized sending a major detachment from Virginia to bolster Bragg. In fact, Davis wanted Lee himself to go and assume command, but Lee declined on several grounds, which the president accepted. In late August Davis summoned Lee to Richmond to discuss the matter, without reaching a resolution. Davis knew what he wanted, but he resisted exercising his authority to force on his best general something that Lee opposed. Lee wanted to launch another offensive against the Army of the Potomac. But in early September Knoxville fell, and it appeared that two Yankee armies would now be free to concentrate against Bragg. The situation was becoming desperate. Davis considered opening up southwestern Virginia by sending its troops to Bragg, but in the end he won over Lee, who agreed to send Longstreet's I Corps to the West. Davis pressed Lee to go with it, but the general demurred yet again, and the president dropped the matter.[15]

Even as he valiantly tried to build up Bragg to meet the advancing threat, Davis felt increasing concern for the health of the high command in the Department of Tennessee. Repeated complaints against Bragg were coming to him now. Fathers encouraged their sons to desert or not return from furlough, and one even wrote to Davis accusing him of obstinacy in retaining the "imbecile" Bragg while ignoring the best men in the army—Beauregard, Gustavus Smith, and especially Johnston. "In Gods name stop your foolish attachment for such men as Bragg," the father wrote, "before a revolution within a revolution should take off your head." Despite ignoring such obvious malcontents, the president still felt concerned enough to send Preston Johnston to look at matters for himself on September 3, asking him to confer freely with all the generals in the army, not just Bragg. The increasing rumblings of discontent had inevitably reached Davis that summer. Bragg's health was not good, which, combined with his frail mental stability, left him hardly fit to command the army should a battle come, or so thought Polk and Hardee. The latter actually brought up the possibility of forcibly relieving his commander, but nothing came of it. Polk went even further, questioning the judgment of his old friend the president. "I am somewhat afraid of Davis," he wrote in August. "I do not find myself willing to risk his judgment." Davis relied too much on his own judgment and would not listen to "minds in the land from whom he might obtain counsel worth having," meaning, of course, Polk himself. "He is proud, self-reliant," wrote the supposedly devoted friend from Sidney Johnston's "set," "and I fear stubborn." Davis would have been wounded to the core had he known of Polk's words, especially since in early September he was trying to keep Bragg from bringing about a court-martial charging Polk with disobedience of orders at Perryville.[16]

The lack of full and timely information in Richmond became critical by the first week of September. Davis believed that Rosecrans intended to try to maneuver Bragg into evacuating Chattanooga, when in fact he was already doing exactly that, but communications were so poor that the information lag hampered the president in providing effective assistance. This, plus the knowledge of the unrest in the army high command, left him no alternative. At the beginning of September, Colonel Johnston had suggested that Davis himself go to the Army of Tennessee to see its condition. Of course, since Johnston was in constant communication with several anti-Bragg men, he probably hoped the visit would produce a change in commanders. Davis may have thought of going right away. On September 4 he obtained for himself a passport, required for leaving Richmond's limits, where security precautions restricted travel, yet he did not actually decide to make the trip until almost three weeks later. By then Rosecrans's advance had forced Bragg out of Chattanooga and into north Georgia, and on September 19–20, they met at Chickamauga. There, for once, Bragg's army did a better job of fighting with an enemy than with itself. After two days of battle a combination of daring and luck and Davis's sending of Longstreet gave Bragg the most crushing victory ever inflicted on a Yankee army, sending Rosecrans flying back to Chattanooga. Only Bragg's hesitance and the stiff rearguard resistance of General George H. Thomas and a few stubborn Federals prevented the entire destruction of Rosecrans's army. Bragg leisurely pursued him to lay siege.[17]

At first elation over the victory allowed Davis to reconsider plans for going to Tennessee. He had much to do in Richmond and could ill spare the time. But as soon as the fighting with Rosecrans ended, the war within the Army of Tennessee erupted with renewed fury. Bragg feuded with Lieutenant General D. H. Hill, whom Davis had sent to replace Hardee, still in Mississippi. He relieved Polk for disobedience of orders. Davis refused to allow Bragg to do so, saying that only Richmond could relieve a general, whereupon Bragg promptly preferred charges against Polk, hoping to get rid of him via court-martial. Soon a host of conflicting reports appeared on Davis's desk as Bragg, Polk, and their several supporters waged a war of words. Polk himself, while backbiting the president for his poor judgment, appealed to him out of friendship to relieve Bragg and save the army. Soon Longstreet and Buckner joined the fray. On October 4 a petition signed by twelve generals, including Longstreet, Hill, and Buckner, was sent to Davis, calling for Bragg's removal. The army's high command had slipped into chaos.[18]

By then Davis was on his way in person, and in the War Department the clerk John B. Jones commented that "the President cannot arrive in the field a moment too soon." In fact, he had sent Chesnut around October 1 to see if affairs had not improved since the victory, but after falling under the influence of Polk while stopping in Atlanta, Chesnut quickly accepted that Bragg was at fault, and further discussions with others when he reached the army left him in no doubt. "Your immediate presence in this army is urgently demanded," he wired Davis on October 5.[19]

Davis made up his mind instantly and left Richmond by train early the next morning. He went quietly, taking only one or two friends with him, among them Pemberton, who had been in Richmond the past few weeks. Incredibly, turning a deaf ear to all the calumny heaped on the general, Davis hoped to find a place for Pemberton with Bragg, perhaps to replace Hill or Hindman in their command, though Bragg had already relieved the latter and replaced him with Breckinridge. Hill, whom Bragg found "despondent, dull, slow" and prone to "constant croaking," he would have been happy to replace. But Pemberton? Nothing better revealed the knee-jerk reflex that criticism of one of his friends produced in Davis than this obstinacy—this insistence on overriding all opposition and continuing to sustain Pemberton. Ironically, he was going to try to do it by forcing Pemberton into an army already plagued with other friends whom Davis insisted on sustaining in the face of opposition and failure. It was a habit going back years and now beyond reform.

Often it was said of Jefferson Davis that he understood and judged his enemies much better than he did his friends. Now he went about proving it.[20]

Davis and Pemberton reached Atlanta on October 8, and there Polk met them, intent on having the first access to Davis's ear, which his old friend readily granted. Immediately the bishop-turned-general gave his side of events at Chickamauga, putting "the brand of falsehood" on Bragg's charges of disobedience. Davis agreed with him, then pleaded with him to smooth over his differences and return to his corps, offering to have the charges against him dismissed. But Polk refused. He wanted the court-martial, for it would air publicly the material that he and the other malcontents had gathered to discredit Bragg. Frustrated, the best Davis could do was to persuade Polk to be reassigned elsewhere, as he refused ever to serve under Bragg again.[21]

The next morning Davis boarded a train for Marietta, where Bragg then made his headquarters. The night before he had asked Breckinridge and Longstreet to come down and join him for the ride, that they might "speak more freely than here" in Atlanta. During the ride he undoubtedly heard much the same thing from them that he heard from Polk, though Longstreet was by far the more vitriolic. Indeed, Chesnut, now with Davis, found Breckinridge remarkably open, with "nothing narrow, nothing self-seeking" about him, a refreshing change from the rest of those turbulent generals. Davis would not forget Breckinridge's openness.[22]

When Davis reached Marietta later that day, he first wired to Varina, now back in Richmond, of his safe arrival. Then he closeted himself for some time with Bragg, and it became immediately apparent that Davis had no intention of relieving the general or of even considering such a change. Indeed, before leaving Richmond Davis intimated to Seddon that he would not consider replacing Bragg, and the reason was obvious, as he told Polk in Atlanta. The only alternatives were Joseph Johnston, Beauregard, and perhaps Longstreet. Otherwise some junior officer would have to be made a full general and that would bring a fresh storm of protest from the other generals' partisans. Consequently when Bragg offered to resign during their October 9 meeting, Davis refused him.[23]

But then the president asked to call in the corps commanders, ostensibly to discuss what should be done to recover Chattanooga and bag Rosecrans and his army. Apparently neither Davis nor Bragg made any announcement of the outcome of their private meeting, and the generals believed that the subject of Bragg's tenure was still an open question. Consequently, when the president asked for comments after a discussion of strategy, Longstreet spoke out boldly in calling for a change of commanders, and Buckner and Hill followed his lead. If Davis was surprised, he should not have been. Bragg had quite probably gotten in the first shots during their prior interview. Then Hill prejudiced their case by letting his irascible temper get the better of him and in some manner giving offense to Davis. Though they calmed and were on good terms again by the end of the meeting, the president undoubtedly felt betrayed to a degree. The previous summer he had stood by Hill, or so he thought, in sending him to a corps command with Bragg in spite of rumors that Hill had criticized him. But Hill's intemperance now, added to Bragg's antipathy, lessened him in Davis's eyes.[24]

Clearly Davis found the meeting getting out of hand, not to mention the embarrassment to Bragg, who heard all this, and the aggravation to Davis at hearing his friend thus criticized to his face. Somehow the president terminated the conference, though inconclusively, and with the dissident generals still feeling that their views might have some effect. Almost immediately afterward rumors began to spread through the camps that Davis intended to stand by Bragg. The next day the subordinates loyal to Bragg had their say when Davis asked their views. Undoubtedly Davis needed to hear some supportive testimony in order to justify in his own mind the decision he had already made. These generals tried to convince him that the army's troubles lay only with Polk and Buckner and Hill and that the disaffection did not extend beyond them. Davis was happy to accept that, even when a ride along the lines showed him otherwise. He got loud cheers from many units, but when he rode past Breckinridge's division, accompanied by Bragg, the men stood respectfully at attention "but not a man opened his mouth." Nevertheless, that evening Davis told Bragg emphatically that he intended to stand behind him.[25]

For another day Davis continued the pretense of not having made a decision. He spoke again with Longstreet and Buckner, the latter telling him that Bragg was "wanting in imagination," a man who in a crisis "will lean upon the advice of a drummer boy." Riding along the crest of Lookout Mountain, overlooking Chattanooga, Buckner again urged Davis to oust Bragg. Longstreet said the same thing in an interview that he recalled being "exciting, at times warm." He introduced the warmth by suggesting that Joseph Johnston should be placed in command. Davis was already sick of this kind of talk, for Chesnut had told him that "every honest man he saw out west thought well of Joe Johnston." Davis did not want to hear that. He became agitated, started to ramble about the politicians and armchair generals whose carping beset him, and clearly wanted to turn the discussion in another direction. Longstreet read his mood and they switched to matters of appointments, which Davis left unresolved when he took the general's hand and left him. Longstreet found his hand warm and his smile gracious, "but a bitter look lurking about its margin, and the ground-swell, admonished me that clouds were gathering about head-quarters."[26]

The next day Davis disspelled all doubt. He had heard enough of complaining and backbiting about his friend Bragg. Worse, when Bragg had consulted his subordinates about Pemberton joining the army, they unanimously advised against assigning him a position, certainly because of his unpopularity in the Confederacy and probably also because the most likely spot would be as a replacement for Bragg's opponent Hill. It was time to speak out for his friends. Davis could not help Pemberton without forcing him on Bragg, which he would not do, but in a brief speech on October 12 he praised the army commander and brushed aside all "shafts of malice" that had been directed against him. Two days later he issued a written address to the army, praising them for their services, exhorting them to renewed gallantry and sacrifice, and promising that after the war "the highest meed of praise" would go to those who quietly and unassumingly did their duty. In an obvious admonition to the discontented generals, he added that the "bitterest self-reproach" would haunt the memory of those who allowed "selfish aspirations to prevail over a desire for the public good. . . . He who sows the seeds of discontent and distrust prepares for the harvest of slaughter and defeat."[27]

"Mr. Davis got more than he came for," said one of Longstreet's staff officers, and indeed he did. Davis found himself forced to take sides, and in the end he came down squarely for Bragg. Indeed, even before he left the army on October 14, Davis began to sustain Bragg in his counteroffensive against his generals. Having heard Polk assail Hill earlier, then hearing more from Bragg and sensing his own ire aroused by the crusty general, Davis readily agreed to allow Bragg to relieve him of his corps command, and Bragg did it the day after the president departed. Hill later protested in writing of his unfair treatment, but Davis declined to admit that he had a point worthy of contention. When Davis transferred Polk to Mississippi in order to get him out from under Bragg, Hill pointed out that the bishop was being rewarded in spite of charges of disobedience, whereas he himself was being persecuted. Again Davis turned a deaf ear. Hill protested that he was relieved for objecting to Bragg as commander of the army, but Davis asserted that the real reason was his performance at Chickamauga. Only twenty-three years later would he admit to Hill that poor relations with Bragg lay behind the removal. Thus the president made himself a party to a shabby vendetta and did so in violation of his own oft-stated claim that a good general should not be relieved just because of a single poor performance on the battlefield. He had sustained Bragg through several defeats, and Lee as well, and stood by Polk after more than one failure as a subordinate. But when Bragg planted a flimsy accusation on Hill of failure at Chickamauga, even though the battle was a resounding victory, Davis countenanced his dismissal. Besides breaking his own rule, he played the hypocrite, supporting Polk for the same cause that got Hill relieved. Worst of all, Davis lied to Hill or knowingly dodged the truth. When the general charged that the reason for his relief was his lack of confidence in Bragg—which of course covered the whole range of his objections to his commander—Davis took refuge in hairsplitting, replying that "that reason was not given to me in the note through which Genl. Bragg recommended your removal." Of course it was not, else Bragg would have looked the fool in official correspondence that could be made public. But Davis knew the real reason, as he later confessed to Hill, though the admission did not erase his shame over his part in Bragg's self-destructive little melodrama.[28]

Even as Davis continued his trip, on to Alabama, Bragg continued to work at disrupting and destroying his opposition. The president stopped in Selma on October 18 and there made his customary speech about sacrifice, the bravery of the state's sons, the futility of looking to Europe for aid, and the inevitability of Confederate victory and independence if only everyone united in the effort. Though he seemed not to have much stomach for speaking after leaving Bragg's army, perhaps too disturbed by what he had seen, he continued to play a part in the war within the Army of Tennessee. Davis went on to Mississippi to meet with Johnston and Hardee, and while there he officially switched Hardee and Polk, thus sending the former back to Bragg and the latter to Johnston. Then the president went to Montgomery, where he met with Polk again personally, and now in open and very friendly discussions dealt with the situation in Mississippi. Indeed, having just come from headquarters intrigue with Bragg, Davis may have caught the fever a bit, for when Polk boastfully promised he could do great things if Johnston did not get in his way, Davis intimated that Johnston might not be in the way much longer, if at all. In fact, he rather thought that the hesitating Johnston would be happy to have someone relieve him of responsibility, and if not, then the president might give Polk his own independent department. Clearly Davis intended to take care of his friends.[29]

From Montgomery Davis returned to Atlanta, accompanied by Polk, and along the way he officially put an end to the charges brought against Polk by Bragg. This done, he turned from friend to foe, leaving Atlanta on October 29 for Charleston, and Beauregard. Even after the success at Battery Wagner, Davis remained critical of the general. "The President is still scrutinizing Beauregard," the clerk Jones observed on July 31, looking for points to challenge in his reports and complaining repeatedly of being left ill informed. "Omitting all notice of the defense (so far) of the batteries," said Jones, "the attention of the President seems fixed on what the general omitted to do; or what he might, could, or should have done." But now when he reached Charleston on November 2, Davis barely conferred with Beauregard at all. Instead he went through a lengthy celebratory procession, no doubt uncomfortable at having to share the leading carriage with the cold and formal general. They rode through streets filled with cheering crowds, past ornamental displays of captured Yankee trophies and Confederate military handiwork, and on to the city hall. It was the best reception Davis had seen yet on his tour, marred only by the realization that much of the cheering was also for Beauregard, the city's darling.

He made yet another speech, one much different from those out west, and one that Beauregard could not help but regard as critical of himself. Davis was heard to say that he came to see firsthand the situation, "and by personal observation acquire some of that knowledge which would enable him to understand more clearly the reports which would be submitted to him." Could anyone listening see that as other than an inference that Beauregard's report had been insufficient or unintelligible? He said not a word about the defense of Battery Wagner, and in referring to the recent unsuccessful bombardment of Sumter by Yankee batteries on other nearby islands, he highly praised the fort's commander but said nothing of Beauregard. Then, in saying that he believed the Yankees would never take Sumter or the city, he almost breached security by commenting that even if the enemy got past their conventional defenses, they had "other means" of defense that he would not refer to. He meant, of course, torpedoes and land mines, and the new semisubmerged torpedo boats like the *David* that had only recently attacked the blockading fleet off the harbor. It was an unwise reference but one calculated to invigorate his audience. And should Charleston ever fall, he said, then he hoped that the city's people would destroy it themselves first, leaving only "one mass of rubbish," as he wished Vicksburg's people had done. Was this rhetoric or did Davis now truly prefer utter destruction to defeat? "It is only a question whether you leave it a heap of ruins or a prey for Yankee spoils," he said, to which voices in the crowd cried out, "Ruins, ruins."

Then in closing, unwittingly or not, he struck at Beauregard yet again. He called for fraternal feeling, for "casting away all personal consideration. . . . He who would now seek to drag down him who is struggling, if not a traitor, is first cousin to it," he asserted. "He who would attempt to promote his own personal ends," said the president, "is not worthy of the Confederate liberty for which we are fighting."

Beauregard was incensed. "May God forgive him," he raged in a letter. "I fear I shall not have charity enough to pardon him." Invited to a dinner that evening in Davis's honor, Beauregard had declined, stating pointedly that he observed only "official" relations with the president. "I cannot participate in any act of politeness which might make him suppose otherwise." And that had been before Davis even arrived in Charleston to make his speech. Ironically, in Richmond there was speculation that the reason for Davis's making this long trip was "to cultivate a renewal of lost friendships," and that he lingered long in Charleston "in social intercourse with Gens. Beauregard and Wise, who had become estranged." That this was ever any part of Davis's intention is doubtful, and if it was, he certainly failed with Beauregard.[30]

He also failed with Brigadier General Henry A. Wise. Davis never enjoyed cordial relations with the former governor of Virginia. Wise displayed a turbulent, unstable nature, ever ready to explode in bitterly cynical sarcastic invective against those who met his disfavor. His unhappiness with Davis went back before the war, yet Davis made him a brigadier in June 1861, solely for political reasons. He carped at his superiors, constantly pressed for promotion, and showed no ability in the field. Worse, when his son died in February 1862 while under his command, Wise blamed the Richmond government, Secretary Benjamin, and even Davis for failing to support him and causing his son's death. By September 1863 he had become sufficiently a nuisance that the War Department sent him to Beauregard's "department of refuge," as the Creole called it.

There, near Mt. Pleasant, Davis came to visit with Wise and others on November 3, probably relishing the chance to get into the country. He would regret it. At first the president and the general spoke affably enough, and Davis teasingly traded horses with him when they took a ride around Wise's camps. Wise challenged him to a race, and that Jefferson Davis could never turn down. They put out at full speed, Wise taking an early lead on Davis's horse, but then toward the end of the run the president cut a corner very close, regained the lead, and won. Exhilarated as he always was by riding a good horse, Davis essayed to make one of his rare witticisms, saying that Wise's mount was the best and fastest of the two but had been "badly ridden." The general responded with a taunt that he would report Davis to his deacon for running a "prancing horse race." "Thus were we joking," Wise said later, "and he beginning the banter." But then Wise went too far, not appreciating the rigid sense of dignity in the man confronting him.

Newspapers reporting Davis's reception in several cities during his tour had occasionally mentioned his being kissed by young ladies in welcoming committees, not at all an uncommon occurrence for Davis or any other prominent dignitary. "He has a good, mild, pleasant face," a young lady in Savannah said after seeing him there on October 31, "and, altogether, looks like a President of our struggling country *should* look." Enthusiastic young ladies kissed such men. But Davis could be uncommonly prudish about such things. Varina had recently spoken with the president's doctor, A. Y. P. Garnett, who happened to be on his way to see his father-in-law, Henry A. Wise. She asked him to take her love to old Wise, and now the prickly general pointedly said to Davis that it seemed interesting that Varina should send her love to him, while her husband had been "smooching all the women in the South." Davis took it well at the moment, but soon after he got back to Richmond he changed his mind. Perhaps Varina, prone to jealousy, objected to those newspaper reports, and when Wise reminded Davis of the joke in a subsequent letter, a minor controversy ensued, leading Wise to conclude, referring to the Davises, that "they are a *little, low, vulgar* people. . . . Jeff has played *Turk* with his wife, undertaken *Mock* dignity with me, and he has caught it." Promising that "I shall poke my lips out at him—*bussing* fashion—in private and public wherever the fair opportunity is afforded," the none-too-stable Wise concluded that the whole affair with Davis "shows further that there is a screw loose in him."[31]

Davis must have felt an unaccustomed relief when he finally arrived in Richmond again on the evening of November 7. After the turmoil of Bragg's army, the snub by Beauregard, the boorishness of Wise, and the constant tension of the past month, the usually oppressive capital seemed calm by contrast, especially with Congress in adjournment and not due to start a new session for a month. As he unpacked to settle into his home and office again, he may well have wondered what he had accomplished. Indeed, many still wondered what he intended in the first place. Though he would say that he went to see things for himself, to gather information, it had largely proved to be something other than that. He gathered and heard much, but what he did not wish to countenance he rejected, and in fact his actions flew in the face of the overwhelming preponderance of the evidence. The outcry against Bragg, both before and during his trip, came unanimously from all his corps and many of his division commanders, yet Davis sustained him. Bragg and others clamored against Polk, yet Davis protected him. Despite all the outcry across the nation, the president had tried to sustain Pemberton by getting him a place with Bragg, perhaps even countenancing Hill's dismissal in hope of creating a vacancy for Pemberton should Bragg change his mind about him. At the same time he had done nothing for Beauregard, allowed the sacrifice of Hill with whom he was already on distant terms, and left Bragg clearly under the impression that he had carte blanche to deal with his other foes.

In Richmond, clerk Jones judged from the press accounts that "his austerity and inflexibility have been relaxed, and he has made popular speeches wherever he has gone." Even the press praised him for making the tour, perhaps in part because after the disasters at Gettysburg and Vicksburg he tried for awhile to subordinate his pride and make himself available to editors, even welcoming them "with smiles." Yet many felt uneasy that Davis retained Bragg, as Jones said, "in spite of the tremendous prejudice against him in and out of the army." A more caustic observer expressed the sentiments of the real doubters. "He retains his favorites long after they have blundered themselves out of the confidence of all their troops & would rather lose a battle or give up a state than admit that Jeff Davis could have made an injudicious promotion." The accusation was overstated, of course, and off the mark. But it touched the target, for the great western tour came down, in the end, to a blow for the president's friends and against his enemies.[32]

Davis looked "pretty well" when he resumed his duties on November 9, but his relief at returning to Richmond proved short-lived. His problems followed him even on his return home. In Savannah he learned that Grant had come to relieve the siege of Chattanooga, despite Longstreet's efforts to prevent it, and now Bragg charged Longstreet with disobedience of orders. Davis called it a "bitter disappointment." He wanted a full report, told Bragg to get an explanation from Longstreet, and sent Chesnut back to Tennessee to investigate in person. It was too late to help. Bragg was already at work completely reorganizing his army to break up the support his opponents enjoyed in their own commands, shifting their regiments around so that units loyal to the likes of Breckinridge, Longstreet, and others no longer reported to them. As for Buckner, with Davis's assent, Bragg reduced him from command of the Department of East Tennessee to being only a division commander. The army's high command almost went into shock. Worse yet, with only Longstreet now left as an outspoken opponent among his corps commanders—the returned Hardee was discreet, and the newly elevated Breckinridge had not spoken out publicly in some time—Bragg went after him irrationally by accepting Davis's suggestion of sending him and his command away from the army and off to attack the Yankees in Knoxville. The move did reflect a modicum of strategy discussed by Bragg and Davis—the hope that driving the Yankees out of Knoxville would prevent Grant, now in command at Chattanooga, from breaking out of the besieged city. But it also weakened the Army of Tennessee by one-third, leaving the remainder, entrenched along the heights of Missionary Ridge and Lookout Mountain, spread thin. Yet the generals felt confident that they could hold their seemingly impregnable perch against all comers.[33]

Davis still felt concerned by Bragg's lack of a serious strategy. He had the enemy almost bottled up in Chattanooga yet did not know what to do next. Lee in Virginia impressed on the president the need for the Army of Tennessee to do more than await Grant's next movement. The Yankees were bringing in reinforcements and supplies for an attempt to break out of Chattanooga. If Bragg did not act soon, Grant would. To aid him, Davis asked Joseph Johnston to send more reinforcements from Mississippi, but predictably Johnston "strangely misapprehended the orders given by me," said Davis. While trying to get more out of Johnston, Davis also secured the willingness to assist of General Samuel Jones, now commanding the Department of Southwest Virginia. Yet still Bragg had no plan. When Davis visited the army all their strategic discussions failed to produce a consensus, and now they paid for it in lost time and opportunities. Every day Grant grew stronger.[34]

And every day Bragg grew weaker, not in numbers but in spirit. His war on his own army cost him dearly now. Early in November Howell Cobb visited the army, and reported to Davis that he thought the internal strife was then limited to Bragg and Longstreet, and that Bragg had the confidence of the army as a whole. But Cobb was alone. Other reports soon reached Davis from Missionary Ridge that the army "loathes" its commander. "For heaven's sake put a man at the head of that army in whom it will have confidence," pleaded one correspondent. More disturbing was the report of a friend Davis asked to visit the army in mid-November. Desertion was increasing. The troops disliked Bragg, and especially his ill-advised reorganization separating them from their old commanders. In the office next to the president's in Richmond, Preston Johnston saw it all and commented that "the Bragg imbroglio seems to intensify."[35]

But it was too late to do anything about it. Davis had made the decision to leave Bragg in place and to allow him to deal with the disaffection in his army as he chose. That fateful—and terrible—decision taken, there was little the president could do other than try to get reinforcements to him. Besides, Davis could hardly forget about Lee, who himself faced an uncertain situation in northern Virginia. Lee and his opponent, General George G. Meade, had done little more than spar during the months after Gettysburg. Lee, in particular, had been too shattered after the losses in the battle, and spent months rebuilding his army and his command system. In late July the armies almost met again at Manassas Gap, and again near Bristoe Station in September and October, but they never came to serious blows. Now in November Meade crossed the Rappahannock and captured several hundred Rebels, then drove on toward the Rapidan, with Lee falling back before him. Obviously concerned, Davis turned his attention from Tennessee and left for a visit with Lee on November 21. He stayed for three days, inspecting the troops and conferring with Lee on what he intended to do in the face of nearly twice his numbers. They went to church together. More and more frequently, now that he had been baptized and confirmed, Davis turned to his religion for comfort.[36]

He would need it. Probably not until he returned to Richmond on the evening of November 24, or early the next day, did the president see the telegrams from Bragg. The news started good, with a report that Longstreet was supposed to be driving the Yankees into their defenses at Knoxville. That much of their plan—such as it was—seemed to be working. But then came a telegram sent late on November 25. The Confederates had been driven off of Lookout Mountain and most of Missionary Ridge "in considerable disorder," and the whole disorganized force was retreating into Georgia. At first the telegram came over the wires unintelligibly, but everyone soon knew its purport. In three days of fighting, Grant had steadily driven Bragg until, on the last day, in the face of a full frontal assault up the slopes of Missionary Ridge, a panic seized most of the army and the men simply fled. It was the most humiliating defeat yet suffered by Confederate arms. "The belief is general that Bragg will retreat," the clerk Jones wrote that day. Bragg had been "in a fog" for months, he thought. "If disaster ensues, the government will suffer the terrible consequences, for it assumed the responsibility of retaining him."[37]

Davis was silent immediately after receiving the news. There was little he could say, of course. He tried to find more reinforcements for Bragg, even as he struggled to learn more of what had happened. And he had to brace himself for the storm of angry protest sure to come. Indeed, just the day after the disaster rumors spread of a break in the cabinet, where a supposed majority had favored removing Bragg and now reminded Davis of the fact. Certainly the question of Bragg staying in place any longer was resolved by these latest events. On November 29 the general himself asked to be relieved, and Davis did not argue with him. Yet, unable ever to let go of enemies within, Bragg immediately commenced a last campaign against Breckinridge and others, charging the Kentuckian especially with drunkenness during the battles for Chattanooga. The charge was invented, showing more of Bragg's instability than maliciousness, and Davis seems not to have given it credence, for he soon brought Breckinridge to Richmond for conferences and then assigned him to command Lee's vital left flank in the Department of Southwest Virginia, relieving the ineffective Jones.[38]

For the moment Davis gave command of the Army of Tennessee to Hardee, but he knew he would have to find another permanent commander. Hardee made it clear that he would not accept more than temporary command. He knew his limitations, and he also knew the poisoned atmosphere that Bragg left as a legacy. Davis was disappointed in his response. He liked Hardee and probably would have risked promoting him to full general for the post, even if it meant slighting his seniors. But Hardee's refusal put him in a corner. At a cabinet meeting on December 2, the president surely discussed what should be done. Unfortunately, Seddon missed the meeting, staying home with a daughter who died a few days later, and Davis probably went to his home to confer with him. The alternatives available now were the same ones Davis had tried so often before to avoid. His first choice was Lee. Even though considerable skirmishing broke out along Mine Run as Meade crossed the Rapidan and tried to force Lee back onto Richmond, the campaign quickly sputtered out and the Yankees retreated. Davis felt desperate. With Congress convening on December 7, he had to do something decisive before it assailed him, as it inevitably would. The day before he asked Lee once more if he would go to the Army of Tennessee. The next day Lee again respectfully declined, showing his own perception of affairs in the Army of Tennessee by adding that he feared he would not get "cooperation" from its officers.[39]

The remaining alternatives pained Davis beyond description. It must be either Beauregard or Johnston, and he was not sure which evil was the lesser. Even as Davis offered the command to Lee, capital rumormongers speculated that Beauregard would have the command. Lee had gingerly suggested the same, but Davis could not face the prospect. He avoided the decision for a day or two, then summoned Lee to Richmond on December 8 and spent much of the next week closeted with him and Seddon, trying to change the general's mind yet again. The matter was heating up rapidly. Congress had reconvened, and the president's critics, led by Foote in the House, were already going for his throat. Before news of Bragg's relief became official, a delegation called on Davis to demand it, suggesting as well that Johnston be appointed in his place. Davis told them of Bragg's removal. On December 9, as Lee arrived for conferences, Foote started proceedings to launch an investigation into the loss of Chattanooga. In his message to the new session, Davis placed most of the blame on "misconduct by the troops" and quickly turned to foreign affairs and other cabinet departments. Foote violently arraigned Davis for being himself the cause by his obstinate retention of Bragg. Not content with this, Foote went on to the matter of another friend of Davis's, Pemberton, and attacked the President for the loss of Vicksburg. Then he charged him with Longstreet's expedition to Knoxville. "The President's visits to the army have never brought out any good," said Foote, going on to accuse Davis of "gross misconduct in retaining his favourites in office, and with partialities and prejudices, which, if persisted in longer, will prove fatal to our cause." Not satisfied to omit a blow at any of the president's friends, Foote went on to assail Northrop, a man who had been "a curse to the country." A few days later, while Davis was still trying to persuade Lee to go to the army in Georgia, Foote introduced more resolutions calling for investigations both of Vicksburg and Chattanooga, his clear aim being to embarrass and discredit Davis.[40]

Though Davis always maintained that he felt impervious to external pressure, undoubtedly he sensed the fire growing in Congress even as he felt Lee's resistance gradually overcoming him. On December 14 Foote spoke yet again, now proposing a resolution asking Davis to depose any commander who did not possess the confidence of the army and the people. Such a measure would virtually have removed any power of decision from Davis, placing commanders at the whim of public opinion, to which not even Lee was immune. Foote brought out the measure to show that Davis alone was to blame for Bragg. But Bragg had been gone more than two weeks. Why was there no successor? "Why is Johnston not now appointed?" he asked. "Why is not Beauregard?" "The country is tired of the delay," he fumed, "and every moment becomes more and more perilous."[41]

Loath as he was ever to agree with Foote, Davis had to do so in at least the last respect. He could not wait. That Lee would not take the command was clear by December 14. Moreover, Lee, too, now seemed to favor Johnston, having seen Davis put Beauregard entirely out of the equation. There was no alternative. Even Polk wrote to advise Johnston's appointment. In a final cabinet meeting on December 14 or 15 the whole matter was thrashed out again and at length, as usual. Some still preferred Hardee, but he had irrevocably removed himself from consideration. Seddon and one or two others spoke for Johnston, but Benjamin, who would never lose his own prejudice against the general, countered, probably with Beauregard. The longer the meeting went, and the more evident it became that no acceptable candidate could get a majority, they all—no doubt excluding Benjamin—slowly came to Johnston as the only available choice. Davis finally agreed himself, needing to have his cabinet reach the conclusion first in order to relieve his own mind should the decision prove to be as unfortunate as he feared. Seddon watched as, "with doubt and misgiving to the end," the president gave the command to his enemy Johnston, "not as due exaltation on this score, but as the best on the whole to be obtained." On December 16 Davis notified Johnston of his assignment. Thus did he give command of the Confederacy's second-most-important army to a man whom he detested, and for no reason other than an inability to find another candidate less odious or willing to take the job. Nor could Davis take any comfort from a report by Preston Johnston ten days later, before the new commander reached the army in Dalton, Georgia. Perhaps playing to the president's prejudices, young Johnston claimed that the army expected little from the new man and actually would have preferred Hardee or even Bragg. Davis would have, too, for only days after appointing Johnston, he received a copy of an article from an Alabama newspaper, in which the writer severely castigated Davis for failing to appoint Johnston. Now that he had done so, the matter was moot. Still, the president could not help taking time to annotate the clipping with crosses in the margins "to mark falsehoods." He sent it on to Seddon on Christmas Day. Jones received it in the War Department and wondered why Davis bothered to send or even note it, since Johnston had been appointed and the matter was ended. But for Jefferson Davis it would never end.[42]

There was cold cheer for Christmas in Richmond that winter. Despite the occasional welcome expression of confidence in his administration, ill tidings struck Davis from every front. Preoccupied as he was by military affairs, he could not entirely ignore his civil cares as president. Clerks in the capital complained of starvation and freezing, and the clerk Jones warned Davis that he feared a repeat of the bread riots if food shortages could not be assuaged by opening government warehouses to the people. " 'The Ham the Lamb the Jelly & the Jam' are now of the past," a friend told the president. "It is now 'Small Hominy sometimes called Grits.' " Women complained that they were "out of employment. . . , out of bread, and out of spirits," and could not get jobs because they were not young and pretty. Fathers with four or more sons in the army wrote pleading for the president not to take more of their "seed corn" from them. As men tried to print enough treasury notes to buy things, counterfeiters proliferated, and Davis could not help himself when it came to pardoning them or commuting their death sentences. Nor could he bring himself to approve the executions of army deserters when they were men who simply went home to get in a crop for their suffering families. At one stroke he pardoned more than thirty from the small army in Mississippi. Amid all the hardship and suffering, the unrelenting course of retreat and defeat, the tender, hidden side of Jefferson Davis's nature had to find some small victory in little acts of mercy.[43]

Mercy is what the president needed for himself now. It had been an abysmal, cursed year. Tennessee was entirely gone, and with it the Kentucky dream. Louisiana east of the Mississippi remained lost, and with Vicksburg went much of Mississippi. Lee's brilliant success at Chancellorsville had not kept the enemy out of Virginia after all, and the disaster at Gettysburg postponed yet again, and perhaps permanently, the hopes for Maryland. Foreign relations continued to be almost nonexistent, and Britain was starting to show tacit signs of hostility. The economy was in dreadful shape, and only loans kept it going. The people were tiring, losing their heart. Even the women, to whom Davis turned time and time again for their spirit, were weakening in their resolve.

Worst of all, perhaps, though he could neither see nor admit it, Davis's performance as chief executive had been woefully inadequate. Through much of 1862 he rose to the occasion, thinking and acting with prudence, frequent vigor, and even occasional open-mindedness. But now, in the year just past, he could not sustain his rise above himself. The whole mess in the West, the loss of Murfreesboro, the fall of Vicksburg, and then the disaster of Missionary Ridge came down in the end to a few insurmountable frailties. His antipathy to Beauregard and Johnston ruled the war that year, assisted by his accompanying inability to make objective judgments about his friends—his unyieldingly blind devotion to Bragg and Pemberton. Circumstances, many beyond his control, and logic, from which he could only occasionally waver, had given him a disappointing set of men from which to choose his commanders. The failings were not all his. But as president, he had the power to try to overcome them, which he did not, or to try to work around the system forcing him to choose from among them, which he would contemplate only reluctantly. Only Lee and the detested Beauregard had saved him from defeat on all fronts. And once again he had retreated into personal feuds and controversy, lecturing Johnston repeatedly and at length and building a private file on the general, while at the same time using his influence to try to protect Pemberton, Polk, and Bragg. His involvement in the D. H. Hill affair would have brought down his own disparaging condemnation had it been committed by someone else, even against a foe.

He had ceased to be presidential for the most part, and reverted to being Jefferson Davis. Even if he had been more active and decisive, forcing Johnston to go earlier to Mississippi, forcing him to take command at Vicksburg, the city might have fallen. Even if he had forced Johnston to supersede Bragg in the fall, the positions around Chattanooga would have been just as indefensible. Even if he had placed Johnston in one of those commands and Beauregard in the other—or Lee in either—the numerical superiority of the enemy could still have made the outcome the same. Davis's failure was that he prejudiced his chances of success by consistently adhering to a man whose record gave cause to expect little but defeat. At the same time, out of personal antipathy and his old stubborn refusal to be moved by popular opinion, he would not take the chance with men who had victories to their credit. Granted that with Cooper too old, Sidney Johnston dead, and Lee needed in Virginia, his remaining full generals were flawed at best, Davis consistently tied his fortunes to the one who was demonstrably the worst of the lot. And when the president more than once conceived the commendable and potentially beneficial notion of sending Lee to the West, he backed away. Davis did not hesitate to compel Johnston to accept the overall western command against his wishes; that was simply forcing his own will on a man he did not like. But he could not make himself order Lee to the Army of Tennessee when the latter begged off. Again and again the inconsistencies in his official conduct came down to his very consistent personal demeanor toward friend and foe.

The war was lost now. Though Davis could neither see nor admit so if he did see it, increasing numbers of others in the South felt it. Perhaps there was never a real chance of success if Lincoln pressed his advantages relentlessly. The loss of the Mississippi split the Confederacy in two, and the Yankees who defeated Bragg were poised to drive toward Atlanta, splitting the remainder in half. The always chimerical notion of European recognition and aid was more remote than ever, and Davis himself advised his people to forget it. Even conscription could not fully replenish their losses, and his armies would never again be as large as they had been in 1862, growing ever smaller while the enemy's only increased. He had found one great general, who would not leave Virginia where at best he sustained a status quo while the war was being lost in great chunks out West, and Davis would not order him to go there. Meanwhile, Yankee victories in Mississippi and Tennessee allowed Lincoln to find Grant, Sherman, George Thomas, and Philip Sheridan. None were Lee's equal on the battlefield; all were the better of Davis's other alternatives.

Davis had to answer for much of it, and as the awful year came to an end, his foes prepared to lay everything at his feet. They would gloatingly parade his faults before the public, even while they twisted and distorted his strengths to deny him the credit he deserved for his few accomplishments. Now, with 1864 looming ahead, even as Jefferson Davis was losing his war for Confederate independence, he entered the opening battles of another war destined to last the rest of his life, and beyond to posterity, the battle for vindication of his reputation and his place in history.

One of the first shots was a real one. Shortly before Christmas, during an evening ride, Davis heard a bullet whistle past his head. Davis himself rode instinctively toward the origin of the gun's report, and soon a mentally ill man was found whom Davis believed to be the would-be assassin. But since robberies and murders had become commonplace in Richmond, as thousands of indigent refugees from the war flooded its streets, the bullet may not have been intended for Davis, or if so the guilty man may not have known who he was shooting at. Then again, perhaps he did. It mattered little to Davis at the moment. He had the man sent to Lee to become a soldier where he could shoot at the enemy in blue. Before long a dozen disabled soldiers would form an informal guard at the Executive Mansion. But behind him the unknown rifleman left a host of others prepared less openly, but more accurately, to open fire on their beleaguered president.[44]

Not Mine, Oh, Lord, But Thine

Lights and music gave the Executive Mansion a gay aspect on New Year's Day. The president and first lady held a reception attended by most of Richmond's luminaries. Ives and Browne appeared in full military regalia, acting as ushers, while Chesnut stayed at Varina's side through most of the evening. Her father had died nine months before, yet still she wore black, though her mood was vivacious as she and her husband shook hands with every guest who passed through. Hundreds came into the house, from senators to soldiers. Davis knew that he needed to reach out to his people, but extending his hand to a man in front of him was about as far as he could go. Perhaps some came in simply to get out of the bitter weather, the coldest of the winter, but all clasped his hand, so that Davis's arm remained stiff for three days and Varina could not bear the slightest touch to her hand. Davis's foes in Richmond charged that he held the public reception solely in hopes of recovering some popularity, but if so he paid for it, and it did not work. The very next day, after a painfully freezing night, rumors swept the capital that a dictator was needed to save the country, and some believed that Davis had only lost what popularity he already had.[1]

That bitter cold night proved a fitting introduction to the cold and bitter days ahead. Lean and hollow-cheeked, Jefferson Davis went forth to meet his foes. Ironically, in the days ahead some proved to be his friends. Under the pressure of overwork and almost constant calumny in the press, most of his cabinet ministers felt their nerves fray by the dawn of 1864, and some began to war among themselves. Mallory and Benjamin entertained a hearty dislike for one another, and most of the ministers to some degree resented the secretary of state for his self-important manner, and for his obvious position as Davis's favorite. Then Reagan and Memminger commenced a feud, as the Post Office Department ran out of paper for printing stamps and Treasury refused to supply funds for the purchase of more from abroad. Davis himself had to intercede to terminate the "controversy between the Depts," as he called it. Reagan also got into a squabble with Seddon in January, and the president almost had to intercede yet again. Meanwhile Memminger put more business on the president's desk when he refused to yield to officers arresting employees charged with crimes, and then again, on January 2, got into a disagreement with Seddon over manpower. Memminger took his complaint to Davis, who took it back to Seddon, then took Seddon's reply back to Memminger, then took Memminger's counterresponse to the War Office and left it there with recommendations to find ways to "avoid these controversies." Meanwhile, rumors circulated that Seddon intended to resign, and some newspapers charged that Memminger and the rest were personally profiting by engaging in an illegal cotton trade with the Yankees. Before the summer Memminger would resign in disgust.[2]

While he struggled to keep his cabinet working together, the president faced even tougher challenges from his governors. Those west of the Mississippi, now isolated from Richmond, he left to Kirby Smith. Of the rest, the sometimes troublesome Letcher left office on January 1, replaced by Davis's friend and supporter General William Smith. The only real trouble spots were North Carolina and Georgia. Davis tried to court good relations with Governor Zebulon Vance of North Carolina, but with only mixed results. Vance quarreled with him over appointments and commissions, both within and outside the state, but Davis mainly had his way. Their real fight came over using the power of suspension of habeas corpus, which Davis did sparingly and under authority from Congress. Still, when that Congress in early 1864 prepared a new authorizing act, Vance exploded. A typical correspondence of escalating heat and innuendo ensued between Vance and Davis, one largely meaningless since Davis never suspended the writ in the governor's domain. Though strained, their relations did not impede their cooperation.[3]

Not so with Brown of Georgia. The governor opposed Davis over conscription, and their ensuing correspondence showed two men of remarkably like tendencies, as each struggled for the last word. When Davis published it, an enraged Brown attacked him anew on a host of issues, and later fought with him over the proper defense of Georgia in the spring campaign. Brown was a humorless controversialist, savoring argument for its own sake and enjoying goading the president into what he called an "exhibition of temper." Even with Howell Cobb and William

Browne trying to mediate, their relations steadily worsened. Reagan later recalled that "Governor Brown gave him more trouble than the Governor of any other State."[4]

But of course it was Congress that really went for Davis, at least a very vocal minority who took every opportunity to use any setback in the field to thrash Davis and his policies. At least his bitter foe Toombs no longer sat in the body, though that did not keep him from loudly denouncing and vilifying the president. As for those who gathered in Richmond for the new session commencing in December, Davis privately agreed with friends who averred that, on the whole, the group of senators and representatives lacked intelligence. They could not see the necessity imposed on him to take strenuous measures to defend the Confederacy. He saw habeas corpus, conscription, and other enactments allowing the impressment of farmers' produce and livestock, taxation, and more as weapons in the overall war. His opponents saw them as weapons to use against Davis. Ironically, Jefferson Davis, the great prewar champion of sectional and local rights, now had to act as perhaps the leading nationalist in the Confederacy. He saw what others like Brown, blinded by their states' rights dogma, or Foote, blinkered by hatred of Davis, could not see: The only way to preserve those states' rights in the long run was to surrender many of them now to achieve victory.[5]

After the opening salvos of December, mostly from Foote, Davis could expect more of the same in the New Year. Still, on January 2, despite the cold and the soreness in his arm, he hosted a delegation from the House at eight in the evening, even though it was a Saturday, a day and time when he ordinarily did not conduct business. Quite probably they came to discuss a joint resolution on the war to be introduced two days later, calling for "unselfish and patriotic cooperation" from everyone in order to achieve independence. No one would argue with that. But some in that delegation must also have spoken with Davis about more disturbing affairs in the Capitol. During the first few weeks of the session just past, three especially troubling matters arose in debate, all of them showing a premeditated purpose to strike at Davis and embarrass if not discredit him. Not surprisingly, the leading speaker in the House on most of them was Henry S. Foote.[6]

On December 15, even as Johnston was about to be ordered to the Army of Tennessee, the whole matter of command in the West came onto the floor. Correspondence dealing with the nature of Johnston's command over Bragg and Pemberton had been requested, and Davis provided extracts showing consistently that he expected Johnston to assume actual field command when necessary, and that Johnston himself had repeatedly sustained Bragg. The president's friends hoped that this might quiet his opponents, but it could not stop Foote. He leapt on the fact that they had been given only "garbled extracts," and accused Davis of being "ungenerous and unmanly" by not producing the entire correspondence. In fact, Johnston himself was working behind the scenes, hoping that publication of all of his letters to and from Davis would show where lay the responsibility for the loss of Vicksburg. He met and corresponded frequently with Wigfall in the Senate and Foote in the House, providing them with documents. Finally on January 29 Davis sent the House all of his correspondence for May, June, and July 1863, to or from Johnston, and this time not in extract. He left out Johnston's point-by-point reply to his long scolding letter of July 15, though logically it should have been included. By omitting it Davis seemed to have the last, definitive word, and as justification for leaving it out he specifically noted the House's instructions definitely fixing the inclusive dates for the correspondence it wanted to see. Johnston's reply was dated August 8, 1863, and therefore outside the boundaries. But the general advised his friends in Congress of his letter, along with other material going as far back as November 1862, and in the forthcoming June the House required all of this, which amounted to dozens more documents. Fortunately, Congress adjourned the session on February 18, so little time remained to thrash the issue, but it continued long after adjournment as both sides used the press to publish the correspondence, with Johnston fearing that Davis was getting the better of him in print.[7]

More embarrassing for Davis was the matter of former Quartermaster General Colonel Abraham C. Myers. Davis gave him the post on April 15, 1861, with the rank of lieutenant colonel. Subsequently Myers gained promotion to a full colonelcy and performed competently. Indeed, he became rather popular in Richmond, unlike his counterpart Commissary General Northrop, but almost certainly he became a victim of the warfare among the capital's wives. Mrs. Myers did not care for Varina, and there ensued what Mary Chesnut called a "ladies war" between them, culminated by Mrs. Myers's referring to the swarthy Varina as "an old squaw." The remark became commonplace in every parlor in the city, to the Davises' considerable chagrin. How much this influenced the president toward Myers is uncertain, though his relations with men like Johnston and Wigfall often seemed to parallel Varina's with their wives. The remark was made in the spring of 1862, yet Davis seems to have shown no disposition against Colonel Myers for nearly a year. In March 1863, however, Congress authorized a brigadier's pay and rank for Myers's office, expecting that Davis would so appoint him. But the president surprised them all by relieving Myers and replacing him with Brigadier General A. R. Lawton. Explaining that Myers had never been more than a "temporary" appointee, Davis argued that Congress's action gave him no choice but to appoint someone of commensurate rank. Most, however, saw in his act either a petulant response to Congress's pressure to promote Myers, or else the seizure of a technicality to oust a man whom he disliked personally but could not charge with sufficient shortcomings to dismiss otherwise.

Davis and Congress fought over the issue at the time, but now this winter it arose anew as the Senate demanded all the documents in the case and Wigfall arose to charge that since the Senate never confirmed Lawton's appointment, Myers was still legally quartermaster general. Worse, Davis insulted the Senate by not responding directly but by having Seddon reply instead. Wigfall accused Davis of cheating that body of its constitutionally mandated confirmation powers, and later introduced a resolution declaring Lawton not authorized to perform the duties of his office. But even when seventy-six members of the House signed a letter asking Davis to sustain Myers, Davis refused to move, as always refusing to consider anything when a group of people sought to pressure him. Lawton would remain in place and eventually got his confirmation, while a move by Wigfall to vote a censure of Davis never came to pass.[8]

Davis could still win battles like these, but each one cost him, as did a memorandum from the officers of the Army of Tennessee sent to suggest measures for improving its efficiency. In the main it called for keeping all troops then in service in the army for the duration of the war, regardless of expiration of enlistments. Moreover, it called for drafting all males between ages fifteen and sixty for varying degrees of military service, and for ending most exemptions and furloughs, while placing blacks in service as noncombatants. Thirteen generals, including Hardee and Breckinridge, signed it, along with scores of colonels and lesser officers. Foote immediately attacked the proposal, while paying great respect to the officers proposing it, and he used it as an excuse to get to his favorite theme, Davis's usurpation of power. If Congress acted on this memorandum, it would give the President power to draft virtually every man in the nation, giving him more power "than any monarch now living." Foote asserted that experience had shown that Davis would not use the power wisely. Worse, he knew men in this chamber and in the Senate who actually advocated making Davis a virtual dictator for the duration of the war. Foote proclaimed that they must all oppose any such measures that would add to Davis's "present dangerous capacity for mischief." "The President will have to show himself a little more free from his strange and unreasonable partialities and prejudices," said Foote, "before he could yield him any increase of his military capacity." Should they have to resort to a dictator, then they ought not to look at Davis but Lee.[9]

Then there were the legislative assaults on Davis's powers. In December the Senate entertained a resolution limiting cabinet appointments to the term of the sitting Congress, and forcing Davis to make his appointees undergo confirmation with every new Congress. "This is a direct attack on Mr. Davis," observed Robert Kean in the Bureau of War, but fortunately it did not pass. In late January the Senate rebuked Davis for lecturing it over the matter of nominations for promotions, implicitly saying that his own powers in the matter were not absolute. Perhaps most ominous of all, this being the last session of the First Congress, Davis's opponents strove to postpone action on a number of administration measures until the first sitting of the Second Congress, to be elected later in the year. Almost everyone took it for granted that the makeup of the new Congress would be even more hostile to Davis.[10]

The whole business became distressingly public. "It looks like war between the Executive and the Senate," clerk Jones wrote in his diary on January 19, and a week later he saw the breach widening. "As the session advances the President loses friends and now hardly has any," wrote Robert Kean of the Bureau of War late in December 1863. He overstated the case, for Davis consistently had enough of a majority in both houses to carry most of his program. But he did lose friends. Wigfall was already long gone, though his violent opposition only became embarrassingly public during this session. Then Davis unwisely went off on a tirade about problems with the state of Virginia during a private meeting with Senator R. M. T. Hunter of the Old Dominion, sending him away miffed and bitter. Already shifting gradually to the opposition, Hunter moved more rapidly after Davis's foolish lack of common sense in abusing the man's state to his face.[11]

It was no wonder that Davis seemed melancholy and distant to many who met him that winter. He often rode alone now in the evenings, "to indulge his thoughts in solitude in the suburbs of the city," thought Jones, who occasionally saw him. Colonel Browne felt sufficient concern for Davis that he detailed a guard to follow him. Besides the presumed assassination attempt, there had been a recent try at arson at the Executive Mansion, and several close to the president feared for his safety. Still Davis tried to extend himself to the public, if only haltingly, by opening his house to visitors every Tuesday evening. Receiving every guest courteously with an extended hand and saying "I am glad to meet you here to-night," still Davis was distant, absentminded. One evening he saw the clerk Jones, whom he had known for three years in the War Department, and said "*we* have met before" as if the realization were startling. A few weeks earlier during another evening, Davis and Mary Chesnut walked back and forth in the huge dining room at the Executive Mansion, engrossed in what she called the "saddest" of conversations. She saw easily how the multiplying cares and difficulties besetting the Confederacy bore him down, believing that he appreciated them all better than any other, as indeed he did. She found his voice perfectly modulated, but "I think there is a melancholy cadence in it which he is unconscious of as he talks of things as they are now."[12]

Varina and the children were his chief, perhaps his only, solace, besides his long solitary rides. Mallory looked on smilingly as he saw that the president's little ones "regarded him as their pleasantest playmate" and that all children regarded him as a favorite. Margaret was nine in February, and Jefferson Jr. turned seven the month before. Little Joseph would be five in April, and the infant William was just past his second birthday. The president doted on them, sometimes singing old Indian songs, to their delight. "Cora wankee shangmonee, sheereerra notty hiee, notty hiee," he murmured to them in his sweet baritone. The meaning counted for little—the act meant much. And Varina was pregnant again, expecting that summer, and she seemed to blossom almost in reverse ratio to her husband's lowering moods. "She is so clever, so brilliant indeed, so warmhearted, and considerate toward all who are around her," wrote Mrs. Chesnut. "After becoming accustomed to the spice and spirit of her conversation, away from her things seem flat and tame."[13]

Like most others in the Confederacy now, the Davises felt the pinch of wartime shortages. In January the president sold two slaves to raise $1,612, and two months later parted with three of his horses to fetch another $7,330. They had to buy their own provisions just like any other citizens, and thus Davis forced himself to part with all but an essential mount or two. Varina sent her carriage and team to be sold as well, fetching $12,000, though sympathetic citizens repurchased and returned it to her. Meals at the Executive Mansion took on an austere character, with breakfast often little more than hot ersatz coffee, some corn cakes or pones, bread, and a small dish of fat bacon fried crisp. Davis himself might be late to the table, often not retiring until nearly sunrise, and his indifference to food increased as the war went on. Even little luxuries like a gift of real butter rarely tempted him, and often he simply forgot to eat entirely. As spring approached, Varina took to bringing him a lunch basket every afternoon to make certain that he ate while she waited. Friends did what they could to brighten the home life of the first family, sending sherry or theater tickets. Some gifts that did not nourish the body stirred his spirit. In January General William Preston gave Davis the pistol worn by Sidney Johnston at Shiloh. And there were days when the president still looked and felt presidential. That spring Virginia Clay chanced to see him walking with the handsome Kentucky generals Breckinridge and Buckner. "Can a cause fail with such men at the head?" she asked herself.[14]

It would not fail for want of attention from Davis, certainly. While his health steadily declined that winter and spring, while his enemies in Congress and in the statehouses carped away at him, he kept doggedly on with the task that always occupied his chief time and attention—the armies and the war. Perhaps because of his health, or else from slowly realized experience, he tried to cut back a little on all the details he handled. To eliminate many of the constant petitions to commission generals, he suggested to Seddon that they make public the manner in which they selected such officers. Moreover, he started sending recommendations for such appointments to Seddon, to discuss later in conference. After more than a year of working together, Davis continued to feel comfortable with the Virginian, who rarely if ever challenged his president. The Chief also engaged Preston Johnston in making précis of reports and recommendations, to reduce the load of all the documents Davis had to read and study.[15]

Some issues he already knew quite well, for they would not go away. The subject of enlisting Negroes persisted. While some suggested emancipating the South's slaves and sending them to Liberia to get rid of them, others continued to press for raising black troops. In January Davis got word that he would soon receive a proposal from the Army of Tennessee calling for the conscription of blacks as soldiers, with the promise of freedom for those who served. Its author was Major General Patrick R. Cleburne. When Davis learned of the petition, signed by a number of the ranking officers in that army, he immediately saw its explosive potential and tried to bury the document in the War Department files and keep news of it out of the press. To hint at abolition would be to undermine the very "right" for which they had seceded and gone to war, regardless of the compelling argument in favor of tapping this source of manpower. The antipathy for free blacks, especially armed to fight with or against white men, was too great. If Davis needed confirmation of this, he got it in April when the cavalryman Nathan Forrest attacked and captured Fort Pillow, Tennessee. In the process, some of his men spontaneously shot down black Union soldiers, many of whom had thrown down their arms and surrendered. There would be a few other such massacres later this year, making it all the more evident that having blacks don the gray was one experiment that Confederates were not yet ready to try.[16]

Yet in February Davis tried another experiment that was nearly as risky and destined to bring down a virtual avalanche of indignation all across the Confederacy. He called Braxton Bragg to Richmond. Even Bragg's implacable foe Polk had confessed that he thought the general would make a good inspector general or do good service in some other staff capacity in the capital. But Davis had something even higher in mind for him. He appears to have timed his announcement carefully. On February 18 Congress adjourned, with the next session not due until May 2. At the same time the president discontinued his Tuesday evening receptions, suggesting, as some suspected, that they were aimed at members of Congress. Then on February 23, with Congress safely out of the way for nearly three months, he ordered that Bragg take office as commanding general "charged with the conduct of military operations in the armies of the Confederacy."[17]

The outrage erupted immediately. The capital press crucified Davis. "When a man fails in an inferior position," the *Whig* editorialized with dripping sarcasm, "it is natural and charitable to conclude that the failure is due to the inadequacy of the task to his capabilities, and wise to give him a larger sphere for the proper exertion of his abilities." Daniel's *Examiner* called the news "a bucket of water on a newly kindled grate." Having failed repeatedly in the command of a single army, was Bragg now to command all of them? Kean found that "quite a buzz" persisted in Richmond, as people on all sides assailed "an illustration of that strong common sense which forms the basis of the President's character." Privately, some wondered if Bragg did not inwardly gloat in thus once more beating popular opinion. Perceptively, Jones wondered if Davis's being "naturally a little oppugnant" to public opinion had anything to do with Bragg's appointment.[18]

In fact, there was some logic to the assignment. What first brought Bragg to Davis's favorable notice back in 1861 was his organizational effort at Pensacola, and then after Beauregard left his army after Shiloh, Bragg ably reorganized and trained the command. Completely unsuited by temperament, health, and ability to be a field commander, Bragg still possessed the attributes of an excellent staff officer. He could take much of the paperwork load from Davis's desk. He could be useful in the work of coordinating logistical support for the armies and in finding and raising the ever-needed reinforcements. Of course, Davis would not allow him unilaterally to plan strategy or issue important strategic instructions to Lee, Johnston, or Kirby Smith. Bragg would join with the president and the cabinet to discuss such especially important matters, and his counsel would be valuable but not decisive.

Thus, in intent and practice, Davis did not envision a role for Bragg any more significant than that of Seddon or Cooper. Rather, he would relieve each of some duties. The uproar over fear of what Bragg would do as commanding general, then, was largely unjustified. But the man in the street and the soldier in the ranks could not know that, and whatever the intellectual logic of putting Bragg in Richmond might be, its emotional impact on the Confederacy was profound and revealed just how completely inadequate was Jefferson Davis's ability to weigh the merits of his own loyalty to friends versus Confederate morale. At times the Chief's utter unawareness of the consequences of such acts—or his refusal to countenance those repercussions—could be positively mystifying. His waiting for Congress to adjourn shows that he knew there would be massive indignation that could only do harm to himself and, thereby, his war effort. Going ahead with the appointment in spite of it all shows just how far short he fell of requirements for a national leader.

The furor over Bragg would subside, but the appointment haunted Davis for the rest of the war, and as always the criticism left him ill tempered, especially given his declining health. His mood did not improve when, on March 1, sitting in his office, he heard the distinct sound of cannon and small arms fire not far from the city. It left him in a "bad humor," and he would have been in worse had he known that but for fortune, some of those shots might have been aimed at him. A botched raid on Richmond—its intent being to free Yankee prisoners held in the city's prisons and to "kill or capture" Davis and his cabinet—got within a few miles of the capital. One of the leaders, Colonel Ulric Dahlgren, fell in the skirmishing, and Confederates took from his body papers confirming his intent. General Fitzhugh Lee delivered these in person to Davis, who quickly released them to the press in order to show what a rabble of plunderers and assassins they faced in Lincoln's armies. Immediately afterward he called a cabinet meeting to discuss what measures should be taken.

The majority of his counselors favored executing all or some of the prisoners taken from Dahlgren's command as an admonition to Federal authorities. The discussion became more heated than some members recalled at any other session, naturally enough since all of them could have felt the enemy's bullets. Davis appears to have opposed rather strenuously the notion of shooting unarmed soldiers who had only been following their orders. Nevertheless, he agreed in the end to withhold a final decision until Lee could be consulted on what effect he thought such executions would have. Since one of Lee's own sons was then a prisoner in enemy hands, his fear of retaliation no doubt influenced his dissenting reply, and there the matter ended. But beneath the surface something stayed with Davis from the incident. The enemy—he had to presume with Lincoln's sanction—had introduced a terrible new element into the war, a game at which more than one could play.[19]

In fact, the war assumed a more and more sinister aspect that winter, well before active campaigning commenced. One enterprising inventor offered the president "a flying machine" that he promised could destroy enemy forces on the ground and seas, and have the Rebels "thundering away at all their principal cities and towns." Things of that sort Davis regarded as little more than eccentric curiosities, but there were more practical ways to carry the war to the enemy—and without having to send Lee on another invasion. Long inclined to overrate the disaffection in northern Indiana, Illinois, Ohio, and elsewhere, Davis believed that such areas were hotbeds of Southern sympathizers. In fact, while vocal and near violent opposition to Lincoln did run high there, it was based on opposition to the war rather than love for the Confederacy, but Davis could not know that.

Tantalizing reports came to Davis regularly that a secret society, the Knights of the Golden Circle, thrived all across the North, its members organized, armed, and anxious to revolt against Lincoln. Late in February Polk sent his friend the same news gathered from a scout; then early in March Davis received full intelligence of a society 490,000 strong, spread throughout seven Yankee states, but especially powerful in Illinois and Indiana. They promised to sabotage Union communications and supply if provided with necessary funds. While Davis was not such a fool as to jump at every promise of great things—he had received similar promises throughout the war, always accompanied by a request for funds—still the persistence of these reports and what he could see for himself in the Northern newspapers brought through the lines convinced him and his cabinet that here was a chance to accomplish something. But Davis looked to a grander result than mere sabotage. If he could place agents and funds in Canada, just across the line from the disaffected areas, he might be able to boost the growing peace movement in the North in time to deny some of those states to Lincoln in his fall reelection bid. Defeat Lincoln on a peace platform, and the victor, whomever it might be, could be brought to the peace table with an offer to end the war in return for Confederate independence.

The notion misgauged both the support for Lincoln and the overwhelming commitment by now of Northerners to reconstruct the Union and put down the rebellion. But operating only on the basis of what information he had, Davis's idea possessed merit. Moreover, he gained rapid and ready support in his cabinet and Congress. The latter gave him a $5 million secret service fund in mid-February, and a few days later he appointed his first commissioner, James P. Holcombe, to go to Canada, chiefly to help escaped prisoners get back to the South. Later in March and April Davis chose formal commissioners. Oddly enough, one whom he appointed was his sometime friend and more-often foe, Jacob Thompson. Not always a savory character, Thompson carried with him rumors of past financial chicanery when he served as Buchanan's secretary of the interior, and certainly Davis knew firsthand of Thompson's slipperiness in Mississippi politics. Perhaps he felt that this somehow suited the man for clandestine and slightly unchivalric espionage service. Perhaps as a check on Thompson, Davis also appointed his very trusted friend Clement Clay as a co-commissioner. In fact, neither was his first choice, for several others turned down the appointments. Since Thompson and Clay's mission involved basing themselves on foreign soil, Davis brought Benjamin into their discussions, and together the two spent long hours verbally instructing the commissioners on their duties. In the end, however, Davis had to leave much to their own discretion as they would be far away and beyond immediate control. Davis sent them on their way with $1 million and his trust in their "zeal, discretion and patriotism." Specific measures would be up to them.[20]

Otherwise, in foreign affairs Davis ceased to take an active role, having in his own mind sincerely given up hope that Europe would grant recognition to the Confederacy until it was obvious that such assistance was not needed anyhow. In fact, in April Britain issued a formal protest at Davis's efforts to purchase, build, and outfit privateering vessels in the shipyards of Birkenhead and Liverpool. Yet the protest did not come through ordinary diplomatic chanels, since England did not recognize the new nation, and it referred to the "so-called" Confederate States in a manner that Davis found offensive, however diplomatically correct. Warming to his response, Davis warned that any future communications so addressed would be refused. As for Britain's pleas of observing strict neutrality, Davis accused Victoria's government of using it as "a mere cover for actual hostility." Using a queer but typical twist of logic, Davis argued that if Britain were really neutral, then it would not allow the subjugation of the South. In other words, to the president's way of thinking, to be neutral England must take sides with him. Then, after accusing Britain's rulers of acting with "treacherous, malignant hostility" and of raising "specious arguments" on the subject of the privateers, Davis proceeded to dodge the issue entirely, thus sidestepping the sole purpose of the protest and avoiding having to make an admission or denial of what, in fact, the Confederacy was most certainly doing. In an attempt to add some measure of insult of his own, Davis did not send the response over his own name, but had Harrison write and sign it as his private secretary.

In fact, through the whole course of diplomatic efforts, the only glimmer of recognition—and that meaningless—came from the Vatican, when Pius IX addressed a letter to the "Illustrious and Honorable President," expressing a hope for peace between the peoples of America. Confederates tried to seize on this as having great significance. The foolish old Dudley Mann, who engineered the correspondence, called it "a positive recognition of our Government." Davis and Benjamin were not fooled. Still they tried other means, though closer to home now. In January 1864 Davis appointed General William Preston envoy to Mexico, where a puppet emperor installed by the French would soon sit uneasily on the throne of a nation troubled by a civil war of its own. Hoping that the sympathetic Emperor Maximilian might have some influence with the court of Napoléon III back in Paris, Davis dispatched a man who had briefly served as minister to Spain for Buchanan. Besides, sending Preston out of the country would get him out of the president's hair. Preston went first to France, since Maximilian himself had not left Europe for Mexico. Though the envoy may have met briefly with the emperor-to-be, it accomplished nothing, and Preston himself never even saw the land of the Montezumas. And his suggestions that recognition of the Confederacy would allow it to help prevent Yankee aggression against Mexico rang hollow to men who remembered that in 1846 it was Southerners, not Northerners, who pressed most hotly for war with Mexico, and that among those most eager to swallow great chunks of the country had been a younger Jefferson Davis. Glumly Davis commented to young ladies with whom he walked on March 20 that "we have no friends abroad!"[21]

Thus diplomacy was a pantomime they must walk through, but Davis saw reality well enough to know that the only recognition he could hope for would be an admission of Confederate independence by the Union and from Lincoln or his successor. The only diplomats who could win that would be his generals. As spring approached, the maps on the wall told him what to expect. Grant had been given overall command of all Union armies, leaving Sherman in charge of the forces facing Johnston in north Georgia. Grant was with Meade in northern Virginia. Banks had a smaller but substantial army based in New Orleans, and other lesser enemy forces were dotted in Arkansas, Mississippi, and the South Carolina coast. Banks and the others west of the Mississippi could be expected to operate against Kirby Smith, Sherman to move toward Atlanta, and Grant and Meade toward Lee.

To meet what was to come, Davis had more than ever to husband and concentrate his dwindling resources. The complete enemy control of the Mississippi made effective control of or cooperation with the Trans-Mississippi extremely difficult if not impossible. Thus Davis could only continue to sustain Kirby Smith's complete autonomy as both military and civil authority in his department, merely chiding him from time to time to observe Confederate laws on impressment and the like. If Smith could turn back the Yankees on his fronts, he might be called on for reinforcements for Mississippi or armies further east, but any such movement would be difficult at best. Then the spring campaigns got off to an early start, with Smith the first objective. In March, Banks and a small army of men and gunboats started up Louisiana's Red River, headed toward Shreveport. A few days later another Union army started south from Little Rock to link with Banks. If successful, they could cut the Trans-Mississippi in two. Kirby Smith already had his hands full, and Davis could do nothing more than wish him well.

That left the president staring at a war largely reduced to two factors, Johnston and Lee. Johnston, of course, offered the greater concern. Early in February Davis sent his aide Colonel Browne to Dalton to inspect the army and report on its condition, as well as to take a hard look at the new commander. On the whole Browne returned encouraging news. "The army is in excellent spirits," he said on Valentine's Day. The men seemed well provided for in food and equipment, showed good training in their drill, and carried good arms. Late morning reports showed 41,500 of all branches present for duty, with only the artillery seriously wanting. Best of all, Browne found a full month's supply of rations waiting in Atlanta. The railroads of northern Georgia, while rickety and frail, could handle the movement of men and matériel, and even Governor Brown was being cooperative now that his own state was threatened. Matters offered much room for improvement, of course. Horses were in poor condition, artillery ammunition proved of uneven quality, and many men still needed bayonets. Besides his official report, Browne also sent Davis a confidential appraisal of Johnston, whom he found very courteous and even communicative. But Davis wanted to know what plans the general entertained for the spring campaign, and Browne reported that Johnston stayed silent, "although I gave him many opportunities to speak freely." Davis would have expected as much. Browne did infer that Johnston felt himself unable to attack Sherman at Chattanooga and warned the president to expect demands for reinforcements soon.

But then came the worrying part. Johnston liked his army, and his men liked him. "But he does not seem to be sufficiently impressed with the importance of getting ready to strike before the enemy is prepared to assume the offensive," warned Browne, "nor does he seem to have any well matured plan of operations." Johnston hinted that he might move into east Tennessee, perhaps to draw Sherman away from Atlanta, but he would say no more, and even his corps commanders confessed to Browne that they were "equally in the dark." Relations with his high command were good and cheerful, Hardee being well pleased. But Hindman, commanding Breckinridge's old corps, threatened resignation because a new lieutenant general was being assigned to supersede him, John B. Hood.[22]

Hood was almost entirely Davis's doing. Indeed, Davis had played a major role in Hood's career from the early part of the war. In March 1862 Davis promoted him over several other senior colonels to make him a brigadier in command of a Texas brigade, then saw that promotion justified on successive battlefields as Hood proved to be an able combat leader. Davis first met him on the Peninsula in May 1862, when Johnston was retreating before McClellan, and perhaps the sad-eyed young general's calm impressed the president. Certainly his later conduct caught Davis's eye, especially his wounding at Gettysburg and then his lightning performance at Chickamauga, where Hood lost a leg. Davis resolved almost immediately to make Hood a lieutenant general, but there was a problem. No promotion could be made without there first being a vacancy, and none immediately existed. None, that is, until the convenient ousting of D. H. Hill, whose own nomination to the rank had not yet been confirmed by the Senate. Thus Davis probably had a motive of his own in mind when he allowed Bragg to relieve Hill. It would take another three months before the Senate acted on Hood's promotion, but Davis had his way.[23]

Hood came to Richmond to recuperate from his Chickamauga wound and immediately fell into capital society, which lionized the one-legged hero. The influential Kentucky lobby—Buckner, Breckinridge, Preston, and others—especially promoted their fellow native son, and thus Hood came into frequent contact with Davis. Very soon a close relationship grew between them. Naturally enough Davis admired Hood as a fighter, a man of quick action who constantly advocated the offensive. But there was a more sinister side to their growing bond. Mary Chesnut saw a lot of "Sam" Hood, as friends called him. "General Hood's an awful flatterer," she observed. He told Davis what the president liked to hear, praised his military sagacity, and on one occasion even begged Davis to come lead the Army of Tennessee in person, saying, "I would follow you to the death." Mary Chesnut, hearing the remark, chided Hood not to stay in Richmond too long: "You will grow to be a courtier." Hood's flattery of Davis had nothing to do with his promotion to lieutenant general, but certainly it helped during January and February 1864 to win him the president's regard and confidence. Davis let him use his carriage, took him on evening rides in place of Preston Johnston, and even attended church with him. Some now believed that Davis expected Hood to spy on Johnston for him in the Army of Tennessee. Davis probably did not ask it, but certainly Hood would do it in the days ahead, and the president would see in Hood's carping commentary on Johnston nothing more than a brave fighting general's frustration with a hesitating commander. Davis never recognized Hood's underlying ambition.[24]

But this lay in the future when Browne concluded his confidential letter that the Army of Tennessee was in "magnificent order & spirits" and cheered Davis loudly whenever Browne passed. Obviously the president's criticism of its performance at Missionary Ridge had been forgotten in the euphoria over Bragg's removal and Johnston's arrival. Now at last they had a commander in whom they felt confidence. If only Davis could share their enthusiasm, but what he heard once Hood reached Dalton did not encourage him. As far back as December, Davis told Johnston that he expected an offensive as soon as the break in winter weather allowed. Two months later, at the end of February, Johnston revealed his usual studied obtusity by asking the War Department if it still wanted him to advance, even urging that they must move quickly. He asked to have Polk sent to him from Mississippi, Beauregard's spare men from South Carolina, and Longstreet's from East Tennessee, where he remained after failing to take Knoxville.

Bragg, in place in Richmond, responded, confirming that Davis wanted an offensive and reminding Johnston politely that the preparations he now called for should have been commenced weeks before. Davis wanted Johnston to interpose his army between Chattanooga and Knoxville, isolating the latter and forcing its defenders to meet him in the open field. Thereafter Johnston could move on the line of communications to Chattanooga and perhaps even force its evacuation and the consequent recovery of middle Tennessee as far as Nashville. It was an ambitious plan, and Davis was willing to send Longstreet, Polk, and troops from Beauregard to swell Johnston's numbers to 75,000 or more. It was also a concentration more complex and ambitious than any tried before, depending heavily on timing and coordination that the Confederacy's crumbling railroads could hardly provide. In theory it could work; in practice it stood only a remote chance.

That chance would be lessened even more by its dependence on Johnston, and now Hood arrived to find the commander talking of withdrawal from Dalton. When Johnston heard Davis's plan, either from Bragg or perhaps verbally from Hood, he saw its weaknesses, and suggested instead that being numerically inferior, his best chance was to strike at Sherman in response to his advances, in other words an offensive-defensive. While it offered few chances of any decisive advantage, it was more practical than the grand concentration, and Johnston would adhere to this basic notion for the rest of his tenure. Hood wanted more, however, and began sending letters back to Davis and Bragg, alternating flattery and expressions of his devotion with hints that he felt more aggressive than Johnston. "I am eager for us to take the initiative," he told the president, "but fear we will not do so." Hood may not yet have had a private agenda, but he well knew Davis's prejudice against Johnston and did not hesitate to play to it occasionally.

Meanwhile, the debate in cabinet sessions and in meetings with Lee and even Longstreet continued through March and April, as Davis and Bragg stuck to their hopes for an offensive, while Lee wanted Longstreet back with him. Davis sent other observers to Dalton to see to Johnston's artillery and again urge taking the offensive. Johnston, in turn, sent his own representative to Davis to promise that he, too, wanted to take action but that he needed more men and could not operate with Davis's ambitious plan. Meanwhile, Hood kept writing, telling Bragg and Davis that "I have done all in my power to induce General Johnston" to take the offensive. Johnston would not, as indeed he probably could not, but Davis no longer trusted any representation from the general, especially now that he had the sympathetic Hood at headquarters and the ever-critical Benjamin feeding his prejudice in the executive offices.[25]

How much more thankful Davis felt to have Lee in Virginia. He did not complain, he did not plot, he did not talk to the newspapers, and even when he did not bring the president victories, still Davis found that he could not fault the conduct of his campaigns. Many of these winter days Lee spent in Richmond, meeting first with Davis and Seddon and then with Bragg after his appointment. Most of Davis's discussions with Lee centered on organizational matters. Samuel Jones proved unpopular and ineffective in southwest Virginia and would have to be replaced. Incredibly, some around him urged Davis to put his aide Custis Lee, now a brigadier, in the position, and Davis offered him the post. To send a completely inexperienced commander to such a difficult post was foolish. Lee's father agreed, and Breckinridge assumed the command instead. Davis and Lee also debated at length what to do with Longstreet, deciding before the early spring that he should rejoin the Army of Northern Virginia. Longstreet, a good soldier with rather too much taste for politics, pushed his brief familiarity with Davis too far when he questioned one of the president's promotions and got a stern rebuke for his "highly insubordinate" conduct. As always, Davis prodded Northrop and others to keep Lee's men fed, while trying to find replacements for the men lost on so many battlefields. Both tasks became increasingly difficult that winter.[26]

More than anything, Davis talked with Lee of what to do in the coming campaign. The plan for an invasion of Tennessee by Johnston was first on the table, and in the main Davis sought Lee's counsel on its feasibility. Ever cautious and diplomatic, Lee consistently deferred to the opinions of Johnston, who had the best vantage for judgment from his position at Dalton. Besides, as March came quickly to a close, Lee became convinced that the greatest enemy pressure would be applied to him, else why would Grant himself have come east to join Meade? He advised Davis that now it was imperative to get Longstreet back to him and also asked that Beauregard's small army be brought from South Carolina to guard Richmond. Meanwhile, Lee would advance to the Rappahannock and hope somehow to meet the enemy and turn it back. Davis agreed that it was the best they could hope to do, especially if they were to defend Richmond. Davis had said two years before that he did not think the capital all that important strategically: But for its factories, its worth was mostly symbolic. However, the Confederacy had lost so much else in the past year that symbolism now assumed larger proportions, while the rail center at Petersburg a few miles south of the capital could be vital to any future concentration or shifting of troops between theaters. The best place to defend Richmond, Davis decided, was on the Rappahannock.[27]

Thus matters stood as April came to a close. Kirby Smith was already scrambling to counter Banks on the Red River. Johnston could not or would not budge from Dalton to preempt Sherman's expected move out of Chattanooga. And Lee awaited the coming of Meade and Grant. At least Davis may have felt some satisfaction at bringing Beauregard up out of his stronghold in Carolina. That general had occupied himself during much of the winter with keeping alive his old hatred of Davis by a steady campaign of letter writing, leading one friend of the president's to refer to the "Beauregard clique" as a pack of "pestilential conspirators" who had to be stopped. Bringing the Creole to Virginia would put him under Davis's eye, and that might help control him. Beauregard arrived at Weldon, Virginia, on April 22, taking command of all of the state south of the James, as well as North Carolina. He had to guard the back door to Richmond, including any attempt to land on the Peninsula and approach the capital along the route tried by McClellan in 1862. While he and Davis did not meet immediately, the president made it clear that his shoulder remained cool to the general. When Beauregard suggested to Bragg that he would be happy to cooperate under Lee's command, should he have to be brought north of the James, Davis dashed off a hot reply that Lee would command in such an instance thanks to superior rank and not Beauregard's sufferance or voluntary subordination. Davis did not forget the snub of Charleston the previous fall.[28]

Meanwhile, a minor success in taking Plymouth, North Carolina, brought a measure of relief, though its military import was small. The news had "a wonderful effect on the President's mind," said Richmonders. Nevertheless, with all the tension of planning for the excruciating imponderables of the spring, the failure to eat well or regularly, the nights without sleep, and the constant sense of being besieged within as well as without, Davis's health slipped steadily. By April 23 his friends the Reverend Minnegerode and General William N. Pendleton told him that "your nervous system is at present outraged by labor & anxiety." The long hours of working through the night must stop. Could he not "devolve all the smaller matters upon some of your accomplished aids & give your own care to only the great matters of vital moment?" They begged him to take rest and exercise.[29]

Varina saw it too, as she always did. His only release at times was his family. In the children especially he took solace, for they robbed his mind of its cares for a few minutes each day. As a result, he indulged them constantly. Many an important meeting with Lee or a cabinet official came to a temporary halt when little Willie burst into the room or the children raced around the house in play with Nickie. Joseph was his father's special favorite. The president delighted in hearing the little boy say evening prayers at his knee. Davis might be in a meeting, entertaining guests, or about to leave on a long evening ride to see Lee. No matter, when bedtime arrived, Joseph came padding down the stairs to the entrance foyer in his nightgown, walked to his father wherever he sat or stood, and kneeled to say his prayer. Jefferson Davis rested his hand on the boy's head, bent down, and whispered the prayer with him. "This child was Mr. Davis' hope and greatest joy in life," Varina would say. It was almost as if "le man," the long-dead little Samuel, had been returned to him.[30]

On the morning of April 30, as usual, Davis barely ate before going to his office. It was a warm day, and all the windows in the house stood open, the breeze fluttering the curtains. Varina's sister Margaret, who was visiting with them, left for a carriage ride with Mary Chesnut. The president conducted some business through the morning, sent a telegram to Polk in Alabama telling him how to handle captured runaway slaves, and issued an order placing James Chesnut in command of the militia of South Carolina in the current emergency and with Beauregard being withdrawn to Virginia. Probably he worked at perfecting the wording of his message to the first session of the Second Confederate Congress, due to assemble on May 2, and he may have met with Clay and Thompson before they departed for Canada. The morning passed quickly, as they all did. About 1 P.M., as usual, Varina appeared with her covered basket bearing his lunch. She had just lifted the napkin and begun spreading their fare when a servant came running into the second-floor office shouting that little Joe had fallen from the first-floor balcony.

Varina had left the children playing in one of the rooms downstairs when she prepared her husband's lunch. Apparently they wandered out onto the balcony at the back, and Joseph began climbing on the railing at the far left corner. He lost his footing or grip and went plummeting almost twenty feet from the top of the rail to the brick pavement at the ground-floor level. Little Jeff found him. "Joe wouldn't wake up," he cried to his Irish nurse Catharine before she ran to tell the Davises. When the parents reached their boy's side, he still breathed but was insensible, the terrible injuries to his head and body obvious. In minutes he died, even while his brother Jeff knelt at his side and prayed.

Varina became hysterical. Throughout the afternoon and into the evening passersby could hear her shrieking inside the house. Even when Margaret Howell and Mary Chesnut arrived well after nightfall to learn the terrible news, Varina still screamed. Burton Harrison brought a doctor soon after the accident, but there was nothing to be done for Joseph, and Dr. Garnett attended to Varina instead. Through the day and into the evening friends came to stand vigil in the house, to help with the children, and to comfort Varina.

Of Jefferson Davis they saw almost nothing. As others carried the body of his lifeless son to a second-floor room to be laid out for the funeral, the president's iron will took control to keep him from breaking down. "Not mine, oh, Lord, but thine," he muttered as he gazed on his boy's face. For almost three hours after the tragedy he sat with Varina, saying this again and again. Shortly before 4 P.M. a courier arrived with a message from Lee. The enemy appeared to be moving up reinforcements in his front. An offensive against him was imminent. He needed reinforcements of his own. Davis opened the dispatch and stared blankly at it for a few minutes without seeing the words. Finally he returned to the moment and looked at Varina. Obviously disoriented, he asked her if she had just read this to him. Then he read it for himself and tried to write a response. The words would not come and finally he cast it aside. "I must have this day with my little child," he exclaimed in heartbreak. He went upstairs, and those who called for the rest of the day and long into the night never saw him. Yet they knew he was there, for all night long, through the gloomy hours before the funeral, they heard the president's ceaseless tread as he paced back and forth in his room.[31]

They buried little Joseph the next day in Richmond's Hollywood Cemetery in a lot offered them at no cost by the sympathetic managers of the burial ground. Hundreds of children from the capital came to the ceremony, piling Joseph's grave high with flowers and green boughs. Davis gave himself this one day, Sunday, to mourn his son and comfort Varina. But on Monday he was back in his office, attending to Lee, Johnston, Smith and all the rest. His personal tragedy could not slow the war by a minute. Yet even his self-control could not keep his thoughts from wandering. Richmond was full of refugee families now, many reduced to poverty. Somehow many of these little beggar boys and girls took to visiting Harrison and Johnston and the other aides in their office, even though Harrison had to spank one occasionally. Trying mightily to contain his grief and longing, Jefferson Davis struggled to continue the cause, while now and then from just the other side of the wall came the cruelly taunting sound of the laughter of children.

In September Davis would have the balcony from which little Joseph fell torn down.[32]

28

I Love My Friends and I Forgive My Enemies

The day after little Joe's funeral, President Davis greeted a new Congress with what amounted to a "state of the Confederacy" message. It was hard to put a good face on affairs. Foreign hopes were more remote than ever. "Every avenue of negotiation is closed against us," he stated matter-of-factly. No reasonable hope for a change in European attitudes existed, nor did the enemy give any indication of relaxing its fixed intent of conquest and complete subjugation. Neither would Lincoln exchange prisoners with the South, thus imposing the double burden of caring for Yankees taken in battle, as well as denying the return of Confederate prisoners to their armies. Davis could not understand Lincoln's cruelty in allowing his soldiers to languish and die in Rebel prisons, though Davis ascribed their high death rate to "homesickness" and "hopelessness of release" rather than poor food and abominable sanitation.

In the economy inflation had assumed runaway proportions despite attempts to control the paper money supply. Davis did not even refer to the Justice Department or to Reagan's domain. He alluded only briefly to naval affairs, and even his report on military affairs received less attention than his complaints against England, France, and the other powers. He did try to offer expressions of hope, but they sounded feeble as he pointed to a string of recent successes in the field that spring, all of them of minor scale and not of lasting consequence.[1]

It was one of the briefest messages to Congress that Davis ever delivered, no doubt reflecting both the discouraging state of affairs and also his own preoccupation with his recent tragedy. Davis did not tell them anything about the evolution of his own efforts in recent months, of how he had increasingly come to act both as secretary of war and general-in-chief. He personally issued the orders that commenced the organization of militia reserves in South Carolina, Richmond, and elsewhere. He himself managed the matter of Longstreet's position in East Tennessee, even bypassing Lee, to whose army the former's corps still belonged. Davis orchestrated the reinforcement of Polk in Mississippi in February and March as he resisted a raid by Sherman, and after the Yankees had gone it was Davis who personally ordered Polk and most of his command to join Johnston's army in Georgia. In Virginia, Davis took charge of coordinating Breckinridge's efforts to hold onto the Shenandoah with Lee's movements east of the Blue Ridge, while also overseeing pulling reinforcements from other regions to add bulk to the Army of Northern Virginia. He also stepped into Mallory's territory occasionally, taking an interest in the construction of ironclads for the defense of Mobile. And when he had to be tough, Davis showed that his patience was not inexhaustible, as in March when he relieved both the army and navy commanders at Wilmington, North Carolina, on the same day.[2]

The increased level of Davis's direct involvement reflected Seddon's increasingly poor health, a probable unwillingness to give Bragg a free hand, and Davis's own perception of just how desperate the situation had become. This, combined with his unshaken confidence in his own ability and judgment in military matters, made it imperative that he take an even greater hand in managing the armies. The events of the days immediately following his message to Congress only underscored this. On May 4 Grant and Meade crossed the Rapidan and began advancing deeper into Virginia, intent on taking Lee and his army out of the war for good. As the ensuing Battle of the Wilderness raged, Sherman started to move against Johnston, and within days the Army of Tennessee evacuated Dalton and started to retreat on the defensive. On May 8 Grant sent his cavalry on a raid toward Richmond, and the next day the Yankees on the Peninsula, commanded by Davis's onetime supporter Benjamin F. Butler, began to advance toward Richmond. Another raid moved deep into the Shenandoah Valley, and out in the Trans-Mississippi, Banks presumably still campaigned along the Red River, though communications were so slow that Davis could not be certain of what happened out there.

Johnston's abandonment of Dalton deeply disappointed the president. He could only hope that the general intended to turn and fight the Yankees on better ground farther in Georgia, though when he expressed this to Lee, Davis put little conviction in his words. Johnston had disappointed him too often. Kirby Smith would deal with Banks on his own. Breckinridge, too, must look out for himself now. About Lee, of course, Davis never felt a doubt, even when day after day of relentless pressure by the Federals slowly forced the Virginia army back from the Wilderness to Spotsylvania.[3]

Besides trusting Lee enough to leave things in his hands, the president quickly found his own hands full in Richmond. By May 10 Butler's advance posed such a severe threat that Davis himself rode the seven miles to Drewry's Bluff, on the James below Richmond. There local defense forces from the capital tried to maintain a flimsy line of resistance. Davis had previously asked Beauregard to bring reinforcements from Petersburg, but on seeing the situation for himself he peremptorily ordered it done. Meanwhile, apparently mistrusting Beauregard, Davis continued to deal directly with the commander at the bluff until the Creole arrived. In fact, Beauregard took his time, not arriving until four days later, after unnecessary and petulant delay.[4]

Much happened during those days. On May 11 the cavalry raid sent by Grant came within less than six miles of Richmond, and near Yellow Tavern a hot engagement broke out. Davis could hear the firing from his office and wired to Lee, "I go to look after defence." He rushed to his office at home and took his pistols in hand. Varina and the children prayed as he made ready to leave, while little Jeff suggested that his own pony ought to be saddled that he might ride to battle with his daddy. Varina could see in her husband's eyes how he "bitterly regretted his executive office" at times like this, "and longed to engage actively in the fight." Yet the battle was done before the president could arrive, and what met him was word of the mortal wounding of General Jeb Stuart, Lee's premier cavalryman. The next day, in Richmond, Davis visited the bedside of the dying hero, spending perhaps a quarter of an hour with him and praying with Varina that he might yet live. But then he had to return to Drewry's Bluff once more, since Beauregard had not yet arrived. Varina saw his anxiety, though he would not speak of it. Already rumors flew through the city that the president was preparing his own evacuation of the city and that the capital would have to be abandoned. "This is the time to try the nerves of the President and his counselors!" the clerk Jones confided to his diary.[5]

No one found Jefferson Davis's nerves wanting. As in the May two years before when the enemy threatened the capital, the president displayed the calm and bravery that even his bitterest foes could not deny. "He never appeared to greater advantage," said the commander of the reserves at the bluff. "Calm, self-contained, cheerful, hopeful, determined, he was an inspiration." Indeed, he believed that the president was ready to assume command personally. Beauregard's arrival, while tardy, put an end to the necessity for that, though on May 14 Davis still believed that "affairs here are critical." He had already withdrawn every organized brigade from South Carolina and Georgia to come to Petersburg and beyond for the emergency.[6]

Feeling ill that day, Davis stayed at home until late morning, when Bragg came in with news that Beauregard was finally in command at Drewry's Bluff. Moreover, the Creole proposed one of his customary impractical plans for a grand concentration, this time calling for Lee to fall back and send him reinforcements for an attack on Butler. Then Beauregard would turn around and bring his forces to Lee to push back Grant. Davis and Bragg both wisely rejected the scheme; then the president rode out to Drewry's Bluff personally, where he again turned down the impractical plan and instead ordered Beauregard to attack Butler immediately with his existing force. Unfortunately, to Beauregard "immediately" meant proposing a three-day delay. Worse, Davis found that one of Beauregard's first acts on arriving was to pull many of his men out of their earthworks on his flank in order to concentrate their numbers. Davis challenged this, but on hearing the Creole's explanation, he said little further, "according to my uniform practice never to do more than make a suggestion to a general commanding in the field," as he would later recall. Of course, Davis's direct orders to attack Butler were certainly something more than suggestions.[7]

Early on May 16, expecting to observe an attack, Davis arose early and rode to Beauregard's headquarters. Some speculated that he intended to embarrass the general, perhaps by relieving him and taking command personally, though others felt Davis wanted to be outside the city in order to flee if the battle should go against them. Disheartened by news from Bragg and Pemberton, now a lowly lieutenant colonel of artillery, Davis had decided to return to Drewry's Bluff in person to confirm their report of the day before—a report perhaps intentionally pessimistic thanks to their shared dislike of Beauregard.

Postmaster General Reagan joined the president for the ride, and the sound of firing accompanied their short journey. By the time Davis arrived, Beauregard had already enjoyed some success in pushing Butler back, or so he thought. For several hours through the morning Davis stayed at headquarters, listening to the desultory firing in the distance and waiting for Beauregard's attack, which never came. Briefly during the morning Federal shells actually started coming down near headquarters, one striking the earth at the president's feet. He and Beauregard calmly walked aside, though eventually Reagan and other officers persuaded Davis to leave the field entirely for a time.

The fighting died down to a lull early in the afternoon, while Davis and Beauregard waited for a flanking command to make the assault that he expected would dislodge the enemy and commence the victorious general attack. The general, the president, and Preston Johnston were actually standing atop the abandoned earthworks in their front, listening, when the sound of a distant cannon finally came. "Ah, at last," cried Davis. But then they heard nothing more. The flank attack failed to materialize, and the battle ended inconclusively. The best Beauregard could do was to pursue Butler as he withdrew the next day, eventually trapping him in a bend formed by the James and Appomattox rivers. Beauregard sewed him into that pocket with a line of earthworks that did not succeed in destroying Butler, as the Creole had boastfully hoped, but that at least prevented the Federal from moving. That same day Davis met with his cabinet and proclaimed not quite a victory but still a limited success, and they much needed one. Reagan chided Davis again for exposing himself on the field the day before. The president acknowledged that no particular service he could render required him to be on the scene, but protested almost plaintively that "it would have been an unpleasant thing, to ride off under fire."[8]

Though disappointed that better results did not come of the small fight at Drewry's Bluff, still Davis took some encouragement. At least this one threat to Richmond would not plague him now. He even allowed Beauregard some latitude on the Peninsula, saying, "You will be best able to judge" in conducting further operations in that area. Through much of the rest of the month he allowed Custis Lee and Davis's nephew John Taylor Wood to act as his eyes with Beauregard. Happily, too, though Stuart's death came as a terrible blow, Yellow Tavern did turn back Grant's cavalry raid, removing another threat to the capital. Better yet, at New Market on May 15, Breckinridge repulsed the threat to the Shenandoah and would soon be on his way with his tiny army to reinforce Lee.[9]

This left, for the moment, only Meade as a threat to Virginia—the greatest of all—and he was haltingly pushing Lee back, though at great cost. Still Davis felt unbounded confidence in his one great general, as he repeatedly expressed to his cabinet. Mallory recalled that Davis regarded Lee "as standing alone among the Confederate soldiers in military capacity." When Davis spoke of Lee, said Mallory, "All others were, in comparison to him, beginners." As a result, though he stayed in constant communication with Lee, Davis rarely tried to suggest as much to him as he did to Beauregard or Johnston. Once the threat from Butler abated, and as Lee slowly retired closer to Richmond, Davis frequently rode to the army. The president's spirits rose and fell alternately depending on what he saw and heard at headquarters. Especially disturbing to him were the stories that Lee recklessly exposed himself and even tried to lead troops into battle personally before he was persuaded otherwise. Davis had lost too many of his great generals by now—Stonewall Jackson, Stuart, and of course, Sidney Johnston; he must not lose Lee. "Don't expose yourself," the president implored the general he now called "my dear friend." Yet Davis himself took constant risks in his rides to visit

Lee, often going alone. On one journey, a young soldier on the road fell in with him and stayed at the president's side long after they had passed the boy's regimental camp. Davis kindly asked if the soldier should not turn back, but he responded that he had come along to protect Davis. "You ought to have a guard with you," he said, but Davis nevertheless kept riding alone.[10]

Inevitably Grant and Meade pushed Lee farther and farther. By early June the armies stood at Cold Harbor, just ten miles northeast of Richmond, and there the Federals brutally exhausted themselves in wasted frontal assaults on Lee's lines. Davis took heart from the repulse but also believed that Grant would not make the same mistake again. On June 8 the president rode to the defenses along the Chickahominy, midway between the armies and the capital. In looking over the ground and considering the events of the past few days, he told Lee that Grant would next try to "embarrass you by flank movements." One of the defenders on that line even claimed later that Davis predicted the startling movement Grant commenced on June 12, when he secretly moved the Army of the Potomac out of its lines in front of Lee and south, across the James, suddenly to approach Richmond and Petersburg from the south. Perhaps so, though given Grant's long history of a preference for flank movements, such an expectation did not require a great deal of prescience. Since Grant's move took even Lee completely by surprise, it is probable that Davis suspected only a local tactical flank move rather than the startling strategic shift made by the Federals.[11]

When not with the army, Davis spent long hours with his cabinet and Bragg, sometimes using up whole days in discussions. In the evenings Davis sat at home with his family, still lost in thought over little Joseph or puzzling out in his mind how next to counter the enemy. Varina often heard him murmuring phrases from a favorite hymn: "I'll strengthen thee, help thee, and cause thee to stand," he sang, "upheld by my righteous, omnipotent hand." Later, after everyone retired, Davis still sat up every night, his only company a cat named Maryland. "My Maryland," he called this cherished animal, "the companion of my nightly vigils in the interests of Southern Independence." With genuine pain he sent the pet out of the city as a gift to a friend when provisions became so scarce he could not feed it any longer.[12]

As the president spent those lonely hours, stroking his Maryland, hearing the occasional night guns of the armies in the distance, his thoughts turned with increasing anxiety to the West. Throughout May and into June he received nothing but disappointing reports. He had hoped that Johnston would attack Sherman and thereby prevent that general from sending reinforcements to Grant. Instead, Johnston abandoned Dalton without a fight and started pulling back. There followed a succession of defensive battles in which Johnston, heavily outnumbered, took high ground, tried to retard Sherman's advance, and then inevitably pulled back yet again before being outflanked. Given the disparity of odds, Johnston could have done little else. By the first week of July, he was within five or six miles of Atlanta.[13]

Davis watched it all in despair, an anguish enhanced when word came on June 14 that his old friend Polk was dead, killed by a Yankee cannonball. It all only seemed to confirm the lack of confidence the president felt in Johnston, though he did at least pay lip service to Johnston's having a better grasp of the situation on the scene than Davis could from a distance in Richmond. Worse, in cabinet and in private the president now heard an almost-constant harangue of Johnston. At seemingly every opportunity, Benjamin criticized the general. Mallory thought hostility to Johnston and Beauregard to be the secretary of state's "favorite theme." "We'll never have a fight of his army as long as Johnston keeps at the head of it," Benjamin would say, or "Johnston is determined not to fight; it is of no use to reinforce him, he is not going to fight." Week after week Davis heard his friend's incessant "Why didn't Johnston do this & why didn't Johnston do that?"[14]

The general's customary uncommunicativeness and lack of a clear plan of action made Benjamin's insinuations the easier to accept, especially given Davis's prejudice toward Johnston. On July 9 he finally ordered Bragg to go to Atlanta and confer with Johnston, and meanwhile he received a visit from Senator Benjamin Hill of Georgia, just come from Johnston's headquarters. Hill was one of Davis's most ardent supporters in Congress, and the president would listen to him. The senator had taken it upon himself to visit Johnston in June, and there he heard the general's view of the situation. In short, Johnston could not attack Sherman. All he could do would be to send a large cavalry raid against his supply lines. If successful, the raid would force the Yankees to retire or, said Johnston, give battle in the open ground on the Confederates' terms. If only Davis would order the cavalry to him from other departments, it would all work, he promised. Of course, it was mostly wishful thinking. Sherman was not a man to be turned aside by a few thousand cavalry, even if it did temporarily cut his communications, as he would demonstrate before long. And that such a severance would force the Yankees to come out of their works and fight on Johnston's "terms" was an exercise in pure wishful thinking. Besides, Sherman had been trying to fight Johnston in the open repeatedly, but the Confederate would not come out. In his current position just above the Chattahoochee River, Johnston implied to Hill on June 30, he could hold out against the enemy for nearly two months.[15]

Hill reached Richmond on July 9 or 10, and immediately Davis welcomed him at his home. When Hill repeated Johnston's views, the president went into a typically lengthy and detailed explanation of why the general was wrong at every point, especially on the availability of reinforcements from other areas. Indeed, Johnston was in error about affairs beyond his immediate vision and command, just as Davis never fully understood the limited possibilities against Sherman. But when Hill came to the promise to hold the Chattahoochee line for up to sixty days, Davis handed him a telegram just received announcing that the general had already abandoned the river and pulled closer to Atlanta. How much more evidence must he have, Davis may have thought, of Johnston's unfitness for command?[16]

More would come. Soon reports from Bragg came back. "I find but little encouraging," he said on first arriving, and two days later he reported that citizens were evacuating Atlanta. As for Johnston, in two interviews the general did not ask Bragg's advice or counsel, and the latter came away to telegraph Davis that "I cannot learn that he has any more plan for the future than he has had in the past." The next day, in response to Bragg's information, Davis wired Johnston directly asking to be informed of the current military situation "and your plan of operations so specifically as will enable me to anticipate events."[17]

By this time, July 16, Davis was already anticipating events on his own. Four days earlier he told Lee frankly, "*Genl. Johnston* has *failed* and there are strong indications that he will *abandon Atlanta*." "It seems necessary to *relieve him* at once." In fact, relieving Johnston had been on Davis's mind for at least a week and perhaps longer. Part of Bragg's assignment in going to Atlanta was to report on Johnston's fitness for command, and Davis may even have authorized him to remove Johnston. Certainly he gave Bragg some authority, but the timid general declined to take it. Instead, he reported in full on July 15 that Johnston had repeatedly opposed giving battle throughout the campaign, as had Hardee, and that only Hood of the corps commanders favored an aggressive policy. Since Hardee was the senior corps commander, Bragg warned that turning the command over to him would avail no change in policy. "If any change is made Lieutenant-General Hood would give unlimited satisfaction," said Bragg, though he qualified his endorsement by saying that Hood was neither a genius nor a great general, but simply better than anyone else available.[18]

Bragg's qualified endorsement of Hood may not have been entirely spontaneous. At least as early as July 12, Davis himself proposed Hood to Lee as a possibility, though he had not yet decided anything. Indeed, the president was showing his frequent tendency to postpone decision, even though the crisis of the hour called for quick action. While proposing Hood to Lee, Davis also considered Bragg as a possible successor, though not to be taken seriously. Of course, in principle Davis opposed making any change of commanders during an active campaign, just as he had opposed relieving Bragg the year before while he faced the enemy. "It is a sad alternative," the president told Lee, "but the case seems hopeless in present hands." "We can conquer a peace against the world in arms, and keep the rights of freemen, if we are worthy of the privilege," he told Varina. They had to show that worthiness on the battlefield. Toward that end the president once again considered taking the field himself. To Varina, and probably to no one else, he confided a desire—perhaps even an intent—to take command of Johnston's army personally, and use it in tandem with Lee to fight what he called "one great battle" that would be decisive.[19]

Like all his previous thoughts about donning uniform, these proved to be only daydreams. While Bragg told Davis what he probably wanted to hear from Atlanta, Davis fought his own battle in cabinet. There would be little dissent: Benjamin detested the general. Seddon felt chagrined at having backed his appointment in the first place and now anxiously wanted him out, believing that the cabinet was unanimous in agreeing. Mallory probably disagreed, however, as in fact he disagreed more often than any others with the president. The exact views of the rest are unknown, but none seems to have offered firm resistance. In fact, Davis's hardest task was in convincing Lee of the necessity of relieving Johnston, and he never entirely succeeded, despite sending Seddon to meet personally with him in the matter. Moreover, Lee doubted Hood's capacity for army command, and Lee had observed him intimately. Yet Hood impressed Davis and ably impressed Bragg, partially by misrepresenting his own and Hardee's actions during the campaign to date. Bragg, of course, felt little love for Hardee, who had been outspoken in opposition to him in previous years, and Davis knew from past experience of Hardee's reluctance to accept the army command. The only other corps commander available was the newly promoted A. P. Stewart, a good man but hardly yet experienced at the head of a corps, much less an army. The only man available seemed to be Hood, unless Davis were to turn to men from other departments with even less experience, take one of Lee's corps commanders from him, or turn in the distasteful direction of Beauregard.[20]

Seddon believed that Johnston might have kept the command, even at this late hour, if he had presented Davis with some kind of a plan, or anything to show that he would do more than simply react to Sherman's actions. Indeed, Seddon and others also believed that Davis himself still resisted relieving the general and at heart did not want to do so. Undoubtedly they mistook his opposition in principle to such a removal at such a time for a reluctance to rid himself of Johnston, when in fact Davis put the general in that position only as the least of several evils, and his correspondence throughout the entire campaign revealed a continuing and growing distaste for him. Now, at last, Johnston settled the matter for him when he responded to the president's demand for a statement of his plans. He had none. "My plan of operation must," said Johnston, "depend upon that of the enemy." It was the same old story. Worse, Johnston spoke of holding Atlanta for only another day or two. "This evasive answer to a positive inquiry," one cabinet member said to Hill, "brought the President over." Johnston must go.[21]

The next day Davis sent a terse telegram informing Johnston of his relief, and that he was to turn over the command to Hood, whom he had promoted to the temporary rank of full general. The rank could not become permanent without action by Congress, which was in recess. Unfortunately, signs indicated that a severe battle was imminent as Sherman readied an advance on Atlanta itself. There could hardly be a worse moment to change commanders, as Davis should have known, but neither Bragg nor Johnston gave him good information. Even Hood, along with Hardee and Stewart, asked Johnston to hold up announcing his relief until after the fight and retain command until then. But Johnston had his orders, and he gave the army to Hood on July 18.[22]

Few alternatives were available to Davis. While critics then and later would severely castigate him for removing Johnston, they did so chiefly because of Johnston's exalted reputation rather than his actual performance, which had been lackluster since the first Manassas. He rarely risked anything, gained little, and habitually avoided responsibility. As a subordinate he was consistently uncommunicative, noncommittal, slow to follow instructions, and frequently insolent. Indeed, the lobby that formed itself around Johnston, and which then and later did so much to create his reputation as a great genius, could point to very little that specifically supported their claims. Instead, they used him as yet another tool in their war against Davis, arguing what Johnston would have done had the president supported him. Indeed, so pervasive was the myth of Johnston's genius that even many of Davis's friends, such as Kirby Smith and Richard Taylor, regarded his relief as a mistake. Yet Davis's only mistake with Johnston was assigning him to the command in the first place and then retaining him while he gradually lost most of north Georgia. If the president could set aside his dislike of the man enough to give him the command, then he should have been able to do the same by installing Beauregard instead, and the Creole at least had several small victories to his credit around Charleston in 1863. Furthermore, where Johnston never had a plan, Beauregard always had at least one if not more, impractical though they might be. Very likely Beauregard could not have stopped Sherman either, but Davis would have been better served by him than by Johnston.

And now, with the enemy on the threshold of Atlanta, almost anyone would have been better than Hood. Beauregard might have achieved much. More to the point, following his crossing of the James, Grant tied Lee's army down to a siege in and around Petersburg, leaving the Army of Northern Virginia immobile. Now was the time to send Lee himself to the West, whether he liked it or not. Beauregard could ably command the defense of the earthworks in Virginia, leaving Davis's best general to try to do something with the only remaining large mobile field army east of the Mississippi. By replacing Johnston with Hood, Davis only compounded one mistake with another, and capped them both by keeping his best man in a post that suffocated his abilities.

It did not take Davis long to discover that he would have his problems with Hood, too. "Confident language by a military commander is not usually regarded as an evidence of competency," Johnston wrote Davis in a parting shot aimed at Hood's boastfulness. The new commander had done an able job of promoting himself to Richmond as an aggressive fighter, and at least succeeded in winning Davis's qualified confidence. Varina, though she shared a common misconception that her husband was a shrewd judge of men, still saw that "he was apt to be misled by some of the qualities he admired and infer the rest, and was thus sometimes mistaken in his judgment." Davis admired Hood's combativeness, and mistakenly inferred that a good fighter could be an effective army commander. But problems arose right away. Hardee felt immediately miffed on two counts—that the army command was not offered to him and that it went to Hood, his junior in grade. Early in August Hardee asked to be relieved "from an unpleasant position." Just because he declined the army command the previous winter did not mean that he declined it for all futurity. Worse, he felt no confidence in Hood. Neither did General Samuel G. French, who also asked to be relieved. Davis could only plead with Hardee that this was not the time to let personal or professional motivations stand in the way of the needs of the country. "Let your patriotic instincts answer," he begged. Hardee persisted, and finally in September Davis gave in, assigning him to command in South Carolina and eastern Georgia.[23]

By that time Atlanta was lost. Hood proved to be a better fighter than thinker. In July and August he launched four major attacks on Sherman, each one failing, and the last one cost him his route of retreat. He had no choice but to evacuate the city on September 1. The news disheartened Davis terribly. There had been hope that a failure by Sherman would add enough impetus to the war weariness in the North to lead to Lincoln's defeat for reelection in November. Thompson and Clay had been making considerable efforts to encourage disaffection in the northern and midwestern states, and Grant's being bogged down in a siege at Petersburg had helped. But Sherman's taking of Atlanta almost certainly reversed all that. From September on it appeared increasingly clear that Lincoln would be reelected and that no change in Yankee war aims would ensue.

Moreover, the fall of Atlanta gave Davis serious cause to question

Hood's capacity. Bragg was no longer on the scene, having continued on to Montgomery and Charleston after leaving Atlanta. By now men in the Deep South were showing themselves distinctly uncooperative with Bragg. Governor Thomas Watts of Alabama positively refused even to meet with Bragg except as a courtesy to Davis. Yet the president had to know the true state of affairs in Hood's army, and in the region the Army of Tennessee was mandated to defend. Then there was the concern for loyalty. Unionism had always run high in the mountain regions of the South, but in the face of defeat and retreat, disloyalty was spreading. Newspapers in North Carolina openly avowed reunification with the North. Reports came that Texans in the army thought of themselves as discontented stepchildren of the Confederacy, and brigade commanders complained to him that numbers of their men were joining secret "peace societies" with names like the Heroes of America, dedicated to reunification. Worse yet, reports came to Davis that Governor Brown of Georgia was considering dealing with Sherman to make a separate peace for his state, effectively abandoning the Confederacy. With Davis and Brown barely on civil terms already, it was imperative that they understand each other completely on such an important matter. Davis decided to make yet another trip to the West.[24]

He hoped at first to leave on September 20, but business may have kept him in Richmond for another day, so that, accompanied by his aide Lee and Francis Lubbock of Texas, Davis did not reach Hood's headquarters until September 25. Immediately they went into extended conference, one of the first matters discussed being Hardee, whom Davis now agreed to reassign. The president felt heartened to see the morale of the army improving after its recent disaster and, hoping that its numbers could be augmented by returning absentees, he suggested strategy to recover what had been lost. Davis advised raiding the railroads in Sherman's rear, cutting up his supply and communications, and forcing him to retire northward or else drive straight for the Atlantic coast, while Hood struck at his exposed rear with his cavalry and planted himself in front of Sherman, requiring the Yankees to attack him in an entrenched position. The plan did not differ materially from the only real strategy Johnston had proposed, the difference now being that Johnston had refused to try it without reinforcements that were not available, whereas Hood was willing.[25]

That subject of reinforcements was much on Davis's mind now. Governor Brown had withdrawn from Hood the 10,000 Georgia militia loaned to him during the defense of Atlanta, and Davis hoped through Howell Cobb to persuade Brown to make them available again, along with an estimated 15,000 other men exempted because Brown claimed them as state officials. In this he would fail, but at least he did not have to address the more worrying specter of Georgia making its own separate peace with the Union. Brown received Sherman's proposal on the matter but did not act, nor did Vice President Stephens, who also came into the controversy. But they did not entirely reject Sherman's idea either, and it caught hold elsewhere. Vance of North Carolina called for a convention of the Confederate governors in Augusta on October 17, and Brown hoped that there he might introduce the matter. Happily it came to nothing.[26]

Davis discussed one other matter with Hood before he left his headquarters. His mind was not yet fixed on the matter, but the president considered reviving the "super command" that Johnston had held the year before. It would embrace Hood's army and that of Richard Taylor, under the old designation Military Division of the West. Now even more than before it made a desperate kind of sense, for only in coordination and concentration was there any hope of salvaging the situation between the Mississippi and the lower Atlantic. Taylor commanded the Department of Alabama, Mississippi, and East Louisiana. Hood commanded the adjacent Department of Tennessee and Georgia. The new commander of the division would not relieve either of them of their army commands, except when immediately present with one army or the other, just as Davis had repeatedly instructed Johnston in 1863. Johnston, of course, was out of the question for such a command, however, and this, at last, had forced Davis, after more than three years, to look again toward Beauregard.[27]

Beauregard probably came to Davis's mind soon after the fall of Atlanta. Hood was a good fighter but needed mature supervision. Beauregard could provide that, and from the first, as the idea developed in the president's mind, he probably envisioned the Creole basing himself with the Army of Tennessee. Indeed, when Davis asked Lee to inquire after Beauregard's willingness to accept such an assignment, it appears that Davis initially had in mind relieving Hood and specifically assigning Beauregard to the Army of Tennessee. Learning of his assent, Davis wanted Beauregard to meet with him on his way to see Hood, but the general could not do so. In any case, after his meeting with Hood, Davis decided to retain him in immediate command and asked him how he would feel about Beauregard. Hood did not object. As a result on October 2 Davis issued the order after a meeting with his old adversary in Augusta. Beauregard acted cordially toward the president, though each must have felt inwardly wary of the other. Beauregard had to realize that Davis had simply run out of generals, and now had no alternative but to turn to him. Then, too, this was not exactly a field command, though Beauregard could make it one in an emergency. Otherwise he was to perform an advisory and coordinating function.

As usual, Davis was not too specific about powers and responsibilities, but he did say that "wherever present with an army in the field you will exercise immediate command of the troops." His doing so would not relieve the immediate commander of that army of duty, only of responsibility, since all orders from Beauregard to the army would go through its commanders, Hood or Taylor. Perhaps it occurred to Davis that in this wise he would not have to relieve any more generals of command, to a storm of public protest, while if a battle were lost while Beauregard was present as supercommander, the blame might attach to him rather than to Davis and his generals. Davis should have known better, for by now anything that went awry would be laid at his door.[28]

Sending Beauregard off to confer with Hood, Davis continued a series of morale-boosting speeches he began at Macon on September 28. They were all of a piece, and at Macon, Montgomery, Columbia, and Augusta he adhered repeatedly to the same theme. Though he met them in a time of adversity, the cause was not lost. Without stating names, he struck at Johnston for giving up much of Georgia, and at Brown for accusing Davis himself of abandoning the state. "I love my friends and I forgive my enemies," he said only half in truth. This was not the time and he was not the man to "have any friends to reward or enemies to punish." Had he not just given an important new command to Beauregard, who appeared on the stand with him at Augusta on October 5? Davis even paid tribute to the general's patriotism, and Beauregard responded in kind. Time and time again, however, in every speech Davis appealed for the absentees to return to the ranks, for the cowards and skulkers to stiffen their spines and enlist, and for the "croakers" and carping critics who abused him and his generals to turn their anger on the enemy by taking up arms themselves. He also repeatedly stressed that there could be no reconciliation with the Yankees. He had tried more than once to bring about peace without subjugation, and was rejected. How could any state, by itself, hope to do better? Sherman could and would be beaten, if they all strove together. Look at what Lee achieved against similar odds in Virginia, he told them. And look not at their battles lost, like the man who saw not the sun because of a speck upon it. Rather, look at all they had won, and take heart from their achievements against such dreadful odds. "Be of good cheer," he told the audiences over and over again. "In homely phrase, put your shoulder to the wheel, and work while it is day."[29]

Following his October 5 speech in Augusta, Davis returned to Richmond, exhausted by his third and last trip to the army in the West. As he might have predicted, his foes took every word of his addresses and attacked him for them. Brown's partisans were the most vociferous in damning the president for criticizing their governor on his own soil. Johnston's friends, especially Wigfall, condemned Hood as Davis's puppy and favorite, and even Beauregard's supporters looked suspiciously upon their hero's ambiguous new posting. Yet Davis did have his own partisans as well, and he could take comfort from their cheering words. It was comfort that he needed, for once again Varina saw him "quite feeble" from his exertions. Yet immediately he returned to his killing office routine, working from 10 o'clock in the morning until 7 or 8 in the evening, usually without eating unless she brought him that hamper. Often she found him deep in discussions with Lee, or feverishly doling out correspondence and other duties to his aides. The Chief's staff had dwindled by now, no doubt in response to the wishes of some of his aides to see active service, and criticism that Davis kept too many able-bodied men out of the ranks. His nephew Wood he sent away on naval service. Joseph Davis had already gone to the front, and occasionally now Custis Lee did the same. Browne was in Georgia on a temporary conscript-raising assignment that seemed to become permanent, and Chesnut was down in South Carolina now. This left only Ives, who fell ill that summer, and Preston Johnston. Back in June Davis also appointed Lubbock to be an aide, specifically to advise him on affairs in the far-off Trans-Mississippi. It reflected a tendency of the Chief's to use some of his aides as specialists—Lubbock for the Far West, Lee for Virginia, Chesnut for the lower Atlantic, and Johnston for the Army of Tennessee and Kentucky matters. To the extent that he sought their counsel, it was sound policy, but none of them, except perhaps Johnston, appears to have exerted real influence with the president. He made his own decisions, and all his aides seem to have developed a good ear for what he would wish to hear and for what it would be impolitic to say. To Davis's credit, all of them developed a fierce loyalty to their Chief.[30]

While Varina and his aides, along with the faithful secretary Burton Harrison, tried to lighten Davis's burden, the work he imposed on himself relentlessly continued. He involved himself continually in minor matters like transfers of lower-level officers, promotions, and assignments: "Nine-tenths of the President's time and labor consist of discriminating between applicants for office and for promotion," the clerk Jones complained a few weeks before. At the same time he would not turn away inconsequential civil complaints and petitions and actually made the load heavier for himself unwittingly in his Macon speech when he told his audience that he read every letter he received. It resulted in a flood of new correspondence—all of which he dutifully handled. Then there were his commanders in the field. Without consciously realizing it, Davis compromised the very military system he had set up by allowing his favorites in subordinate commands to go around official channels to correspond directly with him. Polk, Browne, Pemberton, Smith, and more commonly corresponded directly with the president rather than through their immediate commanders or the secretary of war. It only made more work for Davis.

There was some comfort at home. When not off with a basket full of dainties for the wounded soldiers in Richmond's hospitals, Varina gave him constant attention. On June 27 she gave birth to Varina Anne, their last child, and a baby in the house always gave her husband cheer, though some of the society dames of Richmond seemed to take offense when little Varina's mother had to leave them for the child. In her tart Western way, Varina retorted that she "reckoned the President's babies required attention as well as other people's." Many an hour before he went to office or after he returned, Davis spent with the new one, perhaps in the small room that Varina decorated with the innumerable handmade wooden chains and statues carved and sent to her by Confederate soldiers held in Yankee prisons. And even in his office during working hours, Davis could not turn away a child. Perhaps it reminded him of his favorite, the departed Joseph, when three-year-old Willie came into his room and sat in his lap or at his feet, anxiously waiting for his father to drop a pen for him to pick up or send him to fetch a book. When his mother scolded the boy, his ever-indulgent father responded that "you will not grudge me our grave little gentleman's company when you know how I enjoy his presence."[31]

With Willie at his knee, Davis labored through the piles of orders and correspondence. Despite his continuing protestations that everything he did was in the interests of the cause, and not from personal motive, still he indulged a few very human sympathies. Unaccountably, since he had not lived there for forty years, he devoted inordinate attention to the protection of Woodville, Mississippi, from the enemy. Perhaps it was the entreaties of "do not let us be abandoned" that came from his cousins and nephews. Perhaps it was his parents' graves that he wished to preserve inviolate. Other tugs at ties from his early life came when Davis learned that two sons of his old friend John Kinzie, from Fort Winnebago days, had been captured. Ironically, one of them had served on the staff of another old friend, the hated Yankee General David Hunter. Davis assisted a relative in getting to see them.[32]

The subject of men sentenced to death for desertion and other summary infractions continued to occupy the president's mind, and by now he drew considerable criticism for his softheartedness. "The broadcast, inevitable interposition of his prerogative of pardon," complained Beauregard's protégé General Thomas Jordan, "made it plain to the men of the army that there was the fullest immunity for desertion." The opposition press, especially the *Richmond Examiner*, also took up the cry, yet the president continued granting stays of execution. Indeed, earlier in the year he ordered Lee to suspend all such executions pending Davis's opportunity personally to examine their individual cases. Attorney General George Davis complained that "it was the most difficult thing in the world to keep Mr. Davis up to the measure of justice. He wanted to pardon everybody."

Yet with increasing frequency, Davis decided to allow an execution to proceed, whether from the specific nature of the offense, or—much less likely—in response to pressure to be stern. When he concluded not to interfere, however, he nonetheless ordered his generals to give the condemned sufficient time to prepare himself for death. Perhaps the hardest words he had to write as president were those: "I decline to intervene," he would pen. "Sentence to be carried out." Furthermore, despite his bold and occasionally sanguinary public utterances, Davis could not make himself take a ruthlessly retaliatory course toward the enemy. In the Trans-Mississippi, especially Missouri, as well as in northern Virginia, partisan warfare took on very ugly colors, and more than once a Yankee commander summarily hanged captured Rebel guerrillas. Immediately a clamor arose for retaliation in kind, and some Confederates, including even Lee, sanctioned such executions as a means of preventing further outrages by the enemy. But when members of his cabinet pressed Davis for a retaliation policy, and that captured Federals held in Richmond's Libby Prison should be executed, man for man, in payment for Rebels hanged, Davis balked. If he could get a Yankee officer who so murdered Rebel soldiers, said Davis, "I would hang him high as Haman." "But I have not the heart to take these innocent soldiers taken prisoners in honorable warfare, and hang them like convicted criminals." The president refused to set an official policy and left it to his generals in the field. "If they say hang," he declared, "I will forego my individual views."[33]

Even when unwell, Davis kept working. Often Lee was closeted with him that fall, discussing plans, or even talking of the inevitable shortages. In August the president of the Confederate States of America actually devoted himself to trying to find soap for the soldiers of his armies. And if he needed any reminder of the chronic shortages of everything, he need only look at the stationery beneath his pen. His own had run out, and by September he was writing on Treasury Department paper, crossing out the heading with his pen and and writing "Executive" in its place.[34]

Weightier problems confronted the president in departments with different letterheads. Memminger finally resigned in June, and finding a new treasury secretary proved difficult. Reflecting a growing lack of confidence in Seddon, as well as an awareness of the war secretary's poor health, Davis offered him Memminger's post, but Seddon declined. So did several others until, finally, George A. Trenholm, a banker from South Carolina, accepted the position in July. The change did not help fiscal matters, already in disarray, for the Confederacy was running out of money and out of things to sell.[35]

Even more problems confronted Davis from the War Department. After years of being treated largely as a cipher, General Cooper took offense at his position. "I am not simply a bureau [officer] as some view me," he protested, and Davis had to take pains to improve the Adjutant General's image with his officers in the field. Calling him "Chief of Staff of the whole army," the president admonished Seddon that Cooper was not to be treated merely as "an organ for the transmission of the instructions and inquiries" of the Secretary of War. Yet one officer in the War Department observed that Cooper's advice, when sought by Davis, "was seldom acted on," and the old general "was left severely at his own specialty and gradually came to act only as he was regarded—an excellent Adjutant who had not a word to say beyond the routine of his office." Nothing changed for Cooper in the end, and his suffering may well have been due to his being yet another of Davis's friends. As Seddon felt himself falling increasingly out of favor, he became more and more chilly toward Cooper.[36]

Northrop, perennial bone of contention, continued to be a liability. Thirty years before, Davis declared that "I have always thought Lieut. Northrop rather pertinacious than yielding in his opinions." Somehow Davis had thought that obstinacy a virtue, but now he began to see otherwise. Even the ever-diplomatic Lee complained of inefficiencies in the supply system, though never actually naming Northrop as the culprit. Everyone else did not show such reluctance, and after more than three years of universal complaint, Davis was tired. Northrop should be chasing after soap, not the president. Davis actually took his old friend to task earlier that year for losing two herds of cattle ordered to Lee. More and more, as Northrop himself confessed, he and Davis met only "for me to render explanations and to meet difficulties which are naturally prone to give rise to irritations." By early August, perhaps betraying the siege mentality that occasionally beset him, Davis became suspicious that Northrop's friendship for him had changed. Practically a slave to consistency himself, Davis could not understand or forgive inconsistency in others, especially in the behavior of his friends toward him. "After every defection of a friend he suffered keenly," Varina observed, and now Davis felt that Northrop, whom he had loyally sustained for decades, was turning against him. On August 6, in a tense and heated meeting, Davis lashed out at his friend, accused him specifically of attempting to confuse him on a matter at hand, and in general of treating the president shabbily. Unable to say anything, Northrop accepted it quietly as Davis peremptorily dismissed any discussion, and soon left. Having once thought Northrop "incapable of feigning anything," Davis felt shock at seeing—or thinking that he saw him—dissembling now.[37]

Yet later that day Davis sent a note of apology to Northrop and in November would actually nominate him for a brigadier's commission, despite his own doubts of the man's capacity and the universal outcry about his inefficiency. Blind as always in such matters, Davis had only recently insisted to Vance that "promotions of officers have been guided *exclusively* by military considerations, and that they have almost invariably been made upon the recommendations received from their fellow-soldiers and commanders." Yet he would have been hard pressed to produce any such encomiums from soldiers or officers for Northrop, and once his promotion was known, the complaints only escalated, especially when Northrop assumed an even more imperious than normal attitude. Like Bragg and Polk and others, Northrop was a problem that Davis simply would not see and would not solve.[38]

Part of the reason in this instance is that Davis came more and more to see Seddon as the overriding problem, both for his friend Northrop and for Cooper. Serious rumors of a breach between them went through the War Department back in May. Seddon reportedly told a friend that he found Davis "the most difficult man to get along with" that he had ever known. In June Davis "ranted and scolded" at Colonel Gorgas for trying to draft a law that infringed on his presidential prerogatives, and clashed with Seddon over appointments of quartermasters and commissaries. While Robert Kean in the Bureau of War noted in June that Davis "seems to possess a most unenviable facility for converting friends into enemies," Davis himself began confiding to others a desire to rid himself of Seddon. Yet when Seddon confronted Davis with these stories, they had a full discussion of their differences, supposedly concluding with Davis's assurance that there was no one else in the War Department whom he would prefer to have in Seddon's place. It was a conditional endorsement at best, and reflected the swings of temper that Davis suffered now, just like his explosion at Northrop.

Indeed, barely a day after his upset with the commissary general, the president collided with both Seddon and Cooper over the minor matter of an appointment for a commissary to settle his accounts. Davis gave Seddon a "cutting rebuke" for issuing the instructions "by order of the President," saying imperiously that it was a great presumption for anyone other than himself to use such language. Perhaps Davis had forgotten that when he was a secretary of war, he had used the same form, incurring Winfield Scott's wrath. Davis soon calmed again, but clearly Seddon's tenure was threatened. On September 20 Davis dispatched his aide Johnston to southwest Virginia to see General Breckinridge relative to certain "verbal instructions" from the president. Davis had used such emissaries in the past to sound out potential cabinet appointees, and Johnston may have been on just such a mission now.[39]

Observers saw these acts and moods in isolation, and as they affected themselves or their departments particularly. If any of them could have seen it from Davis's point of view, they might better have understood him now. They were losing the war. Davis would never admit that, perhaps not even to himself, but the signs were plain, and all of the blame was falling on him, a man whose whole makeup was based upon the assuredness that in any situation, he was right and without blame. So many trusted friends had let him down or turned on him—Wigfall, Yancey, Joseph E. Johnston—and now others like Northrop and Cooper seemed hostile to him. The new Congress showed unfriendly colors during its first session, and the second session due to commence on November 7 could be expected to do the same. The governors, especially Brown and Vance, were flirting with treason in their opposition and their independence and he could not make them understand that to win *national* freedom, they must for a time yield some of their precious states' rights. Even his vice president, Stephens, stood clearly with his enemies now, declaring that he believed Davis preferred the re-election of Lincoln to that of his opponent McClellan. Davis bristled at this, fearing that it would damage Confederate efforts to defeat Lincoln in November. Demanding an explanation from Stephens, he got a long one, and Davis replied that he would not enter into any lengthy controversy since it would be neither useful nor becoming. Having said that, he then went ahead to write a letter of more than 4,000 words in response, with the same old point-by-point lecturing that he had used on so many before Stephens. More than once he passed points by saying that "I cannot spare the time to refute" them, then went right on and spent the time anyhow. The two had seen each other no more than two or three times in the past two years, as Stephens petulantly absented himself from Richmond, and Davis just as petulantly refused to keep the vice president informed even of the most important matters. Certainly it did not help that Stephens hailed from Georgia, that hotbed of opposition. At one point Davis actually forbade his aides even to discuss Georgia in his presence.[40]

Then there was Bragg. His sycophancy, his ill temper and jealousy, his presumed spying and attempts to take credit for the ideas of others, made his name anathema in the War Department. Men like Kean took quiet glee in little triumphs, as in August when Kean noted that "Beauregard had made Bragg eat dirt" over a dispute. "Bragg gets worse and worse, more and more mischievous," Kean declared on September 25. "He resembles a chimpanzee as much in character as he does in appearance." Davis had found by now that the office of general-in-chief was not working, or at least not with Bragg as incumbent. The man generated respect from no one and hostility from almost everyone. Others in the War Department detested him, and Davis himself was actually doing the work of the position anyhow. Bragg had become little more than an adviser. By October, as Federal threats to the vital North Carolina blockade running port of Wilmington mounted, Davis decided to send Bragg there to assume command personally. He still held his title as general-in-chief, but in effect the president reduced him to command of the newly designated Department of North Carolina. When Bragg left Richmond on October 17, observers felt immediate fears that Wilmington would now surely be lost, but delight, nevertheless, "that this element of discord, acrimony, and confusion is withdrawn from here."[41]

More and more plagues settled on the president as the long months of weary siege at Petersburg continued. He could not escape the massive problem of prisoners of war, especially with the Yankees' refusal to exchange. As much as it drained Confederate resources to provide for Yankee prisoners, Davis needed even more the tens of thousands of Confederates held in Northern compounds. He even approved a scheme of his nephew Wood's and others to make a raid on the Point Lookout, Maryland, prison camp to free Southerners held there, but was soon mortified to hear the contemplated raid spoken of on the streets. In the face of the leak, he had no choice but to cancel the plan. And as conditions deteriorated in his own prisons, Davis could do little. Hearing disturbing reports of affairs at Georgia's massive Camp Sumter at Andersonville, and feeling genuine sympathy for suffering prisoners, Davis ordered General John H. Winder, the capital's provost marshal, to go there in person to assume command. But Winder's first report in August was terribly disheartening. There were 32,000 men crammed into a stockade designed for 10,000, with every manner of sanitary and supply problem imaginable. It distressed Davis immeasurably, for however much he condemned the enemy's leaders, he consistently regarded the average Billy Yank as merely a soldier innocently obeying orders. Knowing of the suffering of these men now, he met with Lee one afternoon to discuss the practicality of trying to relocate most of them to the Trans-Mississippi, where beef and other provisions were plentiful. Lee pointed out that their own men in the ranks suffered from the same want as the Yankee prisoners, coolly advising the president, "Do not distress yourself."[42]

Yet if this was not supposed to distress Davis, everything else did. Lincoln won reelection in November despite efforts from Canada that had been futile at the outset. Thompson and Clay, along with others Davis sent to assist them, were consistently misled about the extent of disaffection in the North, and the presumably formidable Knights of the Golden Circle proved to be almost a fiction. They, in turn, gave Davis an imperfect understanding of what could be achieved, and he supported them with funds and men to the extent possible. He approved a scheme for releasing prisoners at Johnson's Island that came to nothing and even fell under the spell of an apparently unstable minister who proposed that their efforts had failed because "God has been against" Thompson and the "unholy" associates with him. The Reverend Kenzey Stewart got Davis's authorization for $20,000 to organize a raid on the

Elmira, New York, prison compound. It is even possible that in September Davis authorized Captain Thomas Conrad and a small group of men quietly to infiltrate Washington to study the possibility of capturing President Lincoln and bringing him back to the Confederacy as a hostage for the release of Confederate prisoners of war. Years later Conrad claimed that when he presented the idea to Davis, the president sent him to Benjamin and Seddon with instructions for them to facilitate his plan, though Davis always denied any such scheme. Lincoln was a "Western" man, he said, and would certainly resist, preferring death to capture. Certainly the capture of a high civil official did not exceed the boundaries of civilized warfare. After all, Davis could still well remember the sounds of the firing as Dahlgren's raid came so perilously close to Richmond, its intent to kill or capture the president and his cabinet.[43]

None of these and other schemes came to fruition, nor did an abortive attempt at peace negotiations instigated by New York newspaperman Horace Greeley, though Davis leapt at the possibility, only to see the correspondence in the episode embarrassingly spread in the newspapers. Then came more bad news in the aftermath of Lincoln's reelection, this time from his own side of the lines. When he left Hood and Beauregard in early October, Davis believed that they were all agreed on plans for coming operations. But in the days that followed Hood acted largely on his own, not consulting Beauregard, and finally devising an entirely new strategy. He dreamed of marching north, recovering Tennessee, and even moving into Kentucky to the Ohio. Sherman, now marching his army across Georgia on the way to the Atlantic, would have to follow him. If he did not, Hood could turn and race to reinforce Lee in a drive against Grant, and then together they could move against Sherman. It was a wildly impractical idea, reminiscent of some of Beauregard's schemes, though that general opposed the plan. Nevertheless, he did not try to hinder Hood but only informed Davis of Hood's intentions, leaving it to the president to agree or demur.

Learning of it after the fact, and with Hood already in motion, Davis did not call him back, though he confessed that "I consider this movement into Tennessee ill-advised." He felt that Sherman would regard Hood's move as "of minor importance," as indeed he did. Rather than turning his whole army back, Sherman sent only a part of it, led by General George Thomas, and in bloody battles at Franklin on November 30 and at Nashville on December 15–16, Thomas effectively smashed Hood's army in its last great battles. Davis gave Hood only occasional tactical advice during the campaign, and though he neither planned nor approved the operation, still the immediate outcry after the defeats laid the blame to him. "The President will suffer," war clerk Jones wrote after Franklin, as indeed he did. He probably also censured himself privately. A year or two earlier, Jefferson Davis would never have allowed Hood to launch such a campaign unilaterally. Not even Lee's great invasions of the North jumped off without prior presidential and cabinet approval. And once the campaign was under way, Davis felt increasing doubts about Hood's generalship, even tallying the total casualties Hood suffered in his first ten weeks in command and comparing them—unfavorably—with those of Johnston's last ten. That Davis allowed Hood to proceed shows just how distracted and exhausted he was by now.[44]

Only the Trans-Mississippi failed to send the president bad news this fall, and that mainly because of the dismal state of communications. One letter from Texas took a full year to reach him, and much of Kirby Smith's correspondence arrived four months late, chiefly revealing that general's pique when Davis ventured to criticize some of his imperious actions. Alas, far more timely news came of Sherman's march to the sea and of his capture of Savannah on December 21. Davis had feared losing Savannah less than he feared a failure to resist successfully Sherman's march, but now both were accomplished facts. In anticipation of the emergency, Davis extended Beauregard's supercommand to include Hardee's department, and the Creole soon went to Savannah and then Charleston to see to their defense. Still revealing a distrust of Beauregard, Davis sent the recovered Colonel Ives to Charleston to "keep me advised." Meanwhile Davis sent Bragg to Augusta late in November to aid in defending that city, and then sent him right back to Wilmington three weeks later. The president was acting as general-in-chief and secretary of war all in one, and now relying only on Lee for military advice.[45]

Only in Virginia was there even minor success, and that was limited. Breckinridge was succeeding in holding onto his department, but the Shenandoah was lost decisively to Sheridan in October. Meanwhile, Grant spread ever-widening arcs of works around Petersburg and Richmond, threatening to encircle the capital and cut off all routes of supply and escape. Only the coming of harsh weather slowed his operations, but Davis knew they would resume in the spring.

"Alas for President Davis's government!" Jones lamented on December 17. "It is now in a painful strait." "His enemies are assailing him bitterly, attributing all our misfortunes to his incompetence." Indeed, the opponents escalated their attacks anew, and from Canada Clay advised his wife not to set foot in Richmond or to attempt to contact Davis. "He is in a sea of trouble," wrote the old friend. "Congress is turning madly against him." Clay doubted that the president had any reliable friends in Congress any longer, while adding that "he has less and less power to intimidate his enemies, and they grow more numerous every day." They seemed to be gathering around him like jackals at a wounded lion. Wigfall, ever the ringleader, was making plans for action to remove all military power from the president's hands, and he hoped to get together with Brown and Vance for a renewed call for a convention of the states "to take the best next step for the accomplishment of the object." What Wigfall's true object might be, few could say. Even though Congress was back in session, the Texan would not arrive until after the New Year. Only then would the president know what his enemies had in store for him.[46]

The unrelenting mental and physical pressure became too much for Jefferson Davis. By mid-December the "sea of trouble" was drowning him, and his health failed. Rumors of his illness swept through the capital's streets on the fifteenth. Some said it was "an affection of the head," others that it was severe neuralgia. Wilder rumors said that he was dying, even dead, and many did not fail to note that Vice President Stephens had come to the city for the first time in months. Could he be waiting to assume the presidency in the wake of Davis's death? Others maintained that Davis was not ill or dead at all, and that the stories were only circulated to gain sympathy for the beleaguered chief executive. But by December 19 Davis was back at work, pasting together remnants of battalions and companies to make a new regiment in Mississippi. Too ill to go to his office, he worked at home and took refuge in the petty details in which he always found sanctuary from the great issues he could not solve. "It is difficult to get his attention to any business just now but *appointments*," the War Office found on December 22. On Christmas Eve the clerk Jones noted bitterly that "the President is hard at work making majors, etc." Davis had to feel that he accomplished something. With the war collapsing around him, at least he could still give promotions to deserving men, winning a hundred tiny administrative battles to distract his fevered brain from the greater losses everywhere else.[47]

Christmas 1864 came clear and pleasant, with a beautiful white frost over the sidewalks and shrubbery of Richmond. Boys stole their fathers' rifles and shotguns and fired precious rounds into the air to celebrate the day, and the people of the capital evinced a need to be jolly and even intemperate after a season of such woe. The less frolicsome continued to complain about the president even on that day, some declaring that Davis should be deposed and Lee made dictator. "Every one felt the cataclysm which impended," remembered Varina.

In the Executive Mansion, the Davises tried to make this, their fourth war Christmas, a day for the children. Varina scraped and improvised to make a mince pie and a little ersatz eggnog 'for the servants. The children rummaged through their large room on the second floor for eyeless dolls, broken tops, three-legged horses, and other discarded toys to be sent to the orphans of the city for their holiday, while Varina worked with civic women to find candies, a few little delicacies, and even a Christmas tree for the unfortunates.

The evening before, the family invited neighboring children in to help string apples and popcorn for their tree, while a neighbor molded tiny candles to place in the boughs. Homemade paper cornucopias held sweets sent by a confectioner, and Varina made quite a party for the young people out of rolling and pasting the cones with little love poems written on them. Then the lady cake and gingersnaps were passed around, and they all drank the eggnog. Little Jeff took a sip from his mother's cup, then said to his father, "Now I just know this is Christmas."

The president himself, still unwell, no doubt felt relief when all the guests left and just the family remained. Then they stuffed their stockings, one for each member of the family, as well as the aides. The next morning it was the children who were up first, and early, racing to their stockings. The president and his wife came in due time, confronted by a cheery holiday greeting from the servants who, if they said it before their masters did, were entitled to a gift. When they got to their own stockings, Varina discovered that her husband had found for her six cakes of soap, a book of poetry (printed on wallpaper due to scarcity), and other things sent by admirers. Varina gave Jefferson a pair of chamois riding gauntlets sent to her by a Virginia woman, along with little love letters from each of the children.

After breakfasting they walked to St. Paul's Episcopal Church to hear the Reverend Minnegerode's sermon, and then back to the Executive Mansion for their afternoon dinner of roast turkey and beef, followed by mince pie, plum pudding, and a life-size hen of spun sugar nesting on blancmange eggs. Their chef had husbanded ingredients for weeks and more to make this one feast. The children and the aides reveled in it and ate until their stomachs tugged at their buttons.

President Davis, if he ate at all, did so sparingly. His holiday lay in watching little Jeff, Willie, Maggie, and six-month-old Winnie enjoy a day when the war seemed forgotten. Then, their dinner done, the Davises went back to the basement of St. Paul's, where the tree decorated for the orphans was unveiled. They all sang songs, then gave the ersatz presents to the children of the city. Feeling more joy than he had in months, Davis became so enrapt in the scene that he turned Santa to help pass out the presents but made a confusion of it as he gleefully gave anything that came to hand to any outstretched arm. Varina pulled him away and assigned him the task of untangling two little ones who had wrapped themselves up in a popcorn string. Yet Davis could not restrain himself. Here there were no croakers and carpers, no discordant generals or dissident politicians. Here he was making everyone happy. Unwinding the tots from their string, he crept back to the great tree whenever Varina looked away and stole the apples from its boughs, giving them to the smallest children in the hall. Varina saw him all the same, but she also saw the brief expression of joy that transformed his face, and she could not begrudge him his few moments of contentment and happiness.

That evening they went to a "starvation party," at a neighbor's, where the shortages preempted any thought of refreshments. Davis and Varina watched a host of crisply attired young officers and their ladies dance through the dark hours to the songs from a piano in the drawing room. Then it was back down Clay Street to their home. The beautiful day could not last forever. Rain commenced falling, and the sky turned dark and ominous again, matching the returning mood of the city. For Jefferson Davis, as for the Confederacy, Christmas had been only an interlude. When he awoke in the morning—if he slept at all—the war was still there.[48]

Faction Has Done Much

Snow blanketed the ground on New Year's Day 1865. It was a Sunday, and President Davis went to St. Paul's to hear Minnegerode preach. Convalescing nicely now, he still wore a woolen cap when leaving the house, probably to keep the cold from tormenting the residual neuralgia in his head. Nothing could help the troubled mind inside, however. "Another year has gone and the new one brings to us no cessation of our bitter trials," he wrote to his sister Amanda a week later. "We are here in a constant state of excitement from the proximity of the Enemy in superior numbers." Yankee raids on railroads made it hard to feed Lee's men, and the number of skulkers and shirkers who continued to stay out of the military service "have a heavy responsibility for the prolongation of [the] war," he wrote. In his troubled heart, now, Davis thought more and more of his family that he had not seen in so long. Uncertain mails delayed letters from Joseph for some time. As for Amanda, "am[i]d many and grievo[us] [respo]nsibilities my heart turns [with] increasing desir[e] [to] the sister who from childhood has been to me the memory of all that was good and generous."[1]

Indeed, this same day the president wrote more letters to other family members, unable to draw his thoughts away from Mississippi and happier times. He needed those thoughts to carry away from Richmond. As he left the house each morning about 9:30 and walked down Twelfth Street to the Capitol Square, then across its graveled paths to the executive offices in the Treasury Building between Main and Franklin Streets, the attacks of his enemies seemed to strike him from all sides. "The malcontents," as he called them, had seized upon the restlessness occasioned by the length of the war and were urging men not to comply with his conscription and subsistence procurement measures. "Magnifying every reverse and prophesying ruin they have produced public depression," he said, "and sown the seeds of disintegration." He saw full well the irony that some of these men, onetime nationalists of the Federalist school, now "invoke the cause of *State rights* to sustain a policy which in proportion to the extent of its adoption must tend to destroy the existence of the States of our Confederacy and leave them conquered provinces." It was, he lamented, a "perversion of truth to the maintenance of error as now appears in the conduct of those who assume the guise of state rights men to sink the States by the process of disintegration into imbecility and ultimate submission to Yankee despotism."[2]

While Davis pondered the fact that he, the onetime champion of localism, now stood practically alone as a Confederate nationalist, evidences of the spread of disaffection came continually to his attention. In Breckinridge's department disloyal men had actually declared the Free State of Southwest Virginia, with their own governor, general, and militia. In North Carolina's western reaches Confederate authorities could no longer maintain any meaningful control over the population. Howell Cobb wrote him from Georgia of the "deep despondency in the public mind extending in too many instances to disaffection." Hood's disaster and Sherman's march to Savannah dispirited the people and had been siezed upon by Davis's enemies like Brown and Stephens. "The teachings of those who are hostile to the administration have prepared the way for all this dispondency and disaffection, to be concentrated to a feeling of opposition to your administration." Cobb had never been one of those malcontents but generally a good friend to the president, and when he wrote of such ill feeling, Davis listened. Even if the president could turn his back on these expressions, he could not hide from the fact that by now every Confederate state but South Carolina had seen regiments of volunteers form and take service—in the Union army.[3]

Davis's own friends could see much of the part he had played in bringing this about. On New Year's Day the clerk Jones noted in his diary that "the President is considered really a man of ability, and eminently qualified to preside over the Confederate States, if independence were attained and we had peace. . . . But he is probably not equal to the role he is now called upon to play." It was a common sentiment among Davis's friends. Reuben Davis thought him well equipped for "rulership in a settled and powerful government." Where "a firm, strong hand to guide, and a polished intellect" were needed, Davis would have succeeded. "A revolution calls for different qualities," he believed, and among them was flexibility. "Gifted with some of the highest attributes of a statesman," said Reuben Davis, Jefferson Davis "lacked the pliancy which enables a man to adapt his measures to the crises." The president, instead, tried "to bend the crises to his measures." Jones echoed these sentiments. "He has not the broad intellect requisite for the gigantic measures needed in such a crisis." Worse, Davis could not leave behind him his personal prejudices and would not court the friendship of the men like Yancey and Brown, who made the revolution. "The consequence is that many of these influential men are laboring to break down his administration." Indeed they were. The calls for Lee to depose Davis continued into the new year, though the general would have none of it, and clerks in the War Department spoke intemperately of wanting to see revolution, and the deposing of the president. The spiteful Toombs declared to an equally disaffected General Gustavus Smith that "nothing can save us but the overthrow of Davis & that must come quickly."[4]

But it was in Congress that Davis's chief antagonists were to be found. "Now when we require the brain and heart of the country in the legislative halls of the Confederacy and of the States all must have realized how much it is otherwise," he lamented on January 8, "and if there be a growing spirit of opposition to continued effort it is I think to be attributed to the bad conduct of those whose official position made it their duty to cultivate confidence and animate patriotism." Congress did not disappoint him, and Wigfall led the way, backed by a Senate majority now hostile to the president. Indeed, on January 20, Speaker of the House Thomas Bocock of Virginia met privately with the president to tell him that the delegation from the Old Dominion was considering a proposal of a resolution of no confidence in the cabinet, and warning him to be ready.[5]

In the end their efforts achieved little other than to make both Congress and the president lose some dignity. Wigfall ranted on so that even his friends begged him to forget his hatred of Davis in the interests of the cause. Mary Chesnut, watching Wigfall's antics, lamented that the Texan from whom they had hoped so much "has only been a destructive." In a series of resolutions, Wigfall tried to curb the president's control of the army and navy both. He also introduced a resolution calling for Benjamin's resignation, which failed, and threw his support to a January 9 bill calling for a general-in-chief. This battle Davis fought and in the end won, to a degree, for accompanying resolutions called for the reinstatement of Johnston to the Army of Tennessee and Beauregard to the South Carolina, Georgia, and Florida command. By working through his friends in Congress, Davis got the bills modified so that Beauregard was not mentioned at all, and the wording about Johnston only expressed a sentiment that should he be reinstated, such a move would "be hailed with joy" by the army. As for the general-in-chief legislation, it was eventually revised to a form that Davis found inoffensive, and passed. There was a common assumption that Davis would appoint Lee to the position, and so he did, on February 6. Some observers regarded the measure as a condemnation of Davis, as it was surely intended by Wigfall and others, yet the president emerged with his authority over the military undamaged, for the legislation gave the general-in-chief no specific powers and still left Davis with the right to appoint his staff.[6]

By early March the troublesome Congress was wearing itself out, with little productive to do, and more often engaged in minor squabbles of the sort that had beset the Confederate government almost from the outset. Debates largely covered setting a time to adjourn, as many felt anxious to get home before Grant's grip on Richmond trapped them in the capital. After minor parting shots at Davis, including sending a committee to demand information as to his future plans and further attempts to curb his appointive powers, Congress finally adjourned on March 18 with not even a quorum present. One of the Senate's final actions was a failure to override a presidential veto, after which it received a message from Davis lamenting politely that Congress would not stay in session longer to attend to the legislation he felt necessary to sustain their cause. In the House not even this pitiful last jab from the opposition could be mustered.[7]

"I hope the badgering of congress does not annoy you," Joseph wrote his brother the day after the adjournment. "Much of it I am convinced is from personal resentment." While the attacks did bother Davis more deeply than he let on, outwardly he remained calm during the session, even to the point that some thought him subdued by his opponents. Yet he raged inside as always when questioned or challenged. "Faction has done much to cloud our prospects and impair my power to serve the country," he told Cobb's wife on March 30. He gave Wigfall and the others faint credit for having loftier motives, but it sounded insincere. "The indulgence of evil passion against myself injures not the individual only but the cause also of which I am a zealous though feeble representative." He hoped against hope that his opponents would discover their mischievous error in time to repair the damage they were doing to the cause. When the Senate published a rejoinder to his final message to them before their adjournment, lamenting that more work needed to be done, he accused them of calculating to destroy public confidence. Worse, he said, "No opportunity was afforded to me to reply and correct the many mis-statements." As always, he believed he could destroy his enemies by having the last word. "Whether truth can overtake falsehood has always been doubtful," he lamented, "and in this case the race is most unequal."[8]

Yet however much Davis decried the individual influence of the men who railed against him, and it was considerable, the fact remained that from first to last they were collectively impotent. The opposition never mounted a serious challenge to any of his important legislation. Conscription, martial law, suspension of habeas corpus, taxation, and a host of other issues came out of Congress just as Davis wanted them. Never did a majority in the House stand against him, and only in this final session did the Senate opponents outnumber his supporters. In the entire four years since the Provisional Congress first sat, only one Davis veto was overridden, and that one a petty matter of the franking privilege for newspapers.

The opposition never succeeded in amounting to an "opposition" but remained first to last a petty group of squabbling, self-important, second-rate politicians with nothing to bind them together other than what Reuben Davis called "ignoble jealousies" and "unworthy enmities." Jefferson Davis made the ideal foil for them, for not only did his well-known weaknesses give them ample targets for their barbs, but his inability as a diplomat and unwillingness to try any personal politicking with them guaranteed that any breaches opened would only widen. "Resenting opposition with the unalterable resentment of a reserved, proud and self-centred nature," said Reuben Davis, "it was not a possibility with him to recognize the justice of such opposition, even when proved by the fatal results of a contrary policy." And this Davis was one of the president's friends, yet he admitted frankly that he found Jefferson Davis obstinate, guided by his prejudices for and against men, "unbending in his conviction," and continually sustained by the "serene approval of his mind and conscience." Worse, while he would not try to appease his foes individually, as a group they presented no focused target for attack. They had no program, no policy, no alternatives—in short, no tangible issues that Davis could concentrate against. Consequently, if he responded at all it could only be to the individuals, which only enhanced the personal nature of the discord. By its very nature, the political atmosphere of the Confederacy presented a winless situation not even a brilliantly gifted executive could have overcome. Davis, lacking such gifts, never had a chance.[9]

The opposition did achieve one victory, or so they thought, but in fact they probably simply allowed Davis to do something he had considered for some months anyhow. The rumors of Seddon's unstable tenure in the War Department never abated from the past fall, and by mid-January they appeared with renewed frequency, accompanied now by expectations that Breckinridge would be appointed in his stead. It helped that the Kentuckian had been called to Richmond for unknown reasons and was staying at the home of an influential citizen. Then the Virginia congressional delegation met on January 16 to discuss the no-confidence resolution that Bocock warned Davis of four days later. Seddon learned of the meeting first, however. Stung that fellow Virginians would speak of him thus, Seddon gave Davis his resignation on January

18, effective with the appointment of a successor. Two days later Assistant Secretary of War John A. Campbell also resigned, that Davis might completely reorganize the War Department. Immediately the president began to receive urgings from influential friends that he appoint Breckinridge.[10]

Rumors of Seddon's resignation hit the streets by January 21, but so did rumors that Davis refused to accept it. Hunter apparently tried to talk Seddon out of the move, as the opposition had looked favorably on his being in Davis's cabinet earlier on, and intimates still knew of Seddon's dissent with many of Davis's policies. Others called on the president directly and asked that the resignation not be accepted. The Virginia delegation had stepped on its own foot, for in espousing the no-confidence measure, the only cabinet member they injured was their fellow Virginian Seddon. Davis withheld acting on the resignation for almost two full weeks, but finally on February 1 he accepted it, though not without noting that he did not recognize that Congress had any power to influence the tenure of executive officials appointed constitutionally by the president. His protest was largely for effect, since Seddon wanted to resign anyhow because of poor health. By releasing the correspondence in the whole matter to the press, Davis allowed it to look as if Virginia congressmen had tried to usurp executive authority but only harmed one of their own and got a scolding from the president in the bargain. It was a small victory over the opposition, and a warning as well that Davis could fight back effectively on occasion and knew how to use the press if he had to.[11]

There was another reason that Davis delayed accepting Seddon's resignation. He did, indeed, want Breckinridge for the position. In fact, he had considered the Kentuckian as far back as late 1861, and probably again in the fall of 1864 when relations with Seddon were breaking down, explaining Preston Johnston's mission to southwest Virginia to see the general. Breckinridge made good sense from many standpoints. Having been the South's candidate in the presidential election of 1860, he enjoyed enormous popularity with the public. Almost every faction in the military and government circles respected and admired him. Lee thought very highly of the man who had protected his flank in the Shenandoah the previous spring and summer, and of the few victories—minor at that—of the past fall and winter, several had been Breckinridge's. Better yet, he was widely respected in the troubled remnant of the Army of Tennessee, being the only one of the dissident generals to emerge with an enhanced reputation after the wars with Bragg. Even Beauregard and Johnston thought highly of him, as had Sidney Johnston. The still-influential Kentucky lobby fawned upon him, naturally, and in fact his only bitter enemy in the whole Confederacy seemed to be Bragg.

There lay one of the problems: Breckinridge could hardly be expected to work effectively with Bragg. Indeed, rumors even suggested that the Kentuckian made Bragg's dismissal a condition of accepting the post, but Davis did not have to go that far. Thankfully, Lee's appointment as nominal general-in-chief effectively removed Bragg from the War Department. Besides, he was still in North Carolina and would remain there. But Breckinridge also had another condition: Northrop had to go. Here was a real problem for Davis. He could hardly abandon a friend, though he knew Northrop to be a heavy liability. Yet he needed Breckinridge, who brought a level of civil and military stature to the War Department that none of his predecessors approached. According to an official close to Davis, the Kentuckian made it clear that "on condition that he was to be a positive, and not a passive, chief of the Department," he would take the portfolio. By January 30 the president gave in. Even before Davis sent Breckinridge's name to the Senate for confirmation, on February 6, he relieved Northrop and temporarily put Breckinridge's friend Eli Bruce of Kentucky in place as commissary general. Soon after taking office, Breckinridge formally relieved Northrop and put General Isaac M. St. John in his place. Within a month the commissary system was winning praise from Lee and others for being better run than at any time during the war.

Certainly Davis took comfort from this upswing in War Department affairs. He and Breckinridge were not close, never had been, and never would be, but they respected each other. This benefit came at a price, however. Breckinridge was no cipher like Walker or Seddon, to be dominated at will by the president. Arguably the Kentuckian enjoyed greater personal popularity in the South than Davis, and many spoke of him as a successor should the nation last long enough to elect another president. Moreover, though eminently diplomatic, still Breckinridge was strong-willed and not accustomed to being dominated by anyone. His conditions for accepting the portfolio showed his independence, and Davis's acceptance of those conditions, as well as his choice of Breckinridge in the first place, evidenced a number of concessions on his part. Congress liked Breckinridge and even invited him to a seat in its deliberations. Thus the new secretary could be expected to win friends for the administration. Furthermore, the appointment represented a tacit yielding of some of Davis's jealously guarded executive prerogatives in the War Department. As subsequent events would show, henceforth Breckinridge, not the president, ran that department. Indeed, before long people would speculate that Breckinridge was running more than just his department—perhaps even the government itself. Yet one man in the government complained that it came too late, "like sending for a competent physician when the patient was already physicked and poulticed to death by quacks."[12]

Davis would not have accepted such a person in his cabinet if he had not been tired, worn down by the years of strain, opprobrium, and constant controversy. He fell ill again in early February, and most who saw him commented on his feeble appearance and often distracted state of mind. Even as he struggled to deal with the crisis in his War Department, other old foes haunted him anew. Gustavus Smith seemed to keep popping up in positions of minor authority and in January took command, under Hardee, of a subdistrict in Georgia. Davis quickly assigned Howell Cobb to the region so that he would rank Smith and could prevent any recurrences of the problems that general had created on the Peninsula—and, no doubt, to deny his old antagonist any real authority. Worse was the case of Joseph E. Johnston. Like Davis's old fevers, he never really went away. Barely a month after he relieved the general back in July, Davis learned that Johnston and his followers were working assiduously as "something like an organised band" to publicize a defense of the general's operations. They kept the newspapers continually supplied with inflammatory letters demanding the general's reinstatement and charging Davis with personal enmity, which by this time, of course, was entirely true. Davis fought back as well as he could, first attempting to hold up publication of Johnston's report of his operations before Atlanta due to its "potential for controversy," and then by building a massive dossier on Johnston's military conduct going all the way back to First Manassas. He did the latter when Congress started to call for Johnston's report and he wanted to be ready to append to it all the documentation necessary to show that he had been justified in his treatment of that general throughout the war.[13]

In the end Davis thought better of sending the 4,500-word review of Johnston's career to Congress, but the controversy raged on just the same when Hood's report of his operations arrived. While Hood castigated Johnston's conduct of the campaign prior to his relief, implying much blame for Hood's own later failures, still Davis was not pleased with the document, knowing that it would only stir the pot of controversy, as indeed it did. Davis spent a whole day discussing it with his cabinet but turned it over to Congress quickly enough since it still supported his own position toward Johnston. Meanwhile, he gave Johnston's report to the Senate but only with an appended protest that it should not be published. Davis could tell that the tide ran against him. From all quarters came urgings that the general be reappointed to replace Hood. "Genl Johnston is the man to restore confidence in the army—and country," the trusted Howell Cobb advised early in January. "Nothing you could do in this respect would command more cordial and universal approval than the restoration of Johnston." Friends in Alabama feared that Davis would never recover his lost popularity if he did not put Johnston in command again, and even his brother Joseph admitted that

he "regreted deeply the removal of Genl. Johnson and hope his restoration may silence the clamor if it does not restore our loss."[14]

Once again Davis had to yield, but Lee and Breckinridge made it
easier for him. Lee, now general-in-chief, suggested to the secretary of
war that Beauregard, facing Sherman in the Carolinas, was in poor
health and might not be physically up to the task before him. That
department had no one else who could replace him, as even Hardee was
ill. Lee said that Johnston was the only officer who would be suitable and
that he would assign him to the command "if he was ordered to report
to me." Breckinridge then suggested that Lee specifically request Johnston, which he did. Thus Davis could now quiet his enemies by allowing
Johnston to resume a field command once more, without appearing to
have backed down. He was simply showing his faith in his general-in-
chief by granting his wishes, though he would still tell a supporter in
Mississippi that he did so "in the hope that General Johnston's soldierly
qualities may be made serviceable to his country when acting under
General Lee's orders, and that in his new position those defects which I
found manifested by him when serving as an independent commander
will be remedied by the control of the general-in-chief."

Davis took no pleasure in seeing Johnston resume field command,
especially since by relieving Beauregard he would automatically accede
to leadership of the remnant of the old Army of Tennessee. Hood had
resigned of his own accord in January. The episode may even have
strained Davis's relations with Lee briefly, for Lee had always been a
forthright supporter of Johnston, though never a member of the clique
of conspirators scheming for that general's restoration. A few days after
the appointment of Johnston, Davis heard rumors said to be based on
Lee's views on the destruction of private property to keep it out of the
hands of the enemy. He asked Lee to come and see him "if you can spare
the time." Lee could not spare the time. Within the past week Charleston
and Columbia had been lost to the Federals, Bragg evacuated Wilmington, and Lee himself advised Davis that it might be necessary to abandon
Richmond to avoid losing his army. Lee was too busy just then to come
talk with the president about tobacco and cotton. Moreover, Davis called
Lee to him frequently for conferences, and the general probably tired of
the interminable discussions without conclusions and of the plans and
dreams that revealed an increasing unwillingness to address the reality
of their situation. When the general said that he could not come, Davis
felt hurt and showed it in a sharp response: "Rest assured I will not ask
your views in answer to measures," he said. "Your counsels are no longer
wanted in this matter." Sensing that he had hurt the president's feelings,
Lee went to see him after all, and though their correspondence temporarily took on a cool tone, the injury was soon forgotten. By this time,

Davis just needed to talk to Lee for security and support. He needed to have his friend with him for comfort.[15]

Fleeting glimmers of hope appeared from other quarters this winter, the most promising coming out of a seemingly insignificant request from Francis P. Blair of Maryland. He wanted to cross the lines to Richmond to try to retrieve some personal papers supposedly taken from his home during a Confederate raid. The seventy-three-year-old editor had known Davis before the war, and thus he now addressed the president directly. But his simple note of request proved to be a blind "to answer enquiries as to the object [of] my visit." In an accompanying letter he explained that he had a plan that he hoped might bring about peace, and he wanted to discuss it with Davis before approaching Lincoln. Davis told him to come, and on January 12 they held a long and cordial discussion.

Blair explained that he came without credentials or any authority to speak for the United States. He simply read aloud a letter he had intended sending, while Davis listened in silence. In short, he heard the old editor propose that both warring sides cease firing and unite to support the Monroe Doctrine, to which both adhered. Davis asked him to be more specific, and Blair proposed that the United and Confederate States might join in driving the French out of Mexico. That would require a treaty between North and South, of course, and Davis protested that for four years Lincoln consistently refused to receive any accredited commissioners. But, without saying where he got that impression, Blair believed Lincoln might negotiate now, and when Davis observed that passions and animosities might be too high for Confederates to restore friendly relations, Blair reiterated that nothing would bind the two sides together more than fighting against an external enemy. The president made it clear that a cease-fire must be the first step "toward the substitution of reason for passion." Making joint war against Maximilian's regime might hasten friendship, he added, but that was in the future. They had to deal with the immediate problems before them, though Davis could not resist giving a little lecture, with historical allusions, designed to impress Lincoln with how expensive and onerous it would be for the North to garrison and police the South should it be subjugated. Peace with independence would be cheaper and easier for all parties. Davis assured Blair of his willingness to negotiate and to send peace commissioners "with a view to secure peace to the two countries."[16]

Blair remained in Richmond for two days, probably meeting again with Davis, perhaps even recalling their acquaintance when the president was a schoolboy at Transylvania. He then returned to Washington, conveyed Davis's expressions to Lincoln, and soon arrived back in

Richmond again. The president met with him on January 22, and Blair handed over a letter in which Lincoln expressed his own willingness to receive any agent sent to discuss "securing peace to the people of our one common country." Davis saw at once the irreconcilable difference that still remained. Lincoln spoke of "our one common country"; the Confederate spoke of "the two countries." Each held a basic position that excluded compromise with the other.

Lincoln had also protested that his own political troubles in the North would get worse if he tried normal political negotiations with the Confederacy, suggesting that perhaps Lee and Grant could meet to arrange a cease-fire that would serve as prelude to more far-reaching discussions. Davis readily agreed to this, and Blair went back to Washington, only to find that on further reflection, Lincoln could not leave it to the generals. That got them back to sending a commission.

Davis brought all this before his cabinet on January 27, and the ensuing discussion went on for hours. Benjamin, particularly, looked skeptically on the idea and probably pointed out the apparent incompatibility of Lincoln's reference to one nation while Davis spoke of two. Nevertheless the president would not walk away from any chance of stopping the war, even if it might seem an unrealistic dream. Consequently he turned the discussion to the selection of commissioners. Mallory suggested Vice President Stephens, to which both Davis and Benjamin immediately objected, though Davis had consulted with Stephens the day before on Blair's proposal. Davis would naturally oppose Stephens from personal reasons growing out of their estrangement; Benjamin would oppose him because Davis did. Yet Mallory offered compelling arguments, not least of which was that Lincoln and Stephens had been friends. In the end the vice president was included, along with R. M. T. Hunter, representing the Senate, and John A. Campbell, currently still assistant secretary of war.[17]

Since all the principals were then in Richmond, and since Davis was already ill and probably held the cabinet meeting at his home, he called the three commissioners to the Executive Mansion on January 28. The meeting would have been stiffly formal, for none of the three thought highly of Davis by then. Stephens well knew that Davis had not wanted him on the commission, and the vice president himself thought it all a waste of time. Further, Stephens was backing resolutions in the Senate just then that called for a convention of all the states to determine a peace policy—one reason that the president may have been willing to give in to Mallory's initial suggestion. The commission would at least get Stephens out of the way for awhile.

Davis gave them verbal instructions, while Benjamin sent William J. Bromwell, a clerk in the State Department, over with three drafts of a letter of instruction to the commissioners. They had left by the time

Bromwell arrived. Asking after the president's health, the clerk handed him the sheets for his signature. Davis read each copy, thought for a moment, and then said, "There is something wrong here." He questioned Benjamin's wording on a small point and then himself went on to declare, "It will never do to ignore the fact that there are *two* countries instead of but *one common country.*" "We can't be too particular on that point." Davis made the corrections in pencil on one copy, while Bromwell burned the other two in the fire grate before returning to the State Department to prepare the new versions of the letter. "He has cut it up considerably," the clerk said to Benjamin, who was also at work despite its being a Saturday. "Just like him," Benjamin responded, then turned to another clerk and said, "I never saw such a man in my life." Apparently the sycophantic secretary of state did not scruple at criticizing his president behind his back. Moreover, shown Davis's corrections, Benjamin dismissed the first as of no consequence, saying, "It doesn't matter what his objections are, we will have something *now* that he *will* sign." But when it came to the substantive issue of the one-country–two-country business, Benjamin exclaimed, "That is the very point that I tried to avoid." With visible agitation he predicted that "the whole thing will break down on that very point" and that Lincoln's minions would never even allow the commissioners to cross their lines with any reference to two countries in their credentials. "But go on," he told Bromwell. "Copy them over—you will see how it will be." Clearly Benjamin felt no enthusiasm for the whole project even before it started.[18]

Benjamin proved to be right. The reference to countries did pose a problem, along with other considerations. In the end, the commissioners met with Lincoln at Hampton Roads, and nothing came of their discussions. Everything stuck on the one issue of reunion. Lincoln would accept nothing less and would not stop hostilities short of an end of the war, disbanding of Confederate armies, and a recognition of the Emancipation Proclamation and subsequent legislation ending slavery. Lincoln knew he was winning the war. There could be no reason now for backing away from victory.

The commissioners returned and delivered their report to Davis on February 5. They all met, along with Benjamin, Mallory, and perhaps others, at the Executive Mansion in an informal session. Benjamin soon lost his temper again and ranted about the "folly" and "weakness" and "danger" of having anything further to do with Lincoln or such terms. Davis seemed immediately to adopt Benjamin's language, and Mallory soon concluded that the secretary of state decidedly influenced the president against any consideration at all of this chance for ending the war. If it was lost anyhow—as Mallory, Breckinridge, and many others believed—then yielding short of utter defeat might at least get them more lenient terms than otherwise. But Davis evidently feared—or actually told Mallory—that his opposition in the Senate was so strong that it would crucify him if he went to it with any proposal to abandon the war while they still had armies in the field. At the same time Mallory believed that the Senate could have passed a resolution calling for peace, and that thus relieved of the responsibility for initiating such a move, Davis could have approved and peace been achieved. Mallory erred. At almost this same time, a group of senators called on Davis and suggested opening negotiations with Lincoln for the surrender of the Confederacy. Somehow Davis did not know they came by Senate authority and took them simply for men acting on their individual initiative. He became indignant at such a proposal coming from men of their stature, and they left thinking the interview entirely unsatisfactory. Only sixteen years later did Davis actually learn that they had been an official senatorial delegation, but as he said in 1881, "The pain would have been intensified if I had known that my struggles to save our cause & country were being thus paralysed by the Confederate Senate."[19]

Jefferson Davis simply would not countenance that his desperate cause did not still have a chance. Yet he would cling to hopes for a negotiated peace. Two weeks after the Hampton Roads commissioners returned, Federal General E. O. C. Ord proposed to Longstreet via flag of truce that Lee and Grant should call a cease-fire, during which the leading officers and their wives should call on each other, easing tensions, while the generals-in-chief sought some military solution that could in turn lead to a political solution, perhaps even to peace without defeat. Breckinridge endorsed the idea and discussed it with Lee, Longstreet, and Davis around February 26. Davis held little hope for the plan but empowered Lee to take any measures he saw fit "to enter into such an arrangement as will cause at least temporary suspension of hostilities." By now, if not before, Davis was convinced that there was no way to achieve peace without either defeating the North or being utterly defeated themselves, and he so expressed himself to Lee. "The President is very pertinacious in opinion and purpose," the general told an associate, possessing a "remarkable faith in the possibility of still winning our independence." He might better have called it pure obstinacy, if not a retreat from reality, but the president was constitutionally incapable of admitting defeat in anything.

Indeed, he even thought that in the failure of the Hampton Roads conference he could find a tool to lever the people of the Confederacy into greater commitment. The very day after the commissioners' report reached his hands, he allowed it to be published in the Richmond press, thinking that this new proof of Lincoln's intention to accept nothing but subjugation might stiffen the all-but-flaccid resolve of his people. In transmitting a copy of all the correspondence and the final report to the Senate, Davis even insisted that the commissioners add words to their report that would say Lincoln insisted on the South recognizing emancipation and accepting subjugation. This was, he said, "to influence the people." Stephens and the others balked, and in the end, they won. Later Davis also published the correspondence on the abortive Ord-Longstreet effort, all with a view toward influencing the people to continue their resistance.[20]

To some degree it worked. Many Georgians took renewed conviction, not so much from hope for their cause as from anger that Lincoln had also ruled out dealing individually with any of the Southern states, ruining the hopes still held by many, including Brown. Members of the Virginia legislature called on Davis at his office in the Treasury Building to offer their aid in drafting any new legislation he might desire. They came away with an impression of a president with "a heart full of heroic fire and that felt no fear." As the news of the failure of the peace mission hit the streets of Richmond, war clerk Jones believed that "now the South will soon be fired up again." General Wise spoke in the city, and Governor Smith as well, and regiments and brigades began passing resolutions condemning any reunion. "There is a more cheerful aspect on the countenances of the people in the streets," said Jones on February 6. "All hope of peace with independence is extinct—and valor alone is relied upon now for salvation." Everyone he spoke to in the capital believed that the South would now muster anew its military strength "and strike such blows as will astonish the world." Coincidentally, it was on this day that Breckinridge officially took office, and Jones asserted that "every effort will be made to popularize the cause again."[21]

For once in his career, Jefferson Davis had engineered a stunning public relations victory. The release of the Hampton Roads material showed everyone exactly what the Confederacy faced, seemingly crystallizing what remained of their spirit of independence. Given the initial momentum that he sensed, Davis acted even more uncharacteristically by deliberately following up his advantage with personal politicking. On the evening of February 6, as Governor Smith ran a public meeting to adopt resolutions condemning Lincoln and his measures and reaffirming their resolution to resist, President Davis appeared unannounced and uninvited. Indeed, he still wore his working suit and probably left his office spontaneously when he learned of the gathering. At once he walked to the front of the meeting hall to greet Governor Smith, who turned the meeting over to him. Extemporaneously, and with a smile of satisfaction on his lips as he read their attitude, he spoke to the Virginians for half an hour. He applauded their "new courage and resolution," their renewed feeling of patriotism and commitment. If the rest of the South would only follow their lead, he promised, then they "stood now upon the verge of successes, which would teach the insolent enemy who had treated our propositions with contumely, that in that conference in which he had so plumed himself with arrogance, he was, indeed, talking to his masters." Though still visibly unwell, he delivered what even his foe Edward Pollard of the *Examiner* termed "a powerful and eloquent address." He made special capital of the recently enacted legislation in Washington amending the Constitution to abolish slavery and did not hesitate to paint a picture of Lincoln demanding the humiliating subjugation of the South and planning massive retaliations at the gallows, even though Lincoln had explicitly stated to the commissioners that he would show extra leniency in any punishments that might be apportioned to leaders of the rebellion. Now if only the men of the Confederacy would rush to the armies, he promised great victories in the field. Indeed, according to Pollard and others, Davis even predicted that before the end of June, the North would be coming to him asking for peace.

These and other sentiments Davis also expressed three nights later at an even larger meeting that he helped arrange, this time with Hunter, Stephens, and Benjamin present. Even Davis's detractors did not deny his boldness and conviction as he predicted ultimate Confederate triumph, however much some of them, like Stephens, thought the president's predictions "the emanation of a demented brain." "Brilliant," Stephens said of Davis's performance, "but little short of dementation," while Pollard found the predictions "boastful, almost to the point of grotesqueness." "He is a good political speaker," John B. Jones attested that same day, "and will leave no stone unturned to disconcert his political enemies in Congress and elsewhere—and their name is legion."[22]

One of those foes was Stephens, who, even though he attended the second rally, refused to speak to the crowd. Almost immediately afterward, however, he told Davis in person that he was going home and would not return to Richmond. He would take no further part in the Confederate government and no more role in the opposition to Davis. He would stay home and await the end.

Years later Stephens looked back on that speech by Davis at Richmond's African Church, and speculated on what Davis could have been thinking of when he predicted bringing the Union to its knees by summer. It may have been dementia, but Stephens also wondered if perhaps Davis was "relying on something I and the world generally knew nothing about." The vice president thought Davis might have been thinking of some of his Canadian schemes or an uprising of the disaffected people in the North. But these were all dead issues by now. Stephens also speculated that Davis's confidence might have had something to do with a plan for "the abduction of the heads of their Government." Unquestionably such a scheme had been suggested to Davis several times during the war, and Thomas Conrad quite possibly went to Washington in 1864 to investigate the possibility of effecting Lincoln's capture. He may not have done so at Davis's request, but by January 1865, when Conrad asked for and received a payment in gold authorized by Davis, the president had to know of his activities. Furthermore, Davis was sending other agents into the enemy capital. On March 1 he met with Franklin Stringfellow, a daring young Virginia cavalryman and scout, and entrusted to him a mission still shrouded in mystery, but as a result Stringfellow went to Washington and made it his business to stay at Vice President Andrew Johnson's hotel and to become well acquainted with an officer who was very close to Lincoln, to whom he made an unspecified "proposition." Nothing came of Stringfellow's mission, apparently, but he worked independently of Conrad, who was himself back in Washington by the end of February and sending military intelligence out to Richmond. Seddon, too, had had some involvement in these clandestine affairs, which were for the most part financed by Benjamin's department. Chiefly they were aimed at gathering information and encouraging opposition to Lincoln in his own city. But there can be no doubt that Conrad, at least, had worked with people in the Federal capital towards an abduction scheme, and there may even have been attempts that failed due to a change in Lincoln's daily routine. There can be little doubt that Davis at least knew of these plans, while certainly he did not originate them. Certain, too, is the conclusion that Davis approved, or else he could have put a stop to Conrad and others at this point and certainly would not have authorized the financing of their efforts. How much Davis knew, and how deeply he involved himself, however, will never be known.[23]

If Jefferson Davis did actively lend himself to any such plans, it is a measure of how desperate he felt the situation to be, no matter how much confidence he tried to show. Foreign recognition was deader than ever. Lincoln would not negotiate on any basis other than submission to Union authority. Efforts at disrupting the North from within produced only insignificant results. And the military situation was awful. Only in the Trans-Mississippi did a Confederate army have room for maneuver, though the enemy slowly squeezed Kirby Smith. The past fall he had launched the last real Confederate offensive west of the great river when he sent Price and a small army composed mostly of cavalry on a raid into Missouri. The Yankees turned it back, and by the approach of spring Smith watched his army slowly dwindle as desertion, hunger, and disease sapped it daily of its manpower. Davis had been mildly critical of Smith's inaction after the close of the Red River campaign, and now in early March Smith responded, showing his hurt and hinting that he would not object to being relieved. Instead, Davis contemplated expanding his already massive command, suggesting to Lee, as general-in-chief, that Smith assume control of Confederate territory on the east side of the Mississippi as well, no doubt hoping this would facilitate the ability to move reinforcements across the stream to augment Johnston. Smith never got the chance to try it.[24]

Elsewhere in the Confederacy the tale of woe did not even stop for the winter. Before appointing Lee general-in-chief and Breckinridge secretary of war, Davis continued trying to do both jobs himself. He attempted to reinforce Hardee at Charleston and even considered breaking up the Army of Tennessee in order to send part of it to Hardee, and the balance to Richard Taylor's army in Mississippi. But then Hood resigned, and Davis gave the army to Beauregard, leaving him wide discretionary powers as to its movements. But events came too quickly. Sherman could not be stopped. Beauregard had gone to Charleston himself and soon advised Davis that it must be evacuated to save Hardee's command. Then the day after the Confederates lost both Charleston and Columbia, Davis asked Lee himself to go to South Carolina. Lee had to demur, but Davis sent another emissary to convey his views on the future conduct of Beauregard's operations. But then Beauregard's health and the uncertainty of his own intention for future operations convinced Lee to replace him with Johnston.

Lee may have been nominally in charge now, and the president certainly conferred with him on even minor military matters, but Jefferson Davis still could not stay out of war business, and especially when it concerned Joseph E. Johnston. He made it clear that he wanted Lee not just to advise but to direct the troublesome general, or else he believed nothing productive of good would be forthcoming. Davis would have felt even more uneasy had he known that Johnston viewed the cause as hopeless now and, as he later claimed, only accepted the command in the belief that they could have no objective now but to hold out for fair terms of peace, "for the Southern cause must have appeared hopeless then, to all intelligent and dispassionate Southern men." Johnston assumed command on February 25, and within two weeks Davis found him withdrawing again, with a view toward abandoning Raleigh, North Carolina, to the foe. To do so threatened much of North Carolina and even opened southern Virginia to Sherman. Yet Davis, who did not know and probably would not have been willing to see that Johnston had little choice, did not take the general to task himself. He appealed to Lee to give Johnston "specific instructions to avert so great a calamity."[25]

Lee himself struggled to avert calamity by then. Grant nearly had him completely surrounded. He appealed repeatedly to Davis to order troops from Kirby Smith to come east, though by now such a transfer was logistically almost impossible. Since Smith had proved reluctant or ineffective at sending reinforcements, Davis even toyed with the idea of sending Bragg to the Trans-Mississippi to supersede him. Lee never responded to the suggestion, probably because there was not time. He needed men right away, and needed them in the East where they could help him hold off Grant and help Johnston keep Sherman from marching north to join Grant, for once that happened all resistance would be pointless.[26]

It was the desperate need for manpower that finally forced Jefferson Davis to face a question presented to him repeatedly since before the firing on Fort Sumter. "Is it not time to enlist the negroes," one Confederate had asked him back in September 1864, "upon the condition if necessary of freedom after the war?" On Christmas another acquaintance had been even more frank. Thanks to conscription, "the white men who now comprise our armies are the mere dregs of the noble armies," he argued. "They will surrender you next spring." The president's petitioners felt that up to two-hundred-thousand blacks could be turned into efficient soldiers, led by white sergeants and officers. They could be given their freedom in return and sent to colonize the Western territories after the war.[27]

Davis had resisted the notion throughout the war, thinking it at first unnecessary and later impractical, not to mention the fact that it tended to undermine the institution of slavery itself, the very foundation of their cause. He had tried to prevent widespread knowledge of the petition from Cleburne in late 1863 and did not rise to any of the legislative attempts to revive the subject during 1864. Yet Davis had come out for impressing slaves for noncombatant service. Then, in a message to Congress in November, he took a greater step, proposing a "radical modification" in Confederate theory. Until then slaves had been impressed for limited periods of time for the benefit of their labor. But then they were returned to their masters. Davis suggested that in future such noncombatant blacks be taken entirely, and their masters compensated financially. Then, to get the best and most willing service from them, the government should reward the slaves with emancipation at the end of the war. He made it clear that he suggested their use only as workers, but added that if the question ever came to a decision between arming slaves and putting them in the ranks or accepting defeat, "there seems no reason to doubt what should then be our decision." It was the president's first public avowal that arming blacks could become a necessity. He may have said nothing more than he intended at that moment, or he may have been attempting gradually to clear a path for an even more radical move. Surely Davis knew that Southerners in the main would recoil from emancipation or armed blacks in their armies. They would have to be led slowly to accept any such step.[28]

An initial storm of outrage flew at the president from the press after that November message, but he weathered it and saw also considerable support. Governor Smith of Virginia endorsed the idea, and so did Governor Henry W. Allen of Louisiana. Meanwhile, as evidence that Davis now was willing to see and use the slave as almost any kind of tool necessary to help achieve independence, he called his old friend Congressman Duncan Kenner of Louisiana. In a private meeting sometime in December, the president recalled a proposal Kenner had made to him almost two years before that the Confederacy should offer to abolish slavery in return for recognition from England and France. Davis had rejected the idea then; now he was willing to give it a try. Appointing Kenner a special minister to the European courts, he sent him on his way authorized to make the offer in January 1865. It came to nothing, for France would not act without England, and Britain had many issues besides slavery keeping it from granting recognition. It was probably just as well, for if the offer had been accepted, Davis had no way of making good on his promise. Abolition in his government could only be accomplished by the individual votes of the separate state legislatures. Perhaps he hoped that the carrot of recognition would be so appetizing that the states would swallow the stick of emancipation in the same gulp. By late March he pretended the offer had never been made and even argued its impracticability.[29]

Yet it was all a part of a slowly evolving policy change toward slavery and the slaves. Slavery and slavery alone was what brought the Confederate States together, however much they might try to argue more elevated arguments about states' rights. No other substantive issues bound them in 1861, and since then it was only the war, the Yankee enemy at their gates, and Jefferson Davis that held them together. Davis, too, went to war to defend his section's right to its own institutions, meaning slavery. But by late 1864 he had come to see a higher goal. The war, the years of struggling against enemies foreign and domestic, produced a new allegiance in him. Still an ardent Mississippian, he had become an even more ardent Confederate nationalist, as in his mind and heart he made the Confederate cause his cause. From that vantage now, almost any interest became secondary, even the one great issue that gave birth to the Confederacy. Preserving slavery had become secondary to preserving his new nation.

Thus the failure of the Hampton Roads conference could not have come at a more propitious time. In the wave of renewed enthusiasm produced by that revelation of Union war aims—and well orchestrated by Davis—many other Confederates finally saw slavery as secondary to independence. It was no accident that when Benjamin spoke at the African Church on February 9, he made what Jones called "a significant and most extraordinary speech." He forthrightly advocated recruiting blacks for the armies at once. "Let the negroes volunteer, and be emancipated," he told them, undoubtedly prodded by Davis as well as by his own convictions. The timing was perfect. The resistance the notion would have met a few months before stood radically diminished by the current situation, and Davis capitalized on this by emphasizing to everyone the necessity of such a course. "We are reduced to choosing whether the negroes shall fight for us or against us."

Congress debated the issue endlessly, but not until March 13 did it finally approve raising black soldiers. The act allowed Davis to accept slaves offered by their masters, to organize them into units as large as brigades, and even to pay them the same wages given to white soldiers. However, Congress made it clear that such service would not change the relation of slaves to masters "except by consent of the owners." In short, there would not be emancipation unless it came voluntarily from the slave owners. Davis saw clearly enough that this provided no incentive for a black man to fight. Consequently he waited until five days after Congress adjourned before he promulgated the new legislation, and then he simply added a provision of his own requiring the owner of any slave taken into the service to provide manumission papers. The president would worry about congressional reaction to that if and when Congress ever reconvened. Unfortunately the measure came so late in the day that it accomplished next to nothing. On April 1 Davis complained to Lee that he was laboring "without much progress to advance the raising of negro troops." He hoped to implore the governors to use their influence to persuade masters to contribute their black men. In fact, a few black units did start to muster and train in Richmond, but too late. Davis lamented that passage of the legislation had taken so long. If enacted much earlier, he felt it might have put thousands of men in Lee's ranks. Yet it had taken too long to convince other leaders away from their belief that the black was not capable of fighting efficiently and obediently as a soldier. Arguing with one senator sometime prior to final passage, Davis even declared that "if the Confederacy falls, there should be written on its tombstone, 'Died of a theory.' "[30]

On the same day that he told Lee of his difficulties in raising black units, Jefferson Davis addressed an even more immediately pressing question. Everyone asked him, "Will we hold Richmond?" He answered one and all that "if we can, it is purely a question of military power." That power was all but gone by then. Lee made a heroic effort to break Grant's siege lines late in March, hoping either to drive him back or at least allow Lee to escape to join with Johnston. The attempt failed, and by this same April 1 the need to evacuate was imminent. Indeed, for almost six weeks now Lee had been advising the president to prepare for a probable abandonment of the capital. At once Davis authorized Breckinridge to start shipping supplies and nonessential War Department archives west to Danville, along the line of probable withdrawal for Lee. Davis seemed to feel little interest in the subject or else could not face it, and when the secretary of war raised the issue in cabinet of how much time they needed for an orderly evacuation, he received little or no comment from the president.[31]

When Davis met with Lee, Longstreet, and Breckinridge late in February to discuss the Ord peace suggestion, Lee told the president that he felt convinced that he would have to abandon Richmond but that he might be able to hold his position for another two weeks. Davis clung to this and any other ray of hope, though he conceded that Richmond might have to be abandoned and expected in such an event to remove the capital to Danville. Meanwhile, to the rest of Richmond's inhabitants Davis's aspect of determination remained unchanged. Though those who saw him in church on Sundays noted that he looked thin and sallow, still his good eye shone brightly. When he talked with friends on public events, he still impressed them with his quiet manner and easy conversation, bowing his head slightly to emphasize his points. "I never saw quiet determination more strikingly manifest in any person than in Jeff. Davis," an Irishman wrote in his diary after meeting the president on March 13. "Altho toil & watchfulness had told upon his physical strength the lustre of his spirit is undimmed." Richmonders who saw him on his afternoon rides with Johnston and others marveled at his composure, "seeming as cheerful as if each day did not have its calamity."[32]

That spirit and determination by now were a part of the ethic that kept him going. Fully believing that there could be no reconciliation with the North on any terms, he long before accepted the conclusion that "we are fighting for Independence, and that, or extermination, we *will* have." There was too much bitterness, too much blood shed between the sections. "I despair of seeing any harmony in my time," he had said the previous July. "Our children may forget this war, but *we* cannot." Within him by now there was a fatalistic resignation even to the idea of a Southern armageddon. "The war came," he said, "and now it must go on till the last man of this generation falls in his tracks, and his children seize his musket and fight our battle." He had long ago crossed a river over which he could not return.[33]

Admirable as the president's conviction and determination were, others in Richmond that March regarded him as deluded and his cause as lost, and they began working quietly on their own to halt the war short of extermination. Breckinridge seemed to be their leader and coordinated what efforts were made. Soon after taking office he surveyed his department's bureau heads for their assessment of the situation, and the reports proved to be uniformly gloomy. Campbell advised asking for terms of surrender in early March, and Breckinridge asked Lee for a frank expression of his sentiment. When all these pessimistic reports were in hand, Breckinridge presented them to Davis on March 13, hoping that it would prod the president to ask Congress to make terms before it adjourned. Nothing came of the effort, but Breckinridge continued holding meetings with influential leaders. Stating his belief that all hope was gone, he hoped to make surrender as painless and honorable as possible. He also expressed a belief that in such an event Davis would not consent to escape the country but would insist on sharing the lot of his defeated people. Breckinridge feared that Davis's fate in such an event would be hanging.[34]

By the end of March almost all officials had left the capital. Only Davis and his cabinet remained. When Lee's breakout attempt failed on March 25, it was evident to all that within days Grant would cut off the last route of escape toward Danville. The tension told on Varina. She evidenced an increasing tendency to bitterness and sarcasm, criticizing even her friends. One visitor described her "bitter malevolent tongue," found her "very unamiable," and avoided the woman he called "the tigress." Her husband surely understood her mood and knew that it was probably heightened by his telling her sometime during the last week of March that she and the children must leave Richmond. Once the army evacuated the defenses around the city, the president would have to make his own headquarters in the field, not a suitable place for his family. She argued and pleaded to stay with him but he remained adamant. While he instructed her to start packing, he sent a note to Gorgas asking that he provide fifty cartridges for a small Colt revolver and send them immediately. Davis asked Burton Harrison to accompany Varina and the children, who would be joined by her sister Margaret, their black maid and coachman, and the daughters of Treasury Secretary Trenholm. They were to take with them nothing but their clothing. Everything else must be left, even food. The Davises had little hard cash, but the president kept one five-dollar gold piece for himself and gave the balance to Varina to help finance the trip. While their ultimate destination depended on circumstances, Davis told Harrison to take them to Charlotte, North Carolina, first, while to Varina he confided that they might ultimately need to go on to Abbeville, South Carolina, where they could stay with his friend Armistead Burt. In the last extremity, he wanted her to get to the Florida coast and from there to sail to Cuba or even Europe.

Just when Davis gave her the pistol is unclear, but there was nothing uncertain in his intent. He showed her how to use it. Fearing that she might be subjected to unspeakable humiliation if taken, he told her to "force your assailants to kill you" rather than submit to capture and what might follow. If nothing more, this fear revealed the president's state of mind during the last days in Richmond. More revealing yet is what he said to Varina when he saw them all off at the Danville railroad late on Friday, March 31. It was a tearful farewell. A special train awaited them, with only two cars to carry the family and friends. He accompanied Varina aboard her car and there took leave of his children. Davis almost broke down in front of them. Varina believed that he was "bowed down by despair." Little Jeff begged his father to stay with them. Maggie clung convulsively to him, refusing to let go. To Varina he said, "If I live you can come to me when the struggle is ended, but I do not expect to survive the destruction of constitutional liberty." Varina believed him, thinking as she left that "it was evident he thought he was looking his last upon us."

Still fighting back his own tears, Davis left the car and walked with young Harrison for a few minutes, giving him the very latest news from Lee and asking him to return to Davis—wherever he might be—as soon as the family was safely deposited at Charlotte. That done, there was nothing left for Davis but to watch and wave as the train finally pulled out of the station at ten o'clock. In a separate car was the pair of carriage horses that they had sold the previous year to raise money. They and the carriage had brought $12,000 at the sale, which Davis deposited in the Farmers Bank of Virginia, but then concerned citizens repurchased the animals to give them back to Varina. So rushed was her departure, and so distracted the president's mind, that they utterly forgot to draw that $12,000 out of the bank.[35]

No one was with him now but his aides Johnston, Lubbock, and Wood. He probably slept little if at all that night, and the morning, All Fools' Day, brought nothing but more gloom. In an engagement outside Richmond at Five Forks, Lee lost a vital road junction, reducing his available avenues of escape to one. He could hold no more than hours now. Lee and Davis had been able to meet only infrequently during these last days. The danger on his line prevented the general from leaving. Yet occasionally they did talk privately or over dinner with the Reverend Minnegerode and others. The Episcopal minister could not but note that "it was sad to see these two men with their terrible responsibilities upon them and the hopeless outlook." When Lee arrived during one dinner, the others retired and "left them to consult in lonely conference."[36]

Davis turned to Minnegerode frequently now for comfort, just as more and more he turned to the Almighty for support. Typically, once the president decided on committing himself to religion, he did it wholeheartedly and without further question. To Davis there was a God, a god that intervened in the affairs of men, who rewarded the worthy and punished the wicked. In earlier days he sometimes blamed Confederate failures on divine displeasure with the South, and now in these closing hours of the Confederacy he revealed an inclination that the Confederate constitution should not have stopped at recognizing God but should have gone on to express its belief in "the Saviour of Mankind" and perhaps even that the document should specifically have countenanced Christianity. Might this, he may well have wondered, have saved his dying nation?[37]

The following day, Sunday, April 2, Davis turned to God again as he walked out on a crisp, beautiful morning to St. Paul's for services. He sat, alone now, in his regular pew, following the services prior to communion. He listened as the choir sang the hymn "Jesus, Lover of My Soul," then waited for Minnegerode's sermon. After a few minutes the sexton walked down the aisle from the front of the church and gently touched Davis on the shoulder to get his attention. He handed the president a paper and whispered to him that it came from Breckinridge at the War Department just a block away. When Davis opened it, he saw that it was a copy of a telegram received from Lee less than an hour before. The enemy had broken through his lines, endangering the last remaining avenue of escape. To save his army he had to evacuate immediately. At best he could hold his position only until nightfall. Quietly Davis rose, put on his overcoat, and walked out of the church with the sexton. In the next half hour, the sexton returned again and again, calling other members of the government and military from their pews. Before long the congregation, who witnessed all this, began spontaneously rising and leaving the church in groups. Even when Minnegerode appealed to them to come back, they continued to wander out to learn what had happened, though most surely suspected well enough. Richmond must be abandoned.[38]

I *Cannot* Feel Like
a Beaten Man!

When Davis walked up that aisle, all eyes in the church were on him. To most he appeared calm and self-controlled, while others saw his face so rigidly set in its expression that "we could read nothing." The news may have surprised the president less than might be expected. Reagan had been at the War Department early that morning watching the incoming telegrams, and he read Lee's first notice of the disaster as soon as it arrived. At once he set out to find Davis himself and soon encountered Colonel Lubbock walking with the president, both on their way to church. Reagan told Davis of Lee's news, but since the first telegram promised more information later, Davis went on to St. Paul's, where he got a second telegram, making it absolutely clear that they must abandon their position that night.[1]

Once he left the church, Davis walked immediately toward the executive offices between Franklin and Main, and there he shortly gathered his cabinet, along with the mayor and Governor Smith. The president read Lee's dispatches to them all, explained the situation briefly, and ordered them to pack the records of their departments and prepare to evacuate the city. He left it to Breckinridge to arrange their transportation to Danville but still could not entirely give up hope, saying to them that he expected Lee to link with Johnston to defeat Grant and Sherman separately.[2]

Davis himself spent much of the rest of the day in his office, packing and trying to attend to last-minute needs for sending supplies ahead on Lee's anticipated line of retreat. His aides soon moved most of Davis's papers to the Executive Mansion to do the actual packing there in a trunk left by Harrison. They also looked around the house for other personal papers of the president's and went into his office on the second floor to gather more items found on the table. Meanwhile, the Chief stayed at his labors at least until five o'clock that afternoon, when Breckinridge sent word that Lee believed their road would be secure until the next morning. The secretary of war also told the president that a special train would carry the government away that evening. He should be at the Danville station by 7 P.M.[3]

Davis left his executive office for the last time soon thereafter, and walked back to his home. Many people stopped him in his walk to ask what was happening and what they should do. In the Capitol square he advised one acquaintance to leave the city as quickly as possible, while to some ladies met on the path he tried to put a better face on it, saying that he hoped Hardee might arrive to save Lee. That was either a delusion or a lie, for Hardee was several days' march away. To everyone he met, Davis appeared as he did to Reagan that day, full of "calm and manly dignity, his devotion to the public interest, and his courage."[4]

The Chief found a bustling scene of activity when he walked in the front door of the house on Clay Street. Some of his aides still worked at packing what could be taken; Ives and other hangers-about got drunk. Now Davis himself addressed the matter of the family's furniture. Hurriedly he scribbled a note, leaving out words and making others barely legible, authorizing housekeeper Mary O'Melia to pack and store the furnishings as best she could. Davis did not entirely trust her, however. Many people feared that even being associated with Davis possessions might invite Yankee punishment, and the president seems to have feared that O'Melia might simply destroy or abandon things instead of placing them in safekeeping. As insurance, he asked a friend to watch her, but even then he privately warned Varina to "count on nothing as saved which you valued." In fact, most of the personal items had been sold by Varina at a public sale before she left. As a result, Davis had to concern himself only with packing some personal things of his own. He found a valise and was busily putting little heaps of clothing and papers into it when his old friend Clement Clay arrived. Together they finished what packing the president had to do, and then Clay left.

With only a few minutes before he must leave for the station, Davis walked around the Executive Mansion one last time. Its walls inspired a host of memories of the past four years—the gay receptions, the happy, quiet times with the family, the Christmas holidays, the births of Willie and Winnie. His own study still echoed with the voices of his generals and cabinet ministers. The second-floor nursery looked barren without the children's toys, and the bedroom had already become desolate without Varina. Carrying his valise downstairs, he looked once more at the parlor and drawing room where the flower of Southern society had sparkled and the dining room that once entertained scores of guests beneath its ornate high ceiling. Pulling aside the green brocade drapery at a rear window, he could see where the balcony had been from which little Joseph fell to his death. As he walked back to the small library at the front of the house, perhaps in his mind's ear he heard the sound of his own footsteps from his office above, the sound of his fevered pacing on the terrible night that his favorite child died.[5]

Yet Davis resisted the melancholy. In the library he sat on a divan and talked with his aides. They found him "sad, but calm and dignified." At least he had these trusted young men around him. And, dark as the hour appeared, still Davis was finally getting out of the capital and onto the road, a prospect that always brightened his spirits. For all the uncertainty ahead, he did not shrink from it. In a few minutes a carriage arrived to take him to the station. He stepped outside, lit a cigar, and left.[6]

Davis reached the depot to find only Breckinridge there, overseeing the final preparations of the overloaded train. The two spoke for several minutes, agreeing that the secretary of war would remain behind to manage the rest of the evacuation. He would ride out of the city with an escort and try to join Lee on his retreat. Shortly the rest of the cabinet arrived and took their seats, while Davis remained with Breckinridge. Delays in the scheduled departure held the train for fully three hours, during which the president consulted with Breckinridge and others on roads for a supply train to meet Lee on his route. Not until 11 P.M. did Breckinridge finally escort Davis to his seat in the crowded presidential car. Even then, after the secretary of war remounted his horse, he and Davis spoke for a few minutes more through the window. Probably they discussed the anticipated contingency of trouble with Yankee raiders along the road to Danville. A boxcar on the train carried mounts for the leading officials, and the men themselves were armed in varying degrees. Just now Davis might have welcomed a fight.[7]

Then the train slowly pulled away into the darkness. Happily Davis could not see the chaos behind him as the capital erupted in a near riot of looting and destruction. Things were bad enough in his car just then. Nearly thirty men crowded the seats, with only the wife of Treasury Secretary Trenholm to brighten the company. They spoke in low, hushed tones. Reagan stayed silent, thinking to himself that all aboard were "oppressed with sorrow," as he chewed his tobacco and whittled absently on a stick. Benjamin displayed his usual jaunty temperament, predicting that all was not lost. Mallory remained silent, reflecting on the ships about to be blown up in the James River to prevent their capture. Trenholm, ailing and nervous by nature, nursed a headache while his wife Anna tended to him. Wood and Preston Johnston tried to sleep, but Lubbock regaled those willing to listen with stories of Texas, which some aboard the car believed might be their ultimate destination, there to make a last stand with Kirby Smith.[8]

Looking calm as always, Davis rarely spoke unless spoken to, and most were content to leave him in peace. The train moved slowly over the poor roadbed, doing barely more than ten miles an hour at times, and there were frequent stops at which people gathered to gawk at the president and shake his hand. Early the next morning one crowd cheered him but he could do no more than wave, his face in the window showing the toll that the last twenty-fours had taken on him.[9]

Thanks to all the delays, Davis and his government did not reach Danville until 5 P.M. on April 3, preceded by another, earlier train loaded with baggage and soldiers. The arrival of the first train alerted Danville's citizens to what would be coming later, and a large crowd waited at the depot to greet Davis when he stepped off the car onto the platform. Major William Sutherlin offered his home to Davis and his staff. Mayor James Walker and the town council gave him a warm welcome and escorted him to the Sutherlin house. There Davis and members of his cabinet had their first hot meal since leaving Richmond. Before retiring that night, Davis sent a telegram off to Varina to tell her that he had escaped the capital safely. He also made inquiries as to the whereabouts and condition of Lee and his army, but could learn nothing.[10]

Rising in the morning, the president found much to do in his new "capital." He expected to be able to establish his government there more or less securely for Lee to be able to make a junction with Johnston and interpose the combined army between Danville and Grant. The city seemed defensible, and one of Davis's first acts was to assign engineer A. C. Rives the task of surveying the city's defenses to make recommendations on further works needed. The morning of April 4 he also called a meeting with all of his cabinet present. They discussed the details of setting up their government offices in the spaces available. Davis made it clear that he hoped this would be a temporary location, but still they must all go on with their work.

The president also believed it imperative to inform the nation that the government still lived and the cause was not lost. He probably thought over the details of a message during the long dark hours aboard the train. Now, leaving the cabinet to its duties, he went to Sutherlin's library and sat down to prepare an address "to the People of the Confederate States of America." Here was his dilemma: How to state forthrightly the current situation without giving cause for despair? How to inspire the people to greater efforts, to convince them that they could still win their independence?

"It would be unwise, even if it were possible," he began, "to conceal the great moral, as well as material injury to our cause that must result from the occupation of Richmond by the enemy." Yet they must not allow their energy, spirits, or efforts to falter or wane. Moreover, for all that they gave up in abandoning Richmond, "the loss which we have suffered is not without compensation." Indeed, Richmond had been a drain on Lee's ability to move. Freed from the need to defend the city, that great general could now maneuver in the open field where he always performed his best, and he could strike the enemy telling blows. Furthermore, while Yankees believed that to take Richmond was to win the war, continued resistance now would demonstrate the falseness of their premise and contribute to renewed war-weariness in the North and might even admonish the Yankees that the war must be "abandoned if not speedily brought to a close."

"We have now entered upon a new phase of the struggle, the memory of which is to endure for all ages," he said. They no longer needed to tie themselves to the defense of cities "important but not vital to our defense." Now they were free to move where they would with their armies, striking and destroying small detachments of the enemy, operating in the interior of their own country with the aid of the people. They would require the enemy to send expeditions far from his bases to reach them. Then Confederate numbers, though reduced, could still strike decisively. "Nothing is now needed to render our triumph certain," he promised, "but the exhibition of our own unquenchable resolve. . . . Let us but will it, and we are free."

His whole heart and soul were still in the cause, he told them. He would never consent to abandon a foot of Confederate soil, and if driven out of Virginia, he would be back. "Again and again we will return, until the baffled and exhausted enemy shall abandon in despair his endless and impossible task of making slaves of a people resolved to be free."[11]

President Davis was announcing a policy of partisan warfare on a grand scale. Unable to meet the enemy on even terms, his forces would take to the hills, to snipe at and pester the Yankees until they simply got tired and gave up. No doubt he was inspired in his confidence in this scheme by the success of the partisans during the Revolution and by the feats of Colonel John S. Mosby in northern Virginia. But the patriots of 1776 had European powers backing them, and tangled with a foe distracted by other global conflicts. As for Mosby, he achieved much, but he never kept the Federals from coming back into his territory time after time, and he only succeeded to the extent he did thanks to the remarkable succor and support of the civilian population. What Davis did not realize, or would not admit to himself, was that on a large scale it could not work. Driven from their port cities and manufacturing centers, Confederates would have to subsist in the higher mountainous regions of the South, chiefly Appalachia, living entirely off the land and its people. Yet these were the most destitute sections of the country, and furthermore thay also harbored all of the growing hotbeds of disaffection and all the old strongholds of Unionism. Davis's cause enjoyed the least support in exactly the regions he now expected to shelter his forces. The mountains could not feed his armies; the mountaineers would not accept them. Given the high level of disloyalty already in practice, at best he could expect the enemy to be given a constant stream of information on his whereabouts and numbers. At worst, espionage, sabotage, and pro-Union partisan activities against his armies would escalate into a war on a second front in his own rear. Davis had been given enough information by his own agents during the past year to have some grasp of this danger, but either he was not told enough, or else he simply refused to accept it. Years later, looking back on his message, he confessed that "viewed by the light of subsequent events, it may fairly be said it was over-sanguine." That was as close to an admission of error as Davis ever came.[12]

In any event it mattered little, for only a handful of Confederates ever read the message, at least before its content became moot. The Danville paper published it, but few other journals received it in time. Finishing his message, Davis probably called on his cabinet ministers to see how their arrangements were coming, and continued to make inquiries after Lee. By the next day, April 5, he still had heard nothing, and the anxiety began to tell on him. He continued trying to run the war, since Breckinridge still had not come in, but the efforts were mere form and meaningless. He actually snapped at his brother-in-law Richard Taylor in Mississippi, telegraphing him in considerable displeasure over the removal of a subordinate in command of a small district. Davis ordered a replacement and advised Taylor that the new man "will not be removed without authority." He also tried to coordinate General Cobb with others in Georgia and Alabama for the defense of southwestern Georgia and even ordered Beauregard to come to Danville to superintend the laying out of its new defenses.[13]

It troubled him not to know of Varina and the children. Though she sent him letters, they did not arrive in time to allay his anxieties, and he felt little certainty that his own letters and telegrams reached her. He tried to tell her what he could of recent events, but the news was unrelentingly bleak. "I weary of this sad recital and have nothing pleasant to tell," he lamented on April 5. Happily, the next day there came a note from Varina, though its content must have disturbed him. She had sent it from Charlotte the day before yet misdated it by two days, and thereafter she spoke in halting, barely coherent sentences. "We are in doubt," she cried. Twice she said "we hope to make F. safely," meaning Florida. At least the children were well, and she had money for their travel. But she trembled for his safety, imploring him not to try to make a stand against the enemy east of the Mississippi, and advising that he not even travel with an escort for fear it would attract attention to him. When he wrote back to her, Davis did not let on that he was disturbed by the state of mind shown in her note, but it must have troubled him. During those days the Sutherlins noted an increasingly careworn and anxious look about the president.[14]

These were hectic but pleasant hours for Davis's staff. "We had a good time at Danville," Preston Johnston thought. Sharing the Sutherlins' hospitality proved to be very comfortable. A host of assorted officers came through the town, the flotsam of the collapsing war in Virginia. Troublesome Humphrey Marshall of Kentucky saw Davis briefly, and the president met others as he frequently rode around Danville's defenses, repeatedly commenting on their poor layout. Throughout, Davis fidgeted at the lack of news from Lee. All he heard was a telegrapher's report on April 5 that the Army of Northern Virginia was believed to be fighting somewhere near Amelia Court House. But the next day numbers of fugitives from Lee's army began to filter into Danville. They brought little news, but their presence bespoke a desperate situation with Lee. Davis decided to order the train carrying the remnant of the Confederate Treasury farther south, to Charlotte, North Carolina, for safety. On April 7 Davis sent an officer off to the east to find Lee and bring back a firsthand report.[15]

The president's hostess grew more concerned as she watched him day after day. He was uniformly "pleasant and agreeable and self-possessed," she thought, but he would not eat or partook but little while his aides ravenously consumed her cooking. His only solace seemed to come from listening to a mockingbird that sang outside his window in the mornings and from afternoon conversations with Sutherlin in his library. Davis's mood swung rapidly from optimism to resignation, then back again, and from the present to the past. He spoke of his love of farming, recalled fondly his Mexican War days, then recounted the fall of Richmond, at the same time expressing his unshakable confidence in Lee. "I think under all the circumstances we have done the best we could," the president went on. He spoke of the resources against them, and rehearsed his old inner debate about taking young boys into the armies to fight, "grinding seed-corn" as he called it. One evening, sitting up late smoking cigars under the trees in front of the major's house, Sutherlin cautioned Davis to look to his own safety. Grant was before him and Sherman in his rear. "Do not delay so in your journey," said Sutherlin. "Let your movements be as rapid and veiled as possible."

Davis was unmoved. Taking his cigar from his mouth and exhaling a plume of smoke, he said, "Major, I comprehend the situation exactly. It is all clear before me and I would not evade it if I could. For myself I care nothing—it is my dear people that I am thinking of—what will become of my poor people!"[16]

Events unraveled quickly after that. On April 8, a Saturday, news finally came from Breckinridge reporting that he had been with Lee and left him the day before at Farmville: "The situation is not favorable." Then that evening came more news. Davis and his cabinet sat in session in Sutherlin's dining room when a servant announced someone to see the president with important news. It was young Lieutenant John S. Wise, son of General Wise, and Davis summoned him to the meeting immediately. Here was the first person to come directly from Lee's head-quarters. As Wise entered and stood at the far end of the dining table all eyes turned to Davis at the other. Davis asked him for his report, and the young officer made it quickly and concisely. Lee had met with disaster at Sayler's Creek, losing a third of his army. With the enemy pressing from several sides, he could no longer retire toward Danville but must move toward Lynchburg instead, several miles to the north. It was his only available line of march. Davis listened in silence, then asked a number of questions.

"Do you think General Lee will be able to reach a point of safety with his army," asked Davis.

"I 'regret to say, no," replied the lieutenant. "In my opinion, Mr. President, it is only a question of a few days at furthest."

Wise saw Davis and the others shudder. The president asked him to remain, and after the cabinet meeting concluded, he took the boy into the drawing room to get more details on Lee's condition. As Wise spoke, Davis stood at a window, peering out into the dark night. He asked the boy to go back to Lee in the morning to take dispatches.[17]

Sunday Davis went to church. Then in the afternoon he finally received his first telegram from Lee, but it was three days old and told him nothing he did not already know. Immediately he wired back with what news he had of Johnston and the other fronts, and of the conditions at Danville. He still prayed he would not have to leave Virginia soil and expressed the impractical hope that Lee might win some kind of victory. Davis should have known as well as anyone that after the Sayler's Creek losses Lee had barely thirty thousand men left, while Grant pursued him with twice that number, many of them swift-moving cavalry. Yet what else could Davis do? Happily the return of Burton Harrison that evening cheered him with recent news of Varina and the children. At least they were well and comfortably established at Charlotte. Davis dined with Harrison and some of his cabinet at the Sutherlins' that night, their talk all of the recent news of Lee's predicament. "The President had never seemed so poised or self-confident," his hostess would recall. When she asked if a surrender by Lee would signal the end of the war, Davis dismissed the idea. "We'll fight it out to the Mississippi River," he declared. It was only a question of time. They would keep on fighting "to the end, beyond the end."[18]

Davis continued trying to perform the routine duties of his office the next day, making appointments, looking after railroad communications, and more. When a report arrived that Yankee cavalry were believed to be coming toward Danville from the west, reserves quickly went out to the still inadequate works around town. Harrison found the government in a "turbulent uproar all the time" that day, with a host of matters to attend to. Still, "as nothing like sounds of battle could be heard in the country round about, we inferred that the situation had been improved."[19]

Davis gathered his cabinet for a late luncheon at the Benedict House, where he made his executive offices, the rain outside preventing them from going even the short walk to the Sutherlins' for their meal. As they started to dine, no doubt discussing the situation of Lee and plans for the future, a messenger called Davis from the table. In the hallway he met Captain W. P. Graves, the man he had sent out three days before to find and report on Lee. It was disaster. The day before, Graves reported, Lee had been forced to surrender himself and all of his army but for some cavalry at Appomattox Courthouse. The Army of Northern Virginia no longer existed. A stunned and incredulous President Davis returned to the dining room and handed Graves's written report around the table. They all read it in silence.[20]

At once Davis sat down again and the balance of the meal—which most managed to eat despite the news—constituted a cabinet meeting once more. With the army in Virginia now extinct, they must evacuate Danville immediately, and determined to withdraw to Greensboro, North Carolina, to be near Johnston and the remaining army in the East. The rest of the afternoon became a flurry of activity as the secretaries and their clerks once more packed their archives and loaded the boxcars of yet another train. "An age seems to me to have passed," Harrison wrote of those hours two days later. Davis sent Johnston a terse telegram announcing Lee's surrender, only hinting that he would be moving the government south to join him. Indeed, Davis had left Johnston woefully ill informed during the past several days, apparently not even warning him of an impending evacuation of Richmond and failing entirely to coordinate his supposed junction with Lee, which Johnston could hardly effect if he did not know where Lee was.

Of course Davis felt distracted and overlooked much. The shock of the news, feared but never really expected, proved to be almost too much for him. He spent part of the afternoon simply pacing back and forth "evidently in great excitement" in the Sutherlin yard, just as once he paced in his second-floor office in Richmond. Gorgas believed that the news overwhelmed the president momentarily, and Mallory agreed that Davis had never in his heart really accepted the possibility of Lee surrendering.[21]

Yet by that evening, as the preparations approached completion, Jefferson Davis's iron self-control won out again, and Preston Johnston found him "as collected as ever." He thoughtfully gave Mayor Walker a testimonial letter thanking him for the hospitality of the city. He wired to Beauregard to disregard his earlier instructions and join Johnston instead. That evening he returned to the Sutherlin house and personally broke the news to his hostess, almost whispering that he must leave Danville as quickly as possible. After packing, he gave her a pen as a memento, and then around 9:30 a carriage arrived to take him to the depot for another journey. The Sutherlins begged him to take a thousand dollars in gold they had hoarded for some time, but Davis only broke into tears at their generosity. "I cannot," he protested. "God bless you and yours." Then he got into his carriage and left for the depot.[22]

The trip to the train was depressing, in keeping with the occasion. Rain poured down and mud clung to the wheels of the carriage, while all along the road Davis could see the remnants of bits and pieces of Lee's army that had escaped, along with the confusion of yet another capital being abandoned. When Davis reached the train he encountered more delays. Burton Harrison arranged the seating on the crowded presidential car. He set aside a whole bench for Davis and then posted himself to prevent any but authorized personnel from boarding the car. Somehow General Gabriel Rains got access to Davis, however, pleaded for seats for himself and his daughters, and the president agreed, sharing his own bench with one of the general's girls. There they all sat for another two hours waiting for the engine to be readied. Davis and his ministers were silent, "full of gloom at the situation," said Harrison, and "wondering what would happen next, and all as silent as mourners." But not the general's daughter. Revealing an irrepressible loquacity, she chattered at the president constantly. Was not the weather terrible? When would the train get going? What a shame about General Lee! While Davis said not a word, the garrulous girl asked him innumerable questions and pestered him unmercifully until an explosion at the other end of the car caught all their attention, and they looked forward to see a soldier bounce into the air with his hands clasping his smoking trouser seat. He had been carrying one of General Rains's torpedoes in his pocket and foolishly sat on a stove. At least it shut up the daughter, and Harrison could write to Varina that "I have some sad and many amusing stories for the next time I see you."[23]

It was close to midnight when the engine finally lumbered off toward Greensboro. The train moved with agonizing slowness and did not arrive until late the next afternoon. In the process they missed by barely half an hour a Yankee raiding party that burned a trestle bridge over which they had just passed. When Davis got word of the narrow escape from interception by the enemy, he laconically dismissed it by saying that "a miss is as good as a mile."[24]

The president found an altogether different sort of welcome in Greensboro. The town reeked with long-standing Unionism, and as a result, there were no welcoming crowds and few offers of accommodations. Indeed, most of the government party wound up having to make their living quarters in their railroad cars, and the president only got quarters in town by sharing rooms with his nephew Wood and his family, already living there. At that, Wood's landlord repeatedly demanded to know when Davis would be leaving, fearing retaliation if Yankee raiders later learned that the Rebel president had stayed under his roof. Still, Harrison believed that "we are a fixture for the present," and even tried to assure Varina that they were all "comfortably fixed." Preston Johnston came closer to the mark, when he wrote to his wife Rosa that by contrast to the "good time" had in Danville, they "got along" in Greensboro.'[25]

Just hours after Davis reached Greensboro, Beauregard came in on a train, and immediately walked to the boxcar where government operations were trying to get under way. Davis gave him a cordial welcome; then the two went immediately into discussion. Speaking in low tones at one side of the car, Beauregard gave Davis an utterly pessimistic picture of affairs, concluding that further resistance was hopeless. Davis seemed unaffected by everything he said. The president actually proposed that the Confederacy could still survive by exerting every effort and concentrating all its remaining resources, though it might have to do so west of the Mississippi. Beauregard went away amazed at Davis's "visionary hope."[26]

Indeed, the president still did not despair. Just as they had during the darkest days in Richmond in 1862, his determination and courage shone at such adverse moments, though guided now by what Beauregard and others more and more openly regarded as a detachment from reality, perhaps even from reason. Davis wrote to Governor Vance asking him to come to Greensboro to provide moral influence to revive the spirit of the people, an obvious reference to the decided lack of patriotism that Davis saw here. "We must redouble our efforts to meet present disaster," the president insisted. "An army holding its position with determination to fight on and manifest ability to maintain the struggle will attract all the scattered soldiers and daily, and rapidly gather strength."[27]

The army he spoke of, naturally, was Johnston's, then near Raleigh. At midnight on April 11 Davis sent the general a letter suggesting that he come to Greensboro immediately. Johnston arrived the next morning, and Davis summoned him and Beauregard to a cabinet meeting in the government passenger car. There Davis set the tone of the meeting by opening with a brief address announcing that he expected to build a large army by luring back to the ranks all those who had straggled but whose patriotism would get the better of them now. He also expected to find even more men in the ranks of those conscripted who had not yet donned the uniform. Beauregard and Johnston both told him the notion was clearly impractical, but Davis dismissed discussion, neither asking nor answering questions. Then he adjourned the meeting with the announcement that the secretary of war was expected that afternoon at last.[28]

Breckinridge did indeed arrive late that afternoon and, finding Davis at Wood's lodgings, he went to him at once with confirmation of Lee's surrender. Despite all the previous news of the event, Breckinridge's assurance still came as a hard blow. As late as that morning Davis had still hoped that somehow Lee and part of his army might have escaped. Now after hearing from the secretary of war, Davis called another cabinet meeting for the next morning at 10 A.M. When all were gathered, excepting Trenholm, now too ill to leave his quarters, Davis gave them the latest news. "Though I was fully sensible of the gravity," Davis later remarked, "I did not think we should despair." Consequently he asked Beauregard and Johnston to come to the meeting, not expecting to discuss with them anything relating to negotiations or cease-fires, but to get their views on what could be done with the forces at hand "as a military problem."

Davis did not know that the generals and members of his cabinet had an agenda of their own for this meeting. Breckinridge and Mallory met with Beauregard and Johnston the night before, heard their views, and agreed that it was time to ask Sherman for terms. Breckinridge promised to give Johnston, as senior officer, a chance to state his opinions in the forthcoming meeting, and now Johnston did just that. It had been an ordinary cabinet meeting until then, Davis even digressing into old stories and unrelated matters as had been his wont in earlier days, as if the Confederacy was not collapsing around them. When finally he did come around to their reason for gathering, after almost two hours, he prefaced the generals' entrance by saying that "of course we all feel the magnitude of the moment." Recent disasters were terrible, but all was not lost. "We can whip the enemy yet, if our people will turn out. We must look at matters calmly, however, and see what is left for us to do. Whatever can be done must be done at once. We have not a day to lose."[29]

In this frame of mind, Davis was not ready for what Johnston proceeded to say. "It would be the greatest of human crimes for us to attempt to continue the war," Johnston said in opening. The Yankees outnumbered them by more than ten to one, and what few material resources remained to sustain even their small armies in the field were pitiful, and might be overrun by the enemy at any time. There was

616 / THE HOUR

nothing to do but open negotiations with Sherman immediately. When Johnston finished, Davis said nothing but asked Beauregard for his views, and heard him concur. Through it all, Davis sat quiet, almost motionless, nervously folding and unfolding a piece of paper in his hands. He could hear the spite in Johnston's voice, imagining his old enemy to be rejoicing inwardly now at this one last act of cowardice, this act of vengeance against the president. Indeed, how bitter it was to have to sit there before his cabinet and have no generals left to turn to but the two who, to his mind, had lost the war for him. Anger grew within the president as Reagan and others noted a funereal atmosphere descend on the room. Finally Davis asked the cabinet for their views. Reagan went first, and concurred with the generals, and so did all the rest except Benjamin. In the face of a clear majority against him, Davis showed his agitation as he argued against seeking terms. The Yankees had never shown any disposition to negotiate in the past. As recently as February, the Hampton Roads conference had failed. Why should Lincoln change now? Johnston suggested that they not look immediately toward civil negotiation but that he simply ask Sherman for an armistice temporarily, in order for the civil authorities later to discuss actual terms. They would thus stop the killing now and leave the more difficult questions for later.

Davis disapproved even of this, but with the majority of his cabinet against him, he decided to yield. As with the decision to put Johnston back in command of the Army of Tennessee, he could face making a distasteful choice only if he could take refuge behind the wishes of Lee or this vote by his cabinet. Now Davis dictated to Mallory a letter to Sherman containing the substance of Johnston's suggestions. That done, he turned away from the subject and asked Johnston for his anticipated line of retreat, in order to arrange for supplies along the route. Clearly Davis expected Johnston's army to stay mobile and had no notion of a surrender just yet. As long as he had armies in the field, hope yet lived. An armistice, if granted, would buy him time, and if the Federal authorities rejected any negotiations over civil terms—as he confidently expected—then that would show his generals and his cabinet that there was nothing to do but continue resistance, just as Hampton Roads had shown the rest of the nation. When he adjourned the meeting, Davis had not a thought of surrender.[30]

Still Davis left the meeting depressed. Now he was alone. All of his cabinet save Benjamin no longer stood with him, and even the secretary of state's support was probably more habit than conviction. His highest-ranking field officers were his two most implacable foes, one of whom deserted an army when he commanded it and the other too fearful or cautious to use an army. The people he saw now had no stomach for the fight and no love for the cause. He was tired and had been ill again in Danville. Then that evening an actual dispatch from Lee finally reached the president, and it told in the general's own words of his surrender. It arrived while the president and others sat in conference in Wood's rooms. Davis had recovered a bit from his mood of earlier that day and still talked of continuing the fight with Kirby Smith. But after he handed Lee's note to the others, Davis turned away and broke down, weeping bitterly. "He seemed quite broken," one of them remembered, "by this tangible evidence of the loss of his army and the misfortune of its general." Respectfully, they all silently filed out of the room and left their weeping president to himself.

The bitterness was still with him the next morning when General Bonham came by on his way to Charlotte and offered to take a letter to Varina. There was little time to write. "Everything is dark," he wrote in obvious dejection. "I have lingered on the road and labored to little purpose," he continued. Now he would try to join her if possible. Meanwhile, she should "prepare for the worst." At last it was sinking in that the end might be near. Sensing the same, his cabinet now pressed him to leave Greensboro. They were all too exposed there. Trenholm was too ill to continue, and Davis assumed his duties, getting the Treasury on the road again. Wagons and ambulances were found for most of the government officials, for the rail line ended at Greensboro and they must go overland to Charlotte. Davis, Mallory, Reagan, and Breckinridge would ride horseback, along with a few others, including a small military escort the secretary of war assembled from various bits of cavalry commands that had attached themselves to the procession here and at Danville. Breckinridge would do double duty from now on, still acting in his cabinet capacity, but also assuming command of the troops and the march.[31]

Amid the heavy rainfall, the mud at their horses' hooves, and the depressed mood of the president, theirs made a sad procession as it rode out of unfriendly Greensboro. Looking at Davis and Breckinridge, riding side by side, one resident could not but admire the "graceful forms and dignified countenances of the two horsemen." Some shed tears as the ghostly government rode south.[32]

The rain made travel slow, and the wagons and ambulances delayed them even more. By 5 P.M. they had gone barely ten miles to Jamestown, where the party camped for the night. Davis and Breckinridge rode to a house atop a nearby hill to ask for lodging, accompanied by Harrison and the aides. They got a good meal for a change, but when it came time for sleep, their host somehow mistook General Cooper for the president and escorted him to the guest room, leaving the rest to sleep on the floor in front of the fireplace. Eventually he also found a bed for Davis.

In the morning their host made up for his slip of the night before by giving Davis a splendid young filly to replace his tired mount. But the road that day proved no more hospitable, and they traveled even less distance than the previous day. By nightfall on April 15 they camped in a grove a few miles outside Lexington. Davis presented different moods to those around him, or perhaps they read their own feelings in his features. Mallory found him still depressed, apparently losing hope, but Burton Harrison recalled that "during all this march Mr. Davis was singularly equable and cheerful; he seemed to have a great load taken from his mind, to feel relieved of responsibilities, and his conversation was bright and agreeable." Harrison, who knew Davis more intimately, was closer to the mark. Whenever he got back into the saddle, Davis's spirits lifted, and especially in adversity. The president was born for moments like this, even if his heroic determination should have been outweighed now by a clear vision of the true state of affairs. He could think clearly out in the open—and being on the move, making plans, dealing with emergency, all brought out those reserves of spirit and courage that first emerged on the fields of Monterrey and Buena Vista. Outnumbered again, in danger of being cut off or surrounded once more, he could become lighthearted, even jovial, reminiscing about the old days, talking of horses and dogs, quoting Sir Walter Scott. Along the route he pointed out plants and birds to his companions, told their stories, and spoke of farming and the prominent men he had known. The execrable condition of the muddy pike beneath them set him off on a discourse on road building. Yes, he had lost Richmond, but that gave him freedom, and so did being relieved of defending Virginia, though he grieved for the noble Old Dominion and for Lee. But he still had armies, and now that he was no longer encumbered with the running of a massive government and its bureaucracy, he undoubtedly expected before long to take command in the field himself. He knew Johnston and Beauregard had no fight left in them. If he could himself get to the interior of the South and rally the patriots from their homes, he could merge them with the Army of Tennessee and the other remnants and lead them to victory. No wonder that his mood lifted as he rode toward Charlotte. Jefferson Davis was planning another "V."[33]

When he arrived near Lexington, Davis received dispatches from Johnston. One notified him that Sherman had agreed to a meeting, while the other asked that Breckinridge come to confer with him. This was good news of a sort. If Sherman was willing to talk, then hostilities might cease for at least a few days, giving Davis more time. The request for the secretary of war did not specifically say why Johnston wanted Breckinridge there, but in his official capacity he could discuss a cease-fire embracing all Confederate forces, whereas Johnston could only speak for his own army. Davis decided to send him, and Reagan as well, since the postmaster general had already drafted proposed terms for negotiation and could represent them to Sherman, if possible.[34]

They rode on to Salisbury the next day, and it was probably there that telegrams from Breckinridge caught up with him. The secretary of war had reached Greensboro that morning, and by 11 A.M. Johnston and Sherman were in discussions. Breckinridge expected that he might be asked to participate within a few hours. Davis wired back that the Kentuckian should join him at Charlotte when the meetings concluded. Davis passed the night in a local home, his affable mood manifestly recovered. He drank tea on the porch of the house of a local clergyman, talking cheerfully until well after dark, keeping an unlit cigar in his mouth. The next day he actually enjoyed a pleasant ride to Concord. The people offered a cordial welcome now, and better yet, Davis expected to find Varina and the children still in Charlotte when he arrived. As they approached the town, Davis had Harrison send a courier forward to tell Varina of their coming, and the same man met Davis again on the outskirts of town with the sad news that she had left several days before.

Still, when Davis rode into Charlotte at last, intending to make his capital here for the immediate future, his spirits remained high. Yet there was a problem finding accomodations for the president. Though the residents were friendly enough to everyone else, they, too, feared retaliation from the enemy. In the end, one man, ironically a Yankee from Massachusetts named Lewis Bates, offered to share his home and table with Davis. Since Bates had mistakenly gone to the depot, expecting Davis to arrive by train, a local officer met him instead. When the president rode up to the house, he found telegrapher William Johnston on the front step, and there they waited while the officer went to the back of the house to enter and unlock the front door. In only a few seconds a crowd of people and soldiers, drawn by the remarkable cavalcade passing through their streets, gathered in front of the Bates house. They shouted greetings to Davis and called for a speech. It was more than two months since his African Church addresses. Perhaps he could put some spirit back into the people by speaking out again. Though unprepared, Davis spoke to them for a few minutes, thanking them for their hospitality, thanking the soldiers for remaining true to their oaths. Yes, Lee had surrendered and the prospects looked bleak, but "the cause is not yet dead, and only show by your determination and fortitude that you are willing to suffer yet longer, and we may still hope for success." For himself, while he admitted many errors in the past four years, he took back nothing, and now he promised to "remain with the last organized band upholding the flag." Jefferson Davis would never quit.[35]

Just as he finished and placed his foot on the second step, ready to enter the unlocked door, J. C. Courtney, another telegraph operator, ran up to Davis and handed him a wire just received from Breckinridge. He opened it and read: "President Lincoln assassinated in the theatre in

Washington." It went on to say that Davis's old friend Seward had been stabbed and was believed mortally wounded. Davis read it in silence, then handed it to Johnston, saying, "Here is a very extraordinary communication." Voices in the crowd demanded to know the news, and Davis told Johnston to read it to them. A few cheered, but most remained quiet, some even dumbfounded.

At the moment, Davis himself probably did not believe it. He knew too well how many times stories of his own death had been circulated. These were confused times, with the wildest sort of rumors gaining credence. He would await hearing more from Breckinridge before he fully credited the story. When Mallory joined him, Davis said he thought it probably untrue. Others recalled that Davis said nothing at all at the news. Harrison heard not a sound from him, and only once inside the house did Davis comment to Mallory that *if* the story should be true, "I fear it will be disastrous for our people, and I regret it deeply." Davis would not pretend to shed tears for Lincoln himself. But at his death, Andrew Johnson became president of the United States, and Davis remembered all too well the malignant feeling that that poor, hardscrabble Tennesseean had manifested toward himself and the old-line Southern aristocracy and its leaders. He could expect less from Johnson than from Lincoln, and on that score alone the news disturbed this president.

There is no reason at all to question the sincerity of Davis's expressions about Lincoln's death, nor is there ground to suspect that he had either foreknowledge of or involvement in the murder of his opponent. At this point Davis probably did not even suspect that Lincoln's death at the hand of John Wilkes Booth might have a distant connection to those kidnapping plots that Davis almost certainly knew of, if he did not condone them. By March 1865 his agents in Washington were beyond Davis's reach or control, and by April Booth and his friends, originally participants in the kidnapping scheme, were beyond the control of Davis's agents. In the evolution from kidnapping to killing, Booth acted alone. Jefferson Davis would have recoiled from assassination just as he shrank from retaliatory executions of Federal soldiers. Indeed, one witness said that Davis gave a stern look of reproof when a cheer in the crowd met the news.[36]

Undoubtedly shaken by the telegram, Davis prepared for a lengthy stay in Charlotte. Lubbock, Wood, and Preston Johnston made their quarters with him in the Bates house, and young Johnston soon found Bates a very genial host. "Living splendidly," he wrote to his wife in a few days. "All good things to eat and drink." The Lincoln murder haunted them for a few days, especially when Davis attended local church services the following Sunday and thought the preacher, in denouncing the assassination, seemed to be directing his remarks at the president's pew.

But otherwise the week in Charlotte was at times almost a restful interlude. Davis met frequently with Brigadier General John Echols, the local department commander, a tall, hearty, capable officer whose bad heart had led him to try to leave active service the previous fall. Only Davis's persuasion then had kept him in the field, though he reassigned Echols to this point of relative inactivity.

Working chiefly with Echols, Davis feverishly tried to consolidate the few brigades of soldiers in the region. Most were cavalry, chiefly from Kentucky and Tennessee. They needed saddles, equipment, and forage for their horses. Echols needed artillery to guard river crossings, and Davis ordered Beauregard to forward it from Greensboro. With a view toward his anticipated move to the West, Davis wired to General Cobb in Georgia for him to proceed with new organizations of refugees and other available men. Davis could meet them on the way and take them across the Mississippi. He also kept a watchful eye on Yankee raiding parties in South Carolina, through which he expected to pass. Indeed, while his route would depend much on the enemy and local circumstances, Davis had to travel south some considerable distance before he could turn west, perhaps near Macon. Then he hoped to march straight across Georgia, Alabama, and Mississippi, meeting Richard Taylor's army near Mobile if possible. The whole combined force, along with Johnston's Army of Tennessee, of course, would have to hammer its way across the Mississippi to Kirby Smith in Louisiana. If it worked, he would have an army of more than one hundred thousand. They would be hungry, ill equipped, largely cavalry, and cut off from any logistical support, but while they lived, so would the Confederacy.[37]

Davis became a familiar sight on the streets of Charlotte, in his gray suit and low-crowned crepe-covered hat. "He alone, of all that vast crowd," said a soldier present, "seemed to retain the majesty and self-possession of his character, and to rise with the emergencies of that dreadful hour." He remained cheerful, and the presence of several hundred troopers and the activity of coordinating men, weapons, and supplies buoyed his spirits higher than at any time since he left Richmond, and as his spirit rose, so did his almost unquenchable optimism. Talking with Burton Harrison one afternoon, Davis declared, "I *cannot* feel like a beaten man!"[38]

Inevitably that mood must be crushed. While Davis worked out of a hastily prepared office in the Bank of North Carolina building, news arrived of the fall of Mobile and other cities. More and more of the soldiers in Charlotte simply vanished into the North Carolina hills. On April 18, before arriving at Charlotte, Davis received a telegram from Breckinridge announcing that Sherman and Johnston had reached an agreement. The president ordered him to come to Charlotte at once to provide full particulars of the conference, but disrupted trains and enemy patrols delayed Breckinridge's arrival until Saturday, April 22. He found Davis sitting in the doorway of the Bates house.

The president's first question was about the Lincoln news. Breckinridge confirmed that it was true. Then the secretary of war handed Davis a copy of the agreement signed by Johnston and Sherman. It was more than he feared and less than he hoped. Johnston, Reagan, and Breckinridge had collaborated to present suggestions to Sherman, and when the Federal general sifted the acceptable from the unacceptable, they arrived at a far-reaching document that in effect sought to end the war everywhere. It called for a universal armistice, the disbanding of Confederate forces and the turning over of their arms to the state arsenals, the recognition of existing state governments as soon as leaders took oaths of allegiance, a general amnesty, and the speedy reestablishment of Federal courts with full recognition of the personal and property rights of Southerners. Davis had authorized Johnston to discuss a cease-fire and negotiations for his army only, and now Davis saw an agreement that virtually dissolved the Confederacy and reconstructed the Union. He immediately called a cabinet meeting for that evening in his office.[39]

The president explained to those present the nature of the agreement and allowed each to read the document. While he heartily disapproved of the settlement himself, he may not have expressed that dissent, though they could hardly fail to note it in his manner. Once again he faced a terrible decision, one he did not want to make, though it might be inevitable in any event. If that were to be the case, then once again he wanted the decision to be made by his cabinet and not unilaterally by himself. He, and he alone now, actually had the power to make the decision, but in moments like these that constituted a personal defeat for Jefferson Davis, he had not the courage. He asked each of them to give him a written statement the next day, detailing whether or not the peace terms should be accepted, and if so, how they were to be implemented. It was the only time during the war that Davis asked his ministers to put their views in writing, and the fact that he later kept their replies in his personal baggage confirms that he wanted their papers as a dossier to defend himself in the future against any charges that it was he who gave up. These documents would prove that Jefferson Davis never gave up.[40]

Davis spent a troubled night. He probably knew the responses the morrow would bring. To his credit, he neither censured nor denounced those who believed the cause to be lost. He was long-since accustomed to standing alone in his beliefs. But he distrusted these terms and their timing. Grant had been generous to Lee, but Davis was convinced it was only because Grant feared that offering less would induce Lee to keep fighting. Davis still did not know or understand that Lee had been utterly surrounded with no option but capitulation. Johnston sat in an entirely different situation. He could still move and still fight, and thus Davis no doubt believed that Sherman's equally generous terms betrayed not magnanimity but a fear that Johnston could continue fighting. As long as the enemy feared that, then he must keep fighting and the Confederacy might live.

Feeling very alone now, Davis had no one to turn to but Varina, and he was not certain of her whereabouts. She had been several days ahead of him all along the route. Leaving Charlotte on April 13 when she heard rumors of a raid on the place, she moved south to Abbeville, South Carolina, and the Burt home. Yet Davis had not heard from her for days, probably since he left Greensboro, and now he worried. On the morning of Sunday, April 23, after the church service during which the minister seemed to look at Davis while speaking of the Lincoln murder, the Chief called Harrison to him and told him to prepare to ride south to find Varina.[41]

While his secretary got ready, Davis wrote his wife a letter that poured out all the pain and anger and heartbreak of recent events that he could not share with anyone else. He could not disguise that Lee's surrender had destroyed his hopes. If Lee could have escaped, then the plan to join with Johnston might have been effected and they "would have been today on the high road to independence." Even if all the stragglers from Lee's army who escaped the surrender had come back "we might have repaired the damage," though Davis exaggerated their number to forty thousand, more than had been in Lee's whole army when he left Richmond.

Now "panic has seized the country." All along his route he saw store-houses pillaged by lawless soldiers. As for Johnston and Beauregard, he called them "hopeless" and complained that "their only idea was to re-treat." Men were deserting in large numbers, and worse, many threw away their weapons. Even if he could raise another army now, Davis despaired of being able to arm it. He told Varina that at that moment he awaited the written statements from his cabinet ministers on the Sherman-Johnston cartel. The terms were "hard enough," he thought, though there was nothing of humiliation in them, and the state governments would remain intact with constitutional rights guaranteed. Yet whatever his cabinet advised, he doubted that Washington would accept them, for they went too far.

"The issue is one which it is very painful for me to meet," he went on:

> On one hand is the long night of oppression which will follow the re-turn of our people to the "Union"; on the other, the suffering of the women and children, and carnage among the few brave patriots who

would still oppose the invader, and who, unless the people would rise en-masse to sustain them, would struggle but to die in vain. I think my judgment is undisturbed by any pride of opinion, I have prayed to our Heavenly Father to give me wisdom and fortitude equal to the demands of the position in which Providence has placed me. I have sacrificed so much for the cause of the Confederacy that I can measure my ability to make any further sacrifice required, and am assured there is but one to which I am not equal—My wife and my Children—How are they to be saved from degradation or want is now my care.

Jefferson Davis was ready to quit . . . almost. He hoped that Varina might get to Mississippi somehow and then cross to Texas or else sail to some foreign port. Meanwhile, he would keep his cavalry escort together. "I can force my way across the Mississippi," he hoped. If once there he found nothing that he could do in the Trans-Mississippi, then he would go to Mexico "and have the world from which to choose a location."

It was hard to close. "Dear Wife, this is not the fate to which I invited [you] when the future was rose colored to us both." He trusted that she would bear the hardship as she always had. Only he would reproach himself for the past. "There may be better things in store for us than are now in view," he said, "but my love is all I have to offer, and that has the value of a thing long possessed, and sure not to be lost."

His letter done, Davis told Harrison to ride first to Abbeville, and gave him an introduction to Burt, noting that his secretary would also fill him in on recent events, though "I am sorry that he will have little to tell which it will be pleasant for you to hear." Given the present prospect of things, Davis expected that he would himself follow in only a few days. Meanwhile, amid the scenes of disintegration and shambles, Davis, incredibly, turned to the solace of petty tasks, promoting and appointing staff officers for Joseph Johnston though that general's army was all but surrendered.[42]

There were no surprises in the statements from his cabinet. To a man they advised accepting the agreement with Sherman, and Reagan even argued that slavery might still be preserved to them, since the constitutional amendment abolishing it had not yet been ratified. If the Confederate states were quickly accepted back into the Union—or treated as if they never left—then their votes could stop the Thirteenth Amendment. No doubt still believing that Washington would reject Sherman's terms, Davis agreed to go along with his cabinet, if for no other reason than to buy more time. While the cabinet was in session, Governor Vance finally arrived in Charlotte and Davis invited him to join the meeting. Revealing his own belief that accepting Sherman's terms would not put an end to hostilities, Davis immediately went to work on the governor.

"Mr. Davis appeared still full of hope," Vance remembered. He talked boldly of the move to the Trans-Mississippi, there to continue the fight with Kirby Smith as a nucleus. He wanted Vance to come with them and to influence North Carolina soldiers to follow. The governor could not help but admire the president's earnestness and his "most dauntless spirit." But he met Davis's remarks with silence, and so did the rest of the cabinet. Having just presented their views, and having heard the president accept terms for a general armistice and disbanding of the armies, a return to peace, how could he in the next breath talk of fighting on? They did not share Davis's conviction that the Sherman agreement was a waste of time. Finally Breckinridge spoke out frankly and said Davis was not dealing candidly with Vance. In the current state of affairs, any hope of effecting Davis's Western plans was extraordinarily dim and impractical. For his part he would not advise Vance to abandon his state, but rather urged him to remain and share his people's fate and do the best he could for them. Revealing just how thin now was the line between resolution and resignation, Davis sighed and gave in. "Well, perhaps, General," he said, "you are right." That ended it, and Vance soon left.[43]

Only minutes after concluding the meeting, Davis sent Johnston a wire that the terms were approved. But then that evening came news that Davis anticipated, but not so quickly. Washington had rejected the cartel. Sherman informed Johnston that hostilities would recommence in forty-eight hours. He could only offer the same terms given by Grant to Lee, and that was for the unconditional surrender of the Army of Tennessee. Davis asked Breckinridge to advise Johnston on getting as many of his men mounted as possible to get them away from Sherman during the balance of the cease-fire. They could still get to Charlotte and join the movement to the southwest. Johnston's cavalry, commanded by General Wade Hampton, could certainly get away, and Hampton had been in direct correspondence with Davis for some days expressing an unwillingness to be bound by any surrender. Moreover, after his discussion with Johnston at Greensboro, Davis and the general had agreed on a line of retreat, and the president had started arrangements for supplies to be awaiting the army or its remnants.

But Johnston balked. Seeing the opportunity for ending all bloodshed cut off, he could at least end it for this army. The next day, pointedly declining to communicate with Davis at all, he notified Breckinridge that his generals believed the troops would not fight again and thought the plan of escaping to the southwest impractical. "We have to save the people, spare the blood of the army, and save the high civil functionaries," said Johnston. The best he could—or would—do would be to send cavalry to provide an escort for getting Davis out of the country. Without waiting for a response, he reopened negotiations with Sherman for the surrender of his army. To Davis it was the final insult in a relationship that had brought him nothing but dismay from this turbulent general for almost four years. Yet in these final moments, he played Johnston's game after a fashion, by himself refusing to send any peremptory instructions to the man directly. Only Breckinridge communicated with the general, and as for Hampton, Davis bypassed Johnston by giving him direct authorization to leave the army and avoid the surrender. By April 26 Johnston had surrendered, in what the president ever after regarded as willful disobedience of orders. It would be hard to imagine a more fitting end for this valiant but strife-ridden army. For Lee, final defeat matched the career of his command: smooth, honorable, dignified. The Army of Tennessee and Johnston went down riddled with strife and acrimony to the last.[44]

Davis must have been livid with rage at Johnston, but when he called the cabinet to a meeting in Trenholm's room, which the treasury secretary was too ill to leave, witnesses saw only a president and advisers "bowed in sorrow." They met on April 26, in the full knowledge that Johnston's army would be gone in a matter of hours. Their course was obvious. Davis told them they must leave quickly and make their way to South Carolina, then Georgia, and so on to the Mississippi, in a broad sweep through the Lower South that would leave Sherman behind and evade Yankee raiders in the interior. Attorney General George Davis asked that he be allowed to resign now, since he had orphaned children to look after. Remembering his own pledge that his family was the one sacrifice he would not make for the Confederacy, Davis accepted the resignation without prejudice. Old General Cooper, too ill to continue the arduous journey, also asked to be left behind. Sadly the president bade a farewell to his old friend. Preston Johnston moaned, "I fear the spirit of the people is broken," and his friend Wood noted pathetically, "We are falling to pieces."[45]

Almost immediately after the cabinet meeting closed, the evacuation commenced. As they approached the Catawba River and the South Carolina border, Trenholm could go no further. He met with Davis and the others a last time and gave the president his resignation. Davis accepted it in warm and even touching terms, then crossed the river and rode on. He soon appointed Reagan to take Trenholm's portfolio temporarily, meeting his protest with what may have been a bit of dark humor when he added that in their current condition, there was "not much for the Secretary of the Treasury to do. and there is but little money left for him to steal."

After the night passed uneventfully, they rode on the next day, April 28, and those about him noted that the president's spirits rose once more. He generally rode in the front of the procession, accompanied either by Breckinridge or Reagan, and the secretary of war himself sometimes rode in advance to find lodgings for Davis each night. South

Carolinians proved to be far more hospitable than their neighbors to the north, and Davis spent nights between clean sheets and ate hearty meals for which the rigors of the journey gave him an appetite once more. Often Davis tried to leave behind some token of thanks for the kindness of his hosts. At the home of a woman who gave him water and introduced her little son as his namesake, the president presented the boy with a small gold coin from his pocket, afterward noting to Reagan that it was the last hard cash he had. "I was particularly struck with Mr. Davis's generosity," Reagan recalled.

Davis might have had cause to regret that little gift, for when they reached the Broad River to make camp that evening, the members of the government commenced a jocular comparison of their worldly fortunes in the wake of the war. Of them all, only Reagan, whose home was in far-off Texas, had any idea that he might still own something. The rest knew or believed that their homes and farms and property had been confiscated or destroyed. Davis then commented rather sadly that he found it gratifying that no member of his cabinet "had made money out of the war, and that they were all broke and poor." For himself, he now had nothing more than some almost-worthless Confederate scrip.[46]

Whenever they stopped now, people flocked to see the dusty, worn, but somehow noble remnant of the Confederacy. Davis delighted in the children that he took on his knee. He told them stories, gave them little mementos, and found joy in the smiles of the little ones. As they rode southward, he regaled his companions with stories of Mexico and his early days, and inevitably turned his discussion to horses and how to care for and love them as he did. At every river crossing he was full of advice on where to ford and how to do it safely, and at every little hamlet they passed, there were reminders of earlier, grander days, when the poor folk appeared with flowers and wreaths. His nephew Wood found it "flattering but sad." Others found their hearts in their throats as they watched such pitiful echoes of the ovations he once received in Montgomery and Richmond, and sadder still to see Davis clinging tenaciously to his belief in ultimate triumph amid these scenes of desolation and defeat. "Poor President, he is unwilling to see what all around him see," wrote a boy from the old First Virginia Infantry. "He cannot bring himself to believe that after four years of glorious struggle we are to be crushed into the dust of submission." But others saw something different. Micajah H. Clark, a young clerk from Davis's office in Richmond, recalled of this ride that "to me he appeared incomparably grander in the nobleness of his great head and heart, than when he reviewed victorious armies returning from well-won fields." Perhaps Clark understood what Davis felt. So long as he did not himself give up, the Confederacy lived.[47]

* * *

On the morning of April 29 they crossed the Broad and made for Unionville, South Carolina. All the ghosts of the war seemed to haunt this flight out of Virginia. Johnston and Beauregard, who had brought him so much grief and bitterness, had been there to taunt him one more time. Sidney Johnston, long gone, lived on in his son William Preston, who loyally stayed by Davis's side just as his father would have done. Now in Unionville Davis met one more—the one who, though still a friend, had brought him the greatest difficulty of all. Braxton Bragg, with nowhere else to go and at Davis's request, joined the procession. It was fitting that he should be in at the end. "What an eventful month this has been," young Johnston wrote as they passed through South Carolina.

The people continued to show manifest respect and even affection for their president. This section of South Carolina had been almost untouched by the war. There had been no Yankee marauders pillaging and destroying, and no great season of want had set upon these people. Thus they did not regard their president as the agent of woe that others saw, but as a revered leader. They brought him strawberries and fresh milk and flowers. They cheered as he passed. And they moved him to tears.[48]

At last they made Abbeville early on May 2, to find the warmest welcome yet. "The whole town was thrown open to the party," said Clark. Davis immediately found his old friend Burt inviting him to his home, and telling him that Varina and young Harrison, with the children, had left just two days before. Through the rest of the morning and the early afternoon, Davis talked with Burt and mingled with the cavalrymen and the teamsters handling the baggage train, as had become his wont, trying to maintain their morale. Then at 4 P.M. he called a meeting in the dining room of the Burt mansion.[49]

There was an evident and significant change in the composition of this gathering. The cabinet was not included. They had met for the last time in Charlotte, or perhaps on the bank of the Broad, for a brief business discussion about giving Treasury to Reagan. Now Davis turned to his generals, the men commanding the remnants of cavalry brigades composing the large escort on the journey. Before him at the table sat General Basil W. Duke and Colonel William C. P. Breckinridge, both leading Kentucky brigades. There was General Samuel W. Ferguson of South Carolina, and Generals John C. Vaughn and George G. Dibrell and their Tennesseeans. Bragg sat at the president's right hand, and John C. Breckinridge on his immediate left. Significantly, Breckinridge was here now in his capacity as a general and not as secretary of war. More significantly, even though Bragg outranked him by two full field grades, Breckinridge was clearly in command. Just as Davis realized that his civil government no longer had a function and his cabinet were now mere symbols, so also did he seem to recognize that the military hierarchy no longer mattered. Reliability, not rank, signified now.

"I had never seen Mr. Davis look better or show to better advantage," Duke would say. His spirits seemed high, he showed a bit of his old humor, "and the union of dignity, graceful affability, and decision, which made his manner usually so striking, was very marked in his reception of us." It might have been the president of old, sitting with his counselors in the cabinet room or meeting his grandly caparisoned generals in the dining room of the Executive Mansion, talking of the great victory at Manassas or the Seven Days, and planning how next to discomfit the enemy and win independence. Davis may have been acting a part now, hoping by his demeanor to infuse spirit and confidence into these men and their by-now-unstable commands. More likely he was the same president he had always been, seeing not defeats but temporary setbacks on the road to success. They must discuss that road now.[50]

As if this were just another of the old cabinet meetings, Davis opened by digressing, speaking of the journey, of South Carolina, perhaps of many things but the war. He needed to do so in order to put himself at ease with what he was about to say next. Then he came to it: "It is time, that we adopt some definite plan upon which the further prosecution of our struggle shall be conducted," he opened, and thus his reason for calling them together. With what Duke thought rather an arch smile on his face, the president continued that he thought he should do nothing now "without the advice of my military chiefs." The irony was almost too much for some of them. A man who had commanded hundreds of thousands and led the most glittering commanders of the age now called a handful of obscure brigadiers and one colonel his "chiefs." Duke liked to think it a compliment, but was not certain, when their whole combined command amounted to less than a good brigade by 1862 standards.

Davis asked for a statement of the condition of their men, and when the officers finished, he hit them with an even greater surprise. The cause was not lost, he said, any more than their grandfathers' cause had been lost in the darkest days of the Revolution. "Energy, courage, and constancy might yet save all . . . Even if the troops now with me be all that I can for the present rely on, three thousand brave men are enough for a nucleus around which the whole people will rally when the panic which now afflicts them has passed away." So saying he asked for their suggestions on the future course for continuing the war.[51]

When he finished, he looked at five dumbfounded faces before him and saw them glancing at each other with expressions of amazement and trepidation. None could believe what he had heard. There was a silence, the kind of silence Davis had seen before in recent cabinet meetings when he made similar expressions. It did not bode well. Finally someone had to speak, and since etiquette allowed the most senior officer the final word, the most junior, Colonel Breckinridge, had to begin. He was probably brief, but he said without equivocation that there was no war to continue. They were beaten, and it was only with effort that he held his command together. Duke was next, and he did not hesitate to agree with Breckinridge. All hope was gone, and any attempt to continue the war would only be cruel, bringing additional and pointless suffering. A guerrilla war such as Davis proposed would inevitably lead to greater evils than it could justify. They would be a burden to their people and brigands to the enemy. Dibrell said much the same when his turn came, and so did Ferguson, saying that their command was "too small for the thousands which I knew already surrounded us," and he doubted his outfit's stability. Vaughn, the senior brigadier, said nothing to contradict the others.

An annoyed Davis asked them why, given their feelings, they remained in the field, and unanimously they replied that they were there solely to ensure his safe escape from capture. To that end they would ask their men to stay in the field as long as necessary, even if they must risk battle. But emphatically they said they "would not fire another shot to continue hostilities."

Talk of his own safety made Davis bristle. He would entertain no such subject, he said abruptly. Johnston had sent word from the first conference with Sherman that both generals wished him to leave the country and save himself. Davis rejected such ideas then and he rejected them now. Then he made yet another appeal to their patriotism, hoping that he could stir them as he had stirred audiences before. In what Duke called a "spirited and exceedingly eloquent speech," he begged them not to give up, appealing to "every sentiment and reminiscence that might be supposed to move a Southern soldier." They must accept his views, he pleaded. He was Jefferson Davis. He was right.

There was nothing they could say. For minutes the room heard nothing but silence. Duke, at least, feared that to say anything more in contradiction of the president might lead to an altercation. They probably looked at each other, but certainly not at Davis. If they had, they would have seen the high color in his face from his earlier anger slowly fade. The longer the silence lasted, the more pallid he became. Almost perceptibly he seemed to sink in his chair, to age. However much the others felt his disappointment, they could not say a word. Finally he crossed a divide in his heart. This was the end. If these men would not stand by him, none would. Painfully he stood. With evident bitterness in his voice, he cried that all was indeed lost. Without adjourning the meeting, he absently turned to leave, but moved so feebly and falteringly that he might have fallen had not General Breckinridge jumped up to take his arm and lead him to a room where Davis fell on a bed, crushed and devastated, to fall into the sleep of mental and emotional exhaustion. "I have the bitterest disappointment in regard to the feeling of our troops," he wrote Varina that evening, "and would not have anyone I love dependent upon their resistance against an equal force." By 9 P.M., he intended to remain only an hour longer. He wanted only to find her and the children.[52]

Breckinridge and Bragg said nothing during the meeting, though it is more than probable that the secretary of war had already discussed what might occur with some of the commanders beforehand, explaining their unanimity. Now both he and his old adversary Bragg seconded their views. Asking them to poll their commands for volunteers to continue the journey, Breckinridge made it clear that henceforward this was not a retreat from the enemy or a trek to join forces to the west. They had but a single purpose: to get Jefferson Davis to safety out of the country.[53]

It was 11 P.M. that night when Davis heard Breckinridge enter his room to tell him it was time to continue the flight. Federal patrols were too close now, and they could not afford to spend the night. Refreshed somewhat by his sleep, the president probably welcomed getting back into the saddle again, even for a long and difficult night ride. Besides, the sleep—and probably much wakeful reflection—had taken some of the sting from the afternoon's meeting and its result. Perhaps he was not beaten after all, Davis thought. The fact that these generals would not stay with him did not mean that others would not. After all, these were but three thousand men in arms, while west of the Mississippi there were ten times that number, and even more with Richard Taylor. The cause was not lost everywhere, just here in the East. Better yet, if this large escort would not fight on, then he could detach himself with a smaller party and move much faster. When Breckinridge informed him that he intended to organize and personally lead diversionary parties to draw pursuing Federals away, the president probably still protested. His will to resist returned again. General Duke looked in on Davis again that evening, and though he found him occasionally irritable, he saw nothing that smacked of defeat. If the president agreed that afternoon that all was lost, it was a temporary resignation. "He seemed to cling obstinately to the hope of continuing the struggle in order to accomplish the great end of Southern independence—his whole soul was given to that thought, and an appearance of slackness upon the part of others seemed to arouse his indignation." Davis would not even speak of escape now. "I think the very ardor of his resolution prevented him from properly estimating the resources at his command," said Duke. More to the point, at this, the most critical moment in his life, with the burden of four years of leading his people in a bitterly destructive war, preceded by more than a decade of leading the Southern rights cause that brought about the war, Davis simply could not make a decision. That old tendency to indecision reemerged, exaggerated by the emotional stress of the moment, and there was no Samuel or Joseph Davis there to tell him which way to go. Constantly, rather, he wavered back and forth across the line between resignation and resistance.[54]

Only about half the cavalry escort volunteered to continue the march, and all of that remainder, at least, clearly understood that they rode but for a single goal, and that was getting their president to safety. During the first hours of the all-night ride, Breckinridge must have had to impress this on Davis yet again, as the two rode side by side for some time. The secretary of war also broached to Davis at least one escape plan, proposed to him by a pair of young Kentuckians, and undoubtedly continued to urge the general idea of leaving the country by whatever means necessary. Sometime during the night Davis finally agreed.[55]

By morning they came to the Savannah River and crossed into Georgia, where breakfast at a farmhouse refreshed them after the difficult ride. Before reaching the Savannah, Breckinridge was called back to the rear of the three-mile-long column, neither he nor Davis having any suspicion that they would never meet again. Now Benjamin decided that it was time for him to make his own escape attempt. Probably only for Davis's benefit, Benjamin agreed that his mission would be to get to Cuba and the Bahamas for diplomatic business, after which he would meet the president in Texas to continue the fight. In fact, the charming secretary of state intended to leave the Confederacy behind him entirely, confiding to Reagan that he was getting as far away from America as possible "if it takes me to the middle of China." After a rest, the balance of the party remounted and rode into Washington, Georgia.[56]

It was past noon when Davis dismounted at the J. J. Robertson home in the Bank of Georgia building. Exhausted from the ride, Davis accepted their hospitality and immediately went to his room to sleep. His coming had attracted much notice, especially among soldiers in town who had been with the Army of Tennessee during his visits to the army in better times. They recognized the suit of plain gray cut in military style, the pants stuffed into black cavalry boots, and the gray felt hat with the wide strip of crepe. He still looked like their president.[56]

If Davis slept at all that afternoon and evening, his rest must have been interrupted by fits of wakeful reflection. Still he continued crossing and recrossing the line of resolution. The tiny command with him was breaking down. Breckinridge sent forward word that morning that the men at the Savannah refused to go farther, and since they were guarding the train carrying the remnant of the treasury that had been following, he had seen no choice but to pay them to prevent their looting the wagons. Hundreds expressed a determination to stay where they were and surrender to the first passing Yankees. Many just threw away their weapons. Breckinridge advised yet again that Davis prepare to make good his escape. Now, here in Washington, Mallory tendered his resignation, written back in Abbeville the day before, and to Davis's own eyes it was evident that the cavalrymen with him were uncertain and might melt away, too.[57]

The next morning Jefferson Davis took command once more, his indecision at an end. He summoned young Micajah Clark to him and gave him a commission as acting treasurer, ordering him to issue pay to the remaining troops in Washington and take charge of getting the rest of the Treasury to safety. Once this was done, Davis intended to leave them all behind. He narrowly missed seeing Varina and Harrison, who left Washington only hours before he arrived, and his own purpose was not to catch up with them immediately. Believing that the increasing number of enemy patrols in the region had but a single goal—his capture—he felt that Varina's safety for the moment was best served by their being apart.[58]

He called a conference with the remnant of his commanders, civil and military. Reagan, Mallory, Quartermaster General A. R. Lawton, Duke, and a few other officers, probably including young Johnston, Lubbock, and John Taylor Wood, attended. Davis brought up the subject of dissolving the government. Even though he was president, he did not have the authority to do so, he argued. The Confederacy was the creature of the several state legislatures, and only the action of the states could disassemble the nation. Instead, since resistance was clearly impracticable in this region now, he decided to disband the government temporarily. They could reassemble in the Trans-Mississippi if they all made their escapes, he said. For himself, he intended to move straight south, below points believed occupied by the enemy. Then—not knowing that Taylor had already surrendered—he would turn west and head straight for Taylor's army in Alabama. After that, he would be on to join Kirby Smith.[59]

"It is all over," Lawton said when he left the meeting. "The Confederate Government is dissolved." Davis left the session in good spirits. It had been not so much a meeting as a forum for an announcement, for Davis told those present what he intended to do. He was tired of the past two weeks of counselors and generals telling him what to do. Now he called for Captain Given Campbell of Kentucky and asked him to furnish ten picked volunteers to continue the journey. All the rest of the troopers would be left here in Washington. Sometime before noon Davis called his party together in the middle of the street. Besides Campbell and his ten, there were the president, Wood, Lubbock, Johnston, and a few others, making no more than twenty. As they left, a tearful scene ensued when Davis said farewell to Mallory and the others remaining behind, especially the loyal cavalrymen who had stayed with him all this way, and from whom he now parted at his own wish, not theirs. Then the riders left. Behind them one young Kentuckian felt "the stillness of a benediction." Tears flowed down cheeks weathered and grizzled by years of hard campaigning. "Many a veteran sighed and gazed prayerfully upon the little cavalcade until it passed from view."[60]

They traveled swiftly now, and by the morning of May 5 had covered more than twenty miles. Then they rode another thirty that day, making camp outside Sandersville, Georgia. But Davis fretted that they did not cover even more ground, so the next morning he left the accompanying wagon train and rode ahead with Reagan, Johnston, and others. "He seems yet hopeful," one young man wrote of the president. Behind him he left Clark and the remnant of the Treasury, while Davis's aides and Reagan accepted some traveling money from the acting treasurer. Davis took nothing himself. They rode hard all day on May 6, and when they heard stories that Varina was not far ahead of them on the road, they rode even harder. Reagan's horse threw a shoe that afternoon, and while a smith repaired it, Davis heard from a bystander that a party of bushwhackers had set out to waylay a traveling party that matched perfectly the description of Harrison, Varina, and their company. When Johnston returned from a ferry over the Oconee River with much the same story, Davis mounted again instantly. "This move will probably cause me to be captured or killed," he said to the others. "I do not feel that you are bound to go with me, but I must protect my family."[61]

They rode without rest the balance of the day, and when some of the soldier escort's horses gave out, Davis continued with his aides. Not knowing which road Varina might have taken, they tried several, looking for wagon tracks. The moon was high and dawn not more than two or three hours away when Davis encountered some dismounted men on the road who said they had seen a wagon camp a few miles farther along the road. Davis took them for the bushwhackers and believed that his small escort discouraged them from proceeding with their marauding design. A few minutes more and the president heard a voice in the moonlight call out, "Halt, who comes there?" "Friends," Davis shouted back, and then he saw Burton Harrison step out of the gloom.[62]

Joyful in the reunion with his family, Davis rode with Varina in her ambulance all the next day, even though attaching himself to this wagonbound party necessarily slowed his progress dramatically. Repeatedly Varina begged him to leave her. "Cut loose from your escort," she had told him. "Go swiftly and alone." She, too, still clung to hopes of continuing the cause in the Trans-Mississippi. "It is surely not the fate to which you invited me in brighter days," she said, recalling his earlier apology to her, "but you must remember that you did not invite me to a great Hero's home, but to that of a plain farmer." She did not complain of anything but the faint hearts of these people in the eastern Confederacy. She wanted to go to England and put the older children in school. Then she would return to Texas with Winnie and William and join him there, "once more to suffer with you if need be." "This people are a craven set," she complained. "They cannot bear the tug of War." She even feared that in the Trans-Mississippi there would be difficulty at first. Without saying so, she hinted that he must assume dictatorial powers. "But you have now tried the 'strict construction' fallacy," she said. "If we are to require a Constitution, it must be much stretched during our hours of outside pressure if it covers us at all."[63]

Here truly was a woman with the spirit to match her husband's. If Davis might have disagreed with her radical idea about forgetting states' rights and assuming total power, in the end he could not argue with the logic of separating himself from her again. He could continue nothing if he were captured, and staying with his family slowed him and exposed them to risk of injury should they encounter a Yankee patrol. After breakfast on May 8, Davis and his party rode off ahead of Harrison and Varina, passing the night in a deserted house outside Abbeville, Georgia. Their progress had been so slowed by rain that Varina and the wagons actually caught up with them. Harrison entered the house to find the president lying on the floor, wrapped in a blanket, trying to sleep. Reports indicated the Yankees were closing in, and Davis advised Harrison to keep the wagons moving. He and his party would catch up in the morning, their mounts too jaded now to ride again. All night the wagons kept on, accompanied by a fierce storm punctuated by bolts of lightning. Before morning Davis and his escort remounted and soon caught up with the wagons, and together they pressed on through the weather until five that afternoon. They had just crossed a little creek when they decided to make camp for the night.[64]

Davis fully intended to leave Varina and the wagons yet again that night, to ride on and recover the time lost thanks to the storm. But all the horses desperately needed time to rest and recover from the past two grueling days. After Johnston rode into Irwinville to buy some eggs and other supplies, he came back with more stories of roving bands of lawless renegades, and Davis decided to stay in the camp for the night. They pitched tents, one for the president and his wife, another for the children, while the rest of the men slept on the damp ground under the sky. Most, like Harrison, were so exhausted that they fell asleep as soon as they lay down, and none knew a thing until just before dawn. In the nighttime silence, the exhausted sleepers did not hear the sounds of nearly three hundred men slowly stalking through the woods to within only a few hundred yards of the camp.[65]

A rifle shot awakened them in the dim predawn light. The Davises' black coachman James Jones was perhaps the first actually to see the

Yankee cavalrymen almost completely surrounding the camp. He ran first to Harrison, then to Wood and others. Then came more firing, and the sound of cavalry charging up the road from the south. "We were taken by surprise, and not one of us exchanged a shot with the enemy," said Harrison.

Jones rushed to the president's tent, where he found that Davis had slept in his clothes, removing only his boots and coat. When he first yelled that the Yankees were coming, Davis did not believe him, thinking it was the renegades. But he ordered his horse brought up immediately, saying, "I still have authority enough I hope to prevent our people from robbing my wife." He pulled on his boots and stepped outside. There, in the half light, he could see the profiles of the horsemen in the distance and knew at once that the servant had been right. He stepped back inside the tent to tell Varina, and she immediately begged him to flee while he still could. The cavalry were yet some distance off, and their movement into the encampment seemed disorganized and desultory. There was time. Indeed, John Taylor Wood determined to make his escape, but first he ran to the Davis tent to point out a swamp barely one hundred yards away. If Davis could get to it, he might disappear.

Again and again Varina pleaded with him to leave while he could. It was time for a quick decision, but Davis took what he called "a few precious moments" before settling his mind. Flight was not in his nature. Even though these attackers were organized Federal cavalry, he still feared what might happen to Varina. The firing had ceased quickly, however, and now the Yankees simply wandered through the camp and wagons in the dim light. She could probably not hope to conceal her identity, though they all had a preagreed story that they were Texans heading for home. But there seemed less to fear of outrages or humiliation from organized enemy soldiers than Davis had thought when he gave her the pistol in Richmond more than a month before. This, and the unshakable conviction that he could still do some good if he got to Texas, finally persuaded Davis to escape.

In the darkness inside the tent, he reached for his overcoat, grabbing instead Varina's dark gray raglan, or short-sleeved cloak. He barely had stepped outside when Varina rushed out and threw her black shawl over his head and shoulders. He already had spurs on his boots as he quietly walked off toward the swamp and safety, though his horse was in the opposite direction and now surrounded by Yankees. Varina, meanwhile, sent one of her servant women running after Davis with a bucket in hand, as if going for water, thus hoping the Federals would think the two walking together were innocuous enough. When Corporal George Munger of the Fourth Michigan Cavalry approached, Varina tried to distract him in conversation while the president continued in his deliberate walk.

Quite probably Munger, and one or two others who joined him, mistook the two people walking away from the tent both for women, for Davis still had the shawl on his head and the raglan draped down from his shoulders in a manner not unlike a dress. But then he saw the glint of spurs in the gathering light. Munger may have called to Davis to halt once or twice, but finally he rode his horse over to confront Davis and once more demanded that he stop, this time aiming his carbine at the president.

When the trooper appeared before him, Davis reached back and dropped both shawl and raglan from his head and shoulders. He may have said something defiant at the same time, and perhaps took a step toward Munson, who drew back the hammer on his carbine. Back at the tent, Varina saw the weapon drawn level with her husband and immediately ran to him, grasping him from behind to keep him from advancing any farther toward Munson. Davis later said that he intended to risk the man's fire, throw him from the saddle, and then ride his horse to freedom. In the heat of the moment, it is more likely that his old fighting instinct emerged, that he saw nothing more than a man with a gun whom a reflex within him said to attack.

Varina ended any such thoughts. Her presence slowed him; any attempt now would have no advantage of surprise, and any discharge of Yankee guns might hit her instead. "God's will be done," Davis murmured. He turned around and led Varina back to their tent. After seeing her inside, he walked beyond to a camp fire to try to burn away some of the cold and damp of the morning. A few minutes later the women started cooking breakfast for the children.[65]

Munson may have realized who his prisoner was as soon as the shawl dropped from Davis's head, for his face was well known in the country, North and South, though his features—gaunt from exertion, his normally smooth cheeks stubbled—must have looked like anything but the studio portraits and engravings so widely circulated. And if Munson had recognized him right away, it is hardly likely that he would have been allowed to sit by a camp fire instead of being placed under immediate guard. Still, once troopers began going through the wagons, it became apparent that important people were with this caravan, and inevitably the Federals knew that they probably had the man they were looking for. Half an hour or more after the episode began, Colonel Benjamin Pritchard rode up to the captives, having put an end to the firing, which tragically proved to be Federals firing at each other. When he gathered his prisoners before him, many of his men were already looting the captives' bags. Soldiers took the breakfast prepared for the Davis children, and most of his aides were relieved of their money, saddles, horses, and other effects.

Davis watched it all in helpless silence. But when the Yankee commander appeared, Davis stepped forward and demanded to know if Pritchard commanded these men. Yes, came the reply, and what should he call the man now addressing him? he asked. The president responded that Pritchard might call him whatever he chose. Sure of his man now, the colonel retorted that he would call him "Davis." After a moment or two, the prisoner admitted that that was indeed his name.

It was all over now, absolutely and irrevocably finished. No escape to Florida, no boat to Texas, no Kirby Smith and resistance in the Trans-Mississippi—no hope of holding out long enough in the West to persuade, as he now hoped, the enemy to allow the Southern states back into the Union with all their rights and without retaliation, confiscation of property, and civil disabilities on former Confederates. He had never intended to leave the Atlantic states until all organized troops had either gone west or been dissolved. Indeed, some thought he never intended to leave at all—that he wanted to be captured or even killed, rather than face defeat.

But such a course was not in the man. As he showed Corporal Munson, Jefferson Davis was a fighter to the end. If he courted capture, he need not have exposed himself and others to a pointless flight. If he courted death, he could have found Federals in a host of places to accommodate him. Certainly he did not want escape to Cuba or Europe, for Sherman had offered that and Davis rejected it, and Benjamin and Breckinridge would soon achieve it for themselves. But such a course would prevent him from reaching the Trans-Mississippi, and that unshakable goal provides the only consistency to Davis's actions for the past two weeks. Disheartened and depressed by Johnston's surrender, and then by the opposition of his cabinet and his generals, he repeatedly gave up hope, he said—but only hope for the war in the East. Never by word or deed did he abandon the dream of joining with Kirby Smith. While he may have told Breckinridge and others that he assented to escape the country, he said so only to quiet them. He could not force them to fight on, but they could not force him not to keep fighting, and his trail all the way to Irwinville is consistent with a design to get far enough into the deep Southern interior that he could safely turn west toward Alabama. Only weather and Varina slowed his journey enough for Federals to close in. But for them and any chance encounters with Yankees on the road, he might well have reached southern Alabama, only to find Taylor's army surrendered. With great daring and energy—which he had—and great luck, he might still have reached the Mississippi. It is well that he did not, though, for it would have broken his heart. There was no more fight in the soldiers west of the river than in those east of it. Just the day before Davis's capture, when stories of his trying to reach Kirby Smith reached the soldiers of the Trans-Mississippi, one man wrote, "His efforts will all be in vain. . . . The soldiers are disheartened, & disgusted, and determined not [to] sacrifice their lives to gratify anyboddys ambition." Davis probably could not have reached the Mississippi before May 26 at the earliest, just in time to learn that Kirby Smith had surrendered in New Orleans.[66]

Some of this Davis could not know for many days, or even years. For the rest, the shock of the moment prevented immediate realization. But now, standing before Colonel Pritchard, Davis's instincts took over once more. "I cannot feel like a beaten man," he had said to Harrison. Now Pritchard saw his prisoner "suddenly draw himself up in true royal dignity," and then exclaim in proud, defiant tones, "I suppose you consider it bravery to charge a train of defenseless women & children but it is *Theft*—it is *Vandalism*."[67]

The war might be over, but the postwar battles were now about to begin. For Jefferson Davis, ex-president of the Confederate States of America, the fight must go on.

31

There Is the Gridiron
We Have Been Fried On

"I would have heaved the scoundrel off his horse as he came up, but *she* caught me around the arms."

Inside her tent, Varina could be heard sobbing. William Preston Johnston found the Chief sitting on a camp stool by the fire. "This is a bad business, sir," he said, while Jefferson Davis still muttered defiantly about his thwarted escape attempt. While Johnston assured him that it would have proved useless, Davis shivered in the cold and complained that Munson did not give him back the raglan. Johnston found and gave him his own in its place.[1]

The whole party set out for Macon, Georgia, and the headquarters of Major General James Wilson, commanding in the region. The next day Pritchard encountered other units from his brigade, who brought with them news of a one-hundred-thousand-dollar reward for the capture of Davis and others believed involved in the assassination of Abraham Lincoln. Pritchard showed the notice to Davis, and Harrison watched him as he read it "with a composure unruffled by any feeling other than scorn." Already the jubilant captors had taunted and teased the Davis family, singing the favorite lyric, "We'll hang Jeff Davis from a sour apple tree," and speaking profanely in front of Varina and the children. Once word of the reward reached their ears, they became even more insulting, Davis remembering every word and boiling over at the insult he was helpless to redress. More than once he exchanged words with Pritchard, who did try, without success, to control his men's mouths. Davis also took the colonel to task for not allowing the family to stay together after dark, and when Pritchard replied hotly, Davis virtually accused him of cowardice by saying he would not speak that way with impunity to Jefferson Davis if he were not a prisoner. In response Pritchard said something about the bravery of a man who would hide behind woman's clothing. Davis may not have understood at first just what he meant.[2]

They reached Macon on May 13, and the escort took Davis to a hotel used by Wilson as his headquarters. By contrast with the treatment from Pritchard's troopers, Davis could not fail to notice that the guard outside the hotel stood at attention and moved to present arms as he passed by, a welcome bit of respect from honorable enemies. More courtesy awaited inside. Wilson provided a spacious room for the Davis family, along with an excellent meal, after which the general sent an invitation to call on him. The two spoke of West Point, where Cadet Wilson had seen Senator Davis in the late 1850s. Wilson found Davis "quite cheerful and talkative," even though when the topic turned to his future, the Mississippian expressed a belief that his captors would expend every effort in prosecuting him for treason. Yet Davis felt a conviction that they would find no legal or constitutional grounds for such action. Perhaps it was this last seemingly incredible notion, from the man who led a separatist movement that had cost four years of war and hundreds of thousands of lives, which led Wilson to wonder. "The thought struck me once or twice that Jefferson Davis was a mad man," he wrote hours after the meeting. "The indifference with which he seemed to regard the affairs of our day savored of insanity." Very likely Davis did present an appearance of disorientation, Wilson noting that "his whole demeanor showed no dignity or great fortitude." The events of the past days would have left any man distracted and not at his best. But what Wilson mistook for indifference to the occasion was almost certainly more than that. He was encountering Jefferson Davis's cocksure certainty that his position was legally unassailable.[3]

Indeed, Davis evidenced much more interest in the possibility of being tried for treason than in the charges of complicity in the Lincoln murder, which he almost shrugged off. Wilson asked him if he had been informed of the charge. "I have," said Davis, "and there is one man who knows it to be a lie." When the general asked who that man might be, Davis told him Andrew Johnson, "for *he* knows that I would a thousand times rather have Abraham Lincoln to deal with, as President of the United States, than to have *him*." Despite his declaration on leaving the Senate in 1861 that he left all his colleagues with nothing but goodwill, Davis obviously had not included his old foe Johnson in that amnesty.[4]

Wilson acceded to his prisoner's request that the balance of the journey to Washington—for he believed that to be his destination—be by ship rather than the taxing roads of the South. They lost no time. Four hours after arriving at Macon, Davis and the rest boarded railroad cars, still guarded by Pritchard, and prepared to set out for Atlanta. Most of the others were kept separated from the Davises now, but as the family sat in their car, Jefferson and Varina suddenly saw familiar faces step aboard. Clement Clay had also been named in the assassination charges, along with others in the Canadian mission, and now he and his wife were also prisoners. Davis rose and embraced Mrs. Clay. "This is a sad meeting, Jennie," he said, as she sat beside him for the all-night ride to Atlanta.[5]

Mrs. Clay thought Davis rather ashen faced when she first saw him, but by the next morning they were all worn and fatigued from the train ride and the tension of their situation. Only the children slept, and during the night the adults were aroused from their fitful nodding by a stop to take aboard other prisoners. Meals were brought to them in the car, but with the windows shut tight to prevent any thought of escape, the air inside soon became intolerable. Yet they were kept in the car in Atlanta while it was shifted to a different rail line for the trip to Augusta, where they arrived around sunset on May 14. Without a moment's delay, carriages took them the few miles to the Savannah River and a steamer bound to Savannah itself. More than twenty-four hours later they arrived, joined now by Vice President Stephens and Major General Joseph Wheeler. Though they reached Savannah at one o'clock in the morning, still Pritchard shifted the prisoners without rest to another steamer three hours later, and then when they reached Hilton Head Island, a major base for the Federal blockading fleet, he put them aboard the steamer *Clyde*. At 3 P.M. that afternoon, May 16, accompanied by the steam sloop USS *Tuscarora*, they steamed off northward along the Atlantic Coast.[6]

Even though their constant shifting and jostling was at an end, Davis found the journey anything but pleasant. His eye pained him severely, as it had off and on ever since the last days in Richmond, and often he wore the little woolen skullcap that somehow helped with his facial neuralgia. The heavy seas did not help, leaving many aboard seasick, though Davis himself seems not to have been affected. Varina and Virginia Clay sometimes bathed his temples with cologne, which seemed to ease the pain.

At least their captors allowed the ex-president the freedom of the deck during much of the voyage. In tense times, given enough space, Jefferson Davis always paced, and now he walked up and down the wooden deck, often carrying his baby Winnie in his arms, trying to forget himself in the moments of cheer brought by her giggling. He spoke frequently with Reagan, Wheeler, and the others and had his first conversations with Stephens since the vice president left Richmond back in February. Old enmities seemed forgotten as the two discussed their predicament and the future of the South. "It was evident that he felt his relief from responsibility," said Wheeler, "and amid all his trials and troubles he evidently enjoyed the pleasure of having a few days which he could so entirely devote to his family."

Their accommodations proved to be comfortable enough, staterooms for most of them, and good food. The ship's officers gave them newspapers, and now Davis learned for the first time that several conspirators accused in the Lincoln murder were even then about to be tried, though the actual assassin, John Wilkes Booth, had been killed attempting to escape. But these were only believed to be the actual perpetrators of the plot. Davis, Clay, and the others were widely held to be the true originators of the heinous crime. If Davis discussed the subject at all, it was with the same contemptuous dismissal that he manifested before Wilson.

Incredibly, though Pritchard and the rest of the Federals aboard the *Clyde* treated their captives courteously, still the Yankees feared some last-gasp Rebel move to retake Davis and the others. Even though the Confederacy had virtually disintegrated, with no resistance at all left east of the Mississippi, rumors of a powerful ironclad ram, the CSS *Stonewall*, prowling in the area, gave them pause. In fact the ram was nowhere near them, having steamed into Havana to surrender to Cuban authorities several days before. But the men having charge of Davis felt they could take no chances. They removed all the axes normally kept at stations on deck to Pritchard's room, leading Davis to exclaim with disgust to Virginia Clay, "Cowards! They're afraid of this handful of Confederate men!" As usual Davis saw only his own point of view. The Federals feared the *Stonewall*, but in a naval battle with a presumably superior vessel, even these weak old men could distract the crews if they wielded axes in their hands. Even the guns of the *Tuscarora* remained trained continually on the *Clyde*.

Indeed, more than cannon may have taken aim at the prison ship, for aboard the *Tuscarora* a mock court took place at which the jurors tried Davis for Lincoln's murder. They found him guilty and detailed an ensign of reputed marksmanship to shoot the Confederate when he next presented himself as a target. The ensign loaded an Enfield rifle and took aim through an air port one sunny afternoon, finding Davis sitting on the deck of the *Clyde* in a chair. But somehow he could not pull the trigger, as he later told the episode, and then Winnie ended any further attempt when she ran into her father's lap and spoiled the target.

By noon on May 19 the *Clyde* reached Hampton Roads and moved to anchor off Fort Monroe. The prisoners remained aboard ship for the next few days while Federal authorities determined their final destinations. Late on May 20 a tug came alongside and took Johnston, Lubbock, and Wheeler and his staff off to be shipped to another fort in Delaware for incarceration. Later on Stephens and Reagan went aboard the *Tuscarora* to be transported to Fort Warren in Massachusetts. When

Stephens left the *Clyde*, he went to say farewell to Davis, who could not utter a word. "He seemed to be more affected than I had ever seen him," Stephens wrote in his diary the next day. He simply squeezed Stephens's hand and murmured good-bye in a tone that evinced "deep feeling and emotion."

By the afternoon of May 22 only Davis, Clay, Harrison, and their families remained. It was a sultry, rainy day. Davis, as usual, paced restlessly about the deck, looking exceedingly depressed to Virginia Clay, though he could still pause to give little lectures on the causes of the poor weather or the birds that perched on the rails. That morning Davis received notification to prepare to be transferred to a tug, and that told him all he needed to know of his destination. Fort Monroe would be his prison, and Clay's.

Varina and the children walked to the gangway with her husband when the time came. He whispered to her not to show tears or any sign of weakness, while he himself betrayed little or no emotion, though the flush of his face spoke for his excitement. Kissing her in farewell, he whispered in her ear his promise that he had nothing to do with Lincoln's death or "any other deed unworthy of a soldier, or of, our cause." Then he stepped aboard the tug for the trip to shore.[7]

Jefferson Davis spent the next 720 days as an inhabitant of Fort Monroe, in conditions of varying severity and consideration, yet most of which he and his supporters then and later would onesidedly regard as abominable. To be sure, at the outset he had no reason to be thankful to his jailers. They took him to Casemate Number 2, specially prepared to be his cell while he awaited whatever trial the government might decide on. Almost immediately, the first and greatest indignity that he would suffer at Federal hands beset him. Brigadier General Nelson A. Miles, a soldier of unquestioned daring and bravery, but with a character of occasionally lesser stature, took the assignment of being Davis's jailor, with a free hand to act as necessary to ensure the prisoner's security and behavior. Fort Monroe, however well armed and protected, still lay on Virginia soil. Word of the *Stonewall*'s surrender at Havana had not yet reached Hampton Roads. Confederates, though surrendered, were everywhere around the fort and nearby Newport News and Norfolk, and the war was not yet over, with Kirby Smith and a few other small commands that remained in the field. The idea of an escape, or of an external attempt to engineer a breakout, might have seemed absurd given the manpower in the fort and the physical condition of the prisoner. But these were unsettled times, and the prisoner himself, despite his depression, still displayed a haughty defiance in his demeanor. Miles, a man uncommonly concerned about his reputation, would take no chances of losing his prisoner. With Washington's discretion to do so, he sent men into Davis's cell on May 23 to fix leg irons to his ankles.

Davis could not believe it at first, then he protested and may even have offered brief physical resistance, though there was nothing he could do. One man, not an eyewitness, said that Davis broke down and sobbed. Perhaps he did, but never in front of his jailers. However distressed he might be, he was too proud ever to give them that satisfaction. When an outcry against the shackling spread quickly throughout the North, Secretary of War Edwin M. Stanton almost immediately ordered them removed, and in the end Davis suffered the humiliation of the irons for only five days. Ironically, they did him more good than harm, for almost at once a glimmer of sympathy appeared in the Yankee press and among influential men who recoiled at seeing a state prisoner treated in this fashion, though the subsequent embarrassment to Miles probably accounted for his adopting an increasingly cold attitude toward his prisoner.[8]

"Our beloved *President* is in chains," Virginia Clay moaned when she first heard the news, though by then the shackles had been removed. But there were to be more indignities, and some of them calculated. A series of abusive letters were sent to Davis in the first weeks after his imprisonment, some taunting him by sending Confederate notes for his defense fund, others from blacks congratulating him on his captivity and their freedom, and a few even suggesting that he be banished, hanged, or sent to Libby Prison in Richmond to suffer the horrors supposedly inflicted on Federal soldiers held there. Worst of all, however, was the attempt to humiliate him by asserting that when he tried to escape the Federals at Irwinville, he did so by wearing a woman's clothing. No one at the time spoke of this, though the mistake was natural enough given the shawl on his head and shoulders and the long, flowing raglan of Varina's that he wore. Indeed, his aide Wood wrote in his diary shortly after making his own escape that he believed Davis adopted a woman's guise, and lamented the fact. None of Pritchard's men made any such accusation, but rumors caused by the dim light and the confusion of what Davis did have on soon spread to other troopers not immediately on the scene. By May 13, while Davis himself was on the train to Atlanta, Wilson passed the story on to Washington, and an immediate sensation spread through the Yankee press. This was a story with powerful potential, and Stanton gleefully gave it to the newspapers and strove to support it with eyewitness testimony, which many of Davis's actual captors, hoping to claim a share of the $100,000 reward, were naturally happy to "recall." There could be no more fitting end to punctuate the utter defeat of the Confederacy than to rob it of its last chance for a dignified demise by having its president run in ignominy with skirts about his heels.

On May 23, while her husband was being shackled, Varina received a visit from Pritchard, who came with orders to take the raglan. Ignorant of the intent behind the act, Varina freely admitted that it was the garment Davis wore. The next day he came back and this time took the shawl, though apparently Varina by now had some inkling of the story, and Davis himself seems to have heard a cryptic reference to it from Wilson back in Macon. Now, after seeing the newspapers, they understood all too well. "A peal of inextinguishable laughter goes ringing round the globe," cackled one editor. "Davis, with the blood of thousands of brave and noble victims upon his soul, will go down to posterity, cowering under a petticoat, the object of mingled horror and derision."

Unfortunately, the Union War Department faced a bit of potential embarrassment of its own when finally it saw the raglan and shawl. While the raglan was, indeed, a woman's, it was virtually identical to the same garment worn by thousands of men as a waterproof or rain garment, and almost exactly like Davis's own, which was taken from his tent on May 10. As for the shawl, while again a woman's, it signified little, for men, too, commonly wore shawls to stay warm, as had the late President Lincoln. There was no dress, no petticoat, no bonnet or hoop skirt, as the exaggerated stories soon claimed. Rather than spoil a story with excellent propaganda value, Stanton decided not to reveal the true garments to the public but put them in a War Department safe, where they would languish for generations. Meanwhile, he simply adapted the story slightly by saying that Davis had worn not a dress, but a woman's cloak and shawl. The denigrating effect on Davis as a heroic figure could be just as great, and that was the objective—to diffuse latent Southern spiritual resistance by eliminating any possible idols as rallying points, just as the Federals buried Booth in an unmarked grave to prevent the site from becoming a "holy" place for diehard Rebels.[9]

While the overwhelming majority of Confederates never believed the canard about dresses and petticoats, Jefferson Davis nonetheless felt keenly the humiliation of the lie, which only helped to depress him even more. However much he tried to present a resolute front, the mental anguish of imprisonment, added to the burden of the now-incontestable realization of utter Confederate defeat, wore him down dangerously. His prison doctor, John J. Craven, saw him daily and noted his condition. "I found him very feeble," reported the doctor after his first visit on May 24, "prematurely old—all the evidence of an iron will, but extremely reduced in physical structure." Subsequent visits revealed only a gradual decline in the prisoner's state. It did not help that Davis, an insomniac to begin with, could hardly get any sleep under the conditions imposed by Washington. A light was kept burning in his cell all night, with inspections by an officer of the guard at fifteen-minute intervals. Davis could not leave his casemate for any purpose, and sentinels actually stood inside his area of confinement at all times, with orders not to speak if spoken to. It is no wonder, then, that he sickened, mentally and physically. This was security, not the studied cruelty that later accusations would claim, but the effect on Davis was the same. By midsummer the prisoner appeared despondent, his facial neuralgia reappearing. Craven found that his hearing and sight were failing, and Davis himself complained of memory loss. He lost even more weight, the tone of his skin and muscles turning soft and weak. He had trouble walking, could not eat, and could not digest what he did consume. By late July even Miles was concerned, finding that Davis spent all his time sitting in a chair or reclining on a couch and would not walk or take other exercise. He asked, and received, permission to allow the prisoner to leave the casemate to take walks in the open air, accompanied by the general himself. At the same time, he was ordered to remove the lights and guards from the casemate, to give him books and papers to read, and to take any other measures to ease his condition compatible with security. "It is not the desire of this Government to subject him to any hardships not essential to his secure detention." While Preston Johnston, still in his own cell at Fort Delaware, declared his belief that the Yankees intended to let Davis die in prison, President Johnson sent a personal representative to Fort Monroe to make certain that Davis's health had not become dangerous.[10]

Gradually Davis improved, thanks to Craven's changes in his meals, cooked by the doctor's wife, and the exercise provided by Miles, though the prisoner took no pleasure in the general's company on his walks. By mid-August Davis asked for permission to write to Varina, and though he underwent a brief bout with erysipelas along with facial lesions and a carbuncle on his right leg, still he showed signs at least of stabilizing his overall condition, though it still was not good. By the end of August he took exercise every day, and while Miles thought he showed improvement, the more sympathetic Dr. Craven feared the opposite. He found Davis dull and despondent. "He is evidently breaking down," said Craven, and he blamed much of it on the dampness of the casemate cell. He and Miles both recommended removing Davis to other, drier quarters, and President Johnson immediately approved. On October 2 Davis left the casemate for the last time and moved to Carroll Hall, to an airy and pleasant second-floor room recently the quarters of an artillery officer. Even before the move Craven found Davis completely recovered from his recent illness, though still much reduced in general condition. Thereafter for nearly a year, with variations, his condition remained much the same.[11]

The opportunity at last to correspond with Varina gave Davis what little cheer he could take during the first year of his confinement. Miles issued him paper for each letter, with orders to speak only of family matters and a warning that his letters would be screened by the attorney general before they were mailed. He first wrote on August 21, reassuring her that his condition was not too bad. Of his future, or of what the government planned to do with him, he knew nothing. But he did know of some of the slanders being repeated and hoped that one day he might have the chance to refute them. Future letters continued in the same vein, occasionally complaining of lack of sleep or illness, but mostly taking a reassuring tone, along with a bit of resignation bordering on martyrdom. "If I alone could bear all the suffering of the country, and relieve it from further calamity," he wrote in September, "I trust our Heavenly father would give me strength to be a willing sacrifice." Henceforward, and for some time to come, Davis viewed himself in the Christlike role of one who took upon himself punishment for the supposed sins of millions. There was nothing inconsistent in such an assumption, for all of his public life Jefferson Davis had protested that he did not want the life he led, but that he gave himself to his public only at their insistence, from his sense of duty.[12]

It would be almost exactly a year before authorities allowed Varina actually to see her husband. His first visitors were legal counsel and the Reverend Minnegerode, who came to him on December 9 and gave him the sacrament. Minnegerode found Davis in good health, but the following spring he suffered a relapse, the neuralgia set in again, the sleeplessness aggravated by the constant shifting and banging of sentinels outside his door, and then the onset of his old fever once more. Word of his weakening condition reached Varina, and she immediately started anew a campaign to see him, appealing directly to President Johnson. On April 26, 1866, Johnson granted that permission, as war passions had subsided considerably, and mature reflection and absence of evidence had by then all but eliminated serious belief that Davis was a participant in the Lincoln conspiracy. Now he was simply a state prisoner, though still accused of treason.[13]

Varina entered his second-floor room in Carroll Hall on the morning of May 3, 1866, in a reunion both joyful and pathetic after a separation of forty-nine weeks. She found his condition alarming and his surroundings not much less so. Bugs inhabited his mattress. His tablecloth was nothing but an old copy of the *New York Herald*, never his favorite journal. He took his water from a horse bucket, used a chair for his washstand, and sat in another with a short leg that made it wobble under him. Davis himself found his quarters unobjectionable, but then he knew them by comparison to the casemate. He had a few books, including some works by the historian Bancroft, Washington Irving's life of Washington, a few novels, and the Bible, to which he turned with regularity.[14]

For the next three months Varina made regular, often daily visits, in time being allowed to take her meals with Davis, and found that fresh meat, dairy products, and fruits and grains were provided for him in good variety. Lack of exercise continued to be a problem, and that was relieved on May 25, when the authorities granted him the freedom of the grounds inside Fort Monroe from dawn until sunset in return for his parole of honor not to attempt to escape. By early June, Craven's replacement Dr. George Cooper reported Davis in better condition than at any time he could recollect, his appetite improving, his nerves calming. Varina's proximity must have had much to do with his turnaround, and it is no surprise that when she left at the end of July to join others lobbying for his release on bond, his fevers returned for a time, partially induced by the summer heat but also the result, no doubt, of Varina's absence.[15]

Throughout those months in the fort, regardless of his health, Davis watched events in the reunited nation with keen interest. "Though neither a spectator nor an actor," he told Varina in November 1865, "a life spent more in the service of my country than in that of my family, leaves me now unable to disengage myself from the consideration of public interests." He believed that the South had been betrayed at the war's end by the treatment of the victors, with men disenfranchised, property confiscated, and the state governments not immediately recognized and the states readmitted to the Union. Despite Varina's and his own later claims that he opposed the expatriation movement that took up to ten thousand former Confederates to Mexico and more distant lands after the collapse, Davis at the time approved of the motives of Confederate soldiers who found that they could not submit to rule by their former enemies. In his own mind he entertained notions that, if ever released, he would make a home in some other country. Yet he worried over one class of people who could not leave, the freed slaves. In his very first letters to Varina he asked after the family servants, praying that their fidelity could somehow be rewarded. Learning that Federal authorities had seized Brierfield and turned it into a home for recently freed blacks, he worried that his own former slaves might be pushed out, and now expressed a feeling that civil rights should be granted to all the freed blacks. He had always favored accepting their testimony in courts, an attitude adopted from his brother Joseph. "The negro is unquestionably to be at last the victim," he wrote of the war's aftermath. It might be possible to hold onto a modicum of the old good feeling that he believed existed between white and black before emancipation, but "to be successful, the policy must be as far removed from the conservatism that rejects everything new, as from the idealism which would retain nothing which is old." Competition would inevitably pit white against black now, and he believed that the latter, being intellectually and morally inferior, must inevitably suffer. Freedom, he feared, would be a cursed blessing to the Negro.[16]

Davis even had a chance to hear some of the opening salvos of the historical controversies over conduct of the war that would occupy public print for the next several generations, some of them involving him prominently. In October 1865 Beauregard's old chief of staff and partisan Brigadier General Thomas Jordan launched one of the very first Confederate attacks on Davis as president with an article in *Harper's New Monthly Magazine*. It rehearsed all the old arguments between Beauregard and Davis, reawakened the Manassas controversy, the animosity toward Northrop and Benjamin, the Johnston feud, and more, concluding that Davis had cost the South its independence through his obstinacy and pettiness. "Jefferson Davis for four years illustrated, like his monarchical prototypes, that no two natures are so widely oposite and unlike as the willful and the wise." "What a brute," Varina complained of Jordan when she read the article. It was some time before Davis saw it, confessing himself "at a loss" to see how Jordan could make a case that Davis's interference had lost the "game." "The unfortunate have always been deserted and betrayed," he told Varina, reverting to his role as martyr. With almost blatant hypocrisy he told her that "after faithful self-examination it is permitted to me to say, I have not done to others as they do unto me." Thus he dismissed the campaigns against Johnston and Beauregard, the feud with Yancey, and his shabby treatment of D. H. Hill. *He* would not seek to blame *his* failures on others by creating false scenarios. "There is no occasion, now, to make Frankensteins." "If the records are preserved," he said, they would dispose of all "romances past, passing, and to come." Davis did not refer to the records of the Confederacy by accident. One of his concerns during the flight from Richmond had been their preservation, though at the moment he did not know of their whereabouts or if they survived. But already in the recesses of his mind he certainly studied the possibility of one day using whatever archives remained to tell the "true" story of the rise and fall of the Confederacy, *his* story.[17]

By August 1866 attitudes in the North showed a marked change from the year before. Immediately after his capture, Davis was the object of innumerable entreaties to President Johnson to have him speedily tried and hanged for Lincoln's murder. At least one innovative citizen suggested that, instead, Davis should be sent around the country dressed in female attire and put on display for ticket sales. Yet pleas for clemency also cluttered Johnson's desk, and not just those from Southern pens, especially after the embarrassing shackling episode. Some offered constitutional arguments, pointing out the long-held notion that a man acting under the mandate of a state legislature could not be guilty of treason, and Davis had acted under the mandate of eleven such bodies. Others pleaded that for the sake of a harmonious repatriation of the former Confederates, leniency toward Davis and others would best serve the interests of North and South. Finally, the revelation in April 1866 that the evidence supposedly connecting Davis to the Lincoln murder was all fabrication and perjury removed the cause for much of Northern hostility toward the Confederate president. It was shortly after this that the stringent rules of his daily life in prison began to relax, starting with his parole to the freedom of the fort's grounds. Matters improved even more after August, when General Miles received orders to turn over command to a successor. Stories, often exaggerated, of the harsh treatment accorded Davis won sympathy for the prisoner, while making Miles unpopular and even controversial. Davis detested Miles. "The damned ass," he once called him to his guards. "The miserable ass!" Under Colonel H. S. Burton, Davis found a more agreeable regime. Burton allowed visitors much freer access to the prisoner, and soon Davis clasped again the hands of Preston Johnston, General John B. Gordon, and others who came to talk of old times and new. Varina was allowed to live in the fort with Davis, and sometimes they actually entertained visitors at dinner, raising their glasses to "toast the dead." In November Davis renewed his parole, with an accompanying relaxation of his restraints, and though his health took a temporary turn for the worse, his doctor believed it to be caused more by mental anxiety than his actual physical condition. After eighteen months as a prisoner his anxiety was not from worry over his captivity but nervous excitement and anticipation over when he might be released.[18]

Davis expected from the first that he would not be held indefinitely, expecting imprisonment only until his captors should bring him to trial, and almost from the first moment his friends began working to arrange his defense. Legal counsel was no problem. Sympathetic Northerners contacted the noted New York attorney Charles O'Conor late in May 1865 asking him to be Davis's legal counsel, and he promptly agreed, soon being joined by several others who would assist in the defense. Davis's friends began raising funds to pay for his defense as well, looking first toward moneys remaining in Confederate hands at the end of the war. This proved to be disappointing. In England, Benjamin and Breckinridge attempted to collect the balance of the diplomatic funds left with Jacob Thompson in Canada, but Thompson refused to turn it over, keeping at least one hundred thousand dollars for himself, and perhaps several times that amount never accounted for.

The dishonorable behavior of Thompson would not have surprised his old fellow Mississippian Jefferson Davis, but the conduct of another trusted friend must have pained him. Micajah Clark and the train carrying the Confederate Treasury finally reached Florida late in May, only to learn of Davis's capture and the dissolution of their government. The only remaining use for the specie still in his charge as acting treasurer would be for Davis's defense or other needs, and he proposed to the others guarding it to pay each a fair share, then deposit the lion's share in England. But others balked, especially Captain Watson Van Benthuysen and his two brothers. After a hot argument, they prevailed by sheer numbers, forcing a larger division among themselves, but promising to take $6,190 in trust to be handed over to Davis or Varina at the first opportunity. But Van Benthuysen kept all of it for more than two years. Burton Harrison approached him about it in March 1866 and quarreled severely with him, gaining nothing. Only in the summer of 1867 did Harrison take him to task again, this time finding that "his conscience and his acquaintances trouble him about the matter." Yet even then, he only turned over to Harrison the equivalent of $1,071 in gold, and Davis's secretary accepted it as the best he was likely to get. The reason the whole episode hurt Jefferson Davis, and that he never forgot it, is that Van Benthuysen was Joseph Davis's nephew by marriage.[19]

Still, the funds necessary for Davis's defense came together from whatever sources, including Benjamin's sending Varina the equivalent of half a year's salary for the president. The greater question was when he would be tried, and for what. Davis believed at first that the North felt "blood thirsty" toward him, and within days of arriving at Fort Monroe he asked to see his old friend Seward or Francis P. Blair, perhaps expecting that Seward, at least, would give him a fair hearing in memory of their former intimacy. Seward, still recovering from an assailant's attack and perhaps believing that Davis actually had something to do with it, made no response.[20]

Soon enough the shape of the charges against Davis became manifest. In May 1865 a Federal court in Virginia charged him with treason, but the indictment was lost and so a court in Washington issued another, only to have it quashed, the prevailing opinion being that any indictment and subsequent trial should take place in a place where the treason was committed, namely a former Confederate state. Thus another court in Norfolk indicted Davis again in May 1866, the specification being that on June 15, 1864, in and around Richmond, within the jurisdiction of this Federal court, Davis incited citizens—Beauregard's command—to resist the lawful authority of the United States, meaning Grant's army.[21]

At first, once the court handed down the indictment, it appeared that a trial might come that summer, or at least an initial arraignment appearance in a Richmond court. Davis was not a civil prisoner, but in the hands of the military. The whole question of jurisdiction became muddy, for initially the government intended to try him by military commission, as it had tried the Lincoln conspirators. The collapse of that case against Davis made such a trial untenable now. Then Davis's health seemed not to be up to what would undoubtedly be a lengthy trial, though coincidental with his indictment, Davis's conditions improved. The opportunity to give his parole in exchange for greater freedom may have owed as much to a desire to diffuse sympathy for Davis's condition in any civil court appearance as to the dictates of his health.

While the civil and military authorities wrestled with questions of jurisdiction, Chief Justice Salmon P. Chase settled the matter for the moment when he announced that he could not attend the summer session of the court. Thus they postponed Davis's appearance until the fall term. Now O'Conor and the others petitioned the attorney general to release Davis on bail. Three prominent and sympathetic Northern businessmen, Cornelius Vanderbilt, Horace Greeley, and Gerrit Smith, volunteered to put up between them $1 million, but it was declined on the grounds that Davis was still a military prisoner and thus not liable to bail. Indeed, bail and security now seemed to be the chief reason for keeping Davis at Fort Monroe rather than turning him over to Virginia authorities, though even beyond that it was becoming evident that Washington did not know what to do with him, and the longer he remained a prisoner, the more difficult the situation became. With the Lincoln murder accusation out of the way, the only outstanding charge against Davis was treason—a civil, not a military, offense. Yet the army continued to hold Davis. Had the Virginia court demanded that he be remanded to its custody, the army would have had no choice but to comply, but security was better at Fort Monroe than in a state prison; Davis's health could be better monitored; and as long as he remained in the hands of the military, he could not be bailed, while the subject of bail would have to arise immediately if he were in civil hands and not speedily brought to trial. Yet the civil case against Davis was not ready for trial. Moreover, there were questions of whether he could ever be tried on the treason charge. President Johnson had already issued amnesties for most of the men who bore arms for the Confederacy and left the door open for applications for pardon by almost all others. None of the military leaders were imprisoned any longer, and of the high civil officials, even Stephens had been released. Of the cabinet, only Memminger and Trenholm remained in custody, and they would be pardoned before the end of the year. Indeed, Davis was almost alone now as a state prisoner, and President Johnson had even hinted that he should apply for pardon. It would save the government the difficulty of what would undoubtedly be a long and acrimonious trial, contributing nothing to healing the wounds between the sections. It was an eventuality foreseen long before, when Sherman had suggested, echoing a sentiment of Lincoln's, that it would be better for everyone if Jefferson Davis had simply escaped.[22]

But he did not escape, and they had to deal with him. When Varina left that summer to meet with O'Conor, she reported to her husband that the attorney general seemed favorably disposed toward him and even that the president expressed friendly sentiments. In mid-August O'Conor actually hoped to achieve something within a few days, but it came to naught. Johnson was up against heavy resistance within his own party, the more radical Republicans, including Stanton, showing vigorous hostility to his more pacific reconstruction measures. Thus Davis became something of a pawn in the greater power struggle in Washington. Even if Davis applied for pardon and Johnson granted it, the act would still have been political suicide, and Davis would never beg pardon in any case. To do so would have been an admission of guilt.[23]

That summer a serendipitous publication of a book added materially to the growing momentum for the government to do something in the Davis case. Dr. Craven had kept a diary and notes of his conversations with Davis during 1865, and turned them over to Charles G. Halpine, a popular writer, to make them into a book. Halpine, however, had his own motives. A Democrat friendly to Johnson's mild reconstruction views, Halpine thought that a book highlighting the cruelty to Davis by his Republican-backed military captors would discredit the radicals and aid Johnson. The president approved, and within months *Prison Life of Jefferson Davis* appeared, to become a major sensation. Though published over Dr. Craven's name, Halpine's authorship was well known. He presented an idealized portrait of Davis as a tragic hero—a man with nothing but love in his heart, who even shared the crumbs of his bread with a mouse, "the only living thing he had now power to benefit"— cruelly treated by Miles.[24]

It was all an appeal for leniency for Davis and other former Confederates, and it served Johnson's purpose admirably, stirring a renewed swell of sympathy for the prisoner. Ironically, Davis himself detested the book and broke his friendship with Craven forever, for Halpine engrafted enormous fictions on a few grains of fact, and that Davis could never forgive even if the book did work to his benefit. Yet the portrait of the prisoner languishing away waiting for the trial that never came had something of Dumas or Hugo about it, appealing to the romantic imaginations of Americans. Thus when the fall session of the Virginia court failed to sit after all, another outcry ensued, and Washington could not fail to listen. With Davis's health always precarious, what if he should die in military custody? Then there would be the devil to pay, not just in the South but even internationally. Greeley began using the editorial pages of his influential *New York Tribune* to champion the cause of Davis's speedy trial or release on bail, and more and more of Davis's friends urged him to apply for pardon, having cause, they thought, to expect that Johnson would grant it. But he always refused. "Confident of the justice of our cause, and the rectitude of my own conduct," he would say, "I declined." If Jefferson Davis had been right in 1861, then he was right now, and he wanted a trial in open court in order to prove—as he could always prove such things to his own satisfaction—that secession was not treason and that the war had been but self-defense.

There is no better proof of the utter myopic isolation in which Davis's intellect worked than this naive belief. Through thousands of years of history, with which he was thoroughly familiar, and in the civil wars of his own time in Europe, countless thousands lost their freedom, property, and their lives in the wake of failed separatist movements. It was what happened when bloody wars engendered high passions and when winners had power over losers. By contrast, only one Confederate, Major Henry Wirz, the commandant of Andersonville's prison camp, lost his life to Yankee retaliation, while relatively few forfeited indefinitely either property or civil rights. It had been the mildest end to a civil conflict in all of history, yet Davis believed even this unwarranted and actually maintained that the victor owed apologies to the vanquished. In court he could prove that the South had been right, that *he* had been right.[25]

Davis never got his trial, but he would get his freedom. The appeals for leniency continued to flow into Washington, with more and more influential men championing Davis's cause, not so much out of love for the prisoner as a concern for the constitutional process guaranteeing the right to speedy trial. As the spring of 1867 approached, the prisoner neared the end of two years of confinement without the chance to face his accusers. Trying and convicting Davis for treason might not be a travesty of justice, but letting him languish year after year certainly was. Secretary of War Stanton, one of the chief spokesmen for the radical faction in Washington, seemed to be the last remaining stumbling block, and Varina approached him through one of his close friends, who finally persuaded him that with Johnson leaning toward turning Davis over to civil authorities, and the attorney general and the secretary of the treasury favoring it, Stanton had little ground for objection, especially since no one now claimed that Davis was subject to military law. Stanton relented, saying he would not object to handing Davis to Virginia civil authorities. "At last I can see some little way into the millstone which weighs us down," Varina wrote her husband on April 9, 1867, somewhat mixing her metaphors. Two weeks later, writing from Baltimore, she reported, "People seem to agree on your immediate release." Much started to happen in a short span of time. Davis's beloved old friend Franklin Pierce made a special trip to Fort Monroe to visit him. Though the exact nature of his visit is unknown, most at the time speculated that it touched on his impending trial or release. Certainly the visit buoyed Davis's spirits; he had never lost his reverential love for the man who had been *his* president.[26]

On April 28 President Johnson strongly hinted yet again that he would grant a pardon if Davis applied, regardless of the storm of criticism that would ensue. Then on May 4 O'Conor made application for a writ of habeas corpus requiring the military at Fort Monroe to hand over the prisoner to Virginia authorities. It was granted, and O'Conor asked Burton Harrison to take it to Richmond to be signed and attested and then to take it to Burton at Fort Monroe. Harrison left at once, secured the proper signatures, then went to Fort Monroe on Friday, May 10. Presenting the writ to Colonel Burton, he received an assurance that there would be no difficulty with compliance. Harrison spent that night with Davis in Carroll Hall, the last night of his imprisonment, and it must have been a bittersweet occasion, the second anniversary of their capture. He helped the Chief and Varina pack their belongings for the trip to Richmond.

If not a triumphal progress, still the next day's journey up the James must have raised Davis's spirits. Burton imposed no guards upon him, continuing to honor his parole, and showing uncommon courtesy and consideration. Along the banks of the river people gathered to cheer and wave, and flowers came aboard at stops, all attesting to the reverence Virginians still felt for their former leader. At Richmond itself, Davis was given the same rooms at the Spotswood Hotel that he occupied when he first came to the city as president in 1861. The well-wishers almost exhausted Davis as they came to pay their calls, Harrison looking on anxiously all the while. "No stranger would suppose the quiet gentleman who receives his visitors with such peaceful dignity is the State prisoner around whose dungeon so many battalions have been marshalled for two years," the secretary wrote two days later. "Everyone has called, bringing flowers and bright faces of welcome to him who has suffered vicariously for the millions." Davis was not the only one saw himself as Christ-like.[27]

It was almost anticlimactic when they entered the courtroom on Monday, May 13, and went before Judge John Underwood. Ironies crowded around him like old friends. The United States District Court now used the building that two years before housed the Treasury and Confederate executive offices. Davis's own former set of rooms there now hosted the men who would pass judgment on him. Here, surrounded by walls that once held the maps he used to plan the campaigns of mighty armies, Jefferson Davis at last heard Burton formally remand him to civil custody. The first step to freedom had been taken.[28]

The rest followed quickly. O'Conor asked that Davis's trial commence immediately, to which the government prosecutor replied that he was not prepared to prosecute the case at this term. After lengthy prefatory remarks covering the constitutional ground, O'Conor then asked that Davis be released on bail, the bond posted by Greeley and a host of others who pledged themselves in the defendant's behalf. Neither the district attorney nor the government counsel raised objection to releasing Davis on bond, suggesting one hundred thousand dollars as an appropriate sum. Judge Underwood, whom some had feared would take a tough stance, proved to be anything but harsh. He delivered a little speech of his own about peace, harmony, and reconciliation; tried to justify somewhat the necessity for Davis's long incarceration; and then promptly granted the motion for bail. Greeley and the other sureties stepped forward and signed the bond, and Underwood ordered Davis to be released pending trial before the November session.[29]

The courtroom exploded in an uproar of applause and cheering. Onlookers threw open windows to shout the news to the street, and Harrison a few days later told Preston Johnston that "it was for a time the most exciting drama I ever expect to see in a court room." So tumultuous was the uproar that O'Conor feared the excitement would be too much for Davis, whose emaciation left him pitifully weak and suffering from a lassitude that Varina thought very noticeable. He was fully bearded now, though most of it had gone gray, and his onetime attorney general, George Davis, in the courtroom himself, found the ex-president to be "only the shadow of his former self." They half led, half carried the frail man down to the street and put him in a carriage to his hotel. There Varina awaited him, along with the Reverend Minnegerode. Davis asked that they all pray with him in thanksgiving.[30]

Congratulations and good wishes poured in from around the country. All his old Confederate associates sent their best. Pierce, knowing better than most of his friend's condition, asked that Davis come to his cabin in New Hampshire and spend a few months recuperating. James Mason suggested Niagara, Canada, instead, now a haven for a small community of high-ranking Confederate expatriates including, at times, Breckinridge, Early, and Mason himself. In fact, Canada had been Davis's intended goal for some time, since his older children lived there in the keeping of Varina's mother in Montreal. Yet getting there was exhausting. Almost immediately after his release, he went with Varina, Harrison, and Winnie and Willie to New York, hoping to rest briefly before continuing the journey. But the press of visitors proved so great that after thirty-six hours he was completely broken down. Harrison had to handle him the way he picked up the children who had haunted the aides' offices in Richmond. "I didn't quite 'spank' him," Harrison told Preston Johnston, but he carried Davis bodily to a carriage and drove him out of town to O'Conor's country place for a few days of rest. Even then Harrison worried, seeing the Chief feeble and apathetic to everything. As soon as possible they left for Montreal, and happily no one along the way recognized the invalid with the gray beard. At last he saw Margaret and little Jeff once more and took up lodging at a small boardinghouse at 247 Mountain Street, on Mountain Terrace.[31]

Davis remained only a few days in Montreal, however, before he left for Niagara to see Mason and the others. His old friend Charles Helm, former Confederate agent in Havana, came to accompany him on the journey, and Mason, Early, and others joined them in Toronto. On May 30 they all reached Niagara and a warm welcome. Just across the Niagara River they could see Fort Niagara, New York, and the Stars and Stripes fluttering above it. Breckinridge, when he sojourned in Niagara, came in order to be able to see that flag, hoping one day to return to his home. Davis looked at it now and commented bitterly, "Look there, Mason, there is the gridiron we have been fried on."

Though he stayed but a few days, the visit greatly cheered Davis, and he found some hours to forget the bitterness as he talked and joked with his old friends. He preferred not to speak of his imprisonment, and the rest did not press him. Yet even though he could feel himself getting better in the cool, bright days in the untroubled little village, he longed to return to his children in Montreal. Mason tried hard to persuade him to stay, but in the end gave in to what he told Davis was "the perverse habit of having your own way."[32]

Once reunited in Montreal, the Davis family made the best of their reduced circumstances. Social invitations abounded, though he accepted few and spent most of his time in their small house, often lost deep in distracted thought and occasional depression. All who met him came away with an impression of a broken man, careworn and emaciated, with sunken cheeks and hollow eyes. Only children seemed to draw him out of himself. For the rest, he reportedly told one friend that he wished he could disappear from view entirely and spend the balance of his days in seclusion from all but family and friends. Unhappy with their residence, the Davises looked for another with the aid of friends, moved to a new place in Montreal, and then in October moved again to Lennoxville in eastern Quebec, where little Jeff boarded at school. Here Davis found more in the way of rest. "This is a very quiet place and so far agreeable to me," he wrote Helm, but could not describe it further. "A village tavern is a thing which you can comprehend without a description," he said. There he boarded at a tavern for nearly a month. Varina left to visit her ailing mother.[33]

Much occupied Davis's mind as he recuperated, took long walks, read, and talked with his Canadian neighbors. Immediately he needed money, for the salary Benjamin sent Varina did not last long, and he resented having to accept the charity of friends who helped pay for his family's lodging. He tried through Harrison to recover the money from Van Benthuysen, with only limited success, and inquired of Mason and other former diplomats about remaining funds abroad, with even less result. Besides needing money, he also grew restless at inactivity and cast about for some employment. Ruling out a return to a settled life in Mississippi so long as his trial remained pending, he looked into moving to England, where he thought he might form a business association in Liverpool, probably with a firm formerly connected with the Confederacy. Nothing came of it, and in any case, everything depended on his trial. Expected first for the November term, it soon became evident in communications from O'Conor that it would be postponed until the following spring. "I am still at a loss to the purpose of the U.S. Govt. in relation to myself," he said in September, and he remained so.[34]

Davis did toy with one way of filling his idle hours. Barely a week after his release rumors spread in the United States that he intended to write a book "giving a history of the Secession movement, the Southern struggle, and his own adventures from December 1860, to May, 1867." Even hostile press speculated that such a book "would be a really valuable contribution" if the author could write honestly and without prejudice. Probably Davis had conceived the idea of a book while yet in prison, though it remained an undeveloped thought. Then Joseph suggested that he write something, and in Canada Varina encouraged him to go ahead with it. Yielding, he obtained from storage in the Bank of Montreal a collection of his papers and books that Margaret Howell had managed to conceal in her trunk, and he started to go through them. He did not stay with it for long. He came to an April 9, 1865, telegram he had sent to Lee, and that brought back at once all the anguish of the loss of the Army of Northern Virginia and the tale of disaster that it inaugurated. Closing the book, he stood and began the old pacing, his face showing how upset he was. "Let us put them by for awhile," he told Varina finally. "I cannot speak of my dead so soon."[35]

I Seem to Remember More Every Day

When Jefferson Davis left Canada in November, bound for Richmond and his trial, he could hardly have guessed that he embarked on two journeys—one the quest for the justice before the law that he believed he could secure and the other a search for someplace where he belonged, some permanent home, that would last nearly ten years. The first trip proved pointless. Arriving in Richmond, he met with Lee for the first time, then sat in the courtroom listening to Lee give testimony in his case, all the while expecting this to be the beginning of the trial. But when Lee finished, the government attorney asked that the trial be rescheduled for March 1868 without even hearing Davis. The defendant, released on his own recognizance, was bitterly disappointed though still free.[1]

There was nothing to do now but kill time. Davis spent a few days at the home of General Isaac Trimble, outside Baltimore, until Varina could join him. Then they determined to pay visits through the South, especially in New Orleans and Mississippi. But first they sailed for Havana, both for the warm winter climate and to look into any remaining Confederate funds left there by Helm or by Benjamin when he passed through in 1865. On their arrival, friends found Davis worn and pale, "hardly recognizable." He stayed through Christmas, perhaps recalling his earlier visit after another personal tragedy, and then went on to New Orleans, always his favorite city in the South. Within a few days he was finally back in Mississippi. Davis stopped briefly at Woodville, receiving a warm welcome from old friends and relatives, and then went on to Vicksburg, where at last, after so many years, he saw his brother Joseph once more. The joy of the reunion was marred, however, when he went downriver to Davis Bend. So much had changed. Hurricane was gone, and though Brierfield still stood, the plantation itself lay in miserable condition. Moreover, it no longer belonged to him. Legally, of course, it never had, Joseph always retaining title. That may have saved it from absolute confiscation by the Yankees during the war. They had operated it for a few years as a freedmen's home, but late in 1866 the title reverted unconditionally to Joseph. Unfortunately, he needed money and could no longer manage the plantations himself. Consequently, he sold both Hurricane and Brierfield to his friend and former slave Ben Montgomery and his sons. No Davis ever lived at Davis Bend again.[2]

This did not entirely please Jefferson Davis. From prison he had authorized Joseph to sell the plantation if necessary, though legally the brother hardly needed such authorization. But Joseph gave the Montgomerys such liberal terms, and crop reverses prevented them from meeting even those, that income from the sale was paltry. Jefferson Davis needed money and was not happy with the situation. When Joseph drew a will a year later desiring his executors to continue to extend liberal terms to Montgomery, Jefferson Davis—one of the executors— did not approve and urged Joseph to take back the land and sell it to someone else. His attitude toward blacks had never been as enlightened as Joseph's, and in the years after the war it would retreat a little more, perhaps as a result of finding himself homeless and dependent on charity while his former slaves lived in his home. "Poor creatures," he said of his onetime slaves this season. "They do not fail so much in warmth as in consistency of feeling, and their gratitude is of the kind which is felt for favors to come." In other words, Negroes were still children, to be cared for and nurtured but not to be trusted entirely.[3]

White Mississippians made up for Davis's disappointments at Brierfield, and there came urgings that he should one day serve the state yet again. To all such suggestions he replied that if in his current situation he could not help Mississippi anymore, at least he could not hurt it either. He could, in fact, do nothing so long as his indictment and trial hung over his head, and he soon left Mississippi to go to Richmond, hoping on O'Conor's advice that he might have his day in court in April. It did not come. Johnson was even then in the throes of his impeachment problems, and the government did not want to risk more than one sensational trial at a time. Instead it simply drew up a new indictment in March and began taking testimony before a grand jury. Once again, though he was in Richmond, Davis was not called to testify, and the case was put off until May. But during the months to come, Davis received one notification after another from O'Conor of additional postponements, from May to June and then to October. There was nothing Davis could do but return to Canada and wait.[4]

He never stopped worrying about some kind of occupation. The previous summer he investigated a copper mine in Canada in which friends offered him a share, and, hoping to make something from it, he invested two thousand dollars in a half interest, though its prospects did not immediately improve. Virginia's Randolph-Macon College offered him its presidency shortly after his return to Canada, but Davis forthrightly declined it out of fear that his name being associated with the college would, at that time, do it more harm than good. Until his legal questions were resolved, Davis felt it would be almost impossible to find honorable employment without compromising his employer. Until then he would just keep looking. More and more often now, references comparing himself to Mr. Micawber from *David Copperfield* crept into his correspondence, as he waited for "something to turn up."[5]

The waiting almost turned to despair. That summer in Canada he took a wretched fall down a staircase while carrying Winnie, ending on the floor of the hotel in Lennoxville with two broken ribs and friends fearful for his life. When his recovery seemed to take too long, a doctor prescribed an ocean voyage, and Davis quickly resurrected his idea of establishing a Liverpool cotton and tobacco commission partnership with an English friend. Varina prayed that something might come of it, as much for his mental health as their material support. "He looks wretchedly," she confided to Howell Cobb, "and I think much of his indisposition is induced by his despair of getting some employment."[6]

The summer's trip to England did, indeed, do much to restore Davis in health and spirit, though not in fortunes. Prominent British statesmen lionized the ex-president of the Confederacy, and old friends like Benjamin gave a good example of men who could dismiss painful memories of the past, a lesson Varina wished her husband could learn. Being constantly the guest of one dignitary after another, at least the Davises did not have to depend upon their meager funds to survive, yet by December, with the children in school and business prospects still uncertain if not gloomy, Davis decided to remain longer and rented rooms in London. Thereafter he went to Paris to visit with old Dudley Mann and John Slidell, and there—showing his pique that France never granted recognition to the Confederacy—he declined an invitation to visit the Emperor Napoléon III. He did accept the hospitality of his old political foe William Gwin, however, now like so many others living in exile. Davis played the tourist, admiring the Greek marbles in the Louvre and paying homage to the paintings of Titian, Raphael, and David, though he balked at expressing any admiration for the portraits by Rubens. He showed a special fondness for the ink sketches of Gustave Doré. As he walked the boulevards and gardens of Paris, he often remarked on the artworks everywhere in that glorious city, though he detested the equestrian statue of Joan of Arc in the Tuileries. "Brave little Joan," he lamented, "they have mounted her up there with such long stirrups that the poor child can barely touch them by stretching down her toes." Revealing a well-developed Francophobia, he would ever after say that "no Frenchman ever could design an equestrian statue properly."[7]

In the coming months Davis visited Switzerland, journeyed through Scotland, touched down in Wales, and all the while improved his constitution by long walks and rides in the invigorating British air. But nothing came of his business hopes, and after more than a year abroad he faced the realization that he might have to go back to the United States to make a living. At least he could go back without fear now, for during his absence the government continued to show no disposition to bring him to trial. By October 1868 O'Conor believed there was a chance that a *nolle prosequi* was in the offing, essentially a declaration not to prosecute. On the last day of November, Davis's counsel petitioned to quash the indictment and then proposed to the court that Davis had already been punished for his supposed crimes before the trial, thanks to the constitutional amendment that excluded him and others from certain rights of citizenship. On December 5 Chief Justice Chase dismissed the indictment, agreeing that since punishment had already been inflicted by the Fourteenth Amendment, the case could not be tried ex post facto. When President Johnson issued a Universal Amnesty that same Christmas, the road was open to a full pardon, if Davis chose to apply for one.[8]

It was not the resolution of his case that Davis wanted. He would always believe that he could have vindicated himself, and thereby vindicated the South as well, in court. It is well for him that it never went to trial, however, for certainly he would not have prevailed. His arguments would have been the same that he presented interminably in his Senate speeches. He never convinced anyone of his idea of the legal relation of the states to the Union then, and there is no reason to expect that he would have found a more sympathetic audience in a jury in a Federal courtroom later. They had heard it all before, and Jefferson Davis would have invited for himself only another bitter defeat. Moreover, he would never have accepted the justice of any adverse verdict.

At least now he could honorably and without fear attempt to repair his fortunes back in the United States, and a tempting offer appeared that could not have been better timed. Former Tennessee Governor Isham Harris wrote to offer Davis the presidency of the Carolina Life Insurance Company of Memphis, and at a negotiable salary of between twelve and twenty thousand dollars per annum. Davis at first felt some hesitancy, fearing the "persistent hostility" of Northerners to anything connected with him, but Harris and others in the company prevailed. At last Davis would have something to do. At last he could take care of his family. Leaving the children in school, and Varina to care for them, he returned alone to the United States in September.[9]

Insurance companies and railroads, especially, sought out former high-ranking Confederates to be figurehead executives during the late 1860s and 1870s. Breckinridge, Forrest, Echols, and a host of others would all tread the same path that Davis now tried to walk, and generally with no more long-run success. Davis threw himself into the work with his usual commitment, and almost as a first order of business began engaging old friends as agents—Bragg in Texas, Gilmer in Georgia. Involving such inexperienced military men in business affairs did not help, and the business climate made things worse. Speculation was on the rise in the wake of the war, the banking system was not sound, and the gathering signs of a collapse were there to be seen. A financial panic hit the nation late in 1872 and continued through the following year, wiping out a host of insurance companies. The Carolina survived after a fashion, but only by dint of its board selling out at a ridiculous compensation to another firm, against Davis's wishes and without even his knowledge. Mortified, he resigned his presidency, finding himself once again out of employment and in debt. Another failure.[10]

The years in Memphis proved trying for many reasons. The separation from Varina and the children lasted for nearly a year, and though his own health improved, Varina's letters indicated that hers suffered. Yet, unwilling to pull the children out of school in midyear and unable to provide a proper home just yet, Davis held off going back to England to bring them home until the late summer of 1870. Even then he could barely afford the trip. Attempts to sell his copper mine stock and some land he still owned in Mississippi produced nothing. "When I returned to Missi. I found everything I had destroyed or scattered," he lamented to a friend. "It was new to be in debt and new to be without resources." During the past year he had saved enough from his salary to meet most of his debts connected with Brierfield, chiefly taxes, even though he had lost its ownership and occupancy. But he complained that "you never knew me so dull and tedious." The constant concern over money oppressed him.[11]

More oppressive was his brother Joseph's condition. The elder Davis would be eighty-six years old in December 1870, if he lived that long, but his frail health became increasingly uncertain. Jefferson Davis already felt bitter that Joseph's trusted servant Jack had abandoned the old man the previous winter while he was ailing. "Jack has disappointed me and weakened the little faith I had in the fidelity of a free negro," Davis complained, calling his behavior "worse than could have been expected of a *human being*." Still Davis hoped that his brother's health would hold while he went to England to fetch his family. He sailed on August 10 and remained through October, and it was in London that a letter from his niece Lise Mitchell brought the dreaded news that Joseph Davis had died on September 18. "How bitter are the waters in which I am overwhelmed," Davis cried. And the news got no better, for when Davis returned, leaving Varina and the children to follow on a later vessel, he learned that in his absence Robert E. Lee, too, had gone to final rest. "He was my friend," Davis mourned, "and in that word is included all that I could say of any man."[12]

Perhaps because of their long separation during his imprisonment, and then the year spent away from him abroad, Varina resisted all attempts to persuade her to go to a healthier climate in the summer of 1871, though eventually Davis prevailed. The next year, however, she was not to be moved, even though she was ill—suffering chiefly from a frayed nervous system—from a variety of causes through much of the season. Davis blamed Memphis in part. "I cannot commend the climate of this place if there is any tendency to disease," he warned friends. Yet he and Varina survived. Alas, little Willie did not. In mid-October he came down with diphtheria, and in a matter of days the boy, not yet twelve years old, succumbed. Davis had been away on business and only returned as his son was sinking. "I thought of the bright boy I had left at home, the hope and pride of my house," he lamented a few days after the tragedy. "I have had more than the ordinary allotment of disappointment and sorrow." Varina was distraught, while Davis met the death of his fourth son as stoically as possible. Two months later, with Christmas approaching, he still confessed, "I am too sad to enter into the joyeties of this festive season." His Christmas wish to friends that year was the pitiful hope, "May God spare you such sorrow as our's."[13]

The following year brought little cheer. The Carolina failed, Varina's nerves and depression did not improve, Maggie became seriously ill, and Davis had to send all of them away to better climates for the summer. By September he was writing to Varina that "the tide of my fortune is at the lowest ebb." Then his sister Lucinda Stamps died, capping the horrid year. Again at loose ends, Davis thought of moving to Louisville, tried to sell his mining stock again, and even pursued the thought of going to Texas, but it all came to nothing. His own health took a downward turn again in the fall, the old fever came back, and as he described it, "For some days the scale seemed equally balanced between life and death." Then, when just recovering, he went outside in the cold and suffered a relapse, this time involving the old eye affliction again. His doctor suggested another sea voyage. Downhearted by the unrelenting woes of Memphis, he resolved to go.[14]

Not until January 1874 did Davis finally steam out of New Orleans bound for England. Varina came to wish him good-bye, but she could not go along. Separated from him so much over the years, she seemed suddenly better able to handle it all in good cheer, and besides, her "precious Banny" wrote to her several times a week wherever he went. Yet it was hard for Davis to leave, especially "without definite purpose," as he put it. He was going for his health, but he had as well the feeling of an aimless wanderer. For all that he enjoyed his stay overseas, visiting again with old Mann and other exiled friends, Davis found it all to little point. He investigated the possibility of associating himself with British insurance companies but it came to nothing, and by May he confessed that "days have grown into weeks" without avail. At least his health recovered remarkably, but when he returned at the end of May he had to admit that "I have no settled plans." He rejoined Varina in Memphis. "And so we wait," he said, "like McCauber [Micawber] for something to turn up."[15]

He was sixty-seven years old that June, almost penniless, and with no tangible prospects. Most of what he had owned went into Brierfield, and he never really owned that, though it had always been his brother's intention that he should. He seemed to have little alternative now but to try to recover his plantation despite the provisions of Joseph's will. He filed a suit against Joseph's heirs, claiming that his brother's intent all along had been for him to have Brierfield, a contention that few in the family contested and that even Ben Montgomery supported. It proved to be the beginning of a long and increasingly acrimonious feud between Davis and his once-beloved niece Lise Mitchell and her brother, Joseph's grandchildren and surviving heirs. Before it was over, the Montgomerys were also caught up in it, thanks to their inability to keep up with the interest payments due on the purchase of the plantations. A judge dismissed Davis's suit early in 1876, but of course that could not stop him. He filed an appeal, and in April 1878 the state supreme court found in his favor. That done, he immediately filed to foreclose on the mortgage held by the Montgomerys, now drastically in default. Not until September 1881, however, did the property finally come back into Jefferson Davis's hands, more than twenty years after he left it to go to Montgomery. And even then, it would bring him no support.[16]

By the time he recovered Brierfield, many other changes in Davis's life had altered his outlook considerably from what it had been in 1874. There were more investigations of railroad ventures and mining opportunities, especially in Arkansas and Texas. He even considered moving to Texas when offered another college presidency, but Varina so loathed the idea that in the end he declined. At least he began to assume a modest public posture again, as invitations to address veterans' groups and agricultural fairs started coming in his mail. He had first made a public address back in November 1870, at memorial services for Lee, then spoke again in 1873 to the Virginia Historical Society, only to arouse a minor controversy when he condemned the enfranchisement of blacks and other repressive measures imposed after the Reconstruction acts of 1867, averring that had the South known what was in store for it, Confederates would never have surrendered. Like all Southerners, he loathed the military occupation and other effects of Reconstruction that became manifest after those acts were passed; like most Southerners, he would not countenance the idea that the acts were encouraged after two years' experience showed a disinclination in the Southern states, especially regarding the position of blacks in the new society, to accept the verdict of the war.[17]

By mid-1875 something, at last, appeared to have "turned up," and it suited both Davis's pecuniary needs and also his continuing desire to help rebuild the South. Mississippians had again asked him to accept a senatorial seat, but he declined because he could not do so without being pardoned, and that he would never request. When friends suggested electing him in spite of his disfranchisement, he still demurred. "Insult and violence, producing alienation between the sections, would be the only result," he protested. "I am too old to serve you as I once did." Indeed, he sought to avoid involvement in any sort of controversy with federal authorities, even asking to be excluded from a current bill to pay pensions to Mexican War veterans rather than see himself become an issue as one entitled to such a federal emolument. But then came an invitation from the Mississippi Valley Association, a new British concern that hoped to induce foreign emigration to the South and to develop a commercial trade directly between New Orleans and the ports of Europe, carried in company-owned holds. "Poverty compels me to seek for whatever employment may serve my needs," he told a friend that year.[18]

The only good news was the January 1876 wedding of his daughter Maggie to J. Addison Hayes of North Carolina, a young man who would come to be almost a son to Jefferson Davis. And the Mississippi Valley Association started off well, with a salary of at least six thousand dollars to keep the family going. He put his son Jefferson Jr. into the Virginia Military Institute and moved Varina and Winnie to New Orleans, where the association made its headquarters. Soon business required yet another trip abroad to raise capital in Britain, and that is where the association failed. But the Davises enjoyed their sojourn at first, placing Winnie in a German school for young ladies, and then Varina's health broke once again. By now her bouts with clearly psychosomatic nervous ailments—the result of years of emotional upheavals and of more years of semipoverty, along with the deaths of three of her children—were almost constant. And she was not yet fifty. Watching the gradual aging of her husband, seeing his pain and humiliation at being unable to make a steady living for them, she took refuge in her depressions.

By November Davis decided to return to the South. Varina remained behind, too unwell to travel, but he had to settle affairs with the Mississippi Valley Association and get on with some kind of work that would provide an income. Yet when he returned to New Orleans he confessed to Varina that "I do not know how long will be my stay here and have nothing definite in view." There was faint hope of an embryonic savings-and-loan company, but he did not even try to appear enthusiastic on that score. Almost as an afterthought he closed the letter by saying that, in the absence of anything else, he could "join Maj. Walthall at Mobile and push forward the memoirs."[19]

The old idea of writing his own story of the Confederacy never entirely left Davis's mind during the years that passed since he turned away from it in tears. Already the memoirs of other actors on that stage were coming into print, including those of enemies like Joseph E. Johnston, and it seemed incumbent on Davis as the premier leader of the Lost Cause to present his own view, both for posterity and also to put Johnston and others in their place. Varina and Joseph both urged him to the task when he got out of Fort Monroe. Mann implored him in 1869 to "prepare your *Book*," showing that Davis continued at least to discuss the idea with friends, and Mann's further plea to "bring out your first volume" implies that even at that early day, Davis envisioned a massive tome requiring more than one volume. Or perhaps it was just self-awareness on Davis's part, for never could he make an argument succinctly, and any book of his on the Confederacy and his conduct of its affairs was destined to be argumentative. In 1870 Preston Johnston joined the chorus, asserting, "You owe it to yourself not to die without vindicating the truth of history."

By December 1873 rumors spread widely that Davis was, in fact, working on his memoir, though most assuredly he was not. However, he had continued in a desultory fashion the gathering of some of his scattered papers, along with statements from former associates relating chiefly to the more controversial matters such as his capture. The failure of the Carolina and the death of Willie interrupted further progress, but late in 1874 he found the subject more and more on his mind. For some reason, Davis appears to have doubted either his ability or his stamina for the task on his own, but in November of that year he called to mind Major W. T. Walthall, who first came to his attention in 1870 as a defender of the cause, and who by early 1871 was an agent for the Carolina. Davis knew him to be working on a history of the Army of Tennessee, and continued association convinced Davis, with his usual poor judgment of character, that Walthall would be a good man to assist him with his own memoir. In April 1875 Walthall himself proposed that he aid Davis with "fragmentary labor" in preparing the work. Davis's own assistance in critically reading the manuscript of Preston Johnston's biography of his father no doubt further whetted his appetite for telling his own story, but the ever-present press of financial affairs forced him to continue postponing it.[20]

Finally, in the fall of 1875, Davis and Walthall came to an informal agreement. Walthall approached publishers on behalf of Davis, starting with Turnbull Brothers of Baltimore, then Lippincott and D. Appleton. Negotiations took several months, and Davis left almost all of it to Walthall, his chief concern being that he not be rushed into print. "We are not seeking an 'opportune time' for publication," Davis advised, "but mainly desiring to vindicate our cause." Finally, during his summer stay in England in 1876, Davis accepted a proposal from Appleton and authorized Walthall to enter into a contract. Chiefly, Appleton engaged to pay Walthall a stipend plus expenses for his efforts in "the preparation of the work," and Walthall, for his part, was to get the work done in a timely fashion but no later than July 1, 1878. Compensation for Davis was to come from royalties on sales of the finished book.[21]

When Davis arrived back in New Orleans in December 1876, he needed to find a place to work where Varina could join him when she was well enough to make the voyage. He thought first of locating a small house somewhere on the Mississippi or on a Louisiana beach "to get books and papers together for the work always in contemplation." Looking yielded nothing that took his eye, but he did pay a visit to a lifelong friend of Varina's, Mrs. Sarah Dorsey, who had a house in New Orleans. She invited him to visit her in January at her home, Beauvoir, near Biloxi, Mississippi, and when he did and discussed his proposed memoirs with her, she promptly suggested that he take rent-free residence in a cottage on her property. It was exactly what he needed, though he insisted on paying her fifty dollars a month for board for himself and his servant Robert Brown. He was tired of charity.[22]

Davis commenced work almost at once. Alterations to the cottage or pavilion quickly set off separate bedroom and study, with shelves for his books and papers, and Davis furnished it simply with a bed and writing desk and some rush mats on the floors. Daughter Maggie sent some things; his nephew General Joseph Davis provided a table and chairs, as well as the desk; and he was ready to begin. "The soft air, here, is delicious," he said. Within the sound of the surf, untroubled by the turbulent outside world, here he could relive and recount the stirring and heartbreaking scenes of past years.[23]

Within a few weeks his books had arrived, along with his son Jefferson Jr., recently expelled from the Virginia Military Institute, much to his parents' chagrin. Though of good heart, the boy had never carried either the drive or the intellect of their other children. Now Davis kept him to help where he could in the work at hand. Before February was well under way, the writing began. Mrs. Dorsey, somewhat infatuated with both Davis and the idea of writing a book, offered to be his amanuensis, an arrangement that, thanks to his eyesight, suited Davis admirably given his frequent difficulty in writing. By the third week of February, despite a bout of illness, Davis was dictating his first copy.[24]

Davis and Walthall divided the work, apparently, in a distinctive manner. Davis would write the great matter on constitutional issues, secession, states' rights, and the like, while Walthall was to handle the bulk of the correspondence in gathering documents and statements from surviving participants. Nor did Walthall's work stop there. He was to do a fair amount of the actual writing as well, working from notes and sketches provided by the "author." Davis would write what he called "a skeleton," leaving it to his associate to "add all the muscle, flesh & sinews needful." It was a remarkable way to proceed, and entirely out of character for Jefferson Davis, who in times past refused to allow newspapers to publish extracts of his letters and speeches for fear of being misrepresented. Yet now he was allowing another man to put whole paragraphs in his mouth. Of course, Davis and Walthall met often, discussing the author's ideas, so Walthall should know his master's views on the issues being discussed. And Davis could also count on reading all the copy produced and making corrections before sending it to Appleton.

Still, the arrangement ran counter to Davis's character, and moreover it also ran at variance with his lifelong habit of immersing himself in detail and minutiae. Now he would paint only with a broad brush, leaving Walthall to add the color and detail. Davis also had much to do in cajoling reminiscences from old associates, which helped encourage such a division of labor. Furthermore, though Walthall was not an especially experienced writer, still he certainly had more practice at writing for commercial publication than Davis. And beyond question, the matter of dignity entered the equation. Davis constantly felt the pressure not to stoop beneath the office he once held in seeking employment. He received much criticism, including his own, for entering the insurance business, for ex-presidents did not go into commerce on leaving office. Writing was surely a more dignified task, yet only one American president to date, James Buchanan, had written a memoir, and that reportedly with considerable outside assistance. While others like Johnston and Hood scrambled to write their own works, Davis could seem aloof in a fashion, above the crowd, by engaging an assistant to do the common work of the book while he devoted himself only to what a president should devote himself—the great men and issues. Yet incontestably, in the end the overriding reason for leaving so much work to Walthall had to be economic. This way the job could be finished quickly, and royalties could start coming in.[25]

Every week at first Sarah Dorsey packaged what Davis wrote and gave it to Walthall. Some weeks, when he was ill, Davis could produce but a few pages, and then only with her constantly begging him to stay with it. At the same time he had to study the letters, diary extracts, newspapers, and other documents from the 1860s that his correspondence and Walthall's brought in the mail. The first matters turned to revealed those that he found most sensitive. Within two months of starting, he was deeply into the Manassas controversy once again, gathering sources to prove that the failure to pursue the Federals after the victory was not his fault. A month later he began seeking material to aid in a defense of Bragg. At the same time he sought from Benjamin and others their recollections of the discussions surrounding the Hampton Roads peace conference, and soon afterward commenced collecting all the official telegrams and correspondence between Breckinridge, himself, and Joseph E. Johnston relating to the surrender of the Army of Tennessee, a surrender that he ever after maintained was against orders. He frequently sent Walthall traveling to collect materials, as well as to interview Harrison, Preston Johnston, and others, while he kept on with his writing. Varina's absence worried him, and then in June his new grandson died in infancy, further impeding his ability to work. Always Mrs. Dorsey prodded him to continue, though sometimes when he dictated, she could see that "it [was] with only a forced interest." Still, however slowly, the "Reminiscences" progressed.[26]

In time, after Walthall moved to the coast as well, he came for whole days at a time to work with the president, and when Davis did not feel up to either writing or dictating, he simply spoke freely to Walthall and left it to him to set down later the substance of what he said. There was much of frustration in the work. Many associates like Breckinridge were already dead, their papers lost or dispersed. Others did not respond or else evaded on controversial issues. And yet more, Davis lamented, had already forgotten what happened as he recollected events. "There seems to be no reliance due to the memories of our friends," he told Walthall sadly after a year of work had passed. "Men remember their own acts, and vanity often magnifies their part."[27]

On through the balance of 1877 and 1878 the work continued, interrupted frequently by illness, trips to look after the continuing Brierfield suit, and occasional visits to Varina. Though she returned to the country, she did not, would not, live at Beauvoir. The trouble began almost as soon as Davis commenced working on his memoir. In March, while Varina still remained ill in Europe, he told her he was spending three or four hours a day dictating "for a book of reminiscences of my public career." That was bad enough, but he went on to say that it was Mrs. Dorsey who took his dictation. Always in the past Varina acted as his amanuensis. Worse, the public press soon carried the story that Mrs. Dorsey assisted Davis, with no mention of the ailing and forgotten wife. Then, when Davis continued to write of his own improving health and that "Mrs. Dorsey is kind and constantly attentive," Varina exploded. Already short and petulant as she indulged her hypochondria, she now dwelled on any word or phrase in her husband's letters that would allow her to exaggerate her self-pity. She had lost so much—home, children, cause, youth—all she had now was her place as wife of Jefferson Davis, and even the honor of that was endangered by another woman taking the role in its writing that properly belonged to her. When Davis told her he thought of calling the work *Our Cause*, she waspishly commented that even as "a matter of sympathy" he had not deigned to tell her anything of its plan or scope. Finally, when Mrs. Dorsey repeatedly asked that Varina come live with them when she returned to America, Varina made her feelings perfectly clear. "I do not desire ever to see her house," she wrote in September. "Nothing on earth would pain me like living in that kind of community in her house." Everywhere people asked Varina what part of the book Mrs. Dorsey was writing, her role having been exaggerated from amanuensis to coauthor, and when confronted by such questions, Varina felt "aggravated nearly to death." She actually accused the woman of lying to the press and claiming that she was writing portions of the book. Varina wanted Davis to leave Beauvoir and write somewhere else. If not, he could stay, but when she returned to the South she would live elsewhere until the book was done and Davis himself could leave Biloxi.[28]

Here was an added strain Davis did not need. Middle age and years of hardship were bringing out some of those qualities in Varina that so troubled him in their first years together. Happily, he had acquired perspective and patience by now in dealing with Varina. He made no complaint, constantly expressed his love for her, and when finally she felt well enough to travel home in October 1877 and went to live with their daughter Maggie Hayes in Memphis, Davis patiently went to her and tried to persuade her to join him at Biloxi. Adamantly she refused. "In the course of human events I shall probably go down to Mr. Davis's earthly paradise temporarily," she said sarcastically. "He inclines to the 'gentle hermit in the dale' style of old age—so behold we are a tie—and neither achieves the desired end."

By the beginning of April 1878, the Davises had spent a total of ten days together during the entire preceding seventeen months. Their correspondence remained ever loving and intimate, but Varina refused to come to him, and health and work prevented him from going to her. Then she finally began to consider at least visiting him in New Orleans, and at the same time he offered to leave Beauvoir and settle elsewhere if she would only join him. Thus they gravitated back together, and in the end Varina swallowed her pride and moved to Biloxi in July. Better yet, the reminiscences that she once regarded as her enemy now became her own passion. Months earlier she despaired of enjoying better times until "the history" was done, even wishing that he had never started it, "since it has been, and must ever be, such bitter, *bitter work*." But now Mrs. Dorsey diplomatically gave up her role in the work, and Varina took over receiving her husband's dictation, and delighting in hearing him sing in his room as he worked among his papers. Within a few weeks her spirits rose, she set aside her largely invented prejudice against the Gulf coast, and they were happy.[29]

Years of heartbreak should have warned them never to hope for too much happiness. Within a few months a yellow fever epidemic swept the Mississippi Valley, and in October it claimed as a victim their fourth and last son, Jefferson Jr. "The last of my four sons has left me," a shattered Davis wrote at the news. "I am crushed under such heavy and repeated blows." Varina immediately became prostrate with grief and renewed illness. Mrs. Dorsey tenderly cared for her. And when Davis himself felt a recurrence of his old facial pain, he did not complain. Rather, he welcomed it, "for the distraction it creates from less endurable or irremediable ills."[30]

Like a reed in the wind, Jefferson Davis might be bent but could not be broken. He forged ahead with the work on his memoir. For reasons he did not completely fathom, Walthall proved to be slower at the work than expected. The original contract with Appleton called for the work to be done on July 1, 1878, yet Walthall was nowhere near completion, and furthermore the agreed-on money had all been advanced to him. Appleton wanted their book, and soon. Walthall finally had to agree to arbitration with the publisher, and a new agreement was reached, extending his contract for an additional six months starting January 1, 1879, with the stipulation that he submit one-sixth of the work each month in return for additional compensation. This also placed a renewed burden on Davis to work even harder. At first, after his son's death, he could not work at all, but simply sat in his chair all day, saying nothing more than "I do not know why I suffer so much." But the challenge revived him quickly, and by early 1879 he was declining invitations, pleading being too busy on his book.[31]

In the end, Walthall disappointed everyone. July 1 came, and it was not done. Davis verbally extended the major's contract on December 1, but still there seemed to be little progress. Indeed, Davis himself paid little attention to Walthall's activity, surprising given that he was ultimately responsible and that the major was supposedly his assistant. The manuscript existed in some form as early as mid-1878, but there it sat while Walthall, having been paid most of what he hoped to get for his work, turned his attention to other matters. Finally Appleton sent a representative to see Davis in February 1880, admitting that they did not "believe he [could] ever complete the work on his present plan." When J. C. Derby arrived at Beauvoir he found Davis "in blissful ignorance of the progress of his work," trusting entirely to Walthall. In fact, Davis confessed that he only occasionally saw a few odd pages of what Walthall had produced and suggested that Derby call directly on Walthall. When he did, he found barely enough copy for half the first volume of the now projected two-volume work, and much of that was not ready for an editor. Derby took the partial manuscript back to Davis, who was shocked that there was so little of it. "I was but little better prepared then yourself to find how little had been done," he confessed.

Mortified, Davis said he was determined nevertheless to fulfill his contract, since he could not afford to pay back the eight thousand dollars that had been advanced to Walthall. Derby, an old acquaintance, suggested that he send Judge W. T. Tenney of New York, a facile and experienced writer, to help speed the work. Davis quickly agreed. Tenney would help get the second volume done. Meanwhile, Walthall, under protest, signed yet another agreement binding him to finish the first volume no later than May 1 and paying him in promissory notes redeemable only when the manuscript was completed. He was to turn over all material gathered for the second volume immediately to Davis.

Thus the pressure was on. Davis converted a room at Beauvoir exclusively for the use of Walthall, so that he could work under his master's eye, with daily checks on his progress. Anxious to complete the manuscript on time, he prodded the major constantly. "In the pressure which resulted from bad conduct of my assistant," he lamented later, "much of the last part of my work was done hastily." Inevitably, Walthall rushed, became careless, and left out much that Davis would rather have seen included. Still, by May 1 Walthall was done. Quite probably Davis had time to give the manuscript no more than a cursory glance through the pages before posting it to Appleton. On May 5 they acknowledged receipt of the first volume of *Personal Memoirs of Public Events*, the tentative title. There and then Walthall's connection with the work ceased. Varina gave a conditional sigh of relief at completion of the first volume. "The weary recital of the weary war," she lamented, was depressing to them both.[32]

While the book remained Jefferson Davis's consuming passion now, and as Judge Tenney arrived to take over Walthall's room for the work on volume 2, the blessed Mrs. Dorsey continued to be his benefactor from the grave. She died on July 4, 1879, with Davis near her bedside, she having moved to New Orleans. The previous March Davis bought Beauvoir from her for $5,500, giving her his note payable on future dates, but her death came before the first part of the note fell due. Only then did he discover that in her will she had left Beauvoir and three small plantations, along with all the rest of her property, to Davis, "my most honored and esteemed friend." It was not a princely bequest. The rent on the plantations was modest, though it provided a steady income, added to what Davis could take out of crops at Brierfield once it passed back into his hands. Mrs. Dorsey left debts that had to be paid from her estate, and that cost Davis money at first. But now he owned his home, "a pleasant residence," he called it. Relatives contested Mrs. Dorsey's will, and ugly rumors circulated for a time of there being something more than friendship between her and Davis, but they soon died, and a court upheld the will.[33]

Davis remained consumed by his book. Preston Johnston assured him that the book "will to a great extent *sell itself*," but the author believed that only by making it as thorough and exhaustive as possible would he tell the story properly and achieve the anticipated sale. He succeeded in retrieving some of the papers looted from Brierfield during the war and feverishly continued the work of calling for more documents from Early, Richard Taylor, Pemberton, Bragg's widow, and more. Unfortunately, the deeper he got into the second volume, the more he discovered that Walthall had left undone. Then, with a heavy deadline hovering over himself and Tenney, he had to rush the work of copying and compiling the material assembled. On top of this came requests from old Confederates who asked that he not fail to mention them in his work. It was all a task greater than he could ever have imagined. "We were told long ago that of making books there was no end," he wrote to Derby. "I am making the first experiment in that manufacture and am very desirous to bring it to an end."[34]

By the end of 1880, Davis was rushing at a feverish pace to finish. Finally, one night in April 1881, after a leisurely afternoon in the sea breezes, Davis sat down and started dictating to Varina. Commencing at 8 P.M., he went on speaking long into the night. "It has been shown in previous pages," he said, asserting that he had proved the inalienable right of state self-government and secession. He spoke of the Lost Cause. "When the cause was lost, what cause was it?" he asked. His answer: "Not that of the South only, but the cause of constitutional government, of the supremacy of law, of the natural rights of man." He spoke of his object in writing the work, the attempt to prove the right of secession, and that the resulting war was one of "aggression and usurpation" by the United States. Yet he told Varina to write further that "in asserting the right of secession, it has not been my wish to incite its exercise: I recognize the fact that the war showed it to be impracticable." But, he added, "this did not prove it to be wrong." How typical of the man who never admitted error.

He spoke a few words more, then fell silent. It was 4 A.M. Varina thought he was perhaps dozing and asked him if he wanted to continue. It took him a moment to reply, "I think I am done."[35]

After Tenney went over the last copy, they rushed the manuscript of the second volume to Appleton, and at once the typesetting began. Even then Davis continued gathering material and figures to be inserted in New York. Now he encountered the frustrations an author endures *after* the book is written. He had to scramble to get photographs of his leading aides and officials and associates. He found that the publisher, concerned about the massive size of the book and its already-high investment, decided to eliminate some portions, including a biographical preface into which Davis and Walthall had put much labor. He also learned that the editors quibbled about some of his spellings, for example, preferring "saber" to the old-fashioned "sabre" that Davis espoused. Unwilling ever to yield a point where he believed himself correct, he gave in, but insisted that the very last line in the book after his conclusion should be a statement that the publisher accepted full responsibility for the spellings therein. How like Jefferson Davis![36]

By June 3 the two volumes, now titled *The Rise and Fall of the Confederate Government*, were off the press and on their way to the nation's bookstores. By every measure but one, it was a terrible book. Rambling, disjointed, discursive, and forever disputatious, it spoke for all the personality quirks that had made Davis himself so disliked by many who knew him. Antipathy toward Beauregard, Johnston, and Gustavus Smith in particular permeated the book, Johnston most of all. Not surprisingly, but still uncharitably, Davis denied any skill at arms to his old foes in blue, while glossing over or ignoring entirely the manifest flaws in his favorites like Bragg and Northrop. It was the same Davis who had ruled in Richmond, protecting his friends and flaying his foes. Just as bad, throughout the work the logic of his arguments was the same as it had always been, which is to say almost none at all other than the automatic assumption that his opinion, whatever it might be, was the right one. Stating his position as fact, he thereafter built his arguments to their "proof" by using such "facts" as givens, and not as mere opinions.

The organization of the work was forever digressing as Davis wandered off the subject, rather as he had in his cabinet meetings, and often to display his admittedly prodigious capacity for classical allusions and quotations from world literature. It suffered from an excess of pre-1850 history of exactly the sort that always elongated Davis's Senatorial speeches. Moreover, a considerable part of its 1,561-page bulk was taken up with extended verbatim quotes and extracts from letters and documents, loosely strung together with connecting text. This undoubtedly reflected some of the rush to publish, though the first volume done by Walthall revealed a far greater excess. Tenney's second volume, by contrast, was much more smoothly put together, though done in a fraction of the time available to his predecessor. The latter volume also devoted much more space to events on the battlefield than the first and was entirely superior to the first in construction.

It would be difficult to tell with certainty just which portions actually came from the pen or mouth of Jefferson Davis himself and which from Walthall and Tenney based on Davis's notes or discussions. It is clear that much of what Davis intended to include was left out, and in the rush he almost certainly did not have—or take—time to give the finished manuscript a careful reading. Indeed, his sight may not have allowed him to.

When Virginia Clay wrote to protest that her husband's important mission to Canada with Thompson was ignored, Davis could not believe her at first until he looked in the index himself and then scanned the book in a fruitless search. "I had expected to find so much," he lamely apologized, later claiming that "some of the manuscript was not printed." As the months wore on, he would receive a number of complaints from those whose roles in the Confederacy he had ignored. Incredibly, thanks to his unusual working relationships with Walthall and Tenney, his own distractions with other matters, and the hurry to get into print, Jefferson Davis never knew the exact contents of his great work until *after* it was published.[37]

The one saving grace of *Rise and Fall* was its rich load of anecdotal and personal reminiscences. There was the sound of Sidney Johnston's step on the floor below Davis's sickchamber. There are Davis's own recollections of standing under fire with Joseph E. Johnston and Lee in May 1862. There is his own account of the heartbreaking retreat from Richmond to Irwinville. Sandwiched between undistinguished secondary accounts of battles and campaigns that he did not witness, and in whose planning or execution he often took little part, Davis placed these little gems of memory. To be sure, any recollection by Davis was likely to be defensive, even self-serving if it touched one of his innumerable controversies or his conduct of the war, but there they were just the same, and largely—if not entirely—in his own words. And his exposition and justification of the compact theory of government and the argument for secession, while unconvincing, are still among the best to be found.

Alas *Rise and Fall* provided almost a metaphor for its author's postwar life. Disorganized, rambling, without direction, often bitter, and always argumentative, it was not a credit to Davis, and it was not the book he would have written in earlier years, before the accumulated weight of a lifetime of sorrows and disappointments. Moreover, it proved to be largely an economic failure. By the end of 1881 he complained that Appleton failed to send him his royalties due, and two years later he still complained that he did not even know the figures for copies sold and royalties owing him. In fact, sales were not good. The book proved to be expensive for its time, prices ranging from $10 to $20 depending on the binding, rather high for those, especially in the cash-poor South, who might find it interesting. Appleton apparently did not make the kind of sales effort that Davis expected. "With parental partiality" Davis confessed that he thought the book would sell itself in the South and that the publisher would pursue sales in the North, but friends complained to him that they could not find the book to buy it. Given the fact that the eight thousand dollars or more paid to Walthall was to come out of Davis's royalties, the fact that the publisher charged Davis interest on the money advanced Walthall, and that his royalty rate was 10 percent of the sales price on each set, Davis probably had to sell at least six thousand sets just to pay the advances and interest. Chances are that he never himself realized a cent from the work. Like the Carolina and the Mississippi Valley Association, it was one more enterprise that failed economically. Though he claimed he did not do it to make money, the experience left him soured on Appleton and, for a time, on publishing itself. During the remainder of his life, there is little evidence that he took great pride in *Rise and Fall*, nor could he be greatly encouraged by the reviews, which tended to show the same partisanship evidenced in the book itself. Perhaps it was still too soon for Davis or the United States to take a dispassionate, objective look at the "late unpleasantness." Davis himself, of course, had never been objective about much of anything in his life.[38]

Almost immediately after sending off the manuscript of the second volume, Davis borrowed enough money to go to Canada to arrange for publication there; then, in the summer, he and Varina sailed to Europe to bring Winnie back home and to visit Mann, Benjamin, and other old friends. He had not seen his daughter in five years, and the reunion gladdened his heart. Here for three months he rested from the years of labor on the book and gradually became philosophical about the unlikelihood of its ever becoming remunerative. "My book was cumbrous and sold at a dear rate," he would say, adding with a touch of humor that profits to a writer seemed to be generally on the order of zero divided by two.[39]

Yet if Davis looked forward to anything like tranquillity after finishing *Rise and Fall*, he soon discovered his error. No sooner did the family return to the United States in December than he saw himself attacked in the newspapers, his accuser none other than his old foe Joseph E. Johnston. Davis's memoir had largely been a rejoinder to

Johnston's 1874 book, and now Johnston rebutted, but on an entirely new field not connected with the military controversies that had divided him and his president. He intimated now that Davis had retained for his own uses large portions of the Treasury specie that accompanied the fleeing Confederate government in 1865. Worse, Johnston seemingly made the accusation on information gained from Beauregard. It all grew out of an interview Johnston gave to a reporter, and a figure of $2,500,000 in missing funds was mentioned. Preston Johnston, Van Benthuysen, and a number of friends quickly published denials on Davis's behalf, and eventually Johnston himself claimed to have been misreported. Davis did not at first read the newspaper articles, but when they were brought to his attention he must have boiled. However, he stayed quiet and did not respond, either publicly in the press or privately to Johnston. Some years before Davis adopted a stance that would have served him well had he assumed it during the war. Whatever charges were made against him, he determined, even from ex-Confederates, he would not speak in his own defense. Certainly he would not restrain his friends from responding for him, but he believed that even noticing any such calumnies would be to give them more credence than they deserved. Furthermore, always concerned for the dignity of the cause he still felt he represented, he decried all the petty squabbling that went on among former Confederates.

Yet Davis did draw lines. So far as he was concerned, Joseph E. Johnston no longer existed. He would not notice him. But when invited to attend the dedication of a statue of Lee in Richmond, Davis declined and made it quite clear that his reason for declining was that Johnston would also be on the platform. As the years went on, it became more difficult for Davis to maintain his stance of silence. When Beauregard's memoirs appeared in 1884, all the old controversies with him revived again, and for a time Davis wanted to write a rebuttal to the general's "egotism & malignity." In the end he thought better of it. "I should not answer the assailments of Confederate officers," he told Early, even though Beauregard, for his part, never stopped speaking of Davis as "that malignant old man" and "a calumniator who had little regard for *truth*." Davis did form something of an alliance with Early, himself one of the most bitter and venomous Confederate controversialists of the postwar years, who tried to make up for his shortcomings on the battlefield by assuming the mantle of protector of the memory of the Lost Cause. Happily, Davis maintained sufficient distance not to be drawn into the undignified and destructive vendettas that Early pursued well into the next century.[40]

Davis's differences of opinion and controversies did not confine themselves to former Rebels. In 1881, when the War Department published the first volume in a massive 128-book collection of documents of both sides during the war, Davis objected to its title, *War of the Rebellion.* Theirs had been no rebellion, he maintained. When Yankees castigated him he responded. Young Theodore Roosevelt compared Davis to Benedict Arnold in an 1885 writing, and though Davis did not make his retort public, still he responded by writing the future president that he had "too low an estimate of you to expect an honorable retraction of your slander." One year earlier Davis got into a more heated matter with William T. Sherman, when the Union general said in a speech that he had seen documents proving that Davis actually conspired not for secession but to rule the whole United States. Davis challenged him to produce any such documents, but Sherman, who had probably spoken in an enthusiasm or exaggeration of the moment, could not. He claimed that the papers in question had been lost in the Chicago Fire, but Davis was not so easily put off. In the end he labeled Sherman a "base slanderer" and an "imbecile scold." Two years later, when told that Sherman might also be present, he almost declined to attend the unveiling of a statue of his dearest friend, Sidney Johnston. These dedications and unveilings could be awkward things for men who engaged in postwar controversies.[41]

Yet Davis could be charitable even to a foe, if that man had fought him honestly and, to his mind, honorably. Davis had certainly never felt any great admiration for U. S. Grant, and never met him unless their paths crossed momentarily at Monterrey. He thought Grant's generalship during the Civil War uninspired and clumsy, mere bludgeoning of a weaker foe. Indeed, Davis reportedly maintained that the greatest of the Union generals was McClellan, though he did not say why. Perhaps it was because Lee was rumored to have felt the same. More likely it was because McClellan fought the slow, timid kind of war the Confederates could easily best. Psychologically, the foe defeated is always the superior of the foe triumphant. But by mid-1885 all the world knew that Grant was fighting a losing battle with cancer and racing against his own death to finish his memoirs. Just days before the general drew his last breath, Davis agreed to trade a set of *Rise and Fall* for Grant's two-volume *Personal Memoirs.* At the same time, when asked for his comments on the dying Yankee's military career, Davis feelingly declined. He gave two reasons. "Gen. Grant is dying" was the first. For the second, though Grant had come into the Confederacy as an invader, still "it was with an open hand." He neither burned nor pillaged like Hunter and others, and after the war he "showed no malignity to Confederates." "Therefore," said Davis, "instead of seeking to disturb the quiet of his closing hours, I would, if it were in my power, contribute to the peace of his mind and the comfort of his body." That was the kind of charity and humanity that ran so deep within Jefferson Davis, which his other traits so often kept hidden or prevented others from seeing.[42]

Davis could not, of course, remain indifferent to the other public events in the reunited nation, for a great deal of what happened grew out of the war that still consumed so much of his time. The harsh Reconstruction dismayed him immeasurably. "I had at one time hoped that the spirit of vengeance might be allayed by making me a scapegoat for the South." Once Federal troops were withdrawn and the much-exaggerated "carpetbag" rule came to an end in Mississippi, he was jubilant. "Mississippi is again governed by Mississippians," he exclaimed. Truth, he prayed, was coming again to the fore. Now he saw the great issue before the nation to be a continuation of the one great debate of his life—their fathers' interpretation of the Constitution versus "the unrestricted will of the majority." To renewed appeals for him to seek a pardon and the removal of his political disabilities, however, he still said no. To do so would be to admit that the United States had had the power to disfranchise him in the first place, while others would believe it a prelude to his seeking a Senate seat: "Where I will say to you I have not the least disposition to go." He believed that the truth of the position he and the South had taken would triumph in the end. Meanwhile, he said, " 'the mills of the Gods grind slowly.' "[43]

As for national politics, Davis was incensed when "an ass" proposed to pay blacks reparations for their servitude. Unable to vote, he took little interest in elections, but in 1880 he showed a distinct preference for the former Union General Winfield S. Hancock, and found it deeply "humiliating" when James A. Garfield, a Republican, won the presidency instead. As a rule, when he spoke out at all on anything touching public policy, Davis called for reconciliation. He repudiated any thought of ever attempting secession again. The war had settled that, for better or worse. "Be obedient and good citizens," he counseled, "and if *Secession* ever comes again, let it come from the North." Yet he also rejected the so-called "New South." "There *is* no *New* South!" he declared in 1887. "No, it is the *Old* South rehabilitated, and revivified by the energy and virtues of Southern men."[44]

During the 1880s Davis made himself more and more available for attending commemorative celebrations, with invitations coming from all over, even from Yankee states like Iowa and from conventions of blacks. Unable to go to Richmond in December 1887 for the cornerstone laying of the grand equestrian monument to Lee, he did not miss the unveiling of the Albert Sidney Johnston statue in New Orleans a few months before. "This is *your* day of remembrance as well as mine," Preston Johnston told him. When Davis appeared on the stand on the anniversary of Shiloh, the crowd's applause became so insistent that—though not scheduled to speak—he had to say a few words.[45]

Whenever he could get away from illness or involvement with Brierfield to attend a reunion of old friends or Confederates, Davis tried to go. In 1879 he considered going to a reunion of his 1828 West Point class. Two years later he had, with sorrow, to miss a reunion of Mexican War veterans, but he never failed to take an interest in any achievement of members of his old First Mississippi Rifles, saying, "It fills my heart with joy few other things could give." In 1878, speaking before a meeting of the Association of the Army of Tennessee, he accepted an honorary badge of membership, then gave them a moving and eloquent speech, part of it almost in a whisper, as he upheld states' rights but avoided all manifestations of rancor, indulging only in a little "quiet irony." And it gratified Davis considerably at such meetings that he saw manifestations of a return of fraternal feeling between North and South. When Bowdoin College notified him that his honorary degree was still on its rolls, he felt a degree of genuine pleasure.[46]

In 1887 Davis passed his eightieth birthday, though with his occasional lapse of certainty he would withhold celebrating it until a year later. Freed from the serious want and near penury of the decade before, still he could not sit idly and enjoy an untroubled old age. He worked intermittently to rebuild Brierfield, occasionally going there in person to work on the levee and oversee the crops, but it was ever a losing proposition and by 1886 he was deeply in debt over the plantation. He also found himself taking up the pen yet again, partly for remuneration but more for truth as he saw it. He wrote a number of articles for the *North American Review* and *Belford's Magazine* on Confederate topics, though of course controversy was bound to dog his efforts. First he researched and wrote a lengthy defense of the charges growing out of the horrors of Andersonville, and with it a vindication of commandant Henry Wirz, who paid with his life for what happened in that prison camp. Davis delivered his article for the $250 promised and was scheduled to do another on Lee when the *Review* published an assault on Davis by the distinguished British general Sir Garnet Wolseley, soon to be commander in chief. Davis immediately wrote a response to the "European stripling," castigating him as a soldier "without an earned record of ability." Clearly there was still fire in the old man, even at eighty-two when he replied to Wolseley.

Appleton would find that out in 1889 when Davis again took them to task over unpaid royalties from *Rise and Fall*. He believed that they owed him at least forty thousand dollars, and a publishing friend in New York agreed. He demanded that the dispute go to arbitration, asserting a belief that "there was a hostile power in your house creating unfriendly action in my case." Perhaps to urge the publisher to some action, Davis held up submission of articles he had contracted to write for Appleton's *Cyclopedia of American Biography*. He should have known better. Writers rarely win battles with publishers, and he was no exception. He would not live to see the *Rise and Fall* arbitration settled, and as for his articles for that company's *Cyclopedia*, when he saw them in print he was mortified to see that his essay on Zachary Taylor had been altered, while the essay on himself was full of myths and slanders, including the old canard that he had eloped with Knoxie Taylor. Then, when he saw his reply to Wolseley in the *Review*, he found that it had been altered, presumably to make it less insulting to the viscount. That alone incensed Davis. When he learned that the *Review*'s editor also wanted to alter the Andersonville piece to take out a reference to Nelson Miles as a "heartless vulgarian," Davis demanded the return of the manuscript. He turned it over to his new friend James Redpath, formerly of the *Review* but now connected with *Belford's Magazine*. There it would appear, though not until a month after the author's death.[47]

It was Redpath, too, who helped set Davis on the road to writing another book. During a visit to Beauvoir in 1888, he persuaded Davis to undertake a task that the ex-president had been hoping someone else might tackle—the writing of a concise history of the Confederacy. Davis must have set to work almost at once, and by October 1889 his *Short History of the Confederate States* was completed in manuscript form. The title may have been a misnomer, for when published the following year it ran to 517 pages. Davis found the work congenial, especially with Redpath's help and encouragement. He already had most of the necessary raw materials in his study after the *Rise and Fall* research, and Varina, as always, was happy to take his dictation. Though of less value historically than *Rise and Fall*, still it was a superior work from a literary standpoint, relatively free from the rancor and controversy of the former work, and less defensive except on the touchy subject of treatment of prisoners of war, a feature reflecting Davis's recent preoccupation with his Andersonville article. Hard on the heels of finishing the *Short History*, Davis began writing and dictating to Varina his own memoirs, intending to cover his whole life and not just the Confederate years.[48]

Those long hours of traveling back into memory were pleasant ones for Jefferson Davis. Rosemont offered his earliest recollections. Sadly, he could call to mind only a little of his father Samuel. As occasionally throughout his life, he changed his mind about his year of birth, celebrating his eightieth birthday in 1888 rather than the year before, leading his old friend David Rice Atchison to remark, "It's singular how old men lose track of the years and make themselves either much older or much younger than they really are. . . . I couldn't explain it in Davis."

Yet there was so much that Davis could never forget. "Disfranchised as I be," he said in 1887, "the love of my life for the Constitution and the liberties it was formed to secure, remains as ardent in age as it was in youth." He still adhered as he always had to the maxim that "the world is governed too much." Yet he was not unmindful of the effects his advancing years had both on his memory and his attitudes. "It is said to be the weakness of age to think all things are worse than they were," he had said to an old friend. "Perhaps that is what ails me." Perhaps he had lived too long. So many others were gone: Lee, Jackson, Sidney Johnston, Breckinridge, Bragg, Polk, Cooper, Howell Cobb. The list seemed endless. He had outlived so many. Perhaps that is what made him turn so often to those who always gave him joy and hope—Winnie, and Maggie's son Jeff. "In bringing up a child think of its old age," he admonished a friend, for "children are the tomorrow of society."[49]

It was the young ones who gave him the most delight at Beauvoir in these last years. Winnie was his delight. He walked with her along the beach, talked with her while he futilely nursed a live oak near the house that never quite prospered. He spoke of fencing, and of how he thought it a fit exercise for the grace and form of girls, wandering off into reminiscences of the fencers he had known at West Point in his youth. Every evening they played backgammon and euchre, using buttons as their treasure, each hoarding and counting their little piles as if they had been gold. The neighbor children, too, gave him undeniable pleasure, and he specially liked to tease them by asking if they would like to come home with him. Given the affection that Davis always brought out in children, often they did want to accompany him. To all of them he presented the gentlest aspect of a kindly grandfather, and enjoining that kindness upon them, even to the point of asking them not to tread needlessly on the tiniest creatures. "Is there not room in the world, little daughter," he said once to Winnie as she nearly stepped on a beetle, "for you and that harmless insect, too?" Occasionally they even rode, his carriage as erect as when he sat a dragoon's horse.

Old friends came to visit, even former Yankees. Special delight attended any visit from dear old William S. Harney after he moved to Pass Christian, Mississippi. Loved for more than fifty years, Harney came frequently and Davis gladly confessed how "cheered" he felt when they talked of the old days at Fort Crawford, of the races and the dogfights and their near duel. Again and again for years Harney came, their separation by the war entirely forgotten.[50]

If something of the old formality still remained, Davis proved to be a genial host. When a guest was expected, he waited at the front gate to walk him or her through the yard, and if he was busy, Varina met them instead. There visitors found a small but cosy parlor filled with photographs, miniatures, and engravings of members of the family, living and dead. One of Davis's beloved dogs, perhaps the Newfoundland, curled sleepily by the fireplace in the winter. When Davis himself was not at work writing, he might take the visitor to his study, actually the small building outside the main house where he first lived when renting from Mrs. Dorsey. Visitors could admire his large collection of books and the little statues and other mementoes that crowded the room, but there were always polite yet firm requests not to touch or disturb anything. If Davis happened to be at work writing in his study, no one could disturb him, not even family. But when free from his labors, he would pull a couple of chairs up to the parlor windows to catch the sea breezes or take his guests outside to sit on the veranda, where he could be as charming and as talkative as they wished.[51]

With his family, he was much the same husband and father that he had always been. He encouraged Winnie's interest in art and had a room adjacent to his study converted into a studio for her. He hummed and sang about the house, chiefly old ballads, especially "Annie Laurie" and "Mary's Dream," and perhaps "The Last Rose of Summer." He loved the works of Chopin, asking often for Winnie to play them on the piano, but lighter comic opera, and especially the works of Gilbert and Sullivan, he absolutely detested, no doubt finding them vulgar. He never gave up certain of the old formalities, notwithstanding the inconveniences of age. Despite Varina's suggestions that he come to the dinner table in his dressing gown when there were no guests or his health troubled him, he refused ever to appear improperly dressed, regarding it as disrespectful to his wife. And well into his eighties, when most elderly people are happy to have their years entitle them to any available seat, he still sprang up to offer his to guest or visitor. Into the evenings he still liked to read aloud to Winnie or his grandson, even though his sight grew dim and his hearing dull.[52]

Winnie was his joy, and the darling of the South as well. Thanks to her birth during the war, she came to be called the Daughter of the Confederacy and as such held a special place in the attention and affection of her people. Her every move would be watched paternally by millions, and in an era when a young woman could find herself idealized, Winnie bore special responsibilities to be the perfect daughter and, it was expected, the perfect wife. Well-meaning protectors of the Lost Cause even expressed a hope that through her a sort of Confederate royal bloodline might be preserved and passed on, suggesting to Davis that she should marry some grandson of Lee or Jackson, Sidney Johnston or Breckinridge. While Davis never expressed a particular preference regarding a husband for Winnie, still he naturally assumed that she would marry some young Southern man. Thus it came as quite a shock in September 1888 when a young man from New York arrived at Beauvoir and told Davis that he wished to marry his daughter. They had met during her visits with friends in the North, and love grew, nurtured by a long correspondence. Davis did not say what he thought when he first met young Alfred Wilkinson, but he was sufficiently taken with the fellow not to refuse him outright. In fact, further acquaintance gave cause for close friendship between Davis and Wilkinson, and Varina, too, came to care for the young man. By the spring of 1889 consent had been given, and Winnie became engaged. They all knew that marriage to a Yankee would raise a storm of indignation from old diehard Confederates. But then, fear of controversy had never deterred Davis in the past. Besides, there was something poetic, symbolic of the restoration of good will, in his girl and a Northern boy starting a new life together. Indeed, the storm did come, and Davis dealt with it as he handled all storms, largely by ignoring it all. He had made up his mind that marrying Wilkinson was the right thing for Winnie. That ended all further discussion.[53]

Happy for Winnie, happy in his work of writing, Davis enjoyed these last years perhaps more than any of his life, and certainly more than any since the war. He rarely joked anymore and never had been a great humorist, though Varina noted that after 1865 even that stopped. But he was cheerful. He delighted in his walks along the beach, studying the flounder and the seashells. Besides his Newfoundland, he bought a collie in 1884, and the dogs became his constant companions. He stroked their heads gently and affectionately, and took them with him on his daily walks along the Gulf Shore. Rain or shine, he could be seen there every day, throwing driftwood sticks into the surf for the dogs to run and fetch. Winnie walked with him when she could, listening enrapt to his tales of the early days, of the Indians, the Academy, Mexico, of the boyhood in Woodville that memory made charmed. She asked him once what he would choose to do if he could live his life over again. Turning to her with a soft smile and the light twinkling in his good eye, he said without a moment's hesitation, "I would be a cavalry officer, and break squares."[54]

Inevitably the end had to come. He turned eighty-two in June 1889, his health as variable as it had always been, yet for a man so dogged by illness, his constitution showed remarkable tenacity. Like the man himself, his body refused to give up in spite of trial after trial. Throughout the 1880s he had his bouts with the fevers, rheumatism, the neuralgia, the inflamed eyes. In the fall of 1887 he suffered a heart ailment that many expected to kill him, but he sprang back, and by the next summer reporters at his birthday celebration found him straight and erect, his old military training and service still evident in his gait and demeanor.

By November he decided that he needed to pay another visit to Brierfield to see his agent John Trainor. The plantation never did produce what he felt it should, and from time to time he had taken a boat upriver to look after its improvements and inspect his crops as well as to scrutinize the manager farming it for him. Varina did not want him to go now, but when he insisted, saying that his health was excellent, she agreed, only begging that he take her with him. He would only be gone a few days, he said. She should stay at Beauvoir.

He went to New Orleans to take passage, but even before he boarded he felt the winter chill settling into his chest. By the time the boat reached Brierfield's landing, Davis felt too ill to be moved. They took him on to Vicksburg, and then after several hours' rest, he went back to Davis Bend. By now acute bronchitis had set in, and perhaps a touch of the old malaria as well. He lay for three days in bed at Brierfield, weakening rapidly. Trainor wired to Varina that he seemed desperately ill, and then on November 12 Davis himself sent her a brief note that was only just better than coherent. "Nothing is as it should be," he told her. He was disappointed not even to be able to look at the plantation. He would return home on the morrow if able. "I have suffered much but by the help of the Lord—."

The next day they carried him to the steamboat *Leathers*, named for an old friend of Davis's and one of the river's most famed captains. Trainor's little niece Alice asked the invalid to sign her autograph book, and then the boat steamed south. Once he was in New Orleans, Davis's physicians took him to the home of another old friend, Jacob Payne, out in the city's lovely Garden District. There in a ground-floor room looking out on the garden, Varina nursed him when the doctors pronounced him too ill to be taken home. There for the next three weeks she tenderly gave him crushed ice, beef tea, milk, and the few other things he could digest. There on the street outside the crowds gathered respectfully almost daily when the word spread in the city that the old chieftain was fighting his last battle.

He thought of many things, but especially of his barely begun memoirs. He may have dictated a little to Varina even as he lay ill, no doubt thinking of Grant's feverish race with mortality to finish his own memoirs. But his strength could not stand the test now. "I have not told what I wish to say," he complained weakly to Varina. He wanted to speak of Polk and Sidney Johnston. "I have much more to say of them," he told her. "I shall tell a great deal of West Point, and I seem to remember more every day."

It was almost certainly pneumonia that attacked him now. He had known so many enemies, yet never feared a one of them. Nor did he fear this one. "I am not afraid to die," he told Varina on December 5. Indeed, there were even signs that once again he might recover. Davis may never have beaten foes like Foote, Lincoln, Toombs, and Wigfall, though he outlived enough of them to claim some victory. But always, in the end, he had defeated his own ill health. Perhaps he would beat it again. By the afternoon everyone around him felt cheered by his improved color and vigor, as he teased his doctor and took what was obviously a deep and refreshing nap.

He awoke shivering with chills early in the evening and could not be made comfortable. Varina tried to give him some medicine, but he turned it aside politely but firmly. "Pray excuse me," he told her, "I cannot take it." Within a few minutes he appeared to sleep again, but when his physicians came to his bedside it was apparent that he had lapsed into a coma.[55]

He saw them no more, nor did they know now where he was and what he saw—perhaps nothing. But perhaps he had some lingering sense of himself, some realization that he was leaving that racked old body and that world in which he rarely felt truly at ease. Perhaps in his religious faith he knew that he was going elsewhere now. Maybe he even saw the path, and at the end of it a bright patch of Mississippi field filled with horses and dogs, and romping with them there the beloved Sidney Johnston. So many of those he loved had gone before him. Surely they would all be there. And if he scanned their welcoming faces, he might have given way to a little smile of secret delight. For here Joseph E. Johnston was nowhere to be seen.

33

May All Your Paths
Be Peaceful and Pleasant

Friends and old associates began trying to judge Jefferson Davis's place in his times well before final sleep closed that one good eye on his last sight of Varina. Barely had he taken office as Confederate president before admirers predicted that he would be remembered as one of the great men of the age. Thereafter estimates of him jumped up and down in time with the fortunes of the South and the prejudices of his would-be judges. In 1889, as the nation watched at his bedside, the verdicts continued unabated. Though he would not have been judged at all but for his public career, still one after another of the arbiters of his image in posterity could not separate their views from attitudes felt toward him personally. More than most prominent men of his era, Davis's outer self could not be isolated from the inner man.

To the multitude who knew him only as a figure on a podium or as a cool stare in a short interview, Jefferson Davis was at best a puzzle, a bewildering maze of contradictory traits defying definition or understanding. To those few who knew him intimately, and especially to Varina, he presented a case of wonderful consistency in all his attitudes and acts. He was what his blood and his environment had made him, and to those who got past his all-too-often infuriating outward manifestations, there was an arresting internal symmetry to the man.

Within Davis dwelled a host of character and personality traits commonplace in men and women of all times and places. What set him apart is that he seemed to have more than most, and to an exaggerated degree. Where others might be dedicated, he was committed. Where others felt enthusiasm, he felt passion. Where others were determined,

689

he was obstinate. Moreover, Janus-like, there were two faces to all these qualities in Davis, for better and worse, and it is when they approached the extremes that were a part of his personality that those around him felt baffled by seeming inconsistencies.

The unswerving loyalty that made him the truest friend a man could have also made him susceptible to rank cronyism and to manipulation by flatterers if they returned that loyalty. The bravery that won the envy of a generation at Monterrey and Buena Vista turned to reflexive combativeness and an instinct to fight first and think later. The often-keen insight that made him an excellent judge of his enemies was so exclusively tuned to be critical that he would not turn it on those he loved, making him a dreadful judge of his friends. The dignity with which he customarily bore himself, and with which he sought to invest his office and his country, he could not control when face-to-face with an individual, and hence he seemed cold and aloof. When Jefferson Davis found a good man, as with Lee, he stood by him even in the face of criticism, in spite of storm and controversy; unfortunately, when he found a bad man like Bragg, he stood by him, too. The determination and dedication that ennobled him turned easily to obstinacy. The clarity of vision that made him almost the first to admit that foreign recognition would not come to the Confederacy made him almost the last to admit defeat as he continued to see what others abandoned.

No one could question his remarkable intelligence, his great powers for study and retention, yet in exhausting all sides of a question he often so filled himself with conflicting data that he could not make a decision. He was thorough in almost everything he did, down to the smallest detail—too many details, and too small. With his keen command of forms and laws, he could spot the tiniest anomaly in a system or argument; yet he so loved such minutiae that he could not tear himself away from the little matters to attend to the big ones. His was a touchingly compassionate heart. No one who had suffered all that he did in life could fail to be compassionate. Yet understanding pain so well himself made him weak and hesitant in inflicting it on others like Bragg and Pemberton when the health of his cause demanded. For a man of such frequent volatility, he was remarkably patient, yet so often that patience was misplaced to the detriment of the Confederacy, as with his sustaining Joseph E. Johnston long after he had demonstrated his unsuitability for command.

Few men of his age and place entertained such enlightened views toward the treatment and condition of slaves, and the potential "improvability" of the Negro, yet the view was largely abstract, and he retained a fundamental distrust of the intellect, reliability, and "humanity" of the black man. Few men looked with such fascination upon advances in technology and innovation, yet he would not countenance that the fundamental nature of things like the Constitution could evolve. He had a very open intellect, and a very closed mind.

Davis rarely if ever held failure in battle against one of his generals, yet his prejudice toward Beauregard after he failed Sidney Johnston's memory kept the fourth-ranking officer in the Confederacy virtually out of the war for its last three years. The iron will with which he controlled himself through so many trials could break down entirely in discussion, allowing his temper so to run away with him that he nearly went to the dueling field with his own friends. Davis often said he wished he had become a lawyer. With his grasp of laws and his attention to detail, he would have made a good litigator; with his inability to keep from escalating the heat of debate when challenged, the natural combativeness of courtroom debate would inevitably have led him to become either a very experienced duelist or very dead before his time. Few men could be more generous in granting accolades to others; few men could be more insistent on having the last word to themselves. He took inordinate pride in his consistency in all things, believing it one of his finest attributes, yet he could condemn consistency of principle in an opponent and was himself, in fact, consistently *in*consistent in his actions. He damned hypocrisy and was himself, all too often, a hypocrite. He detested liars and demagogues, yet when under the sway of these extremes of character, he could appeal to the meaner side of men, prosecute vendettas, and twist the truth into what can only be called lies.

All these traits dwell in abundance in humanity. Everyone manifests at least some of them without being regarded as enigmatic or mysterious. And viewed away from the personalities involved, nothing is particularly difficult in understanding them. Are not the most compassionate people always those most reluctant to injure the feelings of others? Are not those who rigidly seek to control their angers and emotions the same ones whose outbursts, when they come, are the most passionate? Are not those who strive commendably to see all sides of an issue also the ones who have the most difficulty making up their minds? The fact that a coin has two faces does not mean that one side contradicts the other. Without the obverse, there would be no reverse, and personalities are no different. That Davis seemed to be a mystery to people in his own time and later is due simply to the fact that he showed such an abundance of these two-sided traits and that he had the misfortune to live in the public scrutiny. Every generation produces innumerable Jefferson Davises who escape the labels of *enigma* and *mystery*. They don't come under the glass for study; he did.

The man who came to Montgomery to lead a revolution in 1861 brought with him the accumulated traits, attributes, and attitudes of fifty-three years of living under the unifying and overriding influence of one single paramount force—insecurity. Certainly all humans are insecure to greater or lesser degrees. Jefferson Davis was more so than most, and its effects on him were seemingly exaggerated by his insecurities being played out before millions on a national stage. It was not a failing in him any more than in other humans; the problem for Davis was that in the great event of his life and of his generation, it helped to guide him to failure. However much that failure may have been preordained, the fact that a man of his mold guided the cause ensured that then and thereafter his guidance and that failure would be inextricably intertwined.

It requires little imagination to see that insecurity guiding Davis in so many of his thoughts and acts. Where it came from originally must inevitably remain largely conjecture, but it probably developed in him as it does in all men and women. Some came to him in the nature of his species. Given that, Samuel Davis undoubtedly accounted for much of its development. Old enough to be the boy's grandfather when Jefferson was born, Samuel Davis was certainly upright and responsible but also remarkably undemonstrative and self-contained, rarely speaking at home even with his family. Certainly he was not abusive and loved his children. Just as certainly, he never knew how to show his affection. What could be more touching and revealing than the fact that in later years Jefferson Davis always remembered as something remarkable one occasion when his father hugged him? As a result, the boy grew up starved for affection, which came chiefly from his mother, and when told that his father had died in 1824, young Davis responded in a letter that devoted but three sentences to Samuel, and the balance to family matters and his going to West Point. Years later Davis spoke of Samuel as a man he barely knew. What could be more revealing than the subsequent succession of father figures whom Davis adopted almost worshipfully? Zachary Taylor, John C. Calhoun, perhaps even Andrew Jackson and Martin Van Buren from afar, and looming over all the rest, Joseph E. Davis. Even the reverential friendship for Franklin Pierce and Sidney Johnston may have had more of filial love in it than camaraderie. With all of these men, Davis did what boys do with their fathers. He idealized them into paragons of infallibility. Even when they represented political opinions that he condemned contemptuously in others, still he found a way to rationalize such failings in his heroes. Only in middle age did he free himself of his hero-making, but by then the impulse redirected him toward idealizing his friends instead. Always he needed someone to look up to.

Samuel, and even more Joseph, also encouraged the development of that streak of irresolution that so often frustrated Davis's contemporaries. As Mallory and others complained, he was indecisive, and it went all the way back to youth. It was Samuel who decreed that he would go to school at St. Thomas. Back in Woodville when young Davis decided to quit school, he changed his mind three days later. When he left for Transylvania he wanted to finish there and go on to law school, but he let Joseph persuade him to go to West Point instead. After less than a year in the army he wanted out. Then he changed his mind; then three years later he wanted to resign again but let Joseph talk him out of it. In 1835 it was Joseph again who persuaded him to leave the service and take up planting, yet when Davis resigned he could not do it decisively but withheld his resignation for four months. Once he committed himself wholeheartedly to planting after Sarah's death, the resolution lasted only two years before he sought a commission to get back into the army. Once in Congress, he served but six months before seeking the colonelcy of the First Mississippi, but after Monterrey he wanted to return to Washington. Barred from that, he returned to the war, then vacillated back and forth between staying and leaving after Buena Vista, nor could he decide to accept or reject Polk's commission as a brigadier without consulting Joseph and Taylor. Back in politics, he categorically rejected the notion of running for governor, got a senate seat, then four years later resigned it to run for the governorship. Then he let Pierce persuade him to accept a cabinet post for four years as Secretary of War, the only political office he ever held in which he served out a full term. And through all of his political career, down to his swearing in as president of the Confederacy, he maintained that he took office against his wishes, and only out of a duty to the people who elected him.

It is a classic portrait of insecurity, of a man almost wandering through life allowing others to make his decisions for him. The matter of duty was very real in his later years, and undoubtedly a factor in his allowing the public to determine his life after 1847, but even that plea that he made so often can also be seen as an excuse for not deciding his career for himself. To the very end of his life, he continued to vacillate on matters relating to his career. He hated the army when he was in uniform, and sought repeatedly to find a way out. Yet by 1861 he regarded the military as his true calling, and in old age he revelled for hours in fond recollections of a life he once viewed with distaste. Given his life to live over, he would be a "cavalry officer, breaking squares," he told Winnie, now looking back fondly on a life he had been only too happy to leave at the time.

Corollary to the indecisiveness produced by his insecurity was his behavior when he did make a a decision. He could be inflexible to the point of rigidity. It developed early in life. Varina saw it at their first meeting, noting his "way of taking for granted that everybody agrees with him." Having decided that he was right, he could not admit the possibility of error. It is an old story with people who find decisions troublesome. Uncomfortable with committing themselves, once committed they must remain rigid in that resolution. When they cannot make decisions, as Davis often could not, it is from a deep inner fear of error and responsibility. The death of Sarah Taylor taught Jefferson Davis a painful lesson about error and responsibility. To cope with that, he had either to avoid decisions, or else commit himself to them so irrevocably that he could not admit of the possibility of error. Often as not, however, he preferred to allow others to appear to make those decisions for him, as with those last painful cabinet meetings during the flight from Richmond. That way, at least, he absolved himself of responsibility and guilt. Thus, too, is explained his hypersensitivity to criticism, his compulsion to lecture dissenters at exhausting length, and the spite running toward vindictiveness that he showed toward his most outspoken critics. With such a fragile inner grasp on his resolution, such a morbid fear of error and responsibility for what might go wrong, he could only cope by refusing to countenance fallibility. Being questioned on that score constituted one of the most mortal threats he could encounter.

The consistency that Davis so prided himself on has been said to be "the hobgoblin of little minds." Perhaps so, but in his case it had nothing to do with intellect, and everything to do with insecurity and indecision. Having once chosen a course, whether it be expansionism, Episcopalianism, or any other position, he adhered to it inflexibly. To alter or change was to admit initial error, and thus he viewed the work of others whom he admired. Thus the Constitution came in perfect form from its framers and was not to be changed or evolved at the hands of later generations. Thus his inflexible rooting in the past. Ironically, this same devotion to a higher consistency is what accounted for his inconsistency in everyday acts. No one could number the times that Davis protested that he made his military appointments on merit only, only to turn around and give commissions to the inexperienced sons of old friends or favored old associates like Polk. His violations of his own rule regarding seniority in the commissions of men like Joseph E. Johnston, Twiggs, W. H. T. Walker, and others were alarmingly numerous. But they were not inconsistent, for in them Davis was remaining true to what was in his mind a higher consistency, his loyalty to friends.

And that loyalty itself, perhaps his most admirable trait for all the problems it brought him, owed much to his insecurity, to the need to attach himself to people permanently, to have fixed points in his life. He needed to admire people, and those whom he admired would have his loyalty for life. What he gave, he expected in return. Save only the deaths of his sons and the death of the Confederacy, none of life's adversities hurt him more than to see a friend turn against him. This, too, helps account for his having relatively few intimate personal friendships with men. Davis was always warm with women, children, and slaves, and they in turn warmed to him. He could be open with them because they were no threat. In his society all were his inferiors, and they could not and did not challenge him. But with men it could be another matter. A man could question his infallibility, his judgment, his consistency, or anything else he chose to doubt, and Davis could do nothing about it other than fight back, even to the duelling ground if necessary. Thus he never could handle or manage strong-willed or independent men, for inevitably they would come to question his rectitude on something, and that touched too close to the central uncertainty that he strove so hard outwardly to overcome.

From his insecurity, too, stemmed the trait that drove so many to near distraction, his obsession with handling petty details himself. Breckinridge often told the story of his escape from Florida to Cuba in an open boat, when during a storm they almost capsized and drowned thanks to a friend's holding rigidly to the tiller and sail rope even though the wind in the sail was swamping them. The man later explained that he thought he ought to hold on tightly to everything lest anything "get the better of him." Davis was the same. Oppressed by the feeling of responsibility for the War Department under Pierce, and the Confederacy later on, he was compelled to immerse himself in managing even the smallest matters lest one of them get the better of him. Moreover, Davis had somewhat the bureaucrat's turn of mind, delighting in rules and regulations and often taking refuge behind them. Nothing so delights the bureaucratic mentality as routine paperwork. A clean desk at the end of the day left a warm feeling of accomplishment, of well-being, a feeling that could make up for failure on a much grander scale. Unfortunately, in his need to assuage his insecurity by accomplishing things, Davis often did not recognize the difference between doing business and just being busy.

This was the man whom delegates to Montgomery chose to lead their nation in 1861, and when he arrived to take his oath, he brought all this with him to his task. For the next four years and more these traits could be seen in operation to both the benefit and the detriment of the Confederacy, and it is on this record that Davis's place in history must be judged. The challenge is to make that judgment free of the prejudices that his less admirable traits naturally engender without being overswayed in the opposite direction by a certain natural sympathy that must go to any man thrust into such a terrible situation. Moreover, such a judgment must from the outset be weighed in the light of the incontestable fact that Jefferson Davis was unsuited by personality and character to be a chief executive. Varina knew it, and in one of those occasional penetrating personal insights, Davis knew it himself.

Dwelling on all the factors that left him ill-equipped to be lead a nation would serve little purpose and only reiterate so much that has gone before. Suffice it to say that demonstrably he did not possess the managerial skills necessary, from his penchant for becoming bogged down in detail, to his interference in the daily work of his department heads, to his inability to subordinate his own ego in order to get what he needed out of troublesome commanders, to his distant and aloof demeanor and image that gained him the respect, but never the love, of Confederates. He could not have been a great popular leader even if he had wished to be. A man who would not relax into informality with his own wife at the table could hardly be the "man of the people" that nineteenth-century Southerners needed to inspire their loyalty and enthusiasm.

Taking into consideration his manifest disabilities for the job, then, Davis emerges as more successful than could have been expected in the administrative aspects of his presidency. Excepting for the secretary of war, he generally allowed his cabinet secretaries to run their departments without excessive interference, and some like Reagan and George Davis he never meddled with at all. After setting some initial funding policy, Davis left Treasury to its incumbents; and after he early on foresaw that European recognition would be a pipe dream, he left State to Benjamin. Even with Mallory he did not intrude himself obsessively, though only because it was so obviously and exclusively a land war. His secretaries got from him the support they needed in appropriations from Congress, and by and large their programs, and his, prevailed. Indeed, in spite of the growth of a bitter and, at the end, dangerous opposition, still President Jefferson Davis never met a serious challenge from Congress and no organized threat at all from the critics out in the Confederacy at large. Only a concerted conspiracy by all or most of the governors could have damaged his policy severely, but he managed to stay on sufficiently good terms with most of them that the Browns and Vances could never gather substantial support. And even from them, in the end, he usually got what he asked for, though it came at a high price in goodwill.

Inescapably, it is not Davis the administrator but Davis the war president whom history judges. The manifest ways in which all his character strengths and flaws influenced the conduct of that conflict from campaign to campaign, from victory to defeat, have long been matters of record, studied from the war years themselves through the rest of his life and beyond. It is the larger picture that must be addressed. But first a touchy distinction must be made. Any final verdict on Davis as war president must be predicated on the assumption that the Confederacy could not have won the war under the conditions it faced. The material and manpower resources arrayed against it were simply too overwhelming. Barring completely unforeseeable events, only a massive intervention by European powers or the loss of the will to use its own resources to full victory could have cost the Union the war. Even a failure by Lincoln to win reelection in 1864, in which Davis put considerable hope, would not have influenced the outcome, for he would still have held office and pursued his policy until March 4, 1865, by which time the South was on its knees. No successor, not even McClellan, would have walked away from the victory in that circumstance. Thus Davis cannot be judged because he did not win what could not be won. Rather, the only reasonable measurement of him as a war leader is the extent to which his leadership either hastened or postponed the inevitable denouement. And even that is a complex question, elusive of answer.

Beyond cavil, Davis prolonged successful resistance in the Eastern theater, if for no other reason than one single fact—his unswerving and unyielding support of Robert E. Lee. It is often forgotten that Lee came to command with an unenviable war record behind him. Many thought him timid, others believed he was not committed to the cause, and in Virginia and South Carolina especially critics derisively called him "Granny Lee" and "Spades Lee." Davis was not obliged to give him command of the Army of Northern Virginia when Joseph E. Johnston took a wound, and possibly he would not have but for his own prejudice toward Gustavus Smith, and Smith's own nervous disorder. But once Lee was in command, Davis quickly realized his worth and stood by him, even though he confided to Varina that Lee did not achieve on the Peninsula all that Davis had hoped. Through the near loss of most of his army at Antietam and the crushing defeat at Gettysburg, the president never once wavered in his attachment to Lee. Furthermore, by resisting the clamor to send Lee to the troubled Army of Tennessee, Davis kept in place the man who knew his army and his countryside better than any other. Moreover, Davis listened to Lee, in time taking his counsel almost as if it had come from the lips of Sidney Johnston himself, whom he always believed might have been an even greater general had he lived. Davis did not interfere with Lee's army, gave him the generals he wanted for his corps and divisions, and bent every effort to send him the regiments he needed. In the understanding and rapport they achieved, and in the way they cooperated, Davis and Lee formed a civil-military team surpassing any other of the war, even Lincoln and Grant.

Equally beyond question, and sadly, west of the Appalachians Davis hastened the inevitable. For the loss of the Mississippi he bore far too much direct responsibility, from the inexplicable appointment of the inexperienced and inept Polk to command its northern end in 1861, to the strategic blindness that refused to believe that New Orleans could be threatened from below. Quite possibly it was not within his power to command sufficient resources to prevent New Orleans' fall. But by refusing to countenance the danger in spite of repeated entreaties from the commander on the spot, he failed even to try, and then sought to cover his culpability by shifting the blame to Lovell. Almost as bad, though the loss of Vicksburg may have been inevitable, Davis only sped its fall by setting up a command system that Joseph E. Johnston refused to use and on which Davis inexplicably imposed no direct orders of his own. The Yankees had mighty ironclad gunboat fleets by 1863, ships that repeatedly proved themselves largely immune to stationary fortifications. Consequently those river bastions would have fallen eventually. By placing the bumbling Polk in a position in which he shattered the Kentucky neutrality that protected the northern end of the river, and by himself bungling the defense of the southern end, Davis helped give the great river to the enemy months before it might otherwise have been taken. By failing to issue direct orders when Johnston refused to act, Davis also lost an army in the surrender of Vicksburg. The blame is not his alone, but he cannot escape a portion of the guilt.

Unhappily, Davis must bear full responsibility for what he allowed to happen in the Army of Tennessee. None can say if Sidney Johnston was a good choice or bad in late 1861, nor is it possible to say with certainty that the removal of Beauregard in the summer of 1862 was a bad move. He simply did not command long enough to show what he could do. Nor was putting Bragg in his place immediately an error. Even after the failure of the Kentucky Campaign in October 1862, Davis still did not err in retaining Bragg. After all, Lee's northern invasion that season failed, too. Generals did lose battles. But after Murfreesboro, when Bragg lost not only the battle but the confidence and goodwill of his high command as well, Davis should have removed him. The excuses that Johnston expressed confidence in Bragg, and that there was no one else available as a replacement, are feeble, the kind of rationale that Davis often used to absolve himself of responsibility. He had already lost faith in much of Johnston's judgment, and as for other available army commanders, there was Beauregard. But now, and for the balance of the war, Davis's unreasoning hostility to that man governed his command decisions in the West.

Worse, largely because Beauregard was his only alternative, Davis remained patient with Joseph E. Johnston even after his sloth and obtuseness helped cost them Vicksburg and Pemberton's army. Patience was a virtue not always manifest in Davis, but with Johnston he extended it beyond reasonable limits, and the only feasible explanation is that he regarded Johnston as the least of evils, the others being sending Lee to the West or giving command to Beauregard. It was a poor basis at best for making decisions that could affect the life of his nation.

Once in command, Johnston complained that Davis did not give him the support that he gave Lee, even intimating that the president wanted to see him fail. If Davis did withhold succor, it owed much to the general's own habit of keeping his commander in chief ill informed. Davis had many demands and few resources, and he could not send them to a man who could not or would not tell him how he planned to use those resources. Given the fact that he should never have entrusted the command to Johnston in the first place, Davis did for him about what he could do, and when he relieved him in July 1864 after the loss of all of northwestern Georgia, it was not before time, though too late. Thereafter the appointments of Hood, then Beauregard, then Johnston, were merely the dying echoes of mismanagement that had crippled that unfortunate army two years before. What the Army of Tennessee *might* have done under good leadership in protecting the Confederate heartland is pointless speculation. With the exception of one bright spot in the accidental victory at Chickamauga, however, what did happen was an unbroken tale of opportunities and territory lost. Ultimately the blame must belong to Davis, though it might not have been otherwise no matter whom he put in command. Lee was one of a kind, as Davis himself intimated to his brother Joseph. It was a fortunate age that had one great captain, he said. He needed a dozen.

As for the far West, the often forgotten Trans-Mississippi, Davis did what he could, which was to set up a semidictator in Kirby Smith and leave the territory to him. The Confederacy's chances would have been much improved if Texas, Arkansas, and western Louisiana had never seceded. The Mississippi made the best border defense of all. By having to attempt to retain all that vast territory, Davis had to divert resources that were desperately needed east of the river. Certainly most of the manpower and matériel used in Kirby Smith's domain came from that department, but the drain of anything from elsewhere Davis could not afford. In the end, his management of the Trans-Mississippi mattered no more to the outcome of the war than did the department itself. And by the same token, naval affairs barely signified for the Confederacy. Mallory's only decisive hope was in breaking the blockade, but the attitude of Britain and France rather quickly made it apparent that even in that event they did not intend to intervene. Thus the blockade became diplomatically insignificant and important to Davis only for the constriction it placed on the importation of war supplies. Even that proved not to be significant so much as worrying, for by 1865, by and large, there was no shortage of weapons and rations, even despite the worst efforts of Northrop. The critical shortage was in men.

The structure that Davis erected to support the armies and generals in the field, though controversial in his own time and later, may have done more good than harm. The system of departments shifted and evolved in reaction to the changing fortunes and positions of the armies, and is a credit to the president's willingness to adapt policy to fit circumstances. And though Beauregard, Johnston, and others condemned Davis for his policy of dispersal, for trying to defend every square inch of Confederate soil in preference to concentration, the record does not support their claims. Davis readily ordered Kirby Smith to use his department's forces to cooperate with Bragg in the Kentucky invasion of 1862. It was Davis who persuaded Lee to part with Longstreet in 1863 for the Chickamauga and Knoxville campaigns. And it was the president who authorized Lee to coordinate the smaller territorial commands of Breckinridge and John Imboden to his own movements in protecting the Shenandoah in 1864. To be certain, there were instances of men of the stamp of Van Dorn who refused to cooperate outside their departments, even when ordered to by Davis, but the fault lay with the men, not the system: Those same generals made poor subordinates even when officially attached to another army.

If Davis failed in his system, it lay in managing the smaller departments too tightly and the larger commands too loosely, most especially in his so-called Division of the West, the superdepartment created for Johnston and later commanded by Beauregard. So often accused of interfering with his generals and hampering their activities, in fact Davis consistently declined to issue direct orders to his major commanders or to take a decisive hand in their operations once in the field, Johnston excepted. If anything, he should have introduced himself more forcefully into the conduct of the Division of the West, especially because of Johnston. Contrary to the complaints of Johnston and some others, the superdepartment was not at all unwieldy given the technology of the time. Communication between Tullahoma and Vicksburg by telegraph was "instantaneous" by the standard of the era, meaning information could be transmitted and received within hours or less. Even given the dreadful hodgepodge of incomplete rail lines and varying track gauges that slowed train traffic in the South, still a whole division could be shifted seven hundred miles from the Mississippi to Knoxville in less than two weeks by rail and steamboat, and troops from central and eastern Alabama to Vicksburg, more than three hundred miles, without even changing trains and in a matter of days. The Division of the West was big and clumsy, but it was not unmanageable. Rather than try, Johnston sat in his headquarters and grumbled, played dumb, and prejudiced any efforts he might make by defeating himself. Jefferson Davis's mistake was allowing such a situation to continue for almost six months while he tried persuasion and patience with Johnston, thereby leaving Vicksburg to its fate.

In the matter of the overall military strategy of the Confederacy, as conceived and implemented by Jefferson Davis, authorities then and later would differ widely. But viewed from afar, and with the benefit of hindsight, it would be difficult to conceive of another better calculated to postpone the inevitable. Given that Yankee armies were going to invade the South, Davis had only two basic alternatives. He could adopt the "defensive-offensive" that he implemented, trying to hold as much of his nation as possible and then making occasional thrusts and combinations against targets of opportunity, or he could adopt the Beauregard plan of abandoning substantial areas of the Confederacy in order to achieve massive concentrations of divisions with which to invade the North or engage in all-or-nothing slugfests with Sherman or Grant on Southern soil.

Both approaches were flawed, the latter more so, for it only addressed one dimension of the president's responsibilities and only the most obvious of his enemies. To follow Beauregard's schemes and strip whole departments of their troops, abandoning them to the enemy with the notion of reclaiming them after the big decisive battle was fought elsewhere, ignored a host of hidden enemies. Unionism was rampant throughout much of the Confederacy, and especially in those more remote departments that were the same ones the concentrationists would give up. In such areas Lincoln's forces would be welcomed not as conquerors but as friends, and dislodging them again with a sympathetic population behind them would have been doubly difficult. Furthermore, to give up without defense any part of the Confederacy was political dynamite, as witness the explosion of Brown in 1864 when it looked as if Georgia was going to be abandoned without a fight. Any such abandonment would cost Davis vital support in enlistments and produce from that state, and even should the ground be recovered subsequently, the damage to morale and confidence in the government would have been irreparable.

No. Even if it was impractical to hold the entire Confederacy, Jefferson Davis had at least to try, for political if not military reasons—and in the Confederacy, they were usually one and the same. On the other hand, the defensive-offensive had a built-in limitation on what it could achieve. The concentration theory promised great rewards, but only after potentially fatal risks. One crushing victory might not win the war for the Confederates, but one crushing massive defeat could end it for them. By contrast, the defensive-offensive took only small risks in return for the chance at relatively small gains. It was not the sort of policy that won open field wars. It was the kind of approach that allowed an underdog to stay alive as long as possible in the hope of wearing down the opponent's will to continue, as with the colonists during the Revolution. And in the final analysis, as long as he could keep the Confederacy alive, Jefferson Davis was winning. Beauregard's was the audacious approach, Davis's the prudent. Ironically, in his heart and instinct, Davis preferred Beauregard's bold all-or-nothing strategy. But as a president, Davis had to serve many interests, and to his credit he kept his own daring and combative instincts under firm rein.

Only in the last days of the war, when Yankee advances made both approaches moot, did Davis yield his sound strategic sense and in desperation give himself up to the impractical, and suicidal, notion of taking to the hills and continuing the war on a partisan basis. Had Confederates done so, the Yankees would not have needed to go after them. The warfare that would have ensued between Confederate soldiers and Unionist civilians in the hardscrabble Piedmont regions of the interior would have done the job for Grant and Sherman. Indeed, much of the ill feeling of later Reconstruction might have been averted, for Southerners would have been too busy feuding among themselves to find time to hate the Yankees. Fortunately, Breckinridge, Reagan, and most of the rest saw the folly of such a plan and guided Davis away from it, and for a change even Johnston showed wisdom. Of Davis's occasionally stated wish late in the war to see the South laid waste and Confederates dead to the last man rather than surrender, little can be said. It is the wish of most leaders of dying causes.

A single question remains. Should Davis have taken a field command himself? Could he have done better than Bragg, Johnston, Pemberton, Hood, or Beauregard, or even Sidney Johnston? While on several occasions Davis definitely considered donning a uniform, and even more often daydreamed of it, there is nothing to suggest that at any time he came close to actually deciding to do so. It is to his credit, for no matter what the constitution suggested in potential, in fact a president had no business on a battlefield leading troops. The commander in chief section of the Constitution was framed specifically with Washington in mind, and more generally conforming to the notion that the military must always be subordinate to the civil authority. The president is thus a commander in a civilian, not a soldierly, capacity, or at least that was the intent. As chief executive, Davis bore a host of responsibilities, of which the army was only one. Neither he nor the Confederacy could afford to have him out in the field playing general when he was needed in Richmond to coordinate Congress, the executive departments, and the governors in the overall effort to keep those armies supplied and fighting.

Furthermore, and this must have occurred to Davis, should he fall in battle, Alexander H. Stephens would have become president, a move that definitely would have shortened the war, and not to the benefit of the Confederacy. Given his combative instincts, Davis almost certainly would have been a frontline general like his hero Sidney Johnston, and that would have meant repeated exposure to enemy bullets. Even if he survived the fire of battle, there is nothing to suggest that Davis would have made an effective army commander. His sole combat experience was in leading a few hundred Mississippi volunteers in two small battles, and in reacting to circumstances encountered rather than molding circumstances to suit his purpose. There was a world of difference between that and commanding fifty thousand or more on a front so wide it covered miles and could not all be seen at any one time by its commander. Davis's whole military fame rested on a few minutes of personal heroism and an ability to use his own bravery to inspire others who saw him. Neither was a great asset to an army commander, as Lee's primarily behind-the-lines leadership attested. Moreover, just as Davis could not avoid quarrels with his civilian subordinates, he would undoubtedly have encountered even more among the hot-tempered and ambitious corps and division commanders of the Army of Tennessee, while his administrative penchant for detail might have bogged him down interminably in the minutiae of running a field army. Strategically, at least, there is everything to suggest that he would have thought and moved swiftly and with decision; tactically, once in command on a battlefield, there is nothing to support a prediction of either success or failure.

Somewhere in all this lies the basis of a final tally, a telling judgment on Davis's impact for better or worse on the brief life of the Confederacy. Working against him from the start was his own temperamental disqualification for the job. Working against him, too, was the enormous disparity in the challenge facing him versus that confronting his opponent. Lincoln commenced the war with staggering advantages. His whole government was in place and operating; Davis's had to be created overnight almost from nothing. Lincoln had an established professional army, albeit small and dispersed; Davis had only hastily raised militia and volunteers, haphazardly armed and equipped and barely trained. Lincoln had the instincts of a great executive; Davis had the administrative instincts of a bureaucrat. The Union enjoyed such overwhelming superiority in resources and manpower that it could fight the war with one hand, while with the other it expanded railroads, built universities, and pressed foreign trade around the world; the Confederacy, from the first, had to commit every resource, every sinew, every calorie, to the war, and still it was not enough. And Lincoln was Lincoln, a man of myriad quirks and failings, who yet could govern his weaknesses; Davis was Davis, and was governed by them.

The war was decided in the West. While for three years the armies in Virginia preserved little more than a status quo, in Tennessee, Mississippi, and Georgia the advances of the Union forces split the Confederacy east of the great river in half, ruined much of its hard-pressed industrial base, dispirited its people, and ravaged its armies. Only in the West did the great Yankee army commanders emerge—Grant, Sherman, Sheridan, Thomas. Only after they emerged out there did Grant and Sheridan come to Virginia, and only then did the status quo in the Old Dominion shift irrevocably toward defeat. Thus, by his manifest contributions to Confederate defeat and Union victory in the West, Davis must be judged to have stunted overall the military longevity of the South.

But there is more to the calculation. Without a civil infrastructure supporting those armies in the field, Confederate arms would not have outlasted the first euphoria after Manassas. More than anyone else, Jefferson Davis built the system and organization that kept those armies in the field another four years. Cajoling the governors, dominating Congress, having the courage to call for and enforce conscription, taxation, and the impressment of agricultural produce did not make him popular, but it kept the legions manned, armed, fed, and moving. Moreover it was Davis who, more than anyone else, accounted for what little sense of Confederate nationalism grew in the South. It came at the price of some of his cherished states' rights beliefs, and cost him the goodwill of men like Stephens, Brown, Toombs, Vance, and more. Yet without that sense of nationalism, how much less might he have gleaned from the trouble states like Georgia and North Carolina? And if one of the other prime contenders for the presidency had gotten the post instead, could Toombs or Stephens or Howell Cobb have done any better, or even as well? Of the first two, certainly not. They and the Confederacy would have died of states' rights in little more than two years. Though Cobb may be another matter, it remains an unknown. Thus, for all Davis's flaws as an executive, without his performance of his civil functions as president, the Confederacy would not have lasted until 1865.

Thus there are debits and credits in the ledger, and in the balance the latter must somewhat outweigh the former. As president, for all his faults and all the damage he did in the West, Jefferson Davis prolonged the life of his infant nation beyond what any likely competitors could legitimately have been expected to achieve. And it needs to be noted that, had their roles been reversed, and Davis led the North and Lincoln the South, the Union would still have won. Not even Lincoln could have achieved Confederate independence, though with his human and executive skills he would certainly have done a better job than Davis. But that is because Lincoln was truly a great man. Jefferson Davis was a good man, possessed of elements of greatness, but few of them suited for the impossible task he was called to perform.

The Southern people sensed this somehow. During the war and afterward they never loved Davis as they loved Lee, nor did they venerate him as they did Jackson. But they respected him with an odd kind of stubborn pride that almost matched his own. That he led them to defeat, few charged him with responsibility. Rather, they remembered him for his unyielding resolve, for his refusal to admit defeat, for his determination to fight on and on even after the cause was not only lost but crushed. His was the uncompromising spirit of Andrew Jackson, of John C. Calhoun, of the heroes of the Alamo, of men who never gave up no matter the odds. Then, too, he was their martyr, crucified in the shackles and dungeon of Fort Monroe in atonement for all of them. He was the man who struggled for twenty-two years afterward to maintain the dignity of their cause and their sacrifice. He did not just lead them—he suffered with them, losing more himself than most Confederates lost. And however old and frail he became, he remained erect, unbent, and unbowed, proud and unrepentant to the end. Like Lee, somehow Davis became ennobled by defeat. He who could never be their hero in the 1860s had two decades later become the most admired and venerated man in the South.

That is why they came day after day to stand out on Camp Street to await news and perhaps catch a glimpse of their dying chieftain. Perhaps a few still stood on the sidewalks that December 5 as midnight approached and Varina and the doctors gathered at his bedside. She held his hand. A few other relatives came in the late hours. His breathing grew gradually more faint. Midnight came and went, and at 12:45 A.M. on December 6, 1889, the life that had been so troubled and turbulent ended in the sweetest of peacefulness.

The funeral on December 11 was perhaps the largest ever seen in the South, with estimates of the mourners rising to two hundred thousand and above. Veterans of the Army of Northern Virginia and the Army of Tennessee accompanied the caisson bearing the president to Metarie Cemetery. When open to view, the casket revealed Jefferson Davis clad in a suit of Confederate gray, quite probably cut from cloth sent him by Jubal Early eight months before. His pallbearers recalled the days when Confederate banners brazenly challenged the winds of the South—Buckner, Gordon, Francis T. Nicholls, Robert Lowry—generals all. Thomas Watts, for more than a year attorney general in Davis's cabinet, came from Alabama. In their old chieftain's hands they saw flowers. When the casket was closed, they draped over it a silken flag of the Confederacy. Atop the banner they placed his old saber from Monterrey and Buena Vista.[1]

Every state in the South tried to claim the remains for its own, but Varina chose to have him interred in the Army of Northern Virginia tomb at Metarie. Yet three years of entreaties followed, and in the end she could not deny the fitting logic of sending him to Hollywood Cemetery in Richmond, there where he had led the cause, and where his beloved little Joseph lay. In May 1893 he returned to Richmond for the last time, to rest among other presidents and with Jeb Stuart, John Pegram, his old friend David R. Jones, and nineteen other Confederate generals. For a man who had spent so much of life uncertain of what he wanted to do and of where his destiny lay, Jefferson Davis came at last to that one spot above all where he belonged.

Behind him he left the women. His daughters gave portraits in happiness and sorrow. Margaret Hayes lived into the next century, and happily. Through her came the only descendants of her father to carry forward the blood and the pride of his name. But poor Winnie saw her engagement to young Wilkinson shatter when economic collapse in the 1890s destroyed his fortunes. They drifted apart. Never marrying, and never of robust health, she lived on as "the daughter of the Confederacy" until she died in 1898, still a young woman of thirty-four.

Varina lived on for sixteen years of widowhood, hardy, independent, imperious to the end. She filled her first months of grief by writing her own massive memoir of her husband, assisted by his friend Redpath. In many ways a better book than *Rise and Fall*, it is the best intimate look at Jefferson Davis to survive, though there was so frustratingly much that she did not tell. Less defensive than her husband, she did not shrink from addressing some of his flaws and weaknesses, though always presenting him rather in the cast of classical heroes by asserting that "Mr. Davis failed from the predominance of some of these noble qualities." Yet one cannot help catching just a hint here and there of Varina getting her own back, of a bit of loving revenge taken by tweaking ever so gently at the pride of the man she so loved, who kept her so subdued through the exuberant years of girlhood that she gave to an older man. But of pride she had her own full share, and based squarely on the man to whom she gave her life. Through all her last years she amended her name, living and finally dying as Varina Jefferson-Davis.[2]

All but forgotten, another young woman was left behind when the president made his last journey. Young Alice Trainor never suspected that when Jefferson Davis signed her little memory book at Brierfield on November 13 he was writing his last mortal words. They expressed the wish of a man who so often found happiness and contentment elusive, who never achieved the peace and retirement from worldly affairs that he so cherished until his last years and his final rest. "May all your paths be peaceful and pleasant," he had written to her, "charged with the best fruit, the doing good to others."[3]

Notes

Abbreviations in the Notes

Because a number of sources appear with great frequency, the following abbreviations have been adopted:

JD	Jefferson Davis
JED	Joseph E. Davis
VD	Varina Davis
WPJ	William Preston Johnston
MC	Museum of the Confederacy, Richmond, Virginia
JDA	Jefferson Davis Association, Rice University, Houston, Texas
LC	Library of Congress, Washington, D.C.
NA	National Archives, Washington, D.C.
TU	Howard-Tilton Library, Tulane University, New Orleans, Louisiana
UA	University of Alabama, Tuscaloosa
Citizens' File	Confederate Papers Relating to Citizens or Business Firms, Record Group 109, National Archives
Officers' File	Confederate Papers Relating to Army Officers, War Department Officials, and Other Individuals, Record Group 109, National Archives
Davis vs. Bowmar	Jefferson Davis vs. Joseph H. D. Bowmar et al., Warren County, Mississippi, Chancery Court, July 3, 1874–January 8, 1876
Life	*Life and Reminiscences of Jefferson Davis by Distinguished Men of His Time* (Baltimore, 1890).
Memoir	Varina Davis, *Jefferson Davis, Ex-President of the Confederate States of America: A Memoir By His Wife*, 2 volumes (New York, 1890).

707

OR U.S. War Department, *War of the Rebellion: Official Records of the Union and Confederate Armies,* 128 volumes (Washington, D.C., 1880–1901).

ORN U.S. Navy Department, *Official Records of the Union and Confederate Navies in the War of the Rebellion,* 31 volumes (Washington, D.C., 1894–1927).

PJD Haskell M. Monroe and James T. McIntosh, eds., *The Papers of Jefferson Davis,* Vol. 1, 1808–1840 (Baton Rouge, 1971).

James T. McIntosh, ed., *The Papers of Jefferson Davis,* vol. 2, June 1841–July 1846 (Baton Rouge, 1974).

James T. McIntosh, ed., *The Papers of Jefferson Davis,* vol. 3, July 1846–December 1848 (Baton Rouge, 1981).

Lynda Lasswell Crist, ed., *The Papers of Jefferson Davis,* vol. 4, 1849–1852 (Baton Rouge, 1983).

Lynda Lasswell Crist and Mary Seaton Dix, eds., *The Papers of Jefferson Davis,* vol. 5, 1853–1855 (Baton Rouge, 1985).

Lynda Lasswell Crist and Mary Seaton Dix, eds., *The Papers of Jefferson Davis,* vol. 6, 1856–1860 (Baton Rouge, 1989).

Rise and Fall Jefferson Davis, *Rise and Fall of the Confederate Government,* 2 volumes. New York, 1881.

Rowland Dunbar Rowland, ed., *Jefferson Davis, Constitutionalist: His Letters, Papers and Speeches,* 10 vols. (Jackson, Miss., 1923).

Strode, *Letters* Hudson, Strode, ed., *Jefferson Davis, Private Letters, 1823–1889* (New York, 1966).

Tarpley Colin S. Tarpley, *A Sketch of the Life of Jeff. Davis* (Jackson, Miss., 1851).

A Word About the Citations

In the interests of brevity, all individuals whose correspondence is cited are identified by their full names in the first citation only, unless some possibility of confusion could arise. In citations of papers in libraries and archives, the full location of the institution is listed only in the first reference, unless a possible confusion could ensue.

In citations from the sources listed above as *OR* and *ORN,* it should be noted that references are as follows: *OR,* I, 20, pt. 2, p. 56 = *OR,* series I, vol. 20, part 2, page 56; and *ORN,* II, 3, p. 300 = *ORN,* series II, vol. 3, page 300.

Where no part number is given, only one part exists.

Chapter 1 There My Memories Begin

1. *PJD,* vol. 6, p. 170.
2. *PJD,* vol. 1, p. lxvii. This family history is taken from pp. 488ff. and is in places conjectural.

3. Robert McElroy, *Jefferson Davis, The Unreal and the Real* (New York, 1937), vol. 1, p. 2.

4. *PJD*, vol. 1, p. 511; vol. 6, p. 170.

5. *PJD*, vol. 1, pp. lxvii–lxviii.

6. *PJD*, vol. 1, pp. lxviii, 512.

7. Ibid., p. 512; "The Mount Vernon of Kentucky," *Confederate Veteran* 11 (July 1909), p. 327.

8. McElroy, *Davis*, vol. 1, p. 3; *PJD*, vol. 1, p. 512. While most twentieth-century biographers have accepted Davis's late-life emendation of his birth year from 1807 to 1808, it seems unwarranted and somewhat illogical. Throughout his life he repeatedly came back to the 1807 date, even as late as 1882, when he told his West Point friend Crafts Wright that he had just turned seventy-five (JD to Wright, June 13, 1882, Davis Papers MC). Furthermore, in all his West Point muster-roll appearances from 1824 onward, the age shown is consistent only with an 1807 date of birth (*PJD*, vol. 1, pp. 17, 29, 47, 52, 58, 89, 93, 103). Moreover, in his 1850 campaign biography by his friend Colin S. Tarpley, an underappreciated document that shows clear signs of close collaboration with Davis, 1807 is the year given (Tarpley, p. 4). Further, it should be noted that when Davis began to change the date, it was at the urging of "family members," few if any of whom had been present at his birth. Almost certainly his brother Joseph is the one who influenced him. But is it to be assumed logically that a young man growing up with parents present to observe his birthday would not know his own age and not get the accurate date from those who had been in the best position to know—his mother and father? Hardly.

9. "Mount Vernon of Kentucky," p. 327; "Jefferson Davis's Birthplace," *Confederate Veteran* 11 (December 1903), p. 544; *PJD*, vol. 1, p. lxviii.

10. Nannie Davis Smith, "Reminiscences of Jefferson Davis," *Confederate Veteran* 38 (May 1930), p. 178; *PJD*, vol. 1, p. lxviii.

11. "Rosemont Plantation," *Southern Accents* 10 (March–April 1987), pp. 139, 141; McElroy, *Davis*, vol. 1, p. 4.

12. *PJD*, vol. 1, p. lxix; Rowland, vol. 10, p. 79.

13. Thomas C. DeLeon, "The Real Jefferson Davis in Private and Public Life," *Southern Historical Society Papers* 36 (1908), pp. 76–77; *PJD*, vol. 1, p. 305; vol. 6, p. 544.

14. *PJD*, vol. 1, p. lxxii; *New York Herald*, August 11, 1895.

15. *New York Herald*, August 11, 1895.

16. *PJD*, vol. 1, pp. lxviii, lxxiii.

17. Ibid., pp. lxviii, lxxii.

18. Ibid., p. 5; DeLeon, "Real Jefferson Davis," p. 81; *Memoir*, vol. 1, pp. 8–9n.

19. *PJD*, vol. 1, pp. lxix, lxxii.

20. *New York Herald*, August 11, 1895.

21. Jonathan Daniels, *The Devil's Backbone* (New York, 1962), pp. 6–7.

22. *PJD*, vol. 1, p. lxx; Daniels, *Backbone*, pp. 115, 188, 217, 222.

23. *PJD*, vol. 1, pp. lxx–lxxi, 3n.

24. Ibid., pp. lxxii, 3.

25. Ibid., pp. lxxi–xxii, 4; V. F. O'Daniel, *A Light of the Church in Kentucky* (Washington, D.C., n.d.), pp. 191, 193–94; *Memoir*, vol. 2, p. 305.

26. William M. Lytle, comp., *Merchant Steam Vessels of the United States* (Mystic, Conn., 1952), p. 3; *PJD*, vol. 1, pp. lxxii–xxiii; WPJ to Rosa Johnston, Au-

gust 5, 1862, Mason Barret Collection of Albert Sidney and William Preston Johnston Papers, Howard-Tilton Memorial Library, TU.

27. *PJD*, vol. 1, pp. lxxii–xxv.
28. Smith, "Reminiscences of Jefferson Davis," p. 178; Tarpley, p. 6; Rowland, vol. 3, p. 464; JD to Lise Mitchell, February 7, 1884, Lise Mitchell Papers, TU.
29. A. R. Kilpatrick to J. F. H. Claiborne, May 2, 1877, Claiborne Collection, Mississippi Department of Archives and History, Jackson; WPJ to Rosa Johnston, May 22, June 10, 1862, Mason Barret Collection.
30. Tarpley, p. 6; *PJD*, vol. 1, p. lxxvi.
31. Ibid., p. lxviii, 4.

Chapter 2   Boys, Put Away That Grog

1. *PJD*, vol. 1, p. 7n, 9n. The controversy over the time Davis spent at Transylvania is ably discussed in the work cited, and settled.
2. G. W. Ranck, *Guide to Lexington, Kentucky* (Lexington, 1883), n.p.; *Memoir*, vol. 1, pp. 29–31.
3. *PJD*, vol. 1, pp. lxxvi, 9.
4. Ranck, *Guide*, n.p.; *A Catalogue of the Officers and Students of Transylvania University* (Lexington, Ky., 1824), pp. 5, 6, 13, 14, 17.
5. Margaret Wager, *The Education of a Gentleman* (Lexington, Ky., 1943), pp. 5–6, 9; *PJD*, vol. 1, pp. lxxvi–xxvii.
6. Wager, *Education*, p. 10n.
7. *Life*, pp. 109–10; *Memoir*, vol. 1, pp. 27–29.
8. *Memoir*, vol. 1, pp. 28, 29.
9. Ibid., pp. 30–31.
10. Wager, *Education*, pp. 33, 35; *PJD*, vol. 1, p. lxxviii.
11. *PJD*, I, pp. 5, 12n, 512.
12. Ibid., vol. 1, pp. 5, 11; *Memoir*, vol. 1, p. 32.
13. *PJD*, vol. 1, p. 11.
14. Ibid., vol. 1, p. lxxix, vol. 3, p. 455; Christopher Rankin to John C. Calhoun, January 7, 1823, Secretary of War, Register of Letters Received, vol. 16, "Register of Cadet Applications," Record Group 107, NA.
15. *PJD*, vol. 1, pp. lxxviii–lxxix.
16. Ibid., p. 4.
17. Walter L. Fleming, "Jefferson Davis at West Point," *Publications of the Mississippi Historical Society* 10 (1909), pp. 247–67; broadside, "United States Military Academy, Studies and Class Books," JDA.
18. *PJD*, vol. 1, pp. 16, 21, 97–98.
19. Ibid., pp. 17–19.
20. Fleming, "Davis at West Point," pp. 247–67; *PJD*, vol. 1, p. lxxx.
21. *PJD*, vol. 1, p. 14. JD's report of his offenses and JED's admonition about the guardhouse do not survive, but are inferred from JD's January 12, 1825, letter to his brother, here cited.
22. Ibid., vol. 1, pp. 27, 98.
23. Fleming, "Davis at West Point," pp. 247–67; Albert E. Church, *Personal Reminiscences of the Military Academy* (West Point, N.Y., 1879), p. 19.
24. Samuel P. Heintzelman Journal, May 22–23, June 17, 1825, Virginia State Library, Richmond; *PJD*, vol. 1, p. 31n.

25. *PJD*, vol. 1, pp. 30, 33, 36, 37, 38n, 39–41.
26. Ibid., vol. 1, pp. 23, 43–44.
27. Church, *Personal Reminiscences*, pp. 75–76, 80.
28. *PJD*, vol. 1, pp. 21, 28; Board of Visitors, USMA, *Report, June 22, 1825* (West Point, N.Y., 1825), p. 150.
29. *PJD*, vol. 1, p. 29; *Memoir*, vol. 1, p. 51.
30. Ibid.; *Chicago Times*, August 29, 1886; *New Orleans Daily Delta*, September 12, 1852.
31. *PJD*, vol. 1, pp. 47, 48, 50, 51, 99; *Memoir*, vol. 2, p. 305.
32. Ibid., vol. 1, pp. lxxx–lxxxii.
33. Ibid., vol. 1, p. 52; *Memoir*, vol. 1, pp. 53–54.
34. *Memoir*, vol. 1, p. 52; *PJD*, vol. 1, pp. 53–54; Strode, *Letters*, p. 187.
35. *PJD*, vol. 1, pp. 55, 60–61, 64, 68, 75–84, 99; *Memoir*, vol. 1, p. 54. It is as sumed that Varina's version of JD's role in the eggnog affair came from JD himself.
36. *PJD*, vol. 1, pp. 81, 82, 88.
37. McElroy, *Davis*, vol. 1, p. 19; *PJD*, vol. 1, pp. 89, 100, 101, 102, 109.
38. Lynda Lasswell, ed., "Jefferson Davis Ponders His Future," *Journal of Southern History* 49 (November 1975), p. 520.

Chapter 3   Something of a Martinet

1. *PJD*, vol. 1, pp. 103, 104, 106.
2. *Memoir*, vol. 1, p. 55; H. E. Mitchell, "History of Jefferson Barracks," Missouri Historical Society, St. Louis, p. 11. There are some indications that JD had a servant named David at this time.
3. Lasswell, "Future," p. 521; Mitchell, "Jefferson Barracks," p. 11.
4. *PJD*, vol. 1, pp. 117–19.
5. Edward A. Coffman, *The Old Army* (New York, 1986), p. 49; Lasswell, "Future," pp. 520–21.
6. *Milwaukee Sentinel*, February 3, 1891; *Memoir*, vol. 1, pp. 59–60, 62.
7. *PJD*, vol. 1, pp. 121, 123; John Wentworth, *Fort Dearborn, An Address* (Chicago, 1881), p. 28; WPJ to Rosa Johnston, August 28, 1862, Mason Barret Collection.
8. *PJD*, vol. 1, p. 127; *Memoir*, vol. 1, pp. 58–59; G. W. Jones in *Life*, pp. 108–9.
9. *Memoir*, vol. 1, pp. 63–64; L. V. Reavis, *Life of General William Selby Harney* (St. Louis, Mo., 1878), p. iv; Lasswell, "Future," p. 522; WPJ to Rosa Johnston, June 9, 1862, Mason Barret Collection.
10. Susan B. Davis, *Old Forts and Real Folks* (Madison, Wis., 1939), pp. 261–62.
11. Milo M. Quaife, "The Northwestern Career of Jefferson Davis," *Journal of the Illinois State Historical Society* 16 (1923), pp. 1ff.; *PJD*, vol. 1, pp. 134, 144–45, 153, 156, 164.
12. *PJD*, vol. 1, pp. 182–83, 193; WPJ to Rosa Johnston, June 10, 1862, Mason Barret Collection; JD to T. C. Reynolds, November 12, 1882, *Autograph Bulletin* (December 1920), p. 48.
13. *PJD*, vol. 1, pp. 202–3; Tarpley, p. 8.
14. *PJD*, vol. 1, p. 206; *Milwaukee Sentinel*, February 3, 1881; *Memoir*, vol. 1, p. 81; WPJ to Rosa Johnston, June 10, 1862, Mason Barret Collection; Harris D. Riley, "Jefferson Davis and His Health, Part I," *Journal of Mississippi History* 49 (August 1987), pp. 183–84; *Memoir*, vol. 2, p. 305.

15. *PJD*, vol. 1, pp. 210, 217–18, 220; *Memoir*, vol. 1, pp. 86–89; WPJ to Rosa Johnston, August 5, 1862, Mason Barret Collection.
16. *PJD*, vol. 1, pp. lxxvii, 233, 246–48; *Memoir*, vol. 1, p. 91.
17. *PJD*, vol. 1, pp. 240–41n, 250.
18. Ibid., vol. 1, pp. 252–54, 297, 483–84; *New York Herald*, August 11, 1895.
19. *PJD*, vol. 1, p. 259; JD to Lise Mitchell, March 21, 1873, Mitchell Papers.
20. N. Matson, *Reminiscences of Bureau County* (Princeton, Ill., 1872), pp. 112–14; *St. Louis Globe-Democrat*, January 3, 4, 1883.
21. *PJD*, vol. 1, pp. 244, 251n, 346, 443; *Memoir*, vol. 1, pp. 94–96.
22. *PJD*, vol. 1, pp. 264–65; *Memoir*, vol. 1, p. 149.
23. Tarpley, p. 9; *PJD*, vol. 1, pp. 271–72, 285n.
24. *PJD*, vol. 1, pp. 283, 289–91.
25. Ibid., pp. 479–80.
26. Ibid., pp. 293, 299, 307–8.
27. Ibid., pp. 308–9; *New York Herald*, August 11, 1895.
28. *PJD*, vol. 1, pp. 303, 304, 360–61, 375.
29. Ibid., pp. 313, 315, 318.
30. Ibid., pp. 321, 365–66, 372.
31. Ibid., p. 395; WPJ to Rosa Johnston, May 22, 1862, Mason Barret Collection.
32. *PJD*, vol. 1, pp. 325, 330-31, 395; Grant Foreman, *Pioneer Days in the Early Southwest* (Norman, Okla., 1926), pp. 124–33; *Memoir*, vol. 1, pp. 146–47, 155–56; WPJ to Rosa Johnston, August 5, 1862, Mason Barret Collection; Tarpley, pp. 9–10. While there is some variation and embellishment in the accounts by Johnston, Varina, and Tarpley, still they are so close that the stories are surely not an invention.
33. *PJD*, vol. 1, pp. 331–32; *Memoir*, vol. 1, p. 154.

Chapter 4   We Have Taught Them a Lesson

1. *PJD*, vol. 1, p. 317.
2. Ibid., pp. 368, 419, 426–27.
3. Ibid., pp. 391, 421.
4. Ibid., pp. 361, 366, 370–71, 375.
5. Ibid., pp. 342, 343, 345–56; *Memoir*, vol. 1, pp. 161–62; McElroy, *Davis*, vol. 1, p. 32.
6. *PJD*, vol. 1, pp. 341, 346.
7. Ibid., pp. 358–59, 362, 371, 375, 381.
8. Ibid., p. 371.
9. Ibid., pp. 354, 381, 419, 425.
10. Ibid., pp. 350, 358–59, 360, 363–64, 366.
11. Ibid., pp. 360–75, passim.
12. Ibid., pp. 377–81.
13. Ibid., p. 402.
14. *Memoir*, vol. 1, pp. 162–63, says that JD resigned because of his impending wedding. Presumably this is what JD told Varina. She omits entirely any mention of his court-martial and may not have known of it.
15. *PJD*, vol. 1, pp. 389–90, 396.
16. Ibid., pp. 342, 399–400, 406n; Harris Dickson, "Marse Jeff Davis," *Collier's* 51 (March 5, 1938), p. 54; Dennis Murphree interview with Florida Heulett,

1931, WPA Slave Interviews, Warren County, Mississippi, JDA. The Dickson oral history, heavily embellished by the interviewer, must be used very cautiously.

17. Dickson, "Marse Jeff," *Collier's* 51 (February 19, 1938), p. 54; Davis vs. Bowmar, n.p.
18. *PJD*, vol. 1, pp. 355, 397, 401–2, 403, 410–11.
19. *Memoir*, vol. 1, p. 162; *PJD*, vol. 1, pp. 406–10.
20. Florida Heulett interview, JDA; Dickson, "Marse Jeff," *Collier's* 51 (March 12, 1938), p. 56; *Memoir*, vol. 1, pp. 164–65.
21. *Memoir*, vol. 1, p. 163; Janet S. Hermann, *The Pursuit of a Dream* (New York, 1981), pp. 6, 26; *PJD*, vol. 2, pp. 244–45n.
22. Dickson, "Marse Jeff," *Collier's* 51 (March 12, 1938), pp. 56–57; Davis vs. Bowmar, pp. 408–14.
23. *Memoir*, vol. 1, p. 163; Dickson, "Marse Jeff," *Collier's* 51 (March 12, 1938), p. 57.
24. *PJD*, vol. 1, pp. 474–75.
25. *Memoir*, vol. 1, pp. 164–65; *PJD*, vol. 1, p. 408n. Riley, "Health, Part I," p. 185, concludes that malaria is what they had, and he is the most authoritative student to date of Davis's diseases.
26. Hudson Strode, *Jefferson Davis, American Patriot* (New York, 1955), pp. 104–5.
27. *Memoir*, vol. 1, p. 165; *PJD*, vol. 1, p. 414. By this time JD's problem with his right eye was common knowledge in the family (*PJD*, vol. 1, p. 477).
28. *Memoir*, vol. 1, pp. 165–66. Varina says it took three weeks for JD to sail to Havana, but in that time a ship could have crossed the Atlantic, let alone the scant two hundred miles from New Orleans to Cuba. She also says that JD went to New York and Washington after leaving Havana, but clearly she confuses this with his Northern visit in the winter of 1837–38. Besides, having gone to Havana for his health to escape winter, he would hardly then go to New York in the dead of winter's cold.

Chapter 5 Toughing It Out

1. Hermann, *Pursuit*, pp. 3–4, 11–12, 14–16, 23–26.
2. *New York Herald*, August 11, 1895; *Memoir*, vol. 1, p. 171.
3. *Memoir*, vol. 1, pp. 176–77.
4. *Rise and Fall*, vol. 1, p. 518; *Memoir*, vol. 1, pp. 174–79. Though Varina's portrait of JD's treatment of slaves is certainly glowing, it is entirely in keeping with the actions of his brother and model JED, and almost certainly not embellished.
5. *New York Herald*, August 11, 1895; *Memoir*, I, pp. 177–78.
6. *New York Herald*, August 11, 1895.
7. *Harper's Weekly Illustrated Newspaper*, January 9, 1858; interview with Burton N. Harrison, n.d., Burton Harrison Papers, LC; *New York Herald*, August 11, 1895; Tarpley, p. 12; *Memoir*, vol. 1, pp. 171–72, vol. 2, pp. 302–4.
8. *New York Herald*, August 11, 1895; *PJD*, vol. 1, pp. 406–7.
9. *PJD*, vol. 1, pp. 106–7, 520; *Memoir*, vol. 1, p. 173.
10. *PJD*, vol. 3, p. 456.
11. *New York Herald*, August 11, 1895.

12. *PJD*, vol. 1, pp. 416, 417, 432; *Memoir*, vol. 1, p. 177.

13. *PJD*, vol. 1, pp. 434–35, 445. JD left no explicit statement of intent to rejoin the army, but it is apparent from statements by and to him in that winter's correspondence.

14. *PJD*, vol. 1, pp. 434–35, 444–45, 527n6; *Memoir*, vol. 1, pp. 166–69; *Life*, pp. 118–20.

15. *PJD*, vol. 1, p. 445.

16. Ibid., pp. 448–49, 450, 453, 456, 462; Davis vs. Bowmar, p. 419.

17. *PJD*, vol. 1, pp. 468, 470–71; vol. 5, p. 475.

18. Ibid., vol. 1, pp. 463, 468; vol. 2, pp. 10, 34, 311, 719.

19. Ibid., vol. 1, p. 455.

20. Ibid., vol. 1, pp. 455, 464–65; vol. 2, p. 279.

21. Ibid., vol. 1, pp. 467, 470.

22. Ibid., vol. 2, pp. 15, 20–21, 23, 30.

23. Ibid., pp. 41–42; John D. Van Horne, "Jefferson Davis and Repudiation in Mississippi," *Southern Historical Society Papers* 41 (September 1916), pp. 50–52.

24. *PJD*, vol. 2, pp. 35–36, 697.

25. Reuben Davis, *Recollections of Mississippi and Mississippians* (New York, 1889), p. 166.

26. *PJD*, vol. 2, pp. 48–49n, 697–99.

27. Ibid., pp. 44–45, 47, 695; Davis, *Recollections*, p. 166.

28. *PJD*, vol. 2, p. 49.

29. *Memoir*, vol. 1, pp. 190–91; *PJD*, vol. 2, p. 58.

Chapter 6   How Little Do We Know That Which We Are

1. *Memoir*, vol. 1, pp. 51, 191–92; *PJD*, vol. 2, p. 53n.

2. *Memoir*, vol. 1, pp. 192–93, 198.

3. Ibid., pp. 197–98; *PJD*, vol. 2, pp. 120–21.

4. *PJD*, vol. 2, pp. 127–28.

5. Ibid., pp. 58, 68–75.

6. Ibid., pp. 119, 131.

7. Ibid., pp. 139–40, 153; *Memoir*, vol. 1, p. 198.

8. *PJD*, vol. 2, pp. 165, 175–88, 194.

9. Davis, *Recollections*, pp. 197–98.

10. *Memoir*, vol. 1, p. 215; Davis, *Recollections*, pp. 196–97. A fragment of a written speech by JD survives from this period in *PJD*, vol. 2, pp. 706–7.

11. *Memoir*, vol. 1, pp. 198–99, 214–15.

12. *PJD*, vol. 2, pp. 166, 176; *Memoir*, vol. 1, p. 213.

13. *PJD*, vol. 2, pp. 180, 185, 188, 190, 194, 197, 207, 216–17.

14. Ibid., pp. 218–21.

15. Ibid., pp. 226, 708–10.

16. Ibid., pp. 173, 225; McElroy, *Davis*, vol. 1, p. 56.

17. *PJD*, vol. 2, p. 234.

18. Ibid., vol. 1, p. 199; vol. 3, p. 456; *Memoir*, vol. 1, p. 199.

19. *Memoir*, vol. 1, p. 200; Strode, *Patriot*, 138n.

20. *Memoir*, vol. 1, pp. 202–3; *New York Herald*, August 11, 1895; *PJD*, vol. 2, pp. 255, 258–59.

21. *PJD*, vol. 2, pp. 280–83.
22. *Memoir*, vol. 1, p. 205; *PJD*, vol. 2, pp. 283–84.
23. *Memoir*, vol. 1, pp. 205–6; *PJD*, vol. 2, pp. 290–91n.
24. *PJD*, vol. 2, pp. 290, 292–94, 302n.
25. *Memoir*, vol. 1, p. 206.
26. *PJD*, vol. 2, pp. 307–8, 313, 315, 357–59.
27. Ibid., p. 315.
28. Ibid., p. 329; Riley, "Health, Part I," pp. 198–99.
29. *PJD*, vol. 2, p. 327.
30. Ibid., pp. 324, 328, 699.
31. Ibid., pp. 316, 334, 336, 342, 347.
32. Ibid., p. 356.
33. Ibid, pp. 357–60.

Chapter 7   I Make No Terms, I Accept No Compromise

1. *Memoir*, vol. 1, p. 208.
2. Ibid., p. 198; *PJD*, vol. 2, pp. 353–54n.
3. *Memoir*, vol. 1, pp. 208–12, 214; *PJD*, vol. 2, pp. 370, 375.
4. *Memoir*, vol. 1, pp. 215–20; *PJD*, vol. 2, pp. 373–74.
5. *PJD*, vol. 2, pp. 379, 381; Henry W. Hilliard, *Politics and Pen Pictures at Home and Abroad* (New York, 1892), p. 132.
6. *PJD*, vol. 5, p. 475; U.S. Congress, *Congressional Directory for the First Session of the Twenty-Ninth Congress* (Washington, 1846), pp. 36, 40; *Washington Daily Union*, January 6, 1846.
7. *Memoir*, vol. 1, p. 225; *PJD*, vol. 2, pp. 419–20.
8. *PJD*, vol. 3, p. 457; vol. 2, pp. 474–75; *Memoir*, vol. 1, pp. 225–26. See *PJD*, vol. 2, for most examples of constituent requests.
9. *PJD*, vol. 2, pp. 420, 422; vol. 3, p. 457; *Memoir*, vol. 1, p. 267.
10. *PJD*, vol. 2, pp. 389–90.
11. *PJD*, vol. 2, p. 421.
12. *PJD*, vol. 2, pp. 438–39, 454, 457–59.
13. Tarpley, p. 16; *Memoir*, vol. 1, pp. 229, 245; Burton Harrison interview, Harrison Papers; *New York Herald*, August 11, 1895; *Columbus* (Ga.) *Southern Standard*, September 24, 1853; Christian Eckloff, *Memoirs of a Senate Page* (New York, 1909), p. 209. There is much confusion as to when Adams actually complimented JD, Varina placing it after his May exchange with Johnson, Winnie placing it during an exchange at West Point, and Burton Harrison placing it after JD's euology over Calhoun, though by that time Adams had been dead two years. JD's Oregon speech—his first major address and only his second appearance on the House floor—is the most likely occasion, especially since Adams liked to size up freshmen early. Furthermore, by the time of any of the later proposed occasions, Davis was already well known to Adams thanks to their Smithsonian service together.
14. *PJD*, vol. 2, pp. 397, 563–64, 575–76, 577n.
15. "A Day and Night with 'Old Davy,' " *Missouri Historical Review* 31 (January 1937), p. 133.
16. *PJD*, vol. 2, pp. 404, 410.
17. Ibid., pp. 499–515 passim.

18. Ibid., pp. 394, 475, 537.
19. Ibid., pp. 525–30, 540–43.
20. Ibid., pp. 577–78, 582–83.
21. Ibid., pp. 415–16.

Chapter 8   The War Is Probably Over

1. *PJD*, vol. 2, p. 641.
2. Ibid., pp. 609–10, 636.
3. Ibid., pp. 615, 617, 627–28, 632, 634n.
4. Ibid., pp. 641–42; vol. 3, pp. 457–58.
5. *Memoir*, vol. 1, p. 32.
6. Ibid., pp. 252–53; *PJD*, vol. 2, pp. 666, 675, 700.
7. *PJD*, vol. 2, pp. 670–71, 673n.
8. Ibid., pp. 675, 700. JD's acceptance dated June 20 is almost certainly meant to read June 30.
9. *PJD*, vol. 2, p. 693.
10. Ibid., p. 695; *Memoir*, vol. 1, p. 284.
11. *Memoir*, vol. 1, pp. 284–85; *PJD*, vol. 3, p. 16.
12. *Memoir*, vol. 1, p. 285.
13. *PJD*, vol. 3, p. 11; vol. 2, p. 695.
14. *Memoir*, vol. 1, p. 285.
15. *PJD*, vol. 2, p. 223n; vol. 3, p. 30n; *Natchez Courier*, October 13, 1847.
16. *New Orleans Picayune*, July 10, 1846; *Holly Springs* (Miss.) *Guard*, July 3, 1846.
17. *PJD*, vol. 3, pp. 11, 12–13.
18. Ibid., pp. 13–14.
19. Tarpley, pp. 18–19; *PJD*, vol. 3, p. 16.
20. *PJD*, vol. 3, pp. 14–15.
21. Ibid., pp. 16–17; Franklin Smith Diary, August 18, 20, 1846, Mississippi Department of Archives and History.
22. Smith Diary, August 24, 1846; *Memoir*, vol. 1, p. 290; *Chicago Times*, August 24, 1886.
23. John S. Weems, *To Conquer a Peace* (New York, 1974), p. 213; *PJD*, vol. 3, p. 21.
24. Weems, *Conquer*, p. 209.
25. *PJD*, vol. 3, p. 100.
26. Smith Papers, vol. 16, pp. 29, 33, Latin American Collection, University of Texas, Austin; St. George L. Sioussat, ed., "Mexican War Letters of Col. William Bowen Campbell," *Tennessee Historical Magazine* 1 (1915), p. 155.
27. *PJD*, vol. 3, pp. 25, 101; Robert E. May, *John A. Quitman* (Baton Rouge, 1985), p. 157.
28. *PJD*, vol. 3, pp. 25, 101.
29. *Vicksburg Tri-Weekly Whig*, July 17, 1847.
30. *PJD*, vol. 3, p. 87.
31. Ibid., p. 57; *Jackson* (Miss.) *Southron*, October 26, 1846; *Vicksburg Tri-Weekly Whig*, July 17, 1847.
32. Smith Diary, October 22, 1846; *The Vedette* 5 (January 20, 1884), p. 7; *PJD*, vol. 3, p. 102.
33. *PJD*, vol. 3, pp. 26, 103; *Vicksburg Tri-Weekly Whig*, July 13, 1847; *Jackson Mississippian*, July 23, 1846.

34. *PJD*, vol. 3, p. 104; *Yazoo City* (Miss.) *Whig*, November 27, 1846; *Woodville* (Miss.) *Republican*, November 7, 1846.
35. *PJD*, vol. 3, pp. 36–37, 105.
36. Ibid., vol. 3, pp. 28–29, 105–6; *Vicksburg Sentinel*, November 2, 1846.
37. *Jackson Southron*, October 28, 1846; *The Vedette* 2 (December 15, 1880), p. 5; *Washington Daily Union*, October 31, 1846; *Lafayette* (La.) *Louisiana Statesman*, June 26, 1850.
38. *Holly Springs Gazette*, November 28, 1846; *Memoir*, vol. 1, pp. 304–5.
39. Weems, *Conquer*, pp. 232–33.
40. *PJD*, vol. 3, pp. 22–23; WPJ to Rosa Johnston, August 24, 1862, Mason Barret Collection.
41. *History of the War Between the United States and Mexico* (Philadelphia, 1848), p. 90.
42. *PJD*, vol. 3, p. 24.
43. *Memoir*, vol. 1, p. 308; *Carrolton* (Miss.) *Democrat*, September 30, 1846; *Natchez Courier*, October 7, 1846; Eleanor Damon Pace, ed., "The Diary and Letters of William P. Rogers, 1846–1862," *Southwestern Historical Quarterly* 32 (April 1929), p. 266.
44. Pace, "Rogers," p. 267; *Jackson Mississippian*, July 23, 1847; *Vicksburg Tri-Weekly Whig*, July 13, 1847; *PJD*, vol. 3, p. 30n.
45. Sioussat, "Campbell," pp. 154–55.
46. *PJD*, vol. 3, pp. 88, 115.
47. Smith Diary, October 22, 1846.

Chapter 9   Boys, Fire, and at Them with Your Knives!

1. *Memoir*, vol. 1, p. 310; *PJD*, vol. 3, pp. 53, 56.
2. *Vicksburg Whig*, November 5, 1846.
3. *PJD*, vol. 1, pp. 77–79, 80–83, 85, 86–88.
4. Ibid., pp. 56, 93–95.
5. Weems, *Conquer*, pp. 274–75.
6. *PJD*, vol. 3, p. 112; vol. 1, p. lvii; Weems, *Conquer*, pp. 279, 299.
7. Weems, *Conquer*, pp. 283–85.
8. *PJD*, vol. 3, pp. 115, 118.
9. Pace, "Rogers," p. 274.
10. *PJD*, vol. 3, pp. 139–40.
11. Pace, "Rogers," pp. 276–77.
12. *Memoir*, vol. 1, p. 341; *PJD*, vol. 3, p. 140.
13. *Harper's Weekly Illustrated Newspaper*, January 9, 1858; Oram Perry, *Indiana in the Mexican War* (Indianapolis, 1908), p. 304.
14. *PJD*, vol. 3, pp. 140–41; *Memoir*, vol. 1, p. 344; Riley, "Health, Part I," p. 189; Tarpley, p. 20.
15. *PJD*, vol. 3, p. 141ff; H. Montgomery, *The Life of Major General Zachary Taylor* (Auburn, N.Y., 1847), pp. 346–47; G. N. Allen, *Incidents and Sufferings in the Mexican War* (Boston, 1848), n.p.
16. *Memoir*, vol. 1, pp. 335–36.
17. *PJD*, vol. 3, pp. 141–42.
18. *The Vedette* 1 (February 1880), p. 12.
19. *PJD*, vol. 3, pp. 142, 148; Jacob Neff, *Thrilling Incidents of the Wars of the*

United States (Philadelphia, 1848), p. 573; Henry W. Benham, *Recollections of Mexico and the Battle of Buena Vista* (Boston, 1851), p. 17; *Matamoros* (Mexico) *American Flag*, March 31, April 10, 26, 1847.

20. *PJD*, vol. 3, pp. 142, 148; Neff, *Incidents*, p. 573; Benjamin F. Scribner, *Camp Life of a Volunteer* (Philadelphia, 1847), p. 65.
21. *PJD*, vol. 3, pp. 142–43; Scribner, *Camp Life*, p. 65.
22. *Matamoros American Flag*, March 31, 1847; Scribner, *Camp Life*, p. 65; Neff, *Incidents*, p. 574.
23. *PJD*, vol. 3, pp. 143, 148.
24. Weems, *Conquer*, pp. 309–10; Robert F. Lucid, ed., *The Journal of Richard Henry Dana, Jr.* (Cambridge, Mass., 1968), vol. 1, p. 344; Benham, *Buena Vista*, pp. 23, 24.
25. Samuel G. French, *Two Wars* (Nashville, 1901), p. 82; *Matamoros American Flag*, April 10, 1847.
26. *PJD*, vol. 3, pp. 122–23; *Memoir*, vol. 1, pp. 316–18.
27. *Memoir*, vol. 1, pp. 332–33, 334–35; *Lafayette Louisiana Statesman*, June 26, 1850; Lucid, *Dana*, vol. 1, pp. 343–44.
28. *Memoir*, vol. 1, p. 351; *PJD*, vol. 3, pp. 148n, 149n, 151n, 164.
29. *PJD*, vol. 3, pp. 165–66.
30. Ibid., pp. 172–73, 176.
31. Smith Diary, December 15, 1846; *PJD*, vol. 3, pp. 169, 170, 173, 186–87.
32. *PJD*, vol. 3, pp. 175–76, 185–86, 190.
33. Ibid., pp. 181–82, 184, 417.
34. Ibid., pp. 203, 205–6.
35. Ibid., pp. 192, 193–94, 207, 215–16; *Natchez Courier*, August 25, 1847.
36. *PJD*, vol. 3, pp. 190–91, 196–97.
37. Davis, *Recollections*, p. 247; *PJD*, vol. 3, pp. 199, 201, 211.
38. *PJD*, vol. 3, pp. 225–26.

Chapter 10   The Days of the Confederation Are Numbered

1. Riley, "Health, Part I," p. 190; *PJD*, vol. 3, p. 419.
2. *PJD*, vol. 3, pp. 96n, 238–39.
3. Ibid., vol. 5, pp. 475–76; vol. 3, pp. 302–3.
4. Ibid., vol. 2, p. 86n; vol. 3, p. 246n.
5. U.S. Congress, *Congressional Directory for the First Session of the Thirtieth Congress* (Washington, D.C., 1848), p. 22; *PJD*, vol. 3, pp. 240n, 248–50.
6. *PJD*, vol. 3, pp. 253–54.
7. *PJD*, vol. 3, p. 86n; vol. 6, pp. 51–52.
8. *Congressional Directory*, n.p.
9. *Chicago Times*, August 29, 1886; Oliver Dyer, *Great Senators of the United States Forty Years Ago* (Freeport, N.Y., 1872), pp. 123–24; E. F. Ellett, *Court Circles of the Republic* (Philadelphia, 1872), p. 490; *New York Herald*, August 11, 1895.
10. Tarpley, p. 24.
11. *PJD*, vol. 3, pp. 254–56, 257–60.
12. Ibid., pp. 254, 266–67, 292.
13. Ellett, *Court Circles*, p. 490; Dyer, *Great Senators*, p. 124; Tarpley, p. 26; *Congressional Directory*, p. 22; *PJD*, vol. 3, pp. 302–3.

14. *PJD*, vol. 3, pp. 277, 278–79, 287; Ellett, *Court Circles*, p. 490.
15. *PJD*, vol. 3, pp. 266, 286, 292–93, 318, 319–20, 324n.
16. Ibid., pp. 314, 315.
17. Rowland, vol. 1, pp. 217–19.
18. *PJD*, vol. 3, pp. 330–31.
19. Ibid., vol. 3, p. 443.
20. Ibid., vol. 3, pp. 332–73, passim.
21. Rowland, vol. 1, pp. 40–45.
22. *PJD*, vol. 5, p. 476; vol. 3, pp. 316–17, 447.
23. Ibid., vol. 2, pp. 246–47n; Frank Everett, Jr., Floor Plan of Brierfield, JDA; Jessie Abbott Hite, Reminiscences, ca. 1916, Old Court House Museum, Vicksburg, Miss.; Davis vs. Bowmar, pp. 260–61, 263–65, 495–96.
24. *PJD*, vol. 3, p. 476; vol. 3, pp. 374–75, 379; Rowland, vol. 1, pp. 215–16.
25. U.S. Congress, *Congressional Directory for the Second Session of the Thirtieth Congress* (Washington, D.C., 1849), pp. 22, 23.
26. *PJD*, vol. 5, p. 477; vol. 4, pp. 3, 15–17.
27. Ibid., vol. 3, p. 452; vol. 4, pp. xxxi, 315.
28. Ibid., vol. 4, pp. xxxi, 8–9; Rowland, vol. 1, pp. 224–26.
29. Rowland, vol. 1, pp. 226–36.
30. *PJD*, vol. 4, pp. 7–8.

Chapter 11   The Assurance That I Am Right

1. *PJD*, vol. 2, p. 246; Dickson, "Marse Jeff Davis," *Collier's* 51 (March 12, 1938), p. 59.
2. *Memoir*, vol. 2, pp. 302, 304; *PJD*, vol. 5, p. 479; vol. 4, p. 364; Walter L. Fleming, "Jefferson Davis, the Negroes and the Negro Problem," *Suwanee Review* 16 (1908), pp. 408, 413; Florida Heulett interview.
3. *PJD*, vol. 4, pp. 20, 22–23; Rowland, vol. 1, pp. 236–43.
4. *PJD*, vol. 4, p. 25.
5. VD to Mrs. W. B. Howell, December 27, 1849, Jefferson Davis Papers, University of Alabama, Tuscaloosa.
6. Rowland, vol. 1, pp. 246, 250–53.
7. *PJD*, vol. 3, p. 62.
8. Ibid., vol. 4, pp. 63–70; *Baltimore Sun*, February 2, 1850.
9. Holman Hamilton, *Prologue to Conflict* (Lexington, Ky., 1964), pp. 33–34.
10. *PJD*, vol. 4, pp. 71–72, 76n; WPJ to Rosa Johnston, May 22, 1862, Mason Barret Collection.
11. Rowland, vol. 1, pp. 263–308, passim.
12. "A Night with 'Old Davy,'" p. 133; *Vicksburg Weekly Sentinel*, February 22, 1850; Strode, *Patriot*, p. 223.
13. Donald F. Tingley, "The Jefferson Davis–William H. Bissell Duel," *Mid-America* 27 (July 1956), pp. 146–55; *PJD*, vol. 4, pp. 79–81; *Springfield* (Ill.) *State Register*, February 28, 1850; *Baltimore Sun*, March 1, 1850; *New York Herald*, March 4, 1850.
14. *PJD*, vol. 4, p. 59n; *Memoir*, vol. 1, pp. 412–413.
15. *PJD*, vol. 4, p. 82.
16. *Memoir*, vol. 1, pp. 447–48.
17. Strode, *Patriot*, p. 225; *Washington Union*, March 14, 1850.

18. *Vicksburg Weekly Sentinel,* March 8, 1850; Rowland, vol. 1, pp. 309–10; *PJD,* vol. 1, p. 88.
19. *Memoir,* vol. 1, pp. 457–58, 462–63.
20. *PJD,* vol. 1, pp. 101–108; *Port Gibson* (Miss.) *Herald and Correspondent,* June 14, 1850.
21. *PJD,* vol. 1, p. 117; *Vicksburg Weekly Whig,* June 5, 1850; Rowland, vol. 1, pp. 323, 338, 347.
22. Rowland, vol. 1, p. 378; *Port Gibson Herald and Correspondent,* July 12, 1850.
23. *PJD,* vol. 4, p. 120n.
24. *Port Gibson Herald and Correspondent,* July 19, 1850.
25. *PJD,* vol. 4, pp. 123–24.
26. *Baltimore Sun,* January 4, 1850; *New York Herald,* February 25, 1850; *PJD,* vol. 5, p. 479; William J. Rhees, ed., *The Smithsonian Institution: Journals of the Board of Regents* (Washington, D.C., 1879), pp. 59–60.
27. Hamilton, *Prologue,* pp. 109–11.
28. *PJD,* vol. 4, pp. 124–25; Rowland, vol. 1, pp. 473, 502–4.
29. Rowland, vol. 1, pp. 486, 512–13, 514, 521–22.
30. *PJD,* vol. 4, pp. 132–33; Hamilton, *Prologue,* pp. 138, 148.
31. *Aberdeen* (Miss.) *Monroe Democrat,* September 25, 1850; *New Orleans Louisiana Courier,* March 31, 1851; *New York Daily Tribune,* December 8, 1899; Rowland, vol. 1, p. 546.
32. New York, *Daily Tribune,* December 8, 1899; *New York Herald,* August 11, 1895.
33. *Vicksburg Weekly Sentinel,* October 23, 1850; *Yazoo Democrat,* October 17, 1850.

Chapter 12   I Will Meet Force with Force

1. *Jackson Mississippian,* October 25, 1850; *Yazoo Democrat,* October 31, 1850; *Vicksburg Weekly Whig,* October 30, 1850; *PJD,* vol. 4, pp. 135–37.
2. *Jackson Southron,* November 1, 1850; *PJD,* vol. 4, pp. 135–36.
3. *Jackson Flag of the Union,* December 6, 1850; Tarpley, pp. 27–28; Rowland, vol. 1, p. 599.
4. *PJD,* vol. 1, p. 140.
5. Ibid., vol. 5, p. 480.
6. Rowland, vol. 2, pp. 1, 11; *PJD,* vol. 4, pp. 154–55; *Jackson Mississippian,* January 31, 1851.
7. Rowland, vol. 2, pp. 22, 23, 27.
8. *PJD,* vol. 4, p. 172.
9. Ibid., vol. 4, pp. 167–70, 175–76; *Port Gibson Herald and Correspondent,* February 14, 1851.
10. *Washington Union,* March 7, 1851; Rowland, vol. 2, p. 66ff.
11. *PJD,* vol. 4, pp. 179–81; Robert J. Ward to JD, February 16, 1861, Jefferson Davis Papers, TU.
12. *PJD,* vol. 4, p. 181.
13. Rowland, vol. 2, pp. 72–81; *Columbus* (Ga.) *Southern Standard,* June 7, 1851.
14. *Memoir,* vol. 1, p. 467; *Columbus* (Miss.) *Primitive Republican,* June 19, 1851.
15. *Woodville Republican,* June 17, 1851; *PJD,* vol. 4, pp. 218–19.
16. *Columbus Southern Standard,* July 27–31, 1851; *New Orleans Louisiana Courier,* August 1, 1851; *Port Gibson Herald and Correspondent,* July 25, 1851; *New Orleans Delta,* June 22, 1851.

17. *PJD*, vol. 4, pp. 219–20; *Memoir*, vol. 1, pp. 469–70.
18. *Woodville Republican*, August 5, 1851; *PJD*, vol. 4, p. 223.
19. *Memoir*, vol. 1, p. 470; *PJD*, vol. 4, pp. 219, 223.
20. Rowland, vol. 2, p. 84; *Memoir*, vol. 1, p. 470; *PJD*, vol. 4, pp. 222–23.
21. *Memoir*, vol. 1, p. 470; *PJD*, vol. 4, pp. 224–25; Rowland, vol. 2, p. 86.
22. *PJD*, vol. 4, pp. 231–32; *Whig Almanac* (New York, 1852), p. 18.
23. *PJD*, vol. 4, pp. 227–28.
24. *Columbus Primitive Republican*, November 6, 1851; *Jackson Mississippian*, November 7, 1851; *New Orleans Delta*, November 14, 1851; *Washington Southern Press*, November 11, 1851.
25. Davis, *Recollections*, pp. 320–21; *PJD*, vol. 4, pp. 232–33.
26. Rowland, vol. 2, pp. 108, 123; *PJD*, vol. 4, pp. 237n, 249n.
27. Rowland, vol. 1, pp. 125ff.; *PJD*, vol. 4, p. 250n; *Natchez Mississippi Free Trader*, March 24, 1852.
28. Rowland, vol. 2, pp. 171–72; *Washington Southern Press*, March 18, 1852; *Memoir*, vol. 1, pp. 474–75; *PJD*, vol. 5, p. 481.
29. *PJD*, vol. 4, p. 62; VD to Margaret Howell, March 4, 1852, Davis Papers, UA.
30. *PJD*, vol. 4, pp. 275, 291; *Memoir*, vol. 1, pp. 477–80.
31. Rowland, vol. 2, p. 175; *PJD*, vol. 4, pp. 295–96.
32. *PJD*, vol. 4, pp. 120n, 301n; Washington Green to JD, September 15, 1863, Officers' File.
33. *PJD*, vol. 4, p. 301; Roy F. Nichols, *Franklin Pierce* (Philadelphia, 1931), p. 216.
34. *PJD*, vol. 4, pp. 307–8.
35. *Memoir*, vol. 1, p. 476.
36. Rowland, vol. 2, p. 179; *PJD*, vol. 5, pp. 3–4.
37. Nichols, *Pierce*, p. 238; *Memoir*, vol. 1, p. 477.

Chapter 13 I Am Paying Dearly Indeed

1. *Memoir*, vol. 1, pp. 265–66, 533.
2. Frank J. Welcher, *The Union Army 1861–1865* (Bloomington, Ind., 1989), pp. 1–3; JD to Fitzhugh Lee, April 5, 1877, in Fitzhugh Lee, "Sketch of the Late General S. Cooper," *Southern Historical Society Papers*, 3 (May–June, 1877), pp. 274–75.
3. Rowland, vol. 2, p. 292.
4. *New Orleans Picayune*, January 7, 1853; *Aberdeen Weekly Independent*, February 19, 1853; *Vicksburg Tri-Weekly Whig*, February 19, 1853; *Jackson Flag of the Union*, March 11, 1853.
5. Casimir Bohn, *Bohn's Hand-Book of Washington* (Washington, D.C., 1861), p. 38.
6. *New York Times*, March 15, 1853; *Vidalia* (Miss.) *Concordia Intelligencer*, April 9, 1853.
7. *PJD*, vol. 5, pp. 16–17, 18.
8. Ibid., pp. 21, 97n; Thomas Jordan, "Jefferson Davis," *Harper's New Monthly Magazine* 31 (October 1865), p. 610.
9. *PJD*, vol. 5, pp. 94–96.
10. Ibid., pp. 64–65, 197, 479–80; *New York Times*, June 4, 1857.
11. *PJD*, vol. 5, pp. 88–89, 291–92, 454; vol. 6, pp. 166–67; Rowland, vol. 2, pp. 374–76.

12. Rowland, vol. 2, pp. 221, 357–58, 460; *PJD*, vol. 5, p. 146n.
13. *PJD*, vol. 5, p. 114; Rowland, vol. 2, pp. 473, 475–82, 487, 488–89, 491–525, 574–75, 590–91; vol. 3, pp. 1–10, 11–25, 36–39, 43; E. A. Hitchcock, *Fifty Years in Camp and Field* (New York, 1909), pp. 406–8, 417–18.
14. *Harper's Weekly Illustrated Newspaper*, January 9, 1858; *Raymond* (Miss.) *Hinds County Gazette*, February 25, 1857; *New York Times*, September 22, 1855.
15. *PJD*, vol. 5, p. 46n; Godfrey Weitzel to Thomas Young, May 12, 1882, Godfrey Weitzel Papers, 1639-ACP-1884, NA; Charles Roland, *Albert Sidney Johnston* (Austin, Tex., 1964), pp. 170–71.
16. Robert Utley, *Frontiersmen in Blue* (New York, 1967), pp. 34–35n.
17. Ibid, pp. 32, 36; Rowland, vol. 2, p. 23.
18. *New Orleans Daily Delta*, January 10, 1857; Rowland, vol. 2, p. 292; *PJD*, vol. 5, p. 62; vol. 6, pp. 72–91, passim.
19. *New York Herald*, April 17, May 4, 1856; *New Orleans Daily Crescent*, May 21, 1861.
20. *PJD*, vol. 4, pp. 385–89; *Memoir*, vol. 1, p. 526; *New York Herald*, December 19, 1853.
21. *PJD*, vol. 5, p. 419; Robert Utley, *Frontier Regulars* (New York, 1973), pp. 145–46, 177–78.
22. *PJD*, vol. 6, pp. 63–67.
23. Utley, *Frontier Regulars*, pp. 53–55.
24. *PJD*, vol. 5, pp. 10, 17, 155.
25. *PJD*, vol. 5, p. 22n.
26. *New Orleans Daily Picayune*, May 2, 1856; *PJD*, vol. 5, p. 49; Nichols, *Pierce*, p. 274; Jefferson Davis, "Reminiscences of Pierce and Cabinet," 1877, Jefferson Davis Papers, Louisiana Historical Association Collection, TU.
27. *PJD*, vol. 5, pp. 48–49, 168.
28. Rowland, vol. 2, pp. 194–95; *Richmond Daily Enquirer*, November 11, 1853; *Life*, pp. 33–34.
29. *PJD*, vol. 5, p. 176; vol. 6, pp. 7–8, 195–96; "Recent Acquisitions of the Manuscript Division," *Quarterly Journal of the Library of Congress* 24 (October 1967), p. 277.

Chapter 14   Hasten Slowly, and Be Temperate in All Things

1. *Baltimore Sun*, May 30, 1853; *PJD*, vol. 5, p. 46.
2. *Washington Union*, July 14, 1853; *New York Times*, July 14, 1853; *PJD*, vol. 5, pp. 28–32; *Richmond Daily Enquirer*, July 23, 1853.
3. *Vicksburg Tri-Weekly Whig*, May 14, 1853; Statement of Harris D. Riley, n.d., JDA; Riley, "Health, Part I," pp. 193–94; *Jackson Mississippian*, January 12, 1858; *New Orleans Daily Delta*, September 12, 1852; Eckloff, *Memoirs*, p. 209.
4. U.S. Congress, *Directory of the Thirty-Third Congress, First Session* (Washington, D.C., 1854), n.p.; *PJD*, vol. 5, pp. 28, 44; *Memoir*, vol. 1, pp. 534–35.
5. *PJD*, vol. 5, pp. 68–69, 72–73.
6. U.S. Congress, *Congressional Directory of the Thirty-Fourth Congress, First Session* (Washington, D.C., 1856), n.p.; U.S. Congress, *Directory of the Thirty-Fifth Congress, First Session* (Washington, D.C., 1857), n.p.; George Brown, *Washington: A Not Too Serious History* (Baltimore, 1930), p. 222; *Baltimore Sun*,

August 19, 1853; *Washington Union*, August 23, 29, September 4, 1853; *Natchez Courier*, June 15, 1855; George M. Battey, Jr., *A History of Rome and Floyd County* (Atlanta, 1969), pp. 241–42.

7. *New York Herald*, June 20, September 25, 1855; *Woodville Wilkinson Whig*, February 9, 1856; *New York Times*, May 1, September 22, 1855.
8. Rowland, vol. 2, pp. 277–79; *Augusta* (Ga.) *Chronicle*, November 4, 1853; *Woodville Wilkinson Whig*, January 28, 1854; *New York Times*, March 18, 1857.
9. *PJD*, vol. 5, pp. 9, 10, 14, 35, 37n, 55; vol. 3, p. 22n; *New York Herald*, January 18, 1854.
10. *PJD*, vol. 5, p. 97; *New York Times*, March 10, 1855; *Washington Evening Star*, March 24, 1855; *Natchez Courier*, June 7, 1855.
11. *Baton Rouge Daily Advocate*, November 15, 1855; *Natchez Courier*, December 4, 1855; *Jackson Semi-Weekly Mississippian*, November 16, 1855; *New York Herald*, November 1, 1855; *PJD*, vol. 5, pp. 138, 140, 141, 148; vol. 6, p. 44; *New Orleans Daily Delta*, October 21, December 7, 1855.
12. Robert W. Johannsen, *Stephen A. Douglas* (New York, 1973), pp. 404–10; William C. Davis, *Breckinridge: Statesman, Soldier, Symbol* (Baton Rouge, 1974), pp. 102–6.
13. Mrs. Archibald Dixon, *True History of the Missouri Compromise and Its Repeal* (Cincinnati, 1899), pp. 457–60; *Rise and Fall*, vol. 1, p. 28; Davis, *Breckinridge*, pp. 107–9.
14. *PJD*, vol. 5, pp. 67–68; Davis, *Breckinridge*, pp. 118–19.
15. *New York Times*, May 1, 22, 1855; *Natchez Courier*, June 21, 1855.
16. *New York Times*, September 7, 1855; *New York Herald*, September 25, 1855; *New Orleans Daily Delta*, May 30, 1856; Nichols, *Pierce*, pp. 430–34.
17. *New York Herald*, November 29, 1855.
18. *PJD*, vol. 6, pp. 25–26.
19. Ibid., vol. 5, pp. 78–81, 198; *New York Herald*, January 28, 1854.
20. *PJD*, vol. 5, pp. 80–81, 138; Robert E. May, *The Southern Dream of a Caribbean Empire* (Baton Rouge, 1973), pp. 61–62, 119; Rowland, vol. 4, p. 80.
21. *PJD*, vol. 6, pp. 39–40, 46–47.
22. Ibid., vol. 6, p. 44.
23. *New York Tribune*, March 16, 1857; *New Orleans Daily Delta*, March 21, 1857; *PJD*, vol. 5, pp. 112–13.
24. *PJD*, vol. 6, p. 590; *Chicago Times*, August 29, 1886.
25. *New York Herald*, October 23, 1856; *PJD*, vol. 6, pp. 54–55, 504; Rowland, vol. 3, pp. 63–64; George G. Henry to JD, May 9, 1861, Letters Received by the Secretary of War, Record Group 365, NA.

Chapter 15 A Pretty Good Secessionist

1. *PJD*, vol. 6, pp. 102–3, 109, 111–12; *Memoir*, vol. 1, pp. 529–30, 570–71.
2. *PJD*, vol. 6, pp. 115n, 540–42; *Washington National Intelligencer*, March 19, 1857.
3. Strode, *Letters*, pp. 89–90; *PJD*, vol. 5, p. 543; Joseph B. Lyman, Sketch of Jeff Davis, 1863, Joseph B. Lyman Papers, Yale University.
4. *PJD*, vol. 6, pp. 117–25.

5. Ibid., pp. 131–32.
6. *Memphis Daily Appeal*, September 11, 13, 15, 1857; *PJD*, vol. 6, p. 137; J. L. Goodloe, "Reminiscences of the University of Mississippi," *University of Mississippi Magazine* 26 (December 1902), pp. 23–24.
7. *PJD*, vol. 6, pp. 137–40, 152–54, 160–61; *New Orleans Daily Delta*, October 10, 1857.
8. *New York Herald*, September 18, 1857; *PJD*, vol. 6, p. 134; *Washington States*, October 1, 1857.
9. *PJD*, vol. 6, pp. 115, 550–51; *New York Tribune*, January 9, 1858; *New York Times*, January 23, 1858.
10. Rowland, vol. 3., pp. 169–75.
11. *Jackson Mississippian*, January 12, 1858.
12. *Natchez Mississippi Free Trader*, March 1, 1858; *Washington States*, February 4, 1858; *Richmond Enquirer*, February 2, 1858.
13. *PJD*, vol. 6, pp. 169–71; *Memoir*, vol. 6, pp. 575–80; Virginia Clay-Clopton, *A Belle of the Fifties* (New York, 1905), p. 69.
14. *Jackson Mississippian*, March 9, 1858; *Washington Evening Star*, March 29, 1858.
15. *Jackson Mississippi and State Gazette*, June 9, 1858; Ellett, *Court Circles*, p. 496; *Natchez Mississippi Free Trader*, June 14, 1858; *PJD*, vol. 6, p. 172.
16. Rowland, vol. 3, pp. 218–28; *PJD*, vol. 6, p. 200; *Washington Union*, July 4, 1858; *Washington States*, July 10, 1858.
17. *Harper's Weekly Illustrated Newspaper*, January 9, 1858; *Jackson Mississippian*, January 23, 1858; *New York Times*, June 7, 1858; *PJD*, vol. 6, pp. 191, 196, 197–98, 200; *Washington States*, June 9, 1858.
18. Riley, "Health, Part I," p. 194; Strode, *Letters*, p. 470.
19. Rowland, vol. 3, pp. 271–73.
20. *Memoir*, vol. 1, pp. 586–95; Carolina Vose, "Jefferson Davis in New England," *Virginia Quarterly Review* 2 (October 1926), pp. 557–68.
21. *New York Herald*, July 14, 1858; *Richmond Enquirer*, July 20, 1858; *New Orleans Daily Delta*, July 31, 1858.
22. *Charleston Mercury*, July 30, 1858.
23. *Memoir*, vol. 1, pp. 593–94; Rowland, vol. 3, pp. 315ff., 348.
24. *New Orleans Daily Delta*, June 24, 1858.
25. Rowland, vol. 3, pp. 339ff.; *PJD*, vol. 6, pp. 227–29.
26. *PJD*, vol. 6, pp. 229–31, 251–52, 253.
27. Rowland, vol. 3, pp. 376ff., 387, 392–93.
28. Ibid., vol. 3, pp. 501ff., 514.
29. Ibid., pp. 498–99.
30. Eckloff, *Memoirs*, pp. 209–10; Mary J. Windle, *Life in Washington* (Philadelphia, 1859), p. 267; David Bartlett, *Presidential Candidates* (New York, 1889), p. 297; *New York Daily Tribune*, December 8, 1889.
31. *Memoir*, vol. 1, p. 264; *New Orleans Sunday Delta*, January 10, 1858.
32. Rowland, vol. 3, pp. 570–74; *PJD*, vol. 6, pp. 604–5.
33. Strode, *Letters*, pp. 108–9.
34. *PJD*, vol. 6, pp. 226, 241–42; Strode, *Letters*, pp. 108–9.
35. *PJD*, vol. 6, p. 247; Strode, *Letters*, p. 110.
36. Riley, "Health, Part I," p. 201; *PJD*, vol. 6, p. 613.
37. Rowland, vol. 4, pp. 61–88.
38. *PJD*, vol. 6, pp. 259, 261–64; Rowland, vol. 4, pp. 93–94.

Chapter 16 We Have Piped But They Would Not Dance

1. *Rise and Fall*, vol. 1, p. 41.
2. *PJD*, vol. 6, p. 618; Rowland, vol. 4, pp. 95, 107–8.
3. *PJD*, vol. 6, pp. 267–68, 619; *Rise and Fall*, vol. 1, p. 41.
4. Rowland, vol. 4, pp. 1, 36, 204, 205, 344, 382, 460, 515.
5. *PJD*, vol. 6, pp. 194, 273–76.
6. Rowland, vol. 4, pp. 203–4.
7. Ibid., vol. 4, pp. 250–80, 331, 348–60, 367–70; *Rise and Fall*, vol. 1, p. 43.
8. *Memphis Daily Avalanche*, January 27, 1859; *PJD*, vol. 6, pp. 264–65, 270–71, 276–77.
9. *PJD*, vol. 6, p. 277.
10. Edward Mayes, *Lucius Q. C. Lamar* (Nashville, 1896), p. 83.
11. *PJD*, vol. 6, pp. 289–94.
12. JD to Caleb Cushing, June 25, 1860, Caleb Cushing Papers, LC; *PJD*, vol. 6, pp. 661, 664; *Louisville Courier-Journal*, May 18–19, 1875, November 17, 1887; *Rise and Fall*, vol. 1, p. 52; J. Henley Smith to Alexander H. Stephens, August 18, 1860, Alexander H. Stephens Papers, LC; *Washington Daily National Intelligencer*, July 25, 1860; *Washington Constitution*, June 27, 1860; Davis, *Breckinridge*, p. 226.
13. Davis, *Breckinridge*, pp. 224–27; Smith to Stephens, August 18, 1860, Stephens Papers; Roy F. Nichols, *Disruption of American Democracy* (New York, 1948), pp. 318, 334–35.
14. John C. Breckinridge to S. L. M. Barlow, June 30, 1860, S. L. M. Barlow Papers, Henry E. Huntington Library, San Marino, Calif.; *Memoir*, vol. 1, p. 685.
15. *PJD*, vol. 6, p. 585; Morris Schaff, "The Spirit of Old West Point," *Atlantic Monthly* 99 (March 1907), pp. 471–72.
16. *PJD*, vol. 6, 295ff, 364–66, 630; Rowland, vol. 4, p. 158.
17. *PJD*, vol. 6, pp. 368–70.
18. *Rise and Fall*, vol. 1, pp. 57–59; Rowland, vol. 2, p. 202; Davis, *Recollections*, p. 391.
19. *PJD*, vol. 6, pp. 371–72.
20. *Rise and Fall*, vol. 1, p. 59; *PJD*, vol. 6, pp. 375–76.
21. Rowland, vol. 4, pp. 201–2, 559–60; *PJD*, vol. 6, pp. 622–23.
22. *PJD*, vol. 6, pp. 376–77; Rowland, vol. 4, pp. 544–45, 552–53.
23. Davis, *Recollections*, pp. 396–99; *PJD*, vol. 6, pp. 377–78; Rowland, vol. 4, pp. 555–57, 561; Library of Congress Loan Record, Jefferson Davis, January 1861, Receipt Book K, 4, Library of Congress Archives, LC.
24. *PJD*, vol. 6, pp. 669–70.
25. Ibid., pp. 669–70; *Rise and Fall*, vol. 1, pp. 68–69, 199.
26. Rowland, vol. 4, pp. 510, 564–65; *Rise and Fall*, vol. 1, pp. 204–5.
27. Harris D. Riley, Jr., "Jefferson Davis and His Health, Part II," *Journal of Mississippi History* 49 (November 1987), p. 261; JD to Eli Whitney, January 2, 1861, Box 571, Mississippi Department of Archives and History; *New York Herald*, February 4, 1861; JD to Edwin DeLeon, January 8, 1861, Edwin DeLeon Papers, South Caroliniana Library, University of South Carolina, Columbia.
28. *New York Herald*, January 10, February 4, 1861; *Richmond Examiner*, January 18, 1861; Rowland, vol. 5, pp. 1ff.

29. *Memoir*, vol. 2, p. 3n; JD to George Lunt, January 17, 1861, Schoff Collection, University of Michigan, Ann Arbor; JD to Clement C. Clay, January 19, 1861, Clement C. Clay Papers, Duke University, Durham, N.C.
30. U.S. Congress, *Congressional Globe*, Thirty-sixth Congress, Second Session (Washington, D.C., 1861), p. 327; Check, January 7, 1861, Casemate Museum, Fort Monroe, Virginia; WPJ to Rosa Johnston, May 22, 1862, Mason Barret Collection.
31. Francis Pickens to JD, January 9, 1861, JD to Pickens, January 10, 1861, Executive Council Journal, Letter Book 32, South Carolina Department of Archives and History, Columbia; William H. Trescott and Laurence M. Keitt to JD, January 9, 1861, James Buchanan Paper, Pennsylvania Historical Society, Philadelphia; Rowland, vol. 5, pp. 36–37, 40; *Washington States and Union,* January 18, 21, 1861.
32. *PJD*, vol. 6, pp. 672–73; J. E. B. Stuart to JD, January 15, 1861, Citizens' File; Robert Ransom to JD, January 19, 1861, P. M. B. Young to JD, February 6, 1861, Record Group 109, NA; *Baltimore Sun,* January 10, 1861; Rowland, vol. 5, p. 45.
33. *New York Herald,* January 15, 1861; JD to Isaac Hayne, January 15, 1861, Hayne to Pickens, January 1861, JD to Pickens, January 20, 1861, Pickens to JD, January 23, 1861, South Carolina Executive Council Letter Book, 59–61.
34. *New York Herald,* January 11, 1861; OR, I, 52, pt 2, p. 10; JD to Clay, January 19, 1861, Clay Papers.
35. Rowland, vol. 5, pp. 37–39, 40–45; *New York Citizen,* April 6, 1867.
36. *Memoir*, vol. 1, pp. 696–99; Rowland, vol. 5, pp. 40–45; JD to Anna Ella Carroll, March 1, 1861, Anna Ella Carroll Papers, Maryland Historical Society, Baltimore.
37. W. T. Moore, "A Journey with Jefferson Davis," *Confederate Veteran* 11 (March 1903), pp. 115–16; *Chattanooga Press,* January 24, 1885; *Memoir*, vol. 2, pp. 6–7.
38. *Vicksburg Weekly Whig,* February 6, 1861; Proclamation, January 23, 1861, Series Z, Private Mss., Jefferson and Varina Davis Collection, Mississippi Department of Archives and History; *New Orleans Delta,* January 27, 1861; *Memoir*, vol. 2, pp. 7–10.
39. *Memoir*, vol. 2, pp. 11–12, 18; *Richmond Dispatch,* January 28, 1861; *Washington States and Union,* January 24, 1861; *New York Herald,* January 31, 1861; Robert Ward to JD, February 16, 1861, David Papers, TU.
40. JD to Alexander M. Clayton, January 30, 1861, Cross Collection, University of Florida, Gainesville.
41. *Memoir*, vol. 2, p. 18; JD to John F. Callan, February 7, 1861, JDA.

Chapter 17 I Saw Troubles and Thorns Innumerable

1. JD to Callan, February 7, 1861, JDA; John J. Pettus to JD, February 7, 1861, Davis Papers, TU.
2. Thomas C. DeLeon, *Belles, Beaux and Brains of the '60's* (New York, 1909), p. 50.
3. "Thomas R. R. Cobb—Extracts from Letters to His Wife," *Southern Historical Society Papers* 28 (1900), p. 281; Alexander H. Stephens, *A Constitutional View*

of the Late War Between the States (Philadelphia, 1868–70), vol. 2, pp. 329–33; Stephens to Linton Stephens, February 23, 1861, Alexander H. Stephens Papers, Southern Historical Collection, University of North Carolina, Chapel Hill.

4. "Cobb—Extracts," p. 282; Stephens, *Constitutional View* 2, pp. 329–33; *Rise and Fall*, vol. 1, pp. 238, 239, 240; David H. Twiggs, "Presidency of the Confederacy Offered Stephens and Refused," *Southern Historical Society Papers* 26 (1908), pp. 141–44.

5. "Cobb—Extracts," pp. 281, 282–83.

6. *Memoir*, vol. 2, pp. 18–19.

7. Ibid., vol. 2, p. 19; *Vicksburg Weekly Whig*, February 13, 1861; *New Orleans Times-Democrat*, February 16, 1902.

8. *Vicksburg Weekly Whig*, February 13, 1861; *New York Times*, February 22, 1861; *Memoir*, vol. 2, p. 21.

9. JD to VD, February 14, 1861, Townsend Collection, Huntington Library; Rowland, vol. 5, p. 46; *New Orleans Delta*, February 14, 1861.

10. JD to VD, February 14, 1861, Townsend Collection; *Vicksburg Weekly Whig*, February 20, 1861; *Atlanta Intelligencer*, February 20, 1861; JD to VD, February 20, 1861, Jefferson Davis Collection, MC.

11. *Atlanta Gate-City Guardian*, February 16, 1861; John Oliver to James Wilson, May 18, 1865, Entry 38, Record Group 110, NA.

12. *Atlanta Intelligencer*, February 18, 1861; *Atlanta Gate-City Guardian*, February 18, 1861; Thomas H. Watts, *Address on the Life and Character of Ex-President Jefferson Davis* (Montgomery, Ala., 1889), p. 14.

13. *Memphis Daily Appeal*, February 21, 1861; *New York Herald*, February 23, 1861.

14. *Atlanta Intelligencer*, February 20, 1861; JD to VD, February 20, 1861, Davis Collection, MU.

15. Rowland, vol. 5, pp. 49–53.

16. *Atlanta Intelligencer*, February 21, 1861; JD to VD, February 20, 1861, Davis Collection, MC; "Cobb—Extracts," p. 281.

17. "Cobb—Extracts," p. 283; *Harper's Weekly Illustrated Newspaper*, March 9, 1861; *Augusta* (Ga.) *Daily Constitutionalist*, February 21, 1861.

18. "Cobb—Extracts," pp. 283–84; Richmond, *Enquirer*, February 15, 1861; *New Orleans Daily Delta*, February 10, 1861.

19. *Natchez Courier*, February 12, 1861; *New York Citizen*, April 20, 1867; *Washington Evening Star*, March 14, 1861.

20. *Washington Evening Star*, February 19, 1861; "Cobb—Extracts," p. 283.

21. *Rise and Fall*, vol. 1, pp. 242–43; Robert Toombs to JD, February 19, 20, 1861, Davis Papers, TU; Clay-Clopton, *Belle*, p. 157; JD to Howell Cobb, February 21, 1861, Jefferson Davis Collection, Chicago Historical Society; JD to Howell Cobb, February 25, 1861, Record Group 109, NA; John H. Reagan, *Memoirs* (New York, 1906), pp. 109–110.

22. C. Vann Woodward, ed., *Mary Chesnut's Civil War* (New Haven, 1981), p. 8; *Memoir*, vol. 2, p. 37; DeLeon, *Belles*, p. 48; *The First White House of the Confederacy* (Montgomery, 1986), pp. 2ff; *New Orleans Daily Picayune*, April 9, 1861; *Charleston Daily Courier*, March 9, 1861; *New York Tribune*, April 10, 1861.

23. *Memoir*, vol. 2, pp. 11, 38; Henry D. Capers, *The Life and Times of C. G. Memminger* (Richmond, 1893), p. 330; Henry P. Beers, *Guide to the Archives*

of the Confederate States of America (Washington, D.C., 1968), p. 62; *New York Citizen*, April 20, 1867.

24. *Mobile Tribune*, 1861 clipping in Scrapbook #4, W. T. Walthall Papers, Mississippi Department of Archives and History; *Richmond Enquirer*, March 30, 1861; *New York Citizen*, April 13, 1867.

25. William McWillie to JD, April 5, 1861, E. Kirby Smith to JD, February 28, 1861, Wiley P. Harris to JD, March 30, 1861, Officers' File; P. G. T. Beauregard to JD, February 10, 1861, P. G. T. Beauregard Papers, Duke; James Condon to JD, February 11, 1861, CSA Papers, LC; G. W. Lee to JD, February 18, 1861, Letters Received by the Confederate Secretary of War, chap. 9, Record Group 109, NA; A. Gerard et al. to JD, February 18, 1861, Davis Papers, TU; Ephraim Parker to JD, March 13, 1861, Felix Hargell Collection, University of Georgia, Athens.

26. Mariana Jones et al. to JD, April 23, 1861, A. G. Miller to JD, February 18, 1861, Charles Edwards to JD, March 15, 1861, N. S. Reeves to JD, April 12, 1861, T. Gaszynsky to JD, April 1, 1861, John Teas to JD, April 1, 1861, R. G. Davidson to JD, May 11, 1861, chap. 9, Record Group 109; G. W. Yerby to JD, March 16, 1861, Record Group 365, NA; W. T. Howell and T. H. Hatcher to JD, April 20, 1861, Davis Papers, TU; George Bickley to JD, April 3, 1861, Sam Richey Collection, Miami University, Miami, Ohio; *Montgomery Advertiser*, April 15, 1861.

27. WPJ to Rosa Johnston, May 22, 1862, Mason Barret Collection.

28. William H. Chase to JD, February 20, 1861, Citizens' File; JD to Howell Cobb, March 1, 7, 1861, Jefferson Davis Papers, Record Group 109; Henry Heth to JD, April 17, 1861, Officers' File; Lucius B. Northrop to JD, March 16, 1861, Davis Papers, TU.

29. JD to Beverly Tucker, April 16, 1861, Beverly Tucker Papers, University of Virginia, Charlottesville; John Hancock to JD, April 15, 1861, Jefferson Davis Papers, LC; A. L. Humphries to JD, April 5, 1861, Chapter IX, D. L. Yulee to JD, March 1, 1861, Officers' File, Record Group 109; T. B. J. Hadley to JD, April 6, 1861, CSA Records, Volume 46, LC.

30. JD to George Howard, April 1, 1861, Autograph File, Frederick Dearborn Collection, Harvard University, Cambridge, Mass.; Henry Wise to JD, May 15, 1861, Chapter IX, Virginia Delegation to JD, April 2, 1861, H. S. Foote, Jr., to JD, April 29, 1861, Davis Papers, Record Group 109; WPJ to Rosa Johnston, May 31, 1862, Mason Barret Collection; John B. Jones, *A Rebel War Clerk's Diary* (Philadelphia, 1866), vol. 1, p. 74.

31. JD Notes, March 16, 1861, Jefferson Davis Papers, Transylvania University, Lexington, Ky.; Pay Record, March 28, 1861, Davis Papers, TU.

32. William H. Russell, *My Diary North and South* (New York, 1954), pp. 93–95; William H. Russell, *Pictures of Southern Life* (New York, 1861), p. 20; *New York Citizen*, April 13, 1867; DeLeon, *Belles*, p. 49; *Mobile Tribune*, clipping in Scrapbook #4, Walthall Papers.

33. *Memoir*, vol. 2, p. 40; *Vicksburg Weekly Whig*, April 17, 1861; *New York Times*, May 30, 1861; *Richmond Enquirer*, April 27, 1861; *Richmond Whig*, April 27, 1861; *New Orleans Crescent*, April 4, 1861.

34. Louis T. Wigfall to JD, February 18, 1861, Jefferson Davis Papers, Schoff Collection, University of Michigan, Ann Arbor; Wigfall to JD, February 20, 1861, Jones Autograph Letters, Duke; *New York Times*, February 28, 1861.

35. Rowland, vol. 5, pp. 56–57; James M. Mason to JD, February 12, 1861,

Schoff Collection; Isaac Hayne to JD, February 18, 1861, G. A. Baker Catalog #34, 1939, p. 8.

36. Pickens to JD, February 20, 1861, JD to Pickens, February 22, 1861, Executive Council Letterbook, pp. 107, 108; Rowland, vol. 5, pp. 58–59.
37. *Rise and Fall*, vol. 1, pp. 268–73; Rowland, vol. 5, p. 61; *OR*, I, 1, p. 273.
38. John Cannon to JD, April 3, 1861, Chapter IX, John A. Campbell to JD, April 3, 1861, JD to Campbell, April 10, 1861, Citizens' File, Record Group 109.
39. *Rise and Fall*, vol. 1, p. 278; *New Orleans Daily Delta*, April 10, 1861.
40. *New York Tribune*, April 9, 1861; *Montgomery Advertiser*, April 9, 1861.
41. Samuel W. Crawford, *The Genesis of the Civil War* (New York, 1887), p. 421; Pleasant Stoval, *Robert Toombs* (New York, 1892), p. 226.
42. *OR*, I, 1, p. 297; Wigfall to JD, April 10, 1861, G. A. Baker Catalog #34, 1939, p. 8.
43. *OR*, I, 1, pp. 13–14, 301, 305, 306; *New York Citizen*, May 4, 11, 1867.
44. *OR*, I, 1, pp. 308–310; JD to Pickens, April 13, 1861, Executive Council Journal Letterbook, 1861, South Carolina Department of Archives and History; Alfred Roman, *The Military Operations of General Beauregard* (New York, 1884), vol. 1, p. 52.
45. *Memoir*, vol. 2, p. 80; *Baltimore Sun*, April 15, 1861; Frank Moore, comp., *The Rebellion Record* (New York, 1861), vol. 1, Documents, p. 188; *New York Citizen*, May 11, 1867; *Charleston Courier*, April 26, 1861; *Richmond Dispatch*, April 22, 1861; Howell Cobb to JD, April 22, 1861, Officers' File.

Chapter 18   We Will Make a History for Ourselves

1. *Rise and Fall*, vol. 1, pp. 292, 297.
2. Wigfall to JD, February 18, 1861, Jones Autograph Letters.
3. Wise to JD, February 22, 1861, Officers' File; *Memphis Daily Appeal*, February 19, 1861; Mason to JD, April 21, 1861, Schoff Collection; Rowland, vol. 5, pp. 63–65.
4. Mason to Davis, May 6, 1861, Jefferson Davis Papers, Duke; *New York Citizen*, May 18, 1867; Isham Harris to JD, April 20, 1861, Dearborn Collection; John Ellis to JD, April 25, 1861, John Ellis Papers, Southern Historical Collection.
5. *Charleston Daily Courier*, April 25, 1861; J. W. Woltz to JD, April 17, 1861, chap. 9, Record Group 109; *Vicksburg Weekly Whig*, April 17, 1861; Campbell to JD, April 23, 1861, Citizens File; "Cobb—Extracts," p. 285.
6. Moore, *Rebellion Record*, vol. 1, Documents, pp. 188–89.
7. Campbell to JD, April 28, 1861, Citizens' File.
8. Rowland, vol. 5, pp. 67–84.
9. Woodward, *Chesnut*, pp. 11, 12; "Cobb—Extracts," pp. 284–85; Thomas R. R. Cobb to Marion Cobb, February 28, March 2, 1861, Thomas R. R. Cobb Collection, University of Georgia, Athens.
10. *OR*, IV, 1, pp. 117, 247.
11. JD to Braxton Bragg, April 3, 1861, William Palmer Collection, Western Reserve Historical Society, Cleveland, Ohio.
12. Bragg to JD, April 7, 1861, Palmer Collection; *Charleston Daily Courier*, May 18, 1861; *Richmond Dispatch*, May 20, 1861; *New York Times*, May 22, 23,

1861; Charlotte Wigfall to Halsey Wigfall, May 23, 1861, Louis T. Wigfall Papers, LC; JD to Bragg, May 23, 1861, Goodspeed's Catalog #373, 1943, item 71.

13. Undated clipping, Scrapbook #4, Box 25, Walthall Papers; Clay-Clopton, *Belle*, p. 158; *Richmond Examiner*, May 24, 1861; *New Orleans Daily Crescent*, May 14, 1861.

14. Thomas O. Moore to JD, May 9, 1861, Davis Papers, Duke.

15. Bragg to Davis, May 18, 1861, Jefferson Davis Papers, Emory University, Atlanta; ———Brooks to JD, May 13, 1861, Documents in the *OR*, Record Group 109, NA.

16. Henry C. Wayne to JD, May 10, 1861, Davis Papers, MC.

17. JD to John Letcher, April 22, 1861, JD to Joseph E. Johnston, May 2, 1861, Executive Papers, Virginia State Library, Richmond; Leonidas Polk to JD, May 14,.1861, *The Collector* 47 (November 1932), n.p.; JD to Polk, May 22, 1861, in William M. Polk, *Leonidas Polk, Bishop and General* (New York, 1893), vol. 1, pp. 352–53.

18. WPJ to JD, April 26, 1861, Dearborn Collection; WPJ to Rosa Johnston, August 24, 1862, Mason Barret Collection.

19. *New York Times*, May 30, 1861; *New Orleans Daily Crescent*, May 24, 1861; Jones, *Diary*, vol. 1, p. 36.

20. Woodward, *Chesnut*, p. 25; *Richmond Whig*, May 6, 1861; Clay-Clopton, *Belle*, p. 158; *New Orleans Daily Picayune*, April 24, 1861; *Charleston Daily Courier*, May 14, 1861; *Richmond Dispatch*, May 4, 1861; *Richmond Enquirer*, May 14, 1861; *New Orleans Daily Crescent*, May 14, 1861.

21. James D. Richardson, comp., *The Messages and Papers of Jefferson Davis and the Confederacy* (Washington, D.C., 1905), vol. 1, pp. 60–62; "Cobb—Extracts," p. 286.

22. Roger Pryor to JD, April 25, 1861, Davis Papers, TU; O. P. Baldwin to JD, May 4, 1861, Pritchard von David Collection, University of Texas, Austin; Pickens to Milledge L. Bonham, July 7, 1861, Milledge L. Bonham Papers, South Caroliniana Library; A. T. Bledsoe to JD, May 10, 1861, Dearborn Collection; Bledsoe to JD, May 11, 1861, Davis Papers, Duke.

23. *Richmond Dispatch*, May 9, 1861; JD to John J. Byrd, May 9, 1861, Palmer Collection; *Richmond Examiner*, May 28, 1861; *Memoir*, vol. 2, pp. 74–75; *New York Citizen*, June 1, 1867.

24. *Memoir*, vol. 2, pp. 74–75, *Richmond Examiner*, May 29, June 6, 1861; *Augusta Daily Chronicle and Sentinel*, May 28, 1861; *New York Tribune*, June 2, 1861; JD to Robert E. Lee, May 28, 1861, Letters and Telegrams Received by Robert E. Lee, chap. 2, Record Group 109.

25. *Richmond Whig*, May 30, 1861; *New Orleans Delta*, June 5, 1861; *New York Tribune*, June 2, 1861.

26. *Baltimore Sun*, June 10, 1861; *Richmond Examiner*, May 31, 1861; *Richmond Whig*, June 1, 1861; *Richmond Enquirer*, June 3, 1861; *Augusta Daily Chronicle and Sentinel*, May 30, 1861.

27. *Richmond Enquirer*, June 4, 1861.

28. *Richmond Examiner*, May 31, June 3, 1861; *Richmond Whig*, June 1, 3, 1861.

29. *Richmond Whig*, May 31, June 3, 10, 1861; *Charleston Courier*, June 21, 1861.

30. Samuel J. T. Moore, Jr., *Moore's Complete Civil War Guide to Richmond* (Richmond, 1978), p. 24; L. Q. C. Lamar, "The Confederate State Department," *The Independent* 53 (September 19, 1901), p. 2221.

31. "Cobb—Extracts," p. 286; Howell Cobb to Mrs. Cobb, May 18, 1861, Cobb Family Papers, University of Georgia; Joseph Brown to JD, June 7, 1861, Governor's Letterbook 45, Georgia Department of Archives and History, Atlanta; JD to Brown, June 8, 1861, Documents in the OR, Record Group 109.
32. Brown to JD, July 8, 1861, Governor's Letterbooks; JD to Brown, July 11, 1861, Documents in the OR, Record Group 109.
33. OR, IV, 1, pp. 419–20; JD to Letcher, July 9, 1861, Benjamin Gratz Collection, Pennsylvania Historical Society.
34. William L. Yancey to JD, February 27, 1861, Citizens File; WPJ to Rosa Johnston, May 22, 1862, Mason Barret Collection; Beauregard to JD, July 2, 1861, Microfilm 618, Record Group 109; Harris to JD, July 13, 1861, Isham Harris Papers, Tennessee State Library and Archives, Nashville; JD to Harris, July 17, 1861, Richey Collection.
35. P. T. Scroggs to JD, July 1, 1861, chap. 9, Record Group 109; Wise to JD, August 28, 1861, Dearborn Collection.
36. Polk to Mrs. Polk, June 10, 1861, Leonidas Polk Papers, University of the South, Suwanee, Tenn.; JD to William M. Polk, December 15, 1879, Leonidas Polk Papers, Southern Historical Collection.
37. Richmond Enquirer, June 13, 1862; Mason to JD, April 21, 1861, Schoff Collection.
38. R. M. Smith to JD, May 9, 1861, Davis Papers, TU; Charleston Daily Courier, June 6, 1861; J. N. Ragsdale to JD, June 28, 1861, Richey Collection; OR, II, 2, p. 18; James W. Cole to JD, June 16, 1861, chap. 9, Record Group 109.
39. JD to JED, June 18, 1861, Mrs. J. D. Marrett.
40. Ibid., OR, I, 2, pp. 943–44: Beauregard to JD, June 16, 1861, P. G. T. Beauregard Papers, LC.
41. Beauregard to JD, June 12, 1861, Davis Papers, Emory; William C. Davis, Battle at Bull Run (New York, 1977), p. 65; Woodward, Chesnut, pp. 80, 83, 85, 129.
42. F. Hodges to JD, July 8, 1861, Davis Papers, Record Group 109; Woodward, Chesnut, p. 84; "Old Fell" to ?, July 10, 1861, Joseph Rubenfine List #66, n.d., p. 6; New York Tribune, July 15, 1861; Richmond Dispatch, July 18, 1861.
43. JD to JED, June 18, 1861, Mrs. J. D. Marrett; Richmond Dispatch, July 18, 1861; New York Citizen, June 8, 1867; Polk to Mrs. Polk, June 10, 1861, Polk Papers, Suwanee.
44. Beauregard to JD, July 11, 1861, Joseph E. Johnston to JD, June 26, 1861, Davis Papers, Emory.
45. JD to Joseph E. Johnston, July 10, 1861, Documents in the OR, Record Group 109; JD to Joseph E. Johnston, July 13, 1861, Jefferson Davis Papers, Huntington.
46. James Chesnut to JD, November 2, 1861, Schoff Collection; JD, Memorandum on P. G. T. Beauregard's Manassas Report, Documents in the OR, Record Group 109; Beauregard to JD, July 17, 1861, Davis Papers, TU.

Chapter 19 We Have Taught Them a Lesson

1. JD endorsement on Beauregard to JD, July 17, 1861, Beauregard to JD, July 18, 1861, Davis Papers, TU; Rowland, vol. 5, p. 111.

2. *New York Citizen*, September 14, 1867; *Rise and Fall*, vol. 5, p. 348; Rowland, vol. 5, pp. 111–18.
3. R. A. Pierson to William Pierson, July 19, 1861, Pierson Family Papers, Kuntz Collection, TU; Rowland, vol. 5, pp. 118–19; *Rise and Fall*, vol. 1, p. 348.
4. JD to G. W. C. Lee, July 21, 1861, Richard Frajola Catalog, July 10, 1983, p. 16; *Life*, p. 153.
5. *Rise and Fall*, vol. 1, pp. 349–50; Gary Gallagher, ed., *Fighting for the Confederacy* (Chapel Hill, 1989), p. 54; Joseph E. Johnston, *Narrative of Military Operations* (New York, 1874), pp. 53–54; *New Orleans Daily Picayune*, July 27, August 4, November 5, 1861; *New York Herald*, August 2, 1861.
6. *Rise and Fall*, vol. 1, p. 351.
7. Gallagher, *Fighting*, pp. 57–58; *Rise and Fall*, vol. 1, pp. 354–56; JD to Samuel Cooper, July 21, 1861, Documents in the *OR*, Record Group 109; *New York Citizen*, September 14, 1867; Incident relative to Mr. Davis' telegram announcing our victory, n.d., Beauregard Papers, LC.
8. JD to E. H. Andrews, July 25, 1861, Svenette Dinkins, Jackson, Miss.; *Memoir*, vol. 2, p. 111; *Rise and Fall*, vol. 1, pp. 359–61.
9. *Richmond Enquirer*, July 24, 26, 1861; *New Orleans Daily Picayune*, July 27, 1861; Jones, *Diary*, vol. 1, p. 66; *New York Citizen*, September 21, 1867; *Charleston Daily Courier*, July 24, 1861; *Charleston Mercury*, July 30, August 7, 1861; Resolution, August 6, 1861, Confederate Collection, Earl Swem Library, William and Mary University, Williamsburg, Va.
10. Riley, "Health, Part II," pp. 267–68; *Richmond Examiner*, September 13, 30, 1861; *New York Herald*, September 5, 1861.
11. Jones, *Diary*, vol. 1, p. 66.
12. Joseph E. Johnston to JD, July 24, August 3, 1861, Joseph E. Johnston Papers, Duke; Beauregard to JD, July 25, 1861, Davis Papers, TU.
13. Toombs to Stephens, June 21, 1861, in Myrta L. Avary, ed., *Recollections of Alexander H. Stephens* (New York, 1910), p. 67; Toombs to JD, September 1, 1861, Robert Toombs Papers, Duke; Jones, *Diary*, vol. 1, pp. 74, 78, 79.
14. *New York Citizen*, May 25, 1867; *Charleston Daily Courier*, August 17, 1861.
15. Woodward, *Chesnut*, pp. 85, 120, 127, 167; *New York Citizen*, May 25, August 24, 1867.
16. *Journal of the Congress of the Confederate States of America, 1861–1865* (Washington, D.C., 1904–1905), vol. 1, p. 461; *Rise and Fall*, vol. 1, p. 307.
17. *Memoir*, vol. 2, pp. 138–40.
18. Ibid., pp. 144–53.
19. JD to Joseph E. Johnston, September 14, 1861, Davis Papers, TU.
20. *Memoir*, vol. 2, pp. 150n, 157–58.
21. *OR*, I, 53, p. 635; WPJ to Rosa Johnston, August 24, 1862, Mason Barret Collection; *PJD*, vol. 5, pp. 309–10, 377, 440, 432; vol. 6, pp. 402, 644–45, 665; Roland, *Johnston*, p. 240; Rowland, vol. 8, pp. 257–58.
22. Rowland, vol. 5, pp. 120–21.
23. Beauregard to JD, August 10, 1861, in Roman, *Beauregard*, vol. 1, pp. 123–24; Woodward, *Chesnut*, p. 124; Jones, *Diary*, vol. 1, p. 89.
24. Woodward, *Chesnut*, p. 124; Beauregard to William Porcher Miles, September 4, 1861, in Roman, *Beauregard*, vol. 1, p. 483.
25. Jones, *Diary*, vol. 1, pp. 71–72, 89.
26. Woodward, *Chesnut*, p. 130; *OR*, I, 5, p. 920.

27. *New Orleans Picayune*, October 11, 1861; Joseph E. Johnston to JD, August 23, 1861, Jones Collection, Duke.
28. JD to VD, October 2, 1861, Davis Papers, MC; G. W. Smith, Council of War at Centreville, October 1, 1861, Jefferson Davis Collection, Beauvoir Shrine, Biloxi, Miss.; *Rise and Fall*, vol. 1, pp. 451, 453; Jordan, "Jefferson Davis," p. 615.
29. *Rise and Fall*, vol. 1, pp. 445–48; G. W. Smith to JD, October 14, 1861, G. W. Smith Papers, Duke.
30. *Natchez Daily Courier*, October 26, 1861; *New York Tribune*, October 8, 1861; *Charleston Daily Courier*, October 7, 1861; *Richmond Examiner*, June 4, 1861.
31. *Memoir*, vol. 2, p. 163; *Washington National Intelligencer*, September 24, 1861; *Charleston Daily Courier*, September 6, 1861; Jones, *Diary*, vol. 1, p. 55.
32. *Charleston Daily Courier*, September 24, 1861; *Charleston Mercury*, September 28, 1861; *Washington National Intelligencer*, October 7, 15, 1861; *New Orleans Daily Crescent*, September 23, 1861.
33. Rowland, vol. 5, pp. 142–43, 150–51; Beauregard to JD, October 22, 1861, Beauregard Papers, Duke.
34. Rowland, vol. 5, 163–64.
35. *Rise and Fall*, vol. 1, pp. 368–69; Rowland, vol. 5, pp. 157–65.
36. Beauregard to JD, November 7, 1861, Jones, Georgia Portfolio, vol. 2, p. 109, C. C. Jones Papers, Duke; JD on Beauregard's Manassas Report, Documents in the OR, Record Group 109; Chesnut to JD, November 2, 1861, Schoff Collection.
37. *Charleston Mercury*, November 4, 1861; Jones, *Diary*, vol. 1, p. 90.
38. WPJ to Rosa, August 20, 1861, Mason Barret Collection.
39. Rowland, vol. 8, p. 232; William Preston Johnston, *The Life of General Albert Sidney Johnston* (New York, 1879), p. 291.

Chapter 20   Sidney Johnston's Step

1. *Memoir*, vol. 2, p. 12; *OR*, I, 5, pp. 9, 13–14, 53, 690.
2. Ibid., vol. 1, 4, pp. 362, 368–69.
3. JD to Polk, May 22, 1861, Polk, *Polk*, vol. 1, pp. 352–53.
4. *OR*, I, 3, p. 691.
5. *OR*, I, 4, pp. 180, 189; Polk to JD, September 6, 1861, Robertson Tabb to JD, September 6, 1861, Davis Papers, TU.
6. WPJ to Rosa Johnston, August 24, 1862, Mason Barret Collection; *New York Times*, April 7, 1887; *OR*, IV, 1, p. 600.
7. F. Lane to JD, September 6, 1861, chap. 9, Record Group 109; Jacob Thompson to JD, September 6, 1861, Schoff Collection; *New York Citizen*, August 17, 1867; *OR*, I, 3, pp. 687–88.
8. Moore to JD, September 6, 7, 1861, JDA.
9. G. W. Smith to JD, September 3, 1861, Schoff Collection; Rowland, vol. 5, p. 137.
10. Mansfield Lovell to JD, October 18, 1861, Davis Papers, Emory; Jacob Payne to JD, October 24, 1861, Davis Papers, Duke; Rowland, vol. 5, p. 137.
11. JD to Samuel R. Anderson, June 11, 1861, *Washington National Intelligencer*, April 26, 1862; *OR*, I, 4, p. 405; *Richmond Daily Dispatch*, October 28, 1861; Rowland, vol. 5, pp. 151–52.

12. Reynolds to JD, June 3, 1861, Dearborn Collection; Reynolds to JD, June 3, 1861, Davis Papers, TU.
13. Payne to JD, October 24, 1861, Davis Papers, Duke; James L. Morrison, ed., *The Memoirs of Henry Heth* (Westport, Conn., 1974), pp. 159–60; Rowland, vol. 5, p. 197.
14. Pickens to JD, November 24, 1861, Francis Pickens Papers, South Carolina Department of Archives and History; Herschel V. Johnson to JD, November 11, 1861, Read Collection, University of Georgia.
15. Rowland, vol. 5, pp. 166–68.
16. Colin J. McRea to JD, April 17, 1861, Officers' File; C. G. Memminger to JD, April 20, 1861, Denver Public Library.
17. Richardson, *Messages and Papers*, vol. 1, p. 123; E. A. Pollard, *Life of Jefferson Davis* (Philadelphia, 1869), p. 175; Raphael Thian, *Register of Issues of Confederate States Treasury Notes* (Washington, D. C., 1880), pp. 173–80.
18. Mark Valentine to JD, July 16, 1861, Letters Received by the Secretary of War, Record Group 365, NA.
19. *ORN*, II, 3, pp. 1191–95.
20. A. D. Mann to JD, April 20, 1861, Dearborn Collection; Mann to JD, November 4, 1861, Citizens File; Daniel W. Johnson to JD, September 30, 1861, William Seward Collection, Rush Rhees Library, University of Rochester, New York.
21. Pierre Rost to JD, July 20, 1861, Davis Papers, Emory; Mann to JD, November 4, 1861, Citizens File; DeLeon to JD, October 30, 1861, JDA.
22. Yancey to JD, December 30, 1861, Davis Papers, Emory.
23. Rowland, vol. 5, p. 171; Jones, *Diary*, vol. 1, p. 103.
24. Neill S. Brown to JD, September 22, 1861, Davis Papers, Duke; *Natchez Daily Courier*, September 27, 1861.
25. D. Morris to JD, January 26, 1862, Davis Papers, TU; *Charleston Daily Courier*, November 13, 1861; *Charleston Mercury*, November 5, 1861.
26. Ambrosio J. Gonzales to JD, March 20, 1862, Davis Papers, Duke; Northrop to JD, March 6, 1862, Citizens File; Mary Ellis to JD, March 6, 1862, Officers' File; M. W. Philips to JD, January 9, chap. 9, Record Group 109.
27. Jordan, "Jefferson Davis," p. 616; Richard Gatlin to JD, September 6, 1861, Carded Records of Confederate Engineers, Chapter III, Anderson to JD, March 7, 1862, Harvey Jones to JD, March 8, 1862, chap. 9, John J. Chipley to JD, January 5, 1862, David Currier to JD, March 4, 1862, Microfilm 437, Record Group 109; *Memoir*, vol. 2, p. 305.
28. M. C. Harmon to JD, September 20, 1861, Microfilm 618, William Dunbar to JD, January 7, 1862, chap. 9, Record Group 109; J. A. McNutt to JD, December 27, 1861, Davis Papers, TU; JD to Virginia Moon, n.d., Filson Club, Louisville, Ky.
29. Fairfax Harrison, ed., *The Harrisons of Skimino* (New York, 1910), p. 231; William Tyler to JD, February 15, 1862, Officers' File; JD to George Davis, September 15, 1861, Lawrence O. Branch Papers, Duke; Gaspar Tochman to JD, September 19, 1861, Davis Papers, Duke; JD to James Seddon, January 31, 1862, Bruce Family Papers, Virginia Historical Society, Richmond.
30. N. Van Bail to JD, October 2, 1861, JD to Judah P. Benjamin, January 18, 1862, H. R. Walker to JD, January 7, 1862, Ed Jegou to JD, January 18, 1862, chap. 9, Record Group 109; JD, Salary Warrant Register, CSA Papers, LC.

31. *Richmond Examiner*, January 2, 1862; Charles Davidson to Evaline Davidson, January 17, 1862, Charles E. Davidson Papers, Virginia Historical Society; Stephen R. Mallory Diary, September 27, 1865, Stephen R. Mallory Papers, Southern Historical Collection.

32. Mallory Diary, September 27, 1865; Dallas, *Morning News*, April 30, 1897; *New York Citizen*, June 22, September 21, 1867.

33. Mallory Diary, September 27, 1865.

34. Ibid.

35. Ibid., October 6, 1865.

36. Ibid.

37. Watts, *Address*, n.p.; *Dallas Morning News*, April 30, 1897; Mallory Diary, October 6, 1865.

38. Mallory Diary, September 27, 1865.

39. *Charleston Daily Courier*, October 12, 1861; JD to Clay, March 14, April 3, 1862, Clement C. Clay Papers, Alabama Department of Archives and History, Montgomery; *Richmond Examiner*, November 11, 1861; Emma Lyon Bryan Reminiscences, Virginia Historical Society; Lamar, "State Department," 2223.

40. *Charleston Daily Courier*, November 11, 1862.

41. George Davis to JD, February 19, 1862, Davis Papers, Emory; *Memoir*, vol. 2, pp. 180–83.

42. Jones, *Diary*, vol. 1, p. 111; Broadside, "President Jefferson Davis's Inaugural Address," February 22, 1862, JDA.

43. Jones, *Diary*, vol. 1, p. 111.

Chapter 21   The Drooping Cause of Our Country

1. *OR*, I, 4, pp. 193, 194.

2. *OR*, I, 4, p. 430; St. John R. Liddell, "Liddell's Record of the Civil War," *Southern Bivouac*, New Series 1 (December 8, 1885), pp. 417–19.

3. Benjamin to Beauregard, January 26, 1862, JD to Albert Sidney Johnston, n.d., 1861, Mason Barret Collection.

4. JD to Polk, February 7, 1862, Miscellaneous Correspondence, Record Group 109.

5. WPJ to Rosa Johnston, August 20, 1861, February 14, 1862, Mason Barret Collection.

6. JD to A. S. Johnston, February 18, 1862, A. S. Johnston to JD, February 20, 1862, Telegrams Received and Sent, War Department, Record Group 109; Jones, *Diary*, vol. 1, p. 111.

7. A. Wright to JD, February 24, 1862, Davis Papers, Duke; Tapp to JD, February 24, 1862, von David Collection; A. B. Bacon to Davis, February 25, 1862, List 481, Duke; L. C. P. Smith et al. to JD, February 25, 1862, W. H. McCardle to A. G. Brown, March 1, 1862, Davis Papers, TU.

8. JD endorsement on Clayton to JD, March 2, 1862, Carnegie Book Shop Catalog #346, 1975, item 94; Edward W. Munford, "Albert Sidney Johnston," n.d., Mason Barret Collection; Gustavus A. Henry et al. to JD, March 8, 1862, Civil War–Confederate Collection, Tennessee State Library and Archives.

9. Rowland, vol. 5, pp. 203–6.

10. Benjamin to JD, March 8, 1862, Davis Papers, Duke; Benjamin to JD, March 11, 1862, Microfilm 523, Record Group 109; WPJ to Rosa Johnston, May 24, 1862, Mason Barret Collection; *New York Citizen*, June 8, 1867; Gideon Pillow to JD, March 24, 1864, Microfilm 618.
11. Rowland, vol. 5, pp. 215–6.
12. *OR*, IV, 1, pp. 997–98.
13. John D. Imboden to——Frazier, March 2, 1862, Robert E. Lee Papers, Petition, March 8, 1862, chap. 9, Record Group 109; *OR*, I, 51, pt. 2, p. 511; Rowland, vol. 5, p. 220; Committee of Safety to JD, March 8, 1862, Davis Papers, Duke.
14. *Richmond Examiner*, February 24, March 6, 20, 1862.
15. "A Friend" to JD, April 2, 1862, chap. 9, Record Group 109.
16. R. M. T. Hunter to JD, February 17, 1862, CSA Papers, LC; JD to Benjamin, March 19, 1862, chap. 9, Record Group 109; George W. Randolph to JD, March 20, 1862, Dearborn Collection; *New York Citizen* August 17, 1867.
17. Rowland, vol. 5, p. 225.
18. Ibid., p. 225; Earl Van Dorn to JD, March 30, 1862, Officers' File.
19. *OR*, I, 10, pt. 2, p. 381; Rowland, vol. 5, p. 381; JD to Camille Polignac, April 5, 1862, Palmer Collection.
20. *Memoir*, vol. 2, p. 230; William Preston to JD, April 7, 1862, Mason Barret Collection.
21. JD to Van Dorn, April 7, 1862, Autographs, Miscellaneous, American, Pierpont Morgan Library, New York; Beauregard to JD, April 7, 1862, CSA Papers, LC; WPJ to Rosa Johnston, May 4, 1862, Mason Barret Collection.
22. WPJ to Rosa Johnston, May 3, 1862, Mason Barret Collection.
23. Randolph to JD, April 12, 1862, Microfilm 523, Record Group 109; Edward W. Munford to JD, May 10, 1862, Johnston Family Papers, Filson Club; WPJ to Rosa Johnston, May 3, 1862, Mason Barret Collection; Jones, *Diary*, vol. 1, p. 120.
24. *OR*, I, 10, pt. 2, pp. 385–92.
25. WPJ to Rosa Johnston, May 19, July 20, 1862, Mason Barret Collection.
26. Ibid., August 24, 1862, WPJ to Preston, May 22, 26, 1862, Mason Barret Collection.
27. WPJ to Rosa Johnston, June 12, 1862, Mason Barret Collection; *OR*, I, 10, pt. 1, pp. 780–86.
28. JD to VD, June 3, 13, 21, 1862, MC.
29. WPJ to Preston, July 20, 1862, Preston to WPJ, June 14, 1862, Mason Barret Collection.
30. Rowland, vol. 5, p. 274.
31. *OR*, I, 6, pp. 641–42; *Rise and Fall*, vol. 2, pp. 210, 224; Rowland, vol. 5, p. 279.
32. J. C. Ives to JD, June 16, 1862, JD to Bragg, July 16, 1862, Bragg to JD, June 17, 1862, Davis Papers, TU; Rowland, vol. 5, p. 283; Mallory Diary, June 21, 1862.
33. Preston to WPJ, June 14, 1862, Mason Barret Collection; Beauregard to Thomas Jordan, July 12, 1862, Beauregard Papers, Duke.
34. WPJ to Rosa Johnston, July 4, 1862, Mason Barret Collection; *OR*, I, 10, pt. 1, pp. 782–84.
35. Albert Pike, Circular, July 3, 1862, JD to Van Dorn, March 20, 1862, Davis Papers, TU; JED to JD, May 22, June 6, 1862, Davis Papers, Transylvania.

36. JD to JED, February 21, 1862, *Washington Daily Morning Chronicle*, May 13, 1864; T. H. Holmes to JD, May 4, 1862, *Flying Quill*, April 1941, item 462.

37. J. E. Johnston to JD, February 16, 1862, Johnston Papers, William and Mary; Benjamin to JD, December 16, 1880, Kuntz Collection, TU; Johnston, *Narrative*, p. 96; Rowland, vol. 6, p. 494.

38. Thomas Bocock to JD, March 10, 1862, chap. 9, Record Group 109; *OR*, I, 5, pp. 1079, 1083–84, 1088.

39. *OR*, I, 5, pp. 527–28, 1096; JD to ?, 1880, Goodspeed's Catalog #378, June 1944, p. 10.

40. John D. Phelan to JD, September 9, 1861, Richey Collection.

41. Johnston, *Narrative*, p. 109; *Memoir*, vol. 2, p. 196; *Rise and Fall*, vol. 1, p. 464; *OR*, I, 11, pt. 3, p. 392.

42. *OR*, I, 11, pt. 3, pp. 396–97, 405, 409.

43. Jones, *Diary*, vol. 1, p. 120; *OR*, I, 11, pt. 3, p. 414.

44. *OR*, I, 11, pt. 3, p. 420; J. E. Johnston to JD, April 4, 1862, Davis Collection, Emory; Jones, *Diary*, vol. 1, p. 117.

45. JD to Van Dorn, April 7, 1862, Autographs, Miscellaneous, American, Pierpont Morgan; Brown to JD, April 12, 1862, Governor's Letterbooks, 1861–1865, Georgia; *Rise and Fall*, II, pp. 86–88.

46. *OR*, I, 11, pt. 2, p. 485.

47. Randolph to JD, May 7, 1862, Davis Papers, Duke.

48. WPJ to Rosa Johnston, May 8, 1862, Mason Barret Collection.

49. *Memoir*, vol. 2, pp. 269–301; "The Religious Life of Jefferson Davis," *Confederate Veteran* 35 (October 1927), pp. 375–76; Charles Minnegerode to Mrs. Josiah Gorgas, May 6, 1862, Josiah Gorgas Papers, University of Alabama.

50. *Harper's Weekly Illustrated Newspaper*, June 7, 1862.

51. JD to William Browne, May 8, 1862, Davis Papers, Record Group 109; WPJ to Rosa Johnston, May 8, 1862, Mason Barret Collection; *Memoir*, pp. 268–69; *OR*, I, 11, pt. 2, p. 508.

Chapter 22   We Could End the War

1. *Memoir*, II, p. 739; *New York Citizen*, June 22, 1867; WPJ to Rosa Johnston, May 10, 1862, Mason Barret Collection.

2. Burton Harrison notes, April 19, 1862, chap. 9, Record Group 109; WPJ to Rosa Johnston, May 22, 1862, Harrison to WPJ, March 6, 1866, Mason Barret Collection; Harrison to JD, March 12, 1862, Harrison Papers; *New York Citizen*, June 22, 1867.

3. WPJ to Rosa Johnston, May 12, 14, 1862, Mason Barret Collection; *OR*, I, 11, pt. 2, pp. 507–8; J. E. Johnston to JD, May 24, 1862, Davis Collection, Emory; JD to J. E. Johnston, May 25, 1862, Clements Library, University of Michigan.

4. JD to VD, May 13, 1862, MC.

5. JD to VD, May 16, 1862, MC.

6. JD to VD, May 19, 1862, MC; *Rise and Fall*, vol. 2, pp. 101–2; J. E. Johnston to Wigfall, November 12, 1863, Wigfall Papers.

7. *OR*, I, 11, pt. 2, pp. 523–24.

8. Reagan, *Memoirs*, pp. 138–39; *Rise and Fall*, vol. 2, p. 103.

9. Reagan, *Memoirs*, p. 139.
10. *Rise and Fall*, vol. 2, p. 120; *OR*, I, 11, pt. 2, pp. 526, 530, 536; WPJ to Rosa Johnston, May 22, 24, 1862, Mason Barret Collection.
11. VD to JD, May 26, 30, 1862, Jefferson Hayes-Davis, Colorado Springs, Colorado.
12. *Rise and Fall*, vol. 2, pp. 121–23; WPJ to Rosa Johnston, June 1, 7, July 20, 1862, Mason Barret Collection; JD to VD, June 2, 1862, MC; Reagan, *Memoirs*, p. 140; *Dallas Morning News*, April 30, 1897.
13. *Rise and Fall*, vol. 2, p. 129; WPJ to Rosa Johnston, June 1–2, 1862, Mason Barret Collection; JD to VD, June 2, 1862, MC.
14. *Rise and Fall*, vol. 2, p. 131.
15. *OR*, I, 5, p. 1099.
16. WPJ to Rosa Johnston, June 1–2, 1862, Mason Barret Collection; *Rise and Fall*, vol. 2, pp. 133–34.
17. Rowland, vol. 5, p. 264.
18. WPJ to Rosa Johnston, May 22, 29, June 7, 9, 1862, Mason Barret Collection; JD to VD, June 13, 1862, MC.
19. JD to VD, May 12, 1862, Davis Papers, Transylvania; JD to VD, June 3, 13, 1862, MC; WPJ to Rosa Johnston, August 26, 1862, Mason Barret Collection; VD to JD, June 3, 1862, Jefferson Hayes-Davis.
20. WPJ to Rosa Johnston, May 8, 24, 29, June 9, 1862, Mason Barret Collection.
21. Harrison notes, Harrison Papers; Passport of JD [May 1862], MC.
22. WPJ to Rosa Johnston, May 8, 26, June 7, 9, 10, 12, July 27, 1862, Mason Barret Collection.
23. JD to VD, June 13, 1862, MC; Rowland, vol. 5, p. 272.
24. Harrison notes, Harrison Papers; JD to VD, June 21, 23, 1862, MC.
25. *Dallas Morning News*, April 30, 1897; *Rise and Fall*, vol. 2, pp. 140–44; *Memoir*, vol. 2, pp. 316–17.
26. *Rise and Fall*, vol. 2, pp. 149–50.
27. Harrison notes, Harrison Papers; *Dallas Morning News*, April 30, 1897; Rowland, vol. 5, pp. 290–91.
28. VD to WPJ, June 5, 1862, Mason Barret Collection; VD to JD, June 3, 12, 1862, MC; VD to JD, July 6, 1862, Jefferson Hayes-Davis.
29. VD to JD, June 26, July 6, 1862, Jefferson Hayes-Davis.
30. Ibid., June 26, 1862.

Chapter 23 The Vicious and the Selfish

1. JED to JD, October 7–8, 1862, Davis Papers, Transylvania; R. W. Woolley to WPJ, August 4, 1862, Mason Barret Collection.
2. JD to Pickens, January 11, 1862, Microfilm 618, Record Group 109; Moore to JD, July 23, 1862, JD to Moore, September 29, 1862, Thomas O. Moore Papers, Louisiana State University, Baton Rouge; Moore to JD, September 12, 1862, Dearborn Collection; *New York Herald*, July 2, 1865.
3. Woodward, *Chesnut*, pp. 206, 334.
4. Ibid., pp. 159, 194; *Richmond Examiner*, February 24, 26, March 20, May 19, 1862.
5. WPJ to Rosa Johnston, August 4, 1862, Mason Barret Collection.

6. *Richmond Examiner*, May 19, 1862; Woodward, *Chesnut*, p. 215.
7. Woodward, *Chesnut*, p. 215; WPJ to Rosa Johnston, June 7, 1862, Mason Barret Collection.
8. *New York Herald*, July 2, 1865.
9. JD to John Forsyth, July 18, 1862, Richey Collection.
10. WPJ to Rosa Johnston, May 22, 1862, Mason Barret Collection.
11. JD to Bonham, June 24, 1862, Bonham Papers; *Charleston Mercury*, November 5, 1861.
12. *New York Citizen*, April 13, August 17, 1867; G. W. Smith to JD, February 23, 1863, Dearborn Collection.
13. WPJ to Rosa Johnston, May 19, July 20, 1862, Mason Barret Collection; Bragg to JD, July 31, 1862, C. C. Jones Georgia Portfolio, Duke; Rowland, vol. 5, p. 312.
14. WPJ to Rosa, July 20, 1863, Mason Barret Collection; Rowland, vol. 5, p. 312.
15. John W. DuBose, *The Life and Times of William Lowndes Yancey* (Birmingham, Ala., 1892), vol. 2, pp. 650–53; Rowland, vol. 5, pp. 231–32.
16. JD to Clay, March 14, 1862, Paul Richards Catalog #59, p. 18; JD to Clay, April 25, 1862, Davis Papers, TU; Yancey to JD, April 17, 1862, Yancey and Clay to JD, April 21, 1862, William L. Yancey Papers, Alabama Department of Archives and History; Yancey to JD, April 17, 1862, Citizens' File.
17. Rowland, vol. 5, p. 234; Yancey to JD, May 5, 1862, University of Michigan.
18. DuBose, *Yancey*, vol. 2, p. 678; Rowland, vol. 5, p. 498.
19. DuBose, *Yancey*, vol. 2, pp. 743–44.
20. Yancey to JD, May 6, June 26, July 11, 1863, Yancey Papers; Rowland, vol. 5, p. 498; DuBose, *Yancey*, vol. 2, pp. 745–52.
21. DuBose, *Yancey*, vol. 2, p. 750.
22. Bell I. Wiley, *The Road to Appomattox* (New York, 1968), pp. 100–101.
23. Thomas R. R. Cobb to Marion Cobb, January 24, 26, February 1, 1862, Thomas R. R. Cobb Collection, University of Georgia.
24. Rosser H. Taylor, ed., "Boyce-Hammon Correspondence,"*Journal of Southern History* 3 (May 1937), p. 349.
25. Thomas R. R. Cobb to Marion Cobb, January 24, March 16, 1862, Thomas R. R. Cobb Collection.
26. Charlotte Wigfall to Louly Wigfall, June 11, 1861, Wigfall Papers; Woodward, *Chesnut*, p. 136.
27. Woodward, *Chesnut*, pp. 86, 104, 143; Wigfall to Clay, May 16, 1862, Clay Papers; Wigfall to J.E. Johnston, May 1862, Wigfall Papers.
28. Woodward, *Chesnut*, pp. 136, 433.
29. Ibid., pp. 79, 121, 138–39.
30. WPJ to Rosa Johnston, June 10, 1862, Mason Barret Collection; *New York Citizen*, August 24, 1867; Burton Harrison interview, Harrison Papers; *Dallas Morning News*, April 30, 1897.
31. Rowland, vol. 5, pp. 459–60; Jones, *Diary*, vol. 1, p. 181; Mallory Diary, September 27, 1865.
32. WPJ to Rosa Johnston, May 19, 1862, Mason Barret Collection; E. A. Pollard, *The Lost Cause* (New York, 1866), p. 656.
33. Wilfred B. Yearns, *The Confederate Congress* (Athens, Ga., 1960), p. 222; *Memoir*, vol. 2, pp. 160–61; Rowland, vol. 5, p. 246.
34. *Memoir*, vol. 2, p. 163.

35. Jones, *Diary*, vol. 2, p. 330; *Memoir*, vol. 2, p. 164.
36. JD to Kirby Smith, July 28, 1862, E. Kirby Smith Papers, Southern Historical Collection; JED to JD, June 13, July 10, September 1, 1862, Jefferson Hayes-Davis.
37. WPJ to Rosa Johnston, June 7, August 26, 28, 1862, Mason Barret Collection.
38. *New York Herald*, July 2, 1865; W. N. Haldeman to WPJ, July 22, December 4, 1862, Mason Barret Collection; *Charleston Mercury*, November 5, 1861.
39. *Charleston Daily Courier*, November 11, 1861.
40. Pollard, *Lost Cause*, pp. 282–83; WPJ to Rosa Johnston, May 19, 1862, Mason Barret Collection.
41. WPJ to Rosa Johnston, May 22, 1862, Mason Barret Collection; Richardson, *Messages and Papers*, vol. 1, pp. 219–27; *New York Citizen*, September 21, 1867.
42. *Dallas Morning News*, April 30, 1897; "Cobb—Extracts," p. 299; Thomas R. C. Cobb to Marion Cobb, November 17, 1862, Thomas R. R. Cobb Collection.
43. Richardson, *Messages and Papers*, vol. 1, pp. 205–6.
44. Thomas R. R. Cobb to Marion Cobb, April 24, 1862, Thomas R. R. Cobb Collection; JD to Benjamin, April 26, 1862, CSA Papers, LC.
45. VD to WPJ, August 7, 1862, Mason Barret Collection; *Memoir*, vol. 2, pp. 919–20.
46. Wiley, *Road to Appomattox*, p. 10; WPJ to Rosa Johnston, July 1, August 24, 1862, Mason Barret Collection.

Chapter 24 To Strike Another Blow

1. VD to WPJ, August 7, 13, 1862, WPJ to Rosa Johnston, August 14, 1862, Mason Barret Collection; Margaret Davis to JD, August 28, 1862, Davis Papers, Alabama.
2. VD to JD, July 6, 1862, Jefferson Hayes-Davis; WPJ to his daughter, August 3, 1862, WPJ to Rosa Johnston, August 26, 1862, Mason Barret Collection.
3. WPJ to Rosa Johnston, August 15, 28, 1862, Mason Barret Collection.
4. Ibid., August 15, October 9, 24, November 10, 27, December 7, 1862; Chesnut to JD, October 19, 1862, Davis Papers, TU.
5. *OR*, I, 11, pt. 1, p. 939; George Carter to JD [April 1862], Items Received, Quartermaster General, S. H. Goetzel & Co. to JD, October 20, 1862, E. Griswold to Randolph, October 15, 1862, Henry Rupell to JD, September 18, 1862, chap. 9, Record Group 109.
6. Brown to JD, October 15, 1862, chap. 9, Record Group 109.
7. *Memoir*, vol. 2, p. 326; WPJ to "Henny," October 1862, Mason Barret Collection.
8. *New York Citizen*, June 22, 29, 1867; DeLeon, *Belles*, pp. 117–18; VD to WPJ, August 7, 13, 1862, WPJ to Rosa Johnston, August 26, 1862, Mason Barret Collection; Gallagher, *Fighting*, pp. 89–90.
9. Johnston, *Narrative*, p. 97; Rowland, vol. 5, p. 225; JD to JED, July 7, 1862, Davis Collection, Emory.
10. *OR*, Atlas, plate 165.

11. Thomas Snead, "With Price East of the Mississippi," C. C. Buel and R. Johnson, eds., *Battles and Leaders of the Civil War* (New York, 1887–88), vol. 2, pp. 724–26.
12. WPJ to Rosa Johnston, August 15, 1862, Mason Barret Collection; Holmes to JD, August 28, November 9, 1862, T. H. Holmes Papers, Duke.
13. Cooper to JD, November 28, 1862, chap. 9, Thompson to JD, December 5, 1862, Officers' File, Record Group 109; W. S. Oldham to JD, October 13, 1862, CSA Papers, LC.
14. JED to JD, June 13, 1862, Jefferson Hayes-Davis; JED to JD, July 10, September 1, 1862, Davis Papers, Transylvania.
15. *OR*, I, 15, pp. 14, 794–95.
16. *OR*, I, 17, pt. 2, pp. 707, 715.
17. WPJ to Rosa Johnston, August 3, 6, 1862, John S. Bransford to WPJ, November 24, 1862, WPJ to Preston, February 19, July 20, 1862, Haldeman to WPJ, July 22, December 4, 1862, Mason Barret Collection.
18. *OR*, I, 17, pt. 2, pp. 645, 656.
19. *OR*, I, 17, pt. 2, pp. 628, 655.
20. *OR*, I, 16, pt. 2, pp. 745–46; JD to Kirby Smith, July 28, 1862, Kirby Smith Papers.
21. *OR*, I, 16, pt. 2, p. 741; WPJ to Rosa Johnston, August 15, 1862, Mason Barret Collection.
22. JD to Kirby Smith, July 28, 1862, Kirby Smith Papers; *OR*, I, 12, pt. 3, pp. 931, 935, 938–39, 945.
23. *Rise and Fall*, vol. 2, p. 329.
24. *OR*, I, 19, pt. 2, pp. 590–91, 598–99, 600, 602–3, 604–5.
25. G. W. C. Lee to JD, September 25, 1862, Dearborn Collection; Rice W. Payne to JD, September 21, 1862, Davis Papers, TU; Jones, *Diary*, vol. 1, pp. 153–54; Rowland, vol. 5, p. 346.
26. William Crump et al. to JD, October 7, 1862, Clayton to JD, October 11, 1862, Davis Papers, TU.
27. William J. Hardee to WPJ, August 27, 1862, Mason Barret Collection; JED to JD, September 1, 1862, Davis Papers, Transylvania.
28. Preston to WPJ, September 18, 19, 1862, Mason Barret Collection.
29. WPJ to Rosa Johnston, October 11, 1862, Mason Barret Collection; Jones, *Diary*, vol. 1, p. 154, 164, 165, 171, 173, 174; JD to Bragg, October 17, 1862, L. S. Ruder Collection, Beauvoir.
30. JD to Kirby Smith, October 29, 1862, Kirby Smith Papers; Kirby Smith to JD, October 20, 1862, Dearborn Collection; Preston to WPJ, November 22, 1862, George B. Hodge to WPJ, November 17, 1862, WPJ to Rosa Johnston, October 27, 1862, Mason Barret Collection.
31. Jilson P. Johnson and G. A. Henry to JD, October 20, 1862, Davis Papers, TU; WPJ to Rosa Johnston, October 16, 27, 1862, Mason Barret Collection; Thomas Bragg Diary, October 30, 1862, Southern Historical Collection; George Brent Diary, November 2, 1862, Palmer Collection; JD to Kirby Smith, October 29, 1862, Kirby Smith Papers.
32. JD to Kirby Smith, October 29, 1862, Kirby Smith Papers; Kirby Smith to JD, November 1, 1862, Davis Papers, Record Group 109; Polk to JD, November 3, 1862, Davis Papers, TU; *OR*, I, 16, pt. 2, p. 981; Hardee to WPJ, November 19, 1862, Mason Barret Collection.

33. *OR*, I, 20, pt. 1, p. 698; JD to Kirby Smith, October 29, 1862, Kirby Smith Papers; Kirby Smith to JD, November 19, 1862, chap. 9, Abraham Buford, Compiled Service Record, Record Group 109.
34. Clayton et al. to JD, October 11, 1861, Van Dorn to JD, December 8, 1862, JD to Bragg, October 17, 1862, Ruder Collection.
35. D. W. Yandell to WPJ, November 8, 1862, Mason Barret Collection; JD to Kirby Smith, October 29, 1862, Kirby Smith Papers.
36. Jones, *Diary*, vol. 2, p. 163; JD to Kirby Smith, October 29, 1862, Kirby Smith Papers.
37. *OR*, I, 20, pt. 2, p. 493; Johnston, *Narrative*, pp. 148–49.
38. *OR*, I, 52, pt. 2, pp. 496–97.
39. J. D. Bradford to JD, June 23, 1862, Davis Papers, MC; JD endorsement, October 23, 1862, William A. Blount to JD, November 3, 1862, D. R. Williams to JD, November 6, 1862, Polk to JD, November 29, 1862, chap. 9, Record Group 109; Kirby Smith to JD, November 3, 1862, Davis Papers, Record Group 109; WPJ to Preston, December 6, 1862, Mason Barret Collection.
40. John B. Magruder to Randolph, October 18, 21, 1862, chap. 9, Record Group 109; WPJ to Preston, December 6, 1862, Mason Barret Collection.
41. R. G. H. Kean to Randolph, July 18, 1862, Henry Fitzhugh to JD, October 23, 1862, chap. 9, Record Group 109; George G. Shackelford, *George Wythe Randolph and the Confederate Elite* (Athens, Ga., 1988), p. 149; Edward Younger, ed., *Inside the Confederate Government* (New York, 1957), p. 31.
42. Randolph to JD, August 11, 1862, von David Collection; Randolph to JD, October 1, 1862, Microfilm 523, Record Group 109.
43. Shackelford, *Randolph*, pp. 144–45; Younger, *Inside*, pp. 29–31; Frank Ruffin to Randolph, November 13, 1862, Francis G. Ruffin Papers, Virginia Historical Society.
44. Randolph to JD, November 15, 1862, Edgehill-Randolph Collection, University of Virginia, Charlottesville; WPJ to Rosa Johnston, November 18, 1862, Mason Barret Collection; Bledsoe to JD, November 19, 1862, Davis Papers, Duke.

Chapter 25   I Mourn over Opportunities Lost

1. Jones, *Diary*, vol. 1, p. 190; Younger, *Inside*, p. 35.
2. Jones, *Diary*, vol. 1, p. 191; Younger, *Inside*, pp. 31–32; *New York Citizen*, August 17, 1867.
3. Bledsoe to JD, November 19, 1862, Davis Papers, Duke.
4. G. W. C. Lee to JD, November 17, 1862, Davis Papers, Record Group 109; Jones, *Diary*, vol. 1, p. 192; Younger, *Inside*, p. 33.
5. W. S. Featherstone to JD, October 25, 1862, chap. 9, Record Group 109; *OR*, I, 21, p. 1015; Rowland, vol. 5, pp. 376, 384.
6. Rowland, vol. 5, pp. 384–86; Pettus to JD, December 1, 1862, Davis Papers, TU; JD to Moon, December 1862, Miscellaneous Manuscripts, Jefferson Davis, Filson Club; Jones, *Diary*, vol. 1, p. 210; Younger, *Inside*, p. 33; WPJ to Preston, December 6, 11, 1862, Mason Barret Collection.
7. Rowland, vol. 5, p. 384; *New York World*, December 26, 1862.
8. Bragg to JD, March 5, 1863, Davis Papers, Record Group 109; John S.

Jackman Diary, December 13, 1862, LC; *New York World*, December 26, 1862; JD to VD, December 15, 1862, Davis Papers, MC; Nathaniel C. Hughes, ed., *Liddell's Record* (Dayton, 1985), pp. 102–3; Brent Diary, December 12, 16, 19, 1862, Palmer Collection; *Life*, p. 310.

9. J. E. Johnston to Wigfall, December 15, 1862, Wigfall Papers; JD to VD, December 15, 1862, Davis Papers, MC; Rowland, vol. 5, p. 386.
10. JD to VD, December 15, 1862, Davis Papers, MC; Seddon to JD, December 13, 1862, Lee's Official Telegrams, Duke; Seddon to WPJ, December 15, 1862, Mason Barret Collection; *OR*, I, 21, p. 1062.
11. Memorandum of a contract, December 20, 1862, Charles H. Collins Collection, Colorado College, Colorado Springs; David Pierson to William H. Pierson, December 24, 1862, Pierson Family Papers, Kuntz Collection; Rowland, vol. 5, pp. 386–89.
12. *New York Times*, January 14, 1863.
13. WPJ to Rosa Johnston, December 30, 1862, January 4, 6, 1863, Mason Barret Collection; Jones, *Diary*, vol. 1, pp. 229, 232; Rowland, vol. 5, pp. 390–95.
14. J. E. Johnston to JD, December 31, 1862, Johnston Papers, William and Mary; WPJ to Rosa Johnston, January 6, 9, 1863, Preston to WPJ, January 26, March 13, 1863, Mason Barret Collection; Polk to JD, February 6, 1863, Davis Papers, TU.
15. JD to Bragg, January 14, 1863, Davis Papers, TU; *OR*, I, 23, pt. 2, pp. 613–14.
16. J. E. Johnston to JD, January 1863, Johnston Papers, William and Mary; Rowland, vol. 5, p. 396; John C. Pemberton to JD, January 5, 1863, Thomas Madigan Catalog, 1937; *OR*, I, 23, pt. 2, p. 624.
17. *OR*, I, 23, pt. 2, pp. 626–27, 632–33.
18. VD to JD, December 21, 1862, Jefferson Hayes-Davis; *OR*, I, 23, pt. 2, p. 614.
19. J. E. Johnston to JD, March 2, 1863, Johnston Papers, William and Mary; Woodward, *Chesnut*, p. 268.
20. WPJ to Rosa Johnston, January 28, 1863, Mason Barret Collection.
21. Ibid., January 6, February 8, 12, 17, 24, 1863, Mason Barret Collection; Jones, *Diary*, vol. 1, pp. 269–70; JD to Senate, January 26, 1863, Davis Papers, TU.
22. WPJ to Rosa Johnston, January 6, 1863, Mason Barret Collection; Rowland, vol. 5, pp. 396–415.
23. Stephens to JD, January 26, 1863, chap. 9, Record Group 109; Pardon, May 11, 1863, CSA Papers, LC; Bragg to JD, June 9, 1863, Browne to JD, June 17, 1863, President's Letterbook, TU.
24. Bragg to JD, March 26, 1863, University of Michigan; Blanton Duncan to JD, January 21, 1863, Davis Papers, Duke; Jones, *Diary*, vol. 1, p. 342; "A Mississippian" to JD, February 20, 1863, Richard Davis to JD, February 21, 1863, Davis Papers, MC; Rowland, vol. 5, p. 441.
25. Seddon to JD, February 16, 1863, Lists of Nominations for Government Positions, Tennessee and Alabama Congressmen to JD, February 2, 1863, Officers File, Record Group 109; JD to Clay, April 2, 1863, JD to Virginia Clay, May 9, 1863, Clay Papers; JD to Thomas Devereaux, February 12, 1863, Davis Papers, MC.
26. Jones, *Diary*, vol. 1, pp. 280, 284; Douglas O. Tice, " 'Bread or Blood': The

Richmond Bread Riot," *Civil War Times Illustrated* 12 (February 1974), pp. 12–18.
27. Jones, *Diary*, vol. 1, pp. 285; *Memoir*, vol. 2, pp. 374–75; Tice, "Bread Riot," pp. 18–19.
28. Jones, *Diary*, vol. 1, pp. 286–87.
29. Ibid., pp. 287–88; Seddon to JD, April 8, 1863, JD to G. W. C. Lee, April 8, 1863, Officers' File; *OR*, I, 23, pt. 2, pp. 757–61, 24, pt. 3, pp. 709, 713.
30. WPJ to Preston, April 22, 1863, WPJ to Rosa Johnston, February 5, 1863, Mason Barret Collection; Phelan to JD, April 25, 1862, chap. 9, Record Group 109; JD to Virginia Clay, May 2, 1863, Clay Papers; Jones, *Diary*, vol. 1, pp. 293; Holmes to JD, January 20, 1863, Telegrams Received and Sent, Adjutant and Inspector General, Record Group 109; Zebulon Vance to JD, February 2, 1863, Dearborn Collection; Reynolds to JD, February 26, 1863, von David Collection; R. W. Johnson et al. to JD, February 2, 1863, Davis Papers, Duke; Holmes to JD, February 12, 1863, Private Correspondence of T. H. Holmes, chap. 2, Volume 358, Record Group 109; *OR*, I, 22, pt. 2, pp. 798, 871.
31. *OR*, I, 25, pt. 2, pp. 700, 752, 756, 765, 768, pt. 1, p. 805; *Memoir*, vol. 2, pp. 382–83; Jones, *Diary*, I, pp. 308, 321.
32. Pemberton to JD, April 11, 1863, JD to "Col. B. G.," May 1, 1863, Davis Papers, Record Group 109; Pemberton to JD, April 30, 1863, G. A. Baker Catalog #34, 1939.
33. Augustus Garland to JD, January 30, 1863, University of Michigan; Peter B. Starke to JD, May 11, 1863, Davis Papers, Duke; *OR*, I, 23, pt. 2, pp. 825–26.
34. *OR*, I, 24, pt. 3, p. 890; A. M. Paxton to JD, May 21, 1863, John A. Orr to JD, May 22, 1863, Davis Papers, TU.
35. Pettus to JD, May 28, 1863, Microfilm 618, Record Group 109; JD to JED, May 7, 31, 1863, Lise Mitchell Papers.
36. Johnson to JD, June 15, 1863, University of Michigan; Walter Lord, ed., *The Fremantle Diary* (Boston, 1954), pp. 168–69.
37. Reagan, *Memoirs*, pp. 150–53; *OR*, I, 27, pt. 1, pp. 75–77, pt. 3, p. 931; Seddon to Vance, June 5, 1863, Governors' Papers, North Carolina Archives, Raleigh; Brown to JD, June 23, 1863, Governor's Letterbook, 1861–1865, Georgia Department of Archives and History.
38. Anna Farrar to JD, June 20, 1863, Davis Papers, Duke; Jefferson Bradford to JD, June 5, 1863, Davis Papers, MC.
39. JD endorsement, June 24, 1864, Davis Papers, Record Group 109.
40. JED to JD, June 22, 24, 25, 1863, Davis Papers, Record Group 109; Seddon to JD, June 16, 1863, Davis Papers, TU; WPJ to Preston, May 28, 1863, Mason Barret Collection; Jones, *Diary*, vol. 1, pp. 339, 367, 370; Frank E. Vandiver, ed., *The Civil War Diary of General Josiah Gorgas* (University, Ala., 1947), p. 47; James Sinclair to JD, July 4, 1863, Citizens' File.
41. Jones, *Diary*, vol. 1, pp. 370–71; Seddon to JD, July 7, 8, 1863, Davis Papers, TU; *Memoir*, vol. 2, p. 392.

Chapter 26   The Clouds Are Truly Dark over Us

1. *OR*, I, 51, pt. 2, pp. 752–53; *Memoir*, vol. 2, pp. 397–99.
2. Pemberton to JD, July 14–15, 16, 1863, Davis Papers, TU; Pemberton to JD,

July 19, 1863, Telegrams Received and Draft Telegrams Sent, Adjutant and Inspector General, G. W. Lee to JD, July 27, 1863, chap. 9, Record Group 109.

3. William Brandon to JD, August 8, 1863, University of Michigan; Harris to JD, August 12, 1863, Pemberton to JD, August 17, 1863, Davis Papers, TU.

4. *Providence Journal*, November 24, 1863; JD to Pemberton, March 11, 1864, John C. Pemberton Papers, Southern Historical Collection.

5. Vandiver, *Gorgas*, p. 50; WPJ to Rosa Johnston, July 15, 1863, WPJ to Preston, July 17, 1863, Mason Barret Collection; *OR*, I, 24, pt. 1, p. 196.

6. *OR*, I, 24, pt. 1, pp. 202–7.

7. Ibid., pp. 209ff.; John Withers to JD, July 25, 1863, Davis Papers, TU.

8. *OR*, I, 24, pt. 3, p. 1076; Rowland, vol. 5 pp. 587–88, 596; vol. 6 pp. 1–13.

9. WPJ to Rosa Johnston, August 5, 1863, Mason Barret Collection; Wigfall to Clay, July 13, 1863, Clay Papers, Duke; Mrs. Johnston to Mrs. Wigfall, August 2, 1863, Wigfall Papers.

10. Pemberton to JD, July 29, 1863, Dearborn Collection; JED to JD, August 15, 1863, Davis Papers, Transylvania; Robert Melvin to JD, July 22, 1863, John Duncan to JD, September 7, 1863, Davis Papers, Duke; L. Norris to JD, August 19, 1863, JED to JD, October 29, 1863, Davis Papers, TU.

11. Rose Greenhow to JD, July 19, 1863, Davis Papers, TU.

12. O. G. Edward to JD, July 20, 1863, J. H. M. Barton to JD, July 29, 1863, W. C. Bibb to Seddon, July 29, 1863, Leonidas Walthall to JD, August 11, 1863, chap. 9, Record Group 109; Benjamin F. Bolling to JD, July 24, 1863, Negroes in Military Service of the United States, Record Group 94, NA.

13. Rowland, vol. 5, p. 555; *OR*, I, 24, pt. 1, pp. 193, 200; George P. Kane to JD, July 17, November 24, 1863, Davis Papers, TU; H. C. Durham to JD, August 17, 1863, Record Group 153, NA; Jones, *Diary*, vol. 5, p. 24.

14. Simon Buckner to JD, July 8, 1863, Simon Buckner Collection, Huntington Library; Bragg to JD, July 13, 1863, Letters and Telegrams Sent by Braxton Bragg, Record Group 109; Polk to JD, August 9, 1863, Polk Papers, Duke.

15. *OR*, I, 30, pt. 4, pp. 529–30; Rowland, vol. 6, pp. 19, 20, vol. 5, p. 598; Clifford Dowdey and Louis Manarin, *The Wartime Papers of R. E. Lee* (Boston, 1961), p. 596.

16. G. Preston Williams to JD, September 2, 1863, chap. 9, Record Group 109; Jones, *Diary*, vol. 2, p. 51; JD to WPJ, September 3, 1863, Library, Washington and Lee University, Lexington, Virginia; Polk to Stephen Elliott, August 15, 1863, Polk Papers, Duke; Bragg to JD, October 1, 1863, Palmer Collection.

17. *OR*, I, 30, pt. 4, pp. 602–4; Rowland, vol. 6, p. 30; WPJ to Preston, October 3, 1863, Mason Barret Collection; Passport, September 4, 1863, Davis Papers, MC.

18. Bragg to JD, October 1, 1863, Palmer Collection; Bragg to JD, September 25, 1863, C. C. Jones Georgia Portfolio, vol. 2, Duke; JD to Bragg, October 3, 1863, Davis Papers, TU; Jones, *Diary*, vol. 2, pp. 65–66; Polk to JD, September 27, 1863, Dearborn Collection.

19. Jones, *Diary*, vol. 2, p. 66; *OR*, I, 52, pt. 2, p. 538.

20. *Washington Evening Star*, October 12, 1863; Rowland, vol. 7, p. 321.

21. Polk to JD, October 8, 1863, Davis Papers, Duke; Thomas L. Connelly, *Autumn of Glory* (Baton Rouge, 1971), pp. 242–43.

22. Rowland, vol. 6, pp. 57–58; JD to John C. Breckinridge, October [8], 1863, Cohasso, Inc., Catalog, October 1977; Woodward, *Chesnut*, p. 483.
23. JD to VD, October 9, 1863, "An Interesting Batch of Telegrams," *Confederate Veteran* 2 (April 1894), p. 111; Connelly, *Autumn*, p. 243.
24. James Longstreet, *From Manassas to Appomattox* (Philadelphia, 1896), pp. 465–66; D. H. Hill to JD, November 16, 1863, D. H. Hill Papers, North Carolina Department of Archives and History; Rowland, vol. 6, p. 81; *Memoir*, vol. 2, p. 363n.
25. Woolley to WPJ, November 28, 1863, Mason Barret Collection; Jackman Diary, October 10, 1863; Connelly, *Autumn*, p. 245.
26. "Last Surviving Lieutenant General," *Confederate Veteran* 17 (February 1909), p. 83; Longstreet, *Manassas to Appomattox*, pp. 466–68; Woodward, *Chesnut*, p. 482.
27. Rowland, vol. 6, pp. 61–62; vol. 7, p. 321; Davis, *Breckinridge*, p. 382; Connelly, *Autumn*, p. 245.
28. G. Moxley Sorrell, *Recollections of a Confederate Staff Officer* (New York, 1905), p. 201; *OR*, I, 30, pt. 2, p. 148; Rowland, vol. 6, p. 81; Hill to JD, November 16, 1863, Hill Papers; JD to Hill, December 24, 1886, Robert Batchelder Catalog #43, 1983, item 110.
29. *Providence Journal*, October 26, 1863; Jones, *Diary*, vol. 2, p. 76; Polk to JD, October 25, 1863, Davis Papers, TU; William D. Gale to Mrs. Gale, October 27, 1863, William D. Gale Papers, Southern Historical Collection.
30. *OR*, I, 30, pt. 2, p. 70; Beauregard to JD, October 2, 1863, Officers' File; Jones, *Diary*, vol. 1, p. 392; vol. 2, p. 89; Rowland, vol. 6, pp. 73–78; Beauregard to Augusta J. Evans, November 25, 1863, Beauregard to William Aiken, October 31, 1863, War Department Collection of Confederate Records, NA.
31. Wise to A. Y. P. Garnett, November 17, 1863, JD to Garnett, November 10, 1863, Garnett to JD, November 11, 1863, Garnett-Wise Family Papers, Southern Historical Collection; Josephine Habersham Diary, October 31, 1863, quoted in Hudson Strode, *Jefferson Davis, Confederate President* (New York, 1959), p. 489.
32. Jones, *Diary*, vol. 1, p. 379, II, pp. 88, 90, 91, 93; Lyman, "Sketch of Jeff Davis," 1863, Lyman Papers.
33. Jones, *Diary*, II, p. 93; Rowland, vol. 6, p. 73; Bragg to JD, October 22, 1863, Davis Collection, Emory.
34. Rowland, vol. 6, pp. 80-81, 82, 87–88.
35. Howell Cobb to JD, November 6, 1863, Davis Collection, Emory; John Thompson to JD, November 13, 1863, chap. 9, Record Group 109; G. A. Henry to JD, November 17, 1863, Civil War Collection, Tennessee State Library and Archives; WPJ to Preston, November 10, 1863, Mason Barret Collection.
36. G. W. C. Lee to JD, November 18, 1863, University of Michigan; Jones, *Diary*, vol. 2, p. 101.
37. Bragg to JD, November 21/22, 1863, Letters and Telegrams Sent by Braxton Bragg, chap. 2, Record Group 109; Bragg to JD, November 25, 1863, G. A. Parker Catalog #34, 1939; Rowland, vol. 6, p. 90; Jones, *Diary*, vol. 2, p. 104.
38. Rowland, vol. 6, pp. 91, 92; Jones, *Diary*, vol. 2, p. 106; Bragg to JD, November 30, December 1, 1863, Palmer Collection; Bragg to JD, December 8, 1863, Davis Papers, TU.

39. JD to Seddon, December 2, 1863, James Seddon Papers, Duke; Rowland, vol. 6, p. 93; *OR*, I, 31, pt. 3, p. 792.
40. Jones, *Diary*, vol. 2, p. 110; R. E. Lee to JD, December 7, 1863, Davis Papers, TU; Rowland, vol. 6, pp. 96, 128; "Proceedings of the First Confederate Congress," *Southern Historical Society Papers* 50 (1953), pp. 21–24, 28–29, 37.
41. "Proceedings of the First Confederate Congress," p. 49.
42. Rowland, vol. 8, p. 351; WPJ to JD, December 26, 1863, Davis Papers, TU; JD endorsement, December 23, 1863, CSA Papers, LC; Jones, *Diary*, vol. 2, p. 119.
43. Herschel V. Johnson to JD, August 6, 1863, Davis Papers, Duke; T. P. A. Bibb to JD, September 25, 1863, Jones to JD, September 30, 1863, Mrs. C. V. Baxley to JD, January 18, 1864, John J. Henley to JD, January 20, 1864, chap. 9, T. C. Mackin to JD, October 28, 1863, Officers' File, JD to Seddon, October 19, 1863, Microfilm 618, Robert Collier and H. C. Warsham to JD, October 31, 1863, Adjutant and Inspector General Letters Received, Record Group 109, NA; Pardons, July 13, August 4, 1863, CSA Papers, LC.
44. *Life*, p. 42; Jones, *Diary*, vol. 2, p. 120; Harrison, *Harrisons of Skimino*, p. 234.

Chapter 27 Not Mine, Oh, Lord, But Thine

1. Woodward, *Chesnut*, pp. 524–25, 526; Jones, *Diary*, vol. 2, pp. 122–23, 136.
2. Mallory Diary, October 6, 1865; Reagan to JD, October 2, 1863, CSA Papers, LC; Rowland, vol. 6, p. 56; John H. Reagan, Memorandum, August 7, 1863, University of Michigan; Reagan to JD, February 1, 1864, C. C. Jones, Autographs and Portraits, p. 144, Duke; Memminger to JD, July 7, 1864, Letters Received, Adjutant and Inspector General, Memminger to JD, January 2, 1864, chap. 9, Record Group 109; Jones, *Diary*, vol. 2, p. 124; J. G. Humphries to JD, September 16, 1863, Richey Collection; Memminger to JD, June 2, 1862, Dearborn Collection.
3. JD to Vance, July 26, 1863, Governors' Papers, North Carolina.
4. Browne to Seddon, February 9, 1864, Microfilm 618, Record Group 109; *OR*, IV, 1, pp. 1133ff, 1156ff, 2, pp. 2–3; Reagan, *Memoirs*, p. 161.
5. David Lewis to JD, September 9, 1863, Keith Read Manuscripts, University of Georgia; Reuben Davis to JD, December 11, 1863, Citizens' File.
6. Harrison to House of Representatives, January 2, 1864, Citizens' File; "Proceedings of the First Confederate Congress," p. 177.
7. "Proceedings of the First Confederate Congress," p. 55; *OR*, I, 24, pt. 1, pp. 189ff, 237.
8. *OR*, IV, 3, pp. 318–22; Woodward, *Chesnut*, p. 437; Younger, *Inside*, pp. 89–90, 126, 127, 130; "Proceedings of the First Confederate Congress," pp. 109–12, 307–9, 422.
9. "Proceedings of the First Confederate Congress," pp. 141–47.
10. Younger, *Inside*, pp. 126, 133; Richmond, *Enquirer*, January 25, 1864.
11. Jones, *Diary*, vol. 2, pp. 132, 134, 139; Younger, *Inside*, pp. 127–28.
12. Jones, *Diary*, vol. 2, pp. 125, 134, 136; Woodward, *Chesnut*, p. 532.
13. Mallory Diary, September 27, 1865; *Memoir*, vol. 2, p. 305; Woodward, *Chesnut*, p. 429.
14. John Handy to JD, January 26, 1864, S. Root to JD, March 19, 1864, R. D.

Ogden to JD, April 7, 1864, Davis Papers, Duke; Receipt, March 7, Preston to JD, January 9, 1864, Davis Papers, TU; *Memoir*, vol. 2, pp. 529–30, 913; Clay-Clopton, *Belle*, p. 173.

15. Alabama Legislature to JD, August 20, 1863, General and Staff Officers' Files, Ed O'Neal Compiled Service Record, Record Group 109; J. G. M. Ramsey to JD, January 6, 1864, Citizens' File; WPJ to Rosa Johnston, February 3, 1864, Mason Barret Collection.

16. Alex Fitzpatrick to JD, January 1, 1864, von David Collection; Harris to JD, January 16, 1864, Dearborn Collection; Seddon to J. E. Johnston, January 24, 1864, Johnston Papers, William and Mary.

17. Polk to JD, November 1863, Polk, *Polk*, vol. 2, p. 316; Rowland, vol. 6, p. 164; Jones, *Diary*, II, pp. 152, 157-58; JD to Seddon, February 23, 1864, chap. 9, Record Group 109.

18. Richmond, *Whig*, February 25, 1864; Richmond, *Examiner*, February 25, 26, 1864; Younger, *Inside*, p. 138; Jones, *Diary*, II, pp. 158–59.

19. Jones, *Diary*, II, pp. 164, 166; *Memoir*, II, p. 471; Reagan, *Memoirs*, p. 182.

20. R. Finley Hunt to JD, January 26, 1864, chap. 9, Record Group 109; Jones, *Diary*, vol. 2, p. 155; *OR*, IV, 3, p. 174; Rowland, vol. 6, pp. 204–6, 220; *Journal of the Confederate Congress* 6, p. 845; JD to J. P. Holcombe, February 19, 1864, JD, Warrant, April 25, 1864, CSA Papers, LC.

21. *Memoir*, vol. 2, pp. 445–48, 475–82; *OR*, II, 3, pp. 973–74; Jones, *Diary*, vol. 2, p. 175.

22. Rowland, vol. 6, pp. 236–37; Browne to JD, February 14, 1864, Dearborn Collection; Browne to JD, February 14, 1864, Richey Collection.

23. Rowland, vol. 5, p. 253; *OR*, I, 52, pt. 2, p. 555.

24. Woodward, *Chesnut*, pp. 519, 527, 565.

25. Browne to JD, February 14, 1864, Richey Collection; *OR*, I, 32, pt. 2, p. 799, 808–9, pt. 3, pp. 606–8, 614–15, 781; Longstreet, *Manassas to Appomattox*, pp. 544–46; Rowland, vol. 7, pp. 227–30.

26. "Correction of Errors," *Southern Historical Society Papers*, 11 (December 1883), p. 563; *OR*, I, 32, pt. 3, p. 738.

27. *OR*, I, 33, pp. 1282–83.

28. Hodge to WPJ, April 5, 1864, Mason Barret Collection; *OR*, I, 33, pp. 1326–28.

29. Jones, *Diary*, vol. 2, p. 191; William Pendleton to JD, April 23, 1864, William Pendleton Papers, Duke.

30. "Religious Life of Jefferson Davis," p. 376; *Memoir*, vol. 2, pp. 496–97.

31. Rowland, vol. 2, pp. 238–39; *Memoir*, vol. 2, pp. 496–97; Bryan Reminiscences; Woodward, *Chesnut*, pp. 601–2.

32. Certificate, May 3, 1864, Davis Papers, MC; Rowland, vol. 6, pp. 238–39, 267; Woodward, *Chesnut*, p. 602; Harrison to WPJ, May 24, 1867, Mason Barret Collection; Jones, *Diary*, vol. 2, p. 285.

Chapter 28   I Love My Friends and I Forgive My Enemies

1. Rowland, vol. 6, pp. 239–44.

2. Ibid., pp. 180, 181–82, 200, 202–3, 238, 243, 246, 247, 249, 265.

3. Ibid., 258.

4. *Memoir*, vol. 2, p. 509; Rowland, vol. 6, pp. 249, 250.

5. Rowland, vol. 6, p. 250; *Memoir*, vol. 2, pp. 498, 500; Jones, *Diary*, vol. 2, pp. 207, 209.
6. *Memoir*, vol. 2, p. 911; Rowland, vol. 6, pp. 251, 252.
7. *Memoir*, vol. 2, pp. 511, 516–19; Jordan, "Jefferson Davis," p. 618.
8. Jones, *Diary*, vol. 2, p. 212; *Memoir*, vol. 2, pp. 514–20; *Dallas Morning News*, April 30, 1897.
9. Rowland, vol. 6, pp. 258–59; Harrison to WPJ, May 28, 1864, Mason Barret Collection.
10. Mallory Diary, December 8, 1865; *Memoir*, vol. 2, p. 493; Rowland, vol. 6, p. 253.
11. Rowland, vol. 6, p. 269; *Memoir*, vol. 2, pp. 912–14.
12. Harrison to WPJ, May 28, 1864, Mason Barret Collection; JD to "My Dear Madam," May 25, 1864, Sotheby, Parke Bernet Catalog, June 20, 1979, pt. 3.
13. Rowland, vol. 6, pp. 255, 256–58, 284.
14. Ibid., pp. 283, 284; Mallory Diary, December 8, 1865.
15. Rowland, vol. 6, pp. 286, 288, 291; *Rise and Fall*, vol. 2, pp. 557–61.
16. *Rise and Fall*, vol. 2, pp. 560–61.
17. *OR*, I, 38, pt. 5, pp. 878, 881, 882.
18. Rowland, vol. 6, pp. 291–92, 293; *OR*, I, 39, pt. 2, pp. 712–14.
19. Rowland, vol. 6, p. 292; *OR*, I, 52, pt. 2, p. 692; *Memoir*, vol. 2, p. 494.
20. Rowland, vol. 8, pp. 352–53; Mallory Diary, December 8, 1865; Younger, *Inside*, pp. 165–66.
21. Rowland, vol. 8, p. 253; vol. 6, p. 295; *Rise and Fall*, vol. 2, p. 561.
22. Rowland, vol. 6, pp. 295–96.
23. J. E. Johnston to JD, July 18, 1864, G. A. Baker Catalog #34, 1935; *Memoir*, vol. 2, p. 919; *OR*, I, 38, pt. 5, pp. 987–88.
24. Jones, *Diary*, vol. 2, p. 289; Younger, *Inside*, p. 175; Bragg to JD, August 16, 1864, Braxton Bragg Papers, Duke; Rowland, vol. 6, pp. 194–96, 280–81, 307, 402ff; James A. Clanton to JD, May 31, 1864, chap. 9, Record Group 109; Guy Bryan to JD, July 20, 1864, Davis Papers, TU.
25. Rowland, vol. 6, pp. 340, 341, 344, 345; Hardee to JD, September 27, 1864, Dearborn Collection; *Rise and Fall*, vol. 2, pp. 565–67; JD to Hugh Davis, January 8, 1865, Mary Stamps Papers, Southern Historical Collection.
26. *Rise and Fall*, vol. 2, p. 566.
27. Rowland, vol. 6, pp. 344–45.
28. *OR*, I, 39, pt. 2, p. 846; Rowland, vol. 6, pp. 340, 344–45, 348–49, 368; *Rise and Fall*, vol. 2, pp. 566–68.
29. Rowland, vol. 6, pp. 341ff, 345ff, 347ff, 348, 356ff.
30. Jones, *Diary*, vol. 2, p. 300; *Memoir*, vol. 2, pp. 573–74; Rowland, vol. 5, pp. 276–77, 300, 301.
31. Jones, *Diary*, vol, 2, p. 275; Bryan Reminiscences; *Memoir*, vol. 2, p. 814.
32. Rowland, vol. 2 pp. 223, 278; Hugh Davis, William Stamps, et al, to JD, June 26, 1864, Davis Papers, TU; Hodge to JD, July 9, 1864, chap. 9, Record Group 109; Nellie Gordon to JD, September 1, 1864, Davis Papers, MC; Seddon to JD, September 23, 1864, private collection.
33. Jordan, "Jefferson Davis," p. 620; Rowland, vol. 6, pp. 208–9, 324; S. Jones to JD, August 15, 26, 1864, Davis Papers, TU; *Life*, p. 218; Watts, *Address*, pp. 15–16.
34. Harrison to WPJ, September 14, 1864, Mason Barret Collection; Rowland, vol. 6, p. 310.

35. Rowland, vol. 6, pp. 275–76; Younger, *Inside*, pp. 162, 167.
36. Bradley Johnson to Cooper, July 23, 1864, JD endorsement, July 26, 1864, Officers' File; *New York Citizen*, July 20, 1867.
37. *PJD*, vol. 1, p. 394; JD to Northrop, January 4, 1864, William J. Rucker Collection, University of Virginia; *Memoir*, vol. 2, p. 919; Northrop to JD, August 6, 1864, Dearborn Collection.
38. JD to the Senate, November 26, 1864, Dearborn Collection; Rowland, vol. 6, p. 194; Landon Haynes to JD, November 30, 1864, Officers' File.
39. Younger, *Inside*, pp. 153, 154–55, 156, 161, 171–72; Jones, *Diary*, vol. 2, p. 262; Rowland, vol. 6, p. 340.
40. Rowland, vol. 6, pp. 409, 439ff; Harrison to WPJ, July 21, 1864, Mason Barret Collection.
41. Younger, *Inside*, pp. 172, 175, 177; Rowland, vol. 6, p. 361.
42. Rowland, vol. 6, pp. 267, 285, 287, 291; *New York Citizen*, July 27, 1867; *Memoir*, vol. 2, pp. 573–74; *OR*, II, 7, pp. 541ff.
43. Thompson to JD, September 12, 1864, Dearborn Collection; Rowland, vol. 1, p. 401; JD to Thompson, October 15, 1864, Joseph Holt Papers, LC; Kensey J. Stewart to JD, November 30, 1864, Confederate War Papers, Volume 24, NA; Thomas N. Conrad, *A Confederate Spy* (New York, 1892), p. 69. Any discussion of JD's involvement in the Lincoln abduction plans must be speculative and inconclusive, though given his occasional association with Conrad and his funding of the spy's efforts, it is hard to conclude that Davis was entirely in the dark on the plan.
44. JD to Hugh Davis, January 8, 1865, Stamps Papers; Clay to JD, July 25, 1864, Clay Papers, Duke; *Rise and Fall*, vol. 2, pp. 569–70; Rowland, vol. 6, pp. 398–99, 413; Jones, *Diary*, vol. 2, pp. 347, 349; JD, Memorandum, November 19, 1864, Davis Papers, TU.
45. Rowland, vol. 6, pp. 323, 327, 410–11, 416, 423, 425; Beauregard to JD, December 20, 1864, Beauregard Papers, LC.
46. Jones, *Diary*, vol. 2, pp. 356–57; Clay Clopton, *Belle*, p. 239; Lewis to JD, December 30, 1864, Read Manuscript Collection.
47. Jones, *Diary*, vol. 2, pp. 355, 359, 362, 364.
48. Ibid., p. 364; *New York World*, December 13, 1896.

Chapter 29   Faction Has Done Much

1. Jones, *Diary*, vol. 2, p. 372; Browne to JD, December 29, 1864, Davis Papers, TU; JD to Amanda Bradford, January 8, 1865, Percival Beacroft, Jr., Collection of Davis Papers, Rosemont, Woodville, Mississippi.
2. JD to Hugh Davis, January 8, 1865, Stamps Papers; *Life*, p. 39.
3. Rowland, vol. 5, pp. 436–37; Howell Cobb to JD, January 6, 1865, Cobb Papers, Duke.
4. Jones, *Diary*, vol. 2, pp. 372–90; *Life*, pp. 207–8; Toombs to G. W. Smith, March 25, 1865, David Battan Catalog #19, 1977, p. 3.
5. JD to Hugh Davis, January 8, 1865, Stamps Papers; *OR*, I, 46, pt. 2, p. 1118.
6. Wade Hampton to Wigfall, January 20, 1865, Wigfall Papers; Woodward, *Chesnut*, p. 698; "Proceedings of the Second Confederate Congress," *Southern Historical Society Papers* 52 (1959), pp. 168–73, 178–83, 190–91, 199–204,

218–22, 246–51, 261–63; *Journal of the Confederate Congress* 4, pp. 457–58; Jones, *Diary*, vol. 2, p. 392.

7. "Proceedings of the Second Confederate Congress," pp. 497–99.

8. JED to JD, March 19, 1865, Davis Papers, Transylvania; Jones, *Diary*, vol. 2, pp. 379, 393; Rowland, vol. 6, pp. 524–25.

9. *Life*, pp. 211–13.

10. Jones, *Diary*, vol. 2, p. 389; Seddon to JD, January 18, 1865, University of Michigan; Campbell to JD, January 20, 1865, Dearborn Collection; M. J. Leovy to WPJ, January 24, 1865, Mason Barret Collection.

11. Jones, *Diary*, vol. 2, pp. 393, 394, 395, 396; Rowland, vol. 2, pp. 458–59; *Richmond Enquirer*, February 15, 1865.

12. Jones, *Diary*, vol. 2, pp. 390, 394–95, 403, 423; *New York Citizen*, August 24, 1867; Younger, *Inside*, p. 200; Rowland, vol. 7, p. 356.

13. William P. Chilton to JD, February 2, 1865, Citizens' File; Browne to WPJ, January 1, 1865, Mason Barret Collection; Memminger to JD, August 23, 1864, Cooper to JD, February 5, 1865, Dearborn Collection; *OR*, I, 47, pt. 2, pp. 1304–11.

14. Nelson Lankford, ed., *An Irishman in Dixie* (Columbia, S.C., 1988), p. 43; Howell Cobb to JD, January 6, 1865, Cobb Papers, Duke; Clay-Clopton, *Belle*, pp. 236–37; JED to JD, March 19, 1865, Davis Papers, Transylvania.

15. Dowdey and Manarin, *Wartime Papers*, pp. 905, 906; *OR*, I, 47, pt. 2, p. 1303; Rowland, vol. 6, p. 488; Charles S. Venable to W. S. Taylor, March 29, 1878, Virginia State Library; John B. Gordon, *Reminiscences of the Civil War* (New York, 1903), pp. 131–34.

16. Rowland, vol. 6, pp. 432–33; *Rise and Fall*, vol. 2, pp. 612–16.

17. Francis P. Blair to JD, January 22, 1865, Davis Papers, TU; *Rise and Fall*, vol. 2, pp. 616ff; Mallory Diary, December 8, 1865.

18. William J. Bromwell, memorandum, January 28, 1865, Causten-Pickett Papers, LC; *Rise and Fall*, vol. 2, pp. 617ff.

19. Rowland, vol. 6, pp. 466–78; Mallory Diary, December 8, 1865; JD to F. W. Pumphrey, February 14, 1881, Robert Lee Traylor Papers, Virginia Historical Society.

20. Rowland, vol. 6, p. 489; *OR*, I, 46, pt. 2, pp. 1264–65; Longstreet, *Manassas to Appomattox*, p. 584; Gordon, *Reminiscences*, p. 393; *Richmond Examiner*, February 7, 1865; Younger, *Inside*, p. 202.

21. *Life*, pp. 40–41; Pollard, *Lost Cause*, pp. 658–59; Jones, *Diary*, vol. 2, pp. 410–11.

22. Richmond, *Examiner*, February 7, 1865; Jones, *Diary*, vol. 2, pp. 411, 414; Pollard, *Lost Cause*, p. 685; Avary, *Stephens*, pp. 183, 241.

23. Avary, *Stephens*, p. 183; Jones, *Diary*, vol. 2, pp. 398, 436; Thomas Conrad to JD, January 1865, Davis Papers, Duke; Franklin Stringfellow to JD, n.d. [1880], Franklin Stringfellow Papers, University of Virginia.

24. Rowland, vol. 6, pp. 445, 447, 448, 451, 456–57, 464–65, 481, 482–84, 509, 510–11.

25. Johnston, *Narrative*, p. 372; Rowland, vol. 6, p. 512.

26. Rowland, vol. 6, p. 521.

27. H. Kendall to JD, September 16, 1864, C. B. Leitner to JD, December 31, 1864, Edward Pollard to JD, January 13, 1865, chap. 9, Record Group 109; Alex W. Cooper to JD, December 25, 1864, Davis Papers, Duke.

28. Rowland, vol. 6, pp. 394–96.
29. Ibid., pp. 518–19.
30. Jones, *Diary*, vol. 2, p. 415; Rowland, vol. 6, pp. 482, 513, 526; *OR*, IV, 3, p. 1161; *Rise and Fall*, vol. 1, pp. 518–19.
31. Rowland, vol. 6, p. 527; *OR*, I, 46, pt. 2, p. 1257.
32. Lankford, *Irishman in Dixie*, pp. 42, 47–48; Jones, *Diary*, vol. 2, p. 426.
33. Edmund Kirke, *Down in Tennessee and Back by Way of Richmond* (New York, 1864), p. 269f.
34. Rowland, p. 577; *Louisville Courier-Journal*, June 8, 1875.
35. Lankford, *Irishman in Dixie*, pp. 48–49, 60; *Memoir*, vol. 2, pp. 574–77; JD to Gorgas, March 29, 1865, Josiah Gorgas Collection, Alabama Department of Archives and History; Harrison, *Harrisons of Skimino*, pp. 225–27; Mrs. Armistead Burt to VD, April 10, 1865, Davis Papers, MC; JD to J. W. Jones, June 24, 1883, Davis Papers, Duke.
36. *Life*, pp. 232–33.
37. Rowland, vol. 6, p. 512.
38. *Life*, pp. 234–36; Lankford, *Irishman in Dixie*, p. 82; Dowdey and Manarin, *Wartime Papers*, pp. 924–25.

Chapter 30 I *Cannot* Feel Like a Beaten Man!

1. Mrs. Roger A. Pryor, *Reminiscences of Peace and War* (New York, 1904), p. 354; Reagan, *Memoirs*, pp. 196–97; Reagan, account of the evacuation of Richmond, undated clipping in Virginia Clay Scrapbook, Clay Papers, Duke; Dowdey and Manarin, *Wartime Papers*, p. 925.
2. Mallory Diary, April 2, 1865; Reagan, *Memoirs*, pp. 197–98.
3. Rowland, vol. 7, pp. 548–49; Davis, *Breckinridge*, p. 503.
4. Herman P. Baum, "Life of James A. Duncan," B. D. thesis, Emory University Library, pp. 15–16; Jones, *Diary*, vol. 2, p. 466; Reagan account, Clay Scrapbook.
5. *Life*, pp. 42–43; Rowland, vol. 6, pp. 532–33, 561; Clay-Clopton, *Belle*, pp. 244–45; JD to Mary O'Melia, April 2, 1865, *Southland*, II (February 1898), pp. 64–65; *Memoir*, vol. 2, p. 574.
6. *Life*, pp. 42–43.
7. William H. Parker, *Recollections of a Naval Officer* (New York, 1883), pp. 350–52; Mallory Diary, April 2, 1865; "Resources of the Confederacy in 1865," *Southern Historical Society Papers* 3 (March 1877), pp. 110–11.
8. Anna Trenholm Diary, April 2, 1865, George A. Trenholm Papers, South Caroliniana Library; Stephen R. Mallory, "Last Days of the Confederate Government," *McClure's Magazine* 16 (December 1900), pp. 104–05; Reagan, *Memoirs*, p. 198.
9. H. W. Bruce, "Some Reminiscences of the Second of April, 1865," *Southern Historical Society Papers* 9 (May 1881), p. 209; John S. Wise, *End of an Era* (Boston, 1900), p. 415.
10. Trenholm Diary, April 3, 1865; Edward Pollock, *Illustrated Sketch Book of Danville, Virginia* (Danville, 1885), pp. 51–52; Rowland, vol. 6, p. 538.
11. A. C. Rives to JD, April 10, 1865, Davis Papers, Duke; *Rise and Fall*, vol. 2,

p. 676; John H. Brubaker, III, *The Last Capital* (Danville, 1979), pp. 27–28; Rowland, vol. 6, pp. 529–31.

12. *Rise and Fall*, vol. 2, p. 677.
13. Rowland, vol. 6, pp. 532–42.
14. Ibid., pp. 527–28, 533.
15. WPJ to Rosa Johnston, April 8, 1865, Mason Barret Collection; Humphrey Marshall to JD, January 6, 1884, Davis Papers, MC; Brubaker, *Last Capital*, p. 34; Pollock, *Sketch Book*, p. 56.
16. Brubaker, *Last Capital*, pp. 39, 43–44; *Montgomery Daily Advertiser*, October 10, 1865.
17. *OR*, I, 46, pt. 3, p. 1339; Wise, *End of an Era*, pp. 444–48.
18. Rowland, vol. 6, pp. 541–42; Harrison, *Harrisons of Skimino*, p. 228; Brubaker, *Last Capital*, p. 52.
19. Rowland, vol. 6, pp. 542–43; Harrison, *Harrisons of Skimino*, p. 228; Harrison to VD, April 12, 1865, Edwin M. Stanton Papers, LC.
20. Pollock, *Sketch Book*, pp. 58–59; Harrison to VD, April 12, 1865, Stanton Papers; Mallory, "Last Days," p. 107.
21. Harrison to VD, April 12, 1865, Stanton Papers; Rowland, vol. 6, pp. 542–43; Pollock, *Sketch Book*, pp. 63–64; Vandiver, *Gorgas*, p. 180; Mallory, "Last Days," p. 105.
22. WPJ to VD, April 12, 1865, Stanton Papers; Rowland, vol. 6, p. 543; Brubaker, *Last Capital*, pp. 57–58; *Montgomery Daily Advertiser*, October 10, 1865.
23. Harrison, *Harrisons of Skimino*, pp. 229–31; Harrison to VD, April 12, 1865, Stanton Papers.
24. Harrison to VD, April 12, 1865, Stanton Papers; Brubaker, *Last Capital*, p. 61.
25. Harrison, *Harrisons of Skimino*, pp. 232–33; Harrison to VD, April 12, 1865, Stanton Papers; WPJ to Rosa Johnston, April 22, 1865, Mason Barret Collection.
26. Roman, *Beauregard*, vol. 2, pp. 389–92.
27. JD to Vance, April 11, 1865, Ellis E. Jensen Autograph Collection, State Historical Society of Wisconsin, Madison.
28. Rowland, vol. 6, pp. 543–44; Johnston, *Narrative*, pp. 396–97.
29. WPJ to Rosa Johnston, April 12, 1865, Mason Barret Collection; *Rise and Fall*, vol. 2, pp. 679–80; Mallory, "Last Days," p. 240.
30. Johnston, *Narrative*, pp. 398–400; Reagan, *Memoirs*, pp. 199–200; Mallory Diary, n.d.; Mallory, "Last Days," pp. 240–42; *Rise and Fall*, vol. 2, pp. 680–82.
31. Robert E. Lee, Jr., *Recollections and Letters of General Robert E. Lee* (New York, 1904), pp. 156–57; Rowland, vol. 6, pp. 545–56.
32. *Greensboro Patriot*, March 23, 1866.
33. Trenholm Diary, April 15, 1865; Harrison, *Harrisons of Skimino*, pp. 239–40.
34. *Rise and Fall*, vol. 2, p. 683; Reagan, *Memoirs*, p. 201.
35. Rowland, vol. 6, pp. 547–48; vol. 9, pp. 157–58; John Taylor Wood Diary, April 18, 1865, Southern Historical Collection; Harrison, *Harrisons of Skimino*, pp. 241–42; *Memoir*, vol. 2, p. 627; "Last Address of President Davis, CSA," *Confederate Veteran* 22 (July 1914), p. 304; *Lynchburg Daily Virginian*, August 31, 1866.

36. Rowland, vol. 9, p. 158; vol. 6, p. 551; Basil W. Duke, *Reminiscences of General Basil W. Duke* (Garden City, N.Y., 1911), p. 383; Mallory, "Last Days," p. 244; *Lynchburg Daily Virginian*, August 31, 1866.

37. WPJ to Rosa Johnston, April 22, 1865, Mason Barret Collection; Harrison, *Harrisons of Skimino*, p. 243; David McIntosh to JD, April 19, 1865, Pegram-Johnson-McIntosh Family Papers, Virginia Historical Society; Rowland, vol. 6, pp. 553, 555–57.

38. *Lynchburg Daily Virginian*, August 31, 1866; Harrison, *Harrisons of Skimino*, p. 243; Wood Diary, April 19–23, 1865.

39. *OR*, I, 47, pt. 3, p. 809; Davis, *Breckinridge*, p. 515.

40. Mallory, "Last Days," p. 245; Rowland, vol. 6, pp. 577, 585.

41. WPJ to A. Y. P. Garnett, September 19, 1865, Mason Barret Collection; JD to Jubal Early, April 30, 1888, Early Family Papers, Virginia Historical Society; VD to JD, April 7, 1865, Davis Papers, Duke; Strode, *Letters*, pp. 152–55; Harrison, *Harrisons of Skimino*, pp. 243–44.

42. Rowland, vol. 6, pp. 559–62; Breckinridge to JD, April 24, 1865, Microfilm 474, Record Group 109.

43. Rowland, vol. 6, pp. 562, 568, 585; Clement Dowd, *Life of Zebulon B. Vance* (Charlotte, N.C., 1897), pp. 485–87.

44. Rowland, vol. 6, pp. 552–54, 563; *OR*, I, 47, pt. 3, p. 835; *Rise and Fall*, vol. 2, p. 689.

45. Michael Ballard, *A Long Shadow* (Jackson, Miss., 1988), p. 109; Mallory, "Last Days," p. 245; WPJ to Rosa Johnston, April 26, 1865, Mason Barret Collection; Wood Diary, April 24, 1865.

46. Trenholm Diary, April 26, 1865; Reagan, *Memoirs*, pp. 209–10; Rowland, vol. 6, pp. 564–65; *Life*, p. 261; *Baltimore Sun*, December 1889 clipping, "Mr. Reagan's Recollections," Dallas Historical Society, Dallas, Texas; *Dallas Morning News*, April 30, 1897.

47. *Memoir*, vol. 2, p. 587; Wood Diary, April 28–30, 1865; Joseph T. Durkin, ed., *John Dooley, Confederate Soldier* (Washington, 1945), p. 198; Mallory, "Last Days," p. 246.

48. Mallory, "Last Days," p. 246; Wood Diary, May 1, 1865; Micajah H. Clark, "Retreat of the Confederate Cabinet," *Southern Historical Society Papers* 26 (1898), p. 100; WPJ to Rosa Johnston, April 30, 1865, Mason Barret Collection.

49. Clark, "Retreat," pp. 100–101; Given Campbell, Memorandum of a Journal Kept Daily During the Last March of Jefferson Davis, April 28–May 2, 1865, LC.

50. Basil W. Duke, "Last Days of the Confederacy," *Battles and Leaders*, vol. 4, p. 764.

51. Duke, "Last Days," p. 764.

52. Ibid., p. 765; Rowland, vol. 8, pp. 161–62, 188–89; vol. 7, pp. 586–89; Samuel W. Ferguson, "Escort to President Davis," *Confederate Veteran* 16 (June 1908), p. 263; Duke, *Reminiscences*, p. 385.

53. Duke, "Last Days," pp. 764–65; JD to WPJ, April 5, 1878, Breckinridge Family Papers, LC.

54. Rowland, vol. 8, p. 171.

55. WPJ to Rosa Johnston, May 3, 1865, Mason Barret Collection; John W. Headley, *Confederate Operations in Canada and New York* (New York, 1906),

pp. 433–34; Rowland, vol. 8, p. 251; Reagan, *Memoirs*, p. 212; Duke, "Last Days," p. 766.

56. *Rise and Fall*, vol. 2, p. 694; Reagan, *Memoirs*, p. 211; Jackman Diary, May 3, 1865.

57. Rowland, vol. 6, pp. 586–89.

58. Micajah H. Clark, "The Last Days of the Confederate Treasury," *Southern Historical Society Papers* 9 (December 1881), p. 544; *OR*, I, 49, pt. 2, p. 1277.

59. *Rise and Fall*, vol. 2, p. 697.

60. Ballard, *Long Shadow*, p. 132; Campbell Journal, May 4, 1865; Headley, *Operations*, p. 437.

61. A. J. Hanna, *Flight Into Oblivion* (Richmond, 1938), p. 90; Reagan, *Memoirs*, p. 217; Harrison, *Harrisons of Skimino*, pp. 252–54.

62. Harrison, *Harrisons of Skimino*, pp. 253–54.

63. Campbell Journal, May 7, 1865; Rowland, vol. 6, pp. 566, 567, 589–90.

64. Harrison, *Harrisons of Skimino*, pp. 254–55; Rowland, vol. 8, p. 54.

65. Harrison, *Harrisons of Skimino*, pp. 257–60; WPJ to Rosa Johnston, July 7, 1865, Mason Barret Collection; Wood Diary, May 10, 1865; Chester Bradley, "Was Jefferson Davis Disguised as A Woman When Captured," *Journal of Mississippi History*, 36 (August, 1974), p. 243f; JD to W. M. Green, May 8, 1872, in *St. Louis Post-Dispatch*, January 22, 1937; VD to JD, n.d., recollection of capture, Davis Papers, TU.

66. *Memoir*, vol. 2, p. 615; WPJ to Garnett, September 19, 1865, Mason Barret Collection; David Pierson to William H. Pierson, May 9, 1865, Kuntz Collection.

67. *OR*, I, 49, pt. 1, pp. 536–37.

Chapter 31   There Is the Gridiron We Have Been Fried On

1. WPJ to W. T. Walthall, July 14, 1877, *Southern Historical Society Papers*, 5 (March 1878), p. 120.

2. Notes on capture of Jefferson Davis, n.d., Harrison Papers; *Memoir*, vol. 2, p. 642; VD to JD, notes of capture, Davis Papers, TU.

3. *Rise and Fall*, vol. 2, p. 703; *Memoir*, vol. 2, p. 643; James P. Jones, ed., "Your Left Arm: James H. Wilson's Letters to Adam Badeau," *Civil War History*, 12 (September 1966), pp. 243–44.

4. W. T. Walthall, "The True Story of the Capture of Jefferson Davis," *Southern Historical Society Papers* 5 (March 1878), pp. 116–17.

5. *OR*, I, 49, pt. 1, p. 537; Clay-Clopton, *Belle*, pp. 256–57.

6. Clay-Clopton, *Belle*, pp. 256, 258.

7. Ibid., pp. 259–62; *Memoir*, vol. 2, pp. 648–52, 704n; Alexander H. Stephens Diary, May 15–21, 1865, quoted in "Alexander H. Stephens' Prison Life," *Confederate Veteran* 1 (June 1893), pp. 169–71; *Life*, p. 313; Virginia Clay Diary, May 16–22, 1865, Clay Papers, Duke; "Mysteriously Restrained," *Confederate Veteran* 1 (May 1893), p. 145.

8. *Memoir*, vol. 2, pp. 653–59; *OR*, II, 8, pp. 571, 577.

9. Virginia Clay Diary, May 24, June 2, 1865, Clay Papers; Wood Diary, May 10, 1865; Bradley, "Disguised," pp. 248ff; *OR*, I, 49, pt. 1, pp. 536–37; Kathleen Collins and Ann Wilsher, "Petticoat Politics: The Capture of Jefferson Davis," *History of Photography* 8 (Fall 1984), pp. 237–43.

10. *OR*, II, 8, pp. 564–65, 710–12, 740; Riley, "Health, Part II," p. 281; *Memoir*, vol. 2, pp. 699–702; WPJ to Rosa Johnston, July 5, 1865, Mason Barret Collection.

11. *OR*, II, 8, pp. 719–20, 736, 740, 746, 761; Anna Craven to JD, April 19, 1879, Davis Papers, MC.

12. Strode, *Letters*, pp. 168, 178.

13. *OR*, II, 8, pp. 835, 900, 904–5, 910.

14. Ibid., p. 904; *Memoir*, vol. 2, p. 759; Strode, *Letters*, pp. 189–90, 208.

15. *OR*, II, 8, pp. 924–25; The Prison Life of Jefferson Davis," *Southern Historical Society Papers* 32 (1904), p. 345.

16. Strode, *Letters*, pp. 207–8; JD, notes, April 1866, Davis Papers, MC; *Memoir*, vol. 2, pp. 816–17; Fleming, "The Negro Problem," pp. 418–23; William Hanchett, "Reconstruction and the Rehabilitation of Jefferson Davis: Charles G. Halpine's *Prison Life," Journal of American History* 56 (September 1969), p. 287.

17. Jordan, "Jefferson Davis," p. 619; VD to WPJ, October 3, 1865, Mason Barret Collection; *Memoir*, vol. 2, p. 737; Strode, *Letters*, p. 189.

18. Jonathan T. Dorris, *Pardon and Amnesty Under Lincoln and Johnson* (Chapel Hill, N.C., 1953), p. 283; *OR*, II, 8, pp. 841, 974; *Memoir*, vol. 2, pp. 772–73, 774–76; JD, Parole, November 3, 1866, Davis Papers, MC.

19. Davis, *Breckinridge*, pp. 560–61; *Memoir*, vol. 2, p. 879; Watson Van Benthuysen to Harrison, October 31, 1867, Harrison to Van Benthuysen, August 20, 1867, Harrison Papers.

20. Breckinridge to WPJ, September 17, October 8, 1865, Mason Barret Collection; Strode, *Letters*, p. 171; *OR*, II, 8, p. 573; JD to Clay, January 2, 1866, private collection.

21. Rowland, vol. 7, pp. 150–52.

22. Ibid., pp. 164–65.

23. Strode, *Letters*, p. 250.

24. Hanchett, "Reconstruction," pp. 281–89.

25. *New York Tribune*, November 21, 1866.

26. Strode, *Letters*, pp. 266, 267; *Leavenworth* (Kans.) *Daily Times*, May 23, 1867.

27. Rowland, vol. 6, pp. 97–98, 99–101; Strode, *Letters*, p. 269.

28. *Life*, p. 39.

29. Rowland, vol. 7, pp. 169ff.

30. Harrison to WPJ, May 24, 1867, Mason Barret Collection; *Memoir*, vol. 2, p. 797; *Life*, pp. 240–41.

31. Rowland, vol. 7, p. 103; Harrison to WPJ, May 24, 1867, Mason Barret Collection.

32. A. J. Clark, "When Jefferson Davis Visited Niagara," *Ontario Historical Society Papers and Records* 19 (1922), pp. 87–89; *Memoir*, vol. 2, p. 797; Rowland, vol. 7, p. 111.

33. *Leavenworth* (Kans.) *Daily Times*, July 17, 1867; JD to Charles J. Helm, September 15, October 30, 1867, JD to Sarah Helm, October 10, 1867, Mrs. Wert E. Chapman, Louisville, Kentucky.

34. JD to Van Benthuysen, July 5, 1867, JD to Harrison, September 4, 1867, Harrison Papers; Rowland, vol. 7, pp. 114, 115–16; JD to Charles Helm, September 15, 1867, Chapman.

35. *Leavenworth Daily Times*, May 22, 1867; JD to JED, July 22, 1867, Mitchell Papers; *Memoir*, vol. 2, p. 798.

Chapter 32   I Seem to Remember More Every Day

1. Rowland, vol. 7, pp. 176–77.
2. Sarah Brewer, "Recollections of Jefferson Davis," *Confederate Veteran* 1 (July 1893), p. 195; *Memoir*, vol. 2, pp. 803–4; *Woodville Republican*, January 18, 1865; Hermann, *Pursuit of a Dream*, pp. 103–4.
3. JD to Lise Mitchell, November 30, 1867, Mitchell Papers.
4. JD to James Howry, February 8, 1868, Howry Family Papers, LC; Charles O'Conor to JD, February 14, March 11, April 27, May 27, 1868, Davis Papers, MC.
5. JD to JED, July 22, 1867, Mitchell Papers; JD agreement with F. W. Terrill, July 11, 1867, John C. Blackwell to JD, June 9, 1868, JD to Blackwell, June 15, 1868, Davis Papers, MC; JD to Sarah Helm, July 31, 1874, Chapman.
6. *Memoir*, vol. 2, p. 805; Rowland, vol. 7, p. 243.
7. *Memoir*, vol. 2, pp. 807–10; *New York Herald*, August 11, 1895.
8. *Memoir*, vol. 2, p. 810; O'Conor to JD, October 16, November 3, 1868, January 6, 1869, Davis Papers, MC.
9. Harris to JD, May 27, July 20, 1869, M. J. Wicks to JD, July 17, 1869, Davis Papers, Alabama Department of Archives and History; JD to Harris, June 22, 1869, Diane J. Rendell Catalog, n.d.
10. JD to Jeremy Gilmer, November 24, 1869, Davis Papers, MC; JD to Bragg, December 1, 1869, Braxton Bragg Papers, Rosenberg Library, Galveston, Texas.
11. JD to Sarah Helm, May 17, 1870, Chapman.
12. JD to Lise Mitchell, December 30, 1869, August 9, 20, October 24, 1870, Mitchell Papers; Rowland, vol. 7, p. 284.
13. JD to Sarah Helm, October 29, December 14, 1872, Chapman; *Memoir*, vol. 2, pp. 814–15.
14. JD to Sarah Helm, April 7, October 20, 1873, Chapman; Strode, *Letters*, p. 369.
15. Strode, *Letters*, p. 383; JD to Sarah Helm, May 9, July 31, 1874, Chapman.
16. Hermann, *Pursuit of a Dream*, pp. 201–4, 206–7, 211.
17. Rowland, vol. 7, pp. 364ff.
18. *Memoir*, vol. 2, pp. 816–18, 823, 825; *The Vedette* 8 (May 1886), p. 10; Rowland, vol. 7, p. 413.
19. Strode, *Letters*, p. 439.
20. Mann to JD, March 6, September 18, 1869, Davis Papers, Alabama; Rowland, vol. 7, pp. 265, 286, 294, 338–39, 380, 409, 422.
21. Rowland, vol. 7, pp. 459, 464, 487, 492, 496, 508, 516; Walthall to JD, October 16, 1883, May 21, 1888, Walthall Papers.
22. Strode, *Letters*, pp. 440, 446.
23. Ibid., p. 447.
24. Ibid., p. 450; Rowland, vol. 7, p. 523.
25. Rowland, vol. 7, pp. 523, 527.
26. Ibid., pp. 523, 525, 527, 528, 530, 536, 540–41, 544, 558.
27. Ibid., vol. 8, pp. 32, 33, 116.
28. Strode, *Letters*, pp. 451, 453, 461–63.
29. Ibid., pp. 467, 475–78; *Memoir*, vol. 2, p. 305.
30. Ibid., pp. 490–92.
31. Memorandum of agreement, December 14, 1875, Memorandum of pro-

posed "Compromise," December 13, 1878, Walthall to D. Appleton & Co., December 11, 1878, Walthall Papers; *Memoir*, vol. 2, p. 826; JD to Gorgas, February 10, 1879, Gorgas Papers.

32. Walthall to JD, May 21, 1888, Agreement, February 14, 1880, JD to Walthall, April 22, 1880, D. Appleton, receipt, May 5, 1880, Walthall Papers; J. C. Derby, *Fifty Years Among Authors, Books and Publishers* (New York, 1884), pp. 494–96; JD to J. C. Derby, February 22, 1880, Davis Papers, Duke; JD to Virginia Clay, July 30, 1882, Clay Papers, Duke; Strode, *Letters*, p. 500.

33. Rowland, vol. 8, p. 403; JD to Derby, February 22, 1880, Davis Papers, Duke; Sarah Dorsey, deed, March 20, 1879, Mary Wilson McRee Papers, Clayton Library, Biloxi; Deed Book 16-328, Harrison County, Miss.

34. WPJ to JD, April 14, 1880, Davis Papers, MC; *Chicago Times*, August 9, 1880; JD to S. D. Lee, April 28, 1882, S. D. Lee Papers, Southern Historical Collection; Rowland, vol. 8, p. 363.

35. *Memoir*, vol. 8, pp. 829–30; Strode, *Letters*, p. 507; *Rise and Fall*, vol. 2, pp. 763–64.

36. Rowland, vol. 8, pp. 594, 598; *Rise and Fall*, vol. 2, p. 764.

37. JD to Virginia Clay, July 12, 30, 1882, Clay Papers, Duke; "Davis and Davidson," *Southern Historical Society Papers* 24 (1896), pp. 287–89.

38. JD to Derby, December 15, 1881, Aaron J. Cooke Collection, University of Michigan; JD to Derby, December 3, 1883, JD to Donn Piatt, April 23, 1889, Davis Papers, MC.

39. *Memoir*, vol. 2, p. 831; Strode, *Letters*, p. 508; JD to VD, June 1, 1881, Davis Papers, Transylvania; JD to Margaret Davis Hayes, July 18, 1881, Jefferson Hayes-Davis; JD to W. J. Tenney, November 15, 1881, University Archives, Notre Dame, Indiana; JD to Virginia Clay, February 25, 1882, Clay Papers, Duke.

40. *New Orleans Times-Democrat*, December 22, 1881, January 12, 1882; *Memoir*, vol. 2, pp. 848–49, 854, 858; JD to John W. Jones, June 24, 1883, JD to Jubal Early, November 2, 1884, Davis Papers, Duke; Beauregard to Leona Queyrouze, February 15, 1891, Leona Queyrouze Papers, Kountz Collection.

41. JD to L. Q. C. Lamar, May 3, 1881, L. Q. C. Lamar Papers, Emory University; JD to Theodore Roosevelt, September 29, 1885, in Joseph A. Bishop, *Theodore Roosevelt and His Time* (New York, 1920), p. 41; "President Davis in Reply to General Sherman," *Southern Historical Society Papers* 14 (1886), pp. 260ff; WPJ to JD, March 11, 1887, Davis Papers, MC.

42. *Life*, pp. 57–58, 265; M. H. Seth to JD, July 20, 1885, Paul Hayne to JD, August 8, 1885, Davis Papers, MC.

43. JD to James Lyons, May 15, 1879, James Lyons Papers, Southern Historical Collection; *Pascagoula (Miss.), Democrat-Star*, June 13, 1879; *Nashville American*, September 18, 1879; JD to D. H. Hill, August 27, 1887, Robert Batchelder Catalog #43, 1983, item 111.

44. W. R. Vaughan to JD, August 25, 1883, Davis Papers, MC; JD to Mann, July 16, 1880, Palmer Collection; JD to Nahum Capen, November 22, 1880, John Heise Catalog #2477, 1937, p. 4; Watts, *Address*, pp. 16, 17.

45. JD to C. M. Robinson, June 18, 1879, newspaper clipping, JDA; Benjamin Singleton to JD, May 18, 1881, John T. Wood to JD, December 1, 1887, WPJ to JD, March 11, 1887, Davis Papers, MC; *New York Times*, April 7, 1887.

46. Crafts Wright to JD, March 21, 1879, Davis Papers, MC; JD to Thomas H. Taylor, February 7, 1881, Joseph Rubenfine Catalog #83, item 17; *The*

Vedette 1 (May 15, 1880), p. 10; B. H. Lee to James T. Harrison, July 11, 1878, in "A Note of Jefferson Davis," *Journal of Mississippi History* 31 (July 1964), p. 149; *Memoir*, vol. 2, pp. 904–5.

47. JD to Lise Mitchell, 1884, Mitchell Papers; JD to Constance Harrison, May 24, 1886, Harrison Family Papers, University of Virginia; Donn Piatt to JD, June 28, July 9, 1889, Davis Papers, MC; JD to D. Appleton & Co., January 31, 1889, Robert Batchelder Catalog #11, n.d., item 85; JD to T. K. Oglesby, August 6, 1889, copy in JDA; Rowland, vol. 10, pp. 98, 161; Jefferson Davis, "Andersonville and Other War Prisons," *Belford's Magazine* 4 (January 1890), pp. 161–78; (February 1890), pp. 337–53.

48. Rowland, vol. 9, p. 470; vol. 10, pp. 158–59.

49. "A Day and Night with 'Old Davy,'" p. 132; *Memoir*, vol. 2, pp. 891–95; JD to Nahum Capen, November 22, 1880, Heise Catalog #2477, p. 4; JD to ———, April 20, 1883, Gary Hendershott Catalog, n.d.

50. *New York Herald*, August 11, 1895; W. S. Harney to JD, March 15, 1879, Davis Papers, MC; JD to E. G. W. Butler, May 13, 1884, Minnesota Historical Society, St. Paul.

51. Derby, *Fifty Years*, p. 499; *Life*, pp. 55ff.

52. *Life*, p. 55; *New York Herald*, August 11, 1895.

53. Theodore Nunn to JD, April 1, 1887, Davis Papers, MC; Strode, *Letters*, p. 560.

54. JD to W. W. Garig, March 2, 1884, New York Public Library; *New York Herald*, August 11, 1895.

55. Riley, "Health, Part II," pp. 284–86; Strode, *Letters*, pp. 560–61; *Memoir*, vol. 1, pp. 41–42.

Chapter 33   May All Your Paths Be Peaceful and Pleasant

1. *Life*, pp. 68–84; Early to JD, April 17, 1889, Davis Papers, MC.

2. *Memoir*, vol. 2, p. 923.

3. Rowland, vol. 10, p. 164.

Bibliography

Manuscripts

Alabama Department of Archives and History, Montgomery
  Clement C. Clay Papers
  Jefferson Davis Papers
  Josiah Gorgas Collection
  William L. Yancey Papers
University of Alabama, Tuscaloosa
  Jefferson Davis Papers
  Josiah Gorgas Papers
Percival Beacroft, Jr., Woodville, Mississippi
  Davis Collection
Beauvoir Shrine, Biloxi, Mississippi
  Jefferson Davis Collection
  L. S. Ruder Collection
Mrs. Wert E. Chapman, Louisville, Kentucky
  Charles J. Helm Papers
Chicago Historical Society
  Jefferson Davis Collection
Clayton Library, Biloxi, Mississippi
  Mary Wilson McRee Papers
Colorado College, Colorado Springs
  Charles H. Collins Collection
Museum of the Confederacy, Richmond, Virginia
  Jefferson Davis Papers
Dallas Historical Society, Dallas, Texas
  "Mr. Reagan's Recollections"
Jefferson Davis Association, Rice University, Houston, Texas
  Jefferson Davis Miscellaneous Papers

Frank Everett, Jr., Brierfield Papers
Florida Heulett Interview, 1931, WPA Slave Interviews, Warren County, Mississippi
Harris D. Riley Statement, n.d.
Denver Public Library, Denver, Colorado
C. C. Memminger Letter
Svenette Dinkins
Private Collection
Duke University, Durham, North Carolina
P. G. T. Beauregard Papers
Lawrence O. Branch Papers
Clement C. Clay Papers
Howell Cobb Papers
Jefferson Davis Papers
Theophilus H. Holmes Papers
Joseph E. Johnston Papers
Jones Autograph Letters
Charles C. Jones Papers
R. E. Lee's Official Telegrams
William Pendleton Papers
Gustavus W. Smith Papers
Robert Toombs Papers
Emory University, Atlanta, Georgia
Jefferson Davis Papers
L. Q. C. Lamar Papers
Filson Club, Louisville, Kentucky
Jefferson Davis Letters
Johnston Family Papers
Miscellaneous Manuscripts: Jefferson Davis
University of Florida, Gainesville
Cross Collection
Casemate Museum, Fort Monroe, Virginia
Jefferson Davis Collection
Georgia Department of Archives and History, Atlanta
Governors' Letterbooks
University of Georgia, Athens
Cobb Family Papers
Thomas R. R. Cobb Collection
Felix Hargell Collection
Keith Read Manuscript Collection
Harvard University, Cambridge, Massachusetts
Frederick Dearborn Collection
Jefferson Hayes-Davis, Colorado Springs, Colorado
Davis Family Papers
Henry E. Huntington Library, San Marino, California
S. L. M. Barlow Papers
Simon Buckner Collection
Jefferson Davis Papers
Townsend Collection

Library of Congress, Washington, D.C.
  P. G. T. Beauregard Papers
  Breckinridge Family Papers
  Given Campbell Journal
  Causten-Pickett Papers
  Confederate States of America Papers
  Caleb Cushing Papers
  Jefferson Davis Papers
  Burton Harrison Papers
  Joseph Holt Papers
  Howry Family Papers
  John S. Jackman Diary
  Library of Congress Archives: Loan Receipt Books
  Edwin M. Stanton Papers
  Alexander H. Stephens Papers
  Louis T. Wigfall Papers
Louisiana State University, Baton Rouge
  Thomas O. Moore Papers
Mrs. J. D. Marrett
  Private Collection
Maryland Historical Society, Baltimore
  Anna Ella Carroll Papers
Miami University, Miami, Ohio
  Sam Richey Collection
University of Michigan, Ann Arbor
  Aaron J. Cooke Collection
  Jefferson Davis Letters
  John H. Reagan Memoranda
  Schoff Collection
Mississippi Department of Archives and History, Jackson
  J. F. H. Claiborne Collection
  Jefferson and Varina Davis Collection
  Franklin Smith Diary
  W. T. Walthall Papers
Harrison County, Mississippi, Court House, Biloxi
  Deed Books
Missouri Historical Society, St. Louis
  H. E. Mitchell, History of Jefferson Barracks
Minnesota Historical Society, St. Paul
  Jefferson Davis Letter
National Archives, Washington, D.C.
  Record Group 94
    Negroes in Military Service of the United States
  Record Group 107
    Secretary of War, Register of Letters Received,
    vol. 16, "Register of Cadet Applications"
  Record Group 109
    Jefferson Davis Papers
    Robert E. Lee Papers

Godfrey Weitzel Papers
Compiled Service Records: Abraham Buford
General and Staff Officers' Files: Ed O'Neal
Confederate Papers Relating to Army Officers, War Department Officials, and Other Individuals
Confederate Papers Relating to Citizens or Business Firms
Confederate Records of Confederate Engineers, chap. 3
Confederate War Papers, vol. 24
Documents in the O.R.
Letters Received by the Confederate Secretary of War, chap. 9
Letters and Telegrams Sent by Braxton Bragg, chap. 2
Letters and Telegrams Received by Robert E. Lee, chap. 2
Microfilm 437, 523, 618
Miscellaneous Correspondence
Private Correspondence of T. H. Holmes, chap. 2, Volume 358
Telegrams Received and Draft Telegrams Sent, Adjutant and Inspector General, chap. 9
Telegrams Received and Sent, Adjutant and Inspector General
Telegrams Received and Sent, War Department
Record Group 365
Letters Received by the Secretary of War
New York Public Library
Jefferson Davis Letter
North Carolina Department of Archives and History, Raleigh
Governors' Papers
D. H. Hill Papers
Southern Historical Collection, University of North Carolina, Chapel Hill
Thomas Bragg Diary
John Ellis Papers
William D. Gale Papers
Garnett-Wise Family Papers
Stephen D. Lee Papers
James Lyons Papers
Stephen R. Mallory Papers
John C. Pemberton Papers
Leonidas Polk Papers
E. Kirby Smith Papers
Mary Stamps Papers
Alexander H. Stephens Papers
John Taylor Wood Papers
University of Notre Dame, South Bend, Indiana
University Archives
Old Court House Museum, Vicksburg, Mississippi
Jesse Abbott Hite Reminiscences
Pennsylvania Historical Society, Philadelphia
James Buchanan Papers
Benjamin Gratz Collection
Pierpont-Morgan Library, New York, New York
Miscellaneous Autographs Collection

University of Rochester, Rochester, New York
   William Seward Collection
Rosenberg Library, Galveston, Texas
   Braxton Bragg Papers
South Carolina Department of Archives and History, Columbia
   Executive Council Journals and Letterbooks
   Francis Pickens Papers
South Caroliniana Library, University of South Carolina, Columbia
   Milledge L. Bonham Papers
   Edwin DeLeon Papers
   George A. Trenholm Papers
University of the South, Suwanee, Tennessee
   Leonidas Polk Papers
Tennessee State Library and Archives, Nashville
   Civil War–Confederate Collection
   Isham G. Harris Papers
University of Texas, Austin
   Pritchard von David Collection
   Latin American Collection: Smith Papers
Transylvania University, Lexington, Kentucky
   Jefferson Davis Papers
Tulane University, New Orleans, Louisiana
   Mason Barret Collection of Albert Sidney and William Preston Johnston
       Papers
   Jefferson Davis Papers
   Kountz Collection
       Pierson Family Papers
       Leona Queyrouze Papers
   Louisiana Historical Association Papers
       Jefferson Davis Papers
   Lise Mitchell Papers
   President's Letterbook
Warren County Court House, Vicksburg, Mississippi
   Jefferson Davis vs. Joseph H. D. Bowmar et al.
Virginia Historical Society, Richmond
   Bruce Family Papers
   Emma Lyon Bryan Reminiscences
   Charles E. Davidson Papers
   Early Family Papers
   Pegram-Johnson-McIntosh Family Papers
   Thomas G. Ruffin Papers
   Robert Lee Traylor Papers
Virginia State Library, Richmond
   Executive Papers
   Samuel P. Heintzelman Journal
   Walter Taylor Papers
University of Virginia, Charlottesville
   Edgehill-Randolph Collection
   Harrison Family Papers

William J. Rucker Collection
Franklin Stringfellow Papers
Beverly Tucker Papers
Washington and Lee University, Lexington, Virginia
    William Preston Johnston Papers
Western Reserve Historical Society, Cleveland, Ohio
    William Palmer Collection
William and Mary University, Williamsburg, Virginia
    Confederate Collection
State Historical Society of Wisconsin, Madison
    Ellis E. Jensen Autograph Collection
Yale University, New Haven, Connecticut
    Joseph B. Lyman Papers

Autograph Dealer Catalogs Quoting Jefferson Davis Documents

Autograph Bulletin. N.p., December 1920.
Baker, G. A. Catalog No. 34. N.p., 1939.
Batchelor, Robert. Catalog No. 11. N.p., n.d.
———. Catalog No. 43. N.p., 1983.
Battan, David. Catalog No. 19. N.p., 1977.
Carnegie Book Shop. Catalog No. 346. N.p., 1975.
Cohasso, Inc. Catalog. N.p., October 1977.
The Collector 47. N.p., November 1932.
Flying Quill. N.p., April 1941.
Frajola, Richard. Catalog. N.p., July 10, 1983.
Goodspeed's Book Shop. Catalog No. 373. Boston, 1943.
———. Catalog No. 378. Boston, June 1944.
Heise, John. Catalog No. 2477. N.p., 1937.
Hendershott, Gary. Catalog. N.p., n.d.
Madigan, Thomas. Catalog. N.p., 1937.
Rendell, Diane J. Catalog. N.p., n.d.
Richards, Paul. Catalog No. 59. N.p., n.d.
Rubenfine, Joseph. List No. 66. N.p., n.d.
———. Catalog No. 83. N.p., n.d.
Sotheby, Parke Bernet. Catalog. N.p., June 20, 1979.

Newspapers

Aberdeen (Miss.) *Monroe Democrat,* 1850
Aberdeen Weekly Independent, 1853
Atlanta Gate-City Guardian, 1861
Atlanta Intelligencer, 1861
Augusta (Ga.) *Chronicle,* 1853
Augusta Daily Chronicle and Sentinel, 1861
Augusta Daily Constitutionalist, 1861
Baltimore Sun, 1850–53, 1861

Baton Rouge Daily Advocate, 1855
Carrolton (Miss.) Democrat, 1846
Charleston (S.C.) Daily Courier, 1861
Charleston Mercury, 1858, 1861
Chattanooga Press, 1885
Chicago Times, 1880, 1886
Columbus (Ga.) Southern Standard, 1851, 1853
Columbus (Miss.) Primitive Republican, 1851
Dallas Morning News, 1897
Greensboro (N.C.) Patriot, 1860
Holly Springs (Miss.) Gazette, 1846
Holly Springs Guard, 1846
Jackson Flag of the Union, 1850, 1853
Jackson Mississippian, 1846–47, 1850–51, 1858
Jackson Mississippi and State Gazette, 1858
Jackson Mississippi Free Trader, 1858
Jackson Semi-Weekly Mississippian, 1855
Jackson Southron, 1846, 1850
Lafayette (La.) Louisiana Statesman, 1850
Leavenworth (Kans.) Daily Times, 1867
Louisville Courier-Journal, 1875, 1887
Lynchburg Daily Virginian, 1886
Matamoros (Mexico) American Flag, 1847
Memphis Daily Appeal, 1857, 1861
Memphis Daily Avalanche, 1859
Milwaukee Sentinel, 1881, 1891
Mobile Daily Advertiser, 1865
Mobile Tribune, 1861
Montgomery Advertiser, 1861
Nashville American, 1879
Natchez Courier, 1846–47, 1855, 1861
Natchez Daily Courier, 1861
Natchez Mississippi Free Trader, 1852, 1858
New Orleans Daily Crescent, 1861
New Orleans Daily Delta, 1852, 1855–58, 1861
New Orleans Daily Picayune, 1856, 1861
New Orleans Delta, 1851, 1861
New Orleans Louisiana Courier, 1851
New Orleans Picayune, 1846, 1853
New Orleans Sunday Delta, 1858
New Orleans Times-Democrat, 1881, 1902
New York Citizen, 1867
New York Daily Tribune, 1889, 1899
New York (Harper's Weekly Illustrated Newspaper), 1858, 1861
New York Herald, 1850, 1853–58, 1861, 1895
New York Times, 1853–58, 1861, 1887
New York Tribune, 1857–58
New York World, 1862
Pascagoula (Miss.) Democrat-Star, 1879
Port Gibson (Miss.) Herald and Correspondent, 1850

Providence (R.I.) *Journal,* 1863
Raymond (Miss.) *Hinds County Gazette,* 1857
Richmond (Va.) *Daily Dispatch,* 1861–65
Richmond Daily Enquirer, 1853, 1858
Richmond Enquirer, 1858
Richmond Examiner, 1861–65
Richmond Whig, 1861–65
St. Louis (Mo.) *Globe-Democrat,* 1883
St. Louis Post-Dispatch, 1937
Springfield (Illinois) *State Register,* 1850
Vicksburg (Miss.) *Sentinel,* 1846
Vicksburg Tri-Weekly Whig, 1847, 1853
Vicksburg Weekly Sentinel, 1850
Vicksburg Weekly Whig, 1850, 1861
Vicksburg Whig, 1846
Vidalia (Miss.) *Concordia Intelligencer,* 1853
Washington Constitution, 1860
Washington Daily Morning Chronicle, 1864
Washington Daily National Intelligencer, 1860
Washington Daily Union, 1846
Washington Evening Star, 1855, 1858, 1861, 1863
Washington National Intelligencer, 1857, 1861–2
Washington Southern Press, 1851–2
Washington States, 1857–8
Washington States and Union, 1861
Washington Union, 1850–51, 1853, 1858
Woodville (Miss.) *Republican,* 1846, 1851, 1865
Woodville Wilkinson Whig, 1854, 1856
Yazoo City Democrat, 1850
Yazoo City Whig, 1846

Official Publications

Journal of the Congress of the Confederate States of America, 1861–1865. 7 vols. Washington, 1904–5.
"Proceedings of the First Confederate Congress." *Southern Historical Society Papers* 50, 1953.
"Proceedings of the Second Confederate Congress." *Southern Historical Society Papers* 52, 1959.
Richardson, James D., comp. *The Messages and Papers of Jefferson Davis and the Confederacy.* 2 vols. Washington, 1905.
United States Congress. *Congressional Directory for the First Session of the Twenty-ninth Congress.* Washington, D.C., 1846.
———. *Congressional Directory for the First Session of the Thirtieth Congress.* Washington, D.C., 1848.
———. *Congressional Directory for the Second Session of the Thirtieth Congress.* Washington, D.C., 1849.
———. *Congressional Directory of the Thirty-third Congress, First Session.* Washington, D.C., 1854.

————. *Congressional Directory of the Thirty-fifth Congress, First Session.* Washington, D.C., 1856.

————. *Congressional Directory of the Thirty-fifth Congress, Second Session.* Washington, D.C. 1857.

————. *Congressional Globe.* Thirty-sixth Congress, Second Session. Washington, D.C., 1861.

United States Navy Department. *Official Records of the Union and Confederate Navies in the War of the Rebellion.* 31 vols. Washington, D.C., 1894–1927.

United States War Department. *War of the Rebellion: Official Records of the Union and Confederate Armies.* 128 vols. Washington, D.C., 1880–1901.

Books

A Catalogue of the Officers and Students of Transylvania University. Lexington, Ky., 1824.

Allen, G. N. *Incidents and Sufferings in the Mexican War.* Boston, 1848.

Avary, Myrta L., ed. *Recollections of Alexander H. Stephens.* New York, 1910.

Ballard, Michael. *A Long Shadow.* Jackson, Miss., 1988.

Bartlett, David. *Presidential Candidates.* New York, 1889.

Battey, George M., Jr. *A History of Rome and Floyd County.* Atlanta, 1969.

Beers, Henry P. *Guide to the Archives of the Confederate States of America.* Washington, 1968.

Benham, Henry W. *Recollections of Mexico and the Battle of Buena Vista.* Boston, 1851.

Bishop, Joseph A. *Theodore Roosevelt and His Time.* New York, 1920.

Bohn, Casimir. *Bohn's Hand-Book of Washington.* Washington, D.C., 1861.

Brown, George. *Washington: A Not Too Serious History.* Baltimore, 1930.

Brubaker, John H. *The Last Capital.* Danville, Va., 1979.

Buel, C. C., and R. Johnson, eds. *Battles and Leaders of the Civil War.* 4 vols. New York, 1887–88.

Capers, Henry D. *The Life and Times of C. C. Memminger.* Richmond, 1893.

Church, Albert E. *Personal Reminiscences of the Military Academy.* West Point, N.Y., 1879.

Clay-Clopton, Virginia. *A Belle of the Fifties.* New York, 1905.

Coffman, Edward A. *The Old Army.* New York, 1986.

Connelly, Thomas. *Autumn of Glory.* Baton Rouge, 1971.

Conrad, Thomas N. *A Confederate Spy.* New York, 1892.

Crawford, Samuel W. *The Genesis of the Civil War.* New York, 1887.

Crist, Linda Lasswell, ed. *The Papers of Jefferson Davis, Volume 4, 1849–1852.* Baton Rouge, 1983.

Crist, Linda Lasswell, and Mary Seaton Dix, eds. *The Papers of Jefferson Davis, Volume 5, 1853–1855.* Baton Rouge, 1985.

————. *The Papers of Jefferson Davis, Volume 6, 1856–1860.* Baton Rouge, 1989.

Daniels, Jonathan. *The Devil's Backbone.* New York, 1962.

Davis, Jefferson. *Rise and Fall of the Confederate Government.* 2 vols. New York, 1881.

Davis, Reuben. *Recollections of Mississippi and Mississippians.* New York, 1889.

Davis, Susan B. *Old Forts and Real Folks.* Madison, Wisc., 1939.

Davis, Varina H. *Jefferson Davis, Ex-President of the Confederate States of America: A Memoir by His Wife.* 2 vols. New York, 1890.

Davis, William C. *Battle at Bull Run*. New York, 1977.
―――. *Breckinridge: Statesman, Soldier, Symbol*. Baton Rouge, 1974.
DeLeon, Thomas C. *Belles, Beaux and Brains of the '60's*. New York, 1909.
Derby, J. C. *Fifty Years Among Authors, Books and Publishers*. New York, 1884.
Dixon, Mrs. Archibald. *True History of the Missouri Compromise and Its Repeal*. Cincinnati, 1899.
Dorris, Jonathan T. *Pardon and Amnesty Under Lincoln and Johnson*. Chapel Hill, N.C., 1953.
Dowd, Clement. *Life of Zebulon B. Vance*. Charlotte, N.C., 1897.
Dowdey, Clifford, and Louis Manarin, eds. *The Wartime Papers of Robert E. Lee*. Boston, 1961.
DuBose, John W. *The Life and Times of William Lowndes Yancey*. 2 vols. Birmingham, Ala., 1892.
Duke, Basil W. *Reminiscences of General Basil W. Duke*. Garden City, N.Y., 1911.
Durkin, Joseph T., ed. *John Dooley, Confederate Soldier*. Washington, 1945.
Dyer, Oliver. *Great Senators of the United States Forty Years Ago*. Freeport, N.Y., 1872.
Eckloff, Christian. *Memoirs of a Senate Page*. New York, 1909.
Ellett, E.F. *Court Circles of the Republic*. Philadelphia, 1872.
The First White House of the Confederacy. Montgomery, Ala., 1986.
Foreman, Grant. *Pioneer Days in the Early Southwest*. Norman, Okla., 1926.
French, Samuel G. *Two Wars*. Nashville, 1901.
Gallagher, Gary, ed. *Fighting for the Confederacy*. Chapel Hill, N.C., 1989.
Gordon, John B. *Reminiscences of the Civil War*. New York, 1903.
Hamilton, Holman. *Prologue to Conflict*. Lexington, Ky., 1964.
Hanna, A.J. *Flight Into Oblivion*. Richmond, 1938.
Harrison, Fairfax, ed. *The Harrisons of Skimino*. New York, 1910.
Headley, John W. *Confederate Operations in Canada and New York*. New York, 1906.
Hermann, Janet. *The Pursuit of a Dream*. New York, 1981.
Hilliard, Henry W. *Politics and Pen Pictures at Home and Abroad*. New York, 1892.
History of the War Between the United States and Mexico. Philadelphia, 1848.
Hitchcock, Ethan A. *Fifty Years in Camp and Field*. New York, 1909.
Hughes, Nathaniel C., ed. *Liddell's Record*. Dayton, Ohio, 1985.
Johannsen, Robert W. *Stephen A. Douglas*. New York, 1973.
Johnston, Joseph E. *Narrative of Military Operations*. New York, 1874.
Johnston, William Preston. *The Life of General Albert Sidney Johnston*. New York, 1879.
Jones, John B. *A Rebel War Clerk's Diary*. 2 vols. Philadelphia, 1866.
Kirke, Edmund. *Down in Tennessee and Back by Way of Richmond*. New York, 1864.
Lankford, Nelson, ed. *An Irishman in Dixie*. Columbia, S.C., 1988.
Lee, Robert E., Jr. *Recollections and Letters of General Robert E. Lee*. New York, 1904.
Life and Reminiscences of Jefferson Davis by Distinguished Men of His Time. Baltimore, 1890.
Longstreet, James. *From Manassas to Appomattox*. Philadelphia, 1896.
Lord, Walter, ed. *The Fremantle Diary*. Boston, 1954.
Lucid, Robert F., ed. *The Journal of Richard Henry Dana, Jr*. 2 vols. Cambridge, Mass., 1968.

Lytle, William M., comp. *Merchant Steam Vessels of the United States.* Mystic, Conn., 1952.

McElroy, Robert. *Jefferson Davis, The Unreal and the Real.* 2 vols. New York, 1937.

McIntosh, James T., ed. *The Papers of Jefferson Davis, Volume 2, June 1841-July 1846.* Baton Rouge, 1974.

———. *The Papers of Jefferson Davis, Volume 3, July 1846-December 1848.* Baton Rouge, 1981.

Matson, N. *Reminiscences of Bureau County.* Princeton, Ill., 1872.

May, Robert S. *John A. Quitman.* Baton Rouge, 1985.

———. *The Southern Dream of a Caribbean Empire.* Baton Rouge, 1973.

Mayes, Edward. *Lucius Q.C. Lamar.* Nashville, 1896.

Monroe, Haskell M., and James T. McIntosh, eds. *The Papers of Jefferson Davis, Volume 1, 1808-1840.* Baton Rouge, 1971.

Montgomery, H. *The Life of Major General Zachary Taylor.* Auburn, N.Y., 1847.

Moore, Frank, comp. *The Rebellion Record.* 12 vols. New York, 1862–68.

Moore, Samuel J. T., Jr. *Moore's Complete Civil War Guide to Richmond.* Richmond, 1978.

Morrison, James L., ed. *The Memoirs of Henry Heth.* Westport, Conn., 1974.

Neff, Jacob. *Thrilling Incidents of the Wars of the United States.* Philadelphia, 1848.

Nichols, Roy F. *Disruption of American Democracy.* New York, 1948.

———. *Franklin Pierce.* Philadelphia, 1931.

O'Daniel, V.F. *A Light of the Church in Kentucky.* Washington, n.d.

Parker, William H. *Recollections of a Naval Officer.* New York, 1883.

Perry, Oram. *Indiana in the Mexican War.* Indianapolis, 1908.

Polk, William M. *Leonidas Polk, Bishop and General.* 2 vols. New York, 1893.

Pollard, E. A. *Life of Jefferson Davis.* Philadelphia, 1869.

Pollock, Edward. *Illustrated Sketch Book of Danville, Virginia.* Danville, 1885.

Pryor, Mrs. Roger A. *Reminiscences of Peace and War.* New York, 1904.

Ranck, G.W. *Guide to Lexington, Kentucky.* Lexington, 1883.

Reagan, John H. *Memoirs.* New York, 1906.

Reavis, L. V. *Life of General William Selby Harney.* St. Louis, 1878.

Rhees, William J., ed. *The Smithsonian Institution: Journals of the Board of Regents.* Washington, 1879.

Roland, Charles. *Albert Sidney Johnston.* Austin, Tex., 1964.

Roman, Alfred. *The Military Operations of General Beauregard.* 2 vols. New York, 1884.

Rowland, Dunbar, ed. *Jefferson Davis, Constitutionalist. His Letters, Papers and Speeches.* 10 vols. Jackson, Miss., 1923.

Russell, William H. *My Diary North and South.* New York, 1954.

———. *Pictures of Southern Life.* New York, 1861.

Scribner, Benjamin. *Camp Life of a Volunteer.* Philadelphia, 1847.

Shackelford, George G. *George Wythe Randolph and the Confederate Elite.* Athens, Ga., 1988.

Sorrell, G. Moxley. *Recollections of a Confederate Staff Officer.* New York, 1905.

Stovall, Pleasant. *Robert Toombs.* New York, 1892.

Strode, Hudson. *Jefferson Davis, American Patriot.* New York, 1955.

———. *Jefferson Davis, Confederate President.* New York, 1959.

———. *Jefferson Davis, Private Letters, 1823-1889.* New York, 1966.

Tarpley, Colin S. *A Sketch of the Life of Jeff. Davis.* Jackson, Miss., 1851.

Thian, Raphael. *Register of Issues of Confederate States Treasury Notes.* Washington, D.C., 1880.

United States Military Academy Board of Visitors. *Report, June 22, 1825.* West Point, 1825.

Utley, Robert. *Frontier Regulars.* New York, 1973.

———. *Frontiersmen in Blue.* New York, 1967.

Vandiver, Frank E., ed. *The Civil War Diary of General Josiah Gorgas.* University, Ala., 1947.

Wagers, Margaret. *The Education of a Gentleman.* Lexington, Ky., 1943.

Watts, Thomas. *Address on the Life and Character of Ex-President Jefferson Davis.* Montgomery, Ala., 1889.

Weems, John. *To Conquer a Peace.* New York, 1974.

Welcher, Frank J. *The Union Army 1861–1865.* Bloomington, Ind., 1989.

Wentworth, John. *Fort Dearborn, An Address.* Chicago, 1881.

Whig Almanac. New York, 1852.

Wiley, Bell I. *The Road to Appomattox.* New York, 1968.

Windle, Mary J. *Life in Washington.* Philadelphia, 1859.

Wise, John S. *End of an Era.* Boston, 1900.

Woodward, C. Vann, ed. *Mary Chesnut's Civil War.* New Haven, 1981.

Yearns, Wilfred B. *The Confederate Congress.* Athens, Ga., 1960.

Younger, Edward, ed. *Inside the Confederate Government.* New York, 1957.

Articles

"A Day and Night with 'Old Davy.' " *Missouri Historical Review* (January 1937).

"Alexander H. Stephens' Prison Life." *Confederate Veteran* (June 1893).

"An Interesting Batch of Telegrams." *Confederate Veteran* (April 1894).

"A Note of Jefferson Davis." *Journal of Mississippi History* (July 1964).

Bradley, Chester. "Was Jefferson Davis Disguised as a Woman When Captured?" *Journal of Mississippi History* 36 (August 1974).

Brewer, Sarah. "Recollections of Jefferson Davis." *Confederate Veteran* 1 (July 1893).

Bruce, H. W. "Some Reminiscences of the Second of April, 1865." *Southern Historical Society Papers* 9 (May 1881).

Clark, A. J. "When Jefferson Davis Visited Niagara." *Ontario Historical Society Papers* 19 (1922).

Clark, Micajah H. "The Last Days of the Confederate Treasury." *Southern Historical Society Papers* 9 (December 1881).

———. "Retreat of the Confederate Government." *Southern Historical Society Papers* 26 (1898).

Collins, Kathleen, and Ann Wilsher. "Petticoat Politics: The Capture of Jefferson Davis." *History of Photography* 8 (Fall 1984).

"Correction of Errors." *Southern Historical Society Papers* 11 (December 1883).

"Davis and Davidson." *Southern Historical Society Papers* 24 (1896).

Davis, Jefferson. "Andersonville and Other War Prisons." *Belford's Magazine* 4 (January and February 1890).

DeLeon, Thomas C. "The Real Jefferson Davis in Private and Public Life." *Southern Historical Society Papers* 36 (1908).

Dickson, Harris. "Marse Jeff Davis." *Collier's* 51 (February 19, March 5, 12, 1938).

Ferguson, Samuel W. "Escort to President Davis." *Confederate Veteran* 16 (June 1908).

Fleming, Walter L. "Jefferson Davis, the Negroes and the Negro Problem." *Suwanee Review* 16 (1908).

———. "Jefferson Davis at West Point." *Publications of the Mississippi Historical Society* 10 (1909).

Goodloe, J. L. "Reminiscences of the University of Mississippi." *University of Mississippi Magazine* 26 (December 1902).

Hanchett, William. "Reconstruction and the Rehabilitation of Jefferson Davis: Charles G. Halpine's *Prison Life*." *Journal of American History* 56 (September 1969).

"Jefferson Davis' Birthplace." *Confederate Veteran* 11 (December 1903).

Jones, James P., ed. "Your Left Arm: James H. Wilson's Letters to Adam Badeau." *Civil War History* 12 (September 1966).

Jordan, Thomas. "Jefferson Davis." *Harper's New Monthly Magazine* 21 (October 1865).

Lamar, L. Q. C. "The Confederate State Department." *The Independent* 53 (September 19, 1901).

Lasswell, Linda, ed. "Jefferson Davis Ponders His Future." *Journal of Southern History* 41 (November 1975).

"Last Address of President Davis, CSA." *Confederate Veteran* 22 (July 1914).

"Last Surviving Lieutenant General." *Confederate Veteran*, 17 (February 1909).

Lee, Fitzhugh. "Sketch of the Late General S. Cooper." *Southern Historical Society Papers* 3 (May–June 1877).

Liddell, St. John R. "Liddell's Record of the Civil War." *Southern Bivouac*, new series, 1 (December 1885).

Mallory, Stephen R. "Last Days of the Confederate Government." *McClure's Magazine* 16 (December 1900).

Moore, W. T. "A Journey with Jefferson Davis." *Confederate Veteran* 11 (March 1903).

"The Mount Vernon of Kentucky." *Confederate Veteran* 11 (July 1909).

"Mysteriously Restrained." *Confederate Veteran* 1 (May 1893).

Pace, Eleanor Damon, ed. "The Diary and Letters of William P. Rogers, 1846–1862." *Southwestern Historical Quarterly* 32 (April 1929).

"President Davis in Reply to General Sherman." *Southern Historical Society Papers* 14 (1886).

"The Prison Life of Jefferson Davis." *Southern Historical Society Papers* 32 (1904).

Quaife, Milo M. "The Northwestern Career of Jefferson Davis." *Journal of the Illinois State Historical Society* 16 (1923).

"Recent Acquisitions of the Manuscript Division." *Quarterly Journal of the Library of Congress* 24 (October 1967).

"The Religious Life of Jefferson Davis." *Confederate Veteran* 35 (October 1927).

"Resources of the Confederacy in 1865." *Southern Historical Society Papers* 3 (March 1877).

Riley, Harris D. "Jefferson Davis and His Health, Part I." *Journal of Mississippi History* 49 (August 1987).

———. "Jefferson Davis and His Health, Part II." *Journal of Mississippi History* 49 (November 1987).

"Rosemont Plantation." *Southern Accents* 10 (March–April 1987).

Schaff, Morris. "The Spirit of Old West Point." *Atlantic Monthly* 99 (March 1907).

Sioussat, St. George L., ed. "Mexican War Letters of Col. William Bowen Campbell." *Tennessee Historical Magazine* 1 (1915).
Smith, Nannie Davis. "Reminiscences of Jefferson Davis." *Confederate Veteran* 38 (May 1930).
Southland 2 (February 1989).
Taylor, Rosser H., ed. "Boyce-Hammond Correspondence." *Journal of Southern History* 3 (May 1937).
"Thomas R. R. Cobb—Extracts from Letters to His Wife." *Southern Historical Society Papers* 28 (1900).
Tice, Douglas O. " 'Bread or Blood': The Richmond Bread Riot." *Civil War Times Illustrated* 12 (February 1974).
Tingley, Donald F. "The Jefferson Davis-William H. Bissell Duel." *Mid-America* 27 (July 1956).
Twiggs, Davis H. "Presidency of the Confederacy Offered Stephens and Refused." *Southern Historical Society Papers* 26 (1908).
Van Horne, John D. "Jefferson Davis and Repudiation in Mississippi." *Southern Historical Society Papers* 61 (September 1916).
The Vedette 1 (February 1880).
—— 1 (May 15, 1880).
—— 2 (December 15, 1880).
—— 5 (January 20, 1884).
—— 8 (May 1886).
Vose, Caroline. "Jefferson Davis in New England." *Virginia Quarterly Review* 2 (October 1926).
Walthall, W. T. "True Story of the Capture of Jefferson Davis." *Southern Historical Society Papers* 5 (March 1878).

Index